ATLANTIC
OCEAN

B A H A M A S

Camagüey Archipelago

Jigüey Bay

Ciego
de Ávila

★ Ciego de Ávila

★ Camagüey

Camagüey

Las Tunas

★
Las Tunas

Holguín
★

Nipe Bay

Holguín

Guacanayabo
Gulf

Bayamo
★

Granma

Santiago
de Cuba

Guantánamo

★ Guantánamo

★ Santiago
de Cuba

Guantánamo
Bay

Guantánamo Bay
Naval Base
(U.S.A.)

Windward Passage

HAITI

JAMAICA

CUBA

ALAN WEST-DURÁN, *editor in chief*

EDITORIAL BOARD

SCRIBNER WORLD SCHOLAR SERIES

VOLUME 1

A-K

CUBA

ALAN WEST-DURÁN, *editor in chief*

CHARLES SCRIBNER'S SONS

A part of Gale, Cengage Learning

GALE
CENGAGE Learning

Detroit • New York • San Francisco • New Haven, Conn • Waterville, Maine • London

GALE
CENGAGE Learning

Cuba
Alan West-Durán, Editor in Chief

For product information and technology assistance, contact us at
Gale Customer Support, 1-800-877-4253.
For permission to use material from this text or product,
submit all requests online at **www.cengage.com/permissions.**
Further permissions questions can be emailed to
permissionrequest@cengage.com

While every effort has been made to ensure the reliability of the information presented in this publication, Gale, a part of Cengage Learning, does not guarantee the accuracy of the data contained herein. Gale accepts no payment for listing; and inclusion in the publication of any organization, agency, institution, publication, service, or individual does not imply endorsement of the editors or publisher. Errors brought to the attention of the publisher and verified to the satisfaction of the publisher will be corrected in future editions.

LIBRARY OF CONGRESS CATALOGING-IN-PUBLICATION DATA

Alan West-Durán, editor in chief.
    v. cm. -- (Scribner world scholar series)
    Includes bibliographical references and index.
    ISBN-13: 978-0-684-31681-9 (set : alk. paper)
    ISBN-10: 0-684-31681-1 (set: alk. paper)
    ISBN-13: 978-0-684-31682-6 (v. 1 : alk. paper)
    ISBN-10: 0-684-31682-X (v. 1 : alk. paper)
    [etc.]
1. Cuba. I. West, Alan, 1953-

F1758.C9485 2012
972.91--dc22   2011012007

Gale
27500 Drake Rd.
Farmington Hills, MI, 48331-3535

ISBN-13: 978-0-6843-1681-9 (set)   ISBN-10: 0-6843-1681-1 (set)
ISBN-13: 978-0-6843-1682-6 (vol. 1)   ISBN-10: 0-6843-1682-X (vol. 1)
ISBN-13: 978-0-6843-1683-3 (vol. 2)   ISBN-10: 0-6843-1683-8 (vol. 2)

This title will also be available as an e-book.
ISBN-13: 978-0-6843-1684-0 ISBN-10: 0-6843-1684-6
Contact your Gale, a part of Cengage Learning, sales representative for ordering information.

Printed in the United States of America
1 2 3 4 5 6 7 16 15 14 13 12

EDITORIAL AND PRODUCTION STAFF

EXECUTIVE VICE PRESIDENT
Frank Menchaca

VICE PRESIDENT AND PUBLISHER
James P. Draper

PRODUCT MANAGER
Stephen Wasserstein

PROJECT EDITORS
Rebecca Parks, Scot Peacock

EDITORIAL SUPPORT
Lawrence W. Baker, Sheila Dow,
Julie Mellors, Alexander Polzin,
Jennifer Stock

EDITORIAL ASSISTANTS
Chelsea Arndt, Hillary Hentschel,
Marit Rogne

ART DIRECTOR
Kristine Julien

COMPOSITION
Evi Seoud

IMAGING
John Watkins

MANUFACTURING
Wendy Blurton

**RIGHTS ACQUISITION AND
MANAGEMENT**
Jackie Jones, Robyn V. Young

TECHNICAL SUPPORT
Marc Faerber, Michael Lesniak, Mike Weaver

COPYEDITORS
Judith Culligan, Gretchen M. Gordon,
Anne C. Davidson, Jessica Hornik Evans, Michael
Levine, Mary H. Russell, David E. Salamie, Drew
Silver

PROOFREADERS
John Fitzpatrick, Carol Holmes, Laura Specht
Patchkofsky, Amy L. Unterburger

TRANSLATORS
ASTA-USA Translation Services, Dick Cluster,
Comms Multilingual, Mark Schafer

TRANSLATION VERIFICATION
Elizabeth Campisi, Dick Cluster,
Pablo Julián Davis, Cola W. Franzen, Dawn Gable,
Lourdes Gil, Heriberto Nicolás García, Ana M.
Sanchez

CAPTIONS
Judith Culligan

CROSS-REFERENCES
M. Karen Bracken

CUSTOM GRAPHICS
XNR Productions, Inc.

INDEXER
Laurie Andriot

PAGE DESIGN
Kate Scheible Graphic Design, LLC

TABLE OF CONTENTS

G

H

I

J

K

L

Introduction

Few countries in the world have received the kind of political, scholarly, and journalistic attention that Cuba has throughout its history. Literally, hundreds, if not thousands, of books have been published about the largest of the Caribbean islands, including numerous biographies of Cuba's two most prominent figures, Fidel Castro and José Martí. Much of what has been written of the post-1959 revolutionary period has generated debate and controversy.

The island has demonstrated a bracing cultural vitality over its turbulent history: Cuba has been surprisingly open to foreign cultures (Africa, Europe, Asia) and yet exhibits a profound sense of nationalism. The diversity of its culture is matched by a struggle for its unfulfilled potential, burst asunder by one of the most radical revolutions in the twentieth century. Because of this dramatic re-insertion into the world stage at the height of the Cold War, Cuba is refreshingly paradoxical: Even as the country seems suspended in time or in the midst of the ruins of something that has ended, it has creatively generated a highly sophisticated cultural and social space where pre-modern religious rituals coexist with postmodern blogging, where non-market egalitarianism collides with capitalist consumption tastes.

THE COMPLEXITY OF HISTORY AND WORD CHOICE

Because of the interest and passions unleashed by their history, Cubans are "bilingual": They speak not only Spanish, but also "history as a second language," in the words of poet Dionisio Martínez. Cuban history is spelled in full caps, like tabloid headlines. There are many headlines, and this cacophony of voices and polarized interpretations challenged us as editors to create a civil dialogue and a linguistic, cultural, and conceptual translation that would present a rich, complex, and vibrant portrait of Cuba.

Currently, historical memories seem to be measured in days and weeks rather than years or decades; however, Cubans have a long memory, not surprising for a small Third World country that has had to deal with major powers (Spain, the Soviet Union, and the United States) over decades or centuries. It is this long, intricate, and sometimes troubled memory—and its many different voices—that this reference book tries to document and make intelligible to the reader.

The avalanche of literature on, by, and about Cuba reminds us of a mordant quip by American bandleader Duke Ellington: "You can say anything you want on the trombone, but you gotta be careful with words" (in Lock, p. 219). Cuban poet Virgilio Piñera, in his poem "La isla en peso" (Island in the Balance), speaks to the difficulty of defining Cuba, even for Cubans: "An entire people can perish from light or from the plague.... My people, so young, you don't know how to make order!/ My people, so divinely rhetorical, you don't know how to tell a story!/ Like light or childhood you do not have a visage" (p. 46). Ellington's advice and Piñera's poem are prudent reminders that words not only matter but have enormous resonance and implications. When the subject is Cuba sometimes words are lobbed like ideological grenades, reducing a rich symphony of voices to a shouting match between two sides.

For example, in a 2011 *New York Times* op-ed piece Cuban blogger Lizabel Mónica described how the different terms used to refer to the April 1961 U.S.-backed invasion of Cuba reflect the differing perspectives of this event. It is known in the United States as the Bay of Pigs Invasion; in Cuba it is the Battle of Playa Girón. For the Cubans, the event was a military invasion with support by the CIA: hence those who were defeated were imperialist mercenaries. For Cuban exiles, those who fought in Brigade 2506 seeking to overthrow Fidel Castro's government are seen as Cuban patriots fighting for freedom against a tyrant. While not all moments of Cuban history are so dramatically charged, it does alert us to some of the pitfalls of writing about Cuba and the hidden or not so hidden assumptions made in the words used to describe the island's history and culture. These assumptions or mistranslations of history can provoke misunderstanding, hostility, even violence.

When we speak about Cuba it should be understood as well that its meaning extends beyond the geographical territory of the island. There are over 1.2 million Cubans or Cuban-Americans in the United States, and tens of thousands living in Puerto Rico, Spain, Mexico, and Venezuela, with smaller populations scattered around the world. They constitute a significant diaspora, making important contributions in economics, culture, politics, sports, media, and ideas to a "greater Cuba." This being said, this book's emphasis is tilted toward the island, since eighty percent of the Cuban population still lives there.

WHY SO MUCH INTEREST IN CUBA?

Why so much interest in Cuba? Is it the "David vs. Goliath" political drama that erupted in 1959 that pitted a defiant Caribbean island against the most powerful nation on the planet? Is it the ideological and historical confrontation between capitalism and socialism? Is it the natural beauty of the island, which collides with its rebellious history? Is it the long relationship between Cuba and the United States, fueled by political ambition, travelers, and tourists that have seen the island as friendly neighbor, ripe fruit, or protectorate? Is it the appeal of Cuban music over two centuries, which has had a long and seductive relationship with the United States? Is it due to a persistent curiosity about a place that has been off-limits for U.S. travelers for over five decades? Is it the lure of utopian change symbolized by the Cuban Revolution?

Ever since the Enlightenment's promise of liberty, equality, and fraternity by way of the French Revolution, many thinkers have addressed the possibility of a different kind of society, free of want, exploitation, inequality, and domination. These ideals have animated many reformers and revolutionaries who seek an alternative kind of power. Cuba's utopian history is not recent, nor only related to the Marxist tradition, but rooted in both a Latin American tradition and its own longings to fulfill its national ideals, expressed by some of its key intellectual and political figures. Even the collapse of European socialism (Soviet Union and allies) between 1989 and 1991, not to mention the economic changes in China and Vietnam (opening up to global commerce, market reforms) have not completely eliminated these utopian impulses. As French philosopher Paul Ricoeur said: "A society without utopia would be dead, because it would no longer have any project, any prospective goals" (1986, p. xxi). For all their shortcomings and failures, twentieth-century revolutions, of which Cuba is clearly an example, speak the utopian language of the unfulfilled promises of the Enlightenment project. When the Berlin Wall was torn down almost everyone predicted Cuba would follow suit; some twenty-three years later the island has resisted against all odds. Conversely, those who claim that Cuba has run its course and spent its political capital, see the island from the perspective of the burgeoning group of *transitólogos* ("transitionists" often with a political agenda), those who are devising scenarios for Cuba's transition to a post-socialist society, often using comparative experiences from post-Communist Eastern Europe or ex-military regimes of Latin America. From a North American perspective, what Cuba has attempted to do over the last half century confronts us, challenging our way of looking at issues of equality, social justice, the individual and society, the commodification of daily life, race relations, North-South relations, the arts, health care, education, and politics, to name only the most visible. As editors we wanted to give more reliable tools to the reader to assess whether Cuba's lessons in these areas are positive, negative, or a mixture of both, knowing that these appraisals will shift over time.

Cuba's history, of course, did not begin in 1959 with the Revolution, and this publication is insistent in covering the Colonial period (1492–1898) and the Republican period (1902–1959) in the major articles, not only because they help illuminate the present, but because they deserve to be studied and explained in their own right. Despite its relative youth as an independent country at just a little more than a century, Cuba's roots are deep and go back centuries to Spain, Africa, Asia, the Americas, and the indigenous peoples who were the original inhabitants of the island.

A DIFFERENT KIND OF REFERENCE BOOK ON CUBA

The initial idea for this project was called an "encyclopedia," yet as the publication was conceptualized and refined the need to have a traditional type of encyclopedia with thousands of entries, biographies, etc., not only seemed repetitive of previous efforts but unnecessary. As editors we wanted to present the long view of what has made Cuba what it is today, not simply focus on the current moment.

The concept then evolved to combining a panoramic portrait of Cuba achieved through long "survey" essays, with a series of shorter and more focused "counterpoint" pieces. In this regard this reference book operates both as a mural and as a mosaic: It accentuates broad outlooks with incisive particulars. The long essays are on major topics like Economics, Food, Tobacco, Race, Sexuality, Faith, Gender, Cuban Thought and Cultural Identity, Literature, Language, and more than a dozen more. The counterpoints are associated with the big topics but focus on something specific: a date in history, a town or city, a work of art or literature, a film, a piece of music. For example, within the general category of "Sugar" (which covers the Colonial, Republican, and Revolutionary periods) there is a related article that speaks about how sugar has been represented in Cuban art, literature, song and popular culture. The topic of literature includes key counterpoints that cover important novels, poetry, or plays, like José Lezama Lima's *Paradiso* (1966) or Reinaldo Arenas's *The Color of Summer* (1991). Key works or emblems of Cuban society were selected as counterpoints. Their subject matter, perspective, and historical importance helped define Cuba's unique identity. We hope because of their brevity and themes, they offer a livelier approach to Cuba's creativity and identity.

The idea then was not to attempt an up-to-the-minute collection of information on Cuba—a thankless task, given the 24/7 information cycle—but to have the interested reader find out about the economic, historical, political, and cultural forces that have shaped Cuba and make it what it is today: from a colonial outpost in Spain's empire, to a sugar-producing juggernaut in the nineteenth century, to a troubled twentieth-century republic, and more recently an embattled revolutionary island since 1959. In an electronic age, a printed text fixes a point in time; the editors wanted that point to be a gathering place where people would be exposed to information, ideas, and knowledge that can become guides to other, renewed and multifaceted sources. Central to both long articles and counterpoints was the need to contextualize Cuba's rich history and culture to counter the simplistic, dismissive, frivolous, or shortsighted popular images of the country. Unlike a traditional encyclopedia, there is no assumption—tacit or overt—that these two volumes have all the answers about Cuba. On the contrary, the editors saw this project more along the lines of helping the reader ask the right questions about Cuba. We sincerely hope the reader will learn a great deal about the country, but more important is that consulting *Cuba* will take the reader on further journeys to explore the island's culture, history, and society with a particular discernment.

DIVERSE VIEWPOINTS

A key feature of this publication is the high participation of Cuban contributors living on the island. This was an exciting and challenging aspect of the project since it meant navigating the worlds between Cuba and the United States, always an undertaking fraught with differences, misunderstandings, and mutual suspicions. Fortunately, the drawbacks were far outweighed by their contributions; it has made the project a more rounded and nuanced view of the island's rich if sometimes baffling reality. This is not the first time scholars and artists from inside and outside the island have collaborated, but it is the first involving a major reference work in English.

In putting together an editorial team we sought to have input from the island, Cubans abroad, plus a host of Latin American, Caribbean, North American, and European scholars who are experts on the subject of Cuba. In addition, an independent historian created chronology sidebars for key articles to highlight important events. These scholars brought their decades of experience and scholarship to topics and issues that were sometimes controversial and contested. Despite the commitment to achieve consensus on difficult issues, there are perspectives in the publication that not everyone shared. Still, the authors were asked to express and discuss differences on matters that had antithetical viewpoints, and not merely take sides.

These different viewpoints have been organized to dispel some of the more hardened notions about Cuba and its people: that Cubans are anti-American, that the two sides between pro- and anti-Castro populations are monolithic blocs, that the one-party state in the island has not seen any substantial changes or reforms since the 1960s, that island Cubans do not want better relations with the United States, that Cuba's pre-1959 history should only be regarded as the prelude to the revolution led by Fidel Castro. Equally important is to recognize that not all Cubans want to leave Cuba, that post-1959 Cuba is not an unmitigated disaster, that not all Cubans in exile support the embargo (blockade), that the Cuban diaspora is pluralistic and not uniformly right-wing.

Cuba, however, elicits great passion from those who write about it, be they Cuban or not. Damián Fernández has written eloquently about this, devoting an entire book to the subject of the politics of passion and affection with regard to Cuba. In it, he warns against two dangers: seeing a false opposition between reason and emotion, especially in the political realm, and overlooking the role of emotion in analyzing the role of interests in politics. As he says: "Social life has an emotional infrastructure, and so do political systems" (p. 2). This book does not shy away from these passions or the emotional infrastructure of history; *Cuba* embraces them while avoiding the settling of scores. This emotional undertow might cause discomfort for some readers, but this discomfort reveals much about Cuba.

Given the contested terrain of Cuban history and politics, there are a great many issues on which scholars and Cubans passionately disagree: the Bay of Pigs Invasion (Batalla de Playa Girón), the Cuban Missile Crisis (Crisis de Octubre), negotiations between the U.S. and Cuban governments, immigration, the Mariel Boatlift, Cuba's involvement in Africa, the Rafter Crisis, the Helms-Burton bill, the Elián González Affair, the embargo (or *bloqueo*), congressional or executive restrictions on travel or remittances to Cuba. At a policy level there are profound disagreements on political philosophy (type of system, elections, etc.), economics (role of markets, private property, the state, entrepreneurship), human rights, reproductive rights, and privacy, among others.

These differences need not lead to despair, nor obscure the difference between information and knowledge. Information is something that can be stored, shared, used, and reused by many people; there is a public dimension to information that also lends itself to being packaged and re-articulated into "morsels" and made available to large numbers of people. Knowledge, on the other hand is more focused on an individual knower (Blair p. 2). Knowledge involves context, a bigger picture, a conceptual breadth, as well as personal-intellectual experience. While information can be compiled, knowledge requires a kind of apprenticeship through time. *Cuba* has both information and knowledge, but its editors are keenly aware that the distinction between the two can sometimes be hazy. One person's information can be deemed as just non-factual ideology by another. This does not mean that one should give up and simply conclude that gathering or disseminating information on Cuba is hopeless, or that knowledge about the country is inevitably tainted by ideological bias. It does, however, remind us that these differences are not ephemeral and challenge us to be doubly conscious of the fact that these difficulties are not going away anytime soon. It is by engaging these differences that the reader will see a more complete understanding of Cuba emerge.

THE CHALLENGE OF TRANSLATION

These differences came to the fore during the translation of work by Cuban scholars to English. The difficulty in translation was not just in the transition from Spanish to English but also in the capturing of historical or cultural nuances that might be understandable to a Cuban audience but lost on a U.S. reader. At times one word could not capture the complexity or the nuance and an explanation was necessary; this was often the case when translating (or having to explain) certain words from the Afro-Cuban religious lexicon like *orisha*, *cajón al muerto*, or *casa-templo*. In other instances it was an issue of political-historical interpretation; for example, traditionally the war between Spain and the United States in 1898 has been called the Spanish-American War or Hispanic-American War, which leaves out any Cuban agency in this matter. However, the conflict began in 1895 as the War of Independence for Cuba, and the three-year struggle was a reprise and renewal of the Ten Years' War that began in 1868; thus Cuban scholars call it more accurately the Spanish-American-Cuban War or just War of Independence.

Or when referring to the U.S. embargo, now over fifty years old, island Cubans use the word *bloqueo* (blockade), a much stronger term that evokes an image of war (with naval blockades, combat). Blockade also means that it goes beyond just a U.S.-Cuba issue and that the United States has tried to convince other countries to follow suit and support their policy. For those living in Cuba, the embargo is an act of economic warfare, used in conjunction with political and military threats to overthrow their government. So in many instances we have placed both words together to indicate these perspectives. Translation is not only a matter of linguistic difference, but cultural and/or conceptual difference, too. In this regard *Cuba* serves as a translator at all three levels.

In Paul Ricoeur's comments on translation he speaks of a state of "linguistic hospitality," where the translator "acknowledges the difference between adequacy and equivalence" and that equivalence can be achieved without total adequacy. This is where the translator can find a degree of happiness: "Linguistic hospitality, then, [is] where the pleasure of dwelling in the other's language is balanced by the pleasure of receiving the foreign word at home, in one's own welcoming house" (2006, p. 10). As editors we strove not only to create a linguistic hospitality but also a cultural and conceptual hospitality, where the reader can dwell in Cuba and where Cuba can dwell in our home as well.

As editors we proposed to "translate" what might seem untranslatable: ideas, themes, and polemics that seem unbridgeable. Cuban-American author Gustavo Pérez Firmat affirms that Cuban identity is transient, not one of essence, translational and not foundational (p. 157). If so, did the Cuban Revolution change it to a foundational identity? Or is there something about Cuba that makes it untranslatable to the United States or the new global order? Is Cuba somehow opaque in global eyes or is it a source that can shed light and understanding on important global issues and problems? As editors we would like to think the latter, while acknowledging the former.

The word "translation" always conjures up issues of faithfulness and betrayal, two words that underline much of the discourse on Cuba. For many Cubans who have left the island, the Revolution was not faithful to its original ideals and has betrayed its promises; those who have remained in Cuba see those who have departed as being unfaithful to their country, betraying its sovereignty and its utopian potential. This adherence to faithfulness or betrayal in the extra-linguistic sense (the gulf between an ideal and its realization) is echoed in the language-translation realm (bridging the gulf between two languages and cultures); both see translation as ultimately unattainable, or at best an impossible approximation, as an activity that leads to failure. Still, this pessimism does not take into account that the activity and meaning of translation (linguistic, cultural, conceptual) can be rich and enabling precisely because it is something always unfinished, something that will never be perfect. In effect, the challenge is to try again and create a new or better translation, turn it into an emblem of hope and not of failure. It is in this spirit of hope, of a linguistic, cultural, and conceptual hospitality, instead of hostility, that the editors of *Cuba* have tried to bring to its readers the rich, perplexing, and ever-changing reality of Cuba.

ACKNOWLEDGEMENTS

Any project of this magnitude requires the dedication and perseverance of many people. First, I want to thank Frank Menchaca, Executive Vice President of Gale, for proposing that it happen; it is the fifth time we have collaborated on a publication and hopefully it will not be the last. ¡Gracias, Frank! Stephen Wasserstein as Project Manager was a constant source of insight and advice, as was Jim Draper, the Publisher. Rebecca Parks, the Project Editor, was a joy to work with; her valuable comments, her patience, hard work, and equanimity were exceptional. I also want to acknowledge the invaluable editorial assistance offered by Jose Viera, Guillermo Jiménez, María del Carmen Barcia, and Manuel J. Suzarte, all in Cuba. Though I don't know them personally, I want to thank the copyeditors and the translators for their valuable work in making a difficult topic eminently readable.

The editors of this project all made this work possible: Lou Pérez, Jr., María de los Angeles Torres, César Salgado, Víctor Fowler, and Marel García-Pérez, as well as Holly Ackerman, our Contributing Editor. Their dedication to Cuba and this project have been inspiring and helped me keep my sanity. Finally, to Ester Shapiro, who shared with me on a daily basis all of the joys and frustrations of this amazing and emotional experience, while always providing insight. I dedicate this book to the memory of my mother and father, who deeply loved Cuba (and did not return after leaving in 1960) and to all Cubans, no matter where they live. To all, ¡gracias y aché!

Alan West-Duran
Editor in Chief

WORKS CITED

Blair, Ann. *Too Much to Know: Managing Scholarly Information Before the Modern Age.* New Haven, CT: Yale University Press, 2010.

Fernández, Damián J. *Cuba and the Politics of Passion.* Austin: University of Texas Press, 2000.

Lock, Graham. *Blutopia: Visions of the Future and Revisions of the Past in the Work of Sun Ra, Duke Ellington, and Anthony Braxton.* Durham, NC: Duke University Press, 1999.

Martínez, Dionisio D. *History as a Second Language.* Columbus: Ohio State University Press, 1993.

Mónica, Lizbel. "You Say Bay of Pigs, I Say..." *New York Times* (16 April 2011).

Pérez Firmat, Gustavo. *The Cuban Condition: Translation and Identity in Modern Cuban Literature.* Cambridge, U.K.: Cambridge University Press, 1989.

Piñera, Virgilio. *La isla en peso, obra poética.* Barcelona, Spain: Tusquets Editores, 2000.

Ricoeur, Paul. *Lectures on Ideology and Utopia.* New York: Columbia University Press, 1986.

Ricoeur, Paul. *On Translation.* New York: Routledge, 2006.

LIST OF CONTRIBUTORS

NORMA ABAD MUÑOZ

Writer, Advisor, Director of Radio Programs

Member, Unión de Escritores y Artistas de Cuba (UNEAC)

MARK ABENDROTH

Mentor, School of Graduate Studies

Empire State College, SUNY

HOLLY ACKERMAN

Librarian for Latin America & Iberia

Duke University

ANTONIO AJA DÍAZ

Director, Professor, Centro de Estudios Demográficos, Universidad de La Habana, Havana, Cuba

Director, Programa de Estudio sobre Latinos en Estados Unidos, Casa de las Américas

MARÍA EUGENIA ALEGRIA NÚÑEZ

Independent Scholar

Cuba

OLAVO ALÉN RODRÍGUEZ

Ethnomusicologist

Cuban, Afro-Cuban, and Caribbean Studies

CARMEN ALMODÓVAR MUÑOZ

Member

Unión de Escritores y Artistas de Cuba (UNEAC)

AURELIO ALONSO

Deputy Director

Casa de las Américas, Havana, Cuba

ALEJANDRO ANREUS

Associate Professor of Art History and Latin American/Latino Studies

William Paterson University

UVA DE ARAGÓN

Associate Director, Cuban Research Institute (retired)

Florida International University

JORGE LUIS ARCOS

Adjunct Professor of Literature

Universidad Nacional de Río Negro, San Carlos de Bariloche, Argentina

PAQUITA ARMAS FONSECA

Member, Unión de Escritores y Artistas de Cuba (UNEAC)

Member, Unión de Periodistas de Cuba

JOSSIANNA ARROYO-MARTÍNEZ

Department of Spanish and Portuguese, African and African Diaspora Studies

University of Texas, Austin

CARIDAD ATENCIO

Poet and Essayist

Researcher, Centro de Estudios Martianos de La Habana, Havana, Cuba

MARÍA DEL CARMEN BARCIA ZEQUEIRA

Senior Professor, Casa de Altos Estudios Don Fernando Ortiz, Universidad de La Habana

Senior Academic, Academia de la Historia de Cuba

Havana, Cuba

RUTH BEHAR

Professor, Department of Anthropology

University of Michigan, Ann Arbor

EMILIO BEJEL

Professor of Latin American Studies, Department of Spanish and Portuguese

University of California at Davis

CARMEN BERENGUER HERNÁNDEZ

Historian

Bibliography Specialist, Biblioteca Nacional José Martí, Cuba

MARÍA-CECILIA BERMÚDEZ

Historian, Member, Grupo de Estudios Cubanos

Unión de Escritores y Artistas de Cuba (UNEAC)

ANKE BIRKENMAIER

Professor, Department of Spanish and Portuguese

Indiana University

PETER C. BJARKMAN

Cuban Baseball Historian

www.baseballdecuba.com

MELISSA BLANCO BORELLI

Lecturer in Dance and Film Studies, Department of Dance, Film and Theatre

University of Surrey, United Kingdom

DENISE BLUM

Assistant Professor, School of Educational Studies

Oklahoma State University

VELIA CECILIA BOBES LEÓN

Professor

Facultad Latinoamericana de Ciencias Sociales, Sede México

NATALIA MARÍA BOLÍVAR ARÓSTEGUI

Writer, Researcher

Unión de Escritores y Artistas de Cuba (UNEAC)

PHILIP BRENNER

Chair, Council on Latin America

American University

P. SEAN BROTHERTON

Department of Anthropology

Yale University

RUFO CABALLERO

Former Professor, Universidad de la Habana, Havana, Cuba

Former Professor, Instituto Superior de Artes (ISA), Cuba

ANA CAIRO

Member

Unión de Escritores y Artistas de Cuba (UNEAC)

LUISA CAMPUZANO

Emeritus Professor, Facultad de Artes y Letras, Universidad de La Habana, Havana, Cuba

Founder and Director of the Women's Studies Program, Casa de las Américas

ZAIDA CAPOTE CRUZ

Instituto de Literatura y Lingüística

Havana, Cuba

DAVID C. CARLSON

Assistant Professor, Department of History and Philosophy

University of Texas-Pan American

ODETTE CASAMAYOR-CISNEROS

Assistant Professor, Department of Modern and Classical Languages

University of Connecticut-Storrs

ANA VICTORIA CASANOVA

Musicologist, Researcher, Centro de Investigación y Desarrollo de la Música Cubana

Member, Unión de Escritores y Artistas de Cuba (UNEAC), Havana, Cuba

ENVER M. CASIMIR

Visiting Assistant Professor, Latin American Studies

Gettysburg College

LUCIANO CASTILLO

Head of the Mediateca "André Bazin" of the Escuela Internacional de Cine y TV de San Antonio de los Baños

Member of the Unión de Escritores y Artistas de Cuba (UNEAC) and the Asociación Cubana de la Prensa Cinematográfica, Havana, Cuba

SIRO DEL CASTILLO

Caribbean Commissioner

Comisión Latinoamericana por los Derechos Humanos y Libertades de los Trabajadores y Pueblos (CLADEHLT)

NORMA DEL CASTILLO ALONSO

Tobacco Research Institute

San Antonio de los Baños, Artemisa, Cuba

MARIELA CASTRO ESPÍN

Director

Centro Nacional de Educación Sexual (CENESEX), Cuba

ILIANA CEPERO-AMADOR

Independent Curator

Stanford, California

MICHAEL CHANAN

Professor of Film and Video, Department of Media, Culture, and Language

Roehampton University, London

GRACIELA CHAO CARBONERO

Member, Unión de Escritores y Artistas de Cuba (UNEAC)

Havana, Cuba

JUSTO ALBERTO CHÁVEZ RODRÍGUEZ

Principal Researcher, Instituto Central de Ciencias Pedagógicas

Professor, Academia de Ciencias de Cuba

ROBERTO COBAS AMATE

Museo Nacional de Bellas Artes

Havana, Cuba

MARIO COYULA-COWLEY

Architect; Distinguished Professor, Faculty of Architecture

Instituto Superior Politécnico José Antonio Echeverría (ISPJAE/CUJAE), Havana, Cuba

GRACIELLA CRUZ-TAURA

Associate Professor, Department of History

Florida Atlantic University

MAYRA CUÉ SIERRA

Adjunct Professor

Universidad de La Habana, Havana, Cuba

JULIA CUERVO HEWITT

Associate Professor of Spanish and Portuguese, Department of Spanish, Italian, and Portuguese

Pennsylvania State University

EMILIO CUETO

Independent Scholar

MARÍA CARIDAD CUMANÁ GONZÁLEZ

Adjunct Professor, Department of Arts and Letters

Universidad de La Habana, Havana, Cuba

GUILLERMINA DE FERRARI

Associate Professor, Latin American and Caribbean Literature

University of Wisconsin-Madison

HÉCTOR DELGADO

Professional Photographer

Havana, Cuba

DANAE C. DIÉGUEZ

Assistant Professor, Department of History and Media Theory

Facultad de Arte de los Medios de Comunicación Audiovisual del Instituto Superior de Arte; Universidad de las Artes, Cuba

JORGE DUANY

Professor, Department of Sociology and Anthropology

University of Puerto Rico, Río Piedras

ILAN EHRLICH

Assistant Professor, Division of Arts, Humanities, and Wellness

Bergen Community College

VICTORIA ELI RODRÍGUEZ
Professor, Department of Musicology
Universidad Complutense de Madrid, Spain

ROSA MIRIAM ELIZALDE
Editor
Cubadebate

EUMELIO M. ESPINO MARRERO
Director of Development
Instituto de Investigaciones del Tabaco de Cuba

CARLOS ESPINOSA DOMÍNGUEZ
Assistant Professor, Department of Foreign Languages
Mississippi State University

NORGE ESPINOSA MENDOZA
Poet, Playwright, and Gay Activist
Revista Extramuros, Centro Provincial del Libro y la Literatura, Havana, Cuba

REINALDO ESTRADA ESTRADA
Research Assistant
Fundación Antonio Núñez Jiménez de la Naturaleza y el Hombre, Havana, Cuba

TONY ÉVORA
Musicologist, Painter
Valencia, Spain

ALBERTO FAYA
Singer-Songwriter, Co-Founder of the Nueva Trova Movement
Radio and Television Writer and Commentator

JORGE FEBLES
Professor and Chair of Department of Languages, Literatures and Cultures
University of North Florida

JULIE M. FEINSILVER
Senior Research Fellow
Council on Hemispheric Affairs (COHA)

ANTONIO ELIGIO FERNÁNDEZ
Independent Artist and Art Critic
Vancouver, Canada

RAÚL FERNÁNDEZ
Professor, School of Social Sciences
University of California, Irvine

SUSAN J. FERNANDEZ
Associate Professor, Department of History

University of South Florida, St. Petersburg

TOMÁS FERNÁNDEZ ROBAINA
Senior Professor and Researcher
Biblioteca Nacional de Cuba; Universidad de La Habana, Havana, Cuba

JAVIER FIGUEROA
History Department
University of Puerto Rico, Río Piedras

LUDÍN B. FONSECA GARCÍA
Director, Casa de la Nacionalidad Cubana, Bayamo, Cuba
Member, Unión Nacional de Historiadores de Cuba, Unión de Escritores y Artistas de Cuba (UNEAC), Academia de Historia de Cuba

AMBROSIO FORNET
Member
Unión de Escritores y Artistas de Cuba (UNEAC)

JORGE FORNET
Director del Centro de Investigaciones Literarias
Casa de las Américas, Havana, Cuba

VÍCTOR FOWLER CALZADA
Poet and Essayist
Member, Unión de Escritores y Artistas de Cuba (UNEAC)

CELESTE FRASER DELGADO
Associate Professor, Department of English
Barry University

REINALDO FUNES MONZOTE
Adjunct Professor, Department of History, Universidad de La Habana, Havana, Cuba
Fundación Antonio Núñez Jiménez de la Naturaleza y el Hombre

DAVID F. GARCÍA
Director of Charanga Carolina and Professor of Ethnomusicology, Music Department
University of North Carolina at Chapel Hill

GUADALUPE GARCÍA
Assistant Professor, Department of History
Tulane University

ALEJANDRO GARCIA ÁLVAREZ
Professor, Universidad de La Habana, Havana, Cuba

Member of Unión de Escritores y Artistas de Cuba (UNEAC), Academia de la Historia de Cuba, and the Asociación de Historiadores de América Latina y el Caribe (ADHILAC)

ROLANDO GARCÍA BLANCO
Researcher, Museo Nacional de Historia de las Ciencias "Carlos J. Finlay"
Member, Unión de Historiadores de Cuba, Unión de Escritores y Artistas de Cuba (UNEAC), and Academia de la Historia de Cuba

JUAN ANTONIO GARCÍA BORRERO
President, Cátedra de Pensamiento "Tomás Gutiérrez Alea"
Member, Unión de Escritores y Artistas de Cuba (UNEAC)

AUGUSTO C. GARCÍA DEL PINO CHEN
Historian
Unión Nacional de Historiadores de Cuba (UNHIC)

ORLANDO F. GARCÍA MARTÍNEZ
Independent Scholar
Cienfuegos, Cuba

MERCEDES GARCÍA RODRÍGUEZ
Principal Researcher and Senior Professor, Casa de Altos Estudios Don Fernando Ortiz, Universidad de La Habana, Havana, Cuba
Member, Academia de la Historia de Cuba, Asociación de Historiadores Latinoamericanos y del Caribe (ADHILAC), Unión de Escritores y Artistas de Cuba (UNEAC), and Unión Nacional de Historiadores de Cuba (UNHIC)

MAURO G. GARCÍA TRIANA
Historian
Unión Nacional de Historiadores de Cuba (UNHIC)

GLADYS MAREL GARCÍA-PÉREZ
Senior Researcher, Academia de Ciencias de Cuba. Specialist in Women and Gender Studies
Director, Grupo de Estudios Cubanos, Unión de Escritores y Artistas de Cuba (UNEAC)

ALBERTO GARRANDÉS
Novelist and Critic
Havana, Cuba

RADAMÉS GIRO

Independent Researcher and Principal
Editor

Ediciones Museo de la Música, Cuba

GISELLE VICTORIA GÓMEZ

Independent Curator

Researcher, Instituto Cubano de
Investigación Cultural (ICIC) Juan
Marinello, Havana, Cuba

MAGDA GONZÁLEZ GRAU

Television Director

Member, Unión de Escritores y Artistas de
Cuba (UNEAC)

JULIO CÉSAR GONZÁLEZ
LAUREIRO

Specialist in Services, Processes, and Data
Analysis, Universidad de La Habana,
Havana, Cuba

Member, Unión de Escritores y Artistas de
Cuba (UNEAC)

FLORA GONZÁLEZ MANDRI

Emerson College

JULIO CÉSAR GONZÁLEZ PAGÉS

Professor

Universidad de la Habana, Havana, Cuba

GUILLERMO J. GRENIER

Professor, Department of Sociology

Florida International University

JULIO CESAR GUANCHE
ZALDIVAR

Essayist and Professor

New Latin-American Cinema Festival

RAMIRO GUERRA

Dancer, Choreographer, and Essayist

Founding Director, Conjunto Nacional de
Danza Moderna de Cuba

Founding Member, Unión de Escritores y
Artistas de Cuba (UNEAC)

GUSTAVO GUERRERO

Université de Cergy-Pontoise, France

LAURA G. GUTIÉRREZ

Associate Professor, Department of Spanish
& Portuguese

University of Arizona

PATRICK J. HANEY

Department of Political Science

Miami University, Oxford, Ohio

KATRIN HANSING

Associate Professor, Black and Hispanic
Studies

Baruch College, City University of New
York

EVGENIJ HAPERSKIJ

Council on Hemispheric Affairs

ORLANDO HERNÁNDEZ PASCUAL

Writer, Poet, Researcher, Art Historian,
Art Critic, Havana, Cuba

Member, Unión de Escritores y Artistas
de Cuba (UNEAC) and International
Association of Art Critics (AICA–
Southern Caribbean)

RAFAEL M. HERNÁNDEZ
RODRIGUEZ

Chief Editor

Temas. Ideología, Cultura, Sociedad

MARTA HERNÁNDEZ SALVÁN

Assistant Professor of Spanish, Department
of Hispanic Studies

University of California, Riverside

MAITÉ HERNÁNDEZ-LORENZO

Adjunct Professor, Instituto Superior de
Arte, Havana, Cuba

Member, Unión de Escritores y Artistas de
Cuba (UNEAC)

LINDA S. HOWE

Associate Professor of Spanish, Department
of Romance Languages

Wake Forest University

JORGE RENATO IBARRA GUITART

Assistant Researcher

Instituto de Historia de Cuba

GLENN JACOBS

Associate Professor of Sociology

University of Massachusetts-Boston

HÉCTOR JAIMES

Associate Professor, Department of Foreign
Languages and Literatures

North Carolina State University

GUILLERMO JIMÉNEZ SOLER

Lawyer, Historian

Unión de Escritores y Artistas de Cuba
(UNEAC); Member of Academia de la

Historia de Cuba

CATHERINE KRULL

Associate Dean, Faculty of Arts and Science

Queen's University, Canada

JENNIFER LAMBE

Department of History

Yale University

CARRIE LAMBERT-BEATTY

John L. Loeb Associate Professor of the
Humanities, Department of History of
Art and Architecture; Department of
Visual and Environmental Studies

Harvard University

SAUL LANDAU

Professor Emeritus

California State University, Pomona

ZOILA MERCEDES LAPIQUE BECALIS

Member, Academia de Historia de Cuba;
Unión de Escritores y Artistas de Cuba
(UNEAC)

Doctora Honora of Instituto Superior de
Arte

MARTA LESMES ALBIS

Researcher, Instituto de Literatura y
Lingüística "José Antonio Portuondo
Valdor"

Professor, Universidad de La Habana,
Havana, Cuba

JOHN M. LIPSKI

Department of Spanish, Italian, and
Portuguese

Pennsylvania State University

ANA M. LÓPEZ

Associate Provost, Office of Academic
Affairs; Director, Cuban and
Caribbean Studies Institute

Tulane University

FÉLIX JULIO ALFONSO LÓPEZ

Professor, Colegio Universitario San
Gerónimo de La Habana, Havana, Cuba

IRAIDA H. LOPEZ

Ramapo College of New Jersey

VIRGILIO LÓPEZ LEMUS

Poet, Essayist, Professor, Principal
Researcher, Senior Fellow

Academia de Ciencias de Cuba

JACQUELINE LOSS

Associate Professor, Department of Modern and Classical Languages

University of Connecticut

BONNIE ADORNO LUCERO

University of North Carolina at Chapel Hill

CARLOS M. LUIS

Retired Professor, St. John Vianney College Seminary

Art Critic, Arte al Día

WILLIAM LUIS

Gertrude Conaway Vanderbilt Chair in Spanish and Editor of Afro-Hispanic Review, Department of Spanish and Portuguese

Vanderbilt University

HUMBERTO MANDULEY LÓPEZ

Independent Scholar

Havana, Cuba

LILLIAN MANZOR

Associate Professor of Spanish; Director, Cuban Theater Digital Archive

University of Miami

INÉS MARÍA MARTIATU

Cultural Critic and Narrator

Havana, Cuba

JUAN A. MARTÍNEZ

Professor and Chair, Department of Art and Art History

Florida International University

URBANO MARTÍNEZ CARMENATE

Chairman of the Scientific Council of the Provincial Directorate of Culture

Museo Provincial Palacio de Junco, Matanzas, Cuba

FERNANDO MARTÍNEZ HEREDIA

Principal Researcher; Director General

Instituto Cubano de Investigación Cultural Juan Marinello, Havana, Cuba

LUIS MARTÍNEZ-FERNÁNDEZ

History Department

University of Central Florida

JORGE MARTURANO

Assistant Professor, Department of Spanish and Portuguese

University of California, Los Angeles

MARGARITA MATEO PALMER

Teacher, Consultant

Instituto Superior de Artes, Havana, Cuba

LUZ M. MENA

Assistant Professor, Women and Gender Studies

University of California, Davis

ROBERTO MÉNDEZ MARTÍNEZ

Member, Unión de Escritores y Artistas de Cuba (UNEAC)

Member, Academia Cubana de la Lengua

ADRIANA MÉNDEZ RODENAS

Professor, Department of Spanish and Portuguese

University of Iowa

ELIO MENÉNDEZ

Sportswriter

Havana, Cuba

JUAN MESA DÍAZ

Adjunct and Visiting Professor at Universities in Cuba, Canada, and Spain

Member, Unión de Escritores y Artistas de Cuba (UNEAC)

IVOR MILLER

Research Fellow, African Studies Center

Boston University

NANCY RAQUEL MIRABAL

Associate Professor, Latina/o Studies

San Francisco State University

NIVIA MONTENEGRO

Professor, Department of Romance Languages and Literatures

Pomona College

OSCAR MONTERO

Professor, Department of Languages and Literatures

Lehman College, City University of New York

HORTENSIA MONTERO MÉNDEZ

Curator of Cuban Art

Museo Nacional de Bellas Artes (MNBA), Havana, Cuba

DANNYS MONTES DE OCA MOREDA

Art Critic and Curator

Centro de Arte Contemporáneo Wifredo Lam and the Havana Biennial

MATÍAS MONTES HUIDOBRO

Professor Emeritus, Department of European Languages

University of Hawaii

INÉS MORALES

Florida International University

ESTEBAN MORALES DOMÍNGUEZ

Professor of Economics and Political Science, Universidad de La Habana, Havana, Cuba

Member, Unión de Escritores y Artistas de Cuba (UNEAC)

PEDRO MORALES-LÓPEZ

Professor, Universidad Pedagógica Nacional, Bogotá, Colombia

Member, Unión de Escritores y Artistas de Cuba (UNEAC), the Asociación Cultural Yoruba de Cuba, and the Asociación Colombiana para el Avance de la Ciencia

FRANCISCO MORÁN

Associate Professor of Spanish, Foreign Languages and Literatures

Southern Methodist University

NANCY MOREJÓN

Writer, Poet

Havana, Cuba

ISABEL MOYA RICHARD

Director

Editorial de la Mujer

MIRTA MUÑIZ EGEA

Professor, Universidad de La Habana; Member, Consejo Nacional de la Asociación Cubana de Comunicadores Sociales

Member, Sección de Radio y Televisión, Unión de Escritores y Artistas de Cuba (UNEAC)

ROBERT L. MUSE

Lawyer

Law Offices of Robert L. Muse

JOSHUA H. NADEL
Assistant Professor, Department of History
North Carolina Central University

CONSUELO NARANJO OROVIO
Researcher
Instituto de Historia, Consejo Superior de Investigaciones Científicas-Centro de Ciencias Humanas y Sociales-Antillas, Madrid, Spain

ROBERT C. NATHAN
Institute for the Study of the Americas
University of North Carolina at Chapel Hill

YOEL CORDOVÍ NÚÑEZ
Researcher
Instituto de Historia de Cuba

ILEANA OROZA
Lecturer, School of Communication
University of Miami

VÍCTOR JOAQUÍN ORTEGA IZQUIERDO
Writer and Journalist
President, Equipo Nacional de Historia del Deporte de Cuba
Member, Unión de Escritores y Artistas de Cuba (UNEAC); Unión de Periodistas de Cuba; Unión Nacional de Historiadores de Cuba

RICARDO L. ORTÍZ
Director of Graduate Studies; Associate Professor of U.S. Latino Literature and Culture, Department of English
Georgetown University

FRANK PADRÓN
Critic, Essayist, and Writer
Havana, Cuba

MELINA PAPPADEMOS
Assistant Professor of History & African American Studies
University of Connecticut, Storrs

SILVIA PEDRAZA
Department of Sociology and Program in American Culture
University of Michigan

LISANDRO PÉREZ
Professor and Chair, Department of Latin American and Latina/o Studies

John Jay College of Criminal Justice, City University of New York

ENRIQUE PÉREZ DÍAZ
Writer, Researcher, Editor in Chief
Havana, Cuba

GUSTAVO PÉREZ FIRMAT
David Feinson Professor of Humanities, Department of Latin American and Iberian Cultures
Columbia University

GRAZIELLA POGOLOTTI
President, Fundación Alejo Carpentier
General Counsel, Unión de Escritores y Artistas de Cuba (UNEAC)

ANTONIO JOSÉ PONTE
Writer, Vice Director
Diario de Cuba

OLGA SARINA PORTUONDO ZÚÑIGA
Professor, Universidad de Oriente
Historian, City of Santiago de Cuba

GERALD E. POYO
Professor and Chair, Department of History
St. Mary's University, San Antonio, Texas

SANTIAGO PRADO PÉREZ DE PEÑAMIL
Researcher and Television and Film Director
Televisión Cubana, Instituto Cubano de Radio y Televisión

PATRICIA PRICE
Associate Professor, International Relations
Florida International University, Miami

YOLANDA PRIETO
Professor Emerita, School of Social Science and Human Services
Ramapo College

ROLANDO PUJOL
Professional Photographer
Havana, Cuba

E. CARMEN RAMOS
Department of Art History
University of Chicago

ALBERTO RAMOS RUIZ
Festival Programmer, Festival Internacional del Nuevo Cine Latinoamericano de La Habana
Havana, Cuba

CARLOS EDUARDO REIG ROMERO
Independent Researcher, Havana, Cuba
Member, Unión de Escritores y Artistas de Cuba (UNEAC)

FRANCISCO REY ALFONSO
Historian of the Gran Teatro de La Habana
Havana, Cuba

DEAN LUIS REYES
Independent Scholar
Havana, Cuba

ARCHIBALD R. M. RITTER
Professor, Department of Economics and Norman Paterson School of International Affairs
Carleton University

PEDRO PABLO RODRÍGUEZ
Centro de Estudios Martianos de La Habana
Havana, Cuba

REINA MARÍA RODRÍGUEZ
Poet
Cuba

LAURA ROULET
Independent Scholar
Bethesda, Maryland

JORGE RUFFINELLI
Professor, Director of Department of Iberian and Latin American Cultures
Stanford University

ENRIQUE SAÍNZ
Senior Researcher
Academia Cubana de la Lengua

DAVID SARTORIUS
Assistant Professor, Department of History
University of Maryland

PAUL A. SCHROEDER RODRÍGUEZ
Professor and Chair, Department of Foreign Languages and Literatures
Northeastern Illinois University, Chicago

RICHARD SCHWEID
Independent Scholar
Barcelona, Spain

YESENIA SELIER
Center for Latin American and Caribbean Studies
New York University

ANA SERRA
Associate Professor of Spanish and Latin American Studies, Department of Language and Foreign Studies
American University

ESTER R. SHAPIRO
Associate Professor, Psychology Department
University of Massachusetts, Boston

NOHEMY SOLÓRZANO-THOMPSON
Assistant Professor of Spanish, Spanish Department
Whitman College

ARTURO SORHEGUI D'MARES
Historian
Havana, Cuba

GONZALO SORUCO
Associate Professor, School of Communication
University of Miami

ANN MARIE STOCK
Professor of Hispanic Studies and Film Studies, Department of Modern Languages and Literatures
College of William and Mary

K. LYNN STONER
Associate Professor, Department of History
Arizona State University

JEAN STUBBS
Professor, Institute for the Study of the Americas
University of London

NED SUBLETTE
Center for Postmambo Studies

MANUEL JORGE SUZARTE
Specialist, U.S.-Latin American Relations and Migratory Studies
Grupo de Estudios Cubanos; Unión de Escritores y Artistas de Cuba (UNEAC)

SUSAN THOMAS
Assistant Professor, School of Music
University of Georgia

ARACELI TINAJERO
Associate Professor
The City College of New York and the Graduate Center

MARÍA DE LOS ANGELES TORRES
Director and Professor, Latin American and Latino Studies
University of Illinois, Chicago

OMAR VALIÑO CEDRÉ
Director of the Cuban Theater Magazine Tablas

SARA VEGA MICHE
Specialist in Cuban Film and Posters
Cinemateca de Cuba

JOSÉ VEGA SUÑOL
Member, Unión de Escritores y Artistas de Cuba (UNEAC)
Holguín, Cuba

CARLOS VENEGAS FORNIAS
Instituto Cubano de Investigación Cultural Juan Marinello

Havana, Cuba

MARÍA DEL CARMEN VICTORI RAMOS
Independent Scholar
Miami, Florida

RACHEL WEISS
Professor, Department of Arts Administration and Policy
School of the Art Institute of Chicago

ALAN WEST-DURÁN
Associate Professor, Department of Languages, Literatures and Cultures
Northeastern University

ESTHER WHITFIELD
Assistant Professor of Comparative Literature, Department of Comparative Literature
Brown University

ROBERT WHITNEY
Associate Professor of History, Department of History
University of New Brunswick (Saint John)

THOMAS C. WRIGHT
Distinguished Professor, Department of History
University of Nevada, Las Vegas

OSCAR ZANETTI
Universidad de La Habana, Havana, Cuba
Member, Unión de Escritores y Artistas de Cuba (UNEAC); Academia de la Historia de Cuba

ROBERTO ZURBANO
Essayist, Editor, and Cultural Critic
Director, Fondo Editorial Casa de las Américas, Havana, Cuba

A

AFRO-CUBAN SPIRITUALITY IN THE ART OF MANUEL MENDIVE

Hortensia Montero Méndez

The integration of Afro-Cuban themes in the art of Manuel Mendive Hoyo with particular emphasis on two versions of his Los hijos del agua conversando con un pez.

Manuel Mendive Hoyo (b. 1944) was born in Luyanó, Havana, in a humble home where he received the Afro-Cuban Yoruba traditions, starting with its rhythms and songs in their native tongue. He graduated from the Academia San Alejandro in 1963, and in 1964 he held his first exhibition. His assemblages of discarded materials and carved wood reproduce the iconic symbols and aesthetic codes typical of the iconography of religious systems of African origin. Mendive appropriated the imagery, ceremonies, and symbols of the Yoruba pantheon to develop a creative process based on the rituals of Regla de Ocha (Santería), re-creating this mythological imaginary from a domestic perspective.

Natalia Bolívar notes that the Yoruba achieved the most important urban development in tropical Africa with a level of artistry unparalleled on the continent. In Cuba, they shaped the culture with their colorful religious beliefs. Their pantheon of deities known as *orishas* attracts many scholars and remains vital and influential to this day (Bolívar Aróstegui). With a seemingly primitive language that moves beyond the anecdotal thematically, technically, and in terms of resources and materials, Mendive uses the Yoruba iconographic tradition and ritual and reinforces his commitment to the religion. In doing so, he reclaims Cuban origins based on an expansive, holistic conception of national identity.

The works Mendive exhibited at Havana's Twenty-third Salón de Mayo (July 1967) show his interest in contextual relationships that expand the field of art, with a transgressive attitude toward conventional artistic traditions based on the syncretism of Caribbean, European, and African cultures and an artistic confrontation with the problems of the individual in a collectivist society. Mendive blends sculpture, dance, and body painting, together with theatrical resources—acting, gesturing, mimicking, music—to create living sculptures, an imaginary of man and nature, and an atmosphere that integrates the popular and the liturgical.

A self-referential artist whose conceptual discourse interrelates environment, tradition, and religious syncretism, Mendive reveals in his work an autochthonous edge within Cuban heritage. He reinvents the cultural habitat through suggestion and fable in the everyday lives of believers. Gods and mortals, real and unreal beings, coexist in his work. They are dreamlike visions of an allegorical universe of mythical interconnection and fertility among humans, flora, and fauna. Mendive defines crucial aspects of Cuban cultural identity, based on a humanistic cosmogony that incorporates human feeling. He is fascinated by his ancestral culture's power of synthesis and attracted by the poetic evocation of its spirits and the energy transmitted by nature. He creates powerful structures that reflect a transcultured heritage of African origins and expresses his vision through simple and direct language.

Mendive focuses on the connection between water as a source of life and as a mediator of broad symbolic connotations. The recurring image of a rooster signifies masculinity, the spirit of Eros, and virility personified in Shangó, god of Regla de Ocha, or Ikú, a representation of death.

Los hijos del agua conversando con un pez (Children of the Water Conversing with a Fish, 2001) is an image of idealized love that juxtaposes memory and experience with imagination and reveals the magical-religious traditions in Mendive's artistic motifs. The work has a powerful emotional impact. It expresses the artist's worldview of communion with nature, religion, and art through an aesthetics focused on the connection between the individual and his natural

■ *See also*

Faith: Regla de Ocha and Ifá

Language: Lucumí

Visual Arts: Revolutionary Period

1

environment. The confluence of these factors (nature, religion, art) produces a metaphorical inspiration that is reinforced in the authenticity of a religious creed (Ocha or Santería) deeply rooted in the practice of the believer, a practice intertwined with the Afro-Cuban religious veneration characteristic of Cuba's island reality. The viewer is invited to see things differently, as Miguel Barnet explains: "His eyes, as through the *mpaka* conga, see in the everyday the raw material of the extraordinary" (Barnet 1987, p. 3). Mendive's work encourages the viewer to ponder the idea of coexistence and what is at risk for different types to inhabit the same space.

The painting itself evokes the ocean waves and Yemayá, on the surface and in the marine depths, all in shades of blue. Yemayá signifies the mother whose children are like the fish. The six figures (three with fans) on the surface look out at the viewer and are accompanied by seven ducks, Yemayá's favorite food. Just below the undulating surface there is a fish, and below the fish there are seven (the number of Yemayá) human figures in profile, three obviously female and one of them obviously pregnant, their arms extended out and upward, all looking or gesturing toward the fish with their mouths open. The figure below the fish is kneeling, as in an act of reverence. On the surface of the sea there are two small figures in small boats. The painting achieves a union of the natural (sea), animal (fish and duck), human, and divine worlds. As in other paintings by Mendive, the heads are disproportionately large, highlighting the importance of the head in the religious world of Ocha.

The sculpture of the same name, *Los hijos del agua conversando con un pez* (2002), made of wood, metal, and oils, depicts a human figure in a rowboat looking at and speaking with an enormous fish that is positioned on the side of the boat. They communicate in an expressive and contemplative code that eludes the viewer: The sculpture is simple, intimate, and mysterious. The boat is at sea, represented by the waves of metal from which hang chains—a powerful reference to the transatlantic slave trade as well as to Yemayá (one incarnation of Yemayá is Achabá, who wears a silver chain around her ankles). The chains also evoke Olokun, who is chained at the bottom of the sea by Olofi, causing Yemayá to rise to the surface. In this sculpture, Mendive achieves a type of mystic materialism.

These two works are connected to two other sculptures by Mendive that deal with Yemayá: *Hijo de Yemayá con caldero* (Son of Yemayá with Cauldron, 2002) and *Dentro de mí, los peces y las aguas tranquilas* (Within Me, the Fish and Calm Waters, 2002). The former depicts a blue-faced figure in profile with a duck on its head, as if Yemayá had seated herself atop it; where the stomach should be there is a cauldron that looks like a *nganga* (a ritual metal pot that contains magical items and substances). Here Mendive takes the spiritual aspect of the head and unites it with

■ *See also*

Diasporas: Cubans Abroad, Post-1959

Visual Arts: Revolutionary Period

the body. The second sculpture is a dark blue reclining female with a duck on her head. Mendive highlights the figure's breasts and the arm covering her belly to evoke the *orisha* of motherhood and a mood of reverence, tranquility, and spirituality. The base of the sculpture is blue and encrusted with seashells. Myth and history, the natural and supernatural, all converge in these works.

Mendive's contribution to Cuban art reflects a sustained, methodical labor over the course of decades. The social impact of his work extends beyond the traditional setting of the gallery, reaching ever more widely through performance and popular participation, contributing to the international renown of Cuba's visual arts.

BIBLIOGRAPHY

Barnet, Miguel. *La pintura de Manuel Mendive. Para el ojo que mira.* Inaugural speech, Museo Nacional de Bellas Artes, Havana, 8 August 1987.

Bolívar Aróstegui, Natalia. *Los orishas en Cuba.* Havana: Ediciones Unión, 1990.

Morejón, Nancy. "Manuel Mendive y el azoro." *Para el ojo que mira.* Catalog. Havana: Museo Nacional, Palacio de Bellas Artes, 1987.

■

LA ANUNCIACIÓN (ANTONIA EIRIZ)

Alejandro Anreus

An expressionist painting by one of the leading artists to emerge in the 1960s.

Born in the Havana suburb of Juanelo, Antonia Eiriz (1929–1995) was apprenticed to a dressmaker at the age of thirteen. From 1953 to 1957, she attended the Academia de San Alejandro on a scholarship. While a student at the Academia, she had a son with the artist Manuel Vidal (b. 1929). Throughout the 1950s, she was close to the painter Guido Llinás (1923–2005) and the group Los Once, which introduced abstract expressionism to Cuban art. From 1960 to 1968, Eiriz produced a series of paintings, drawings, prints, and assemblages consisting of ugly, menacing figures; these critiqued established notions of Western culture and revolutionary Cuba. Her work, which can be defined broadly as neofigurative, had much in common with other work produced in Latin America in the 1960s, such as the art of the Otra Figuración group in Argentina, Jacobo Borges (b. 1931) in Venezuela, and the Nueva Presencia painters in Mexico. They all shared gestural and improvisational strategies as well as sources in film, photography, and mass-media advertising. Their vision of the world and society tended to be negative and critical.

The pessimistic view of society inherent in Eiriz's work was not well received by the Cuban government. In 1960 to 1961, her graphic work illustrated nine issues of the polemical literary weekly *Lunes de Revolución*. In 1964, Eiriz exhibited a large body of her work under the title *Pintura/Ensamblajes* (Painting/Assemblies) at the Galería de La Habana. This exhibition demonstrated the consolidation of her pictorial language, in which a tragic and dramatic intensity is expressed through the grotesque. By the end of 1968 Eiriz had stopped painting; the following year she resigned her job teaching at the Cubanacan art school and began to teach papier-mâché workshops to children and neighborhood groups.

In the early 1990s, she began to suffer from depression, and in 1993 she was given permission to visit her family in Miami, Florida. Shortly after arriving in Miami, she requested and was granted political asylum. After twenty-five years of not painting, she began again with great intensity in 1993, producing more than seventy-five works on canvas and paper during the next three years. Her new subjects reflected not only the turmoil she had left behind in Cuba, but the more intolerant and sinister aspects of exile in Miami. She died in Miami in 1995.

La Anunciación (The Annunciation) is Antonia Eiriz's best known and most reproduced work. Painted in 1964, the work hangs prominently in Cuba's Museo Nacional. Eiriz recalled the painting's genesis:

Guido Llinás was very important for me as a teacher. He would say to me, "You have to paint." One day he showed me a modern annunciation by a Mexican woman painter. It had a black angel. It occurred to me that I wanted to paint one also. I looked at other annunciations, by Leonardo. Giotto's work was very helpful in matters of color, the blues, the weeping angels in the Scrovegni chapel in Padua, Fra Angelico's work in matters of texture. I wanted to paint a modern annunciation. The figure of the woman is not classical, she is a popular figure. The sewing machine? Perhaps because I was a seamstress; I would sew children's clothes.

La anunciación (1964) by Antonia Eiriz (1929–1995). *La anunciación* (The Annunciation), an expressionist painting by Antonia Eiriz, dissects conventional notions of the blessedness of pregnancy and motherhood, replacing them with the daily struggle of working women and their fears of death and nothingness. COLECCIÓN MUSEO NACIONAL DE BELLAS ARTES, LA HABANA, CUBA

A Chilean painter, upon seeing this painting at the National Museum, told me that it was a portrait of my mother, but I did not paint it thinking of her, and in reality it looks like her.

Blanc p. 1

La Anunciación is a pictorial tour de force that depicts a skeletal angel of death accosting a pregnant woman who sits at her sewing machine. The angel is about to touch the woman's shoulder; the woman draws back into her chair and away from the angel. The angel wears a crude crown and has battered wings. The woman is dressed modestly. She sits in a chair that is heavy and worn, and the sewing machine is a 1940s Singer model. The surface of the entire painting is rough and thick. The angel of death is painted in dirty grays and browns, with red highlights on the face. The screaming face of the pregnant woman is a thick mask of black, gray, and white. The overall coloristic neutrality of the painting is anchored by the red table where the sewing machine sits. This work, like the rest of the artist's, subverts the tradition of the theme. Instead of the joy and grace of the annunciation, fear and death are depicted here.

The painting critiques the roles and conditions of women: pregnancy, motherhood, and backbreaking humble labor such as sewing. This is done within the context of a revolutionary society that in 1964 was struggling with machismo. *La Anunciación* also contains an autobiographical component: The woman looks like the artist's mother, and she is a seamstress and a single pregnant woman like Eiriz herself. In *La Anunciación* Eiriz dissects the conventional notions of the blessedness of pregnancy and the promised future happiness of motherhood, replacing them with the daily struggle of working women linked to fears of death and nothingness, all of which seems to draw into question the expected optimism of life in revolutionary Cuba.

Other works by Eiriz from the years 1960 to 1968 that were critical of Cuban life and customs include *El vaso de agua* (The Glass of Water, 1963), *Ni muertos* (Not Even Dead, 1963), *La muerte en pelota* (Death in the Baseball Game, 1966), and *Una tribuna para la paz democratica* (A Tribune for Democratic Peace, 1968).

BIBLIOGRAPHY

Anreus, Alejandro. "The Road to Dystopia: The Paintings of Antonia Eiriz." *Art Journal* 63, no. 3 (Autumn 2004): 4–17.

Blanc, Giulio V. Unpublished interview with Antonia Eiriz. First draft, 19 February 1994. Giulio V. Blanc papers, Archives of American Art, Smithsonian Institution, Washington, DC.

Martínez, Juan A. "Antonia Eiriz in Retrospect." *Antonia Eiriz: Tribute to a Legend*. Exhibition catalog. Fort Lauderdale, FL: Museum of Art, 1995.

THE APONTE REBELLION: 1811–1812

David Sartorius

A series of revolts by slaves and free people of color that challenged slavery and colonial rule.

The Aponte Rebellion refers to a series of revolts across Cuba led by slaves and free people of African descent in the early months of 1812. Unrest in Havana became identified with the free black carpenter José Antonio Aponte (c. 1750s/1760s–1812), and although there is no conclusive evidence that the various rebellions were related to each other or to Aponte, they collectively acquired the moniker bearing his name. Taken together, the uprisings constituted one of the largest and most visible threats to slavery and colonial rule in Cuba before the gradual movements toward slave emancipation and national independence that came many decades later. In the era of Latin American independence movements, the aftermath of the Haitian Revolution, and the Age of Revolution throughout the Atlantic world, the Aponte Rebellion made evident the potential for popular resistance to the political, legal, racial, and class stratification that accompanied Cuba's ascendancy as a slave society.

WAVES OF UNREST

The unfolding of the various episodes of the Aponte Rebellion reveals patterns of violence targeted at sugar plantations and the white authorities who ran them, followed by heightened public anxiety and countered by violent repression. As central as Aponte and the Havana rebellion became to the authorities' investigation and to the historical memory of the events, the revolts of 1812 began in eastern Cuba, starting in January on plantations outside Puerto Príncipe (later known as Camagüey). There, slaves on the Najasa estate burnt their owner's house and killed three white supervisors. Unrest spread to four other sugar plantations and prompted an armed response by the local militia, the Spanish army, and fearful citizens. The suppression of the rebellions was accompanied by news of rebels who had eluded the authorities and sought to incite unrest in the neighboring eastern cities of Holguín and Bayamo. Extensive surveillance and interrogations, indeed, uncovered two fugitives from Puerto Príncipe in the house of a free man of color in Bayamo, which suggests the movements' coordinated efforts. Mostly, government inquiries prompted by the example of Puerto Príncipe and by a fearful populace successfully unearthed and disabled plans for rebellions in Bayamo and Holguín.

By the time that these acts of resistance had been contained in the eastern part of the island, other

CHRONOLOGY OF EVENTS

1804: The Haitian Revolution ends with the creation of the Republic of Haiti.

1806: Sebastián Francisco de Miranda launches the Venezuelan independence movement.

1808: Napoleon conquers Spain.

1809: Several thousand refugees from Santo Domingo arrive in Cuba.

1810: Cuba's Junta Superior rejects the invitation from the Caracas Junta to join the revolt against Spain; suspected opponents to Spanish rule, including the free black carpenter José Antonio Aponte, expelled from militia.

1811: The Spanish government under Napoleon's brother, Joseph, abolishes slavery, but the Cuba government rejects the ban.

1812: January: Slave revolts in eastern Cuba.

1812: February: Rebellion spreads to Havana.

1812: March: José Antonio Aponte arrested and imprisoned in La Cabaña; the Cádiz Cortes issues the Constitution of 1812.

1812: 9 April: Aponte hanged and then beheaded, his head displayed in an iron cage in front of his Havana house. Hundreds more arrested through rest of year and 34 executed.

1817: Spain's King Ferdinand VII reintroduces slavery.

1886: Slavery abolished in Cuba.

rebellions began outside Havana. In the middle of March, a group of slaves and free people of color destroyed the Peñas-Altas estate and killed several white residents before continuing on to three neighboring plantations and burning cane fields. An armed response by the local white population, similar to the one in the east, overcame the insurgencies and sent rebels fleeing. The months that followed witnessed the apprehension, imprisonment, punishment, and execution of many individuals believed to have carried out the various crimes and acts of insubordination. Whether the uprisings around Havana had a clear link to those in Puerto Príncipe, Bayamo, or Holguín remains unclear, but authorities were quick to view them as a coordinated effort to threaten the stability of slavery and colonial rule in Cuba.

Foremost among the detained suspects was José Antonio Aponte, whom other individuals had identified as a leader in organizing the revolts. Aponte's personal history reveals the possibilities and limitations of free people of African descent in early nineteenth-century Cuba. Just as many other free men and women working in the skilled trades in Cuban cities, Aponte worked as a carpenter in Havana. But Aponte was also a teacher who maintained a small library in his house. He had been a captain in Havana's militia for free *morenos* (blacks), an institution in which his father and grandfather had also participated and a marker of status and mobility for many urban free men. In fact, Aponte had traveled beyond Cuba as a member of his regiment during the American Revolution, assisting in Spanish defensive maneuvers; however, he was discharged from the militia in 1810 based on suspicions of his involvement in an anticolonial conspiracy led by a white Freemason.

While evidence of his direct involvement in African-derived religious practices is obscure, some scholars believe that Aponte may have belonged to the Changó-Tedum, one of Havana's *cabildos de nación*, or fraternal societies of slaves and free people alike organized around African ethnic affiliations. Other individuals identified as leaders of the unrest, however, had clearly documented ties to *cabildos* in the various cities. These institutions had been central to planning resistance in Bayamo during festival days, when Catholic celebrations provided an opportunity to gather. During the planning of the Havana revolts, Aponte had hosted several meetings in his house, where he also had his carpentry shop. Several testimonies cited Aponte as the author of a declaration of independence from Spain in March that had been nailed to the palace of the captain general, Cuba's highest colonial authority, vowing to "vanquish the arrogance of our enemies" (Childs p. 156). Aponte was arrested in March 1812 and held at La Cabaña, a fortification across the bay from Havana's bustling center.

INVESTIGATING THE REBELLIONS

One of the central pieces of evidence found in the search of Aponte's house was a book of drawings that authorities used to piece together the possible origins of the insurgency. The symbolic richness of the book evinced the wide range of Aponte's knowledge and interests, even if its status as evidence of the ideological or logistical underpinnings of the unrest was never ascertained. Images of George Washington (1732–1799), Abyssinian kings, and the Spanish monarch Carlos III (1716–1788) added political depth to the descriptions of Aponte's house, which featured more politically provocative portraits of Haitian leaders Toussaint Louverture (c. 1743–1803), Jean-Jacques Dessalines (c. 1758–1806), Jean François (c. 1765–1805), and Henri Christophe (1767–1820).

Less than a decade after the conclusion of the Haitian Revolution, which ended slavery and colonial rule in the Caribbean's most profitable European colony, authorities were quick to interpret references to Haiti as challenges to political and social order. Scenes from Aponte's own life and those of his relatives appeared in the book of drawings, as well as renderings of streets and fortifications and schematic images of black soldiers defeating white ones. Aponte's book,

La Fortaleza de San Carlos de la Cabaña. The entrance to La Fortaleza de San Carlos de la Cabaña, an eighteenth-century Spanish fortress in Havana. Aponte was imprisoned in La Cabaña following his capture. © DANITA DELIMONT/ALAMY

known only through descriptions in the investigative record, became a focal point in the process of judging and punishing suspects, as the political ideas it indexed informed the lengthy interrogations of countless individuals. For Aponte himself, the book sealed his fate as the figure on whom government officials could easily lay blame. Two weeks after authorities searched Aponte's house, the presumed leader of the rebellion was hanged and beheaded on 9 April, and as an example to those who might seek to follow in his footsteps, his head was displayed in an iron cage in Havana.

Thirty-four individuals were executed as a result of the government's investigation of the uprisings that constituted the Aponte Rebellion. Hundreds of suspects were arrested, many of whom were tortured and whipped during their interrogations. This brutality clouds the historical record of the events, as testimony taken by slaves and free people during the investigation likely came in response to or with the threat of physical pain.

Yet common themes appeared in the information gathered by authorities—that cabildos provided crucial spaces for slaves and free people to gather and plan resistance and that the backgrounds of participants were remarkably diverse, including urban and rural inhabitants, African- and Cuban-born, and people of various African ethnic and linguistic affiliations. Executions and whippings of the accused were conspicuous public affairs, demonstrations of state authority calculated to calm the fearful white population and

deter other Cubans of African descent from planning more rebellions. Other suspects and prisoners were sent to Florida, where they served prison sentences. In addition to punishing those accused of organizing the rebellions, the government simultaneously rewarded those individuals who denounced the subversive activity. Town councils bought the freedom of helpful slaves, often funded by donations from local residents in appreciation for the swift suppression and punishment of the rebellions. Thus, the Spanish government attempted to persuade its African-descended subjects that continued loyalty to colonial rule could represent a more advantageous path than rebellion.

Explaining the various uprisings later known as the Aponte Rebellion continues to challenge scholars. The concerted efforts of colonial authorities were insufficient to destroy the travel and communication networks of slaves and free people of color that made planning an island-wide conspiracy a distinct possibility. Yet it remains unclear if the various uprisings were coordinated.

Several events may have catalyzed the resistance. The promulgation of a Spanish constitution in 1812 sparked rumors that the delegates to the parliament in Cádiz had agreed to declare slaves free. Other rumors variously cited the king of England, the king of the Kongo, and the so-called king of Haiti (likely a reference to Haitian emperor Henri Christophe) as the emancipating authorities. Indeed, the recent example of the Haitian Revolution may have offered inspiration to those slaves and free people who might have heard about it—perhaps from newly arrived refugees from the neighboring island. Interrogated suspects' identifying distant kings thus referred to recognized authorities far less immediate than slave owners or local officials.

Plotting the Aponte Rebellion along the timeline of the Age of Revolution raises questions about the influence of European political ideologies on the slave and free colored populations in Cuba. Certainly, ideas about slave emancipation and national sovereignty might have been comprehended through Enlightenment discourses of freedom and rights, but not necessarily so. The testimonies of individuals suspected of participation in the uprisings suggest that long-standing Spanish colonial institutions such as militias and cabildos, as well as royalist political idioms and the idealized image of a benevolent monarch, may have been as generative of rebellious sentiment as the revolutionary ideologies circulating throughout the Atlantic world. The overseas travels of figures such as Aponte and memories of Africa—re-created and reinterpreted by cultural institutions and practices in Cuba—offer evidence that slaves and free people of color were not isolated from political and ideological developments beyond the island.

AFTERMATH AND SIGNIFICANCE

The long-term effects of the Aponte Rebellion were varied. For slave owners and landowners eager to accelerate the pace of the slave trade and sugar production in Cuba, the fear instilled by the uprisings sent a powerful message about the potential for popular resistance by a rapidly changing slave population and a free population whose mobility and privileges were always conditional. For colonial officials, the rebellion prompted harsher measures of surveillance and social control for the African-descended population. Restrictions on travel, associational life, and public meetings for slaves and free people along with an increased Spanish military presence attempted to limit the potential for the Aponte Rebellion to repeat itself.

But African-descended Cubans were not the only inhabitants whose autonomy was compromised in the aftermath of the rebellion. As independence movements in mainland Spanish America dissolved ties between the colonies and their metropole, Cuban Creole elites, whose counterparts elsewhere often represented the vanguard of anticolonial sentiment, may have been less enthusiastic about the political and social instability that independence might bring. Many of them agreed that remaining under colonial rule offered the best opportunities for increased wealth through sugar production, with Spanish legal and military authority providing a check on the increased potential for resistance as African slaves arrived in Cuba in ever-greater numbers.

Yet challenges to Spanish rule and slavery continued, and the Aponte Rebellion remained a powerful symbol of the possibility of a coordinated popular movement. Officials who investigated the suspected conspiracy of slaves, free people of color, and British abolitionists of 1844 called *La Escalera* reviewed the official records of the Aponte Rebellion as a model for their own procedures. References to the Aponte Rebellion appeared in the 1839 masterpiece, *Cecilia Valdés*, by Cirilo Villaverde (1812–1894). Writers supportive of Cuban independence from Spain cited the rebellion as an example of early separatist sentiment, and intellectuals during the Cuban Revolution referred to the rebellion as they looked to the island's past for early examples of potentially radical transformations of Cuban society and politics.

BIBLIOGRAPHY

Childs, Matt D. *The 1812 Aponte Rebellion in Cuba and the Struggle against Atlantic Slavery.* Chapel Hill: University of North Carolina Press, 2006.

Franco, José Luciano. *La conspiración de Aponte.* Havana: Consejo Nacional de Cultura, Publicaciones del Archivo Nacional, 1963.

Franco, José Luciano. *Las conspiraciones de 1810 y 1812.* Havana: Editorial de Ciencias Sociales, 1977.

García Rodríguez, Gloria. *Conspiraciones y revueltas: La actividad política de los negros en Cuba (1790–1845).* Santiago, Cuba: Editorial Oriente, 2003.

Palmié, Stephan. "'For Reasons of History': José Antonio Aponte and His Libro de Pintures." In *Wizards and Scientists: Explorations in Afro-Cuban Modernity and Tradition.* Durham, NC: Duke University Press, 2002.

Yacou, Alain. "La conspiración de Aponte (1812)." *Historia y Sociedad* (Puerto Rico) 1 (1988): 39–58.

THE ART OF RENÉ PORTOCARRERO

Carlos M. Luis

One of Cuba's most prolific painters of the twentieth century.

René Portocarrero (1912–1985), born in the El Cerro neighborhood of Havana, was one of the most prolific of all Cuban painters, with close to 10,000 works attributed to him. His vast oeuvre is divided into overlapping periods in different media. Often the painter repeated themes portrayed in series such as *Interiores del Cerro*, which he started in 1943 and returned to in the 1960s. Portocarrero was first and foremost a colorist: By his own account, no color or combination of colors was foreign to him. He also frequently experimented with new forms of expression, surprising visitors to his studio. The result was a lavish variety of subjects that included interiors of Cuban mansions,

■ *See also*

Havana: Architectural Development and City Planning

The Orígenes Group and Journal

Visual Arts: Republican Period

landscapes, mythological beings, flowers, carnivals, and masks.

Portocarrero became an autodidact after abandoning his studies at the Academia San Alejandro. In 1934, he presented his first solo exhibition, a collection of drawings at the Lyceum in Havana. In 1937, he participated in El Estudio Libre de Pintura y Escultura founded by the painter Eduardo Abela (1889–1965) in order to create an independent studio dedicated to creative experimentation. During that period, he joined a circle of young intellectuals surrounding the great poet José Lezama Lima (1910–1976), and he eventually became Lezama Lima's collaborator and one of his closest friends. Portocarrero's poetry collection *Distante voz y signo* was published in *Verbum*, a magazine edited by Lezama Lima (three issues, 1937–1938). In 1939, a book of Portocarrero's drawings and text titled *El sueño* (The Dream) was published, demonstrating the poetic inclinations that constitute one of the most distinctive features of his work. The magazine *Espuela de Plata* (1939–1941), founded by Lezama Lima, the art critic Guy Pérez de Cisneros (1915–1953), and several others, became an important venue for poets and artists articulating a new voice in Cuba. Portocarrero was one of its most assiduous contributors, illustrating all its issues. Lezama Lima, in turn, wrote three seminal essays about Portocarrero's painting.

Between 1941 and 1943, following the trend of the new generation of Cuban painters, Portocarrero began to produce work intended to shape the Cuban identity. In 1943, an important year in the development of his art, he executed his murals in the church of the town of Bauta, near Havana, where his friend Angel Gaztelu (1914–2003) was the parish priest. In the same year, he participated in an important exhibition of Cuban art at the Museum of Modern Art in New York, organized by Alfred Barr Jr., and he began work on his celebrated series *Interiores del Cerro*.

In 1944, Lezama Lima and several other painters and poets founded the magazine *Orígenes*, which ran until 1956. Portocarrero joined its staff, illustrating a number of its covers. He also mounted an extensive exhibition of his works at the University of Havana. The following year, he traveled to the United States and opened an exhibition of his work, *Mitologías imaginarias*, in the Julian Levy Gallery in New York City. Over the next few years, he traveled to Haiti, France, Holland, England, and Italy, and he showed his work in group or solo shows in galleries in Washington, São Paulo, Paris, Sopot (Poland), and Havana. He continued to work on his various painting series, including *Los Brujos* (1944), *Arlequines* and *Tiros al Blanco* (1950), *Máscaras* (a portfolio with twelve lithographs, 1955), *Catedrales* (1956), *Color de Cuba* (1962), *Ciudades* (1962), *Retratos de Flora* (1966), *Figuras Ornamentadas* (1968), *Carnavales* (1970), *Transfiguración y Fuga* (1982), and many more. An important exception

to his work on series was the single large oil painting *Homenaje a Trinidad* (1951), as of 2010 in the collection of the Museo Nacional de Bellas Artes in Havana. During these years, he also illustrated several books written by his friends: *Trailer de sueños* (1947), by Enrique Labrador Ruiz (1902–1991); *La fijeza* (1947), by Lezama Lima; *Gradual de laúdes* (1955), by Angel Gaztelu; *Cuentos completos* (1962), by Onelio Jorge Cardozo (1914–1986); and *Paradiso* (1986), by Lezama Lima.

His seminal series *Los interiores del Cerro* marked a turning point from the depictions of peasants and Cuban landscapes, favored by the first wave of avantgarde painters, to urban representations of the Cuban national identity. Executed first in watercolors, then in oils, Portocarrero's series reflects the poetics of the group of intellectuals that came to be known as the *origenistas* (after the magazine *Orígenes*). Portocarrero and two other painters associated with the *origenistas*, Mariano Rodríguez (1912–1990) and Amelia Peláez (1896–1968), were heralded by Lezama Lima as the best interpreters of the Cuban ethos.

In 1947 another *origenista*, the poet Eliseo Diego (1920–1994) published a long poem, "En la calzada de Jesús del Monte," which mentions a number of decorative domestic objects also depicted in the *Interiores del Cerro* of Portocarrero, including the movable screens known as *mamparas*. Both Diego and Portocarrero evoke a sense of intimacy and nostalgia with their poetic depictions of these objects, thus establishing a link between the written word and the painted image. In addition, both of the Havana neighborhoods Jesús del Monte and El Cerro were known for their distinctive fin-de-siècle architecture. Portocarrero reproduced particular architectural features of his city in some of his series, embellishing them with a pointillist treatment reminiscent of the Byzantine mosaics. Series depicting the cathedrals and other features of Havana became in his hands poetical transformations of an architecture that represented a pictorial counterpart of the baroque style employed in the poetry of Lezama Lima. In that sense, both men departed from the national identity paradigms in order to create a utopian vision of the Cuban urban landscape.

The importance of René Portocarrero in the development of Cuban art is long established; his contribution to Latin American art is a matter for separate analysis. During his long career, Portocarrero created much work with a rich iconography that crossed the national borders of Cuba. The acknowledgment of this came when he received an award for the totality of his work presented at the São Paulo Biennial of 1963. This award recognized his accomplishments in creating works in a vast array of styles, while maintaining a poetical current that unified them. For this, Portocarrero has remained an undisputed master of his generation.

BIBLIOGRAPHY

Lezama Lima, José. "Homenaje a René Portocarrero." In *Obras Completas*, vol. 2. Madrid: Aguilar, 1977.

Lezama Lima, José. "René Portocarrero y su eudemonismo teológico." In *Obras Completas*, vol. 2. Madrid: Aguilar, 1977.

Pérez Cisneros, Guy. "Enlace de líneas en Portocarrero." *Espuela de Plata* (August 1941).

Pérez Cisneros, Guy. "Exposiciones: Lo Atlántico en Portocarrero." *Orígenes* 1 (Spring 1944).

Portocarrero, René. "Distante voz y signo." *Verbum* 1, no. 2 (1937).

Portocarrero, René. "Indicación." *Máscaras*. Havana: Alberto Ruiz de Villa, 1955.

Portocarrero, René. *Exposición Antológica, Museo Español de Arte Contemporáneo de Madrid*, December 1984–January 1985.

Pogolotti, Graziella, and Ramón Vázquez Díaz. *René Portocarrero*. Havana: Editorial Letras Cubanas, 1987.

AUTOBIOGRAPHY OF A SLAVE (JUAN FRANCISCO MANZANO)

William Luis

The first and only autobiography written by a slave in Spanish America.

The slave poet Juan Francisco Manzano (1797–1853) wrote his autobiography in 1835 at the request of Domingo del Monte (1804–1853), Cuba's most important literary critic at a time in which slaves were denied a formal education. Manzano, a house slave, taught himself to read and write by copying the letters that one of his masters, Don Nicolás de Cárdenas y Manzano, had discarded. He described the fluctuations of life under slavery, over which he had no control. He first narrates how his first mistress, Doña Beatriz de Justiz, treated him as if he were a white child; however, he reports that, after her death, a new mistress, the Marquesa de Prado Ameno, often punished him as a common slave for no apparent reason.

PURPOSES OF THE NARRATIVE

The autobiography had at least three intended readers: Domingo del Monte, who asked the slave to write about his experiences; the Marquesa de Prado Ameno, who often accused him of stealing and disobeying her; and the captain general, the maximum legal authority on the island, who was assigned to protect physically abused slaves. With this manuscript, the slave intended to provide his own testimony of the unjust punishments he suffered. At the end of his autobiography,

Manzano introduced the voice of a free black house servant to articulate the legal slavery discourse of the period (Luis 2007, p. 114). A friend of the Manzano family counseled the slave to flee the marquesa's abuse and present his case before the captain general. The reader assumes that Manzano was successful, since sometime after writing this text, he was employed by Don Tello de Mantilla and María de la Luz de Zayas. However, besides making a case for his innocence and integrity, Manzano also used the autobiography to showcase his skills and talents.

VERSIONS OF THE AUTOBIOGRAPHY

Though Manzano was indeed able to write about his life, there are different versions of his autobiography, each offering its own version of the events surrounding this unique individual. To make the autobiography clear to a broad reading public, Del Monte in 1839 asked Anselmo Suárez y Romero (1818–1878) to correct Manzano's manuscript. That same year Del Monte gave the British arbiter in Mixed Court, Richard Madden, an antislavery portfolio to present at the next meeting of the Anti-Slavery Society in London, which contained antislavery materials, including a version of Manzano's autobiography and poems. One year later, Madden translated the autobiography as *Life of the Negro Poet,* and with some of Manzano's poems, some of Madden's own compositions, and interviews with Del Monte, he published it in London as *Poems by a Slave in the Island of Cuba* (1840).

Though Suárez y Romero's corrected version circulated among the members of the Del Monte salon, this and Manzano's authored copy were lost. An original manuscript was not made available until one century later, when José Luciano Franco published *Autobiografía, cartas y versos de Juan Francisco Manzano* in 1937, transcribed from a copy handwritten by Manzano himself, now preserved at the Biblioteca Nacional José Martí in Havana. This manuscript shows that Manzano wrote with great difficulty; he made numerous grammatical and syntactic errors. But it also demonstrates the slave's courageous effort to accept, understand, and even master European culture and its system of writing.

Yet in a way, Manzano's autobiography is also an oral text, as it relies on mnemonic strategies associated with an oral tradition known to him and other slaves. Manzano wrote phonetically, without regard to standard orthography, and did not distinguish between homologous phonemes with different graphic representations, often confusing the *c* and *s*, *l* and *r*, *g* and *j*, and *v* and *b*, and omitting the silent letter *h*.

History of the Alterations Some scholars wonder whether Del Monte controlled Manzano's writing, whether Madden altered or embellished the autobiography, and whether the version published by Franco is an accurate reproduction of the manuscript housed in Havana's Biblioteca Nacional José Martí. These

■ *See also*

Literature: Nationalist and Reformist Literature, pre-1850

Literature: Poetry in the Colonial Period

Literature: Testimonial Literature

Race: Slavery in Cuba

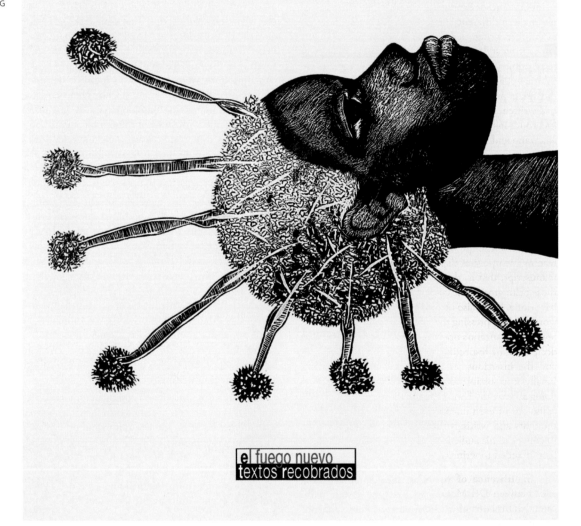

Juan Francisco Manzano
Autobiografía del esclavo poeta
y otros escritos

Edición, introducción y notas William Luis

el fuego nuevo
textos recobrados

questions were addressed in *Juan Francisco Manzano: Autobiografía de un esclavo y otros escritos* (2007). The study reproduces a manuscript found in the 1980s in the Beinecke Library at Yale University, handwritten by Nicolás Azcárate, which contains a copy of the version Súarez y Romero was asked to correct. This edition also transcribes more faithfully the manuscript housed in the Biblioteca, the same one Franco published.

An overview of the Manzano manuscript archived in the Biblioteca reveals a text written in an elegant calligraphy in accordance with the importance given to penmanship in that period; in the manuscript, Manzano states that he imitated Don Nicolás's handwriting. But even in this holograph there is no single Manzano manuscript. Instead, there is, first, a script in Manzano's handwriting with his own corrections. Some corrections are found within the sentence, as when Manzano copies a word incorrectly and replaces it with a similar word or expression. However, there are annotations in a different hand, revealing the intervention of another writer, perhaps a copyeditor with a different writing style and calligraphy, who may have been responsible for the interlineations. These and other findings suggest that in his 1937 publication, Franco did not reproduce accurately what Manzano himself had written. Instead, Franco revised the manuscript by incorporating the additions and cancellations of both Manzano and the copyeditor.

Manzano's original is thus a single manuscript and many manuscripts at the same time. It can be read as a palimpsest, except that the first writing, the one made by the poet's hand, has not been totally erased. His writing and the corrections and additions exist simultaneously and share the same time and space. Therefore, the manuscript can be read in multiple ways. One reading incorporates all of the writings contained in the manuscript, that is, those attributed to Manzano, and those belonging to the copyeditor, as Franco appears to have done. It can also be read by restoring the cancelled words and suppressing the interlineations, perhaps thus revealing Manzano's original intent. Likewise, it can be deciphered by respecting the corrections, the deletions, and the insertions, as the copyeditor had intended. Finally, it is possible to perceive Manzano's writings by doing away with all the changes, thus revealing an early conscious or even unconscious moment in Manzano's thoughts and writings that indicates what he wanted to convey to his audience and the manner in which he first intended to write it.

Significance of the Changes The correspondence between Del Monte and Suárez y Romero indicates that the latter often corrected Manzano's grammar. Though this is the manuscript that circulated among the members of the Del Monte literary circle, it is now possible also to determine the editorial changes that altered Manzano's narration of his life. A comparison of the Azcárate version of the autobiography and the manuscript at the Biblioteca shows how Suárez y Romero

eliminated many of the happy moments under slavery, rearranged the chronology of lived events, and shortened the narrative. This version coincides in both form and content with the one Madden translated. Manzano's Biblioteca original and Suárez y Romero's Azcárate version follow the same sequence of events until the passage that describes a sleepy Manzano, here working as the Marquesa de Prado Ameno's page, who inadvertently drops the lantern he is holding while riding on the back of the coach. The slave jumps off the moving carriage, retrieves it, and makes a valiant but failed effort to get back onto the horse-drawn vehicle. When Manzano arrives on foot to his mistress's property, the overseer punishes him severely. After this incident, the two manuscripts diverge. The original describes the following scenes: (1) The marquesa gives Manzano a coin for a beggar; Manzano exchanges it for one that Don Nicolás has given him but, when asked, the master does not recognize it as his. (2) Manzano visits his mother without authorization. (3) The marquesa accuses Manzano of stealing another coin; this one is trapped between the table boards, and the slave dislodges it when cleaning the table.

While the three mentioned scenes in the original can be interpreted as a ploy by Manzano, that is, that the slave is really attempting to deceive the marquesa—and the reader—and keep her money, the Suárez y Romero version underscores the brutal punishment and sufferings of the slave. It does not narrate the events mentioned above, as described in the original manuscript, but others of a more serious character: (1) Manzano is severely punished for picking a leaf from the geranium plant; the punishment is so severe that the slave needs six days to recover. (2) Manzano's mother attempts to buy her son's freedom, but the marquesa keeps the money and does not free Manzano. (3) Manzano is accused of stealing a capon; for this alleged offense, he is brutally beaten. Manzano tries to escape but is captured with the help of tracking dogs and injured in the process. He is summarily whipped twenty-five times and is subjected to nine consecutive days of punishment. Later, the overseer, Manuel Pipa, admits to having eaten the capon.

The changes highlighted here in the Suárez y Romero version alter appreciably Manzano's autobiographical text, his actions, and his life. According to the Suárez y Romero rendition, Manzano's life did not unfold as the slave indicates in his autobiography, but as it is reproduced in the corrected version. Though the alterations can be construed as an attempt to modify or embellish the author's life, Manzano is conscious that his autobiography does not accurately describe his life; he conveys this information to the reader in a footnote that underscores the oral nature of the autobiography. The note appears toward the end of the original manuscript, after Manzano enjoys the protection of Don Nicolás and his wife, Doña Teresa, and helps the sick, such as Don José María, but must abandon that lifestyle and return to work for the Marquesa de Prado Ameno. The note states that at this juncture the author remembers that the episode with the geranium happened in fact after his stay at the sugar mill, when his mother attempted to buy his freedom but died three months after. This note is omitted from the Suárez y Romero version.

Suárez y Romero corrected the autobiography to make it accessible to members of the Del Monte literary circle. He concentrated on events mentioned in Manzano's footnote, but instead of placing them where Manzano had suggested, that is, after the marquesa's request that Manzano return, he inserted them even earlier, before she gives the slave a coin for the beggar. In so doing, Suárez y Romero further modified the chronological order of the author's experiences. In the Suárez y Romero/Azcárate transcription, the incident with the geranium, the mother's attempt to buy her son's freedom, and the affair with the capon happen after the events that have here been described in the original: that is, the coin that Manzano was to give the beggar, the unauthorized visit to see his mother, and the second coin that was trapped in the table. It is not until after these unfortunate events that Suárez y Romero's rendition narrates moments of happiness, when the slave lives with Estorino, a friend of the marquesa, and with Don Nicolás.

The changes Suárez y Romero introduced in Manzano's autobiography are connected to the slave's life but also speak to other events unfolding during the period. Suárez y Romero's version heightens the slave's suffering and punishment and diminishes the mix of good and bad experiences under slavery. Instead, it groups together all of the difficult and cruel moments and augments the tragedy of the slave's life. While the narrative detailing the incident with the coins could be construed as a ploy that cast aspersions on Manzano's honesty, the Suárez y Romero version starts with the geranium episode and leaves no doubt that the slave was punished for no apparent reason, thus setting the tone for reading the other events. At the end of the autobiography, Manzano escapes to the city. In Suárez y Romero's version, Manzano finds momentary sanctuary with his benevolent masters and then appears to be permanently delivered from suffering by his escape to Havana, finally liberating himself from the yoke of the Marquesa de Prado Ameno. It is the Suárez y Romero rendition that makes Manzano's escape more urgent and necessary and takes the strongest possible antislavery stance.

Manzano wrote a second part of his autobiography, which Suárez y Romero gave to Ramón de Palma to copy. However, this continuation of Manzano's life was lost while in De Palma's possession and as of 2010 had not been found.

OTHER WRITINGS; LATER YEARS

One year after Manzano wrote his autobiography, he was invited to read his autobiographical poem "Treinta años" (Thirty Years) at one of Del Monte's literary

■ *See also*

Literature: Nonfiction in the Republican Period

Sugar: Republican Period

The Sugarmill (Manuel Moreno Fraginals)

sessions, before purchasing his freedom. More than 180 members of Havana's high society contributed to the subscription that secured Manzano's manumission. Manzano was a known poet; he published *Poesías líricas* (1821) and *Flores pasageras* (1830) and many other compositions in the magazines of the period and also wrote the play *Zafira* (1841). However, in 1844, both Manzano and Del Monte were accused of participating in the revolt by slaves and free blacks known as the Escalera (Ladder Conspiracy). Del Monte died in exile in Madrid in 1853. Manzano spent a year in prison before being exculpated; after that, he never wrote again. Despite Manzano's many accomplishments, few Cuban scholars—even in the early twenty-first century—are willing to see a slave poet as a central pillar of Cuba's national literature.

BIBLIOGRAPHY

Azougarh, Abdeslam, ed. *Juan Francisco Manzano: Esclavo poeta en la isla de Cuba.* Valencia, Spain: Episteme, 2000.

Burton, Gera C. *Ambivalente and the Postcolonial Subject: The Strategic Alliance of Juan Francisco Manzano and Richard Robert Madden.* New York: Peter Lang Publishing, 2004.

Franco, José Luciano, ed. *Autobiografía, cartas y versos de Juan Francisco Manzano.* Havana: Municipio de La Habana, 1937.

Franco, José Luciano, ed. *Obras.* Havana: Instituto Cubano del Libro, 1972.

Friol, Roberto. *Suite para Juan Francisco Manzano.* Havana: Editorial Arte y Literatura, 1977.

Luis, William. *Literary Bondage: Slavery in Cuban Narrative.* Austin: University of Texas Press, 1990.

Luis, William, ed. *Juan Francisco Manzano: Autobiografía del esclavo poeta y otros escritos.* Madrid: Iberoamericana, 2007.

Mullen, E. J., ed. *The Life and Poems of a Cuban Slave: Juan Francisco Manzano, 1797–1854.* Hamden, CT: Archon Books, 1981.

Schulman, Ivan, ed. *Autobiografía de un esclavo.* Madrid: Guardarrama, 1975.

AZÚCAR Y POBLACIÓN EN LAS ANTILLAS (RAMIRO GUERRA)

Carmen Almodóvar Muñoz

A highly significant comparative study that promoted debate over a basic problem in the Cuban economy.

Ramiro Guerra (1880–1970) is one of the most authoritative voices of twentieth-century Cuban historiography. His work has received much comment, not always favorable, but both his followers and his detractors acknowledge its importance.

In 1944 the Cuban writer Carlos Rafael Rodríguez published in *Cuadernos de historia habanera* (Reports on Havana History) the essay "El marxismo y la historia de Cuba" (Marxism and Cuban History), in which he analyzed liberal-leaning historians, most particularly Guerra. Rodríguez asserted that "if one does not take Ramiro Guerra into consideration, Cuba's new history will not be able to be written" (Rodríguez p. 29). Other Marxist intellectuals who agreed with this appraisal include José A. Portuondo, Pedro Deschamps, and Julio Le Riverend.

Regardless of his views on history, Guerra—an educator, historian, and journalist born in the little town of Batabanó, on the southern edge of Havana Province—did not go unnoticed by more mainstream scholars of national history, for he was a great pioneer who gave new life to Cuban historical studies during the 1920s. On par with Guerra were the eminent Cuban scholar Fernando Ortiz (1881–1969) and Emilio Roig (1889–1964), the historian of the city of Havana and author of *Historia de la Enmienda Platt* (History of the Platt Amendment, 1951). Their work opened up new paths into Cuban historiography.

ORIGINS OF THE WORK

Azúcar y población en las Antillas (Sugar and Population in the West Indies, 1971) is not crafted in the same way as Guerra's other works—*Historia de la nación Cubana* (History of the Cuban Nation, 1921–1925), *Manual de historia de Cuba* (Manual of Cuban History, 1938), and *Guerra de los diez años* (The Ten Years' War, 1950–1952)—all of which are required reading for research on colonial Cuba. It is the journalist Guerra, whose dynamic articles draw the reader in, offering new information with elegance and precision, that comes to the fore in the anthological *Azúcar y población en las Antillas*.

The long-standing conservative newspaper *Diario de la Marina* had the support of Spanish business and industry and, generally speaking, enjoyed great prestige for its contributions from noted Cuban intellectuals. During the 1920s, under the management of José Ignacio Rivero (1895–1944), *Diario de la Marina* included a literary supplement edited by José Antonio Fernández de Castro (1887–1951), who promoted the literature of the movement known as *vanguardism*. Emilio Ballagas (1908–1954), Alejo Carpentier (1904–1980), Nicolás Guillén (1902–1989), Miguel Navarro Luna (1894–1966), José Zacarías Tallet (1893–1989), Félix Pita Rodríguez (1909–1990), José Carlos Mariátegui (1894–1930), and other representatives of Cuban and Spanish American literary avant-garde movements all wrote for the newspaper's *Suplemento Literario Dominical* (Sunday Literary Supplement).

The articles that led to *Azúcar y población en las Antillas* originally appeared in the *Diario de la Marina* from May through August 1927. Initially, Guerra did not plan to collect these critical articles into a book; the

Ramiro Guerra (1880–1970). In *Azúcar y población en las Antillas* (1927), Ramiro Guerra analyzes the destructive activity of sugar estates in the West Indies. COURTESY OF THE CUBAN HERITAGE COLLECTION, UNIVERSITY OF MIAMI LIBRARIES, CORAL GABLES, FLORIDA

idea emerged as he went along. He put up the money to produce the first edition in 1927. The influential publishing house Cultural S.A. printed it in 1935 and undertook a new edition in 1944; both those editions include a prologue, footnotes, and epilogue by the author. It was reprinted in 1961 by Editorial Lex, with an appendix by José Antonio Guerra Debén on the sugar industry's recent socioeconomic evolution, and republished in 1970 by Ciencias Sociales, with an introduction by Manuel Moreno Fraginals, author of the controversial *El Ingenio* (1964). In the early 2000s, *Azúcar y población en las Antillas* continued to be reprinted because it contains a wealth of firsthand information on an important theme in Cuba's economic history.

To fully understand its influence, *Azúcar y población en las Antillas* must be evaluated within the historical context in which it originated. The new Cuban Republic was badly affected by the economic crises that began to emerge in 1920. It also was wrestling with internal political conflicts and near total dependence on the U.S. government, to which it was bound by signed agreements.

When Gerardo Machado became president of the Republic in 1925, he indicated that he would govern with an iron hand and preclude attempts to create an environment conducive to socioeconomic change. The Cuban middle classes watched with apprehension the increasing U.S. encroachment, which they saw as deleterious to their interests. U.S. expansion into the sugar industry had reached completion, and all the harmful features of a plantation economy, which Fraginals had described in his 1970 introduction to *Azúcar y población en las Antillas*, were evident. The voices of the Thirties Generation that denounced the leadership of Machado had reached beyond the university campuses. In this atmosphere, Guerra believed that the results of his research would be useful to the country, and he gave himself passionately to the project, but he did not foresee that it would become a formidable weapon of war for many of his fellow citizens.

CONSEQUENCES OF THE *LATIFUNDIO*

In *Azúcar y población*, a comparative study of Cuba and the British colony Barbados, Guerra analyzes the Cuban sugar industry phenomenon, which had become an integral element of plantation policy in the Caribbean, and establishes the differences between the two nations' processes of sugar industry expansion. The fundamental problem of the Cuban economy is analyzed in detail in *Azúcar y población* using historical data and contemporary circumstances linked to the international experience of imperialist domination. The student leader Julio A. Mella (1903–1929), who founded the Liga Antiimperialista de las Américas (Anti-Imperialist League of the Americas), contributed to the dissemination of this debate.

Guerra supplemented his comparative study with the works of other researchers published during the 1920s in order to present a more complete view of the evolution of the *latifundios* (large estates) at the core of the plantation industry. In particular, he consulted Charles S. Higham's *The Development of the Leeward Islands under the Restoration, 1660–1668* (1921), James A. Williamson's *The Caribbean Islands under the Proprietary Patents* (1926), Vincent T. Harlow's *Colonising Expeditions to the West Indies and Guiana, 1623–1667* (1925), and William Law Mathieson's *British Slavery and Its Abolition: 1823–1838* (1926).

Guerra focused his attention on the large estate, concentrating on a set of factors related to the futility of the fight waged by the large Cuban sugar estate against the U.S. socioeconomic organization. He reflected intelligently on Cuba's serious problems related to the ownership of land—such as the disappearance of independent rural landowners—and the difficulties faced by the mass of workers paid absurdly low wages. He stressed that low-cost imported labor was destructive to small- and mid-sized land ownership.

The results of his exhaustive research alarmed him, and he felt obligated to warn Cuban society of the threat hanging over the nation. The predominance of large properties in the Cuban countryside, the destruction of colonies as a social sector, the immediate impoverishment of the rural population, and the long-term impoverishment of the entire country led Guerra to sound the alarm in Cuba. *Azúcar y población* put an end to the conspiracy of silence that protected the large sugar estate and its consequences,

as the author—prompted by an intense patriotic nationalism—put the controversial issues of the *latifundios* in the dock.

Although the book lacks cohesion in places, that does not detract from the work's merits when considered in its entirety. *Azúcar y población* admirably summarizes the destructive activity of the sugar estates in the West Indies, the historical process of appropriation and division of Cuban land, the development of the island's big sugar estates, their socioeconomic effects, and their helplessness in the face of foreign competitors. Guerra also proposes a national plan of action against the latifundios.

RECEPTION

Raúl Roa, author of the influential *Bufa subversiva* (Subversive Farce, 1935), correctly asserted in 1950 that *Azúcar y población* had contributed to "the formation of the nationalist consciousness that characterized the popular movement, which attempted—with some success—to transform the foundations of the Cuban economy" (Roa p. 159). Because of his peasant origins and because he was a teacher rather than a pedagogue or scholar, Guerra was the right person to undertake a scientific study of the roots of the national historical process. Cuba's tragedy—the management of its national wealth by foreign interests—took on a new dimension through Guerra's voice, which laid bare the nation's anguish at a momentous time.

Guerra's warning did not fall on receptive ears among the nation's middle-class landowners, but it was much welcomed by the more radical elements in the country's political opposition. Once the issue had been raised, it captured the attention of intellectuals and particularly the members of the Thirties Generation: Julio A. Mella (1903–1929), Rubén Martínez Villena (1899–1934), and Pablo de la Torriente Brau (1901–1936) all responded with writings of their own.

Since *Azúcar y población* first appeared in Cuban bookstores much of the information it contains has been updated or rewritten with greater precision, based on new research conclusions. Though one may not agree with some of Guerra's interpretations or conclusions, the long-term value of the work cannot be denied. In *Azúcar y población* Guerra subscribes to a line of thought—initiated by José Martí and continued by other historians—that defends economic independence as the indispensable basis of political independence. *Azúcar y población* is one of Guerra's most significant works because of the crucial issues he addresses and because he brought it to the public at an opportune time.

BIBLIOGRAPHY

Almodóvar Muñoz, Carmen. *Antología crítica de la historiografía Cubana*. Havana: Editorial Pueblo y Educación, 1989.

Deschamps, Pedro. "Ramiro Guerra: Maestro e historiador." *Gaceta de Cuba* (December 1970): 1–6.

Guerra, Ramiro. *Azúcar y población en las Antillas.* Havana: Editorial Ciencias Sociales, 1970.

Le Riverend, Julio. "Ramiro Guerra: Recuento y significación." *Revista de la Biblioteca Nacional José Martí* (January 1980): 113–126.

Piqueras, José Antonio. "Introducción." In *Diez nuevas miradas de historia de Cuba*, edited by José Antonio Piqueras. Castelló de la Plana, Spain: Universitat Jaume I [James I University], 1998.

Roa, Raúl. *Guerra de los diez años en su viento sur.* Havana: Editorial Selecta, 1953.

Rodríguez, Carlos Rafael. "El marxismo y la historia de Cuba." In *Letra con Filo.* Havana: Editora Política, 1987.

B

See also

Governance and Contestation: Colonial Period

Spain's "Discovery" of Cuba: 1492

Ten Years' War: 1868–1878

BARACOA

Jorge Renato Ibarra Guitart

The history of the town of Baracoa.

Baracoa, located near the easternmost part of Cuba, was one of the landing sites in Cuba of explorer Christopher Columbus's first voyage in 1492. Nearly twenty years later, it became the first Spanish colonial settlement founded in Cuba. According to the census of 2002, Baracoa had 81,256 inhabitants, predominantly mestizo, a mix of Spanish, French, native, and African peoples.

GEOGRAPHY AND DEMOGRAPHY

Baracoa's bay is surrounded by mountains, with El Yunque being the tallest in the region. This natural barrier has helped the area to retain its pristine natural environment, which is marked by palm trees, lush vegetation, and beaches, in addition to the rivers Miel, Duaba, Yumurí, and Toa. Located here is the Alejandro de Humboldt National Park, named for the German explorer Alexander von Humboldt (1769–1859) who studied the island in the early 1800s.

Before the arrival of Christopher Columbus, the natives who populated the Baracoa region had the highest production levels on the island and the largest population demographic. Ethnic Taínos eventually dominated the area, displacing the Siboneyes to the west, although there were some instances of ethnic mixing. These tribes were skillful in agriculture, pottery, and stone polishing. Some 333 archeological sites have been discovered, of which 271 have been identified as ethnic Taínos. These aborigines, like others in the Caribbean region, based their diet on the cassava root, or yucca. These communities lived under the authority of a leader or chief. The hierarchy was matriarchal, with inheritance passing through the female line (García p. 21).

SPANISH CONQUEST, INDIGENOUS RESISTANCE

Columbus arrived at what would become the site of Baracoa on 27 November 1492. He noted the relatively high population and suggested the Spanish begin a settlement there. Columbus erected a cross at the entrance of the port; it was named La Cruz de Parra (The Cross of the Vine). The icon, rich in legends, can be found in the Church of Baracoa (Hartman). When Columbus set sail on 4 December, he recognized that he had been very lucky to find this promised fertile land abundant in fresh water and able to support agriculture (Pérez p. 148).

The conquest of Cuba began in the middle of 1510 by Spanish conquistador Diego Velázquez, who soon after founded the first Spanish settlement in Cuba at the site of Baracoa, named Nuestra Señora de la Asunción (Our Lady of the Assumption) by the Spanish. This colony, which was a small town, a capital, as well as an episcopate, apparently was founded at the end of 1510 or the beginning of 1511. The rugged geography made it difficult to use Baracoa as a seat of administration for the rest of the island, however. The Dominican priest, Father Bartolomé de las Casas, requested that it be dissolved because it was located "between the highest mountain ranges...and the angry seas." Bartolomé de las Casas was also concerned about the Spanish mistreatment of the indigenous population. The town was not abandoned, but as soon as Velázquez founded the town of Santiago de Cuba around 1515, the capital was moved there because of its favorable geographic location (Pichardo pp. 12–16). For centuries thereafter, Baracoa dedicated itself to livestock farming and subsistence agriculture.

Indigenous uprisings against Spanish rule in the area were initiated by Chief Hatuey, who was burned at the stake sometime close to the founding of Baracoa. Afterward, when Spanish troops in the area left to support the conquests of Mexico and Florida, the number of revolts increased. Documents directed to the Spanish Crown confirmed that "this land is lost... because there are many rebel Indians." Baracoa was set ablaze by insurgent Indians, who built forts in the mountains that survived for ten years under the

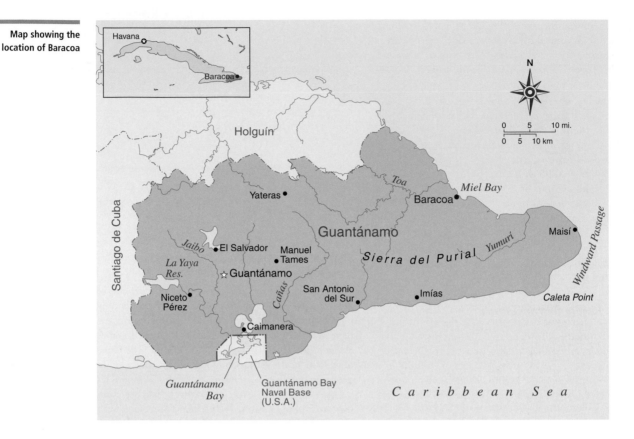

leadership of Chief Guamá until they were flattened by Spanish troops in 1532 (Ibarra pp. 17–20).

COMMERCIAL IMPORTANCE

In its early centuries, Baracoa was isolated from the principal lines of official commerce. This opened the way for harassment by pirates and corsairs and facilitated smuggling in the area. The first literary work in Cuba was produced, the epic poem "La Florida" (1602), by Fray Alonzo de Escobedo. It describes the author's sea voyage from Baracoa to Havana (Agencia Cubana de Noticias). Around the end of the seventeenth century, the town flourished as a support point for fleets of merchant ships that stopped over in Havana and needed to cross the Bahama Channel. Baracoa later experienced a population increase when French refugees fled to Baracoa from nearby Haiti during the Haitian Revolution in 1791.

One of the earliest shipments of bananas in the Americas left from Baracoa en route to the United States in 1804 (Reynolds p. 39). This export business marks the beginning of commercial development in the region. By the 1870s a fruit exportation group existed in the area. This consortium formed links with U.S. businesses that later engendered the much celebrated United Fruit Company (Di Giorgio p. 11). Banana commerce increased in the first years of the 1800s, but around the middle of the nineteenth century production shrank for several reasons. First, Cuban bananas competed in the global marketplace with bananas exported from other Latin American countries. Second, Cuban bananas were susceptible to invasion of plant diseases that affected the harvest. Third, Cuban farmers began to shift to the production of the more lucrative sugarcane crop. Similarly the coconut palm was affected by disease and diminished in importance compared to the coffee bean and cacao, cacao receiving more favorable prices (García pp. 120–177).

MILITARY IMPORTANCE

In the second quarter of the eighteenth century, the construction of military fortifications was ordered, and they were built quickly because of the threat of conflict with the English. Between 1739 and 1742, three important forts were built: Matachín, la Punta, and El Castillo de Seboruco. In 1807 the British prepared an attack on Baracoa, but Spain knew about it in advance and had troops waiting at the walls to meet the British with a barrage of fire. The attack was successfully repelled. By order of Queen María Cristina de Habsburgo y Lorena, the city of Baracoa received a coat of arms on 20 September 1838 (Castro 1977, pp. 48–49; De las Cuevas 1924, pp. 73–74).

Rebel forces in Baracoa struggled against Spanish colonialism into the nineteenth century. During the Ten Years' War (1868–1878), important battles for independence were led by Baracoan general José Policarpo Pineda Rustán, a subordinate of Supreme Commander Máximo Gómez (Castro pp. 74–75).

Rebels under the command of General Antonio Maceo took control of Baracoa in 1877, who in turn convincingly defeated the Spanish troops of the prince of the Royal House of Spain, Brigadier Francisco de Borbón (Cardosa 1977, p. 2).

Many important revolutionary expeditions made landings in the Baracoan region, such as those of Francisco Estrampes in 1854 and Limbano Sánchez in 1885. Both attempts were repulsed by Spanish counterattacks. However, the struggle for independence was revived in 1895 with the expeditions of José Martí and Máximo Gómez in Playitas and Antonio Maceo in Duaba, as well as those of Francisco Sánchez and Carlos Manuel de Céspedes y Quesada. The expedition of Calixto García at Maraví Beach in 1896 was also important. Baracoans fighting the Spanish under the leadership of Félix Ruenes supported all of these expeditions. A few days after Martí disembarked in Playitas, he wrote, "We saw ourselves in the arms of Félix Ruenes's Baracoan guerrillas.... I found myself for sure when I was among these intelligent Baracoans" (Vidal). On the other hand, the autonomist alternative to the Cuban colonial dilemma had a significant following, and its supporters won the local elections and maintained a certain hegemony that began to wane only with Maceo's landing at Baracoa (De las Cuevas 1924, pp. 99–100; Castro 1977, pp. 84–85).

REVOLUTIONARY CHANGE

The economic instability generated levels of poverty among the Baracoan peasants, who around 1945 found themselves, according to the description of Martín Gutiérrez, "in a great state of need and backwardness." These peasants lived crowded together in huts under poor hygienic conditions and suffered growing illiteracy rates (Gutiérrez 1945, pp. 79–83).

On 27 December 1958, forces from the Rebel Army's Second Eastern Front, who were fighting the regime of Fulgencio Batista, took the city of Baracoa (López 2008). When Batista was overthrown in 1959, a phase of socioeconomic transformation began. Baracoa benefitted from the revolutionary government's social programs, including literacy campaigns; rural medical assistance; agrarian land reforms, which redistributed land among workers; and the construction of La Farola, a road through the mountains that linked Baracoa with the rest of Cuba (Rodríguez). In the twenty-first century, Baracoa, the mecca of cocoa production in Cuba, had trouble maintaining high cocoa production due to low prices, the aging and decreasing numbers of cocoa farmers, old technology, lack of reliable means of transportation, and mismanagement of the land, structures, and labor (Lescaille).

BIBLIOGRAPHY

Agencia Cubana de Noticias. "Baracoa inspiro pasajes de la primera obra literaria cubana." *La Demajagua* (Granma province). 25 August 2010. Available from http://www.lademajagua.co.cu.

Cardosa Arias, Santiago. "La toma de Baracoa, audaz acción del General Antonio Maceo." *Granma*. 7 January 1977.

Castro Lores, José Ignacio. *Baracoa: Apuntes para su historia*. Havana: Editorial Arte y Literatura, 1977.

De las Cuevas, Ernesto. *Baracoa ante la historia*. Baracoa: La Crónica, 1924.

Di Giorgio, Robert, Ruth Teiser, and Joseph Di Giorgio. *The Giorgios from Fruit Merchants to Corporate Innovators*. Berkeley: Regional Oral History Office, Bancroft Library, University of California, Berkeley, 1986.

García, Alejandro. *La costa cubana del guineo: Una historia bananera*. Havana: Editorial de Ciencias Sociales, 2008.

García, Ivette. "Los pueblos originarios y la regionalidad histórica del extremo oriente de Cuba: ¿Capítulo cerrado o deuda de la historiografía y la cultura cubanas?" In *Nuevas voces... Viejos asuntos: Panorama de la reciente historiografía cubana*. Compiled by Ricardo Quiza. Havana: Editorial de Ciencias Sociales, 2005.

Gutiérrez, Martín. *Baracoa: La Primada y la postrera*. Havana: Editorial América, 1945.

Hartman, Alejandro. *Los días de Colón en Baracoa*. Costa el Azahar, Spain: Diputación Provincial de Turismo, 1995.

Ibarra Cuesta, Jorge. "Las grandes sublevaciones indias desde 1520 hasta 1540, y la abolición de las encomiendas." In *Aproximaciones a Clio*. Havana: Editorial Ciencias Sociales, 1979.

Lescaille Durand, Lisván. "¿La hora del cacao?" *Juventud Rebelde*. 25 June 2010. Available from http://www.juventudrebelde.cu.

López Castellanos, Richard. "Entrada del Ejército Rebelde en Baracoa." 27 December 2008. Available from http://www.radiobaracoa.cu.

Pérez Guzmán, Francisco. *La aventura cubana de Cristóbal Colón*. Havana: Editorial de Ciencias Sociales, 2006.

Pichardo, Hortensia. *La fundación de las primeras villas de la Isla de Cuba*. Havana: Editorial Ciencias Sociales, 1986.

Baracoa, Guantánamo Province. Baracoa's bay is surrounded by a mountainous barrier that has helped the area retain a pristine natural environment marked by palm trees, lush vegetation, and beaches. SVEN CREUTZMANN/GETTY IMAGES

Reynolds, Philip Keep. *The Banana: Its History, Cultivation, and Place among Staple Foods.* Cambridge, U.K.: Riverside Press, 1927.

Rodríguez Rivera, Alipio: *En el hocico del Caimán.* Havana: Ediciones Unión, 1985.

Vidal Martínez Utria, Andrés. "Baracoa en la visión política y militar de José Martí." 4 December 2008. Available from http://www.radiobaracoa.cu.

■ *See also*

Governance and Contestation: Colonial Period

Spain's "Discovery" of Cuba: 1492

Spanish-American-Cuban War: 1898

Ten Years' War: 1868–1878

BAYAMO

Ludín B. Fonseca García

History of the city of Bayamo.

The city of Bayamo is the capital of Granma province, located in the far southwest corner of Cuba. The area has a history of resistance to foreign invaders that extends back even to the sixteenth century, when the indigenous population fought with the Spanish conquistadors as they attempted to settle Bayamo in the early 1500s. This history continued as Bayamo residents defied Spanish colonial authorities in the seventeenth, eighteenth, and nineteenth centuries; fought for Cuba's independence toward the end of the nineteenth century; and conspired with Fidel Castro against the regime of Fulgencio Batista in the twentieth century. The city also became an important commercial trading center.

EARLY POLITICS, GOVERNMENT, AND CRIME

For over four centuries, Bayamo was the site of important events in the formation of Cuban national identity. In 1603, the pirate Gilberto Girón (d. 1604) captured Bishop Juan de las Cabezas Altamirano (1565–1615) on the Yara hacienda. Bayamo residents rescued the bishop, and the capture and decapitation of the smuggler provided the central theme for what many considered the first work of Cuban literature, the epic poem *Espejo de paciencia* (Mirror of Patience; 1608), by Silvestre de Balboa (1563–1649).

Bayamo's position on the coast made it an ideal location for smuggling. Spanish authorities in Havana attempted a crackdown on organized smuggling by launching an offensive that included trying suspects. In December 1603, captain general Pedro Valdés appointed Melchor Suárez de Poago to charge and transfer to Havana members of Bayamo's oligarchy involved in smuggling. Bayamo residents took control of all land and river routes to prevent the removal of the accused and appealed to Spanish king Philip III, demanding that they be tried locally. The legal process was eventually aborted, and the soldiers withdrew. Smuggling persisted as a way of life in Bayamo for nearly two centuries.

These were not the only events that demonstrated the role the people of Bayamo played in Cuban history.

In 1795, inspired by the ideas of the Enlightenment, Nicolás Morales (1745–1812), a free black man and owner of a small farm, launched an abortive pro-independence revolutionary effort. In 1810 Joaquín Infante (b. 1780) drew up a constitution for the island. But Bayamo resistance continued; indeed, since the seventeenth century, a tradition of resistance there to colonial political and administrative restrictions, of battle against the privateers and pirates, and of defiance of Crown regulations on the contraband trade became formative of Cuban character. In these attitudes can be found the beginnings of Cuban national identity.

POETRY

In the first half of the nineteenth century, various figures from Bayamo helped shape the transformation of the dominant schools of poetry. Juan Clemente Zenea (1832–1871), the foremost representative of the second generation of Romantics, restored the sense of *buen gusto* (good taste) to Cuban poetry. José Fornaris (1827–1890), founded *siboneísmo*, a movement that used poetry to defend the indigenous heritage as a component of Cuban culture. In 1851, Francisco Castillo Moreno (d. 1867), along with Fornaris and Carlos Manuel de Céspedes del Castillo (1819–1874), composed "La Bayamesa," considered by many to be the first Cuban song.

RELOCATION AND CONTRIBUTIONS OF BAYAMO RESIDENTS

Resistance to Spanish colonial authority resulted in hundreds of Bayamo residents being sent into exile by Spanish authorities during the eighteenth and nineteenth centuries. Others left the country in search of a better life and excelled in their new locations as political and cultural organizers. In Colombia, Manuel del Socorro Rodríguez (1758–1818) founded newspapers and other cultural institutions; he is recognized there as the father of Colombian journalism. Manuel Cedeño (1780–1821) left for Venezuela and fought alongside Simón Bolívar to emancipate South America, attaining the rank of major general. In Guatemala, José Joaquín Palma (1844–1911) wrote the words to that country's national anthem, and José María Izaguirre (1828–1905) founded and headed the Escuela Normal de Guatemala (Teacher Training College of Guatemala).

THE STRUGGLE FOR INDEPENDENCE

Cuba's last pro-independence movement began on 2 August 1867, when Francisco Vicente Aguilera (1821–1877), Francisco Maceo Osorio (1828–1873), and Pedro Figueredo Cisneros (1819–1870) founded the Comité Revolucionario de Bayamo (Revolutionary Committee of Bayamo). On 14 August 1867, Figueredo composed the lyrics and music of the "Himno patriótico cubano" (Cuban Patriotic Anthem), which came to be identified with the independence movement.

At the Demajagua sugar refinery on 10 October 1868, Céspedes del Castillo proclaimed Cuba's independence and freed his slaves, thus launching

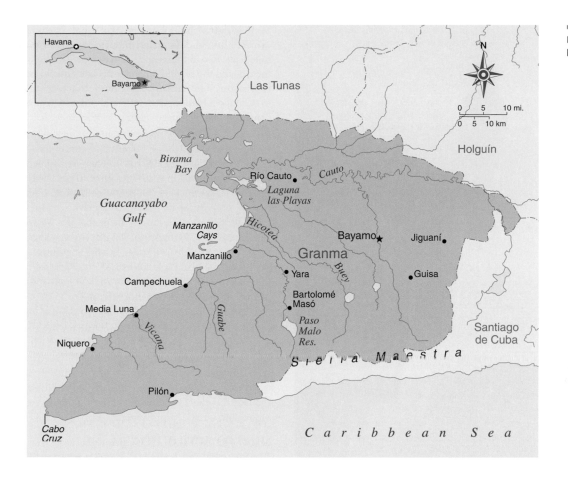

Map showing the location of Bayamo

what became the Ten Years' War. On 17 October, Spanish troops laid siege to Bayamo, and two days later, Céspedes established a provisional government in Bayamo, representative and democratic, in which both Spaniards and mulattoes could participate, alongside *criollos*. On 20 October, with the city in the hands of the pro-independence faction, Bayamo was declared the provisional capital of the uprising. Figueredo performed for the people assembled in the plaza of the Parroquial Mayor (Main Parish Church) the march he had composed months earlier, which became the Cuban national anthem. Late in 1868, several laws were enacted to improve the quality of life for the city's inhabitants, among them hygiene measures to ensure public health and establishment of free and mandatory elementary schools for all children, regardless of race. The Milicias Cívicas (Civic Militia) was organized to defend the city against Spanish troops. *El Cubano libre*, the first pro-independence newspaper, circulated freely. On 27 December 1868, Céspedes signed a decree that conditionally abolished slavery, setting the stage for total abolition, and orders were issued to seize blacks who were property of declared enemies of the uprising. The Ejército Libertador (Liberation Army) welcomed slaves freed by their owners at the same time that it increased the compensation given to property holders who freed them.

On 12 January 1869, after the pro-independence movement had been in power for eighty-two days, and faced with the imminent arrival of Spanish troops, the residents of Bayamo set fire to the city. They preferred to destroy the city and move to the countryside—where many would die of hunger, sickness, and repression by the Spanish—rather than live under the Spanish yoke. This act came to symbolize the Cuban struggle for freedom.

During the nineteenth century, the people of Bayamo fought for Cuban independence for thirty years, joining the Ejército Mambí, the guerrilla army in the Guerra Grande (Big War) (1868–1878) and the Guerra Chiquita (Small War) (1879–1880). On 24 February 1895, they responded to the call of José Martí (1853–1895) to join the anti-colonial struggle and headed for the countryside with the Mambí troops. On 28 April 1898, when Bayamo was captured by troops led by insurgent general Calixto García (1839–1898), it became the first Cuban city to be liberated from Spanish rule. Spain ceded control of all of Cuba later that year to the United States.

REPUBLIC OF CUBA ESTABLISHED

The United States governed Cuba as a protectorate until 20 May 1902, when the republic of Cuba was officially established. A series of weak Cuban governments, however, ensured that the United States

Statue Honoring Carlos Manuel de Céspedes (1819–1874). Bayamo native Carlos Manuel de Céspedes co-wrote one of Cuba's firsts songs "La Bayamesa." © IAN NELLIST/ ALAMY

Sierra Maestra. On 21 October 1957, eight youths were executed for standing against Batista. Bayamo played a significant role in this chapter of national liberation. In the city and the surrounding countryside, intense military actions were carried out by rebel detachments led by Captain Orlando Lara (1936–1966) and Comandante Camilo Cienfuegos (1932–1959).

On 1 January 1959, the Revolution toppled Batista's rule. On the night of 2 January, Castro arrived in Bayamo; from the City Hall balcony, he gave a speech to the people gathered in what later came to be called the Plaza de la Revolución. The people of Bayamo offered massive support for the measures decreed by the revolutionary government, among them the first Agrarian Reform Law (1959). In April 1961, the city sent a youth contingent to teach in the nation's literacy campaign. Well over 24,000 of Bayamo's 143,487 residents learned to read and write (Pérez Figueredo and Tornés Mendoza p. 55; Cuban Tribunal Superior Electoral p. 351).

During the first years of the Revolution, the economy of the region, based primarily on livestock, was strengthened with the improvement of pastures and the introduction of more productive breeds. At the same time, an effort unprecedented in the history of Bayamo was made to diversify agriculture and industry by the introduction of new farming techniques and genetic improvements.

MILITARY ACTION IN CUBA AND ELSEWHERE BY BAYAMO RESIDENTS

Thousands of people from Bayamo have participated in the struggles by the Cuban people to protect their sovereignty and in international missions—both civil and military—around the world. In April 1961, more than thirty people from Bayamo fought against invading CIA-backed Cuban exiles in Playa Girón during the Bay of Pigs invasion. In 1965, Ramón Alcolea Aguilera (b. 1933) became the first person from Bayamo to participate in a military mission outside Cuba when he traveled to the Congo as a member of the Patricio Lumumba Battalion. After 1975, many volunteers from Bayamo went to Angola to support its struggle for independence, which was being threatened by the government of South Africa.

BAYAMO IN THE LATE TWENTIETH AND EARLY TWENTY-FIRST CENTURY

The political-administrative division of 1976 recognized Bayamo as the capital of Granma province. The city was chosen because of its central location in the province and its historical leadership since the conquest and colonization of the island. Also in 1976, a new constitution was approved, and elections were held to choose members to the Asamblea Municipal del Poder Popular (People's Power Municipal Assembly). In the early twenty-first century, Bayamo had reached high levels of artistic and cultural development, due to the creation of new educational centers—among them, the Band School, the Fine Arts Academy, and the Professional

remained heavily involved in Cuba economically and politically. Discontent manifested itself in workers' strikes, which were violently repressed by the authorities. On 30 November 1930, the Communist Party of Bayamo was founded, and in September 1933, the first Workers and Peasants Soviet in the Americas was established at the Mabay sugar mill, an indication of the political maturity being attained in the region.

On 10 March 1952, Fulgencio Batista (1901–1973) staged a coup d'état in Cuba. On 25 July 1953, rebel leader Fidel Castro Ruz (b. 1926) arrived in Bayamo to finalize the details of an operation to be carried out the following day. The attack there on the Carlos Manuel de Céspedes barracks failed, but the support the rebels received from the people of Bayamo allowed many of them to escape execution by Batista's soldiers.

When Castro landed in Los Cayuelos, Niquero, on 2 December 1956, the residents of the city offered information and supplies to the rebel troops operating in the

Art School—which, along with other distinguished institutions, including the Casa de la Nacionalidad (Cuban Nationality House), serve the cultural needs of the municipality's more than 220,000 inhabitants.

BIBLIOGRAPHY

Cuban Tribunal Superior Electoral. *Censos de Población, Viviendas y Electoral. Informe General 1953*, Havana: P. Fernández y Cía, 1955.

Lacalle Zoquest, Enrique Orlando. *Cuatro siglos de historia de Bayamo*. Bayamo, Cuba: Editorial Bayamo, 2010.

Lago Vieito, Ángel, and José Yero Masdeu. *San Salvador de Bayamo: Sigue el misterio*. Bayamo, Cuba: Editorial Bayamo, 2002.

Lago Vieito, Ángel, Ángel Velásquez Callejas, Nelson Oliva Rodríguez, et al. *Bayamo en el crisol de la nacionalidad*. Bayamo, Cuba: Ediciones Bayamo, 1996.

Maceo Verdecia, José. *Bayamo*. Bayamo, Cuba: Editorial Bayamo, 2009.

Martínez Carbonell, Isolda. *Bayamo: Economía y dominación (1899–1902)*. Bayamo, Cuba: Editorial Bayamo, 2005.

Novel é Ibañez, Dionisio. *Memoria de los sucesos ocurridos en la insurrección que estalló en la ciudad de Bayamo en octubre de 1868*. Granada, Spain: Imprenta de la Viuda de Puchol, 1872.

Pérez Figueredo, Damiana, and Sonia Tornés Mendoza. *Bayamo: La Revolución en el poder, 1959–1965*. Bayamo, Cuba: Editorial Bayamo, 2006.

Reinaldo Ramos, Magdeline. *La mujer bayamesa*. Miami, FL: Ediciones Relámpago, 2010.

Riera Hernández, Mario. *Bayamo Político, 1898–1956*. Havana: Imprenta Modelo, 1957.

Rodríguez Expósito, Cesar. *Hatuey: El primer libertador de Cuba*. Havana: Editorial Cubanacán, 1944.

Seara Ricardo, Isabel. *Los comercios en Bayamo, 1899–1929*. Bayamo, Cuba: Editorial Bayamo, 2004.

Velázquez Callejas, Ángel. *La hacienda ganadera de Bayamo, 1800–1850*. Havana: Editorial de Ciencias Sociales, 1996.

BAY OF PIGS INVASION: 1961

Augusto C. García del Pino Chen

The failed U.S. attempt to overthrow the revolutionary government in Cuba in 1961.

During 1960, relations between Cuba and the United States worsened. The revolutionary laws applied by the Cuban government affected U.S. economic interests in Cuba, and the United States responded with punitive measures. After the failure of a series of muddled actions meant to overthrow the revolutionary government and influenced by Cold War considerations, in October 1960 President Dwight Eisenhower made the decision to implement a military invasion plan, to be carried out by forces made up of Cuban emigrés that the CIA had trained, outfitted, and advised.

The Bay of Pigs invasion (also known to Cubans as the Battle of Playa Girón for the beach on which much of the fighting took place) has been referred to as "the perfect failure"; it has been cited as an example of a U.S. government agency (the CIA) getting out of control and taking over the reins of the nation's foreign policy. The result profoundly affected President John F. Kennedy and triggered a new series of aggressions—and Cuban and Soviet countermeasures—that led to the missile crisis of October 1962.

The military objective of the Bay of Pigs invasion was to establish a beachhead by means of an amphibious operation with strong air support, set up a provisional government, and ask for direct intervention from the United States. The invaders did have good reason to believe they would get help from the U.S. armed forces (Johnson p. 68). Given its complexity and level of specialization, the plan for the invasion—Operation Pluto—was very likely drawn up by experts at the Pentagon, with participation by the CIA.

The Bahía de Cochinos (Bay of Pigs) was selected because it was located in an almost totally uninhabited region where there was a landing strip the invaders could use for their aircraft. In addition, marine conditions in this area are excellent; its coastline offers numerous beaches (Instituto Cubano de Hidrografía pp. 168 et seq.) that would facilitate landing operations.

The composition of the invasion force, known as Brigade 2506, was similar to that of a U.S. Marine regimental landing team, although it was smaller. The plan was to supplement this unit with additional elements that would complete its military capabilities; all told, with air and naval forces, some two thousand men took part in the invasion.

FORMATION OF THE INVASION FLEET

To form the invasion fleet, the CIA acquired two infantry landing craft, the *Blagar* and the *Barbara J.*, equipping them for standby; thirty-six aluminum boats; and two rubber rafts. The acquisition of six cargo ships, which were necessary for transporting personnel and equipment to the beaches, required a high level of secrecy; the selection was left to a shipping company, García Lines, which had its main office in New York, with branches in Louisiana and Texas. With its ships registered in Liberia, it made regular trips among the ports of the United States, Central America, and Havana, where it also had offices and substantial business (Archivo Nacional de Cuba, pp. 14 et seq.). One of its ships, the *Río Escondido*, was used on different occasions to take directors of anti-Revolution organizations out of Cuba. The CIA freighted the ships, paying $600 per day for each one, in addition to other expenses, and a guarantee of adequate naval coverage for the operation.

■ *See also*

Cuban Embargo

Cuban Missile Crisis: October 1962

Diasporas: The Politics of Exile in the Early 1960s

Governance and Contestation: The Cuban Revolution

Political Perspectives on Prisoners in Cuba

CHRONOLOGY OF EVENTS

1960: January: The CIA creates the Cuba Task Force.

1960: February: Cuba signs a trade agreement with the Soviet Union.

1960: March: President Dwight Eisenhower approves covert operations against Cuba aimed at overthrowing Castro.

1960: May: Cuba establishes diplomatic relations with the Soviet Union.

1960: June: Cuban exiles form the Frente Revolucionario Democrático Cubano (FRDC) to resist Fidel Castro; Cuba begins nationalizing U.S. oil companies operating in Cuba.

1960: July: U.S. Congress passes the Sugar Act, eliminating Cuba's sugar quota; Cuban government announces that it will nationalize all U.S. businesses.

1960: September: Fidel Castro speaks at the United Nations General Assembly in New York.

1960: October: U.S. begins economic embargo of Cuba; President Eisenhower orders invasion of Cuba by CIA-trained Cubans.

1961: January: U.S. breaks diplomatic relations with Cuba.

1961: 9 April: Anti-Castro forces concentrate at Puerto Cabezas, Nicaragua.

1961: 15 April: Cuban airfields bombed, destroying eight Cuban fighters.

1961: 17 April: Anti-Castro forces land at the Playa Girón, the Bay of Pigs.

1961: 19 April: Anti-Castro forces defeated.

1961: 5 May: U.S. National Security Council determines to work for the overthrow of Castro.

1961: November: President John Kennedy approves Operation Mongoose.

1962: December: Kennedy approves exchange of $53 million worth of medicines and baby food for 1,100 men captured at Bay of Pigs, meets with the survivors at the Orange Bowl in Miami.

1986: Last Bay of Pigs prisoners released.

The U.S. Navy provided landing craft for vehicles and personnel, as well as utility vessels. This completed the Naval Tactical Group. Later, the Joint Chiefs of Staff approved the use of a landing craft dock vessel for the operation, so that the landing craft could be moved into the Bay of Pigs.

In 1960 hundreds of Cuban exiles were recruited in the United States and Central America and sent to training camps in Guatemala, where they were integrated into the assault Brigade 2506. Aircraft to be used in the operation was supplied to the CIA by the Alabama National Guard (particularly the B-26 bombers). Cargo planes were employed before the Bay of Pigs struggle in air supply operations aiding contra revolutionary armed groups inside of Cuba.

Starting in early 1961, various outlets of the foreign press, mostly from the United States, published news about the training camps in Guatemala (Thomas p. 1304). That is why, at the main points along the southern coast where landings could be made, small garrisons of the National Revolutionary Militia were situated and provided with communications equipment. Their primary mission was to send out information about any military action as soon as it took place.

THE CROSSING

Cargo ships were concentrated in Puerto Cabezas, Nicaragua, on 9 April 1961. The final embarkation of provisions and brigade personnel started on 10 April, and the ships were armed with artillery. All these activities were completed by 12 April.

On 13 April, CIA officials handed over to the leadership of Brigade 2506 precise, updated information on Cuban defenses, and specified the missions included in Operation Pluto. Landing points were designated, in U.S. military fashion, Blue Beach, Red Beach, and Green Beach, which corresponded to Playa Girón, Playa Larga, and Caleta Redonda, respectively.

The departure of the ships started that same day and continued into the early hours of 14 April. The ships crossed by various routes that converged in the Cayman Islands, from which they proceeded to a point three miles south of Playa Girón, during the final hours of 16 April. U.S. Navy destroyers and submarines escorted the fleet—at a distance—the whole way. The dispersed pattern of navigation of the naval convoy concealed its nature, since it did not work as a group until it arrived in the vicinity of the landing area.

The landing vessel *San Marcos* moved the landing craft, along with their cargo, from Vieques, Puerto Rico, toward the Bahía de Cochinos. The secondary landing, which had to be carried out from the vessel named *La Playa*, some 50 kilometers east of Guantánamo in eastern Cuba, failed on two occasions because of a lack of decisiveness on the part of the commanding officer; he had postponed the landing until 19 April, to take place in the Casilda region, but that never transpired.

AIR-SEA ACTION

Air activities began on 15 April at 6 a.m. with simultaneous attacks on the San Antonio and Ciudad Libertad airfields, as well as the Santiago de Cuba civilian airport. As a result of the attack, eight Cuban planes were destroyed on the ground, some of which were inoperative (Carreras pp. 99 et seq.). For their part, the Cuban defenses brought down one attacking plane and damaged another four. The day after the bombardment, at the burial of the Cuban victims, Prime Minister and Commander-in-Chief Fidel Castro proclaimed the Revolution's socialist nature and declared a general state of alert and mobilization.

On 15 and 16 April, a Cuban counterintelligence operation, with popular participation, broke up the internal support plan for the invasion when several thousand people throughout the country who could have lent their support were arrested.

On 16 April, just before midnight, fighting took place on Playa Larga and Playa Girón when the National Revolutionary Militia clashed with landing forces. The militiamen on the beaches achieved their objective, alerting their commands and delaying the invaders. The leaders of Brigade 2506 decided to suspend the landing at Caleta Redonda, landing the additional fighters instead on Playa Girón as reinforcements. This failure to fulfill the plan of operation meant that the distant access points on the right (east) end of Playa Girón were not occupied by the invading forces and the area of beachhead was considerably reduced. Nevertheless, they were able to go in and occupy the town of Girón at 2:30 a.m.

On 17 April, at 5:30 a.m., only half the forces, with their support weapons, had landed at Playa Larga. With daylight approaching, the captain of the *Houston*, anticipating an attack by Cuban planes, asked for authorization to put out to sea and return during the night. This he received, but shortly thereafter he was ordered back to continue the landing. Meanwhile, two aircraft carriers, a helicopter carrier, several destroyers, and a landing ship were waiting in the vicinity of the Cayman Islands.

On 17 April at dawn, Castro, as leader of military operations, ordered the Revolutionary Air Force to initiate attacks against the cargo vessels. Meanwhile, a group of planes was sent to Cuba from Happy Valley in Puerto Cabezas, Nicaragua, to drop off the parachute battalion that was to occupy advantageous positions in Brigade 2506's zone of operations. The tactical thinking was that it would give the brigade a considerable advantage since "the government forces would have to advance toward the beaches along the only two narrow roads, crossing 10 kilometers of impassable swampland that would make the march the equivalent of the crossing of the Thermopylae Pass (Castro p. 292).

PARATROOP LANDINGS

The airborne operation was carried out at dawn; the paratroopers who landed in the area northeast of Girón took control of the junction where the San Blas highways came together. The company that landed in the area north of Playa Larga had barely touched down when it had to fight Militia Battalion 339, which prevented it from consolidating its positions and joining up with those invaders who had already seized the town, resulting in yet another failure in implementing Operation Pluto.

The Revolutionary Air Force's attacks began at dawn. In less than three hours, the *Houston* was badly burned and damaged and the *Río Escondido* sunk off Playa Girón. At the same time, the infantry landing craft *Barbara J.* suffered considerable damage.

Immediately afterward, the troopships *Atlantic* and *Caribe* withdrew at full steam. The standby ship *Blagar* and the utility landing craft also withdrew from the theater of operations.

Over the course of the day on 17 April, the invading forces lost several B-26s in battles with the Revolutionary Air Force and in mishaps. The Cuban ship *Baire*, a former U.S. sub chaser that was part of the Revolutionary Navy, was partially sunk after being attacked by the invading air force. During the night, a new attempt to bombard the air base at San Antonio de los Baños, in the vicinity of Havana, failed.

During operations, the infantry landing craft *Blagar* and the utility landing craft were situated 30 nautical miles south of Cuba, waiting to unload provisions for the ground forces. The *Atlantic* joined them at 1645 hours on 18 April and began the transfer of supplies and munitions to other boats, which it concluded at 2200 hours. The *Caribe*, whose crew refused to continue with the action, never returned. CIA headquarters ordered the *Blagar* to escort the utility landing craft up to Playa Girón, but its crew would agree to do so only under the protection of a U.S. destroyer. This operation was finally cancelled, and the plan to supply provisions to the brigade was not carried out.

On 17 April, three C-46 cargo planes took off from their Nicaraguan base. Their mission was to drop off equipment and supplies at the Girón airstrip—which was under the invaders' control—but they retreated when confronted by Cuban planes. Nevertheless, they were able to make some parachute supply drops at a later time. That same day, the Girón airstrip was bombed on two occasions by the Revolutionary Air Force, which carried out a second attack on

Landing points of the Bay of Pigs invaders. American-supported forces were reported to have invaded Cuba in April 1961 at the following sites: (1) southern Las Villas Province; (2) the Bahía de Cochinos (Bay of Pigs) area; (3) western Pinar del Río Province; (4) Baracoa; (5) northern Matanzas Province; (6) the Santiago area; and (7) the Isle of Pines. AP IMAGES

Bay of Pigs prisoners. Prisoners captured by revolutionary forces during the Bay of Pigs invasion stand in line on the Playa Girón in April 1961. Around 1,200 members of Brigade 2506 were taken prisoner. GETTY IMAGES

the *Houston*, which was half sunk. During the night, the Brigade 2506 pilots, who had lost nine bombers, were replaced by U.S. instructors, so that the missions scheduled for 19 April could be carried out.

THE END OF THE INVASION

On the morning of 19 April, Brigade 2506's air force lost control of its airspace once artillery fire from the Cuban Granma base and the Revolutionary Air Force brought down three of its B-26s, two of which were manned by American pilots. At approximately 3 p.m., a part of the Brigade 2506 forces found itself cornered in the town of Girón, under attack by artillery and aerial fire.

The U.S Navy destroyers *Eaton* and *Murray* received the order to give support to a re-embarkation operation; each of them moved to two thousand meters off the coastline (Fernández Álvarez p. 255), thus entering Cuban territorial waters. Confronted with a combined artillery and air assault by Cuban forces against the retreating boats of Brigade 2506, the destroyers moved out to sea. The Revolutionary Air Force, the artillery, and tanks continued to fire on the brigade forces, causing them to disperse.

On 19 April at 5:30 p.m., the Revolutionary National Army and Militia forces, after almost 65 hours of combat, retook the invaders' last positions, bringing the Battle of Playa Girón to an end.

After Brigade 2506 was defeated at Playa Girón and all operations were ended, the García Lines ships that had not been sunk were sold, and the company was dissolved. Some of the attacking aircraft

that survived the operation were handed over to the air force of General Anastasio Somoza, dictator of Nicaragua. Others continued to be used by the CIA for new military actions.

The defeat of Operation Pluto left the U.S. government in a difficult political situation. Some 114 members of Brigade 2506 had died in combat, as had 176 in the Revolutionary Armed Forces. Around 1,200 members of Brigade 2506 were taken prisoner. In March 1962, after several failed attempts to arrange a prisoner exchange, 1,179 of the prisoners were found guilty of treason and sentenced to 30 years in prison. In December 1962, 1,113 of them were freed in exchange for $53 million in food and medical aid financed by the U.S. government. The members of Brigade 2506 were welcomed back to Miami by President Kennedy himself.

On 21 April 1961, Kennedy took responsibility for the failed mission. The very next day he entrusted General Maxwell Taylor with an investigation into it (Political Directorate Ministerio del Interior pp. 38 et seq.) Some days later, he removed CIA administrators and some members of the Joint Chiefs of Staff from their posts.

Numerous reasons have been put forward for the failure of the invasion, including failure to carry out the full plan of operation, the loss of the *Houston* and the *Río Escondido*, the nonparticipation of the *Lake Charles* (a ship that did not arrive on time), the loss of air supremacy, the lack of coordination with the exiled leadership, and the lack of intelligence about the Cuban forces' actual military capabilities. Perhaps the most serious error was underestimating the Revolution's political support and its ability to resist an invasion.

In spite of the Taylor report and one that came later, President Kennedy, who wanted to show that he had not been weak when it came to confronting communism, authorized Operation Mongoose in November 1961. Its plans included sabotage, assassination attempts against Fidel Castro, and psychological warfare, all for the purpose of causing an uprising against the Cuban government. Although Playa Girón resulted in a military defeat for the United States, Kennedy's persistence in relation to Cuba paved the way for the October 1962 missile crisis.

BIBLIOGRAPHY

Archivo Nacional de Cuba. *Registro Mercantil*. Vol. 523. Libro de Sociedades.

Carreras Rolas, Enrique. *Por el dominio del aire: Memorias de un piloto de combate (1943–1988)*. Havana: Editora Política, 1995.

Castro, Fidel. *Cien horas con Fidel: Conversaciones con Ignacio Ramonet*. 2nd ed. Havana: Oficina de publicaciones del Estado, 2006.

Del Pino Díaz, Rafael. *Amanecer en Girón*. Havana: Dirección Política de las FAR, 1969.

Escalante Font, Fabián. *La contrarrevolución en los primeros años de la Revolución cubana*. Havana: Imagen Contemporánea, 2008.

Fernández Álvarez, José Ramón. "Playa Girón." In *Memorias de la Revolución*. Vol. 2, edited by Enrique Oltuski Ozacki, Héctor Rodríguez Llompart, and Eduardo Torres-Cuevas. Havana: Imagen Contemporánea, 2008.

Instituto Cubano de Hidrografía, Rolando Díaz Aztaraín, ed. *Derrotero de las costas de Cuba*. Vol. 2, *Región maritima del sur*. Havana: Editorial Científico-Técnica, 1989.

Johnson, Haynes. *The Bay of Pigs: The Leaders' Story of Brigade 2506*. New York: Norton, 1964.

Kornbluh, Peter, ed. *Bay of Pigs Declassified: The Secret CIA Report on the Invasion of Cuba*. New York: New Press, 1998.

Martínez Valverde, Carlos. "Desembarco." In *Enciclopedia general del mar*. 2nd ed. Vol. 3, edited by José M. Martínez-Hidalgo y Terán. Barcelona: Garriga, 1968.

Molina, Gabriel. *Diario de Girón*. Havana: Editora Política, 1983.

Morales Pérez, Salvador E. *Cuba en rebeldía: Del Moncada a Girón*. Morelia, Michoacan, Mexico: Instituto de Investigaciones Historicas-UMSNH, 2009.

Nixon, Richard M. *Six Crises*. Garden City, NY: Doubleday, 1962.

Nixon, Richard M. *Seis crisis*. Translated by Jesús de la Torre. Barcelona: G.P., 1967.

Pino Machado, Quintín. *La batalla de Girón: Razones para una victoria*. Havana: Editorial de Ciencias Sociales, 1983.

"Plan Pluto." Museo de la Revolución, Fondo de Archivo Playa Girón.

Political Directorate Ministerio del Interior. *Playa Girón: La gran conjura*. Havana: Editorial Capitán San Luis, 1991.

Prendes Quintana, Álvaro. *En el punto rojo de mi kolimador: Cronicas de un aviador*. Havana: Editorial Letras Cubanas, 1982.

Soto Valdespino, Juan J., ed. *Historia de una agresión*. 2nd ed. Havana: Ciencias Sociales, 1977.

Thomas, Hugh. *Cuba, or, The Pursuit of Freedom*. Updated ed. New York: Da Capo, 1998.

Wise, David, and Thomas B. Ross. *The Invisible Government*. New York: Random House, 1964.

Wise, David, and Thomas B. Ross. *El gobierno invisible*. Havana: Ediciones Venceremos, 1965.

Wyden, Peter. *The Bay of Pigs: The Untold Story*. New York: Simon and Schuster, 1979.

C

CAR CULTURE

Richard Schweid

The Cuban love affair with the automobile.

Between the end of the Second World War in 1945 and the Cuban Revolution in 1959, many Cubans subscribed to the U.S. model of middle-class success. Ownership of a Detroit-built automobile was an important sign of having achieved it. During those years credit was available to almost anyone with a steady job, and many Cubans took advantage of it. In 1957, over fourteen thousand new cars manufactured in the United States were sold in Cuba, and some two hundred thousand cars were registered on the island, according to a 1958 national vehicle census (reported in the magazine *El Automóvil de Cuba*).

Some fifty thousand of those same vehicles were still in use in 2010, although not a single spare part was shipped to Cuba from the United States between October 1960 and late 2010. The continued existence of those cars is even more surprising given that most of them were built using planned obsolescence engineering methods to assure they would need to be replaced after a few years.

Every Cuban over seven years of age knows a number of official revolutionary slogans, like *¡Patria o muerte!* (Fatherland or Death) or *¡Venceremos!* (We Shall Be Victorious). However, the real slogan of the Revolution during the following fifty years of scarcity has been *Hay que resolver*, which could be translated as "A solution has to be found." Nowhere has this make-do attitude been more rigorously applied than in keeping the cars running on Cuban streets and highways. The joke goes that the only original thing left on many of them is the serial number.

Among those Detroit-built cars still on the road are some that many younger North Americans have never even heard of, including Plymouth, Packard, Studebaker, and Nash Rambler. In contemporary North America, these extinct brands built in the heyday of Detroit's extravagantly designed vehicles would be treated like fine works of art—protected from the elements, pampered, polished, and treasured as collector's items. In Cuba, they are put to work on a daily basis, and hard work it is, too. Sometimes they serve as revenue producers for their owners who rent them out to tourists or for weddings or films. In many cases, they serve as collective taxis, crossing and re-crossing the deteriorated streets of Havana or Santiago de Cuba under a brutal sun. As few people have their own automobiles, car pooling is common, and people frequently approach strangers' cars at stoplights and ask for rides. The Detroit models are appreciated for their ample interior space. They may have enema-bag hoses for fuel lines, dishwashing detergent for brake fluid, gaskets cut from tin cans, and their high-octane engines modified to burn diesel, but they are still running, still able to carry people from one place to another.

For all their love of automobiles, Cubans have never built them on the island. The first cars in Havana, beginning in 1898, came from France, with names such as Rochet-Schneider, Panhard-Levassor, and De Dion-Bouton. U.S. manufacturers initially had trouble breaking into the market. An article in the December 1904 issue of *Motor Age* reported from Havana:

> There are a few Whites and some Oldsmobiles, but American machines generally are not in favor owing to the failure of some early samples, three of which by the way were owned by the United States ambassador [Herbert Squiers], who, despite his hard luck, is still intent on discovering a car on which he can depend. Demonstrations will be necessary before our cars can be marketed satisfactorily.

That changed for good a decade later, in 1913, when the first Model T Fords arrived in Cuba from Michigan. With dependable performance and reasonable prices—in 1916, a Model T cost $365 in

■ *See also*

Cuban Embargo

Havana: Urban and Social History in the Twentieth Century

The World and Cuba: U.S. Culture in Cuba

Vintage automobile in Trinidad, 2009. In 1957, more than 14,000 new cars manufactured in the United States were sold in Cuba, and 200,000 cars were registered on the island in 1958. Some 50,000 of those same vehicles registered in 1958 were still in use in 2010. PAUL PIEBINGA/ PHOTODISC/GETTY IMAGES

this century. . . . I think it has a moral influence because it's a means to add to a woman's independence, and it creates certain responsibilities that were completely unknown before."

For both men and women, driving in those years was more fraught with peril than in the early 2000s. In the country, asphalt highways were nonexistent, and city streets were in poor condition. An editorial in the monthly magazine *El Heraldo del Chauffeur* in March 1925 complained, "The individuals who have to use a car for their occupations know what it is to drive in Havana. The humble, plebian, democratic *fotingo* falls into potholes, bounces into them, sinks into their depths, occasionally to founder."

When Gerardo Machado (1871–1939) was elected Cuba's fifth president in 1925, he promised better highways, and by the time he left office in 1933, the Carretera Central (Central Highway) was completed, stretching 672 miles across the island from Pinar del Río in the west to Guantánamo Province in the east. Car sales dropped during the Second World War (1939–1945), when steel was diverted for military purposes, but at war's end, sales picked up again, and the streets of postwar Havana were as congested with makes and models from Detroit as any stateside city. Gabriel Míguez Deus opined in a May 1951 article in *El Automóvil de Cuba*: "Our beautiful city, Havana, is an immense garage, where the parking and driving of each automobile means resigned patience and finely honed skills, now that our principal avenues are congested with automobiles, buses, and trucks."

In 1958, 60 percent of adult Cubans were functionally illiterate, less than half of urban homes had indoor plumbing, and more than five thousand beggars worked the city streets daily. Havana also had the highest per capita sales of Cadillacs of any city in the world. The dealership was owned by Amadeo Barletta (1894–1975), who also owned a newspaper and a television station in Batista-era Havana. Cars, and the ancillary businesses that kept them on the road, generated a lot of business across the island, and many people in both Cuba and Detroit assumed that even after the Revolution toppled the rule of Fulgencio Batista (1901–1973) in January 1959, the new regime would not drastically alter automotive commerce on the island. After all, *los barbudos* (the bearded revolutionaries) appreciated a nice car as much as the next person. When fleeing Cubans left behind their cars, they were parceled out among the Revolution's chosen, with Fidel Castro claiming an Oldsmobile and Che Guevara a Chevrolet. However, a September 1959 speech by Castro, reported in *Revolución*, presaged otherwise: "The country must import what it needs in the way of basics, what it needs in the way of food . . . but the nation cannot afford the extravagance of importing Cadillacs or luxury items of any kind."

Havana—Ford soon became the leader in Cuban auto sales. The first models had three pedals, two for forward and one for reverse, and they were called Foot 'n Go, contracted in Spanish to *fotingo*, which is what all Model Ts were subsequently called. Havana's first taxi service was begun in 1914 by Ernesto Carricaburu with a fleet of ten Model Ts.

Slowly, Cubans adopted motorized transport, including trucks, buses, and tractors. By the 1930s, cars were in widespread use, among women as well as men. The first woman in Havana to have a driver's license received it in 1917, and by 1930, the island had over sixteen thousand registered vehicles and numerous female drivers. In April of that year, a young woman from Havana told *A.C.C.*, the monthly magazine of the Automobile Club of Cuba: "I think a woman who drives an auto has made a step forward in

By the end of 1960, Amadeo Barletta had decamped with his family to the Dominican Republic, and automotive commerce of any kind with the United States was nonexistent. Transport became a major concern for Cubans. Over the subsequent decades, cars from the Soviet bloc—Ladas, Skodas, Volgas, and Moskviches—supplemented the North American cars left on the island when the blockade went into effect. The Eastern-bloc wheels were given to party faithful, to members of the military, and to other deserving citizens, although they could not be bought or sold and belonged, ultimately, to the state. Many of the parts from these cars were modified for use in keeping the ever-dwindling fleet of Detroit machines on the road. Détente between East and West arrived under the hoods of Havana even while the Cold War raged.

European and Asian automakers are well-represented in Havana. Mercedes-Benz, Peugeot, Toyota, and Mitsubishi mostly sell cars to the state to be used by rental agencies, high-ranking party officials, or in various other ways. As of 2010, the number of cars registered in Cuba, like almost all statistics about quotidian life, is harder to find than a 1957 Edsel, but there is no doubt that an appetite and appreciation for four-wheeled vehicles remains alive and well.

BIBLIOGRAPHY

Castro Ruz, Fidel. "Comparencia de Fidel 'Ante La Prensa.'" *Revolución*, 19 September 1959.

"El Censo Nacional de Vehículos de 1958." *El Automóvil de Cuba*, June 1958, pp. 57–59.

"Cuban Automobile Trade Shows Marvelous Increase." *Motor Age*, 15 February 1906, p. 21.

"The Cuban Road Race." *Motor Age*, 29 December 1904, p. 3.

"La Habana se ofrece los ojos de las turistas como un enorme peligroso lugar de accidentes." *El Heraldo del Chauffeur*, March 1925, p. 24.

Míguez Deus, Gabriel. "Automovilismo en Cuba: Su Desarrollo y sus Asociaciones Imperfectas." *El Automóvil de Cuba*, July 1951, p. 149.

Pérez, Louis A., Jr. *On Becoming Cuban: Identity, Nationality, and Culture*. Chapel Hill: University of North Carolina Press, 1999.

Ramet, Simone. "Entrevista." *A.C.C.* [Automóvil Club de Cuba], April 1930.

Schweid, Richard. *Che's Chevrolet, Fidel's Oldsmobile*. Chapel Hill: University of North Carolina Press, 2004.

Classic cars in Cuba. American-made cars still on the road in Cuba include some that many North Americans have never heard of, such as Packard, Studebaker, and the Nash Rambler. The automobiles parked on this Cuban street include (left to right): a 1956 Plymouth sedan, a 1957 Chevrolet 210 station wagon, a 1951 Ford Crestliner, and a 1952 Chevrolet station wagon. © PAUL MANNIX

CECILIA VALDÉS (CIRILO VILLAVERDE)

Jossianna Arroyo-Martínez

The most important novel of nineteenth-century Cuba.

Cirilo Villaverde (1812–1894), author of the famous novel *Cecilia Valdés,* was born in the western province of Pinar del Río and grew up on a sugar plantation where his father was a physician. He moved to Havana, where he studied philosophy and law in the San Carlos seminary; later he abandoned his law career to dedicate himself to teaching, writing, and journalism. Between 1837 and 1847, he published his first short stories and short novels such as *Engañar con la verdad* (To Deceive with the Truth, 1838), *El espetón de oro* (The Golden Spear, 1838), and the first part of *Excursión a Vueltabajo* (Excursion to Vueltabajo), a project that he finished in 1842. His first romantic novel, *El espetón de oro,* was produced the first year he joined Domingo del Monte's *tertulia* (gathering), a literary salon of writers who assembled, first in the city of Matanzas and later in Havana, to read, write, and disseminate Cuban culture. Antonio Benítez Rojo (1988) described del Monte's *tertulia* as the most significant event in Cuban letters in the mid-nineteenth century. When Cuba was denied permission to open a Cuban academy of letters in 1834, del Monte's *tertulia* became one of the few places where writers could meet. Del Monte, who came from an aristocratic family that owned a sugar mill, was a reformist who believed in the gradual abolition of slavery. The *tertulia* was visited by Ramón de Palma (1812–1860), Félix Tanco y Bosmeniel (1797–1871), the black poet Juan Francisco Manzano (1797–1854), and Anselmo Suárez y Romero (1818–1878), among many other writers. Slavery—mainly the relationship between masters and slaves in Cuba—became the most important theme for these writers.

BEGINNINGS OF *CECILIA VALDÉS*

Villaverde wrote the first version of his novel, titled simply *Cecilia Valdés,* in 1839. Published in the magazine *La Siempreviva,* this version was only twenty-five pages long. It tells the story of Cecilia, a ten-year-old mulatto girl whom Villaverde claimed he met around 1824, who is seduced by a young white man, Leonardo Gamboa. At the end of the story she disappears, probably becoming Leonardo's lover. Later that same year, at the request of a friend, Villaverde developed this story into a 200-page novel and added the subtitle *La loma del Ángel* (Angel's Hill).

Villaverde put aside the story of Cecilia and undertook other writing projects. He also became involved in the anti-Spanish activities of General Narciso López (1797–1851), who recruited Cuban exiles in New York and attempted several filibustering expeditions from the United States to free Cuba from Spanish colonialism. Villaverde was sentenced to prison in 1848, but he escaped and fled to New York the following year. For several years he worked as López's secretary. When López was executed by Spanish military forces in 1851, Villaverde again took up journalism and teaching. In 1858, he briefly returned to Cuba after nine years' absence. He published his novel *Dos amores* (Two Loves, 1858) and tried to go back to his manuscript about Cecilia Valdés. That same year he returned to the United States, and after that, he never went back to Cuba. After 1868, Villaverde's writing became more politically engaged with the cause of Cuban independence. Rodrigo Lazo (2002) traced Villaverde's political and writing trajectory during his forty-five years of exile in New York. Politically active as a member of la Junta Revolucionaria de Cuba y Puerto Rico, Villaverde became the editor of the journal *El Espejo*, which also published Spanish-language books about Cuba. Deeply involved with his wife, Emilia, in political clubs and activist pro-independence writings, mostly in the journal *La Revolución*, Villaverde became an important leader in the Cuban exile community in the United States.

CECILIA VALDÉS AND THE CUBAN NATION

The first edition of *Cecilia Valdés, o la Loma del Ángel: Novela de costumbres cubanas*, Villaverde's second (and final) version of the story, appeared in 1882. In contrast to his earlier romantic story, the 1882 novel is a critique of slavery, law, and colonialism in nineteenth-century Cuba. In his prologue to the second edition, Villaverde states that the novel took him more than forty years to write because of "his dedication to patriotic dreams" (p. 5). Villaverde focuses his historical narrative on the period from 1812 to 1831, when Spanish censorship, abuses of law, and the inequalities created by colonial black slavery defined social relations. Although the novel has strong overtones of *costumbrismo* (the literary interpretation of local everyday life, costumes, and manners) in its depiction of customs, dress, talk, and manners of the Cuban upper, middle, and slave classes, *Cecilia Valdés* could be best described as a realist novel. Critics such as Manuel de la Cruz (1885) praised the novel for its accurate depictions of life in early nineteenth-century Cuba; however, others such as Martín Morúa Delgado (1891) criticized its graphic depictions of slavery and public executions and the author's depiction of mulatto characters. Villaverde represents historical mulattoes from 1830s Cuba such as writer Gabriel de la Concepción Valdés, or the tailor Francisco Uribe, with the purpose of giving a realist account of race relations. Costumbrismo figures mostly in the opening scenes when white creoles, mulattoes, and blacks interact at the *bailes de cuna* (black and mulatto dance balls), in Uribe's tailor shop, and elsewhere in the racially and socially mixed Havana. Some characters, such as Malanga, the black *curro* (a well dressed, street-smart black man associated with petty crimes and gang violence) come close to folkloric caricature, yet Villaverde conveys their deep social and psychological nuances, and some characters' dress, language, and social status are thoroughly described. Leonardo Gamboa is a white creole attracted to all things Cuban—including *bailes de cuna* and Cecilia Valdés. For mulatto characters such as José Dolores Pimienta and the tailor Francisco de Uribe, language and social interaction reflect the middle-class status that the mulatto-artisan class had during this period. Most of these characters (such as the tailor Uribe) are based on historical figures, for Villaverde wanted to accurately depict the rebellion and social discontent of free mulattoes that led to the incarceration or execution of many during the court process that followed the conspiracy of La Escalera (1843–1844). Similarly, characters such as María de Regla and Dionisio Gamboa give voice to the cruelties of slavery.

Cecilia Valdés's rebellion is expressed in her passion for the aristocratic white man, Leonardo Gamboa, who happens to be her half-brother. A daughter of Don Cándido and Rosario Alarcón (a free-born mulatto woman), Valdés is not officially recognized by him. Her last name of "Valdés," given to all illegitimate children in Cuba, marks Cecilia as "other." The threat of racial miscegenation is represented through the theme of incest (Cecilia and Leonardo do not know they are related). Desired by all men, including the mulatto musician and tailor José Dolores Pimienta, she knows that Leonardo Gamboa can offer her social status and respectability; a marriage to José Dolores, a dark-skinned mulatto, would be a step down socially.

CUBANIDAD AND THE TRAGIC MULATTA TROPE

Cecilia is a passionate, assertive, and beautiful woman who embodies the essence of *cubanidad* (the essence of "Cubanness" or a way of being Cuban). Doris Sommer (1993) and Vera Kutzinski (1993), among others, have argued for the importance of the mulatta character in the representation of *cubanidad*. For Sommer, Cecilia and Leonardo represent the consolidation of the Cuban nation, yet, as it happens in novels in which mulatto characters are involved in the national narrative, this consolidation—their marriage—never happens. Leonardo leaves Cecilia to marry Isabel Illincheta, a white woman from the sugar aristocracy. Cecilia, a representative of Cuban womanhood, is extremely feminine, assertive, passionate, and driven; she stands in contrast to Isabel, who represents white-dominant, traditional Christian values and Protestant work ethic. Leonardo's decision to marry Isabel is led by reason rather than passion, for their union will finally consolidate the Gamboa family's aristocratic position. (Don Federico will become a count.) In desperation, Cecilia orders José Dolores Pimienta to kill Isabel in order to prevent Leonardo's marriage, but he ends up killing Leonardo instead. Cecilia, pregnant with Leonardo's baby, ends her days in prison.

Even though the novel ends tragically for Cecilia, her character does not fit easily with the so-called tragic mulatta trope. Suzanne Bost writes that "unlike the chaste heroines of Elizabeth Livermore and Frances Harper," Cecilia Valdés is not tragic (p. 105). Under slavery, black women were victims of the white masters' desire. Raped and abused by their masters, black slave women did not own their own bodies or their sexuality. Whereas many U.S. and Brazilian tragic mulattas are passive, pure, chaste characters, Cecilia is strong-willed, assertive, sexually active, and driven. For Brazilian white-creole authors such as Aluísio Azevedo (*O Mulato*, 1881) and Bernardo Guimarães (*A Escrava Isaura*, 1875), a sexually-driven mulatta embodies characteristics associated with black women as objects of desire of the white master. Thus, the master-patriarchal-racial discourse represents black women as sexual and unruly beings. Thus, traditional or romantic tragic mulattas for Brazilian and U.S. authors are chaste, pure, and passive. They represent traditional feminine values associated with white women. Cecilia's independence and sexual assertiveness locate her in a different position. Cuba did not have anti-miscegenation

Cirilo Villaverde (1812–1894). Cirilo Villaverde's novel *Cecilia Valdés* (1882) is a critique of slavery, law, and colonialism in nineteenth-century Cuba. COURTESY OF THE CUBAN HERITAGE COLLECTION, UNIVERSITY OF MIAMI LIBRARIES, CORAL GABLES, FLORIDA

laws like the United States, but laws still serve the interests of powerful white-creole men like Don Cándido or Leonardo. Cecilia openly denounces the hypocrisy of Cuban patriarchal-white supremacy laws and the social consequences of colonial slavery. A victim of sexual exploitation like her own mother Rosario Alarcón, Cecilia makes the mistake of falling in love with Leonardo—and attempting to use this love to change her economic circumstances. For these actions, she represents a threat to the social and class hierarchies of colonial society, and she is imprisoned by the society that produced her.

VILLAVERDE'S POLITICAL AND SOCIAL MESSAGE

Villaverde ends his novel with a critical commentary about the absurdity of Spanish laws, holding the government under Spanish rule accountable for slavery, corruption, and social inequality. Thus, the final version of *Cecilia Valdés* demonstrates Villaverde's commitment to Cuba's independence and sovereignty. Like Cecilia, the Cuban mulatto nation is exploited for its resources and ends up a prisoner of Spanish colonialism. The marriage of Leonardo and Isabel does not materialize, and the novel ends with a somber note on the political future of Cuba under Spanish rule. At novel's end, Isabel also embodies the good female master, representing Villaverde's view on improving master-slave relations. Although the political discourse seems anticolonial, Villaverde settles for a traditional-reformist position on slavery, similar to that promoted by Domingo del Monte and his *tertulia* in the 1830s. Villaverde endorsed the view of slavery as a necessary evil that sustained the Cuban economy. Villaverde dedicated the last years of his life in New York to activist journalism, pedagogy, and the cause of Cuban independence. He died in New York City in 1894.

BIBLIOGRAPHY

Alvarez, Imeldo. *Acerca de Cirilo Villaverde: Selección, prólogo y notas de Imeldo Alvarez*. Havana: Letras Cubanas, 1982.

Arroyo, Jossianna. *Travestismos culturales: Literatura y etnografía en Cuba y Brasil*. Pittsburgh, PA: Editorial Iberoamericana, 2003.

Benítez Rojo, Antonio. "Azúcar/poder/literatura." *Cuadernos hispanoamericanos* 451–452 (1988): 195–215.

Bost, Suzanne. *Mulattas and Mestizas: Representing Mixed Identities in the Americas, 1850–2000*. Atlanta: University of Georgia Press, 2005.

Holland, Norman S. "Fashioning Cuba." In *Nationalisms and Sexualities*, edited by Andrew Parker, Patricia Yaeger, Mary Russo, and Doris Sommer. New York: Routledge, 1992.

Homenaje a Cirilo Villaverde. Havana: Comisión Nacional Cubana de la UNESCO, 1964.

Kutzinski, Vera. *Sugar Secrets: Race and the Erotics of Cuban Nationalism*. Charlottesville: University of Virginia Press, 1993.

Lazo, Rodrigo. "Filibustering Cuba: Cecilia Valdés and a Memory of Nation in the Americas." *American Literature* 74, no. 1 (March 2002): 1–30.

Ortiz, Fernando. *Los negros curros*. Havana: Pensamiento Cubano, 1986.

Ramos, Julio. "La ley es otra: Literatura y constitución de la persona jurídica." In *Paradojas de la letra*, by Julio Ramos. Caracas: Ediciones Excultura, 1996.

Sommer, Doris. *Foundational Fictions: The National Romances of Latin America*. Berkeley: University of California Press, 1993.

Villaverde, Cirilo. *Cecilia Valdés*. Foreword and edited by Iván A. Schulman. Caracas: Biblioteca Ayacucho, 1981.

CHE GUEVARA AND THE NEW MAN

Ana Serra

Che Guevara's model for Cuban revolutionaries as explained in his essay "El socialismo y el hombre en Cuba."

The term *New Man* was introduced and extensively explained by Che Guevara (1928–1967) in the essay "El socialismo y el hombre en Cuba" ("Socialism and Man in Cuba"), first published as a letter to the editor in the 12 March 1965 edition of the Uruguayan journal *Marcha*. After that, the document was republished and quoted countless times, and the "New Man" became associated with Guevara himself as a popular model for all Cubans to follow. The idea that a new era required creating a new human being was not entirely novel at the time Guevara was writing; in fact, the concept of the "New Man" had been popular since the Enlightenment in Europe and was central to the Soviet revolution in Lenin's writings as well as to the Chinese Cultural Revolution. Nevertheless, the mythical status of Guevara, the resonance of the Cuban Revolution in Latin America and the rest of the world during the Cold War, and the long life of the Cuban regime gave the term *New Man* a central location and meaning in Cuba. Guevara's ideas on the New Man were extremely influential in the Cuban Revolution and provided the backing for many of the regime's policies.

THE "OLD MAN" AND "NEW MAN" MODELS

Guevara's writing in "Socialism and Man in Cuba" is clear and convincing, styled to reach what he expected would be a large audience. By the time this essay was published in Cuba, Guevara knew that he was resigning from his position in the Ministry of Finance in order to carry out the internationalist mission of the revolution in Congo. Therefore, the essay can be read as a sort of farewell manifesto, in which Guevara attempted to set down his legacy. The essay spells out all the concepts that he had been emphasizing from

Billboard celebrating Che Guevara, near Havana, 15 October 1997. A roadside billboard displays the slogan "Tu ejemplo vive, tus ideas perduran" (Your example lives, your ideas endure), alongside an image of Che Guevara. Such revolutionary slogans grace numerous billboards in Cuba, and the idea of imitating revolutionary behavior remains strong. STEPHEN FERRY/LIAISON/GETTY IMAGES

his various positions in the Cuban government: the relationship between the individual and the masses and the vanguard, indirect and direct education, the law of duty versus the law of value, moral incentives versus material incentives, artistic creation, conscience, and sacrifice.

Most importantly, in "Socialism and Man in Cuba" Guevara described the "New Man" as a counterfigure to the "Old Man" of capitalism, which the new Cuba was leaving behind. In order to build socialism, and ultimately communism, the New Man would be responsible for changing pre-1959 Cuba, which suffered from high levels of consumerism, worker alienation, and a lack of national purpose. The island was beset by social ills typical of so-called Third World nations such as unemployment, social inequality, racial and gender discrimination, corruption, prostitution, and organized crime. Rather than following the capitalist mentality of the law of the jungle, the New Man would focus on the common good. As Guevara wrote this essay in the early years of the revolutionary government, the New Man was an "unfinished product," an ideal to work toward every day (Guevara p. 5).

Guevara barely mentioned women in his reflections. Granted, in Spanish the term *hombre* (man) includes both men and women; nevertheless, it is significant that in this essay Guevara referred to women specifically only when he wrote that "the leaders of the revolution have children . . . who are not learning to say 'daddy.' They have wives who must be part of the general sacrifice of their lives in order to take the revolution to its destiny" (Guevara p. 15). In later years, after

the Family Code (1975) and the campaign for the inclusion of women in the labor force (mid-1970s), the concept of the New Woman was invoked, but in this essay Guevara revealed a strictly male-centered idea of Cuban identity that reinforced a stereotypical idea of masculinity based on strength, will power, and endurance. To some extent, Guevara cannot be faulted for not being a feminist in the 1960s, after Cuba had emerged from a brutal right-wing regime, but many critics are disappointed by Guevara's lack of vision in gender matters.

TEACHING THE CUBAN MASSES

According to Soviet views on socialism that Cuba was loosely following at the time of Guevara's writing, a regime first built socialism by gradually transforming the means of production and ensuring the distribution of wealth favorable to the working classes and the peasants. The evolution of scientific, productive, and cultural forces led to the culmination of the process: communism. In Cuba, however, leaders wanted socialism and communism to be built at the same time, appealing to Cuba's exceptionalism and the primacy of revolutionary consciousness over the objective conditions of the Revolution. Such a profound and swift transformation of society required heroic measures that needed to be supported by a completely new way of thinking—a new consciousness, and a new type of human being: selfless, firm in his convictions, and resolute. In order to introduce this new way of thinking, ensure that it was well understood and implemented, and reinforce its currency at all levels of society,

Guevara wrote that "society as a whole must be converted into a gigantic school" (Guevara p. 6). What Guevara meant was that the New Man with his new way of thinking would permeate all levels of life. For instance, during the late 1960s—and more so in subsequent decades—the regime encouraged Cuban artists and writers to use their art to teach the main ideas of the Revolution and proper revolutionary behavior. The 1970 Ten Million–Ton Sugar Campaign offered the opportunity to prove the effectiveness of voluntary labor in a socialist regime, which was a key idea behind the concept of the "New Man." After the failure of this campaign, upon which Cuba had depended to pay its debts to the Soviet Union, the gigantic school of society became stricter, as it were, accepting only one way of teaching and one textbook—a narrowly defined set of revolutionary principles. Fidel Castro seemed to be supporting Guevara's ideas when at the 1971 First National Congress of Education and Culture he announced: "There will only be room here—without any kind of hesitation…for the revolutionaries.… For us, a revolutionary people in a revolutionary process, there is value in cultural and artistic creations inasmuch as they are useful for the people…our evaluation is political" (Nuiry Sánchez p. 118). The 1970s ushered in the so-called "grey years," representing a hardening of cultural policy that fortunately began to change during the Special Period that started in the early 1990s.

Guevara's model of society as a gigantic school offered both a direct and an indirect method of education. According to Guevara, the direct method used propaganda or straight instruction to spread the ideas of the Revolution, just as every Cuban campaign articulated its objectives by means of catchphrases and slogans. This is consistent with Guevara's thought that, in a class society, education reflects the biases of its governing classes and that, after 1959, it should reflect the ideals of the Revolution (and the lower classes). When Guevara wrote this essay he was describing pedagogical strategies that had been put into practice since the beginning of the Revolution. For instance, 1961 was the Year of Education, which implemented the Literacy Campaign and introduced the slogans "Estudio, Trabajo y Fusil" (Study, Work, and Rifle) and "Venceremos!" (We Will Win!). The campaign's reading primers had chapter titles such as "Fidel es nuestro líder" (Fidel Is Our Leader) and "La tierra es nuestra" (The Land Is Ours). The relationship between the literacy teacher and the student was based on their learning from each other, which illustrates the concept of indirect education, what was later called *emulación* (imitation).

In the context of the Literacy Campaign, the teachers that were sent to the far reaches of the Sierra were encouraged to imitate the simplicity and allegedly genuine revolutionary spirit of the peasants, while students were supposed to learn the civilized ways of the teacher. In later years, factory workers, for instance, were encouraged to imitate their most committed colleagues to ensure that the production objectives of the factory were met. Rather than competing against one another, indirect education shows that one makes progress by imitating other people's positive behavior. Overall, the gigantic school was supposed to install a top-down system of teaching in which doctrine was clear from straight instruction, and revolutionary behaviors such as selflessness, sacrifice, voluntarism, and internationalism were made standard with modeling and imitation. In practice, the gigantic school became less strict in the 1990s. Classic Cuban slogans such as 1968's "100 años de lucha" (100 Years of Struggle), which commemorated the hundred years of the fight for independence, gave way in the late 1990s to "No cojas lucha" (Pick Your Battles) as resources became scarce and people adapted to hardship with a sense of humor. Nevertheless, revolutionary slogans—mostly quotations from Guevara, Castro, and leaders of the Cuban independence movement such as José Martí (1853–1895), Antonio Maceo (1845–1896), Carlos Manuel de Céspedes (1819–1874)—continued into the early 2000s to grace billboards in Havana and the provinces, and the idea of imitating revolutionary behavior persisted, especially among people who lamented the weakening of the strong commitment of earlier decades.

USE OF LANGUAGE AND ITS IMPLICATIONS

Guevara's use of Christian imagery and expressions in his essay is striking. Not only does he pronounce his ritual greeting of "Ave María Purísima"—a reference to the Virgin Mary as the epitome of purity—before "Patria o Muerte" (Fatherland or Death) at the end of his letter, but he also refers to contemporary intellectuals suffering from "the original sin" of not being true revolutionaries, and he writes at length about the many sacrifices involved in becoming the New Man. In describing a life of sacrifice he brings to mind the unflinching discipline of Ignatius of Loyola (1491–1556), with whom Guevara must have been familiar (Geirola pp. 125–176). The final objectives of sacrifice are very different for Guevara, but his message still blends with Christianity in a broad sense when he refers to love for humanity as the revolutionary's guiding principle (Guevara p. 15). These passages and those that refer to the needs of daily life that revolutionaries will have to neglect, such as providing new shoes for their children (Guevara p. 16), are often quoted as demonstrating Guevara's humanity and sympathy for the common man (e.g., Pogolotti). Guevara strongly believed that a leader or party member should have no more privileges than a worker. At the same time, he showed steely resolve for enforcing revolutionary principles by promoting moral rewards (that is, the satisfaction of working for the common good) rather than material rewards. The idea of moral rewards can be identified with Christian virtue, yet, for Guevara, violence was an integral part of the life of the New Man. He believed that guerrilla fighting was a rite of passage for true revolutionaries, and he is reported to have chosen a box of bullets and not a doctor's kit when he had to lighten his load during his guerrilla fight in Cuba (Guevara p. 6). But Guevara's heroic death in the Bolivian campaign and the photographs of him that were taken at the time—which resembled classical paintings of Jesus after he was taken down from the cross—contributed further to his being identified with Jesus as a sacrificial and saving figure.

When describing the structure of command in the Revolution, Guevara specifically identified Castro as the head of the "immense column" that is marching on, followed by the party's core group of leaders, and finally, "the people in its entirety" (Guevara p. 16). This image makes clear that power in the Revolution was hierarchical, and, most importantly, that individual differences were supposed to be put aside in pursuit of the common goal. The New Man thus became a figure that must override all distinctions of race, ethnicity, and gender. In practice, this meant that the New Man was automatically white, male, and heterosexual. By deemphasizing discussions on gender, ethnicity, and race that were considered divisive, the regime did not sufficiently advance the specific demands of women, blacks, or homosexuals (Bunck; De la Fuente; López Vigil; Lumsden; Molyneux; Serra). What is more, because the New Man represented vanguard revolutionaries, and Cuba aspired to be the model for all of Latin America, Guevara's doctrine is at least partly responsible for the erasure of racial, ethnic, and gender differences in revolutionary movements that took Cuba as their starting point, such as the Ejército Guerrillero de los Pobres in Guatemala and the Sandinistas in Nicaragua. The archetypal New Man fell decidedly out of favor and was replaced by an emphasis on diversity in Latin American political movements such as the Ejército Zapatista de Liberación Nacional (EZLN, Zapatista Army of National Liberation; 1994–c. 2009), or the Movimiento al Socialismo (MAS, Movement for Socialism) of Evo Morales, beginning in 2005. In Cuba, however, the New Man was adapted and refashioned according to the needs of the Revolution, but without losing its essential traits.

THE NEW MAN IN THE REVOLUTION AND BEYOND

Guevara's assassination in Bolivia in 1967 prompted revolutionaries to identify him with the New Man at a time when Cuba was entering a financial crisis and needed models of sacrifice. After Guevara's death, 1968 became the Year of the Heroic Guerrilla, and schoolchildren were taught the motto "Seremos como el Che" (We Will Be Like Che). The failure of the Ten Million–Ton Sugar Campaign in 1970 necessitated use of the New Man to provide justification for new economic policies. During campaigns in the late 1970s to integrate more women into the labor force, the "New Man" was dressed as a "New Woman." The

"New Man" model was employed again to promote a return to core revolutionary values during the Rectification campaign in 1986, when Cuba, rejecting the political and economic measures proposed by Soviet leader Mikhail Gorbachev (b. 1931), embarked on its own campaign to reinvigorate socialism. After the fall of the Soviet bloc in 1989, and during the period of tremendous scarcity and exodus that became known as the Special Period, Guevara was still identified with the New Man, which was presented variously as a model to follow, a figure to question, or an object of parody.

One of the earliest and most popular reactions to the concept of the New Man was the 1994 Cuban film *Fresa y chocolate* (*Strawberry and Chocolate*), directed by Tomás Gutiérrez Alea (1928–1996) and based on the short story "El lobo, el bosque y el hombre nuevo" (The Wolf, the Forest and the New Man, 1991), by Senel Paz (b. 1950). The film depicts the clash between Diego, a homosexual character who is a devoted Cuban and a good revolutionary in his own fashion, and David, a heterosexual and narrow-minded revolutionary who does not understand the wealth of Cuban culture. In addition to attempting to widen public discourse on key issues such as religion, art versus propaganda, and critical thinking versus institutionalized literature, the film proposes a more inclusive model of the New Man, one possessing David's commitment to the Revolution as well as Diego's sensitivity and intimate knowledge of Cuban tradition. Though the film depicts a sort of reconciliation or forgiveness between the two characters, Diego is ostracized by the regime because of his homosexuality and his views on art and feels he has to leave the country. *Fresa y chocolate* opened up discussion about homosexuality and whether there is room for different sexual orientations and religious beliefs in the idea of the New Man. After the late 1990s, homosexuality became a common topic of discussion in Cuba, though critics such as Emilio Bejel and José Quiroga charge that homosexuals continued to be presented as marginal to the institutionally defined Cuban nation, and that the rectification of homophobic cultural practices was insufficient.

Late 1990s cinematic representations of the New Man have illustrated the implications of the strict, one-size-fits-all model for Cuban men. Elpidio, one of the protagonists of Fernando Pérez's celebrated film *La vida es silbar* (*Life Is to Whistle*, 1998), is an Afro-Cuban man who challenges his mother, named Cuba, to explain why she had demanded perfection of him. Elpidio regrets that he was unable to meet his mother's ideal, and, as a result, she dismissed him as "un marginal, un vago, un vicioso" (a marginal man, a bum, a junkie) and left the country, leaving him behind. With this, Pérez reminds viewers that the ideal of the Cuban New Man not only erased ethnic and racial differences, but also branded such differences as objectionable or unacceptable in the context of the nation in revolution. In addition, it must be noted that the character that functions as Elpidio's conscience in the film is an image of the Cuban singer Bola de Nieve (Ignacio Villa, 1911–1971), who was black, homosexual, and supportive of the Revolution. Pérez's Elpidio is one of the most important representations of an Afro-Cuban individual who aspires to be a New Man, and he is given the chance to protest against the strong demands that this model of identity imposed on Cubans.

Some post–Special Period Cuban novels assert that the desire of youths for the so-called marginal, the abnormal, and the illicit stems from years of being subject to the ideal of the New Man. As one father puts it in Leonardo Padura's novel *La neblina del ayer* (The Fog of Yesterday, 2005):

> they were bent on making us better human beings.... I have a name for this, "historical exhaustion." From so much experiencing the exceptional, the historical, the transcendent, people get tired and want normalcy. Since they cannot find it, they seek abnormality.... [The youth] do not want to belong and be forced to be good. Most importantly, they do not want to be like us, their parents. We are a shitty failure.

p. 199

Numerous young Cuban novelists and short story authors of the 1990s revealed a need to write about what hitherto had been considered marginal or even counterrevolutionary. A prime example is Ena Lucía Portela (b. 1972), whose very style of writing resists traditional models of narration. In her novels and short stories, characters are marginal, and plots are fragmentary and digressive. In *Cien botellas en una pared* (One Hundred Bottles on a Wall, 2002), for example, Portela depicts the relationship between a practitioner of Santería and her paranoid husband and a lesbian Jewish emigrant woman who is a successful writer. Portela's female characters are very different from the "New Woman" whose defining characteristic was devotion to the Revolution and hard work, both in the context of heterosexual pairings in families and in the fields or the factory.

As of 2011, it was hard to predict whether the "New Man" model would continue to lead Cubans in the twenty-first century. Leadership on the island was precarious, and political slogans had lost their strength. For some, the idea of the New Man remained steeped in nostalgia, having been a source of inspiration for generations; for others, the New Man was an imposing figure who cast a shadow over those who were not able to, or who refused to, conform to his example. Fifty years after the Revolution, Cuba had become a society where the ideal of the New Man was not realized, and the Old Man was no longer dominant. Because of their history, Cubans were equipped for a model of society that shunned the destructive values of capitalism and neoliberalism, as they tried to create a sense of meaning and stability. But it was clear that if the "New Man" model were to survive in the twenty-first century, as Guevara aspired, it would have to represent differences in gender, sexual orientation, and race.

BIBLIOGRAPHY

Bejel, Emilio. *Gay Cuban Nation*. Chicago: University of Chicago Press, 2001.

Bunck, Julie Marie. *Fidel Castro and the Quest for a Revolutionary Culture in Cuba*. University Park: Pennsylvania University Press, 1994.

Castañeda, Jorge. *Compañero: Vida y muerte del Che Guevara*. New York: Vintage español, 1997.

Cheng, Yinghong. *Creating the "New Man": From Enlightenment Ideals to Socialist Realities*. Honolulu: University of Hawaii Press, 2009.

De la Fuente, Alejandro. *A Nation for All: Race, Inequality, and Politics in Twentieth-Century Cuba*. Chapel Hill: University of North Carolina Press, 2001.

Duchesne Winter, Juan. *La guerrilla narrada:Acción, acontecimiento, sujeto*. San Juan, Puerto Rico: Ediciones Callejón, 2010.

Geirola, Gustavo. *Teatralidad y experiencia política en América Latina, 1957–1977*. Irvine, CA: Gestos, 2000.

Guevara, Ernesto. *Socialism and Man in Cuba*. New York: Pathfinder Press, 1989.

Guevara, Ernesto. *Pasajes de la guerra revolucionaria*. Havana: Editorial de Ciencias Sociales, 1999.

López Vigil, María. *Ni paraíso ni infierno, Cuba*. Managua, Nicaragua: Vigía, 1999.

Lumsden, Ian. *Machos, Maricones, and Gays: Cuba and Homosexuality*. Philadelphia, PA: Temple University Press, 1996.

Medin, Tzvi. *Cuba: The Shaping of the Revolutionary Consciousness*. Boulder, CO: Lynne Rienner, 1990.

Molyneux, Maxine. "State, Gender and Institutional Change: The Women's Federation of Cuba." In *Hidden Histories of Gender and the State in Latin America*, edited by Elizabeth Dore and Maxine Molyneux. Durham, NC: Duke University Press, 2000.

Nuiry Sánchez, Nuria, ed. *Pensamiento y política cultural cubanos. Antología*. 2 vols. Havana: Pueblo y educación, 1987.

Padura, Leonardo. *La neblina del ayer*. Barcelona: Tusquets, 2005.

Paz, Senel. *El lobo, el bosque y el hombre nuevo*. Mexico City: Era, 1991.

Pérez, Fernando. *La vida es silbar*. Havana: Instituto Cubano de Arte e Industria Cinematográficos, 1997.

Piglia, Ricardo. "Ernesto Guevara: Rastros de lectura." In *El último lector*. Madrid: Anagrama, 2005.

Pogolotti, Graziella. "Apuntes para el Che escritor." *Casa de las Américas* 46 (January–February 1968): 152–155.

Portela, Ena Lucía. *Cien botellas en una pared*. Barcelona: Mondadori, 2002.

Quiroga, José. "Homosexualities in the Tropic of Revolution." In *Sex and Sexuality in Latin America*, edited by Daniel Balderston and Donna J. Guy. New York: New York University Press, 1997.

Saldaña Portillo, María Josefina. *The Revolutionary Imagination and the Age of Development*. Durham, NC: Duke University Press, 2003.

Serra, Ana. *The "New Man" in Cuba: Culture and Identity in the Revolution*. Gainesville: University Press of Florida, 2007.

CHE GUEVARA, SOCIAL AND POLITICAL THOUGHT

Alan West-Durán

The political, military, and economic thought of one of Cuba's revolutionary leaders and its legacy.

Ernesto Guevara de la Serna (1928–1967) was born in Argentina, fought in Bolivia and the Congo, and traveled to almost every country in Latin America, along with the Soviet Union, China, and Africa. Even so, his fate is inextricably linked with Cuba and its revolution. Guevara came to Cuba via his observed experiences of poverty, social inequality, and class injustice in his travels through Latin America in 1951 and 1952, captured in the Walter Salles film *The Motorcycle Diaries* (2004). Guevara's political consciousness was further awakened by the CIA-sponsored overthrow of Guatemalan president Jacobo Arbenz Guzmán (1913–1971) in 1954, an event he witnessed. In 1955 Guevara met Fidel Castro in Mexico and joined the 26th of July Revolutionary Movement. Though recruited as a doctor, Guevara soon showed his skills as a leader and military tactician. In late 1958 he led the battle of Santa Clara, the decisive blow to the Batista regime, which collapsed on 1 January 1959.

As a key figure in the revolutionary government, Guevara oversaw the tribunal that prosecuted war crimes committed under the Batista regime, and in 1961 he became director of the Ministry of Industry. He was also later sent on various diplomatic missions to the Soviet Union, China, and Africa. In 1965 Guevara assumed command of an unsuccessful guerrilla group in the Congo. He returned to Cuba in December 1965 and secretly prepared a mission to Bolivia, where he arrived in November 1966. Lacking local support—the Bolivian Communist Party withdrew from the plan—the guerrilla insurrection failed. Guevara was wounded, captured, and assassinated on 8 October 1967.

Despite his reputation as a man of action, Che Guevara left a considerable written testimony of his life and thought: *Guerrilla Warfare: A Method* (1960), *Reminiscences of the Cuban Revolutionary War* (1963), *The Bolivian Diary* (1968), and a host of articles and speeches that have been published in various collections. A man with a voracious intellect, Guevara was a keen reader of Latin American writers, including the Chilean poet Pablo Neruda; the Uruguayan essayist José Enrique Rodó; the Ecuadorean novelist and playwright Jorge Icaza; the Cuban José Martí, a writer and symbol of the independence movement; and Alejo Carpentier, a Cuban novelist. Guevara was also well-versed in works by Marx, Lenin, Mao, and other authors in the socialist tradition, such as José Carlos Mariátegui of Peru, Aníbal Ponce of Argentina, Vo Nguyen Giap of Vietnam, Oskar Lange of Poland, and Ernest Mandel of Belgium, not to mention his contemporaries Frantz Fanon of Martinique and Regis Débray of France. Guevara was a self-declared Marxist-Leninist who critically examined these political traditions. As committed as he was to building socialism, Guevara was not an orthodox thinker and was often critical of Soviet policy; he was influential on a host of economic, political, and cultural matters.

PATHS TO LIBERATION: REVOLUTIONARY WARFARE

The forceful ouster of Arbenz by the CIA was crucial to Guevara's thinking that true social change in Latin America could be achieved only through violence. The Algerian War (1954–1962), the Korean War (1950–1953), the Vietnamese struggle for independence (1945–1975), and African decolonization only confirmed those views.

In *Guerrilla Warfare* Guevara puts forth three principles that came out of the Cuban Revolutionary War (1956–1959): (1) "Popular forces can win a war against the army"; (2) "It is not necessary to wait until all conditions for making a revolution; the insurrectional nucleus [*foco insurreccional*] can create them"; and (3) "In underdeveloped America, the countryside is the basic arena for armed struggle" (1967, p. 27). Compared to what Latin American communist parties argued, these policies were heretical at the time because they suggested, first, that a popular struggle can win through political and military means by outmaneuvering a conventional army and had to be rurally based, and, second, that not all the material, political, and social conditions had to be aligned for a revolutionary movement to be successful. Finally, it meant that the revolution need not be led by a communist party, which was the case in Cuba's guerrilla war.

Guevara's emphasis on the guerrilla insurrection led some critics to dismiss his ideas as embracing *foquismo* (focalism, or the theory of armed insurrection by guerrilla *foco* [nucleus]) tends to overlook the patient political networks that must be built to sustain a revolutionary movement. Guevara never denied these political necessities, despite his evident impatience at making them come about in Bolivia. Guevara also never argued that the guerrilla foco alone would be able to overthrow the government, knowing that eventually these irregular forces would have to function like a regular army to defeat the state's military. The success of the foco would depend on generalized discontent among the population as well as demoralization and the breakup of the army.

In his travels Guevara had seen the enthusiasm of the Bolivian revolution of 1952 and the role of labor militancy in achieving the nationalization of foreign-owned mines. Several factors led Guevara to try out his revolutionary strategy in Bolivia: widespread discontent with the regime of General René Barrientos, who had seized power in a 1964 coup; long-standing resentment against U.S. interference in Bolivian affairs; dismal poverty, illiteracy, and social inequality; a high degree of trade union militancy; an ineffectual Bolivian military; and finally the country's strategic geographic location as the so-called heart of South America, sharing borders with Brazil, Paraguay, Argentina, Chile, and Peru. If Bolivia warmed to the revolutionary tide, its example would radiate outward to the whole continent.

Havana sponsored the Tricontinental Congress (1966) in support of liberation movements in Asia, Africa, and Latin America. At its second congress, in April 1967, Guevara delivered his famous message ("Create Two, Three, Many Vietnams"), publicly stating that imperialism should be dealt simultaneous decisive blows all over the world. Sensing the difficulty of this planetary task, Guevara quoted Fidel Castro: "Of what difference are the dangers to a human being or a people, or the sacrifices they make, when at stake is the destiny of humanity?" (2003, p. 362).

Despite Guevara's failed mission in Bolivia, Cuba's example had an inspirational impact on Latin America. Guerrilla *focos* came into existence in Colombia (1961), Venezuela (1961), Nicaragua (1961), Argentina (1964), and Peru (1962 and 1965), with urban guerrilla movements in Uruguay (1965), Brazil (1968), and Argentina (1970). All were home-grown and would have appeared with or without Cuba's example. Every one of them failed, except for one: Nicaragua's Frente Sandinista de Liberación Nacional (FSLN) overthrew the Anastasio Somoza regime in 1979.

BUILDING SOCIALISM: THE ECONOMIC DEBATE

From 1962 to 1965 Guevara was central to an intense and polemical economic debate on how to build socialism in Cuba. The debate included Carlos Rafael Rodríguez (head of the Agrarian Reform Institute), Alberto Mora (minister of foreign trade), Marcelo Fernández Font (president of the National Bank), and Luis Alvarez Rom (minister of finance), and two foreign Marxist economists, Charles Bettelheim and Ernest Mandel. The chief themes were centered on economic policy, political economy, and Marxist theory in the building of socialism. Central to the economic debate was whether firms would be allowed financial autonomy or would operate under a budgetary system and whether to reward with material or moral incentives.

Guevara favored the budgetary finance system (BFS) over autonomy. Enterprises were not supposed to function on profit that they kept; instead, their surplus would be centrally managed in an account for firms of a similar type. Although conscious of the importance of material incentives, Guevara favored moral incentives as the catalyst to production.

Guevara was also opposed to allowing the law of value, the epitome of capitalism, to operate as a guiding mechanism in Cuba's socialist economy. There were to be no commodity exchanges between state enterprises, and cost-cutting instead of profits was to be the key to evaluating a firm's performance. Prices were adjusted for basic or social needs and not based solely on market criteria.

For Guevara, socialism was not merely a mechanism for producing goods a little more fairly, but for building a new type of society and creating a "New Man." His "New Man" was a rejection of the values of capitalism: selfishness, lack of empathy, class envy, prejudices, materialism, and violence. Socialism's "New Man" meant a human being that was selfless, showed solidarity with the poor and oppressed, and upheld ideals of social justice and equality. Work was motivated not by money but by moral incentives and the social utility and degree of moral and creative fulfillment of one's labor. These moral criteria applied equally to voluntary labor such as cutting cane or building public housing on weekends. In an interview Guevara expressed his view:

> Economic socialism without communist morality does not interest me. We are fighting against poverty, yes, but also alienation....Marx was equally concerned...[with what] he called...a "fact of consciousness." If communism fails to pay attention to the facts of consciousness, it may be a method of distribution, but it is no longer a revolutionary morality.

Löwy p. 59

After Guevara's death, Cuba's economic policy alternated between embracing and rejecting his economic thought. The late 1960s embraced it, especially the so-called revolutionary offensive of 1968, which closed all remaining small, private businesses, as well as the government's 1970 plan for a 10-million-ton sugar harvest; both of these policies had highly disruptive economic consequences. From the early 1970s to the mid-1980s the pendulum swung the other way: In 1972 Cuba joined the Council for Mutual Economic Assistance (CMEA, or Comecon), the Eastern Bloc common market, and in 1986 Guevara's ideas were embraced anew as Cuba observed the Soviet Union, under the Communist Party leadership of Mikhail Gorbachev, drifting toward capitalism. In the 1990s, as the economy went into survival mode, policy swung toward market measures, but in the early 2000s there was renewed interest in Guevara's ideas as derived from his *Apuntes críticos a la Economía Política* (2006), a series of notes and commentaries he made on the Soviet *Manual of Political Economy* in 1966, plus other notes as well as minutes to the meetings held during the Great Debate (1962–1964). Guevara found both the manual and Soviet economic policy mechanistic, rigid, and undemocratic in its top-down approach; his highly critical predictions about the demise of the Soviet Union were prescient. In these notes one can also glimpse an outline of a vision of socialist democracy that he never fully worked out.

Any sweeping remarks about Guevara's economic-political thought and the Cuban economy are at best tentative. Measured by capitalist standards (high productivity, variety and quality of goods, ability to consume through credit, technical innovation, and sophisticated telecommunications), the record of command economies—Cuba included—is at best modest and at worst dismal. But if one views matters from a nonmarket perspective, with capitalism seen as engendering exploitation, inequality, social polarization, and environmental destruction and prone to market busts and booms, violence, and war, Cuba's economy appears more benign. None of this needs obscure the fact that Cuba's economy has remarkable similarities with the history of other socialist experiments: bureaucracy, inefficiency, and waste; bottlenecks and shortages of goods; shoddy products, poor incentives for workers, pilfering of state resources, and corruption. These ills of socialist economies were not created by Che Guevara (indeed they preceded his tenure as minister of industry), but the hasty implementation of some of his ideas and the foolhardy insistence of policy makers to gloss over economic realities are troubling.

GUERRILLA THEORIST, ECONOMIST OF SOCIALISM, AND POLITICAL THINKER

By all regards Guevara was an accomplished and sometimes brilliant military mind. As a guerrilla soldier and strategist he has been widely read, studied, and admired for his will and tactical flexibility despite the crucial mistakes in the Congo and Bolivia; in the latter case, he paid with his life. Guevara's tricontinental outlook was aimed at sparking two, three, or more insurrections that would tie up the military capabilities of Western imperialism and was less focused on any one national struggle. Guevara's internationalism was predicated on support from the Soviet Union and China to wage these struggles—yet it was not always forthcoming, a fact of which he was highly critical. In this regard he gave new emphasis and a greater moral charge to the idea of proletarian internationalism. In the early 2000s, that strategic bastion had vanished. Time had not proved that the guerrilla path was a viable option except in Central America, where the Sandinistas triumphed in Nicaragua (1979) and the Farabundo Martí National Liberation Front (FMLN) in El Salvador evolved into a political party to participate in elections (2009). In other cases, such as Peru, a twelve-year guerrilla war against the government cost over 70,000 lives and devastated the country.

Guevara's exhortation for social change has taken a more peaceful route as countries such as Venezuela, Bolivia, Ecuador, Nicaragua, Uruguay, and Argentina have taken turns to the left, all through the ballot box. The one exception is Mexico's Zapatista National Liberation Army, which originated as an armed insurrection in 1994 but as of 2011 was no longer a guerrilla movement that sought state power. Yet the Zapatista movement's leader, known as Subcomandante Marcos, said in 2006: "Che reminds us of what we have known since Spartacus, and sometimes forget: in the struggle against injustices humanity finds a course that teaches it, makes it better, and more human" (Besancenot and Löwy p. 120).

As an economic thinker, Guevara remained relevant in the early 2000s to Cuba as it carves out an independent socialist path in a world without the former Soviet Union and Soviet bloc countries, and with China and Vietnam firmly on the road to being capitalist economies. In the early twenty-first century Venezuela and Bolivia experimented with a different kind of noncapitalist development, sometimes known as twenty-first-century socialism to distinguish it from its twentieth-century version (command economy, one-party political systems, limited social and technological innovation).

Critics of Che Guevara tend to see him as a hopeless romantic with a destructive bent, a relic from the 1960s who is best forgotten. For many around the globe who do not see globalization as an unmitigated blessing, his sharp critique of inequality, power imbalances, and economic exploitation still ring true. For Cuba, he remains a powerful presence, his thought deeply rooted in Cuban history but with a universal message, fiercely realistic and mystically hopeful, offering a complex, humanistic vision of society that is painfully aware of the limits and contradictions of social emancipation.

BIBLIOGRAPHY

Anderson, Jon Lee. *Che: A Revolutionary Life*. New York: Grove Press, 1997.

Ariet, María del Carmen. *Che: Pensamiento Político*. Havana: Editora Política, 1988.

Besancenot, Olivier, and Michael Löwy. *Che Guevara: His Revolutionary Legacy*. New York: Monthly Review Press, 2009.

Dosal, Paul J. *Comandante Che, Guerrilla Soldier, Commander, and Strategist, 1956–1967*. University Park: Pennsylvania State University Press, 2003.

Guevara, Ernesto Che. *Obra revolucionaria*. Edited by Roberto Fernández Retamar. Mexico City: Ediciones Era, 1967.

Guevara, Ernesto Che. *Che Guevara Reader, Writings on Politics and Revolution*. Edited by David Deutschmann. Melbourne: Ocean Press, 2003.

Guevara, Ernesto Che. *Reminiscences of the Cuban Revolutionary War*. Melbourne: Ocean Press, 2006.

Guevara, Ernesto Che. *Guerrilla Warfare*. Breinigsville, PA: BN Publishing, 2007.

Löwy, Michael. *The Marxism of Che Guevara: Philosophy, Economics, Revolutionary Warfare*, 2nd ed. Lanham, MD: Rowman & Littlefield, 2007.

Martínez Heredia, Fernando. *Che, el socialismo y el comunismo*. Havana: Casa de las Américas, 1989.

Silverman, Bertram, ed. *Man and Socialism in Cuba: The Great Debate*. New York: Atheneum, 1971.

Taibo, Paco Ignacio. *Guevara, Also Known as Che*. Translated by Martin Michael Roberts. New York: St. Martin's Press, 1997.

Yaffe, Helen. *Che Guevara: The Economics of Revolution*. Basingstoke, U.K.: Palgrave Macmillan, 2009.

■ *See also*

Governance and Contestation: Insurrection, 1952–1959

Governance and Contestation: The Republic: 1902–1952

CIENFUEGOS

Orlando F. García Martínez

The history of the city of Cienfuegos from its beginnings as a largely French settlement to its role in the Revolution of 1959.

Cienfuegos was founded on 22 April 1819 under the Spanish flag led by Luis De Clouet Pietre (d. 1848) (Edo Llop pp. 15–18). Among the adult colonists were thirty-one Frenchmen (including two from Hispaniola), three Germans, one Italian, and the rest Spaniards. By December of that year there were 231 residents recorded in the town: 165 French, 31 Americans, 18 Irish, 3 Germans, 1 Genoese, 1 Belgian, and only 12 Spaniards. For a decade, immigration continued from the United States, France, and Spain as well as ports along the Gulf of Mexico, the Caribbean, and Cuba, all of which sealed its urban expansion and unique cosmopolitan air.

In 1829 the town received the title of Villa of Cienfuegos (Village of Cienfuegos), named in honor of Captain General José Cienfuegos (1763–1825), the driving force behind the project. These were times of coexistence between free laborers and slaves, Africans and *criollos*, in a society dominated economically by immigrants. The white French population continued to dominate, with the French families close to De Clouet achieving the greatest degree of power and influence.

In Cienfuegos, the regional sugar boom provoked a significant demographic jump. In thirty years, the number of sugar mills grew to exceed 100 (Edo Llop p. 282). In 1862 the plantation labor force reached 10,644 slaves, 822 Chinese coolies, 55 Yucatan natives, 150 middle-class blacks, and 430 white employees. The population of the jurisdiction reached 54,511. The construction of a rail line between Santa Clara and Sagua la Grande fueled the development of the sugar towns of Lajas, Palmira, and Cruces. The port-sugar-rail triangle definitively inserted the Cienfuegos region into the plantation economy of western Cuba.

URBAN DEVELOPMENT AND ARCHITECTURE

This city was built upon innovative criteria for urban development and architecture and has a layout that reflects neoclassical urban planning and architectural concepts, adapted to the Laws of the Indies and influenced by inspiration from the Enlightenment and the French and North American experiences. The plan took the shape of a square with 25 blocks of some 330 feet (100 meters) per side, each block being divided into 10 lots that demarcated broad streets. The Plaza de Armas was located in the center, with the city hall, church, customs house, and other public buildings and households of the local hierarchy situated around it (Martín Brito pp. 10–11).

La Villa expressed modern urban planning concepts in its entranceways and sidewalks, which followed the lines of the facade. The construction of tree-lined avenues on Arango and Vives Streets and the Plaza de Labra were in keeping with the proposals of Baron Georges-Eugène Haussman (1809–1891) for Paris, reinforcing the idea of privileging public space. The cemetery buildings, with their vertical niches around their perimeters, reflected the concepts of hygiene and respect for hierarchical placement, and the specific typology in the construction of religious and public buildings reinforced the urban order and hygiene governed by municipal regulations. Alongside the sea were the docks, large warehouses, and workshops owned by the principal merchants.

Slavery, sugar, and trade produced the fortunes of the Cienfuegans, some of whom built sumptuous homes in the neoclassical style that merged three functions: home, office, and business. Of these mansions built in the 1870s, those belonging to José Quesada and Manuel Blanco stand out. In 1881 José García de la Noceda built his mansion, adding a balcony in order to enjoy the view of the sea.

In 1880 Cienfuegos received the title of "city." From then on, the elegant lines of the facades, in the form of blocks, continued to typify the main streets, and it was at this time that the Paseo del Prado (Prado Avenue), with its porticos, became the backbone of the municipality. Pediments, cupolas, and balconies sprang up in the urban space, lending harmony to the original architectural assembly. Engineers and master craftsmen had been adding elements of other styles to the predominant neoclassical motifs, heralding a certain eclecticism that would endure in the new buildings (Millán p. 6). Ancestral estates, almost always of wood and showing a notable North American influence, were built in places meant for vacationing in the area around Cayo Carenas, Punta Gorda, and Castillo de Jagua, the

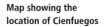

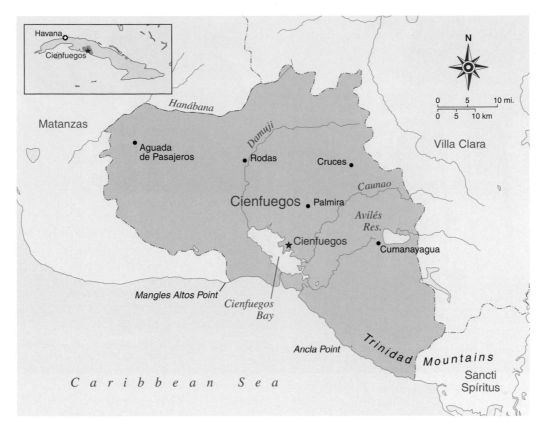

fort where the Spanish regrouped in order to attack the English, who had taken Havana in 1762. The identifying elements that bind together, give life to, and maintain the dynamism of the Cienfuegos tradition are built out of the tensions between a *criollo* vernacular heritage and incorporated neoclassical motifs.

The construction of the Jesuit school Nuestra Señora de Monserrat and the Terry Theater speaks of changes in architecture, education, and culture. When the Republican period began, the city maintained its urban centrality and strengthened its eclecticism with the majesty of the Palacio de Valle, the San Lorenzo School, the retirement home, and the Acea Cemetery, whose eclectic facades are reminiscent of Greco-Roman classicism and whose garden-type layout expressed North America's growing influence. The proliferation of American Protestant religions brought with it the construction of schools and churches. The Atkins Botanical Garden appears as a sign of this northern presence in Cienfuegos.

The continuity of this dialogue assimilated the modernity of art nouveau, art deco, and rationalist architecture without changing the roots that had defined neoclassicism as the main symbol of Cienfuegos's identity. In the nineteenth century, Cienfuegos became an "exceptional example of a representative architectural collection of new ideas of modernity, hygiene, and order in the urban planning developed in Latin America" (Millán pp. 4–5). More than a century later, the historic urban center became part of a UNESCO World Heritage Site (Millán p. 5).

ETHNIC AND RACIAL MIXTURE

The *cienfueguero* reflected the idiosyncrasy and feeling of belonging to Cienfuegos: The inhabitants created symbols rooted in their various cultural influences and generated the fusion and exchange of things from the Spanish and French with those of the *criollos*, Africans, Americans, Europeans, and Chinese. At first the indigenous mixed with the European and the African. The creation of the city's crest in 1831, the publication of the first local history in 1846 and another in 1862, and the flag inspired by the French tricolor hoisted during the insurrection for independence—all these provide evidence of a distinct identity with many cultural roots recognized by other Cubans, who began to refer to the region as the *Pearl of the South.*

The French and European families made notable scientific and cultural contributions to the life of Cienfuegos. Memories remain of the French settlers' fine cuisine and their interest in fashion, theater, dance, and music. In addition, pastimes and customs from North Americans—from baseball, cycling, and gymnastics to the taste for comfort and luxury—are part of the local fabric thanks perhaps to the urban upper and middle classes.

The black community witnessed an intense religious syncretism among African ethnicities, a situation that was most strongly expressed in the city and among the Congo, Lucumí, and Arará *cabildos*. No one can deny the underlying African influence in Cienfuegos. This cultural presence drew from Catholic Christianity and Western European customs and gave rise to a new system of Cuban beliefs, forming important centers of worship in Palmira, Lajas, and Cienfuegos. This tradition remains highly applicable even into the early twenty-first century, with the popular musical symbol Benny Moré (1919–1963) (Fuentes Guerra pp. 43–44).

On the one hand, the right to free association favored the process of racial mixing and transculturation, and on the other, it slowed national integration by creating separate groups of Spaniards (divided into regional associations), Cubans, Asians, workers, landowners, women, and men. In the absence of a nation and in the process of building a national culture, traditions were created in the style of Guanaroca (the Eve figure of the indigenous Siboney people), the Dama Azul (Lady in Blue), and the Venus Negra (Black Venus). A Cienfuegan Cuban identity was imagined, beginning first with the French and Spanish, and later the Cuban stew—the *ajiaco*, Fernando Ortiz's metaphor—in which all the members of the imagined community have a place.

Life in the rebel camps between 1868 and 1898 erased the racial and class barriers of the colony and created a different perspective, dimension, and flavor for the spicy *ajiaco* that went into configuring the Cuban nation and its national identity. Cubanness, in Cienfuegos, emerged from this whole process of racial blending, syncretism, the formation of associations, and the struggle for independence. The Cienfuegan collective identity assumed the distinct traits of the city, a place defined by idiosyncrasy and local character. The city residents, of different origins and cultures, recognized themselves as Cienfuegans, the first step toward feeling Cuban.

POPULAR REVOLT IN CIENFUEGOS

In the early morning of 5 September 1957, the leadership of the 26th of July Revolutionary Movement (MR-26-7) and a group of sailors from the Southern Naval Division in Cayo Loco led the popular uprising in the city of Cienfuegos against the regime of Fulgencio Batista (1901–1973). That day, several groups of low-ranking sailors surrendered the guard posts to the Southern Naval District in Cayo Loco and granted entry to the leaders and soldiers of the 26th of July Movement, who had previously been quartered in various houses throughout the city. The rebels were paralleling the frustrated attempts organized first to support the expedition of the yacht *Granma* in November 1956 and later to create a guerrilla front in the mountains of Escambray during the spring of 1957. The September action was the first step of a plan of coordinated revolt, with conspiratorial nuclei in several military units from Havana, seconded by clandestine soldiers of the Movement in the capital and the province of Las Villas.

Supporters took to the streets in droves at the news of the uprising in the most important naval enclave of the southern coast and the taking of the Maritime Police and the National Police Station by commandos made up of sailors and MR-26-7 combatants. In the centrally located Martí Park, people converged from all sectors of Cienfuegan society, especially students, workers, the poor, and the unemployed. This strong popular support quickly exhausted the ammunitions taken from the three central garrisons that had been overtaken by the rebels. Many backers were left waiting for a weapon, as it was proving impossible to defeat the Rural Guard on the periphery of the city.

However, calm reigned in the rest of the Republic on 5 September, because conspiring leaders from the national navy had decided to postpone the start of the revolt. The Cienfuegans remained distanced from the decisions made in Havana and were out of contact with Faustino Pérez and the other leaders of MR-26-7, whose soldiers tried to distract the forces of Batista in Havana and other parts of Las Villas province. By midday, the air force was showering machine-gun fire on the rebel positions, and soldiers were able to advance on Cienfuegos with the help of borrowed cars.

Still, the revolutionary leaders placed their hopes on the national uprising. At midday there was fighting downtown against superior forces. By nightfall Batista's military had retaken Cayo Loco and the Maritime Police. Fighting continued only on the outskirts of Martí Park. Around 10 p.m. on 5 September, the resistance at the police headquarters ceased, followed by the fall of Colegio San Lorenzo, the last bastion of the rebels. Prisoners taken during the battle of Colegio San Lorenzo were executed. Close to fifty combatants died in the popular uprising, which demonstrated the divide that existed among members of Batista's armed forces, the strength of the clandestine movement in the cities, and the popular support for the armed struggle to restore democratic rule and the Constitution of 1940 (García Martínez 2007, pp. 17–18).

Fourteen months later the Cienfuegan revolutionaries provided important support to the guerrillas of MR-26-7, the Revolutionary Directorate of March 13, the Organización Autentica, the 2nd National Front of Escambray, and the invasion unit of the 26th of July Revolutionary Army, commanded by Ernesto "Che" Guevara (1928–1967). The fall of the Batista regime led to the entrance of the 2nd Front guerrillas into Cienfuegos on 1 January 1959, headed by Commander William Morgan (1928–1961).

The days between August 1959 and December 1965 were characterized by an intense armed confrontation with the revolutionary government of Fidel Castro (b. 1926) in the mountains of Escambray and throughout urban Cienfuegos. A large portion of the 150 counterrevolutionary groups rising up in Las Villas province were defeated by Fidel's forces in this part of the central southern region of Cuba.

In the 1970s and 1980s, Cienfuegos received large investments to turn it into an industrial center. The Juraguá nuclear facility, the Carlos Manuel Céspedes thermoelectric plant, and the Carlos Marx cement plant were begun in those decades. The latter was the first cement producer in the country, while the electric plant provided more than 10 percent of the country's electricity. These projects were affected by the Special Period, and the nuclear facility was never completed. By contrast, tourism became central to the city's economy in the late twentieth and early twenty-first centuries, with Cienfuegos's bay, architectural jewels, and Martí Park being the main attractions.

BIBLIOGRAPHY

Atkins, Edwin F. *Sixty Years in Cuba: Reminiscence of Edwin F. Atkins.* New York: Arno Press, 1980.

De la Fuente García, Alejandro. *A Nation for All: Race, Inequality, and Politics in Twentieth-Century Cuba.* Chapel Hill: University of North Carolina Press, 2001.

Edo Llop, Enrique. *Memoria histórica de Cienfuegos y su jurisdicción.* Havana: Ucar, García y Cía, 1943.

Ferrer, Ada. *Insurgent Cuba: Race, Nation, and Revolution, 1868–1898.* Chapel Hill: University of North Carolina Press, 1999.

Fuentes Guerra, Jesús. "El sincretísmo en los sistemas de creencias cubanos de sustrato africano." *Ariel: La revista cultural de Cuba* (January 2005): 43–50.

García Martínez, Orlando F. "Estudio de la economía cienfueguera desde la fundación de la Colonia Fernandina de Jagua hasta mediados del siglo XIX." *Islas* (Universidad Central de Las Villas), nos. 55–56 (September 1976–April 1977): 117–170.

García Martínez, Orlando F. "El alzamiento popular del 5 de septiembre de 1957 en Cienfuegos." Special issue, *Ariel: La revista cultural de Cuba* 10 (2007): 3–18.

García Martínez, Orlando F. *Esclavitud y colonización en Cienfuegos, 1819–1879.* Cienfuegos, Cuba: Ediciones Mecenas, 2008.

Ibarra Cuesta, Jorge. *Patria, etnia, y nación.* Havana: Editorial de Ciencias Sociales, 2007.

Martín Brito, Lilia. "El proceso de urbanización en Cuba y las Leyes de Indias." *Ariel: La revista cultural de Cuba* 3 (January 2000): 5–11.

Martínez Heredia, Fernando, Rebecca J. Scott, and Orlando F. García Martínez, eds. *Espacios, silencios y los sentidos de la libertad: Cuba entre 1878 y 1912.* Havana: Ediciones Unión, 2001.

Millán Cuétara, Irán. "Reconocimiento mundial para una perla." *Ariel: La revista cultural de Cuba* 8 (April 2005): 4–9.

Pérez, Louis A., Jr. *Ser Cubano: Identidad, nacionalidad, y cultura.* Havana: Editorial de Ciencias Sociales, 2006.

Piqueras, José Antonio. *Sociedad civil y poder en Cuba: Colonia y poscolonia.* Madrid: Siglo XXI, España Editores, 2005.

■ *See also*

Music: 1900–1945

Music: Afro–Cuban
Religious Influence on
Cuban Popular Music

CLASSICAL COMPOSERS: ALEJANDRO GARCÍA CATURLA

Radamés Giro

One of the founders of twentieth-century Cuban music.

Alejandro García Caturla (1906–1940) seems to have been born with a talent for being everywhere at once. He demonstrated his ability to move in the most varied directions. He learned both music and law with the speed of light; cultivated the most dissimilar friendships imaginable; authored copious correspondence as well as articles for *Musicalia* magazine; gave lectures; produced a rich body of work as a composer that marked him as a pioneer in the use of Afro-Cuban roots and ingredients; was a judge who resolved many disputes and, in dispensing justice, sealed his own fate. He married a black woman, which was uncommon for someone of his social class, and fathered ten children. It is nearly impossible to believe he did all this in the mere thirty-four years of his life. He was born in the city of Remedios in the former province of Las Villas on 7 March 1906. He died in Remedios, assassinated by a convict, on 12 November 1940.

BEGINNINGS

From an early age García Caturla was interested in music, studying violin in Remedios, voice in Havana with the Italian singers Tina Farelli (1879–1966)

Alejandro García Caturla (1906–1940). Composer Alejandro García Caturla produced a rich body of music that marked him as a pioneer in the use of Afro-Cuban ingredients. COURTESY OF THE CUBAN HERITAGE COLLECTION, UNIVERSITY OF MIAMI LIBRARIES, CORAL GABLES, FLORIDA

and Arturo Bovi (1868–1953), and harmony, counterpoint, and fugue with the Spanish conductor Pedro Sanjuán (1886–1976). He was a violinist in the Orquesta Sinfónica de La Habana (Havana Symphony Orchestra) and played viola for the Orquesta Filarmónica de La Habana (Havana Philharmonic); as a tenor he performed in the Tercer Concierto Típico Cubano (Third Concert of Traditional Cuban Music) in the capital's Payret de La Habana theater, singing his *criolla* titled *Mi amor aquel* (That Love of Mine) and, with José de Castro, the duet from the first act of the opera *La Gioconda* by Amicare Ponchielli (1834–1886). He also played piano accompaniment for silent films in several Havana movie houses and both founded and directed the University of Havana's Caribe jazz band.

PARIS, BARCELONA, AND PARIS AGAIN

Having amassed this background of both knowledge and experience, García Caturla traveled to Paris in 1928 in order to study with the eminent composer and teacher Nadia Boulanger (1887–1979), then a professor at the École Normale de Musique de Paris. Boulanger recognized the beehive of ideas churning in the mind of her young student, which she determined to channel without doing violence to the creative imagination of this disciple who wanted to learn everything at once.

His compulsion to experience all that Paris could offer led him to attend the productions of the Ballets Russes and the Ballet Espagnol. Through Cuban writer Alejo Carpentier (1904–1980), García Caturla met the filmmaker Georges Sadoul (1904–1967), the writers Louis Aragón (1897–1982) and Robert Desnos (1900–1945), and the composer Edgar Varèse (1883–1965). The Maurice Senart publishing house issued his compositions *Danza lucumí* (Yoruba Dance) and *Danza del tambor* (Dance of the Drum).

García Caturla returned to Cuba equipped with the tools to compose the pieces then simmering in his mind. He joined the Asociación Latinoamericana de Compositores (Latin American Composers' Association) and began a correspondence with the U.S. composer Henry Cowell (1897–1965), who had by invitation of the International Society for Contemporary Music (ISCM) premiered several of his own works in Cuba and became the promoter of Caturla's works abroad.

In 1929 García Caturla returned to Europe, this time accompanied by Eduardo Sánchez de Fuentes (1874–1944), both traveling as delegates to the fourth Festival Ibero-Americano de Música Sinfónica de Barcelona (Ibero-American Music Festival in Barcelona), where they premiered their *Tres danzas cubanas* (Three Cuban Dances) under the direction of Catalán Mario Mateo and won one of the festival prizes. In Barcelona he met Spanish musicologist Adolfo Salazar (1890–1958), composers Rodolfo (1900–1987) and Ernesto Halffter

(1905–1989), and conductor Bartolomé Pérez Casas (1873–1956).

From Barcelona, García Caturla moved on to Paris, now in the company of Mexican composer Manuel M. Ponce (1882–1948). There he presented his piece *Dos poemas afrocubanas* (Two Afro-Cuban Poems), with words by Alejo Carpentier, premiering it with himself at the piano at the Salle Gaveau in Paris. This was soon followed by the premiere of his *Bembé* (*fiesta* in African-derived Cuban slang), conducted by Marius François Gaillard (1900–1973), this time without Caturla's presence. Later, U.S. conductor Nicolas Slonimsky (1894–1995) directed *Bembé*, *Tres danzas cubanas*, *Fanfarrías para despertar espíritus apolillados* (Fanfare to Wake Up the Old and Drowsy), and *Primera suite cubana* (First Cuban Suite).

BACK HOME

In 1932 Caturla founded the Sinfónica de Caibarién (Caibarién Symphony Orchestra), with which he presented works by Wolfgang Amadeus Mozart (1756–1791), Claude Debussy (1862–1918), Maurice Ravel (1875–1937), Igor Stravinsky (1882–1971), George Gershwin (1898–1937)—with himself at the piano in *Rhapsody in Blue*—Henry Cowell, and Manuel de Falla (1876–1946), as well as his own compositions.

Alejandro García Caturla employed the most advanced composition techniques of the era, adapting them to his expressive purposes. Only briefly was he under the influence of Debussy, Erik Satie (1866–1925), Darius Milhaud (1892–1974), Falla, and Stravinsky. His most notable contribution was his working with material from the Afro-Cuban musical tradition, from which he borrowed stylistic elements that matched his expressive needs, culture, and sensibility. As an artist, he accepted no laws other than those of his intuition.

In his article "Symbolic Possibilities of Afro-Cuban Music," he asserted: "The exuberance, color, power, freshness, forcefulness, and rhythmic richness of Afro-Cuban music lend themselves perfectly, in all senses, to the meaning and content of the symphonic genre, as well as to its ideology and needs. With an astonishingly varied quantity of rhythms, Afro-Cuban music possesses all the requisites for a triumphal entry into the symphonic field" (Henríquez p. 178).

WORKS

The song *Mari-Sabel* (1929), for voice and piano, is one his most beautiful by virtue of its melody, rhythm, harmony, and style. From a structural point of view, the work unfolds in a mood of richness, with a heterogeneous relationship between song and accompaniment. The lyrics, by Caturla himself, unfold unpretentiously and in accord with the atmosphere of black Cuban life they evoke; they can be located within the Afro-Cuban poetics later made famous by Nicolás Guillén (1902–1989) who popularized them with his outstanding qualities as a poet and his fertile imagination.

García Caturla's *Mulata* (1933), also for voice and piano, uses a text by Guillén that presents one of the many social problems faced by blacks in the Cuban republic: the social inferiority complex. But beyond its emphasis on the racial problem, the work contains the poetic symbolism of the black soul evoked by Guillén and captured by Caturla in his unique song. *Mulata* is similar to *Mari-Sabel* in style and expression, in its aesthetic world, but the aural realities are different, as is the lacerating dramatic quality of Guillén's poem with the same title:

> Ya yo me enteré, mulata,
> mulata, ya sé que dise
> que yo tengo la narise
> como nudo de cobbata.
>
> [Mulatta, I already know
> what they say about me
> that I've got a nose
> like the knot in a tie.]

The poem is a playful evocation of the street idiom most closely associated with Cubans of color; it contains invented modifications, like *narise* for *naríz*, for purposes of rhyme and atmosphere.

Caturla handles Afro-Cuban rhythms with equal effectiveness even without the use of percussion, as can be heard in *Primera suite cubana* (1931), for piano and eight wind instruments. This is one of his most rigorous works both in style and in its use of the most diverse elements of Cuban folkloric music, including son and rumba. "Folklore's importance is not in its subject matter, but in its spirit. And that spirit resides inside the composer, not outside" (Carpentier 1994, p. 49).

Berceuse campesina (Country Berceuse, 1939), his final work, is a synthesis of the ingredients in the historical development of Cuban music up to that time: Afro-Cuban in the insistent drumming of the left hand and Hispanic in the melody played with the right. Thus Caturla culminated his development of a style in which nothing was alien to him. If the rhythm of his music is tenacious and at times frenetic, that is because it reflects an enormous ancestral strength as well as the interior demon that possessed him—the Afro-Cuban rhythm with which he created his symphonic works, all touched with a power of seduction and an aura of secular mystery.

What has allowed him to so outlast his period? Caturla was an alert musician, an artist never complacent, in constant struggle, who committed himself to infusing Cuban music with a distinct nationality. As a man, musician, and artist he created himself; he

■ *See also*

Music: 1900–1945

Music: Afro–Cuban Religious Influence on Cuban Popular Music

was a man and a musician ahead of his time, which is why he endures as a composer. His life and works attracted so much attention that Mexican musicologist Gerónimo Baqueiro Foster (1898–1967) did not hesitate to declare him one of the three musical geniuses produced by Latin America; the other two were Heitor Villa-Lobos (1887–1959) of Brazil and Silvestre Revueltas (1899–1940) of Mexico (Marinello p. 22). Along with fellow Cuban musician Amadeo Roldán (1900–1939), Caturla introduced modern symphonic music to Cuba. Thanks to him, Cuban classical music then found its way into the repertoires of the most demanding orchestra conductors in other lands. His importance as a composer, one always ahead of his time, has been proved—hence the surprising currency of his works as contemporaneous of a different age.

Those attempting to analyze Caturla's works with the usual theoretical tools will find only a trace of what is there, because harmonic analysis, the rules of counterpoint, and the formulas of composition are of little or no use in measuring the value of his music. If Caturla owes anything to the European avant-garde of his era, that debt remains encased in the strength and originality of his work, because his music is order, strength, and freedom.

SELECTED DISCOGRAPHY

Dos poemas afrocubanos. Lyrics by Alejo Carpentier and Nicolás Guillén. Performed by Phillis Curtin (soprano) and Gregory Tucker (piano) (1929).

Leyendas. Obras inéditas de Alejandro García Caturla. Performed by María Victoria del Collado (piano) and Alfredo Muñoz (violin).

Lullaby (*Berceuse campesina*): *Danza del tambor.* Performed by José Echániz.

Preludio corto. Performed by Henry Brant.

Primera suite cubana. Performed by Orchestre National de la Radiodiffusion Française (1931).

BIBLIOGRAPHY

Béhague, Gerard. *Music in Latin America: An Introduction.* Englewood Cliffs, NJ: Prentice-Hall, 1979.

Carpentier, Alejo. *Temas de la lira y del bongó.* Havana: Editorial Letras Cubanas, 1994.

Carpentier, Alejo. *Music in Cuba.* Translated by Alan West-Durán. Minneapolis: University of Minnesota Press, 2001.

Cowell, Henry. "Sones de Cuba." *Modern Music* 8 (January–February 1931): 445–447.

García Caturla, Alejandro. *Correspondencia.* Edited by María Antonieta Henríquez. Havana: Editorial Arte y Literatura, 1978.

Henríquez, María Antonieta. *Alejandro García Caturla.* Havana: Ediciones Museo de la Música, 2006.

Marinello, Juan. *Imagen de Silvestre Revueltas.* Havana: Publicaciones Sociedad Cubano-Mexicana de Relaciones Culturales, 1966.

■

CLASSICAL COMPOSERS: AMADEO ROLDÁN

Ana Victoria Casanova

A composer who upended Cuban concert music in the third decade of the twentieth century.

Amadeo Roldán, the distinguished Cuban composer, violinist, and orchestra conductor, revolutionized and modernized the repertoire of concert music in Cuba in the mid-1920s. He was the first to compose avant-garde symphonic works using Cuban and Afro-Cuban melodies and rhythms.

Roldán's compositions brought him universal recognition and laid the foundations for the emergence of autochthonous works within the most modern movements of the first half of the twentieth century. As a musician and conductor, he founded and directed groups dedicated to the performance and premiers of contemporary music of the time, as well as works in a range of styles from Cuba and the rest of Latin America.

LIFE

Amadeo Roldán Gardes (1900–1939) was born by chance in Paris, where his parents, Moisés Roldán, a Spanish businessman, and Albertina Gardes, from Cuba—both residents of Madrid—were visiting the Universal Exposition. He began studying music at a very early age and had contact with Cuban music, as his mother would play works by Manuel Saumell (1818–1870) and Ignacio Cervantes (1847–1905) on the piano as well as songs of the celebrated eastern Cuban group El Cocoyé. In 1908 Roldán entered the Conservatorio de Música y Declamación de Madrid where, two years later, he began to study the violin. Seven years later he graduated with a degree in performance and won the conservatory's first prize as well as the Sarasate Prize named after the eminent Spanish violinist Pablo Sarasate (1844–1908). At the age of only seventeen, he founded the Orquesta Filarmónica de Madrid, and by 1918, he was performing as a soloist in various cities in Spain.

Roldán arrived in Cuba at the age of nineteen. Soon afterward, he held the position of first violin in a range of orchestras belonging to Spanish and opera review companies. He also played in various nightclubs in Havana, such as the Hotel Inglaterra, where he began composing *Fiestas galantes*; the cabaret El Infierno, where he composed several parts of his two ballets; and the Hotel Lafayette, where he met important Cuban intellectuals from the Grupo Minorista, among them Alejo Carpentier (1904–1980).

Roldán held the position of first viola in the Orquesta Sinfónica de La Havana, founded by Gonzalo Roig (1890–1970) and Ernesto Lecuona (1895–1963) in 1922. When Pedro Sanjuán (1886–1976), the Spanish orchestra conductor, arrived in Cuba a year later, he founded a second symphonic organization, the Orquesta Filarmónica de La Habana, in which Roldán held the position of first violin. In addition, Sanjuán became his teacher, and his influence was decisive in the subsequent trajectory of Roldán's work.

In 1924 Roldán put together and founded the Cuarteto de La Habana, which for three years specialized in the performance of modern music. He also conducted the Filarmónica from 1932—when Sanjuán returned to Spain—until 1938. At the same time that Roldán was carrying out these activities, he taught and conducted at a variety of institutions, such as the Conservatorio de la Filarmónica and the Conservatorio Municipal de La Habana, which subsequently bore his name. He raised academic standards at these schools and modernized the curricula. In addition, he belonged to the Pan-American Association of Composers, where he directed the West Indies Section. Roldán died at the young age of thirty-eight. It represented an incalculable loss for Cuban culture.

WORK

Amadeo Roldán began composing at the age of sixteen. In this first stage of his career, which lasted until he was twenty-five years old, his works showed a marked influence of French impressionist music. Among these compositions are the *Gran suite*, for classical trio; *Fugue* and *Cuarteto en do* (Quartet in C) both for string quartet; the orchestral pieces *Escena sinfónica* (Symphonic Scene) and *Scherzo*; and *Recitativo* (Recitative) for piano and string quartet.

Roldán also wrote for voice and piano using verses from outstanding poets such as the avant-garde Cuban writer Mariano Brull (1891–1956), the Spanish modernist Francisco Villaespesa (1877–1936), and the French symbolist poet Paul Verlaine (1844–1896), from whom he took the title for one of his early works, *Fiestas galantes*, a homonymous collection of eight songs from 1923, considered by composers to be his "first piece" (Gómez p. 34). Other compositions are the unfinished opera *Deirdre*, *Sonata en mi* (Sonata in E) and *Dos danzas cubanas* (Two Cuban Danzas) for violin and piano, and *Amanacer en el mar* (Dawn over the Ocean), *Prelude*, *Romanza sin palabras* (Wordless Ballad), and *Cervantiana* for piano.

In the 1920s Roldán joined Afrocubism, the aesthetic, humanist movement that sought to revalue the presence of the African elements in Cuban culture that were precursors of that culture and that had been suppressed for so long. From this point on, influences from earlier Yoruba, Bantu, or Abakuá music began to appear in his works, along with other types of music born in Cuba, such as *son* and *rumba*. They were expressed in a language characterized by the most up-to-date concepts of timbre, instrumentation, polyrhythm, and polytonality of the times.

Furthermore, he used traditional Cuban percussion instruments in his symphonic works and developed a graphic notation for them, paying attention to the techniques and effects of execution employed to play each one. In this last regard, Roldán made a technical contribution of worldwide import. When other composers—Edgar Varése (1883–1965) in his work *Ionisation* (1931), for example—wanted to write out the rhythms of Cuban percussion instruments, they needed to use the graphic system Roldán had invented (Neyra p. 14).

The focus of his musical production, decidedly folklorist in the broadest sense, went beyond the limited field of Afro-Cuban music. As he indicated in a letter to Henry Cowell, his goal was

> to revitalize the folklore of our countries, not to create works of a purely local or national character, but as a universalizing project.... American musicians, masters that we are of such rich and varied melodic and rhythmic foundations as those that exist in each of our countries, let us seek to disseminate our art across the continent, let us use American modes of expression, let us develop, let us give life to our own essentials—in a word, let us make autochthonous American art.

Gómez pp. 168–169

In 1925, under the baton of Pedro Sanjuán, *Obertura sobre temas cubanas* (Overture on Cuban Themes) made its premier. This event located Roldán in the aesthetic avant-garde of the time, for it constituted "a work in which the use of national themes as the basis of a symphonic construction inaugurated a new stage in history" (Martín p. 123).

A year later he had his first great success with his musical treatment of folkloric and national stylistic elements in *Tres pequeños poemas: Oriental* (Three Short Poems: From the East), inspired by *cocoyé*, a type of music from eastern Cuba; *Pregón* (Merchant's Call), based on an authentic street vendor's song; and *Fiesta negra* (Black Festivity), with a range of elements from Afro-Cuban music.

His ballets *La rebambaramba* (1927) and *El milagro de Anquillé* (Miracle at Anquillé, 1928), with librettos by Carpentier on Afro-Cuban themes, were performed for years as symphonic suites. The former was taken on tour through Europe by Nicolás Slonimsky (1894–1995) and played by the Orquestra Strara in the Salle Gaveau in Paris. It also caught the interest of Sergey Diaghilev (1872–1929), director of the Ballets Russes, "but his death cut short the idea of presenting this ballet" (Gómez p. 68).

In 1928 Roldán completed three works whose titles and instrumentation displayed a broad vision of Cuban folklore. They were *Danza negra* (Black Dance), for voice and seven instruments (clarinets in B minor and A, two violas, bongo, maracas, and cowbell), with poetry by the Puerto Rican poet Luis Palés Matos (1898–1959), premiering a year later in the Salle Gaveau in Paris under the direction of Marius François Gailard (1900–1973); *Dos canciones populares cubanas* (Two Popular Cuban Songs), for cello and piano, titled *Punto criollo* (Criollo Punto) and *Guajira vueltabajera* (Peasant from Vueltabajera); and *A Changó* (For Changó), for a laud quartet.

Poema negro (Black Poem), for string quartet, and the *Rítmicas* (Rhythmic) series date from 1930. *Rítmicas I-IV* were composed for wind quintet and piano, whereas parts *V* and *VI—En tiempo de son* (Son Tempo) and *En tiempo de rumba* (Rumba Tempo)— were written for an ensemble of instruments characteristic of Cuba, composed of claves, cowbells, maracas, *quijadas* (donkey jawbones used as percussion instruments), *guiro* (percussion instrument made from a gourd), bongo, Cuban timbales, timpani, *bombo* (Cuban bass drum), and *marímbula* or double bass. These last two *Rítmicas* placed Roldán at the forefront of the national and international avant-garde, as they constituted "two of the first works in the world written for a percussion ensemble" (Neyra p. 14).

He later produced, among other works, a collection of eight songs using poetry by Nicolás Guillén (1902–1989). They are titled *Motivos de son* (Son Motifs), for voice and eleven instruments; *Tres Toques* (*De marcha, De rito, De baile*) (Three Beats [March, Ritual, Dance]), for orchestra; *Curujey*, also with poetry by Guillén, for chorus, two pianos, and percussion instruments; as well as three compositions for piano: *Mulato* (Mulatto) and *Dos piezas infantiles* (Two Children's Pieces), namely *Canción de cuna del niño negro* (Black Boy's Lullabye) and *El diablito baila* (The Little Devil Dances).

■ *See also*

Music: Music since 1959

The Music of Ernesto Lecuona

DISCOGRAPHY

New World Symphony. *Tangazo. Music from Latinamerica* (1993).

BIBLIOGRAPHY

Carpentier, Alejo. "Amadeo Roldán–Alejandro García Caturla." In *Music in Cuba*. Minneapolis: University of Minnesota Press, 2001.

Diaz, Henríquez y Piñeiro. *Amadeo Roldán Testimonios*. Havana: Letras Cubanas, 2001.

Gómez, Zoila. *Amadeo Roldán*. Havana: Editorial Arte y Literatura, 1977.

Henríquez, María Antonieta, and José Piñeiro Díaz. *Amadeo Roldán: Testimonios*. Havana: Editorial Letras Cubanas-Museo Nacional de la Música, 2001.

Kuss, Malena. "Cuba: A Quasi-Historical Sketch." In *Music in Latin America and the Caribbean: An Encyclopedic History*, edited by Malena Kuss. Vol. 2: *Performing the Caribbean Experience*. Austin: University of Texas Press, 2007.

Martín, Edgardo. *Panorama histórico de la música en Cuba*. Havana: Cuaderno C.E.U. Universidad de La Habana, l971.

Moore, Robin. *Nationalizing Blackness: Afrocubanismo and Artistic Revolution in Havana, 1920–1940*. Pittsburgh, PA: University of Pittsburgh Press, 1997.

Neira, Lino. "Rítmicas V–VI de Amadeo Roldán: Golpe al centro de a percusión." *Revista Clave* 8, no. 1 (2006): 12–17.

■

CLASSICAL COMPOSERS: LEO BROUWER

Ana Victoria Casanova

Famous guitarist and composer of twentieth-century Cuban music.

The prolific Cuban composer Leo Brouwer (b. 1939) made major contributions to contemporary world music in the second half of the twentieth century. Considered one of the greatest guitarists of all time, Brouwer is also regarded as one of the most significant composers for that instrument. He also composed over three hundred works for other instruments. Acclaimed as a conductor, he has led orchestral groups in Cuba, Europe, and the Americas, including the Symphony Orchestra of Cordoba (Spain), the Philharmonic Orchestras of Liège and Berlin, the BBC Chamber Orchestra and Symphony Orchestra, the Chamber Orchestra of Toronto, and the Toronto Symphony Orchestra.

EDUCATION

Brouwer's family included noted Cuban musicians, including his paternal grandmother the composer Ernestina Lecuona (1882–1951) and his paternal great uncle the composer and pianist Ernesto Lecuona (1895–1963). His mother, a member of a women's orchestra, played a variety of instruments and sang. His father was an amateur guitar player. Leo began to play the guitar at the late age of thirteen, first under the tutelage of his father. Later, and for just three years, he studied with Isaac Nicola, who immersed him in a world previously unknown to Leo. Mirta de Armas quotes Brouwer as saying: "Nicola's discovery had a huge impact on me. I remember...how he took the guitar and played music I had never heard before in my life: Gaspar Sanz, Luis de Milán and, later, Fernando Sor [1778–1839] and Tarrega" (p. 34). Brouwer performed for the first time in 1955 at the Lyceum Lawn Tennis Club of Havana.

Thereafter Brouwer went to the United States. He attended the Juilliard School of Music in New York and the University of Hartford in Connecticut, before returning to Cuba in 1960. Among his teachers in that era were Stefan Wolpe, Joseph Iadone, Isadora Fredd, Vincent Persichetti, and J. Diemente (Giro pp. 71–72).

WORKS

Brouwer began composing at the age of sixteen on the instrument with which he felt the closest connection: the guitar. His first works include *Preludio* (Prelude), *Pieza sin título no. 1* (Untitled Piece No. 1), and *Danza característica* (Typical Dance). He gradually expanded his compositional range to include other instruments. In 1959 *Ritual*, his first composition for symphony orchestra, appeared, a choreographic sketch in which he reformulated fragments of Afro-Cuban music of Yoruba origins. Brouwer has made many contributions to the guitar repertoire with regard to the use of an innovative aesthetic, the adoption of new technical resources, and the enrichment of its language with forms of expression particular to traditional Cuban instruments like the *laúd* and the *tres*.

Outstanding among his many compositions for guitar is *Elogio de la danza* (In Praise of Dance, 1964), which was originally commissioned for a ballet by the Cuban choreographer Luis Trápaga and was staged internationally by famous choreographers such as Maurice Bejart (1927–1980). Post-serial and aleatory works such as *La espiral eterna* (The Eternal Spiral, 1970) and the earlier *Canticum* (1968) also took on great significance. This last piece was considered by the Catalan guitarist Emilio Pujol to represent a new starting point in modern composition for the guitar, similar to the impact of *Homenaje a Debussy* (Homage to Debussy, 1920), by Manuel de Falla (1876–1946) (Giro p. 76).

As of the early 2000s, Brouwer had composed for piano, cello, viola, violin, flute, percussion set, and trumpet; he had written for solo instrument and chamber or symphonic orchestra and for choral groups and various chamber ensembles. His incidental music for plays and films also stands out, with nearly one hundred scores for Cuban films, among them *Lucía* (1968), *Memorias del subdesarollo* (*Memories of Underdevelopment*, 1968), and *La última cena* (*The Last Supper*, 1976).

Over the years, Brouwer adopted various types of languages and compositional techniques. A pioneer in the use of aleatory and electroacoustic music in Cuba, his *Sonagrama I* (for prepared piano), from 1963, constitutes the first aleatory piece composed in Cuba. Two years prior, after he appeared at the Warsaw Autumn Festival, his compositional concepts underwent a transformation. "It wasn't a question of novelty," Brouwer notes, "as I remember circulating recent recordings of [German composer Karlheinz] Stockhausen, [French composer Pierre] Boulez, and [U.S. composer Morton] Feldman, among others, in Havana four years earlier; rather, it was the continuity of contact, the saturation of the ear" (Brouwer, p. 65).

Brouwer used the technical and aesthetic qualities of those composers to develop new styles of music. Through these influences and throughout the evolution of his work, Brouwer introduced a broad range of authentic forms for expressing the Cuban essence in contemporary world music.

Toward the end of the 1960s, the search for a more accessible avant-garde music led Brouwer increasingly deeper into postmodernism. *La tradición se rompe…pero cuesta trabajo* (Tradition Can Be Broken…But It Takes Work), a work for symphony orchestra in which the composer built in an unusual form of audience participation, dates from these years.

According to Brouwer, his postmodern works are directly related to the essence of his country that musically has absorbed a vast array of styles, rhythms, and genres from Europe, Africa, the United States, the Middle East, and Asia:

> Cuba…exists on a foundation made up of a blend of cultures. This superimposition of ways of life creates a typology that, ever since the end of the sixteenth century, has been known as *criollo*. Totality, integration, plurality, blend—and therefore, richness—form the true roots of our idiosyncrasy, which is directly connected to the essence of postmodernism.
>
> *Brouwer p. 49*

Among the many compositions in this vein, the *Concierto de Lieja* (Liège Concerto, 1980) for guitar and orchestra represents a synthesis of all the techniques and languages Brouwer employed previously. By 1980 the constant search for better communication had led the composer to employ a heightened lyricism and minimalist techniques.

Brouwer has also written many orchestrations, transcriptions, and versions over a very wide spectrum of the repertoire of international music. Outstanding examples include his versions of songs by Gonzalo Roig (1890–1970), Jorge Anckermann (1877–1941), and Eliseo Grenet (1893–1950), along with two ragtime pieces by Scott Joplin (1868–1917). *Pantomima* (Pantomime) and *Farruca*, from Manuel de Falla's (1876–1946) ballets *El amor brujo* (Love, the Magician) and *El sombrero de tres picos* (The Three-Cornered Hat) are also noteworthy pieces in this category. In addition, in *From Yesterday to Penny Lane* (1986), for guitar and string orchestra, Brouwer re-created and restructured songs by John Lennon (1940–1980) and Paul McCartney (b. 1942) in the characteristic modalities and tendencies of composers representative of various eras in the evolution of world music.

RELATIONSHIP WITH OTHER ARTS

The close connection between Leo Brouwer's compositions and other arts, such as literary and visual arts, appear in his catalog with a universal vision and an all-encompassing range of aesthetics and eras (baroque, classical, romantic, twelve-tone, contemporary, rock, jazz, Cuban). These convergences with non-musical artistic genres could be a response to extra-musical subject matter that is far from being merely programmatic. The precepts of modular theory—the

Leo Brouwer (b. 1939). Cuban guitarist and composer Leo Brouwer receives the tenth SGAE Tomás Luis de Victoria Award for Latin American music at the San Fernando Royal Academy of Fine Arts in Madrid, 25 November 2010. © EPA/GUSTAVO CUEVAS/CORBIS

central aspect of the artistic conceptions of Paul Klee (1879–1940) and Wassily Kandinsky (1866–1944), among others—with regard to geometric forms, color, proportion, dimension, and structure are reflected in a large number of Brouwer's compositions, not only those directly related, through their titles, to literary and visual works of art.

For example, the composition *Manuscrito antiguo encontrado en una botella* (*Ancient Manuscript Found in a Bottle*, 1983) for violin, cello, and piano, is based on the "The Lotus and the Bottle," a story by the nineteenth-century U.S. author O. Henry (1862–1910); *El Decamerón negro* (The Black Decameron), for guitar (1981), is inspired by African tales collected by Leo Frobenius (1873–1938); and *El reino de este mundo* (*The Kingdom of This World*, 1968), for wind quintet; and *Los pasos perdidos* (The Lost Steps, 1999), for double bass and percussion, are connected to the magical realism of the novels of the same names by Alejo Carpentier (1904–1980).

With regard to painting, the *Bocetos* (Sketches) series, for piano—begun in 1961 and taken up again in 2006—was inspired by works of Cuban painters such as Raúl Milián, René Portocarrero, Nelson Domínguez, Eduardo Roca (Choco), Manuel Mendive, Fernando Cabrera Moreno, Roberto Fabelo, Carlos Enriquez, and Raúl Martínez. A similar connection also appears in *Cuadros de otra exposición* (*Pictures from Another Exhibition*, 2000), whose various parts were conceived as music for certain paintings by Hieronymus Bosch (1450–1516), Eugène Delacroix (1798–1863), Francisco Goya (1746–1828), Amedeo Modigliani (1884–1920), Wilfredo Lam (1902–1982), and Robert Rauschenberg (1925–2008).

STYLES AND TRENDS

Brouwer's compositions include an extraordinarily broad spectrum of musical styles, trends, and genres from around the world. In them he combines traditional and avant-garde principles, which are reflected in a wide variety of languages and in the highly heterogeneous musical forms he employs.

References to folk and popular music appear in Brouwer's work through an extensive amalgamation of genres from Cuba and other countries in the Americas, Europe, and, to a lesser extent, Asia. Their presence, often more implicit than explicit, manifests itself through essential manners of expression and abstractions and in a very peculiar use of inflection, articulation, endings, and sound textures. In this sense, it should also be noted how Brouwer uses particular forms for organizing contents and structures of sonic material. In this regard, the distribution in polytimbric and polyrhythmic bands becomes especially relevant, characteristic of the diverse forms of Cuban and Afro-Cuban aesthetic languages and, by extension, of an entire, essentially Caribbean and Afro-Caribbean, culture.

The universality achieved in Leo Brouwer's musical language emerges precisely from its proximity to the aesthetic expressions and traditions native to Cuba and the Caribbean and perhaps in the New World as a whole. Nevertheless, his creative and compositional techniques are rooted in the most contemporary languages born of highly diverse philosophies and aesthetic currents from the second half of the twentieth century. Without a doubt, this pluralistic musical language positioned him as the foremost creative artist, or the most important composer, in contemporary Cuban music.

SELECTED DISCOGRAPHY

Colección: La obra guitarrística de Leo Brouwer (2001).

De Bach a Los Beatles (2000).

Leo Brouwer 1939: Integral Cuartetos de Cuerda (2010).

Leo Brouwer: Antología Selecta (2003).

Leo Brouwer: Homoludens (2004).

BIBLIOGRAPHY

Armas, Mirta de. "La guitarra habla cubano." In *Revista Revolución y Cultura* (December, January, February 1976): 52–54.

Brouwer, Leo. *Gajes del oficio.* Havana: Editorial Letras Cubanas, 2004.

Giro, Radamés. *Leo Brouwer y la guitarra en Cuba.* Havana: Editorial Letras Cubanas, 1986.

Hernández, Isabelle. *Leo Brouwer.* Havana: Editora Musical de Cuba, 2000.

CLASSICAL COMPOSERS: TANIA LEÓN

Susan Thomas

Cuban-born composer and conductor.

Multifaceted composer, conductor, pianist, arts advocate, and educator, Tania León has been an established international artist since beginning her professional career in the United States in the late 1960s. Born in Havana in 1943, León began studying piano as a child and later earned two degrees from the Conservatorio Peyrellade: a bachelor's degree in theory and solfège in 1961 and one in piano in 1963.

León was a concert pianist in Cuba when, in 1967, she immigrated to the United States. She settled in New York City, where she entered New York University, earning two degrees in piano (B.S. 1971, M.S. 1975). About a year after her arrival in New York, León joined the Dance Theatre of Harlem, first as a rehearsal pianist and then as music director, a position she held from 1969 to 1980. León utilized all of her skills as pianist, conductor, and composer with the Dance Theatre, and her tenure as music director had a lasting impact on the organization. She established the Dance Theatre's music school (1970) and orchestra (1975) and composed four ballets premiered by the group: *Tones* (1970), *The Beloved* (with Judith Hamilton, 1972), *Haiku* (1973), and *Dougla* (with Geoffrey Holder, 1974). She later described her involvement with the Dance Theatre of Harlem as one of the most formative experiences in her professional career, describing it as having shaped "the Tania that I am right now" (Spinazzola p. 4).

León's conducting career began in 1971 with a performance at the Festival of Two Worlds in Spoleto, Italy, by the Dance Theatre of Harlem accompanied by the Juilliard Orchestra. After that she began to concentrate on conducting, studying with Laszlo Halasz, Vincent La Selva, Leonard Bernstein, and Seiji Ozawa. In addition to conducting the Dance Theatre, she began to receive invitations to conduct other prominent ensembles, including the Buffalo Philharmonic (1970, 1975), the Symphony of the New World (1974), and the BBC Northern Orchestra (1976). By the 1990s, she was a sought-after guest conductor, appearing with such major ensembles as the Orchestra of the Metropolitan Opera (1990, 1996), the National Symphony Orchestra of Johannesburg (1992), the Gewandhausorchester Leipzig (1995), and the New York Philharmonic (1996). She also has conducted a more popular repertoire. In 1977 to 1978, she served as the music director for the Broadway production of *The Wiz*, and in 1996, she served as music director for *The Lion King* for Walt Disney Theatricals.

In the late 1970s she and the composers Julius Eastman and Talib Rasul founded the Brooklyn Philharmonic Community Concert Series, establishing León as a force for promoting minority composers and performers and for broadening music's role in the community. A tireless advocate for new music and especially that by Latin American composers, León served as the new music advisor to Kurt Mazur and the New York Philharmonic, and until 2001 was the Latin American music advisor to the American Composers Orchestra (ACO). Her work with the ACO led her to found the annual music festival Sonidos de las Americas (Sounds of the Americas), which began in 1994 in New York City by showcasing the work of Mexican composers.

León's compositions reflect a multitude of compositional, stylistic, and personal influences. Her highly individualistic works draw from Cuban and Latin American dance rhythms, jazz, and gospel music, as well as the Western art music tradition. Her work shows a tendency toward angular melodic writing and uses colorful and often surprising orchestration. León's writing is technically proficient, and her harmonic language shows the influence of twentieth-century atonal and serial composition. Music critics frequently place her works in the tradition of modernist composers such as Igor Stravinsky, Charles Ives, and George Crumb, yet it is also important to view her contributions in light of Cuban modernists who blended contemporary compositional methods with local music style, such as Amadeo Roldán (1900–1939), Alejandro Caturla (1906–1940), and Hilario González (1920–1996).

One of the most prominent characteristics of her work and the one most often mentioned by critics as evidence of her Cuban heritage is her use of rhythmic layering. This characteristic can be seen in her work for chamber orchestra, *Ácana* (2008), which combines shifting rhythmic layers with birdcalls and animal sounds, placing the listener into a vibrant Caribbean soundscape. Her widely acclaimed *Drummin'* (1997) for orchestra and percussion ensemble and *Indígena* (1991) for large chamber orchestra illustrate her integration of popular Cuban and Caribbean rhythms. The sixty-minute *Drummin'* is a multimedia work that juxtaposes Afro-Caribbean, Native American, and pan-Asian percussion ensembles, orchestral percussion, and a chamber orchestra alongside choreography by Bebe Miller, video art by Philip M. Jones, and an onstage mirror installation that reflects and refracts musicians, dancers, and images. One of the few musical or theatrical works to explore the cultural diversity of South Florida, *Drummin'* chronicles the history of Miami, exploring in sound, movement, and visual art the shaping of the city by various immigrant cultures. The opening of *Indígena* evokes Stravinsky, with angular woodwind flourishes interrupted by bursts of percussion and a brief marching ostinato (repeated motive) in the bassoon that recalls

■ *See also*

Diasporas: Afro-Cubans in the Diaspora

Music: Afro-Cuban Religious Influence on Cuban Popular Music

Music: Music since 1959

The Rite of Spring. The work's opening also references jazz, introducing blue notes and the melodic texture and harmonic vocabulary of post-bebop jazz. Approximately halfway through the work, however, the sudden appearance of a static G-major triad announces a major shift in texture, and the work shifts into *comparsa* (carnival) mode, with the trumpet leading an orchestral parade of polyrhythms closer and closer through a prolonged crescendo and even playing a riff from "La Jardinera," an authentic *comparsa* melody.

León is also known as an accomplished composer for the voice. Her published works demonstrate her interest in and commitment to diversity and inclusion. *Singin' Sepia* (1996), a cycle of songs about slavery and diaspora, was recorded by soprano Tony Arnold and Continuum in 2008. León frequently set to music the poetry of female writers, as she did in *Singin' Sepia* as well as in *To and Fro* (1990), *Reflections* (2006), *Atwood Songs* (2007), and her choral compositions *Rezos* (2001) and *Estampas* (2008). León's opera *Scourge of Hyacinths* (chamber version, 1994; full opera, 1999) was written on a libretto coauthored with the Nobel Prize-winner Wole Soyinka based on his radio play. The opera, set in an unnamed authoritarian country, tells the story of three political prisoners being held in a prison surrounded by a lagoon choked with water hyacinths. The hyacinths represent corruption, and their tangles prevent the literal escape of the prisoners and also serve as a metaphor for the prisoners' inability to appeal for justice. The score references Yoruba and Afro-Cuban religious music, using the religious theme as a plot catalyst and the music's rhythmic drive to move the action forward. The complete opera premiered in 1999 at the Grand Théâtre de Genève, Switzerland, as part of the official celebrations commemorating the fiftieth anniversary of the Universal Declaration of Human Rights.

Although known for its major impact on contemporary classical music in Latin America, Europe, and the United States, León's work did not receive comparable recognition in Cuba. In October 2010, for the first time in over forty years, she was invited to return to Cuba in her professional capacity as a musician. Her works were performed during the II Festival Leo Brouwer de Música de Cámara in a special session honoring Cuban composers in other lands. With this invitation, Cuba joined other nations in recognizing and celebrating the work of this important force in contemporary classical music.

■ *See also*

Cuban Embargo

Cuban Thought and Cultural Identity: Socialist Thought

Food: Food Shortages and Gender

Food: Revolutionary Period

The Ration System in Cuba

Television: Television since 1959

BIBLIOGRAPHY

Alzola, Concepcion Teresa. *Trayectoria de la mujer cubana*. Miami: Ediciones Universal, 2009.

Briscoe, James R. *Contemporary Anthology of Music by Women*. Bloomington: Indiana University Press, 1997.

Gray, Anne K. *The World of Women in Classical Music*. La Jolla, CA: Word World Publishing, 2007.

Iturralde, Iraida. "In Search of the Palm Tree: An Afternoon with Tania León." In *Cuba: Idea of a Nation Displaced*, edited by Andrea O'Reilly Herrera. Albany: State University of New York Press, 2008.

Koskoff, Ellen, ed. *Music Cultures in the United States: An Introduction*. New York: Routledge, 2005.

Mendoza, Sylvia. *The Book of Latina Women*. Avon, MA: Adams Media, 2004.

Piñero Gil, Carmen Cecilia. "La riqueza multicultural en la composición de Tania León." *La Retreta* (Costa Rica) special issue, *Tania León en Madrid* (February–April 2008).

Piñero Gil, Carmen Cecilia, and Eulalia Cecilia Piñero Gil. "*Scourge of Hyacinths* de Tania León y Wole Soyinka. La universalidad del discurso postcolonial." *Revista Canaria de Estudios Ingleses* (Tenerife) 35 (November 1997): 185–193.

Ramos López, Pilar. *Feminismo y música: Introduccion critica*. Madrid: Narcea, S.A. de Ediciones, 2003.

Reyes, Adelaida. *Music in America*. Oxford, U.K.: Oxford University Press, 2005.

Spinazzola, James M. "An Introduction to the Music of Tania León and a Conductor's Analysis of *Indigena*." D.M.A. diss., Louisiana State University, 2006.

COCINA CUBANA: NITZA VILLAPOL

Antonio José Ponte

Cuba's longest-running cooking show and its celebrity hostess.

Nitza Villapol (1923–1998), familiarly known as Nitza, was the host of a television cooking program that ran for decades and the author of a cookbook perennially republished and pirated. Many consider her to be the epitome of Cuban cooking. She is known particularly for promoting the integration of the cuisine of other Latin American countries into Cuban cooking. She also showed Cubans how to cook under the constraints of Cuba's food rationing program by creating simple meals that required few ingredients.

Nitza was named after the Nitsa River in the Ural Mountains by her father, Francisco Villapol, a communist and admirer of the Soviet revolution, who believed the name to be faithful to the Russian. The Villapol branch of the family had emigrated from Spain to Cuba in the late 1870s, settling in Cienfuegos. Nitza herself was born in New York in 1923, into the well-off Villapol Andiarenas family, who had emigrated from Cuba for political reasons. Her earliest memories were of Washington Heights, and her first gastronomic memory was of American ice cream and candy. She had polio as a child. Her family returned to Cuba when she was nine or ten.

Nitza studied abroad after graduation from high school, although sources differ about her college curriculum. Some say she received a doctorate in education in 1948, whereas others state that she studied diet and nutrition at the University of London in the early 1940s. In 1955 she took courses at Harvard and the Massachusetts Institute of Technology.

STARTS *COCINA AL MINUTO*

Villapol began broadcasting her cooking show *Cocina al Minuto* (Cooking in a Minute) on 3 July 1951 on the Unión Radio TV channel. Her first recipe was a flan de pescado. Her assistant Margot Bacallao was her constant companion in front of the camera throughout the show's run.

Villapol was not the first Cuban to host her own cooking show. Cuban television offered several cooking programs from the time it started broadcasting, including *Teleclub del Hogar* (*Home Teleclub*) that featured information on fashion, exercise, makeup, society, cooking, and cocktails with co-host Dulce María Mestre covering the cooking segments. Rival channels soon produced similar programs: *Cocina Frigidaire* (Frigidaire Cooking, with Ana Dolores Gómez Kemp, 1951), *Cocina Popular* (Popular Cooking, with Amada Cañizares, 1954), *Cocina Mágica Hotpoint* (Hotpoint Magic Cooking, with Italian chef Borchosechi, 1954), and *El Postre de Hoy* (Today's Dessert, with Dulce María Prats, 1955). There were also numerous cookbook authors: Ana Dolores Gómez, Nena Cuenco de Prieto, Carmencita San Miguel, María Radelat de Fontanills, María Antonieta de los Reyes Gavilán, and María Teresa Cotta de Cal (who wrote a very popular manual about using the pressure cooker). But none of these authors or TV hosts enjoyed Nitza Villapol's long and even posthumous celebrity.

Villapol's television cooking show stayed on the air for more than forty years, making it the longest-running show in Cuban television history. Observers of her career have lamented that her tenure on television was never registered in the Guinness Book of World Records. According to Ciro Bianchi Ross (2002), the only show to last longer was NBC's *Meet the Press*. Villapol's show moved from one channel to another over the years, and its schedule varied (it was broadcast daily for a long time then went to three times a week and finally to Sundays only), but it never changed its name, *Cocina al Minuto*, which was also the title of her best-known book, first published in 1954. Her practice of writing down cooking secrets, collecting recipes, and clipping recipes from newspapers and magazines may have encouraged her to create her own cookbook.

"You don't even know how to fry an egg?" asks the book flap of the 1958 edition, coauthored with Martha Martínez. "Do you think you'll never learn how to cook? You're fooling yourself. You know how to read, and you'll know how to cook when you read *Cocina al minuto*."

ABILITY TO ADAPT CUISINE TO CHANGING TIMES

One of the reasons for Villapol's enduring tenure was her ability to adapt her program to the radical changes that took place in society following the Cuban Revolution in 1959. In those first days after the Revolution in January 1959, Cuban television was busy with nonstop reporting on the many current events. Cloistered on the set where she did her program, Villapol cooked for the broadcasters.

The efforts of Cuba's revolutionary government to institute a socialist society brought drastic changes to the country, which also affected Villapol's show. The revolutionary government began to nationalize domestic industries, including the Cuban television industry in 1961, resulting in the exodus of the channel's owner and board of directors. More drastic was the Cuban government's decision to nationalize foreign companies, including those that had formerly advertised on Villapol's show. The government was now her only sponsor. Her eggs were no longer distributed by La Dichosa; her rice was not Gallo brand; her oil was not El Cocinero. Instead eggs, rice, and oil transformed into generic, unbranded goods distributed by the government. They came close to the archetype of ingredients or underwent a curious transformation into Platonic ideals: whatever eggs, rice, or oil came in, whatever eggs, rice, or oil she was given—that was what she used. Any indication of production and sales processes had been erased from the language: Goods seemed to be donated rather than sold. Cuba fed and clothed itself, detached from any connection to money.

The U.S. government responded to Cuba's nationalization program by imposing a trade embargo on Cuba in October 1960. Cuba's isolation from trade with the United States and its allies restricted the flow of food into Cuba. The Cuban government responded by instituting a ration program. Many food items were in short supply or unavailable.

Other cooking hosts were not able to adapt to these changes and were forced out or left voluntarily. Villapol, by contrast, embraced the revolutionary principles and responded by changing her approach to recipes. "I just switched the terms around," she admitted. "Instead of asking myself what ingredients I needed to make this or that recipe, I started asking what recipes could be made with the products that were available" (Bianchi Ross).

Like any seasonal chef, she concentrated on the ingredients people could find in the markets. A prudent decision was made to air the show once a week. That was when Nitza Villapol became legendary. She appeared before the cameras as the epitome of culinary imagination. She represented a cuisine of substitution, given over to metaphors. She cultivated the art of shortcuts and tricks.

ADVOCATE OF THE REVOLUTION AND CUBAN CUISINE

Villapol had spent more than one-third of her life in an era of scarcity. Starting from the few things that were available, she attempted to put together the most delicious of spreads. In addition to dealing with the socialist economy, she had to confront Cuban food prejudices. In a book written after his 1970 visit to Cuba, Nicaraguan poet and priest Ernesto Cardenal (b. 1925) remarked that much of the island's agricultural bounty was not utilized. The country was experiencing terrible shortages, and yet Cubans would not consider eating many of the foods enjoyed by neighboring countries.

Nitza Villapol fought against this narrowmindedness. She showed her viewers that some Latin American cuisines made a sort of vegetarian *ropa vieja* (literally *old rags*), a stew traditionally made using long-simmered tough cuts of beef, but using green plantain peels instead. She introduced the public to some of the revolutionary government's innovations in the fishing industry, such as tilapia. Her talent for improvisation led some to falsely suggest that she would go so far as to make steak out of a cleaning rag or make pizza with melted condoms instead of cheese.

Another persistent rumor tied Nitza Villapol more closely to the administration of Cuba's ration program. Though it could not be proved, many believed that she served on the commission that determined which goods and how much of them would be available in the ration books. She may have been consulted as a dietician and nutritionist by the commission. In her prologue to the 1980 edition of *Cocina al minuto*, Villapol aligned her beliefs with the official discourse of the Cuban government, stating that the embargo was to blame for the food shortages. In addition to the substitution of ingredients in that edition, advertisements were replaced with political propaganda, including an epigraph quoting the founder of communism Friedrich Engels. She maintained that Cuba's first inhabitants had a rich culinary culture. She accused the Spanish conquerors of not properly appreciating indigenous recipes. She expounded on the evils of trade with the United States (when such trade existed) and sang the praises of Soviet flour and friendship.

Fernando Ortiz (1881–1969) wrote that the Cuban nation is an *ajiaco*, a stew with many ingredients. Villapol set the moment Cuban cuisine was born as being that moment when Spanish cooking did away with garbanzos in favor of the local mélange of the ajiaco. At a time when the official discourse shunned local idiosyncrasy in order to more closely associate with the Soviet Union, she highlighted national characteristics. Her conformity led some to accuse her of trying to shore up the revolutionary government, justifying it with recipes.

Villapol was an engaging celebrity whose face was routinely seen in magazine ads. However, off-camera she reportedly did not like to cook, often eating alone at the bar of the Emperador restaurant. Like comedians who refuse to crack a joke offstage or specialists who keep their professional secrets to themselves, she avoided cooking when she was not in front of the cameras. She was an expert at rounding out dishes into meals and was certainly well versed in her field, but she preferred to leave the actual work to Margot. Villapol lived with her mother in a modern apartment in the Vedado neighborhood, and one journalist who visited there at lunchtime, sent on a mission to interview her, discovered that the midday meal consisted only of commercially produced mashed plantains.

Television executives decided to take *Cocina al Minuto* off the air in 1993. Later on they changed their minds (or perhaps the executives themselves had changed), but by then Villapol was not strong enough to appear on television. At her funeral five years after the show's demise, there were very few mourners, her celebrity all but forgotten by the public.

BIBLIOGRAPHY

Works by Nitza Villapol

Cocina al minuto. Havana: Talleres de Roger A. Queralt-Artes Gráficas, 1954.

Cuban cookbook = cocina cubana. México: Tolusa, 1973; Compañía de Publicaciones, 1975.

Cocina al minuto. Havana: Editorial Orbe, 1980.

Cocina cubana. Santiago de Cuba: Editorial Oriente, 1991.

Cocina cubana. 3rd ed. Havana: Editorial Científico-Técnica, 1992.

Los dulces de Cuba. Havana: Editorial Científico-Técnica, 1996.

Desde su cocina: más de 350 recetas de la obra de Nitza Villapol. Havana: Editorial Científico-Técnica, 1999.

Las mejores recetas de la cocina cubana. Algete Madrid: Mestas Ediciones, 2002.

The bilingual cocina criolla. Mexico: Ediciones Zocalo, 2003.

Secondary Works

Bianchi Ross, Ciro. "Nitza Villapol: La mujer que escribía de cocina." Juventud Rebelde (31 March 2002). Available from http://www.lajiribilla.cu

Cardenal, Ernesto. *En Cuba*. Buenos Aires: Ediciones Carlos Lohlé, 1972.

López González, Marcos E. *Nitza Villapol: Breve historia de su vida*. Madrid: Nitza Villapol, 2005.

Ortiz, Fernando. "Los factores humanos de la cubanidad." *Revista Bimestre Cubana* 14, no. 2 (March–April 1940): 161–186.

Pérez Sáez, Dora. "Margot Bacallao, la mejor cocinera de la TV cubana." *Juventud Rebelde* (14 May 2009). Available from http://www.juventudrebelde.cu.

THE COLOR OF SUMMER (REINALDO ARENAS)

Jacqueline Loss

The great Cuban writer's fantastic, satirical history of the Cuban Revolution.

El color del verano, o, nuevo jardín de las delicias (1991; best known in its English translation, *The Color of Summer, or, the New Garden of Earthly Delights*, 2000) is the fourth in the five-novel series that Reinaldo Arenas called his *Pentagonía* (an invented word combining *pentalogía* [pentalogy] and *agonía* [agony]). This fantastic verbal adaptation of *The Garden of Earthly Delights* (the triptych representation of paradise, orgy, and hell, painted by the late fifteenth and early sixteenth-century Dutch master Hieronymus Bosch) exposes the mechanisms through which the Cuban revolution holds on to power, using the literary intelligentsia as an arm in its struggle to do so.

The five *Pentagonía* novels follow the trials and transformations of one protagonist throughout Cuban history. In *Celestino antes del alba* (1967; *Singing from the Well*, 1987), he is a young boy growing up in the rural Oriente province during Fulgencio Batista's second period of rule (1952–1958), who defers his lyrical talents to avoid the violence of a grandfather who considers poetry to be a thing for sissies; in the experimental *El palacio de las blanquísimas mofetas* (1980; *The Palace of the White Skunks*, 1990), he becomes Fortunato, an adolescent who attempts to escape the repression of his family by joining Fidel Castro's guerillas in the late 1950s; in *Otra vez el mar* (1982; *Farewell to the Sea*, 1986), he turns into Héctor, an unhappily married homosexual vacationing on the outskirts of Havana, living under the institutionalized revolution that is coming to resemble the authoritarian Batista regime he had previously condemned. In *The Color of Summer*, this protagonist morphs into the tripartite character Gabriel/La Tétrica Mofeta (Skunk-in-a-Funk)/Reinaldo. Gabriel is the heterosexual son who returns to a resentful and sexually repressed mother in his hometown of Holguín. Skunk-in-a-Funk is a bitchy and gloomy queen referred to as "she," for whom the rest of the world is just as transgendered. Reinaldo is the somber "persecuted" writer. Finally, the protagonist is transformed into the anonymous narrator in *El asalto* (1991; *The Assault*, 1994), the only *Pentagonía* avatar who survives his agony—by murdering the nation's leader, who is his own mother. Francisco Soto, a scholar who has written extensively on Arenas, aptly categorizes the pentalogy as a homosexual *bildungsroman* (a coming-of-age novel) and as a *künstlerroman* (a making-of-the-artist novel). The unconventional, nonlinear, and multiplying fictional registers in all five of Arenas's novels challenge the

■ *See also*

Literature: Fiction in the Revolutionary Period

Peruvian Embassy Crisis and the Mariel Boatlift: 1980

Sexuality: Gay and Lesbian Representation in Cuban Art, Film, and Literature

Sexuality: Revolutionary Period

Sexuality: The UMAP Camps

Reinaldo Arenas (1943–1990) in Paris, 6 June 1986. *The Color of Summer,* published posthumously in 1991, is the fourth novel in a five-part series that Reinaldo Arenas termed *pentagonía.* © SOPHIE BASSOULS/SYGMA/CORBIS

norms and expectations of historical progress viewed as instrumental in both communism and capitalism.

THE COLOR OF SUMMER AS TESTIMONY AND MENIPPEAN SATIRE

Although *The Color of Summer* is the fourth in the *Pentagonía* series, it was the last to be written, during Arenas's final days as he was battling AIDS. As was the case with *El palacio de las blanquísimas mofetas* and *Otra vez el mar*, some chapters of *The Color of Summer* were first written in Cuba and confiscated by the authorities and later rewritten in exile. By placing the action of the novel in the future in the year 1999, the artist transcends his own illness, as he resurrects Cuban artists from different centuries to give testimony to a violent and passionate so-called secret history of the author's nation and its people.

In the author's foreword, uniquely located in the middle of this novel, Arenas explains that homosexuals are treated so poorly in Cuba because Cubans in general possess a despicable attitude toward beauty: "I have suffered not only my own horror, but also the horror of all those who have not even been able to publish their horror" (p. 254). These words capture the extent to which Arenas's *Pentagonía* in general, and *The Color of Summer* in particular, are a kind of collective testimonial, a memoir with many voices interwoven into the narrative. In this respect it both resembles and subverts the *testimonio*, a genre for which Casa de las Américas established a competition in 1970. The novel's frequent depiction of prominent Cuban and international figures participating in gay sex as the rest of the country—men and women alike—acquiesce to such sex/power relations puts a rather different spin on that genre from what that Cuban cultural institution had in mind.

Arenas's literary agent, Thomas Colchie, has explained that the "cyclonic"/episodic structure of *The Color of Summer* was, in part, "born out of necessity. Arenas did not know exactly how long he had to live. So each vignette is, in fact, carefully structured as a complete entity unto itself, just in case it might suddenly be the last" (p. xxiii). Told through several distinct points of view that revolve around the country's preparation in 1999 for a carnival celebrating the fiftieth (rather than the fortieth) anniversary of the 1959 revolution, *The Color of Summer*'s meandering plot and wild mixing of genres (including the satirical drama, the epistolary novel, the essay, the tongue twister, and the *refranero* [collection of proverbs]) manifests a death-defying edginess and hilarity that connect the novel to the tradition of Menippean satire. The official Cuban intolerance of the 1960s and 1970s that led to sending homosexuals and other "social scum" to labor in agricultural-military camps to be "rehabilitated" (actions for which, in 2010, Fidel Castro apologized) comes most directly under fire in the novel. Once imprisoned under the charges of "indecent behavior" and "ideological deviation" but really as a punishment for smuggling writings out of the country, Arenas becomes a close-up observer of sexual and power relations in prison. These and other anecdotes are narrated in Arenas's memoir *Antes que anochezca* (1992; *Before Night Falls*, 1993) in a straightforward fashion, and in a more absurdist and fragmented one in *The Color of Summer*.

Numerous personages from Cuban literary, political, and artistic history are caricatured in *The Color of Summer*. Arenas speaks in the voice of diverse writers, including the Countess of Merlin (1789–1852), and spoofs the internationally renowned Cuban writer Severo Sarduy, whom Arenas considered his greatest literary rival, by nicknaming him "Zebro Sardoya." The talents of the novel's villain Fifo, an "affectionate" nickname for Fidel, lie in his ability to aggrandize revolutionary triumphs. An initial playlet, titled "The Flight of Gertrudis Gómez de Avellaneda: A Light Comedy in One Act (of Repudiation)," focuses on one of the nineteenth century's most canonical writers, who departed Cuba for Spain in 1836. However, in this dramatization, Gómez de Avellaneda defies orders to participate in carnival festivities and, as a punishment, finds herself out at sea among guardian sharks trained by Fifo. Alternating the perspective between the Malecón seawall mobbed by Fifo's supporters repudiating her and the Key West shores where Cuban exiles implore her to follow their lead, this hilarious and horrific comedy somewhat anticipates the Elián González affair in 2000 that brought the most melodramatic and tragic aspects of the island's and exiles' divisions to the fore. Another pawn in this battle is

José Martí, known as the "Apostle of Cuba," who floats in the straits while reciting his own poetic verses critical of the United States. La Avellaneda is insulted until she sinks. Such dramatizations foreground the hypocrisies involved in the forging of communities, about which the excluded Arenas was suspicious.

The destinies of Cuban homosexuals and the rest of the islanders overlap in *The Color of Summer*. The first group migrates abroad to enjoy greater freedom and escape prejudice and persecution, while the latter quarrel so much that they end up on a piece of land in the middle of the sea, detached from Cuba. In a concluding metafictional gesture, the protagonist puts the novel's manuscript into bottles that he throws into the sea. The ever-present sharks that guard the island against its citizens' attempts to escape swallow them up, along with the author.

THE SPECTACLE OF HOPE

The Color of Summer contrasts Cuba's image as the beacon of hope and solidarity in the international sphere in the 1960s and 1970s with the internal repression it endured during that same period. In coalition with intellectuals and artists, everyday citizens, grouped together in Committees for the Defense of the Revolution, harassed and at times assaulted those whose behavior was judged to be incommensurate with the revolutionary cause. Many renowned regime intellectuals are satirized in the novel, often under fictionalized names: novelist Alejo Carpentier appears as Alejo Sholejov, a name that links him to the Soviet Mikhail Sholokhov, a practitioner of socialist realism, a writing style despised by Arenas; Halisia Jalonzo is the name Arenas gives to the Cuban prima ballerina and choreographer Alicia Alonso, portrayed as a right-hand woman of Fifo. *The Color of Summer* also spotlights those leftist sympathizers who support a fraught revolution to feel better about themselves. In Arenian fashion, *feeling better* is sexualized.

Arenas turns stale intellectual history into an international orgy in which geography is inscribed onto bodies. The gigantic phallus of the character nicknamed "The Key to the Gulf" belongs to Lázaro Carriles, based on Arenas's real-life long-term friend, Lázaro Gómez Carriles. However, "the key to the Gulf" also refers to Cuba's position at the Gulf of Mexico's entrance, making it seem as if the very nation receives fellatio when "kings, bishops, working men, soldiers, young Communists, young terrorists, cloistered nuns, virgin young ladies" perform oral sex on Lázaro as Fifo masturbates and monitors from a hot air balloon above (Arenas 2001, p. 440). As a trade-off for such indulgence, some of the foreigners, like Argentina's president and Canada's prime ministress, confer favors upon Fifo. Simultaneously, the Bulgarian embassy opens its doors to Cuban asylum seekers. When, as a result, chaos erupts, it becomes obvious that foreigners' projections onto Cuba and the reality of Cubans' lives are entirely distinct. Clearly this section alludes to the Mariel Boatlift, which is how Arenas left the island in 1980.

CARNIVAL AND MIGRATION

The novel's quasi-psychological report on Fifo ridicules the Revolution's attempt to supplant family with the nation through sexualizing the leader and his relatives. The spawn of a great-great grandfather whose utmost sexual pleasure was sodomizing "a *male* horse," a mother who was as promiscuous as she was Catholic, a father who would rape almost anything, and under the influence of priests who admired his backside, Fifo could not help but engage in a wide range of behavior. As a bugger, queen, and womanizer, the nation's leader, the novel suggests, was obliged to pacify his anxieties through abolishing homosexuals and prostitutes within his dominion.

Russian theorist Mikhail Bakhtin suggests that the function of carnival within the Renaissance social system is as the limited space of permissible transgression, in which the oppressed explode the power structure and undergo degradation and regeneration. Bakhtin's interpretation helps to elucidate *The Color of Summer*. Officialdom's victims, largely *locas* (homosexuals) in Arenas's view, "scream" by outing their fellow citizens for secret "queer" activities and/or working for state security. The sobriety of intellectual discourse is ridiculed in the title of Fifo's speech at "The Grand Oneirical Theological Political Satirical Conference," attended by, among others "the President of the PEN Club of Germany, Herr Günter Greasy," "the President of Mexico, the head of the Syrian Institute of Sports, the chancellor of World University in Santo Domingo, and the writer Carlos Puentes" (Arenas 2001, p. 392). Arenas's temporally and geographically motley list sets the stage for carnival.

The Color of Summer refuses to give in to the consequences of exclusion and silencing. When a scheduled participant is turned away at the door of the conference salon, his Latin (sacred?) discourse on the modern world's condemnation of pleasure is instead delivered by the Queen of Holland: "We have lost all meaning because we have lost paradise, and we have lost paradise because pleasure has been condemned" (Arenas p. 397). Odoriforous Gunk's theorization on the collective experience of fairies is fraught with both pain and pleasure regarding the impossibility of realizing a place for desire:

> A homosexual is an aerial, untethered being, with no fixed place, no place to call his own, who yearns to return to...—but, my friends, he knows not where. We are always seeking that apparently nonexistent place. We are always in the air, keeping our eyes peeled. Our aerial nature is perfect, and so it should not be strange that we have been called *fairies*. We are fairies because we are always in the air, in the air that is not ours because it is unpossessable, though at least it is not bounded by the walls and fences of *this* world.

> *Arenas 2001, p. 400*

The exile's abundant suffering and loneliness incite Arenas to use the first person plural—"we." Furthermore, the local epithet *pájaro* (fairy) becomes a locus for an alternative deterritorialized community that, always searching, is in a perfect condition.

ADAPTATIONS

In 2000, the renowned New York-based painter and filmmaker Julian Schnabel brought Arenas's beautiful suffering to screen in *Before Night Falls* (2000), a biopic that drew from Arenas's memoir, anecdotes, *Celestino antes del alba, El mundo alucinante* (1969; *Hallucinations*, 1971) and *The Color of Summer*. In some scenes, the director appropriates a strategy of collage from Arenas. For instance, in one passage from *The Color of Summer* titled "Impossible Dreams," the narrator says, "I dreamed of an enormous balloon pulled by all the grackles in Lenin Park, and I would ride inside the balloon and travel far, far away, so far away" (Arenas 2001, p. 270); in Schnabel's cinematographic rendering, partygoers attempt to escape the island in a hot air balloon, full of hope, only to crash pathetically into the seawall. While some of the more blatant homosexual aspects of *The Color of Summer* are not as evident in the film, *Before Night Falls* is successful for calling greater attention to this writer not only internationally, but in Cuba as well, where the director Manuel Zayas explored the marginalization of homosexuals through documenting Arenas's life on the island in *Seres extravagantes* (Odd People Out, 2004).

Rebellious, irreverent, and raunchy, Reinaldo Arenas was one of the major voices of Cuban literature in the post-1959 era. Politically, culturally, sexually, he was an outlaw in Havana, Miami, and even New York. Abilio Estevez quotes Arenas as saying, "The world and I are at war." His weapons were his imagination and an almost lethal humor. Despite his solitary stance Arenas was fully immersed in Cuban literary tradition. Arenas, whose work turned apocalypse into *choteo* (mocking, satirical play), left an enduring legacy for Cuban and non-Cuban readers.

BIBLIOGRAPHY

Arenas, Reinaldo. *El color del verano, o, nuevo jardin de las delicias*. Miami: Ediciones Universal, 1991.

Arenas, Reinaldo. *The Color of Summer, or, The New Garden of Earthly Delights*. Translated by Andrew Hurley. New York: Penguin, 2001.

Bakhtin, Mikhail. *Rabelais and His World*. Translated by Hélène Iswolsky. Bloomington: Indiana University Press, 1984.

Canaparo, Claudio. *The Manufacture of an Author: Reinaldo Arenas's Literary World, His Readers and Other Contemporaries*. London: Centre for Latin American Cultural Studies, King's College, 1997.

Colchie, Thomas. "Introduction." In *The Color of Summer, or, The New Garden of Earthly Delights*, translated by Andrew Hurley. New York: Penguin, 2001.

Díez Cobo, Rosa María. "El color del verano o Nuevo jardín de delicias, de Reinaldo Arenas: Humor negro y carnaval narrativo." *Espéculo* 35 (March–June 2007). Available from http://www.ucm.es/info/especulo/numero35/index.html.

Epps, Brad. "Proper Conduct: Reinaldo Arenas, Fidel Castro, and the Politics of Homosexuality." *Journal of the History of Sexuality* 6, no. 21 (1995): 231–283.

Estévez, Abilio. "Between Nightfall and Vengeance: Remembering Reinaldo Arenas." In *Bridges to Cuba/Puentes a Cuba*, edited by Ruth Behar, 305–313. Ann Arbor: University of Michigan Press, 1995.

Ette, Ottmar, ed. *La escritura de la memoria: Reinaldo Arenas, textos, estudios y documentación.* Frankfurt: Vervuet, 1992.

Hurley, Andrew, and Jacqueline Loss. "Afterword." In *The Color of Summer, or, The New Garden of Earthly Delights*, translated by Andrew Hurley. New York: Penguin, 2001.

Loss, Jacqueline. *Cosmopolitanisms and Latin America: Against the Destiny of Place.* New York: Palgrave, 2005.

Miaja de la Peña, María Teresa, ed. *Del alba al anochecer: La escritura en Reinaldo Arenas.* Madrid: Iberoamericana; Frankfurt: Vervuert, 2008.

Molinero, Rita. "Arenas en el jardín de las delicias." In *Reinaldo Arenas: Recuerdo y presencia.* Miami: Universal, 1994.

Salgado, César A. "Reinaldo Arenas." In *Latin American Writers: Supplement I*, edited by Carlos A. Solé and Klaus Müller-Bergh. New York: Scribner's Reference 2002.

Sánchez, Reinaldo, and Humberto López Cruz, eds. *Ideología y subversion: Otra vez Arenas.* Salamanca, Spain: Centro de Estudios Ibéricos y Americanos de Salamanca, 1999.

Soto, Francisco. *Reinaldo Arenas.* New York: Twayne, 1998.

Valero, Roberto. *El desamparado humor de Reinaldo Arenas.* Coral Gables, FL: North-South Center, University of Miami, 1991.

CONSTANTINO ARIAS: HAVANA'S PRE-REVOLUTION PHOTOGRAPHER

Iliana Cepero-Amador

Constantino Arias (1920–1991), a prolific Cuban photographer who depicted social, artistic and political events during the pre-Revolution era.

In the 1940s and 1950s, Havana was the perfect city for leisure. It combined natural beauty, a sophisticated culture, friendly people, and above all, a dazzling nightlife replete with Hollywood movie stars, flashy millionaires, famous artists and intellectuals from the United States and Europe, American gangsters, and tourists. This colorful and conspicuous group frequented Havana's beaches in the morning, mingled over cocktails with the local bourgeoisie in early afternoon, flocked to the fabulous nightclubs at night, and, in the early hours of the morning, watched amazing performances in beach cabarets.

Beneath this happy and glittering face of the capital there was turbulence. Havana was also a city of shantytowns, illiteracy and poverty, rampant prostitution, gambling, and drugs. It was a city shaken by student riots and workers' strikes. The origins and motives for this discontent were diverse: uncontrolled corruption in the government, gangsterism, and a rapid succession of dictatorships in a very short time (Gerardo Machado, 1927–1933, and Fulgencio Batista, 1933–1934 and 1952–1959). After his first coup in 1933, Batista had become the most powerful man in the island, with absolute control of the military. During his first period serving as president (1940–1944), he had established strong relationships with organized crime in the United States, and those links were strengthened after he established his dictatorial regime in 1952. Notorious American mobsters ran casinos, hotels, and racetracks in Cuba, and their businesses were so profitable that an era of economic prosperity took shape.

These were the years when photographer Constantino Arias (1920–1991) was active. Entirely self-taught, he learned the art of his medium in the darkroom he shared with some members of the Cooperativa Fotográfica. At that time, Cuba's photography scene was narrow and extremely competitive. Securing a full-time position at a prestigious publication or setting up a studio required certified training, good connections, and often a lot of money. Lacking all of these prerequisites, Arias was essentially a freelance photographer (*lambiero*)—he was an itinerant photographer working for himself, taking pictures of birthdays, weddings, baptisms, and all sorts of street and social events.

PHOTOGRAPHING HIGH SOCIETY

In addition to being part of the troop of Havana *lambieros* who scraped together a living, Arias had a poorly paid but steady job as the official photographer of the Hotel Nacional from 1941 to 1959. The hotel served as his headquarters and most stable source of income. He set up a small darkroom in one of the bedrooms, for which he paid 100 pesos a month. Under his exclusive contract with the hotel, Arias was required to take photos almost every five minutes. He shot whomever and whatever he came across and anyone who asked for his picture to be taken. He wandered around the building taking souvenir photos for tourists, mostly from the United States, who were enjoying the amenities of this luxurious establishment. Another of his duties was to photograph all celebrities who visited the Nacional; these images were used to promote the hotel.

Arias's routine was hectic. In addition to working at the hotel, he began his mornings by checking the social columns of the newspaper for announcements of the day's most prominent social activities—a wedding joining wealthy families, the presentation of a debutante, an important reception, the arrival of a foreign movie star, or a celebrity-filled party. Then he rushed off to the venue, laden with heavy equipment, in the hopes of arriving before his competitors. Arias quickly developed his shots in order to sell them to the guests at the event or to be the first to offer the pictures to a magazine or newspaper (though there was no guarantee that the pictures would sell).

POLITICAL LEANINGS

Social events and celebrities were not Arias's only subjects. He was involved in political issues, and at times he worked for ideologically radical publications such as the newspaper *La Calle* in 1956, and the University of Havana magazine *Alma Mater* from 1952 to 1959. From early 1940, he also published in *Bohemia*, a journal of reformist and progressive views. In 1943, together with the journalists Carlos Lechuga (1918–2009) and Enrique de la Osa (1909–1997), he began to work on "In Cuba," a section of *Bohemia* that examined the most controversial topics of the day. Arias also befriended student political leaders (stealing steaks from the hotel restaurant for them) and Eduardo Chibás (1907–1951), a politician who actively denounced corruption, and he was a member of Chibás's Partido Ortodoxo and the 26th of July movement.

These competing interests help to explain the wide range of Arias's vision, as he methodically chronicled several themes that symbolized the power struggles and the conspicuous social and racial divisions in the island. Generally, his subjects were enjoying the comfortable ambience of the Hotel Nacional and attending familial and commemorative upper-class events; his subjects were also living the lives of the poor, the marginal nightlife in and around the Rumba Palace cabaret, and those involved in the country's political instability. Shooting indefatigably, Arias was able to sell his flattering and innocuous pictures and keep for himself the more controversial images—especially those that were corrosive in content and style. In these he found a suitable outlet to express more openly his political leanings and his secret enthusiasm for Afro-Cuban popular culture.

METHOD AND STYLE

Arias's method resembled that of the American photographer Arthur Fellig (Weegee, 1899–1968)—a so-called flash-and-run approach, for which Arias used a Speed Graphic camera and 4 × 5-inch negatives. Later he switched to a Rolleiflex and 6 × 6-inch negatives. The continual use of the flash (which gives a frozen brilliance to the foreground and immerses the background in darkness) and the rapidity with which he worked produced highly realistic photographs with a great degree of immediacy.

Many photos at the Hotel Nacional were taken at nighttime, in the elegant casino where gamblers were dressed in evening clothes and an atmosphere of decadence prevailed. Other shots are amusing, such as a photo of a woman in a bathing suit reclining on a chair and covering her face with a hat. Arias's access inside the hotel allowed him to go up to the rooms, making possible pictures such as one of a completely naked voluptuous blonde sitting on the floor while looking at herself in a mirror. The woman—an American guest—did not seem to mind posing for the photographer, and he took advantage of the situation, printing seven images of her.

The photographs of the Hotel Nacional portray an effervescent world of luxury, licentiousness, and carelessness. Batista and his cohorts had great ambitions for Havana as a destination for gambling and unrestrained sexual liberty; Arias's photographs document this Caribbean proto–Las Vegas. Yet, in those pictures not intended for sale, Arias's sitters seemingly are unaware of his presence, enabling him to capture, for example, the vulgarity and artificiality in a middle-aged couple fully dressed in evening attire, walking the hallways of the hotel.

THE RUMBA PALACE BAR

In tandem with the lavishness and dubious morality at the Hotel Nacional, the marginalized racial hedonism that reigned in the city was represented in Arias's photographs at the Rumba Palace Bar. Along the western beaches of Havana (Playas de Marianao), there was an array of third-rate bars and cabarets frequented by poor blacks, prostitutes, blue-collar workers, bohemians, and American tourists. Those cabarets were not safe, and sometimes the nights ended in a bloody fight.

These venues were cultural hotbeds of musical experimentation. The musicians worked from 9 p.m. until the early hours of the morning, and they were poorly paid, but the long hours made them virtuoso performers. Many famous Cuban musicians (including Benny Moré, Barbarito Diez, Miguelito Valdés, Celeste Mendoza, La Lupe, and Rita Montaner) went there to jam after finishing their gigs in the elegant clubs of the city. The cabarets of the Playa de Marianao were also places in which *la rumba* was danced and perfected. Far from the stiffness of the local bourgeoisie and the wealthy tourists who attended their performances in the respectable clubs, Cuban musicians and dancers found in those marginal bars a feeling of liberation and inspiration. A genuine Afro-Cuban culture was forged there.

El Chori (Silvano Shueg Hechevarría), a prodigy on the timbales (*pailas criollas*, Cuban drums), was the star of the Rumba Palace. Though he never cut a record or traveled outside Havana, celebrities passing through Havana (Errol Flynn, Ernest Hemingway,

María Félix, Josephine Baker, Pedro Vargas, and Marlon Brando) went to see him. Arias was one of his fans, too, and his photographs at the Rumba Palace were created out of pure enjoyment and admiration for El Chori rather than for commission. His characteristic expressionist style suited the marginal but stimulating environment of the club: its ramshackle construction and makeshift décor; the overtly sexual contortions of the rumba dancers on the dance floor (and on the tables); the energy of the musicians of El Chori's band; and the shady look of the nightclub's clients. The Rumba Palace series illustrates how musical virtuosity, sexual license, and disdain for social norms informed a way of life and an authentic culture of entertainment.

■ *See also*

The Cuban Revolution of 1959

Gender: The Women's Suffrage Movement in Cuba

Governance and Contestation: The Republic: 1902–1952

Platt Amendment

The World and Cuba: Cuba and the United States

STREET LIFE

Arias combined the realities of everyday life with political activism. He prowled the streets of Havana photographing people overwhelmed by poverty: the beggars, the people living in the slums, the unemployed. Strong black-and-white contrasts, close-ups, and a feeling of improvisation give a rough quality to these photos. There is a whole gallery of characters battered by hard circumstances. A homeless man known in Havana as the Parisian Gentleman (José María López Lledín, 1899–1985) sits on the grass and faces the camera with the tenderness that made him a beloved figure among *habaneros*. A gravedigger hollowing out a trench confronts the photographer with rage; it seems as if he is digging his own grave. An old black woman who works as a maid in a white household is captured in the cramped kitchen of her own home, surrounded by battered pots and pans, brewing coffee with a cloth colander and a can fashioned into a cup; she stares at the camera with an air of resignation and, at the same time, dignity. In one of Arias's most distressing images, a troubled homeless woman sleeps on the ground at the foot of a hospital wall in Havana, overwhelming the viewer with her insanity and destitution. That image signified the fundamental wrongs of Cuban society that Arias strove to highlight in radical periodicals of the era.

Arias photographed electoral posters and police on the street, as well as street demonstrations by workers and university students. Unlike his images of the Hotel Nacional and the Rumba Palace, these shots were taken in daytime and from a distance. Arias wanted to convey a different idea—purity and solidarity among this rebellious sector of the population. His protesters exude an attitude of unity and determination. Arias shared their determination in his belief that a drastic solution to social inequalities was urgently needed.

Because of his status as a freelancer and because of his irrepressible drive to represent all aspects of Havana's life, Arias produced one of the most interesting and certainly one of the most comprehensive collections of photos of Cuba's last republican era. In taking the pulse of a mesmerizing and glamorous city, he realized that a huge upheaval was only a matter of time.

BIBLIOGRAPHY

Bartolomé Barguez, Carlos, personal communication with author, March 2007.

González, María Josefa, personal communication with author, March 2007.

Martínez, Mayra A. "Constantino, testimonio de sus fotos." *Revolución y Cultura* (July 1986).

■

CONSTITUTION OF 1940

Robert Whitney

The Constitution of 1940 and its judicial and political principles for a democratic and sovereign nation-state.

The Constitution of 1940 cannot be understood without understanding the political and economic crisis of the late 1920s and 1930s. The Cuban revolution of 1933 transformed Cuban politics. The experiences of revolutionary struggle and mass mobilization changed the way most Cubans viewed the relationship between the nation and the state. Indeed, many of the popular demands of 1933 became the constitutional edicts of 1940.

POLITICAL CONTEXT AND BACKGROUND

In September 1933, a loose coalition of radical activists, students, middle-class intellectuals, and disgruntled lower-rank soldiers formed a provisional revolutionary government. This coalition was directed by a university professor, Ramón Grau San Martín (1887–1969). Grau's government promised a new Cuba with social justice for all groups and social classes. Grau also made the commitment to abrogate the Platt Amendment, though that did not happen until he had been ousted from power in 1934. The government gave women the vote, instituted the eight-hour work day for workers and a minimum wage for cane cutters, and promoted compulsory arbitration between employers and unions. A Ministry of Labor was created and a nationalization of labor law was passed, which established that 50 percent of all workers in agriculture, commerce, and industry had to be Cuban citizens. The Grau government made agrarian reform a priority.

Grau's provisional government survived until January 1934, when it was overthrown by an equally loose coalition of conservative civilian and military elements. Led by a young sergeant, Fulgencio Batista y Zaldívar (1901–1973), this movement was supported by the United States. To many Cubans at the time, it appeared that the country would become and remain a dictatorship, but this did not happen. Batista understood that after the coup of 1933, in order for any government to rule effectively, it must reflect popular concerns. He also believed that because Cuban political and economic life was so dominated by the

United States under Franklin D. Roosevelt, Cuba would have to evolve toward democracy. The central issue was how, and under whose authority, democracy would be established. Cuba had several civilian presidents between 1934 and 1940, but it was Batista and his army and police that held the strings of power throughout the period. Yet, Batista saw himself as a leader of the revolution of 1933, not as a counter-revolutionary, and though his revolutionary credentials can certainly be disputed (as his contemporaries noted), Batista believed it was his duty to bring order and democracy to Cuba. Cuban governments between 1934 and 1940, therefore, were not democratic, but as the decade came to a close, there were clear signs that Batista was more attuned to the political trends of the time than his enemies—and many of his friends—gave him credit for.

After 1937, Batista's politics took a decidedly populist turn. Under his supervision, the state redistributed wealth taken from capitalists' profits and used it to pay for social programs and labor policies that responded to popular demands. Batista had long promised that he eventually would oversee free and fair presidential elections and a new constitutional convention. In 1938, Batista legalized the Communist Party, which by that year had abandoned its revolutionary program in favor of a popular front against so-called bourgeois democracy. When congressional elections were held on 15 November 1939, political alignments did not correspond to clear ideological differences. Rather, two electoral coalitions emerged, one that supported Batista as a presidential candidate and the other that did not. The anti-Batista forces were dominated by the Partido Revolucionario Cubano (PRC-A, or Auténtico), led by Grau San Martín. The other members were the Republican Action Party of Miguel Mariano Gómez, the Democratic Republican Party led by the elderly conservative former president Mario Menocal (1866–1941), and the ABC Party. The Auténticos were the largest single group that opposed Batista, but internal divisions undermined their unity of purpose. The pro-Batista camp included the Liberal Party, the Unión Nacionalista, the Partido Realista, and the Partido Unión Revolucionaria (the name used by the Communist Party at the time). The organizational backbone of Batista's coalition, however, was made up of his loyal followers within the army and police and the Communist Party, especially its increasingly strong Federation of Cuban Workers (CTC).

What divided these two coalitions was not the question of whether Cuba needed democracy and a strong state but who would build that state and how they would do it. The intense enmity many felt toward Batista stemmed from his role in overthrowing Grau San Martín in 1933. The Auténticos and several other smaller nationalist groups were angered that Batista (and his Communist allies) had robbed them of their opportunity to lead Cuba toward democratic and nationalist reform in 1933. Although the PRC-A was the single most popular political party in Cuba, it had been founded between 1934 and 1936 at the height of Batista's postrevolutionary repression; consequently, in the four years leading up to 1940, the party's internal divisions and Batista's police kept the party organizationally off balance and many of its leaders in exile.

Yet despite the divisive and frequently violent legacy of 1933, the overall trend after 1937 was toward greater democracy. This move was driven by the realization of all political tendencies—each in its own way—that the Cuban state had to have a more solid institutional and constitutional foundation. Of course, it was not inevitable that Cuban politicians would choose democracy as the best means to strengthen the state: In the late 1930s and early 1940s, fascist and corporatist ideologies pulled other Latin American governments in the opposite direction. But authoritarianism had little resonance with Cubans, given Cuba's history of popular and nationalist insurgencies that stressed social and racial equality and the influence of American president Franklin Roosevelt's New Deal liberalism. What helped make this consensus a reality was that the country's economic situation favored relative political stability. Wartime conditions provided Cuban producers with a stable sugar market, especially in the United States, and the investment climate in Cuba improved for American capitalists. Although seasonal unemployment continued to generate hardship for workers in the sugar sector, market stability meant that chances of getting a job for the next *zafra* (late summer or early fall harvest) were better than in pre-1940 harvests. The relations among trade unions, employers, and the state, though not always peaceful, were better than ever before. Tourism, again mostly from the United States, increased dramatically, and there were greater opportunities for Cuban small- and medium-sized businesses to gain a foothold in local and national markets. The income from this commerce made it possible for governments to pay for popular projects and provide employment for larger sections of the population.

It is important to emphasize, however, that although the overall trend was toward democracy, the revolutionary violence and gangsterism that plagued Cuban society in the 1930s lasted well beyond 1940. Most political groups, but especially those more or less affiliated with various Auténtico factions or with Joven Cuba, used armed violence to intimidate or gain leverage with rivals. To complicate matters, both the army and police had extralegal armed groups that acted outside formal command structures and were loyal to one or more political factions or to none at all. Much of this armed violence and intimidation was motivated by a desire to gain access to government and/or criminal patronage networks that would provide people with jobs or other tangible benefits. But because violence was often accompanied by revolutionary slogans and demands for justice and political honesty, it is understandable why many Cubans became both confused and cynical about politics. Thus, Cuban politics leading up to 1940 was marked by a contrast between, on the one hand, the popular desire for democracy and constitutional stability, and on the other hand, widespread anxiety and cynicism about the sincerity of all politicians.

THE CONSTITUTIONAL CONVENTION

The constitutional convention, which opened on 9 February 1940, was presided over by the respected Cuban statesman Carlos Márquez Sterling (1898–1991) and Ramón Grau San Martín. Batista, as usual, stayed in the shadows while still making his presence known. The choice of Grau was recognition that as fractious as the Auténticos were, they had widespread support. Indeed, overall, the balance of power within the convention tended to go against Batista and his allies. In total, there were seventy-six delegates, with the largest numbers going to the PRC-A (18), the Liberal Party (16), the Democratic Republicans (15), the Unión Nacionalista (9), the Communist Party (6), and the ABC (4). Grau's role was to oversee the debates regarding the judicial role and limits of the constitutional assembly, and much of the language and political tone of the constitution was inspired by the Auténticos. Needless to say, these debates were marked by intense public arguments and backroom dealing. It took two months and eight days for the assembly to approve fifty of the eventual 286 articles, and Grau was blamed for much of the political haggling and delay. In contrast, when Carlos Márquez Sterling chaired many of the sessions, the remaining statutes were approved in relatively quick order, perhaps because he was a less polarizing figure than was Grau.

THE CHARACTER OF THE CONSTITUTION

The character of the 1940 Constitution was very much a product of the times, fitting into the larger pattern of the evolution of welfare-state capitalism that emerged before and after World War II (1939–1945). Although the constitutional statutes clearly refer to Cuba's own historical and political traditions, the influence of American New Deal liberalism, Spanish republicanism, and anti-imperialist and populist ideologies in Peru, Mexico, Venezuela, Argentina, and Chile influenced many delegates. And though the ABC Party was no longer as large or as influential as it had been ten years earlier, two of its four delegates—Jorge Mañach (1898–1961) and Joaquín Sáenz—were highly respected intellectuals, and their ideas about the need for a strong state that could oversee and balance competing social classes and interest groups were incorporated into the constitution.

The most important statutes of the Constitution of 1940 established the right of all Cubans to vote in free and fair elections, the use of referendums on issues of singular national importance, the need for the state to prevent unemployment, compulsory social insurance and compensation for workplace accidents, pensions, a minimum working age, the eight-hour day, and a forty-hour work week. Political movements that were based on sex, race, and class were not allowed, though the practical interpretations of exactly what *equality* meant were highly contentious. The state was given the power to suspend political rights for a period of forty-five days if and when national security was threatened. The state reserved the right (which it never used) to limit the extent of cane growing and harvesting if it weakened Cuba's market position or if the size of *latifundia* (extensive and often underutilized private land holdings) threatened to hurt small *colonos* (peasants). The right to expropriate privately owned land in the national interest was also stipulated, but again, this provision was never used.

Ironically, two of the most significant features of the constitution were conceived and written by bitter adversaries, the Auténticos and the Communists. The Communists played a leading role in pushing the statutes on racial equality and making them as specific and concrete as possible. No one objected to general and vague statements about the equality of all Cubans, but once the Communist delegates (half of whom were black or mulatto) insisted that the courts and legislative branches enforce racial equality, there was sharp opposition from more conservative groups. Though the Communist proposals were eventually defeated, the very fact that institutional racism in Cuba was publicly debated at all—with many of the debates broadcast on national radio—was unprecedented, and as a result the Communist Party gained both respect and support.

The second important change brought about by the Constitution of 1940 was the power of the state to assert greater sovereignty over citizenship, labor, and immigration. Between 1916 and the 1930s, sugar companies brought in mostly Haitian and British West Indian labor to cut and harvest cane and Americans to work as managers and technicians. Prior to the 1930s, Cuban governments had neither the will nor the ability to change this situation. But when sugar markets contracted in the late 1920s, Cuba no longer needed foreign labor for the annual sugar harvests, and with the mass unemployment and nationalist protests of the 1930s, demand to nationalize the Cuban working class became both popular and feasible. It is for this reason that Batista retained Grau's original 1933 labor legislation and why most of that legislation became constitutional law. The constitution stipulated that the majority of the Cuban working population must be Cuban by birth. Employment preference was given to naturalized citizens with family members born on the island. Exceptions were made in cases in which Cubans could not be found to fill indispensable technical positions, but the constitution stipulated that whenever possible, Cubans must be given the opportunity to apprentice for these positions. The constitution declared that immigration policy must be entirely under the patrimony of the state and that the importation of foreign labor should not have a detrimental impact on Cuban society.

HISTORICAL AND POLITICAL SIGNIFICANCE

The importance of the Constitution of 1940, as indicated by subsequent history, was not found in what it actually said or accomplished but rather in what it promised and why those promises had to be made in the first place. Not only did the constitution promise equal rights and democracy, but, for the first time in the island's history, Cuba was, judicially speaking, a sovereign nation-state. Once the Platt Amendment was abrogated in 1934, Cuba was in constitutional limbo. The U.S. State Department acknowledged that the source of much political instability was Cuba's humiliating semi-sovereign status. Of course, after 1940 Cuban economic dependence on the United States continued to be a source of debate and tension, but now the legitimacy of the Cuban state was based on its own constitutional sovereignty rather than on approval of U.S. ambassadors or the State Department. How Cuban politicians used and abused that sovereignty would become the central political irritant for the next twenty years.

With the end of World War II in 1945 and a return to insecure market conditions, the 1940 political consensus quickly unravelled. Without the stable and lucrative source of state revenue from the U.S. wartime market, the economic foundation for political stability disappeared. After 1945, Cuban political discourse retained its democratic and populist form, but politics became increasingly violent and corrupt. When Ramón Grau San Martín and the Auténticos were elected in 1944, almost any semblance of the idealism of 1933 had gone. What made the post-1940 debates more than rhetorical verbiage, however, was that constitutional principles could be, and were, interpreted in potentially radical ways. In large measure, this is what the struggles of the late 1940s and 1950s were all about.

■ *See also*

Diasporas: Introduction

Diasporas: Waves of Immigration Since 1959

Miami

Peruvian Embassy Crisis and the Mariel Boatlift: 1980

The World and Cuba: Cuba and the United States

BIBLIOGRAPHY

Álvarez Martens, Berta. "La constituyente de 1940 es una leccíon de madurez nacional : El período 1935–1940 en la historia de Cuba." In *La imaginación contra la norm: ocho enfoques sobre la república de 1902*, edited by Julio César Guanche. Havana: Ediciones la Memoria, Centro Cultural Pablo de la Torriente Brau, 2001.

Argote-Freyre, Frank. *Fulgencio Batista: From Revolutionary to Strongman*. New Brunswick, NJ: Rutgers University Press, 2006.

Carreras, Julio A. "La institucionalidad republicana: Estado, Nación y democracia." In *La imaginación contra la norma: Ocho enfoques sobre la república de 1902*, edited by Julio César Guanche. Havana: Ediciones la Memoria, Centro Cultural Pablo de la Torriente Brau, 2001.

Chang Pon, Federico. "Reajustes para la estabilizzación del sistema neocolonial." In *La neocolonia: Organización y crisis desde 1899 hasta 1940*, edited by Instituto de Historia de Cuba. Havana: Editora Politica, 1998.

Del la Fuente, Alejandro. *A Nation for All: Race, Equality, and Politics in Twentieth Century Cuba*. Chapel Hill and London: University of North Carolina Press, 2001.

Fitzgibbon, Russell H. "Cuba." In *The Constitutions of the Americas*. Chicago: University of Chicago Press, 1948.

Gellman, Irwin F. *Roosevelt and Batista*. Albuquerque: University of New Mexico Press, 1973.

Ibarra, Jorge. *Prologue to Revolution: Cuba, 1898–1958*. Boulder, CO: Lynne Rienner Publishers, 1998.

López Civeira, Francisca. *La crisis de los partidos políticos burgueses en Cuba, 1925–1958*. Havana: Ministerio de Educación Superior, 1990.

Pérez, Louis A., Jr. *Army and Politics in Cuba, 1898–1958*. Pittsburgh, PA: Pittsburgh University Press, 1976.

Pérez, Louis A., Jr. *On Becoming Cuban: Identity, Nationality, and Culture*. Chapel Hill and London: University of North Carolina Press, 1999.

Pérez-Stable, Marifeli. *The Cuban Revolution: Origins, Course and Legacy*. New York: Oxford University Press, 1993.

Sims, Harold D. "Cuba." In *Latin America Between the Second World War and the Cold War, 1944–1948*, edited by Leslie Bethell and Ian Roxborough. Cambridge, U.K.: Cambridge University Press, 1992.

Thomas, Hugh. *Cuba, or the Pursuit of Freedom*. London: Eyre & Spottiswoode, 1971.

Whitney, Robert. *State and Revolution in Cuba: Mass Mobilization and Political Change, 1920–1940*. Chapel Hill and London: University of North Carolina Press, 2001.

CUBAN ADJUSTMENT ACT

Siro del Castillo

A 1966 U.S. law regarding Cuban immigration that fed tensions between the United States and Cuba.

Within the U.S.-Cuba conflict, ongoing since 1959, the issue of Cuban migration, legal and illegal, to U.S. territory has always been a thorny one, full of subtleties and the source of numerous crises between the United States and Cuba. It has also been the impetus for bilateral discussions and agreements. Although these efforts have failed as of 2011 to provide a solution that is satisfactory for those involved, they have helped prevent more serious consequences and, on several occasions, have facilitated the implementation of procedures allowing legal and orderly immigration of Cubans to the United States. However, illegal immigration has not been halted.

Before 1966 most Cubans entered the United States with nonimmigrant visas issued by the U.S. embassy in Havana. Later, under U.S. government instructions, Cubans received the status of "indefinite voluntary departure" (Dominguez p. 502). After diplomatic relations were broken, the two airlines flying between Havana and Miami were instructed to grant a visa waiver to travelers from Cuba. Six months after arriving in the United States, Cuban immigrants were granted indefinite parole. The U.S. desire to offer refuge to people fleeing Communist regimes was central to its Cold War policies. The Refugee Relief Act of 1953 made specific provisions for those fleeing Communist or Communist-controlled countries because of fear of persecution due to race, religion, or political opinion. (These provisions were later eliminated following approval of the Refugee Act of 1980, just one month before the Mariel Boatlift crisis.) On the basis of the 1953 law, in 1961 and 1962 only 1 percent of the Cubans requesting visa waivers were refused. After the Cuban Missile Crisis in 1962, the U.S. government suspended flights from Cuba to the United States. This action led to an increase in illegal departures from Cuba by sea and an attendant increase in loss of life. To address this problem, the Cuban government opened up the port of Camarioca to Cubans who wished to emigrate. The renewal of special flights to the United States in 1965 sparked the second wave of Cuban immigration (1965–1973). By 1966 the U.S. government sought to revise its open-door policy so as to normalize and regulate Cuban immigration, a process that culminated in the Cuban Adjustment Act of 1966.

ENACTMENT AND CONSEQUENCES

From 1959 to 1965, close to 274,000 Cubans arrived in the United States. The original purpose of the Cuban Adjustment Act, as signed into law by President Lyndon B. Johnson in 1965 and enacted in 1966, was to make it possible for most of these Cubans to remain. Thus the law allowed Cubans who had entered U.S. territory illegally to legalize their status. The migratory agreement established what has been called the Varadero-Miami air bridge, across which thousands of Cubans traveled without risking their lives. As a result of this first migratory agreement between the two countries since the Revolution, more than 250,000 more Cubans arrived on U.S. shores.

The Cuban Adjustment Act (Public Law 89–732, 2 November 1966) stated:

> Notwithstanding the provisions of section 245(c) of the Immigration and Nationality Act the status of any alien who is a native or citizen of Cuba and who has been inspected and admitted or paroled into the United States subsequent to January 1, 1959, and has been physically present in the United States for at least one year, may be adjusted by the Attorney General, in his discretion and under such regulations as he may prescribe, to that of an alien lawfully admitted for permanent residence.

According to Cuban authorities, no migratory procedure was followed by the first 70,000 of the 274,000 Cubans who entered the United States; thanks to the agreement, from 1965 to 1973 the 250,000 Cubans who left Cuba did so legally and

with both governments' approval and consent. As Hugh Thomas noted in his book *Cuba, or, The Pursuit of Freedom* (1998), for many Cubans the road to government-authorized emigration was filled until the moment of their departure with obstacles and obligatory work on state-owned farms.

There are various myths surrounding the Cuban Adjustment Act and much confusion both inside and outside Cuba as to the truth behind its implementation. For example, as Siro del Castillo observes in a 2009 article, many do not know that the U.S. government denied permanent residency to thousands of Cubans under the provisions of the law. This was the case for the 125,000 Cubans who entered the United States during the Mariel Boatlift exodus in 1980 and remained in legal limbo for more than five years because they were classified as *entrants*. They attained their legal status, along with thousands of Haitian refugees who had also arrived illegally in 1980, only as a result of Section 202 of Public Law 99–603 of 1986, also known as the Cuban-Haitian Entrants Adjustment Act. (Some observers have pointed out that Haitians and Cubans have received extremely different treatment from the U.S. government, with naturalization and asylum rates for Cubans in certain years twenty times higher than the rates for Haitians.) (Laguerre pp. 87–89).

Subsequent to enactment of the Cuban Adjustment Act, prompted by migratory crises such as the Mariel Boatlift of 1980 and the Rafter Crisis of 1994, the two governments signed partial migratory agreements in 1984, 1987, 1994, and 1995. The U.S. government pledged to grant 20,000 visas annually to Cubans to travel to the United States, but from 1984 to 1994, it issued only 6.8 percent of the promised number, according to a 2002 paper by Max J. Castro. These agreements reestablished commitments and formal channels for ordered, legal migration, but they never handled in-depth the complex problems involved. One of the problems that these agreements approached only in a limited manner is that of Cubans whom U.S. immigration authorities branded *excludables* and who received final deportation orders. Another is that of Cubans who entered U.S. territory illegally. Cubans are considered excludables if they have been tried and convicted in U.S. courts for serious crimes, if they lose their permanent residency because they violated current immigration laws, or if they lose their U.S. citizenship because they committed perjury during their naturalization procedures. The only agreement that dealt with the problem of excludables was that signed in 1984, when the Cuban government agreed to repatriate 2,746 people who had left the country through the port of Mariel; but as of 2011, fewer than 1,800 had been repatriated. In 2006, according to official government figures released to the press, 29,079 Cubans had been given final deportation orders, and unofficial estimates in 2010 totaled more than 40,000

(Chardy p. 14A). However, none of them could be repatriated because there was no bilateral agreement on this subject.

The 1999 implementation of what is known as the *wet-foot, dry-foot* policy, which is an administrative measure rather than an actual law, emerged when it became impossible for authorities to deport Cubans who had reached dry land. Such deportations had not been stipulated in the 1994–1995 migratory agreements, which covered only the repatriation of Cubans who were intercepted by U.S. authorities on the high seas while trying to enter the United States illegally. Moreover, in two separate court cases (*Zadvydas v. Davis et al.* in 2001 and *Clark v. Martinez* in 2005), the Supreme Court ruled that the Immigration and Naturalization Service could not detain an alien indefinitely.

In periodic bilateral meetings held to evaluate fulfillment of the agreements, the Cuban government called for the repeal of the Cuban Adjustment Act; the U.S. government repeatedly urged Cuba to accept the repatriation of Cubans declared inadmissible because they entered the country illegally or were declared excludables. However, no understanding had been reached on these matters as of 2011. Repeal became more complicated with passage of the Helms-Burton Act in 1996, a law intended to reinforce the U.S. embargo against Cuba and which stipulated new conditions for revision of immigration laws. In a proclamation issued in July 2000 by the National Assembly of People's Power on the Cuban Adjustment Act—stated with even greater emphasis in a *Granma* newspaper editorial—Cuban authorities declared that "in the context of the economic war against the Cuban Revolution, U.S. immigration policy has been one of the most important instruments of U.S. hostility toward the island." The Cuban government charged that the Cuban Adjustment Act was the main cause of continued illegal immigration, aggravated by the emergence of criminal human trafficking using motorboats.

According to the Web site of the Cuban Ministry of Foreign Affairs, "The highest expression of the United States' criminal, immoral and discriminatory immigration policy toward Cuba is the Cuban Adjustment Act, the monstrous legislation adopted in 1966 for the clear purpose of encouraging illegal departures of Cuban citizens to that country." The Cuban government viewed the act as one prong of the embargo, a set of economic, political, and migratory policies intended to weaken Cuba and promote attempts to leave the country without government authorization.

The normalization of U.S.-Cuban migratory policies would be a great step forward in the overall normalization of bilateral relations. From 2009 to 2011, the two countries held four meetings on migratory policy, but no new agreements were reached.

Siro del Castillo, Caribbean Commissioner of the Latin American Commission for the Human Rights and Liberties of Workers and Peoples, advocated for an agreement on deportations that would eliminate the need to apply the Cuban Adjustment Act. According to Castillo, every Cuban entering or attempting to enter the United States illegally, on land or sea, should be detained and deported to their country of origin, like any other illegal immigrant. The Cuban Adjustment Act would then only apply to the immigration status of those who have entered the country legally, or have been inspected and paroled. If there were the possibility of immediate deportation, there would be no need to parole them, which is the basis of the Supreme Court decision.

Castillo pushed for the permanent normalization of U.S.-Cuban migratory practices that reflects both sides' interests. The United States must eliminate all policies that encourage illegal emigration or desertion on the part of Cuban workers in third countries, and the Cuban government must standardize its migratory laws and procedures in accordance with universally accepted standards. This would be a great step forward in the overall normalization of bilateral relations.

BIBLIOGRAPHY

Aja, Antonio, and Miriam Rodríguez. "Antecedentes." Centro de Estudio de Alternativas Políticas (CEAP). *CubavsBloqueo.* Available from http://www.cubavsbloqueo.cu/Default.aspx?tabid=2195.

Castro, Max J. "The New Cuban Immigration in Context." *The North-South Agenda* 58 (October 2002). Available from http://www.revistainterforum.com/english/pdf_en/58AP.pdf.

Chardy, Alfonso. "Some Exiles Fearful of Deportation." *Miami Herald* (3 August 2006): 14A.

Commissioner's Memorandum on Eligibility for Permanent Residence under the Cuban Adjustment Act Despite Having Arrived at a Place Other than a Designated Port of Entry. 19 April 1999. Available from http://www.uscis.gov/ilink/docView/afm/html/afm/0-0-0-1/0-0-0-26573/0-0-0-31937.html.

"Current or Recent Alien Adjustment Provisions: Cuban Adjustment. Public Law 89-732, November 2, 1966, as Amended." Available from http://www.state.gov/www/regions/wha/cuba/publiclaw_89-732.html.

Del Castillo, Siro. "La Ley de Ajuste Cubano: Mitos y Realidades." *Viernes* 15, no. 7 (August 2009). Available from http://democraciacristiana.info/derechoshumanos/emigracion/79-la-ley-de-ajuste-cubano-mitos-y-realidades.html.

Dominguez, Jorge I. *La política exterior de Cuba (1962–2009).* Madrid: Editorial Colibrí, 2009.

"Editorial del Periódico *Granma* [27 November 2001]: Trescientas mil personas protestaran hoy en la tribuna Antiimperialista 'José Martí'." Available from http://www.cubavsbloqueo.cu/Default.aspx?tabid=2205.

Estevez, Roland. "Modern Application of the Cuban Adjustment Act of 1966 and Helms-Burton: Adding Insult to Injury." *Hofstra Law Review* 30, no. 4 (Summer 2002): 1261–1298.

Illegal Immigration Reform and Immigrant Responsibility Act of 1996. Public Law 104-208, Section 606, Conditional Repeal of Cuban Adjustment Act. Available from http://www.uscis.gov/ilink/docView/publaw/html/publaw/0-0-0-10948.html.

Immigration Reform and Control Act (IRCA). Public Law 99-603, 100 Stat. 3359, enacted 6 November 1986. Available from https://www.oig.lsc.gov/legis/irca86.htm.

Laguerre, Michel S. *Diasporic Citizenship: Haitian Americans in Transnational America*. New York: St. Martin's Press, 1998.

Ministry of Foreign Affairs, Republic of Cuba. "Acerca de la Ley de Ajuste Cubano." Available from http://www.cubaminrex.cu/Enfoques/lac_acerca.htm.

"Proclama de la Asamblea Nacional del Poder Popular de la República de Cuba sobre la Ley de Ajuste Cubano." 12 July 2000. Instituto Cubano de Amistad con los Pueblos (ICAP). Available from http://www.icap.cu/medidas/proclama_asamblea_nac.html.

Refugee Relief Act of 1953. U.S. Statutes at Large, Public Law 203.

Talamo, Javier. "The Cuban Adjustment Act: A Law under Siege?" *ILSA Journal of International & Comparative Law* 8, no. 2 (Spring 2002): 707–724.

Thomas, Hugh. *Cuba, or, The Pursuit of Freedom*. 2nd ed. New York: Da Capo Press, 1998.

CUBAN COUNTERPOINT: TOBACCO AND SUGAR (FERNANDO ORTIZ)

Jean Stubbs

Foundational twentieth-century text on transculturation for understanding Cuban thought and identity.

Cuban Counterpoint: Tobacco and Sugar was published in Spanish in Havana in 1940 and in English in New York in 1947. It has since been published in several editions in Spanish, in Italian in 1982, and in German in 1987, and a facsimile second edition was set in English in 1995. Destined to become the most famous work of Cuban ethnologist and ethnomusicologist Fernando Ortiz (1881–1969), and long the only work of his available in English, its examination of the impact of Cuba's two principal commodities on Cuban society laid the cornerstone for Ortiz to introduce his concept of transculturation. In the early 2000s, it is seen as a foundational text for understanding not only Cuban history, culture, and identity, but also the Caribbean and Latin America, and more broadly the contemporary globalized world.

THE TEXT, AND TRANSCULTURATION

Counterpoint is an unorthodox, erudite treatise in two parts. The first is an eighty-page title essay, narrating the contrasts between tobacco and sugar as the central agricultural products of Cuba. It begins with allegorical reference to the literary medieval dispute of Carnival and Lent, *Don Carnal* and *Doña Quaresma*, in the book *Libro de buen amor* (1330), by the poet Juan Ruiz, Archpriest of Hita (c. 1283–c. 1350), to set the scene for a drama personifying dark tobacco and white sugar: Don Tabaco and Doña Azúcar. Ortiz affirms:

> Out of the agricultural and industrial development of these amazing plants were to come those economic interests, which foreign traders would twist and weave for centuries to form the web of our country's history, the motives of its leaders, and at one and the same time, the shackles and the support of its people. Tobacco and sugar are the two most important figures in the history of Cuba.

> *1995, p. 4*

Striking contrasts are made:

> Tobacco requires delicate care, sugar can look after itself; the one requires continual attention, the other involves seasonal work; intensive versus extensive cultivation; steady work on the part of a few, intermittent jobs for many; the immigration of whites on the one hand, the slave trade on the other; liberty and slavery; skilled and unskilled labor; hands versus arms; men versus machines; delicacy versus brute force. The cultivation of tobacco gave rise to the small holding; that of sugar brought about the great land grants. In their industrial aspects tobacco belongs to the city, sugar to the country. Commercially the whole world is the market for our tobacco, while our sugar has only a single market. Centripetence and centrifugence. The native versus the foreigner. National sovereignty as against colonial status. The proud cigar band as against the lowly sack.

> *1995, pp. 6–7*

Binary categories are also metaphorical: quality and quantity, power and resistance, desire and repression, dark and light, masculine and feminine, tradition and modernity, *criollismo* and cosmopolitanism, independence and dependence, sovereignty and intervention.

Tobacco was the uniquely Cuban transcultural product—satanic, sacred, magical, masculine, and desirable. Sugar represented the most destructive features of foreign capitalism, and while powerful and masculine, in Cuba it was dependent and feminized even as it modernized. Yet the capitalism "that is not Cuban by birth" was also reducing everything to the same common denominator:

> The landowner is disappearing from the vegas, and the *guajiro* is joining the ranks of

the proletariat, becoming undernourished, poverty-stricken, preyed upon by intestinal and social parasites. The economic system of tobacco is gradually approaching that typical of the sugar industry, and both are being strangled by heartless foreign and native tentacles.

1995, p. 69

The utopian ending to the tale, "because there never was any real enmity between sugar and tobacco," is the counterpoint born of the contrasts, the possibility of a fruitful marriage and happy offspring, jauntily symbolized as alcohol.

The second part of the text, five times the length of the first, comprises what Ortiz originally titled "Complementary Chapters" and changed to "Additional Chapters" in the 1963 second revised Cuban edition in Spanish. Subtitled "Transculturation of Havana Tobacco and the Beginnings of Sugar and Negro Slavery in America," this second part contains twenty-five numbered chapters. Chapter I, "*On Counterpoint* and Its Complementary Chapters," is only three short paragraphs, the first of which reads:

> The preceding essay is of a schematic nature. It makes no attempt to exhaust the theme, nor does it claim that the economic, social, and historical contrasts pointed out between the two great products of Cuban industry are all as absolute as they would sometimes appear. The historic evolution of economic-social phenomena is extremely complex, and the variety of factors that cause them to vary greatly in the course of their development; at times there are similarities that make them appear identical; at times the differences make them seem completely opposed. Nevertheless, fundamentally the contrasts I have pointed out do exist.

1995, p. 97

The following paragraphs frame the remaining four hundred pages in two groupings of chapters, one titled "Transculturation of Havana Tobacco" (Chapters II–X, XIX–XXII, XXV) and the other "The Beginnings of Sugar and of Negro Slavery in America" (Chapters XI–XVIII, XXIII, XXIV).

The opening of Chapter II, "On the Social Phenomenon of 'Transculturation' and Its Importance in Cuba," only five pages long, introduces the real history of Cuba as that of its intricate transculturations. Incessant migrations were accompanied by uprootedness, deculturation, exculturation, inculturation, and neoculturation, and the process as a whole is best expressed as transculturation, itself constantly mutable.

An eclectic array of chapters follows, some a paragraph or so in length, others much longer, advancing information and arguments to ground the initial texts. Chapters III–X on tobacco include short ones—on the seed, Cuban tobacco's low nicotine content, the news of tobacco's virtues taken to Europe by a Spanish Jesuit priest, tobacco and cancer, and how the tobacco of the Amerindians was discovered in Cuba by Europeans—and two on tobacco among the indigenous Amerindians and the transculturation of tobacco. The former is longer than the initial counterpoint essay, and the latter almost as long and far longer than the earlier chapter on transculturation.

While the work is known for its opening essays on counterpoint and transculturation, it is in Chapter X that Ortiz elaborates how tobacco underwent one of the most extraordinary processes of transculturation: the rapid spread of the plant and its radical change in social significance as it passed from the cultures of the New World to the Old. Ortiz expounds on how the tobacco of Amerindians was taken up by blacks and by white sailors before traveling the world; makes comparisons with chocolate, tea, and coffee; and delves into religion and inquisition, liturgy and literature, music and dance, magic and myth.

Chapters XI–XVIII redirect attention to sugar: short ones on terms associated with sugar and sugar's beginnings in the Americas precede a long chapter on the beginnings of the trade in black slaves to the Americas, linked to sugar, and what befell Fray Bartolomé de Las Casas (1484–1566) for having argued in favor of bringing Africans to replace the labor of the indigenous people who faced extinction in the wake of the Spanish conquest. This is followed by short ones on immigrant settlement in sugar, the privileged capitalism of the sugar mill, and the first trans-Atlantic shipment of sugar.

The remaining chapters are uneven in length, but in the main short: four on tobacco, two on sugar, and a final one on tobacco. Chapters XIX–XXII comprise one on tobacco terms prefacing a longer one on how Cuban tobacco conquered the world, followed by two on rolled tobacco and Havana cigar manufacture. Chapters XXIII and XXIV on sugar recount the first rebellion of blacks in 1503 and the enemy beet. The final Chapter XXV is on the Havana cigar, the best in the world, and its seal of quality, introduced in 1889 in legitimate defense against imitations the world over.

The English editions have a simplified chapter format and modified headings. Thus, the second part is titled "The Ethnography and Transculturation of Havana Tobacco and the Beginnings of Sugar in America" and contains only twelve chapters, the first of which is "On Cuban Counterpoint" and the second "The Social Phenomenon of 'Transculturation' and Its Importance." Then follow Chapters 3–7 on tobacco, Chapters 8–11 on sugar, and a final Chapter 12 on how Havana tobacco conquered the world.

Chapter format aside, Ortiz applies transculturation more to tobacco than sugar and then the two transculturate; and, whereas sugar and tobacco recede to the background of the initial narrative of transculturation, they are very much present in all the other chapters. However, just as the point of departure is fiction—the battle between Don Carnival and Dame Lent—so contained within the contrasting parallels of tobacco and sugar are the poetry and the music of *controversia* in the peasant *décima* brought to Cuba by Canary Island immigrants and the African *punto,* to fashion a baroque-style fugue, or counterpoint. The more Ortiz writes about tobacco and sugar, the more he explains Cuban history, culture, humor, and musicality.

THE TEXT IN CONTEXT, NEW TRANSCULTURATIONS

Counterpoint was written as Ortiz turned sixty and was the culmination of his earlier scholarship but also a rupture. Having started with an Italian- and Spanish-influenced criminalistic outlook, his fascination with what he once termed "the Afro-Cuban underworld" led him to adopt a more humanistic approach to the mixing of cultures, rejecting acculturation as a one-way process in favor of two-way transculturation.

Ortiz lived the historic transition between centuries, mainly in Cuba but also abroad, caught up in the intellectual shifts of his time. He studied law, served as a diplomat, ran for office for the Liberal Party, and was then drawn to progressive cultural movements such as the Grupo Minorista and Afro-Cubanism. From the 1920s to the 1940s, he educated himself in a range of disciplines, including anthropology, sociology, history, and music. His influences were many, but *Counterpoint* engaged most with the work of Polish-born British functionalist anthropologist Bronislaw Malinowski (1884–1942), who had coined the term *acculturation,* and with whom he had been in contact since Malinowski's first visit to Havana in 1929. Malinowski wrote the introduction to *Counterpoint,* praising Ortiz as a modern functionalist who knew the value of history.

Ortiz shared many Cuban intellectuals' concern about the situation of the nation since the end of Spanish colonial rule in 1898, especially the crisis-ridden 1930s, and the relative silence surrounding *Counterpoint* after its publication has been attributed to its criticism of the foreign presence, something highlighted by nationalist Cuban historian Herminio Portell Vilá (1901–1992) in his prologue.

After *Counterpoint,* Ortiz researched more fully the African presence in Cuban folklore, music, and theater; and post-1959 revolutionary Cuba saw a flourishing of folklore, dance, and music

Fernando Ortiz (1881–1969). Cuban ethnomusicologist Fernando Ortiz (seated) meets with Prime Minister Óscar Gans (left) and Ricardo Riaño. COURTESY OF THE CUBAN HERITAGE COLLECTION, UNIVERSITY OF MIAMI LIBRARIES, CORAL GABLES, FLORIDA

groups and institutions in the best Ortiz tradition. Re-editions of his prolific work included *Counterpoint*, with the 1963 revised edition, including a new prologue by Cuban historian Julio Le Riverend (1912–1988), replacing that by Portell Vilá, who had by then left Cuba for the United States. Among those furthering his scholarship were Manuel Moreno Fraginals (1964) and Jean Stubbs (1985) on sugar and tobacco; Rogelio Martínez Furé, Nancy Morejón, and Diana Iznaga on culture; and Miguel Barnet, who in 1995 became the director of the new Fernando Ortiz Foundation in Ortiz's former Havana home.

More of Ortiz's work became available in English: *The Batá in Cuba* (1980), "The Afro-Cuban Festival 'Day of the Kings'" (in Bettleheim 2001 [1993]), and "On the Relations between Blacks and Whites" (in InterAmericas and in Pérez Sarduy and Stubbs 1993). *Counterpoint,* however, was the most acclaimed. Elevated with other Latin American masterpieces—notably *The Cosmic Race* (1925) by Mexican José Vasconcelos (1881–1959) and *The Master and the Slaves* (1933) by Brazilian Gilberto Freyre (1900–1987)—it became part of a 1990s revival in cultural and anthropological studies in the Americas. Uruguayan writer and critic Angel Rama (1926–1983) in the early 1980s questioned cultural exchange within a power framework in his work on transculturation in Latin American narrative, and this was developed by Mary Louise Pratt (1992) through the notion of *contact zones* for transculturation, where cultures interact from asymmetric positions of domination and subordination, for an end product of false harmony.

In the context of modernism, postmodernism, and postcolonialism, Cuban American scholars interpreted transculturation differently. Gustavo Pérez Firmat (1989) valued Ortiz's conceptual and textual counterpoint of literal and figurative contrasts but, most importantly, Ortiz's view of Cuban national identity as translational and not foundational. It was not difficult to see how powerful a current of thinking this was for Cuban émigrés, legitimizing their Cuban identity as opposed to their civil status. For Antonio Benítez-Rojo (1989), Western scientific thinking would see much of *Counterpoint* as absurd, irrational, fantastic, but was that so from the margins of power? Benítez-Rojo interpreted transculturation through chaos theory (whereby in nature order and disorder are not the antithesis of each other but rather mutually generative phenomena). Like the Guyanese writer Wilson Harris (b. 1921), Benítez-Rojo argued that, in the sociocultural fluidity and apparent disorder of the Caribbean, there emerges an island of order. This repeats itself, in the paradoxical sense of chaos discourse, whereby every repetition entails the unpredictable flux of transformative change, transition, and return in cultural and racial mixing.

The stage was set for new critical editions of *Counterpoint*, by Enrico Mario Santí (1992) in Spain and Fernando Coronil (1995) in the United States. Santí situated his examination of the text in the interest non-Western cultures generated in post–Cold War globalization. He compared *Counterpoint*, in which tobacco is good and sugar is bad, with the work of Luis Eduardo Nieto Arteta (1913–1956) in Colombia, for whom tobacco was bad and coffee good, and Celso Furtado (1960–2004) in Brazil, for whom coffee was good and sugar bad——and one might add Barickman (1998), whose Bahian counterpoint is one of sugar, tobacco, and cassava. Santí also highlighted transculturation as a literary play James Joyce–style, and neo-baroque in approach, akin to the later work of Ortiz's Cuban contemporary Alejo Carpentier (1904–1980) and the incursion into smoke on film by Cuban émigré Guillermo Cabrera Infante (1929–2005).

Coronil heralded *Counterpoint* as ahead of its times, fashioning binary opposites as tropes for events, ideas, and interpretations in flux. He applied the postmodernist maxim that each reading of the book opens up a different book: Ortiz would have welcomed a perspective that "recognizes its provisionality and inconclusiveness, the contrapuntal play of text against text and of reader against author . . . engaging in this transcultural exchange, as Ortiz's book does, in counterpoint with the historical conditions of its own making" (Coronil in Ortiz 1995, p. xi). This was the text's attraction over half a century later, in a much-changed world "in which globalising forms of capital accumulation and communication are met both with transnationalizing and reconfigured nationalist responses, have unsettled certainties associated with the belief in modernity" (Coronil in Ortiz 1995, p. xii).

One dimension of the revival was the concern over Ortiz's giving primacy to harmony over conflict, especially of the races. Mirrored in Pedro Pérez Sarduy and Jean Stubbs's *AfroCuba* (1993), which included English translations of Ortiz and others who had been inspired by him (including Tomás Fernández Robaina, Tomás González, and Argeliers León, along with Martínez Furé and Morejón), this became highly charged in Cuba's crisis of the 1990s. In their later *Afro-Cuban Voices* (2000), the title of the introduction—"The Rite of Communion"—was taken from Ortiz, but as a beacon for their message and that of others, as they grappled with a more conflictual terrain of racial paradigms facing Cuba in the new millennium.

Interpretations continued to vary widely, as seen in Mauricio Font and Alfonso Quiroz's *Cuban Counterpoints* (2005), the product of a symposium, including scholars from on and off the island held in New York in 2000 to mark the sixtieth anniversary of *Counterpoint*. Suffice it to mention four contributions: Ricardo Viñalet wrote of Ortiz's version of a novel by Canary Island writer Benito Pérez Galdós (1843–1920), told with the irony and implausibility of chivalrous tales of old, suggestive of Ortiz's later allegorical start to *Counterpoint*. Stubbs highlighted old and new global counterpoints between on- and off-island Cuban tobacco and unforeseen transculturations. Enrique Pumar decried economic sociologists for overlooking *Counterpoint* when it speaks to the concept of embeddedness in currency in development studies. Rafael Rojas located *Counterpoint* nationalisms in the rift between those who believed that without sugar there would be no Cuba and contemporaries such as Ramiro Guerra (1880–1970) and Emilio Roig de Leuchsenring (1889–1964) demanding an end to sugar latifundia; drawing on the interpretations of George Yudice, Román de la Campa, Peter Burke, and Coronil, he differentiated Ortiz's transcultural nationalism from the ethnic nationalism of Vasconcelos.

In the early 1990s, Puerto Rican Arcadio Diaz-Quiñones compared the Hispanic-Caribbean national discourse of Puerto Ricans Antonio Pedreira (1899–1939) and Tomás Blanco (1897–1975) with Cubans Ramiro Guerra, Jorge Mañach (1898–1961), and Ortiz, signaling the destruction wrought by colonialism and plantation and U.S. intervention, and calling for a project of national cultural regeneration against the sugar latifundia. Yet there is little scholarship that compares *Counterpoint* with work on the material and symbolic role of key commodities in other national histories. In Puerto Rico, comparisons could be made with the 1940s work of Raymond Christ on sugar expropriating the coffee peasantry and the ensuing struggle of a landless proletariat; with John Auguelli in the 1950s comparing sugar and tobacco in the Eastern Highlands; and with Angel Quintero Rivera in the 1980s on the urban-rural dichotomy, or plantation-counterplantation tension, in the formation of Puerto Rico's cultural identity.

Most intriguing, perhaps, is an example that predates *Counterpoint* by almost a century, which is the work of Dominican Pedro Francisco Bonó (1828–1906). Emilio Rodríguez Demorizi is credited with rescuing Bonó from oblivion in the 1960s, and Bonó's thinking has permeated Dominican intellectual thinking into the early 2000s. Bonó introduced concepts of class, race, capitalism, and inequality into Dominican history and mounted a spirited defense of the peasantry in the central Cibao Valley, arguing that tobacco was democratic in contrast to oligarchic cacao. His anger was also directed against the encroaching sugar industry in the south, driven by land concessions to exiled Cubans (and Puerto Ricans) and its impact on the dispossessed. Sugar was capitalist and foreign, tobacco nationalist; the patriotic liberalism of the Cibao contrasted with the conservatism and foreignness of the south.

And so, in the globalized world of the twenty-first century, but with no cut-and-dried unambiguous blueprints, *Counterpoint*'s legacy must and will continue.

BIBLIOGRAPHY

Barickman, Bert Jude. *A Bahian Counterpoint: Sugar, Tobacco, Cassava, and Slavery in the Recôncavo, 1780–1860*. Stanford, CA: Stanford University Press, 1998.

Benítez-Rojo, Antonio. *La isla que se repite: El Caribe y la perspectiva posmoderna*. Hanover, NH: Ediciones del Norte, 1989. Translated by James Maraniss as *The Repeating Island: The Caribbean and the Postmodern Perspective* (Durham, NC: Duke University Press, 2001).

Bettleheim, Judith, ed. *Cuban Festivals: A Century of Afro-Cuban Culture*, rev. ed. Kingston, Jamaica: Ian Randle Publishers and Princeton, NJ: Marcus Wiener Publishers, 2001. Originally published as *Cuban Festivals: An Anthology with Glossaries*. New York: Garland, 1993.

Font, Mauricio A., and Alfonso W. Quiroz, eds. *Cuban Counterpoints: The Legacy of Fernando Ortiz*. Lanham, MD: Lexington Books, 2005.

InterAmericas. *Miscelanea II of Studies Dedicated to Fernando Ortiz (1881–1969)*. New York: InterAmericas, Society of Arts and Letters of the Americas, 1998.

Moreno Fraginals, Manuel. *El ingenio: complejo económico cubano del azucar*, 3 vols. Havana: Comision Nacional Cubana de la UNESCO, 1964. Translated by Cedric Belfrage as *The Sugar Mill: The Socio-Economic Complex of Sugar, 1760–1860*. New York: Monthly Review Press, 1976.

Ortiz, Fernando. *Contrapunteo cubano del tabaco y el azúcar*. Havana: J. Montero, 1940. Translated by Harriet de Onís as *Cuban Counterpoint: Tobacco and Sugar*. Introduction by Bronislaw Malinowski; prologue by Herminio Portell Vilá; new introduction by Fernando Coronil. Durham, NC: Duke University Press, 1995.

Ortiz, Fernando. *The Batá in Cuba: Selected from the Writings of Fernando Ortiz*. Translated by John Turpin III and B. E. Martínez. Oakland, CA: Institute for the Study of Ancient African Traditions, 1980.

Ortiz, Fernando. *Contrappunto del tabaco et dello zucchero*. Translated by Cesco Vian. Milan: Rizzoli, 1982.

Ortiz, Fernando. *Tabak und Zucker: Ein kubanischer Disput*, abridged. Translated by Maral Meyer-Minnemum. Frankfurt: Insel Verlag, 1987.

Pérez Firmat, Gustavo. *The Cuban Condition: Translation and Identity in Cuban Literature*. New York: Cambridge University Press, 1989.

Pérez Sarduy, Pedro, and Jean Stubbs, eds. *AfroCuba: An Anthology of Cuban Writing on Race, Politics and Culture*. Melbourne: Ocean Press and London: Latin American Bureau, 1993. Translated as *AfroCuba: Una antología de escritos cubanos sobre la raza, la política y la cultura*. San Juan: University of Puerto Rico, 1998.

Pérez Sarduy, Pedro, and Jean Stubbs, eds. *Afro-Cuban Voices: On Race and Identity in Contemporary Cuba*. Gainesville: University Press of Florida, 2000.

Pratt, Mary Louise. *Imperial Eyes: Travel Writing and Transculturation*. London: Routledge, 1992.

Stubbs, Jean. *Tobacco on the Periphery: A Case Study in Cuban Labour History, 1860–1958*. New York: Cambridge University Press, 1985. Translated as *Tabaco en la periferia: El complejo agro-industrial cubano y su movimiento obrero 1860–1959*. Havana: Editorial de Ciencias Sociales, 1989.

CUBAN EMBARGO

Robert L. Muse

Shifting rationales for a policy in effect since 1962.

In 1962 the U.S. president John F. Kennedy imposed a comprehensive embargo on Cuba that prohibits all financial transactions between U.S. citizens and Cuban nationals. This action followed President Dwight Eisenhower's embargo on Cuban sugar imports in August 1960. Kennedy's embargo remained in place as of 2011. To the extent the U.S. embargo on Cuba has been modified over the years, it has only been made harsher, most recently with the expressed purpose of the overthrow of the Cuban leader Fidel Castro (and later his brother Raul Castro) and to put an end to the Cuban Revolution. (An exception to this general rule of an ever-stricter embargo was congressional authorization in 2000 of U.S.-origin food sales to Cuba.)

The embargo on Cuba is so broad that it even prohibits all but a few U.S. citizens from traveling to that country. The stringency of the overall embargo on Cuba is perhaps best exemplified by this fact: Cuba is the only country in the world that the United States prohibits its citizens from visiting. The U.S. Government Accountability Office states: "The embargo on Cuba is the most comprehensive set of sanctions on any country, including the other countries designated by the U.S. government to be state sponsors of terrorism" (Amnesty p. 5).

Why has the embargo lasted so long? And why is it arguably more deeply embedded in U.S. laws and policies now than at any time in its history?

In part, the embargo's durability can be attributed to artful lobbying of the U.S. Congress by a politically conservative segment of Cuban Americans based in Florida, who dream of a return to their island properties. Another explanation is the annoyance that the Cuban Revolution's heated defiance of the United States seems to engender in every American president. Whatever the reason, the embargo has been maintained, endorsed, and extended on a bipartisan basis by eleven presidents in succession: five Democrats and six Republicans.

For Cubans, who employ the term *bloqueo* (blockade), and not *embargo*, the persistence of this policy is an act of economic warfare, an infringement of the island's sovereignty, and a daily symbol of political hostility.

THE ORIGINS AND RATIONALES OF THE EMBARGO

The trade embargo in 1960 began as a coercive exercise to achieve compensation for property expropriated by the government of Cuba from U.S. corporations and citizens. Basically, trade and other benefits from the United States were conditioned, by Congress, on Cuba's settling the outstanding expropriation claims. Those expropriations remained unsettled as of 2010, but no U.S president has ever sought actively to resolve the issue through negotiations. So it cannot accurately be said to be the current basis for the embargo.

Quickly after the Revolution, with the worsening of relations and the invasion of the Bay of Pigs (1961), the United States reoriented its embargo policy to serve as an economic weapon to weaken Cuba and rid it of its leader and government. In effect, a two-track policy was taken: the open track (embargo, expulsion from Organization of American States, and so forth) and a covert (and sometimes not so covert) policy (involving military means such as sabotage, arming groups, and carrying out attacks, bombings, strafings, and the like).

The Cuban Missile Crisis in 1962 produced a national security dimension to United States–Cuba relations. That incident led to President Kennedy's strengthening of the embargo as a means of denying dollars to Cuba that could, in its role of Soviet ally, be used for purposes inimical to the interests of the United States.

From the mid-1960s to the late 1980s, other reasons for the embargo were offered: to contain Cuba and the spread of its revolution elsewhere (particularly Latin America and the Caribbean) and to break its strong ties to the Soviet Union.

Employing the rationale of containment and Cold War anti-Sovietism, the Supreme Court in the case of *Regan v. Wald* (1984) upheld the ban on U.S. citizens traveling to Cuba. The Court's decision was based on evidence from the U.S. Department of Defense that Cuba would use revenue from U.S. travelers to support leftist insurgencies in Latin America. However, Cuba's economy collapsed in the early 1990s as its trade relations with the Soviet Union and the Eastern Bloc vanished. As a result Cuba withdrew active support for revolutionary movements in Latin America. Cuba's change of position made no difference to U.S. embargo policy. As of 2010 the courts relied on *Regan v. Wald* for the proposition that the ban on travel to Cuba is justified by the U.S. government's policy of denying hard currency to that country.

But that is demonstrably not U.S. policy, as evidenced by the fact that the U.S. government licensed over $2 billion a year in currency flows to Cuba as of 2010. The flow consisted of remittances and authorized travel by Cuban Americans to the island to visit relatives. If the U.S. government honestly believed that the dollars of U.S. travelers would be used by Cuba in ways harmful to U.S. national security, it presumably would not license the conveyance of $2 billion annually to that country.

A fifth rationale for the embargo took hold in the 1990s and remains in effect as of 2011. It is the displacement of the government of Cuba and the forced inducement of political and economic change in that country. The Helms-Burton Act of 1996 explicitly conditions an end to the embargo on Fidel and Raul Castro's no longer holding power in Cuba, along with the legalization of all political activity, the release of political prisoners, the dissolution of Cuba's Department of State Security, the commitment to hold free and fair elections within eighteen months (with multiple parties and under international supervision), and an end to interference with U.S. broadcasts to Cuba.

Helms-Burton opened a new chapter in the history of the embargo on Cuba by extending the embargo's reach to third countries and their citizens. U.S. sanctions programs historically have been limited to individuals and companies clearly subject to U.S. jurisdiction. The Helms-Burton Act constitutes a serious departure from traditional U.S. sanctions programs in that it seeks to assert jurisdiction over nonnationals and properties that are located outside U.S. territory. It does this by subjecting persons who invest in certain properties in Cuba to various penalties, including denial of entry into the United States. The extraterritoriality of the act matters. When a nation prohibits its nationals from trading with a certain country, the proper analysis requires asking whether it is good policy. But when a nation legislates with respect to other countries' nationals' activities in third countries, the correct analysis requires asking whether it is legal.

Under international law, the answer to the question about nationals' activities is no. Intercepting and deflecting third-country nationals' trade or investment in Cuba is not properly described as an embargo—rather, it is a blockade. This is precisely the point Cuba intends to make when it refers to U.S. trade and investment sanctions as constituting a *bloqueo*, rather than an embargo. To Cubans, therefore, Helms-Burton represents a flagrant violation of international law, undue interference in Cuba's internal affairs, and a return to so-called "big-stick" policy through economic means.

Many European countries (and Canada) rejected the internationalization of Helms-Burton, and the United Nations has voted to condemn the embargo every year since 1992, with the 2010 vote being 187 to 2 in favor of lifting the blockade. Pope John Paul II condemned it and asked the United States to lift the embargo during his 1998 visit, and even prominent Cuban dissidents such as Elizardo Sánchez and Vladimiro Roca have voiced their opposition to U.S. sanctions. The Cuban exile community is roughly divided on the question, and among supporters of the embargo almost half agree that the policy has failed.

Amnesty International, an organization that has often been highly critical of Cuba on human rights, issued a 2009 report on the economic and social ramifications of the embargo. Aside from condemning the embargo as a violation of international law, the report outlines the damage wrought, especially in the area of medicine and health. The report quotes a U.N. official: "The negative impact of the embargo is pervasive in the social, economic and environmental dimensions of human development in Cuba, severely affecting the most vulnerable socioeconomic groups of the Cuban population" (Amnesty p. 13). The American Association for World Health issued a report in 1997 that also details the negative impact of the embargo on Cubans. The report directly blamed the embargo's restriction on the sale of medicines and medical equipment to Cuba for an increase in patients going without essential drugs and doctors performing medical procedures without adequate equipment.

THE COST OF THE EMBARGO

President Barack Obama has said, "Our guiding light . . . is libertad; whether there's greater freedom inside Cuba" (quoted in Talev and Clark). It cannot be coincidental that he used the word *libertad*. It comes directly from the title of Senator Jesse Helms's 1996 legislation, thereby confirming that the current embargo is not based on U.S. national security concerns but instead continues to rest on a rationale of regime change and political reform in Cuba. This observation prompts the obvious reflection that the United States has based no other embargo on such a rationale. If it did, such key trading partners as China and Saudi Arabia would find themselves embargoed.

The embargo has cost Cuba billions of dollars in lost trade opportunities with U.S. business. Likewise

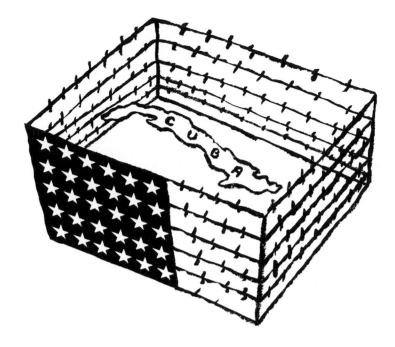

Cartoon about the Cuban embargo. American illustrator Robert Neubecker depicts the American embargo on Cuba as a form of imprisonment. ROBERT NEUBECKER

U.S. businesses have lost revenue from trade with Cuba. Estimates of the value of the lost trade range from $1.5 to $5 billion (and tens of thousands of jobs) to the United States. For Cuba the estimates are $700 million annually, and for 1960–2010 between $40 and $50 billion. U.S. companies also find themselves unable to invest in Cuba, thereby losing out to European and Canadian enterprises. For Cuba, the embargo has meant an ever-increasing cost for its food imports, as well as hampering agriculture (especially inputs).

There is a human cost in Cuba to the embargo insofar as U.S. trade and investment would ameliorate to a degree the deprivations Cubans have been subjected to since the end of the trade relationship with the Soviet Union. Another cost of the embargo since it was made extraterritorial in the 1990s is the amount of inward investment it may have thwarted from third countries. This has certainly cost ordinary Cubans thousands of jobs.

These human costs increased even more with the Bush administration restrictions (2004) on Cuban American visits and remittances, including people-to-people visits to Cuba. Cuban Americans were only allowed to visit the island once every three years, could only send a maximum of twelve hundred dollars per family in remittances, and the definition of the family members who could be visited was narrowed by the new law. Although the Cuban exile community favored being tough on the Cuban government, many saw these restrictions as a true hardship for Cuban families, especially their loved ones on the island.

THE U.S. PRESIDENT'S AUTHORITY TO MODIFY THE EMBARGO

The prospects for purely legislative initiatives that seek to lift the embargo on Cuba, or any part of it, are dismal. This state of affairs predates the Republican gains in Congress in 2010 and results from a realignment that has brought many Democrats into the pro-embargo camp. Those votes are secured through targeted political action committee (PAC) contributions and must be viewed as more or less permanent as of early 2011.

Because a change in Cuba policy will not originate in Congress, it follows that it will have to come from Obama or a future president. The question is when and how. Cuba will inevitably adopt further economic restructuring in 2011. All that is required is for the president to declare that changes under way in Cuba are positive and greet them with encouraging responses. By broadening educational travel to Cuba in January 2011, President Obama gave such a response.

A bilateral trade gesture may be the next logical step. It could take the form of a simple rule change that would license the importation of Cuban-origin agricultural products. Such a step would simply reciprocate U.S. producers' current access to the Cuban market, thereby making it a largely uncontroversial action.

By making such changes, the United States could begin the incremental process of building the foundation for a negotiated normalization of relations with Cuba, which could provide a context for ending the embargo.

The United States has predicated the lifting of the embargo on unilateral concessions by Cuba: regime change, a reorientation of its foreign policy, release of political prisoners, and complete overhaul of its economy. Cuba, by contrast, uses the embargo-blockade as a way of encouraging national unity and patriotic affirmation and at times as a means of deflecting criticism for the economic ills of the country.

As a superpower, the United States often acts as if it can influence or dictate the fate of smaller countries such as Cuba. But Cuba is not a political, economic, or military threat to the United States, even if the reverse is perceived as so in Cuba. The United States has solid relations with Vietnam and China, two countries run by Communist parties. The Cold War has ended, and yet dismal relations between the United States and Cuba persist; the embargo plays a key role as a potent symbol of intransigence. Greater trade, increased cultural and scientific exchange, new business ventures, technological and educational collaborations, and eventually full and normal relations will be of mutual benefit to both countries.

BIBLIOGRAPHY

American Association for World Health. *Denial of Food and Medicine: The Impact of the U.S. Embargo on the Health and Nutrition in Cuba*. Washington, DC: American Association for World Health, March 1997.

Amnesty International. "The U.S. Embargo against Cuba: Its Impact on Economic and Social Rights." London: Author, 2009.

Benjamin, Jules R. *The United States and the Origins of the Cuban Revolution: An Empire of Liberty in an Age of National Liberty*. Princeton, NJ: Princeton University Press, 1990.

Coleman, Jonathan, for the U.S. International Trade Commission. "U.S. Agricultural Sales to Cuba: Certain Economic Effects of U.S. Restrictions." Office of Industries Working Paper, U.S. International Trade Commission (Washington, DC), June 2009.

Cuervo, P. T. *Informe de Cuba sobre la resolución 61/11 de la Asamblea General de las Naciones Unidas: "Necesidad de poner fin al bloqueo económico, commercial, y financiero impuesto por los Estados Unidos de América contra Cuba."* Havana: Juventud Rebelde, 2007.

Franklin, Jane. *Cuba and the United States: A Chronological History*. Melbourne: Ocean Press, 1997.

Haney, Patrick Jude, and Walt Vanderbush. *The Cuban Embargo: The Domestic Politics of an American Foreign Policy*. Pittsburgh, PA: University of Pittsburgh Press, 2005.

Krinsky, Michael, and David Golove. *United States Economic Measures against Cuba: Proceedings in the United Nations and International Law Issues.* Northhampton, MA: Aletheia Press, 1993.

Miranda Bravo, Olga. *The USA versus Cuba: Nationalizations and Blockade.* Havana: Editorial José Martí, 1996.

Murray, Mary. *Cruel and Unusual Punishment: The U.S. Blockade against Cuba.* Melbourne: Ocean Press, 1993.

Rennack, Dianne E., and Mark P. Sullivan. *U.S.-Cuban Relations: An Analytic Compendium of U.S. Policies, Laws, and Regulations.* Washington, DC: Atlantic Council of the United States, 2005.

Spadoni, Paolo. *Failed Sanctions: Why the U.S. Embargo against Cuba Could Never Work.* Gainesville: University Press of Florida, 2010.

Talev, Margaret, and Lesley Clark. "Education Initiative Has Eye on Latino Vote." *Miami Herald*, 19 October 2010. Available from http://www.miamiherald.com/2010/10/19/1881765/education-initiative-has-eye-on.html.

U.N. General Assembly. *Necessity of Ending the Economic, Commercial, and Financial Embargo Imposed by the United States of America against Cuba: Report of the Secretary-General.* New York: United Nations, 2009.

CUBAN MISSILE CRISIS: OCTOBER 1962

Rafael M. Hernández Rodriguez

An event that shaped the conflict between Cuba and the United States.

The Cuban Missile Crisis of 1962 (or the October Crisis, as it is referred to in Cuba) is one of the most important events in the history of the relationship between the United States and Cuba. The pattern created at that time, with its burden of negativity and its void, has molded the logic of this relationship and framed all discussion of it into the early 2010s.

Most students of the Cuban Missile Crisis are not students of the history of Cuba or of its relationship with the United States (Abel; Allison; Blight and Welch; Garthoff 1989, 1980; George; Munton; Pachter). In analyzing the crisis, these writers point to the bilateral Soviet–United States relationship as the explanatory key for everything that happened, or could have happened, in 1962. A reexamination of the crisis that includes the role of Cuba and its perspective, in contrast, provides clearer insight into its nature and alternatives presented at the time, as well as, in general, the dynamics of the Cold War, particularly in the Third World.

Medium-range Ballistic Missile Base, San Cristóbal. Reconnaissance photos taken by the United States in October 1962 revealed a ballistic missile base in San Cristóbal in western Cuba. HULTON ARCHIVE/GETTY IMAGES

See also

Bay of Pigs Invasion: 1961

Diasporas: The Politics of Exile in the Early 1960s

Governance and Contestation: Insurrection, 1952–1959

The World and Cuba: Cuba and Socialist Countries

The World and Cuba: Cuba and the United States

PUTTING MISSILES IN CUBA: MYTHS AND REALITIES

The crisis erupted publicly on 22 October, when U.S. president John F. Kennedy appeared on television—one week after an American U-2 spy plane photographed Soviet bases in Pinar del Río—to give an ultimatum to the Soviet Union to remove the nuclear missiles it was placing in Cuba. Kennedy and the American public found the Soviet decision to install nuclear missiles to be deceptive, inexplicable, and aggressive, placing the world in danger of nuclear war over the course of thirteen days (Kennedy). This is the first myth. The truth is that the decision, however risky, was not inexplicable and its origins lay outside the Soviet Union.

How was the decision arrived at? From the time of Playa Girón (the Bay of Pigs invasion) in April 1961, both Soviet and Cuban intelligence had strong evidence that the United States had chosen to implement a strategy that would lead to a direct military attack against the island to accomplish the task that had been stymied at that time. U.S. agencies had begun to recruit a growing number of Cubans and train them in their own military units; to practice landing maneuvers on the island of Vieques, Puerto Rico; and to covertly implement a new strategy of action against Cuba, under the code name Operation Mongoose, whose emphasis was on the infiltration of armed groups into Cuban territory. These forces were intended to accomplish what the Bay of Pigs had failed to do: Take control of a territory, declare a provisional government, and demand official U.S. intervention. Although the Cuban government did not have details of this plan, its penetration into Cuban counterrevolutionary organizations revealed that the plan was in progress (Escalante). Cuba requested conventional military support from the Soviet Union in order to dissuade the United States from its intentions, and the Soviet government offered to place in Cuba medium- and intermediate-range nuclear-armed missiles. The Soviets were taking this unique opportunity for a military and geopolitical move: to show they could deploy missiles near the U.S. border, the same way the United States had missiles surrounding the Soviet Union, and to challenge the exclusive U.S. control over their sphere of influence. These missiles were much more than Cuba needed, but they certainly would be an effective deterrent against a possible attack.

The Cuban leadership accepted this offer and proposed the signing and official announcement of a Soviet-Cuban Mutual Defense Treaty. The Soviet Union responded that there was no need to make such an announcement before the missiles were installed, since U.S. intelligence would not discover them. The MRBM (Medium Range Ballistic Missile, the R-12, known to NATO as the SS-4) had a 1,200-mile range; the IRBM (Intermediate Range Ballistic Missile, or R-14, known to NATO as the SS-5) had a 2,200-mile range. Forty-two MRBMs were installed; the IRBMs never reached Cuba, although the nuclear warheads of the first did.

The second myth is that of the thirteen days. Although the Soviet Union and the United States reached an oral agreement on 28 October, the U.S. government maintained low-altitude flights over the island until 15 November and contemplated specific plans to attack Cuban air bases on 17 November, among other measures, such as the reinforcement of the blockade (Garthoff 1980, p. 34). The heavy tension and U.S. military actions did not begin to let up until at least 20 November. Both U.S. and Soviet forces were on high alert until 22 November, when the military blockade of Cuba was lifted. However, political uncertainty—and with it the danger that the United States would reconsider its promise made to the Soviet Union on 28 October not to invade Cuba—existed until the Soviet Union and the United States notified the United Nations that their talks had ended (the United States never accepted that all of its conditions had been met, including on-the-ground supervision) on 7 January 1963.

In the early 2010s it is known that Soviet anti-aircraft troops deployed in Holguín brought down a U-2 on Saturday, 27 October, an act that pushed military tensions to red alert and nearly provoked an attack on Cuba; it is also known that the Soviet government decided to remove the missiles in exchange for the public promise from the United States not to invade Cuba, along with the secret one to remove U.S. Jupiter missiles deployed in Turkey. Considering all of these facts, it would appear that the initiative was always on the side of the Soviet Union, in unleashing the events, carrying them to their most critical point, and bringing the situation to an end. Based on this partial perspective, the United States was limited to playing a rational defense, making a show of moderation and realism. However, this reading is true only to the extent to which the crisis is understood as a chess match between the two superpowers. In reality, this was a more complex event that, if it can be compared to a game in some way, would perhaps be like a strange game of cards played on several tables at the same time, with the active participation of the allies of the principal players, and even of numerous onlookers (i.e., important sectors of the population).

THE CRISIS

The crisis was dangerously sparked when the Soviet Union began to handle the decision to install nuclear missiles in Cuba in a politically erratic manner. This period extends at least through the demobilization of Soviet troops in Cuba under the bilateral agreement between the United States and the Soviet Union. While risky, this decision was neither illegal nor insane and could have been accomplished without necessarily and inevitably leading to a crisis that would place the world on the brink of nuclear war.

The first of two factors that complicated the situation and that caused it to end in a crisis was the disproportionate U.S. reaction regarding the real military significance of the ballistic missiles for the strategic balance with the Soviet Union. Even the Defense Department staff member responsible for evaluating the scale of this threat, Raymond Garthoff, has recognized that the U.S. response was decided upon before there was a precise military evaluation available (Garthoff 1980). This response was fundamentally derived from political policy considerations (Hampson), due to the symbolic effect of Soviet bases on the U.S. policy of regional exclusivity. The second factor was the Soviet tactic of first concealing the presence of the missiles and then limiting itself to stating that they were defensive, instead of openly reaffirming the right of Cuba and the Soviet Union to locate arms on the island that they considered necessary for their defense, based on Cuba's right to choose its allies, just as the United States had, and even moving forward with the publication of the text of the military accord, the rough draft of which had been approved by the two governments.

Once started, the crisis dragged on and became deeper, coming to a poor resolution not just because of the factors discussed above but also because the Russians did not bring the question before the United Nations, where it would have been debated multilaterally on the basis of international law, and because the Russians accepted the U.S. terms, ignoring Cuba as a belligerent party and necessary actor in any negotiation.

DEVELOPMENT OF THE DRAMA

The Kennedy administration reacted according to the model of not appearing weak against communism. Another failure like the Bay of Pigs would have been a disaster for the administration—as Robert Kennedy commented to the president in a secret memo on 1 June 1961 (Schlesinger p. 480). The measure adopted to confront the crisis, the quarantine (naval blockade), did not have a serious military effect; rather, it was a stalling tactic to make the Soviets react. According to close advisors of Kennedy, if the Soviets had successfully installed nuclear missiles in Cuba, the political consequences would have been dangerous for the United States, insofar as the Soviet Union would have proved its ability to act with impunity in the heart of its region of vital interest. But the quarantine was largely counterproductive because it created the conditions for an unanticipated complication and it was not diplomatically effective. The U.S. response, supported by illegal, threatening, and highly risky actions—the naval blockade, low-altitude flights over the island, and the reiterated ultimatum—decisively contributed to drawing the situation toward the brink of nuclear war.

On the other side, more than a few incongruent moves were also committed. Once the bold strategy of placing the missiles on the island had been decided upon, Khrushchev did not know how to deal politically with the situation that was created. He downplayed the fact that the installation was legal, as if he had not calculated the possible consequences or thought that Kennedy would easily accept everything. From Fidel Castro's point of view, this approach reflected the Soviet leaders' profound ignorance of the political psychology of the United States. The daring Soviet move—debatable in itself, but coherent within the logic of a larger strategy—was replaced along the way with a search for a quid pro quo. Enthusiasm flagged, and the morale that inspired the original decision was affected to a significant extent.

The Cubans worried—as is clear from letters sent by Castro to Khrushchev on 26 and 30 October 1962 (Chang and Kornbluh)—about the gravity of the consequences of any hostile, uncontrolled, or deliberately provocative action. In particular, on the island, people felt a sense of great danger that the United States would launch a preventive attack against the Soviet bases and the high probability that this could in fact become the trigger for a nuclear conflict. Placing himself inside the logic of the U.S. leaders, Castro was certain that, in the long run, the preventive strategy implied a first strike against the Soviet Union. This somber certainty, which weighed on the mind of Kennedy at that same time, was not seen with clarity by the Soviet leaders in Moscow. The lack of a crisis atmosphere in the Soviet Union—such as existed, although with different characters, in Cuba and the United States—led them to handle the issue as a regional confrontation, revealed in their labeling of the conflict as the Crisis of the Caribbean. They thought it would not escalate, since supposedly

neither of the parties would be propelled to attack the continental territory of the other. As Andrei Gromyko and other Soviet actors of the time reiterated in a conference about the crisis held in Moscow in 1989, the Soviet government believed that the situation was serious but did not think that it was really on the brink of nuclear war. Years later and after these revelations, it seems clear that the Cuban leaders interpreted the implacable logic of events and the potential margin of U.S. negotiation more clearly than was appreciated from Moscow.

THE RESOLUTION

Deliberately, the Soviet Union decided not to involve Cuba in the negotiation process. On one hand, the Soviets thought that the attack against the island was virtually in progress and that they could not risk introducing any element that would complicate and in effect delay the conclusion of an agreement with the United States. They had every reason to think so, given the level of risk in objective terms.

On the other hand, the predominant sentiment in the Executive Committee (EXCOM) of the U.S. National Security Council (NSC) was dictated more by fear in the face of the imminent danger of nuclear war than by a certainty in the effectiveness of their actions. The prevailing military perceptions in this organization inexplicably overestimated—as they later realized—the weight of the missiles in Cuba for creating an unfavorable nuclear imbalance between the Soviet Union and the United States. The truth was that, even after the installation of the missiles, the U.S. arsenal continued to surpass that of the Soviets by several times in terms of the number and power of its nuclear delivery vehicles. If it had followed that logic, the United States would have launched a massive attack against several million Cubans and 40,000 Soviet soldiers in Cuba based on false assumptions. Would the military leaders and the government in Moscow, who held the decision-making power regarding strategic missiles on the island, have stood for that? And even if they had, would the Soviet generals in Cuba, who had discretionary authority over the use of tactical nuclear missiles deployed on the coasts to confront a possible invasion, have accepted the same fate? Nearly thirty years after this event during a conference in Havana in 1992, U.S. veterans of the crisis (and the Cubans themselves) confirmed the existence and the number of nuclear warheads that had arrived on the island.

The Soviet Union kept the Cuban government in the dark with respect to the content of their conversations with the United States. The Soviets were probably fearful of an emotional response from Cuba because of the fear of an attack from the United States. They believed that under this tremendous tension the Cubans would not be moderate and realistic. However, the Cubans never broke the agreement to maintain Soviet control over the bases, they did not hinder the dismantling of the missiles, they allowed low-altitude flights over the island until 15 November, they received the UN secretary general and explained to him their willingness to negotiate, they maintained the highest level of communication with Soviet military leaders in Cuba, and they publicly presented an agenda containing their main national security concerns with respect to the United States: End the economic embargo, cease attacks by sea and violation of air space, and return the Guantanamo naval base. This was not a maximalist plan, nor was it excessive in terms of basic international law.

As it had not been involved in the negotiating process, Cuba did not accept supervision of the dismantling of the missiles on the ground, nor did it yield to the idea that the low-altitude flights would continue indefinitely, for fundamental reasons of national security. In all other aspects, Cuba actively cooperated to achieve an end to the crisis.

THE CONSEQUENCES

Twenty years after the crisis, in 1982, the nuclear race had given rise to such a powerful Soviet naval force that the Soviets had achieved nuclear parity and the capacity to annihilate all the cities in the United States several times over, without the need for bases in Cuba—something it could not have done with the missiles in 1962.

The understanding that put an end to the crisis managed to stop the nuclear collision in progress, but it did not establish an instrument for stable peace in the region. It was a simple oral commitment between two leaders, both gone from office within two years, which was never translated into an official agreement or treaty of mandatory compliance.

President Kennedy's rejection of a direct invasion of Cuba did not protect the Revolution from other types of aggression. It did not achieve the comprehensive preservation of Cuban national security, a problem that had not been resolved as of 2011. On several occasions, U.S. presidents, such as Ronald Reagan, and other high-level officials have explicitly ignored the existence of that commitment.

The conflict was not brought to the United Nations, which could have been useful in promoting a multilateral approach, since international consensus—and particularly that of the nonaligned and certain influential Latin American countries—favored a negotiated solution. According to some sources, the diplomatic reaction of the United States in private was not inflexible, but rather showed an inclination to negotiate the situation. Within this multilateral framework, a constructive conversation on resolving the crisis could have been initiated.

While the diplomatic maneuvers needed for a safe landing were in progress, the letters of Khrushchev and Kennedy of 27–28 October hastened a formula for an emergency landing. Thus, the accord was not the product of a settlement based on principles, but rather a result of the fears of both parties, and was a pragmatic accommodation based on mutual concessions. It was a lost opportunity to resolve a conflict whose very high human, material, and political costs—not only at the bilateral level between the two parties but also regionally in Latin America, the Caribbean, and Africa—affect people still.

BIBLIOGRAPHY

Abel, Elie. *The Missile Crisis*. Philadelphia: Lippincott, 1966.

Allison, Graham T., and Philip Zelikow. *Essence of Decision*. 2nd ed. New York: Longman, 1999.

Blight, James G., and David Welch. *On the Brink: Americans and Soviets Reexamine the Cuban Missile Crisis*. New York: Hill and Wang, 1989.

Chang, Laurence, and Peter Kornbluh, eds. *The Cuban Missile Crisis, 1962: A National Security Archive Documents Reader*. New York: New Press, 1999.

Diez Acosta, Tomás. *La Crisis de los Misiles, 1962: Algunas reflexiones cubanas*. Havana: Verde Olivo, 1997.

Diez Acosta, Tomás. *October 1962: The "Missile" Crisis as Seen from Cuba*. New York: Pathfinder, 2002.

Garthoff, Raymond L. "American Reaction to Soviet Aircraft in Cuba, 1962 and 1978." *Political Science Quarterly* 95:3 (Fall 1980), 434.

Garthoff, Raymond L. *Reflections on the Cuban Missile Crisis*. Rev. ed. Washington, DC: Brookings Institution, 1989.

George, Alice L. *Awaiting Armageddon: How Americans Faced the Cuban Missile Crisis*. Chapel Hill: University of North Caroline Press, 2003.

Hampson, Fen Osler. "The Divided Decision-Maker: American Domestic Politics and the Cuban Crises." *International Security* 9, no. 3 (Winter 1984–1985): 130–165.

Hernández, Rafael. "Treinta días. Las lecciones de la Crisis de octubre y las relaciones entre los Estados Unidos y Cuba". In *Otra guerra: Ensayos cubanos sobre estrategia y seguridad internacional* by Rafael Hernández Rodríguez. Havana: Ciencias Sociales, 1999.

Hernández, Rafael. "La lucha entre lo nuevo y lo viejo fue en todas partes: Entrevista al General (r) Fabián Escalante." *Temas* 56 (October–December 2008).

Kennedy, Robert F. *Thirteen Days: A Memoir of the Cuban Missile Crisis*. New York: Norton, 1999.

Munton, Don, and David A. Welch. *The Cuban Missile Crisis: A Concise History*. New York: Oxford University Press, 2007.

Pachter, Henry M. *Collision Course*. New York: Praeger, 1963.

Schlesinger, Arthur M., Jr. *Robert Kennedy and His Times*. Boston: Houghton Mifflin, 1978.

THE CUBAN REVOLUTION OF 1959

Gladys Marel García Pérez

The factors underlying Fulgencio Batista's decision to surrender the presidency and flee Cuba.

Fulgencio Batista (1901–1973), president of the Republic of Cuba (1940–1944; 1954–1958), ruled Cuba with an iron fist after assuming power in a 1952 coup. He was determined to follow through with his strategy to stay in power until 24 February 1959, the date on which he was to hand the presidency over to Dr. Andrés Rivero Agüero. To accomplish this, he decided to reinforce the Leoncio Vidal regiment at Las Villas by dispatching an armored train carrying troops from Havana and Matanzas, along with reinforcements from Oriente. The failure of this plan and the outcome of the battle of Santa Clara were key factors in his decision to surrender the presidency and flee Cuba.

FULGENCIO BATISTA AND AMBASSADOR EARL SMITH

In spite of the disagreements among top political and military leaders of the regime, Cuban institutions, and the government of the United States, Batista was determined to stay in power. In looking back on the events that converged to influence Batista's decision on the last day of 1958, and even right up to the very early morning of January 1, 1959, one can identify the outcomes of that critical period, the scenarios and actors playing out the conflict, and the thought processes of the military leadership, the U.S. government, and the revolutionary insurgent movement.

The United States upheld the policy of diplomacy and avoidance of military intervention, but several converging factors led the Department of State and the Central Intelligence Agency to draw the conclusion that Fulgencio Batista had to leave Cuba. These factors included electoral shenanigans, increased repression, the people's reaction in support of the insurrectionist movement, the increasing deterioration of the system, the public opinion campaign in Cuba and overseas on behalf of the rebel forces, and the risk to the sugar harvest and U.S. interests in Cuba.

Ambassador Earl Smith was the person charged with delivering a message to Batista that was couched in diplomatic terms, but unambiguous: The U.S. State Department was convinced Batista had to leave Cuba without delay in order to hand over the reins of the government, which was losing control over the situation and could not survive for much longer (Smith pp. 171–177).

Once again, the State Department sought to broker the establishment of a civil and military junta or governing board, a formula that had been applied successfully after the Revolution of 1933. Indeed, on 12 December, President Dwight D. Eisenhower raised this possibility (Glennon and Landa pp. 281–282).

MILITARY CONSPIRACY: EULOGIO CANTILLO AND FIDEL CASTRO: PACT OR TREASON?

Historians continue in the early twenty-first century to debate whether General Eulogio Cantillo acted as the trustworthy officer trained at the Officers School, loyal to the president of the Republic, or whether he acted on behalf of the interests of the U.S. Embassy in Cuba or whether he betrayed the agreement with the leadership of the Revolution. The testimonies of Fulgencio Batista and Fidel Castro point in all these directions.

Batista had been planning his offensive against rebel forces in the Sierra Maestra since early 1958. He was convinced he could annihilate them with the military capabilities under his command. He operated on the premise that one could fight with the army or without the army, but never against the army.

In February, Lieutenant Colonel Carlos San Martín, the chief of the Operations Section of the Army General Staff, presented a document called "Plan F-F" (the Spanish acronym for "Final Phase" or the "End of Fidel"), which, although not approved, provided the framework for the operational plan for the summer offensive. To this end, in March 1958, General Francisco Tabernilla Dolz, the chairman of the Joint Chiefs of Staff, met with the top military leadership, including the army chief of staff, General Pedro Rodríguez Ávila, and Major Eulogio Cantillo Porras, chief of the Operations Division, who by July would be serving as chief of the Bayamo command post (Castro pp. 10, 12, 585). On 26 March, Cantillo submitted a report on the operational plan and the offensive, in which he reviewed the quality, size, weaponry, organization, health, and morale of the enemy and the army. In his next assessment of the rebel forces, he wrote that their success in capturing units or forcing them to surrender, together with the acquisition of weapons and food, had greatly boosted their morale and made them more daring.

The morale of the army soldiers, by contrast, was extremely low. Several factors had sapped their will, at all levels, to carry on the fight; these included the latest string of defeats, their knowledge that the rebel forces would not deal with them harshly and would respect the physical integrity and morale of soldiers or units who surrendered, and the certain knowledge that to get captured was to end all their problems. To this morale problem was added the lack of rest among frontline soldiers. There was a further problem of entire units that refused to advance or hold the posts assigned to them. Cantillo wrapped up his report saying that all this, along with the lack of supplies and transport, meant he could not renew the offensive (Franqui pp. 540–541).

Having broken the combat morale of the regime's armed forces, in his capacity as chief of the army of

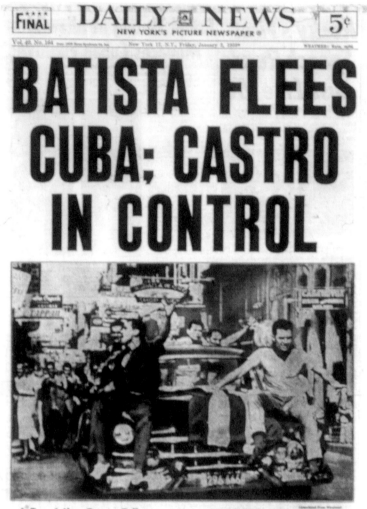

DAILY NEWS

NEW YORK'S PICTURE NEWSPAPER

BATISTA FLEES CUBA; CASTRO IN CONTROL

A Revolution Comes Full. Supporters of Fidel Castro, leader of Cuba's rebels, ride flag-draped car in victory scene through streets of Havana. Their revolution had finally borne fruit: President Fulgencio Batista had been ousted. He fled to the Dominican Republic. —Story on page 3; other pictures in centerfold

"Batista Flees Cuba; Castro in Control." The headline of the 2 January 1959 issue of the *New York Daily News* describes the dramatic turn of events in Cuba. NY DAILY NEWS ARCHIVE VIA GETTY IMAGES

the 26th of July Revolutionary Movement (Movimiento Revolucionario 26 de Julio, or MR-26-7), Fidel Castro informed General Eulogio Cantillo that he would hand over the soldiers that had been captured. Cantillo reported this back to the General Staff, and Batista ordered him to appoint another officer to conduct the negotiations. The defeat of the summer offensive of 1958 demonstrated that the regime's strategy for a military victory was ineffective.

Popular resistance intensified over the next few months, as the clandestine network was strengthened and the rebel forces grew throughout the entire country. The invading columns of the 26th of July Revolutionary Movement advanced on the central province of Las Villas. New fronts opened in central and western Cuba, pushed by the "13th of March" Revolutionary Directorate and the "Second Front" in Escambray, as well as in the north of Yaguajay, Camagüey, and Pinar del Río. The Havana-Matanzas front was also being established (García 2005, pp. 13, 85–164). The Revolution spread throughout the country.

In mid-December, eleven out of sixteen officers of the frigate *Máximo Gómez*, together with the crew, petitioned to transfer their allegiance and materiel to the rebel forces. On 22 December, in the province of Las Villas, Ciro Redondo Column No. 8, together with the 26th of July militias and troops of the Revolutionary Directorate, seized the town of Fomento. The following day, they seized Placetas, a key communications hub of the island, thus completing the encirclement of Santa Clara.

In the meantime, Camilo Cienfuegos was commanding the northern front of Yaguajay and preparing to lay siege to the army headquarters. Rebel operations coincided with the beginning of the sugar harvest and the collection of taxes from the owners of the sugar mills in the heart of the island.

This was the context in which, on 22 December, General Francisco Tabernilla Dolz summoned several generals and colonels to a meeting at which Cantillo reported that circumstances in the Oriente area of operations had taken a turn for the worse. Faced with this outcome, and the gravity of their predicament, the officers agreed to entertain proposals from the rebel leaders for negotiations and to submit them for Batista's consideration. Tabernilla assigned this mission to Cantillo, who arranged a meeting with Fidel Castro.

The meeting between Cantillo and Fidel Castro took place on 28 December, amid all the conspiracies of the army high command in Las Villas and the heat of combat in which the forces under Ernesto "Che" Guevara, assisted by the Revolutionary Directorate, were cutting the island in half. The regime's military strength was collapsing.

Fidel Castro and Cantillo agreed to combine the forces of the revolutionary army and the army of the republic and to operate jointly. The conditions set by the rebel chief was that Fulgencio Batista should not be allowed to escape, try to install a military junta, or encourage a coup d'état or foreign intervention. The parties decided to suspend operations for two days and then to act jointly as of 3:00 p.m. on the afternoon of 31 December. The rebels and the military would occupy the three eastern provinces. While Cantillo took control of the military city of Columbia and detained Fulgencio Batista, Castro would seize the headquarters of Santiago de Cuba.

In the meanwhile, Lieutenant Colonel José Martínez, aide-de-camp of General Cantillo, received instructions to arrange a meeting with the president, disregarding the chain of command; it was thus that Fulgencio Batista became aware of the plot. He immediately summoned the army chief, Pedro Rodríguez Ávila, to order Cantillo to drop the negotiations and to order Martínez to fly to Santiago de Cuba and deliver a personal explanation. But the counterorder arrived too late, and both officers took the flight back to Havana.

Cantillo delivered his report to Batista. As he was about to enter into detail, Batista stopped him with a gesture and said the damage had already been done by the mere fact of the meeting. In Batista's own words, to go and meet the rebel chief, the enemy of the forces under his command, was "more than a show of defeatism, it was defeat itself." He ordered Cantillo to go to Santiago and prevent Fidel Castro from entering the city, to send reinforcements to Santa Clara, and to return to his meeting in Havana (Batista 1960, pp. 128–129).

THE REGIME CRACKS

Fulgencio Batista had not authorized the senior military leadership to seek a truce and negotiate. Upon learning about it, he ordered General Tabernilla to summon the army chief of staff, Pedro Rodríguez Ávila, and the navy chief, Admiral José Rodríguez Calderón. With them present, he admonished Tabernilla, saying that "when an army loses a fight without repelling the assaults of the enemy, and not a day goes by without some of its men turning themselves in, to go and see the enemy chief in order to ask what he wants in order to end the fighting is the same as surrendering" (Batista 1960, p. 129). He blamed him for having made him, Batista, "the object of a very unique coup d'état" (Batista 1960, p. 104). Tabernilla later alleged that he had acted in good faith and had no intention of betraying Batista.

Events now took on a life of their own. In those last days of December, the head of state was well aware of the progressive debilitation of the armed forces. Brigadier General Silito Tabernilla Palmero warned Batista that the situation was dire and that it was useless to fight; the bulk of the forces encamped at Columbia had abandoned the barracks on orders of the General Staff, leaving them utterly vacant and the Military Citadel completely undefended, with its doors shut. In a futile gesture to give a sense of security, Batista ordered the doors to be reopened.

One conspiracy followed another. Several had already been discovered. One of these, at Camp Columbia, entailed marching on the presidential residence on 27 December while Batista was dining with the main service chiefs, some ministers, and congressmen, and taking them prisoner. But this plot failed (Batista 1960, pp. 104–106, 131).

THE BATTLE OF SANTA CLARA AND BATISTA'S FLIGHT

The battle of Santa Clara, between 29 December and 1 January, involved rebel forces of the army of the 26th of July Revolutionary Movement, also known as the rebel army, and the troops of the 13th of March Revolutionary Directorate. Although the latter were headed by Faure Chomón and Rolando Cubela, it was Commander Che Guevara who commanded the entire force, including his Ciro Redondo Column No. 8 and the militias of the movement.

While the Revolutionary Directorate troops assaulted the Rural Guards' Thirty-first Garrison, forcing its surrender, the troops from the 26th of July army laid siege to the police station and the military trench works. Throwing Molotov cocktails (gasoline-filled bottles set on fire), they captured the military armored train along with its twenty-two wagons, machine guns, and ammunition. Meanwhile, El Vaquerito (Little Cowboy), the teenage leader of the Suicide Platoon, forced various points in the city to surrender (Guevara Vol. 2, pp. 267–269).

The main cities, Santa Clara along with Cienfuegos and its port, were now isolated and under siege. Only the Thirty-first Squadron at the police headquarters and in the vicinity of the regimental garrison fought on, but once the armored train had surrendered there was no longer any possibility of reinforcements from ports to the north or south. The assault on Santa Clara accelerated the implosion of the regime (Barquín Vol. 2, pp. 868–869).

THE REGIME'S DOWNFALL

On 31 December, the president lunched with his wife, Marta Fernández, in the intimacy of the private quarters of the Presidential Palace. He gave her instructions to be ready for the possibility of leaving the country, a decision he would make known to her before bidding adieu to the old year at their Columbia residence. He then departed for his farm, Kuquine, where he remained in his office during the afternoon and into the night while receiving reports from the operational areas of Oriente and Las Villas (Batista 1960, p. 138). Batista was waiting for the return of General Eulogio Cantillo, in hopes that he had sent troops from Oriente to the regiment holding the center of the island and that he might have been able to prevent Fidel Castro and the rebel forces from gaining control of the city of Santiago de Cuba (Castro p. 706; Franqui p. 707).

In the meantime, on that same night of 31 December, the chairman of the Joint Chiefs of Staff scanned reports from the Santa Clara area of operations on the increasing desertions in the face of an enemy who held the upper hand in morale and enjoyed the determined support of the civilian population. The rebels were operating in Matanzas and Madruga and right up to the outskirts of Havana and the front of Pinar del Río (García 2005, pp. 256–257). The main bridges had been demolished, transportation was paralyzed, fuel and supplies were running out, and the sugar harvest had not yet started. Meanwhile, taxes were being collected in the liberated areas by Pastorita Núñez and in Miami by Haydée Santamaría, a leader of the exile network. Along with Alberto Fernández, they were taxing the sugar-mill owners and using the proceeds to finance the rebels.

Around 10:00 p.m., Cantillo returned from Oriente. He went to Batista's residence in Columbia and told him: "The situation is dire, Mr. President, and decisions need to be made quickly" (Batista 1960, p. 139). Fidel Castro would enter Santiago in a matter of hours, since he knew the troops were defeated. At that point, Batista decided to flee the country, leaving Cantillo in power at the head of a military-civil junta (Batista 1960, pp. 139–140, 143–144). He summoned the senior military leaders with the key commands at Columbia, along with the president-elect, the vice president, and the presidents of the Senate and the Chamber of Representatives, as well as the chiefs of the political parties in the administration and the leaders of Congress. In their presence, he turned over the presidency of the Republic to Judge Carlos Piedra and the military command to Major General Eulogio Cantillo. In this official act, he stated that the senior military leadership and representatives from the Catholic Church, manufacturing, business, and the sugar industry had asked him to resign.

The officers of the army, navy, air force, and police, as well as the country's political leaders, were summoned to the general headquarters of the air force in Columbia, where three transport planes waited to take them out of the country. Fulgencio Batista boarded the DC-4 and from the staircase turned around to give instructions to Cantillo, telling him that the success of negotiations depended on him. It was 2:10 a.m. when his plane took off toward the Dominican Republic (Franqui pp. 681–683).

FULGENCIO BATISTA: SEPTEMBRISM OR THE REVOLUTION OF 4 SEPTEMBER

The military figure of Fulgencio Batista arose from the revolution of the 1930s, when he led a revolutionary junta organized on 4 September 1933, during the mutiny of sergeants, corporals, and enlisted men at the Columbia garrison. At various times, he held either the senior top military command or the presidency of the Republic, during both hard-line (1934–1939) and democratic (1940–1944) regimes, and from 1952 onward on the basis of a coup d'état.

On 4 September 1933, the University Students Directorate (Directorio Estudiantil Universitario or DEU) of the 1930s, which led the civilian movement and the junta, installed a collegiate government known as the Pentarchy. Both forces, acting as the Revolutionary Assembly of Cuba, declared that they "were comprised of the enlisted men of the Army and Navy and civilians from diverse sectors, headed by the University Students Directorate" who were seizing "Power, as a Revolutionary Provisional Government" until such time as a constituent assembly could be held in order to appoint a constitutional government. The nineteen signatories of this document included Batista, who did so as sergeant and chief of all the armed forces of the Republic. The national army surrendered to the uprising, and thus the new constitutional army was born (Riera p. 69; Adam y Silva pp. 484–485; Soto pp. 1–67).

The executive branch was now held by the Pentarchy, which elected Dr. Ramón Grau San Martín as president of the Republic and bestowed the rank of colonel on Batista. The president of the United States, Franklin D. Roosevelt, refused to recognize the government headed by Grau. From this point onward, the history of Cuba becomes convoluted. Washington's attitude changed only after a meeting between Batista and Sumner Welles, who had been dispatched to Havana as a mediator.

The historical-biographical accounts of these facts contradict each other and provide different perspectives as to the question of whether Grau resigned in January 1934 or whether there was a U.S.-backed military coup, since Batista had "moved to the center" in a way that "won him the sympathy and support of the United States." The Columbia garrison in turn gave rise to an administration presided over by Carlos Mendieta, with Batista as the commander of the armed forces (Riera p. 11). There is also a debate between those who consider the generation that carried out the Revolution of 1930 to be the leadership of the popular revolutionary movement and those who argue that it was the generation led by Fulgencio Batista and the Military Septembrism revolutionary action in 1933, also known as the Revolution of 4 September or the Revolt of the Sergeants (García 1998, p. 13; Adam y Silva p. 8; Batista 1973, p. 31).

The years between 1934 and 1939 were marked by political convulsions. Batista directly or covertly dominated Cuban politics and provided continuity to Military Septembrism as the bearer of the symbols representing that date, under the banner of 4 September. During this period, he crushed the insurgent revolutionary movement by ambushing and killing its leader, Antonio Guiteras, and installing a hard-line government. In 1939, he went into military retirement. During these five years, Batista's activities in the national and international arenas followed the constraints set by the U.S. Department of State within the framework of the Good Neighbor policy, because he recognized the need to find economic solutions that would provide greater social and political stability on the island and also prevent outright military intervention.

THE CONSTITUTION OF 1940

Three political parties—the Cuban Revolutionary (Authentic) Party (PRC-A), the ABC Party, and the Revolutionary Communist Union Party—duly unveiled their constitutional platforms in accordance with the electoral code of 1939. A strong current of public opinion developed in support of a constitution that would have far-reaching social and economic content (Instituto de Historia de Cuba p. 384).

Eleven parties then assembled into two electoral blocks. The Democratic Socialist Coalition (CSD), which backed the electoral platform of Fulgencio

Batista, was made up of the Liberal, Nationalist Union, National Democratic Group, National Revolutionary (Realist) Popular Cuban, and Revolutionary Communist Union parties. The opposition block was led by the PRC-A and Ramón Grau San Martín and included the Democratic Republican, Republican Action, and ABC parties. The National Agrarian Party engaged independently.

The Constitutional Convention began in the National Capitol on 9 February 1940 and had two working sessions. Ramón Grau San Martín presided over the first, with Carlos Márquez Sterling presiding over the second.

The language of the constitution was of a progressive nature, reflecting the outcome of the Revolution of 1930. It was, in fact, quite advanced for its time. Its major achievements included the establishment of the moral and legal equality of all people of all races, without discrimination on the basis of race, sex, or class. There were also advances with regard to property ownership and on issues of national independence and economic development. With regard to the National Treasury, the constitution established an Accounting Court and the National Bank of Cuba. It further established regulations to govern the workplace and mandated an eight-hour workday, paid work breaks, and protections for pregnant women. In addition, the constitution provided for equality among citizens and women's suffrage, and it recognized and defended the principles of democracy, egalitarianism, and progressivism in Cuban education. The Constitution of 1940 was promulgated in the National Capitol on 5 June and signed on 1 July in Guáimaro.

REPUBLIC AND REVOLUTION

On 1 January 1959, representatives of Che Guevara established radio contact from the Leoncio Vidal Regiment of Santa Clara with General Eulogio Cantillo, urging him to surrender, since he had betrayed the agreements with the rebel army. Cantillo viewed this as an ultimatum and refused to accept. He declared that he had occupied the leadership of the army following the instructions of the leader, Fidel Castro.

In fact, the units of the armed forces had surrendered unconditionally. Meanwhile, Fidel Castro called for a revolutionary general strike to support these military actions, a strategic objective of MR-26-7 in order to overthrow the regime (Castro p. 6). The strike triggered a general uprising of the population, thus heading off any maneuvers that could possibly stand in the way of an absolute victory by the rebel forces.

The leaders of the movement occupied the military citadel of Columbia in Havana, and Colonel Ramón Barquín replaced Cantillo as commander in chief of the army. A few hours later, Barquín in turn relinquished his command to Camilo Cienfuegos, the commander of the Antonio Maceo Invasion Column No. 2 (Guevara Vol. 2, p. 269), whom Fidel Castro had ordered to assume command of Columbia, and to Che Guevara, the head of the Ciro Redondo Column No. 8, who took over the fortress of La Cabaña.

Commanders Faure Chomón and Rolando Cubela, heading the troops of the March 13th Revolutionary Directorate, did not advance on Havana in tandem with the revolutionary army of MR-26-7. They did so on their own account, occupying positions at the University of Havana, the National Capitol, and the Presidential Palace.

At the same time, throughout the municipalities and provinces of the country, the political leadership of MR-26-7 was appointing government officials, army and police chiefs, and the heads of other institutions. Fidel Castro ordered Camilo Cienfuegos to parlay with the leadership of the March 13th Revolutionary Directorate, in order to hand over the Presidential Palace, and for the revolutionary government to assume power under the presidency of Manuel Urrutia Lleó. Subsequently, Manuel Suzarte of the National Directorate of MR-26-7 was appointed as the government's delegate in the Capitol.

The people had taken to the streets to support the leadership of Fidel Castro and the revolutionary government. A new phase had begun: the transformation from a Republic into a Revolution.

BIBLIOGRAPHY

Barquín, Ramón. *Las luchas guerrilleras en Cuba: De la colonia a la Sierra Maestra*. Vols. 1–2. Madrid: Editorial Playor, 1973.

Batista, Fulgencio. *Respuesta ....* Mexico: D.F., 1960.

Batista, Fulgencio. *Piedras y leyes*. Mexico: Ediciones Botas, 1961.

Batista, Fulgencio. *Dos Fechas: Aniversarios y testimonios, 1933–1944*. Vol. 1. Mexico: Ediciones Botas, 1973.

Camus, Emilio F. "Itinerario de la Revolución del 4 de septiembre de 1933." In *Dos Fechas: Aniversarios y testimonios, 1933–1944*, by Fulgencio Batista. Vol. 1. Mexico: Ediciones Botas, 1973.

Castro Ruz, Fidel. *Por todos los caminos de la Sierra: La victoria estratégica*. Havana: Publications Office of the Council of State of the Republic of Cuba, 2010.

Franqui, Carlos. *Diario de la revolución cubana*. Paris: Ruedo Ibérico, 1976.

García Pérez, Gladys Marel. *Insurrection and Revolution: Armed Struggle in Cuba, 1952–1959*. Translated by Juan Ortega. Boulder, CO: Lynne Rienner, 1998.

García Pérez, Gladys Marel. *Crónicas guerrilleras de Occidente*. Havana: Editorial de Ciencias Sociales, 2005.

Glennon, John P., and Ronald D. Landa. *Foreign Relations of the United States, 1958–1960: Cuba*. Vol. 6. Washington, DC: U.S. Government Printing Office, 1991.

González del Valle, Antolín. *Fulgencio Batista: Trayectoria Nacionalista*. Wilmington, NC: Ediciones Patria, 1980.

Guevara, Ernesto "Che." *Ernesto Che Guevara: Escritos y discursos.* Vols. 1–2. Havana: Editorial de Ciencias Sociales, 1972.

Instituto de Historia de Cuba. *Historia de Cuba.* Vol. 3: *La neocolonia organización y crisis: Desde 1899 hasta 1940.* Havana: Editora Política, 1998.

Le Riverend, Julio. *La República: Dependencia y revolución.* Havana: Editorial de Ciencias Sociales, 1975.

Riera Hernández, Mario. *Un presidente constructivo.* Miami: Colonial Press of Miami, 1966.

Smith, Earl E.T. *El cuarto piso.* San Juan, PR: Cultural Puertorriqueña, Ic, Editorial Corripio, 1963. Originally published as *The Fourth Floor: An Account of the Castro Communist Revolution.* New York: Random House, 1962.

Soto, Lionel. *la revolución del 33.* Vol. 3. Havana: Editorial de Ciencias Sociales, Tomo III, 1977.

Supplementary Sources

Adam y Silva, Ricardo. *La gran mentira, 4 de septiembre de 1933.* Havana: Editorial Lex, 1947.

Busch Rodríguez, Luis M. *Gobierno revolucionario cubano: Génesis y primeros pasos.* Havana: Editorial de Ciencias Sociales, 1999.

Dubois, Jules. "Herald Tribune." In *Diario de la revolución cubana,* by Carlos Franqui. Paris: Ruedo Ibérico, 1976.

Ichikawa, Emilio. *Entrevista con el Sr. Fulgencio Rubén Batista y Godínez, hijo del general Fulgencio Batista y Zaldívar.* Coral Gables, FL: n.p., 2006. Available from http://www.eichikawa.com/entrevistas/ Fulgencio_Batista.html.

Rosell Leyva, Florentino. *La verdad.* Miami: n.p., 1960.

Rosell Leyva, Florentino. "El tren blindado." *La Crónica* (Miami) July–August 1960.

Rosell Leyva, Florentino. "Confirme el acuerdo Batista-Cantillo." *La Crónica* (Miami) 16 August 1968.

■

CUBAN SINGERS IN THE UNITED STATES

Susan Thomas

Three generations of singers who changed Cuban music in the United States.

Celia Cruz, Willy Chirino, and Albita Rodríguez, Cuban singers in the United States, represent three different generations and styles. Cruz (1924–2003) was twenty-two years old at the time of Chirino's birth in 1947, and her recordings as the lead singer of La Sonora Matanzera were part of the musical soundscape of Chirino's boyhood in the small Pinar del Rio town of Consolación del Sur. The child of an attorney and a pharmacist, Chirino led a privileged middle-class boyhood until the 1959 Revolution. In its aftermath, his parents sent him out of the country during Operation

Peter Pan, a joint project of the U.S. Government and the Catholic Church in Miami. In Operation Peter Pan, Cuban children were sent to the United States with the understanding that they would be reunited with their parents when the island returned to its pre-revolutionary status, which was expected to be soon. The thirteen-year-old Chirino arrived in the United States in 1961 just months after Celia Cruz came to the United States via Mexico. Rodríguez, who was born in 1962, represents the third generation by age and a second generation of Cuban immigrants, having arrived in the United States in 1993. As their careers developed in the United States, the three artists generated broad appeal by hybridizing traditional Cuban dance music with a variety of styles and genres, including jazz, rock, pop, and other Latin American genres. They have also done so while navigating their own personal identity politics within the international music industry, the Cuban-American community, and with international audiences as well.

CELIA CRUZ IN CUBA

While Chirino was just a boy at the time of the Revolution, Cruz was a fully fledged musical professional. Cruz grew up in Havana in a family of modest means and began singing as a young girl, despite her father's disapproval. To protect her image, Cruz traveled with a female chaperone until she married Pedro Knight in 1962. While undergoing training as a teacher, Cruz sang in cabarets, recorded Afro-Cuban sacred music, and toured Mexico and Venezuela with the dance troupe Las Mulatas del Fuego. In 1950, her big break came when she replaced Myrta Silva as the lead singer of La Sonora Matanzera, Cuba's preeminent afrocubanista dance band. With La Sonora Matanzera, Cruz became better known, and she was one of the first female singers to record Cuban popular dance music, disproving the notion that women performers made money only through live performances and not by selling records (Cruz p. 50).

In the 1950s, Cruz came to embody the essence of Afro-Cuban popular music and tropical dance music in Cuba and throughout Latin America. Cruz's pre-exile repertoire reflects the afrocubanismo dance music boom that took place in Cuba and throughout Latin America in those years. Her lyrics included Afro-Cuban slang and dialect. The songs referred to Afro-Cuban religion and cultural heritage, used popular dance rhythms, and referred to local personalities such as the herbalist, street vendor, and *babalao* (Santería priest). They also incorporated Afro-Cuban drumming, as in "Azucar negra" (Black Sugar, 1993), "La cumbanchera de Belén" (The Party Girl from Belén, 1958), and the onomatopoetic "Quimboquimbumbia" (1967).

CRUZ IN THE UNITED STATES

At the height of her career in 1959, Cruz arrived in the United States. She found a culture enthralled with rock-and-roll with little interest in Cruz's traditional Latin dancehall style. It took a decade for Cruz's North American career to take off. The cultural impact of the civil rights movement, a resurgence of ethnic pride, and a movement toward a pan-Latin identity all helped Latin music succeed commercially. Record producer Jerry Masucci and his Fania Records provided an urbanized and updated *son*-based dance music that appealed to listeners who had not liked Cruz's traditional Cuban and tropical dance music. Masucci (1934–1997) and Fania produced a hybridized Latin dance music that merged a number of national and regional styles, appealing to Latinos/Latinas of various backgrounds. Revitalized by new arrangements, a marketing strategy that grouped a variety of Latin dance styles together as *salsa*, and, perhaps most significantly, celebrated Latino ethnic identity, Cruz's performances with Fania drew a broad audience.

Collaborating with Fania artists such as Johnny Pacheco and Tito Puente, Cruz became the only female superstar in the emerging salsa industry. She did so by maintaining her traditional Cuban sound as she acquired an increasingly diverse repertoire. Whereas Fania marketed its performers as urban-forward, progressive, and innovative, Cruz continued to approach her music from the traditional, *son*-based performance aesthetic she always had. Throughout her career she maintained that, for her, salsa was simply Cuban music. While her musical aesthetic was traditional, however, her on-stage persona was not. Decked in feathers, turbans, four-inch platform heels, gold sequins, and blond beehive wigs, on the stage she was a visual as well as a musical phenomenon, flamboyantly mixing signs of Afro-Cuban religion, Hollywood, the *rumbera* femme fatale, the capitalist clothes horse, and even the drag queen, leaving Christina Abreu to comment that Cruz "chose to use spectacle rather than sexual appeal to advance her career" (p. 99). Replacing the traditional sexual objectification of female singers with her own performative pleasure, Cruz became a powerful symbol of both female and postcolonial agency and desire.

A critic of the Castro regime, Cruz nonetheless avoided the confrontational political stances of other salsa artists such as the Panamanian Rubén Blades (b. 1948) or the Puerto Ricans Ray Barreto (1929–2006) and Willie Colón (b. 1950), which made their music less marketable to mainstream audiences who did not share their politics (Abreu p. 97). Open about her Cuban nationalist and anti-Castro politics in her personal life, in her music, Cruz's political position was cloaked in symbolism. Her lyrics alluded to the Cuban countryside, island traditions, and a traditional *son* aesthetic. They expressed nostalgia for a pre-revolutionary Cuban homeland. For non-Cubans, such songs could be enjoyed for their musicality alone. For Cuban exiles, however, such songs spoke to the collective longing for a past and a homeland, remembered by some and only imagined by others.

Trained in the theater and cabaret, Cruz was a consummate entertainer, with an uncanny ability to sing to the preferences and desires of different audiences. Onstage she might recognize a Chilean flag in the audience and respond by singing a salsified version of "Gracias a la vida" or even take a request and sing "La Macarena" (Fernández). Her recorded output shows a clear commitment to embrace other Latin American music directly and to bring her own personal Cuban style to some of the best loved tunes of different nationalities, including "Cucurrucucú paloma" (Mexico), "Usted abusó" (Brazil), "Toro mata" (Peru), and "Zambúllete" (Uruguay). Her collaborations with diverse artists, including Johnny Pacheco, Tito Puente, Ray Barreto, Willie Colón, Willy Chirino, Oscar D'León, Cheo Feliciano, Gloria Estefan, and La India, helped to spread her appeal to an increasingly diverse Latino/a and Latin American audience. The same is true for her collaborations with non-Latino performers such as Wyclef Jean, Patti LaBelle, and Dionne Warwick and her participation in the 1992 film *The Mambo Kings*, which attracted new Anglophone listeners to the reigning Queen of Salsa.

If Cruz's success could be attributed to any one factor (beyond the sheer brilliance of her musicality and the joyous vitality of her singing), it might be that she, perhaps more than any other twentieth-century musician, mastered the art of the crossover. She knew how to bridge national styles, generic expectations, nationalist metaphors, and linguistic codes. At the same time, her acts of musical crossing, such as her Spanish adaptations of the Beatles' "Obladi Oblada" or the salsification of "Cucurrucucú paloma" also implicitly acknowledge the tensions associated with both immigrant experience and *destierro* (exile) (Pérez p. 37). In this way, Cruz's crossovers speak not only from margin to mainstream, but also from margin to margin (Abreu p. 101).

WILLY CHIRINO

A generation younger, Willy Chirino shared more with Cruz than his similarly timed arrival in the United States. Like Cruz, his professional career in the United States began in the 1970s with the release of his album *One Man Alone* (1974). The album included Chirino's song "Soy" (I Am), an idealistic personal manifesto that uses pastoral imagery that seems to allude to the Cuban homeland. The song's lack of geographic or cultural specificity, however, made it adaptable to other interpretations, and it was later recorded by more than sixty artists.

Between 1974 and 2010, Chirino recorded twenty-eight albums and his songs were perfomed by other artists on many more. By the 1980s, Chirino was a primary influence on the new Miami Sound, blending salsa with rock and jazz elements, along with some of the Latin pop aesthetic popularized by Gloria Estefan and the Miami Sound Machine. This hybrid

Willy Chirino in Miami, 6 May 2008. Willy Chirino, who arrived in the United States as a teenager in 1961, became one of the primary performers of the Miami sound, which blends salsa with influences from rock, jazz, and Latin pop. ALEXANDER TAMARGO/GETTY IMAGES

sound remained popular; in fact, Chirino's album *Son del Alma* (*Son* from the Soul) won a Grammy award for Best Salsa/Merengue Album in 2006.

Like Cruz, Chirino has been a vocal critic of the Cuban socialist regime; in 2009, for example, he publicly denounced the Colombian singer Juanes for giving a "Paz sin Fronteras" (Peace without Borders) concert in Havana, where he collaborated with state-supported artists Silvio Rodríguez and Amaury Pérez. Chirino published a scathing letter on 12 August 2009, in which he asked whether in the 1980s it would have been acceptable to give a similar concert in Chile collaborating with artists who supported Pinochet's regime or in Cape Town while Nelson Mandela was incarcerated. Unlike Cruz whose songs allude to politics metaphorically or address issues of pan-Latin concern, as in "Pasaporte latinoamericano" (1993), Chirino's exile stance and politics are on full display in his music. "Nuestra día ya viene llegando" (Our Day Is Coming, 1991), for example, expresses the longing for the Cuban government to change hands and for the hardships and separations faced by the Cuban people to end. "Trece de Julio (El mar nos une)" (July Thirteenth [The Sea Unites Us], 2008) similarly speaks to the uniquely Cuban experience. "La Jinetera" (The Jockey [slang for prostitute], 1995) attacks the Castro government for economic policies that force girls to sell themselves in the sex trade. In one of his more prominent political statements, Chirino donated $75,000 of the profits from his song "Habana D.C." (2005) to Hermanos al Rescate (Brothers to the Rescue), an anti-Castro group whose planes were shot down by the Cuban government in 1996.

Chirino has continued to explore his own identity, a project begun with "Soy" (I Am) in 1974. His 1992 album, *Un típicotipo* (An Average Guy),

provides an updated and salsified version of "Soy" preceded by what would become one of his most discussed songs, "Soy un típicotipo." Documenting his own roots as a musician who grew up "on the hyphen" (Pérez-Firmat), the nearly seven-minute long song explores the musical influences that shaped his style. It includes original lyrics and melody spliced with excerpts from the Beatles, Moisés Simons, Jimi Hendrix, and others. It also refers to his roots in traditional Cuban music through changes in rhythm and lyrics that turn the names of famous pre-revolutionary Cuban performers or genres into adjectives that describe his own identity: *matamórico*, *sonoromatancérico*, *chapotínico*. The effect, writes Eliana Rivero, is to give the song a "transnational and syncretic character," noting that the song forces the listener to code-switch at different levels: lyrical, generic, vocal, and rhythmic (p. 213).

ALBITA RODRÍGUEZ

Representing a younger generation than either Cruz or Chirino as well as a subsequent experience of emigration and exile, Albita Rodríguez left Cuba in 1990, traveling first to Colombia and then to Mexico before entering the United States in 1993. The daughter of folk musicians, Rodríguez grew up performing the *música guajira* (country music) of her parents, and by the late 1980s she was one of the island's rising stars of the genre, recording her first album, *Habrá música guajira*, in 1988. In Miami, Rodríguez merged elements of the *guajira* style with salsa, and she successfully spoke to the same nostalgic and pastoral sentiments exploited by Cruz and Chirino. She went beyond the terrain of Cruz and Chirino, however, not only referring to the Cuban countryside in her lyrics but overtly bringing country-style genres such as the *punto* and *guajira* into the Cuban American musical mainstream. In doing so, she brought a new relevance and immediacy to a music that "was even staler in Cuba than it was in Miami" (Rey 117). In this way, she made Cuban country-style music cool for younger listeners whose only exposure to the style might have been Gloria Estéfan's 1993 album, *Mi tierra*, an album whose mainstream success may have helped pave the way for Rodríguez's revival of música guajira.

Rodríguez crossed performative boundaries in much the same way that Cruz and Chirino crossed national and stylistic ones. If Cruz opted for a hyperfeminine glam style that emphasized spectacle rather than sexuality, Rodríguez performed a chameleonic gender play in which she has embodied a number of differently gendered and sexualized identities, from the suit-clad androgyne (mid-1990s) to the femme fatale (late 1990s-early 2000s) to a sort of tropicalized Bette Midler figure (2010) with a "mane of fluorescent orange hair" (Yanez). Rodríguez claims that her visual image was left in the hands of marketing executives, who appear to have cleverly followed a formula of masculine/feminine play most famously associated with female pop artists such as k.d. lang, Madonna, and Annie Lennox, the U.S. pop artist whom Rodríguez most closely resembles. In her transformations, Mario Rey writes, "[Albita] perpetuates a combination of social identities—female, Cuban, rural, émigré, queer—and mediates the often contradictory meanings connected with these social categories" (p. 116).

Rodríguez's gender-bending is not only visual. Unlike nearly all singers of Latin and Cuban dance music, she frequently plays instruments in performance, including the guitar, *trés*, and percussion. Her performance of unconsecrated *batá* drums has drawn particular attention, as only men are permitted to play these Yoruba-derived drums in their sacred context. Thus, Rodríguez's instrumental performing transgresses traditionally gendered musical behavior. It also reveals a generational difference between Cubans like her who were educated in the socialist Cuban arts education system and those who were not. The Cuban state's embrace of musical folklore, for example, and its support of folkloric ensembles such as the Conjunto Folklórico Nacional has resulted in more women being trained on instruments such as trés and batá outside their original social and cultural contexts. Rodríguez's performance on these instruments draws attention to her gendered performance and to her representing a generation of Cuban immigrants whose identity is much more informed by the Cuban socialist state. The presence in Miami of younger émigrés such as Rodríguez required the Cuban exile community to refine its stance and Miami cultural institutions to adapt to these new Cuban-trained musicians and artists. The Madrid-based Habana Abierta (Open Havana) performed in Coral Gables in 2003 shortly after a triumphant concert in Havana (something that previously would have been unthinkable), and Willy Chirino invited them back to Miami for a three-generational megaconcert in 2009 to kick off the tour for his album *Pa'lante* (Forward).

Rodríguez's gendered play also crosses the limits of genre. She abandons the realm of *salsa romántica* that female salseras most frequently inhabit and instead performs the more sexually suggestive, traditionally masculine, and musically aggressive *salsa erótica*. For many queer-identified writers and critics, Rodríguez's arrival on the U.S. Latin music scene was a revelation, offering a transgressive critique of gendered and sexualized normativity that provided a space for previously marginalized listeners such as Darshan Elena Campos "to claim salsa music as [their] own" (p. 52).

Celia Cruz, Willy Chirino, and Albita Rodríguez succeeded in allowing different previously marginalized communities to claim salsa music as their own. Creating hybrid sounds that reach across national and generational divides, the three artists' careers together present a diverse expression of *cubanía* that is vibrant, multifaceted, and musically satisfying.

BIBLIOGRAPHY

"1998 Spirit of Hope Winner Willy Chirino." *Billboard*, April 11, 1998.

Abreu, Cristina D. "Celebrity, 'Crossover,' and Cubanidad: Celia Cruz as "'La Reina de Salsa,' 1971–2003." *Latin American Music Review* 28, no. 1 (Spring–Summer 2007): 94–124.

Aparicio, Frances R. *Listening to Salsa: Gender, Latin Popular Music, and Puerto Rican Cultures.* Hanover, NH: Wesleyan University Press/University Press of New England, 1998.

Aparicio, Frances R. "The Blackness of Sugar: Celia Cruz and the Performance of (Trans)Nationalism." *Cultural Studies* 13, no. 2 (April 1999): 223–236.

Campos, Darshan Elena. "Her Suit Fits: Albita's Performative Postures." In *Beyond the Frame: Women of Color and Visual Representations*, edited by Nefertiti X. M. Tadiar and Angela Y. Davis. New York: Palgrave Macmillan, 2005.

Chirino, Willy. "Willy Chirinohabla de Juanes." F & F Media Corp., August 12, 2009. Available from http://www.ffmediacorp.com/es/Prensa-2/Comunicados-de-Prensa-5/Willy-Chirino-habla-de-Juanes-12-08-09-199.

Cruz, Celia, with Ana Cristina Reymundo. *Celia: My Life*. Translated by José Lucas Badué. New York: Rayo, 2004.

Fernández, Raúl A. "The Course of U.S. Cuban Music: Margin and Mainstream." *Cuban Studies* 24 (1994): 105–122.

Fernández, Raúl A. Interview with Celia Cruz, September 15, 1996. Hollywood, CA: Jazz Oral History Project, Smithsonian Institution.

Guevara, Gema R. "'La Cuba de Ayer/La Cuba de Hoy': The Politics of Music and Diaspora." In *Musical Migrations: Transnationalism and Cultural Hybridity in Latin/o America*, edited by Frances R. Aparicio and Cándida Jáquez with María Elena Cepeda. New York: Palgrave Macmillan, 2003.

Pérez-Firmat, Gustavo. *Life on the Hyphen: The Cuban-American Way*. Austin: University of Texas Press, 1994.

Pérez, Louis A., Jr. *On Becoming Cuba: Identity, Nationality, and Culture*. New York: HarperCollins Publishers, 1999.

Rey, Mario. "Albita Rodríguez: Sexuality, Imaging, and Gender Construction in the Music of Exile." In *Queering the Popular Pitch*, edited by Sheila Whiteley and Jennifer Rycenga. New York: Routledge, 2006.

Rivero, Eliana. "Cuba sí, Cuba no: La fusión de son y rock en la música de Willy Chirino." *Studies in Latin America Popular Culture* 22 (2003), 207–216.

Steward, Sue. "Worlds Apart? Salsa Queen to Pop Princess." In *Girls! Girls! Girls! Essays on Women and Music*, edited by Sarah Cooper. New York: New York University Press, 1996.

Yanez, Luisa. "Documentary Focuses on Art of Popular Cuban Singer Albita." *Miami Herald* December 2, 2010. Available from http://www.miamiherald.com/2010/12/02/1952894/documentary-focuses-on-art-of.html

CUBAN THOUGHT AND CULTURAL IDENTITY

Cuba has brought together many different cultures and ethnicities (for instance, African, European, Middle Eastern, Asian, and American), to form its own unique identity. Its character was also forged in long battles for independence from Spain in the nineteenth century as well as through its volatile relationship with the United States in the twentieth and twenty-first centuries.

Starting with the likes of the religious figure Félix Varela in the nineteenth century, Cuba has had a distinguished set of thinkers and intellectuals who have pondered the Cuban condition in matters related to national identity and culture, and involved themselves with the politics, philosophy, and religions of their times: nationalism, populism, liberal democracy, socialism, Catholicism, Protestantism, positivism, Kantian metaphysics, Hegelian dialectics, pragmatism, existentialism, phenomenology, Orteguian vitalism, and Marxism. In the twentieth century, Cubans began to discuss the importance of Afro-Cuban culture (Fernando Ortiz, Lydia Cabrera, and Rómulo Lachatañeré) and its centrality to national identity, a conversation that continues, sometimes polemically, in the present.

The following section is not just about ideas, though, but also about certain practices: customs that date back centuries to Spanish rule all the way to the revolutionary present. These practices encompass courtship rituals, celebrations, parties, food preparation, weddings, and quinceañeras *(the Cuban fifteen-year-old's equivalent of the American sweet-sixteen parties), friendship, sexuality, a kind of humor known as* choteo, *the influence of U.S. English on the Cuban vernacular, and Cuba's national obsession: baseball.*

CUBAN THOUGHT AND CULTURAL IDENTITY: THE VARIOUS WAYS OF (NOT) BEING CUBAN

Emilio Cueto

What is and what is not Cuban in literature, music, and the visual arts.

During much of the twentieth century, concepts such as *cubanía* and *cubanidad* were frequently discussed among Cuban thinkers, including Jorge Mañach (1898–1961), Ramiro Guerra Sánchez (1880–1970), Fernando Ortiz (1881–1969), Gustavo Pérez Firmat (b. 1949), and Abel Prieto (b. 1950). This essay neither reviews such debate nor adds its own voice to it. Instead, it explores the different ways in which the adjective *Cuban* has been used in diverse contexts and the highly complex, fragmented, and probably distorted picture resulting from its selective and inconsistent application.

Generally, and appropriately, the word *Cuban* designates individuals and things relating to Cuba by virtue of being (1) in or from Cuba; (2) about Cuba; or (3) done by Cubans. These three criteria, however, are not applied consistently. The result is that some things end up considered Cuban whereas related ones may not. This discussion focuses on the fields of literature, music, and the visual arts.

WORKS PRODUCED IN CUBA

Works produced in Cuba are usually labeled Cuban. Following this criterion, all scholars have considered *Espejo de Paciencia* (The Mirror of Patience), the epic poem written in Cuba in 1608 by Silvestre de Balboa (1563–1647/49?), to be the first Cuban literary work. The historian Manuel Moreno Fraginals (1920–2001), however, questions this notion:

> In a formal sense, *Espejo de Paciencia* is a *Spanish* poem written by a native of the Canary Islands who resided in Cuba for a limited time, although referring to an event which took place in Cuban territory and using at times local names for flora and fauna.... But to conclude from its subject matter and the occasional and reduced use of sixteen native words that *Espejo de Paciencia* is an expression of Cuban literature would be like labeling Ercilla's fabulous *Araucana* as "Chilean" (emphasis added).
>
> *Moreno Fraginals p. 357*

Moreno is making a very important point, particularly because Cuba was a Spanish colony for nearly 400 years. Many Spaniards lived and wrote in Cuba, yet not all of their literary production has been considered part of Cuban literature. This begs the question why *Espejo* is considered Cuban while the others are not.

Literary works are not the only objects caught in this dilemma. Spanish poet José Fernández Bremón (1839–1910) disputed the Cubanness of one of Cuba's most iconic works of architecture, El Morro Castle, at the end of Spanish rule in Cuba in 1898 by comparing it to one of Spain's iconic structures constructed by the Moors. He wrote that "The Alhambra will be Moorish even if Spain does not want / And Havana´s Morro Castle will be Spanish unless its stones are removed." So if El Morro Castle was built by the Spanish in Cuba during the period of colonial rule is it Spanish or Cuban—or both? The identification of something as Cuban, therefore, sometimes involves a duality.

Concerning photography, critic Rafael Acosta de Arriba (b. 1953) raises a different, yet related, point: "Rather than talking about 'Cuban photography' I would rather say photography made 'in the country,' since its hybrid nature, borrowings and tendencies, in reference to what is being produced throughout the world, are evident" (p. 183). The larger issue, of course, is whether something with a universal look can be properly or usefully labeled Cuban only because it is made on the island.

WORKS PRODUCED BY CUBANS

The determination of who is (or is not) a Cuban is not always as easy as it would seem. To be born in Cuba normally means that one is a Cuban, although accidental Cubans do happen. The converse is also true. So, for example, famous individuals born abroad are still considered members of the Cuban family, including writers Alfonso Hernández Catá (1885–1940), Pablo de la Torriente (1901–1936), Alejo Carpentier (1904–1980), Cintio Vitier (1921–2009), and Fayad Jamís (1930–1988); musicians Hubert de Blanck (1856–1932) and Amadeo Roldán (1900–1939); sugar tsar Julio Lobo (1898–1983); cinematographer Néstor Almendros (1930–1992); food expert Nitza Villapol (1923–1998); and actress Rosita Fornés (b. 1923).

Others have been labeled Cuban although the connection to the island may be more tenuous. Such is the case of French painter Francis Picabia (1879–1953), born of a Cuban father, who was described as Cuban by Alejo Carpentier. Carpentier said that Picabia was clearly Cuban (or at least Latin American) because of the richness of his lyricism, independence, violence, and *choteo* (humor) (Carpentier).

As a general rule, literary, musical, and artistic compositions by Cubans are considered to be Cuban even if such works are not about Cuba or made in Cuba. Thus, *Oda al Niágara* by José María Heredia (1803–1839), *Pilluelos* by Juana Borrero (1877–1896), and *Ante el Escorial* by Ernesto Lecuona

(1895–1963) are examples of Cuban literature, art, and music, respectively.

However, a unique problem presents itself regarding literature. Cuban-born José-Maria de Hérédia (1842–1905) and Armand Godoy (1880–1964) wrote their poems in French, while Gustavo Pérez Firmat (b. 1949) and Nilo Cruz (b. 1960) express themselves in English. Unlike Belgium or Spain, Cuba is not a multilingual country. Are works written in a language not understood by 90 percent of Cubans part of Cuban literature? What if the works are translated? Italian author Alba de Céspedes (1911–1997) managed to get her *Quaderno proibito* (1952; *The Secret*, 1957) published in translation by Editorial Letras Cubanas, which is reserved for Cuban authors. Did she sneak in because she was the daughter of a Cuban president? Another Italian author, however, fared differently; Italo Calvino (1923–1985) was born in Santiago de las Vegas where he lived until age two, yet no one classifies his work as Cuban. In contrast, the pop singer Gloria Estefan (b. 1957), who also left Cuba as a toddler, is considered to be part of Cuban music.

Language is not the only complicated factor. José Ortega Munilla (1856–1922) was born in Cárdenas, Eduardo Zamacois (1873–1971) in Pinar del Río, and Alberto Insúa (1885–1965) in Havana. Yet, because they lived and wrote mostly in Spain their works are not usually considered Cuban literature. Nor is the work of Caridad Bravo Adams (1908–1990), born in Mexico to Cuban parents, even though she spent several years writing in Cuba (including two *telenovelas* about the heroes of Cuban independence). Somewhat different is the case of Gertrudis Gómez de Avellaneda (1814–1873) who has been included, simultaneously, in both Cuban and Spanish literature.

In his dictionary of Cuban music, scholar Radamés Giro comments that the music of Willy Chirino (b. 1947) is closer to U.S. music (whatever that may be) than to Cuba´s (p. 291). This position draws several interesting questions: Is everything that a Cuban composer writes Cuban music? Can a non-Cuban write Cuban music? Finally, is Cuban music a unique recognizable sound that exists regardless of who writes it and where it is composed?

One might wonder if the contemporary compositions by Aurelio de la Vega (b. 1925) are truly examples of Cuban music, rather than music written by a Cuban. Similarly, one might question why Austrian composer Paul Csonka (1905–1995) could write his Cuban concerto, while the popular guaracha *Cachita*, by Puerto Rican composer Rafael Hernández (1892–1965), is not deemed to be Cuban music even though Hernández himself introduced his *Capullito de Alelí* (Wallflower Bud) to celebrate Cuban Song Day in Havana in 1925. In the same vein, while the *habanera* appears to be a typically Cuban rhythm, the fact is that a good number of habaneras—perhaps most—have been composed in Spain by Spanish artists.

WORKS ABOUT CUBA

Questions about what is universal and what is Cuban are equally relevant in the visual arts. Is there such a thing as Cuban art other than art by Cubans? Books on Cuban colonial art invariably include works done by foreign artists depicting Cuban scenes. The engravings by Dominique Serres (1719–1793) and Elias Durnford (1739–1794) about the seizure of Havana by the British in 1762, the oils by Henry Cleenewerk (1818–1901), the Havana prints by James Gay Sawkins (1806–1878), Hyppolite Garnerey (1787–1858), and Adolf Hoeffler (1825–1898), as well as the various lithographs of Frédéric Mialhe (1810–1881), Leonardo Barañano (b. 1822), Edouard Laplante (b. 1818), and Víctor Landaluze (1828–1889) are typically considered Cuban colonial art.

Yet toward the end of the nineteenth century and into the twentieth century, works with Cuban images done by foreign artists disappear from the scene. Absent are the Cuban works by Winslow Homer (1836–1910), Frederic Remington (1861–1909), and Kiril Tsonev (1896–1961), to cite but a few. The reasons why scholars switched their criteria are not easy to explain. One possible explanation is that the history of eighteenth- and nineteenth-century Cuban art would be short and slim without the foreigners, but they were considered superfluous later on when more Cubans started painting.

Interestingly, this consideration of foreigners as producing Cuban works appears to be more prevalent in the visual arts than in music or literature. Except in the case of Spaniards living in Cuba (whose music and literature are often included as Cuban material), the compositions and literary work of other foreigners are mostly absent from Cuban books even if these works have Cuba as their subject matter. Thus, music inspired by Cuba but written by foreigners during colonial times, as well as the hundreds of habaneras, rumbas, mambos, and congas composed abroad, have not made it into the Cuban canon. Along the same lines, poems written in Spain praising the heroism of Luis de Velasco (1711–1762) while defending Morro Castle from British attack, and novels and theatrical pieces about, or set in, Cuba that were written abroad (e.g., *El don de gentes o La Havanera* by Tomás de Iriarte [1750–1791], *Le Séducteur* by Gérard d'Houvuille [1875–1963], or *Our Man in Havana* by Graham Greene [1904–1991]) have all been excluded.

There are no definitive answers for these questions. It does seem, however, that if a work meets all three criteria (e.g., it is about Cuba, done in Cuba, and by a Cuban) it will usually be considered Cuban. However, if it only meets one of these criteria, chances are that it may be excluded from the canon at one point or another, by one compiler or another.

OTHER MYSTERIES OF CUBAN IDENTITY

Sugar and tobacco are universally associated with Cuba, yet neither is native to Cuba. Cuban coffee ordered at, for example, the Miami airport usually means a mixture of Colombian beans, Miami-Dade County water, and Dominican sugar, prepared in an Italian espresso maker and served by a Nicaraguan waitress in a Chinese cup. Payment is in U.S. dollars, of course.

Cuba´s national flower is the mariposa (*Hedychium coronarium*), which hails from the Himalayas in Asia, while the famous so-called American flamingo painted by John James Audubon (1785–1851) is, in reality, a Cuban specimen. Mexicans, Dominicans, and Brazilians looking at a poster depicting Cuban fruits may legitimately question why they are considered Cuban if those fruits are also indigenous to their countries. And, clearly, travelers outside Cuba should be skeptical when offered *arroz a la cubana* (Cuban-styled rice with fried egg and tomato sauce).

Famous Cuban patriots Felix Varela (1788–1853), Antonio Maceo (1845–1896), and José Martí (1853–1895) were never Cuban citizens; the Argentinean Che Guevara (1928–1967) was, at least for a while; and the Castro government decided that the members of the Bay of Pigs Cuban invasion force should no longer be. For political reasons, Guillermo Cabrera Infante (1929– 2005), Severo Sarduy (1937–1993), Celia Cruz (1924–2003), Olga Guillot (1922–2010), and many other renowned Cuban writers and musicians were excluded from the main dictionaries of Cuban literature and music published in the island during the 1980s. Subsequently, other less myopic publications have made them Cuban again.

The poet Nicolás Guillén (1902–1989) once mockingly described a Cuban baseball team as follows: "First base: Charles Little; Second Base: Joe Cobb; / Catcher: Samuel Benton; Third base: Bobby Hog; / Shortstop: James Wintergarden; Pitcher: William Bot; / Fields: Wilson, Baker, Panther. Yes sir! But, at least, the batboy is Juan Guzmán."

As a Cuban saying has it: "No son todos los que están ni están todos los que son" ("Neither all who belong are here, nor all who are here belong").

BIBLIOGRAPHY

Acosta de Arriba, Rafael. *Caminos de la mirada*. Havana: Ediciones Unión, 2007.

Barquín Cantero, Ramón. "¿Así que eres de Cuba?" *Areíto* (January–March 1975): 23–25.

Carpentier, Alejo. "El cubano Picabia." *Social* (February 1933): 20–21, 57, 61.

Céspedes, Alba de. *Cuaderno prohibido*. Havana: Letras Cubanas, 1991.

Diccionario de la literatura cubana. Instituto de Literatura y Lingüística de la Academia de Ciencias de Cuba. 2 vols. Havana: Letras Cubanas, 1980–1984.

Giro, Radamés. *Diccionario enciclopédico de la música en Cuba*. 4 vols. Havana: Letras Cubanas, 2007.

Guillén, Nicolás. *Las grandes elegías y otros poemas.* Caracas: Biblioteca Ayacucho, 1984.

Moreno Fraginals, Manuel. *Orbita de Manuel Moreno Fraginals.* Havana: Ediciones Unión, 2010.

Orovio, Helio. *Diccionario de la música cubana: biográfico y técnico.* Havana: Letras Cubanas, 1981.

CUBAN THOUGHT AND CULTURAL IDENTITY: COSTUMBRES IN THE ART AND LITERATURE OF THE 19TH CENTURY

Adriana Méndez Rodenas

Depictions of local color and customs in the development of Cuban national consciousness.

During the nineteenth century, Cuban cultural identity evolved out of a gradual process of exchange between *criollos* (creoles)—white descendants of Spaniards—and the descendants of African slaves, manifested in a range of behaviors, from everyday interaction in the marketplace to intimate encounters inside the colonial mansion or rural habitat. Although affiliated by family ties to peninsular Spaniards, Cubans defined their own distinctive set of customs, marital mores, and aesthetic taste. By the early to mid-nineteenth century, the hierarchy of race and class created by plantation society had generated a set of idiosyncratic social types that came to define the national subject. The *calesero* (carriage driver), the *mulata* (mulatta), the fruit-and-vegetable vendor, the *niño* or creole dandy, all strutted down Havana's central plaza in an early display of national pride. Their rituals, dances, language, and forms of courtship are documented in two related contemporary forms: a literary genre, *costumbrismo* (depictions of social customs or local-color sketches), which fulfilled the pedagogic function of defining a national culture; and a visual genre, lithographs and collections of prints, which displayed the local types in their typical settings.

Influenced by the popularity of the genre in Spain, the *costumbrista* or local color sketch developed in Cuba parallel to the development of the local press. The *Papel Periódico de la Habana*, launched in 1790, was the first publication wherein Cuban authors displayed an array of customs and mores, ranging from the depiction of local types to early imprints of life in the plantation (Bueno pp. xi–xii). The flowering of Cuban costumbrista literature occurred between 1830 to 1840, when a series of periodical publications registered an emerging sense of national identity by means of scenes drawn from both rural and urban settings (Bueno p. xiv). In his *Escenas cotidianas* (Everyday

Scenes), Gaspar Betancourt Cisneros (1803–1866) painted the sights and sounds of his native Camagüey, including a deliciously satiric portrait of the twists of tongue and other mannerisms that characterize the use of local dialect (Bueno pp. 31–34).

Two pictorial albums—Frédéric Mialhe's *Isla de Cuba Pintoresca*, published by the Real Sociedad Patriótica from 1839 to 1841, and *Paseo Pintoresco por la Isla de Cuba*, a series drawn by two Spanish artists, Laureano Cuevas and Fernando de la Costa, in 1841–1842 (Cueto pp. xiv–xv, xviii)—established a visual-textual counterpoint depicting Havana and its environs. Images of the bay of Havana, its docks, the tobacco factory, its stately tree-lined promenades, its surrounding *murallas* (walls), its fortresses, monuments, and churches, formed the background for the depiction of social customs during the first quarter of the century in local-color literary sketches.

FERIAS AND FESTIVALS

A typical costumbrista sketch, Cirilo Villaverde's "Jesús María y José" depicted the *barrio* on the outskirts of Havana where the first Cuban *ferias* (fairs) emerged, changed by popular fervor from their Spanish origins as religious festivities into mixed activities of commerce and games described by Villaverde as "un compuesto chocante y horrible" ("a shocking and horrible amalgam"), the primary attraction of which was gambling (p. 112). A variety of tastes, foods, and pastimes is portrayed in this colorful description:

> Veíase asomar por todas aquellas boca-calles, mesas de tijera,...tableros, ruletas pequeñas, retablos, totimundis, juegos de lotería,...en cuanto á juego: ollas de ponche de leche, dulcerías con su toldo á manera de tiendas árabes, pilones de maní, canastas de avellanas y aparadores cargados de jamones, pavos, queso...en cuanto a provisiones de boca...

> [In every side street could be seen evidence of gambling, including folding tables,...chessboards, small roulette wheels, altarpieces, lottery games, and more... As to supplies of food, there were pots full of milk punch, confectioners' shops covered by awnings like Arab tents, heaps of peanuts, baskets of hazelnuts, and sideboards full of hams, turkey, and cheeses.]

> *Villaverde pp. 112–113*

Toward the end of the feria, noisy groups of men and women filled the plaza, giving themselves over to the pleasure of the dance, both singing and dancing to the beat of the unending music. Despite the author's ultimate disapproval of "la exaltacion producida por la música criolla" ("the elation produced by this Cuban music"), since he viewed the frenetic dance as contributing to the disintegration of social and domestic

■ *See also*

Cecilia Valdés (Cirilo Villaverde)

Día de Reyes en la Habana (Víctor Patricio de Landaluze)

Havana: Havana as Cultural Center

Literature: Nationalist and Reformist Literature, pre-1850

Sexuality: The Mulata Figure in the Cuban Imaginary

virtues, it is clear that he also saw crystallized in these cultural practices the culmination of a classically Cuban ritual (Villaverde p. 114).

FOOD AND SOCIABILITY

Other writers of the period depicted the ferias, particularly José Ramón Betancourt in his well-known "Una feria de la Caridad en 189…" (A Popular Feast in Caridad in 189…), a lively account of the celebrations in honor of Cuba's patron saint, Our Lady of Charity, in the neighborhood near Puerto Príncipe, modern Camagüey, which held yearly festivities as the town was named after her. Originally published in the local newspaper *El Fanal,* "Una feria de la Caridad en 189…" saw the light in 1885, with a prologue by Cirilo Villaverde praising the author for his realistic depiction of card games (*el monte*), dances, and creole sociability.

The importance of costumbrista tales for the emergence of Cuban national identity is signaled in José Victoriano Betancourt's "Velar el mondongo," (To Hold a Wake for a Tripe) (González Echevarría p. 52), a sketch published in the 1838 volume of *La Cartera Cubana,* in which the author points out the value of customs and mores in conforming "la fisonomía moral de un pueblo" ("a people's moral physiognomy") (p. 363). With a humble disclaimer as to his literary talent, the author nevertheless affirms his aesthetic intention: "pintar, aunque con tosco pincel y apagados colores [sic] algunas costumbres, bien rústicas [sic] bien urbanas, á veces con el deseo de indicar una reforma, á veces con el de armonizar…" ("to draw, although with rough brushstrokes and dimmed lights, some folkways, both rural and urban, sometimes with the intention of social reform; other times, simply to entertain"). He then goes on to describe his central topic: the transformation of a live pig into a *lechón* (pork roast), while focusing on the intermediate stage when a butcher eviscerates the pig, then cooks and roasts the entrails, a gruesome event followed by drinking, merriment, and dancing (pp. 364–368; González Echevarría p. 52). While in Betancourt's original the ritual is seen as the epitome of country mores, Countess Merlin rewrote the sketch in *Viaje a la Habana* (1840) in order to describe both the barbarity and socializing entailed in the ritual; hence marking the transition between "the raw and the cooked," and a celebration of conviviality and sociability. *The raw and the cooked* is a term borrowed from anthropology, which denotes exactly what is described here: how the pig's entrails are transformed into food, and, in the process, form part of a ritualistic feast that congeals and celebrates Cuban nationality. Though Merlin was a transnational Cuban writer and creole who returned to Cuba after a long residence in France, her rewriting of Betancourt's sketch emphasizes the poetic aspect of popular festivities, what, in her view, erases the grotesque ambience of the scene (Merlin p. 62).

At the opposite end of the social hierarchy, her idyllic images of family life among the Havana sugar aristocracy provide an intimate portrait of domestic life. Merlin's encounter with members of the Montalvo clan captures the moment when the creole gained consciousness of his difference vis-à-vis the Spaniard:

> Uno de los caracteres peculiares de la raza actual de los españoles habaneros, plantas europeas transplantadas á esta isla, es el contraste que existe entre la languidez de estos cuerpos pequeños y delicados,…y el ardor de su sangre que se revela en sus gestos, en los gustos, en la manera de hablar y de discurrir, siempre viva, apasionada é impetuosa.

> [An idiosyncrasy proper to the Spaniards of Havana—a particular race of European plants transplanted to this island—is the contrast between the listlessness of their small and delicate bodies,…and the ardent temperament revealed by their hand gestures, their tastes, and their manner of talking and reasoning, always lively, impassioned, and impetuous.]

> *Merlin p. 17*

These forms of sociability surfaced in a crucial scene in *Viaje a la Habana,* which describes a banquet inside the family home: "Las comidas…tienen siempre un cierto aire de fiesta que las [sic] dan el número de convidados…y la desordenada profusión de los manjares" ("Mealtimes…always have a certain festive air due to the number of guests…and the extravagant array of foods") (p. 14). In what became a recurring motif in Cuban culture, the banquet was an allegory for the emergence of Cuban identity: "Los habaneros comen poco á la vez, como los pájaros; a cualquier hora del día se les encuentra con una fruta o un terrón de azúcar en la boca.… Los señores de la alta clase, á pesar del lujo europeo de sus mesas, reservan la verdadera simpatía para el plato criollo." ("The people of Havana tend to eat in small doses, like birds; at any hour they may be found with a fruit or a lump of sugar in their mouths.… Upper-class gentlemen, in spite of the European luxury of their dinner tables, are really most attached to their creole dishes.") (p. 14). What follows is an enumeration of fruits that recalls the tropical cornucopia that first appeared in *Espejo de paciencia,* Silvestre de Balboa's epic poem of 1609, and suggests a distinctively creole *joie de vivre.* At the banquet, "todo es petulancia, alegría, abandono, delirio; todo el mundo se tutea; las edades y las conversaciones se confunden; todo el mundo es feliz; el corazon se ha encargado de hacer los honores de la fiesta" ("all is presumption, joy, indulgence, frenzy; everyone treats each other as family; generations and conversations blur into one another; everyone is happy; the heart has taken charge of the meal") (p. 16).

POPULAR CELEBRATIONS

Feasts and celebrations surfaced also in ethnographic accounts. The classic work of this genre is Fernando Ortiz's *La antigua fiesta afrocubana del "Día de Reyes"* (The Afro-Cuban Celebration of Three Kings Day, 1925), describing the Epiphany celebration in Havana, when masters released their slaves for an entire day, and the slaves, decked out in elaborate costumes, and grouped in their respective *cabildos* or ethnic mutual aid societies, elected a king and paraded in loud celebration through the streets of Havana (González Echevarría pp. 85–86). On 6 January, *diablitos*, identified as *ñáñigo iremes* (priests) of the Afro-Cuban Abakuá Secret Society, accompanied by an array of dancers, filled the plaza outside the Palacio de los Capitanes Generales, to request an *aguinaldo* or Christmas gratuity from the Spanish Captain-General—staging their ritual celebrations at the seat of colonial authority (Cuervo Hewitt pp. 29–30; González Echevarría p. 85; Mendez Rodenas pp. 219–220). Thus began the tradition of Black Carnival, a collective dance for freedom that emerged as a constant in Cuban history and culture, which "offered one of the most exotic attractions in colonial Havana," due to the diablitos' characteristic hooded costumes and their seemingly erratic movements and behavior (Cuervo Hewitt pp. 31–32). Although the term *diablito* reflects the mistaken attitudes of white society toward Afro-Cuban priests, their "'codified' body language of mimicry and gestures…came to be inscribed in the cultural imaginary and expression of Cuban creole society" (Cuervo Hewitt p. 34). Captured in Mialhe's classic 1848 print, the collective spirit embodied in the Día de Reyes performed acts of defiance against the hegemony of the sugar plantation; hence, the ritual sparked "a new beginning, a new cycle of life" that continued in post-abolition carnivals and well into the Republic, marking the cultural role of carnival "as a masquerade for acts of resistance" (Cuervo Hewitt pp. 33–35).

DEFECTS AND GENIUS

A later collection of costumbrista sketches, *Los cubanos pintados por sí mismos* (Cubans as They Saw Themselves), published in 1852, and "the first anthology of the genre in Spanish America," offered a detailed description of thirty-eight local types (Bueno p. xxii). Later in the century, at the moment when these picturesque types were threatened by the onslaught of modernity, part of this collection appeared as *Tipos y costumbres de la isla de Cuba* (1881), with a prologue by Antonio Bachiller y Morales. Bachiller y Morales recorded the rise of national customs during the "golden period" from 1830 to 1837 (corresponding to the emergence of Cuban literature in the Del Monte circle), only to signal its demise. In order to better convey the distinctiveness of Cuban culture, the criteria for inclusion was "defectos ó genialidades…*peculiares* del pais [sic]," ("defects or genius *characteristic of* the land") rather than traits derived from Europe. Likewise, the figures had to conform to both a local and a universal model, such as the ubiquitous *coqueta* or female flirt (Bachiller y Morales p. 8). The gallery of national types was, in turn, immortalized in the accompanying set of lithographs by Spanish painter Víctor Patricio de Landaluze (1828–1889) (Bachiller y Morales p. 8).

As if anticipating the Independence struggle, costumbrista sketches rounded out the country's historical image: "Los artículos de costumbres tienen que ser auxiliares de la historia" ("Local color sketches must come to the aid of history"), reflecting as well the true imprint of the nation: "cada cuadro es una copia de lo que sucede verdadero ó verosímil: se desciende hasta el tipo individual en el género histórico…" ("each sketch copies what actually happens in realistic or at least likely terms; so historical fiction imitates the entire social scale, all the way down to individual types") (Bachiller y Morales p. 9). Against the backdrop of Cuban history, then, these types served as emblems for an entire period; the calesero, for example, representing a privileged domestic slave in highly embellished dress (Triay pp. 108–109), just as the *quitrín* or *volante*, the two-wheeled carriage that he proudly drove through the streets of Havana, symbolized the urge of the Cuban people toward autonomy: "el carruaje primitivo de esta tierra…donde se busca el dulce descanso como compensacion de la fatiga y de las molestias que causa el sol ardoroso de nuestro clima" ("the primitive carriage used in this land…where we seek sweet respite to make up for the weariness and discomfort inflicted by our climate's burning sun") (Triay p. 106). Mythologized in Landaluze's prints, the calesero and other types collected in *Tipos y costumbres* testify to the gradual transformation of creole sensibility into a sense of national bonding or cohesion.

Many Cuban novelists drew on costumbrista themes in their works, including Cirilo Villaverde's *Cecilia Valdés* (1882), with its magnificent depiction of the *mulata's cuna* or city dance, and his earlier *Excursión a Vuelta Abajo* (1838; 1842), a memoir depicting his nostalgic return to his native Pinar del Río which featured the *guajiro* or country folk as tragicomic stock character. Costumbrista literature absorbed every aspect of life, spanning the movements of Afro-Cuban dance in the plantation, as in Anselmo Suárez y Romero's "Ingenios" (Sugar Mills) (in Bueno, pp. 309–313) and dramatizing the passage to death, as in José Victoriano Betancourt's "El velorio," published in *La Cartera Cubana* in 1839. Full of picturesque detail and humor, these sketches, along with the riveting images drawn by foreign observers, testify to the rich gamut of peoples and places that made colonial Cuba a thriving cultural space.

BIBLIOGRAPHY

Bachiller y Morales, Antonio, et al. *Tipos y costumbres de la isla de Cuba: Colección de artículos.* 1st series. Havana: Miguel de Villa, 1881.

Bachiller y Morales, Antonio, et al. *Paseo Pintoresco por la Isla de Cuba.* 1841–1842. Miami: Herencia Cultural Cubana y Ediciones Universal, 1999.

Betancourt, José Ramón. "Una feria de la Caridad en 189…. Cuento camagüeyano escrito en 1841." Prologue by Cirilo Villaverde. Vol. I. Barcelona: Imprenta de Luis Tasso Serra, 1885.

Betancourt, José Victoriano. "Velar un mondongo." *La Cartera Cubana* (December 1838): 363–368. In *Costumbristas cubanos del siglo XIX.* Edited by Salvador Bueno, 221–226. Caracas: Monte Avila, 1985.

Betancourt, José Victoriano. "El velorio." *La Cartera Cubana* (January 1839): 47–51.

Bueno, Salvador, editor. *Costumbristas cubanos del siglo XIX.* Caracas: Biblioteca Ayacucho, 1985.

Cueto, Emilio. "Los grabados del *Paseo pintoresco por la isla de Cuba.*" In *Paseo Pintoresco por la Isla de Cuba,* by Antonio Bachiller y Morales et al. 1841–1842. Miami: Herencia Cultural Cubana y Ediciones Universal, 1999.

Cuervo Hewitt, Julia. *Voices Out of Africa in Twentieth-Century Spanish Caribbean Literature.* Lewisburg, PA: Bucknell University Press, 2009.

González Echevarría, Roberto. "Reflections on *Espejo de Paciencia.*" *Cuban Studies* 16 (1986): 101–121.

González Echevarría, Roberto. *Cuban Fiestas.* New Haven, CT: Yale University Press, 2010.

Landaluze, Víctor Patricio de, and José Robles. *Los cubanos pintados por si mismos: Colección de tipos cubanos.* Vol. 1. Havana: Imprenta y Papelería de Barcina, 1852.

Los cubanos pintados por si mismos: Colección de tipos cubanos. Edited by Alberto Hernández Chiroldes. 1852. Miami: Editorial Cubana, 1992.

Luis, William. *Culture and Customs of Cuba.* Westport, CT: Greenwood Press, 2001.

Méndez Rodenas, Adriana. *Cuba en su imagen: Historia e identidad en la cultura cubana.* Madrid: Verbum, 2002.

Merlin, Condesa de. María de las Mercedes Santa Cruz y Montalvo. *Viaje a la Habana.* Edited by Adriana Méndez Rodenas. 1844. Doral, FL: StockCero, 2008.

Ortiz, Fernando. *La antigua fiesta afrocubana del "Día de Reyes."* 1925. Havana: Ministerio de Relaciones Exteriores, 1960.

Suárez y Romero, Anselmo. "Ingenios." In *Costumbristas cubanos del siglo XIX,* edited by Salvador Bueno, 309–314. Caracas: Biblioteca Ayacucho, 1985.

Triay, José E. "El calesero." In *Tipos y costumbres de la isla de Cuba: Colección de artículos,* by Antonio Bachiller y Morales, et al. 1st series. Havana: Miguel de Villa, 1881.

Villaverde, Cirilo. "Jesús María y José." In *Paseo Pintoresco por la Isla de Cuba,* by Antonio Bachiller y Morales et al. 1841–1842. Miami: Herencia Cultural Cubana y Ediciones Universal, 1999.

CUBAN THOUGHT AND CULTURAL IDENTITY: COSTUMBRES IN THE REPUBLICAN PERIOD

Carmen Berenguer Hernández

Everyday social customs and traditions in the decades after independence in 1902.

At the start of the twentieth century, Cuba shed its colonial status and moved toward establishing a republic that turned into a so-called democracy controlled by an English-speaking foreign power. Consequently, the formation and maintenance of Cuban customs were characterized by the duality of old traditions of Spanish origin and new, modern ones, coming mostly from the United States.

MODERNIZING THE OLD REFINEMENT

In a classic Cuban historical memoir, *Flor oculta de la poesía cubana* (Hidden Flower of Cuban Poetry), the poets and essayists Cintio Vitier and Fina García Marruz reconstruct what may be the example of greatest refinement in nineteenth-century Cuba: the culture of the folding fan. A selection of short poems written on fans reveals the perspective of a group of illustrious, upper-class Cuban-born whites of a tradition peculiar to the precise time and place, as well as a trace of a dualistic code (open and hidden, public and secret), that was part of the system of courtship during colonial society's final decades. In a parallel fashion, what was perhaps insinuated in one of those fans as it was opened was the complicity of coded language at the moment that the members of the upper class partook of another well-known custom of that period: the stroll, during which a young woman, for her own protection, was always accompanied by her mother or perhaps an aunt. With the decline of that mythic (and mythical) world of elegance, from which the masses—and black people in particular—were excluded, two major transformations of Cuban customs and habits occurred.

The first change occurred in opposition to persistent colonial culture, as both a departure from and a way to overcome it, and involved the formulation and intensification, throughout the period of the Republic, of public discourses on Cuban identity and nationalism discourses, cultural practices, and customs that attempted to project a coherent imaginary of the *Cubanidad* and its representative forms. The second, parallel transformation, later configured as discovery, assimilation, and confrontation, was that effect on Cuban customs of the great social, political, economic, and cultural influence of the United States during that period.

One of the basic requirements for the identity of the new Republic was a symbolic system of patriotic dates that definitively sealed its separation from Spain. National memorial days were created for anniversaries such as 19 May (José Martí's death), 20 May (the establishment of the Republic), 10 October (the start of the first war for independence from Spain), and 7 December (the death of Antonio Maceo). Ties to Spain were maintained in the celebration of 12 October (Columbus Day/La Raza, or Race Day), and cultural holidays such as St. Valentine's Day (14 February) and Mother's Day (the second Sunday in May) were observed. Religious holidays (Catholic saints' days) and dates honored by the political opposition (such as 1 May, Workers' Day) were celebrated by certain groups, but not by the whole country.

Among the most important elements in building Cubans' self-image were those related to their allegedly unique sociability, from informal gatherings (family get-togethers and unannounced visits by friends and acquaintances) to formal relationships at work or in political parties. This open and friendly attitude, typified by the use of the familiar *tu* form instead of the more formal *usted*, as well as slaps on the back, led President Ramón Grau San Martín to a surprising definition of *Cubanidad*: "Cubanidad is love."

In contrast to this idealized view of Cuban sociability, essayist Fernando Ortiz, in his well-known book *Entre Cubanos* (Among Cubans, 1905), issued a devastating criticism of the national cult of friendship, asserting that its most important feature was loyalty to one's *socios* (buddies) above and beyond other responsibilities. This criticism took aim at the connection between social customs and growing political cronyism. Even in the early 2000s, sociability, theoretically beyond class and race, is one of the basic myths of Cuban interpersonal dynamics and social psychology, and the *socio* (sometimes women, but generally men) is a cornerstone of daily life. Years later another essayist, Jorge Mañach, in a lecture titled *Indagación del choteo* (1928), presented what could be called the reverse of the cult of the socio, registering an equally devastating criticism of what he considered the most divisive national custom: *el choteo* (corrosive and irreverent humor), the most implacable taunting of any sort of constructive effort, on both the interpersonal and societal levels.

DEMOCRATIZATION, EXCLUSION

In the 1920s, the musical form known as *son*, native to eastern Cuba, arrived in Havana. The simultaneous birth of radio and the U.S. recording industry's first period of expansion gave the new musical genre a big boost. Listening to and dancing to the *son* became the most democratic and democratizing Cuban pastime; especially among the poor and working class, dancing blurred racial distinctions. The most important national rhythms during the period of the Republic, each with its own style of dancing, were the *son*, the rumba, the mambo, and the cha-cha. In the late 1950s, dancing—which Emilio Roig de Leuschenring defined as "Cubans' unbridled passion"—became

so popular that it spread to hundreds of dance halls around the country. In Havana alone there were more than a hundred, accessible to all social classes. A style of dancing called *casino* emerged during that decade, and soon after that *rueda de casino* (casino wheel), possibly the highest expression of Cuban popular dancing, was born. Rueda de casino is danced in groups with changing partners in a succession of complex steps and interwoven choreography.

By contrast it was also the custom to enjoy free time by attending associations and clubs organized by race and economic status in urban areas. White-only, upper-class societies included the Miramar Yacht Club, the Havana Yacht Club, the Vedado Tennis Club, and the Cienfuegos Yacht Club; a venue for middle-class or affluent blacks was Club Atenas. Another very important type of association was the regional society, whose members were descendents of immigrants from various parts of Spain; these included the Centro Gallego, Centro Asturiano, Centro Balear, and Centro Canario (for Cubans with ancestors from Galicia, Asturias, the Balearic Islands, and the Canary Islands, respectively). The establishment of clubs for mixed-race Cubans (mulattoes) was more complicated. Although in Havana the Malecón seawall was mythified as an example of the democratic use of public space where people of any background could enjoy a stroll, various cities in the country maintained the tradition of segregated public walking. For example, the center of the park or bandstand area where concerts were performed, were reserved for white families.

Bullfighting, a Spanish custom that was identified with colonial rule, was prohibited by the intervening North American government by military order number 187 on 10 October 1899. At the end of the nineteenth century, the North American sport of baseball expanded throughout the country until, by the opening decades of the twentieth century, it was considered the Cuban national sport. Although U.S. ballparks were segregated at that time, in Cuba they were open to all races equally, without privileges or divisions in physical space, such as seating. Even the teams were composed of black and white players, with no discrimination. Also, just as it had done with the *son*, Cuban radio played a major role in making baseball Cuba's national sport. Thus, what had been a sport that Cubans had used to distance themselves from their Spanish heritage in the nineteenth century became popular among all classes and strata of society. Like the *son*, baseball became an element of cultural unity.

The other occasions in which Cuban cultural unity is manifested in public space is on popular feast days, particularly at the carnivals. The most famous carnival celebrations are those held in Santiago de Cuba, Remedios in central Cuba (where the festivities are called *parrandas*), Bejucal (just outside Havana), and Havana itself. The two great cultural contributions of the Cuban Carnival, a celebration lasting several days, were floats and parading dance groups

Cuban comparsa, 1941. Dancers costumed as housemaids parade down the streets of Havana as part of a comparsa. © BETTMANN/ CORBIS

called *carrozas* and *comparsas*, born and developed in poor neighborhoods, some dating back to the late nineteenth century. Crowds of Cubans follow behind the comparsas, dancing in step with the parade, which is known as *arrollar* (*roll* through the streets). At the beginning of the twentieth century there was a public debate about comparsas, which many, from a clearly racist perspective, considered uncivilized. As a result, comparsas were banned from the Havana Carnival until 1937. From then on, despite the inclusion of a final parade of automobiles, which was clearly upper-class and directly connected to the surge in U.S. tourism, the Havana carnival was a moment of cultural splendor, racial intermingling, a stage for the exposition and maintenance of traditions, and bursts of popular creativity. Another popular custom was the election of a *Reina del Carnaval* (Queen of the carnival), which, until the close of the 1950s, took place in the Palacio de Convenciones y Deportes. In addition to those already mentioned, many other cities and towns across the country also celebrate their own carnivals and maintain the traditional mass processions called *romerías*, of Spanish origin.

CUSTOMS AND IDENTITY DURING THE REPUBLIC

The *guayabera* (a type of shirt whose style was redesigned in the 1930s by Lebanese-born tailor Said Selman) provided the solution to the need for symbolic elements that would be visually identified with being Cuban. During the administration of President Carlos Mendieta (1934–1935), the guayabera was declared the national attire, and by the late 1950s, it was accepted as typically Cuban. Furthermore, since the turn of the century, waves of modernization—along with women's entrance into the labor market

and their increased presence in the public sphere—modified fashions and signaled the end of ladies' full-length dresses, with hemlines rising to above the ankle. In the 1930s it became acceptable for women to have short hairstyles, specifically the pageboy, and in the 1950s knee-length skirts became the norm among young women.

Holidays calling for special foods included Christmas Eve, traditionally celebrated with walnuts, almonds, apples, apple cider, and a Spanish nougat called *turrón*, and New Year's Eve dinner, when families gathered for a typical meal of roast piglet, *congrí* (rice cooked with beans), a cooked vegetable, and salad, plus twelve grapes, one for each month of the year. Another New Year's Eve custom—inherited from very old magical thinking—was to throw a bucket of water out on the street at the stroke of midnight, so the water would take away evil. At quinceañeras (fifteenth birthday parties), cake—introduced into Cuba from the United States—became a central part of the celebration. Offering a cup of coffee to any visitor in the home was a mark of sociability.

The intensification of economic, political, cultural, and, generally, social ties with the United States led to changes in eating habits: puddings, pies, powdered soup mixes, Coca-Cola and Pepsi-Cola, cornflakes, and canned goods, among other foods, became normal parts of the Cuban diet. Even Cubans' way of speaking Spanish—beyond the many English words that were incorporated into everyday speech—changed on a syntactic level. The change in foods used led writer José Lezama Lima to note in a 1949 article, "Havana residents have lost taste and pleasure in their food. No Sunday dinners, plans, chefs who only make lunch, canned foods, all this has contributed to an obligatory disregard for good food. Havanans have lost their taste for food."

Among the most traditional boys' games were playing marbles (in all their variants), spinning tops, flying kites both simple and elaborate, and riding a *chivichana* (a wooden board attached to three or four skate wheels) or the more complex *carriola* (a rudimentary, motorless wooden cart). Among girls, the most common games were jacks, hopscotch, and jump rope. Boys and girls together played hide and seek, hot and cold, capture the flag, a team tag game called *burrito 21*, and blind man's bluff, and they competed in sack races and stilt races. Without a doubt, the most popular game played by adults was dominoes, which the whole family enjoyed, plus card and dice games. By the late 1950s canasta and bingo were very popular among the middle and upper classes.

Customs related to courtship centered on two major themes: engagements and virginity. Generally, engagements lasted several years, during which the fiancé was expected to prove the seriousness of his intentions. Virginity was defined as the purity with which the woman was expected to enter into marriage, thereby certifying her family's morality. While these rules pertained to women who had never been married, it is important to remember that one of Cuban women's great victories, after considerable struggle, was the right to divorce, legalized in 1918. Obviously, this meant that, at least for divorced women, the rules of courtship became more flexible and more pragmatic. In a similar fashion, weddings and baptisms in the Catholic Church continued to play an important role within the family and society. The decision to baptize one's children, however, often had more to do with economic motives (association with a wealthy godparent) than with any religious consideration.

BIBLIOGRAPHY

Fariñas Borrego, Maikel. *Sociabilidad y cultura del ocio: Las élites habaneras y sus clubes de recreo (1902–1930).* Havana: Fundación Fernando Ortiz, 2009.

García Marruz, Fina, and Cintio Vitier. *Flor oculta de poesía cubana (siglos XVIII y XIX).* Havana: Arte y Literatura, 1978.

González Pagés, Julio César. *En busca de un espacio: Historia de mujeres en Cuba.* Havana: Ciencias Sociales, 2003.

Iglesias, Marial. *Las metáforas del cambio en la vida cotidiana: Cuba 1898–1902.* Havana: Ediciones Unión, 2003.

Lezama Lima, José. *Tratados en La Habana.* Santa Clara, Cuba: Universidad Central de las Villas, Departamento de Relaciones Culturales, 1958.

Mañach, Jorge. *Ensayos.* Havana: Letras Cubanas, 1999.

Montejo Arrechea, Carmen V. *Las sociedades negras en Cuba, 1878–1960.* Havana: Ciencias Sociales / Centro de Investigación de la cultura cubana Juan Marinello, 2004.

Ortiz, Fernando. *Entre Cubanos: Psicología tropical.* Havana: Ciencias Sociales, 1987.

"El rey de las guayaberas cubanas." *Juventud Rebelde*, August 20, 2008. Available from www.juventudrebelde.cu.

Riaño San Marful, Pablo. *Gallos y toros en Cuba.* Havana: Fundación Fernando Ortiz, 2002.

Roig de Leuchsenring, Emilio. "El baile, desenfrenada pasión del criollo. In *Revista Opus Habana*. Online ed. September 22, 2009. Originally published in *Carteles* 31, no. 17 (April 23, 1950): 82–83. Available from http://www.opushabana.cu.

Vera, Ana, Mona Rosendhal, and Aisnara Perera. "Vida doméstica en Cuba durante los años 50." *Espacio, Tiempo y Forma*, Series V: H. Contemporánea 11 (1998): 297–325. Available from http://e-spacio.uned.es.

Vizcaíno, María Argelia. "La ciudad más bailadora del mundo." *Estampas de Cuba.* Available from http://www.mariaargeliavizcaino.com.

Vizcaíno, María Argelia. "Historia de un mismo baile: Salsa o Casino." *Estampas de Cuba.* Available from http://www.mariaargeliavizcaino.com.

CUBAN THOUGHT AND CULTURAL IDENTITY: COSTUMBRES IN THE REVOLUTIONARY PERIOD

Carmen Berenguer Hernández

The evolution of everyday social customs and traditions since 1959.

There is no doubt that, after independence from Spain, the 1959 Revolution is the most significant political event in Cuban history. Given that it was a socialist revolution, it likely was a process marked by change in customs and habits; however, the Revolution's stages had different ramifications for the understanding of this change. In other words, there has not been a continuum or a single group of innovations since 1959, but instead Cubans have experienced waves of transformation. One possible analytical approach—in addition to tracing a historical continuity from the time of the Cuban Republic or even back to the colonial period—is to describe the customs that emerged during different stages of the revolutionary period and how they have evolved into twenty-first-century customs and practices.

THE BATTLE FOR CULTURE

Customs are part of a country's traditional and popular culture, and as such they are also part of "the set of creations emanating from a cultural community founded in a tradition, expressed by a group or individuals, which recognizes and responds to the community's expectations about its cultural and social identity; [and] mores and values that are transmitted orally, through imitation or in other ways" (Mejuto and Guanche). According to the article devoted to the term in the second edition of the *International Encyclopedia of the Social Sciences*, "tradition" includes a sense of social and cultural patterns—ways of doing things—that occurred continuously in former times (Darity p. 420). As part of a people's traditional and popular culture, traditions, in addition to usage, practices, and behavioral structures that endure through time, may disappear, change and, most importantly, be invented (Hobsbawm pp. 13–14).

Starting with the initial measures taken by the revolutionary government in 1959, concepts and areas of the old system of Cuban customs began to erode rapidly. The political decisions aimed at ending racism (for instance, opening up beaches and recreation centers to black citizens), prostitution (banning brothels, sponsoring projects for former prostitutes to pursue an education and be reincorporated into normal social life), rural poverty (creation of a scholarship program allowing tens of thousands of young people from rural areas to study in Havana), among others—in addition to eroding or interrupting the country's former socioeconomic framework—serve as a measure of how radically traditions were being modified.

Thus, in the dialectic between both temporalities (pre-revolutionary period and the Revolution as such), numerous customs, justly or unjustly, were categorized as typically and intrinsically bourgeois and, therefore, incompatible with the newly initiated process. One example is the diminished prestige of men's suits, previously viewed as a sign of distinction. To fill that symbolic vacuum, toward the end of the 1970s the guayabera shirt came into fashion (in men's and women's versions) as an elegant form of attire, although it turned out to be just a passing fancy that virtually disappeared in the following decade. Perhaps the greatest transformation in how Cubans dressed was the universal adoption of blue jeans by both sexes and all ages and social sectors, for work as well as for casual and elegant occasions. This is particularly striking, considering that before 1959 jeans were worn only for manual labor, and even in the 1970s they were considered a garment whose use was an example of *diversionismo ideológico* (ideological deviation).

THE "NEW MAN"

The Revolution's Marxist ideology strove for a cultural transformation in which the basic component was the "New Man" formulated by Ernesto "Che" Guevara. From this perspective, and in clear conflict with Catholic

Procession of San Lazaro. Two people help a devotee walking on his knees approach the San Lazaro Catholic Church in El Rincón, site of an annual procession that blends Catholicism with aspects of Afro-Caribbean Santería. © VISIONS OF AMERICA, LLC/ ALAMY

ideology, practices such as the celebration of Christmas Eve and Christmas Day (which had been national customs) were officially banned in 1969. Although the ban was lifted in 1998, as a gesture of goodwill during the visit of Pope John Paul II to Cuba, those holidays did not regain their previous strength. This is partially due to Cuba's long economic crisis, which began in the early 1990s, and also to the current high price of foods traditionally served on those dates. Although the same circumstances apply to New Year's Eve dinner, that celebration gained considerable strength in the first decade of the twenty-first century. In contrast, religious pilgrimages such as the those dedicated to Cuba's patron saint, the Virgen de la Caridad del Cobre (Our Lady of Charity of El Cobre, 7 September, and ending at her shrine in Santiago de Cuba), to the Virgen de Regla (Our Lady of Regla, 8 September), and San Lázaro (St. Lazarus, 17 December, and ending at the San Lázaro shrine south of Havana) remain extremely popular among Cubans.

Beyond religion, no area of Cuban tradition was more affected by the Revolution than political practices. Various types of mobilizations, marches, and especially volunteer work were promoted as the best examples of what the "new man" would do freely, rather than out of obligation. Furthermore, many of the dates honored under the previous system of celebration and memory—Christmas Eve, Christmas Day, Columbus Day, Foundation of the Republic Day, to name a few—were no longer celebrated or even mentioned officially, while the acts of the main figures of the Revolution were celebrated. During the last fifty years of Cuba's socialist process, dates such as 19 May, 10 October, and 7 December were honored, while the semantic content of 1 January has changed from New Year's Day to the day the Revolution triumphed. The first of May is celebrated as International Workers' Day; 26 July as the anniversary of the attack on the Moncada Barracks; 8 October as the day Che Guevara died; and 28 October as the day Camilo Cienfuegos died. As a result of its especially close relationship with the Soviet Union, Cuba incorporated into its official calendar the celebration of historical dates such as 22 March (Lenin's birthday); 9 May (victory against fascism in World War II); and 14 November (start of the Bolshevik Revolution). Other dates, such as 20 May (the founding of the Cuban Republic) and 6 August (the dropping of the atomic bomb on Hiroshima) have negative significance. Billboards throughout the countryside that once advertised capitalist products or promoted politicians were subsequently covered with political and ideological messages.

THE NEW LANGUAGE

The semantic devaluing of words associated with the old order led to the replacement of traditional linguistic forms and the emergence of new ones. Words such as *señor* (Mr.) and *señora* (Mrs.) were no longer used in everyday or formal speech and were replaced by the ideology of fraternity signified by *compañero* and *compañera* (comrade). The word *millonario* (millionaire) came to represent a sugarcane cutter who harvested more than a million *arrobas* (equal to 25 pounds) of cane in a harvest year. "Señor" and "señora" did not come back into use until the 1990s, when the economic crisis caused Cuba to turn toward its tourism industry as the country's main source of income. The use of those words as a form of respect was one of the first signs of emerging social differentiation. At the same time, the country experienced a process in which "marginal language has been gaining acceptance," which the literary scholar Nilda Blanco attributes to the nature and depth of the transformations undertaken by the Revolution.

> Language usage furthered this process by permitting, much more easily, the incorporation of words that up until then had been considered marginal in daily speech, while other words were rejected because they were considered "bourgeois," and social strata previously denied the right to education were given a place in society.

This is a controversial issue because—in contrast to bourgeois etiquette and good manners—there are few corresponding rules in socialist society. Indeed, the very idea of good manners is essentially class-oriented.

TRANSFORMATIONS WITHIN TRANSFORMATIONS

The most surprising and unexpected change was in the *quinceañera*, the party thrown for a girl's fifteenth birthday. Before 1959, this occasion was not marked as elaborately as it is in the early 2000s, especially among the poor. It was the Revolution that made it possible for all Cubans to afford the material goods necessary to celebrate *los quince*, as it is called, converting a formerly upper-class observance into a popular one. But in the twenty-first century under the rules of the new economy (under which the island has lived since possession of U.S. dollars became legal in 1995), and without the government's special subsidy for these celebrations, the traditional quinceañera is representative of the new social and economic gap. This indulgence of escapist fantasies is out of reach for teenagers and their families facing hardships and shortages in real life. Something similar could be said of the formal marriage celebration. In the Palacios de Matrimonios (marriage halls) built all over the country, betrothed couples for many years would receive vouchers to purchase clothing for the occasion, food for the party, and a hotel reservation for the honeymoon. However, as testament to the speed with which traditions change, the Cuban press revealed that the rate of marriages in Cuba diminished significantly (68,941 in 1980 compared to 54,969 in 2009) as more people—especially young people—choose to live together without getting married (Pérez Sáez et al.).

Although many traditional games survived the passage of time, lifestyle changes throughout the country reduced their popularity among children. Factors such as the amount of time children spend watching television and expansion of video and computer games conspired against tradition. Even so, marbles, tops, jacks, racing games, hopscotch, and street games of baseball and soccer remained still popular, and adults still enjoyed playing dominoes. The greatest change was among teenagers and young adults, given that computer games were increasingly prevalent, as more and more households gained access to computers.

The Revolution encouraged women to enter the labor market and participate in political, social, and other aspects of the country's transformation, which led to a long crisis in the traditional structure of male-female relationships in which females are submissive, and accompanying values, particularly religious ones. Practices such as long courtships, marriage proposals, church weddings and maintaining one's virginity until the wedding night have diminished to the point of virtually disappearing. In the early 2000s most Cubans get married in civil ceremonies, the age of sexual initiation has dropped to adolescence, and virginity has lost its moral significance.

MUSIC

Although listening to music and dancing remain an important part of cultural life, music produced in Cuba in the early 2000s is only part of the cultural archive that Cubans use. After the birth, internationalization, and penetration of Cuban dance music into the world market and its ultimate transformation into salsa, the concept of the national in music became problematic. From a strictly nationalist perspective, the process meant that the correlation between identity and favorite dance music had blurred. Even so, it is important to mention that the *casino* and *rueda de casino* dance styles danced to musical variants based on the *son*, reached their splendor during the Revolutionary period. This is due, in large measure, to the quinceañeras, at which choreographed dances were staged, and to the Cuban television program *Para bailar* (To Dance), which premiered in 1978. In the early 2000s Cubans preferred to dance to reggaetón, salsa, and so-called timba, a popular hybrid dance music that combines Cuban and African American genres.

Despite the government-owned radio stations' protectionist policies (with quotas for playing mostly Cuban music, in a descending order from international music sung in Spanish and finally to music with lyrics in English and other languages), strong ties with the United States in the past and geographical proximity explain the ready acceptance of U.S. popular dance music on the island. Especially during the 1970s, the act of listening and dancing to music became one more theater of ideological struggle, but this truth conceals a more important and profound culture war: the modernization of culture in its many forms. In this sense, the popularity of rock music, mostly from Europe and the United States, constituted a defeat of hard-line Cuban

CUBAN FOOD IN THE DIASPORA

The Cuban diaspora scattered around the globe retains, remembers, and transforms many elements of Cuban culture: religion, language, courtship rituals, and music, but most especially food.

Shannon Lee Dawdy, in an essay titled "La Comida Mambisa: Food, Farming, and Cuban Identity, 1839–1999," analyzes the formation and coherence over time of what she calls "Cuban national cuisine" and finds a surprising continuity between a cookbook from 1858 and one from 1997: "We can compare nineteenth-century recipes with those in a 1997 cookbook by the well-known Cuban cook, Nitza Villapol. Nearly 70 percent of the recipes in her modern Cuban cookbook correspond to those in the 1858 Cabrisas text." (Dawdy 2002, p. 59). This means that by mid-nineteenth century there is a national cuisine, properly Cuban, even before the country had become independent of Spain. For Dawdy, there are two types of Cuban national cuisine which she defines as follows: ". . .[the] cuisine of *Cuba Grande* dependent on imports, industrial foods, and elaborate technique, as well as a cuisine of *Cuba Pequena*, defined by native produce and influenced by African preparation methods." (Ibid.) It is the latter cuisine that defines Cubans and in the diaspora serves as marker of Cuban-ness.

Traditional Cuban cuisine, eating habits, and the actual foodstuffs themselves continue to exist, but primarily outside of the country in which they originated. As Frédéric Duhart notes in his essay *"Comedo ergo sum. Reflexiones sobre la identidad cultural alimentaria"* (*Comedo ergo sum* [I Eat, Therefore I Am]: Reflections on the Cultural Identity of Eating), we can suggest that the traditions he calls the "cultural identity of eating" "are an identity that materializes in products, cooking techniques, dishes, and consumption modes which are considered 'their own' by those who are part of the culture, and as 'typical' by other people" (Duhart 2002).

Lisa Maya Knauer, in her essay "Eating in Cuban," though speaking about "ethnic restaurants" captures the symbolic value of food that is applicable to the domestic realm of diaspora households: "Ethnic restaurants, I argue, wrap themselves in the language of both heritage and the exotic. They are gathering places, boundary markers and memory palaces for diasporic communities. For 'others,' they invite travel without leaving home" (Laó-Montes y Dávila 2001).

A surprising example can be found in "Yellow Cassavas, Purple Bananas," an essay by Euridice Charon Cardona that "explores the relevance of food in the preservation and re-creation of Cuban identity amongst a group of migrants who have been living in Australia for nearly 30 years." Her research confirms that food is one of the most important economic issues for people who struggle to preserve their identity and customs, and that Australia has a "substantial ethnic food market" which "has facilitated Cuban migrants' maintenance of their previous eating habits, and through this their sense of Cuban identity" (Charon Cardona 2003, p. 149). The relatively small number of Cubans in Australia means that the principal external markers of identity are the Cuban flag, which Charon found displayed at all houses she visited, and the staging of culinary traditions (through invitations to drink a cup of black coffee and be a guest at a Cuban meal).

Even while the group preserves a tradition, it reformulates it and integrates it into the traditions of the new country, within which it lives interactively. Thus, in the United States, the barbecue is turned into a rationale for the traditional Sunday visits to family and friends. At the same time, the cultural models of second and third generation diaspora Cubans transform and incorporate traditions that would have been unthinkable in their parents' or grandparents' generation. This, for instance, explains the phenomenon

nationalism as well as an example of cultural modernization. Conversely, government approval of the New Song Movement, which received and creatively processed those same influences, was an enormous victory.

INFLUENCES OF THE SOVIET BLOC COUNTRIES

Another unexpected aspect of Cuban cultural life resulted from relations with the socialist countries, especially the now-defunct Soviet Union. On one hand, huge cultural differences meant that the Soviet Union and the rest of the Eastern European socialist countries did not greatly influence Cuban customs. On the other

hand, in addition to the symbolic dates added to the official calendar of celebrations, certain customs and objects from those countries remained commonplace in Cuban households. These include *matryoshka* (wooden nesting) dolls and decorated wooden spoons, nostalgia for and collection of Soviet children's cartoons (which Cubans call *muñequitos rusos* or Russian cartoons) shown on Cuban television for many years, abundant tea consumption, the naming of children (thousands of Cubans have Russian names), and even the existence of a small Russian Orthodox religious congregation.

In regard to its customs, the Cuban Revolution demanded that practices and beliefs that crystallized

of the "new Cuban cuisine," which seeks to fuse authentic dishes from the Cuban kitchen with notions of "healthy" eating that are more consistent with vegetarian or low-fat, low-calorie diets (and which have not taken root on the island).

TRADITION AND PERSONAL MEMORY

In spite of all changes and evolution, on special occasions Cuban Americans still prefer to cook and eat traditional Cuban food. Accordingly, when they receive distinguished visitors or even just relatives from the island, it is important to start off the dialogue with an homage to identity. The Cuban novelist Carlos Eire provides a beautiful explanation of how words, food, memory, family, community, loss, the new land, and the resilience and strength of identity all blend together:

> Some words are learned in that very special, very emotionally charged environment of childhood and they carry with them in one's memory whatever the emotional baggage may be. *Frijoles* means more than beans. It means a steaming hot plate of rice and beans and also a nice breaded steak served to you by your mom, back when you were surrounded by all your family. It also means a certain routine, a certain dining room, certain episodes. In my case it means the day that my grandmother's pressure cooker exploded and her entire kitchen was covered in *frijoles negros*. It also means Americans trying to pronounce the word, and always sounding very scatological: "free-hole-ass." It is a word that carries all the comforts of home and is also a reminder of everything you lost. Someday maybe I could compile a dictionary of my

emotional words: *timbiriche, lija, aguacate, embolia, almohada, escaparate, cucaracha, enano, muela, mula, malanga*"

> (Gracia et al. 2008, p. 133)

The emotional resonance of Eire's words reminds us that we are not only what we eat, but that when Cubans eat, no matter where they are, they are re-creating (and digesting) Cuban culture and history.

BIBLIOGRAPHY

Behnke, Alison, and Victor Manuel Valens. *Cooking the Cuban Way: Culturally Authentic Foods, Including Low-Fat and Vegetarian Recipes*. Minneapolis, MN: Lerner Publications, 2004.

Charon Cardona, Euridice. "Yellow Cassavas, Purple Bananas." *Humanities Research* 10:3 (2003), 149–157. Online at http://epress.anu.edu.au/hrj/2003_01/pdf/16_Cardona.pdf.

Dawdy, Shannon Lee. "La comida mambisa: Food, Farming, and Cuban Identity, 1839–1999." *New West Indian Guide/Nieuwe West-Indische Gids* 76, nos. 1 and 2 (2002): 47–80. Online at: http://www.kitlv-journals.nl/index.php/nwig/article/view/3462/4223

Duhart, Frédéric. "*Comedo ergo sum*. Reflexiones sobre la identidad cultural alimentaria." *Gazeta de Antropología* 18 (2002). Online at http://www.ugr.es/ pwlac/G18_15Frederic_Duhart.html

Gracia, Jorge J. E., Lynette M. F. Bosch, and Isabel Alvarez Borland, eds. *Identity, Memory, and Diaspora: Voices of Cuban-American Artists, Writers, and Philosophers*. Albany: State University of New York Press, 2008.

Knauer, Lisa Maya. "Eating in Cuban." In *Mambo Montage: The Latinization of New York*, edited by Agustín Laó-Montes and Arlene Dávila, 425–447. New York: Columbia University Press, 2001.

Carmen Berenguer Hernández

during the nineteenth century around the time of the Cuban Republic be analyzed. From this perspective, the most important was the introduction of new values through modernization. At the same time, U.S. determination to dominate relations with Cuba linked cultural practices to nationalism in a visceral way; after the Revolution triumphed and relations between the two governments became hostile (as part of the Cold War confrontation), customs quickly became a central part of the dispute.

One view is that the Cuban Revolution modernized traditions. This perspective explains the forces of tradition it opposed, the context and the manner in which it worked to impose new customs, and the transformations that occurred after the start of the Special Period. While the triumph of the Revolution marked a critical moment for old customs and relations with the socialist world were the basic condition for establishing new ones, after the disappearance of the socialist camp in the early 1990s, the sudden decline in the Cuban economy shook everyday life to its core. Some of the affected aspects included socializing and gatherings (in areas that experienced more than twelve hours a day without electricity), available foods (a logical consequence of scant imports and minimal domestic production, leading to recipes such as ground banana peel, eggs fried in water, and grapefruit peel steak that were a surreal version of traditional Cuban cuisine), and manners of dress (the widespread use of bicycles as a means of transportation inspired the use of shorts and T-shirts). Once the greatest shortages had passed, the Cuban diet settled back into rice (white, yellow, and mixed with beans), beans (black, red, and white), meat (preferably pork or chicken), tubers (potatoes, yams, manioc, and taro root), vegetables (carrots, cabbage, lettuce, onions, garlic), and fruits (bananas and plantains, oranges, mangoes, mamey). The only nontraditional dishes that have come to occupy an important place in the popular Cuban diet are spaghetti and pizza.

NEW ECONOMY, NEW CUSTOMS

In the mid-1990s, as part of the search for ways out of the crisis, the government opened the country to joint ventures, legalized the possession of foreign currencies, increased tourism, and in general opened the country up to the world. Given that this process coincided with the period in which new information technologies were expanding globally, the impact was total: These radical changes over just half a century made Cuba a veritable laboratory for the study of how traditions depend on and are affected by government policies and economic vicissitudes, while also revealing what practices remain intact or only fluctuate despite the number of variations.

Twenty-first-century Cuba is different from any previous time since the triumph of the Revolution, not only because the fierce cultural battles (such as those related to the transmission and enjoyment of popular music from the United States and the style of wearing long hair) were lost or lost virulence, but because the cultural opening to the world and the increase in the number of computers and other electronic devices to copy music or films serve as the basis, once again, for new transformations. Under the laws of the new economy, importation of Christmas trees and other cheap Christmas decorations comes together with the contribution of private agricultural producers' efforts to facilitate the return of old Christmas Eve and Christmas Day traditions, although with less extravagance. The words *compañero* and *compañera* are used less often, as *señor* and *señora* regain strength, along with all the implied social differentiation. Among men the word *asere* (an Abakuá term meaning *brother* or *friend*) is highly popular as a rhetorical gesture or to indicate the position of the speakers as a marker of proximity. In fashion, following the disappearance of the guayabera shirt, there was an identity crisis in which the use of name-brand clothing came to define elegance, and some well-known companies have opened stores in Havana. Curiously, the government declared the guayabera as the appropriate attire for official activities just as Cuban Americans in Miami did in 1994. Oddly, the guayabera's decline, combined with men's suits going out of style as a sign of distinction, plus the widespread use of blue jeans, T-shirts and shorts, could have resulted in the "development of a national dress code," but this has been defeated by "the U.S. clothing industry and the whole advertising mechanism promoting its products" (Fernández).

Piercing and tattooing, previously considered practices typical only of criminals, have come into fashion, while the press debates graffiti culture and the increase in so-called metrosexuality among young Cuban men. Carnivals and other traditional popular festivals, in the form of carnival, parranda, romeria, and others, have retained their vitality in the rest of the country, but in Havana these celebrations have been paralyzed by a long identity crisis. Right after the triumph of the Revolution, in addition to the *comparsas*, traditional carnival dance groups, floats and clubs belonging to unions and social organizations paraded the carnival streets, but a decline began in the 1980s and continued into the early 2000s. The old practice of choosing a *Reina de Carnaval* (Queen of the Carnival) was transformed into the selection of *la Estrella y sus Luceros* (the Star and Her Bright Stars) where aspiring young girls came from the unions, as well as student and social organizations. However, as an example of a rupture with the past, when *la Estrella y sus Luceros* marched for the last time in 1974 an element of popular expectation disappeared with it, contributing to the loss of the capital's carnival identity. Although they have not regained their old splendor, religious processions were officially permitted in the early 2000s.

Where egalitarian austerity practices were once favored, consumption based on economic difference has gained strength, and a value system organized around the concept of distinction is taking shape. In such a context, trends change quickly. But above it all, Cubans still share a passion for baseball, parties, arriving unannounced at a friend's house, talking and laughing loudly, enjoying a good joke or a double entendre, dominoes (and the game's verbal codes), music and dance, roast pork and a friendly cup of coffee, conversing without maintaining physical distance, and complementing words with an expressive body language that includes touching.

BIBLIOGRAPHY

Alfaro Torres, Rolando. *Juegos cubanos*. Havana: April 2003.

"Aumentan hombres que usan atributos femeninos." *Juventud Rebelde*. 11 November 2007. Available from http://www.juventudrebelde.cu.

Balbuena Gutiérrez, Bárbara. *El casino y la salsa en Cuba*. Havana: Letras Cubanas, 2005.

Barnet, Miguel, and Jesús Guanche. "El carnaval de la Habana: Pasado, presente y futuro." *Catauro* 14 (July–December 2006).

Blanco, Nilda. "Algunas características del español en Cuba antes y después de 1959." *LEA: Lengua española en Aotearoa/Australia* 3 (2004). Available from http://redgeomatica.rediris.es.

Bourdieu, Pierre. *Distinction: A Social Critique of the Judgment of Taste*. Translated by Richard Nice. Cambridge, MA: Harvard University Press, 1984.

Darity, William A., Jr., ed. *International Encyclopedia of the Social Sciences*. 2nd ed. Vol. 8. Farmington Hills, MI: Macmillan Reference USA, 2008.

Fernández, Diana. "Una manera de vestir a la cubana." *Opus Habana* 34 (2008): 4–15. Available from http://www.opushabana.cu.

Hernández, Rafael, ed. "Huellas culturales rusas y de Europa del Este en Cuba." (Panel discussion held 28 May 2009, at the Centro Cultural Cinematográfico, ICAIC.) In *Últimos Jueves: Los debates de Temas*. Vol. 4. Havana: Ediciones ICAIC, 2010. Available from http://www.temas.cult.cu.

Hobsbawm, Eric. "Introduction: Inventing Traditions." In *The Invention of Tradition*, edited by Eric Hobsbawm and Terence Ranger. Cambridge, U.K.: Cambridge University Press, 1983.

Linares, Cecilia, Yisel Rivero, and Pedro E. Moras. *Participación y consumo cultural en Cuba*. Havana: Instituto Cubano de Investigación Cultural Juan Marinello, 2008.

López Cano, Rubén. "Del barrio a la academia: Introducción al dossier sobre timba cubana." *Trans: Revista Transcultural de Música* 9 (2005). Available from http://www.sibetrans.com.

Mateo Palmer, Margarita. "La poética del cuerpo: Tatuaje y escritura." *Catauro* 9 (January–June 2004): 17–38. Available from http://www.ffo.cult.cu/.

Mejuto, Margarita, and Jesús Guanche. *La cultura popular tradicional: Conceptos y términos básicos*. E-book. Havana: Consejo Nacional de Casas de Cultura, 2008.

Miller, Nicola. "A Revolutionary Modernity: The Cultural Policy of the Cuban Revolution." *Journal of Latin American Studies* 40, no. 4 (2008): 675–696.

Orejuela Martínez, Adriana. *El son no se fue de Cuba: Claves para una historia 1959–1973*. Havana: Letras Cubanas, 2006.

Peñate Leiva, Ana Isabel, and Dalgis López Santos. "La Habana: Jóvenes, barrios e identidad. Apuntes desde la investigación social." *Ultima Década* 31 (December 2009): 31–54. Available from http://redalyc.uaemex.mx.

Pérez Rivero, Pedro Teófilo. "El Carnaval de La Habana y la Revolución." 23 November 2009. Available from http://www.archivocubano.org/habana/carnaval.html

Pérez Sáez, Dora, Mayte María Jiménez, Margarita Barrios, and Ana María Domínguez Cruz. "Se acabó la cola en el Palacio de los Matrimonios." *Juventud Rebelde*. Online ed. 6 November 2010. Available from http://www.juventudrebelde.cu.

Ubieta Gómez, Enrique. "Apología del compañero: Antonio Rodríguez Salvador, Tomado de La Calle Del Medio 17." *La Isla Desconocida*, October 11, 2009. Available online at http://la-isla-desconocida.blogspot.com.

Vázquez Muñoz, Luis Raúl. "La palabra exacta." *Juventud Rebelde*, April 2, 2005. Available from http://www.cubahora.cu.

Venegas, Cristina. *Digital Dilemmas: The State, the Individual, and Digital Media in Cuba*. New Brunswick, NJ: Rutgers University Press, 2010.

CUBAN THOUGHT AND CULTURAL IDENTITY: INTERNET BLOGGING

Ileana Oroza

Prominent Cuban bloggers and the challenges they face.

The story of blogging in Cuba is one of contradictions. The nation's rates of Internet and mobile phone penetration are among the lowest in Latin America, but one of its bloggers was named by *Time* in 2008 as one the most influential people in the world. As in the United States, the majority of blogs in Cuba discuss many topics besides politics: culture, sports, relationships, sexuality, spirituality, and personal and social identity. Absent from most Cuban blogs are discussions of fashion and product design and evaluation—almost anything related to consumer goods. In this, the contrast with American bloggers is remarkable: In 2009, 70 percent of bloggers in the United States focused on brands (Dean p. 34).

Cuban bloggers and micro-bloggers conduct spirited online political debates, but few inside Cuba can follow them because private Web access is expensive and restricted by law (a government-issued password is required) and because some of the most critical blogs are blocked internally, placed out of reach for Cuba's readers and the writers themselves.

Some blogs focus on gay life (*CENESEX*); others—Lalita Curbelo's *Negracubana*, for example—on black life in Cuba (*Negracubana* also deals with HIV-AIDS). The Catholic Church sponsors various electronic publications or blogs, among them *Espacio Laical*, a monthly publication that covers not only church issues but current events, economics, ethics, and culture. A 2011 issue included a dossier titled "Where Is the Cuban Model Headed?" Other church blogs are *Palabranueva.net*, by the Archdiocese of Havana; *Bioetica.net*, published by the Centro Bioetica Juan Pablo III; and *Vitral*, by the Archdiocese of Pinar del Río.

Most of Cuba's major print publications, including *Granma*, *Juventud Rebelde*, *Bohemia*, and *El Caimán Barbudo*, have extensive Web presences, as does the Unión de Periodistas de Cuba (UPEC, Union of Cuban Journalists), which offers links to all of their pages from its Web site. Content is not limited to Cuban subjects. For example, *El Caiman Barbudo*, a literary journal, is likely to feature in its book review section reviews of literature from Paraguay and a novel by the Haitian novelist Michele Voltaire Marcelin. Many publications also have active identities on the microblogging site Twitter.

The exact number of bloggers active in Cuba is difficult to determine. The UPEC site links to more than 150 blogs kept by its members, though some of the links lead to sites that have not been updated

■ *See also*

Economy: Special Period

Governance and Contestation: The Cuban Revolution

The Works of Tania Bruguera

for months, which is typical of the blogosphere in general. The UPEC bloggers write on a variety of topics from history and culture to current affairs. When their entries are political they tend to follow the government line, but criticism, though rare, is not wholly absent from these pages. For example, Miguel Díaz Nápoles, writing on the official Web site for the journalists of *Las Tunas*, complained that the sites run by the nation's news outlets simply cut and paste information from their print editions and do not use the Web to its best advantage. He also decried the lack of citizen access:

> In the communication processes of the Cuban Web, such as radio, television and the printed media, there is a high level of institutional and technological mediation, when it should be completely the opposite, to allow the public to have full access to the information sources, keeping in mind that the [traditional] professional profiles are being lost and the receiver [of information] is also the emitter.
>
> *Díaz Nápoles*

Although Web access is tightly controlled in Cuba, not all active Web sites are officially sanctioned, and there may be as many as one hundred unauthorized bloggers in the island (Wilkinson). The Web site *Voces Cubanas*, which identifies itself as "an open space for Cuban residents who want to have a blog," includes links to thirty members, all independent writers whose blogs, when they focus on politics, are critical of the Cuban government and outspoken in their rejection of the restrictions under which they live and write.

The best known among the *Voces Cubanas* bloggers is Yoani Sánchez (b. 1975), who was selected for the *Time* list of influential people in 2008 and whose blog, *Generación Y*, was translated into nineteen languages and in 2010 reportedly received more than a million hits a month (Wilkinson). Despite the worldwide recognition, few people inside Cuba read Sanchez's blog—it was blocked, for the most part—and not all reader responses were positive. These claims and counterclaims are not unusual given the heated debates inside and outside of Cuba about current events and human rights.

Other eloquent writers in *Voces Cubanas* in 2011 included Claudia Cadelo (b. 1983), author of the blog *Octavo Cerco*, who posted a little flag on the door of her Havana apartment calling for "Internet for Everyone" (Wilkinson); Laritza Diversent (b. 1980), a lawyer who discussed legal issues in her blog, *Jurisconsulto de Cuba*; and the photographer and writer Orlando Luis Pardo (b. 1971), whose blog *Boring Home Utopics* was a kind of evolving art performance on the blogosphere. Pardo ran a second, more journalistic blog, *Lunes de Post-Revolución*, and in August 2010 he launched the digital magazine *Voces*, with contributions from writers in and outside Cuba. In an interview with Juan Tamayo of *El Nuevo Herald*, Pardo was quoted as saying that copies of *Voces* had been distributed in Cuba via CDs, flash drives, and the "intranet," a domestic network more accessible than the Internet to more Cubans (Tamayo).

Blogger Yoani Sánchez at her home in Havana, 22 December 2009. Yoani Sánchez, one of Cuba's best-known bloggers, was designated by *Time* magazine as one of the most-influential people of 2008. Her blog, *Generación Y,* was named by Time-CNN as one of the world's twenty-five best blogs of 2009. ARIEL ARIAS/LATINCONTENT/ GETTY IMAGES

Independent bloggers who do not have government approval to use the Internet must find alternative means to access the Web. Most often, they use the computers that hotels make available to their guests, which must be paid for with convertible pesos; sometimes they dictate their blog entries via telephone to friends with Internet access.

In 2010 Sánchez, Cadelo, and Pardo appeared frequently on Twitter, which was made possible by a 2008 change in Cuban law that gave Cubans access to mobile phones and, therefore, to short message service (SMS) technology. Their participation was one-sided, though, because although they could send tweets via SMS, they could not read the Twitter stream or the (sometimes unfriendly) replies that their tweets elicited. Yet the one-way nature of the conversation did not seem to deter these writers. Cadelo, in particular, often put herself at the service of other writers, tweeting links to new postings by fellow *Voces Cubanas* bloggers. Like Sánchez and Pardo, she frequently commented on island events or reported news mostly related to the dissident community—including, on occasion, news of arrests or disappearances. A 2010 video posted on YouTube and announced via Twitter by Sánchez showed a large group of citizens in the eastern town of Banes, accompanied by police, protesting in front of the family home of a noted dissident.

Opposition bloggers and twitterers encountered daily obstacles in their work, but they carried on with energy, compensating for the lack of Internet access with resourceful use of their mobile phones. Sánchez summed up the situation with characteristic humor in an 8 August 2010 Twitter post: "If in #cuba we invented beef *picadillo* without beef and how to bathe without soap, we are now trying the Web without Internet connection."

BIBLIOGRAPHY

Dean, Jodi. *Blog Theory*. Malden, MA: Polity Press, 2010.

Díaz Nápoles, Miguel. "Los paradigmas de la comunicación para Internet en la prensa digital cubana (III)." *Eco Tunero*. Available from http://www.ecotunero.cu/index.php?option=com_content&task=blogcategory&id=28&Itemid=66.

"Latin American Internet Usage Statistics" (2010). *Internet World Stats*. Available from http://www.internetworldstats.com/stats10.htm#spanish–.

Lauría, Carlos, and María Salazar Ferro. "Special Report: Chronicling Cuba, Bloggers Offer Fresh Hope." *Committee to Protect Journalists* (10 September 2009). Available from http://www.cpj.org/reports/2009/09/cuban-bloggers-offer-fresh-hope.php.

Pardo, Orlando Luis. *Lunes de Post-Revolución*. Web site available from http://www.orlandoluispardolazo.blogspot.com.

Tamayo, Juan O. "Cuban Blogger Starts Digital Magazine." *Miami Herald* (20 August 2010). Available from http://www.miamiherald.com/2010/08/20/1784224/cuban-blogger-starts-digital-magazine.html.

Unión de Periodistas de Cuba. Web site available from http://www.cubaperiodistas.cu/.

Voces 1 (August 2010). Available from http://www.scribd.com/doc/35770089/voces1.

Wilkinson, Daniel. "The New Challenge to Repressive Cuba." *New York Review of Books* (19 August 2010). Available from http://www.nybooks.com/articles/archives/2010/aug/19/new-challenge-repressive-cuba/.

CUBAN THOUGHT AND CULTURAL IDENTITY: THE INTERNET EXPERIENCE IN CUBA

Alan West-Durán

■ *See also*

Governance and Contestation: The Cuban Revolution

Radio: Cuban Radio in South Florida

Science and Technology in Cuba

The challenges of using the Internet in Cuba.

Any attempt to understand Internet use and policy in Cuba from a U.S.-bound perspective can be misleading. For example, in the United States Internet usage is measured by how many users are connected, implying that the objective is for all Americans to have a personal computer with Internet access in their home. For Cuba, like many Third World countries, the goal of a computer in every home is too costly and, therefore, unrealistic. Instead, the island emphasizes social use of the Internet, and priority is given to hospitals, scientific and academic researchers, industry, and cultural institutions.

Another common misconception is the assumption that unleashing the full potential of the Internet in Cuba will automatically lead to democratization, possibly even the downfall of the Communist government. This "cyber-utopianism" is premised on a superficial knowledge of Cuban history and an inordinate optimism in technology driving social change. That the Internet has changed Cuba is beyond question, but any beliefs about the cause and effect of information technology on the island must take into account the island's history.

Access to the Internet in Cuba is by no means easy. For example, members of the Unión de Escritores y Artistas de Cuba (UNEAC; Union of Cuban Writers and Artists) pay roughly 10 to 15 CUC (Cuban convertible pesos) a month—a princely sum for most Cubans—for an account that allows thirty hours of access per month. This rate amounts to one hour a day, and sometimes this allotment is shared with family members—the time constraints are almost unimaginable to U.S. users of the Internet. Cybercafés, post offices, and public libraries throughout the nation offer the use of computers with Internet access charged in local currency; although they are more affordable, there are usually lines of people waiting to use them. Cubans compose their emails before they go online in order to save precious (and costly) time. Bandwidth is limited (Internet connections are still via telephone modems, not high-speed broadband), and access often is not available at certain times of the day or even for days at a time. Even in best of times the service is slow, and sending a document or image bigger than a megabyte is next to impossible. A fiber-optic cable from Venezuela that was anticipated to dramatically improve service and accessibility was scheduled to be operational in February 2011, but it was later delayed to the fall of 2011.

Cuba has made a major commitment to bringing the island into the information age, despite major technical and economic obstacles. In 2002 the Universidad de las Ciencias Informáticas (UCI; University of Information Sciences) opened with an enrollment of two thousand students and just a few buildings. By 2010 it had an advanced campus, ten thousand students, and a five-year undergraduate program. The UCI encourages its young *informáticos* to write programs and software that Cuba can use, evading costly purchases from abroad. It works closely with the Joven Club de Computación y Electrónica (JCCE; Youth Club of Computing and Electronics), a national organization that provides services, classes, and support for people interested in learning and using computer skills. The JCCE also publishes a bimonhtly electronic magazine, *Tino*, which has news about computers and the cyberworld as well as articles on software and hardware, interviews, tips, and reviews of blogs. The academic scholar Cristina Venegas described the UCI thus: "Part educational institution, part software factory, UCI not only trains students, but also focuses on authoring code for the open software economy. The expected reach of the products is national and regional in scope" (Venegas pp. 3–4).

According to the Internet World Stats, which uses figures gathered by the United Nations' International Communications Union, Cuba had 1,605,000 Internet users in June 2010, with a penetration of 14 percent. The penetration of mobile phones amounts to 6 percent of the population, according to Lawrence Baker at the telecommunications research Web site BuddeComm. A Cuba study from 2007 states that 5.2 percent of Cubans use a computer at home and almost 90 percent at work or their place of study (Acosta p. 1) Because of the social use of computers, it is difficult to assess true levels of Internet access, but compared to the United States and the European Union, Cuba's rate is low; compared to other Third World nations, Cuba's rate is about average. The Cuban government on many occasions has argued that the restrictions it places on Internet access are a result of the U.S. embargo, which limits its access to the (satellite) technology necessary to develop efficient island-wide Web coverage.

As in the United States, Cubans use Twitter and Facebook to post photos of family members and stay in touch and share information with friends and family. This connection is particularly important for those who have family abroad because telephone calls are expensive.

As of 2011, the U.S. AID program funded independent journalists on the island and, presumably, some bloggers as well. The U.S. Department of Defense has argued that the Internet can be used to further U.S. government objectives, and Secretary of State Hillary Clinton has made major speeches on Internet use and freedom (January 2010 and February 2011). These actions have made the Cuban government nervous about matters of information sovereignty and interference in Cuba's internal affairs. Nonetheless, Cuba continues to promote a computer literate population, despite the numerous technical constraints. This promotion might be more successful if cyber-instruments could be made economically viable for individuals and the government. (For example, Skype service was terminated in Cuba in November 2009—and remained unavailable as of early 2011—not because of government censorship, but because it could not generate income.) Even with the new Venezuelan fiberoptic cable, due to be in service, Cuba will have to juggle the demands and ever-shifting new realities created by cyber-innovation as information technology becomes integral to Cuban society.

BIBLIOGRAPHY

Acosta, Dalia. "Cuba, Emerging Community of Bloggers." Inter Press Service (IPS). October 6, 2008. Available from http://ipsnews.net/news.asp?idnews=44139.

Baker, Lawrence. "Cuba—Telecoms, Mobile and Broadband." BuddeComm. (February 2011). Available from http://www.budde.com.au/Research/Cuba-Telecoms-Mobile-and-Broadband.html.

Clinton, Hillary Rodham. "Remarks on Internet Freedom." U.S. Department of State. January 21, 2010. Available from http://www.state.gov/secretary/rm/2010/01/135519.htm.

Clinton, Hillary Rodham. "Internet Rights and Wrongs: Choices & Challenges in a Networked World." U.S. Department of State. February 15, 2011. Available from http://www.state.gov/secretary/rm/2011/02/156619.htm.

Dean, Jodi. *Blog Theory*. Malden, MA: Polity Press, 2010.

International World Stats: Usage and Population Statistics. June 2010. Available from http://www.internetworldstats.com/car/cu.htm

Valdés, Nelson P. "Cuba: Broadband and Other Such Matters." *Machetera*. November 18, 2009. Available from http://machetera.wordpress.com/2009/11/18/cuba-broadband-and-other-such-matters/.

Venegas, Cristina. *Digital Dilemmas: The State, the Individual and Digital Media in Cuba*. New Brunswick, NJ: Rutgers University Press, 2010.

Wilkinson, Daniel. "The New Challenge to Repressive Cuba." *The New York Review of Books* (19 August 2010). Available from http://www.nybooks.com/articles/archives/2010/aug/19/new-challenge-repressive-cuba/.

CUBAN THOUGHT AND CULTURAL IDENTITY: POPULISM, NATIONALISM, AND CUBANÍA

Jorge Duany

The post-eighteenth-century emergence of the idea of a distinctive Cuban culture.

One of the recurring themes in Cuban thought has been the definition of the island's cultural identity, developed out of a troubled colonial and slave past. Several generations of Cuban intellectuals have sought to interpret their national culture from different historical and ideological perspectives. Expressions of Cuban patriotism became stronger during the early nineteenth century, both in Cuba and its diaspora in the United States, as a growing sense of *cubanía* (Cubanness), articulated by the island's elite, eroded Cubans' attachment to Spain. Initially, many writers limited their concept of the nation to the Cuban-born descendants of Spanish immigrants (the white *criollos* or creoles). Eventually they extended their concept of the nation to blacks and mulattoes, as well as the working classes. During the first half of the twentieth century, essayists often pondered the failure of the Cuban republic to achieve national sovereignty, social justice, and racial equality. Cuba's dependence on the United States was also a constant concern for the island's intellectual elite.

THE LATE COLONIAL PERIOD, 1792–1898

According to the philosopher and educator Medardo Vitier (1886–1960), the origins of Cuba's creole culture lie in the late eighteenth century, when the first "enlightened" colonial institutions were established in Havana. Among these institutions were the San Carlos Seminary (1773), the *Papel Periódico de la Havana* (1790, the first Cuban newspaper), and the Real Sociedad Patriótica de La Habana (1793), later renamed Sociedad Económica de Amigos del País. Cuban thought was increasingly imbued with the philosophical and political ideals of the Enlightenment. During the early nineteenth century, the rifts between Cubans and Spaniards sharpened and a Cuban nationality began to take shape.

An incipient attachment to Cuba's landscape, people, and culture can be traced back to this period, particularly among white, upper-class, Catholic men. Certain key words, such as *patria* (fatherland) and *nación*, circulated more frequently in public discourse. At first, *fatherland* referred to a territory or province within the Spanish empire and did not imply a national consciousness. Cuba was split economically and socially between the western and eastern regions, particularly between Havana and the rest

of the country, and it would thus have been difficult to think of the entire island as a nation. The leading Cuban intellectuals of the first half of the nineteenth century, most of whom were liberal reformers, advocated autonomy under Spanish rule.

To tighten their grip on the island, Spanish colonial authorities censored, imprisoned, and expelled dissidents from Cuba. Consequently, many of the key intellectual figures produced their most important work in exile. Beginning in the 1820s, diasporic experiences often shaped discussions about Cuban identity. Cubanía was largely conceived outside the island, especially among émigrés in the United States.

By the late nineteenth century, romantic ideas about the love and defense of the fatherland had become widespread and justified armed insurrection against Spain. The prolonged wars of independence (1868–1898) widened the gulf between Cubans and Spaniards. According to nationalist philosophers, journalists, and literati, the Cuban people had acquired a unique spirit or soul, a code of moral virtues whose preservation required establishing a sovereign state. For many writers, the development of cubanía also demanded the abolition of slavery, as well as a multiracial coalition of Cubans.

Liberal Reformist Views The wealthy sugar planter and lawyer Francisco Arango y Parreño (1765–1837) was one of the leading spokesmen of Havana's expanding bourgeoisie. In 1792, he authored a foundational political and economic text, *Discurso sobre la agricultura en la Habana y medios de fomentarla* (Discourse about Agriculture in Havana and Ways to Promote It). Written a year after the slave

■ *See also*

Cecilia Valdés (Cirilo Villaverde)

Governance and Contestation: Colonial Period

José Martí: Political Essays

Sab (Gertrudis Gómez de Avellaneda)

Francisco Arango y Parreño (1765–1837). The wealthy sugar planter and lawyer Francisco Arango y Parreño became a leading spokesman for Havana's expanding bourgeoisie. COURTESY OF THE CUBAN HERITAGE COLLECTION, UNIVERSITY OF MIAMI LIBRARIES, CORAL GABLES, FLORIDA

revolt in neighboring Saint Domingue, the *Discurso* proposed numerous incentives for sugar manufacturing in Cuba, including modernizing agricultural technology, teaching scientific disciplines, free trade, European immigration, and importing black slaves. Paradoxically, the *Discurso* also expressed the fear of slave insurrection, which became one of the main preoccupations of nineteenth-century Cuban writers. In 1816, Arango supported the gradual abolition of slavery and its replacement by wage labor. He also favored the so-called whitening of Cuba's population through intermarriage between blacks and whites.

Arango asserted the dominant ideology of members of Havana's creole elite, most of whom remained loyal to the Spanish crown during his time. In 1808, he declared: "We are Spaniards, and we do not belong to the corrupt classes out of whom other nations formed many of their mercantile factories—because that is to what they have reduced their settlements in the Americas—, but a healthy part of the most noble Hesperia [Spain]" (Arango y Parreño vol. 2, p. 18). For Arango, Spain remained *la Madre Patria* (the Mother Country), while Cuba was *la patria amada* (the beloved fatherland). In 1821, he wrote: "I love with the greatest tenderness this land where I was born, and I am always very willing to sacrifice for its sake all that I have and am worth" (Arango y Parreño vol. 2, p. 313).

One of the principal figures of the Enlightenment in Cuba was the Catholic priest José Agustín Caballero (1762–1835). A professor of philosophy and theology, Caballero promoted the reform of scholastic thought to advance colonial science and culture. In 1811, he elaborated the first project for an autonomous government in Cuba. Caballero began his "Exposición a las Cortes españolas" (Exposition to the Spanish Courts) by proclaiming the need for "the salvation of the fatherland," by which he meant Spain, from the Napoleonic invasion of 1808 (p. 214). At the same time, he considered Cuba an overseas territory of Spain. Caballero's model of political decentralization upheld the privileges of the slaveholding elite. It stipulated that only white property-owners ("pure-blooded Spaniards") could vote for Cuba's delegates to the Spanish parliament (p. 232).

The French-Cuban aristocrat María de las Mercedes Santa Cruz y Montalvo, Condesa de Merlin (1789–1852), authored several memoirs, including the three-volume *Viaje a la Habana* (Journey to Havana, 1844). In her travelogue, the countess of Merlin recounted her return to her native city and described its social, economic, and political conditions. She assumed an ambivalent position by defending Spanish colonialism (as well as slavery), while rejecting its abuses on the island. Because of the countess's political ideology, her memoirs have occupied a marginal position in the island's literary canon.

The journalist, philosopher, and attorney José Antonio Saco y López (1797–1879) equally deplored colonial despotism, slavery, and Cuba's annexation to the United States. He preferred a liberal reform that recognized the island's autonomy within the Spanish state and modernized agriculture, communications, health care, and education. In 1850, Saco forcefully defended a Cuban "nationality" as "a people who inhabit the same soil, and have the same origin, the same language, and the same traditional customs" (vol. 3, p. 355). However, Saco did not favor an independent Cuba because of the risk of racial strife. In his view, only whites belonged to the Cuban nation; the growth of the so-called colored people threatened the stability of creole society. Accordingly, he endorsed white immigration "to give the white population a moral and numerical preponderance over the excessive colored one" (vol. 3, p. 177).

José de la Luz y Caballero (1800–1862) was one of the most significant Cuban philosophers and educators of his time. Without advocating the island's independence, he believed in "Love toward all men, but first of all love toward my compatriots" (vol. 1, p. 69). The Spanish colonial government implicated him in an aborted slave uprising, the so-called Conspiración de La Escalera (Ladder Conspiracy) of 1844, and placed him under house arrest for two years. In 1847, Luz y Caballero wrote ironically: "On the question of blacks, the least black of things is black." He also noted, "How slavery contaminates slaves and masters!" (vol. 1, p. 74) and favored its gradual abolition. Luz y Caballero's ethics were a model for a later generation of nationalist writers, notably José Martí, who dubbed him "the silent founder" of the Cuban nation.

The Antislavery Literary Movement The affluent landowner and lawyer Domingo del Monte (1804–1853) is considered the first professional literary critic on the island. He is best remembered for nurturing a Cuban national literature through his *tertulia* (literary salon) in Matanzas and Havana (1834–1843). Among the budding writers he influenced were José María Heredia (1803–1839), Cirilo Villaverde (1812–1894), and Anselmo Suárez y Romero (1818–1878). Del Monte advised novelists to "invent situations and characters that present in more relief the spirit of the times, of the people, and of the characters one wishes to depict" (p. 162). Writing under the pseudonym of Toribio Sánchez de Almodóvar, he published *Romances cubanos* (Cuban Ballads, 1829–1833), exalting the island's rural landscape and *guajiros*, the peasants who descended primarily from Spanish immigrants, as the most authentic representatives of cubanía. Del Monte also encouraged Cuban writers to denounce slavery, which he considered antithetical to the advancement of Cuban culture.

The poet, novelist, and journalist Cirilo Villaverde was one of the most prolific members of del Monte's inner circle. After participating in an anti-Spanish conspiracy, he was imprisoned, but managed to escape to New York City in 1849. Together with other émigrés, such as Gaspar Cisneros Betancourt ("El Lugareño," 1803–1866), Villaverde initially favored Cuba's annexation to the United States. He authored the most emblematic Cuban novel of the nineteenth century, *Cecilia Valdés, o, la Loma del Ángel* (Cecilia Valdés or the Angel's Hill, 1839), which he rewrote while living abroad (1882). This work portrays Cuban society as profoundly divided by race and class, documenting the harsh living conditions of the colored population, both slave and free. Like other foundational novels in Latin America, *Cecilia Valdés* centers on an impossible romance, in this case between an illegitimate mulatto woman and her aristocratic white half-brother.

The émigré poet, playwright, and essayist Gertrudis Gómez de Avellaneda (1814–1873) wrote the first abolitionist novel in Spanish, *Sab* (1841). Its plot revolves around a mulatto slave who falls in love with his master's white daughter, a scandalous topic at the time. Because of its unconventional approach toward interracial romance and criticism of the institution of marriage, the novel was banned in Cuba and was not published there until 1914. Gómez de Avellaneda's pioneering work suggests that unity between whites and blacks is necessary for the consolidation of cubanía. Her text can also been read as an early feminist condemnation of men's subordination of women, which Gómez de Avellaneda compared to that of slavery.

The Emergence of Separatist Thought The Catholic priest and philosopher Félix Varela y Morales (1788–1853) advocated Cuba's independence from 1824. Consequently, Varela was exiled in the United States and was never allowed to return to the island. In his philosophical meditations, Varela extolled patriotism as the most important civic virtue, defined as "the love every man has for the country where he was born, and the interest he takes in its prosperity" (vol. 1, p. 280). Varela was one of the earliest Cuban thinkers to assign a modern nationalist meaning to the word *patria*, as the political incarnation of the attachment to one's country of birth. In 1825, he argued that Cuba should be "an Island in politics as well as it is in nature" and, therefore, have its own sovereign state (vol. 2, p. 200).

The widely acclaimed "Apostle of Cuba," the poet, journalist, and politician José Martí (1853–1895) spent most of his life outside his native land, mainly in New York City. Ideologically, Martí contributed to Cuban nationalism by reaching out to the common people, "los pobres de la tierra" (the poor of the earth). To unite opposition against Spanish rule, he built a multiclass and multiracial movement among Cubans in the United States and on the island. In contrast to colonial tyranny, Martí envisioned a social and racial democracy in Cuba "with all and for the good of all," to cite the motto of the revolutionary newspaper *Patria*. In his often-quoted article *Mi raza* (My Race, 1893), he argued that "a Cuban is more than white, more than mulatto, more than black" (vol. 2, p. 299). Throughout his writings, Martí highlighted the moral virtues of "the Cuban soul," including diligence, generosity, honesty, and dignity (vol. 5, p. 15). For Martí, the affirmation of a Cuban cultural identity was part of the wider struggle against the Spanish colonial regime, as well as the emerging U.S. imperialism.

After his death, Martí became the main icon of cubanía for several generations of Cubans, both on the island and abroad. During the 1920s, he emerged as a national hero for Cubans of various social classes, ethnic groups, and political persuasions. Conservatives, liberals, and radicals claimed Martí as the founding father of the Cuban nation, a selfless patriot and quixotic leader, committed to his country's political and cultural independence. Martí himself was well aware of the foundational character of his words and deeds, through which he carefully crafted an epic narrative and moral utopia of the Cuban nation. His own life ended in the supreme sacrifice for the fatherland, martyrdom. He died in a battle against Spanish forces in 1895.

Antonio Maceo y Grajales (1845–1896) is better known for serving as a general of the revolutionary army than for his ideas about cultural identity. As a freemason, Maceo embraced the principles of the French Revolution—liberty, equality, and fraternity—and sought to apply them to Cuba. In an 1881 letter, he wrote: "I have put before the interest of race, whichever that may be, the interest of Humanity, which is in sum the good that I desire for my beloved fatherland" (p. 160). As a Cuban of African descent, Maceo represented the large number of blacks and mulattoes who participated in the wars against Spain. After his death in combat, Maceo became a symbol of a racially heterogeneous cubanía.

Throughout the nineteenth century, Cuban thought evolved from patriotism to nationalism. During this period, Cuban intellectuals tackled two main problems in defining cubanía: Spanish colonialism and black slavery. By the end of the century, many highly influential thinkers embraced a separatist ideology: Cuba was their fatherland as well as their nation, and this nation should be independent. At the same time, they recognized the need to incorporate African descendants into a broader narrative of the nation. This nationalist and racially inclusive discourse was entrenched in Cuba by 1898, although it was by no means homogeneous.

THE REPUBLICAN PERIOD, 1902–1958

Cuba's independence in 1902 began inauspiciously for many intellectuals who had fought for national sovereignty. The Platt Amendment to the Cuban constitution allowed the United States to intervene in Cuban affairs to protect its economic and political interests. According to both Cuban and U.S. critics, this legal measure turned the island into a "pseudorepublic" or a "neocolony" of the United States. Until its repeal in

1934, the Platt Amendment provoked strong nationalist resentment in Cuba.

Anti-Americanism was one of the main strands in Cuban thought, just as daily life on the island was swiftly Americanized. One of Cuba's foremost literary critics, Cintio Vitier, maintained: "We are victims to the most subtly corrupting [U.S.] influence in the Western world" (Vitier 1970, p. 584). Yet, as Louis Pérez points out, "Many of the values that subsequently gave meaning to Cuban lives, collectively and individually, were of North American origin" (p. 7). During the first three decades of the twentieth century, massive immigration, especially from Spain and other Caribbean islands, also raised difficult questions about the cultural and racial makeup of the nascent Cuban nation.

The Discourse of Republican Decadence and Regeneration The philosopher, educator, and politician Enrique José Varona (1849–1933) was a key transition figure between the colonial and republican periods in Cuban history. He quickly became disenchanted with the republican regime, which in his mind perpetuated colonial practices, such as oligarchic rule and corruption. According to Varona, "Republican Cuba seems like the twin sister of colonial Cuba" (p. 57).

Varona incarnated the "public intellectual" through constant interventions in politics and journalism, while retaining an academic position at the University of Havana. Although he was familiar with the main philosophical currents of his time, he preferred sociological positivism, based on the empirical observation of social life. In a 1905 lecture at the University of Havana, titled "El imperialismo a la luz de la sociología" (Imperialism in the Light of Sociology), Varona urged Cuba's economic, political, and cultural modernization as a "line of resistance" against foreign powers, including the United States. In several essays, he dissected the Cuban national character, underlining such collective vices as indiscipline, mistrust, and arrogance.

In his widely read *Azúcar y población en las Antillas* (1927; *Sugar and Society in the Caribbean*, 1964), the prominent historian, educator, and journalist Ramiro Guerra y Sánchez (1880–1970) recovered the economic project of the creole reformers of the nineteenth century. Like many of his predecessors, he believed that the white rural middle class was the most authentic expression of cubanía. In his view, "Cuba existed as a nation from the time the native-born colonists, who far outnumbered peninsular Spaniards, divided and took possession of the island's territory, tilled, and cultivated it, collectively developing their own economic life, distinct from Spain" (p. 88).

An ideological heir of liberal intellectuals such as Saco, Guerra depicted the *latifundio*, or large landed estate, as the antinomy of a nation of independent property owners. Urging the breakup of rural properties into small farms, Guerra criticized the consolidation of the plantation economy during the early twentieth century. He also decried the importation of Caribbean cane cutters, especially from Haiti and Jamaica, as threats to Cuba's national identity.

Despite his leftist leanings as a young man, the multifaceted writer, university professor, and attorney Jorge Mañach (1896–1961) became increasingly conservative. Mañach expressed the disillusion of many intellectuals with the moral decadence of the early Cuban republic. In his classic essay *Indagación del choteo* (loosely translated, Inquiry into Humor, 1928), Mañach lamented that Cubans mocked all established forms of authority, leading to improvisation, disrespect, and anarchy. In *Pasado vigente* (The Living Past, 1939), he claimed that "the image of full independence had been swindled" (Mañach 1939, p. 19) in Cuba, especially because of the Platt Amendment. In *Historia y estilo* (History and Style, 1944), Mañach declared that the island was "an attempt at a State in a fatherland without a nation" (Mañach 1944, p. 64). He concluded that Cuba was not yet a modern nation in the sense of the free exercise of citizenship rights and duties. Like other contemporary intellectuals, Mañach proposed the moral regeneration of the Cuban people through education.

Afro-Cubanism A lawyer by training and an anthropologist by vocation, the young Fernando Ortiz

(1881–1969) indicted the supposed criminal inclinations of African descendants in his first scholarly publication, *Hampa afro-cubana: Los negros brujos* (The Afro-Cuban Underworld: The Black Sorcerers, 1906). By the 1930s, he had adopted a more benevolent view of Cuban blacks and had become the leading authority on African contributions to the island's national identity. Ortiz's monumental research on African-derived religion, music, dance, and folklore considerably expanded the scope of the Cuban nation. As Ortiz once quipped, "Without blacks Cuba would not be Cuba" (1945–1946, p. 218).

Together with Lydia Cabrera (1900–1991) and Rómulo Lachateñeré (1909–1951), Ortiz spearheaded the search for African roots in Cuban culture. Between the 1920s and 1940s, this wide-ranging movement (known as *afrocubanismo* or *negrismo*) brought together important writers such as Nicolás Guillén (1902–1989), Alejo Carpentier (1904–1980), and Emilio Ballagas (1908–1954); painters such as Eduardo Abela (1889–1965) and Wilfredo Lam (1902–1982); and musicians such as Gonzalo Roig (1890–1970), Ernesto Lecuona (1895–1963), and Alejandro García Caturla (1906–1940).

In his best-known work, *Contrapunteo cubano del tabaco y el azúcar* (Cuban Counterpoint of Tobacco and Sugar, 1940), Ortiz coined the term *transculturation* to describe the fusion of cultural practices of different origins. In a now classic metaphor, he also characterized Cuba as an *ajiaco*, a simmering stew that blended Amerindian, European, African, and Asian ingredients to produce a new cultural concoction.

Furthermore, he distinguished cubanía, the conscious desire to be Cuban, from *cubanidad*, the feeling of belonging to Cuban culture.

Ortiz's ideas about cultural identity have proved extraordinarily productive. Contemporary writers continue to use Ortiz's concepts, especially transculturation. As the famous anthropologist Bronislaw Malinowski acknowledged in his introduction to *Contrapunteo cubano*, the neologism *transculturation* captured the process of cultural exchange better than conventional expressions such as *acculturation* and *diffusion*. Many anthropologists, literary critics, musicologists, and other scholars have appropriated the term to analyze cubanía and other national identities. Ortiz's legacy has extended beyond the island's borders, especially to other Latin American and Caribbean countries.

A creative writer and self-taught ethnographer, Lydia Cabrera (1900–1991) devoted much of her life to documenting the oral traditions of Cubans of African descent. Although she was one of the few white women who belonged to the island's intellectual elite, Cabrera tried to incorporate the standpoint of marginalized blacks into the nationalist canon. In the 1930s, she began gathering and retelling Afro-Cuban folktales, culminating in her landmark study *El monte* (The Wilderness, 1954). In 1958, she was the first non-initiate to publish materials on the origins and myths of the Abakuá secret society or *ñáñigos*.

Cabrera's literary and anthropological work disarticulated the discourse of Cuban culture as fundamentally Hispanic and Catholic. Instead, she argued that Afro-Cubans preserved much of their ancestors'

Carnival preparations, 2009. A member of El Alacrán, one of Cuba's oldest comparsas, reviews the group's street lamps in Havana's El Canal del Cerro neighborhood. The lamps represent Yoruba orishas and must be baptized before the carnival celebrations begin. ADALBERTO ROQUE/AFP/GETTY IMAGES/NEWSCOM

spirituality, characterized by the worship of nature and personified in numerous supernatural beings (the *orishas* or Yoruba deities). For Cabrera, *el monte* (with its multiple connotations of mountain, bushes, forest, and jungle) encapsulated the magical, ritual, and medicinal aspects of Afro-Cuban folklore. A strong African influence persisted in Cuban popular religiosity.

A member of the Cuban Communist Party, the mulatto pharmacist Rómulo Lachatañeré was one of the pioneers of Afro-Cuban ethnography. His book *¡¡Oh, mío Yemayá!!* (1938) was the first systematic attempt to collect the legends of Santería, or Regla de Ocha, as the popular cult of the *orishas* is known in Cuba. In three long articles for the journal *Estudios afrocubanos* (1939–1946), Lachatañeré reconceptualized the religious traditions of African origin on the island, especially those of Yoruba or *lucumí* ancestry. After discarding the biased terms *witchcraft* and *black magic*, he approached Afro-Cuban religions as complex systems of beliefs and customs. His work contributed to recovering Afro-Cuban culture from its practitioners' perspective.

Black Intellectuals' Contributions A growing number of Afro-Cuban professionals probed the limits of racial inclusion in Cuban society from various perspectives. Juan Gualberto Gómez (1854–1933) was a mulatto general of the Cuban war of independence, journalist, and elected official during the republican period. He was a fervent supporter of racial equality and the education of black people. Gómez believed strongly in organizing blacks for collective self-help and defending their civil rights.

Martín Morúa Delgado (1856–1910) was a prominent mulatto politician and journalist. In 1910, as president of the Cuban senate, he proposed an amendment to the Cuban electoral code banning all political organizations based on race or color. Morúa claimed that such an amendment, which was quickly approved by the senate, would promote racial integration and national identity on the island. The Morúa law, as it came to be known, was applied in the violent repression of the Partido Independiente de Color (Independent Colored Party), the first black political party in Cuba, in 1912.

Between 1928 and 1931, the architect and journalist Gustavo Urrutia (1881–1958) published a series of weekly columns in the Havana newspaper *Diario de la Marina*, titled "Ideales de una raza" (Ideals of a Race). In his journalistic writings and radio lectures, Urrutia stimulated black self-esteem through the knowledge of "a racial African heritage, which really deserves as much consideration as the Spanish one" (Urrutia p. 213). At the same time, he did not promote Afro-Cuban religious practices such as Santería or *ñañiguismo*.

The lawyer Juan René Betancourt (1918–1976) denounced Cuban racism from the 1940s. He authored three books and numerous journalistic articles about the so-called black question in Cuba. In 1959, he compiled several of his polemical lectures and essays in *El negro, ciudadano del futuro* (The Black People, Citizens of the Future). Like Urrutia, he sought to lift black self-esteem by highlighting the Afro-Cuban contribution to national identity. Unlike more moderate Afro-Cubans, Betancourt advocated blacks' separate mobilization in Cuba, including the development of black businesses through industrial and trade cooperatives.

The *Orígenes* Group One of the leading intellectuals in republican Cuba was the poet and novelist José Lezama Lima (1910–1976). He founded one of the most prestigious literary magazines in Latin America, *Orígenes* (1944–1956), which published work by such renowned poets as Eliseo Diego (1920–1994), Cintio Vitier (1921–2009), and Fina García Marruz (b. 1923). The magazine also showcased the work of major Cuban painters, including Amelia Peláez (1896–1968), René Portocarrero (1912–1985), and Mariano Rodríguez (1912–1990). The members of the *Orígenes* group distanced themselves from Cuban politics, focusing on aesthetic experimentation and cultivating a transcendental worldview largely informed by Catholicism.

In *La expresión americana* (The American Expression, 1957), Lezama reflected on the origins of Spanish American culture, broadly understood, and by implication Cuban culture. He highlighted the expressive possibilities of the American baroque style, developed toward the end of the eighteenth century. By baroque, Lezama meant the creative appropriation of the Spanish Golden Age by American-born writers and artists of Hispanic, indigenous, and African backgrounds.

In 1958, the poet, essayist, and novelist Cintio Vitier published *Lo cubano en la poesía* (Cubanness in Poetry). This work interpreted Cuba's cultural identity through the major poetic texts written on the island and in the diaspora from colonial times to the 1950s. Vitier detected a peculiar way of being Cuban in the lyrical treatment of the island's nature, vernacular character, and creole spirit. He summarized the literary "essences" of Cubanness in ten recurring themes, including the innocence of the natural scenery, the mythical image of the island, and the remembrance of childhood or nature as a lost paradise. According to Vitier, Cubanness was better represented as "marine and aerial, rather than from the land" (1970, p. 580).

Marxist Approaches The lawyer, writer, and politician Juan Marinello (1898–1977) was the foremost communist intellectual in republican Cuba. Throughout his work, Marinello underscored the Hispanic and Latin American dimensions of cubanía. In his essay "Americanismo y cubanismo literario" (Literary Americanism and Cubanism, 1932), Marinello bemoaned the lack of a specifically Cuban language: "We were born to language, similar to life, without the opportunity of election: when we think, when we exist, the language of Castile is already our unique language. We are through a language that is our own while being foreign" (Augier p. 35). In "Negrismo and mulatismo" (Black and Mulatto Literature, 1933), he argued that Cuban poetry should express a *mestizo* (racially mixed) or mulatto aesthetics to overcome the differences between whites and blacks. Marinello's prerevolutionary writings also included classic studies on Martí, which disclaimed any connection between Martí's thought and socialist principles. In 1962, however, Marinello claimed that the Cuban Revolution had established "fertile communication" with Martí's political, social, and economic ideals (Augier p. 361).

During the 1930s, the young Raúl Roa García (1907–1982) was active in radical student organizations, embraced Marxist ideas, and applied them to Cuban history and culture. Because of his role in the popular revolt against the Machado regime, he was forced to leave the island. Upon returning to Cuba, he worked as an attorney, university professor, and director of culture at the Ministry of Education (1949–1951). Among his initiatives in the government was establishing *cultural missions*, which sponsored theatrical performances, dances, concerts, art exhibits, and films around the island. Lamenting the lack of a cultural policy in republican Cuba, Roa García sought "to bring culture to the masses." In his article "El estado y la cultura" (State and Culture), he wrote that "culture has always been a nourishing source of liberty" (p. 1). One of Roa's main contributions to cubanía was to extend it to the lower classes, especially in the rural provinces.

The republican period (1902–1958) intensified academic and public discussions about cubanía. Nationalist discourse became less elitist and racist, integrating the contributions of working-class people, particularly those of African descent. The anthropological reappraisal of Afro-Cuban culture contributed to an expanded view of national identity. Marxism appealed to some Cuban intellectuals, especially to denounce social injustice and foreign domination. By the mid-twentieth century, the prevailing republican rhetoric of racial fraternity extolled the civic integration of all Cuban citizens, regardless of skin color or social status. Nonetheless, racial prejudice fractured the Cuban population well into the twenty-first century, and black intellectuals continued to denounce racial discrimination.

FROM ELITE TO POPULAR NATIONALISM

Cuban thought about cultural identity became progressively broader after the mid-nineteenth century, particularly after the island's wars of independence and the abolition of slavery. Still, most of the major writers about this topic remained middle- and upper-class white males. Between the 1920s and 1950s, much of Cuba's intellectual elite gravitated toward nationalism, including radical, liberal, and conservative versions. Safeguarding cubanía was a rallying point for numerous literary and artistic

Juan Marinello (1898–1977). Lawyer, writer, and politician Juan Marinello was the foremost communist intellectual in republican Cuba. COURTESY OF THE CUBAN HERITAGE COLLECTION, UNIVERSITY OF MIAMI LIBRARIES, CORAL GABLES, FLORIDA

movements. The threat of U.S. intervention, especially during the era of the Platt Amendment, shaped cultural politics in Cuba. So did lingering racial inequality on the island, which traditionally excluded blacks and mulattoes from the dominant discourse of the Cuban nation. After 1959, writers affiliated with Fidel Castro's revolution would rethink cultural identity from a socialist perspective, while those disaffected with his government, like many of their exiled predecessors, would reformulate the idea of Cuba from afar.

BIBLIOGRAPHY

Primary Sources

Arango y Parreño, Francisco de. *Obras.* 2 vols. Havana: Imagen Contemporánea, 2005 [1862].

Augier, Ángel I., ed. *Órbita de Juan Marinello.* Havana: UNEAC, 1968.

Betancourt, Juan René. *El negro: Ciudadano del futuro.* Havana: Cárdenas, 1959.

Caballero, José Agustín. *Obras.* Havana: Imagen Contemporánea, 1999.

Cabrera, Lydia. *El monte: Igbo finda, ewe orisha, vititi nfinda. Notas sobre las religiones, la magia, las supersticiones y el folklore de los negros criollos y del pueblo de Cuba.* Miami: Ediciones Universal, 2000 [1954].

Cabrera, Lydia. *La sociedad secreta abakuá: Narrada por viejos adeptos.* 3rd ed. Miami: Ediciones Universal, 2005 [1958].

Del Monte, Domingo. "Novela histórica." *Revista Bimestre Cubana* 2, no. 6 (1832): 157–183.

Gómez de Avellaneda, Gertrudis. *Sab.* Havana: Instituto Cubano del Libro, 1973 [1841].

Guerra y Sánchez, Ramiro. *Azúcar y población en las Antillas.* Havana: Ciencias Sociales, 1970 [1927].

Lachatañeré, Rómulo. "El sistema religioso de los lucumís y otras influencias africanas en Cuba." *Estudios afrocubanos* 3, nos. 1–4 (1939): 28–84; 4, nos. 1–4 (1940): 27–38; 5 (1945–1946): 190–215.

Lachateñeré, Rómulo. *¡¡Oh, mío Yemayá!! Cuentos y cantos negros*. Havana: Ciencias Sociales, 1992 [1938].

Lezama Lima, José. *La expresión americana*. Mexico City: Fondo de Cultura Económica, 1993 [1957].

Luz y Caballero, José de la. *Obras*. 3 vols. Havana: Imagen Contemporánea, 2001.

Maceo, Antonio. *Antonio Maceo: Ideología política. Cartas y otros documentos*. 2 vols. Havana: Ciencias Sociales, 1998.

Mañach, Jorge. *La crisis de la alta cultura en Cuba. Indagación del choteo*. Miami: Ediciones Universal, 1991 [1928].

Mañach, Jorge. *Pasado vigente*. Havana: Trópico, 1939.

Mañach, Jorge. *Historia y estilo*. Havana: Minerva, 1944.

Martí, José. *Obras completas*. 26 vols. Havana: Centro de Estudios Martianos, 2001.

Merlin, Condesa de [María de las Mercedes Santa Cruz y Montalvo]. *Viaje a la Habana*. Madrid: Verbum, 2006 [1844].

Ortiz, Fernando. *Hampa afro-cubana: Los negros brujos. Apuntes para un estudio de etnología criminal*. Miami: Ediciones Universal, 1973 [1906].

Ortiz, Fernando. "Por la integración cubana de blancos y negros." *Estudios afrocubanos* 5 (1945–1946): 216–229.

Ortiz, Fernando. *Contrapunteo cubano del tabaco y el azúcar: Advertencia de sus contrastes agrarios, económicos, históricos y sociales, su etnografía y su transculturación*. Madrid: Cátedra, 2002 [1940].

Roa García, Raúl. "El estado y la cultura." *Revista Mensuario de Arte, Literatura, Historia y Crítica* 1, no. 1 (1949): 1–21.

Saco, José Antonio. *Obras*. 6 vols. Havana: Imagen Contemporánea, 2001.

Sánchez de Almodóvar, Toribio (Domingo del Monte). "Poesías del Br. D. Toribio Sánchez de Almodóvar." In *Rimas americanas*, vol. 1, edited by Ignacio Herrera Dávila. Havana: Imprenta de Palmer, 1833.

Varela y Morales, Félix. *Obras*. 3 vols. Havana: Imagen Contemporánea, 1997.

Varona, Enrique José. *Textos escogidos*. Mexico City: Porrúa, 1968.

Villaverde, Cirilo. *Cecilia Valdés, o, La loma del Ángel*. Madrid: Cátedra, 2004 [1882].

Secondary Sources

Benítez Rojo, Antonio. *La isla que se repite: El Caribe y la perspectiva posmoderna*. San Juan, PR: Plaza Mayor, 2010 [1989].

De la Fuente, Alejandro. *A Nation for All: Race, Inequality, and Politics in Twentieth-Century Cuba*. Chapel Hill: University of North Carolina Press, 2001.

Fernández, Damián J., and Madeline Cámara Betancourt, eds. *Cuba, the Elusive Nation: Interpretations of National Identity*. Gainesville: University Press of Florida, 2000.

Hernández, Rafael, and Rafael Rojas, eds. *Ensayo cubano del siglo XX: Antología*. Mexico City: Fondo de Cultura Económica, 2002.

Ibarra, Jorge. *Ideología mambisa*. Havana: Instituto del Libro, 1967.

Ibarra, Jorge. *Nación y cultura nacional*. Havana: Letras Cubanas, 1981.

Moore, Robin D. *Nationalizing Blackness: Afrocubanismo and Artistic Revolution in Havana, 1920–1940*. Pittsburgh, PA: University of Pittsburgh Press, 1997.

Pérez, Louis A., Jr. *On Becoming Cuban: Identity, Nationality, and Culture*. Chapel Hill: University of North Carolina Press, 1999.

Pérez Firmat, Gustavo. *The Cuban Condition: Translation and Identity in Modern Cuban Literature*. New York and Cambridge, U.K.: Cambridge University Press, 1989.

Poyo, Gerald E. *With All, and for the Good of All: The Emergence of Popular Nationalism in the Cuban Communities of the United States, 1848–1898*. Durham, NC: Duke University Press, 1989.

Rojas, Rafael. *Isla sin fin: Contribución a la crítica del nacionalismo cubano*. Miami: Ediciones Universal, 1998.

Rojas, Rafael. *Essays in Cuban Intellectual History*. New York: Palgrave Macmillan, 2008.

Urrutia, Gustavo. "Cuatro conferencias radiofónicas sobre el negro en Cuba." In *Ensayo cubano del siglo XX: Antología*, edited by Rafael Hernández and Rafael Rojas. Mexico City: Fondo de Cultura Económica, 2002.

Vitier, Cintio. *Lo cubano en la poesía*. 2nd ed. Havana: Instituto del Libro, 1970 [1958].

Vitier, Cintio. *Ese sol del mundo moral: Para una historia de la eticidad cubana*. 2nd ed. Mexico City: Siglo XXI, 2002 [1975].

Vitier, Medardo. *Las ideas en Cuba. La filosofía en Cuba*. 2nd ed. Havana: Ciencias Sociales, 2002 [1938].

West-Durán, Alan. *Tropics of History: Cuba Imagined*. Westport, CT: Bergin & Garvey, 1997.

■ *See also*

Cuban Thought and Cultural Identity: Socialist Thought

Economy: Special Period

Gender: Feminism and Masculinity in the Revolutionary Period

CUBAN THOUGHT AND CULTURAL IDENTITY: QUINCEAÑERAS

Giselle Victoria Gómez

Quinceañera, *the fifteenth birthday celebration for young women in Cuba.*

The fifteenth-birthday celebrations for young Cuban females, called *las quinceañeras* (and popularly known as *los quince*), are a mass phenomenon that gathers every level of Cuban society. Key factors in evaluating the impact of *los quince* are the tremendous sense of spectacle at the fiesta itself and in its photographs, the huge sacrifice and effort that many families must make in order to defray the expense, and the existence of a large number of private microenterprises that provide services for the occasion.

RITE OF PASSAGE AND TRADITION

The celebration ceremony for a girl's fifteenth birthday is the traditional mechanism within the family sphere that some contemporary societies in the Americas and in Latin American communities worldwide use in order to mark a girl's change of status from child to woman. Accordingly it is generally recognized as a rite of passage or transition, an initiation.

The origin of this tradition has been associated with the puberty rites of the Aztecs and Mayas in Mexico, the sweet sixteen parties of Anglo-Saxon cultures, and the French *vals de debutantes*. Cuba, however, has an oral history that dates back to a custom of the wealthy colonial families, both Spanish and *criollo*, who would celebrate the fifteenth birthday of their female kin with a lavish feast that served as her introduction to the other families of high society. The rite thus symbolized the initiation of the girl into adulthood, since it was assumed that she was now taking on responsibilities and liberties that she did not previously have. This feast evolved into a display of homage and civility among the wealthy classes, which made certain assumptions (by rendering them explicit) about the socioeconomic status of the girl. The feast thus constituted a mode of social introduction equivalent to laying the foundations for the girl's marriage at some future point. The gowns, the toasts, the *tertulias* (salons that were attended by suitors) were mechanisms for the ideal representation of a fifteen-year-old, as symbolized by the economic backdrop of the event.

Whatever its origin may be, the *quince* is an ancient ritual practice that signified the young girl's introduction to society and her passage to womanhood, duly prepared both socially and physiologically for marriage and motherhood. The girl would already have had her first period and now, at age fifteen, could be assumed to have reached an age where reproduction would not be a physical, psychological, or social risk. From a sociological standpoint, according to Marta Núñez Sarmiento, the Cuban celebration provides a sort of snapshot of the interactions of both sexes during early adolescence that has become socially indispensable.

FIFTEEN MINUTES OF FAME

A customary *quince* celebration in Cuba involves the adolescent girl dressed as a princess, riding through the city with her parents in a vintage automobile from the days of Republican Cuba, festooned with ribbons and balloons, to the nonstop blaring of the klaxon. After the Revolution of 1959 the ceremony was integrated into the horizon of the middle- and lower-income sectors, which appropriated the original practice, turning it into a custom of the masses and thus transforming it into a different cultural product. For decades, some of the measures taken by the revolutionary government to support the celebration included the allocation, through controlled sales, of subsidized products such as cake, refreshments, and beer; the government also provided services such as hall or salon rentals and photographers at prices that were within the reach of the majority. This minimum guarantee of what had formerly been an exclusive brand of the wealthy classes turned the celebration into a pop-culture phenomenon.

Even as it provided the services needed to support the celebration, the state criticized and passed judgment on any ostentatious display, financial extravagance, and the tackiness of trying to appear to be what

Cuban Teenager Celebrating her Quinceañera. Cuban quinceaña celebrations often include ostentatious displays of wealth, including expensive gowns and rentals of vintage cars. © LEO MASON TRAVEL PHOTOS/ALAMY

one is not. The custom was singled out as a throwback to aristocratic-bourgeois roots, and the lavishness was condemned as ideological deviationism. This effort was not entirely in vain. Although in the 1960s and 1970s the grand salon ceremony and fiesta, with its choreographed waltz, went through an impressive boom, during the 1980s the celebration became more austere and introspective. As often as not it was substituted by an opportunity to travel throughout Cuba and the socialist bloc countries. Eventually, however, even though one might have expected the economic decline of the so-called Special Period to present a virtually insurmountable hurdle for the lavish celebrations of the *quince*, the ceremony in the grand salon reappeared with renewed vigor at the end of the 1990s—albeit within a national context that had changed, with new economic actors and a new *imaginarium*.

The renaissance of the lavish feast and waltz is understandable when one considers the historical circumstances of Cuba in the early 1990s: the collapse of the socialist bloc, the start of the Special Period, the decriminalization of the dollar, and the opening of the island to tourism (including families of the diaspora). Other important factors associated with these events served to encourage the circulation of information that was different from that supplied by the official media, such as the installation of dish antennas at certain government centers and for foreign tourists, and the arrival of video equipment and the Internet, albeit in extremely restricted form. These all provided opportunities for greater connectivity between Cuba and the outside world.

Furthermore, the differentiation of classes began to consolidate. Even though Cuba imports technology and equipment from highly developed societies, only people with access to dollars can buy them, at the stores commonly referred to with the English word *shopping*. The new stores sell not only household appliances but also all kinds of home articles, clothing, food, and confectionery. The variety and quality of these products are superior to the offerings at the national currency stores, which lack not just the novelty imports but basic goods altogether. Officially planned sales with coupons were thus publicly replaced by another, less equitable system, in the full knowledge that a worker's salary denominated in the national currency could not provide the purchasing power needed to buy the new items. As an example of this, during the 1990s the dollar reached 120 pesos, while the average salary amounted to 300 pesos a month. Along with the alternative circulation of movies, music clips, and advertising, imported through videocassettes and magazines, as well as the progress in digital technology, these all served to fostered a restatement of aspirations and lifestyles.

As the celebration threaded its way through all these changes, the significance of its practice became woven into the paradoxes of the models for self-representation observed by the fifteen-year-old and her family. The celebration, along with its photographs and video, allows the family to (re)affirm or construct its potential social status, which is turned into a kind of fashionable and obligatory competition. It is symptomatic that what many mothers desire in general is that their daughter should be no less than anybody else; this holds true with regard to the persistence in keeping the *quince* tradition alive and the desire for the daughter's *quince* to be at least as gorgeous, or even more so, than what her mother, grandmother, and other relatives enjoyed. During this play of representations, the family projects the image of a desirable environment and state-of-being. This is an image of happiness that in Cuba is ordinarily attainable through extreme sacrifice, since the subjects involved lack the material assets to support even their own day-to-day existence. If the wages of an ordinary Cuban are not enough to meet the basic needs of the home, they barely begin to defray the expense of the *quince* fiesta or of the photographs, which are quite costly in and of themselves. That single day adds up to a major financial investment.

THE PHOTOGRAPHS REMAIN

The budget needed for all this, with its ephemeral nature, means that for many people the fiesta in the great hall is not as obligatory a gesture as the photographs. These do not come cheap either, but they make it possible to eternalize the rite: at the Cuban celebrations of the *quince,* it is an indispensable cliché to say, "The party will end, but the photographs remain." Fiesta or no fiesta, the photographs are always made. This is probably why the act of getting photographed and the resulting photographs often take on the full symbolic and ritual significance.

All this notwithstanding, the social actors involved (photographers, the fifteen-year-old, and her family) have no predetermined awareness of capturing the rite symbolically through the representation of the girl in front of a camera, as in fact does occur during the waltz, which is organized and practiced for quite some time before the ceremony, in choreographed dancing and a chain of actions. The special waltz of the girl with the paternal figure, who later yields the dance to the boyfriend or friend, is what sets off the dance as homage to the pride in upbringing of the daughter. The conventional dance is a harbinger of permission to have a boyfriend, with the intention that a (good) marriage will in due course arise from the fact. This interconnected chain of activities represents a symbolic moment that serves as an initiation, the rite of passage of girl to woman with all its connotations: from the arms of the father to those of the husband, from the family to society, and so forth. All of this is symptomatic of the power strategies of the family as an institution. Following the waltz are more dances, duly choreographed with fourteen young couples and guided by a variety of musical themes, which are preselected in accordance with current fashion and teenage preferences; these serve to transform the solemn moment of the waltz into entertainment with pop music and reggaetón.

The photography and the video serve to document the spectacle of the ceremony. What sets the Cuban celebration apart in the Latin American context are the photographs produced by the specialized *casas de quince* and photo studios that service the event. The images can be classified according to their time-space context and the similarities among the representations. Classical or traditional photographs repeat (albeit in an updated manner) types of representations from different periods: individual and studio portraits, with the father or the boyfriend, family, and friends, next to the cake, and during the dance (waltz) at the fiesta. Some images imitate the iconography of nineteenth-century photographs, showing the girl dressed in a ball gown, as homage to the colonial dame. Others represent the fifteen-year-old amid digitized fantasy scenarios or glamour shots, including nudes and semi-nudes. Generally speaking, these traditional, classical, and modern typologies all exist within a single album; indeed, these representations (classical and modern) can even be combined in a single photograph. The representation of the colonial dame might be re-created in a Photoshop landscape, and the dress itself might be a montage using that application.

Quite aside from the images of the fiesta as such, within the same album the *quince* photographs typically present the following typologies: classical or period; glamour and erotic; engagement with backdrops (urban and natural landscapes); and montages, which redefine the typologies previously mentioned (for instance, showing the fifteen-year-old set against a virtual landscape with rivers and mountains taken from a Windows screenshot or in Paris beside the Eiffel Tower, and so on). There are of course other specific montage themes, such as advertising (magazine covers or advertisements); star systems and music industry (with entertainers and singers); or religious montages, in which the teenager appears in a saintly pose alongside an icon of the Catholic faith.

The paradigm of the colonial dame derives from Cuban soap operas and the folk photography of the nineteenth century. But the behavior of modern girls is nourished, through an ongoing recycling process, by a variety of images in which official and alternative channels coexist. In this process, the music spectaculars and films that run on Cuban television are not as influential as the—forbidden—use of television antennas, videos, and exchanges with the diaspora, and especially of imported vanity, glamour, and erotic magazines (without underestimating the tortuous and incipient connectivity to the Internet).

FIFTEEN: WHY AND WHAT FOR?

Why is this celebration so important to Cuban families? To synthesize: this ritual, whose symbolic mechanisms are systematized in the photographs and in the fiesta in the grand salon, reflects cultural needs as well as the individual, social, and anthropological self-representation needs of the fifteen-year-old and her parents. It provides for, satisfies, and happily resolves problems that in day-to-day life appear as complex and conflicting. It does so by representing a happy economic situation and by erasing genuine class differences over the course of a single day. The digital photomontage satisfies deficiencies, desire, and aspirations, just as the waltz resolves the endurance of the family institution and patriarchal power. The photos perpetuate the fantasy aspects of the *quince*, resolving generational conflicts and the expressions of sexuality that come with puberty. Furthermore, the photograph is an easily transportable medium (digital photographs in particular); it encourages unlimited circulation and a post-ceremony dissemination process that allows the fifteen-year-old and her family to reaffirm their social status even beyond the circle of their relatives, friends, and neighbors. The value of this celebration is so great that as a general rule it is considered the most important event in the life of a woman, more than even her wedding.

The photography of a Cuban *quince* is a complex phenomenon in which many elements converge in a grand representation. These elements include family and social tensions, in which the rites of the past merge with a postmodern sensibility that appeals to pastiches and recycling; a camera's eye that constructs the image of a heterosexual adolescent and reveals the implicit coexistence of the submission to status symbols and patriarchal power with the converse aspirations of the woman's freedom to embrace her body. This dichotomy is played out when the fifteen-year-old fulfills roles of princess, colonial lady, and religious devotee and is alternately flaunted when she appears as an emancipated modern girl or as a titillating semi-nude virgin. The frailty of Cuba's economy is forgotten in an act of spectacular extravagance, and the ideals of the Socialist Revolution are put to the test against the strength of tradition: a tradition that is constantly reinventing itself.

BIBLIOGRAPHY
Documentaries

Blanco, Manuela. *Todas las muchachitas lo hacen* (2009).

Bernaza, Luis Felipe. *Vals de la Habana Vieja* (1989).

García Espinosa, Julio. *Cuba baila* (1960).

Glatzer, Richard, and Wash Westmoreland. *Quinceañeras* (2005).

Studies

Aldana, María José. "Quince años y vals: Significados a través del tiempo," 2008. Available from http://kabraqan.googlepages.com/mja01.pdf.

Arcaya, Sara. "*La quinceañera*: Performances of Race, Culture, Class, and Religion in the Somerville Community." In *Urban Borderlands*. Cambridge/

Somerville Oral Latino History Project, Fall 2004. Available from Tufts University Digital Collections and Archives: http://dca.lib.tufts.edu/features/urban/MS083.004.002.00013.pdf.

Clarac de Briceño, Jacqueline. "Adolescente, cuerpo, iniciación, nuevo milenio." *Boletín Antropológico* 2, no 49 (May–August 2000): 53–74.

Clarac de Briceño, Jacqueline. "Cultura, lenguaje, mujer." *Otras miradas* 2, no. 2 (December 2002): 88–95. Available from http://redalyc.uaemex.mx/redalyc/src/inicio/ArtPdfRed.jsp?iCve=18320203.

Finol, José Enrique. "De niña a mujer: El rito de pasaje en la sociedad contemporánea." *Cuadernos* 17 (February 2001): 171–185. Available from http://redalyc.uaemex.mx/src/inicio/ArtPdfRed.jsp?iCve=18501711.

Härkönen, Heidi. "Matrifocality in Cuba: A Comparison." Paper delivered at the Congress of the Latin American Studies Association, Rio de Janeiro, Brazil, June 11–14, 2009. Available from http://lasa.international.pitt.edu/members/congress-papers/lasa2009/files/HarkonenHeidi.pdf.

Linton, Ralph. "Status y Rol." In *Antropología: Lecturas*, 2nd ed., edited by Paul Bohannan and Mark Glazer, 187–204. Havana: Editorial Félix Varela, 2005.

Montes de Oca Moreda, Dannys. "Fotógrafas contemporáneas cubanas en la construcción de género e imágenes." *Fotografía cubana* 2 (2009).

Moya, Isabel. "¿Quinceañeras o Vampirezas?" *Mujeres* (March 2, 2006): 18. Available from http://www.mujeres.co.cu/articulo.asp?a=2006&num=273&art=36.

Núñez Sarmiento, Marta. "Cambios en la ideología de género entre mujeres y hombres profesionales en la Cuba de hoy." Available from http://bibliotecavirtual.clacso.org.ar/ar/libros/cuba/cemi/ideologia.pdf. Originally published as "Ideología de género entre profesionales cubanos." *Temas*, 37–38 (April–September 2004): 24–36.

Ortiz, Cristina. "Consuming Identities: How Quinceañera-Related Buying and Spending Practices Help Create and (Re)assert Identities." Paper delivered at the Congress of the Latin American Studies Association, Rio de Janeiro, Brazil, June 11–14, 2009. Available at http://lasa.international.pitt.edu/members/congress-papers/lasa2009/files/OrtizCristina.pdf.

Palencia Villa, Mercedes, and Víctor Gruel. "Algunas visiones sobre un mismo ritual: La fiesta de quince-años." *Temas sociológicos* 11 (2007): 221–240.

Ravelo, Aloyma. "Dime de qué ostentas y te diré de qué careces." *Mujeres* 4 (2005): 75–77.

Rubio, Vladia, and Caridad Carrobello. "Los quince: Vals de las apariencias." *Bohemia* (15 April 2005): 34.

Ruiz Martín del Campo, Emma. "Adolescencia femenina y ritual: La celebración de las quinceañeras en algunas comunidades de México." *Espiral* 7, no. 20 (January–April 2001): 189–222. Available from http://redalyc.uaemex.mx/pdf/138/13802007.pdf.

Saborío Carranza, Mayavel. "La quinceañera, un fenómeno de transculturación e interculturalidad." *Decires* 12, no. 14 (2010): 25–40.

Silva, Armando. *Álbum de familia: La imagen de nosotros mismos*. Bogotá: Editorial Norma, 1998.

CUBAN THOUGHT AND CULTURAL IDENTITY: RADICAL CATHOLICISM AND SOCIAL JUSTICE

Gerald E. Poyo

Cuban Catholic activists and their support of reform and revolution from the late 1920s to the 1960s.

Beginning in the 1930s, Cuban thought and politics were influenced by reformist and even radical intellectual currents and activist trends evident among Catholics in Spain and Latin America inspired by the Catholic Church's social encyclicals. New generations of Cuban Catholic leaders transcended their faith's generally pastoral and moral concerns to engage Cuba's pressing social-civic problems and support movements of reform and even revolution in the 1950s and 1960s.

CATHOLIC ACTION

In the first half of the twentieth century, nationalist, social democratic, and communist ideologies greatly influenced political thought in Cuba, prompting Catholics to more closely explore what their faith said about the socioeconomic issues of the day. Their primary sources of inspiration were the papal social encyclicals *Rerum Novarum* (1891) and *Quadragésimo Anno* (1931), which articulated official Catholic teachings about matters of social concern. Published in response to deepening social tensions and divisions in Europe and the rise of socialism during the nineteenth and early twentieth centuries, the papal documents advocated reforms patterned after the corporatist social traditions that characterized medieval Europe.

Medieval Catholic political thinkers believed that the common good could be achieved through an integrated society subject to a wise ruler and composed of legally autonomous and self-regulating corporations, including towns, military and religious orders, and especially artisan and craft guilds. Informed by these ideas, the encyclicals inspired activist Catholic sociopolitical movements, known as Catholic Action, throughout Europe and later in Latin America. After independence, Cuba's generally discredited official church, which had remained loyal to Spanish colonial authorities, now faced a new era characterized by separation of church and state. Reinvigorated with a new evangelizing mission, Catholic orders founded dozens of schools, bishops encouraged the establishment of lay organizations, and priests and other religious promoted greater engagement with social teachings, laying the foundation for the first Cuban Catholic Action movements in the late 1920s.

In the 1930s, economic depression and revolution in Cuba led to the rise and fall of various governments, transforming the island's political system and bringing workers' issues to the forefront of national discussion. Acknowledging Cuba's intractable social problems, bishops encouraged workers to demand their rights, and they supported the work of Catholic social charities in Havana's worst slums. Charities did not offer permanent solutions to Cuba's social conditions, but they certainly resolved some immediate problems for the poor and contributed to raising consciousness among many middle- and upper-class Catholics about the reality of poverty in Cuba. Father Felipe Rey de Castro (1931–1952), the founder of an important lay organization, Agrupación Católica Universitaria (ACU), fostered a generation of activist laity linking social action to religious transformation. His disciple José Ignacio Lasaga, influenced by Catholic corporatist thought, became a voice for change, advocating union organizing, credit and savings institutions, worker insurance, worker compensation, worker-owned businesses, the prohibition of child labor, and regulation of the workday. Also in the corporatist tradition, the Cuban-born and Spanish-trained Jesuit priest Manuel Foyaca called for a readjustment of Cuban national life through charity and justice rather than social strife and confrontation. Foyaca became the spiritual counselor of men's Catholic Action in 1941 and, at the end of 1942, inspired the formation of the Christian Social Democratic movement, which encouraged activism in support of the church's social doctrines.

HUMANISM AND CHRISTIAN SOCIAL DEMOCRACY

Despite the enthusiasm among many Cuban Catholics for the social encyclicals, most did not embrace the corporatist vision, provoking a theological split among Catholic activists. Whereas Jesuits in Cuba embraced Foyaca and Spanish-inspired Catholic reform traditions, other religious, including Franciscans and LaSalle Brothers, preferred the ideas of the French philosopher and theologian Jacques Maritain (1882–1973), who offered a liberal Christian Democratic alternative. Calling his ideas *integral humanism*, Maritain recognized humanity's need not only for spiritual salvation, but also for a dignified life on earth. He inspired a new generation of Catholic students in Latin America, exemplified by Chile's Eduardo Frei (1911–1982) and Venezuela's Rafael Caldera (1916–2009), who defined the movement as dedicated to democracy, human rights, and development of whole persons in their economic, political, social, and cultural dimensions.

Followers of Maritain in Cuba, including Andrés Valdespino, Rubén D. Rumbaut (d. 2003), and Angel del Cerro, organized the humanist movement of Cuba in December 1950. They considered Maritain's ideas to be consistent with Cuba's new constitution of 1940, a document with clear republican and democratic principles that most Cubans viewed as progressive and, if fully implemented, perfectly capable of addressing many of the nation's social problems. The humanist movement included people of various philosophical and religious traditions who supported socioeconomic reform, and in some ways it reflected Catholicism's growing influence within Cuba's traditionally secular socioeconomic thinking. Though humanism was not a political movement, its adherents sought the transformation of individual and state capitalism into *economic humanism*, a system that favored the moral dimension over the desire for wealth, distribution over production, work over capital, and exchange of traditional private enterprise for a communal system in which all would participate in the ownership, running, and production of enterprises.

Though the Church maintained a firm belief in its essentially spiritual and moral—not political—role, many Catholics in the late 1940s and 1950s increasingly engaged in national discussions about reform and even revolutionary change. Founded in 1948 by Augustinian priests from the United States, Villanueva University facilitated these discussions and expanded Catholic intellectual influence. Catholic Action leaders and several bishops lamented the inherent limitations of the church's considerable charitable initiatives across the island and encouraged social action in support of structural change. Catholic Action evangelized among the working classes and, in 1946, founded Orientación Obrera, headed by the University of Havana law student, José de Jesus Plana. In the following year it became Juventud Obrera Católica (JOC, Catholic Worker Youth), affiliated with an international movement of the same name founded in 1924 in Belgium to improve the condition of Europe's working classes. JOC disseminated Catholic social teachings in its official publication *Juventud Obrera*, and in 1950, it established a women's organization, JOC Femenina, headed by Lydia Maribona, which focused on office and factory workers and domestics.

Catholic activists also concerned themselves with the difficult situation of Cuba's rural poor. In 1945, Enrique Cano urged Catholics to focus on the countryside, where laborers lived in even worse conditions than urban workers. In mid-May 1951, Havana's Cardinal Archbishop Manuel Arteaga (1879–1963) sponsored at Colegio Belén, a prestigious Jesuit school, the Cuban church's first *semana social* (social week), organized by Catholic Action leaders Foyaca, Julio Morales Gómez, Abel Teurbe Tolón, and Miguel Suárez, and focusing on Cuba's agrarian problems. In 1958, ACU published *Por qué reforma agraria?* a disconcerting study that revealed in stark statistical terms the dismal conditions faced by Cuba's rural population. Though the authors did not offer a specific agrarian reform program, they did state categorically that the time had arrived for the nation to stop being the "private feudal estate of the few powerful" and concluded optimistically that within a few years Cuba would no longer be the property of a few, but instead a nation for all Cuban citizens, and that Catholicism would play an important role in transforming the country.

Manuel Artime with another activist, 1960. Catholic activist Manuel Artime (left) enthusiastically supported Cuban agrarian reform until its Soviet-style collectivization goals became clear. He later organized the Directorio Revolucionario Estudiantil to struggle clandestinely. HANK WALKER/TIME LIFE PICTURES/GETTY IMAGES

SOCIAL JUSTICE AND THE REVOLUTION

Catholics also became more openly political after 1956 when Fidel Castro's revolutionary movement against Fulgencio Batista (1901–1973), who had taken over the government in a coup d'état in 1952, took center stage. Perceiving the rebellion to be fully committed to reforming Cuban society for the benefit of the urban and rural poor, hundreds of lay Catholics joined the many middle-class, student, and worker revolutionary organizations confronting the government, including Castro's 26th of July movement. Most Catholic organizations and some bishops condemned the government, eventually demanding that Batista resign, and priests even became chaplains of the various expanding revolutionary fronts in the mountains. When the revolution led by Fidel Castro succeeded in January 1959, Catholics celebrated along with the rest of Cuba's population.

Believing that a new era of social reform had arrived, many Catholic activists, including members of the humanist movement, joined the new revolutionary government, while others supported the revolution in other ways. JOC and other socially conscious Catholic Action lay organizations backed early government measures aimed at improving conditions for Cuba's people, including urban reforms and a radical agrarian law enacted in May 1959. Reassignments of Cuban bishops, including the appointment of a new archbishop in Havana, Evelio Díaz (1902–1984), placed the hierarchy squarely in support of these measures that they considered compatible with Catholic social teaching. The most important Catholic publication in Cuba, the Franciscan journal *La Quincena*, edited by the progressive priest Ignacio Biaín, fully backed revolutionary developments.

Though few initially suspected Jesuit-trained Fidel Castro of being a communist sympathizer, his inclinations became evident during 1959. Revolutionary euphoria among Catholics cooled as collectivist policies guided the implementation of land reform and communists occupied important positions within the government. Despite broad-based Cuban support for the Revolution, Catholics expressed the limits of their support at a large National Catholic Congress in Havana during November 1959. They mobilized hundreds of thousands for a Mass in honor of Cuba's patroness, Nuestra Señora de la Caridad del Cobre (Our Lady of Charity of El Cobre), followed by speeches applauding the government's social reform policies but making clear their own unwavering opposition to communism.

The government responded with intolerance and repression and accelerated radicalization of the economy along collectivist lines, forcing Catholics to choose sides. Some continued to support the Revolution, including Father German Lence, whose organization With the Cross and with the Fatherland held numerous pro-government rallies. Lence and others recognized the Revolution's communist inclinations but did not believe socialism contradicted Catholic social teaching; they believed the Revolution and Catholicism could coexist. Most Catholics, however, became disenchanted, and many joined dissident groups and movements. Intransigently opposed to communism, the lay activist José Ignacio Rasco founded the Cuban Christian Democratic movement to offer a political alternative to the Cuban people, but it was quickly banned, and Rasco fled Cuba. Another activist, Manuel Artime (1932–1977), who enthusiastically worked with Cuban agrarian reform until its Soviet-style collectivization goals became clear, organized the Directorio Revolucionario Estudiantil (DRE, the Student Revolutionary Directorate) to struggle clandestinely, but he too fled. Despite growing Catholic opposition, Cubans remained overwhelmingly supportive of Castro in the early 1960s, leaving the church isolated. Most Catholic activists and intellectuals went into exile, formed anti-Castro organizations, played a significant role in the failed Bay of Pigs invasion, and remained committed to overthrowing the communist system in Cuba.

In 1959, many Cubans influenced by their Catholic social action experiences during the 1930s, 1940s, and 1950s envisioned a noncommunist transformational revolution in their homeland. This hope had the potential to locate Cuban Catholicism at the forefront of a powerful and perhaps quite radical experiment spiritually related to the Latin American Liberation Theology movement, which called on the faithful to pay special attention to the poor and act on their behalf. Even the mainstream Latin American church embraced a strong social agenda at the 1968 Medellín Consejo Episcopal Latino Americano (CELAM) conference, which many Cuban Catholics activists on and off the island endorsed.

But events did not encourage this direction. Though Cuban Catholics remained committed to the social doctrines of the Church, their experience with communism distracted or stifled their commitments to social Catholicism. Those who remained in Cuba hoping to participate as radical and revolutionary Catholics were frustrated and disappointed as orthodox communism's atheism dominated revolutionary thought. Catholics had little choice other than to maintain silence, leave Cuba, or accept communism. A Cuban revolutionary leadership more appreciative and tolerant of the social Catholic traditions of these three decades might very well have inspired broad Catholic support for the revolutionary project. As it was, communism consolidated its hold and became the revolution's sole ideological inspiration, stifling the continuing development of Catholic Action–inspired social thought on the island and in exile.

BIBLIOGRAPHY

Fernández Santalices, Manuel. *Religión y revolución en Cuba: Veinte cinco años de lucha ateísta.* Miami, FL: Saeta Ediciones, 1984.

Fernández Santalices, Manuel. *Presencia de Cuba en el Catolicismo: Apuntes históricos del siglo viente.* Caracas: Fundación Adenauer, Organización Demócrata Cristiana de América, 1998.

Figueroa y Miranda, Miguel. *Historia de la Agrupación Católica Universitaria, 1931–1956.* Havana: 1956.

Kirk, John. *Between God and Party: Religion and Politics in Revolutionary Cuba.* Tampa: University of South Florida Press, 1989.

Payne, Stanley G. *Spanish Catholicism: An Historical Overview.* Madison: University of Wisconsin Press, 1984.

Pérez-Stable, Marifeli. *The Cuban Revolution: Origins, Course, and Legacy.* Oxford, U.K.: Oxford University Press, 1993.

Poyo, Gerald. *Cuban Catholics in the United States, 1960–1980: Exile and Integration.* South Bend, IN: University of Notre Dame Press, 2007.

Suárez Policari, Ramón. *Historia de la Iglesia Católica en Cuba.* 2 vols. Miami, FL: Ediciones Universal, 2003.

CUBAN THOUGHT AND CULTURAL IDENTITY: SOCIALIST THOUGHT

Julio Cesar Guanche Zaldivar

Ideas, prominent figures, and organizations of twentieth-century Cuban socialism.

Socialism has been the ideological signature of Cuban political practice since 1959, but it did not arise from a single philosophy, nor was it the vision of a single man. Socialism was rather a school of thought present in Cuba throughout the twentieth century. Cuban variations of socialism include non-Marxist schools of social reform; alternatives to revolutionary socialism such as anarchism, Stalinism, Trotskyism, and unaffiliated Marxism; populist tendencies; defenders of state socialism; and the socialism of the Cuban Revolution. The common factors in all these schools of thought are the promotion of national sovereignty, the criticism of imperialist relations between the United States and Cuba, and the active defense of social justice.

CUBAN SOCIALISM BEFORE 1959

The work of Cuban nationalist leader José Martí (1853–1895) influenced Cuban socialism from the nineteenth century through the twentieth century, but his thinking cannot be characterized as socialist. Martí radicalized liberalism and steered it toward political democracy and social justice by focusing on popular nationalism and anti-imperialism.

The Appearance of the Ideal Anarchists, moderate social reformers, and Marxists pressed forward in Cuban politics at the beginning of the twentieth century. Anarchists and anarcho-syndicalists organized and held control of the workers' movement until the end of the 1920s and saw several leaders killed—Alfredo López (1894–1926), Margarito Iglesias (d. 1923), and Enrique Varona (d. 1925)—under the regime of Gerardo Machado (1871–1939). They opposed participating in the elections; demanded an eight-hour workday, equal salaries for men and women, and the right to strike; and sought to avoid the bureaucratization of their organizations.

The non-Marxist socialists, notably Eduardo Agüero (1907–1951), Juan Arévalo, Francisco Domenech (1882–1966), and Carlos Loveira (1882–1928), defended social reforms from the perspective of the working world. They achieved groundbreaking victories: the eight-hour workday for government employees, a limit on the workday in stores, the prohibition of child labor for minors under fourteen, and the *Accidentes del Trabajo* (occupational accidents) law, although they did not oppose Machado later on.

One wing of feminism maintained moderate positions in the suffragist battles of the 1920s. Another, radicalized, wing founded the Alianza Nacional Feminista (National Feminist Alliance) and the Unión Laborista de Mujeres (Women's Labor Union.) The socialists—Loló de la Torriente (1907–1983) and Ofelia Rodríguez Acosta (1902–1975), among others—opposed Machado, bourgeois capitalism, and framing the vote as the ultimate goal of their struggle, and called on women to fight for a classless society. In the 1940s, Cuban women, some of them as members of parliament, continued the struggle for better living conditions and social justice. They also worked for these ends within the political parties, creating *secciones femeninas* (women's sections). Carmen Castro Porta (1908–1985), for example, brought advanced ideas of social justice to the Comité Gestor Ortodoxo (Orthodox Administrative Committee), of which she was a member with Eduardo Chibás (1907–1951). In the 1950s, the most radicalized women were at the vanguard of the insurrection against Fulgencio Batista's regime and were members of organizations such as the Frente Cívico de Mujeres Martianas (Martí Women's Civic Front)—Carmen Castro and Aida Pelayo (1912–1998)—and Mujeres Oposicionistas Unidas (Women United in Opposition)—Marta Fraide (b. 1920), Natalia Bolívar (b. 1934), Yeya Restano, and Zoila Lapique (b. 1930).

In the Marxists' camp, the communists broke from the socialists following the triumph of Bolshevism and the creation of the Communist International (CI) in 1919. Carlos Baliño (1848–1926), Julio Antonio Mella (1903–1929), Fabio Grobart (1905–1994), and Alfonso Bernal del Riesgo (1901–1975), among others, unified the disparate groups of communists, establishing the Partido Comunista de Cuba (PCC; Cuban Communist Party) a section of the CI, in 1925. Its leaders would be labor organizers, promulgators of socialism, and anti-imperialists, and they created, among other organizations, the first sugar-workers' union.

The revolutions in Russia and Mexico, the war for the restoration of the Spanish republic, and the New Deal in the United States all influenced Cuban socialisms. Most of the texts published on the island concerning the Soviet Union at that time—whether by liberal authors or unaffiliated figures—shared a common theme: This was not the model for the future. The tendencies that garnered the greatest support followed the socialist-leaning reforms of Mexican nationalist Lázaro Cárdenas (1895–1970) and Franklin D. Roosevelt's social democratic state. Together, they called for a redefinition of Cuba's status with regard to the United States, which a range of authors characterized, until 1933, as a protectorate. It was in that spirit that the Platt Amendment (1901), the law authorizing U.S. military intervention, would be eliminated in 1933.

New Masses and New Socialisms After 1933, socialism burst onto the scene on a grand scale. The two best-known models were those advocated by Ramón Grau San Martín (1887–1969) and Antonio Guiteras (1906–1935). Both men were members of the Gobierno de los Cien Días (Hundred-Day Government, September 1933–January 1934), a provisional government established shortly after the fall of Machado. Grau was appointed president and Guiteras minister of the interior, war, and navy. Fulgencio Batista—who had taken advantage of the September Revolt of the Sergeants—was also in this government, becoming head of a reconfigured Constitutional Army. The government approved new social legislation and seized U.S. companies. Batista, with the support of the U.S. Embassy, overthrew the Grau/Guiteras bloc.

Despite their alliance, the two men were quite different: Grau was a reformer, Guiteras, a revolutionary. Grau proposed a type of social democracy that was opposed to pro-Soviet communism. In 1934, he founded the first modern party of the masses in Cuba: the Partido Revolucionario Cubano (Auténtico), or PRC (Authentic Cuban Revolutionary Party). He promised nationalism, anti-imperialism, and socialism and proclaimed the right to national self-determination, political independence, and economic liberation. Based on that populist platform, he was elected president (1944–1948) by an enormous margin.

Guiteras worked toward socialism through a non-bourgeois, anti-imperialist path of development. In 1934, he formed a radical organization: Joven Cuba (Young Cuba). Its agenda, though not pro-Soviet, sought to create cooperative forms of production, stimulate small industry, socialize the production of state farms through systematic planning, implement agrarian reform, and define the social function of property. Batista ordered Guiteras killed in 1935, but Guiteras had prefigured the program that would be put into practice in 1959: revolutionary nationalism, political radicalism, economic anti-imperialism, and state socialism. His influence can be seen in Fidel Castro's 1953 speech "La historia me absolverá" (1959; History Will Absolve Me).

Family Disputes Among the Marxists In the 1930s, Marxists followed the divergences from Bolshevism: Stalinists, Trotskyites, and unaffiliated Marxists. The Communist Party had a very limited presence in the uprisings of the 1950s, but the successful insertion of pro-Soviet Marxists in the 1959 revolution allowed them to glorify their past. They presented themselves as the force that had driven the revolutionary movement in Cuba until the appearance of Fidel Castro (b. 1926). That position not only undervalued the non-Marxist, leftist nationalists but Trotskyites and unaffiliated Marxists as well.

For his part, the prominent Marxist figure Julio Antonio Mella offered an original line of thinking and political practice. He was cut off from the PCC for having forged alliances with the bourgeois opposition to Machado and for having gone on a hunger strike against Machado, contrary to the judgment of his party. Mella

Ramón Grau San Martìn (right), with Fulgencio Batista, 1944. These two political figures were in conflict with Cuban socialists during the Republican period. GEORGE SKADDING/TIME LIFE PICTURES/GETTY IMAGES

created Cuban Marxism by combining a class analysis with Cuban nationalism: He proclaimed that the national project would be one inherently of the masses.

The subordination of the Cuban Communist Party (PCC) to the Communist International (CI) turned out to be disastrous for the former. It negotiated with Machado an end to a 1933 strike that could have toppled Machado. The PCC believed that by doing so, it could control the course of politics. Its final objective was to gather the forces necessary to install a regime resembling the model established by the Soviet Union. Blas Roca (1908–1987) was elected general secretary of the PCC in 1934. The party fought Grau and Guiteras for the duration of the Gobierno de los Cien Días (September 1933–January 1934), dividing the revolutionary forces, which Batista repressed. Nevertheless, the party successfully negotiated with Batista to get legal status in 1938, to participate in the Constituyente (Consituent Assembly) of 1940, and to create an antifascist front.

Under the influence of militants such as Sandalio Junco (d. 1941), Juan Ramón Breá (1905–1941), Marcos García Villarreal, Charles Simeón, and Bertha García, the Trotskyites did battle from 1920 to 1935. They controlled, at times, the Federación Obrera de la Habana (Workers Federation of Havana), Defensa Obrera Internacional (International Workers' Defense), and the Ala Izquierda Estudiantil (Student Left Wing). In 1933, they joined to form the Partido Bolchevique Leninista (Bolshevik Leninist Party) and continued fighting until around 1940 when they ceased to be a force in the workers' movement. The Trotskyites called for the formation of a single front of workers and *campesinos* (farmers and peasants). They opposed firings and demanded social security for the unemployed, the expulsion of labor leaders who capitulated to the government, and an eight-hour work day. They failed to understand the revolutionary role of the most advanced sectors of the petite bourgeoisie and never held great influence (Soler Martínez 2001). Nevertheless, they left a legacy when they denounced the dictatorial nature of the Soviet regime and the imperialist nature of the relations between the United States and Cuba.

One Marxist school kept its distance from the Soviet Union and became a critic of that experience. Raúl Roa (1907–1982), Aureliano Sánchez Arango (1907–1976), Pablo de la Torriente (1901–1936), and Enrique de la Osa (1909–1997), among others—equally Marxists and nationalists—never joined the PCC and were politically active in a range of organizations. They achieved few practical results—they lived in exile or were repressed on the island—but their writings were noteworthy. They located the origins of the national crisis in the so-called pseudo-democratic condition of the Cuban state and in the nature of what they called the neocolonial economy, and described the agents capable of leading its revolution to victory: all of the elements of society injured and oppressed by the neocolonial regime.

SOCIALISM NEARING 1959

The Constitution of 1940 left the anarchists, the Trotskyites, the Guiterists, and the unaffiliated Marxists behind, murdered by reactionary violence or embroiled in ideological differences. Reformers took advantage of this situation. It was Grau's hour once again. A dissident from Grau's party, Eduardo Chibás (1907–1951), formed the Partido del Pueblo Cubano (Ortodoxo) (PPC[O]; Party of the Cuban People [Orthodox]) in 1947, bringing together the country's most progressive sectors. He shared Grau's social democratic platform but put an emphasis on denouncing corruption, which was considered the national cancer. The PPC(O) was the most likely winner of the 1952 elections, which were prevented by Batista. Several members of the 1959 leadership belonged to this party, among them Fidel Castro.

The Communist Party (CP) in Cuba—starting in 1943, it would be called the Partido Socialista Popular (PSP; Popular Socialist Party)—had various accomplishments in the 1940s: It participated in government, expanded union membership, succeeded in helping the Confederación de Trabajadores de Cuba (CTC; Cuban Confederation of Workers) gain great influence in the daily life of the country, maintained media outlets, and, through figures such as Juan Marinello (1898–1977) and Carlos Rafael Rodríguez (1913–1997) and organizations such as Sociedad Cultural Nuestro Tiempo (Our Time Cultural Society) developed a powerful effort aimed at influencing the intellectual world. The workers' movement acquired visibility, organization, social accomplishments, and status as a powerful interlocutor with the state at the same time it promoted racial equality. Blas Roca, Salvador García Agüero (1907–1965), Lázaro Peña (1911–1974), Jesús Menéndez (1911–1948), and Esperanza Sánchez Mastrapa were respected party leaders.

Following the 1952 coup d'état, the CP was once again repressed by Batista, becoming the illegal opposition. Numerous publications disseminated by U.S. anticommunist organizations circulated throughout the country. The CP sought to gain political support without taking up arms. From that position, its leadership considered the attacks on the Moncada Barracks (1953) carried out by the New Left to be a heroic but false path and the attacks on the Presidential Palace (1957) to be a return to the "putschism" (a secretly plotted and suddenly executed attempt to overthrow a government) of the 1930s. That said, in 1958, the party made alliances with Fidel Castro, and several of its members—without identifying themselves as party representatives—joined the uprising.

Starting in 1940, unaffiliated Marxists had various fates. Their ideal was generally demarxified, turning it into the liberal left wing of capitalism. Those who held civic positions became humanists. Nevertheless, Roa opposed Stalinism in caustic terms and the youth section of Chibás's party distributed his Marxist-friendly platform. The New Left of the 1950s organized itself through the Movimiento Nacionalista Revolucionario (Revolutionary Nationalist Movement); the Frente Cívico de Mujeres Martianas (FCMM; Martí Women's Civic Front); the Movimiento Revolucionario 26 de Julio (26th of July Revolutionary Movement); and the Directorio Revolucionario 13 de Marzo (March 13 Revolutionary Directorate) among other organizations. In 1959, a triumphant leadership framed victory as the common ideological legacy of that spectrum. It defined that legacy as a combination of anti-imperialism and nationalism with social justice and political democracy, which many after 1959 called socialism.

THE SOCIALISM OF THE CUBAN REVOLUTION: THE CONTEXT IN 1959

In 1961, Fidel Castro declared the Revolution to be socialist. The political course of the island ought then to be situated within the process of decolonization and the fight between China and the Soviet Union for hegemony over the communist movement. Cuba went against the tide of international politics. Soviet assistance, similar to aid that country was giving to other Third World countries at the time, faced no criticism by those who asserted, "Fidel, a communist? No—[Soviet leader] Nikita [Khrushchev] is a Fidelist." Fidel Castro became a hero throughout Latin America and Che Guevara (1928–1967) a worldwide symbol, but the differences that distinguished Castroism from Guevarism foreshadowed the global debates of socialism. One segment of the 1968 Left characterized Fidel Castro as a man who preferred the political convenience of the state to the freedoms of revolutionaries. It also celebrated in Guevara the leader who, from a position of power, put revolutionary freedom before the needs of the constituted state. That is why posters from political rallies of 1968 show only Guevara's face.

Western socialists and Marxists critical of the Soviet Union saw in Fidel Castro the drama of an independent politics—Cuba was the sole Latin American country to be a founding member of the Non-Aligned Movement (NAM). In Guevara they found the only Marxist leader in the twentieth century to give shelter to members of the (Trotskyite) Cuban section of the Fourth International; to argue with the socialism of Jean-Paul Sartre (1905–1980), Charles Bettelheim (1913–1906), and Ernest Mandel (1923–1995); to criticize the Soviet Union's policies toward the Third World; and to defend the cultivation of revolutionary processes across three continents. For Latin American revolutionaries, Castro-Guevarism indicated the strategy for victory, showed the viability of the Third World (Ribeiro), signified the triumph of the starving masses of the continent, and indicated the possibility of a socialism that was *sin calco ni copia* (altogether singular).

The underlying discussion was about the nature of the socialism to be created on the island. Two general tendencies appeared after 1961, becoming hegemonic over the course of that decade. They would provide the authentic framework for the discussion among *revolucionarios*: Soviet-inspired Marxist-Leninist socialism and critical Marxist socialism, with a Latin American and Third World lens. Within that arrangement, Fidel Castro occupied a central location. The weight of his figure has been categorical. Both his followers and his opponents agree on one point—his responsibility—for they attribute to him paternity for every success and/or failure. From 1961 on, the schools of Marxist socialism alone occupied the place of all things revolutionary. Noncommunist, nationalist, and social revolutionary groups that had participated in the Revolution but did not want to follow a project supported by Moscow were confined to the symbolic space of so-called reactionaries or counter-revolutionaries.

By 1971, the pro-Soviet school came to dominate the terrain defined at the time as revolutionary. The Marxism arriving in Cuba then was the depositary of "Stalinism without Stalin," which had developed in the Soviet Union after 1956. It had declared Western Marxism and all other heterodoxies to be nonexistent. From that point on, the broad outline of what is understood in the early 2000s as Marxism-Leninism in Cuba took shape. The critical Marxist school was thus limited in its expression. Its main intellectual centers were closed in 1971: the Philosophy Department of the University of Havana and *Pensamiento Crítico*. This journal disseminated critical Marxism (banned in the Soviet Union) and kept watch on Third World geopolitics and, in general, the problems of the underdeveloped world, specifically those of Latin America. That inspiration lives on in *Criterios* and *Temas*, journals that promote critical Marxism in Cuba in the early twenty-first century.

HOPES AND DISAPPOINTMENTS

Socialism, in the sense of social justice, was the foundation that allowed an accumulation of the sort of force and attitudes necessary to prevent the defeat of the Revolution and facilitate the development of an expansive revolutionary process (Martínez Heredia). For this reason it fostered great hope. The leadership decisively expanded the social base of the Revolution: It nationalized land, petroleum refineries, sugar, electricity, telephones, cement, banking, international business, and non-sugar industries; it renewed public life by outlawing prostitution, illegal gambling, and usury; it condemned sexual and racial discrimination; it approved urban reform, developed the literacy campaign, and created the Contingente de Médicos Rurales (brigade of rural doctors); it increased employment opportunities and minimum wages and promoted an economic policy with the control of exchange rates and imports and by seeking out new markets; it resisted the successive attempts by U.S. administrations to undermine the Revolution; and it consolidated consensus for its political position. For leftist sectors, Cuban socialism destroyed the Monroe Doctrine, displayed the advantage of guerrilla warfare over regular armies, contested the assumptions of semicolonial capitalism, articulated the Third World, and corrected the Eurocentric extremes of Marxism. In this way of understanding, the Cuban Revolution was key to the birth of a new Latin America, thanks to its influence on the establishment of the Alliance for Progress (1961) and the developmental policies of the U.N. Economic Commission for Latin America and the Caribbean, its denunciation of the illegitimacy of foreign debt in the 1980s, and the shifting toward the left of the political center of Latin America, visible after 1999.

Nevertheless, the Cuban vision had its setbacks as well. The Marxists Leo Huberman (1903–1968), Paul Sweezy (1910–2004), and Adolfo Gilly (b. 1928) criticized the Cuban mixture of *personalismo* (the glorification of a single leader) and bureaucracy. As they explained it, the former would periodically denounce the latter, destroying the limits that the bureaucracy could set in the face of expanding personal power. Certain characteristics being assumed by the Cuban model were interpreted as Soviet by Western socialists K. S. Karol and René Dumont (1904–2001). Jorge Edwards (b. 1931) added others characteristics in the field of culture to the list. In 1965, Theodore Draper wrote a classic thesis describing his position, which coincided with the perspective of the U.S. State Department: Castroismo was a leader in search of a movement, a movement in search of power, and power in search of an ideology.

Among the authoritarian and pro-Soviet indications were the following: the influence of pro-Soviet Cubans in guiding the revolutionary process; the characterization of ideological dissent as treasonous and the work of so-called the enemy; the officialized nature of all speeches; the legitimacy conferred on Marxism-Leninism and social realism; the reduction of political and civic rights; the linking of country, revolution and socialism; the *burocratismo* (bureaucratization) of the revolutionary process; the high concentration of power in top leadership; the consolidation of the management styles of particular individuals; *voluntarismo* (volunteerism); and monopoly of state property. These interpretations agree on the following common point: Cuban socialism is one applied from above that has established the sovereignty of central power and the absolute priority of the official line while limiting citizen-based organizing.

POSSIBLE DIRECTIONS

The debate around the possible directions that socialism could take was revisited in 1986 by the country leadership, intellectual groups, and the general public in order to correct so-called deviations imported from Moscow. A new conceptualization was expressed in the 1992 constitutional reform that allowed for a renewed socialism with a greater degree of popular participation, the democratic regulation of the market, political freedom and social justice (Valdés Paz). Alternately, it was argued that it provided for the transition to a commercial capitalist regime, given its regulation of property (Domínguez). Other debates marked the first decade of the new century. An opposition platform, with international support, sought to present a social democratic-style proposal, known as Proyecto Varela (Varela Project) to parliament. Parliament judged this proposal to be "antisystemic" and responded by reforming the constitution in 2002 and declaring the "irreversible" nature of the socialism it ratified. In 2006, Fidel Castro stepped down from his government position because of illness, renewing the debate.

In light of this history, it is worth considering scenarios for the future, including, but not limited to, an opening up of socialism, political inflexibility and restriction, the adoption of a Chinese or Vietnamese-style socialist market economy, a collapse or implosion similar to that in the Soviet Union and its satellites, and the overthrow of the government because of a military invasion by the United States or a domestic rebellion (López Segrera). These scenarios could lead to a variety of political models: democratic participatory socialism; market Stalinism; or social democratic or neoliberal capitalism.

The revolutionary hope of Cuban socialists has always been based on one of José Martí's theses: National independence must be bonded with Cubans' personal and social independence. In the early 2000s, that thesis must converse with the agenda of global socialism: ecopolitics, social diversity, economy as a function of life, grassroots democracy, and an international order based on solidarity. As of 2010, the island was full of ideologies that answered more to the political cultures of the time than to categories based in the origins of socialism and communism. Future practice will show if socialism becomes a meeting place for such ideologies. If so, a lack of dialogue would ensure that it becomes a sober, sterile model. In the presence of dialogue, one could anticipate the reinvention of Cuban socialism.

BIBLIOGRAPHY

Cairo, Ana. "Un requiem marxista para la Revolución del 30." Introduction to *Álgebra y Política*, by Pablo de la Torriente Brau. Havana: Centro Cultural Pablo de la Torriente Brau, 2001.

Castro, Fidel. *Fidel Castro: Antología mínima.* Edited by David Deutschmann and Deborah Shnookal. New York: Ocean Sur, 2008.

Domínguez, Jorge I. *Cuba hoy: Analizando su pasado, imaginando su futuro.* Madrid: Colibrí, 2006.

Draper, Theodore. *Castroism: Theory and Practice.* New York: Praeger, 1965.

Dumont, Rene. *Cuba ¿es socialista?* Caracas: Editorial Tiempo Nuevo, 1970.

Edwards, Jorge. *Persona non grata.* Barcelona: Barral Editores, 1973.

Fernández, Frank. *El anarquismo en Cuba.* Madrid: Fundación de Estudios Libertarios Anselmo Lorenzo, 2000.

Gilly, Adolfo. "Cuba entre la Coexistencia y la Revolución." *Monthly Review* (Buenos Aires) 15, November 1964.

Guanche, Julio César. *El continente de lo posible: Un examen sobre la condición revolucionaria.* Havana: Ruth Casa Editorial/Instituto Cubano de Investigación Cultural Juan Marinello, 2008.

Guevara, Ernesto, Ernest Mandel, Charles Bettelheim, et al. *El gran debate sobre la economía en Cuba 1963–1964.* Havana: Ocean Press, 2003.

Huberman, Leo, and Paul M. Sweezy. *Socialism in Cuba.* New York: Monthly Review Press, 1969.

Karol, K. S. *Los guerrilleros en el poder: Itinerario político de la revolución cubana.* Barcelona: Seix Barral, 1972.

López Segrera, Francisco. *La Revolución cubana: Raíces históricas, situación actual, propuestas, escenarios y alternativas.* Barcelona: El viejo topo, 2010.

Stoner, K. Lynn. *From the House to the Streets: The Cuban Woman's Movement for Legal Reform, 1898–1940.* Durham, NC: Duke University Press, 1991.

Martínez Heredia, Fernando. *En el horno de los noventa.* Havana: Editorial Ciencias Sociales, 2005.

Ribeiro, Darcy. "No tener miedo a pensar." *Casa de las Américas* 176 (September–October, 1989).

Rojas, Rafael. *El estante vacío: Literatura y política en Cuba.* Barcelona: Anagrama, 2009.

Rojas Blaquier, Angelina. *El primer Partido Comunista de Cuba.* 2 vols. Santiago de Cuba: Editorial Oriente, 2005–2006.

Soler Martínez, Rafael. "Cuba: comunismo y trotskismo en la revolución del 30." *Santiago* 92 (2001).

Valdés Paz, Juan. *El espacio y el límite: Estudios sobre el sistema político cubano.* Havana: Instituto Cubano de Investigación Cultural Juan Marinello/Panamá: Ruth Casa Editorial, 2009.

CUENTOS NEGROS DE CUBA (LYDIA CABRERA)

Julia Cuervo Hewitt

Cuentos negros de Cuba *and the imaginative rediscovery of the world of Afro-Cuban myths and lore through short stories and fables.*

Lydia Cabrera's *Cuentos negros de Cuba* (Black Stories from Cuba), published in 1936, has had a lasting impact on Cuban literature, ethnological studies, and discourses on Cuban culture and national identity. *Cuentos negros de Cuba* carved a space in Cuban literature for African traditions, myths, rituals, and belief systems that were part of local memories and popular beliefs still unexplored at the time. African legacies in Cuba had been excluded from discourses on the nation by the image of Cuba as a Hispanic society.

Ever since the publication of *Los negros brujos* (Black Sorcerers, 1906), by the anthropologist Fernando Ortiz, Cuban artists and writers had been interested in expressing Afro-Cuba in what came to be known as *negrism* or the *negrismo* movement. However, far from the representations of black Cubans and Afro-Cuban religious rituals by white artists, Cabrera's text was an imaginative rediscovery of oral traditions that were as much Cuban as African. *Cuentos negros de Cuba* was a celebration of the various African traditions in Cuban society.

HISTORY

The text was published first in French translation (*Contes nègres de Cuba*) in Paris in 1936, and then in Havana in 1940, with a prologue by Ortiz. Cabrera said that some of the twenty-three short stories and

■ *See also*

Cuban Counterpoint: Tobacco and Sugar (Fernando Ortiz)

Faith: Abakuá Society

Language: Lucumí

Literature: Fiction in the Republican Period

Race: Afro-Cubanía in the Republic, 1907–1959

Lydia Cabrera (1900–1991). Lydia Cabrera, shown here (second from right) with Afro-Cubans who contributed to her research, carved a space in Cuban literature for the African traditions, myths, and rituals that were part of local memories and popular beliefs. COURTESY OF THE CUBAN HERITAGE COLLECTION, UNIVERSITY OF MIAMI LIBRARIES, CORAL GABLES, FLORIDA

fables in this collection were stories she heard as a child from her nanny and other servants. It is possible that she also heard some of them at the Afro-Cuban community of Pogolotti, where Cabrera began her research on Afro-Cuban religions in the 1920s. The texts are not simple transcriptions of what she heard, as Ortiz proposes, but rather imaginative reconstructions, making use of avant-garde techniques, of a syncretic world of myths and beliefs, traditional European folklore, and oral anecdotes, some of them traceable to Africa.

Cabrera began to write the short stories in *Cuentos negros de Cuba* to entertain her friend, the Venezuelan writer Teresa de la Parra (1889–1936), who was convalescing with tuberculosis. De la Parra died the same year *Contes nègres de Cuba* was published in Paris. Cabrera had been living in Europe since 1927, where she went to study visual art. It is not surprising, then, that her adaptations and reconstructions of the stories she had heard of Afro-Cuban myths and lore would reflect avant-garde styles and literary currents in vogue in the 1920s and 1930s: expressionism, cubism, and especially surrealism. But she also brought to her short stories the irony, sarcasm, and humor typical of Cuban popular culture. After De la Parra's death and the beginning of the civil war in Spain in 1936, Cabrera returned to Cuba and continued her ethnological research on Afro-Cuban religions. In 1948, in Havana, she published a second collection of Afro-Cuban short stories, *¿Por qué? Cuentos negros de Cuba*, in which she included similar fables and short stories on the same themes as in the first collection. In these, however, the avant-garde techniques with which she had experimented earlier gave way to a blend of subtle poetry, popular expressions, and careful documentation, filtered through her imagination.

CHARACTERS

Most of the characters in *Cuentos negros de Cuba* are comparable to animals in African lore and traceable to Afro-Cuban religious anecdotes known as *patakíes*, mythical-religious stories of deities in the Yoruba-Lucumí tradition. Cabrera's representations of them, however, are products of her creativity and poetic imagination.

One of Cabrera's most endearing and complex characters is Hicotea (or Jicotea), a land turtle. Hicotea is Cabrera's adaptation of the mythical African tortoise, the cultural trickster in Yoruba oral traditions, to a Cuban–Afro-Cuban context. Decades later Cabrera dedicated an entire collection of fables, *Ayapá: Cuentos de Jicotea* (1971), to this character, known as Ayapá in the Afro-Cuban Lucumí tradition. However, it was in *Cuentos negros de Cuba* that Cabrera first transformed the complex African trickster (always male) into a *criollo* female, a *comadre*, or comical, lecherous old neighbor who is always envious of others.

This version of Hicotea allows Cabrera to make fun of powerful male figures with social and political authority, such as the Tiger in "Taita Tigre y Taita Hicotea." Here, the small, weak land turtle, Hicotea, uses her wits and malicious machinations to overpower Tiger, despite his physical strength and authority. In "El caballo de Hicotea" (Hicotea's horse), Hicotea is able to convince Horse, her equal, to become her beast of burden. In contrast, Cabrera portrays the female Hicotea as a scoundrel in "Osaín de un pie" (One-foot Osaín), a story faithful to Lucumí traditions and religious beliefs. After fooling a couple, Hicotea begins to eat yams she has stolen from them but is outwitted by the orisha Osaín, in the Lucumí tradition the ancient wisdom or natural forces of the forest.

Some of the stories in *Cuentos negros de Cuba* are variations of anecdotes still circulating in Africa in the early 2000s. "Chéggue" is a variation on a Nigerian song, and "La loma de Mambiala" (Mambiala's Hill) is an anecdote told in many variations and in different contexts, as in the novel *The Palm-Wine Drinkard*, by the Nigerian writer Amos Totuola (1920–1997). Cabrera's fables and stories range from mythical settings, as in "Walo-Wila," to African settings, as in "Chéggue," to vernacular Cuban Creole settings, as in "Apopoito Miama" and "Los compadres." In keeping with the patakíes, in the story "Bregantino Bregantín" Lucumí orishas help overthrow the dictatorial reign of Bull and reestablish order and freedom. Cabrera's lyrical accomplishments are evident in this collection as in the representation of an accomplished love portrayed by the reflection of the rays of the moon over the calm ocean waters ("cuando se besan la luna y el mar"), in "Walo Wila."

MAIN THEMES

Cabrera presents a vision proper of Afro-Cuban belief systems, with the Lucumí predominant, but often she does so from the point of view of the colonial slave. Thus, freedom is a recurring theme. "Chéggue" speaks of boundaries and of the delicate balance of nature, the forces of the forest that humans must respect. In "El caballo de Hicotea," Cabrera constructs a poetics of freedom in the nostalgia of Horse for a time of equality and liberty in which he was his own owner. Horse's loss of freedom causes him to lose his sanity. In "La carta de libertad" (Freedom letter), a fable of why things are the way they are, Dog loses the letter certifying his freedom and is thus destined to be a slave for the rest of his life. In "Suadende," a humorous story about infidelity, Suadende is able to gain her freedom from her extremely jealous husband, who has enclosed her in a remote forest, by running away with another man. Transgression in *Cuentos negros de Cuba* is always punished, but in this case, the writer makes the transgressor not the wife who is guilty of infidelity but the husband who robs his wife of freedom. In "Los compadres," Dolé's infidelity is punished with death, but in "Apopoito Miama," the seductive mulatto woman who steals other women's husbands is saved at the last moment before death by the magic of nature, a crab that hears her lament.

The last short story of the collection, "El sapo guardiero," offers a poetics of love and care. Its characters are an evil witch, tiny twins, and the Old Toad, who represents the ancient spirit of the forest. The Old Toad is a *guardiero*; in slavery times a *guardiero* was an old slave who had become too weak to work and so was sent to live and stand guard at the edge of the forest bordering the plantation. The guardiero slave in Cuban literature is often an icon of ancient African wisdom and knowledge. Cabrera's Old Toad represents ancient wisdom as well as the benevolent forces of the forest, like the orishas in "Bregantino Bregantín"; he is able to save the mythical twins from the evil witch. In a timeless story of good overpowering evil, love is the force that awakens the ancient Toad. "El sapo guardiero" exemplifies the dynamics between power and resistance that are often at play in Cabrera's work, as well as the constant struggle between opposing principles as conceived in Lucumí Afro-Cuban lore.

SYNCRETISM AND HUMOR

"El sapo guardiero" is an example of a religious syncretism characteristic of Cuban society and reflected in Cabrera's fiction. The Old Toad and the twins are based on symbols from the Lucumí belief system in Cuba, whereas the witch is the traditional evil force of European folklore who, like the witch in *Hansel and Gretel*, wants to kill the twins. However, in Cabrera's story the witch is Palera, a Congo practitioner whose magic coincides with Afro-Cuban Palo-Monte rituals. This short story addresses, through the use of irony and religious references, the rivalry that existed in Cuba between Lucumí and Congo belief systems.

Humor in *Cuentos negros de Cuba* is often based on the syncretism it portrays and the juxtaposition of the real and the unreal, the natural and the supernatural, and the colloquial and the learned. Cabrera offers a typical Cuban Creole social context in which African deities and mythical animals coexist, as they do in Lucumí patakíes. She also uses paradox, hyperbole, and absurd images to establish a timeless world in which the impossible is possible and the surreal is real. For example, in "Taita Hicotea y Taita Tigre," the character of Frog at one time had hair and used to perm her hair. Cabrera presents Afro-Cuban religious references, beliefs, symbols, rituals, and deities as part of daily life in a Cuban Creole world. At the same time, humor establishes a distance between the reader and the mythical-magical narrated world. Humor, at times sarcastic, also allows the narrator to criticize society and its vices: arrogance, prejudice, false authority, unmerited power, envy, and jealousy. Cuban society is seen through the eyes of the marginalized and the weak, but also through the eyes of the mischievous author.

Cuentos negros de Cuba, a verbal collage of cultural modes typically Cuban, immediately established Lydia Cabrera's literary talent. Her knowledge of Afro-Cuban lore and religious beliefs and celebration through stories of the rhythm and vitality of the African legacy in Cuba earned Cabrera a permanent place in Cuban literature. *Cuentos negros de Cuba* stands as a watershed moment in Cuban literature.

BIBLIOGRAPHY

Cabrera, Lydia. *Cuentos negros de Cuba.* 2nd ed. Madrid: Ramos, Artes Gráficas, 1972.

Cabrera, Lydia. *¿Por qué? Cuentros negros de Cuba.* 2nd ed. Madrid: Ramos, Artes Gráficas, 1972.

Cabrera, Lydia. *Afro-Cuban Tales (Cuentos negros de Cuba).* Translated by Alberto Hernández-Chiroldes and Lauren Yoder. Lincoln: University of Nebraska Press, 2004.

Carpentier, Alejo. "Cuentos negros de Lydia Cabrera." *Carteles* 28, no. 41 (1936): 40.

Cruz Varela, María Elena. "Arere Marekén: Cuento negro de Lydia Cabrera." *Revista Hispano-Cubana* 10 (Spring/Summer 2001): 85–88.

Cuervo Hewitt, Julia. *Aché, Presencia Africana: Tradiciones Yoruba-Lucumí en la narrativa cubana.* New York: Peter Lang, 1988.

Cuervo Hewitt, Julia. *Voices Out of Africa in Twentieth-Century Spanish Caribbean Literature.* Lewisburg, PA: Bucknell University Press, 2009.

Gutiérrez, Mariela A. *Lydia Cabrera: Aproximaciones mítico-simbólicas a su cuentística.* Madrid: Verbum, 1997.

Gutiérrez, Mariela A. *An Ethnological Interpretation of the Afro-Cuban World of Lydia Cabrera (1900–1991).* Lewiston, NY: Edwin Mellen Press, 2008.

Hiriart, Rosario. "El tiempo y los símbolos en *Cuento negros de Cuba.*" In *Homenaje a Lydia Cabrera*, edited by Reinaldo Sánchez, José Antonio Madrigal, Ricardo Viera, and José Sánchez-Boudy. Miami: Ediciones Universal, 1978.

Marks, Morton. "Exploring *El monte*: Ethnobotany and the Afro-Cuban Science of the Concrete." In *En torno a Lydia Cabrera: Cincuentenario de* Cuentos negros de Cuba: *1936–1986*, edited by Isabel Castellanos and Josefina Inclán. Miami: Ediciones Universal, 1987.

Novas Calvo, Lino. "Los cuentos de Lydia Cabrera." *Exilio* 3, no. 2 (1969): 17–20.

Ortiz, Fernando. *Los negros brujos.* [1906.] Havana: Editorial de Ciencias Sociales, 1995.

Perera Soto, Hilda. *Idapo: El sincretismo en los cuentos negros de Lydia Cabrera.* Miami: Ediciones Universal, 1971.

Rodríguez-Mangual, Edna M. *Lydia Cabrera and the Construction of an Afro-Cuban Cultural Identity.* Chapel Hill: University of North Carolina Press, 2004.

Soto, Sara. *Magia e historia en los "Cuentos negros,""¿Por qué?," y "Ayapá" de Lydia Cabrera.* Miami: Ediciones Universal, 1988.

Valdés-Cruz, Rosa. *Lo ancestral africano en la narrativa de Lydia Cabrera.* Barcelona: Vosgos, 1974.

Valdés-Cruz, Rosa. "Los cuentos de Lydia Cabrera: ¿Transposiciones of creaciones?" In *Homenaje a Lydia Cabrera*, edited by Reinaldo Sánchez, José Antonio Madrigal, Ricardo Viera, and José Sánchez-Boudy. Miami: Ediciones Universal, 1978.

Valdés-Cruz, Rosa. "El mundo del folklore en Lydia Cabrera: Su técnica narrativa." In *En torno a Lydia Cabrera: Cincuentenario de* Cuentos Negros de Cuba: *1936–1986*, edited by Isabel Castellanos and Josefina Inclán. Miami: Ediciones Universal, 1987.

D

DE DONDE SON LOS CANTANTES (SEVERO SARDUY)

Gustavo Guerrero

De donde son los cantantes *and the writing and rewriting of Cuban discourses in the time of* Tel Quel *and the Neo-baroque.*

Severo Sarduy (1937–1993) began writing his novel of *De donde son los cantantes* (From Cuba with a Song, 1967) in 1964 in Paris, having left Cuba five years earlier in December 1959 with a scholarship to study art history in Europe. It did not take him long to settle himself in the French capital and become an active part of Parisian literary life. His encounter with the philosopher and publisher François Wahl (b. 1925), who later became his companion, is among the biographical details that explain Sarduy's rapid success in literary circles. In the early 1960s, Wahl introduced the new arrival into the group of authors and intellectuals who gravitated toward the Editions du Seuil, where Wahl, one of its founders, edited the philosophy, psychoanalysis, and social sciences lists. The connections facilitated by Wahl allowed Sarduy to meet figures such as Jacques Lacan (1901–1981) and Roland Barthes (1915–1980), as well as the group of young novelists and theorists who had recently founded the journal *Tel Quel*. Sarduy became a member of the highly animated French intellectual scene, participating in its discussions and debates and quickly becoming a habitué of the cafés of Saint-Germain-des-Prés.

GENETIC BACKGROUND

The creation of *De donde son los cantantes* is closely tied to this period in Sarduy's life and work. One of his German friends in Paris, the journalist and art critic Werner Spies (b. 1937), helped Sarduy obtain a commission to write a radio play for the Süddeutscher Rundfunk (SDR) in Stuttgart in 1964. Sarduy began working on it in the spring, and within a few months, he had completed a reworking of the tragic story of Dolores Rondón, a popular figure in the Cuban city of Camagüey. Rondón was among the many avatars of the archetypal Cuban mulatto woman, a recurrent figure in the island's literature since Cirilo Villaverde's *Cecilia Valdés* (1839). Well before returning as the subject of a central chapter of *De donde son los cantantes*, Dolores Rondón was thus the basis for a play Sarduy composed for German radio. The play's melodramatic tone must have found a receptive audience among the SDR listeners, because the drama was the first in a series of similar commissions that launched Sarduy's career as a playwright.

According to French genetic criticism, every text bears the traces of its genesis and is to some extent the effect of the conditions under which it is produced. It is possible to read the 1964 commission as presaging what later became *De donde son los cantantes*. On one hand, the novel adheres to a certain Cuban literary tradition that, as in *Cecilia Valdés*, explores the question of collective identity, which unites the disparate elements of Cuba's insular society. On the other hand, it defies and subverts this same national tradition, not by proposing a new model of novelistic or theatrical writing, but by theatricalizing novelistic writing itself, producing a narrative that is an autoreflexive, metafictional object that serves as the vehicle for a critique of representation.

Since its publication in 1967, *De donde son los cantantes* has been interpreted essentially along these two lines. Sarduy's first novel, *Gestos* (1963), clearly belongs to the same tradition of Revolution narratives as Guillermo Cabrera Infante's *Así en la paz como en la guerra* (1960) and *Los años duros* (1966), by Jesús Díaz. But Sarduy's second novel went considerably further in search of a literary lineage. As Roberto González Echevarría observed, it represents a response to the contemporary discourses surrounding the questions of Cuban and Latin American identity that were central to cultural debates about the meaning of the

Author Severo Sarduy (1937–1993) in Paris, 1986. Severo Sarduy's novel *De donde son los cantantes,* published in 1967, reconfigures the traditional elements that contributed to the rise of the Cuban nation and the formation of a Latin American identity. ULF ANDERSEN/GETTY IMAGES

Revolution and the international success of the novelists of the boom that followed it (González Echevarría pp. 98–135).

CUBAN IDENTITY AND TRADITION

In at least three respects, Sarduy's novel constitutes a profound critical break with traditional ways of treating identity issues. The first is the way in which Sarduy reconfigured the three traditional elements that supposedly contributed to the rise of the Cuban nation and the formation of a Latin American identity. After reworking his play about Dolores Rondón to form the basis of the novel's chapter on the African element ("The Dolores Rondón"), he added a chapter on the Chinese of Cuba ("Junto al río de cenizas de Rosa") and another on the Spanish contribution ("La entrada de Cristo en La Habana") before composing the introductory chapter ("Curriculum cubense") and his closing "Note" (Wahl p. 1479). The unexpected chapter on Chinese culture, which occupies the space traditionally reserved for the Taíno aborigines in conventional discussions of Cuban identity, was initially greeted with surprise and even skepticism. As Sarduy confirmed in several interviews, his intention was to question the value of conventional historical narratives about identity while also highlighting the mechanisms of racial exclusion that were used against the Chinese community (Rodríguez Monegal p. 274). Not only had the Chinese been exploited and marginalized throughout the island's history, but their contributions to the formation of modern Cuba were

simply ignored. Sarduy had spent time in Havana's Chinatown during the 1950s familiarizing himself with the plight of Chinese immigrants to the point of identifying closely with them and even claiming Chinese origins for his own family. Incorporating the Chinese into *De donde son los cantantes* was a conscious, voluntary, and completely deliberate choice within Sarduy's critical perspective in the same way that his description of Cuba itself in the book's "Note" represents Cuba as composed of three superimposed cultures instead of a blended culture or cultural *métissage* (miscegenation).

Indeed, the second traditional configuration blatantly challenged by the novel is the celebrated theory of métissage. Rather than following tradition by interpreting the relationships between the three cultures in terms of hybridization, mixing, and fusion, Sarduy's "Note" shows that he postulated the idea of their superimposition and even collage or juxtaposition. He returned later to this question in other texts, such as an essay dedicated to José Lezama Lima (Sarduy 1968, p. 11), but the principle remained constant. The three groups did not give birth to some kind of "cosmic race" in Cuba (to use José Vasconcelos's famous title); instead, they formed relatively airtight blocks or entities that were superimposed on each other, somewhat like the earth's geological strata, without dissolving in a transcultural dynamic of reciprocal give-and-take. As a consequence, the celebration of social, racial, and ethnic equality vaunted by conventional views of the origins of the Cuban nation loses one of its major ideological underpinnings at Sarduy's hands. Furthermore, the very unity of the nation is revealed to be a sham, as is the fraternity between the different groups upon which it depends. Arguably, nothing illustrates Sarduy's opposition to the prevailing discourses with greater clarity than the novel's organization into three chapters that correspond to three cultures that do not necessarily comprise a coherent or organic whole (Guicharnaud-Tollis p. 123).

Sarduy's third break with convention relates directly to the status of the national discourses, which are revealed in *De donde son los cantantes* to be devoid of any rhetorical or historical effectiveness or even any basis for claiming to be the truth about the ties that unite the members of a community. By the time he was writing the novel, Sarduy had been involved with the *Tel Quel* circle for several years, and he regularly attended Roland Barthes's seminars at the École Pratique des Hautes Études de Paris. In fact, Sarduy became close friends with Barthes early in the 1960s, conversing and exchanging ideas with him almost daily. Barthes's perspectives on the relationships between language and society and the forms of representation that establish bridges between them were assimilated into Sarduy's writing very early on, and their influence is stamped on the novel through the transformation of the question of identity into the imaginary object and fantasmatic space of a vast *mythology* in the Barthesian sense of the term. This allowed Sarduy a certain distance from the problematics of identity then at the heart of Cuban and Latin American literary debates, thereby removing the appearance of naturalness that surrounded them so that he could reveal the profound ideological stakes that were involved.

SARDUY'S NEO-BAROQUE

The conception of writing that governed the composition of *De donde son los cantantes* pursued a number of Barthes's ideas, and in turn, it also provided Barthes with some ideas, such as how he first approaches the concept of *jouissance* in his well-known review of the novel (Barthes pp. 15–31). But as "La Dolores Rondón" illustrates, Sarduy drew on the theater and more broadly from baroque Hispanic literature, as the source of the strategy of unmasking illusion and inverting signs that runs through the entire novel (Guerrero pp. 29–46). In 1966, Sarduy published an article in *Tel Quel* on the poetry of Luis de Góngora, which underscored the importance of the baroque paradigm to his thinking at the time. The article illustrates how the baroque served Sarduy as the historical and cultural basis of his critique of representation in modern western literature (Sarduy 1966). The article also was an example of self-conscious, autoreflexive textual production well before it became commonplace, and it is unsurprising that *De donde son los cantantes* strikes the reader as a playful, self-mirroring, decentered artifact in which the stock baroque device of the play within a play is translated via a metafictional turn into the novel within a novel. Sarduy's goal was to critically and simultaneously deconstruct both novelistic discourse and the discourses of Cuban identity, treating them first and foremost as discourses, in other words as clusters of signs, conventions, and scriptural processes and procedures.

The theory of the Latin-American neo-baroque that Sarduy presented in a long article a few years later (Sarduy 1972) derived from this rereading of Góngora and the Hispanic baroque and from Barthes's ideas and those of the *Tel Quel* group. The latter provided the theoretical framework and the concept of textual writing centered on the material and linguistic reality of the text and indifferent to the mimesis of any contents, external or internal, developed by the subjectivity of the author or by his characters. For this reason, the use of reference in *De donde son los cantantes* reveals a will to parody that portrays a theatrical world that is comical and often grotesque. Thus, the overt setting of the final chapter, "Junto al río de cenizas de Rosa," is the formerly celebrated Shanghai, a burlesque theater in Havana's Chinatown, whereas the source for the second chapter, "La Dolores Rondón," is a radio play, and the third chapter, "La entrada de Cristo en la Habana," adopts the form of a carnival parade to narrate the voyage of the three protagonists from deep in Andalusia to the Cuban capital. Furthermore, the title of the third chapter alludes to both James Ensor's painting *L'entrée du Christ à Bruxelles* (1889) and the arrival of Fidel Castro and his *guérilleros* in Havana in January 1959.

In reality, Sarduy summons multiple references without clearly distinguishing them from one another; these include recent and remote Cuban historical events, popular traditions such as Chinese charades, dizain poetry, and Catholic and Afro-Cuban imagery. Most importantly, in his own crazy way, Sarduy uses these and a host of other elements to build a novel whose central topic is the question of identity and its many discourses. In this sense, the forceful, assertive *De donde son los cantantes*—a title taken from the famous *son de la loma* of the Trio Matamoros—signals its aspiration to provide an answer to the Cuban nation's search for its roots. But it is an answer that theatricalizes and demystifies the search itself by reducing it to the search for an illusion or for something whose existence is entirely impossible. This is what the two principal protagonists, in a nod to Heidegger, proceed to tell us, with the failure of their visit to the House of God and their multiple metamorphoses in "Curriculum cubense." Whether it is a question of national identity or other identitary forms, to believe in an ultimate foundation and in the ostensible stability that it could provide is to pursue a delusion or a mirage. Or to cite Roland Barthes, it is merely a mythology that nourishes the always dangerous links between literature, representation, and power.

BIBLIOGRAPHY

Barthes, Roland. "Sarduy: La face baroque." *La Quinzaine Littéraire* n 15, Paris: 28 (1967): 13.

González Echevarría, Roberto. *La ruta de Severo Sarduy.* Hanover, NH: Ediciones del Norte, 1987.

Guerrero, Gustavo. *La estrategia neobarroca.* Barcelona: Edicions del Mall, 1987.

Guicharnaud-Tollis, Michèle. "Ecriture et révolution dans *De donde son los cantantes*." In *Le néo-baroque cubain*, edited by Néstor Ponce. Paris: Editions du Temps, 1997.

Rodríguez Monegal, Emir. *El arte de narrar.* Caracas: Monte Avila Editores, 1977.

Sarduy. Severo. "Sur Góngora." *Tel Quel* 25 (1966): 91–93.

Sarduy. Severo. "Dispersión/Falsas notas (homenaje a Lezama Lima)." *Mundo Nuevo* 24 (1968).

Sarduy. Severo. "El barroco y el neobarroco." In *América Latina en su literatura*, edited by César Fernández Moreno. México: Siglo XXI, 1972.

Sarduy. Severo. *De donde son los cantantes* (1967). Edited by Roberto González Echevarría. Madrid: Cátedra, 1993.

Sarduy. Severo. *Obra completa I y II.* Edited by Gustavo Guerrero and François Wahl. Madrid : Colección Archivos, 1999.

Wahl, François. "Severo de la rue Jacob." In *Obra completa I y II*, by Severo Sarduy. Edited by Gustavo Guerrero and François Wahl. Madrid: Colección Archivos, 1999.

DÍA DE REYES EN LA HABANA (VÍCTOR PATRICIO DE LANDALUZE)

E. Carmen Ramos

A nineteenth-century painting of a Cuban custom supporting a conservative political agenda through racist imagery.

Día de Reyes en la Habana (Three Kings Day in Havana) is one of the best-known nineteenth-century depictions of the Epiphany in Cuba. Painted by the Spaniard Víctor Patricio de Landaluze (1828–1889) likely in the early to mid-1870s, it depicts a local variant of the annual Christian celebration held on 6 January in remembrance of the day when the three kings arrived, bearing gifts to the infant Jesus. As the central scene of the painting readily conveys, in colonial Cuba the Epiphany was commonly associated with slaves and free persons of color who came together for a free day of carnival-like celebration. On this day Afro-Cubans would parade and perform in urban centers—especially Havana—and ask spectators for an *aguinaldo* or Christmas tip. Indeed, this richly detailed painting provides a glimpse of sorts into nineteenth-century Cuba, especially the African diasporic traditions deemed a colorful and exotic facet of colonial daily life. Most scholarship notes and celebrates the ways in which Landaluze captured ethnographic elements of African diasporic culture on the island, but it may be more historically accurate to consider *Dia de Reyes en la Habana* as an indictment of nineteenth-century Cuban society in general and Afro-Cuban culture in particular.

Landaluze was a caricaturist and painter who arrived in Cuba in the mid-nineteenth century and became one of the foremost practitioners of *costumbrismo*, a literary and visual genre in which the character types and customs of a given nation or territory were captured in realistic detail. While there is some debate as to when Landaluze actually arrived in Cuba, archival records in Spain place him there by 1850. Over the course of his thirty-nine-year residence on the island, Landaluze led a paradoxical and multifaceted life and artistic career. Between 1850 and the 1870s, he was affiliated with the volunteer Spanish military force on the island, *los Voluntarios*, which actively defended Spanish colonialism. Starting in 1857 and continuing through the late 1880s, he was a leading caricaturist for and publisher of conservative satirical journals known for their anti-Cuban independence leanings. He also illustrated the two major costumbrista anthologies published on the island: *Los Cubanos pintados por si mismos* (Cubans Depicted by Themselves, 1852), and

the *Tipos y costumbres de la isla de Cuba* (Types and Customs from the Island of Cuba, 1881). His illustrations for the first anthology barely represented distinctive types from the island, but *Tipos y costumbres* especially captured unique Afro-Cuban types such as the *mulata*, or woman of mixed African and European ancestry, and the *ñáñigo*, a member of an all-male Abakuá secret society founded in Cuba in the 1830s. The Afro-Cuban subject of *Día de Reyes en la Habana* more closely relates to this latter period in Landaluze's life and artistic production. The irony of Landaluze's career stems from his own Spanish loyalist political persuasions and the ways in which his work has come to be viewed by later scholars as affirming Cuba's unique culture.

THE IMAGERY OF *DIA DE REYES*

In *Día de Reyes en la Habana*, Landaluze undoubtedly captured aspects of the Epiphany celebration that specifically relate to *cabildo* organizations. *Cabildos* were mutual aid societies sanctioned by the Spanish government that allowed slaves of the same African cultural group to meet and gain emotional sustenance and other sources of support during times of need. These groups helped preserve and reproduce African-based traditions in the New World. In the center foreground of the painting, Landaluze depicts a cabildo carnival group, or *comparsa*. The grouping encompasses the cabildo leadership, namely an extravagantly dressed king (or *capataz*), a queen parading under a parasol accompanied by her entourage, as well as drummers playing Congo-style *yuka* drums, and costumed revelers (Bettelheim p. 323). These revelers—referred to at the time by the disparaging term *diabilitos* or little devils—display African masquerading traditions re-created in Cuba. At the very center of the composition is a male reveler, who wears a feathered and horned headdress, as well as a generously wide vegetable fiber skirt—referred to at the time by the grammatically feminized term *la culona*. Fernando Ortiz has noted that it was once thought that *la culona*, which translates as "big-assed woman," took its name from the way the costume broadens the hips and buttocks of the wearer. Ortiz argued that "culona" was likely the Castilian pronunciation of the Malinke and Mindingo word *kulona*, which means wise and educated (Ortiz p. 25). Toward the right of the canvas, a *ñáñigo*, another costumed reveler not necessarily associated with cabildo life, stands near a stone wall requesting a tip from two female onlookers standing in a balcony above. This figure's pointy-headed and checkered ensemble is almost identical to ritual attires found and worn in parts of modern-day Nigeria and Cameroon (Thompson pp. 260–266). This culturally rich and meaningful detail, however, does not preclude other critical interpretations of this important painting.

Landaluze also carefully staged the scene to convey how African-based traditions were generally held in contempt by many island residents. By carefully composing a tableau of Afro-Cuban revelers and spatially separating white and black figures in the painting, Landaluze

suggests that these revelers lie outside Western norms and, therefore, civilized culture. In the far distance, the dome of a church topped with a cross looms high, providing a contrast between the sanctioned religiosity of Christianity and the profanity of African customs presented in the foreground. Landaluze's white onlookers are visually tethered to their corresponding architectural structure, thereby constituting a physical barrier between white and black. To the left in the canvas is a group of white figures standing behind a large gated and open window. This architectural feature serves to separate and distinguish them from the street-bound ruckus. These figures are not only separated by physical barriers, their bodies manifest the difference between white and black. The white woman, for example, stands erect (as if in disgust) as she extends her hand to place a tip in the king's top hat. This garlanded capataz, alternatively, wears a formal suit and stands in profile. In presenting him in such a way, Landaluze calls attention to his broad nose and

thick lips, nineteenth-century signifiers believed to reveal the primitive nature of African people. The presence of civilized whites, then, establishes the norm or the standard from which to judge the savagery of Afro-Cubans. Even westernized Afro-Cubans, such as the woman in the green dress in the center of the composition, disavow the other revelers. In response to the masked reveler who crouches on the ground on all four limbs, this female figure leans back, cringing, with bent arms and curled fingers as if to suggest fear and repulsion.

SPANISH CONSERVATIVES AND THE TEN YEARS' WAR

It is important to note that *Día de Reyes en la Habana* thematically relates to Landaluze's concurrent political caricatures that address Cuba's first major independence insurrection, the Ten Years' War (1868–1878). In one caricature from 17 October 1869 published in his own journal *Don Junípero*, Landaluze represented the first

Día de Reyes en la Habana (mid-1870s) by Víctor Patricio de Landaluze (1828–1889). *Día de Reyes en la Habana* (Three Kings Day in Havana), a painting by Spanish artist Víctor Patricio de Landaluze, depicts a colonial Cuban variant of the Christian celebration held on 6 January in remembrance of the day when the three kings arrived, bearing gifts for the infant Jesus. COLECCIÓN MUSEO NACIONAL DE BELLAS ARTES, LA HABANA, CUBA

leader of the insurrection, Carlos Manuel de Céspedes, and his supporters celebrating in the manner of Africans in Cuba. Shirtless and wearing a feather headdress and fiber skirt and shaking a pair of maracas, Céspedes is depicted as a *culona* who presides over a topsy-turvy Epiphany celebration in which drunkenness, bestiality, and miscegenation prevail. Caricatures such as this relate to Spanish arguments that the insurrection was a prelude to a race war that would establish a black republic in Cuba. Such provocative relationships between Landaluze's costumbrista painting and caricature suggest that the artist's contributions to Cuban art, culture, and history are indeed much more complex than previously thought. Far from passively ethnographic, Landaluze's work likely represents the artist's desire—and that of the larger, conservative Spanish community of which he was part—to malign Cuban independence efforts by resorting to the discourse of race.

BIBLIOGRAPHY

Bettelheim, Judith. "Caribbean Espiritismo (Spiritist) Altars: The Indian and the Congo." *Art Bulletin* 87, no. 2 (June 2005): 312–330.

Castellanos, Lázara. *Víctor Patricio Landaluze.* Havana: Letras Cubanas, 1991.

López Núñez, Olga. "Víctor Patricio de Landaluze: Sus Años en Cuba." In *Víctor Patricio Landaluze (1830–1889): Colección Museo Nacional de Bellas Artes de La Habana* (exhibition catalog). Bilbao, Spain: Museo de Bellas Artes de Bilbao, 1998.

Ortiz, Fernando. "The Afro-Cuban Festival 'Day of the Kings'," translated by Jean Stubbs. In *Cuban Festivals: A Century of Afro-Cuban Culture,* edited by Judith Bettelheim. Kingston, Jamaica: Ian Randle; Princeton, NJ: Markus Wiener, 2001.

Portuondo, José Antonio. "Landaluze y el costumbrismo en Cuba." *Revista de la Biblioteca Nacional José Martí,* no. 1 (January–April 1972): 51–83.

Sánchez, Reinaldo. "Don Junípero: Vehículo del Costumbrismo en Cuba." *Revista Iberoamericana* 56, no. 152–153 (July–December 1990): 759–768.

Sánchez Martínez, Guillermo. "Landaluze." *Universidad de la Habana*180 (July–August 1966): 83–92.

Thompson, Robert Farris. *Flash of the Spirit: African and Afro-American Art and Philosophy.* New York: Vintage, 1984.

DIÁLOGO AGREEMENT

Guillermo J. Grenier

Events and processes leading up to the Diálogo Agreement as well as the key economic, social and political ramifications.

In September 1978 Fidel Castro extended an invitation to the Cuban community living abroad in the United States, Mexico, Venezuela, and Spain to engage in communication with the Cuban government on issues of mutual interest. The resulting dialogue (*el diálogo* in Spanish) marked an important benchmark in the development of the Cuban American community in the United States as well as in United States–Cuba relations.

The decade of the 1970s had seen the rise of structural changes that offered the opportunity for the Cuban community in exile to become a transnational community. *El diálogo*—referring to the deliberations and negotiations that took place in 1978 between the Cuban exile community and the highest levels of the Cuban government with the U.S. government not too far behind the scene—was the iconic event of the decade. To understand the importance and repercussions of this event, some knowledge about the broader changes occurring during the 1970s is required.

CHANGES IN THE CUBAN AMERICAN COMMUNITY

Despite unresolved questions about the place of Cubans in U.S. society, the 1970 U.S. census reported that there were 560,628 Cubans in the United States, and of these, 252,520 lived in Florida. The post-revolutionary airlift program known as the Freedom Flights, also called the *puente aéreo* (air bridge), which ended in 1973, diversified the Cuban American population throughout the United States, but most of the impact was felt in South Florida. While the earlier refugees were fleeing the threats immediately posed by the Revolution, family reunification and a variety of other reasons motivated the exodus of many within this later group. In its first few years, the airlift brought the remnants of Cuba's upper classes, especially the elderly parents of those who had left in the earlier wave. But by the late 1960s, with the advent of sustained austerity in Cuba, the airlift started to peel away at the middle sectors of Cuba's social class structure: small entrepreneurs, skilled and semiskilled workers, and white-collar employees were leaving as well.

The new arrivals to the United States encountered a different expatriate community than those arriving in the 1960s. It was a community getting accustomed to its life in a new country. During the 1970s, the Cuban community in greater Miami began to acquire an ethnic identity. Civic engagement and concerns about making it in this country characterized much of the community. It was during this decade that the Cuban economic enclave emerged as a solidifying force for the community and the region. Citizenship applications, voter registration, and business activity were on the rise. Civic organizations emerged with Cuban leadership to shepherd the community through the obstacles of being an ethnic minority in the United States. Organizations arose openly proposing a more conciliatory approach to the island, and the community was expressing more openly a desire to try new ways of dealing with the island government. A 1996 study by María Cristina García cites a 1975 *Miami Herald* poll suggesting that 49.5 percent of Cuban émigrés, and presumably most of the later arrivals, would travel to the island if given a chance, and around 46 percent supported the establishment of trade and diplomatic relations with the island.

Among the academic community arose organizations that openly challenged the dominance of the right-wing exile ideology of intransigence and isolation. Perhaps the most significant of these early organizations was El Instituto de Estudios Cubanos, which was founded, and led until her death in 2010, by María Cristina Herrera, a professor at Miami-Dade Community College (later Miami Dade College). The institute brought together Cuban scholars educated on the island, many of whom had participated in the fight against Fulgencio Batista through Catholic youth organizations, as well as younger, U.S.-trained intellectuals who came to be known as *cubanologos*. From its initial meeting in 1969, the Instituto encouraged a plurality of perspectives toward Cuba and the Cuban government. It reflected the changing nature of the community in its openness to less antagonistic approaches to resolving the issues associated with exile.

Young Cubans were also changing the organizational landscape of the Cuban diaspora. Educated in the United States and socialized into the youth movement culture characterizing the 1960s and 1970s, young Cuban Americans organized around different issues from their parents. Some organized around the Cuba issue but, rather than promoting isolation, were interested in establishing and maintaining contact with Cuban Americans throughout the country as well as with the culture of the island as it was developing.

One group, called Areíto, consisting of young, mostly middle-class Cubans who had left the island as children and were raised in various parts of the United States, was among the first to break the isolation imposed on the island by the old-guard exiles. The first contingent of Areíto's Antonio Maceo Brigade (named after the mulatto general of the Cuban War of Independence) spent three weeks on the island in 1977 on what became a historic trip of return. The brigade became a symbol for those in the exile community. Some saw the members as the vanguard of the process of redefining the relationship between the exile community and the island government and inhabitants. Others saw them as traitors whose actions legitimized a dictatorial regime.

CHANGE IN U.S. POLICY

The U.S. policy toward Cuba mirrored the changing nature of the exile community. The geopolitical strategy of détente influenced the establishment of high-level talks, resulting in an anti-hijacking treaty between the two countries in 1973. The effectiveness of the embargo was questioned at the highest level. Several U.S. legislators traveled to the island in the mid-1970s, laying the groundwork for what appeared to be a thawing of relations between the two countries. International support for normalization increased when the Organization of American States voted to lift the embargo on the island in 1975.

The moves toward rapprochement gained more momentum during the Carter administration, as the countries reached agreement on conflicts over fishing rights and maritime boundaries and established interest sections in Havana and Washington that provided limited diplomatic representation. Of most significance for the exile community was President Carter's refusal to renew the restrictions that prohibited travel by American citizens and Cuban Americans to the island as well to spend money while there. The opening up of relations led to the establishment of commercial flights between Miami and Havana in 1978. This momentum toward normalization was slowed, however, due to continued Cuban participation in the conflicts in Angola and Ethiopia.

One series of talks between the United States and Cuba had a broad-ranging impact: Secret negotiations between the Carter administration and the Cuban government resulted in a prisoner release agreement reached in August of 1978 in Cuernavaca, Mexico. The Cuban government agreed to release up to three thousand prisoners, and the United States agreed to process them through the established channels. Because of the perceived intransigence in Cuba's foreign military activity, however, the Carter administration did not want to acknowledge involvement in the negotiations or appear to be soft on communism.

The policies of reconciliation unleashed a reaction from the militant exiles intent on maintaining policies of delegitimization of the Cuban revolutionary government. Public demonstrations against the emerging conciliatory approach erupted in Miami, Florida; Union City, New Jersey; Washington, D.C., and San Juan, Puerto Rico. Anti-Castro paramilitary groups, organized under the umbrella group Coordination of Revolutionary Organizations (CORU), lifted their ban prohibiting bombing within the United States and made the Cuban American community its main target. In 1975 Luciano Nieves, an advocate of peaceful coexistence with the Cuban government, was assassinated. Emilio Milian, a Miami radio commentator who advocated dialogue with Cuba, lost both legs when he triggered a bomb that had been rigged to his car. Cuban exiles were also hatchet men in various terrorist operations organized by Operation Condor, including the assassination of Orlando Letelier, a leading voice in the anti-Pinochet resistance, and his assistant in 1976. Congressional hearings were held to explore the dynamics of terrorist activities in Miami, as more than one hundred bombs

The assassination of Orlando Letelier. Emergency responders investigate the bombed car in which former Chilean diplomat Orlando Letelier and an aide died in Washington, D.C., on 21 September 1976. Cuban exiles participated in various terrorist operations, including the assassination of Letelier, a leading voice in the anti-Pinochet resistance. AP IMAGES

exploded in the Miami area between 1973 and 1976; the FBI nicknamed Miami "the terror capital of the United States."

EL DIÁLOGO

On the island, there was a real, if not consensual, interest within the Cuban hierarchy to take advantage of the opportunities offered by a softening of relations between the two countries. Pioneers such as Lourdes Casals (1938–1981), the first exile to visit the island in 1973, began the conflictive process of reestablishing contacts between exiles and the Cuban intelligentsia. Top-level Cuban diplomats undertook negotiations with members of the State Department and some members of the Cuban community in the United States on issues that were later to become part of the *diálogo* agreements. Bernardo Benes, a banker and former anti-Batista fighter who had turned against the Cuban Revolution during its early years and who had become a pillar of the Cuban exile community, was a key player in framing the negotiating field with the Cuban government. In early 1978, Benes met with Castro in Havana. Benes later wrote that approximately sixteen topics were discussed as points of possible negotiation with the U.S. government: Some dealt specifically with the Cuban community (prisoner release, family reunification), and others were of broader geopolitical significance (willingness to curb support for revolutionary movements, resumption of diplomatic and trade relations). This meeting was followed by a more official meeting between David Aaron, who was the deputy of Carter's national security advisor Zbigniew Brzezinski, and

one of Castro's closest aides, José Luis Padrón. At the meeting, the Cuban emissary conveyed the government's interest in releasing up to thirty-five hundred prisoners if the United States was willing to take them. In future meetings an agreement was forged that was to be implemented as a result of the *diálogo* agreements.

When Castro extended an invitation to the Cuban community abroad in September 1978 to engage in a dialogue with the Cuban government on issues of mutual interest, the biggest surprise to exiled Cubans was Castro's willingness to see the Cuban diaspora as harboring legitimate concerns. The invitation was issued to exiles in the United States, Mexico, Venezuela, and Spain and offered an opportunity to discuss the three major issues of importance to the diasporic community: the fate of political prisoners, the right of Cubans living abroad to visit the island, and a possible establishment of a family reunification program.

The *diálogo* agreements followed the blueprint established by the Benes-Castro discussions of early 1978: At least three thousand political prisoners would be released and allowed to emigrate, with their families, to the United States or other countries; Cubans residing on the island would be allowed to leave to join family in the United States; Cubans in the diaspora would be allowed to visit the island.

In the United States, the dialogue divided the community like no other issue in twenty years of exile. The dialogue was to serve as a reference point dividing true exiles from those not aligning with the dominant right-wing exile ideology. To be labeled a *dialoguero* was to indicate an existence outside of the moral community of exiles for decades to come. The diálogo also offered a new target to those hardliners willing to respond violently against Cubans perceived as violating the right-wing exile ethos; it focused the frustrations of the old-guard militants on a new and accessible target—the so-called traitors in their midst. In 1979 Omega 7, one of the most active militant organizations of the 1970s, claimed credit for more than twenty bombings aimed at the homes and business of prominent dialogueros and issued public warnings vowing to kill any Cuban who traveled to the island. These were not idle threats. Maria de los Angeles Torres documents that in April 1979 Omega 7 claimed credit for the assassination of Carlos Muñiz Varela, a twenty-six-year-old member of the Antonio Maceo Brigade who coordinated the Puerto Rican offices of Viajes Varaderos, an agency that arranged travel to Cuba. In November 1979, in Union City, New Jersey, terrorists killed José Eulalio Negrín, another high-profile dialoguero.

In other countries, the dialogue and its aftermath developed in notably less-conflictive environments. In Venezuela, for example, the labor leader Eduardo Garcia Maure and Monsignor Eduardo Boza Mas Vidal served as interlocutors between the Venezuelan and Cuban governments as diálogo agreements were negotiated and implemented. The result was a peaceful acceptance of thirteen hundred prisoners from the island and no violent retaliation against the Venezuelan dialogueros.

IMPACT OF THE AGREEMENT

On the island, the dialogue resulted in the revisioning of the exile community from *gusanos* (worms) to *mariposas* (butterflies). Ricardo Bofill, a human rights activist living in Havana at the time, remembers the diálogo as important in creating "a favorable atmosphere toward the exiles [and]...a different vision of what transpired in Miami"; the release of the prisoners also "paved the way to denunciations of human rights violations in Castro's jails" (quoted in González-Pando p. 65). Starting in January 1979 and continuing through July 1980, some thirty-six hundred prisoners were released from Cuban jails. Some of those released went on to play significant roles in the development, and moderation, of the exile political culture.

The agreement on family visits resulted in more than 120,000 Cubans visiting the island in a year. Committees to defend and implement the accords of the diálogo sprang up throughout the United States and in Puerto Rico, Venezuela, Mexico, and Spain. In the United States, the Miami-based Committee of 75—headed by Albor Ruiz, a member of the Areíto editorial board—was organized to monitor the implementation of the diálogo accords in the United States and Cuba. The committee concentrated on organizing the exit of political prisoners from the island and assisting the processing of the appropriate visas. Other organizations, such as El Grupo de Reunificación Familiar, worked with Cuban and U.S. officials in coordinating family reunification procedures.

The momentary opening also created an opportunity for organizations to lobby the U.S. government to institutionalize and expand the diálogo by changing policy toward Cuba. In 1979, the Cuban-American Committee, a geographically dispersed group of professionals, presented the State Department with a petition signed by more than ten thousand Cubans requesting a speedy normalization of relations between the United States and Cuba.

The diálogo agreements also played a role in solidifying and expanding the Cuban economic enclave. The legitimization of contact between Cuba and the United States gave rise to travel agencies and associated service providers that catered to the growing number of Cuban Americans traveling and sending packages to relatives on the island. Like everything else associated with the diálogo, such exile tourism deeply divided the Miami community.

Among supporters, some were politically in favor of opening doors to the island, while others simply wished to stay in touch with relatives left behind. As the Cuban businessman Marcelino Miyares noted, "Despite a very vocal opposition to the dialogue by the exile political establishment, thousands went back" (González-Pando p. 64). The vocal opposition, in the meanwhile, emphasized that all contact with the Cuban government served to legitimize and prolong a dictatorial regime.

Perhaps the longest-term impact of the diálogo agreement was the role that it may have had in generating the turmoil within the island leading to the Mariel Boatlift in 1980. A common reading of the impact of the 120,000 exile visitors to the island is that they served to highlight the economic hardships of island residents when contrasted with those who had made the painful decision to leave. For this, if for no other reason, the importance of the diálogo for the development of Cuban community is hard to overestimate. It established the foundation for much of the political, cultural, economic, and social development of the Cuban community for decades.

BIBLIOGRAPHY

Ackerman, Holly. "Different Diasporas: Cubans in Venezuela, 1959–1998." In *Cuba: Idea of a Nation Displaced*, edited by Andrea O'Reilly Herrera. Albany: State University of New York Press, 2007.

Arguelles, Lourdes. "Cuban Miami: The Roots, Development, and Everyday Life of an Émigré Enclave in the U.S. National Security State." *Contemporary Marxism* 5 (Summer 1982): 27–43.

Benes, Bernardo. "Mis conversaciones secretas con Fidel Castro: Memorias." Unpublished manuscript. Available from http://www.latinamericanstudies.org/dialogue/Benes-memorias.pdf .

Committee on the Judiciary. "Terroristic Activity: Terrorism in the Miami Area." Hearings before the Subcommittee to Investigate the Administration of the Internal Security Act and Other Internal Security Laws. Ninety-fourth Congress. Washington, DC: U.S. Government Printing Office, 6 May 1976.

Dinges, John, and Saul Landau. *Assassination on Embassy Row.* New York: Pantheon, 1981.

Forment, Carlos A. "Political Practice and the Rise of an Ethnic Enclave: The Cuban American Case, 1959–1979." *Theory and Society* 18, no. 1 (January 1989): 47–81.

García, María Cristina. *Havana, USA: Cuban Exiles and Cuban Americans in South Florida, 1959–1994.* Berkeley: University of California Press, 1996.

González-Pando, Miguel. *The Cuban Americans.* Westport, CT: Greenwood Press, 1998.

Grenier, Guillermo J., and Lisandro Pérez. *The Legacy of Exile: Cubans in the United States.* Boston: Allyn and Bacon, 2003.

Levine, Robert. *Secret Mission to Cuba: Fidel Castro, Bernardo Benes, and Cuban Miami.* New York: Palgrave Macmillan, 2001.

Martinez, Guillermo, and Helga Silva. "Carter Aides, Cubans Met Secretly." *Miami Herald,* 12 October 1981, p. 1A.

Meluza, Lourdes. "La Causa: Exiles Redirect Their Efforts." *Miami Herald,* 13 April 1986, p. 6C.

National Security Archive. "Posada Carriles Built Bombs For, and Informed On, Jorge Mas Canosa, CIA Records Reveal: CIA Misjudged Posada as 'Not a Typical Boom and Bang Type' Militant: Proposed Posada for 'Responsible Civil Position' in Post-Castro Government: Declassified Documents Identify Posada's Agency Handlers." National Security Archive Electronic Briefing Book, no. 288, 6 October 2009. Available from http://www.gwu.edu/~nsarchiv/NSAEBB/NSAEBB288/index.htm.

Pedraza, Sylvia. "Cubans in Exile, 1959–1989: The State of the Research." In *Cuban Studies since the Revolution,* edited by Damián J. Fernández. Gainesville: University Press of Florida, 1992.

Perez, Lisandro. "Cuban Miami." In *Miami Now,* edited by Guillermo J. Grenier and Alex Stepick. Gainesville: University Press of Florida, 1992.

Perez, Lisandro. "Growing Up Cuban in Miami: Immigration, the Enclave, and New Generations." In *Ethnicities: Children of Immigrants in America,* edited by Rubén G. Rumbaut and Alejandro Portes. Berkeley: University of California Press and Russell Sage Foundation, 2001.

Portes, Alejandro, and Robert L. Bach. *Latin Journey: Cuban and Mexican Immigrants in the United States.* Berkeley: University of California Press, 1985.

Portes, Alejandro, and Leif Jensen. "The Enclave and the Entrants: Patterns of Ethnic Enterprise in Miami before and after Mariel." *American Sociological Review* 54 (1989): 929–949.

Stepick, Alex, Guillermo Grenier, Max Castro, and Marvin Dunn. *This Land Is Our Land: Immigrants and Power in Miami.* Berkeley: University of California Press, 2003.

Torres, Maria de los Angeles. *In the Land of Mirrors: Cuban Exile Politics in the United States.* Ann Arbor: University of Michigan Press, 1999.

℮ DIASPORAS

Diaspora refers to those who leave the country of their birth to settle in foreign lands. People have had many reasons for migrating from Cuba. Some had personal motives for leaving, including the writer Gertrudis Gómez de Avellaneda (1814–1873), who penciled the poem "Al Partir" as she was leaving Cuba for Spain. Her poem set a tone of nostalgia about her homeland that would reflect the feelings of many Cubans living abroad. Other Cubans emigrated to escape political persecution, including Father Félix Varela (1788–1853), an activist who had been sentenced to death for his pro-independence activities, and José Martí (1853–1895), one of Cuba's most revered writers and activists. Most who left Cuba settled in the United States, building sizeable Cuban communities in Miami, New York City, and New Jersey. There, Cubans made important contributions to their new environment, especially in music—mambo and Latin jazz, being notable examples.

The Revolution of 1959 made emigration a particularly divisive issue, both for those leaving and for those staying. Thousands of Cubans opposed to the socialist policies of Fidel Castro's revolutionary government fled the country in the latter half of the twentieth century. His supporters considered those who left to be traitors, while Cubans who made it safely to the United States vocally denounced the Castro regime. After the revolution, Cold War programs established by U.S. presidents hostile to the Cuban government encouraged emigration from Cuba, and exile would become a permanent political identity for many Cubans living abroad.

DIASPORAS: INTRODUCTION

Jorge Duany

Diaspora, one of various terms used to describe Cubans abroad, together with exiles, refugees, émigrés, colonias, *and* transnationals.

Between the early 1800s and the early 2000s, hundreds of thousands of Cubans resettled in the United States and elsewhere. Whether they moved for political or economic reasons, Cubans and their descendants have created diverse and complex communities in other countries. These communities have been given various names that reflect their shifting socioeconomic compositions and political ideologies, as well as the prevailing terminology of the time. This entry reviews how Cubans abroad have been classified, noting that the idea of diaspora illuminates the massive displacement of Cuba's population.

ÉMIGRÉS

Before the Cuban Revolution of 1959, most Cubans abroad were considered *émigrés* who sought employment and better working conditions in the United States. By the 1820s, hundreds of professionals, merchants, and landowners had settled in New York City, Philadelphia, and New Orleans. Large-scale migration from Cuba began in earnest with the Ten Years' War (1868–1878) and continued well after the Spanish-Cuban-American War (1895–1898).

The late nineteenth century was a period of political upheaval and economic difficulties in Cuba, with rising unemployment and cost of living. As a result, many migrated for economic reasons. Most Cubans in the United States were then blue-collar workers, particularly cigar makers. These working-class émigrés laid the foundations of the earliest Cuban communities off the island.

COLONIAS

The Spanish word *colonia* (literally, colony; figuratively, enclave) commonly designated the late nineteenth- and early twentieth-century settlements of Cubans and other Hispanics in the United States. These compact residential enclaves were usually located in coastal cities, near immigrants' workplaces. The first well-defined Cuban colonias, with their distinct neighborhoods, institutions, and leaders, emerged in the 1870s, especially in Key West, Florida. They were all connected to cigar manufacturing, which benefited from a protective U.S. tariff on cigar imports and employed thousands of Cuban immigrants. A vibrant Cuban colonia flourished in Ybor City, near Tampa, between 1886 and 1930. In New York City during the 1920s, the expression *colonia hispana* (Hispanic colony) encompassed Spanish, Cuban, and Puerto Rican immigrants, particularly in East Harlem and the Lower East Side of Manhattan.

EXILES

Beginning in the early nineteenth century, the United States served as a safe haven for political dissidents who supported Cuba's independence from Spain, such as

José María Heredia (1803–1839), Félix Varela (1788–1853), and José Antonio Saco (1797–1879). By the end of the century, growing numbers of Cuban exiles lived in New York City, notably the politician, journalist, and poet José Martí (1853–1895). In the twentieth century, the former Cuban presidents Ramón Grau San Martín (1887–1969), Gerardo Machado (1871–1939), Fulgencio Batista (1901–1973), and Carlos Prío Socarrás (1903–1977) were all exiled in the United States.

After 1959, many Cubans left their country because of ideological differences over the Revolution led by Fidel Castro. Castro's government launched radical socioeconomic and political transformations such as land reform, expropriation of private properties, and restrictions on civil liberties. Disaffection with the Revolution increased when most economic activities were nationalized in Cuba during the 1960s.

An exile ideology emerged among Cubans in the United States, particularly in Miami, characterized by a strong anticommunist sentiment and rejection of and unwillingness to negotiate with the revolutionary regime. For many, their sense of identity (*cubanidad*) incorporated their sense of themselves as reluctant exiles, although some began the ideological transition to immigrants and ethnics. Between the 1980s and the early 2000s, economic motives increasingly drove Cubans abroad, and many of them did not view themselves as exiles.

REFUGEES

Legally, refugees are persons who have fled their country and are unwilling to return there because they fear persecution. The main difference between refugees and émigrés lies in their reasons for moving abroad: The former move primarily because they are estranged from the ruling government, whereas the latter seek a better standard of living. Thus, refugees feel more pushed away from the sending state than pulled by the receiving one. Fearing harassment, torture, incarceration, or sometimes even death, refugees rarely go back to live in their country of birth. Hence, relations between refugees and their relatives back home are often strained or even severed.

In the early 1960s, the U.S. government adopted an open-door policy toward Cubans fleeing what was seen as Communist oppression amid the Cold War with the Soviet Union. Most Cubans received visa waivers without immigration quotas or restrictions; after 1966, they quickly qualified for permanent residence and, later, U.S. citizenship.

However, in 1980, the Carter administration resisted accepting Cuban arrivals from the port of Mariel as refugees. In 1994, President Bill Clinton denied Cubans automatic asylum and began returning those without immigration visas. Nonetheless, the U.S. government continues to grant Cubans a privileged legal status, admitting those who reach U.S. soil and deporting those detained at sea. Between 1997 and 2004, on average, the United States gave asylum to 62 percent of Cuban applicants, compared to only 23 percent of Haitians.

TRANSNATIONALS

Many Cubans abroad can be deemed transnational insofar as they retain strong family ties with their home country. In the late 1990s and early 2000s, émigrés demonstrated transnational practices such as telephoning family in Cuba, visiting the island, and sending money home, albeit on a smaller scale than other Latino groups in the United States such as Dominicans and Mexicans. Among the barriers to Cuban transnationalism are the long-standing U.S. embargo of Cuba, the high cost of traveling there, and ideological differences between Cubans on and off the island. Post-1980 émigrés are more likely than earlier groups to favor cross-border exchanges with Cuba, including sending food and medicine and reestablishing diplomatic ties. Since the late 1980s, increasing social and economic contacts have reinforced transnational kinship networks between Cuba and the United States. The main difference between Cubans and other transnationals has been the entrenched antagonism between Cuban exiles and the Castro government. Consequently, Cubans residing off the island have not been able to participate in the political affairs of their homeland.

DIASPORA

Finally, Cubans meet the standard definition of *diaspora* as a people scattered outside their original territory. They share many of the characteristics of classical diasporas (such as those involving Jews, Armenians, and the Greeks of antiquity), including collective memories and myths about the homeland; a commitment to preserve or recover it; a strong ethnic group consciousness; and a troubled relationship with their host societies. Like other diasporas, countless Cubans harbor the hope of returning home, and they cultivate ties with their compatriots in other places. Specifically, Cubans may be considered engaging in a *victim diaspora*, expelled from their homeland by a traumatic event, the Cuban Revolution. Moreover, Cubans abroad routinely compare themselves to the Jewish diaspora. Diasporic Cubans often claim to belong to an extraterritorial Cuban nation; most oppose the current government on the island. Accordingly, the term *diaspora* has been extended to Cubans dispersed throughout the world.

BIBLIOGRAPHY

Behar, Ruth, and Lucía M. Suárez, eds. *The Portable Island: Cubans at Home in the World*. New York: Palgrave Macmillan, 2008.

Herrera, Andrea O'Reilly, ed. *Cuba: Idea of a Nation Displaced*. Albany: State University of New York Press, 2007.

Poyo, Gerald E. *"With All and for the Good of All": The Emergence of Popular Nationalism in the Cuban Communities of the United States, 1848–1898.* Durham, NC: Duke University Press, 1989.

Rivero Muñiz, José. "Los cubanos en Tampa." *Revista Bimestre Cubana* 74 (January–June 1958): 5–140.

Torres, María de los Angeles. *In the Land of Mirrors: Cuban Exile Politics in the United States.* Ann Arbor: University of Michigan Press, 2001.

DIASPORAS: 19TH CENTURY

Gerald E. Poyo

Integration of nineteenth-century Cuban immigrants in the United States, their response to nationalist interests and developing exile identities.

Throughout the nineteenth century, Cubans immigrated to the United States seeking economic opportunities and fleeing Spanish rule. Cubans established smaller communities in Venezuela, Central America, Mexico, Jamaica, Haiti, and the Dominican Republic, and in Europe they gathered mostly in France and to a lesser extent England, but the favorite destination was the United States. Steamer service regularly transported Cuban immigrants with diverse motives and interests who settled mostly in the port cities stretching along the coast from New Orleans to Boston. Highly unreliable estimates of Cubans living in the United States vary from 20,000 to 100,000, though many more visited for business or vacation. Many Cuban immigrants admired the United States, which represented a welcome contrast to Spanish colonialism. In the United States, they cultivated their nationalist instincts, practiced democracy, participated in the capitalist economy, and integrated and transformed their traditional cultural ways in new community settings.

IMMIGRATION AND WORK

A ten-month British occupation of Havana in 1762 during the Seven Years' War (1756–1763) brought merchants from the English colonies along the North American Atlantic coast into commercial relationships with Cuba, initiating an economic exchange that grew dramatically after Cuba replaced Haiti as the dominant sugar export economy in the Caribbean. Increasing opportunities in the sugar trade and associated enterprises inspired many Cubans to move north from the 1820s through the 1850s. Among them were many members of Cuba's white and upwardly mobile criollo bourgeoisie, including merchants, intellectuals and writers, journalists, doctors, dentists, lawyers, and entrepreneurs of all kinds, who settled in New York, Philadelphia, Baltimore, Boston, and New Orleans.

Criollos continued to immigrate to the United States throughout the century, working in retail stores, banks, restaurants and cafes, bookstores, pharmacies, barbershops, and other enterprises common to large cities. Thousands also travelled to the United States for education, diverting them from the traditional European training Cubans received. These individuals attended fine boarding schools; business, commercial, and technical schools such as Rensselaer Polytechnic Institute; and elite universities such as Harvard and Columbia.

After the U.S. Civil War (1861–1865), an expanding Cuban tobacco and cigar industry broadened the social and racial composition of Cuban emigrants, who traveled in a circular migration between Havana, New York, Louisiana, and Florida, propelled by changing economic circumstances and employment possibilities. U.S.–manufactured Cuban cigars, known as clear Havana cigars for their exclusive use of Cuban tobacco leaf, avoided the high U.S. tariff on manufactured cigar imports from Cuba while benefiting from low tariffs on tobacco leaf from the island's western tobacco-growing region. A handful of small cigar factories in Key West prior to 1868 burgeoned into an important U.S. cigar center, led by Cuban and Spanish entrepreneurs, including Vicente Martínez Ybor (1818–1896), Eduardo Hidalgo Gato (1847–1926), Francisco Marrero, Teodoro Pérez (1857–1927), and others. Factories also appeared in Jacksonville, and (after a fire temporarily destroyed much of the industry in Key West in 1886) in the Tampa Bay area and Ocala. Cigar manufacturing became one of the state's most significant industries.

Florida's tobacco industry towns attracted an ethnically and racially diverse working class. Women also migrated in significant numbers; some accompanied husbands while others arrived on their own, often with children. In Key West, some 10 percent of workers in the factories were women in the 1870s, which at least doubled during the next decades as women experienced greater freedom to seek work in the United States. Neighborhoods and households in Florida's communities remained ethnically coherent and distinct throughout the period, a reality often noted by the Anglo-American press, which commented on their seemingly unusual customs. Cuban cigar workers maintained a strong sense of nationality and developed a seamless transnational identity, thanks to their frequent trips back and forth between Cuba and the United States.

NATIONALISM AND EXILE

Though economic opportunities may have attracted most immigrants in the nineteenth century, many left Cuba for political reasons. Beginning in the 1820s, many Cubans became increasingly disenchanted with Spain's unwillingness to reform its colonial system and grant the island a measure of self-government. Nationalism characterized Cuban communities, which fashioned exile identities reflecting this primary concern. Exile leaders developed highly heterogeneous separatist movements that at times advocated annexation of Cuba to the United States but after the 1870s mostly favored the establishment of an independent republic. From Félix Varela (1788–1853) in the late 1820s to José Martí (1853–1895) in the 1890s, these leaders worked to perpetuate a separatist perspective that even won over many apolitical Cubans. Nationalists developed many of their ideas about Cuba's future while they were in the United States, where they spoke and wrote freely, engaged in debates, and influenced opinion in their homeland.

Hundreds of books and pamphlets, and, most importantly, newspapers debated the merits of separatist propositions and produced a nationalist movement that eventually sparked the independence war against Spain. Popular newspapers included Varela's *El Habanero* (1824–1826), published in Philadelphia and New York; Juan Bellido de Luna's *El Fililbustero* (1853–1855); Enrique Piñeyro's *La Revolución* (1869–1873); Enrique Trujillo's *El Porvenir* (1890–1898), and José Martí's *Patria* (1892–1898) in New York; José Dolores Poyo's *El Yara* (1878–1898) and José Estrada's *La Propaganda* (1884–1888) in Key West, and Ramón Rivero's *Cuba* (1890–1898) in Tampa. These publications, to name just a few, maintained a constant exile discourse among Cubans.

Political organizations and clubs mobilized communities for more than half a century, beginning in the 1840s. Reflecting differing political perspectives and strategic approaches to separatism, these organizations and their leaders supported the revolutionary initiatives of military leaders such as Narciso López (1797–1851), Manuel de Quesada (1833-1884), Maximo Gómez (1836–1905), Antonio Maceo (1845–1896), and Calixto García (1839–1898), among others. The Club de la Habana (founded 1848; New York) advocated Cuba's annexation to the United States; Club Republicano de Cuba y Puerto Rico (founded 1865; New York) raised the banner of Cuba's independence and abolition of slavery; Club Patriótico Cubano (founded 1869; Key West) secured money from tobacco workers for military expeditions to Cuba; La Liga de las Hijas de Cuba (founded 1870; New York) was the first organization to mobilize women for the nationalist cause; Club Nihilista (founded 1883; Key West and New York) sent dynamite to the island to support insurgents; La Convención Cubana (founded 1888; Key West) worked to establish revolutionary cells in Cuba; the Liceo Cubano (founded 1890; Tampa) first invited José Martí to Florida, where he conceptualized and urged the foundation of the Partido Revolucionario Cubano (founded 1892; Key West), which for the first time effectively organized exile political institutions under one umbrella and helped launch the war of independence in 1895. In the Florida communities, Cubans also advanced their nationalist interests by participating in local politics, gaining election to local and state offices, and securing federal jobs, especially in the customs houses.

COMMUNITY AND CULTURE

Cubans in the United States adapted, worked, became citizens, and established vibrant communities where they engaged and debated the diverse ideologies of the day; practiced religious traditions; produced a distinguished body of literature; supported theater and musical arts; and even pioneered baseball in Florida's communities. Nevertheless, their homeland was never far from their thoughts and nationalism influenced almost all aspects of community life.

Cuban cigar workers demonstrated the complexity of actions, motives, and interests that informed Cubans' everyday lives in the United States. Workers led by Manuel Escassi, Santos Benítez, and Ramón Rubiera defended their economic and social interests by organizing unions in Florida and New York, but they also became the most committed constituency in support of Cuban independence. Some labor dissidents skeptical of revolutionary nationalism, such as Ramón Rivero (1856–1908) and Carlos Baliño (1848–1826), urged workers to commit their resources primarily to defending their socioeconomic interests, which complicated matters for the nationalists. The dissidents formed chapters of the Knights of Labor and rejected the nationalist exclusivity of the Cuban immigrant unions. This situation was further complicated when anarchists from Havana such as Enrique Messonier and Enrique Creci organized unions that soon displaced the Knights of Labor and also challenged the nationalists. Though many Cuban workers eventually unified behind the nationalist cause when the possibility of revolution seemed clearer, they never ceased demanding that the nationalist leaders keep their local economic and social interests in mind.

Religion figured prominently in the Cuban communities. Many such as Father Felix Varela (1788–1853), who from the 1820s to 1840s served the Diocese of New York, remained deeply committed to Catholicism, but the Catholic allegiances of others faded during the century as the Church remained uncritical of the Spanish colonial system. In Key West during the 1880s, only a few people regularly attended services at the chapel named after *Nuestra Señora de la Caridad del Cobre* (Our Lady of Charity); most Cuban Christians worshiped in Protestant churches. In New York throughout the 1860s and 1870s, José Joaquín de Palma (1884–1911) led an Episcopalian congregation at Santiago Church, and in Key West Episcopal pastor Juan Bautista Báez and Methodists Enrique Someillán and Manuel Deulofeu led active congregations. Protestants not only opposed Spain but condemned Catholicism as a backward religion. Cubans also practiced African-based religious traditions, especially in Florida, where they practiced openly, though not without occasional criticism from compatriots for giving Americans a so-called bad impression of Cubans. Less interested in religion, many instead participated in the various Masonic rites whose lodges became centers of revolutionary sentiment against Spanish colonialism.

Cubans also supported a thriving artistic community. Writers sold their works in Cuban-owned bookstores such as that of Nestor Ponce de León (1837–1899) in New York and gained distribution in the nationalist newspapers. They often found a following in cigar factories, where *lectores* read to workers as they labored. Important novels published in the United States, including Cirilo Villaverde's *Cecilia Valdéz* (1882), a classic of Cuban literature, and Anselmo Suárez y Romero's *Francisco* (1880), criticized slavery, race relations, and Spanish colonialism. Poetry attracted a following, including José María Heredia's *Poesías* (1825) on the hardships of exile and Miguel Teurbe Tolón's important *El laúd del desterrado* (1858). The most prolific Cuban writer in the United States was José Martí, who published poetry, essays, novels, and other writings. Theater, a mainstay of entertainment in Cuban communities, included drama, comedy, and popular theater and helped maintain a powerful sense of *cubanía* (Cubanness). Cuban musicians, including flutist Guillermo M. Tomás (1768–1933) and pianist Emilio Agramonte (1844–1918), performed regularly in New York.

Baseball was popular among Cubans in Florida. They considered it an enlightened modern pastime worthy of replacing the Spanish tradition of bullfighting in Cuba, giving the sport a political inflection. Florida Cubans learned the game in their communities, and teams from Tampa, Key West, Havana, and Matanzas competed throughout the late 1880s and early 1890s. U.S. born players such as Agustín (Tinti) Molina (1873–1961) and Francisco Andrés Poyo (1872–1961) pioneered baseball in Key West and Tampa and later played, managed, and promoted baseball in Cuba. Throughout the 1890s, baseball also became a vehicle for raising funds for the nationalist cause, and many players joined the insurgent army in 1895.

After Cuban independence in 1898, integration of these communities into North American life accelerated, and a Cuban American ethnic identity slowly displaced the nationalist and exile identity that had prevailed during the previous half century. The Cuban experience in the United States during the nineteenth century established the foundations for an expanding presence in the twentieth, but it also contributed to a Cuban future influenced by the United States, as many returned home after the independence war deeply marked by their North American experiences.

BIBLIOGRAPHY

Casasús, Juan J. E. *La emigración cubana y la independencia de la patria.* Havana: Editorial Lex, 1953.

Mormino, Gary R., and George E. Pozzetta. *The Immigrant World of Ybor City: Italians and Their Latin Neighbors in Tampa, 1885–1985.* Urbana: University of Illinois Press, 1987.

Pérez, Louis A., Jr. *Cuba Between Empires, 1878–1902.* Pittsburgh, PA: University of Pittsburgh Press, 1983.

Pérez, Louis A., Jr. *On Becoming Cuban: Identity, Nationality, and Culture.* Chapel Hill: University of North Carolina Press, 1999.

Poyo, Gerald E. *With All, and for the Good of All: The Emergence of Popular Nationalism in the Cuban Communities of the United States, 1849–1898.* Durham, NC: Duke University Press, 1989.

DIASPORAS: 1930S, 1940S, AND 1950S

Gustavo Pérez Firmat

Cuba's diasporic communities that have spread the distinctive culture of the island throughout the world and particularly to the United States.

Throughout the nineteenth century, many opponents of Spanish colonial rule left Cuba to live in Europe or the United States. During the twentieth century, economic instability combined with dictatorships and revolts forced succeeding waves of Cubans into exile, usually to the United States. In the early 1930s, opposition to the Machado regime intensified, and government forces responded with increased repression and reprisals. Daily violence and the poor sugar harvests led to a depressed economy in which unemployment was high, and thousands of Cubans emigrated to the United States. During the late 1930s and into the 1940s, continued political unrest and economic woes sent others into exile. Roughly 18,000 Cubans were admitted to the United States as immigrants between 1936 and 1950 (Pérez p. 128). As a result of the Cuban Revolution of 1959, nearly half a million Cubans went into exile, most of them to the United States (Pérez 1986, p. 131). Throughout the twentieth century, some exiles returned to Cuba when political and economic scenarios permitted; others, particularly those who left after the revolution led by Fidel Castro, never returned.

No Cuban exports have had a greater impact in the United States than the island's music and dance. Although during the first half of the twentieth century many Americans visited Cuba, particularly Havana, most Americans never saw Cuba. The Cuba they knew, or imagined that they knew, was mainly the Cuban culture that the musicians, composers, and performers who left their country brought with them and that captured the American imagination. In the 1930s and 1940s, the Cuban Tourist Commission capitalized on the singularity of Cuban American ties with the slogan "So near and yet so foreign," in which the pun makes clear that the distance between the countries is

■ *See also*

Economy: Republican Period

Governance and Contestation: The Republic: 1902–1952

The Music of Ernesto Lecuona

cultural rather than physical, a matter of mores rather than miles. This has always been the American perception. Cuba is close but different, a back-of-the-mind country that is almost, but not quite, a fantasy island. In this country, rhythm rules.

THE 1930s AND THE RHUMBA CRAZE

The entertainers who left Cuba in the late 1920s and early 1930s joined Cubans already performing in the United States. Rita Montaner (1900–1958), a popular Cuban singer, pianist, and actress, was well known in New York, where she recorded, filmed, and performed onstage in the Schubert Follies and in Al Jolson's musical *Wonder Bar* (1934) on Broadway. Cuban musicians such as the flutist Alberto Socarrás (1908–1987) were playing in the mostly Puerto Rican club bands of New York City and in downtown society nightclub orchestras. As early as 1925, the Cuban trumpeter Vicente Sigler (1890–1971) organized a New York band that played in hotel ballrooms in Manhattan. The Spanish-born musicians Xavier Cugat (1900–1990) and Enrique Madriguera (1904–1973) arrived in the United States via Cuba in the early 1920s after playing in and leading orchestras in Havana nightspots. But the music these bands played—show tunes and so-called dinner music—was only vaguely Latin in its lyrics or titles.

Then came the rhumba, which permanently changed popular music and dance in the United States. An Americanized, ballroom-style adaptation of the Cuban *son* that bore little relation to the Afro-Cuban *rumba*, the rhumba (or rumba) quickly became a national craze. On 26 April 1930, in New York City, the Don Azpiazú Havana Casino Orchestra played Moisés Simons's *son-pregón* "El Manicero" with vocals by Antonio Machín (1903–1977) and a dance team that demonstrated *rumba* steps for the audience. Simons (1889–1945), a Cuban pianist, composer, and bandleader, was a popular performer in Paris and the United States throughout most of the 1930s; Machín sang and recorded in Cuba, New York, and Europe, where he later settled. Don Azpiazú (Justo Angél Azpiazú, 1893–1943) was a leading Cuban orchestra leader in the 1920s and 1930s. His orchestra had arrived in New York City in early April 1930 and played several dates in the uptown Latin barrio theaters, and hit performances there led to their downtown debut. For the first time, an American audience heard an orchestra that included Cuban instruments (maracas, *claves*, *guiros*, bongos, congas, and *timbales*) play authentic Cuban dance music.

Although "El Manicero" had been recorded in Cuba in the late 1920s by Rita Montaner, Don Azpiazú's orchestral performance was this song's debut in the United States. Azpiazú recorded it as "The Peanut Vendor" in May 1930, and by the next year, the song was a national sensation. Thousands of Americans signed up for rhumba lessons, and the sheet music published by Edward Marks in a simplified version for American musicians sold a million copies during the 1930s. Recording companies and sheet music publishers scrambled to find more tunes to satisfy the growing demand. Edward Marks Company had a large stock of Cuban songs and, by 1932, listed 600 Latin American songs in its catalog; Southern Music Company started a Rhumba Sheet Music Club with the publication of "Green Eyes" (Adolfo Utrera and Nilo Menéndez's bolero "Aquellos ojos verdes").

ERNESTO LECUONA AND LATUNES

Sheet music often played up the Latin atmosphere of the songs with drawings of lovers swooning under tropical moonlit palms, as on the 1935 cover of the music and lyrics for "Havana Heaven" and the 1936 sheet music for "Let Me Dream of Havana," which showed Havana's Morro Castle framed by a palm tree, under an enormous moon in a starlit sky. Sometimes called *latunes*—tunes with a Latin beat and English-language lyrics—these popular songs drew on a variety of Latin American genres, but Cuban rhythms prevailed. The coupling of English words and Cuban rhythms was effective in making these tunes accessible. American couples dancing to these rhythms were enveloped in a Latin atmosphere. Although most Americans never learned to rhumba, in the back of their minds Cuban rhythms, of which the rhumba was only the first, were working their magic.

Some of the most popular Latin melodies were tunes composed by Ernesto Lecuona (1895–1963), one of the few composers and performers who achieved critical acclaim in both the popular and the classical musical worlds. In his early teens, Lecuona played at Havana's Teatro Martí, organized a small orchestra that played in the city's dancehalls, and by 1908 had published his first work, a two-step prophetically titled "Cuba y America." He studied briefly with Maurice Ravel in Paris and, in the 1910s and 1920s, began performing in Europe and the United States. Although Lecuona wrote numerous classical compositions, he is best remembered for his songs, and in his lifetime they frequently outsold tunes by American popular songwriters. "Malagueña," first played in the United States in 1927, for years sold more than 100,000 sheet music copies a year in the United States alone, and in its myriad arrangements for everything from brass band to accordion it became Lecuona's most consistent best seller in the United States. "Siboney" (1929), also an immediate success, was performed by many artists and big bands in the United States. "Andalucia," published in 1930 and reintroduced in 1940 as "The Breeze and I" with English lyrics, had sold nearly 2 million recordings by 1943. His other songs made popular with lyrics in English include "Say Sí Sí" ("Para Vigo me voy"), "Always in My Heart" ("Siempre en mi corazón"), and "Maria My Own" ("María la O"). Sometimes known as the Cuban Gershwin, Lecuona was also a leading film composer, writing scores for numerous American and Latin American films.

DESI ARNAZ, MARACA MUSICALS, AND THE 1940s

Many of the Hollywood musical films of the 1930s and 1940s featured a Latin number, and these maraca musicals often included the conga, which was less a dance than an exercise in group sociability. Imported from Cuba in the late 1930s, the conga was inclusive because anyone could learn the simple steps. The conga line, in which the dancers are physically linked to each other, served as a visually appealing metaphor of Latin-tinged connectedness, and the conga was the inspiration for many latunes such as "Doing the Conga," "Kindergarten Conga," and "I Came, I Saw, I Conga'd." Although it is unlikely that Desi Arnaz (1917–1986) introduced the conga to the United States in his nightclub act in Miami Beach (as he claimed), Arnaz will always be associated with the conga. Arnaz left Cuba in the mid-1930s for Miami to join his father, an exiled Machado supporter. After purchasing a secondhand guitar, Arnaz soon was playing with the orchestra at Miami's Roney Plaza Hotel. After a stint with Xavier Cugat, Arnaz put together his own Latin band in 1937 and two years later made his Broadway debut in George Abbott's *Too Many Girls*, in which he played Manuelito Lynch, a young man from Argentina who is a football prodigy as well as a conga-drumming demon. The climactic scene in the 1940 movie version occurs when Manuelito leads his classmates into a large plaza where a bonfire burns. With the flames spiraling around him, he begins to pound on his conga drum. Picking up the chant, the students form conga lines. The scene cuts to a laboratory where a professor is peering through his microscope: Even the paramecia on the slide are also bumping and grinding to the conga beat—an example of the infectious magic of the conga.

Although Arnaz received good notices for *Too Many Girls*, during the next few years he got only small, mostly non-singing roles in forgettable movies. It was not until his 1946 movie *Cuban Pete*, which borrowed freely from Arnaz's nightclub act, that he landed a lead role. Arnaz, playing a Cuban bandleader, has four songs in the film, including two renditions of the title song. In *Holiday in Havana* (1949), his last film before *I Love Lucy*, Arnaz is a comic *caballero*, a somewhat ridiculous Don Juan. He does sing a tender bolero, "Made for Each Other," but once the song is over he grabs a blanket, says goodnight to his lady love, and goes out to sleep on the porch, which promptly collapses under him. Arnaz always played the Latin lover as good neighbor, the Lothario next door, a role that he would perfect as Ricky Ricardo.

I LOVE LUCY

While filming *Too Many Girls* Arnaz met Lucille Ball (1911–1989), the female lead in the picture, and they married in 1940. In 1950, Ball was approached by CBS, who wanted her to do a television version of her radio show *My Favorite Husband*, in which Richard Denning played her husband. Ball agreed, but only if Arnaz, her real-life husband, took Denning's part. Because the radio program was about an American couple, the network balked, fearing that Arnaz would not be credible as a typical American husband, hardly a suitable role for a conga player from Cuba. After the program's concept was modified to fit Arnaz's background, the network finally agreed. Ball and Arnaz would play a showbiz couple; the husband would be a struggling bandleader whose zany wife would try anything to get into his act. What to call the show remained a problem, however. After much discussion, producer Jess Oppenheimer came up with a clever compromise: *I Love Lucy*. Leaving the spotlight on his more famous wife, the sentence gave Arnaz pride of place without actually naming him—it does take a moment's reflection to realize who is the *I* in *I Love Lucy*. And yet Arnaz's TV persona, Ricky Ricardo, may be the single most influential Hispanic in the history of the United States. Several generations of Americans have acquired many of their notions of how Cuban men behave, how they talk, lose their temper, and treat or mistreat their wives by watching Ricky love Lucy. Not even Fidel Castro has exercised as strong a hold on the American imagination. For millions of Americans, Ricky Ricardo is the quintessential Cuban, charming but volatile, familiar but foreign.

The typical *I Love Lucy* episode centers on some form of competition between Ricky and Lucy. The battle lines are well drawn: on one side, Lucy and Ethel; on the other, Ricky and Fred. Usually the trouble arises from the supposedly irreducible differences between husbands and wives, or men and women. In some episodes, though, the conflict emerges from

Lucille Ball and Desi Arnaz as Lucy and Ricky Ricardo, 1 January 1955. American actress Lucille Ball and her Cuban-born husband, Desi Arnaz, starred in the sitcom *I Love Lucy* from 1951 to 1957. For millions of Americans, Ricky Ricardo became the quintessential Cuban, charming but volatile, familiar but foreign. MPI/ GETTY IMAGES

the clash of cultures. Ricky is not just male, but also Cuban; Lucy is not just female, but also American. In these episodes, the overriding theme is not the war of the sexes but what Lucy called the "battle of the accents." This phrase occurs in "Lucy Hires an English Tutor," an episode from the second season about her efforts to improve Ricky's English. When Ricky tries unsuccessfully to pronounce words such as *bough*, *rough*, *through*, and *cough* (which he pronounces "buff," "row," "thruff," and "coo"), he concludes that because English is a "crazy language," his son will speak Spanish instead. Lucy is having none of that and hires an English tutor. After a few funny scenes in which the tutor, Mr. Livermore, attempts to correct Ricky's diction and accent, the lessons come to an unexpected conclusion: Instead of improving Ricky's English, Mr. Livermore ends up sounding like Ricky. When he launches into an ear-splitting rendition of "Babalú," Lucy calls the whole thing off. "Okay, okay," she says, "it was a battle of the accents and Mr. Livermore lost."

In a show that has been criticized for its ethnocentrism, Lucy's admission of defeat marks an interesting moment. Rather than persisting in her efforts to Americanize her husband, she gives in because, as many episodes make clear, Lucy loves Ricky because he is *not* American. Enlivening every argument and every reconciliation, Ricky's Cubanness is a crucial component in the *I* of *I Love Lucy*. Beginning with the mambo-inflected theme song, Cuba is everywhere, most particularly in the sound of Ricky's voice. For her part, Lucy never tires of bringing up Ricky's nationality and imitating his accent. If Lucy loves Ricky because he's Cuban, Ricky loves Lucy because she is not. What sets *I Love Lucy* apart from other sitcoms, in addition to the talent of its stars, is the aura and allure of Cuban culture. Lucy and Ricky are not, as the reviewers liked to say, a typical middle-class American couple—not because they are not middle-class, but because they are not American; they are Cuban American. In the Ricardo household, the battle of the accents spices the war of the sexes. When Mr. Livermore asks Ricky where he acquired his "odd pronunciation," Ricky replies, "I was born in Cuba, what your 'scuse?" The answer not only puts Livermore in his place, but also provides the excuse, or rather, the explanation for the uniqueness of the show. Those executives skeptical that Americans would accept a Cuban as Lucille Ball's TV husband did not reckon with the singular intimacy of the ties between the two countries. In one respect, *I Love Lucy* is a theater of domestic war; in another, it is the great Cuban American love story, a chronicle of how a Cuban man and an American woman made a life together.

THE MAMBO

Of all the Cuban dances that have migrated to the United States—the rhumba, the conga, the cha-cha-cha—none did so more boisterously, or with more eroticism, than the mambo. The rhumba may have been a rage, but the mambo was madness—mambo mania. Originating in Afro-Cuban religious rituals, where the word referred to the communication between the living and the dead, by the 1930s in Cuba, the mambo had become attached to the final, improvised section of a *danzón*, a nineteenth-century precursor of the rhumba-originating *son*. In the 1940s, Cuban pianist and arranger Dámaso Pérez Prado (1916–1989), severed the mambo from the matrix of the danzón and began to treat it as an autonomous entity. By 1948, he was a well-known figure in Havana's musical circles and had begun experimenting with the mixture of a big-band sound and Afro-Cuban rhythms, though Cuban record companies were not much interested in his music, considering it weird and highbrow. He left Cuba for Mexico and, on 30 March 1949, recorded "Qué rico el mambo," the song that started the mambo craze. "Qué rico el mambo" took the music world by storm, becoming a hit in Mexico and the rest of Latin America. Over the next several years, Pérez Prado recorded dozens of mambos and sold millions of records in Latin America, but the mambo was scarcely known in the United States except among the Latin musicians in the barrio dancehalls of New York City.

Since the 1920s Cuban musicians had been playing and performing with blacks and Puerto Ricans in the bands and dance orchestras of New York's Harlem and the Latin barrio. Mixing of cultures and music was commonplace; both white and black jazz orchestras and big bands contained many Latin players, and the New York mambo emerged from that foundation. By the late 1940s, New York musicians were playing their own versions of the mambo. The Cuban pianist José Curbelo (b. 1917) headed a group that recorded some of the earliest, and the influential Cuban musician Frank Grillo (1909–1984), known as Machito, formed his Latin-jazz band, called Machito and his Afro-Cubans, in New York in 1940. Grillo's brother-in-law, the famed Cuban musician Mario Bauzá (1911–1993), became his innovative musical director, arranger, and trumpeter, and the band recorded a number of Latin-jazz hits. Successfully fusing jazz and Cuban music, Machito's orchestra also triumphed at mambo venues and in the ballrooms of Catskills resort hotels in the 1940s and 1950s. In 1949, the Cuban revue "Las Mulatas de Fuego" performed at the Havana Madrid nightclub in New York and introduced some mambo steps. New York dancers were quick to learn the mambo; at the Park Plaza ballroom at 110th Street, enthusiastic dancers from Harlem and the Latin barrios combined steps from Cuban dances, the jitterbug, and the Lindy Hop.

In 1951, Pérez Prado was discovered in Mexico by the American bandleader Sonny Burke, and the following year, Decca released an album of Burke's mambos, most of them covers of Pérez Prado's arrangements. Encouraged by Burke's success, RCA

Victor switched Pérez Prado from its international to its pop label, and his Latin American success was repeated in the United States. "Qué rico el mambo" became a hit, selling nearly 600,000 copies, and the mambo became widely identified in the United States with the diminutive bandleader from Cuba who wore zoot suits, jumped wildly onstage, and uttered strange guttural sounds. On tour in the United States, Prado played to packed houses, and by the end of 1951, the U.S. mambo mania was going strong. Mambo's new rhythm, a combination of jazz-bop flavor and Cuban *sabor*, proved irresistible. Its reputation as an uninhibited, libidinal dance increased interest in the mambo. A recurring theme in the press coverage was the mambo's seemingly primitive or barbaric dimension, and the mambo was seen as both threat and temptation. The fast, frenetic tempo of the music, the jerky bodily movements, the minimal lyrics and the screeching trumpets, even Pérez Prado's famous grunts, all contributed to the wild eroticism of the mambo.

By 1952, New York's Palladium Ballroom had an all-mambo format, and on Wednesday nights, it featured Mamboscope, the weekly dance fests during which one could mambo all night. Other cities had their own mambo shrines—Chicago had Mambo City, Los Angeles had Ciro's, San Francisco had the Macumba Club. In fall 1954, Tico Records organized *Mambo USA*, a fifty-six-city tour that took the mambo to the U.S. heartland. The forty-strong mambo contingent included Machito, Joe Loco (1921–1988), Facundo Rivero (1912–2002), Miguelito Valdés (1912–1978), Mongo Santamaria (1917–2003), and many other well-known Latin musicians. It did not take long for Tin Pan Alley to jump on the mambo bandwagon, and American tunesmiths began churning out dozens of *mamboids*—songs that were not really mambos though they alluded to them, either musically or in their lyrics, and were in fact amused commentaries on mambo madness. Songs such as "Papa Loves Mambo," a hit for Perry Como, were not mambos at all; rather, they were usually up-tempo, Latin-inflected swing tunes. The mambo elements in these songs typically included some Afro-Cuban percussion, a few screeching trumpet riffs, and above all imitations of Pérez Prado's inimitable grunts. The mambo purists of the day fulminated against mamboids, but during just one week in October 1954, U.S. record companies released no fewer than ten mambo-style recordings.

Cuba was never more evident in the United States than in 1954. Ernest Hemingway was awarded the Nobel Prize in Literature for *The Old Man and the Sea*, a novel about a Cuban fisherman. The top-rated program on television, *I Love Lucy*, chronicled the unpredictable home life of a Cuban bandleader and his ditsy American wife. On the radio, *Bold Venture*, a popular serial set in Havana starring Humphrey Bogart and Lauren Bacall, was in syndication. The Cuban DeCastro sisters (no relation to Fidel Castro) had a hit with "Teach Me Tonight"; the Ames Brothers with the rhumba "The Naughty Lady from Shady Lane" (about a nine-day-old femme fatale); and Dean Martin with "Sway," one of the most popular latunes of all time. And in ballrooms all over the nation, the mambo craze reached a fever pitch.

BIBLIOGRAPHY

Acosta, Leonardo. *Cubano Be, Cubano Bop: One Hundred Years of Jazz in Cuba*. Washington, DC: Smithsonian Books, 2003.

Adler, Barbara Squier. "The Mambo and the Mood." *New York Times Magazine* (16 September 1951): 20.

Andrews, Bart. *The "I Love Lucy" Book*. New York: Doubleday, 1989.

Arnaz, Desi. *A Book*. New York: William Morrow and Company, 1976.

Beardsley, Theodore S. "Rumba-Rhumba: Problema internacional músico-léxico." *Revista Interamericana* 10 (1980–1981): 527–533.

Castellano Gil, José, José Fernández Fernández, Rafael A. Lecuona, and Stanley C. Green. *Ernesto Lecuona: The Genius and His Music*. Laredo, TX: R. A. Lecuona Enterprises, 2004.

Daniel, Yvonne. *Rumba: Dance and Social Change in Cuba*. Bloomington: Indiana University Press, 1995.

Díaz Ayala, Cristóbal. *Música cubana: Del Areyto a la Nueva Trova*. San Juan, Puerto Rico: Editorial Cubanacán, 1981.

Figueroa, Frank. M. *Encyclopedia of Latin American Music in New York*. St. Petersburg, FL: Pillar Publications, 1994.

Leymarie, Isabelle. *Cuban Fire: The Story of Salsa and Latin Jazz*. London: Continuum, 2002.

Orovio, Helio. *Cuban Music from A to Z*. Durham, NC: Duke University Press, 2004.

Pérez, Lisandro. "Cubans in the United States." *Annals of the American Academy of Political And Social Science* 487 (September 1986): 126–137.

Pérez Firmat, Gustavo. *Life on the Hyphen: The Cuban-American Way*. Austin: University of Texas Press, 1994.

Pérez Firmat, Gustavo. "Latunes: An Introduction." *Latin American Research Review* 43, no. 2 (2008): 180–203.

Pérez Firmat, Gustavo. *The Havana Habit*. New Haven, CT: Yale University Press, 2010.

Roberts, John Storm. *The Latin Tinge: The Impact of Latin American Music on the United States*. 2nd ed. New York: Oxford University Press, 1999.

Salazar Primer, Max. *Mambo Kingdom: Latin Music in New York City*. New York: Schirmer Trade Books, 2002.

Shaw, Arnold. *Let's Dance: Popular Music in the 1930s*. New York: Oxford University Press, 1998.

Thomas, Hugh. *Cuba: Or the Pursuit of Freedom*. New York: Da Capo Press, 1998.

Woll, Allen. *The Latin Image in American Film*. Los Angeles: UCLA Latin American Center Publications, 1977.

Woll, Allen. *The Hollywood Musical Goes to War*. Chicago: Nelson-Hall, 1983.

DIASPORAS: AFRO-CUBANS IN THE DIASPORA

Nancy Raquel Mirabal

The communities of Afro-Cubans in the United States and elsewhere that helped define the Cuban nationalist identity.

During the mid- to late-nineteenth century, free people of color left Cuba to organize against Spanish colonialism and slavery. Although only an estimated 10 to 15 percent of the Cubans who left the island were Afro-Cubans, those who migrated to the United States were critical in establishing a definition of *Cubanidad*, a Cuban identity that included race and social equality as central tenets of the nationalist movement.

Cuba was one of the last countries in the hemisphere to abolish slavery (1886) and gain its independence from Spain (1898). Therefore, Afro-Cuban exiles and migrants were involved in exile and migrant revolutionary political movements dedicated to ending slavery and Spanish colonial rule. There were three movements that dominated exile political activity: autonomists, annexationists, and the independence movement. Of the three, the independence movement was the only one to advocate for racial equality and enfranchisement, which attracted Afro-Cubans to it.

The majority of Afro-Cubans who left for the United States settled primarily in New York and Florida and worked in the cigar industry. The torching of plantations and destruction of cigar factories during the Ten Years' War (1868–1878) prompted cigar manufacturers in Cuba to relocate to the United States providing employment for Cuban exiles and migrants. At the same time, the disproportionate number of enslaved Cubans and free people of color involved in the Ten Years' War encouraged Afro-Cubans to see themselves as a necessary part of the nation-building project.

Afro-Cuban women also migrated to work in the cigar industry or work as laundresses, domestic workers, and boarding-house managers. They too were involved in the nationalist and independence movement. However, because women were not allowed formal membership to the political clubs, most of their political work was accomplished through *comités de damas* (women's auxiliaries); some women supported causes as independent *patriotas*, including the respected Paulina Pedroso (1845–1925), who was based in Ybor City, Florida. Although racial equality and enfranchisement were part of the *independentistas'* revolutionary platform, there was little discussion on the rights of women.

The growing number of Afro-Cubans in the United States during the late nineteenth century inspired a more complicated analysis of blackness within the workings of a Cuban nation. According to the nationalist discourse and writings of José Martí, race did not exist, and therefore it was impossible to have racial differences among Cubans. This view inspired Afro-Cubans to publicly challenge slavery, oppose U.S. expansionism and imperialism, and demand that racial equality be an integral part of the Cuban Republic. Rafael Serra and Teofilo Dominguez, as well as the Afro–Puerto Ricans Arturo Schomburg and Sotero Figueroa, worked with the different movements to establish a revolutionary platform based on civil rights and equality. Afro-Cubans published articles in the local exile newspapers and were involved with racially integrated groups in Florida and New York such as the Partido Revolucionario Cubano (Cuban Revolutionary Party), founded in 1892; the Sociedad Republicana de Cuba y Puerto Rico (Republican Society of Cuba and Puerto Rico) formed in 1865 in New York; and El Club de los Independientes (Independents' Club), organized in 1888 in New York. There were also Afro-Cuban clubs, including La Union Martí-Maceo, founded in Ybor City in 1900, and La Liga de Instruccíon, known as the League, founded by Serra, Figueroa, and Martí in New York in the 1890s, with chapters in Florida.

On 24 February 1895, war broke out in Cuba. For three years, insurrections and rebellions continued across the island in the struggle for independence from Spain. The United States intervened in 1898, leading to Spain's cession of control over the island. On 10 December 1898 the Treaty of Paris, which was signed by Spanish and U.S. representatives, handed over Cuba, Puerto Rico, the Philippines, and Guam to the United States. The end of the war signaled a turning point for exile political activity. In less than a year after the war, the Partido Revolucionario Cubano, along with most exile revolutionary clubs, dissolved. The end of the exile nationalist movement was a blow to Afro-Cubans, whose participation in the movement was critical to defining their place within the Cuban diaspora and in a segregated and racist U.S. society. Afro-Cubans found themselves facing a painful and difficult dilemma: return to a Cuba in the making, with no guarantee of social justice and equality, or stay in the United States. Many who returned did so with the strong resolve to effect change in the newly established republic. Those who remained were left to redefine blackness and multiplicity within a segregated society.

Afro-Cuban writers and activists in the United States engaged African American intellectuals and writers in a discussion of alternative meanings of blackness as well as ways to resist segregation, discrimination, and racial violence. They worked closely with Puerto Ricans, Dominicans, West Indians, and Jamaicans in organizing labor unions and creating community networks. Others formed local Cuban clubs as a means to sustain a diasporic Afro *Cubanidad*, an integral element of which was remaining informed about Cuban politics while still negotiating and resisting the racial climate in the United States. Afro-Cuban migrants read, shared, and disseminated copies of *Previsión*, the official newspaper of El Partido Independiente de Color (Independent Party of Color) in Cuba, as well as copies of local African American newspapers.

THE FIRST HALF OF THE TWENTIETH CENTURY

The Morúa Amendment of 1910, which banned the formation of Cuban political parties based on race or color, and the Guerra de Razas (Race War) of 1912 shattered many Cubans' hopes for the creation of a racially just and enfranchised Cuban society. At the same time, racial tensions among white and black Cubans in the diaspora signaled that the often-used rhetoric that all Cubans are Cuban regardless of race was no longer meaningful. Instead, many Afro-Cubans looked to African American institutions, community, and politics, becoming involved in Marcus Garvey's Universal Negro Improvement Association (UNIA), attending historically black colleges and schools, working with African American writers and artists, participating in sports, and performing in African American venues and clubs. They also began to identify deeply with African American ideas, thoughts, and creative expression. As the Afro-Cuban migrant Evelio Grillo noted in his memoir, "My heart and mind belonged to Nat Turner, Frederick Douglass, Harriet Tubman, Sojourner Truth, Paul Laurence Dunbar, John Brown, Paul Robeson, Langston Hughes, W. E. B. Du Bois, Allison Davis, Alain Locke, and the brothers James Weldon and James Rosamond Johnson who wrote 'Lift Every Voice and Sing'" (Grillo p. 17).

During the early 1930s a smaller number of Afro-Cubans left Cuba in protest of the repressive policies of President Gerardo Machado (1925–1933). The majority of these settled in New York, where they became involved in political and cultural clubs and labor unions. Many of these clubs had close ties to labor unions and political organizations in Cuba, establishing a transnationalist connection that would serve as a precursor to a more politicized, widespread Afro-diasporic community. Although smaller in number than previous migrations, this wave proved to be an important network for later migrations of Afro-Cuban musicians, athletes, and writers as well as those seeking factory and garment industry jobs or opening small businesses, restaurants, and bodegas (convenience shops).

It was during the migrations of the 1930s, and 1940s that important Afro-Cuban musicians left Cuba for the United States, including Mario Bauzá, Machito (Francisco Raúl Gutiérrez Grillo), Luciano "Chano" Pozo, Arsenio Rodríguez, and Ramon "Mongo" Santamaría, to name a few. Afro-Cuban musicians greatly influenced and shaped jazz, creating the genres Latin jazz and Cubop. Machito's insistence on naming his band "Machito and His Afro-Cubans" in 1940 signaled the growing power and presence of a distinct Afro-Cuban community in New York. In addition to musicians, athletes, mainly baseball players, including Orestes "Minnie" Miñoso, and boxers, "Kid Gavilan" (Gerardo González) and "Kid Chocolate" (Eligio Sardiñas Montalvo), migrated to the United States. This period would also see the arrival of prominent Afro-Cuban literary figures, such as the poet Nicolás Guillén and Eusebia Cosme, known for her recitations and performances of Cuban poetry. At the same time, Afro-Cuban migrants organized political and social clubs that provided Afro-Cubans with spaces in which to meet, socialize, network, and benefit from being part of a mutual aid society. One of the more important and long-standing clubs to arise in this time was El Club Cubano-InterAmericano, formed in the Bronx in 1945. Afro-Cuban performers, athletes, writers, and club members laid the groundwork for a distinct Afro-Cuban community, one that identified with being both Cuban and part of a larger Afro-diasporic migrant community.

AFTER THE REVOLUTION

The success of the Cuban Revolution in 1959 and the subsequent waves of exiles complicated earlier Afro-Cuban notions of blackness. The revolution changed what it meant to be Cuban in the diaspora. Post-1959 Cuban identity and community were now tied to the Cuban Revolution and communism. Whereas earlier diasporic communities were defined primarily on the basis of being Cuban, now Cuban communities were also defined by politics. For Afro-Cuban migrants who migrated before the revolution and sympathized with elements of the revolution, finding common ground with the first wave of exiles, which consisted of mainly white, upper-class anti-communist Cubans, proved difficult. Geographically, during this period the majority of Afro-Cubans chose to stay in or migrate to the East Coast, in particular New York, a city with a large Afro-diasporic community of Puerto Ricans, Dominicans, Jamaicans, and Haitians. Because the revolution promised to end racism and rectify the racial inequalities of past generations, Afro-Cubans supported it in greater numbers. Those who supported the revolution, connected it to Third World liberation movements and the U.S. civil rights movement. Some, such as the Afro-Cuban writer and activist Lourdes Casal, would change their views of the revolution and create a forum by which Cubans in the diaspora and on the island could communicate and find common ground. An important figure in Cuban exile politics, Casal left Cuba in 1961 and went from being against the Cuban communist regime to sympathizing with the Cuban revolution. She co-founded the Institute for Cuban Studies and the journals *Nueva Generación* (founded in 1972) and *Areito* (founded in 1974). Both publications were based in New York. In 1977 Casal was involved in the Antonio Maceo Brigade, which sponsored trips for young émigrés to Cuba. The following year in 1978 she helped to organize

Ramon "Mongo" Santamarla (1917–2003). Afro-Cuban jazz percussionist Ramón "Mongo" Santamaría performs in New York City's Central Park in 1970. WALTER LOOSS JR./GETTY IMAGES

El Diálogo, which was designed to foster communications between Cubans in the United States and Cuba. These institutions and activities, however, were met with intense criticism and at times, violence. Newspaper offices were ransacked, members were harassed, and their events picketed.

It was not until the Mariel Boatlift in 1980, an exodus that brought an estimated 125,000 Cubans to U.S. shores, and the *balsero* crisis of 1994 that Afro-Cubans left in greater numbers. After the fall of the Soviet Union, Cuba experienced what was known as the Special Period that was characterized by severe economic shortages and chaos. As a result of the Special Period, thousands of Cubans left the island on makeshift rafts. An estimated 15 to 40 percent of Afro-Cubans left Cuba during the Mariel and balsero exiles. According to María Cristina García's 1996 study, only 3 percent of Afro-Cubans left Cuba during the 1960s and 1970s. The arrival of later Afro-Cubans, however, was not welcomed. Whereas the existing Cuban exile community rarely posited or discussed race as part of its cultural or political identity, the later exiles were a more racialized, working-class group.

Public opinion in the United States was less sympathetic to the plight of Cuban exiles and refugees, who were unfairly cast as criminals and deviants. The U.S. government came under pressure to change its policy toward Cuba and Cubans, resulting in the Cuban Democracy Act (1992), which further strengthened the embargo by imposing penalties on American corporations whose foreign subsidiaries traded with Cuba, and Operation Distant Shore (1994), which altered the Cuban Adjustment Act

(1966) by legislating that Cubans needed to arrive on "dry land" to be considered eligible for benefits.

The changes also led to a shift in locations for Cuban resettlement. No longer able to accommodate so many exiles, the city of Miami requested that Catholic Charities, a private network of social service agencies, resettle exiles in cities willing to accept them. These cities included San Francisco; Los Angeles; Santa Fe, New Mexico; Louisville, Kentucky; and Washington, D.C. Some Afro-Cubans opted to stay in their adopted cities, whereas a large number moved to New York City and Miami. For Afro-Cubans who settled in Miami, negotiating a black Cuban identity was not easy. Not easily accepted by the white Cuban majority, Afro-Cubans moved to African-American communities such as Liberty City, where they frequented African-American barbershops, restaurants, and businesses with ease.

In her 5 June 2000 essay on Afro-Cubans in Miami, the Cuban journalist for the *New York Times*, Mirta Ojito, profiled the experiences of two Cuban friends, one white and the other Afro-Cuban who find that their lives in Miami are very different than in Cuba. Shortly after arriving, the friends drift apart with the white Cuban settling comfortably among the white Cuban community and the Afro-Cuban painfully negotiating his blackness and Cuban identity. Not fully accepted by Cubans because of his race, yet not embraced by African Americans because he is Cuban, he ultimately decides, as Ojita tells us, to accept that blackness has a different meaning in the United States and that he is *not* Cuban, but Afro-Cuban.

During the 1990s and the first decade of the twenty-first century, Afro-Cubans left for the United States, Mexico, Canada, Spain, and France. Much like the migrations of the 1940s and 1950s, many of these migrants were athletes, writers, and musicians. They included baseball players Orlando "El Duque" Hernández, José Contreras, and Vladimir Núñez; writer H. G. Carrillo, author of the novel *Loosing My Espanish* (2004); scholar Pedro Perez Sarduy; and journalist Enrique Patterson. In regard to music, the most well-known include the hip-hop group Orishas, which is based in France and has been critical of the Cuban government's claims of a colorblind society; Las Krudas, a lesbian hip-hop group based in the United States, which has been critical of Cuban patriarchy and misogyny; the outspoken and popular musicians Manuel "Manolín" Gonzalez Hernandez, known as El Médico de la Salsa (the doctor of salsa) because he was in medical school in Havana when discovered; the band La Charanga Habanera; and the salsa performer Issac Delgado. El Médico, one of the most popular singers in Cuba and in Miami, is considered a controversial figure, for publicly criticizing the politics that continue, after so many years, to separate Cubans. Famous for his hit "Arriba de la bola," Hernandez has been a strong advocate of dialogue between Cubans in Miami and Havana in an attempt to bridge both communities.

Afro-Cuban artists who left Cuba brought with them strong and important discourses on racism, Cuban identity, sexuality, revolutionary politics, and a future without embargoes, borders, and separation. Echoing the dissatisfaction of later Cuban generations in the United States and Cuba, subsequent Afro-Cuban migrants questioned the viability and sustainability of post-revolutionary politics and forged new directions and discourses regarding Cuban art, politics, and civil society. Despite the invisibility, gaps, and silences within traditional Cuban diasporic historiography, Afro-Cuban migrants and exiles have a long, varied, and rich history in the United States.

BIBLIOGRAPHY

Brock, Lisa, and Digna Castañeda Fuertes, eds. *Between Race and Empire: African-Americans and Cubans before the Cuban Revolution*. Philadelphia: Temple University Press, 1998.

García, María Cristina. *Havana USA: Cuban Exiles and Cuban Americans in South Florida, 1959–1994*. Berkeley: University of California Press, 1996.

Grillo, Evelio. *Black Cuban, Black American: A Memoir*. Houston, TX: Arte Público Press, 2000.

Jiménez Román, Miriam, and Juan Flores, eds. *The Afro-Latin@ Reader: History and Culture in the United States*. Durham, NC: Duke University Press, 2010.

Mirabal, Nancy Raquel. "Scripting Race and Finding Place, African-Americans, Afro Cubans and the Diasporic Imaginary in the United States." In *Neither Enemies nor Friends: Latinos, Blacks, Afro-Latinos,* edited by Anani Dzidzienyo and Suzanne Oboler. New York: Palgrave Macmillan, 2005.

Ojito, Mirta. "Best of Friends, Worlds Apart: How Race Is Lived in America." *New York Times*, 5 June 2000.

DIASPORAS: WAVES OF IMMIGRATION SINCE 1959

Silvia Pedraza

The four major waves of the Cuban exodus from 1959 to 2010, including the policies of both the U.S. and Cuban governments that shaped them.

Over half a century of migration brought around 1.5 million Cuban immigrants to U.S. soil—close to 15 percent of Cuba's population. The exodus was comprised of four distinct waves of immigrants with very different social compositions in terms of class, race, education, family, and values. To understand this exodus, it is necessary to examine certain policies of the U.S. and Cuban governments. The Cuban immigrants arrived in the United States at times when the social and political contexts presented them with vastly different opportunities—such as economic growth or recession, diverse government policy programs, and a warm welcome or cold reception. As a result, they became incorporated to U.S. society in varying ways.

The essential difference between refugees and voluntary migrants lies in their motivations (Kunz 1973). All immigration is the result of both push-and-pull factors (compare Lee 1966); for refugees the *push* is stronger than the *pull*. Political exile is the last step of a process of profound political disaffection (Pedraza 2007). Coerced, and often persecuted, refugees fear for their safety. At the micro level, E. F. Kunz writes of "vintages," or refugee groups that are distinct in "character, background, and avowed political faith" (1973, p. 137). When dramatic changes in the society occur, individuals react differently: Some oppose changes that others support, some call for compromises that to others smell of collaboration. Thus, they leave the country as distinct "vintages." At the macro level, the policies of two governments shape the migration flows.

THE FIRST WAVE: CUBA'S ELITE

Nelson Amaro and Alejandro Portes portrayed the different phases of the Cuban political immigration as changing over time with the exiles' changing principal motivations for leaving. With the unfolding of the Cuban Revolution, over the years, "those who wait" gave way to "those who escape" and then to "those who search." To update their analysis, Silvia Pedraza added "those who hope" and "those who despair" (2007). When the Cuban Revolution in 1959 triumphed over the rule of Fulgencio Batista, the majority of Cubans shared in the euphoria of the Revolution's success, but when the Revolution was radicalized, the exodus of political émigrés took force.

This first wave of migration was composed of Cuba's elite, occurring between 1959 and 1962: "Those who wait" waited for the United States to rescue Cuba from the consolidation of communism only ninety miles away. These upper and upper-middle classes were not tied to Batista's government but were bound to a political and economic structure that, Amaro and Portes underlined, was completely interpenetrated by the demands and initiative of U.S. capital. They were executives and owners of firms, large-scale merchants, sugar mill owners, manufacturers, cattlemen, representatives of foreign companies, and established professionals. Amid the economic and diplomatic war that ensued between Cuba and the United States, they decided to leave. The refugees of this first wave came to the United States driven by Cuba's overturning of the old order and sharp turn toward communism through revolutionary measures such as the nationalization of U.S. industry and agrarian reform laws, all of which entailed serious personal losses: jobs, homes, property, families, friendships, and nation.

In this first stage the exiles' political activity was intensely militant, supporting military counterrevolution against Cuba in actions such as the exiles' invasion of the Bay of Pigs in April 1961. There the 2506 Brigade fought against the Cuban rebel army, waiting in vain for the air cover the United States had promised. The necessary aid did not materialize, and their effort failed (Thomas; Clark).

"Those who escape" were the next group to leave Cuba following further radicalization of the Revolution in the early 1960s. The Catholic Church was silenced after denouncing the communist direction the revolution was taking; the electoral system collapsed when the jubilant crowds chanted around Castro "Elecciones para qué?" ("What do we need elections for?"); and Castro announced he had always been a Marxist-Leninist and would be so until the day he died. These developments sparked an exodus of those from the middle class.

When the private universities and schools began to close in 1961, fears that the children would be educated by the state in communist schools, or even be sent to the Soviet Union, became prevalent. More than 14,000 children were sent alone to the United States through Operation Pedro Pan by their frightened parents (Walsh; Torres). Often the children arrived with nothing other than their names and addresses pinned onto their clothes. At this time the U.S. government initiated the multifaceted Cuban Refugee Program that assisted most of the refugees, helping them to translate their Cuban education and expertise into U.S. credentials (Pedraza-Bailey 1985). This exodus overrepresented the professional, managerial, and middle classes (31%) and clerical and sales workers (33%) (Fagen et al.).

With breathtaking speed, in a couple of years the Cuban Revolution moved through several distinct phases identified by Amaro as democracy, humanism, nationalism, socialism, and Marxism-Leninism. The punitive U.S. policy—cutting the sugar quota, instituting a trade embargo, and backing the exiles' invasion of Cuba—aided the rapidity of this transition. To Fidel and Raúl Castro, the exiles were *gusanos* (worms).

Lourdes Casal observed that although the "highly belligerent" counter-revolutionary movements of the first two phases never actively engaged all exiles, they did draw on the financial and moral support of the majority of exiles who hoped for Castro's overthrow and for their own return to Cuba. When the counter-revolution failed, the Cuban communities became disenchanted with dissident activities and withdrew their support. After the October Missile Crisis in 1962, air travel between Cuba and the United States ceased. The U.S. government provided direct transportation only for the approximately one thousand Cuban exiles who had been imprisoned in Cuba after the Bay of Pigs fiasco, along with their relatives, in an exchange for medicine, medical equipment, food, and money.

During this period, the only Cubans who arrived in the United States had either overstayed their visas in other countries or escaped Cuba illegally in boats and rafts. Half of the arrivals to the United States were blue-collar workers, skilled and unskilled; others were agricultural workers and fishermen (Casal). The Cuban government had introduced food rationing and compulsory military service, spurring the exodus.

THE SECOND WAVE: CUBA'S PETITE BOURGEOISIE

In the fall 1965 a chaotic period ensued when hundreds of boats departed Miami for the Cuban port of Camarioca, where they picked up thousands of relatives to come to the United States. This wave of emigrants was "those who search." In response to President Lyndon Johnson's open-door policy that welcomed refugees from communism, this Cuban exodus was organized and concerted. In 1966, recognizing the need to give legal status to the more than 250,000 Cuban refugees who lived in the United States, the U.S. Congress passed the Cuban Adjustment Act, which allowed Cubans who entered the United States legally to become legal residents one year and one day after arrival. For eight years, beginning in December 1965, the United States and Cuban governments administered an orderly air bridge: The twice-daily *Vuelos de la Libertad* (Freedom Flights) brought 250,000 Cubans to Miami, where the Cuban Refugee Program swiftly processed and relocated them, dispersing them throughout the United States.

Kunz distinguished anticipatory from acute refugee movements. The joint policy of the United States and Cuban governments turned this initially acute exodus into an orderly anticipatory movement. Both governments have often "cooperated with the enemy," as Jorge Domínguez stressed. Throughout this period, the Memorandum of Understanding regulated the departure. Both countries compiled their master lists: in the United States, of those who claimed their relatives in Cuba; in Cuba, of those who requested departure. Jointly, both governments decided who would emigrate through family networks. Cuba barred from exit young men of military service age, as well as professionals and skilled workers, such as doctors (Clark).

Most of the emigrants of this period were working class and petite bourgeoisie: employees, independent craftsmen, small merchants, and skilled and semi-skilled workers. These were some of the leanest and most idealistic years of the Cuban Revolution. To spread access to basic education and healthcare, young, educated Cubans went to live in the countryside, working in public health campaigns and in literacy campaigns to educate poor peasants. At the same time, the impact of the hemispheric trade embargo imposed by the Organization of American States in 1964 resulted in profound economic dislocations. In Amaro and Portes's view, increasingly the immigration ceased to be a political act and became an economic act. Yet their distinction missed the reality that while life in Cuba grew harsh for all, it turned particularly bitter for those who had announced their dissent by declaring their intention to leave. Those who applied to leave lost their jobs and all their belongings, were ostracized as enemies, and were forced to do so-called volunteer work.

The social transformations the Revolution effected—political and economic—were so pervasive that they always *pushed* Cubans; the United States, in facilitating the migration, always *pulled* them. Moreover, the Cuban migration is unique in the extent to which both the U.S. and Cuban governments organized, concerted, and facilitated the exodus (Tabori). Together, Pedraza argued, they set in motion a system of political migration that for many years proved beneficial to both governments. The loss of the educated, professional middle classes indeed proved erosive to the Cuban Revolution, but it also served the positive function of externalizing dissent. At the same time, in the United States, the arrival of so many refugees who "voted with their feet" also served to provide the legitimacy necessary for foreign policy actions during the tense years of the Cold War (Pedraza-Bailey).

By 1970 only 12 percent of the arriving Cuban immigrants were professionals or managers. More than half were blue-collar, service, or agricultural workers (Aguirre). Although Cuban exiles are clearly heterogeneous, the celebrated success story of Cuban immigration often obscures that fact, and it particularly obscures the Cuban poor who live in Miami's *la Southwestcera*. Casal emphasized the costs of the success story, which prevents Cubans from getting a clear picture of their true situation, desensitizes them to the hidden costs of success, and isolates them from other minorities.

Cuban immigrants who arrived after the air bridge ended in 1973 consisted of refugees who previously had lived in Spain and those who made up Cuba's middling service sectors: cooks, gardeners, domestics, street vendors, shoe shiners, barbers, hairdressers, taxi drivers, and small retail merchants (Portes et al.). They left Cuba after Castro launched the Revolutionary Offensive in 1968, confiscating more than 55,000 small businesses. The Cuban government labeled these emigrants *parásitos* (parasites).

With the economic transition to socialism accomplished, in the 1970s the Cuban government cast the shape of the political system. The old idealism and romanticism of the 1960s gave way to what Mesa-Lago called pragmatism (1978). This new phase resulted from the failed mobilization of hundreds of thousands of Cubans all over the island to achieve the national goal of producing 10 million tons of sugar in 1970.

In the United States the Cuban community became far more diverse, with more ideological pluralism. The gap between the political generation that came of age in Cuba during certain critical periods of Cuban history (compare Zeitlin) and that which came of age in the United States under the influence of the civil rights and anti-Vietnam War movements was a chasm. It was a group of fifty-five progressive young people who, in December 1977, first broke through nineteen years of hostility and isolation. The Antonio Maceo Brigade's visit to the island left a profound mark, captured in the documentary *55 Hermanos* (55 Brothers and Sisters, 1978). Widely shown in Cuba, the film gave evidence of the suffering that exile had inflicted on both those who had left and those who had been left behind.

In 1978 discussions between the Cuban government and the Cuban community in exile (known as the "Dialogue") resulted in the Cuban government agreeing to release the political prisoners and to allow Cubans in the United States to visit their families on the island. Yesterday's *gusanos* became respectable "members of the Cuban community abroad." The Cuban community split into opposing camps: those who supported the Dialogue and those who opposed it; those who returned to visit Cuba and those who refused. Still, the political prisoners were released, and hundreds of thousands of Cubans returned to Cuba in the following years, seeking the family they loved and the vestiges of the life they once led.

THE THIRD WAVE: CUBA'S *MARIELITOS*

Few expected the chaotic flotilla exodus in 1980 that lasted from April to September, bringing 125,000 more Cubans to the United States. From Miami, thousands of boats manned by relatives sped to Cuba's Mariel harbor. At times they brought their families; other times they brought whomever angry officials put onto the boats. Toward the end of the period, these people included Cuba's social undesirables: prisoners, mental patients, and homosexuals. The Castro government called them "antisocial elements" and *escoria* (scum). No longer the exiles of the transition from capitalism to communism, they were the children of communism itself. President Jimmy Carter's ambivalent government policy both welcomed them "with open hearts and open arms" and delimited the flow.

Were they "scum"? Robert Bach, Jennifer B. Bach, and Timothy Triplett sampled the *Marielitos* while they were still in the refugee camps: Most were young men, unmarried or unaccompanied, and a higher proportion were black when compared with earlier groups (1981–1982). Their origins were overwhelmingly working class—71 percent were blue-collar workers and bus, taxi, and truck drivers. Indeed, there were some who had been in prison. According to the Immigration and Naturalization Service around 19 percent (24,000) admitted they had been in jail in Cuba. Of those who had been in prison, 5,486 were political prisoners, and 70 percent had been jailed for minor crimes or for acts such as vagrancy or participation in the black market that were not crimes in the United States. The Cuban *Ley de Peligrosidad Social* (Law of Dangerous Social Behavior), introduced in the mid-1970s, had criminalized some forms of dissent, including participating in the black market (buying or selling clothes and food); dodging or deserting military service; refusing to work for the state, particularly in the cane fields; and trying to escape Cuba illegally (Bach et al.). Only 7 percent of those who had been jailed in Cuba were serious criminals (Montgomery). Given their youth, the Marielitos clearly constituted a different political generation (Mannheim). Roughly half of the Mariel immigrants had come of age during the late 1960s or the 1970s, when limits on freedom of expression became particularly acute for artists and intellectuals in Cuba. Moreover, homosexuality was scorned and punished by prison sentence.

At the two poles divided by twenty years of emigration stood two "vintages" that, at best, hardly comprehended each other and, at worst, were hostile (Kunz 1973). A typical 1960 émigré was an older, white executive who had become disaffected by the nationalization of U.S. industry in the early years of the Revolution. A typical 1980 émigré was a young, black bus driver who scarcely would have minded that nationalization. Instead, he might have spent many years believing in the professed goals of the Revolution, until a bout of prison terms for his participation in the extensive black market of the 1970s promoted his disaffection. The early and most recent waves of Cuban immigrants in the United States live side by side but remain aloof from each other, tending to blame each other for having left too soon or stayed too long. As Rieff observed, Cuba is in the heart of the exile—and in the heart of Miami. Cubans suffer a profound nostalgia for the Cuba of memory and desire. But the Cuba they long for is not quite the same Cuba. The early exiles' nostalgia attaches to the Cuba they knew—*la Cuba de ayer* (yesterday's Cuba), before the Revolution; recent exiles long for *la Cuba de hoy* (today's Cuba), of the Revolution.

THE FOURTH WAVE: CUBA'S *BALSEROS*

The Mariel exodus proved so traumatic for both countries that the doors to further migration closed. In the mid-1980s the U.S. and Cuban governments signed a new migration agreement, but in actual practice only around 2,000 visas per year were issued. Cuba's economic crisis reached new depths when communism collapsed in Eastern Europe. Cuba had been overwhelmingly dependent on the Soviet bloc nations for trade and economic subsidies, and the impact of these losses was devastating: a decline in the Cuban national product by one-half, and in investment by two-thirds from 1989 to 1993. Healthcare, education, pensions, and other services established after the Revolution rapidly deteriorated (Mesa-Lago 1994). The economic crisis was so severe that Castro declared it "a special period in a time of peace." This *período especial* was to have been temporary, but it deepened when the United States tightened its embargo on Cuba in 1992 with the Torricelli Act. Abject need and hunger became the reality of Cubans' lives. Cuba managed to survive for a decade until Venezuela's Hugo Chavez came to the rescue, and Cuba opened up the economy to trade, investment, and tourism.

At the same time, the dissident movement grew into a social movement. Despite different political thrusts (e.g., democratic socialist, environmentalist, Christian Democrat), all dissidents in Cuba called for a new democratic opening, a liberalization of political structures. Both Fidel and Raúl Castro adamantly rejected these calls. Hence, both economic and political want drove the emigration of the new Cubans, together with the ever present desire for family reunification.

The new Cuban exodus took several forms (compare Rodríguez-Chavez), with illegal emigration being the primary one. Cubans became so desperate that they left on *balsas* (rafts), risking death from starvation, dehydration, drowning, or sharks. In summer 1994 the political crisis deepened when the Cuban Coast Guard overturned a tugboat of people with powerful sprays of water, killing more than forty adults and children. This was followed by riots on 5 August, when thousands of Cubans protested in the streets of Havana in the largest demonstration of its kind. Castro ordered the Cuban Coast Guard to stop trying to prevent illegal emigration, and immediately, thousands of *balseros* put out to sea in the hopes of reaching Miami. Between July and September the U.S. Coast Guard rescued 33,395 Cubans at sea. One of them, Lizbet Martínez, a twelve-year old girl fleeing Cuba with her parents, played "The Star-Spangled Banner" on her violin for her rescuers (Balmaseda 1994a). "Those who despair" constituted this last wave of migration.

However, abrupt policy changes made the Cubans unwelcome. Under orders from President Bill Clinton and Attorney General Janet Reno, the U.S. Coast Guard intercepted the rafts and diverted them to Guantánamo, where more than 30,000 people lived in tents for many months until they gained entry to the United States. Once again, the U.S. government sought to disperse the new arrivals throughout the United States, though eventually most of them found their way to Florida.

This crisis resulted in the new Migration Accords of 1994–1995, in which the United States promised to actually give at least 20,000 visas per year for Cubans to come to the United States. It also put in place the "wet foot/dry foot" immigration policy, which stipulated that balseros found at sea ("wet foot") would be returned to Cuba, whereas those who had managed to reach land ("dry foot") would be permitted to stay. "Cuba bleeds," headlined Liz Balmaseda (1994b), "and the drops are called rafts." Data from the 2009 American Community Survey show that of the 991,385 persons born in Cuba, 46.3 percent arrived in the United States from 1990 on—about 459,000 (U. S. Census Bureau).

As before, interpretations of the exodus were polarized into two positions. One position held that the emigrants evidenced the loss of legitimacy of the Cuban Revolution, that they discredited it; the other position was that they were propelled by the scarcity of consumer goods and merely embarrassed the Revolution (Fernández). More than a million and a half persons over half a century: Were they political refugees or economic immigrants?

Two different axes determine whether they were political refugees or economic immigrants (Pedraza). First, the motivation of the immigrants defines them as political or economic immigrants—a sociological distinction. Because all societies are simultaneously and inextricably political and economic, Cuba's refugees are, and have always been, both political and economic. But when people grow politically disaffected, when they lose faith and trust in their government and its cause, they can no longer be disposed of as simply economic immigrants. Cuba's refugees have always been fundamentally political.

Second, the governments that regulate their exit and arrival define immigrants as either political or economic immigrants—a legal distinction. Historically, Cubans had been recognized and welcomed as refugees, but with the balseros, for the first time they were defined as aliens attempting to enter the United States illegally. At the other end, in Cuba, for many years those who left were labeled traitors and counter-revolutionaries; later, they were characterized as economic emigrants. The Cuban exodus, over half a century old, has been driven not only by the trauma of revolutionary change in Cuba and the economic hardships it engendered, but also by Cuba's inability to tolerate dissent.

Cuban Raft Crisis of 1994. The economic and political crises of the early 1990s left many Cubans so desperate that they fled on balsas (rafts), risking death due to starvation, dehydration, drowning, or sharks. These emigrants were photographed in 1994 on an overcrowded raft they had dubbed "La Esperanza" (Hope). AP IMAGES/JOSE GOITIA

BIBLIOGRAPHY

Amaro, Nelson, and Alejandro Portes. "Una sociología del exilio: Situación de los grupos Cubanos en los Estados Unidos." *Aportes* 23 (January 1972): 6–24.

Amaro Victoria, Nelson. "Mass and Class in the Origins of the Cuban Revolution." In *Cuban Communism*, edited by Irving Louis Horowitz. New Brunswick, NJ: Transaction Books, 1977.

Bach, Robert L., Jennifer B. Bach, and Timothy Triplett. "The Flotilla 'Entrants': Latest and Most Controversial." *Cuban Studies* 11–12 (1981–1982): 29–48.

Balmaseda, Liz. "Balserita violinista toca pero también escribe como los Angeles." *El Nuevo Herald*, 19 October 1994a.

Balmaseda, Liz. "Cuba Bleeds, and the Drops Are Called Rafts." *Miami Herald*, 17 August 1994b.

Casal, Lourdes. "Cubans in the United States: Their Impact on U.S.-Cuban Relations." In *Revolutionary Cuba in the World Arena*, edited by Martin Weinstein. Philadelphia: Ishi, 1979.

Clark, Juan M. *Cuba: Mito y realidad*. Miami and Caracas: Saeta Ediciones, 1992.

Domínguez, Jorge I. "Cooperating with the Enemy? U. S. Immigration Policies toward Cuba." In *Western Hemisphere Immigration and United States Foreign Policy*, edited by Christopher Mitchell. University Park: Pennsylvania State University Press, 1992.

Fagen, Richard R., Richard A. Brody, and Thomas J. O'Leary. *Cubans in Exile: Disaffection and the Revolution*. Palo Alto, CA: Stanford University Press, 1968.

Fernández, Gastón. "The Freedom Flotilla: A Legitimacy Crisis of Cuban Socialism?" *Journal of Interamerican Studies and World Affairs* 24, no. 2 (May 1982): 183–209.

Kunz, E. F. "The Refugee in Flight: Kinetic Models and Forms of Displacement." *International Migration Review* 7, no. 2 (summer 1973): 125–146.

Kunz, E. F. "Exile and Resettlement: Refugee Theory." *International Migration Review* 15, no. 1 (1981): 42–51.

Lee, Everett S. "A Theory of Migration." *Demography* 3 (1966): 47–57.

Mannheim, Karl. *Essays in the Sociology of Knowledge*. New York: Oxford University Press, 1952.

Mesa-Lago, Carmelo. *Cuba in the 1970s: Pragmatism and Institutionalization*. Albuquerque: University of New Mexico Press, 1978.

Mesa-Lago, Carmelo. "Will Cuba's Economic Reforms Work?" *Miami Herald*, 2 January 1994.

Montgomery, Paul L. "For Cuban Refugees, Promise of U.S. Fades." *New York Times*, 19 April 1981.

Pedraza, Silvia. *Political Disaffection in Cuba's Revolution and Exodus*. New York and London: Cambridge University Press, 2007.

Pedraza-Bailey, Silvia. *Political and Economic Migrants in America: Cubans and Mexicans*. Austin: University of Texas Press, 1985.

Portes, Alejandro, Juan M. Clark, and Robert L. Bach. "The New Wave: A Statistical Profile of Recent Cuban Exiles to the United States." *Cuban Studies* 7, no. 1 (January 1977): 1–32.

Rieff, David. *The Exile: Cuba in the Heart of Miami*. New York: Simon & Schuster, 1993.

Rivas-Porta, Guillermo. "El pueblo Cubano: Protagonista, víctima, y espectador." *Desafíos* 1 (August–September 1994): 4–5.

Rodríguez-Chavez, Ernesto. "Tendencias actuales del flujo migratorio Cubano." *Cuadernos de Nuestra América* 10 (1993): 114–137.

Tabori, Paul. *The Anatomy of Exile*. London: Harrap, 1972.

Thomas, Hugh. *The Cuban Revolution*. New York: Harper & Row, 1977.

Torres, María de los Angeles. *The Lost Apple: Operation Pedro Pan and the Cuban Children's Program*. Gainesville: University Press of Florida, 2003.

U. S. Census Bureau, 2009 American Community Survey. Selected Population Profiles: Country of Birth: Cuba. Available from http://factfinder.census.gov.

Walsh, Bryan O. "Cuban Refugee Children." *Journal of Inter-American Studies and World Affairs* 13 (July–October 1971): 378–415.

Zeitlin, Maurice. "Political Generations in the Cuban Working Class." *American Journal of Sociology* 71, no. 5 (March 1966): 493–508.

DIASPORAS: CUBANS ABROAD, POST-1959

Jorge Duany

The Cuban diaspora, one of the largest refugee movements in recent history following the Cuban Revolution of 1959.

Between 1959 and 2009, approximately 1.5 million Cubans moved abroad. Several generations of Cubans and their descendants have lived in the United States, especially in South Florida, northern New Jersey, and New York. In addition, thousands of Cubans settled in Puerto Rico, Spain, Venezuela, and Mexico. In the late 1990s and early 2000s, Cuban migrants expanded their destinations to other countries of Latin America, the Caribbean, and Europe. As of 2010, the Cuban diaspora was extremely diverse, partly because of successive waves of migration and broadening settlement patterns.

THE GOLDEN EXILES

The massive exodus of Cuban refugees originated with the dismantling of Fulgencio Batista's rule, which lasted from 1952 to 1958. On 1 January 1959, Fidel Castro's overthrow of Batista's government launched the first socialist revolution in the Americas and a large number of exiles. The first to leave Cuba were military officers, government officials, large landowners, and businesspersons associated with the Batista period. As the revolution became more radical, the exodus increasingly included disillusioned members of the middle class, such as professionals and managers, especially those who had been employed by U.S. corporations.

The first post-revolutionary migrant wave between 1959 and 1962 was dubbed the Golden Exile because most refugees came from the upper and middle strata of Cuban society. The majority were urban, well-educated, and white-collar workers. Most were born in the island's largest cities, especially Havana. In addition, the exiles overrepresented the lighter-skinned sectors of the population, mainly of Spanish origin. Many fled for political or religious reasons, fearing persecution by the revolutionary government. Between 1959 and 1962, the U.S. government admitted 248,070 Cubans (Clark p. 75).

Beginning in 1961, the federally funded Cuban Refugee Program provided assistance with professional and vocational retraining, English-language instruction, and college tuition loans. In addition, the program relocated exiles outside South Florida to areas with better employment opportunities at the time. By 1966, the U.S. government had resettled 130,599 Cubans in other states and territories, especially New York, New Jersey, California, and Puerto Rico (Masud-Piloto p. 67; Pedraza-Bailey pp. 40–52). Many exiles later returned to Miami because of its proximity to Cuba, increasing its concentration of Cuban residents and expanding its economy.

During the early 1960s, Cuban refugees settled primarily in Miami. They quickly occupied the Riverside and Shenandoah neighborhoods, at the time a decaying area near the central business district between Flagler and Southwest Eighth Streets, and later rechristened Little Havana or Calle Ocho. This area became increasingly Cuban in its businesses and cultural landscape. Another city that attracted working-class refugees was Hialeah, north of Miami, which became known as Little Marianao, after a Havana suburb. Subsequently, middle-class Cubans tended to move to suburban neighborhoods in southwest Miami and nearby cities such as Sweetwater and Westchester. Little Havana became the symbolic core of Cuban America.

Before 1959, Miami (roughly coterminous with Dade County) was a small town with few Cuban residents. By 1970, one-fourth of Dade County's population was Hispanic, mostly of Cuban origin. Later it became the U.S. city with the largest proportion of foreign-born residents, as well as a hub for international trade, tourism, transportation, and finance. Cuban exiles played a key role in the transformation of Miami from a winter resort into the economic capital of Latin America and the Caribbean.

From the beginning, Cuban exiles in Miami constituted a dense community that resisted geographic dispersion. Predominantly Cuban neighborhoods were increasingly isolated from those of other ethnic groups such as Jews, African Americans, and other Hispanics. This residential segregation coincided with the rise of an ethnic enclave, a spatial concentration of Cuban-owned businesses in a wide range of economic activities catering mainly to the émigré community and employing many compatriots.

Miami's Little Havana. A man uses a pay phone near a Cuban café along southwest 8th Street in the Little Havana district of Miami, Florida, in October 2006. Although many Cubans have moved to suburban neighborhoods in southwest Miami and nearby cities, Little Havana remains the symbolic core of Cuban America. © CARLOS BARRIA/ REUTERS/CORBIS

THE FREEDOM FLIGHTS

The Cuban Missile Crisis in October 1962 interrupted commercial travel between Cuba and the United States. Clandestine migration increased correspondingly, mostly by small craft and makeshift vessels. According to U.S. sources, 6,698 so-called boat people from Cuba arrived in Florida between 1962 and 1965. In addition, 55,916 Cubans were admitted to the United States from other countries such as Mexico and Spain (Ackerman and Clark p. 14; Clark p. 75).

On 28 September 1965, Castro announced that he would permit anyone wishing to leave the island to do so. On 10 October, he opened the port of Camarioca in northern Matanzas, allowing 4,993 persons to depart the country before 15 November (Clark p. 86). Camarioca ushered in a second migrant wave from revolutionary Cuba.

Diplomatic negotiations between Washington and Havana established a regular air bridge between Varadero (a tourist resort east of Havana) and Miami beginning on 1 December 1965. The U.S. government touted the chartered planes as the Freedom Flights. By then, the exodus had become more representative of the island's population. As the number of professionals and managers decreased, the number of blue-collar and service workers increased. Skilled and semiskilled workers, salespersons, and small farmers were the bulk of the immigrants between 1965 and 1973, when Castro cancelled the flights. Shifts in the refugee flow mirrored the impact of revolutionary programs on wider segments of the Cuban population, such as small-scale merchants and artisans. Although most of the Freedom Flights refugees were white and urban in origin, they were predominantly female, older, and less educated than earlier refugees, reflecting travel restrictions imposed by the Castro government. Moreover, economic motives loomed larger during this stage than before. Thus, the Freedom Flights expanded the socioeconomic diversity of Cubans in the United States.

Like their predecessors, Cuban immigrants who arrived on the Freedom Flights settled primarily in Miami, Hialeah, and other cities in South Florida. These cities acquired a distinctive Cuban flavor, as Cuban residents became the largest ethnic group within the local population. Cuban American firms tended to concentrate in retail trade, construction, manufacturing, and professional services. Businesses included restaurants, cafeterias, supermarkets, grocery stores, drugstores, gas stations, bakeries, and other shops. Furthermore, Miami Cubans established their own private schools, churches, theaters, social clubs, tabloids, monuments, and festivals.

A secondary concentration of Cuban émigrés emerged in the adjacent industrial towns of West New York and Union City in New Jersey. This area became known as Little Santa Clara because many exiles were from the province of Las Villas, later called Villa Clara. There the exiles created a strong ethnic community. Most people were employed in blue-collar occupations, particularly as factory workers, and Cuban-owned businesses proliferated, especially along the main commercial thoroughfare, Bergenline Avenue, together with newspapers, religious organizations, social clubs, and political groups. The Cuban community in West New York and Union City dwindled over time as many of their elderly retired in South Florida.

Smaller numbers of exiles established themselves in Puerto Rico, mostly in the San Juan metropolitan area. Cuban migration to San Juan was more selective than to U.S. cities, producing a concentration of upper- and middle-class managers, professionals, and sales personnel. As a result, the socioeconomic profile of Cubans in Puerto Rico resembled that of a so-called middleman minority, specializing in retail trade and professional services.

THE MARIEL BOATLIFT

The third migrant wave, from Mariel harbor to Key West, Florida, took place between 21 April and 26 September 1980. One reason for the Mariel Boatlift was that in 1979, some 100,000 exiles had visited Cuba, renewing contacts with relatives and familiarizing them with economic opportunities abroad. The immediate cause of the exodus was the takeover of the Peruvian embassy in Havana by more than 10,800 Cubans who wanted to migrate. In a reprise of Camarioca, the Cuban government opened the port of Mariel, near Havana, for those who could be picked up by relatives living abroad. When exiles arrived in Mariel aboard private boats and ships, Cuban officials forced them to take unrelated persons, some of whom had been inmates at prisons or psychiatric hospitals, and some who had been identified as prostitutes or homosexuals. Consequently, the Mariel exodus tarnished the reputation of the entire Cuban American community. The boatlift ended abruptly when Castro closed Mariel for further emigration.

The Mariel exodus brought 124,779 Cubans to Key West. Most of the *Marielitos* (as they were pejoratively labeled) were young, single men with a working-class background and an elementary education. Approximately 20 percent classified themselves as black or other (most likely mulattos), compared to only 7 percent of the Cubans who had arrived between 1960 and 1964. Contrary to media reports, less than 2 percent of the Marielitos were common criminals, though 25 percent had been imprisoned for various reasons, including ideological differences with the government and supposedly antisocial behavior such as public displays of homosexuality (Clark et al. p. 7; see also Hernández and Gomis). Thus, the socioeconomic profile of the Mariel exodus departed significantly from those of previous refugee waves, especially those of the early 1960s.

The 1980 boatlift deepened the rifts between old and new Cubans in Miami, where most of the latter group settled. The occupational structure of Cuban Miami became even more heterogeneous than before with the arrival of a large number of service and blue-collar workers. Thus, Miami's exile community became more representative of the entire Cuban population as the inverse relationship between date of departure from Cuba and social status became more visible. The diminutive term *Marielito* itself signaled the public scorn of the new arrivals. Initially, Mariel Cubans faced unemployment, low-paid work, and welfare dependence. Most ended up working for themselves or their compatriots in Miami's Cuban enclave.

THE *BALSEROS*

The fourth migrant wave began during the Special Period in Time of Peace, the official euphemism for Cuba's prolonged economic crisis after the fall of the Berlin Wall in 1989 and the collapse of the Soviet Union in 1991. On 5 August 1994, for the first time in three decades, hundreds of Cubans protested publicly against the government in the streets of Centro Habana in what became known as the *maleconazo* (from El Malecón, Havana's seafront boulevard). On 12 August Castro announced that his government would let those who wanted to leave the country do so in any way they could. For the third time, the Castro regime encouraged a sudden and mass migration to the United States. Thousands took to the sea on anything that floated, creating the *balsero* crisis.

The term *balseros* (rafters) refers to people who attempt to sail across the Florida Straits in home-made rafts, tire tubes, small boats, refurbished vehicles, and other improvised vessels. At least 63,175 Cuban rafters arrived in the United States between 1959 and 1994; during the fall of 1994, unauthorized migration from Cuba broke all records since Mariel. Between 13 August and 13 September the U.S. Coast Guard detained 30,879 Cubans in the Florida Straits (Rodríguez Chávez p. 112). The backdrop of the exodus was the decline in the material conditions of daily life in Cuba, especially food and water shortages, power blackouts, deteriorating public health, and a decaying infrastructure, particularly in housing and transportation. According to Cuban sources, material deprivation and family reunification became the main causes for leaving the country. When interviewed in Cuba, would-be migrants said they wanted to move primarily for economic or personal reasons, especially to join relatives living abroad. According to U.S.-based scholars, economic difficulties aggravated political dissatisfaction with the Cuban government. Once in U.S. territory, most balseros claimed that their chief motivation was the desire for freedom and release from state control.

Compared to earlier migrant waves from Cuba, the balseros were much more representative of the island's occupational structure; the majority belonged to the working class, particularly manual laborers. In addition, most were relatively young, male, light-skinned, urban in origin, and born in Cuba's western provinces, especially Havana. This pattern continued during the first decade of the twenty-first century. The majority of the balseros settled in Miami, although some made it to Union City, West New York, and other U.S. cities. Many of those who moved north eventually returned to South Florida. In contrast to other ethnic groups in the United States, Cubans increasingly clustered in a single location. In 2009, the U.S. Census Bureau estimated that 931,258 Cubans lived in the Miami-Fort Lauderdale-Pompano Beach metropolitan area. Miami grew to have the second-largest Cuban population in the world, smaller than Havana but larger than Santiago de Cuba.

MIGRATION DURING THE SPECIAL PERIOD

During the first decade of the twenty-first century, the diaspora drew primarily on the lower and middle rungs of the labor force, especially unskilled service and blue-collar workers, but it also included a relatively high share of professionals and managers. Thus, the occupational backgrounds of émigrés from post–Soviet Cuba were very diverse. The Cuban migrant flow continued to be primarily oriented toward the United States, especially South Florida. Between 1996 and 2009, more than two-thirds of all Cubans admitted to the United States intended to live in Miami. The operation of social networks that often nurture chain migration, as well as the wide gap in wages and employment opportunities between Cuba and the United States, largely explain this geographic concentration. For economic, cultural, and family reasons, Miami remained the preferred destination for most Cubans abroad.

Nevertheless, the émigré population outside the United States grew steadily after the 1990s. During the Special Period, thousands of Cubans relocated to various Latin American and Caribbean nations, including the Dominican Republic, Chile, and Jamaica, as well as European countries such as Germany, Italy, and France. Canada also became an important place for settlement or sojourning. Several former republics of the Soviet Union, including Russia, Uzbekistan, and Ukraine, attracted sizable numbers of Cubans. Some Cubans followed the trade and tourist routes developed in Cuba after 1989. Consequently, the Cuban diaspora became more widely scattered than ever before.

BIBLIOGRAPHY

Ackerman, Holly, and Juan M. Clark. *The Cuban Balseros: Voyage of Uncertainty.* Miami, FL: Cuban American National Council, 1995.

Aja Díaz, Antonio. "La emigración cubana en los años noventa." *Cuban Studies* 30 (1999): 1–25.

Aja Díaz, Antonio. *Al cruzar las fronteras.* Havana: Centro de Estudios Demográficos/Fondo de Población de las Naciones Unidas, 2009.

Boswell, Thomas D., and James R. Curtis. *The Cuban-American Experience: Culture, Images, and Perspectives.* Totowa, NJ: Rowman & Allanheld, 1984.

Clark, Juan M. "The Exodus from Revolutionary Cuba (1959–1974): A Sociological Analysis." Ph.D. diss., University of Florida, 1975.

Clark, Juan M., José I. Lazaga, and Rose S. Roque. *The 1980 Mariel Exodus: An Assessment and Prospect.* Washington, DC: Council for Inter-American Security, 1981.

Cobas, José A., and Jorge Duany. *Cubans in Puerto Rico: Ethnic Economy and Cultural Identity.* Gainesville: University Press of Florida, 1997.

Eckstein, Susan. *The Immigrant Divide: How Cuban Americans Changed the U.S. and Their Homeland.* New York: Routledge, 2009.

Esteve, Himilce. *El exilio cubano en Puerto Rico: Su impacto político-social (1959–1983).* San Juan, Puerto Rico: Editorial Raíces, 1984.

Fagen, Richard, Richard A. Brody, and Thomas O'Leary. *Cubans in Exile: Disaffection and the Revolution.* Stanford, CA: Stanford University Press, 1968.

García, María Cristina. *Havana USA: Cuban Exiles and Cuban Americans in South Florida, 1959–1994.* Berkeley: University of California Press, 1996.

Grenier, Guillermo J., and Lisandro Pérez. *The Legacy of Exile: Cubans in the United States.* Boston: Allyn and Bacon, 2003.

Hernández, Rafael, and Redi Gomis. "Retrato del Mariel: El ángulo socioeconómico." *Cuadernos de Nuestra América* 3, no. 5 (1986): 124–151.

Martínez, Milagros, Blanca Morejón, Antonio Aja, et al. *Los balseros cubanos: Un estudio a partir de las salidas ilegales.* Havana: Editorial de Ciencias Sociales, 1996.

Masud-Piloto, Félix. *From Welcome Exiles to Illegal Immigrants: Cuban Migration to the United States, 1959–1995.* Lanham, MD: Rowman & Littlefield, 1996.

Pedraza, Silvia. *Political Disaffection in Cuba's Revolution and Exile.* New York: Cambridge University Press, 2007.

Pedraza-Bailey, Silvia. *Political and Economic Migrants in America: Cubans and Mexicans.* Austin: University of Texas Press, 1985.

Portes, Alejandro, and Robert L. Bach. *Latin Journey: Cuban and Mexican Immigrants in the United States.* Berkeley: University of California Press, 1985.

Portes, Alejandro, and Alex Stepick. *City on the Edge: The Transformation of Miami.* Berkeley: University of California Press, 1993.

Prieto, Yolanda. *The Cubans of Union City: Immigrants and Exiles in a New Jersey Community.* Philadelphia: Temple University Press, 2009.

Rodríguez Chávez, Ernesto. *Emigración cubana actual.* Havana: Editorial de Ciencias Sociales, 1997.

Rogg, Eleanor Meyer, and Rosemary Santana Cooney. *Adaptation and Adjustment of Cubans: West New York, New Jersey.* Monograph no. 5. New York: Hispanic Research Center, Fordham University, 1980.

DIASPORAS: THE POLITICS OF EXILE IN THE EARLY 1960s

Javier Figueroa

The exodus of the Cuban population triggered shortly after the Revolution in 1959.

The overthrow of Fulgencio Batista (1901–1973) on 31 December 1958 opened the doors for a new historical process in Cuba. An overwhelming majority of Cubans hoped the event would lead to full-blown economic development, a more equitable distribution of wealth, and a consolidation of national sovereignty. Not everyone, however, shared that dream. Some, including the followers of the ousted president, found themselves in a difficult situation regarding the revolutionary regime. Many feared becoming victims of reprisals and opted to flee the country. Thus an exodus of people from Cuba began, evolving into that political phenomenon known as exile. These Cubans were later followed by other sectors of the population who had enthusiastically welcomed change but had grown hostile to the accelerated radicalism of the Cuban Revolution.

Most of these exiles took up residence in the United States, particularly in Miami, Florida, a city that had been home to Cubans in previous exiles. Miami lies some two hundred miles from Havana. Its attractions include a warm climate similar to Cuba's, but the main reason it became the center of the new diaspora was its closeness to the country left behind. Proximity helped keep alive the wish to return that is integral to the condition of exile. If the men and women who left Cuba in this period considered themselves exiles, it was because of the compelling force of the desire to return.

From the time the exodus of Cubans began in 1959, the exile community transformed itself into one of the centers of opposition to the new regime. The other was located inside Cuban territory and was the main focus of resistance until it was weakened by the failed Bay of Pigs invasion in April 1961. After that, the exile community, which in part had fulfilled the function of rearguard for the domestic underground movement, assumed the leading role in the Cuban opposition struggle.

The concentration of Cubans in Miami made the city a natural political center for the exiles. This population was estimated at over 60,000 Cubans who arrived in different waves and represented various levels of Cuban society. They came to Miami primarily between 1959 and 1962. In October 1962, flights between Cuba and the United States were suspended as a consequence of the Cuban Missile Crisis. This situation brought about a notable decrease in the migratory flow from Cuba to Miami that did not resume until 1965, when airline travel between the two countries resumed.

The community that took shape during the initial years of exile (which later came to be known as the Historic Exile) was heterogeneous, especially in terms of its political objectives. A division existed between those who had supported Batista and those who were opposed to him. The former group achieved a rapid and notable visibility, thanks to the weekly newspaper *Patria* (Homeland), which provided a media outlet for its point of view. The latter group, which became the majority of the exiled population, concurred on certain basic principles such as representative democracy, free elections, freedom of the press, and a free market economy, but was not unanimous in its opinions. The different factions had ideological roots, and dissension predominated among them. They disagreed about various issues, such as the degree of intervention the state should have in the future republic and the role religion should play in society, but the divisions were, above all, the result of following different strong leaders. Some of the political groups operating in the Cuban

diaspora could, however, be classified according to the different ideological tendencies of their political platforms. They included Christian democrats (MDC, MRR, and DRE), social democrats (MRP, JURE, 30 de Noviembre, Agrupación Montecristi, Triple A), and liberals (RECE).

The most important political institution in the Cuban exile community between 1960 and early 1961 was the Frente Revolucionario Democrático (FRD; Democratic Revolutionary Front), an umbrella organization that brought together the principal opposition groups outside Cuba, although it excluded those that were partial to Batista. The Front was founded between May and June 1960, and its first general coordinator was Manuel Antonio de Varona (1908–1992). The origin of the FRD—which had members from the MRR, MDC, and Agrupación Montecristi and Rescate Revolucionario—stems from the U.S. government's interest in overthrowing the Cuban regime. One of the principal responsibilities of the Front was to recruit exiles for Assault Brigade 2506, a military corps conceived by the U.S. Central Intelligence Agency (CIA) to invade Cuban territory. The brigade landed at the Bay

Principal political organizations of the Cuban diaspora (1959–1965)

Table 1

Organization Name	Year Founded	Leadership
Agrupación Montecristi	1960	Justo Carrillo
Alpha 66 (merging of the Alpha 66, Movimiento Revolucionario del Pueblo (MRP), and II Frente Nacional del Escambray)	1961	Eloy Gutiérrez Menoyo
Comandos L	1962	Antonio Cuesta
Consejo Revolucionario de Cuba (merging of Frente Revolucionario Democrático and MRP)	1961	José Miró Cardona
Directorio Revolucionario Estudiantil (DRE)	1960	Alberto Muller Juan Manuel Salvat Luis Fernández Rocha
Frente Revolucionario Democrático (FRD)	1961	Manuel Antonio de Varona
Junta Revolucionaria (JURE)	1961	Manuel Ray Rivero
La Rosa Blanca	1959	Rafael Díaz Balart
Movimiento Demócrata Cristiano (MDC)	1959	José Ignacio Rasco Laureano Batista
Movimiento Insurreccional de Recuperación Revolucionaria	1959	Orlando Bosch
Movimiento Revolucionario del Pueblo (MRP)	1960	Manuel Ray Rivero
Movimiento de Recuperación Revolucionaria	1959	Manuel Artime Buesa
Movimiento 30 de Noviembre	1960	David Salvador
Representación Cubana del Exilio (RECE)	1964	José "Pepín" Bosch
Rescate Revolucionario	1960	Manuel Antonio de Varona
Triple A	1959	Aureliano Sánchez Arango

SOURCE: Javier Figueroa.

of Pigs, in Las Villas province (currently Cienfuegos province), on 17 April 1961, and was defeated by the armed forces of the Cuban revolutionary state.

Prior to this invasion and after some difficult negotiations encouraged by the U.S. government, the FRD forged an alliance with the MRP, led by Manuel Ray Rivero (b. 1924). The accord resulted in the creation of the Consejo Revolucionario de Cuba (CRC; Cuban Revolutionary Council), which became the dominant exile political group from 1961 to 1964, when it ended. The CRC hoped to govern the republic as soon as a regime change in Cuba was achieved. The CRC was presided over by José Miró Cardona (1902–1974) and had the political and financial backing of the U.S. government. Numerous organizations in exile gravitated toward it, as did various public figures who were part of a diverse and not always harmonious universe.

The defeat of Brigade 2506 at the Bay of Pigs was a turning point for the Cuban diaspora. Until then, and particularly inside Cuba's domestic resistance groups, the idea prevailed that the revolutionary regime could be overthrown by means of a popular uprising. After April 1961, the prevailing conviction of the Cuban Revolutionary Council was that this objective could not be achieved without a military intervention led by U.S. forces. Other groups, such as the Directorio Revolucionario Estudiantil (DRE; Student Revolutionary Directorate), Comandos L (Commandos L), and Alpha 66 initiated commando assaults on nearby objectives on the Cuban coasts. The official policy of U.S. president John F. Kennedy ruled out direct U.S. intervention while exploring other options as part of a destabilization plan known as Operation Mongoose. This discrepancy between plans, which became obvious after the Missile Crisis of 1962, helped promote a climate of distrust between many exile militant groups and the U.S. government. José Miró Cardona resigned as president of the CRD in a public letter, reinforcing the prevalent notion among Cuban exiles, that the United States was no longer supporting their cause. Therefore, most of them decided that the only road left open to them was to attack their enemies wherever they were, even if these actions meant the use of terrorist tactics or practices.

The difficulty in achieving a timely regime change in Cuba contributed to the erosion of the policy forged in the initial years of the Cuban diaspora in the 1960s. A number of events compounded the problem, including the decision of the U.S. government to discontinue financial aid to the more violent Cuban exile groups (a decision taken in part when the Vietnam War began to monopolize U.S. attention), Cuba's increasing diplomatic isolation in the Western Hemisphere, and the actions of one of the exile organizations, the Revolutionary Recovery Movement (MRR), which attacked the Spanish merchant marine ship *Sierra Aranzazu* in international waters, having confused it with the Cuban ship *Sierra*

Maestra. Additional divisions were caused by a U.S. government-sponsored plan to relocate part of the Cuban population outside Miami, in an attempt to find work for the exiles.

Part of the legacy of the first stage in the history of the Cuban diaspora was a narrative that exalted the so-called historic exile to heroic levels. It promoted inflexibility as the correct exile political position toward the Cuban government, disseminated the idea that Cubans were betrayed by the United States, and forged a political alliance between the Cuban community and the Republican Party in the United States. Nevertheless, there also appeared in the "historic exile" a political trend that supported the idea of dialogue as the best alternative for fomenting the transformation of Cuba, which serves as a reminder that the diaspora was multifaceted and heterogeneous.

BIBLIOGRAPHY

Arboleya, Jesús. *La contrarrevolución cubana.* Havana: Editorial de Ciencias Sociales, 1997.

Bohning, Don. *The Castro Obsession: U.S. Covert Operations Against Cuba, 1959–1965.* Washington, DC: Potomac Books, 2005.

Figueroa, Javier. *El exilio en invierno: Miguel Figueroa y Miranda; Diario del destierro.* San Juan, Puerto Rico: Librería La Tertulia/Ediciones Callejón, 2008.

García, María Cristina. *Havana USA: Cuban Exiles and Cuban Americans in South Florida, 1959–1994.* Berkeley: University of California Press, 1996.

Pedraza, Silvia. *Political Disaffection in Cuba's Revolution and Exodus.* New York: Cambridge University Press, 2007.

DIASPORAS: IMMIGRANT EXILE POLITICS

Gerald E. Poyo

Cuban immigrants to the United States and their commitment to changing the government in Cuba while advancing their interests in their adopted land.

From the moment Cubans fleeing revolutionary developments arrived in the United States in the early 1960s, exile and ethnic identities fashioned a complicated political experience. Together these identities sought return to Cuba as well as a sense of belonging in the United States. Everyday life for Cubans in the United States involved an intimate interaction between their desire to return home and the reluctant, inevitable integration into a new society. Their engagement with U.S. society did not represent a linear movement from exile to ethnic identity, but rather a parallel and frequently intersecting process, often filled with tension but also mutually supportive and lasting, in which the two identities evolved in the lives

■ *See also*

Cuban Adjustment Act

Cuban Embargo

Diálogo Agreement

Education: Cuban Schools in Miami

Governance and Contestation: The Cuban Revolution

Miami

of the exile generations. Exiles looked to Cuba while their ethnic identity existed in relation to the adopted land, but both strove to maintain cultural identity and change Castro's regime in Cuba. Exile identity served as the basis for developing an ethnic consciousness in the United States, and experiences associated with integration into the United States influenced attitudes about exile and return. This was especially true among Cuban immigrants in Dade County, Florida, and Hudson County, New Jersey; beginning in 1960, their communities were dedicated to overthrowing the government in Cuba. In time they also engaged ethnic politics, participating at the local, state, and national levels, hoping to advance community interests and to influence U.S. policies toward Cuba.

EXILE POLITICS

As a practical matter, Cuban refugees became exiles when they made the decision to remain focused on Cuba, insisting on their eventual return. Exiles expressed a deep grounding in Cuban nationalism and anticommunism, and in the early years exile leaders acted from a revolutionary ethic cultivated for years in Cuba's unruly political climate. Militant instincts persisted in their exile politics, and without hesitation they used violence to achieve political goals. They struggled to overthrow Fidel Castro's government and hoped to return home and build Cuba anew, based on democratic and republican principles embedded in the Constitution of 1940, which most supported. The events associated with departure produced a life-long trauma; it colored worldviews and provided the emotional fuel for an exile frame of reference.

Dozens of political groups conspired against the Cuban government, including followers of Fulgencio Batista, Auténtico politicians who governed Cuba in the 1940s, Ortodoxo leaders who challenged the Auténticos during the same era, leaders of the main labor organizations, industrialists, and many others. Though unified in their opposition to communism, these various organizations represented diverse and often conflicting political persuasions, including Falangists, conservatives, liberals, social democrats, Christian-inspired groups, and even anarchists. Only the U.S. government managed for a time to unite some of them in action against the Castro government.

In 1960 the Eisenhower administration organized Cuban refugees into the Frente Revolucionario Democrático (FRD; Democratic Revoltionary Front), coordinated by former Auténtico politician Antonio de Varona (1908–1992). Representing five distinct political blocs, FRD called for the reestablishment of the Constitution of 1940 and immediate popular elections, linking its activities with dissidents on the island. The United States also funded and authorized the training of a paramilitary force known as the Brigada 2506 to invade Cuba from Guatemala. Members of this force were armed guerrillas who infiltrated Cuba, organized cells, sabotaged government installations, and made numerous assassination attempts on Castro. In January 1961 the newly elected Kennedy administration accelerated the anti-Castro conspiracy, but insisted on a more representative exile organization that included the democratic Left, represented by the Movimiento Revolucionario del Pueblo (MRP; People's Revolutionary Movement), which was led by a former official of the Castro government, Manuel Ray (b. 1924). Though many Cubans in exile characterized the MRP as "Fidelistas without Fidel," under pressure from the U.S. State Department, the FRD and MRP united under the umbrella of the Consejo Revolucionario Cubano (CRC; Cuban Revolutionary Council), led by the short-term first president of the revolutionary government, José Miró Cardona (1902–1974). Besides supporting organizations, the U.S. government funded a radio station and various publications dedicated to overthrowing Castro, including *Cuba Nueva*, which disseminated throughout Latin America carefully argued critiques of Cuban government policies by articulate exile intellectuals such as Angel del Cerro, Rubén Rumbaut, Andrés Valdespino, and Fermín Peinado.

After the failed Bay of Pigs invasion of Cuba in April 1961, followed by the Cuban missile crisis in October 1962, the United States abandoned efforts to invade Cuba but continued funding exile operations through a program known as Operation Mongoose. Several years later the United States stopped funding exiles and moved toward a policy of accommodation with Cuba, leaving the exiles to their own devices. They initiated a radical strategy of harassing and attacking Communist representatives in exile. Throughout the 1970s groups, including the Movimiento Nacionalista Cubano (Cuban Nationalist Movement), Alpha 66, Movimiento Insurreccional de Recuperación Revolucionaria (Insurrectional Movement of Revolutionary Recovery), and Comandos L, attacked Cuban diplomats and assassinated exiles sympathetic to the Communist regime. Perhaps the most dramatic action was the 1976 bombing of a Cuban airline by longtime anti-Castro exile activists; all seventy-three passengers were killed. Among the leaders of this action and others was Luis Posada Carriles, a CIA-trained activist who became a symbol of patriotic virtue for many exiles and of ruthless terrorism for others, including the Cuban government.

Cuban exiles formed an international diasporic network in the United States, Puerto Rico, Venezuela, Mexico, and Spain. Cubans adapted to the realities of their adopted homes but maintained strong relations with each other and lobbied internationally. During the 1960s and 1970s, Cubans in South Florida cultivated relations with Latin America and Spain, to which they were drawn by cultural affinity, economic possibilities, and political necessity. Perhaps the most effective organization in this regard was the Cuban Christian Democratic Party, originally led by José Ignacio Rasco, Enrique Villarreal, and Enrique Ros, which was formed in exile with the intention of eventually establishing its place in a Cuban democratic future. Though exiles found leaders in Latin America fundamentally unresponsive, their experiences nevertheless proved economically and politically valuable as they established lasting contacts and relationships in the region.

This 1960s political activism and its ultimate failure to dislodge the Communist government in Cuba produced enduring exile communities in South Florida and New Jersey characterized by intensity, intransigence, and persistence perpetuated by a powerful media that stressed anti-Communist exile identity for half a century. Political newspapers and magazines circulated widely. In Dade County *Diario de las Americas*, *Patria*, *Réplica*, and *Bohemia*, for example, offered various political perspectives but remained united in their opposition to Communist Cuba. Over the years, virtually every political, cultural, civic, professional, and religious organization of Cuban exiles published a newspaper or newsletter that focused on politics or life in Cuba prior to the Revolution.

The message of the print media was reinforced by community radio and television that reached even larger audiences. In Miami, Spanish-language radio was especially influential and became an integral part of daily life for many. Besides entertainment and nostalgia, radio stations such as La Cubanisima and La Fabulosa offered a constant regimen of political discourse and propaganda that influenced popular thought and action and kept listeners emotionally mobilized against the Cuban regime. Although organizations and media maintained political activism in the communities, the survival of exile consciousness after the consolidation of the revolutionary government in the 1960s ironically had much to do with successful community integration into the economic system and political framework of the United States.

ETHNIC POLITICS

In addition to developing and retaining a powerful attachment to exile identity, Cubans adapted to daily life in the United States. The tensions inherent in their instinctive need to remain connected to Cuban culture and identity while attempting to settle in an alien culture became clear quite quickly. Numerous Cuban leaders, most prominently Bishop Eduardo Boza Masvidal and José Ignacio Lasaga, articulated a strategy of *integration without assimilation*. They recognized the need for Cuban exiles to integrate into their new places of residence but insisted that they remain committed to their culture and identity. Cubans in the United States self-consciously fought assimilation in favor of a pluralistic understanding of their eventual citizenship, diverging from the so-called melting pot model of U.S. society and culture. The civil rights movement and other political and social developments during the 1960s and 1970s provided space for the appearance of ethnic movements among African Americans, Mexican Americans, Native Americans, and others. Arriving at this very moment, Cubans naturally embraced

the ideas of ethnic pluralism as perfectly compatible with their clearly articulated sense of exile identity. They created sufficiently large, economically successful, and ethnically conscious communities in Florida and New Jersey to participate effectively in local, state, and national politics, and they saw no contradiction between their condition as exile Cubans hoping to go home eventually and ethnic citizens obtaining a measure of influence and authority within U.S. society.

Cubans in South Florida first turned to politics to defend their ethnic interests during the 1970s. Inspired by their hope to eventually return to Cuba with children still connected to Cuban identity, many insisted on defending language and cultural rights, which often alienated their American neighbors. Already in the early 1960s, with funds from the Cuban Refugee Program, Cubans in Dade County spearheaded the implementation of public school bilingual instructional programs that became prototypes for the national bilingual movement. These programs encouraged retention of the Spanish language among Hispanic youth and also provided an opportunity for non-Hispanic students to learn Spanish. In 1973, after much lobbying by the Cuban community, Dade County approved an ordinance making the county officially bilingual, and in 1976 the *Miami Herald* began publishing a Spanish-language edition, further heightening the influence of Spanish-speaking people in mainstream South Florida society. Inevitably, this Cuban mobilization in South Florida provoked a backlash in the non-Hispanic community, resulting in a 1980 referendum that overturned the county's bilingual ordinance. This change inspired Cubans to become more involved in local politics; they accelerated their activism in local municipal elections, making strong appeals to ethnic interests as well as Cuban nationalism and anticommunism.

Cubans also adapted their growing sense of ethnic subjectivity to exile goals. In 1980 Jorge Mas Canosa of the exile organization Representación Cubana del Exilio (RECE; Cuban Representation in Exile), with help from Republican Party activists, founded the Cuban American National Foundation (CANF), which blended ethnic and exile politics. Initially a traditional exile activist wholly focused on supporting armed strategies to depose Castro, Mas Canosa was among the first exile activists to lobby Washington, D.C. Identifying congressional representatives willing to resist the growing sentiment that favored dialogue with Cuba, Mas Canosa suggested hard-line alternatives, including isolating Cuba internationally, maintaining the economic embargo, and focusing on human rights violations, among other actions. He did this within the broader context of promoting Republican interests in the Cuban community and promoting his community's ethnic interests within the political system.

Disenchanted with the obvious failure of armed approaches, many exiles supported this shift in strategy. They also participated enthusiastically in state and federal electoral politics in the 1980s, which allowed Cubans to exert direct influence on U.S. policies toward Cuba, as well as domestic policies beneficial to Cuban Americans. In South Florida they did this overwhelmingly as Republicans because they viewed Democrats as too soft on communism, but Cuban political elites in the region also considered the free enterprise philosophy of Republicans compatible with their community's business and entrepreneurial character.

In 1983 three Cubans were elected to Florida's House of Representatives, and the following year Cubans won four more seats on the strength of Ronald Reagan's landslide presidential victory; this level of representation was maintained, more or less, into the early 2000s. In 1985 Florida House member Ileana Ros-Lehtinen gained election to the State Senate, and in 1989 she went to the U.S. House of Representatives. She was joined in the House in 1992 by Lincoln Díaz (who had replaced her in the Florida Senate), in 2003 by Mario Díaz Balart, and in 2008 by David Rivera. From 2005 to 2009 Melquíades (Mel) Martínez served as a U.S. senator from Florida, and in 2010 he was followed by Marco Rubio, who was elected after serving four years as speaker of the Florida House of Representatives. These extraordinary electoral achievements reflected the economic successes of Cuban Americans and also their political experiences in defending ethnic and exile interests.

Cubans in Union City and West New York, Hudson County, New Jersey, also became active in municipal, state, and national politics beginning in the 1980s. Unlike candidates in the Republican enclaves in South Florida, however, Cuban candidates in Hudson County lived in diverse and Democratic Party-oriented working-class communities that included ethnic Europeans and other Hispanics. The most prominent Cuban American politician in New Jersey, Robert Menendez, was born in New York of working-class parents and raised in northern New Jersey. He was mayor of Union City from 1986 to 1992 and a member of the New Jersey General Assembly and the State Senate from 1987 to 1993. In 1993 Menendez became New Jersey's first Hispanic member of the U.S. House of Representatives, and in 2005 he took a seat in the U.S. Senate. Cuban-born Albio Sires served as mayor of West New York from 1995 to 2006, was the first Hispanic speaker of the New Jersey State Assembly from 2002 to 2006, and was elected to the U.S. House of Representatives in 2006. Both Menendez and Sires represented the Democratic Party, which they believed better served the needs of their diverse working-class constituencies. Although the Florida (Republican) and New Jersey (Democratic) congressional delegations disagreed on domestic issues, they generally agreed when it came to maintaining a hard line on Cuba.

POLITICAL HETEROGENEITY

The interplay of Cuban exile and ethnic politics in the United States also produced an alternative, minority perspective in the late 1960s and the 1970s among a younger cohort of Cubans. Arriving as children, adolescents, and young adults, these individuals engaged U.S. society while in their formative years, which

Marco Rubio campaigning in Orlando. Republican candidate Marco Rubio (right) greets former U.S. senator Mel Martinez at a campaign rally in Orlando, Florida, on 1 November 2010. Born in Miami, raised in Las Vegas, and never having set foot in Cuba, Rubio reflects the complex relationship between exile and ethnic identities among Cubans in the United States. JOE BURBANK/ ORLANDO SENTINEL/MCT VIA GETTY IMAGES

influenced their thinking about the Cuban Revolution and their adopted country. Attending universities outside their communities they heard competing interpretations of Cuba and its situation that called into question their elders' attitudes and discourses. The younger generation remained marked by their exile experience but adopted new perspectives and sensibilities, calling on their compatriots to consider the changing realities inside and outside Cuba, the imperative for peaceful coexistence of capitalism and socialism, and the particularly difficult circumstances in Latin America that required thoughtful and creative solutions. Developments in U.S. society, including the civil rights movement, the War on Poverty, the Vietnam War, and emerging identity politics, placed their Cuban experience into perspective. Exemplifying these views, a modest newspaper published in Miami and New York, *Nueva Generación*, rejected armed action and violence as futile, and instead advocated a new sense of political responsibility and dialogue among all Cubans, including Communists and exiles. Some of the younger exiles founded in 1970 the Instituto de Estudios Cubanos (IEC; Institute for Cuban Studies), which advocated academic study and discussion of the Cuban situation. Led by Maria Cristina Herrera, the IEC had an immediate political impact in the Cuban communities, triggering intense and sometimes violent reactions during the 1970s and 1980s when it engaged in direct dialogue with Cuban island scholars on political, economic, literary, and other matters. Prominent U.S.-trained Cuban exile scholars, including the economist Carmelo Mesa Lago, the political scientists Jorge Dominguez and Marifeli Pérez Stable, and the sociologist Lisandro Pérez, among others, played an important role in promoting academic and critical analysis of the Cuban Revolution and the exile communities, as well as advocating dialogue and conversation between them.

Though these ideas caused considerable controversy in the communities still dominated by hard-line discourses, they nevertheless prospered during the 1970s and 1980s, helped along in 1976 by a U.S.-Cuban agreement to establish limited diplomatic contacts through third-party embassies. This opening encouraged the Cuban government in 1978 to invite a delegation of exiles interested in dialogue to meet with Cuban officials, including Fidel Castro. The meetings resulted in the release of 3,600 political prisoners, the reunification of Cuban families, and the initiation of family visits across the Straits of Florida. These events unleashed a spate of assassinations and bombings against the *dialogueros* by hard-line activists, but the practical benefits to the Cuban communities in the United States of visiting Cuba and maintaining active connections with family slowly built support for a more pragmatic attitude toward the Communist government. Even in the hard-line strongholds in Dade County, policies that advocated normalizing relations between Cuba and the United States, lifting the U.S. embargo on Cuba, and allowing uninhibited travel for Cubans as well as

Americans were increasingly accepted. Many organizations adopted these new approaches, and even CANF under the leadership of the founder's son, Jorge Mas Santos, in 2001 embraced greater pragmatism. Nevertheless, hard-line exiles remained firmly in control of important organizations, much of the media, and especially the Cuban American political machines in South Florida. Some liberal Cubans tried their hand at electoral politics in South Florida; in 2008 they hoped to win at least one U.S. congressional seat, but failed to dislodge any hard-line traditionalists. Although most Cubans in the United States supported greater pragmatism in dealing with Cuba, their representatives in the U.S. House of Representatives and U.S. Senate remained committed to the hard-line policies defined in the 1970s and 1980s.

EXILE-ETHNIC PERSISTENCE

For half a century, Cubans in the United States, especially in Dade and Hudson counties, maintained a powerful sense of exile identity that served as the foundation for an ethnic identity that survived among following generations. Perhaps the best institutional illustration of the coexistence and overlapping of Cuban identity perspectives is South Florida's *Nuevo Herald*, owned by the *Miami Herald*, which simultaneously covers the region's Cuban-Hispanic ethnic panorama while providing a continuing platform for exile voices focused on Cuba's past, present, and future. Another example is the election in 2010 of a new generation Cuban, thirty-nine-year-old Marco Rubio, to the U.S. Senate from Florida. Born in Miami, raised for some years in Las Vegas, and never having set foot in Cuba, Rubio reflected the continuing and complex relationship between exile and ethnic identities among Cubans in the United States. His electoral discourse echoed the conservative Republican political ideals of much of the South Florida Cuban ethnic community, but also the traditionally intransigent anti-Castro exile attitudes of the generation of the 1960s and 1970s.

The persistence of an ethnic identity among Cubans in the United States is not difficult to understand, but the survival of an exile identity among those who have never even seen Cuba stemmed from a variety of factors, including the longevity of the Revolution, the continuing arrival throughout the decades of Cubans deeply disenchanted with the situation in their homeland, and the persistence of the Cuban question in national politics. In 1980 more than 100,000 Cubans arrived in the United States in the span of weeks from the port of Mariel, reminding earlier arrivals of their own experiences and reinforcing their determination to overthrow the Cuban government. Although Cubans who arrived after 1980 often brought different perspectives and attitudes that conflicted with the politics of earlier arrivals (they often preferred the pragmatism of dialogue between the nations), they nevertheless reinforced exile identity even as they too found their place in the United

States. The institutionalization of the community's exile and ethnic identities through public and private discourses, organizations, newspapers, radio and television, public monuments and commemorations, and community myths facilitated the generational transfer to people such as Marco Rubio. Many who arrived from Cuba after the 1990s, exhausted from their experience in Cuba and not much disposed to political activism, embraced the exile-ethnic identity of their new communities. New arrivals regularly reinforced the community's awareness of Cuban issues, which inevitably found expression in exile and ethnic forms. Continuing narratives of escape from communism contributed to strong political narratives invoking the rhetoric of arrival, survival, and redemption so common to American discourse and relevant to the complex interaction of exile and ethnic identities.

BIBLIOGRAPHY

Arboleya, Jesus. *La Contarevolución Cubana*. Havana: Editorial Ciencias Sociales, 1997.

Eckstein, Susan. *The Immigrant Divide: How Cuban Americans Changed the U.S. and Their Homeland*. New York: Routledge, 2009.

García, María Cristina. *Havana USA: Cuban Exiles and Cuban Americans in South Florida, 1959–1994*. Berkeley: University of California Press, 1996.

González-Pando, Miguel. *The Cuban Americans*. Westport, CT: Greenwood Press, 1998.

Grenier, Guillermo J., and Lisandro Pérez. *The Legacy of Exile: Cubans in the United States*. Boston: Allyn and Bacon, 2003.

Pedraza, Silvia. *Political Disaffection in Cuba's Revolution and Exodus*. New York: Cambridge University Press, 2007.

Poyo, Gerald E. *Cuban Catholics in the United States, 1960–1980: Exile and Integration*. Notre Dame, IN: University of Notre Dame Press, 2007.

Prieto, Yolanda. *The Cubans of Union City: Immigrants and Exiles in a New Jersey Community*. Philadelphia: Temple University Press, 2009.

Torres, María de los Angeles. *In the Land of Mirrors: Cuban Exile Politics in the United States*. Ann Arbor: University of Michigan Press, 1997.

DIASPORAS: POLITICAL ACTION COMMITTEES AND LOBBY GROUPS

Patrick J. Haney

Lobby groups and political action committees in the United States concerned with U.S.-Cuba relations.

Between 1959 and 2010, the Cuban American population in the United States grew to over 1.5 million, with about two-thirds living in Florida. The population is made up of Cubans who migrated to the United States and second- and third-generation Cuban Americans born in the United States. The geographically concentrated growth of a politically active Cuban American diaspora, located primarily in southern Florida and secondarily in New York and New Jersey, has also provided the opportunity for a range of organized groups to emerge that lobby the U.S. president and Congress on the policy of the United States toward Cuba. Included in the spectrum are political action committees (PACs) that lobby on U.S.-Cuba policy. (PACs are a special type of lobbying group that raises money for the purpose of making donations to political campaigns; *lobby groups* are a general term referring to a range of groups that try to influence the policy process; PACs are one form of a lobby group.) Individuals and groups of individuals who have passionate political interests in U.S. policy toward Cuba organize and personally fund these groups. Their leaders are often referred to as political entrepreneurs because, like a typical business entrepreneur, they are willing to invest their resources with the hope of a return on their investment. In this case, the return would be in the form of policies toward Cuba that are consistent with their own beliefs and interests.

RISE OF THE CUBAN AMERICAN NATIONAL FOUNDATION

While a number of groups formed in Miami in the 1960s and 1970s, the first significant effort to lobby in Washington, D.C., on Cuba policy was made by the Cuban American National Foundation (CANF), formed in 1980. Favoring a strict embargo policy, CANF was founded and led by Jorge Mas Canosa (1939–1997). CANF formed with the help of the Reagan presidential campaign and its subsequent administration and was modeled on the powerful pro-Israel lobby group American Israel Public Affairs Committee (AIPAC). CANF emerged as a dominant force through the 1980s and early 1990s and was generally thought of as the second-most-powerful ethnic lobby group in the United States (second to AIPAC). CANF also set up a political action committee, the Free Cuba PAC, to provide campaign contributions as part of its diverse lobbying efforts. Working in close partnership with the Reagan White House, CANF policy successes included an aggressive approach to Cuba and the founding of Radio Martí and later TV Martí—which Mas Canosa would have a hand in directing (see Brenner; Gunn; Kaplowitz; Haney and Vanderbush).

As the Cold War came to an end during the George H. W. Bush administration, there was an effort in Congress, led by CANF-ally Representative Robert Torricelli (D-NJ), to tighten the embargo on Cuba through the Cuban Democracy Act (CDA). The CDA aimed to reinforce the embargo, which had been largely abandoned with the collapse of

■ *See also*

Cuban Embargo

Radio: Cuban Radio in South Florida

The World and Cuba: Cuba and the United States

the Soviet Union in 1991, by restricting trade with foreign subsidiaries of U.S. corporations and by trying to reach out to the Cuban people in order to foster regime change and a democratic transition. The Bush administration shared the CDA's goals but opposed the measure because, from the administration's perspective, it interfered with the prerogative of the president to set the nation's foreign policy course.

Bush's opponent in the 1992 presidential election, Bill Clinton, went to Miami to give a speech to CANF in which he embraced the CDA, thus making significant inroads in the community. Clinton won the White House, but CANF did not enjoy the same access to the White House as it had during previous Republican administrations. Indeed, Clinton initially seemed interested in altering the landscape of U.S.-Cuba relations by moving toward a policy of constructive engagement. This reversal by Clinton made lobbying more challenging for CANF and shifted the balance toward a range of groups that had long favored dialogue with Cuba. Groups such as the Cuban Committee for Democracy (CCD) and Cambio Cubano formed in 1993, joining the longer-established Cuban American Committee Research and Education Fund (CACREF), the Washington Office on Latin America (WOLA), and the Latin American Working Group (LAWG) in the effort to push for changes to the embargo policy. CACREF was formed in 1976 and helped organize a major petition drive by Cuban Americans calling for more normal relations with Cuba.

LOBBYING EVOLVES IN THE CLINTON ADMINISTRATION

Another sign that CANF's dominance over Cuba policy was eroding can be seen in the 1994 balsero (rafter) crisis that emerged when the Cuban government temporarily withdrew its border guards and permitted mass exit by tens of thousands of people on makeshift rafts. In a matter of days, the Clinton administration altered decades of immigration policy for Cubans seeking entry to the United States in order to stem the flow of rafters. The U.S. Coast Guard was ordered to take the rafters to a safe haven at the U.S. naval base at Guantánamo Bay, Cuba, where their status remained uncertain until they were gradually admitted to the United States over a two-year period.

At the same time in 1994, the United States negotiated an agreement with the Cuban government to stop the exodus and resume border patrols in exchange for a guarantee of a minimum of 20,000 immigration visas per year, including a lottery for those who had no relatives in the United States, thus allowing the Cuban government to regain control over immigration and giving ordinary Cubans a channel for legal exit. In May 1995, the United States and Cuba reached a new migration accord, stating that Cubans picked up at sea by the United States would be returned to the Cuban port of Cabañas, where the Cubans agreed to forgo

any criminal prosecution. Those who subsequently eluded U.S. patrols and made it to dry land were permitted to stay. Prior to announcing the changes in 1994 and 1995, Clinton met with CANF and other Cuban American leaders in order to try to mollify their reaction and prepare them for these concessions. CANF had long claimed to be a political guarantor of unlimited Cuban migration and its members clearly lost face with their constituency when they could not decisively influence U.S. policy.

In 1995, a new move to tighten the embargo began in Congress, led by then-senator Jesse Helms (R-NC), the new chairman of the Senate Foreign Relations Committee, and his staff. The Cuban Liberty and Democratic Solidarity Act, called Helms-Burton after its sponsors, aimed to sharply reduce the Cuban economy by sanctioning non-U.S. companies who were doing business in Cuba with properties owned by U.S. nationals that had been seized following the Cuban Revolution in 1959. For the first time, owners were sanctioned who were not U.S. citizens at the time the properties were seized. CANF helped lobby for the bill but faced opposition in the Clinton White House.

The bill was tabled by Senator Helms after repeated Democratic filibusters until February 1996, when the Cuban air force shot down two civilian aircraft over the Florida Straits. The planes were piloted by Cuban American members of the group Hermanos al Rescate (Brothers to the Rescue), and the four crew members on board were killed. Brothers to the Rescue regularly flew over the Florida Straits spotting rafters and calling for U.S. Coast Guard rescue. In retaliation, the bill moved quickly through Congress and President Clinton signed it, including elements the Clinton administration had previously opposed, such as restricting the president from taking major steps toward normalizing relations without an act of Congress (see Kiger; Morley and McGillion; Torres). Just as CANF's power seemed to be on the rise again, in 1997, Jorge Mas Canosa died. Although it would remain an important player, CANF was not the same without his unifying leadership and single-minded commitment.

CUBAN AMERICANS IN CONGRESS

CANF (and others) worked hard to elect a Cuban American to the U.S. House of Representatives. In a 1989 special election in Miami to fill the seat vacated by Claude Pepper upon his death, Republican Ileana Ros-Lehtinen was elected. She became the chair of the House Foreign Affairs Committee in 2011. Several others joined Ros-Lehtinen in subsequent years, including Florida Republicans Lincoln Díaz-Balart (elected in 1992), his brother Mario (elected in 2002), and New Jersey Democrat Robert Menéndez (elected in 1992). Menéndez would later be elected to the U.S. Senate, and Democrat Albio Sires represented Menéndez's old district. Mel Martínez (R-FL) was elected to the U.S. Senate in 2004, having served in the George

Cuban American National Foundation. Barack Obama addresses the Cuban American National Foundation in Miami on 23 May 2008, during his campaign for the presidency. AP IMAGES/ WILFREDO LEE

W. Bush administration as the secretary of Housing and Urban Development (HUD). Martínez retired in 2009. Republican Marco Rubio, the first Cuban American speaker of the Florida House of Representatives, was elected to that senate seat in 2010. Lincoln Díaz-Balart retired from Congress at the end of 2010; Mario moved to that district and won election to that seat. Both candidates running for the seat vacated by Mario Díaz-Balart in 2010 were Cuban American; Republican David Rivera beat Joe Garcia. Members of the Cuban diaspora thus not only lobby Congress on policy toward the island, they are also members of Congress, who directly shape the contours of U.S.-Cuba policy. Ironically, CANF's success in this regard may also have been part of its weakening. While these legislators have generally pursued CANF's original hard-line stance on the embargo, they see themselves as directing Cuba policy apart from CANF. The exclusive role of CANF was in some ways diminished by these electoral victories.

CONTEMPORARY COMPETITION OVER CUBA POLICY

Lobbying over Cuba policy evolved significantly in the first decade of the twenty-first century as CANF pursued a more nuanced approach toward the embargo: opposed to unilateral lifting of the embargo but in favor of contacts with the Cuban people. This change was in part due to a generational change in leadership. Following Jorge Mas Canosa's death, his son, Jorge Mas Santos, took over leadership of CANF. In 2001,

Mas Santos supported moving the Latin Grammy Awards show to Miami, a decision that alienated some of his father's closest associates and resulted in the resignation of eighteen CANF board members and three prominent staff. CANF's original leadership had rigorously organized opposition to any cultural performance in Miami by artists from the island, claiming that they were representatives of the Cuban government. Mas Santos defended his position as a public display that Cuban American organizations could show tolerance and political maturity.

Many of the defectors from CANF subsequently formed the Cuban Liberty Council (CLC). That group helped to persuade the George W. Bush administration to tighten the restrictions on family travel and remittances to the island in the run-up to the 2004 elections. The group Cuban Democracy Advocates (CDA) was also formed by Cuban-born, American-raised, Spanish businessman Leopoldo Fernández Pujals, to push for a harder stance on the embargo. The U.S.-Cuba Democracy PAC, was founded in 2003 by Mauricio Claver-Carone; it used campaign donations as a way to bring pressure to bear on the embargo policy. Since its founding, this PAC raised and funneled hundreds of thousands of dollars each election cycle into the campaigns of various members of Congress. In the 2010 election cycle, for example, its members raised more than $600,000 and donated over $450,000 to more than 135 congressional candidates (mostly incumbents). It was by far the largest active PAC focused on the embargo at the end of the 2010s. CANF's PAC had mostly ceased to exist by this time.

The New Cuban-American Majority PAC emerged in the 2010 cycle to try to combat the pro-embargo activities of the U.S.-Cuba Democracy PAC. It reflected changes in the Cuban American community, which had become far more skeptical about the embargo and open to dialogue with Cuba. They raised about $85,000 and donated about $30,000 to congressional candidates—small by comparison with other PACs but with potential to grow. A range of business interests also pushed for more trade and travel between the United States and the island. While the Cuban embargo was only one of many issues important to American businesses, their engagement in Cuban policy through lobbying and campaign contributions also altered the embargo's political dynamics. Lobbying on U.S.-Cuba policy is increasingly rich and diverse, reflecting a range of views and interests (see Erikson 2008; Schoultz 2009), but the dynamics of the debate over the proper way to facilitate democratic change in Cuba continue to become more complex and more fascinating.

BIBLIOGRAPHY

Bonachea, Rolando, ed. *Jorge Mas Canosa: En Busca de Una Cuba Libre-Edicion Completa de Sus Discursos, Entrevistas y Declaraciones, 1962–1997.* Miami, FL: North/South Center Press, University of Miami, 2003.

Brenner, Philip. *From Confrontation to Negotiation: U.S. Relations with Cuba.* Boulder, CO: Westview Press, 1988.

Eckstein, Susan. *The Immigrant Divide: How Cuban Americans Changed the U.S. and Their Homeland.* New York: Taylor & Francis, 2009.

Erikson, Daniel P. *Cuba Wars: Fidel Castro, the United States, and the Next Revolution.* New York: Bloomsbury Press, 2008.

Gunn, Gillian. *Cuba in Transition.* New York: Twentieth Century Fund Press, 1993.

Haney, Patrick J., and Walt Vanderbush. *The Cuban Embargo: The Domestic Politics of an American Foreign Policy.* Pittsburgh, PA: University of Pittsburgh Press, 2005.

Kaplowitz, Donna Rich. *Anatomy of a Failed Embargo: U.S. Sanctions against Cuba.* Boulder, CO: Lynne Rienner, 1998.

Kiger, Patrick J. *Squeeze Play: The United States, Cuba, and the Helms-Burton Act.* Washington, DC: Center for Public Integrity, 1997.

Mas Canosa, Jorge. *Jorge Mas Canosa: En busca de una Cuba libre; Edición completa de sus discursos, entrevistas y declaraciones, 1962–1997.* Coral Gables, FL: North-South Center Press, University of Miami, 2003.

Morley, Morris H., and Christopher McGillion. *Unfinished Business: America and Cuba after the Cold War, 1989–2001.* New York: Cambridge University Press, 2002.

Schoultz, Lars. *That Infernal Little Cuban Republic: The United States and the Cuban Revolution.* Chapel Hill: University of North Carolina Press, 2009.

Torres, Maria de los Angeles. *In the Land of Mirrors: Cuban Exile Politics in the United States.* Ann Arbor: University of Michigan Press, 2001.

Vargas Llosa, Alvaro. *El exilio indomable: Historia de la disidencia cubana en el destierro.* Madrid: Espasa, 1998.

DIASPORAS: EXILES IN THE CUBAN POPULAR IMAGINATION

María de los Angeles Torres

The portrayal in Cuban popular culture of those who left Cuba in the wake of the Cuban Revolution.

Between 1959 and 1964 more than 300,000 people left Cuba following the triumph of the Revolution. Families and friends were divided, and staying and leaving became for many signs of loyalty or betrayal. For long periods of time, there was little contact between those who stayed and those who left. Mail service was slow and phone lines were deteriorating, making long-distance telephone calls difficult and expensive. Travel between Cuba and the United States was criminalized by both governments. On the island, maintaining contact with relatives and friends who had left was a sign of ideological weakness, and sometimes those who did were denied certain jobs and educational opportunities. Exiles became the political *others*, a process reinforced by the use of derogatory terms, images, and narratives in political speeches, newsreels, comics, and literature.

EARLY EXILES: THE *GUSANOS*

Initially, Cubans who left the island were called *gusanos* (worms)—a play on words, because the one duffle bag allowed to those who were leaving also was popularly called a *gusano*. The Cuban patriot José Martí had used the term *vil gusano* to describe an enemy. Popular rhymes such as "Pin pon fuera, abajo la gusanera" (Ping-Pong out, down with the worms) were chanted during mass mobilizations. Gusanos were traitors.

After the October Missile Crisis in 1962 the United States suspended flights from Cuba. In 1965 Fidel Castro opened the port of Camarioca and invited families in Miami to come pick up relatives; the camp where people waited to embark was referred to as Gusano Paradise. The theme was repeated in labor mobilizations, as leaflets showing gusanos being beaten by a cane cutter exhorted Cubans to work hard to meet the 10 million-ton goal set for the sugar harvest of 1970.

An enduring exploration of the contradictory feelings about family separations is Tomás Gutiérrez Alea's film *Memorias del subdesarrollo* (Memories of Underdevelopment, 1968). Based on Edmundo Desnoes's novel of the same name, the film follows the thoughts of a wealthy writer, Sergio, who decides to stay in Cuba despite the departure of his family. Although the film is sympathetic to Sergio's choice to remain, it does not fall into easy caricature of those who left Cuba as traitors.

Marta González's *Bajo Palabra: Parolee* (1965) and *Testimonio de una emigrada* (Testimony of an Emigrant, 1974), by Edith Reinoso Hernández, were the first books published after the Revolution that dealt with the subject of those who left Cuba. Both are testimonials of women who find the United States violent and unwelcoming to Cubans. Longing for those who left and recognition of their class and ideological differences are explored in Victor Casaus's 1971 poem "Barbara," in which the narrator remembers how he tried to convince his lover to stay "with feeble arguments" and now laments that little was known about those who had left: "of you we know nothing" (Cardenal 1974). For the next decade, exiles were largely absent from newsreels and popular culture. As Cuba embraced its new revolutionary future, those who had left the island were seen as part of a past best left behind—remnants of a society besieged by corruption, mendacity, and repression.

EXILES RETURN, 1970s–1980s

In the late 1970s young exiles successfully lobbied to be allowed to return to the island. The Antonio Maceo Brigade was born from this group that brought together Cubans who had been born on the island and raised in other parts of the world. The group's return to Cuba in 1977 was recorded in a documentary, *55 Hermanos* (1978), directed by Jesús Díaz. When it was shown in movie theaters in Cuba audiences cried and cheered, watching young exiles visit relatives and travel the island, work on construction sites, and share their heartbreaking stories of physical and cultural displacement and desire to return to their native soil. The official response to the exiles' request for permission to repatriate was also documented: Fidel Castro is filmed saying that the Revolution would best be served by their work outside Cuba. Díaz also published a book, *De la patria al exilio* (Of Homeland and Exile, 1979), based on his film.

Contra viento y marea (Against the Wind and Tide, 1978), a collection of testimonies of exile members of the Areíto group (many of whom were also members of the Antonio Maceo Brigade), received the prestigious Casa de las Américas award for testimonial literature. The young exiles emphasized their experiences with racism in the United States, reinforcing the image portrayed on Cuban television that the United States is a racist country.

On the heels of the brigade trip the Cuban government, with the previous agreement of the Carter administration, initiated a series of conversations with Cuban exiles in 1978. The Dialogue, as the meetings came to be called, resulted in agreements that freed 3,600 political prisoners, permitted their exit from Cuba, and allowed exiles to return to visit their relatives. Gusanos metamorphosed into *mariposas* (butterflies) as more than 100,000 Cuban exiles returned to the island in 1979.

Militant anti-Castro voices were not in favor of dialogue, and they unleashed a backlash in the exile community in the form of assassinations of those who supported these talks and lifting of travel restrictions. In 1979 Carlos Muñiz Varela, one of the founders of the Antonio Maceo Brigade, was killed by an anti-Castro group in Puerto Rico. Luís Adrián Betancourt's book *Por qué Carlos?* (Why Carlos? 1981), published in Cuba, explores Varela's life and death. The exile community became another front in the political struggle, portrayed in the popular late 1970s Cuban television series *En silencio ha tenido que ser* (We Had to Do It in Silence), which follows the story of Sergio, a security agent who is sent to Miami to infiltrate anti-Castro terrorist groups.

Significantly, a more intimate and nuanced view of exile realities was seeping into the Cuban consciousness. As relatives visited the island they were encouraged to bring essential goods to their families in overloaded suitcases. After years of shortages, these gifts challenged the official account that those who had left experienced material hardship in the land of plenty. Cubans humorously transformed the government's portrayal of exiles as traitors with the rhyme "traidor, traidor, traidolares" (traitor, traitor, bring dollars).

Discontent on the island mounted, and in 1980 a group of Cubans crashed a bus through the gates of the Peruvian embassy, resulting in the death of a guard. The Cuban government invited everyone who wanted

Criticism of diaspora Cubans. During the 1960s, Cuban exiles were seen as political "others," a view reinforced by the use of derogatory terms, images, and narratives in political speeches, comics, and literature. This poster, the title of which is translated as "Let Them Go!", depicts Cubans who leave for the United States as rats and insects drawn to garbage. © HOLLY ACKERMAN, PH.D.

to leave to go to the embassy; within thirty-six hours the compound was filled with 10,800 people. The Cuban government then closed access to the embassy, and a week later announced that anyone who wished to leave could register for another boat exodus, this time through the port of Mariel. The Mariel Boatlift lasted until September, bringing more than 125,000 Cubans to U.S. shores. The populace was organized to repudiate those who wanted to leave, and some incidents led to violence. Those departing were portrayed as pariahs, scum, and "limp wrists," words used in Fidel Castro's speech to a mass mobilization billed as "La marcha del pueblo combatiente" (March of the Combatant People) on 19 April. Caricatures of the *Marielitos* drawn by René de la Nuez were compiled in the book *Humor de pueblo combatiente* (Humor of the Combatant People, 1980).

Despite the divisive rhetoric, in 1981 the Cuban exile poet Lourdes Casal (1938–1981) won the Casa de las Américas prize for her book *Palabras juntan revolución* (Words Gather Revolution, 1981). Casal, a U.S.-based academic, was one of the founders of the Areíto group, and she returned to Cuba to die from kidney disease. Among her poems was "Para Ana Veldford," which ends with the lament, "Demasiado habanera para ser newyorkina, demasiado newyorkina para ser—aun volver ser—cualquier otra cosa" (Too *habanera* to be *newyorkina*, too *newyorkina* to be—even to become again—anything else).

After the Mariel Boatlift the imagery of exiles became more tempered. Unlike his first work about the exile community, Jesus Diaz's feature-length movie *Lejania* (1985) portrayed a more ambivalent relationship between those who had left and their homeland. In the film, a mother who left the island ten years previously returns to visit her son. The portrait of the mother is complex, yet she is depicted as having "abandoned her son" and as a racist, though she fully engages with her mulatta daughter-in-law. In a heartfelt moment the mother says, "es duro saber que los muertos no están contigo" ("It's hard knowing that your dead are not close to you"). Interestingly, a cousin who accompanies the mother, movingly recites the Casal poem "Para Ana Velford."

FROM THE 1990s INTO THE EARLY 2000s

The next decade saw the collapse of the Soviet Union and a profound readjustment in Cuban society. Emigration again became central to Cuban reality. Unlike the first wave of emigrants, who have been characterized as "the disaffected," and the second wave—the "scum," the "lumpen proletariat" that socialism had no need of—the émigrés of the 1990s were the children of the Revolution, the heirs of the promise of communism, and often the children of the revolutionary elite. Class differences became stark as those without connections took to the sea in homemade rafts, and the more privileged simply overstayed their tourist visas in countries all over the world. Estela Bravo (b. 1933), an American who had become one of the Cuban government's favored filmmakers, made several documentaries about these exiles, including *Los que se fueron* (Those Who Left, 1980) and *Three Cuban Rafters* (1992). The more affluent were known as "low intensity" exiles, referring to Ronald Reagan's "low-intensity conflict" in Central America, and their exile, *el exilio de terciopelo* (the velvet exile), referring to the Czech Velvet Revolution because they advocated peaceful change on the island and discouraged militarized solutions.

Previously, leaving had been portrayed both as treason and as a purification of the nation, but artists in the 1990s recast the exodus of their friends, family members, and professors as a personal loss, not an overtly political statement. This less ideologically loaded perspective became central to the work of Tania Bruguera (b. 1968), who early in her career re-created the earth sculptures that Ana Mendieta (1948–1985) had made in Cuba. Mendieta, an artist who had been part of Operation Pedro Pan, had been allowed back into Cuba to work, but as exiles fell out of favor her work had been forgotten on the island. Bruguera also focused on the work of Cuban immigrant artists of the late 1980s and early 1990s in her journal *Memoria de la postguerra* (Memory of the Postwar Period, 1993–1994). One of her pieces, *Estadística* (Statistic, 1996), was a large Cuban flag onto which she affixed human hair collected from Cuban residents and rolled into cloth strips, representing the belongings of those who left Cuba for the United States; Bruguera's intent was to show the collective power of the common people as a personal statement of nationalism. *La tabla de salvación* (Life Raft, 1994) was an homage and offering to those who had died attempting to cross from Cuba to Florida on rafts. The raft theme was also central in the work of the Cuban sculptor Kcho (Alexis Leyva Machado, b. 1970), where water becomes a porous border.

Projects produced off the island such as Ruth Behar's *Bridges to Cuba* (1995) and *The Portable Island* (Behar and Lucía Suárez, 2008) and María de los Angeles Torres's *By Heart/ De Memoria* (2003) brought together the works of writers, visual artists, and scholars from both sides of the aquatic divide. Iván de la Nuez's *La isla posible, Cuba* (Cuba: The Possible Island, 1995) and *La balsa perpetua* (The Perpetual Raft, 1998) suggest a way of thinking about *cubanía* free of geographic or ideological constraints. Under the editorship of Ambrosio Fornet, a renowned writer, essayist, and critic, special issues of *La Gaceta* (The Gazette), the official literary magazine of the Unión de Escritores y Artistas de Cuba (UNEAC; Union of Writers and Artists of Cuba), featured articles written by Cubans abroad. Cuba and *cubanía* could exist outside the physical borders of the island.

In *Memorias recobradas* (Retrieved Memories, 2000), Fornet compiled writings from the diaspora, recognizing that off the island there was a vibrant Cuban cultural production. He also explored the depiction of exiles in literature and film in an essay that noted, among others, Pastor Vega's film *Vidas paralelas* (Parallel Lives, 1992) and Ana Rodriguez's *Laura* (1991), a short film in the anthology *Mujer transparente* (Transparent Woman, 1990), which is particularly poignant in its honest reflection of how people who left were mistreated.

The dilemma of leaving or staying became a central theme for Cuban cinema. In the next ten years this theme was explored in the following films: *Fresa y chocolate* (Strawberry and Chocolate, 1993), *Maite* (1994), *La vida es silbar* (Life Is to Whistle, 1998), *Miel para Ochun* (Honey for Ochun, 1991), *Suite Habana* (2003), and *Páginas del diario de Mauricio* (Pages from Mauricio's Diary, 2006).

On the island the difficult economic situation and the importance of remittances became terrain to explore the relationship with those who left. The theme of return and difficult reunions found expression in literature as well as in theater, in productions such as *La visita de la vieja dama* (2010), by Raquel Carrió (b. 1951), which is an adaptation of Friedrich Dürrenmatt's *The Visit*, produced and directed by Flora Lauten and performed by her theater company Buendia. The play tells the story of a young lady wronged and banished from her town who returns years later, now wealthy, and agrees to help the poor townspeople on one condition: She wants the head of the mayor, who made her pregnant and denied his paternity. A similar story about wealth and inheritance inflects the film *El cuerno de la abundancia* (Horn of Plenty, 2008), a comedy by Juan Carlos Tabío (b. 1942).

As independent scholars and intellectuals redefined the imaginary of exile to be inclusive and personal without negating its historical realities, the Cuban government drew distinctions between those who had left long ago and those who were leaving in the 1990s. Cuban Americans were cautiously and selectively allowed to return, whereas recent émigrés were shunned. For instance, when a series of conferences was organized to define who and what is Cuban, Cubans who had left recently were not invited; Cubans who had lived abroad for some time were defined culturally as something else. By the mid-1990s the official terms for those who advocated for change in Cuba were *anti-Cubans* and *ex-Cubans*. Painting criticism in broad strokes, the term *Miami Mafia* often was used to refer to the more conservative exiles.

In 1995 UNEAC and the University of Havana's Center for the Study of Alternative Policies—one of the few centers authorized to study émigrés—organized a conference titled "Culture and National Identity." Participants from the island and abroad suggested an expansive definition of who is Cuban. Ambrosio Fornet lamented that often exiles seemed to simply cease to exist, becoming "ghosts." He asked: "Did we also become ghosts for those who left? Perhaps we will never know who threw the first stone. They, because they dared to declare that *el son* had left Cuba? Or we who refused to accept that they were still Cuban?" (p. 131).

Despite the official negative rhetoric about exiles, the ideological and communicative distance was greatly reduced after 1959: Without denying the ravages of history, the conversation between Cubans on the island and Cubans abroad no longer proceeds along lines of betrayal, invective, and moral platitudes. Dramatic economic reform on the island has compelled many in exile to rethink their relationships with their relatives in Cuba. Unlike the exiles of the 1960s, many of whom had participated in defeating Batista and felt betrayed by the radical course of the Revolution, subsequent waves of émigrés have sought to maintain ties with the island. In turn, those on the island, cognizant of family needs and economic hardships, see their exile relatives with a more humane and nonideological perspective. What was once prohibited—maintaining contact with relatives and friends—has become the norm. The effect has been a less politicized image of émigrés.

BIBLIOGRAPHY

Behar, Ruth, ed. *Bridges to Cuba*. Ann Arbor: University of Michigan Press, 1995.

Behar, Ruth, and Lucía Suárez, eds. *The Portable Island: Cubans at Home in the World*. New York: Palgrave Macmillan, 2008.

Betancourt, Luís Adrián. *Por qué Carlos?* Havana: Editorial Letras Cubanas, 1981.

Cardenal, Ernesto. *In Cuba*. New York: New Directions, 1974.

Casal, Lourdes. *Palabras juntan revolución*. Havana: Casa de las Américas, 1981.

Cuba: Cultural e identidad nacional: Memorias del encuentro. Havana: Unión Nacional de Escritores y Artistas de Cuba, 1995.

De la Nuez, Iván, Juan Pablo Ballester, and Maria Elena Escalona, eds. *Cuba: La isla posible*. Barcelona: Centre de Cultura Contemporania de Barcelona, 1995.

De la Nuez, René. *Humor de pueblo combatiente*. Havana: Editora Politica, 1980.

Fornet, Ambrosio. *Memorias recobradas*. Santa Clara, Cuba: Ediciones Capiro, 2000.

González, Marta. *Bajo Palabra: Parolee*. Montevideo, Uruguay: Ediciones América Nueva, 1965.

Grupo Areito. *Contra viento y marea*. Havana: Casa de la Americas, 1978.

Hernández, Edith Reinoso. *Testimonio de una emigrada*. Havana: Instituto Cubano del Libro, 1974.

Mendieta Costa, Raquel. "La comunidad en la nacion: Para una definicio de esta problematica and la cultura." Paper presented at XVIII International Congress of the Latin American Studies Association, 10–12 March 1994.

"Tania Bruguera: On the Political Imaginary." Art exhibition. Neuberger Museum of Art, Purchase, NY, 2009.

Temas; Cultura, ideología y sociedad 10 (1997).

Torres, María de los Angeles. *By Heart/De Memoria: Cuban Women's Journeys In and Out of Exile.* Philadelphia: Temple University Press, 2003.

■ *See also*

Che Guevara and the New Man

Economy: Special Period

Literature: Fiction in the Special Period

Sexuality: Jinetera in the Special Period

DIRTY HAVANA TRILOGY (PEDRO JUAN GUTIÉRREZ)

Guillermina De Ferrari

A discussion of Pedro Juan Gutiérrez's dirty realist novels in regard to the material conditions of the Special Period and postmodern aesthetics.

The term *dirty realism* was coined by Bill Buford, the editor of the British journal *Granta*, in a 1983 *Granta* issue titled "Dirty Realism: New Writings from America" that collected short stories revealing

Novelist Pedro Juan Gutiérrez, August 2007. Juan Gutiérrez"s *Dirty Havana Trilogy,* first published in Spain in 1998, repudiates beauty in its standard forms and revolts against the grand political projects of the twentieth century. ULF ANDERSEN/ GETTY IMAGES

the unglamorous side of contemporary American life. Although Buford was describing an aesthetic trend grounded in a specific place and time, the term also has been applied to the work Pedro Juan Gutiérrez (b. 1950) wrote in Cuba in the 1990s. Like the stories featured in *Granta*, Gutiérrez's narratives are set in a harsh world, they are written in a crass language, and they deal with characters who "drink a lot and are often in trouble" (Buford p. 4). However, there are three basic differences between *Granta*'s dirty realism and Gutiérrez's. First, the irony is hard to miss in the contrast between the American low-lifes who are "drifters in a world cluttered with junk food and the oppressive details of modern consumerism" and a society defined by the overwhelming scarcity of basic products (Buford p. 4). Second, one of the aspects that make Gutiérrez's realism interesting is its inherent connection with the end of the Cold War. Third, the texts included in *Granta* are not nearly as dirty as Gutiérrez's realist writings.

DETERIORATION OF THE REVOLUTION

Trilogía sucia de La Habana (best known by its English translation, *Dirty Havana Trilogy*) was first published in Spain in 1998 and subsequently in seventeen other countries. The trilogy initiates Gutiérrez's Centro Habana series and serves as a model for all the prose he has published as of 2010. The *Dirty Havana Trilogy* consists of three series of vignettes—"Anclado en tierra de nadie" ("Marooned in No-man's-land"), "Nada que hacer" ("Nothing to Do"), and "Sabor a mí" ("Essence of Me")—of everyday encounters with ordinary people. The stories are connected by the musings of the narrator, a former journalist named Pedro Juan who finds himself immersed in an unexpectedly debasing reality during the deep economic crisis in Cuba after the dissolution of the Soviet bloc—a period known as the Special Period in Times of Peace. In the *Dirty Havana Trilogy* readers follow the narrator in his search for something to eat and something to do while welcoming an astonishing variety of sexual partners and experiences. At a deeper level, this search may be construed as a quest for clarity. The narrator presents himself as a professional, well-read man who has unexpectedly found himself at the very limits of physical and psychological survival during the bleak 1990s. He writes in order to ground himself, to prevent himself from sinking—the original Spanish title for the first vignette series, "Anclado en tierra de nadie" simultaneously evokes a precarious stability and a chaotic insularity. The incidents with neighbors and lovers and other seemingly unremarkable occurrences are related in rich detail and a matter-of-fact tone. What makes the narrator's observations compelling is, in part, the vividness of the portrait he paints of the harsh living conditions that had become the norm in Cuba during the 1990s, as well as the high toll such conditions took on the moral reserves of ordinary people. The aesthetic power of the *Dirty Havana Trilogy* derives from testing the limits of humanity, particularly that of European and academic readers, who constitute Gutiérrez's most immediate audience due to the selective and remarkably slow publication of his works in Cuba.

With frequent references to hunger and excrement, Gutiérrez's prose is uniquely effective at relating political chaos and hopelessness. Following the social anthropologist Mary Douglas (1921–2007) and cultural critics such as Warwick Anderson and Joshua Esty, one may conclude that a scatological aesthetics points to the severe deterioration of a political project that was, in the Cuban case, utopian. The original goals of the Revolution included political autonomy from foreign powers, generalized social justice, and economic modernization. Indeed, at the inception of the revolutionary government, Che Guevara advocated for the moral transformation of society as a basic requirement for a true revolution. He called the new revolutionary citizen the "New Man," a man who would not flinch at making personal sacrifices for the common good. For various reasons, however, the lofty ideals that had sustained the Revolution seemed unattainable four decades later. Indeed, the most striking image of the decay of the socialist state in the *Dirty Havana Trilogy* is found not in the crumbling Centro Havana buildings nor in the overflowing communal and so-called alternative bathrooms, but in the many characters who trade sex for medicines, food, or a place to live (a practice that, in Pedro Juan's world, is not limited to the emerging *jineteras*, the improvised prostitutes who service European tourists). Against the backdrop of this bleak landscape, the text illustrates the astonishing detour of the revolution that sought to bring dignity to the country and to profoundly transform its citizens on a moral level. Given this historical and ideological journey, it is all the more disheartening to see the characters in Pedro Juan's world constantly humiliate themselves and others in their attempts to meet basic needs.

POSTMODERN REALISM

There is little doubt that the *Dirty Havana Trilogy* is dirty, but is it realist? It is possible to follow the traces of the real at many levels: the recognizable neighbors, the references to earlier texts as the series progresses, frequent efforts to quote exact information such as measurements and dates. What is more, the *Dirty Havana Trilogy* complies rather closely with the terms of the autobiographical pact as described by French literary theorist Philippe Lejeune. The protagonist-narrator is named after the author and he too is a journalist: Gutiérrez worked for *Bohemia* and other journals for twenty-six years before becoming unemployed and writing the *Dirty Havana Trilogy*. The author's journalistic signature can be appreciated in the manner in which he weaves the immediacy and the factuality of daily observation into the very texture of the narration—his style is so distinctive that Anke Birkenmaier has called it "a commercial label";

and, in turn, Guillermina De Ferrari describes it as part of a "curated" aesthetics (2007b). Interestingly, the writer-narrator Pedro Juan often equates the terms *dirty* and *realism*. In making his claims to truthfulness, the narrator describes his profession as "revolcador de mierda," that is, "to grab the pile of reality and let it drop at once on the white page" (p. 103) so as to "force others to smell the shit" (p. 85). The writer-narrator's view of his role reveals an attempt to reduce authorial intervention to an absolute minimum, while knocking his readers from their detached, comfortable position by means of sensory overload. His view of reality leads to frequent exaggerations—exaggerations that the narrator categorically denies and local readers inside as well as outside Gutiérrez's texts often find insulting. In an overt transgression of genre expectations, it can be argued that Pedro Juan Gutiérrez's aesthetics is realist *because* it is dirty.

Pedro Juan Gutiérrez's descriptions are as close to raw experience as is possible in a literary representation. Indeed, they demand that the reader engages in the narrative at an intensely physical level. More specifically, Gutiérrez's deliberate descriptions of dirt inflict a certain degree of epistemological violence on the reader of the *Dirty Havana Trilogy*, who is offered no way to sublimate the characters' lives, which revolve around sex, excrement, filth, and moral debasement. The abundance of visceral sensation maintains the reading experience outside preestablished cultural codes, a strategy that is underscored by Gutiérrez's repeated references to smell. According to Laura Marks, "smell is the most mimetic of the senses, because it acts on our bodies before we are conscious of it. Smell requires a bodily contact with the world, which in turn is mediated in the brain in an especially instinctual fashion" (p. 115). Gutiérrez's insistence in delivering reality through the senses (in the narrator's words, "to force others to smell" an unpleasant reality) creates the illusion of a "mimetic contact" that is mediated in the brain at a purely instinctual level. This inexplicable awareness of something being wrong— all the stronger for not being filtered through consciousness—becomes a precodified form of ethical judgment. Pedro Juan Gutiérrez's writing deliberately alters the rules of Kantian aesthetics, which separate intellectual reflection from the most unmediated pleasures and horrors of sensation. As a repudiation of beauty in its standard forms, the *Dirty Havana Trilogy* turns readers against the grand political projects of the twentieth century and at the same time unseats liberal bourgeois readers from their comfortable position. This fall from innocence is what postmodern revolutions should be made of.

BIBLIOGRAPHY

Birkenmaier, Anke. "El realismo sucio en América Latina: Algunas reflexiones a partir de Pedro Juan Gutiérrez." *Miradas* 6 (2004).

Buford, Bill. "Editorial." *Granta* 8 (1983): 4–5.

De Ferrari, Guillermina. "Abjection and Aesthetic Violence in Pedro Juan Gutiérrez's *Trilogía Sucia de La Habana*." In *Vulnerable States: Bodies of Memory in Contemporary Caribbean Fiction.* Charlottesville: University of Virginia Press, 2007a.

De Ferrari, Guillermina. "Cuba: A Curated Culture." *Journal of Latin American Cultural Studies* 16, no. 2 (August 2007b): 219–240.

Gutiérrez, Pedro Juan. *Trilogía sucia de La Habana.* Barcelona: Anagrama, 1998.

Marks, Laura. *Touch: Sensuous Theory and Multisensory Media.* Minneapolis: University of Minnesota Press, 2002.

Whitfield, Esther. "Autobiografía Sucia: The Body Impolitic of *Trilogía sucia de La Habana.*" *Revista de Estudios Hispánicos* 36, no. 2 (May 2002): 329–351.

■ *See also*

Diasporas: Cubans
Abroad, Post-1959

Life on the Hyphen
(Gustavo Pérez-Firmat)

DREAMING IN CUBAN (CRISTINA GARCÍA)

Iraida H. Lopez

One of the earliest novels in English to express the cultural duality of being both Cuban and American.

Published by Alfred A. Knopf in 1992, *Dreaming in Cuban* conveys like few other books what it means to be both Cuban and American. The novel was one of the earliest to address in English the cultural duality one associates with Cuban American and other ethnic writers.

A second generation Cuban American, Cristina García (b. 1958) steered clear of the one-dimensional view of Cubans on both sides of the Florida Straits prevalent in exile literature. García created distinguishable and memorable characters, especially female characters. She also created multiple voices and perspectives via an array of formal narrative devices. Widely reviewed in the U.S. press and nominated for the National Book Award, for which it was a finalist, *Dreaming in Cuban* became essential reading in Latino and Latina literature alongside such coming-of-age narratives as *The House on Mango Street* (1984), by Sandra Cisneros; *How the Garcia Girls Lost Their Accents* (1991), by Julia Alvarez; and *When I Was Puerto Rican* (1993), by Esmeralda Santiago. The first of a trilogy on Cuba, *Dreaming in Cuban* was followed by *The Agüero Sisters* in 1997 and *Monkey Hunting* in 2003.

García's debut novel received much praise. Writing in the *New York Times Book Review*, Thulani Davis called it "a jewel of a first novel" and welcomed García's work as "the latest sign that American literature has its own hybrid offspring of the Latin American school" (p. 14). In an essay, Eliana Rivero asserted that *Dreaming in Cuban* "launched Cuban American

writing by women into stardom." She asserts that "García's writing became emblematic of what it meant to be Cuban American" (p. 117). Even though García left Cuba when she was only two years old and grew up in various non-Hispanic neighborhoods in New York largely disconnected from her Cuban roots, her early work shares some of the characteristics of Cuban American literature. At some point, she felt the need to reconcile her private Cuban self, nurtured by her family, especially her mother, and her public American identity, a need that made García come to terms with her ethnic background (López 1995, p. 103).

A MULTIGENERATIONAL SAGA

This partly autobiographical novel traces the lives of three generations of Cuban women and their families. Celia del Pino's character, the family matriarch, was inspired to a certain extent by García's grandmother, who remained in Cuba. By contrast, Pilar Puente, Celia's granddaughter, who lives in Brooklyn, is a kind of alter ego of the author herself. As her patronymic implies, Pilar Puente (Bridge) serves as a link in the family's transnational history. The special relationship that Pilar and Celia enjoy allows them to communicate by telepathy. Claiming a female genealogy, the author seeks to connect with both the motherland and mother tongue (Davis 2000, p. 64). Lourdes and Felicia, Celia's daughters, live in Brooklyn and Havana respectively. Lourdes is the proud owner of the Yankee Doodle bakery, a sign not only of her material success in the United States but also of her devotion to entrepreneurship and democratic values. She holds conversations on family matters with her dead father, who relays the reasons for Celia's estrangement from Lourdes and who, toward the end of the novel, nudges her to visit Cuba with Pilar. Being an exile, Lourdes at first refuses to return but eventually relents. Meanwhile, her sister Felicia, who is initiated in *santería*, a religious practice in which Yoruba deities are identified with Roman Catholic saints, is driven mad by syphilis contracted from one of her spouses and dies, leaving her twin daughters and her son, Ivanito, under Celia's care. During Lourdes and Pilar's short visit to the island, some Cubans crash through the gates of the Peruvian embassy in Havana; taking advantage of the opportunity to seek asylum, a crowd congregates on the embassy's grounds. Led by Lourdes, Ivanito joins the crowd, hoping to reach the United States.

A NUANCED APPROACH

The family saga occurs in a particular historical period. The main action is set in the 1970s, when the Revolution became further institutionalized through the adoption of the Constitution of 1976, which recognized the Communist Party as the highest leading force in Cuban society. At the same time, the official embrace of the socialist realist style in the arts had such a negative impact on cultural production that the first half of the decade came to be known as the *quinquenio gris* or grey lustrum. These developments, among others, fueled the desire of many to flee the island. The Peruvian embassy incident in April 1980 led to the Mariel Boatlift shortly thereafter, easing the departure of approximately 125,000 Cubans for the United States. Moreover, during this time, planeloads of Cuban exiles returned to visit their relatives on the island after a long period of separation, following an agreement between the Cuban government and representatives of the Cuban community in the United States in November and December 1978. However, the novel covers more ground as a result of the monthly letters, all unsent, that Celia writes to a Spanish gentleman with whom she had a relationship prior to her marriage to Jorge del Pino, Lourdes and Felicia's father. The letters, which help to fill in gaps in the family's history, are dated from 1935 to 1959, the year the revolution came to power and of Pilar's birth three days after Fidel Castro's march into Havana. The family's tribulations are enmeshed with twentieth-century Cuban history. One of García's goals is to portray the impact that these historical events have on individual lives, especially those of women (López 1995, p. 107).

In the field of Cuban American literature, *Dreaming in Cuban* broke new ground. Part of the novel's significance lies in its evenhanded approach to the Cuban divide, as well as to the United States. The novel presents a nuanced view of the Cuban community on both shores. The effort to provide a balanced assessment draws from García's personal experiences, too. Years after fleeing Cuba with her family, she went back to the island to visit her relatives in March 1984. The trip provided her with a larger sociopolitical context that widened her horizons. Two years later, García was appointed Miami bureau chief for *Time* magazine, a position that made her come face-to-face with the intransigent politics of Cuban exiles. Because of her more progressive political leanings, she did not feel welcome in the conservative environment of Cuban Miami.

In the novel, the author, instead of condemning the Cuban Revolution from the outset, introduces a main character, Celia, who, having lived through the 1940s and 1950s, points to the need for radical social reforms in pre-revolutionary Cuba. Some of her comments imply that, given the glaring inequality between the haves and have nots, change was imperative. For this reason, Celia embraces the revolution and lends it her full support. Yet drawing from other characters' experiences, the novel also criticizes the effects of revolutionary upheaval. Lourdes is raped by soldiers who, following a government edict, show up at her door in order to confiscate her husband's dairy farm, while Felicia bemoans the excess of slogans and security that oppress Cubans on the island. Given Lourdes's encounter, it is no wonder that she identifies with other Cuban exiles who, gathering in her bakery, vilify the revolution. Thus, through the characters' perceptions, the author denounces certain aspects of socialist Cuba while casting a more gentle light on others.

Unlike García, Cuban exile writers of an earlier generation often highlighted only the disadvantages of living under the revolution, waxing nostalgic for the Cuba of yesteryear. Many also unconditionally hailed the United States for having provided safe haven. However, as a member of the second generation, García feels entitled to critique the United States as well. It is all too clear that Pilar, for instance, is not so sure that the United States is the land of liberty and opportunity for all. García's work demonstrates the obstacles to effective communication between Cubans on the island and those abroad. These obstacles are partly based on the failure of words to fully capture and communicate a layered experience grounded in a specific reality and thus different from any other. There are several scenes in the novel that draw from García's insights into the limitations of language. Nonetheless, the novelist attempts to represent fairly both points of view.

NARRATING WOMEN

The novel is also significant given its focus on women's perspectives. In García's view, historical accounts gloss over events that project women as subjects, dwelling instead on those that fall entirely within an impersonal, public domain. Female characters in the novel question why history should treat them as the other, failing to take into account their concerns—as if private lives were disengaged from public discourse. Critics have been quick to recognize García's attempt to correct such bias. Speaking of García's contributions, Isabel Álvarez Borland writes: "From the perspective of gender studies, García's text is indeed unique because it becomes a pioneering voice in telling the story of the Cuban diaspora from the point of view of Cuban women" (p. 139). The complexity with which García treats female characters, which makes them capable of being both victims and victimizers, results from her considerable interest in exploring the lives of women confined by a patriarchal social order.

THE FORM OF *DREAMING IN CUBAN*

Dreaming in Cuban is a polyphonic and dialogic novel, and its story is not presented chronologically. Moving back and forth across time (the 1930s and the 1970s, and also within the 1970s) and space (Cuba and the United States), the action is narrated by Pilar and other characters in the first person, although some sections of the novel are written in the third person. Tied to the shift in perspectives is variation in diction and tone designed to distinguish the different narrators. Still, there is generally a lyrical quality to García's prose style that makes the novel enjoyable. Such quality becomes evident in Celia's letters to her ex-lover, which are interspersed throughout the novel.

Given its enduring qualities, it is not surprising that *Dreaming in Cuban* has been the subject of many articles and dissertations. The novel has been analyzed through the lens of feminist and postcolonial theories alike. While some critics draw attention to its connection to

Cuban (Luis) and Cuban American (Álvarez Borland, Luis) literatures, others, without disregarding these connections, emphasize its links to Latino and Latina literature (Dalleo, Rivero). That the novel is open to diverse readings and related to somewhat different but overlapping traditions is proof of the fluid and dual space that writers such as Cristina García occupy in a hybrid and multicultural literature that spans two nations.

BIBLIOGRAPHY

Álvarez Borland, Isabel. *Cuban American Literature of Exile: From Person to Persona.* Charlottesville and London: University Press of Virginia, 1998.

Dalleo, Raphael. "How Cristina García Lost Her Accent, and Other Latina Conversations." *Latino Studies* 3, no. 1 (April 2005): 3–18.

Davis, Rocío G. "Back to the Future: Mothers, Languages, and Homes in Cristina García's *Dreaming in Cuban.*" *World Literature Today* 74, no. 1 (2000): 60–68.

Davis, Thulani. "Fidel Came between Them." *New York Times Book Review* 17 May 1992: 14.

García, Cristina. *Dreaming in Cuban.* New York: Knopf, 1992.

López, Iraida H. "And There Is Only My Imagination Where Our History Should Be: An Interview with Cristina García." In *Bridges to Cuba/Puentes a Cuba*, edited by Ruth Behar. Ann Arbor: University of Michigan Press, 1995.

Luis, William. "Master Codes of Cuban American Culture: Oscar Hijuelos's *The Mambo Kings Play Songs of Love* and Cristina García's *Dreaming in Cuban.*" In *Dance between Two Cultures: Latino Caribbean Literature Written in the United States*, by William Luis. Nashville, TN, and London: Vanderbilt University Press, 1997.

Rivero, Eliana. "Writing in Cuban, Living as Other: Cuban American Women Writers Getting It Right." In *Cuban American Literature and Art: Negotiating Identities*, edited by Isabel Álvarez Borland and Lynette M. F. Bosch. Albany: State University of New York Press, 2009.

DREAMING OF AN ISLAND (MARÍA MAGDALENA CAMPOS-PONS)

Flora González Mandri

A multimedia work of art that expresses the artist's longing for Cuba.

At the core of María Magdalena Campos-Pons's entire oeuvre lies the artistic concept of performance to communicate both personal and cultural displacement. Coming from a family of African descent in Cuba whose father and grandmother were practitioners of Santería, the religious integration of African and Catholic belief systems, the artist (b. 1959) was attentive to the performative nature of her hybrid culture. In Santería ritual, dance, and commemorative practices, a dramatic representation of origins and cultural endurance predominate (Castellanos 1996, pp. 39–50). In Campos-Pons's performances, installations, and large-scale Polaroid photographs she effected a powerful integration of personal and collective identity.

Campos-Pons, born in Matanzas, graduated from Havana's National School of Art in 1980 and Higher Institute of Art. Early in her career she practiced performance art, combining several artistic modes of expression. She incorporated Santería's ability to communicate hidden meanings through multiple ways of signifying (the act of possession and altar making), using contemporary artistic media such as video, music, photography, and performance art. In Cuba, Campos-Pons was a member of the generation of the 1980s, artists who experimented with the postmodern sensibility of mixing artistic strategies from popular art, oral traditions, and religion. Given their international appeal, most of these artists left the island in the early 1990s when the Cuban economy lost its Soviet subsidies and Cuba's revolutionary bureaucracy began to clamp down on independent artistic expression (Fernández 1999, p. 42).

Although Campos-Pons took up residence in the Boston area in the late 1980s when she did graduate work at the Massachusetts College of Art, she still considered herself a Cuban artist working abroad. She professed to occupy an in-between space, between nations, cultures, and artistic forms of expression (González Mandri 2006, pp. 182–185; Enwezor 2007, p. 69). The Cuban art critic Gerardo Mosquera could be describing Campos-Pons when he defined the international installation artist as "a global nomad who roams from one international exhibit to another, his or her suitcase packed with the elements for a future work of art or the tools to produce it in situ" (2002, p. 167). Her multimedia works have been exhibited in many nations, including Cuba, Canada, Mexico, the United States, Europe, Japan, and South Africa. In 2007 she received the Rappaport Prize, sponsored by the DeCordova Museum, which recognizes artistic talent nurtured in New England. The same year, she was featured in a major mid-career solo exhibition at the Indianapolis Museum of Art called *Everything Is Separated by Water.*

Particularly after her arrival in the Boston area, where she married and had a son, Campos-Pons investigated the intersection of autobiography, culture, and memory by using her own image (Hassan 2001, p. 26). Deeply respectful of her African heritage and that culture's emphasis on ritualistic performance to resurrect a deeply troubled past, she often projected her body image in large-scale

Polaroid photographs as if possessed by the spirit of Santería deities or her own ancestors (*Abridor de caminos* [Guardian of the Roads], 1997). By engaging the performative qualities of an African diaspora culture that represents its mythical deities through the accepted images of Catholic saints, the artist used her body as a surface on which to inscribe the history of survival of the Middle Passage and slavery. During the 1990s she produced a series of installations titled *History of a People Who Were Not Heroes*. Ultimately, Campos-Pons used the photographic image as a medium through which she could perform hidden meanings and historical realities.

María Magdalena Campos-Pons. Multimedia and performance artist María Magdalena Campos-Pons, born in 1959 in Matanzas, belongs to a generation of Cuban artists who have experimented with the postmodern strategy of mixing elements from popular art, oral tradition, and religion. PHOTOGRAPH BY MATT KRYGER, COURTESY OF *THE INDIANAPOLIS STAR*

According to Lisa D. Freiman, "Campos-Pons's interest in photography resulted both from her training at Massachusetts College of Art and her growing awareness of postmodern photographers in Cuba and the United States, such as Marta María Pérez Bravo, Lorna Simpson, and Carrie Mae Weems" (Freiman 2007, p. 28). Okwui Enwezor classified her as a "post-conceptual, photo-based artist navigating the treacherous strait of American/Cuban ideological division on the multicultural and diasporic artistic structures that would come to define her work from 1990 onward" (Enwezor 2007, p. 73).

After exploring her cultural and familial connections to the African diaspora for more than a decade, with *Dreaming of an Island* Campos-Pons turned to the subject of the Cuban diaspora. The multi-paneled Polaroid installation suggests the virtues of painting with its blending of multiple shades of blue and its dream-like atmosphere. The artist's subject, wearing a simple summer dress, sits (presumably in Key West, Florida) and contemplates the island of her birth. This narrative of longing occupies only one-third of the piece; six of the photographic panels depict the depths of the sea and conceptually introduce the subject of memory. Particularly for the African and Cuban diasporas, the sea becomes the repository of memory: for the former, the memory of the Atlantic Passage; for the latter, the memory of the Florida Straits, the political chasm that separates Cuba from the United States. Campos-Pons links her personal desire to return to the collective longing of all Cubans through a single strand of her hair.

For women of African descent, hair stands as the metaphor for women's capacity to survive and endure enslavement and discrimination. In conceptual terms, hair roots them to a deep feminine tradition passed from mother to daughter and woman to woman in the act of braiding and remembering (Rooks 2001, p. 286). Campos-Pons honored her ties to the women in her family in her multimedia installations *Spoken Softly with Mama* (1998) and *Meanwhile, the Girls Were Playing* (1999–2000), and in her large-format Polaroid photography *Replenishing* (1998). In her autobiographical poem "The Wife's Monologue," the Cuban poet Excilia Saldaña ties hair to memory in her evocative verse

> braiding and unbraiding
> the tresses of my memory.
>
> *González Mandri and Rosenmeier 2002,*
> *pp. 12–13.*

In *Dreaming of an Island* Campos-Pons braids her hair into vessels of the sea sunk in the waters of the Caribbean. Historically, the image of the ship signifies the traumatic journey of slaves across the Atlantic, but according to Okwui Enwezor, it "also imagines and theorizes their return on the selfsame ship, as the birth of countercultures of modernity" (2007, pp. 70–71). In order to return to the island of her dreams, Campos-Pons fashions multiple canoes, linking her to Cuba's indigenous populations who built seaworthy vessels moving freely from the Caribbean islands to the peninsula of Florida. The canoes also recall the precarious rafts built by many Cubans in the 1990s in their attempts to reach U.S. shores. Most importantly, the multiple canoes link the artist to her Cuban counterparts who, like Sandra Ramos in *La Balsa* (Raft, 1995), Gabriel Gutiérrez in *Isla* (Island, 1999), Agustín Bejarano in his series *Los ritos del silencio* (Rites of Silence, 2003–2006), and Martha Jiménez in *Obstáculo* (Obstacle, 2007), equate the boat with the island itself (see Mosquera 1999).

Dreaming of an Island is a master conceptual work where autobiography, culture, and memory intersect. With this photographic installation, María Magdalena Campos-Pons navigates the deep waters of her inherited diasporas, always returning to her African and Cuban artistic traditions.

BIBLIOGRAPHY

Campos-Pons, María Magdalena. *Everything Is Separated by Water*. Ed. Lisa D. Freiman. New Haven, CT, and London: Yale University Press and the Indianapolis Museum of Art, 2007.

Castellanos, Isabel. "From Ulkumí to Lucumí: A Historical Overview of Religious Acculturation in Cuba." In *Santería Aesthetics in Contemporary Latin American Art*. Ed. Arturo Lindsay. Washington, DC, and London: Smithsonian Institution Press, 1996.

Enwezor, Okwui. "The Diasporic Imagination: The Memory Works of María Magdalena Campos-Pons." In *Everything Is Separated by Water*. Ed. Lisa D. Freiman. New Haven, CT, and London: Yale

University Press and the Indianapolis Museum of Art, 2007.

Fernández, Antonio Eligio (Tonel). "Tree of Many Beaches: Cuban Art in Motion, 1989–1990." In *Contemporary Art from Cuba: Irony and Survival on the Utopian Island*. New York: Delano Greenidge Editions and Arizona State University, 1999.

Freiman, Lisa D. "María Magdalena Campos-Pons: Everything Is Separated by Water." In *Everything Is Separated by Water*. Ed. Lisa D. Freiman. New Haven, CT, and London: Yale University Press and the Indianapolis Museum of Art, 2007.

González Mandri, Flora. *Guarding Cultural Memory: Afro-Cuban Women in Literature and the Arts*. Charlottesville: University of Virginia Press, 2006.

González Mandri, Flora, and Rosamond Rosenmeier, trans. and eds. *In the Vortex of the Cyclone: Selected Poems by Excilia Saldaña*. Gainesville: University Press of Florida, 2002.

Hassan, Salah M. "'Insertions': Self and Other in Contemporary African Art." In *Authentic/Ex-Centric: Conceptualism in Contemporary African Art*, ed. Salah M. Hassan and Olu Oguibe. Ithaca, NY: Forum for African Arts, 2001.

Mosquera, Gerardo. "La isla infinita: Introducción al nuevo arte cubano." *Cuba: Contemporary Art from Cuba: Irony and Survival on the Utopian Island/Arte contemporáneo de Cuba: Ironía y sobrevivencia en la isla utópica*. New York: Delano Greenidge Editions and Arizona State University Art Museum, 1999.

Mosquera, Gerardo. "Alien-Own/Own-Alien: Globalization and Cultural Difference." *boundary 2* 29, no. 3 (fall 2002): 163–173.

Rooks, Moliwe. "Wearing Your Race Wrong." In *Recovering the Black Female Body: Self Representations by African American Women*, ed. Michael Bennett and Vanessa D. Dickerson. New Brunswick, NJ: Rutgers University Press, 2001.

E ECOLOGY AND ENVIRONMENT

Although the frontiers between social sciences and natural sciences have become blurred, very little has been learned about the interaction between human beings and nature throughout Cuba's history. However, scholars have begun to research environmental history, and their essays are helping to reveal the simultaneous evolution of social and natural systems.

The concepts of ecology and environment are often used interchangeably, sometimes generating confusion. Ecology is aimed at changing people's attitudes toward the ecosystems on which they depend for their very existence. Environment, on the other hand, refers to both the physical geography and the ecology of one's surroundings as well as natural, social, and cultural values in a particular place and time that influence current and future generations.

The following essays analyze the interactions between society and nature in the economy, agriculture in general and the sugar industry specifically, cultural affairs, nutrition, and more.

ECOLOGY AND ENVIRONMENT: COLONIAL PERIOD

Reinaldo Funes Monzote

The ecological revolution in Cuba from the inception of Spanish colonialism to independence in 1898.

There is considerable dispute about the size of the Cuban population when colonization began in 1511. The most widely published figures range from 100,000 to 200,000, but various scholars claim larger or smaller densities. Most of the inhabitants lived in agricultural, pottery-making communities dating back about 1,000 years. They used wood in various ways and practiced shifting agriculture, which could have influenced the formation of savannahs. Nonetheless, their impact on the natural ecosystem was minimal, although greatest in the communities of farmers and potters in the central-eastern half of the island. It is thought that, as on other Caribbean islands, the native communities developed complex socioeconomic systems that allowed them to live in harmony with their physical surroundings, preserving their innate resource potential (Watts p. 75).

EUROPEANS' ARRIVAL

Spanish colonization marked the start of an ecological revolution that began with the original population's demographic collapse, a consequence of massacres, slavery, collective suicide, and starvation because they were no longer growing subsistence crops. There is, to some degree, a consensus that the greatest number of native deaths was caused by diseases brought from the Old World such as smallpox, influenza, swine fever, typhus, meningitis, and malaria; because of their having been isolated from the exchange of microbes that occurred over many centuries on the other side of the Atlantic, the natives had no immunological defenses against these diseases (Crosby 1994, pp. 195–216). However, several scholars maintain that the alleged extinction of the natives may have been overstated by certain interests and that the vestigial native population became an important element in the physical and cultural mixture with Spaniards and Africans that resulted in the *criollo*, the basis of new identities (García Molina et. al.; Barreiro).

Columbus and other early chroniclers testified to the exuberance and variety of Cuban vegetation, the vast number and diversity of birds and fishes, and the transparency of the water; they were surprised at how few large quadrupeds and mammals there were on the island. On Columbus's second trip, on the island of Hispaniola, the Spaniards introduced plants and domesticated animals from the Old World's agricultural revolutions. The Spaniards brought seed stocks for wheat, chickpeas, onions, radishes, melon, green vegetables, grapes, fruits, citrus, and sugarcane. The animals included horses, cattle (cows and calves), hogs, sheep, and goats (Crosby 1973, pp. 64–121).

Plants adapted slowly, either because they had difficulty adjusting to the new environment or because the conquistadors did not want to be farmers. However, the newly introduced animals showed an extraordinary capacity for reproduction, especially the cattle and hogs, as well as the dogs, cats, and rats. In the absence of natural predators, the multiplication of European animals had a strong impact on native fauna as well as on the forest undergrowth, and also damaged native subsistence crops. The habitat of saurians, the only native predator, was limited to swampy areas and wetlands.

EXTENSIVE CATTLE RAISING

Once the limited mineral deposits of gold were exhausted, cattle raising became the predominant activity, favored by cattle's rapid reproduction rate, the needs of the continent's colonizers, and the European demand for leather (Marrero pp. 89–104). Before the mid-sixteenth century the councils in the first townships began parceling out land by means of the *merced* (royal distribution) for livestock breeding on extensive plots; cattle ranches were called *hatos* and hog farms were called *corrales*. In 1574 the Cáceres Ordinances established the legal framework for the councils' distribution of farms and ranches, and this system remained essentially unchanged until 1729.

In 1579 the ideal size of these parcels was formalized: 56,280 acres for cattle ranches and 14,070 acres for hog farms. Licenses for crop cultivation were issued for the land closest to the towns, but in time, agricultural fields popped up in the free spaces known as *realengos* between the boundaries of haciendas, and within hacienda boundaries beginning at the limits of sugar mills and tobacco fields, which followed river courses (Le Riverend).

Over time, the original functions of *hatos* and *corrales* intermingled, and often they contained forests and natural grasslands, or grasslands periodically created by clearing for cattle grazing. Usually hogs were kept under trees and fed on the fallen fruit. The forests also provided cattle with fruits, shoots, branches, and reeds to eat during drought periods. Little is known about cattle ranching during the first centuries of colonization before the rise of plantations worked by slaves, which from the mid-eighteenth century sparked a new agrarian and ecological revolution on the island.

Until that time there had been little change in the forest cover, despite the felling of trees for various urban and rural purposes; some researchers have even argued that the forests may have grown, given native depopulation (Matos; Denevan). It is estimated that when the Spaniards arrived, 60 to 85 percent of Cuban territory was tropical forestland, plus added pine groves and other plant formations, and this general panorama, continued through the late eighteenth century. This relative stability is attributed to the fact that woodland exploitation was offset by natural reforestation of other uninhabited areas or that the pace of economic activities allowed for some recovery of the native flora.

SHIPBUILDING

On the cattle ranches, timber was cut for building ships in Havana. Although this selective felling was carried out all over the island, it was most prevalent in the western portion and in central Cuba to a lesser extent (Funes Monzote 2008a, pp. 59–66). In light of shipbuilding's strategic importance, several laws were passed in regard to Cuban forests. Decrees issued in 1622 and 1624 and printed in the *Recopilación de las leyes de los reinos de las Indias* (Code of Law for the Kingdoms of the Indies) prohibited the cutting down of cedar, mahogany, and oak within a distance of 10 leagues (26 miles) east or west of the port of Havana. These restrictions were broadened by a 1748 edict in response to the increasing distance of the timber supply. In addition to increasing the forested area reserved for the navy, it specified more species of trees that could not be felled without a license, including sabicu, chicharron, partridge wood, María wood, and guaicum. In 1772 new requirements were issued for felling trees, and the navy managed to get veto power over land clearing on cattle ranches containing trees that could be used for shipbuilding. Between 1724 and 1796, except during the period when Havana was controlled by the British, a total of 113 ships were built, among them 45 ships-of-the-line and 22 frigates. Six first-rate ships, including the *Santísima Trinidad*, the world's largest at the time, were launched during the last third of that century.

This boom coincided with the upsurge of Havana's sugar industry. The resulting demand for fertile land for cane fields, as well as lumber and firewood, resulted in serious conflicts between sugar mill owners and the leadership of the Spanish Royal Navy. Both parties wanted to control the process of clearing haciendas. One instance of this rivalry was the naval commander's 1783 proposal to establish a new method for preserving woodlands, containing this simple calculation: "If one of the most profitable haciendas is cleared, where the wood has not yet been removed,

Opposite page:
Santísima Trinidad. The *Santísima Trinidad* was launched in Havana on 3 March 1769. It was the world's largest ship at the time.

the King will lose the equivalent of four or five ships in those ashes" (Funes Monzote 2008a, p. 51).

CASH CROPS

Unlike naval shipbuilding, the main resource necessary for cash crops was the soil, not forests. Until the late eighteenth century the most important crops were tobacco and sugarcane, whose agro-ecological and social differences were already becoming evident. Tobacco was a native plant grown mostly on a small scale by free workers. Sugarcane, in contrast, was from the start an exotic plant tended by slave labor in a large-scale, agro-industrial context (Ortiz).

From the seventeenth century, the center of the sugar industry could be found in the vicinity of Havana, given the city's status as a hub of the Spanish imperial fleet and the center of colonial administration. Before 1740 the area's sugar production had its highs and lows, and on occasion it was surpassed by that of tobacco. But its ecological impact was greater than tobacco's because of the huge amount of lumber needed to build sugar mills, carts, and other equipment, and the copious use of firewood to cook the cane juice. The concentration on these crops, sugar and tobacco, neither of which was a source of subsistence, motivated the town council to issue decrees aimed at guaranteeing the provision of foods such as manioc.

The 1739 founding of the Royal Company of Commerce of Havana sparked a gradual upsurge in the founding of sugar mills. This trend was consolidated, owing to the eleven-month occupation of Havana by the British (1762–1763), after which the Bourbon Reforms were undertaken, culminating in the authorization of free trade between Spain and the Indies in 1778. The number of sugar mills in the Havana hinterland grew from about one hundred in the mid-eighteenth century to more than two hundred in 1790, and their average productive capacity also increased. (Funes Monzote 2008a, pp. 41–45). But the great take-off occurred after the 1791 slave revolt in neighboring Haiti, then the top sugar exporter.

From then on, the plantation system thrived in Cuba, built on the direct importation of slaves from Africa (legalized in 1789), free foreign trade (from 1818), and the consolidation of private landownership (in 1819). Particularly important in environmental history is the royal decree of 30 August 1815 that granted individuals the right to chop down forests with total liberty. This put an end to the long conflict between the navy and the Havana sugar mill owners and placed the forests' economic value over the strategic and ecological concerns that had prevailed earlier.

The proliferation of sugar plantations in the Havana area created many environmental problems that later affected the whole island. The most visible of these was intense deforestation and its direct economic consequence—shortages of lumber and fuel.

The areas close to Havana, with depleted forests and exhausted lands, were abandoned in favor of wooded frontier towards the southern plains, the northwestern coast, and above all, the east. There was already talk of a greater local incidence of drought, a decline in other economic activities, and greater food vulnerability as plantations increased their dominance. These effects concerned the colonists and the mother countries of what were known as the Sugar Islands of the Caribbean, whose small land masses required the adoption of better technology in the sugar industry and conservationist measures (Watts; Grove). But in Cuba there was still an abundance of wooded land, and the topographical conditions were favorable for constant increases in the scale of production.

A memoir by the Havana rancher José Ricardo O'Farril warned in 1796 that if preventive measures were not taken, in a few years the closest forest would be 40 leagues (104 miles) from Havana; José Antonio Saco lamented in 1828 that this calculation had been greatly exceeded, and he called for urgent legislation. Looking beyond criticisms of the immediate physical effects, others questioned the soundness of a society dominated by slave plantations and cash crops. One of the early voices of this view was the German explorer and naturalist Alexander von Humboldt (1769–1859), who visited Cuba for almost three months between late 1800 and March 1801 and for just over a month in 1804.

During these stays Humboldt visited Havana sugar mills, where he observed agriculture performed by slave labor, and he tried to find a practical solution to the depleted fuel supply. Later on, in his *Political Essay on the Island of Cuba* (1827), he criticized the creation of Caribbean economies based on sugar and slave labor, writing that the extreme dominance of cash crops, resulting from Europeans' "imprudent activity" in tropical regions, constituted an inversion of the "natural order." Humboldt expressed hope that crop diversification would allow Cuba to follow nature's plan for all large and educated societies. He also noted the widespread complaints of the disproportionate power of Havana as compared to the rest of the island.

Humboldt also observed the rise of the coffee plantations at the dawn of the new century in the eastern mountains near Santiago de Cuba and in the western mountains and flatlands. Immigrants from Haiti played the leading role in this growth. But starting in the 1830s, the coffee plantations declined, and it was even necessary to import coffee to satisfy local demand. These plantations had a strong environmental impact, especially on the mountainsides, but they were on a smaller scale than the sugar mills, and they also had greater crop diversity. Powerful hurricanes in 1844 and 1846 brought about the final crisis of coffee cultivation in the western zone (Pérez pp. 57–82).

CUBAN SUGAR AND THE INDUSTRIAL REVOLUTION

The crisis of the coffee plantations strengthened sugar's predominance in western Cuba and certain parts of eastern Cuba. Despite Spain's treaty with England to end the slave trade by 1820 and despite abolitionist campaigns, the Cuban sugar plantation system based on slave labor entered its period of splendor. Production rose from just over 45,000 tons in 1815 to 750,000 tons in 1875 (Moreno Fraginals pp. 543–544). This boom was partly the result of the proliferation of sugar mills on the western and central plains, in numbers that stabilized at just above 1,000 between 1846 and 1862 (including demolished and rebuilt mills) (Funes Monzote 2008a, p. 130). But above all, the major increase in production was due to the early adoption of technology born of the Industrial Revolution that permitted huge savings in labor and draft animal power.

By the end of the 1820s, steam engines were used in the mills, initially on a limited basis because of high fuel consumption, among other reasons. By 1860 they were being employed in one thousand mills, and their motor power was even greater. The railroad's advent in 1837 signaled a great revolution in the transportation of product to ports. Cuba was one of the first countries in the world—the second in the Americas—to have a railroad, and by 1860 it had a larger railroad network than the rest of Latin America and the Caribbean combined. Not long after that, steamships carried Cuba's growing sugar exports.

The success of Cuba's sugar plantation system was the result of a set of factors related to the transition from an organic, solar-based economy to one based on the use of fossil fuels. The island was one of the first colonial territories to implement modern agribusiness practices and expand the frontiers for the production of food and raw materials, linked to the incipient industrial era (Funes Monzote and Tomich). Predatory agriculture advanced across the forests in search of fuel and virgin lands, but coal was also imported in greater amounts to meet the energy needs of the sugar mills, railroads, and steamships.

The new phase of slave-based plantations included much of the current provinces of Matanzas, Cienfuegos, and northern Villa Clara. Although Havana maintained its importance as an exporting port, the new sugar zones traded directly through the ports of Matanzas, Cárdenas, Cienfuegos, and Sagua la Grande. The hub of this combination of slave labor and industry was situated from 1840 and 1870 on the Colón plains, where many of the mechanized sugar mills were built (Bergad pp. 116–140).

The steam era accelerated the deforestation of constantly increasing areas. Many warned about deforestation's long- and short-term threats to the maintenance of production, as well as economic, climatic, and environmental concerns. Authors of memoirs and other books debated solutions to the demand for fuel and proposed remedies to reverse the loss of soil fertility. Figures of influence in scientific circles such as the Count of Pozos Dulces (1809–1877), Ramón de la Sagra (1798–1871), and Alvaro Reynoso (1829–1888) called for an end to the slash-and-burn system in favor of a science-based agriculture built on fertilizers, irrigation, drainage works, and new agricultural tools. One of the arguments deployed was the perception of the impact of droughts, aggravated by scant rainfall in areas stripped of forest cover (Rodríguez Ferrer p. 290).

Sugar mills' preeminence signified a reduction in indigenous biodiversity. By the time slavery was abolished, there had been a sharp decline in the populations of native mammals, birds, and other species. Juan C. Gundlach (1810–1896), a German ornithologist living on the island, wondered in 1865, "How many Cubans of a certain age recall having seen, as children, an abundance of certain birds that have now disappeared?" (Gundlach p. 179). As ecosystems were simplified by the cultivation of sugarcane, exotic species increasingly were introduced; in many cases, they became identifying elements of the new landscape, such as Guinea grass, mangos, and the Royal Poinciana. Havana's Botanical Garden, established in 1817, played a major role in these plants' acclimatization.

Around 1860 the island seemingly could be divided into two halves: The western half was dominated by sugar plantations, plus tobacco cultivation restricted to areas of Pinar del Río; and the eastern half was dominated by livestock raising and lesser economic activities. Eastern Cuba was certainly not exempt from environmental transformations, but their pace was much slower than in the west. Over time, the livestock region saw the replacement of the original haciendas by more efficient ranches (Monteverde), usually located near towns or in sugar mill areas, which helped maintain the herds of oxen.

In Puerto Príncipe, starting in 1846, Durham, Hereford, and Devon cattle were brought to Cuba from the United States in order to improve the Cuban strain through crossbreeding. Ranchers in Puerto Príncipe, Bayamo, and Sancti Spíritus, among other cities, were at the forefront of this effort. Previously, it had been common in Havana and other cities to introduce horses and donkeys from abroad for urban transportation and mule breeding. Livestock fairs were held periodically in Puerto Príncipe from 1843 to 1868, as well as in other localities.

Juan Pérez de la Riva (2004) used the terms *Cuba A* and *Cuba B* to highlight the differences between the island's western region, dominated by plantations based on slave labor, and the central-eastern region. The contrasts and conflicts between them ultimately played a part in the outbreak of the war of independence in 1868. There is still much to study about this dichotomy from a socio-environmental perspective, but the significant disparity between the two regions, in terms of human intervention in the ecosystem, is beyond question.

MECHANIZED SUGAR REFINERIES

The war, which was fought mostly in the livestock-breeding areas of central and eastern Cuba, came to a close in 1878, marking the initial centralization of sugar refining and the decentralization of cane cultivation into districts that supplied the highly mechanized mills. In western Cuba, the units that were able to adopt new technology consolidated several former sugar mills into one, whereas in eastern Cuba virgin forests were once again occupied. At the renewed outbreak of war in 1895, there were about four hundred mechanized sugar refineries; the previous year's harvest had totaled more than one million tons of sugar for the first time ever (Iglesias).

The increased scale of production was favored by the use of private railroads to transport the raw material to the refineries, as well as by the opening of private docks. The last years of the nineteenth century form a sort of interlude in which the western region moved toward science-based agriculture, accompanied by some diversification into crops such as potatoes, pineapples, and corn (Fernández). In the eastern region, meanwhile, lumber production remained important for ports such as Gibara, Santa Cruz del Sur, and Manzanillo.

In 1876, following several earlier attempts, Spain issued the Woodland Decrees for Cuba and Puerto Rico, foreshadowing modern forestry management, albeit with limited personnel and scant resources. Cuba was divided into three forestry districts under the jurisdiction of the Woodlands Section, which was headed for years by Francisco de Paula Portuondo (1835–1912), a Cuban trained at the forestry school in Spain. This agency's authority was limited generally to government-owned forests, totaling no more than 10 percent of the island's territory, but it also enforced some regulations regarding the exploitation and commercialization of private woodlands (Funes Monzote 2008a, pp. 206–215).

A topic rarely discussed is surface water pollution caused by sugar refineries and other urban industries. In an 1898 file on pollutants dumped into the Sagua la Grande River, the Santa Clara government's health agency proposed that the owners of the Santa Teresa refinery be fined and pointed out the need for legislation to enable effective sanctions on owners of sugar plantations and distilleries that dumped waste into rivers. In the following year the inhabitants of Sagua la Grande filed a major lawsuit against the El Infierno distillery. The engineer Francisco Paradela, on behalf of the Academy of Sciences, confirmed that the distillery had acted improperly, but acknowledged that it was not the only source of pollution, also blaming "the sugar refineries that dump their sugarcane mud and other residues from sugar manufacturing, leather tanneries and factories that dispose of their waste in residential areas, as well as effluents from slaughterhouses and sewers" (Paradela p. 625).

URBAN ENVIRONMENT

Environmental regulation during the colonial period was focused mostly on cities and towns, in the form of municipal ordinances. As early as the sixteenth century, legislation attempted to control access to timber and firewood and to prevent pollution of drinking water and felling of forests at the mouths of rivers (such as the Almendares River in Havana). There were also specific regulations, such as one in 1859, for the cleanup of unhealthy, dangerous, and unpleasant establishments, including manioc starch works, trash and garbage cart depositories, bone char factories, hog corrals, tanneries, and slaughterhouses.

Havana in particular was considered an unhealthy city and a center of the yellow fever epidemics that periodically devastated Europeans newly arrived in the Americas and whose spread was tied to sugar's economic and social network (McNeill). The physician Diego Tamayo estimated in 1893 that more than forty thousand people had died in Havana from yellow fever in the previous thirty years. Other major causes of mortality were tuberculosis, typhoid fever, diphtheria, enteritis, and tetanus. On the basis of statistics from 1892, Tamayo declared that 60 percent of the deaths that year could have been prevented (Tamayo pp. 8–11).

The high incidence of preventable diseases became one of the main targets for criticism of the colonial administration. Havana, as the largest population center, had the biggest problems. An 1890 study emphasized the "alarming nature" of the city's contaminated air, the presence of stables in residential areas, poor conditions in marketplaces and slaughterhouses, the terrible state of sewers and latrines, and pollution of the bay, as well as poor knowledge about hygiene among the population and a frightful lack of concern regarding quarantines (Leyva pp. 8–9). All of this was true, despite the high ratio of doctors to population and the scientific advancement represented by numerous associations, especially the Royal Academy of Medical, Physical, and Natural Sciences of Havana, founded in 1861. Indeed, it was in the pages of the academy's *Annals*, in 1881, that Carlos J. Finlay presented his hypothesis that the female *Aedes aegypti* mosquito was the vector of yellow fever.

In the final third of the nineteenth century, hygiene became a major topic of concern. Central in this effort were the Hygiene Society of Havana (1891–1895) and the Cuban Society for the Protection of Animals and Plants, founded in 1882, which could be considered Cuba's first environmental organization (Funes Monzote 2008b). Its broad objectives included study and experimentation to restore soil fertility, environmental cleanup, diversification of native crops, and adaptation of non-native plants by means of seed and product exchanges with kindred institutions. It organized public exhibitions and sponsored a trip to the Philippines in search of economical plant varieties.

This association denounced acts of cruelty against animals by their drivers and owners and formed commissions to inspect markets, stables, and slaughterhouses. It insisted on the enforcement of established sanctions against the sale of poor-quality animal feed, the possession of sick animals in residential areas, working animals too hard, punishing them too harshly, or slaughtering them in unhealthy conditions. Thus, it was no surprise that the association opposed bullfighting, one of the symbols of cultural identity with Spanish colonialism.

BIBLIOGRAPHY

Barreiro, José. "Survival Stories." In *The Cuban Reader: History, Culture, Politics*, edited by Aviva Chomsky, Barry Carr, and Pamela Maria Smorkaloff, 28–36. Durham, NC: Duke University Press, 2003.

Bergad, Laird. *Cuban Rural Society in the Nineteenth Century: The Social and Economic History of Monoculture in Matanzas*. Princeton, NJ: Princeton University Press, 1990.

Crosby, Alfred W. *The Columbian Exchange: Biological and Cultural Consequences of 1492*. Westport, CT: Greenwood Press, 1973.

Crosby, Alfred W. *Ecological Imperialism: The Biological Expansion of Europe, 900–1900*. 1986. New York: Cambridge University Press, 1994.

Denevan, William M. "The Pristine Myth: The Landscape of the Americas in 1492." In *Annals of the Association of American Geographers* 82, no. 3 (September): 369–395.

Fernández Prieto, Leida. *Cuba agrícola: Mito y tradición, 1878–1920*. Madrid: Consejo Superior de Investigaciones Científicas, 2005.

Frías y Jacott, Francisco de (Count of Pozos Dulces). *Colección de escritos sobre agricultura, industria, ciencias y otros ramos de interés para la Isla de Cuba*. Paris: Jorge Kugelmann, 1860.

Funes Monzote, Reinaldo. *From Rainforest to Cane Field in Cuba: An Environmental History since 1492*. Chapel Hill: University of North Carolina Press, 2008a.

Funes Monzote, Reinaldo. "Los orígenes del asociacionismo ambientalista en Cuba. La sociedad protectora de animales y plantas." In *Naturaleza en declive. Miradas a la historia ambiental de América Latina y el Caribe*, edited by Reinaldo Funes Monzote. Valencia, Spain: Fundación Historia Social, 2008b.

Funes Monzote, Reinaldo, and Dale Tomich. "Naturaleza, tecnología y esclavitud en Cuba: Frontera azucarera y revolución industrial, 1815–1870." In *Trabajo libre y trabajo coactivo en sociedades de plantación*, edited by José A. Piqueras. Madrid: Siglo XXI, 2009.

García Molina, José Antonio, Daisy Fariñas Gutiérrez, and M. Garrido Mazorra. *Huellas vivas del Indocubano*. Toronto: Lugus Libros, 1998.

Grove, Richard. *Green Imperialism: Colonial Expansion, Tropical Island Edens and the Origins of Environmentalism, 1600–1860*. Cambridge, U.K.: Cambridge University Press, 1996.

Gundlach, Juan C. "Revista y catálogo de las aves cubanas." *Repertorio físico natural de la Isla de Cuba*, edited by Felipe Poey. Havana: Imprenta del Gobierno y Capitanía General, 1865–1866.

Humboldt, Alexander von. *Ensayo político sobre la Isla de Cuba*. 1827. Edited by Miguel Ángel Puig-Samper, Consuelo Naranjo Orovio, and Armando García González. Aranjuez, Spain: Ediciones Doce Calles, 1998.

Iglesias García, Fe. *Del Ingenio al Central*. San Juan: Editorial de la Universidad de Puerto Rico, 1998.

Le Riverend, Julio. *Problemas de la formación agraria de Cuba. Siglos XVI–XVII*. Havana: Editorial de Ciencias Sociales, 1992.

Leyva Aguilera, Herminio C. *Saneamiento de la ciudad de La Habana*. Havana: La Tipografía, 1890.

Marrero, Leví. *Cuba. Economía y sociedad*. Vol. 2. Madrid: Playor, 1974.

Matos González, Eliseo. "Breve historia de los montes de Cuba." Havana: Instituto Nacional de Desarrollo y Aprovechamiento Forestal (INDAF). Unpublished, 1970.

McNeill, John. *Epidemics and Geopolitics in the American Tropics, 1640–1920*. New York: Cambridge University Press, 2008.

Monteverde, Manuel. *Estudios prácticos de las condiciones económicas de la industria pecuaria en el distrito de Puerto Príncipe*. Puerto Príncipe, Cuba: El Fanal, 1856.

Moreno Fraginals, Manuel. *El Ingenio. Complejo económico social cubano del azúcar*. Barcelona: Crítica, 2001.

Ortiz, Fernando. *Contrapunteo cubano del tabaco y el azúcar*. 1940. Havana: Editorial de Ciencias Sociales, 1983.

Paradela, Francisco. "Informe sobre la infección de las aguas del río Sagua la Grande por el alambique El Infierno." *Anales de la Academia de Ciencias Médicas, Físicas y Naturales de La Habana* 44 (1907–1908): 620–637.

Pérez de la Riva, Juan. "Una isla con dos historias." In *La conquista del espacio cubano*. 1968. Havana: Fundación Fernando Ortiz, 2004.

Pérez, Louis A., Jr. *Winds of Change: Hurricanes and the Transformation of Nineteenth-Century Cuba*. Chapel Hill: University of North Carolina Press, 2001.

Reglamento sobre establecimientos insalubres, peligrosos e incómodos. Havana: Imprenta del Gobierno y Capitanía General, 1859.

Reynoso, Álvaro. *Ensayo sobre el cultivo de la caña de azúcar*. 1862. Havana: Empresa Consolidada de Artes Gráficas, 1963.

Rodríguez Ferrer, Miguel. *Naturaleza y civilización de la grandiosa Isla de Cuba, o Estudios variados y científicos al alcance de todos y otros históricos, estadísticos y políticos*. Vol. 1. Madrid: J. Noguera, 1876.

Sagra, Ramón de la. *Cuba en 1860 o sea cuadro de sus adelantos en la población, la agricultura, el comercio y las rentas públicas*. París: L. Hachette et Cie, 1862.

Tamayo, Diego. *Reflexiones sociológicas sobre las causas de la mortalidad en La Habana*. Havana: Propaganda Literaria, 1893.

Watts, David. *Las indias occidentales. Modalidades de desarrollo, cultura y cambio medio ambiental desde 1492*. Madrid: Alianza Editorial, 1992.

ECOLOGY AND ENVIRONMENT: REPUBLICAN PERIOD

Reinaldo Funes Monzote

Depletion of natural resources, transition to oil dependency, and the initial efforts of modern conservationism between 1902 and 1959.

The period of the Cuban Republic, declared on 20 May 1902, saw environmental transformations in both urban and rural areas based on practices and policies established during the first U.S. occupation (1898–1902). Some changes began during the occupation, such as vital efforts in disease control and public hygiene; others came later, such as the transition from coal to oil as Cuba's primary energy source and the automobile revolution. In any case, Cuban society's relationship with nature corresponded to the twentieth century's patterns of energy consumption, exploitation and conservation of natural resources, confidence in technology and science, and the rise of the ecology movement (McNeill).

PUBLIC SANITATION

Faced with a critical situation after the war of 1895 to 1898, the U.S. occupiers of Cuba demonstrated their superiority in the area of hygiene and public health, compared to the Spanish colonial administration. Quarantine measures were introduced, and laws were passed to regulate immigration and prostitution, to control infectious diseases, to pave streets and construct the Havana seawall (the Malecón), to control marketplaces and the water supply, and to provide compulsory smallpox vaccinations.

The greatest advance was the eradication of yellow fever, after initially unsuccessful efforts by the occupying government. Carlos Finlay's theory of a biological vector for the disease made it possible to implement effective preventive measures such as prohibiting open tanks and cisterns where mosquitoes could breed. Havana's fight against yellow fever marked the start of the U.S. "colonial public health" policy aimed at safeguarding U.S. interests, protecting its troops and workforce, and justifying its political domination (Espinosa p. 10). William C. Gorgas, the head of the Health Department during the U.S. occupation, wrote in his last report in July 1902 that during its first year in the tropics the United States lost 67 men per 1,000 to illness, and in its last year in Cuba the United States had gained so much experience that its loss was only 7 men per 1,000 (Wood p. 8).

Article 5 of the Platt Amendment obligated the Cuban government to complete "plans already devised or other plans to be mutually agreed upon . . . to the end that a recurrence of epidemic and infectious diseases may be prevented, thereby assuring protection to the people and commerce of Cuba, as well as to the commerce and people of southern United States." Thus, public health and hygiene were a priority for the new republic.

The public health measures were focused on Havana at first, but in 1902 the health authorities began to extend them to the rest of the country. They passed local health ordinances; improved quarantine, immigration, lazaretto, sanatorium, and hospital services; and issued public works contracts to build sewers and pave streets in cities. In 1909 the Ministry of Health and Welfare was established; it was the first government ministry in the world devoted to public health. The resulting rapid decrease in general mortality made Cuba "the healthiest country in the tropics," according to Juan Pérez de la Riva (p. 20). The population of the island rose from 1.5 million inhabitants in 1899 to 6.5 million in 1958, with over 50 percent urbanization (Pérez de la Riva).

The fight against yellow fever in Havana provided a model for similar efforts by the United States in other Latin American countries, the prime example being the campaign led by Gorgas against the disease during the building of the Panama Canal. Widespread tropical diseases contributed to the belief—along with ideas about the white race's alleged superiority—that moderate climates were better than hot ones for the advancement of civilization (Arnold pp. 36–37). These theories were refuted by Cuban intellectuals who considered themselves to be living proof of whites' potential for progress in the tropics, as demonstrated by centuries of Spanish and Portuguese colonial domination (Guiteras).

The tropics became a synonym for vast territories with abundant natural resources that the natives and former colonizers had been unable to exploit. Cuba was at the forefront of the expansion of the U.S. empire because of its geographical location and its historical, economic, and political relationship with its neighbors to the north (Pérez). Indeed, Cuba was featured in the 1914 book *Conquest of the Tropics* that exalted the United Fruit Company's growth, which was rooted in its sugar refineries in eastern Cuba and its banana plantations in Central America (Adams pp. 243–263).

NEW FRONTIERS FOR SUGAR

The sugar industry's renewed march eastward, under the aegis of new political and economic relations with the United States, symbolized that conquest of the tropics in Cuba. The first quarter of the twentieth century was the most intense stage of deforestation because of U.S. corporations' increased control over Cuba's natural environment (Tucker pp. 37–48). The main areas of expansion were Camagüey and Oriente Provinces, where livestock raising continued to be the main activity in an extensive system that maintained large forested zones.

Of course, sugar was not the only factor in the rapid transformation of those territories; it was seconded by forestry and the development of settlements growing other crops. The livestock industry recovered after the war, providing animals used for transportation and later for meat. New bovine breeds such as the zebu were introduced, and the large landed estates that dominated the cattle industry also fueled propagation of the feared *marabú* thorn bush, an exotic invasive plant that had arrived in Cuba at the end of the nineteenth century.

The sugar industry's occupation of the forests was carried out in two phases separated by World War I. The 1914 sugarcane harvest was 2,244,500 tons; in 1925 it totaled 5,200,800 tons. This growth was due to the construction of large sugarcane mills with production levels unprecedented anywhere in the world. From 1900 to 1914 twenty-five new mills opened, and from 1915 to 1926 another fifty appeared. These included the so-called colossus mills, fifteen of which were in Camagüey and twelve in Oriente (Abad pp. 391–428). To supply sugarcane to these units, huge landed estates with private railroad networks were formed. This process had grave socioeconomic consequences such as the establishment of monoculture, the reduction of small landholdings, and the abandonment of subsistence crops. Inseparable from those effects were the ecological and socio-environmental costs: a loss of biodiversity, soil degradation, and diminished food sovereignty.

The United States was not only the main market for Cuban sugar, but also its main producer. U.S. interests increased their share of Cuban sugarcane harvests from 35 percent in 1913 to close to 75 percent in 1927 (Jenks p. 259). Although there were various reasons for extending the sugar frontier into new regions, one of the most important was the persistence of the slash-and-burn system for obtaining high-yield harvests. An American scientist who served for many years as the director of the Santiago de las Vegas Agronomic Station wrote that the virgin lands in Camagüey and Oriente could produce sugarcane for fifteen years or longer without plowing, replanting, or fertilizing, but the lands of Santa Clara, Matanzas, and Havana generally yielded only about five harvests before they had to be replanted (Crawley p. 48).

In the 1899 census Puerto Príncipe (Camagüey) and Santiago de Cuba had 70.5 percent of the highland forests and 64.3 percent of the scrub forests on the island's estates. At least 50 percent of the territory was forested, but this proportion was drastically reduced over the next two decades. In 1923 the head of the Woodlands Department, José Isaac del Corral Alemán, denounced the uncontrolled felling and burning of trees between 1915 and 1920. After diminishing somewhat in 1921 and 1922, this practice gained strength as sugar prices rose. According to Corral Alemán's estimates, the Republic's forested land totaled just 16 percent in 1923, of which

67 percent was in tall woodland areas (Corral Alemán 1923, p. 15).

In 1918 the botanist Juan Tomás Roig wrote that anyone who had visited Camagüey and Oriente ten years earlier would be alarmed "by the rapid disappearance of those magnificent forests that previously could be seen in all directions, and that today have been replaced by cane fields and pastures" (Roig p. 174). Warnings such as this, and particularly from the Forestry Department within the Ministry of Agriculture, prompted the passage of the first measures to slow deforestation. From 1922 to 1924 various decrees were issued to regulate forestry and protect the flora and fauna, but to get to the root of the problem, precepts dating back to the Woodlands Ordinances of 1876 had to be modified in order to restrict the felling of trees on private property. This action resulted in Decree 495 of 13 April 1926, known as the "Prohibición absoluta de hacer talas a hecho en los montes altos del Estado o de particulares" (Absolute Prohibition of Tree Cutting in Tall Woodlands on State-owned and Private Lands), which noted that tree felling on large tracts of land had sparked sentiment in defense of the forests and in favor of reforestation because of the physical benefits of protecting these lands and the wish to end dependence on lumber from abroad when the island could maintain its own supply. A few weeks later, on 3 May 1926, the U.S. Congress approved the Verdeja Act, which limited sugar production and blocked the construction of new sugar mills.

After the flat and hilly lands had been deforested, pressure was concentrated on the mountainous and wetlands areas to harvest their timber, and poor *campesinos* were urged to move to those territories in search of land of their own or other ways of earning a living. By the early 1950s the main enemies of the forest and agriculture were the *campesinos*' slash-and-burn agricultural practices, charcoal making, and fires (sometimes linked to forestry company practices), which increased soil erosion in mountainous areas and dried out the atmosphere (Hermano Alaín pp. 110–112).

TRANSITION FROM CHARCOAL TO PETROLEUM

The sugar interests' final offensive on the forests coincided with Cuba's transition from charcoal to petroleum to supply most of the country's energy. Cuba was one of the first Latin American countries to make this transition (1918–1919), due to the presence of U.S. interests and their adoption of technology that emerged during World War I. By 1925 close to 75 percent of Cuba's fossil fuel was oil—the largest consumption of petroleum of any Latin American country. Cuba also had the greatest total per capita use of fossil fuels in 1925, at 50.09 petroleum-equivalent tons per 100 inhabitants, followed by Chile (49 tons), Argentina (33.3 tons), and Uruguay (29.4 tons) (Folchi and Rubio p. 10). Cuba's first oil well began production in 1915 in Bacuranao; later, small wells appeared in different areas, but the highest annual production averages were barely 30,000 tons from 1955 to 1958. Oil consumption at the end of this period was estimated at 2.3 million tons (Díaz-Briquets and Pérez López pp. 206, 214).

Cuba's transition to petroleum was linked to the development of the internal combustion engine and the expansion of automobile transportation and electricity. Together, these factors favored incipient industrialization in textiles, cement, and chemical fertilizers. By the mid-1950s the island was in twenty-fifth place in the world in terms of per capita electricity consumption, again surpassing all other Latin American countries. However, service reached only 56 percent of the population, with urban areas and sugar mills receiving most of the electricity, to the detriment of nonindustrialized rural areas.

Automobile transportation expanded quickly, but streetcars and railroads lagged behind. Most cars were in urban centers, especially Havana, and belonged to members of the growing middle class. By 1959 Cuba was third in Latin America in private car ownership, with one per forty inhabitants (Marrero p. xxix). The construction of the highway network, especially the Central Highway in the 1920s, stimulated economic activity in some towns and marginalized others that continued to depend on the railroad infrastructure.

In rural areas and in the sugar economy, tractors facilitated land preparation and the use of agricultural machinery, which reduced production costs by 50 percent from the use of draft animals, but there were relatively few tractors in 1958 (9,200 that year). The greatest innovation was the use of trucks to transport sugarcane to the refineries; they gradually replaced the railroad for short and middle distances (Zanetti Lecuona p. 77). Pumps that extracted water from the subsoil made possible some experimentation with irrigation, although on a minor scale.

FORESTRY POLICY AND CONSERVATION OF NATURAL RESOURCES

As conservationist ideas and policies developed internationally in the early 1900s, some Cubans drew attention to the need to manage natural resources rationally (Crawley 1909), but the rapid growth of the economy, and the sugar industry in particular, delayed response to this warning. U.S. corporations had a free hand to use Cuba's resources and convert its forests into cane fields at a time when the United States itself had several national parks, ample forest reserves, and an influential conservationist movement.

The 1926 decree that prohibited felling highland forests was based on the fact that barely 10 percent of Cuba's national territory was forestland at a time when accepted environmental principles dictated that every country should have conserved more than one-third of its surface area as forest. For that reason, the state needed to place limitations on forestry on private lands, in the public interest. One justification for imposing restrictions on the use of private property was that lumber was being used only for crossties and planks, and the rest was wasted because of the practice of "burning down thousands of acres of woodlands, with no benefit to their owners and serious damage to the nation"; admittedly, it was not easy to "suddenly transform the habits of a country from complete freedom to rigorous restriction" (Corral Alemán 1936, pp. 173–175).

Corral Alemán addressed the subject of the devastation of the forests and its dangers in a speech at the 19 May 1928 session of the Havana Academy of Sciences attended by the president of the Republic, Gerardo Machado. In addition to pointing out the immense damage of deforestation in terms of water conservation, climate effects, and impoverished agricultural soil, Corral Alemán discussed endangered animal and bird life. He recalled that during the war, rampant tree cutting had left large tracts of land in such poor condition that they had become useless brush. Forestry resources had been squandered, and thus, he concluded, "we find ourselves impoverished today, in addition to having lost those woodlands that were the pride of the Cuban homeland." His speech ended with proposals such as protecting a forested portion of each province as a reserve for the country's primary woods, as a refuge for wild animals, and a lesson for future generations (Corral Alemán 1928).

After several postponements, in 1930 Decree 495 of 1926 became law and the first Cuban forest reserve, Sierra de Cristal National Park, was created. In addition to protecting the area's forests, the park was established as a refuge for native wild animals and birds to preserve species endangered by excessive hunting. The rivers served as stations for freshwater fish breeding.

The environment was becoming a subject of concern for the government, scientific institutions, and society in general. In 1933 the Conde de Pozos Dulces Forestry School was founded, and in the same year the National Flamingo Refuge was established on the northern coast of Camagüey, including the cays, and killing or capturing flamingoes and destroying their nests was absolutely prohibited. In 1936 that reserve was extended to other areas along the northern and southern coasts of Camagüey and Santa Clara provinces, and a twenty-year ban was placed on the exportation of live animals, excepting those sent to museums or scientific institutions. The Ciénaga de Zapata National Fishing and Hunting Refuge was also created; fishing and hunting of birds and wild animals were prohibited there.

Another presidential order demanded that the state and private citizens reforest lands that were inappropriate for agriculture, lands within 110 yards (100 m.) of riverbanks, streams, and lakes, as well as mountainous areas, coastal zones, and mangroves.

The government also established seedling nurseries in each province for timber-yielding and fruit trees, and an absolute ban on cutting down highland and virgin woodlands for fifteen years.

In 1939 the Topes de Collantes National Park and Forest Reserve was created, and in 1941 the Juan Gundlach National Hunting and Fishing Refuge located on an extensive area near Havana was opened. But despite the establishment of these parks and refuges, the real situation was precarious. A 1956 speech by Abelardo Moreno Bonilla at the Havana Academy of Sciences affirmed that little had been done to create the necessary conditions so that these reserves could fulfill their purpose—not even the most elemental conservationist practices had been undertaken, and the only assistance was provided occasionally by local authorities (Moreno Bonilla).

One factor that hindered legislative efforts was the lack of scientific institutions and researchers devoted to studying nature. At the start of the 1950s a study concluded that the relatively small amount of information about Cuba's natural resources was being compiled unsystematically and without any coordination. With few exceptions, governmental agencies' research was negligent and sporadic; privately funded research was scattered and poorly publicized. The reasons for this state of affairs were a lack of government concern, poor technical preparation, and the absence of an interest in research in government and in the population in general (Chávez).

The small scientific community actively promoted awareness of the need to protect Cuba's natural resources through newspaper articles, legislative proposals, and initiatives such as the creation of the Havana Zoo in 1939. In addition to the few research centers and university departments, there were several organizations that led the way, including the Felipe Poey Cuban Natural History Society (1913), the Geography Society of Cuba (1914), the Geography and History Society of Oriente and the Humboldt Group (both in Santiago de Cuba, 1939), the Speleology Society of Cuba (1940), the Cuban Botanical Society (1944), and the Cuban Society for the Protection of Nature (1949).

Social and political movements also adopted environmentalist stances. One example was the anarcho-naturalist movement in the early 1900s, which rejected advancing capitalism and industrial civilization. The movement's supporters took inspiration from nature as a source of quality, harmony, and solidarity among humans. Their values included the importance of working the land with one's own hands, a healthy diet, vegetarianism, and life in the outdoors. They advocated homeopathy, solar therapy, conscious procreation, and contraception controlled by workers themselves. They criticized the established medical system, which was more concerned with curing illness than preventing it. Naturalism in Cuba was tied to criticism of society, and its goal was to free people from poverty and alienation (Shaffer pp. 126–161).

URBAN ENVIRONMENT: HAVANA

The ecological and socio-environmental dynamics of industrial agriculture were closely tied to environmental changes in urban areas. Although there has been little research on the links between Cuba's urban and rural areas, it is clear that the wealth generated by the sugar industry did not stay in the locales where it was produced: It went mostly to distant metropolises and to Havana.

Despite the improvements in hygiene and public health in the island's largest city in the early decades of the 1900s, slums and pollution persisted, and there was still a shortage of safe drinking water and no efficient garbage collection system. In 1925 the engineer Juan A. Cosculluela pointed out that increased migration from rural areas of Cuba and from other countries helped to offset the poor demographic growth in Havana that resulted from the deterioration of sanitation, which fomented contagious diseases such as tuberculosis, malaria, and typhoid fever. Cosculluela distinguished two phases—demographic growth from the turn of the century until 1915 and downturn after 1915, when the decline in public services resulted in polluted water, dirty streets, and a defective sewer system. The effects of this deterioration were seen in the rise in the incidence of typhoid, which determined the urban health index (Cosculluela). Pollution of Havana Bay was by that time critical, further aggravated by increased oil imports.

Havana's urban development was determined by the economic circumstances of the period. By 1925 it was evident that there were too few landscaped areas in the city and that the street network was incapable of handling the increased automobile traffic. That year, the Ministry of Public Works hired the French landscape architect Jean-Claude Nicolas Forestier (1861–1930) and others to design a master plan for the city in conjunction with a group of Cuban architects and urban planners. Forestier and the members of his team had a certain ecological awareness in step with urbanist movements of that time that attempted to achieve a balance between buildings and nature. As a result, there was a focus on urban parks and especially large landscaped areas along the banks of the Almendares River (Lejeune pp. 168, 184–185; Scarpaci, Segre, and Coyula pp. 51–88).

The project resulted in the creation of the Havana Forest, which initially was to be 5,200 acres (2,100 ha). However, because of an economic crisis that plan was set aside until 1936, when a new design of about 247 acres (a little more than 100 ha) gained the support of the Society of Friends of the City and a presidential decree. By the late 1950s the project remained more a wish than a reality. Residents of Havana's

Vedado district first celebrated Arbor Day (10 April) in 1904, and it became a national holiday in 1926.

In Havana the environmental movement had an elitist tinge; reference was sometimes made to "the ecology of the rich." The urban geography revealed the social and environmental inequality of the city's residents. Middle- and upper-class neighborhoods such as Vedado and Miramar had beautiful parks and broad, tree-lined streets; factories and other polluters were located in working-class and marginal districts. Slaughterhouses, dairies, cosmetics manufacturers, and other industries polluted the rivers, streams, and air, and they posed risks of chemical spills. Slums in impoverished marginal areas and in Old Havana proliferated during the 1930s. After World War II, areas on the outskirts of Havana grew considerably. The population increased from 500,000 inhabitants in 1925 to 1,361,600 in 1958, six times the size of Cuba's next largest city. One-third of Havana's residents lived in poor neighborhoods (Scarpaci, Segre, and Coyula pp. 76–78).

The capital's disproportionate influence in Cuba could be seen in its concentration of industrial activity, tourism, services, and administrative functions. As for environmental issues, Havana continued to have a low index of landscaped areas, calculated at 1.3 square yards (1.1 sq. m.) per inhabitant in late 1950, far from the 21 square yards (18 sq. m.) per capita recommended in accordance with climate conditions. Furthermore, the city only had two-thirds of the necessary per diem water per capita (Scarpaci, Segre, and Coyula pp. 78–80).

In short, the major environmental issues of the Republican Period included sanitation, the expansion of sugar mills to the detriment of forests, and the transition to petroleum and automobiles. These transformations, which influenced demographic and economic growth as well as urbanization, were based on the plundering of the country's natural resources and evident social and environmental injustice. In 1956 the renowned geographer Gerardo Canet reflected the growing concern about this state of affairs and the lack of scientific and technical capacity for the rational exploitation of resources, noting the consequences of the "almost fantastic" promotion of a few plants and animals while destroying the "native garden" for the sake of ephemeral progress and scorning nature's greatest gifts (Canet p. 168).

BIBLIOGRAPHY

Abad, Luis V. de. *Azúcar y caña de azúcar. Ensayo de orientación cubana.* Havana: Editorial Mercantil Cubana, 1945.

Adams, Frederick Upham. *Conquest of the Tropics: The Story of the Creative Enterprises Conducted by the United Fruit Company.* New York: Garden City, 1914.

Arnold, David. *La naturaleza como problema histórico. El medio, la cultura y la expansión de Europa.* Mexico City: Fondo de Cultura Económica, 2000.

Canet, Gerardo. "Ritmo en la formación de los recursos naturales y la población de Cuba." *Revista Bimestre Cubana* 71 (January–June 1956): 164–175.

Chávez Figueredo, Antonio. *Reporte sobre la información disponible de los recursos naturales de Cuba.* Havana: Instituto Panamericano de Geografía e Historia. Proyecto 29. Sección Nacional de Cuba, 1953. Mimeographed.

Corral Alemán, José Isaac. "El problema forestal en Cuba." *Cuba Contemporánea* 32 (1923): 5–30.

Corral Alemán, José Isaac. "La devastación forestal y daños que ocasiona." Fondo Académicos del Archivo del Museo Carlos J. Finlay, Havana. 1928.

Corral Alemán, José Isaac. *Derecho forestal cubano.* Vol. 1. Havana: Imprenta de Fernández y Cía, 1936.

Cosculluela, Juan A. *La Salubridad Urbana. Con especial referencia a la ciudad de La Habana.* Havana: Imprenta Compostela y Chacón, 1925.

Crawley, Josiah T. "Conservación y desarrollo de los recursos naturales de Cuba." *Anales de la Academia de Ciencias de La Habana* 45 (1909): 566–576.

Crawley, Josiah T. "El cultivo de la caña de azúcar en Cuba." *Boletín de la Estación Experimental Agronómica* 35 (Februay 1917).

Díaz-Briquets, Sergio, and Jorge Pérez López. *Conquering Nature: The Environmental Legacy of Socialism in Cuba.* Pittsburgh, PA: University of Pittsburgh Press, 2000.

Espinosa, Mariola. *Epidemic Invasions: Yellow Fever and the Limits of Cuban Independence, 1878–1930.* Chicago: University of Chicago Press, 2009.

Folchi, Mauricio, and Mar Rubio. "El consumo de energía fósil y la especificidad de la transición energética en América Latina, 1900–1930." Paper presented at the Third Symposium of the Latin American and Caribbean Society of Environmental History, Carmona, Spain, April 2006. Available from http://www.helsinki.fi/iehc2006/papers3/Folchi.pdf.

Funes Monzote, Reinaldo. *From Rainforest to Cane Field in Cuba: An Environmental History since 1492.* Chapel Hill: University of North Carolina Press, 2008.

Guiteras, Juan. "Estudios demográficos. Aclimatación de la raza blanca en los trópicos." *Sanidad y Beneficencia* 10 (July–December 1913): 284–299.

Hermano Alaín. "Por la conservación de los bosques en Cuba." *Revista de la Sociedad Cubana de Botánica* 10, no. 4 (October–December 1952): 109–116.

Jenks, Leland H. *Nuestra colonia de Cuba.* [1927]. Havana: Edición Revolucionaria, 1966.

Lejeune, Jean-François. "The City as Landscape: Jean-Claude Nicolas Forestier and the Great Urban Works of Havana, 1925–1930." *Journal of Decorative and Propaganda Arts* 22 (1996): 151–185.

Marrero Artiles, Leví. "Cuba en la década de 1950." In *Geografía de Cuba,* by Antonio García Cubas. New York: Minerva Books, 1966, pp. i–lvii.

McNeill, John. *Something New Under the Sun: An Environmental History of the Twentieth-century World.* London: Penguin Books, 2001.

Moreno Bonilla, Abelardo. "Los refugios naturales y parques naturales: Su importancia en la protección y conservación de la naturaleza." *Anales de la Academia de Ciencias Médicas, Físicas y Naturales de La Habana* 94 (1955–1956): 31–63.

Pérez, Louis, Jr. *Cuba in the American Imagination: Metaphor and the Imperial Ethos.* Chapel Hill: University of North Carolina Press, 2008.

Pérez de la Riva, Juan. "Para saber con cuánta gente contamos." *Cuba* (January 1969): 20–23.

Roig, Juan Tomás. "Breve reseña sobre una excursión botánica a Oriente." *Memorias de la Sociedad Cubana de Historia Natural* 3, nos. 4–6 (January–May 1918): 168–175.

Scarpaci, Joseph L., Roberto Segre, and Mario Coyula. *Havana: Two Faces of the Antillean Metropolis.* Chapel Hill: University of North Carolina Press, 2002.

Shaffer, Kirwin R. *Anarchism and Countercultural Politics in Early Twentieth-century Cuba.* Gainesville: University Press of Florida, 2005.

Tucker, Richard P. *Insatiable Appetite: The United States and the Ecological Degradation of the Tropical World.* Berkeley: University of California Press, 2000.

Wood, Leonard. *Informe Civil del Brigadier General Leonard Wood. Gobernador Militar de Cuba. Enero 1ro. a Mayo 20 de 1902.* Havana: Oficina del Historiador del MINSAP, 1902.

Zanetti Lecuona, Oscar. *Economía azucarera cubana. Estudios históricos.* Havana: Editorial de Ciencias Sociales, 2009.

ECOLOGY AND ENVIRONMENT: REVOLUTIONARY PERIOD

Reinaldo Funes Monzote

The changing relationship of the revolutionary government to Cuba's environment from 1959 to 1990.

The Revolution of 1959 inaugurated a new era in Cuba's relationship with nature, determined by both internal political and socioeconomic processes and global trends in environmental ideas and policies. Generally, two stages can be distinguished: up to the end of the 1980s, when the strategy of accelerated economic development prevailed (without discounting efforts toward the rational exploitation of natural resources); and from the 1990s onward, when a severe economic crisis and the goal of sustainable development converged to inspire strategies with lower impact on the island's agriculture and ecosystems.

HUMAN TRANSFORMATION AND GEOTRANSFORMATION

The Revolution signified a radical change in Cuba's socioeconomic and political processes. Agrarian reform laws of 1959 and 1963 eliminated the private plantations belonging to foreign and domestic corporations that predominated in the sugar and livestock industries. The transfer of these properties to the state, together with the major share of industry and commerce, turned the government into the main actor in the country's economy. Thus, the historic dependency on the United States, whose government established a policy of economic embargo against Cuba, was broken.

Extracting the country from underdevelopment under a dependent capitalist society was the central goal of the Revolution. In order to achieve this end, it was necessary to create the *hombre nuevo* or "New Man," who was responsible for constructing a socialist society. But such proposals could not be achieved without considering the natural resource potential of the island. The transformation of nature thus became a priority within the new socioeconomic projects.

Those ideas soon became a part of the political and ideological confrontation as the Revolution consolidated its alliance with the Soviet bloc countries. Cuba became a prime site in the Cold War, which rekindled the race toward industrialization, economic growth, and attempted conquest of the environment through scientific and technological development. The two sides in the Cold War had parallel policies and laws for the rational exploitation or protection of natural resources (McNeill pp. 331–336).

The optimism that drove the construction of the new society had great influence on revolutionary leaders and intellectuals, in regard to the relationship between society and the environment as in other matters. One historian, reflecting in the 1960s on the signs of a demographic revolution, wrote: "There will never be too many of us, because under Communism the balance between man and natural resources is achieved harmoniously, as part of the dialectic process of transforming nature" (Pérez de la Riva p. 23).

However, the country faced limitations due its lack of natural resources—limited coal, petroleum, and hydropower opportunities, as well as the historical destruction of forest resources. The exploitation of iron ore reserves presented technological difficulties. The principal available resources were the soil and the sun, productive plants and animals, and the marine shelf. But their rational exploitation faced obstacles such as erosion, lack of fresh water, and inadequate scientific potential.

Antonio Núñez Jiménez, the first executive director of the Instituto Nacional de Reforma Agraria (INRA, the National Agrarian Reform Institute), was appointed to address those problems because of his deep understanding of Cuban geography. In 1951, he wrote that when the country was ready, it should confront deforestation, improve its soils, and exploit its groundwater and aquifers, collaborating with specialists in geography, geology, botany, and zoology. His proposals included reforestation along the watersheds and rivers, planting trees to protect against erosion and drought, and constructing dams, aqueducts, and

■ *See also*

Cuban Thought and Cultural Identity: Socialist Thought

Economy: Revolutionary Period

Economy: Special Period

Food: Revolutionary Period

Governance and Contestation: The Cuban Revolution

Sugar: Revolutionary Period

hydroelectric plants where possible. These small transformations "would enrich small geographical areas and in combination they would amount to a grand and positive transformation of Cuba" (Núñez Jiménez 1963, p. 351).

The Revolution tacitly opened up the possibility of putting these ideas into practice. Professional training was encouraged toward this end, as was the creation of research centers and support of foreign scientists. A milestone was the 1962 founding of the Academia de Ciencias de Cuba (Cuban Academy of Sciences), presided over by Núñez Jiménez for ten years. This institution was put in charge of establishing a scientific and technical basis for the rational exploitation of natural resources.

The concept that best expresses the goals set forth is *geotransformation*, an idea that considers the specificities of the Cuban environment, including the incidence of droughts (as in 1961–1962) or floods, like the one caused by Hurricane Flora in 1963. Modification of the environment was not new to Cuba (the Roque Canal, for instance, was built between 1911 and 1914). But during the colonial and neocolonial periods, the "negative transformation of the environment, carried out in order to benefit the exploiters," prevailed; the Revolution launched a period of positive geotransformation: science and technology would determine the changes needed on the island, with geographers playing a central role as engineers of the "new nature," together with other specialists (Núñez Jiménez 1968, pp. 6–7).

Projects included reforestation, construction of dams, terracing to counter erosion, use of solar and atomic energy, submarine agriculture, industrial reuse of water, rechanneling of rivers, and climate control. According to Núñez Jiménez, "the greatest enterprise of the man of the future in communist society will be to strike up the great bloodless campaign to transform the environment." In order to do this, together with the new technology and new science, "the most difficult task of constructing the man of the twenty-first century must begin" (Núñez Jiménez 1968, p. 7).

Pilot experiments were initiated, such as the draining of the Zapata Swamp, which had been considered since the nineteenth century. Other ideas had to be studied, such as the formation of agricultural lands in the seas within the archipelago and in the Gulf of Batabanó, joining the main island of Cuba and the Isla de Pinos (Isle of Pines); the creation of freshwater reservoirs in the Broa Inlet and Nipe Bay; the Cuba beltway channel; and the seeding of clouds to create rain. Most of these were discarded because they were shown to be unfeasible from a technical and economic standpoint or because of their potential ecological impact.

Projects of this type should have promoted accelerated development, especially starting in 1964, when sugar was held as pivotal for other sectors of the economy. Increasing production of the principal export crop would require more land, expanded irrigation, new cane varieties, the use of agrochemicals, and the mechanization of agricultural labor.

THE BLUE-GREEN REVOLUTION

Among the objectives of agrarian reform were fulfilling the historic demand of the peasants for ownership of the land, promoting agricultural diversification, and recovering the richness of forest lands. But the prevailing approach sought to keep undivided the large-scale farming and livestock properties that had previously made up sugar and livestock plantations, so that intensive state-administered agriculture could be established.

The first agrarian reform placed 41 percent of the area of Cuba under state control, a proportion the second law increased to 60 percent (Valdés pp. 93, 129). By 1983, 82 percent of lands belonged to the state sector, while a favorable atmosphere existed for the creation of cooperatives in the private sector. More than 90 percent of farming and livestock production was carried out under socialist forms of production (Valdés pp. 135–146). This favored the reinforcement of the agricultural model known as the green revolution.

The purpose was to increase yields, overcoming limiting factors of climate and geography. In 1968, Fidel Castro proposed remediating the lack of water through reservoirs, excess water with drainage, weeds with machines, pests with herbicides, and hurricanes with windbreaks to protect plantations. He asserted that "when a country located in a tropical climate—and we are undoubtedly going to be the first—is able to control those elements in the environment, it is in a condition to produce three times more per hectare than any of the developed countries in the world" (1994, p. 3).

Agricultural mechanization advanced rapidly. The number of tractors went from slightly more than 9,000 in 1958 to 85,000 in 1990, in addition to increasing their average power from 40 horsepower to 75 horsepower; furthermore, the number of oxen decreased from 500,000 to 163,000, and the number of draft horses from 800,000 to 235,000 (Ríos and Cárdenas). These changes led to problems with soil erosion and compaction, due to inappropriate plowing and cultivation techniques, such as excessive plowing or elimination of protective cover.

In order to increase availability of water, the Instituto Nacional de Recursos Hidráulicos (National Institute of Hydraulic Resources) was created in 1962. In three decades, reservoir capacity was multiplied by nearly 150 times. In agriculture the objective was to provide water to crops at the optimal moment, especially in regard to sugarcane, citrus, rice, and potatoes, whose yields increased. However, its excessive use and insufficient drainage, abuse of underground water pumps, and large irrigation canals generated problems such as salinization of underground water, decreased flow from basins, loss of biodiversity, and the disappearance of coastal ponds (Díaz-Briquets and Pérez-López pp. 123–137).

The large-scale use of agrochemicals characterized Cuban intensive agriculture for decades. From the 1960s to the 1980s, the application of synthetic fertilizers multiplied several times, and the use of chemical pesticides increased greatly, until in the mid-1970s their use began to decline. From 1982 into the early 2000s, integrated pest management, which entails agricultural, chemical, and biological means of control, has been applied as the official policy (Pérez pp. 110–111).

The three-part attack of mechanization, irrigation, and agrochemicals showed results. Sugar production reached its zenith with what was known as the Ten Million Ton Sugar Harvest of 1970, to which great material and human resources were directed. Although the goal was not achieved, a record harvest of 8.5 million tons was reached. In the 1970s, harvests were less than 7 million tons, and during the 1980s they ranged between 7 million and a little more than 8 million tons. These rates were possible because of various factors such as the increase in sugarcane yields by 37 percent and agricultural mechanization, accounting for 66 percent of the harvest and 100 percent of the increase.

Special attention was dedicated to the livestock industry, especially in the pork, poultry, and cattle sectors. An emblematic example was the transformation of the genetic base from beef cattle, which predominated before 1959, to dairy cattle through cross-breeding of the acclimatized Zebu with imported Holsteins or by artificial insemination. The dairy industry was developed in parallel with an increase in milk production, which tripled from the 1960s to the 1980s. This sector relied on a broad network of scientific institutes, mechanization, and modern dairies with milking technology and the most advanced livestock management, and other infrastructural elements.

The high point of this policy is symbolized by a dairy cow named Ubre Blanca (White Udder), that in 1981 became the world record holder, producing 29 gallons (110.9 L) in one day and 7,133 gallons (27,000 L) in one lactation cycle. In addition to fodder and forage, nutrition in this model depended on large quantities of concentrates, mineral salts, fish meal, and other supplements. Cattle herds gradually decreased after the 1970s (Monzote et al. pp. 191–192).

Support for specialization in agriculture and livestock had negative repercussions on several traditional crops: tubers, root vegetables, corn, and beans, which all witnessed decreased production. Others, including pineapple and plantains, experienced production increases, but they did not keep pace with the growing population. However, the production and consumption of vegetables and tomatoes increased, thanks in part to new nutritional habits.

Fishing was also a priority from the beginning, with the creation of a modern fishing fleet for international waters and an increase in the exploitation of the insular shelf. National yields increased from 41,900 tons in 1959 to more than 70 million tons in 1985. At the same time, the manyfold increase in freshwater reservoirs fostered the development of aquaculture. Due to the overexploitation of fishing resources on the island, in the mid-1990s it was estimated that 87.6 percent of its fisheries were in a critical state from a planning perspective and required urgent measures (Baisre pp. 13–14).

INDUSTRIALIZATION, ENERGY, AND MINING

One of the Revolution's priority objectives was to promote industry in order to emerge from underdevelopment, a goal that had been delayed since the mid-1960s because of the renewed emphasis on sugar production and the predominance of the agricultural and livestock sector. Although their greater role and importance in the economy continued, after 1975 industrialization was seen as the basis of Cuba's development strategy. A more balanced redistribution of industry throughout the country was sought as a means to reduce the historical concentration of the industrial sector in Havana.

Investments were preferentially directed toward heavy industry, chemical products, construction materials, and energy, according to the centralized planning model of the Soviet Union and the Soviet bloc. This policy, seeking to accelerate industrialization and rapid urbanization, contributed to serious environmental disruptions in those communist countries, as did factors such as the uneconomical use of natural resources, low efficiency in energy use, and increased emission of contaminants. In Cuba there were fewer environmental impacts due to the geography of the long, narrow island and the preponderance of agriculture over industry (Díaz-Briquets and Pérez López pp. 165–166).

The production of sugar and sugarcane by-products remained the main generator of waste. Agricultural modernization was linked to local production of chemical fertilizers in new factories such as those in Nuevitas and Cienfuegos, which contaminated the water and air around them. Other port cities such as Mariel or Santiago de Cuba faced environmental problems due to the cement industry, which had an annual production capacity of more than 940 million tons in 1958 and 5 million tons by the end of the 1980s, or the oil refineries, such as the one located on Havana Bay.

The energy infrastructure, from the extraction of oil to the generation of electricity, created environmental damage. This is not surprising considering the increase in oil consumption, from 2.3 million tons in 1958 to more than 13.5 million tons in the 1980s. Most of this use depended on external sources, but domestic extraction increased to more than a million tons in 1993. The industrial sector accounted for about 60 percent of consumption, and, of this amount, about half was used to generate electricity, which increased from something more than 400 megawatts in 1958 to more than 3,800 megawatts at the end of the 1980s. At the beginning of the 1990s, electricity reached 95 percent of the country's residents.

The disappearance of the Soviet Union resulted in an abrupt drop of more than 50 percent in oil imports. This reduction contributed to the increased importance of renewable energies and the adoption of a policy of energy-saving with positive balances. In 1994, the Sociedad Cubana para la Promoción de las Fuentes Renovables de Energía (Cuban Society for the Promotion of Renewable Energy Sources, or Cubasolar) was formed (Bérriz and Madruga p. 20), and in 1997 the Programa de Ahorro de Electricidad en Cuba (PAEC; Electricity Savings Program in Cuba) was initiated (Ministerio de la Industria Básica).

Cuba is one of the biggest suppliers of nickel in the world, and surface mining in the north of Holguín generates major impacts. Beginning in 1959, its capacity was increased with the construction of new processing plants, exceeding 46,000 tons of nickel and cobalt annually toward the end of the 1980s. After a temporary drop due to the crisis following the dissolution of the Soviet Union, extraction and processing recovered between 1994 and the early 2000s through mixed enterprises involving foreign capital.

In the areas of operation, nickel mining brought about complete deforestation, erosion of slopes, and contamination of soil, water, and air. In 1980, Raúl Castro proposed legislation to protect the regional landscape in the mining zone, which was enacted as the Law of Natural Resources and Environmental Protection (1981) (Núñez 1998, pp. 465–469). In the years following, some advances were made in the restoration of these degraded mining zones. The fact that some rich nickel reserves are located in the region of the Alejandro de Humboldt National Park, the largest in Cuba, heralds a possible escalation of the conflict between mining and the environment.

ENVIRONMENTAL CONSERVATION AND PROTECTION

In 1959 the Law of Reforestation was enacted, and the Sección de Parques Nacionales e Investigación de Recursos Naturales Renovables (Department of National Parks and Renewable Natural Resource Research) was created. New national parks were created in every province as a means to promote conservation and tourism. The transfer of various new resources from the INRA to the Academy of Sciences in 1963 was a milestone, placing custody of these areas for the first time in the hands of a scientific organization (Samek p. 7). Toward the end of the 1960s, the academy planned a network of forty natural preserves of different categories.

The reforestation plan, directed after 1960 by the Instituto Nacional de Desarrollo y Aprovechamiento Forestal (National Institute of Forest Development and Use), promoted the planting of millions of trees, particularly eucalyptus, pine, and casuarinas, although with only modest success given unsuitable terrain for the selected species and low survival rates. The occasional coordination of these programs with intensive agricultural development had counterproductive results for the native vegetation.

Such was the case with the Brigada Invasora de Maquinaria Agrícola (invasive brigade of agricultural machinery), which sought to prepare tracts of land for agriculture using bulldozers and other heavy machinery. One of its plans in 1968 was the so-called forest grooming, between Tunas and Bayamo, in the Cauto basin, for the purpose of establishing rice and grain fields and extending reforestation. After observing the elimination of natural woodlands by the passing of the brigade, a foreign visitor clarified, "As we are in a planned socialist economy, there is foresight before every action; the ecological balance is not broken with impunity because behind it there is always organized reforestation, rapid construction of the humanized landscape" (Wettstein pp. 71–73).

The creation of new landscapes was also oriented toward cutting distances between urban and rural zones and promoting contact with nature. An example is the restoration of the Havana forest and the creation of Lenin Park (1969–1972) outside the capital. In 1968, institutions appeared that combined recreational and scientific functions, with the initiation of work on the new National Botanical Gardens and National Zoological Park, assigned to the Academy of Sciences. Other plans included the rural schools (1966) that sought to combine education and agricultural work, and the Havana Cordon (1968), designed to encourage cultivation of areas surrounding the city.

Until the end of the 1970s, reforestation efforts achieved little more than a 3 percent increase in forest areas. In 1976, a specific article concerning environmental protection was incorporated for the first time into the Constitution of the Republic, and the following year the Comisión Nacional para la Protección del Medio Ambiente y el Uso Racional de los Recursos Naturales (National Commission for Environmental Protection and the Rational Use of Natural Resources) was created. At the end of the decade a reevaluation of the environmental issue began, as expressed in the campaign from the Sociedad Espeleológica (Spelunking Society) called "Hacia una Cultura de la Naturaleza" (Toward a Culture of Nature) (Núñez 1998, p. 9).

The Law of the Environment and the Rational Use of Natural Resources, passed in 1981, introduced a more modern focus that employs a systematic

Eco-friendly sanitation. A reduction in public transportation in urban areas beginning in the 1990s promoted the use of bicycles and animals for transportation. These sanitation workers gathered trash using a horse-drawn wagon in 2006. FOTO REINALDO FUNES, 2006

and integrated strategy. This legislation was later improved, in line with growing attention to the theme in the international sphere. In 1992, constitutional amendments incorporated the concept of sustainable development in Article 27: "The State protects the environment and natural resources of the country. It recognizes the close ties between sustainable economic and social development in making human life more rational and ensuring the survival, well-being, and safety of future generations."

In 1994 the Ministerio de Ciencia, Tecnología y Medio Ambiente (CITMA, Ministry of Science, Technology, and the Environment), the governing body of the country's environmental policy, was created. One of its initial projects was the National Environmental Strategy, adopted in 1997. That same year, Law 81, the Environment Act, was enacted, granting CITMA broad responsibilities in relation to the evaluation of environmental impacts and environmental permits. This law is considered more ambitious in its goals and details than any comparable legislation in the United States or Western Europe (Houck p. 5).

In the early 2000s the island had a positive shift in balance in relation to the environment. Forest cover had increased to 24.5 percent of the country by 2005, according to official figures. In 1995, the Centro Nacional de Aéreas Protegidas (National Center for Protected Areas) was established, and in 1999 the Protected Areas Act was passed. Some of the more relevant areas appeared during those years, such as the Alejandro de Humboldt National Park (1996), named a World Heritage Site in 2001.

Cuba has three national parks that are designated World Heritage Sites, along with six biosphere reserves and seven sites recognized by the Convention on Wetlands of International Importance (RAMSAR). The national system of protected areas covers 22 percent of the national landscape, although most of it (14.5%) is found in the maritime zone. Eighty areas are of national significance, 183 of local significance, and 7 are special sustainable development regions. As of 2010, more than 260 proposed sites were in the application process.

THE CRISIS OF THE 1990s, AGRO-ECOLOGY, AND TOURISM

After the disintegration of the Soviet Union, Cuban foreign trade dropped by 75 percent, temporarily exacerbated by the reinforcement of the U.S. economic embargo, through the Torricelli (1992) and Helms-Burton (1996) acts. As a result, the first half of the 1990s was marked by a precipitous 35 percent drop in GDP, a decrease in the production of sugar, nickel, citrus, and fish, among other branches of industry and agriculture (Mesa pp. 521–523). The crisis resulted in food shortages and nutritional deficiencies, power outages, and the collapse of public transportation, among other conditions.

Sugar production recorded a continuous drop, influenced by a reduction in agricultural yields. In 2002, seventy sugar mills were shuttered, with seventy-one sugar mills and fourteen syrup processors remaining active. The areas that ceased planting sugarcane switched to livestock, reforestation, or minor crops. Despite efforts to revive the industry on a more efficient basis, it was almost in a state of collapse due to its prolonged undercapitalization (Nova p. 143; Álvarez and Pérez-López, pp. 145–168).

Intensive dairy production suffered a major setback due to a shortage of concentrates and other factors, with high mortality rates in specialized herds. Indicators such as cows in lactation and per-cow yields, milk per hectare, and beef production dropped (González et al. p. 122). An alarming phenomenon was the increased infestation of pasture by invasive bell mimosa trees (known as Marabú), which had previously been controlled with petrochemicals and agricultural machinery.

In the urban environment, the reduction in public transportation promoted alternatives such as the massive use of bicycles and increased transportation with animals, which persist in medium-size and small cities. The obsolescence of the automotive portion of transportation has led to pollution, although at the same time industrial emissions have been reduced due to improved control and technology. These advances include efforts to restore rivers such as the Almendares in Havana and the reversal of the deterioration of the bays. Such efforts are guided by the Grupo de Trabajo Estatal de la Bahía de La Habana (State Work Group of Havana Bay), established in 1998.

One achievement is the promotion of urban agriculture; available spaces are used to establish short-cycle crops, particularly vegetables, with a view toward supplying food to the urban centers. The movement is organized within a 6.2-mile (10-km) radius in provincial capitals, 3-mile (5-km) radius in municipal capitals, and 1.2-mile (2-km) radius in towns with more than 10,000 inhabitants. It is made up of a network of *organopónicos* (small, organic urban gardens), intensive orchards, and yard and patio gardens (Cruz and Sánchez pp. 23–58).

This program formed part of the paradigm shift from conventional agriculture toward a model of reduced consumption based on agro-ecological postulates. This transition was inspired by difficult economic circumstances, signs of stagnation in the previous farming and livestock model, and the conviction of scientists and producers regarding its advantages. It was thus that a movement favoring organic agriculture arose, obtaining positive results (Funes pp. 1–26).

The Cuban experience became a point of reference for defenders of an agricultural model posed as an alternative to modern industrial agriculture dominated by large corporations. In fact, it has been considered the best attempt in human history to switch to organic or semiorganic agriculture (Rosset and Benjamin p. 82). It also involves a broader concern over the implications of oil depletion on the production, distribution, and consumption of food products (Wright pp. 1–41; Miller pp. 229–235).

The transition toward more sustainable agriculture coincided with programs such as the integrated management of drainage basins, for which the Consejo Nacional de Cuencas (National Council of Drainage Basins) was created in 1997. Other national programs covered such subjects as desertification and drought, climate change, and biodiversity. The mountainous zones received special attention through the Manatí Plan and the Integral Forest Farms.

However, the economic recovery beginning in the mid-1990s was based on the strengthening of activities dependent on natural resources. A certain increase in international tourism was in evidence already in the 1980s, but the big jump occurred a decade later. The arrival of foreign tourists rose from fewer than 500,000 in 1991 to about 2.5 million by 2005 (Scarpaci and Portela pp. 112–136).

Sun-and-sand tourism increased the pressure on exploited areas such as Varadero and led to the opening of new areas in different coastal regions. These are fragile ecosystems, such as the island's cays, which suffer various levels of ecological impact. The most dramatic was an over-water highway between Turiguanó and Cayo Coco, which initially dammed the natural flow of sea water. Other problems have to do with the transfer of drinking water over long distances and invasive species of exotic flora and fauna.

The late development of tourism in Cuba's coastal areas, in contrast with the rest of the Caribbean, favored the implementation of smaller-scale projects that seek to harmonize with local ecological conditions. One format that has high potential is ecotourism (Medina and Santamarina pp. 74–88). Before the boom in international tourism, recreational camping was established as an option with minimal infrastructure, making use of local resources in harmony with the landscape.

The new ecological paradigms must coincide with Cuba's state policies, its great human scientific potential, the work of institutions and scientific associations, and its incipient environmentalist organizations, together with international collaboration. This evolution can be seen in contrasts over time, as in the comparison with this statement from 1970—"If we don't dominate the environment, the environment will dominate us"—with this one from 1990: "Humans must adapt to the environment, they must be smart in overcoming the obstacles of the environment" (Castro 1994, pp. 2, 3).

Selling the shells of endangered snails. Sun-and-sand tourism has increased the pressure on Cuba's fragile ecosystems. These necklaces, for sale to tourists, were made from the shells of the endangered Polymitas snail. FOTO REINALDO FUNES, 2007

BIBLIOGRAPHY

Álvarez, José, and Jorge F. Pérez López. "The Restructuring of Cuba´s Sugar Agroindustry, 2002–2004." In *Reinventing the Cuban Sugar Agroindustry*, edited by Jorge F. Pérez-López and José Álvarez. Lanham, MD: Lexington Books, 2005.

Baisre Álvarez, Julio A. *La pesca marítima en Cuba.* Havana: Editorial Científico-Técnica, 2004.

Bérriz, Luis, and Emir Madruga. *Cuba y las fuentes renovables de energía.* Havana: Cubasolar, 1998.

Castro, Fidel. *Ecología y desarrollo: Selección temática, 1963–1994.* 2nd ed. Havana: Editora Política, 1994.

Cruz, María Caridad, and Roberto Sánchez Medina. *Agriculture in the City: A Key to Sustainability in Havana, Cuba.* Ottawa: International Development Research Centre; Kingston, Jamaica: Ian Randle Publishers, 2003.

Díaz-Briquets, Sergio, and Jorge Pérez-López. *Conquering Nature: The Environmental Legacy of Socialism in Cuba.* Pittsburgh, PA: University of Pittsburgh Press, 2000.

Funes Aguilar, Fernando. "The Organic Farming Movement in Cuba." In *Sustainable Agriculture and Resistance: Transforming Food Production in Cuba*, edited by Fernando Funes Aguilar et al. Oakland, CA: Food First Books, 2002.

Funes-Monzote, Fernando. "Cuba: A National-Level Experiment in Conversion." In *The Conversion to Sustainable Agriculture: Principles, Processes, and Practices*, edited by Stephen R. Gliessman and Martha Rosemeyer, 205–237. Boca Raton: CRC Press, 2010.

González, Alfredo, et al. *La ganadería en Cuba: Desempeño y desafíos.* Stockholm: Agencia Sueca de Cooperación Internacional para el Desarrollo; Havana: Instituto Nacional de Investigaciones Económicas; Montevideo: Departamento de Economía, Facultad de Ciencias Sociales, Universidad de la República, Uruguay, 2004.

Houck, Oliver A. "Cuba's New Law of the Environment: An Introduction." In *Cuban Environmental Law: The Framework Environmental Law and an Index of Cuban Environmental Legislation*, edited by Jerry Speir. New Orleans: Tulane Law School; Washington, DC: Center for Marine Conservation, 1999.

McNeill, J. R. *Something New Under the Sun: An Environmental History of the Twentieth-century World.* London: Penguin Books, 2001.

Medina, Norman, and Jorge Santamarina. *Turismo de Naturaleza en Cuba.* Havana: Ediciones Unión, 2004.

Mesa Lago, Carmelo. "Historia y evaluación de medio siglo de políticas económico-sociales en Cuba socialista, 1959–2008." In *Historia de las Antillas.* Vol. 1, *Historia de Cuba*, edited by Consuelo Naranjo. Madrid: Consejo Superior de Investigaciones Científicas (CSIC); Aranjuez, Spain: Doce Calles, 2009.

Miller, Shawn W. *An Environmental History of Latin America.* New York: Cambridge University Press, 2007.

Ministerio de la Industria Básica. *Libro del Programa de Ahorro de Electricidad en Cuba para la enseñanza media.* Havana: Editora Política, 2002.

Monzote, Marta, Eulogio Muñoz, and Fernando Funes-Monzote. "The Integration of Crops and Livestock." In *Sustainable Agriculture and Resistance: Transforming Food Production in Cuba*, edited by Fernando Funes Aguilar et al. Oakland, CA: Food First Books, 2002.

Nova González, Armando. "Redimensionamiento y diversificación de la industria azucarera cubana." In *Reflexiones sobre economía cubana*, edited by Omar E. Pérez Villanueva. Havana: Ciencias Sociales, 2006.

Núñez Jiménez, Antonio. "Transformemos la naturaleza de Cuba en beneficio de sus ciudadanos. Algunas ideas para una futura transformación de la naturaleza en Cuba" [1951]. In *Con la mochila al hombro*, edited by Antonio Núñez Jiménez. Havana: Ediciones Unión, 1963.

Núñez Jiménez, Antonio. *Geotransformación de Cuba.* Havana: Instituto de Geografía, Academia de Ciencias de Cuba, 1968.

Núñez Jiménez, Antonio. *Hacia una Cultura de la Naturaleza.* Havana: Si-Mar, 1998.

Pérez, Nilda. "Ecological Pest Management." In *Sustainable Agriculture and Resistance: Transforming Food Production in Cuba*, edited by Fernando Funes Aguilar et al. Oakland, CA: Food First Books, 2002.

Pérez de la Riva, Juan. "Para saber con cuánta gente contamos." *Cuba* (January 1969): 20–23.

Ríos, Arcadio, and Jesús Cárdenas. "La tracción animal en Cuba: Una perspectiva histórica." In *La tracción animal en Cuba*, edited by Paul Starkey and Brian Sims,

2003. Available in Spanish and English from http://www.recta.org/book/AT.html.

Rosset, Peter, and Medea Benjamin, eds. *The Greening of the Revolution: Cuba's Experiment with Organic Agriculture.* Melbourne: Ocean Press, 1994.

Samek, V. *La protección de la naturaleza en Cuba.* Havana: Instituto de Geografía, Academia de Ciencias de Cuba, 1968.

Scarpaci, Joseph L., and Armando H. Portela. *Cuban Landscapes: Heritage, Memory, and Place.* New York: Guilford Press, 2009.

Valdés Paz, Juan. *Procesos agrarios en Cuba, 1959–1995.* Havana: Ciencias Sociales, 1997.

Wettstein, Germán. *Vivir en revolución: 20 semanas en Cuba.* Montevideo: Editorial Signo, 1969.

Wright, Julia. *Sustainable Agriculture and Food Security in an Era of Oil Scarcity: Lessons from Cuba.* London and Sterling, VA: Earthscan, 2009.

ECONOMY

The subject of the economy has long been the source of sustained scholarly interest, beginning in the eighteenth century. As the essays that follow suggest, developments of the Cuban economy—almost from the outset engaged in global markets—correspond to specific historical periods, bearing on Cuba's relationship to the world at large: from the colonial regime given to ranching, tobacco, mining, and sugar; passing into years of U.S. hegemony, where sugar production was the principal source of foreign exchange; and continuing into the Soviet period.

The transformation from a market economy to a planned economy has characterized developments since the 1959 Cuban Revolution. Examples are efforts to end dependency on foreign exchange generated by a one-crop system and efforts to create new development strategies and reorient trade and commerce relationships using economic logic under socialism. The calamity that befell Cuba after the collapse of the Soviet Union was most profoundly experienced in its economy. The readjustments that followed continued well into the twenty-first century, with uneven results.

■ *See also*

Ecology and Environment: Colonial Period

Food: Colonial Period

Sugar: Representation in Cuban Culture

Tobacco: Cultivation: Botany

Tobacco: Cultivation: Chemistry

ECONOMY: COLONIAL PERIOD

Mercedes García Rodríguez

The development of the ranching, sugar, tobacco, and coffee industries in Cuba as a colony of Spain.

Beginning in 1493, through the papal bull of Alexander VI, Spain regulated the ways and means by which its colonial exploitation in the New World would develop. Three regulations were crucial in the colonization of Cuba and its subsequent economic order:

- The land would be wholly owned by the kings of Spain, and the residents of the colony would be granted land in usufruct by promising to keep them productive;
- The colony would produce only raw materials or certain minimally processed products, reserving the industrial phase of the work for the metropole, an arrangement that produced long-term imbalance between exports and imports; and
- Only Spain was authorized to organize and control the movement of goods to and from the island, and only by ships flying a Spanish flag. The colony could not have its own merchant marine, and Cuba's exporters had to pay high rates to Spanish vessels to place their products in European or American colonies. Businesses had to export products through the metropolis, not individually.

CHRONOLOGY OF EVENTS

1510s: Slavery introduced to Cuba.

1595: Law on Privileges of Sugar Mills aids expansion of sugar production.

1606: Spain prohibits tobacco cultivation in Cuba.

1616: Ban on tobacco cultivation lifted.

1717: Royal monopoly on tobacco established in Havana.

1740: Monopoly on all trade between Spain and Cuba granted to *Real Compañía de Comercio de La Habana*.

1754: Standards and procedures for land ownership formalized.

1764: Royal decree extends right to trade with Spain from Havana to all Cuban ports.

1774: Spanish duties on Cuban imports rescinded.

1784: Spain outlaws trade between Cuba and any country but Spain.

1797: First steam engine in Cuba used at the mill on the Seybabo plantation.

1817: Tobacco monopoly ended; first successful use of steam power in Cuba at Limonar mill.

1837: First railroad in Cuba, Havana to Guines.

1862: Facundo Bacardí begins rum production in Santiago.

1879: First industrial use of a generator at San Joaquín sugar mill, Matanzas.

1886: Slavery abolished in Cuba.

1909: Congress establishes eight-hour day for some workers.

1914–1918: World War I leads to dramatic rise in Cuban sugar prices, a period celebrated in Cuba as *Danza de los Millones*.

1920: Depression hits Cuba, devastating financial system.

1922: U.S. Congress passes Fordney-McCumber Tariff, raising duties on Cuban sugar.

1926: The Verdeja Act attempts to limit sugar production.

1927: Cuba institutes protective tariffs.

1929: Great Depression begins.

1930: U.S. Congress passes Smoot-Hawley Tariff, further limiting Cuban exports to U.S.

1934: Cuba and U.S. sign reciprocal trade treaty.

1937: London Convention on international trade; Cuban Congress passes Law on Coordination of Sugar Activities.

1940: New constitution bans *latifundios*, institutes other economic reforms.

1947: General Agreement on Tariffs and Trade (GATT) international agreement signed under United Nations auspices.

1950: Government establishes agricultural banks.

1959: Cuban Revolution; Castro comes to power, implements agrarian reform law confiscating land owned by large landowners, including those from the U.S.

1960: Nationalization of oil companies and all foreign-owned enterprises; U.S. places embargo on Cuba.

1962: Cuba begins food rationing.

1968: Revolutionary Offensive seeks to virtually eliminate private sector of economy by nationalizing all small businesses and merchants.

1972: Cuba joins Soviet bloc Council for Mutual Economic Assistance (CMEA).

1976: Cuba signs Five-Year Plan of cooperation with U.S.S.R.

1981: Cuba enters into ten-year CMEA program; signs second five-year agreement with U.S.S.R.

1986: Government establishes Rectification Program to increase centralization of economy.

1988: Cuba allows Foreign Direct Investment (FDI).

1990: Government announces Special Period in Time of Peace allowing some free market development.

1991: U.S.S.R. disbands.

1993: Use of U.S. dollars and self-employment legalized.

1995: World Trade Organization (WTO) replaces GATT; Cuba joins WTO.

1992: U.S. Congress passes Torricelli (or Cuban Democracy) Act, extending the embargo of Cuba to food and medicine.

1996: U.S. Congress passes Helms-Burton (or Cuban Liberty and Democratic Solidarity) Act to extend the Cuban embargo to foreign companies.

2000: Cuban food purchases from the U.S. begin considerable increase.

2004: Introduction of Cuban Convertible Currency (CUC), under which U.S. dollars must be converted into CUC.

2006: Raúl Castro becomes acting president, introducing some reforms favorable to small enterprises.

2008: Decree-Law No. 259 makes unused state land available to farmers.

2009–2010: Cuban state announces massive layoffs in the state economy.

Spain's economic subjugation of colonial Cuba continued for four centuries, though some of these rules were modified from time to time. For example, from 1740 until the end of the nineteenth century, land could be purchased from the Crown, and beginning in 1778 new trade regulations instituted by Carlos III allowed Cuba to trade with greater freedom. But these measures did not diminish Spain's control; instead, peninsular economic backwardness toward its colony converted Cuba into a rentier society, where *criollo* sugar planters and landowners imposed their production rhythms while preserving economic bonds created over the centuries.

INITIAL PRODUCTIONS: GOLD AND AGRICULTURE

Gold mining was the first economic activity of the Spanish who settled in Cuba, but it did not last long. By 1550 the panning had been exhausted and most of the natives who worked them had died from diseases brought from Europe, from suicide, or from physical exhaustion from the type of labor imposed on them by their colonizers.

Subsistence agriculture developed alongside gold mining, initially on farms given in usufruct to the early settlers, who produced food for their own consumption and for supply to the Spanish army of conquest.

At that time Cuba served as a supply base where conquest expeditions were organized and launched.

The first farms produced food for their own consumption: cassava, sweet potato, banana, and some other fruits and vegetables. They produced small quantities of tobacco, sugar, and cocoa, and what they did not consume themselves they sold or bartered to the owners of fleets, who then traded them in the cities. Eventually the farms became highly productive in response to the economic incentives of the developing service economy in Havana, which required great quantities of foodstuffs after it became the most important port of call in the Americas, with the responsibility for supplying return fleets and providing food and accommodation to a large number of passengers and sailors in transit from one continent to another.

The cassava produced on these farms became strategically important as it solved the problem of wheat flour shortages in the colony. Colonists used it to make *casabe* (cassava bread), which resembles a large round cracker. The humidity of the sea did not spoil *casabe*, which worked well as a base for other foods such as fish and meat, so cassava became a highly important crop (De la Fuente p. 60).

LIVESTOCK FARMING

Between 1550 and 1620 gold mining came to an end, and the search for a new product to revive the economy began. Subsistence crops for export had become less lucrative as conquered colonies began to produce enough of their own food supplies. The virtual disappearance of the indigenous population was gradually resolved with enslaved blacks from different regions in Africa, who were introduced into the nascent commercial agricultural sector. Numerous attempts to develop a sugar economy had been frustrated by lack of capital and labor shortage. Cattle ranching was the most practical option for the island's population because it required neither large upfront investment nor a great many workers. In addition, there was a lot of land to divide among few families, and the excellent savanna grasses ensured that the cattle introduced by the Spanish would reproduce rapidly.

At first, cattle roamed free and ranchers hunted them, making large profits by selling the meat and skins to other colonies and to Spain. By the middle of the sixteenth century, the meat and leather trade represented 90 percent of the island's exports (Chaunu). By the early seventeenth century ranching was more intensive; herds and pens were introduced, and enormous ranches were dedicated to raising small and large livestock. This development favored the appropriation of land, especially land from the interior of the island (Pérez de la Riva p. 87). With the pens there was greater control of livestock herds and pigs, which were in high demand after 1600 (*Actas del Cabildo Habanero*).

Beginning in 1607 the inhabitants of the interior of the island tried to increase livestock production by establishing *haciendas comuneras* (commoner ranches). These hexagon-shaped ranches produced meat for consumption, traded leather with other colonies, and sold live animals and salted meat as contraband to the English Caribbean.

Livestock production continued to grow over the next two centuries to such an extent that it became the bridge between Cuba's gold mining cycle and its sugar cycle. From its inception at the end of sixteenth century, sugar production grew slowly but steadily until it took off in the second half of the eighteenth century, and it remained the island's main line of production during the nineteenth century (Santamaría García). Throughout the colonial period, stockbreeding fulfilled the island's consumption needs, but it also was a main pillar of support for the sugar industry: Meat was used to feed the slave labor force, animals powered the mills, and even the leather was used for the straps that sealed boxes of sugar.

HAVANA HARBOR IN ECONOMIC DEVELOPMENT

By the last quarter of the sixteenth century the outlines of Cuba's economic evolution were already in place. The essential defining factor in its evolution was Havana harbor and the commercial exchanges that developed because of it. The organization of the fleet system in 1560, and the designation in 1561 of Havana harbor as the largest port of call in the New World, eventually brought the western part of Cuba the same progress and economic growth that the interior enjoyed.

Havana harbor's new mission demanded that the inhabitants of the region supply the fleet. This activity stimulated the production of crops, and the trade generated by the sale of food and other supplies set off an intense process of capital accumulation in the western part of Cuba, beginning with the service economy. Production around the harbor and agricultural hinterland increased (Moreno Fraginals).

Two other factors also contributed to the accumulation of capital in the region: the arrival of money from the royal treasury of New Spain for construction costs, and the arrival of the military to defend the island. The system of defense was conceived around the fact that Havana harbor was a collection point for U.S. gold and silver destined for Spain; this treasure was coveted by pirates and corsairs who infested the Caribbean Sea, and the Spanish fleet was needed to protect these supplies. That reality prompted the construction of an impregnable fortress on the Cuban coast and a wall around Villa Habanera, which turned out to be extremely expensive. Thus, military and construction expenditures for the defense of Cuba required a steady cash injection that came to the island from the treasury of Mexico and helped to lift the island's economy because some of that money was diverted to the construction of mills and warehouses for sugar and tobacco (Pérez Guzmán; De la Fuente).

Another factor in the economic growth of the western area was the money made from shipbuilding in Havana's shipyards, which provided rich income to the region. From 1610 to 1630 there were eight shipyards along the northern coast of Havana; the most productive and important was the Royal Shipyard of Havana, built a few meters from the fortress. In 1608, for example, Havana's accounts took in 5 million reales for the construction of five galleons (De la Fuente).

This initial accumulation of capital from the service and production economy and from naval construction activity stimulated investment in sugar and tobacco in the Havana region. Previously, sugar and tobacco had been grown on primitive ranches for household consumption, but as early as the seventeenth century, and because of increased commercial trade at the port, they emerged as products for export, given the high prices and strong demand in the Spanish and international markets. Havana's oligarchy working from positions in the council and the courts ensured that the central-eastern towns guaranteed, with livestock and food production, the sugar growth of the capital. This arrangement subordinated the region known as Cuba B (the inland, rural region, with little to no urban development and reliant on livestock production) to Cuba A (the sugar-centered west, wealthy and urbanized, growing rapidly from the seventeenth to the nineteenth centuries) (Pérez de la Riva p. 198). These regional differences—which continued into the twenty-first century—resulted from policies that favored the port of Havana with a monopoly of interoceanic trade in order to maximize the geostrategic position of the bay. The affluence of the capital and the reallocation of resources in favor of Havana harbor led the Crown to dismiss the potential of other ports in Cuba, which only became significant after 1778, when the rules of free trade went into effect.

SUGAR PRODUCTION

By 1607 the dominance of Havana in the economy of the island was a *fait accompli* and sugar was gaining ground slowly but steadily. Between 1650 and 1840 new mills built on the lands of former cattle ranches appeared throughout the region. By the middle of the sixteenth century, the sustained growth of sugar production contributed to the demolition of herds and pens, freeing arable land and woodland for the sugar plantations and development of new mills. By the beginning of the nineteenth century, Havana was the sugar capital, the island's most populous, rich, and important city. A high percentage of its exports went to the markets in North America.

There were no appreciable advances in sugar-processing technology until the end of the eighteenth century. The equipment in the mills during the first half of the eighteenth century was rudimentary. The sugar mill itself—the heart of the industry—was the only existing machine in the plant. However, in the 1780s and 1790s new technologies of the Industrial Revolution were introduced in the mills in Cuba. During these years, and only in an experimental way, some wealthy mill owners bought modern equipment for their units, such as *volvedoras* (turners). The first steam engine was installed in a mill in Seybabo, with poor results, around that time (Moreno Fraginals; García Rodríguez 2007).

Similarly, the basic structure of the mills—grinding house, boiler house, and refining house—remained the same from the seventeenth century until well into the nineteenth century. The most notable change was the introduction in the mid-eighteenth century of the French trains, copied from the English, of only one fire in the boiler house, which allowed them to save natural fuel (firewood) by burning *vagazo* (sugarcane bagasse). This technique continued to be used until the mid-nineteenth century, when steam trains, which used steam coils instead of putting pots directly onto the fire, were installed.

Increases in productive capacity characterized sugar production in the eighteenth century. Improvements made in agriculture as well as in manufacturing generated increased sugar production, which in turn satisfied the favorable post–Haitian Revolution market of the 1790s. Cuba filled the void in the world sugar market left by the formerly productive country of Haiti (Fraginals Moreno). From then on, sugar drove Cuba's economy.

The nineteenth century saw real innovations in the manufacturing of sugar. New technologies from the Industrial Revolution were introduced in a more widespread and coherent manner and standardized for the sugar industry. In the 1820s only a few mills had become semi-mechanized by introducing steam-powered engines, which made the mills more powerful, as well as clarifiers, steam trains, and devices that measured the various parameters of production. After 1840 their use increased, and about 20 percent of the country's plantations had installed steam engines (García Rodríguez 2007).

Between 1880 and 1890 steam trains, clarifying components, vacuum evaporators, and especially centrifuges—which eliminated the refining house and standardized the quality of sugar—gave way to mechanized mills that were fundamental to the vast industry that prevailed in western Cuba and in some inland areas into the early twentieth century. These sugar mills were established completely separate from agriculture, and already-free laborers and foreign technicians worked in them (Fraginals Moreno p. 173). These factories installed the latest technologies that eliminated manual tasks, achieving a more streamlined production process.

Typically, throughout the colonial period, sugar and related production was diverse. Various types of mills coexisted: small mills with ten to twenty slaves, medium mills with forty-five to eighty slaves, and the so-called new factory mills with two or more sugar mills and a crew of 100 to 130 slaves (Fraginals Moreno). The new factory mills represented the passage from the traditional sugar mill to a large manufacturing process, a change that entailed an expansion of the crews and equipment and intensive exploitation of the labor force along with the other productive elements in the facility.

In the nineteenth century there was remarkable growth in the number of new sugar mills as the line advanced toward the Havana-Matanzas plain and then invaded Trinidad and other central-eastern regions, particularly Santiago de Cuba. In addition, during this period an essential factor in the dynamics of the sugar industry was added: the railway (Zanetti and García Álvarez).

Most mills in the interior did not become as large or productive as those in the west (Moreno Fraginals p. 96). In 1846 there were 1,442 mills across the island, of which 735 (62%) were in the west, followed by 404 in the central region, and 303 were in the east (Iglesias García 1999). Moreno Fraginals described the nineteenth century as the great national sacrifice for the sake of the sugar plantation. Between 1880 and 1900 sugar production was concentrated in large mechanized mills with advanced technology, and at that same time, a division between agricultural and industrial work was developed. The agricultural stage focused on the sugarcane *colonias* (colonies), within which the so-called *colonato* (sharecropper system) developed. The *colonos* (workers) planted, cultivated, and sent cane to the mill; sugar manufacturing activity was concentrated in the mills, where free workers toiled, many of whom were industry technicians (Iglesias García 2005).

The two wars of 1868 and 1895 affected Cuba's economy in general and sugar in particular, as many medium and small mills in the central-eastern region of the country suffered high losses; in great measure their fields and factories were destroyed by incendiary torches applied by both sides in the conflicts. This was an important factor in the concentration and centralization of capital in the late nineteenth century. Weaker producers were eliminated or their lands expropriated by the competition in foreign markets. Economic and trade relations between Cuba and the United States played a decisive role in this process, especially through mortgage lending, which ended in expropriations when bankrupt sugar producers defaulted on the loans. As an epilogue of the last colonial century, much of the initially *criollo* sugar economy passed from Cuban to foreign hands, especially U.S. ones.

TOBACCO

The tobacco plant was known and cultivated in Cuba before the arrival of Columbus. The indigenous peoples of the island used it in rituals, for healing, and in other ways. Early on, tobacco was cultivated on farms and ranches. In 1603 the crop was banned by royal decree, but the ban was overturned in late 1614, and after that, the production of tobacco continued uninterrupted.

Tobacco fields spread across several regions of the country, particularly Havana (which in the early nineteenth century included present-day Pinar del Río), Matanzas, Trinidad, Santi Espíritus, Remedio, and Santiago de Cuba. The tobacco fields and farms contributed to the dissolution of the old cattle ranches, since the cultivation of the precious leaf resulted in the division of those lands for lease or sale to growers.

During the government of Juan de Salamanca (1658–1663), a royal decree permitted tobacco to be cultivated on the banks of rivers, so that the growers and their crops would not be harmed by any other landowner, an illustration of the Crown's interest in the crop. However, sugar advanced in the second half of the nineteenth century and pushed tobacco production to the westernmost province of Cuba (Pinar del Río), where the soil was particularly well suited for the growing of the precious leaf. Pinar del Río's Vuelta Abajo, Hoyos de Monterrey, and San Juan y Martínez were (and remained in the early 2000s) lands with a great tradition of growing tobacco. They cultivated (and still cultivate) the famous Cuban tobacco, which was manufactured in factories in Havana and transformed into the famous cigars that continue to be renowned for their texture, quality, and aroma.

There was a great demand for tobacco in the form of snuff, and Havana cigarettes became fashionable in the courts of Europe, which encouraged not only its cultivation but also craftsmanship. The snuff was prepared in the so-called tobacco mills on the banks of rivers, especially in Havana and Matanzas, where mill owners used hydraulic power to improve their functioning.

By the end of the seventeenth century, profits from tobacco exports competed with leather and sugar. The excellence of the Cuban leaf rapidly gained international fame, and in 1717 Spain decided to limit Havana's production of tobacco to factories in Spain. It also prohibited rolling tobacco for sale, and years later it also prohibited the production of snuff but without much success. In 1717 a royal decree established the first Factoría General de Tabacos (General Tobacco Factory) in Havana, with branches in other tobacco-producing towns. Its role was to buy tobacco from farmers at a fixed price with money received from Mexico and from the profits from quicksilver (mercury) and to ensure the quality of the crop and its export to Spain. By the middle of the seventeenth century it would be the Royal Trade Company of Havana that had a monopoly on purchase and export of tobacco leaves to Spain. Despite the regulations, the tobacco trade continued as before, and even expanded, but as contraband. Tobacco also was used to buy smuggled goods and slaves first from the French and later on the English, and even to buy technology for the sugar mills (García Rodríguez 2004).

Fig. 79. Tabaksernte auf Cuba.

These trade restrictions ended in 1817, notwithstanding the fact that, by the end of the seventeenth century, some tobacco manufacturing had expanded; there were already two firms in Havana approved for manufacturing and selling tobacco, which also sold the so-called tobacco roll and some snuff. But it was not until the abolition of the restrictions that factories could develop the legendary cigar in Havana and some other towns.

With the birth of cigar factories in the nineteenth century, a new phase of production began, as most of the profits were from manufacturing. Like sugar production, tobacco manufacture was diverse. Along with the large factories of the nineteenth century there were *chinchales* (manufacturers so small they were almost home-based) where the tobacco was coarsely rolled. In 1861 there were 516 cigar factories in Havana, of which only 158 were top-class and quality; each of these employed between fifty to sixty workers. The remaining 358 factories were smaller plants truly diverse in size, operators, production, and quality. Together, they exported about 21 million cigars, which meant large profits for both manufacturers and growers (Iglesias García 1996, pp. 197–199).

The two wars for independence affected tobacco production, but much less so than sugar production. Ironically, many of the small manufacturers survived for a long time, many into the twentieth century, whereas larger businesses fell victim to centralization as the most powerful and wealthy owners attempted to gain control of more brands and factories. They did not concentrate production in fewer facilities, though, because they wanted to maintain the prestige associated with brands and seals of quality given to each factory. Therefore, neither the properties nor the

operators merged—only the capital. However, from 1880 to 1890 there was some reduction in the number of smaller factories, especially chinchales: In 1896 only 106 cigar factories were registered in Havana. The U.S. tariff of 1883 that favored leaf exports over manufactured cigarettes and cigars played a role in the reduction in the number of cigar factories. With this new change in tariffs and market prices, many manufacturers and tobacco growers left Cuba to try their luck in the United States, either moving their factories or simply closing them and leaving the island with their capital. This trend dealt a hard blow to Cuba's production of cigars.

COFFEE

Originally, coffee was produced on Cuban farms for household consumption, but after the Haitian Revolution the number of coffee plantations grew, and productivity grew to meet high demand and excellent prices for the beans. From 1790 to 1818 coffee even competed with tobacco and sugar because the Napoleonic Wars pushed up the price due to the vacuum in the market left by Saint Domingue. Cuban coffee plantation owners, along with those of French origin who immigrated to Cuba, went out of their way to increase production to meet market demand. Planting and preparation for market was done by slave labor, but the production phase did not require large capital investments, so the tobacco industry grew more quickly than sugar did. However, the production level in the colony was ephemeral; in the 1840s the industry virtually disappeared due to the closure of the U.S. market, the major importer, in retaliation for Spain's protectionist tariffs on U.S. flour. When the United States raised import duties on Cuban coffee there was little demand, and it was not until the early twentieth century that the crop recovered.

The major coffee growing areas during the colonial period were located at opposite ends of the island: the mountainous areas of the eastern region, and the mountains of Pinar del Rio in the west. Coffee was also grown in the area of Trinidad. In 1827 there were more than 2,000 coffee plantations on the island, but by 1840 there were fewer than 700, and by 1868 there were only a few.

The economy of Cuba during the colonial era was not only livestock, sugar, tobacco, coffee, and various subsistence crops, but also was interspersed with other products, including coconuts and bananas, which were grown throughout the island, but mainly in the northwestern regions such as Baracoa. The large market for coconuts and bananas was reflected in the export statistics of the international and inter-colonial markets. By the middle of the nineteenth century the exports of bananas and coconuts were large scale, with around 100,000 bunches of bananas shipped in 1843, growing to some 10,000 tons of fruit in 1859, and exports and sales worth more than 110,000 pesos in 1860. Thanks to U.S. demand, Cuba exported to the United States about 500,000 bunches per year, rising to almost 2 million stems a year by 1870, and this level of exports continued into the twentieth century (García Alvarez). In addition, honey, alcohol, and sugarcane spirits brought ample profits in the mid-nineteenth century (La Sagra; García Álvarez; Santamaría p. 77).

In the early 2000s many economic historians question the validity of applying the concept of the plantation colony to Cuba because, even though colonial rule maintained four centuries of specialization in sugar, the island's most exportable commodity, Cuba developed and sustained a level of agricultural diversification in different regions and localities that allowed it to be reborn, like a phoenix rising from its own ruinous ashes. In the Cuban economy of the colonial period, as well as in other eras, the international market situation has always been indisputably important.

BIBLIOGRAPHY

Actas del Cabildo Habanero. Historical Museum of the City of Havana. Books from the years 1600–1762.

Chaunu, Pierre. *Sevilla y América, Siglos XVI y XVII*. Seville, Spain: Universidad de Sevilla, 1983.

De la Fuente García, Alejandro. "Economía, 1500–1700." In *Historia de Cuba*, vol. 1, edited by Consuelo Naranjo Orovio. Madrid: Publicaciones del CSIC, 2009.

García Álvarez, Alejandro. *La Costa cubana del guineo. Una historia bananera*. Havana: Editorial de Ciencias Sociales, 2008.

García Rodríguez, Gloria. "El auge de la sociedad esclavista en Cuba." In *Historia de Cuba: La colonia. Evolución socioeconómica y formación nacional. De*

los orígenes hasta 1867, vol. 1, edited by Instituto de Historia de Cuba. Havana: Editora Política, 1994.

García Rodríguez, Mercedes. *La Aventura de fundar ingenios. La refacción azucarera en La Habana del siglo XVIII*. Havana: Editorial de Ciencias Sociales, 2004.

García Rodríguez, Mercedes. *Entre Haciendas y Plantaciones. Los orígenes Azucareros de La Habana*. Havana: Editorial de Ciencias Sociales, 2007.

Iglesias García, Fe. "El desarrollo capitalista en los albores de la época imperialista." In *Historia de Cuba: Las luchas por la independencia nacional y las transformaciones estructurales (1868–1898)*, vol. 2, edited by Instituto de Historia de Cuba. Havana: Editora Política, 1996.

Iglesias García, Fe. *Del Ingenio al Central*. Havana: Editorial de Ciencias Sociales, 1999.

Iglesias García, Fe. *Economía cubana de fin de siglo*. Havana: Editorial de Ciencias Sociales, 2005.

La Sagra, Ramón de. *Bosquejo económico político de la Isla de Cuba*. 2 vols. Madrid: Edición M. Pita, 1852.

Moreno Fraginals, Manuel. *El Ingenio, Complejo económico social cubano del azúcar*. Vol. 1. Havana: Editorial Ciencias Sociales, 1978.

Pérez de La Riva, Juan. *La Conquista del Espacio Cubano*. Havana: Fundación Fernando Ortiz, 2004.

Pérez Guzmán, Francisco. *La Habana clave de un imperio*. Havana: Editorial de Ciencias Sociales, 1997.

Santamaría García, Antonio. "Evolución económica. 1700–1959." In *Historia de Cuba*, vol. 1, edited by Consuelo Naranjo Orovio. Madrid: Publicaciones del CSIC, 2009.

Zanetti, Oscar, and Alejandro García Álvarez. *Caminos para el Azúcar*. Havana: Editorial de Ciencias Sociales, 1987.

ECONOMY: REPUBLICAN PERIOD

Oscar Zanetti

The organization of the Cuban economy from 1902 to 1959.

During the early decades of the twentieth century, the Cuban economy registered remarkable growth, which was based almost exclusively on the expansion of the sugar industry and related businesses. By the end of the 1920s, however, this highly specialized economic structure was experiencing a crisis; the development of the economy slowed and showed more fluctuations, albeit with an evident trend toward diversification.

THE GROWTH OF THE SUGAR INDUSTRY

In 1899, Cuba emerged from the struggle for independence with a wrecked economy. Sugar output had fallen by more than 70 percent; tobacco output had fallen by 80 percent; and throughout vast areas of the country, it was almost impossible to find a single

■ *See also*

Ecology and Environment: Republican Period

Governance and Contestation: The Republic: 1902–1952

Sugar: Representation in Cuban Culture

Sugar: Republican Period

head of livestock. The census for that year showed a net loss of over 50,000 inhabitants since the previous census of 1887. If, however, one factors in the demographic growth that occurred during the first few years of that timeframe, the loss of inhabitants might well be estimated at 15 percent of the country's population.

This negative assessment makes the speedy recovery that followed all the more surprising. By the time the republic was inaugurated in 1902, the sugar harvest was approaching a record level of slightly more than the one million tons reached in 1894, while tobacco exports had surpassed prewar levels. Meanwhile, massive cattle imports had revived ranching on the island. Although the institutional foundations for this recovery were provided by the U.S. government under military orders (such as those designed to facilitate the appropriation of lands or promote the railroads), the resources for reconstruction came from the island itself, since Washington provided little financing. Of much greater relevance, by contrast, was the role of private U.S. capital, with investors attracted by the collapse in property values and in the value of sugarcane estates and mills in particular. This trend ushered in an investment process that led to the investors' control of the island's key areas of manufacturing and services.

The imposition of the Platt Amendment (1901) as an annex to the Cuban constitution, as well as the stipulation of a reciprocal trade agreement between the United States and the newborn Republic of Cuba at the end of 1902 (in which far-reaching tariff breaks were granted to U.S. goods imported to the island in exchange for preferential treatment for Cuban sugar at U.S. customhouses) set conditions that encouraged even stronger capital flows. In 1913, U.S. firms controlled 38 out of the 171 active sugar *centrales* (where sugarcane is processed) in the country. In that year, these companies produced nearly 40 percent of the harvest, which for the first time surpassed two million tons. Such companies as Cuban American Sugar, United Fruit, and Francisco Sugar had accumulated immense stretches of land in the eastern provinces of the island. These lands were now linked to the western regions by a railroad built by another U.S. company, the Cuba Company. Other infrastructure sectors, such as the ports, also attracted the attention of U.S. investors, as did certain secondary sectors (tobacco, citrus, cement), as well as services, including relatively new services, such as the telephone.

The remarkable economic dynamism fostered by these investments was rounded out by the investments of local capital in the sugar sector and in other branches of the economy (e.g., livestock, agriculture, and the food industry), as well as in trade, where most entrepreneurs of Spanish origin were to be found. Even though their colonial ties had been severed, Spaniards continued to play a prominent role in the economic life of the country, in no small measure due to the robust immigration flows from the peninsula.

Nearly 25,000 immigrants a year provided the human resources that were essential for economic growth.

By 1913, the rising productivity of Cuba's state-of-the-art sugar industry, coupled with trade preferences, allowed the country to displace other foreign suppliers in the U.S. sugar market, which was the destination of 86 percent of the island's sugar output that year. It was to be expected that once U.S. needs for imported sugar had been met, the growth rate for Cuban sugar would slow down, since Cuban producers would now have to compete against the highly protected domestic U.S. output. Indeed, not even the recent resumption of sugar exports to Great Britain was expected to lead to a significant rise in the volume of sales.

The Impact of World War I The outbreak of war in Europe in 1914 completely changed that scenario. Hostilities wrecked sugar-beet production in Europe, causing shortages on the world sugar market that instantly led to rising prices. The new situation greatly enhanced the attractiveness of investment in sugar in the eyes of U.S. capitalists. During the previous decades, such investments had been led by entrepreneurs such as Edwin Atkins (1850–1926) and Manuel Rionda (1854–1943). Now, however, the most powerful American financial interests were poised over the island. By the end of 1915, with $50 million provided by Morgan bank and other Wall Street interests, and within the space of little more than a year, Rionda bought fifteen sugar centrales, encompassing more than 300,000 acres of land, in order to create the Cuba Cane Corporation. By 1919, one year after the end of World War I, this company, which produced more than one-half million tons of sugar a year, was the largest sugar company in the world. Other companies that were incorporated during the war years, such as the Punta Alegre Sugar Company and West Indies Limited, did not attain nearly the same scale as the Cuba Cane Corporation; nevertheless, they were able to position themselves solidly in the constellation of major sugar producers.

The factories that were installed or expanded by U.S. firms, along with a dozen sugar centrales developed with domestic capital, quickly raised the overall capacity of the industry. By 1919, the harvest was reaching the 4.5 million ton mark. The canefields harvested during those years covered nearly two million acres, even though the total extent of lands controlled by the sugar companies was much greater. In order to support this growth in output without a sharp increase in wages, it became necessary to bring in tens of thousands of new day laborers. This contingent was provided primarily by workers imported from the neighboring Caribbean islands, and Haiti in particular; these workers were freely hired with the approval of the Cuban government.

The growth of sugar provided an especially propitious stage for financial maneuvers. Loans increased

Chart 1

**Estimated national revenue compared against the value
of total exports and the value of exports of sugar in Cuba, 1900–1925**

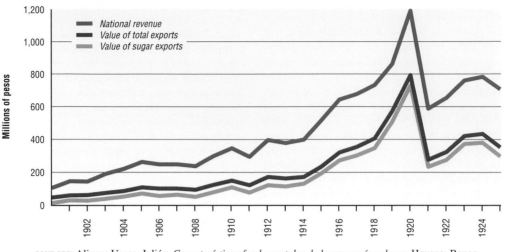

SOURCES: Alienes Urosa, Julián. *Características fundamentales de la economía cubana*. Havana: Banco Nacional de Cuba, 1953, Chart 17. Oscar Zanetti, "El comercio exterior de la república neocolonial," in *Anuario de Estudios Cubanos 1*, Havana: Editorial de Ciencias Sociales, 1975, Chart 5.

from 97.8 million pesos in 1916 to 241 million pesos three years later. During this period, more than twenty-five banking institutions were founded in Cuba. One of these, the Banco Internacional de Cuba, opened 104 branches across the country almost simultaneously. The war also provided a golden opportunity for large U.S. banks, which were able to dislodge their European competitors as the chief financial backers for Cuban output, as much through the direct mortgaging of the harvests of many sugar centrales as through loans to local banks. Encouraged by changes in U.S. laws, entities such as National City Bank of New York, which up to that point had operated quietly as shareholders in certain local banks, could now open branches on the island directly and benefit from the credit boom created by the extraordinary increase in the price of sugar.

Following the outbreak of World War I, the price of sugar rose steadily from 1.93 cents per pound in July 1914 to an average of 4.37 cents in 1916. Nevertheless, once the United States entered the war in April 1917 (followed immediately by its ally Cuba), Washington asserted federal control over the manufacturing and prices of fuels and foods, including sugar. It was thus that, as its so-called contribution to the war effort, Cuba sold its entire harvest at a price set at 4.6 cents per pound, which would be increased to 4.73 cents the following year. Although this figure might have appeared reasonable, it barely compensated for the rising prices Cuba now had to pay for its import bill. This situation generated inflationary pressure on the island, with all its ensuing social unrest.

Crash of the 1920s When the United States scrapped price controls at the end of 1919, the price of sugar took off. By April 1920, the price had increased to 18 cents per pound. Based on these prices, the banks extended virtually unlimited loans to sugar mills and cane-field settlers, eventually in excess of $285 million, a figure that was out of all proportion to the real needs of the country. High prices soon attracted sugar from all over the world to the U.S. market, and by the end of the summer, sugar prices were in free fall. Banks on the island (including Banco Nacional de Cuba, Banco Español de la Isla de Cuba, and other large institutions) were unable to recoup the money that had been loaned so imprudently and, lacking any support from the New York banks, decided to close their doors. After a brief bank moratorium, they were liquidated.

The crash of 1920 not only trashed Cuba's financial system, which fell under foreign (primarily U.S.) control, but it also led to a massive transfer of lands from Cuban estate owners and settlers to these banks. As an example of what happened, in the aftermath of all the bankruptcies and auctions, National City Bank suddenly found that it was the owner of ten sugar centrales. In order to manage them, the bank decided to set up a company, General Sugar Estates, which by 1924 would produce on its own account nearly 250,000 tons of sugar. At the climax of this investment process, the transfer of properties caused by the crash left a total of seventy-four sugar centrales in U.S. hands, which accounted for 60 percent of national output. The encroachment of financial interests was felt even at the very heart of the major U.S. sugar companies,

as old-line promoters, such as Manuel Rionda and James H. Post (1859–1938), were displaced from the boardrooms by banking personalities, such as Gordon Rentschler (1885–1948) and William A. (1841–1922) and Percy Rockefeller (1878–1934).

The financial crash that shook the foundations of the Cuban economy had an especially speculative origin, since at beginning of the 1920s the European sugar-beet industry was still far from making a comeback, and demand continued to outrun supply on world sugar markets. Nevertheless, there was an evident trend toward normalization in the market. Furthermore, there were obvious warning signs, such as the enactment of the Fordney-McCumber Tariff by the U.S. Congress in 1922, which raised duties on Cuban sugar by 0.76 cents per pound. Nevertheless, the large U.S. corporations that controlled the country's key industry were convinced that running their factories at full capacity would place them in an unassailably competitive position. They dismissed the pessimists and chose instead to raise Cuban output by yet another million tons in an effort to wring the highest possible return from their investment on the island. In 1925, a harvest of 5.8 million tons in Cuba coincided with increases in the output of other sugar-producing areas of the world. This glut pulled the price of sugar back down to the perilous threshold of 2 cents per

pound. Of even greater concern, the depressed prices were obviously not just a temporary trend. Faced with the evidence of a saturated market, the U.S. raw-sugar companies, together with a majority of Cuban estate owners, asked the government of President Gerardo Machado (1871–1939) to intervene. His decision to limit the following year's harvest put a decisive end to sugar's growth cycle.

From the standpoint of Cuba's overall economy, the outcome of this expansion is not easy to characterize. On the one hand, there was unquestionably spectacular growth, as shown in the 9.6-percent annual rate of increase for exports. On the other hand, the quality of this progress was questionable: Even as export figures for sugar and sugar by-products multiplied tenfold, tobacco and other export categories barely doubled in sales during that twenty-five-year period. In reality, the single-export nature of the economy became even starker: From an average of 60.3 percent of total exports for the five-year period of 1902 to 1906, sugar rose to 85 percent for the 1921–1925 period, with no change whatsoever in the traditional geographic concentration of exports, of which 80 percent went to the United States throughout this entire period. Domestic production did little to relieve the monotony of this economic landscape. Except for cattle and coffee in the agricultural sector, and certain food products and construction materials in the industrial sector, the progress registered in these other categories was trivial.

The investment interests of U.S. firms was generally confined to sugar and related activities, such as railroads, warehouses, ports, and energy. American investors had little impact on other areas of the national economy. Thanks to the efforts of the industry and of native-born hacienda owners, the production of sugar was state-of-the-art, and the industry in Cuba was among those with the largest capacity for production of cane sugar. Yet, in spite of its vast scale, this process had an extremely limited multiplier effect. Since technology was restricted, the major beneficiary of these investments turned out to be U.S. heavy industry, which supplied the bulk of the machinery and equipment. This set of circumstances, and a tendency not to reinvest profits outside of the sugar industry, led to a drain on capital due to the return on investment. According to some estimates, this drain might well have reached $200 million for the 1921–1925 period alone.

The Cuban contribution to this extraordinary growth in output basically consisted of two factors: land and, in part, labor. At the beginning of the twentieth century, barely one-fourth of the island's arable land was being cultivated. This meant that vast tracts of land, most of unsurpassable quality, were available for the sugar expansion. Given the evolving expansion of industrial capacity, the land factor was critical in order to secure the necessary raw materials. Thus, the sugar companies (foreign companies in particular) rolled out a policy of voracious accumulation, which led to the creation of gargantuan estates. In 1926, the sugar centrales controlled nearly eight million acres, of which barely one-third was sown with cane. This disproportionate accumulation of land, which privileged sugarcane while condemning other crops to be exploited in marginal or less-profitable areas, reinforced single-crop agriculture as the predominant feature of Cuban agriculture and meant low productivity on the land that actually was being sown, even on sugarcane plantations, whose yields tended to be lower than the world average. But the sugar estates, with their vast untilled domains, fulfilled another function: They shut off the peasants' access to land and condemned them to provide at least part of the labor needed to run the cane plantations, although the bulk of the workforce was made up of immigrant day laborers.

The main benefit of the sugar expansion for the Cuban economy as a whole was probably the employment of a substantial number of salaried employees, estimated at some 350,000 by the mid-twentieth century. Given the relatively even geographical distribution of the sugar industry and its high demand for labor, its growth promoted a hierarchy of salaries, even as it restructured and broadened the internal market. Nevertheless, the potential benefits of this process were constrained by an extensive system of paying wages with promissory notes or IOUs. This reduced the cash income of the workers, as well as their freedom as consumers. They were further hampered by the tendency of the U.S. companies to turn their properties into exclusive business preserves. There were also a large number of day laborers from the Antilles whom the *criollo* elites, with their shortsightedness and racism, turned into seasonal workers. All these factors contributed to the drain off of such wages as were being paid.

Undoubtedly, the growth cycle of the sugar industry contributed to the modernization of the Cuban economy by expanding infrastructure, broadening the domestic market, fostering financial and business networks, and introducing new services. This modernization might, in theory, have encouraged multilateral development, and in fact some productive areas in the domestic market were able to take advantage of increased demand or transportation facilities. But these possibilities materialized on a very small scale. The structural framework created by and for the growth of the sugar industry largely hobbled any benefits that might have been obtained. The same trade mechanisms that encouraged the export of sugar served to skew consumption toward imports, and the higher profitability of the cane crop, further heightened under such conditions, encouraged the accumulation of land and the concentration of material and human resources at the expense of other agricultural categories. In addition, given the remittances of the immigrant workers, the capital shifted overseas as profits and dividends, along with other factors, encouraged a system in which the bulk of the surplus value generated during the fat years of sugar in effect turned into capital flight and left the island.

AN EXHAUSTED MODEL FOR GROWTH

Cuba's hard times in the 1920s had their origin in the deep misalignments and changes in the system of international economic relations after World War I. The expansive trend in world trade faded away, to be followed by sharp upturns and downturns that were affected by the vicissitudes of European economic reconstruction, the financial imbalances caused by the war reparations, and above all the protectionist policies adopted by the most developed countries in the face of the twin threats of recession and unemployment.

Cuba, with its sugar industry growth paralyzed after 1925, offers an early case study of the exhaustion of the so-called *export-led, outward-looking* growth model. The direct causes of this phenomenon were, to start with, a series of tariff increases in the United States, which reached their climax in the prohibitive Smoot-Hawley Tariff Act of 1930 and reduced the imports of Cuban raw materials from 4.2 million tons in 1929 to 1.5 million tons in 1933. On top of this were the growing saturation of the international sugar market and the spread of protectionism. Thus began a secular trend toward self-sufficiency among the major sugar consumers, which would restrict demand and fragment the market into preferential areas.

Cuba met these new terms of trade by adjusting its supply of sugar to the requirements of the market. Its main goal was to support prices amid the Great Depression, the global financial crisis of 1929. To this end, the harvests were restricted and international agreements among producers were encouraged, a policy tailor-made for the dominant groups of the main industry of the island. Cuba's sugar harvest was restricted between 1931 and 1958, with the sole exception of the 1944–1952 period, which was marked by the peculiar conditions of World War II (1939–1945) and the postwar period. During these three decades, the average harvest totaled only 4.7 million tons, a figure that was well below the industry's capacity, with underutilization estimated at 25 percent.

This self-restricting policy could be imposed, not on account of its poor direct results, but rather because it dovetailed with the quota system the United States adopted in 1934 to obtain its sugar supply. Although lower than the historical levels, this system guaranteed the place of Cuban sugar in this market and, furthermore, introduced a preferential price that was higher than the world market price, a subtle innovation in the mechanisms of dependence. Despite its stabilizing effects, this quota system, like the one implemented on the world market based on the London Convention (1937), preordained a steady weakening of Cuba's position in global output, as can be seen in Table 1.

The possibility that sugar production could become a factor in overall growth was thus foreclosed by the Cuban state's regulation of the sector. The direct purpose of the state's intervention was to adapt the industry to restricted production conditions by eliminating competition and controlling the free play of market forces, which in the context of a lengthy depression would inevitably have led to the disappearance of less efficient producers. Amid the onslaught of the economic crisis, the proportional distribution of the harvest among all the sugar centrales and sugarcane plantations was meant to preserve the current property-ownership scheme, as well as jobs. As a palliative for serious social tensions, these regulatory activities needed to perform redistribution and equilibrium functions, which were enshrined in the Law on Coordination of Sugar Activities of 1937. This law ensured the survival of the small cane farmers and introduced the principle of adjusting payments within the sector to the price of sugar, using methods that sought to balance the distribution of income but which also led to a slow rise in production costs.

In response to this trend, the most entrepreneurial of the sugar companies made small-scale investments at strategic points along the production chain in an effort to shorten harvest times to match the optimum point in the ripening of the cane. With these resources, it was possible to increase the output of sugar per effec-

Global production of sugar compared to production of sugar in Cuba, 1925–1955
(IN THOUSANDS OF SHORT TONS)

Year	Total global production of sugar	Cuban production of sugar	Percentage of world's sugar produced by Cuba
1925	27,567	5,889	21.1
1930	31,348	5,300	16.6
1935	29,405	3,130	9.6
1940	34,063	3,905	10.9
1945	25,693	3,960	15.3
1950	36,027	6,157	17.0
1955	45,946	6,001	10.8

SOURCE: *Anuario azucarero de Cuba 1959*. Havana: Cuba Económica y Financiera, 1959, pp. 93, 207.

Table 1

tive milling day by approximately one-third; however, since the strategy entailed a reduction in the workers' income, the laborers opposed it and obtained a compensatory formula from the state. The other way to deal with rising costs was to make better use of sugar by-products, with derivatives such as alcohol, chemicals, paper, bagasse fiberboard, and so forth, whose sale would generate supplementary income; however, the majority of entrepreneurs were reluctant to make such investments while prices stayed relatively low.

Thus faced with the stagnation of the sector that for over a century had been the engine of its economic life, Cuban society needed to refocus its development model. From this perspective, the meaning and scope of the crisis that started at the end of the 1920s can best be understood by considering the actual possibilities of carrying out changes that could have revived the country's economic dynamism.

DIVERSIFICATION AND OTHER ALTERNATIVES

At least in theory, the development of the national economy might have been channeled in several different directions, whether by promoting new export categories, by import-substitution strategies, or by some combination of these two variants. In any case, and regardless of which market the output was geared toward, the range of products had to be broadened. *Diversification* thus became the magic word of economic ideology. During these years, the idea of diversification displayed a broad range of facets—from the simple stimulation of subsistence crops on small plots of land to full-scale industrialization—depending on which interests happened to be proposing it as the solution to the country's problems. What diversification meant depended on the circumstances. In this respect, the structural characteristics of Cuban agriculture presented, from the very start, a formidable obstacle. The growth of the sugar industry in the first quarter of the twentieth century had created extreme polarization in land-ownership patterns, concentrated at one end in enormous *latifundios* and fragmented at the other end into many small, unproductive holdings.

Farm Size and Land Productivity This schizophrenic development, far from attenuating, actually intensified after 1925, as can be seen from the available data. Constraints on the data notwithstanding, everything suggests that holdings of fewer than 160 acres (67 ha), which by the end of the 1920s represented two-thirds of the total farms in the country, registered an increase that would bring them close to 75 percent by the 1950s. Holdings of more than 1,000 acres (400 ha) also grew, but only with regard to total land area occupied in comparison with all farms in the country, and not in absolute numbers (they continued to be rare). By 1959, such farms accounted for 73 percent of the farmed area. Thus, something on the order of fifteen million acres were occupied by 3,602 holdings that could be classified as latifundios, of which 52 were on a scale even greater than 35,000 acres. The result of this shifting agricultural structure was a drop in medium-sized holdings (between 160 and 1,000 acres): With regard to the total number of farms, their numbers appear to have shrunk by approximately 15 percent.

The problem of the *latifundio* was not just its size as a holding, but rather the low productivity of its land, which was the result not only of the extensive nature of the crop but also the preservation of vast tracts of uncultivated land. A review of land use by the agricultural census of 1946 (Table 2) provides strong evidence of this situation.

Land misuse was even greater if one factors in the low yields of many crops, which were themselves a direct result of the preservation of the sugarcane latifundios, which held a high proportion of land in reserve, or simply idle, even though there was very lit-

tle likelihood that they would be called upon for a substantial increase in their output. In a context of growing social pressure (the latifundios were banned by the constitution of 1940), the sugar companies tenaciously defended their plantations and even persisted in expanding their properties. The government's timid measures against the cultivation of cane by the mill owners (so-called administrative cane) or its efforts to compel the lease of idle lands (Law 7 of 1948) could easily be dodged by the owners of sugarcane latifundios through the creation of fictitious companies and other legal legerdemain.

The constraints of the domestic market and the relatively low profitability of the noncane agricultural categories thus weakened pressure on the market for land that might have arisen from an interest in using idle terrain. It was only during the 1950s that a record appears of the sugar companies venturing into other agricultural categories, usually cattle-ranching experiments pursued through equally extensive methods.

Yet the cattle-ranching latifundio was precisely the other factor that paralyzed the agricultural resources of the country. There was rapid growth in ranching during the first two decades of the twentieth century, which paralleled that of sugarcane and which left a balance of 4.7 million head of cattle in 1921; after that, however, the figures for livestock stagnate until the end of the 1950s. More than half of the livestock inventory was in the hands of large-scale proprietors, forty of whom in 1940 had accumulated nearly two million acres of pastureland. Cattle ranching, generally pursued on natural pastures, was marked by a low livestock density of approximately one head per every two acres in 1946, and a similarly poor yield with regard to milk production.

The other factor in the low-productivity, polarized structure of Cuban agriculture was the proliferation of *minifundios* (small plots). More than two-thirds of the agricultural holdings in the country in 1946 were farms with fewer than sixty-five acres, predominantly those producing less than $500 a year. From a technical perspective, aside from the constraints on productivity presented by the small scale of these farms, there was also the issue of the control asserted by the great landowners over small and medium-sized rural holdings. In 1946, more than half the farms in the country (and 91% of those under 450 acres) were subject to some type of rent, a situation that affected 38.5 percent of the plotted land area. Rent meant that a substantial share of the farmers' income (more than 20% according to some partial estimates) passed over to the pockets of the landlords.

The economic possibilities of the campesinos were likewise constrained by unfavorable financing and marketing conditions. Bank credit was extended almost exclusively to high-volume agricultural producers, a situation that the emergence of state agricultural banks in 1950 was unable to change significantly. Accordingly,

Use of land in Cuba by size of farm (1945)

Size of farm (acres)	Total (acres)	Cultivated (%)	Pasture (%)	Uncultivated (%)
0–123	4,647,356	39.5	38.3	22.2
124–1,234	7,439,460	23.4	54.4	22.2
greater than 1,235	11,172,704	12.8	36.7	50.5

SOURCE: Cuban Ministry of Agriculture (MINAG). *Memoria del censo agrícola nacional*, 1946. Havana: Cuban Ministry of Agriculture, 1951, p. 380.

Table 2

a majority of the campesinos were at the mercy of moneylenders who provided loans under usurious terms. The constraints on transportation and communications prevented access to the market, placing the farmer in the hands of middlemen, who frequently acquired the harvests for less than one-fourth of what they were worth. These circumstances made financing difficult, even for the small sector of agricultural producers who held farms of between 100 and 350 acres and who showed a greater propensity to use the land intensively, a situation that was reflected not only in the limited machinery for working farms, but also in the extremely low irrigation and fertilization rates.

Nonsugar Agricultural Output and Other Industries Under these conditions, the idea that the export of other agricultural categories could compensate for the stagnation of sugar was little more than a delusion. Tobacco, the traditional little brother of sugar, went through similar vicissitudes on the market. Its output (which was similarly stabilized) went through violent fluctuations during those years, and by the end of the 1950s had barely grown by more than 8 percent over the average level of the 1920s. As a result of a genuine boom in production, coffee broke into the ranks of Cuban exports in the 1930s, but it vanished shortly thereafter amid wild fluctuations that made it possible to renew exports only in 1954. Something similar occurred with sisal, whose fibers began to be exported in the 1930s and reached a record 13,500 tons in 1949, after which sisal exports declined to less than half this figure. Exports of fruits and vegetables were more stable and grew throughout this period, but their value in 1958, at four million pesos, was economically insignificant. With regard to categories for domestic consumption, there were important advances in the production of eggs (national self-sufficiency was virtually attained) and potatoes, which in a little over two decades doubled to reach 130,000 tons. But these are exceptions. Of the country's seventeen primary crops in 1945, eleven had stagnated or lost value by 1950. The production of rice is even more revealing: Its explosive growth made it possible to reduce imports of rice from $52 million in 1953 to only $18.5 million in 1955, but subsequent rice production stagnated under pressure from U.S. suppliers.

Agricultural output for products other than cane was unstable. Even worse, there is evidence of a perverse relationship with sugar, with contractions during sugar booms and revivals during recessions. With more than 60 percent of the country's arable area in sugarcane, Cuba would end the 1950s as the most outstanding Latin American food importer from the United States. Single-crop agriculture was indeed difficult to overcome.

By virtue of the privileges granted to U.S. merchandise in Cuba under the trade-reciprocity agreement, there was practically no category of national output that did not face stiff competition from an American counterpart, leading to the weakness of the

Old brass sign of the Partagás cigar factory. The Partagás cigar company, founded by Jaime Partagás in Havana in 1845, later was purchased by Ramón Cifuentes and his family © JEREMY HOMER/TERRA/ CORBIS

country's industrial base at the end of the expansion of sugarcane. It is estimated that at this time the industrial sector, excluding sugar mills, employed some 26,000 workers distributed across slightly more than 900 installations, among which quasi-artisan workshops were predominant. The late and rather moderate protection provided by the tariff of 1927 could offer only a limited stimulus to the nonsugar sector of manufacturing, since its effects were virtually cancelled out by the severe depression of 1929 and the new reciprocity treaty signed with the United States in 1934, which expanded the concessions for goods imported from the United States.

With such a depressed market, output for domestic consumption grew at a slow and unsteady rate during the 1930s. Some industries that arose under the aegis of the tariff disappeared, while others, such as food preserves, carried on despite remarkable difficulties. Well-established categories, such as beer and cement, overcame the initial contraction, but without recovering their 1929 levels. In the category of shoe manufacturing, while the number of workshops increased, output did not. The most notable exceptions were provided by textiles and condensed milk, which were produced at modern factories backed by foreign financing; the growth of the latter product, in particular, made it possible to substitute almost the full amount of imports.

The manufacturing sector took on new life with the opportunities created by World War II, which strengthened demand while limiting foreign supply to the domestic market. These circumstances, stimulated by government measures that promoted new industries, saw the rise of chemical and pharmaceutical factories, construction materials, diamond-cutting, plastics, and garments. The output of beer, beverages and refreshments, tires, cigarettes, cement, and textiles also rose, with the country's textile industry satisfying 50 percent of the national demand for cotton goods.

This growth, however, was fragile and to some extent an anomaly, since the new industries arose amid severe constraints on the acquisition of capital goods and were marked by low productivity rates and abnormal prices that were determined by shortages. When World War II ended, the Cuban market once again was flooded with cheap American products that displaced local output. There was a sharp contraction in 1948 to which some of the newly created industries succumbed, while others that were long established teetered on the edge of bankruptcy. If national manufacturing was to survive and consolidate, it needed tariff barriers and productivity increases. But protectionism clashed with Cuba's preferential trade system with the United States, which in those years had been ratified under the framework of the General Agreement on Tariffs and Trade (GATT). Faced with any import-substitution effort, the U.S. interests concerned responded with the threat of reprisals against the sugar quota. This, in turn, mobilized the big estate owners and importers to defend the economic model on which their power was based. Short of capital to acquire technologies that would allow for higher productivity, the manufacturers tried to cut their costs by pressuring the government to reduce wages and obtain more favorable terms for hiring. Such demands, however, had a real-life limitation, since a sharp decrease in wage levels and employment would entail both a high political cost and also lead to a contraction in consumption, thus weakening even further the internal market (already tight due to unemployment). All of this made it more difficult to obtain a truly profitable scale in many categories of national production.

Financial Mobilization and a Growth in Manufacturing During the 1950s, industrial development was favored by the financial mobilization that was part of the countercyclical policy of Fulgencio Batista (1901–1973). Nonsugar manufacturing output increased by an estimated 54 percent between 1950 and 1958. Although only a fraction of the investment capital that was mobilized during those years was geared toward manufacturing, it nonetheless made it possible for new categories to appear in this sector, such as glass containers, electrical wire, fertilizer, metal bars, bagasse paper, and others products, some of which were developed with the participation of U.S. capital. Furthermore, the mobilization expanded the productive capacity of certain branches of industries, such as textiles, paint and varnish, food, and oil refining, as well as cement and other building materials. The most notable expansion was in the categories of dairy products and cotton goods, which achieved growth rates of close to 10 percent a year, as well as paint and tires, whose expansion eventually would satisfy most of the national consumer demand. The situation was similar with the production of beer, cigarettes, soaps and detergents, and, to a lesser degree, food preserves and beverages. Mining deserves special mention, particularly with regard to nickel, exploitation of which had begun during World War II by a U.S. company and resulted in the most significant contribution to Cuba's nonsugar exports during this latter stage.

The surge in manufacturing during the 1950s, nevertheless, shows significant irrational features, including geographical location, since 67 percent of the factories built or designed between 1952 and 1956 were located in the capital. In addition, the equipment and machinery at many of these factories, which had supposedly been acquired in the name of state-of-the-art technology, were actually discards from U.S. factories and had productivity rates that were well below the average for that period. Furthermore, 73 percent of the raw materials used in factories after 1953 were imported, which notably limited the effect these materials could have on import substitution. Manufacturing continued to be dominated by small workshops, which employed more than 60 percent of the workers in the sector (Table 3).

As can be seen in Chart 2, the growth in manufacturing during the 1940s and 1950s continued a rising trend that helped reduce the weight of sugar production in national income; it did not, however, fundamentally alter Cuba's economic structure. In 1957, about 21 percent of the labor force was engaged in manufacturing, an obvious increase over the 16.4 percent registered in 1931. This statistic is misleading, however, in that the figure would have been much smaller if industrial workers in the sugar sector were excluded. Another serious problem in national manufacturing was the structure of production: Only 4 percent of the value added was in the metalworking-mechanical sector, which meant total dependence on

Industry structure by number of workers in Cuba (1954)

Number of workers in a factory	Number of industries	Percentage of all industries
less than 5	839	45.1
6–10	330	18.2
11–25	320	17.3
26–100	250	13.6
101–250	67	3.6
250–500	26	1.4
greater than 500	14	0.8

Table 3

SOURCE: U.S. Department of Commerce, *Investment in Cuba*, Washington D.C.: 1956, p. 73.

Evolution of industrial production indexes in Cuba, 1930–1958 (1953 = 100)

Chart 2

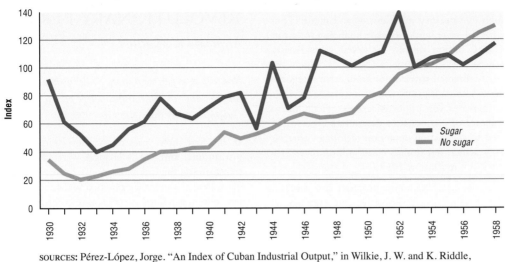

SOURCES: Pérez-López, Jorge. "An Index of Cuban Industrial Output," in Wilkie, J. W. and K. Riddle, *Quantitative Latin American Studies: Methods and Findings*. Los Angeles: UCLA Latin American Center, University of California, 1977.

imports of capital goods to equip the manufacturing sector. If, on top of all this, one adds the narrow local base for supplying raw materials and the weak links between different branches of manufacturing, it becomes possible to understand how truly limited was the economic impact of this disjointed diversification in manufacturing.

Financial Troubles The difficulties in increasing output that could be exported, coupled with the feeble substitution of imports, yielded a negative bottom line in the evolution of Cuba's trade. This problem was further aggravated by the shifting terms of trade between exported and imported goods, which had a negative trend for most of this period. Yet another negative impact on the external financial balance came from the resource flows associated with investments. After 1925, the export of U.S. capital to Cuba was notoriously stagnant, and even though the book value of U.S. investments in Cuba rose by some $330 million during the 1950s, only a relatively small fraction of this amount represented new cash that was actually entering the country. This situation had a negative impact on the category of *return on investments* on the Cuban balance of payments, whose services account was traditionally skewed by items such as shipping; accordingly, between 1925 and 1958, this set of factors yielded a negative balance estimated at $1.034 billion.

The decapitalization process that the sum of these factors produced can only partly explain the low availability of investment capital in the national economy during this period. The low availability of investment was also the result of the low mobility of the capital actually accumulated in the country, as well as the pernicious structure of bank credits geared toward encouraging new production. According to figures from the International Reconstruction and Development Bank in 1951, the savings rate during the sugar bonanza from 1945 to 1949 swung between 12 percent and 14 percent of the gross national product, which represented the accumulation of slightly more than $1.0 billion in the hands of the national private sector, of which approximately $550 million was invested. One-fourth of this figure was destined for construction (chiefly residential), while $360 million went toward the acquisition of capital goods—a tiny amount, when one considers the cumulative need to replace machinery and equipment after the crisis and war years. Of savings not invested, some $300 million was extracted and deposited in U.S. banks or used to acquire property in south Florida, while a similar amount remained in Cuban banks. This distribution in the use of capital reflects the lack of confidence that local capitalists had in the future of the national economy.

Internal financing trends began to change in the early 1950s with the rise of Cuban merchant banks (which had recovered during World War II) and especially after the state bank was founded. Toward 1956 there was a notable expansion in the volume of loans. There were also major changes in how the loans were distributed, since there was a considerable rise in the financing of nonsugar manufacturing, which received a total of $186 million. There was, above all, a steep increase in investments in public securities of $160.9 million, as a result of the mobilization of capital that Batista had decreed in order to dampen the effects of the recession provoked by a new sugar crisis, but which also served for the enrichment of government officials on an unprecedented scale. Private credit was mobilized through compulsory mechanisms and made it possible for the state banks to issue financing for a total of $1.256 billion during the seven years Batista's government was in charge. These funds, which were primarily directed toward nonproductive categories, supported consumption within a context of sharp price increases for imported goods, which caused the balance of payments to deteriorate even further and led to the virtual depletion of foreign currency reserves, which fell from $532.0 million in 1951 to barely $77.4 million in 1958.

As a result of economic processes and behaviors that were not only incompatible but even contradictory between 1925 and 1958, the gross national product grew at an annual rate of little more than 1 percent, providing a prime example of the difficulties standing in the way of a new development path for the Cuban economy.

BIBLIOGRAPHY

Alienes Urosa, Julián. *Características fundamentales de la economía cubana*. Havana: Banco Nacional de Cuba, 1953.

Collazo Pérez, Enrique. *Cuba: Banca y crédito*. Havana: Editorial de Ciencias Sociales, 1989.

Cuban Economic Research Project. *A Study on Cuba*. Coral Gables, FL: University of Miami Press, 1965.

Jenks, Leland H. *Our Cuban Colony: A Study in Sugar*. New York: Vanguard Press, 1928.

Jiménez, Guillermo. *Las empresas en Cuba, 1958*. Havana: Editorial de Ciencias Sociales, 2005.

Ibarra Cuesta, Jorge. *Cuba, 1898–1958: Estructura y procesos sociales*. Havana: Editorial de Ciencias Sociales, 1995.

Le Riverend, Julio. *Historia económica de Cuba*. Havana: Instituto del Libro, 1967.

Márquez Dolz, María A. *Estado y economía en la antesala de la Revolución,1940–1952*. Havana: Editorial de Ciencias Sociales, 1994.

Mesa-Lago, Carmelo. *The Labor Force, Employment, Unemployment, and Underemployment in Cuba: 1899–1970*. Beverly Hills, CA: Sage Publications, 1972.

Pérez-López, Jorge. "An Index of Cuban Industrial Output, 1930–1958." In *Quantitative Latin American Studies: Methods and Findings*, edited by James W. Wilkie and Kenneth Riddle. Los Angeles: UCLA Latin American Center Publications, 1977.

U.S. Department of Commerce, Bureau of Foreign Commerce. *Investment in Cuba: Basic Information for United States Businessmen*. Washington, DC: U.S. Department of Commerce, 1956.

Zanetti Lecuona, Oscar. *La República: Notas sobre economía y sociedad*. Havana: Editorial de Ciencias Sociales, 2006.

ECONOMY: REVOLUTIONARY PERIOD

Archibald R. M. Ritter

Revolution, experimentation, Soviet orthodoxy, and subsidization in this transformative period in the Cuban economy from 1959 to 1990.

In the first three years of the Revolution profound institutional and policy changes were implemented, transforming the Cuban economy from a mixed market system to a centrally planned socialist system. The new system benefited lower income groups, albeit with major economic dislocations. The first development strategy, from 1961 to 1963, aimed at instant industrialization, but it proved unrealistic and was aborted. A second strategy was adopted in 1964 which aimed at a ten-million-ton sugar harvest by 1970. This approach led to the sacrifice of much of the rest of the economy and was terminated in 1970. A more balanced approach was then adopted following Soviet lines, and it produced strong results facilitated by generous Soviet economic assistance. But by 1986 this approach also was running out of steam, and stagnation set in. In response, the Rectification Program was enforced from 1986 to 1990, calling for organizational recentralization, reduced use of market mechanisms, and a reemphasis on moral incentives; again, the results were unsatisfactory. By 1990 the economic meltdown of the first half of the 1990s had begun.

Despite weak economic performance, Cuba's socioeconomic improvement was significant. Indeed, the 1970–1986 period could be called the golden age of Cuban socialism.

THE ECONOMY ON THE EVE OF REVOLUTION

By 1958 Cuba's economy appeared to be reasonably sophisticated relative to other countries in Latin America and the Caribbean. Impressionistic indicators of this assessment are the quality and quantity of Cuba's professional and artistic groups; the quality of the educational and health systems; the physical infrastructure, especially around Havana; and the urban architectural endowment of the time. Although most quantitative data for this period are lacking, available information for 1960 places Cuba as third best in Latin America and the Caribbean for child mortality and fourth best for life expectancy, a reflection of strong nutrition levels, a reasonable health system, and relative prosperity (United Nations Development Program p. 135).

Nonetheless, Cuba faced a number of economic problems, of which income inequities and poverty were the most serious. Again, though data are limited, the contrast between Havana's most opulent neighborhoods and the urban shantytowns and the earth-floor rural *bohíos* (huts) was eloquent testimony to inequalities of income and wealth. Unemployment compounded the poverty problem. During the sugar harvest and the tourist high season of January to April, unemployment normally fell to 9 to 11 percent of the labor force. In the off-season, however, the level rose to 20 or 21 percent because only a small proportion of the 400,000 to 500,000 sugar harvest workers found work for the rest of the year.

Cuba's growth record in the 1950s was mixed but unsatisfactory and insufficient to absorb the yearly increases in the labor force. Real income per capita declined from 1951 to 1954 due to lower sugar production volumes and prices, but it recovered from 1955 to 1958. On the positive side, economic diversification away from sugar in both industry and agriculture proceeded rapidly from 1949 to 1958 at a rate of 5.5 percent per year (Ritter 1974, pp. 45–47).

Finally, Cuba's economic interactions with the United States were intense. From 1955 to 1958 about 74 percent of Cuba's exports were destined for the United States, while 73 percent of its imports came from the United States (Ritter 1974, p. 51). Moreover, the all-important Cuban-U.S. sugar export market and price were controlled in Washington. U.S. enterprises were prominent in Cuba, with just over $1 billion in assets. Although there were important benefits from the U.S. business presence, there were also costs, such as profit repatriation, decision-making in the United States rather than in Cuba, and cultural impacts. Cuban nationalists viewed the asymmetric relationship with concern.

THE ECONOMY IN TRANSITION

When Fidel Castro (b. 1926) came to power in January 1959, his program for the economy was revolutionary and ambitious—if somewhat ambiguous. In his 1953 "History Will Absolve Me" statement, Castro assessed Cuba's socioeconomic failings and put forth a program to deal with income inequities, dependence on the United States, slow economic growth, and unemployment. The program included land reform, nationalization of utilities, improved tax collection, improved health and education, economic diversification, and housing. Later, in December 1956, he stated that "foreign investments will always be welcome here," and he advocated a cure for unemployment "lest it fester and become a breeding ground for Communism" (Ritter 1974, p. 66, citing Coronet). The "Manifesto of the 26th of July Revolutionary Movement," the official blueprint for the redesign of the economy drawn up by Felipe Pazos (1912–2001) and Regino Boti Leon (1923–1999), focused on income distribution, unemployment, Cubanization of ownership patterns, and higher growth rates, but it did not emphasize institutional changes, nor did it discuss the scope of Cubanization or nationalization. The original platform of the Partido Socialista Popular (PSP, Communist Party) also appeared to be moderate, though the PSP undoubtedly was well aware of the Soviet 1950s-vintage economic model. Finally, many who supported Castro in the struggle against Batista had what might be called a business-as-usual blueprint, envisioning a return to pre-Batista normalcy with a mixed market economy and a reestablishment of democracy as defined in the 1940 Constitution.

Institutional Restructuring Change began slowly in 1959 under the first post-Revolution government headed by President Manuel Urrutia (1901–1981), but it accelerated after Fidel Castro took over the presidency in July. The main reforms are listed in Table 1. Of greatest significance in this period was the first agrarian reform law, the key parts of which authorized the expropriation and redistribution of landholdings in excess of 996 acres. The land confiscated included some 480,000 acres owned by U.S. corporations (Kellner p. 58). A provision was made for compensation—thirty-year bonds, at 4 percent interest, with the amount to be based on future tax-assessed value of land—but the compensation was not paid. To administer this law, the Instituto Nacional de Reforma Agraria (INRA, National Institute of Agrarian Reform) was established, and it became the central activist organization in the Revolution, with its own militia to enforce expropriation. It also had its own industries section with Ernesto "Che" Guevara (1928–1967) as chief; in time it became the Ministry of Industries.

In 1960 a whirlwind of nationalizations took place, linked closely to the worsening relations with the United States and the trade embargo. By the end of 1960 the Cuban economy had been transformed into a state-owned economy in which central planning rather than the market mechanism was supposed to be the organizing force (see Table 2).

Meanwhile, effective reforms and expansions in education and health had been taking place. Of special note is the literacy campaign of 1961 that provided functional literacy to about 700,000 adults.

Rupture with the United States and the Embargo The U.S. embargo led to a rapid reorientation of Cuba's international trading relations. As can be seen in Table 3, the Soviet Union quickly replaced the United States as Cuba's chief trading partner, and the socialist countries dominated Cuba's export and import patterns.

Initially, the Revolution's leadership welcomed the U.S. embargo and downplayed its potential negative impacts, arguing that it would hurt the United States more than Cuba (Draper p. 144, citing Ernesto Guevara, Fidel Castro, and Blas Roca). Indeed, the socialist countries did provide a larger market for Cuban sugar than had the United States, and a development assistance program also began so that the worst effects of the embargo were averted.

Table 1

Major economic reforms, 1959–1961

Date	Reform Measure	Specific Objectives
1959 January	Creation of the "Ministry for the Recovery of Misappropriated Assets"	Confiscation of properties of Batista supporters, including 236 businesses
January–May	Elimination of foreign crime syndicates and prohibition of gambling	The Mafia departs; its properties seized by the state
March	Urban Reform Law	Reduction of urban rents, to be based on renters' income levels
April	Vacant Lot Law	Confiscation of unused urban lands
April	Establishment of the Instituto de Ahoro y Vivienda (INAV)	Promotion of housing construction
May	Establishment of the Instituto Nacional de la Industria Turística (INIT)	Promotion of tourism
May 17	First Agrarian Reform Law	Expropriation and redistribution of large estates (30% of cultivated farmland) including 480,000 acres owned by U.S. interests; numerous other components
June	Establishment of the National Institute of Agrarian Reform	Implementation of the agrarian reform; preliminary management of the state sector
July	Tax Reform Law	Rationalization of tax structure and raising revenues
November	Law permitting Ministry of Labor to expropriate firms involved in labor disputes	Takeover of 50 enterprises by March 1960
November	Oil Law, establishment of Instituto Petrolera de Cuba	Institution for managing the oil sector
1960 March	Establishment of the *Junta Central de Planificación* (JUCEPLAN)	Institution preparatory for more centralized planning
June 29	Nationalization of oil companies	
July 6	Law 851, Nationalization of U.S. Properties	Authorizing nationalization of all assets owned by U.S. citizens
	• July 21	• Nationalization of three U.S. sugar mills
	• August 6	• Nationalization of all U.S. sugar mills plus telephone and electricity companies
	• Sept. 17	• Nationalization of U.S.-owned banks
July–Sept.		Nationalization of foreign-owned enterprises
Oct. 13	Law 890	Nationalization of many Cuban-owned enterprises
Oct. 15	Urban Reform Law	Nationalization of non–owner-occupied housing and allocation to former renters under favorable terms
1961	"The Year of Education"	
January	Launch of Literacy Campaign	Objective: universal literacy by December 1961
January	Expansion and structural change in education	Establishment of universal coverage for primary school; expansion of secondary and university education
June	Law for the Nationalization of Education	Takeover of all education by the state

SOURCE: Archibald R. M. Ritter, 2011.

In reality, the embargo had serious consequences despite the socialist countries coming to the rescue. Among the harmful impacts of the embargo were the following:

- The U.S. market for traditional Cuban exports (tobacco, citrus fruit, and coffee) and for new and potential exports was closed;
- because the Cuban economy was based on machinery, equipment, and inputs that were mainly of U.S. origin, the lack of U.S. replacement parts and inputs was damaging;
- the port system, storage facilities, and internal transportation systems were based on short-haul shipping from the United States rather than long-haul ocean freighters, so major disruptions and problems occurred in these areas immediately;
- although Cuba could find substitutes for virtually all products previously imported from the United States, often these were more expensive and/or of poorer quality,

and transportation was usually more costly and time-consuming;

- the termination of U.S. tourism to Cuba was an immediate loss and one that became severe after 1980, when Cuba opened further to tourism.
- the cutoff of financial relations and trade credits with the United States and the eviction from the international financial institutions also hurt Cuba in terms of access to low-cost development loans (from the Inter-American Development Bank and the World Bank) and balance of payments support (from the International Monetary Fund); and
- by its own choice, initially Cuba cut itself off from U.S. direct foreign investment (DFI) and the benefits that accompany this, but when Cuba changed its policy toward DFI in 1982, the embargo prohibited any such inflow from the United States.

THE FIRST DEVELOPMENT STRATEGY: INSTANT INDUSTRIALIZATION, 1961–1963

When the transition to central planning was well advanced and the Revolution's leaders for agreement with they/their began to think of how to promote the development of the economy, they were influenced by four strains of thought. They were inspired first by traditional criticism of the dependence on sugar production and the economic and social structures it engendered. In the words of Fernando Ortiz, "Cuba will never be really independent until it can free itself from the coils of colonial economy that . . . winds itself around the palm tree of our republican coat of arms converting it into the sign of the Yankee dollar" (p. 65). The implication of this view was to diversify out of sugar. Second, the conventional wisdom in Latin America at the time, coming especially from the United Nations Economic Commission for Latin America, was that there was no future for developing countries in primary commodity production because of declining prices vis-à-vis manufactures, which implied that they should industrialize behind protectionist barriers. Third, the Soviet and East European development approaches emphasized not agriculture but industry, along with relative economic autarchy. Fourth, the strategic bias against sugar was strengthened by low sugar prices and some uncertainties regarding future markets, notwithstanding the socialist countries' pledge to purchase 4.86 million tons per year from 1962 to 1965. Finally, the economic inexperience of the Revolution's leaders was an important factor in the decision to promote rapid industrialization. Ernesto Guevara's economic naïveté was illustrated by his euphoric projection of a 12 percent growth rate from 1962 to 1965 and prediction

State ownership shares in the Cuban economy, 1959–1988
(IN PERCENT)

Sector	1959	1961	1968	1988
Agriculture	0	37	74	97
Industry	0	85	100	100
Construction	10–20	80	100	100
Transportation	15–29	92	98	99
Retail trade	0	52	100	100
Wholesale trade	5–10	100	100	100
Banking	5–10	100	100	100
Education	80	100	100	100

SOURCE: Mesa-Lago, Carmelo, Alberto Arenas de Mesa, Ivan Brenes, et al. *Market Socialist and Mixed Economies: Comparative Policy and Performance—Chile, Cuba, and Costa Rica*. Baltimore, MD: Johns Hopkins University Press, 2000, p. 347.

Table 2

that Cuba would be the most industrialized country in Latin America by 1965 (Guevara in Gerassi p. 172).

Though the goal was rapid industrialization, the first directive of the strategy was to assure a high level of sugar production. Elimination of food supply problems and queuing—aiming at ultimate food self-sufficiency—was a second priority. Most important was industrial transformation, with the installation of a wide range of import-substituting industries such as metallurgy, heavy engineering and machinery, chemical products, transport equipment, and even automobile assembly. This was to be achieved not by reduced consumption but by a major investment effort financed by profits no longer being expatriated, foreign exchange earnings from sugar, and Eastern European credits of 357 million pesos. Human efforts were to be mobilized through some participation in planning processes and through socialist emulation.

The strategy failed. The sugar harvest fell from 6.7 million tons in 1961 to 3.8 million tons in 1963, reducing foreign exchange earnings and generating a balance of payments crisis. At the same time, the industrialization program proved unviable because it was import-intensive, requiring imported machinery and equipment, raw materials, intermediate goods, managerial personnel, and repair and maintenance equipment. The record on agricultural diversification is unclear, but by no means robust. The end result was that Cuba became more dependent than ever on sugar exports, on imported inputs of many kinds, and on a new hegemonic partner, the Soviet Union.

Table 3

Cuba's main trade partners, 1955–1990
(TOTAL VALUE IN CURRENT U.S. DOLLARS AND PERCENTAGES OF TOTAL)

Major Sources of Cuba's Merchandise Imports	1955–1958	1960	1965	1970	1975	1980	1985	1990
TOTAL: Millions of U.S. Dollars	692.0	638.0	866.2	1,300.5	3,113.1	4,627.0	7,983.2	7,416.5
Socialist countries (%) of which:	0.3	18.7	76.0	69.4	51.4	78.0	83.7	–
China	0.0	0.2	14.2	5.5	2.8	2.3	2.9	4.5
Soviet Union	0.0	13.8	49.5	52.8	40.2	62.8	71.8	69.0
Rest of the world (%) of which:	99.3	81.3	24.0	30.6	48.5	22.0	16.3	–
Japan	0.6	1.6	0.5	2.4	11.6	3.9	2.7	0.6
Spain	1.7	2.1	5.4	2.0	4.9	3.0	2.2	2.4
United Kingdom	2.7	3.6	5.8	4.5	4.1	1.7	1.3	1.0
United States	73.3	48.5	0	0	0	0	0	0

Major Destinations of Cuba's Merchandise Exports	1955–1958	1960	1965	1970	1975	1980	1985	1990
TOTAL: Millions of U.S. Dollars	700.4	618.0	690.6	1,043.4	2,952.2	3,966.7	5,983.0	5,414.9
Socialist countries (%) of which:	4.1	24.2	77.7	74.5	67.2	70.1	88.9	–
China	0.0	5.2	14.6	7.8	2.7	2.9	2.7	4.9
Soviet Union	3.8	16.7	46.7	50.7	56.3	56.8	74.9	66.4
Rest of the world (%) of which:	95.9	75.8	22.3	26.3	32.8	29.9	11.1	–
Japan	6.1	1.4	3.1	10.2	7.6	2.9	1.3	1.6
Spain	1.7	1.2	4.9	3.9	7.7	1.2	0.8	1.7
United Kingdom	4.1	1.4	1.9	3.9	0.4	0.4	0.5	0.8
United States	63.8	52.8	0	0	0	0	0	0

SOURCE: Oficina Nacional de Estadisticas, Anuario Estadístico de Cuba, La Habana, 1985, pp. 384–391, Naciones Unidas, Comisión Económica para América Latina y el Caribe (CEPAL), and La Economia Cubana, 2000 Cuadro A33 and A34.

THE TEN-MILLION-TON SUGAR STRATEGY, 1964–1970

The failure of the instant industrialization strategy led to a reassessment of Cuba's economic realities and strategic direction. The scarcity of foreign exchange was seen as the fundamental obstacle to economic improvement, in view of Cuba's need for many types of imports for investment purposes. If a central cause of the balance of payments crisis was the low sugar harvests of 1962 to 1963, the obvious solution was to increase sugar production for export. Reinforcing the decision to emphasize sugar were the high domestic value-added and relative cost advantages for Cuban sugar, the higher prices in the international sugar market in 1962 to 1963, and a guaranteed socialist bloc market for five million tons per year at a price of 6.11 cents per pound—well above the world price—from 1965 to 1970.

In these circumstances, sugar, with a production target of ten million tons per year by 1970, became the leading sector designed to generate the savings and foreign exchange earnings that would fuel the economic diversification. Ambitious goals were established for other agricultural export crops, including coffee, tobacco, and citrus fruit, as well as for domestic food crops. But the overriding preoccupation became the ten-million-ton sugar goal, which was characterized by President Castro as necessary for "defending the honor, the prestige, the safety and self-confidence of the country" (9 February 1970).

In order to mobilize human energies for the tasks of the economy—especially for the ten-million-ton harvest—the earlier system based on material incentives, socialist emulation, and voluntary labor was superseded by a more radical Guevaraist approach involving the construction of what was called the

"New Man." The idea behind this was the vision of the Cuban nation as a guerrilla column single-mindedly pursuing a common objective, willingly sacrificing individual interests for the common good, with the esprit de corps, discipline, and dedication of an idealized guerrilla band. To promote this revolutionary altruism, the government used public exhortation and political education, moral incentives instead of material incentives, and proselytizing and enforcement by the party, the Committees for the Defense of the Revolution, and other mass organs of society.

The Revolutionary Offensive of 1968 constituted a further radicalization of economic policy. First, economic institutions were reshaped with the elimination of virtually all of what was left of the private sector (see Table 2). The "New Man" mobilization strategy went into high gear. Despite the close alliance with the Soviet Union and Eastern Europe, reflected in the support given to the Soviet invasion of Czechoslovakia that year, Cuba appeared to be on a Maoist type of trajectory.

In a second simultaneous experiment, a so-called budgetary system of finance was installed under which enterprises were to operate without financial responsibility or autonomy or indeed accounting, neither receiving the revenues from sales of their output nor paying for their inputs with such revenues. Without a rational structure of prices, and without knowledge of their true costs or the value of their output, neither enterprises nor the planning authorities had any idea of the genuine efficiencies of enterprises, of sectors of the economy, or of resource-use anywhere. This situation exacerbated the general problems of running a planned economy, leading to problems of bureaucratization and politicization of the economic administration, as firm managers jostled for resource allotments from the planning authorities. The result of this was pervasive irrationalities and inefficiencies. Again in President Castro's words: "What is this bottomless pit that swallows up this country's human resources, the country's wealth, the material goods that we need so badly? It's nothing but inefficiency, nonproductivity and low productivity" (7 December 1970).

If it had been implemented in a measured way, a strategy to increase sugar production and export earnings would have been reasonable. However, as 1970 approached, implementation of the ten-million-ton target became increasingly forced. Other sectors of the economy were sacrificed as labor, transport capacity, industrial inputs, energy, raw materials, and national attention all focused on sugar. Moreover, a variety of difficulties unique to sugar cultivation and milling also obstructed the achievement of the ten-million-ton target, although a respectable harvest of 8.5 million tons was reached in 1970 following the uneven trajectory earlier in the decade (see Chart 1).

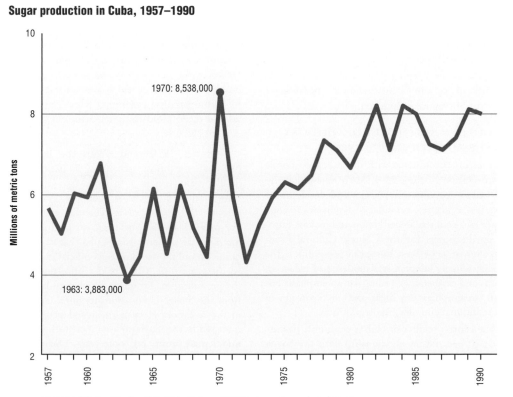

Sugar production in Cuba, 1957–1990

1970: 8,538,000

1963: 3,883,000

Millions of metric tons

SOURCE: Oficina Nacional de Estadísticas (ONE), *Anuario*, various issues.

Chart 1

Chart 2

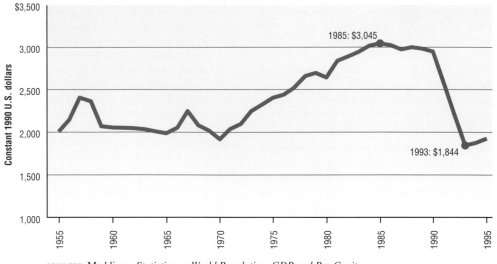

Cuba's gross domestic product per capita, 1955–1995

1985: $3,045

1993: $1,844

SOURCES: Maddison, *Statistics on World Population, GDP and Per Capita.*

The production record in other areas of agriculture was mixed from 1964 to 1970, with many crops (notably vegetables and tropical fruit, milk, coffee, and cotton) declining to below the 1958 levels, and only a few (rice and eggs) surpassing the earlier levels. The picture was also mixed in industry. In aggregate, the volume of output in per capita terms probably declined in 1970—as indicated in Chart 2—despite the record high sugar harvest of 1970.

Perhaps the best summation of the 1964 to 1970 experience came from President Castro himself: "We have cost the people too much in our process of learning. . . . The learning process of revolutionaries in the field of economic construction is more difficult than we had imagined" (26 July 1970).

THE GOLDEN AGE: SOVIET ORTHODOXY AND SUBSIDIZATION, 1970–1985

The problems encountered with the radical economic experimentation of the 1960s led to renewed analysis of Cuba's geoeconomic realities and development alternatives. The obvious course of action was to copy the approaches of the Soviet Union and its East European satellites, rejecting the Chinese Cultural Revolution alternative or West European possibilities. The approach actually adopted was modest and balanced, cautious and deliberative, calling for an emphasis but not an overemphasis on sugar and an expansion of other traditional and new export products.

The central feature of Cuba's economic destiny after 1970 became the relationship with the Soviet Union. Cuba joined the Council for Mutual Economic Assistance (CMEA) in 1972, and its pattern and financing of development became deeply intertwined with the Soviet bloc economies. A variety

of trade, finance, and development aid agreements covered the 1970–1990 period, as summarized in Table 4. The generosity toward Cuba in these agreements was impressive, the payoff being Cuba's support in Soviet international relations, including military interventions in Africa and in the Soviet vision of the future.

The system of economic direction and planning (SPDE) was introduced in 1976, but by 1980 it had been only partly established. Included in the SPDE was an aspiration for self-financing by enterprises and a rational structure of prices for inputs and outputs. However, the new system was subject to a variety of problems, not least of which was its voracious appetite for administrative personnel, which increased from 90,000 to 250,000 from 1973 to 1985 (Mesa-Lago et al. p. 232).

In the 1970s and 1980s the Soviet Union provided the most generous, if partly obscured, development assistance to Cuba (see Chart 3). This subsidization of the Cuban economy occurred mainly through the pricing of merchandise trade products. For many years the Soviet Union paid a ruble price for its sugar imports from Cuba that was a multiple of the prevailing world price at official exchange rates. At the same time, Cuba paid a price that was below the prevailing market price for its petroleum imports from the Soviet Union. Furthermore, Cuba engaged in the re-export of both sugar and petroleum in its trade with the Soviet Union, capturing significant middleman profits for some years. Quantitative estimates place the value of this subsidization at around 23 percent to over 36 percent of national income in the 1980–1987 period, or somewhat less if the overpricing and lower quality of enforced bilateral trade

Major Soviet Union–Cuba economic agreements, 1970–1985

Table 4

Date of Agreement	Period Covered	General Area of Agreement	Main Provisions or Purposes
1972	1972 Onwards	Establishment of Intergovernmental Commission for Economic and Scientific-Technical Cooperation	Economic coordination
1972	1972 Onwards	Membership in Council for Mutual Economic Assistance	Coordinate trade, financial and technical relations with Soviet Bloc
December 1972	1973–75	**Five Soviet–Cuban Accords:** 1. Debt postponement (from trade defecits) 2. 1973–1975 Trade credits 3. Development loan 4. Export subsidies	1. 1960–1972 debt payments postponed interest free, grace period to 1986, 25-year repayment period 2. Same terms as above 3. $362 million for sugar, nickel, textiles 4. Subsidized prices for Cuban sugar and nickel exports to the U.S.S.R.
1976	1976–80	**First Soviet–Cuba Five Year Plan** 1. Continuation of subsidized export prices 2. Development assistance of 1.5 billion U.S. dollars	1. Sugar and nickel exports favored 2. For nuclear power plant and steel mill
1981	1981–90	**Ten Year CMEA Program** 1. Economic development loans of 870 million U.S. dollars 2. Further development credits of 1.8 billion U.S. dollars	1. Low-interest loans for sugar, nickel, nuclear and themal power generation 2. For four new sugar mills and other export sectors
1981	1981–85	**Second Five Year Agreement** 1. Fixed export prices 2. Credits to cover trade deficits	
1984	1985–90	**Long-Term Cooperation Agreement** 1. Strengthen Cuba's integration into CMEA	1. Establishing CMEA joint ventures, promotion of exports to CMEA countries

SOURCE: Mesa-Lago, Carmelo, Alberto Arenas de Mesa, Ivan Brenes, et al. *Market Socialist and Mixed Economies: Comparative Policy and Performance—Chile, Cuba, and Costa Rica.* Baltimore, MD: Johns Hopkins University Press, 2000, pp. 241-244.

with the Soviet Union is taken into account (Ritter 1990, pp. 126 127).

Over and above the subsidization through the pricing of traded goods was the buildup of Cuba's bilateral debt to the Soviet Union, amounting to about US$23.5 billion by 1990. This debt, which will never be repaid, reflected the recurring trade deficits of Cuba with the Soviet Union, as well as the capital account credits provided by the Soviet Union. There were also additional bilateral debts representing recurrent trade deficits with some of Cuba's East European trading partners. Furthermore, there were military credits of an indeterminate magnitude, as well as rental payments for military facilities such as the Lourdes radar base and all of the expenditures of Soviet military procurement and personnel in Cuba. The dramatic escalation of Soviet assistance to Cuba—excluding military assistance—is illustrated in Chart 3. Cuba's development was also financed by borrowing from western countries during this period. Cuba's convertible currency debt increased from US$291 million in 1969 to US$6.45 billion in 1988, with interest on

the debt exceeding 29 percent of convertible currency export earnings (Ritter 1990, p. 138).

THE RECTIFICATION PROCESS, 1986–1990

In April 1986, at the Third Party Congress of the Communist Party, President Castro initiated the Rectification Process (RP), which was intended to correct mistakes he perceived had occurred over the previous fifteen years. Although the real motivation for the RP is not clear, it is perhaps the case that after a decade of improvement, Castro felt that a return to a purer socialism would be possible. Or perhaps he felt that the Soviet-style approach had led to worsening corruption, economic inequalities, and a regression from the ultimate objectives he envisaged for Cuban society.

The RP policies included a shutdown of the farmers' markets and a tightening of restrictions on self-employment, which declined from 1.2 percent of total employment to 0.7 percent by 1990. Further restrictions were placed on private agriculture (see Table 5).

Chart 3

Economic assistance from the Soviet Union to Cuba, 1960–1990

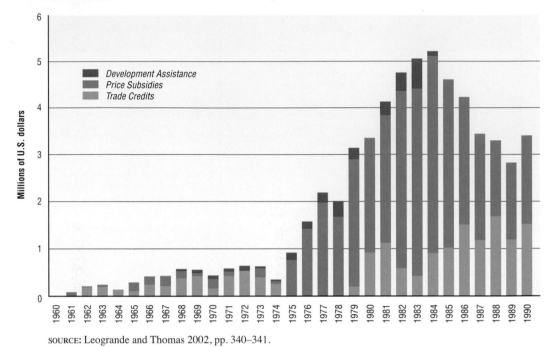

SOURCE: Leogrande and Thomas 2002, pp. 340–341.

Distribution of labor force by institutional forms

	1970	1979	1981	1985	1989
State sector	86.3	93.6	93.4	93.1	94.1
Non-state	13.7	6.4	6.6	6.9	5.9
• Agricultural co-ops	0	0	0	2.1	1.6
• Private farmers	11.0	4.9	3.5	3.2	3.2
• Private salaried	1.5	0.4	0.7	0.4	0.4
• Self-employed and family workers	1.2	1.1	1.5	1.2	0.7
Total	100.0	100.0	100.0	100.0	100.0

SOURCE: Mesa-Lago, Carmelo, Alberto Arenas de Mesa, Ivan Brenes, et al. *Market Socialist and Mixed Economies: Comparative Policy and Performance—Chile, Cuba, and Costa Rica.* Baltimore, MD: Johns Hopkins University Press, 2000, p. 382.

Table 5

Attempts to modify the Soviet-type planning system (SPDE) were in varying stages of implementation by 1990. The basic development strategy continued to emphasize sugar as the main source of foreign exchange, and good harvests continued to be achieved throughout the period (see Chart 1). There was a major push into biotechnology and pharmaceuticals for domestic consumption and export with a massive investment in state-of-the-art research facilities. Priority was given to tourism and to nickel for expanded foreign exchange earnings. A food program was begun in 1986, aiming at sugar harvests of eleven million tons, plus increased citrus fruit for export and increased production of foodstuffs for domestic use, and with grandiose and unrealistic targets for irrigated acreage for rice and sugar, new cattle development centers, new dairies, and so on—all objectives that remained unfulfilled (Mesa-Lago et al. pp. 272–274). A government attempt to target workplace corruption and theft met limited success.

The labor sector continued to be problematic during the RP. Castro again emphasized the importance of moral incentives and criticized material incentives, yet material compensation was given to the military-style brigades that were established for the construction sector as a means of absorbing the surplus labor in enterprises. Part of the problem here was that to avoid rising unemployment, large numbers of low-productivity jobs had been created to absorb the huge cohorts of young people from the baby-boom years who were entering the job market for the first time.

It is hard to judge the economic success of the RP because the development assistance from the Soviet Union began to diminish in 1985, which affected the overall growth rate and stagnated after 1985 (see Chart 2).

SOCIOECONOMIC PERFORMANCE

In general, the performance of the Cuban economy in the 1959–1990 period was problematic and mixed, though income levels by 1990 exceeded pre-Revolution levels. Major improvements had been made in terms of socioeconomic well-being, and most social indicators had improved. The summary of changes in a few key socioeconomic indicators in Table 6 illustrates the absolute and relative improvements achieved in human well-being. Life expectancy and infant and child mortality are summary indications of nutrition, income distribution and poverty, and the quality of a nation's healthcare system. Literacy and educational attainment are key factors in the investment in human capital and in citizen empowerment in a modern economy.

Cuba's ranking for these indicators was strong already in 1960, and, despite improvements in these in the rest of Latin America, Cuba raised its ranking for all five of the socioeconomic indicators vis-à-vis the rest of Latin America (excluding the English-speaking Caribbean). However, Cuba's economic ranking—in terms of the purchasing power of GDP per person—fell well down the list in 1990, placing Cuba fourteenth in Latin America. As a result, Cuba rated 0.711 in the UNDP Human Development Index.

By 1990 the breakup of the Soviet Union and the collapse of communism in Eastern Europe terminated Cuba's special relationship with the Soviet Union and the accompanying subsidization. Cuba's economic meltdown of the early 1990s had begun.

Cuban socioeconomic indicators in comparative perspective

Indicator	1960	1990
Life expectancy at birth (years)	63.8	75.4
Rank in Latin America	#4	#1
Child mortality (under five years), per 1,000 live births	87	17
Rank in Latin America	#3	#2
Infant mortality (under one year), per 1,000 live births	65	14
Rank in Latin America	#3	#1
Adult literacy	(1970) 87	95
Rank in Latin America	#5	#2
Combined primary and secondary school enrollments	(1970) 76	95
Rank in Latin America	#5	#2
Real GDP per capita (purchasing power parity terms)	n.a.	$2,200
Rank in Latin America	n.a.	#14
Human Development Index (HDI)	n.a.	0.711
Rank in Latin America	n.a.	#10
Rank in the world	n.a.	#75

SOURCES: United Nations Development Program (UNDP) 1990, p. 133; UNDP 1992, pp. 135–136.

Table 6

BIBLIOGRAPHY
Primary Sources

Boti Leon, Regino, and Felipe Pazos. "Tesis del Movimiento Revolucionario 26 de Julio." *Revista Bimestre Cubana* (July–December 1958).

Castro, Fidel. "History Will Absolve Me." 16 October 1953. Havana: Editorial de Ciencias Sociales, 1975.

Castro, Fidel. Speech of 9 February 1970. *Granma Weekly Review* (15 February 1970).

Castro, Fidel. Speech of 26 July 1970. *Granma Weekly Review* (9 August 1970).

Castro, Fidel. Speech of 7 December 1970. *Granma Weekly Review* (20 December 1970).

Guevara, Ernesto. "On Growth and Imperialism." In *Venceremos: Speeches and Writings of Che Guevara*, edited by John Gerassi. New York: Macmillan, 1968.

Secondary Sources

Comisión Económica para América Latina y el Caribe (CEPAL). *La Economia Cubana, 2000*. Santiago, Chile: Author, 2000.

Draper, Theodore. *Castroism: Theory and Practice*. New York: Praeger Publishers, 1965.

Kellner, Douglas. *Ernesto "Che" Guevara*. New York: Chelsea House Publishers, 1989.

Leogrande, William M., and Julie M. Thomas. "Cuba's Quest for Economic Independence." *Journal of Latin American Studies* 34 (May 2002): 325–363.

Maddison, Angus. *Statistics on World Population, GDP and Per Capita*. Available from http://www.ggdc.net/MADDISON/oriindex.htm.

Mesa-Lago, Carmelo, Alberto Arenas de Mesa, Ivan Brenes, et al. *Market Socialist and Mixed Economies: Comparative Policy and Performance—Chile, Cuba, and Costa Rica*. Baltimore: Johns Hopkins University Press, 2000.

Oficina Nacional de Estadísticas (ONE). *Anuario Estadístico de Cuba*. Havana: Author, 1985.

Ortiz, Fernando. *Cuban Counterpoint: Tobacco and Sugar*. New York: Random House, 1970.

Ritter, Archibald R. M. *The Economic Development of Revolutionary Cuba: Strategy and Performance*. New York: Praeger Publishers, 1974.

Ritter, Archibald R. M. "The Cuban Economy in the 1990s: External Challenges and Policy Imperatives." *Journal of Interamerican Studies and World Affairs* 32, no. 3 (Autumn 1990): 117–149.

United Nations Development Program (UNDP). *Human Development Report*. Various issues, 1990–1992. New York: Oxford University Press, 1991–1992.

ECONOMY: SPECIAL PERIOD

Archibald R. M. Ritter

Cuba's economic struggles following the end of Soviet subsidization.

From 1990 to 1994, Cuba endured an economic meltdown that resulted mainly from the 75 to 80 percent decline in foreign exchange receipts accompanying the ending of the subsidies from the former Soviet Union (provided through the pricing of imports and exports, credits financing trade deficits, and development aid). Cuba's foreign exchange earnings shrank and imports of consumer goods, energy, raw materials, foodstuffs, and replacement parts and machinery fell sharply, asphyxiating economic activity.

Other factors contributed to the crisis as well. Cuba's export structure had evolved little since 1959, and it remained dependent on sugar for 77 percent of total exports in 1990 (see Chart 1). Cuba lacked access to foreign credit, having declared a moratorium on debt servicing in 1986 and having been excluded from international financial institutions. Its economic system was rigid due to so-called demarketization, centralization, and the suppression of entrepreneurship, which the 1986–1990 Rectification Process did not help. Finally, the U.S. trade embargo was hardened with the 1992 Torricelli Act and the 1996 Helms-Burton Act.

The Cuban economy contracted 34 percent in income per capita from 1990 to 1993 (see Chart 2). The foreign exchange shortage caused a reduction in transportation services and electricity generation, with consequent power blackouts and shutdowns of industry. Domestic food production declined due to

reduced imports of fertilizer, energy, and replacement parts. Levels of savings collapsed to 2.6 percent of GDP, and gross investment fell to 5.8 percent of GDP in 1993. Economic contraction led to reduced tax revenues, increased fiscal deficits, accelerated money creation, and an inflationary spiral. The result was a monetary crisis in which the real purchasing power of the peso declined precipitously, increasing the demand for U.S. dollars and generating a process of so-called dollarization of the economy. Rapid inflation reduced the real purchasing power of budgets in education, public health, and the public sector generally. The real value of average incomes declined catastrophically (see Chart 3).

Citizens responded to the decline in living standards by pursuing self-employment activities, (most of which were illegal at the time), resorting to black-market activities and exchanges, and finding any other means to acquire the U.S. dollars that were vital for survival.

POLICY RESPONSE TO THE ECONOMIC CRISIS

In the face of the crisis, Cuba's leadership in 1990 announced the Special Period in Time of Peace, an era that lasted through to 2010. As the contraction intensified, a range of pro-market policies were adopted (see Table 1).

The reforms also included a reestablishment of fiscal balance with consequent reductions in money creation and inflation, reduced subsidies to enterprises, changes in the structure of the taxation system, state enterprise management modifications, and reductions in military expenditures.

From about 1996 to 2005, few significant reforms were forthcoming. Public policy was designed to contain, if not reduce, the self-employment sector and to freeze any further pro-market initiatives. The leadership and the media were generally hostile to the market-oriented reforms. In a speech in 1997, President Fidel Castro (b. 1926) lamented the pro-market policy moves and implied that they were temporary only—possibly only for the expected duration of the Special Period:

> And thus it was with many things that I'm not going to repeat: commerce, market-determined prices in certain sectors, for certain activities: a proliferation of self-employment. . . . And these are the opinions we have had about these things over the years, never imagining that we would have to learn to live with them for a period of time that is very difficult to predict.
>
> *Castro 1997, p. 8*

Then in 2004, 40 of the 151 varieties of legal self-employment were eliminated for new entrants, though established *cuenta-propistas* (own-account or

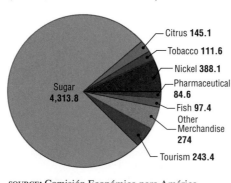

Cuban exports by product shares, 1990
(TOTAL: 5,658 MILLION CUBAN PESOS)

Sugar 4,313.8
Citrus 145.1
Tobacco 111.6
Nickel 388.1
Pharmaceutical 84.6
Fish 97.4
Other Merchandise 274
Tourism 243.4

SOURCE: Comisión Económica para América Latina y el Caribe (CEPAL) 2000, Table A, p. 38.

Chart 1

GDP per capita, 1989–2009
BASE YEAR 1989 = 100.0

Chart 2

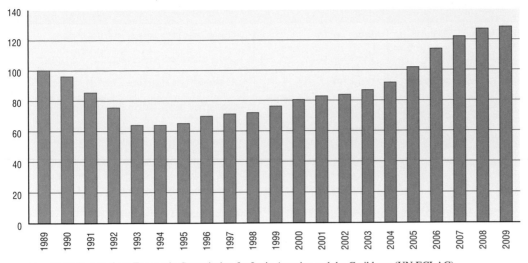

SOURCE: United Nations Economic Commission for Latin America and the Caribbean (UN ECLAC).

Real inflation-adjusted wages, 1989–2009
(IN CUBAN PESOS)

Chart 3

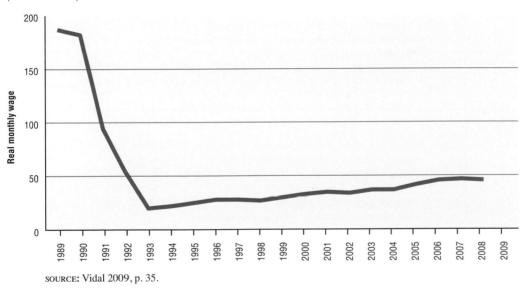

SOURCE: Vidal 2009, p. 35.

self-employed workers) in these areas could continue—if they were able to renew their licenses and avoid infractions.

ECONOMIC MANAGEMENT UNDER RAÚL CASTRO

When Raúl Castro became acting president in July 2006, expectations for reform were heightened by the removal of some irritants to the population, such as denial of the use of hotels and their facilities. Raúl Castro presented critical analyses of work incentives, wage and salary structures and levels, the rationing system, the dual monetary system, and agricultural shortcomings.

The policy changes introduced from 2006 to 2010 are summarized in Table 2. Other policy modifications involved minor step-by-step moves toward greater reliance on small enterprise operating under markets. Two reforms were ambitious, namely the leasing of land to small farmers and the downsizing of the state sector and expansion of small enterprise in 2010.

Table 1

"Promarket" economic reforms, 1993–1997

Date	Legislation	Description
August 13, 1993	Decree-Law 140	Depenalization of the possession of U.S. dollars
September 8, 1993	Decree-Law 141	Liberalization of self-employment
September 19, 1993	Decree 191	Re-establishment of agricultural markets
December 21, 1994	Mining Law	Updating and modification of mining legislation
September 5, 1995	Foreign Investment Law	Updating and liberalization of laws regarding direct foreign investment
October 21, 1995	Decree 192	Establishment of artisanal and industrial product markets
June 3, 1996	Decree-Law 165	Law on export processing zones
May 15, 1997	Decree-Law 172	Law on renting housing or rooms

SOURCE: Comisión Económica para América Latina y el Caribe (CEPAL) 1997, Anexo Legal.

Table 2

Economic reform measures under President Raúl Castro, July 2006–October 2010

Year	Measure
2006	• Permission for Cuban citizens to use tourist hotel facilities • Permission to acquire personal cellular phone contracts • Permission to rent cars previously reserved for foreigners • Relaxation of rules regarding purchase of computers, DVD players, etc. • Resolution on Regulations for Labor Discipline
2007	• Legalization of hard-currency salary supplements to Cuban employees of foreign joint ventures
2008	• Decree-Law No. 259, Long-term leases of unused state land by small farmers • Decree-Law No. 260, Financial incentives to attract teachers back to their profession
2009	• Replacement of Fidel Castro's economic team and resignation of the president of the Central Bank • Proposal to reduce subsidization of rationed products • Replacement of workers' dining facilities with an income increase
2010	• Relaxation of restrictions on private taxis • Experiment with cooperative hair dressing salons and barber shops • Markets for inputs for small farmers • Raising of pension ages from 55 to 60 for women and from 60 to 65 for men • Liberalization of sale of building materials to citizens • Legalization of 99-year leasing of land to foreign tourist companies (Law-Decree 273, Articles 221 and 222.1 (August 13) • Announcement of layoffs of 500,000 state sector workers to be incorporated into self-employment and cooperatives (September 13) • Softening of some regulations for self-employment, plus a 40% tax on gross revenues

SOURCE: Archibald R. M. Ritter, 2011.

ECONOMIC PERFORMANCE: THE EXTERNAL SECTOR

With the termination of Soviet subsidization, Cuba's trade partners shifted from the Soviet Union to the rest of Europe and Latin America. Cuba's geopolitical reality changed again in the 2000s, when Venezuela became the principal trade partner, followed by China. President Hugo Chávez provided support for Cuba through low-cost oil exports, trade and investment credits, and generous foreign exchange payments for Cuban exports of medical services. China became an important source of credit and imports for Cuba.

A central economic constraint during the Special Period was the shortage of foreign exchange. Total exports increased in the 2000s, but merchandise exports actually declined (from CUP5.6 billion [USD6.05 billion] in 1990 to CUP2.4 billion [USD2.59 billion] in 2008), owing partly to the collapse of sugar exports. Merchandise exports did become more diversified—due to the decline of sugar and the expansion of nickel, tobacco products, and pharmaceutical exports. Tourism expanded rapidly over the two decades. Medical and educational service exports expanded quickly in the 2000s, becoming the predominant source of foreign exchange, paid for mainly by Venezuela (see Charts 1 and 4). Family remittances from the Cuban diaspora were a growing source of foreign exchange for Cuba, reaching an estimated USD759 million in 2002 (Barberia 2004, p. 368.)

In 1988 Cuba opened up to foreign direct investment (FDI) in the form of joint ventures with state enterprises. FDI inflows cumulated to USD1.9 billion by 2000 (Pérez-López 2004, p. 151), originating mainly from Spain (tourism and tobacco), Canada (nickel, petroleum extraction), Italy (communications), France (alcoholic beverages), and Mexico.

After having declared a moratorium on its debt servicing in 1986, Cuba lost access to credit in convertible currency—a serious difficulty when the meltdown occurred because Cuba was not a member of international financial institutions. Its convertible currency debt remained fairly constant, but increased in the late 2000s. The debt to Russia as of 1990 amounted to about US$23.5 billion, though Cuba considered it to be zero and not an issue (Ritter 1990).

ECONOMIC PERFORMANCE: THE DOMESTIC ECONOMY, 1994–2000

The reform measures of 1993 to 1995 contributed to an economic upturn by 1995, with recovery accelerating in the mid-2000s (see Chart 2). In 2009, the international recession hit Cuba, transmitted through declining nickel prices, a tourism slowdown, reduced remittances, and reduced subsidization from Venezuela.

Although the Cuban economy surpassed the levels of 1990, the real value of wages in Cuba remained at around 20 percent of the 1989 level (see Chart 3). One possible explanation for this paradox was that Cuba's GDP statistics were dubious: The Oficina Nacional de Estadísticas (ONE) adopted a new approach to measuring GDP and increased the value of so-called government consumption by 76.6 percent—for health, mainly (ONE 2006, Table 2.1.2.30). A second partial explanation is that large portions of the goods and services produced in the economy were pilfered and distributed through the underground economy so that the reduced official revenues did not permit higher wage payments. By 2008, the service sector constituted 64.8 percent of Cuba's GDP (see Chart 5). This reflected the difficulties of increasing production in agriculture and

Cuban exports by product shares, 2008
(TOTAL: 12,506 MILLION CUBAN PESOS)

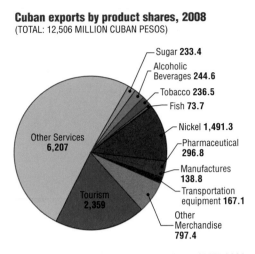

SOURCE: Oficina Nacional de Estadísticas (ONE) 2009, Tables 8.12 and 5.16.

Chart 4

Structure of production in the Cuban economy, 2008
(PERCENTAGE OF TOTAL GDP)

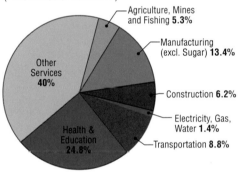

SOURCE: Oficina Nacional de Estadísticas (ONE) 2009, Table 5.7.

Chart 5

manufacturing, as well as the growth of services and changes in their measurement.

Food production was problematic during the Special Period. The downsizing of the sugar sector resulted in large amounts of idled land returning to *marabú*, a noxious weed. The output of food crops fluctuated but did not increase significantly over the twenty-year period, but one bright spot was urban agriculture. Cuba became a major food net importer by 2007 after having been a huge food net exporter in 1990 (see Chart 6).

The passage in 2008 of Decree-Law No. 259, by which long-term leases of unused state land could be granted to small farmers, was envisioned as an important step toward the establishment of a productive agricultural sector. By the middle of 2010, more than 2,273,000 acres (920,000 ha) had been distributed to approximately 100,000 small farmers, though about half the areas were still idle (Hagelburg p. 2).

Chart 6

Cuban exports and imports of foodstuffs, 1989–2008
(EXCLUDING TOBACCO AND ALCOHOLIC BEVERAGES)

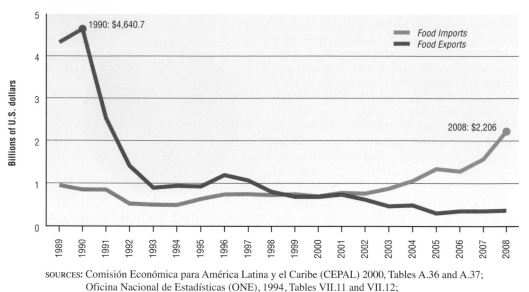

SOURCES: Comisión Económica para América Latina y el Caribe (CEPAL) 2000, Tables A.36 and A.37;
Oficina Nacional de Estadísticas (ONE), 1994, Tables VII.11 and VII.12;
and 2009, Tables 8.12 and 8.13.

The production of sugar, once Cuba's chief product and export, fell sharply to 1.2 million tons in 2010 (see Chart 7). The decline in the 1990s resulted from insufficient reinvestment and the shortage of imported inputs. In 2002, President Fidel Castro shut down 45 percent of the sugar mills and proposed the diversion of sugarcane acreage to other crops. Despite a 2006 program aimed at tripling production, output continued to decline, due mainly to hurricane damages in some years, inappropriate wage incentive levels and structures for eliciting the necessary efforts from workers, breakdowns in old sugar mills, and managerial problems.

Manufacturing output fell after 1989, largely as a result of foreign exchange shortages (see Chart 8). Output for key products such as cement, steel, shoes, and clothing all declined in the 1990–1993 meltdown and did not recuperate in the years of general recovery. During the Special Period, Cuba underwent a partial deindustrialization similar to that of many higher income countries, increasing its imports of manufactured products, most notably from China.

Nickel production increased from 47,000 tons in 1989 to a peak of 76,000 tons in 2005, thanks in part to the joint venture with the Canadian energy company Sherritt International. High nickel prices from 2005 to 2008 provided Cuba with a foreign exchange bonanza. Oil extraction increased from 718 to 2,900 thousand metric tons from 1989 to 2007, supplying about 35 percent of domestic demand by 2007. Natural gas extraction increased from 34 to 1,215 million cubic meters in the same period (Mesa-Lago 2008, p. 5x). These increases also were due largely to Sherritt International, which introduced new extraction technologies and captured the natural gas—previously flared—for thermal electric production and domestic use.

From 1990 to 2006, Cuba was plagued with electrical blackouts. To deal with this problem, in 2006 Castro presented the Revolución Energética, a program for restructuring and reinvesting in the electricity sector that included conservation measures, increased investment in repair and maintenance, new generating capacity in small-sized generators, backup diesel generators, and alternate energy projects. Excluded were the completion of the Cienfuegos nuclear generating plant and coordination with the sugar sector for ethanol production.

CONTINUING PROBLEM AREAS DURING THE SPECIAL PERIOD

When inflation accelerated between 1990 and 1994, Cuban citizens protected themselves by holding U.S. dollars. After the July 1993 legalization of using U.S. dollars, the U.S. currency acquired official status because many goods were available only in dollar stores and some taxes were payable only in dollars. The U.S. dollar was then replaced by the convertible peso (CUC) in 2002.

Citizens are paid for their work in old pesos (*moneda nacional*, MN) but somehow have to acquire dollars or convertible pesos to purchase necessary items (including some foodstuffs, toiletries, and household maintenance supplies) from dollar stores. Because a steadily diminishing number of products

Cuban sugar production, 1985–2010

Chart 7

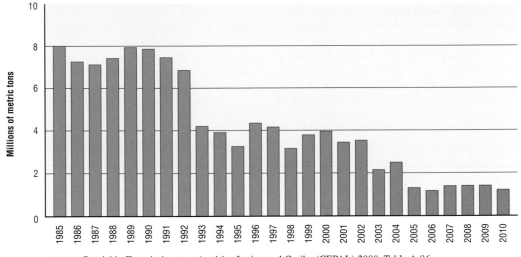

SOURCE: Comisión Económica para América Latina y el Caribe (CEPAL) 2000, Table A.86; Oficina Nacional de Estadísticas (ONE) 2004, Table IX.3, and 2009, Table 11.3.

Index of industrial output (excluding sugar), 1989–2009
(BASE YEAR 1989 = 100.0)

Chart 8

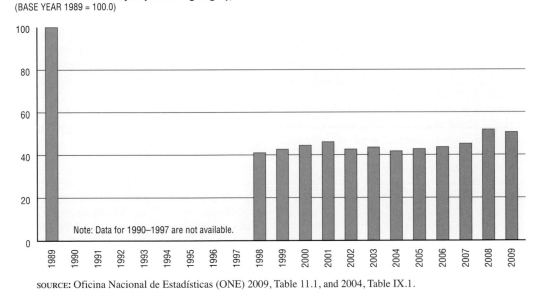

Note: Data for 1990–1997 are not available.

SOURCE: Oficina Nacional de Estadísticas (ONE) 2009, Table 11.1, and 2004, Table IX.1.

necessary for survival have been available through the rationing system for old pesos and a larger number have been channeled through the dollar stores, Cubans have had to chase dollars since the early 1990s. In other words, there has been a strong incentive for people to leave or reduce those economic activities that earn old pesos and enter or expand those that earn dollars or convertible pesos—so engineers are inclined to drive taxis and teachers to seek work in tourism, for example. Citizens with access to U.S. dollars from remittances, foreign travel, or tips from tourists generally have higher real incomes

than those without access, so another consequence of the dual monetary system has been growing income inequality.

The old peso is officially equivalent to US$1.11, but for Cuban citizens it exchanges for 25 to 26 pesos to the convertible peso (CUC), which in turn trades at 1.11 to the U.S. dollar. The value of 1.11 old pesos to the U.S. dollar is thus purely fictional, but is used for official accounting purposes. For remittances transferred in U.S. dollars—mainly from the Cuban diaspora in the United States—the government imposes an additional quasi-tax of 10 percent.

During the Special Period, Cuba continued to have the second most demarketized economy in the world (after North Korea). Though legalized in September 1993, self-employment was discouraged by onerous taxation, regulations, restrictive licensing, and media and political hostility. However, it generated employment and incomes, provided goods and services, paid taxes, utilized domestic resources, and earned foreign exchange. In September 2010, an expansion of self-employment was proposed as a means of absorbing redundant labor from the state sector.

Officially, the rate of unemployment in the late 2000s was approximately 1.7 percent. But the Central de Trabajadores de Cuba (CTC, Workers' Central Union of Cuba) announced on 13 September 2010 that 500,000 redundant state sector workers were to be laid off and reincorporated into the private sector by the end of March 2011 with another 500,000 layoffs to follow (CTC 2010). This announcement implied that underemployment in the state sector was serious, though perhaps less worrisome than the 25.6 to 35.2 percent levels reached between 1990 and 1996, according to estimates of the United Nations Economic Commission for Latin America and the Caribbean (CEPAL 1997, p. 187).

Cuba's gross investment as a percentage of GDP was 8.5 percent in 2008, compared with 21.9 percent for Latin America and the Caribbean (CEPAL 2009, p. 142). Efforts were made in electrical infrastructure, tourist facilities, heritage sites, and some public facilities, though more work was urgently needed. The task of renovating and re-equipping housing, urban infrastructure, water systems, waste management, roads and streets, and the stock of vehicles was huge. Eventually, Cuba's investment effort will have to increase so that economic growth can be sustained, broad-based, and environmentally sound.

DEMOGRAPHY AND HUMAN RESOURCES

Cuba's demographic history since 1990 is summarized in Table 3 and Figure 1. The 1960 to 1970 baby-boom cohorts reached age forty to fifty during the 2000s. Since 1970, the fertility rate has declined steadily, reaching 1.5 births per woman between 2005 and 2010—below the replacement rate—leading to shrinking age cohorts below age forty as of 2010. Some consequences in the drop in birth rate are as follows:

- Cuba's total population changed little from 1990 to 2010.
- The population has aged steadily as new birth cohorts shrink.
- Population is expected to decline when the age 40 to 50 cohorts reach age 60, barring compensating changes in fertility, life expectancy, or migration.
- Cuba experienced a low total dependency ratio (that is the ratio of children and senior citizens to working population) as child dependency declined; consequently, the employed population between 20 and 60 was large, providing a stimulus to economic growth.
- Eventually, the aging population will cause the total dependency ratio to increase, burdening the economically active population for the support of pensioners and their healthcare.

SOCIOECONOMIC PERFORMANCE AND ECONOMIC PROSPECTS

Despite the economic difficulties of the 1990s, Cuba continued to improve its socioeconomic performance in relative and absolute terms, at least as these are measured by the indicators in Table 4. Cuba continued to lead the Latin American countries in infant mortality and the education indicators. In terms of GDP ranking and the UNDP's *Human Development Index*, Cuba continued to improve its performance and standing.

The improvements in education and health indicators and rankings occurred despite weakening of resource allocations and problems in maintaining quality. Cuba's success in these areas was due largely to the quality and quantity of the educational systems built up in the 1960–1990 period and institutional momentum.

In the latter half of 2010, Cuba's economic future became somewhat clearer. After a slow start, the reform process accelerated, pushed forward by the economic slowdown. The Raúl Castro government's downsizing of the state sector, with 500,000 workers to be laid off by March 2011 and reabsorbed—it was hoped—in the self-employment

Basic demographic indicators, 1990–2010

	1990–1995	2005–2010
Total population	10,600,000	11,200,000
Total fertility rate (births per woman)	1.7	1.5
Dependency rates (percent of total population)		
Child dependency	32.8	24.7
Old age dependency	12.7	17.5
Total dependency	45.5	42.2
Rate of natural increase (percent of total population)	0.8	0.4
Net international migration (percent of total population)	-0.2	-0.3

SOURCE: United Nations Development Program (UNDP) 2009, Table L.

Table 3

Cuba's population pyramid, 2010

Figure 1

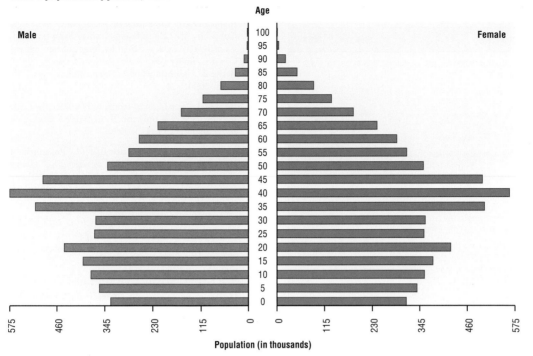

SOURCE: U.S. Census Bureau, 2010.

International economic indicators, 1991–2009
(MILLIONS OF CURRENT U.S. DOLLARS)

Table 4

	1991	1995	2000	2005	2008	2009
INTERNATIONAL TRADE						
Exports: Total	3,563	2,926	4,807	8,963	12,506	
Goods	2,980	1,507	1,692	2,412	3,940	2,458
Services	584	1,419	3,115	6,550	8,506	
Imports: Total	4,702	3,565	5,587	7,823	14,806	
Goods	4,234	2,883	4,816	7,647	14,312	8,963
Services	468	683	771	175	494	
Commercial balance	-1,138	-639	-780	1,140	-2,280	
Remittances		646	740			
DIRECT FOREIGN INVESTMENT						
Cumulative value of DFI		622.10	1,930.90			
Joint ventures (Number)	50	22	392			
Tourism earnings	**243.50**	**1,100.00**	**1,948.30**	**2,398.90**	**2,359.00**	

Note: Blanks indicate that the information is not available.

SOURCE: Pérez-López 2004, p. 151; Oficina Nacional de Estadísticas (ONE) 2009, Tables 8.2 and 15.11.

and cooperative enterprise sector, was a major initiative, begun at the end of 2010. A revised microenterprise policy framework was implemented in October 2010, involving some relaxation of the regulatory structure—permitting restaurants to increase their

seating capacity from 12 to 20, for example. The tax regime was relaxed slightly. It was expected that Raúl Castro would follow a more pragmatic path than did his elder brother. However, at the end of 2010, it appeared unclear as to whether the rather

Cuban socioeconomic indicators in comparative perspective

Indicator	1990	2007
Life expectancy at birth (years)	75.4	78.5
Rank in Latin America	#1	#2
Infant mortality (under one year), per 1,000 live births	14	6
Rank in Latin America	#1	#1
Adult literacy	95	99.8
Rank in Latin America	#2	#1
Combined primary and secondary school enrollments	95	100
Rank in Latin America	#2	#1
Human Poverty Index (UNDP) rank in Latin America	n.a.	#5
Real GDP per capita (purchasing power parity terms)	$2,200	$6,876**
Rank in Latin America	#14	#11**
Human Development Index (HDI)	0.711	0.856**
Rank in Latin America	#10	#3**
Rank in the world	#75	#51**

Note (**): Cuba's GDP estimations lack comparability with the rest of the world because government services are calculated not on the basis of the costs of providing them, but on the basis of some international price, unknown at this time. This deforms the comparison of both GDP and the HDI, which gives a 33.3 percent weight the GDP per capita in purchasing power terms. In its 2010 Human Development Report, a measure of Cuba's GDP in purchasing power terms is not provided, presumably because of concern for its accuracy. This prevents reasonable comparisons with other countries, This table should be considered with this caveat in mind.

SOURCES: United Nations Development Program (UNDP) 1990, p. 133; UNDP 1992, pp. 135–136; UNDP 2009, pp. 171 and 176.

Table 5

BIBLIOGRAPHY

Barberia, Lorena. "The End of Egalitarianism? Economic Inequality and the Future of Social Policy in Cuba." In *The Cuban Economy at the Start of the Twenty-first Century*, edited by Jorge I. Dominguez, Omar Everleny Pérez Villanueva, and Lorena Barberia. Cambridge, MA: Harvard University Press, 2004.

Castro, Fidel. "The Consequences of Neoliberalism Affect Europe Itself, not only the Third World," *Granma International* (23 April 1997).

Central de Trabajadores de Cuba (CTC). "Pronunciamiento de la Central de Trabajadores de Cuba." *Granma* (13 September 2010). Retrieved 2 February 2011 from http://www.granma.cubaweb.cu/2010/09/13/nacional/artic01.html.

Comisión Económica para América Latina y el Caribe (CEPAL). *La Economía Cubana: Reformas estructurales y desempeño los noventa.* 1st ed. Santiago, Chile: Author, 1997.

Comisión Económica para América Latina y el Caribe (CEPAL). *La Economía Cubana: Reformas estructurales y desempeño en los noventa.* 2nd ed. Santiago, Chile: Author, 2000.

Comisión Económica para América Latina y el Caribe (CEPAL). *Balance preliminar de las economías de América Latina y el Caribe.* Santiago Chile, 2009.

Domínguez, Jorge I., Omar Everleny Pérez Villanueva, and Lorena Barberia, eds. *The Cuban Economy at the Start of the Twenty-first Century.* Cambridge, MA: Harvard University Press, 2004.

Hagelburg, G. B. "If It Were Just the Marabú . . . Cuba's Agriculture, 2009–2010." *Cuban Affairs: Quarterly Electronic Journal*, 5, no. 2 (2010).

Mesa-Lago, Carmelo. "The Cuban Economy at the Crossroads: Fidel Castro's Legacy, Debate over Change, and Raúl Castro's Options." Working Paper 19/2008, Real Instituto Elcano, Madrid, 2008.

Mesa-Lago, Carmelo, Alberto Arenas de Mesa, Ivan Brenes, et al. *Market, Socialist, and Mixed Economies: Comparative Policy and Performance—Chile, Cuba, and Costa Rica.* Baltimore: Johns Hopkins University Press, 2000.

Oficina Nacional de Estadísticas (ONE). *Anuario Estadístico de Cuba.* Various years. Available from http://www.one.cu/.

Pérez-López, Jorge. "Foreign Investment in Cuba." In *The Cuban Economy*, edited by Archibald R. M. Ritter. Pittsburgh, PA: University of Pittsburgh Press, 2004.

Pérez Villanueva, Omar Everleny. "The Cuban Economy: A Current Evaluation and Proposals for Necessary Policy Changes." Discussion Paper no. 217, Institute of Developing Economies, Tokyo, 2009.

Ritter, Archibald R. M. "The Cuban Economy in the 1990s, External Challenges and Policy Imperatives." *Journal of Interamerican Studies and World Affairs,* 23, no. 3 (Fall 1990): p. 125.

Ritter, Archibald R. M., ed. *The Cuban Economy.* Pittsburgh, PA: University of Pittsburgh Press, 2004.

timid policy liberalization would permit the sector to expand sufficiently to absorb large numbers of laid-off state sector workers.

A normalization of relations with the United States would be of major economic benefit to both the United States and Cuba. Normalization would lead to a flood of tourists from the United States to Cuba. U.S. exports to Cuba would expand quickly, displacing those of other countries less attractive than Cuba in terms of quality, price, and convenience. Foreign investment and various types of financial inflows to Cuba would promote Cuban economic expansion and diversification (Ritter 2010).

Ritter, Archibald R. M. "Estados Unidos–Cuba: Potenciales implicaciones económicas de la normalización," TEMAS, no. 62–63 (April–September 2010).

United Nations Development Program (UNDP). *Human Development Report*. Various years, 1990–2009. New York: Oxford University Press, 1990–2009.

United Nations, Economic Commission for Latin America and the Caribbean (UN ECLAC).

Preliminary Overview of the Economies of Latin America and the Caribbean. Santiago, Chile: Author, 2000.

United States Census Bureau. International data base. Retrieved 2 February 2011 from http://www.census.gov/ipc/www/idb/country.php.

Vidal Alejandro, Pavel. "Politica Monetaria y Doble Moneda." In *Miradas a la Economia Cubana*, edited by Omar Everleny Perez et al. Havana: Editorial Caminos, 2009.

EDUCATION

Efforts to build a nation and reproduce its cultural unity are most clearly evident in the area of education. Since the nineteenth century, many of Cuba's intellectuals have worked in this field, whether at foundational levels or in universities. Obtaining an education in Cuba was originally a privilege of white male elites at the beginning of the nineteenth century. More recent milestones saw the desire to incorporate the marginalized or neglected (women, blacks, peasants, and the poor) into the classroom; developments in the country's scientific, technical, and cultural fields; and the development of the pedagogical sciences and growth in the complexity and scope of the Cuban educational system during the colonial period, the Republic, and after the Revolution in 1959.

After 1959, the process of emigration and the existence of a Cuban enclave in south Florida imposed a new task on Cuban education, this time concerning the survival of these Cuban transplants' cultural identity and the preservation of their historical memory. In Cuba, the Literacy Campaign (1961) set the stage for changes in education, and afterward educational institutions reached the most distant corners of the country. At the same time, the educational system began a process of increasing complexity that has continued into the twenty-first century.

Two experiences in Cuban pedagogy have an especially unique character: schools in the countryside and international collaboration with Third World countries.

This entry includes the following articles:

EDUCATION: COLONIAL PERIOD

Yoel Cordoví Núñez

The development of education in Cuba before 1898, while under the rule of Spain.

During the first three centuries of the colonial period, education was in the hands of members of the regular Catholic orders, parish priests, and a few private tutors who were often hired by affluent families or by town councils interested in providing education to children of Spaniards and their descendants. But interest in Cuba's public education declined as more attention was given to Spain's colonies in Mexico and Peru, which generated more wealth from the sixteenth century until the independence movement at the beginning of the nineteenth century.

THE BEGINNING OF CUBAN EDUCATION

The earliest reference to an educational institution in Cuba is 1523, the date when Bishop Fray Juan de Witte founded the Scholataria in the Cathedral of Santiago de Cuba. The cathedral school was run by a *maestrescuela* (the administrative and instructional head of a cathedral school) in charge of teaching grammar to the clergy and servants of the church and to all members of the diocese interested in taking lessons. The first Cuban-born *maestraescuala* was Miguel Velázquez, of native Indian and Spanish descent.

In 1607 Bishop Juan de las Cabezas Altamirano founded the Tridentine Seminary in the village of Bayamo, and under Bishop Diego Avelino de Compostela, an extensive period of urban and rural parish construction began. In addition to fulfilling their main role as teachers of Christian doctrine, priests were required to open elementary schools.

The San Francisco de Sales Girls' School was established in February 1689 in Havana. That same

■ *See also*

Economy: Republican Period

Faith: Catholicism

Governance and Contestation: Colonial Period

Literature: Nonfiction in the Colonial Period

year the San Ambrosio school was opened, focusing on grammar and plainchant.

The vast majority of elementary schools on the island consisted of private secular schools. Typically, they were run by free, nonwhite women who taught basic reading, writing, and Christian doctrine to poor children.

Friar Gerónimo de Nosti Valdés, Compostela's successor, successfully finished the construction of Havana's Real Casa Cuna, a school for white children, and the Belén Convent hospital/school run by the Bethlehemites. During Bishop Valdés's term, the San Basilio Seminary was founded in 1722 at the Santiago de Cuba Cathedral. The Real y Pontifícia Universidad de San Gerónimo was founded in September 1728 in the San Juan de Letrán Convent belonging to the Dominican order. As a result of the expulsion of Jesuits from Spanish territory in 1767, the university took over some of the Jesuits' property for its classes.

The statutes for Real y Conciliar Colegio Seminario de San Carlos y San Ambrosio in Havana were established in 1789 under Bishop Santiago José de Hechavarría. The institution's teaching staff brought together Cuba's leading pedagogical theorists from the late eighteenth century through the 1830s.

COUNTERING THE SCHOLASTICS

At the end of the eighteenth century, the Sociedad Económica Amigos del País (Friends of the Nation Economic Society [Santiago de Cuba, 1787; Havana, 1793]) and Cuba's first literary newspaper, *Papel Periódico de la Havana* (1791), began promoting the importance of educational reform on the island. These institutions were authorized in Spain and in Spain's colonies by royal order. The intent was to support Spanish development through the study of economic, cultural, and social phenomena. The schools disseminated Enlightenment views, which conflicted with the mercantilist principles underlying the economic relationship between Cuba and Spain. As such, they were centers of intellectual rebellion as well as learning and teaching. The Sociedad Económica still existed in Cuba in the early twenty-first century.

Among the top opponents of the scholastic philosophy and its instructional method was the San Carlos Seminary professor José Agustín Caballero, who authored *Philosophia Electiva* (1797), as well as several articles of pedagogical guidance. Father Caballero's reformist work was supported and given impetus by Bishop Juan José Díaz de Espada y Fernández de Landa, who endorsed the educational reform movement that had started in the San Carlos seminary as soon as he arrived on the island in 1802.

Among the main advocates of innovative pedagogy was Father Félix Varela, who in 1811 obtained the position of professor of philosophy in the seminary through a competitive exam process, known as an *oposición*. Through his teaching and pedagogical work, he gradually eliminated scholastic and syllogistic methods and incorporated ideas from the European Enlightenment.

Starting with his *Elenco de Filosofía* (Catalog of Philosophy) in 1812, Father Varela called for reflection and analysis as means to secure students' cognitive independence. In addition to the *elencos* that Varela wrote between 1812 and 1819, he published other important pedagogical texts, including *Instituciones de Filosofía ecléctica para el uso de la juventud estudiosa* (Eclectic Philosophical Institutions that Make Use of Studious Youth), *Máximas morales y sociales: Lecciones de Filosofía* (Moral and Social Maxims: Lessons from Philosophy), and *Miscelánea Filosófica* (Philosophical Miscellanea).

Many of his students became distinguished educators who continued to promote his ideas. Among the main exponents were José de la Luz y Caballero; José Antonio Saco, Varela's successor as professor of philosophy in 1821; Nicolás Manuel de Escobedo; and Francisco Ruiz.

The Education Section of the Sociedad Económica was created in 1816 to supervise public education, which had previously been overseen by the society's science and arts class. Following the independence movement in mainland Spanish America, concessions were made to Cuba to coax its loyalty, and the development of public schools expanded. However, these advances were short-lived. By 1824, when Ferdinand VII resumed absolute control of Spain, funds were withdrawn and liberal trends were reversed, which resulted in the closing of some public schools. Religious orders maintained control of school maintenance and pedagogy development, and their resources were concentrated in Havana. An 1833 census showed that out of approximately 190,000 Cubans under the age of fifteen, just over 9,000 were enrolled in school, although actual attendance was much lower (Fitchen p. 109). Education had become an elite phenomenon rather than a public right, and the rural and black sectors of the population were particularly neglected.

Between 1832 and 1833, José de la Luz y Caballero was literary director of the Colegio de San Cristóbal, the so-called Carraguao School, a pioneer school in the application of teaching methods of the day. From 1833 to 1835 he was the school's principal. In December 1833 he presented a report about the Naval School to the Real Junta de Fomento de Cuba (Royal Board of Cuban Development). This report contained a proposal to expand and reform the Naval School in Regla by rechartering it as a scientific institute tailored to suit the country's needs. He also recommended the use of the explicative method he had applied in his classes at San Cristobal for the training of new teachers. In 1835 Luz y Caballero became assistant director of the Sociedad Económica, and in 1839 he was appointed its director. He also served as president of the Education Section for two years.

PUBLIC AND PRIVATE SCHOOLS

In 1842 Spain enacted the General Public Education Act for the islands of Cuba and Puerto Rico. This meant that an official entity, the Inspección General de Estudios (General Educational Program Inspectorate General), presided over by the governor, would now regulate public education in Cuba. It was the first time that the Spanish government assumed responsibility for organizing and funding basic public education, at least in theory. This freed the religious orders and private citizens to turn their attention to expanding the private educational systems that served elites. As a practical matter, control was central but financial responsibility was local, resulting in the chronic underfunding of public education. Due to this growing centralization by the Spanish government, the Education Section of the Sociedad Económica was dissolved in 1846.

Between 1840 and 1850, the great primary and secondary schools proliferated. In addition to the Colegio San Cristóbal, notable institutions included the Colegio Santiago, a school founded in Santiago de Cuba by Juan Bautista Sagarra, and the La Empresa Boys' School established in Matanzas in 1840 by the brothers Pedro, Eusebio, and Antonio Guiteras.

In February 1848 the El Salvador school, home to some of the most important teachers of the nineteenth century, was inaugurated in Havana. It was directed by José de la Luz y Caballero. The institution closed in 1852 because of a cholera epidemic, but it reopened the following year.

Despite the economic- and health-related problems that the school's founder and teacher faced, classes continued. The work Luz y Caballero did as the head of El Salvador was crucial both because of the teaching methods he utilized and because of his commitment to the solid foundation of his students in moral and patriotic values. Upon his death on 22 June 1862, former student and the then–vice principal of the teaching staff, José María Zayas, became the new principal.

The new Public Education Plan, also known as General Concha's Plan, was approved by royal decree on 15 July 1863. This document maintained the basic structure of the General Public Education Act. Public education continued to be managed by the island's governor and his advisory corps, the Junta Superior de Instrucción Pública (High Council of Public Education). Two significant improvements in the 1863 plan were the addition of the category of teacher into the civil service system and the authorization of a system for testing and licensing teachers.

THE TEN YEARS' WAR

In government-controlled areas during the Ten Years' War (1868–1878), private schools whose principals declared support for independence were closed down, whereas schools that showed loyalty to the colonial government remained open. New schools supporting the Crown emerged.

The Cuban teacher Rafael Morales y González stood out during the war. He authored the Public Education Act passed by the Chamber of Representatives of the Cuban Republic in Armas in August 1869, and in 1872 he also wrote a Cuban reader to teach the people within liberated territories to read and write.

The Education Section of the Sociedad Económica was reinstated in November 1872. During the war it founded and supported several schools with funds from private benefactors such as Salvador José Zapata. One of Cuba's top educators, the Matanzas native Manuel Valdés Rodríguez, became the director of this so-called Institución Zapata in 1877. Despite these efforts, at the close of the Ten Years' War schools in the combat zone had been hard hit and were barely functioning. Following the war, Spain

Félix Varela (1788–1853). As one of the main advocates of innovative pedagogy in Cuban education, Father Félix Varela gradually eliminated scholastic and syllogistic methods and incorporated ideas from the European Enlightenment. THE GRANGER COLLECTION, NEW YORK. REPRODUCED BY PERMISSION.

again tightened control of public education by eroding liberal curricula and declaring that the primary purpose of education was to support the "permanent dominion of Spain in the Antilles" (Fitchen p. 113). Promoting loyalty to the Crown and to the Catholic Church would remain the centerpiece of colonial public education in Cuba.

AFTER THE WAR

A royal decree drafted specifically for Cuba on 18 June 1880 stipulated that Spain's educational program and system be instituted on the island. That same year, Enrique José Varona gave philosophical lectures in Havana on logic, psychology, and morality.

Several officially authorized associations emerged after the war. Workers and bosses, blacks and mulattoes, all founded cultural and recreational associations. Teachers, for their part, created the first union organization in 1882, the Asociación de Profesores de la Isla de Cuba. Two years later, in June 1884, they held their first Instructional Convention in the city of Matanzas. Also proliferating were teaching-related publications such as *La enseñanza* (Teaching), *El profesorado de Cuba* (Cuban Teachers), and *La voz del magisterio* (The Voice of the Schoolmaster).

Some of the most important educational institutions created between 1880 and 1898 were the San Manuel y San Francisco school founded in 1886 in Havana, whose principal was Manuel Valdés Rodríguez, and the Isabel la Católica School, purchased by María Luisa Dolz y Arango, a young teacher from Havana. Hers was the first school that prepared girls to obtain a high school diploma. An exceptional educator, Dolz was driven to elevate the status of Cuban women. After Cuba's independence from Spain in 1898, the school's name was changed to María Luisa Dolz.

In 1899 a journal in Havana published an article analyzing the net effect of colonial education, stating that the Crown policy:

> was to restrain the people of the island to the two ideas of loyalty to the Church and subserviency to the Crown, so that the chief lines of public instruction were those of Church doctrine and Spanish history. As a matter of natural consequence the school became simply the drill-room of religion and loyalty, and the graver matters of science, letters, and philosophy of life were eliminated from the educational system.
>
> *Fitchen p. 118*

■ *See also*

Faith: Catholicism

The World and Cuba: U.S. Culture in Cuba

BIBLIOGRAPHY

Calasans Bau, Padre. *Historia de las escuelas pías en Cuba durante el primer siglo de su establecimiento, 1857–1957.* Havana: Burgay y Cia, 1957.

Cartaya Cotta, Perla. *José de la Luz y Caballero y la pedagogía de su época.* Havana: Editorial de Ciencias Sociales, 1989.

Fitchen, Edward D. "Primary Education in Colonial Cuba: Spanish Tool for Retaining the "Isla siempre leal." *Caribbean Studies* 14, no. 1 (1974): 105–120.

García Spring, Santiago. *La enseñanza popular en Cuba desde el descubrimiento hasta nuestros días.* Havana: La Universal, 1926.

García Yero, Olga, Ernesto Agüero, and Araceli Aguiar. *Educación e historia en una villa colonial.* Santiago de Cuba: Editorial Oriente, 1989.

Leyva Lajara, Edelberto. "José Agustín Caballero: El espíritu de los orígenes" (introduction). In *Obras*, by José Agustín Caballero. Havana: Imagen Contemporánea, 1999.

Martínez Díaz, José M. *Historia de la educación pública en Cuba: Desde el descubrimiento hasta nuestros días y causas de su fracaso.* Pinar del Río, Cuba: La Casa Villaba, 1943.

Ortiz, Fernando. *La hija cubana del iluminismo.* Havana: Imprenta Molina, 1943.

Pérez García, Nicolás. *Francisco de Arango y Parreño y la enseñanza en Güines.* Havana: El Siglo XX, 1918.

Pichardo, Hortensia. *Biografía del Colegio de San Cristóbal de La Habana.* Havana: Editorial Academia, 1979.

Sosa Rodríguez, Enrique, and Alejandrina Penabad Félix. *Historia de la educación en Cuba.* 8 vols. Havana: Editorial Pueblo y Educación, 2000–2008.

Torres-Cuevas, Eduardo. *Obispo Espada: Ilustración, reforma, y antiesclavismo.* Havana: Editorial de Ciencias Sociales, 1990.

Torres-Cuevas, Eduardo, Jorge Ibarra Cuesta, and Mercedes García Rodríguez. *Obras. Félix Varela. El que nos enseñó primero en pensar.* 3 vols. Havana: Imagen Contemporánea, Editorial Cultura Popular, 1997.

Zenea y Luz, Evaristo. *Historia de la Real Casa de Maternidad de esta ciudad, en la cual se comprende la antigua Casa Cuna, refiriéndose a sus fundaciones, deplorable estado y felices progresos que después ha tenido hasta el presente.* Havana: Oficina de José Severino Boloña, 1838.

EDUCATION: REPUBLICAN PERIOD

Graciella Cruz-Taura

Educational philosophy and the principle of education for all, integral parts of Cuba's quest to become a modern, independent nation, from 1902 to 1959.

Since the early nineteenth century, when Father Félix Varela (1788–1853), the noted Roman Catholic social reformer, taught Cuba's intellectuals to openly seek national progress through Enlightened education, national identity and educational philosophy have been mutually engaged in Cuba's quest for political independence and modernity. However, it was only in the aftermath of the last war of independence against Spain, during the U.S. military occupation (1899–1902), that Cuban thinkers were first able to formulate a public policy to educate the Cuban people, then 64 percent illiterate (according to the Census of 1899) and devastated by war. The 172,000 students who enrolled in 1902—only about half of the estimated school-age population—represented 10.9 percent of the island's population; children from rural areas were disproportionately without access to schools. For the next six decades, Cuban educators worked to advance learning and the state of schools at the primary, secondary, and tertiary levels of instruction. Their pedagogical vision required private initiatives to counteract the politicians' myopia in the nascent Republic of Cuba.

EDUCATION POLICIES DURING THE FIRST REPUBLIC (1902–1934)

In 1900 the U.S. military government established a Board of Education under the leadership of Enrique José Varona (1849–1933). By 20 May 1902, when the Republic of Cuba was established under a constitution that guaranteed instruction in any subject as a civil right, Varona had arranged the country's first school districts and the creation of nearly 3,600 classrooms. His greatest challenge was not what to promulgate but how to carry out plans with limited resources. The so-called Plan Varona of 1900, which reflected Varona's positivist views, was a four-year secondary school curriculum focused on applied sciences at the expense of the arts and humanities and designed to prepare students for professions in science and engineering. In the absence of adequate textbooks for teaching Cuban history and geography, those disciplines were limited to the European experience. At the completion of the program, a student was granted the degree of *bachiller* (literally a *bachelor* but a secondary-school degree) of Letters and Sciences. Teacher-training initiatives included a summer program for Cuban teachers at Harvard University, and by 1915 normal schools for teachers had opened in each of the six provincial capitals.

By the end of the 1910s, school enrollments were decreasing, and retention was poor: Of 184,560 students in the primary schools in 1919, about 75 percent were enrolled in the first and second grades. The historian Ramiro Guerra (1880–1970), who had attended the Harvard program, was commissioned by the Asociación Pedagógica Universitaria to prepare a policy study on Cuban education. Along with other Cuban scholars, he questioned the Plan Varona. Guerra's nineteen-point *Programa nacional de acción pedagógica* (1922) proposed a major overhaul of the educational system. However, only at the tertiary level would some of the report's recommendations

Enrique José Varona (1849–1933). Philosopher and educational reformer Enrique José Varona served as vice president of Cuba from 1913 to 1917. COURTESY OF THE CUBAN HERITAGE COLLECTION, UNIVERSITY OF MIAMI LIBRARIES, CORAL GABLES, FLORIDA

receive attention, and Plan Varona defined Cuba's official secondary school curriculum with minor revisions until 1941. Arturo Echemendía (1880–1934), a contributor to Cuban educational journals (such as *Cuba Pedagógica, Revista de la Facultad de Letras y Ciencias*, and *Revista de Instrucción Pública*), articulated the need to train a "legion of prepared citizens," a democracy's best minds. In his 1937 study, *Problemas generales de la nueva educación*, he cautioned against a system that promoted the cultural divorce of a scientifically trained elite from the masses, while the latter were limited to a utilitarian and vocational curriculum.

Varona, avowedly anticlerical and a follower of Herbert Spencer, the nineteenth-century English philosopher known for his agnosticism, never obstructed freedom of religion and welcomed the return of Catholic private schools in Cuba after independence. These institutions, which offered instruction beginning in kindergarten and continuing until college readiness, were mostly established in urban settings. With the demise of Spanish power came freedom of worship, and religious schools of various Christian denominations—such as the coeducational Presbyterian school La Progresiva, established in Cárdenas in 1900, and the Central Methodist School in Havana—flourished. Havana's Jewish school, the Talmud Torah Theodor Herzl, opened in 1924 and, by the late 1930s, had become the Colegio Autónomo del Centro Israelita for the primary and secondary instructional levels.

To the students who completed the Plan Varona, whether at public or private secondary institutions, the University of Havana offered a gamut of professional opportunities. Varona had restructured its degree programs to educate the professional class needed to develop and run the country. In 1902 the university granted 80 degrees; in 1927 it granted 625. The number of graduates, however, hardly satisfied the needs of the Cuban nation.

STUDENT ACTIVISM AND REVOLUTION

In 1923 students initiated a university reform movement that revealed the discrepancy between Cuba's political reality and the ideal of the republic anticipated at the time of independence. Inspired by comparable movements in other Latin American nations, the students used protests against the university as a means to criticize society and government. Led by Julio Antonio Mella (1903–1929), the Federación Estudiantil Universitaria (FEU; Federation of University Students) was organized in 1923; its demands dealt with academic issues but also challenged the government over its appointment of faculty through nepotism or political favors, a practice the students criticized as promoting incompetence. The protest began with demands for the resignation of unqualified faculty and for university autonomy. Other student protests soon followed, creating a momentum that spread to other civic groups. These groups' demands for social justice, economic independence, and government transparency echoed those of the university students.

In 1925, when President Gerardo Machado assumed dictatorial powers, student demonstrations turned violent. In 1930 the regime shut down the university and secondary institutes. One month after Machado was ousted, on 4 September 1933, student leaders turned an army revolt into a revolutionary movement that chose as its president Ramón Grau San Martín (1881–1969), a physiology professor at the University of Havana. Varona publicly praised the students' revolutionary defense of the Cuban nation.

TRANSITION PERIOD AND THE NEW CUBA

The Revolution of 1933 was toppled after one hundred days in a military coup led by General Fulgencio Batista (in office for two periods, 1940–1944, 1952–1958), who from 1934 to 1940 effectively controlled the government as the strongman behind hand-picked presidents. During this transition period Cuban and foreign scholars assessed the school system's weaknesses and proposed remedies. New decrees laid out plans to reach more students, diversify curriculum, and offer more secondary school options. Under the 1937 Ley Docente (Education Law), Cuban soldiers were deployed to rural zones to teach in new civic-rural schools where there had never been schools before. The initiative is attributed to Batista, who realized the political expedience of incorporating an education agenda into the new Cuban constitutional order.

In 1940 Batista won the first presidential election to be held under the new Cuban constitution. That document reflected the continuing quest for a modern identity amid the influence of Cuba's own Iberian heritage as well as of the nearby United States. Education specialists sought the convergence of two conflicting traditions that only a few, such as Varela at the Seminario de San Carlos at the turn of the nineteenth century, had been able to reconcile. Thus, Cuba's official education philosophy insisted on scientific pedagogies rooted in the European Enlightenment—fundamentally continuing Varona's line—while remaining imbued with the casuistry of Hispanic Catholic traditions.

In 1944 the government approved a specialized primary school curriculum. To the original core courses were added Cuban history and an integral enrichment program in arts, music, foreign language, health, and physical education. Praiseworthy on paper, the new curriculum required a corps of specialized teachers in a country with rural areas in which breaking ground for the first school was still a dream.

The Plan Remos, a five-year program proposed by the literary scholar Juan J. Remos (1896–1969), became the standard that replaced the Plan Varona. The addition of a fifth year to the secondary school program expanded the core curriculum to include the humanities. New requirements included Cuban history, literature, and geography, as well as the study of the new constitution. For the final year of the *bachillerato*, the students chose a Letters or Science track according to their aptitudes and professional goals. With increasing options to pursue secondary school programs in technical and vocational fields, the bachiller's degree was meant to attract only the advanced and disciplined students most likely to go on to the university.

Article 56 of the constitution, which stipulated that only Cuban nationals could teach courses on Cuba and that only texts written by Cubans could be used in those courses, may have exceeded the nationalist demand to insert Cuban components into the curriculum. In hindsight the measure may seem xenophobic, but it is understandable in the context of its time and place: First, given that the 1940 Constitution was a manifestation of a nationalist project that dated from the early nineteenth century, it is not surprising that at a triumphal hour the drafters of the constitution felt that only Cubans should write Cuban history. Second, private schools were often in the hands of foreigners. The Spanish clergy was well represented in Catholic schools, as were religious orders forced to leave revolutionary Mexico; to a lesser extent, faculty of various nationalities also taught in sometimes bilingual schools. At a moment when Cuban historians were publicizing the excesses of Spanish colonialism and the meddling of the

United States in Cuban affairs (although already siding with the Americans against the Rome-Berlin Axis, formed in 1936 between fascist Italy and Germany), the Cuban educational plan, this time through Plan Remos, was to teach a nationalist, even myth-creating, vision of Cuban history and culture to the nation's youth.

The 1940s brought qualitative changes to the structure of Cuban education. Particularly significant was the opening of technical and vocational schools as well as normal schools and secondary institutes. Yet the reckoning was not good: In 1950, only 50.7 percent of school-age children were enrolled in public schools, which scheduled less instruction to accommodate two 4.5-hour sessions in existing buildings and had reduced core subjects to include the specialized curriculum. Only 4 percent of public school students completed the sixth grade. As noted in a 1954 study by Ramiro Guerra, literacy was at 82.5 percent in Havana province but at 34 percent in easternmost Oriente province and at 21 percent in that province's rural areas. In 1951 the government issued its new twenty-point development plan, which, according to a UNESCO report that year, devoted 27 percent of the nation's budget to education. That same year the World Bank's Truslow Mission issued its *Report on Cuba*, which concluded that the return on the Cuban state's investment in education was disproportionately inadequate because the system was politicized. In other words, political corruption, which included improper allocations of funds and other resources assigned to education, was at the root of results far below expected outcomes. Offering a turnaround plan, the mission prioritized the establishment of a Junta of Education to direct 126 locally elected school districts. The mission's administrative model paralleled the original independent school system of 1900, which was discontinued in 1906 by President Estrada Palma, bowing to partisan demands in an election year.

Among the various curricular changes the University of Havana initiated after 1937, of particular note is the founding of the School of Social Work in 1942, a project spearheaded by Cuban feminist and human rights activist Elena Mederos (1900–1981). This achievement held symbolic importance as a counterpoint to the violent abuse of the university's jurisdictional autonomy by subversive groups, commonly considered gangsters because of the blurred lines between the members' ideological position and their self-promotion, which could include ties to the criminal activities of the underworld.

SCHOOLING IN THE 1950s

After eight years of civilian rule, in 1952 Fulgencio Batista seized power through a coup d'état. Unlike the revolutionary days of 1933, when students lofted Batista to prominence, now university students were the first to demonstrate against his regime. Despite an increase in budget allocations for education, the Batista government was unable to narrow the growing gap between the urban and rural populations' access to education or to answer the demand for quality education and private options.

In 1953, as the nation prepared to celebrate the one-hundredth anniversary of the birth of patriot José Martí, articles in the leading newspaper, *Diario de la Marina*, fueled public outrage at the tragedy of Cuban public education. Ramiro Guerra lamented that the public schools in which he had taught at the turn of the twentieth century, and in which his own children had been well educated, were no longer qualitatively viable: His grandchildren were attending private schools. Echoing his personal experience, private schools expanded in Cuban cities and towns during the 1940s and 1950s. Through its first decade, the Cuban school system maintained its initial momentum of 1900 to 1902, but it never recovered after economic recession began affecting the island in the 1920s. If the culprit had simply been financial, then by the 1940s the public school system should have been thriving along with the developing economy. Taking into account the growth of the school-age population by 253,000 students between 1943 and 1958, the government's allocation of 23 percent of the national budget in 1955 (the highest in Latin America) should have provided some relief to the system. Yet it did not: The percentage of school-age children who registered in public schools stood at 52 percent by the mid-1940s and had not improved by 1958. Policies followed the same politically expedient and nontransparent pattern of the past: As a 1956 UNESCO report indicated, a $20 million loan for school construction assigned only 20 percent of the total to rural schools.

Some analyses, such as those by José R. Álvarez Díaz (1963), Mercedes García Tudurí (1974), and UNESCO annual reports, have argued that the 1950s figures do not reflect all private school enrollments, which by 1958 may have numbered 120,000 to 200,000 students and thus five to eight times the growth since 1934. But those estimates would hardly explain why at least 200,000 students did not enroll in, or had no access to, schools in a country where communication significantly improved during those years. In 1944, for example, 27 private secondary schools had 2,214 students enrolled in the official Plan Remos college preparatory program, and, in 1958, a total of 168 schools reported an enrollment of 14,800 students. Thus private institutions were nurturing some Cuban students while others were consigned to less academically demanding—and, as was becoming increasingly common, politically violence-ridden—public secondary schools. Nevertheless, as García Tudurí notes, these public schools graduated 35,700 students in 1958, not counting the graduates from technical, vocational, and normal schools. The growing university-bound student population is indicative of the school feeder patterns created by new universities, particularly the prestigious Augustinian-run Villanova University. By the late 1950s three more public and eight private universities were operational.

EVE OF REVOLUTION

Cuba's educational system developed along a modern path within the Enlightenment's secular tradition. Academically competitive private schools efficiently delivered the government's established curricula. A growing nationalist, predominantly urban, and educated citizenry deemed the various failures of public schools—particularly in serving rural areas—to be a matter for honest constitutional governments to solve. In the colonial tradition of ¡*Viva el rey y abajo el mal gobierno!* (Long Live the King and Down with Poor Government!), they blamed the political class's gridlocked democracy during the 1940s and the Batista leadership during the 1950s for the inaccessibility to the social and economic fulfillment corresponding to their educational sophistication—or for its lack in the general population (demonstrated by the remaining 23.6% illiteracy rate, the fourth lowest in Latin America).

Statistics and comparative regional analyses indicate that Cuba's educational system was successful at delivering professional classes—impressively so at the tertiary level, increasingly so at the technical secondary level—that did not, however, fulfill the island's social and economic needs as a result of weaknesses at the primary level and discontinuities at the secondary level. The goal of universal access to education stagnated after the first decade of the twentieth century, when the young nation's rising expectations were dampened by political instability and recurrent political violence, a lack of transparency, and the growing pains of development. Critics sought remedies in the context of José Martí's enlightened vision of an educated Cuban citizenry. When the Cuban state offered only rhetoric in support of Martí's project, parents sent their children to private, often religious, schools, asking for scholarships or accepting further strain on their family budgets to cover tuition and related school expenses. As the 1950s came to a close and student activism was on the rise against Batista, many Cubans believed that their schools had finally produced a generation capable of implementing the constitution of 1940 and eliminating malfeasance—as the leaders of the revolution of 1959 promised. That commitment included constitutional guarantees to deliver education for all, while maintaining academic freedom in the attainment of Martí's idealized nation of educated and fulfilled Cubans.

■ *See also*

Health and Health Care: Medical Diplomacy and International Medical Education

BIBLIOGRAPHY

Aguayo, Alfredo Miguel. *Problemas generales de la nueva educación.* Havana: Cultural, S.A., 1936.

Aguayo, Alfredo Miguel. *Tres grandes educadores cubanos: Varona, Echemendía, María Luisa Dolz.* Havana: Cultural, S.A., 1937.

Álvarez Díaz, José R., and Grupo Cubano de Investigaciones Económicas. *Un estudio sobre Cuba: Colonia, república, experimento socialista: Estructura económica, desarrollo institucional, socialismo y regresión.* Coral Gables, FL: University of Miami Press, 1963.

Cartaya Cotta, Perla. "Enrique José Varona Pera." *Palabra Nueva* (May 1999): 26–28.

Commission on Cuban Affairs. *Problems of the New Cuba: Report of the Commission on Cuban Affairs.* New York: Foreign Policy Association, 1935.

Cruz-Taura, Graciella. "Revolution and Continuity in the History of Education in Cuba." *Cuba in Transition* 18 (2008): 168–180.

García Tudurí, Mercedes. "La educación en Cuba." In *La enciclopedia de Cuba*, vol. 6. Madrid: Playor, S.A., 1974.

Guerra, Ramiro. *Un programa nacional de acción pedagógica.* Havana: Imprenta "La Prueba," 1922.

Guerra, Ramiro. *Rehabilitación de la escuela pública, un problema vital de Cuba en 1954.* Havana: Imprenta P. Fernández, 1954.

Report on Cuba: Findings and Recommendations of an Economic and Technical Mission organized by the International Bank for Reconstruction and Development in Collaboration with the Government of Cuba in 1950. Francis Adams Truslow, chief of mission. Baltimore: Johns Hopkins University Press, 1951.

Sorondo y Campanería, Emilio L. *La escuela pública rural: Sus deficiencias pedagógicas y sus deplorables condiciones sanitarias.* Marianao, Cuba: Imprenta L. García Oviedo, 1935.

UNESCO. *Cuba: Annuaire International de l'Éducation*, 13–22. Geneva, Switzerland: IBE, 1951–1960.

U.S. Bureau of the Census. *Report on the Census of Cuba 1899.* Washington, DC: Government Printing Office, 1900.

Vitier, Medardo, ed. *Enrique José Varona: Su pensamiento representativo.* Havana: Editorial Lex, 1949.

EDUCATION: REVOLUTIONARY PERIOD: STAGES OF EDUCATIONAL REFORM

Justo Alberto Chávez Rodríguez

The new changes in Cuban education, post-1959, especially in the areas of enrollment, teacher training, youth retention, major events or campaigns, the transition to a socialist model, and challenges of the post-1989 period.

In Cuba, the educational system contains the following subsystems: preschool; primary education (for 6 to 11 years old); basic secondary education (for 12 to 14 years old); pre-university (for 15 to 17 years old); and higher education, including pedagogical universities. Since 1976 there have been two ministries of education: one for higher education and the other for the rest of the subsystems.

THE BEGINNING (1959–1962)

Before the Revolution the preschool, special, technical, and professional educational systems were in a precarious state, and not everyone had access to primary and secondary education. In a population of 5.5 million, 23.6 percent of those sixteen years of age and older could not read or write, and in rural areas illiteracy was 40 percent. There were only fifteen thousand university students, three public universities, a private university (Santo Tomás de Villanueva Catholic University), and hundreds of trained teachers without schools to work in.

From 1959 to 1962 legislation was aimed at establishing the necessary structures to provide education for everyone. Exceptional measures were taken that were unique in the history of Cuba and possibly in all of Latin America, and integral educational reform was undertaken as an initial effort to create a coherent and harmonized national school system. This period ended when Cuba declared itself a territory free of illiteracy on 22 December 1961. This historic feat was the result of a massive, scientifically organized endeavor. Almost immediately the National Campaign for Literacy and Cuban educational institutions began several post-literacy projects to assure the progressive reduction of residual illiteracy. For example, three weeks after the end of the campaign (4 January 1962), the Department for Special Education was created to assist children with severe physical-movement disabilities or other limitations that impede their attendance in school institutions.

Some of the important educational events of the period are as follows:

- The Ana Betancourt Study Plan to improve education for girls in rural zones was developed in 1961 with 150,000 students registering (Montalván p. 87).
- The voluntary teachers (graduated or not) who went to the mountains numbered 3,000 (later organized in the Brigada de Maestros de Vanguardia "Frank País" ["Frank País" Vanguard Teachers Brigade]) (Castro 1975, pp. 117–120).
- The 6 June Ley de Nacionalización General de la Enseñanza (Law of General Nationalization of Education) established that it is the responsibility of the state to supply free, universal access to education (Castro 1975, p. 118).
- Cuba proclaimed itself a territory free of illiteracy on 22 December 1961 (Montalván p. 95).

- The National Kindergarten program began on 10 April 1961.
- The Escuela Nacional de Arte (ENA; National School of Art) commenced classes with a new concept for Cuban artistic teaching in May 1962.
- The Department of Special Education was created and began the Cuban system of special education on 4 January 1962.

THE TRANSITION TO A SOCIALIST EDUCATIONAL SYSTEM (1962–1975)

The success of the literacy campaign created the conditions for raising the educational level of workers in the cities and the countryside. The most significant achievements were in adult education courses, the battle for the sixth grade (a program to ensure that everyone attained at least a sixth-grade level of education), and the establishment of preparatory schools that made it possible for workers to undertake university studies. University reform, a milestone in Cuban higher education, was carried out in 1962.

In response to social demands, special educational plans emerged. One program concentrated on raising women's educational levels; another established technological centers that offered a degree of organization and dynamism that the Ministry of Education could not provide at that time. The creation in 1962 of the Scholarship Department and a massive scholarship program guaranteed all Cuban citizens free access to education; all of the students' basic needs were subsidized by the state, and thousands of youth from rural zones came to study in the cities, mainly in Havana.

Physical education and extensive athletic training were introduced into the educational program starting at the primary school level and culminating in the School and Youth Sports Games. As a result, Cuba soon moved into the forefront of physical culture and sports and was able to maintain that position for many years, achieving great successes internationally.

The First National Education and Culture Congress in April 1971 made a critical analysis of difficulties in Cuban education. A year later, in April 1972, Fidel Castro stressed the need to carry out a profound revolution in education. Building on the ideas of José Martí, the educational system provided students with strong ties to production and the country's political and social priorities. Cuba organized a program combining academic studies with agricultural and other practical work at all educational levels. Some valuable expressions of the new educational policy were the creation of the Manuel Ascunce Domenech Pedagogical Detachment and the proliferation of basic secondary schools in the countryside, among other educational experiences in the 1970s.

During the 1972–1973 school year, a scientific diagnosis and prognosis of the educational system was carried out with advice from Soviet and East German specialists and with the participation of an outstanding group of Cuban educators. This international contact was fruitful because it offered the island's educators the opportunity to study writings and introduced ways of thinking that would be influential in the formation of Cuban pedagogical policy.

A program known as "School to the Countryside" mobilized students to work from thirty to forty-five days in the countryside, combining academics with work in the fields. This program implemented the principles of linking studies with labor and theory with practice. These tasks were also undertaken by higher education: On that level, combining studies with work and research is an integral part of academic training and directly related to professional life.

In December 1975 the first Congress of the Communist Party of Cuba was held. The Educational Policy Thesis and its corresponding resolution formally identified the island's pedagogy as Marxist-Leninist, while maintaining Martí's theories about education and the legacy of Cuban educational concepts developed throughout the country's history. The first Improvement of the National Educational System was formulated and approved, following careful scientific study.

The following describes some important events of the period.

- Post-literacy projects took mainly two parallel tendencies: a tracking program to give the recently literate a second-grade level of education, and programs to improve adult education for people between third and sixth grades. The latter program, named Workers-Farmers Education, encompassed some 1.5 million workers. The first Workers-Farmers School was opened on 17 July 1963. Throughout these years, and focusing actions on elementary schools and "economically active populations" (16–59 years), illiteracy in this group was gradually reduced to less than 1 percent (InfoCIP).
- In 1964 three Pedagogic Universities opened in Havana, Villa Clara, and Santiago de Cuba (Artiles).
- First Escuela Secundaria Básica en el Campo (ESBEC; School in the Countryside) was unveiled on 26 November 1969. The new modality increased its significance in 1974 with the opening of forty of these new schools (InfoCIP; Artiles).
- The Pedagogic Brigade "Manuel Ascunce Domenech" (1972) was founded. It was made up of tenth-grade students who, under the model of study and work, prepared to be teachers in a moment when the country lived through an "explosion of enrollments" in schools. More than twenty thousand teachers graduated in this project.

- The Destacamento Pedagógico para la Educación Técnica y Profesional (Pedagogic Brigade for Professional and Technical Education) (de las Nieves) was created in 1974.

IMPROVING THE NATIONAL EDUCATIONAL SYSTEM (1976–1990)

The Instituto Central de Ciencias Pedagógicas (ICCP; Central Institute of Pedagogical Sciences), established in 1976, began to play an important role in the application of the educational sciences—among them pedagogy and didacticism—throughout the country. The ICCP led the way in the various stages of the improvement process from 1975 to 1986.

In regard to higher education, it should be noted that the achievements during this period and beyond of Cuban scientists—the immense majority of whom graduated from institutions of higher learning—have been possible, above all, because the government made research a priority, even during moments of severe economic limitations.

The first International Pedagogy Congress in 1986 became an important laboratory for understanding the educational situation in Latin America and the rest of the world; after the downfall of European socialism, links between the Cuban and Latin America pedagogy strengthened, particularly related to experiences of popular and community education. By 2009, Cuba had participated in eleven such congresses.

SURVIVING THE COLLAPSE OF EUROPEAN SOCIALISM (1991–2010)

The disappearance of the Eastern European socialist bloc and the collapse of the Soviet Union, combined with the tightening of the U.S. embargo, drove the country through a serious economic downturn (named "Special Period in Peace Time") and put severe strains on the Cuban educational system. At the same time, without external help, the Cuban educational system turned to its national history and traditions, looking within for an answer to the new circumstances. In the middle of this crisis, even when the Cuban economy shrunk dramatically between 1990 and 1994, not a single classroom was closed, no educators lost their jobs, and the educational process maintained its pre-1989 level of quality. As the scholar Miren Uriarte affirmed: "In the area of education, Cuba's strategy is to 'grow' out of the effects of the economic crisis of the 1990s, keeping the education of the Cuban people at the center of the country's strategies for social development" (Uriarte). Even under these dire circumstances, the Cuban population's average educational level rose from sixth- to ninth-grade level in the period from 1981 to 2002 (Trigésima).

The economic crisis had a massive impact on the Cuban educational system and in the quality of the educational process; hundreds of teachers moved to employment with better benefits, school maintenance declined, and the shortage of materials, equipment, and publications (especially of specialized or technical literature) became a daily reality (Alvarez p. 52). To halt the deterioration of the system, the government ordered an increase of 30 percent in teacher salaries and redistributed students in schools, capping maximums to twenty students per classroom. Perhaps the most evident sign of crisis in the education field was the decline in university registration in the 1988–1994 period (Lutjens).

In a surprising move at the beginning of the 2000s, just when the Cuban economy began to show a slight recovery, Fidel Castro launched a new initiative, which he called "The Battle of Ideas"—a mix of massive political and ideological campaigns geared to educational and cultural projects—based on the concept that the real strength of the Cuban revolution depends on education and culture. After that, the focus was on bringing education in step with the times, privileging the rational use of technology and opening new analytical horizons on the relationship between education and science. The project included the repair of hundreds of facilities and even reached rural schools in very remote areas, some that did not have electricity (2,368 in total); those schools received a photovoltaic solar panel, television, video player, and computer. The mass media, especially television, played an important educational role through the use of educational television to support classroom teaching; to develop this new approach to teaching, all the schools in the country received a television set and video player. A new daily television series, *Universidad para Todos* (University for All) began broadcasting and offering courses in 2000, prepared by experts, to anyone who wanted to study topics such as foreign languages, arts, history, sciences, among others.

A new program was created for the more than 114,000 youth between the ages of 14 and 17 (63.4% of which were girls) who had abandoned school and were not working. It was called "Course of Integral Improvement," under the rubric of "study as work." Youth attended classes, received economic help, prepared for future work, and studied at the university. More than 89,500 youth took part (Canfux 2008, pp. 58, 104). Another program for youths helped members receive training related to their new jobs, giving them stipends and allowing them to study at the university. A third program, "Emerging Teachers," was conceived to fill the lack of teachers in primary and secondary schools; more than ten thousand Cubans were studying at the university under this program as of the early 2000s.

Another aspect of this period is known as the "universalization of higher education," a model that decentralized the teaching-learning process from traditional college campuses onto facilities in local areas. A group of tutors from the original (sponsoring) university monitor the process, local personnel are trained to teach, and the research projects of the students address local problems and concerns. The program was being developed as of 2011 in facilities among 169 municipalities together with a large network of micro-colleges (Ecured).

Cuban professors at all levels have access to various kinds of postgraduate classes, diploma courses, and masters programs especially designed to help them improve their teaching skills. In addition, an extensive system offering doctoral programs in the educational and pedagogical sciences is open not only to Cubans but also to educators from other countries. As of 2011, more than twenty professional Cuban journals (mainly digital) published scientific articles on issues of education in the country.

Some of the important events of the period are as follows.

- The National Department of Educational Software (1996) began.
- The University for Senior Citizens (1999) was created.
- Latin American School of Medicine, with a thousand students coming from Honduras, Nicaragua, and Guatemala, began on 1 March 1999.
- Cuban television began to offer *University for All* courses on 2 October 2000 (InfoCIP).
- The Alvaro Reynoso taskforce for workers in the sugar industry who were affected by the closure of many sugar mills was established in 2002. The workers continued to receive their salaries, study, and train for new work opportunities.
- The number of universities grew from 28 in 1976–1977 to 68 in 2008–2009.
- The University of Computer Sciences (UCI) opened in September 2002.
- Educational Channel (on national TV) began broadcasting in 2002.
- Universalization of Higher Education programs were initiated.
- Networks of specialized pre-university schools (devoted to pedagogy, sciences, sports and technical education) covered all the provinces of the country.

THE FUTURE OF THE CUBAN EDUCATIONAL SYSTEM

The Cuban educational system changed its course after recognizing the need to become a social institution drawing on the most advanced sciences and technologies, coupled with a concept of humanism whose roots extend back to the late eighteenth and early nineteenth centuries. This humanism was driven by the belief that the modern world's severe problems and dangers can only be resolved with education and love of humanity.

Cuba has hundreds of educators and researchers whose work reflects universal and regional thought with an indisputable Cuban imprint. A considerable number of articles and books on education have been published, as well as ongoing research in the field. The Cuban teaching method called "Yo sí puedo" (Yes I Can), conceived to provide a "liberatory education for marginalized populations through South-South collaboration" (Steele p. 38), was created in 2003 and has been practiced in twenty-eight countries and fourteen different languages and praised by UNESCO. More than 3.5 million illiterate people have learned to read and write. According to Elvira Martín Sabina, as of 2009, "30,000 youth from 123 nations are currently engaged in university studies in Cuba," and since 1959, around "50,000 students from 129 different countries" have graduated from different levels of education in Cuba (p. 136).

In *The Cuban Education System: Lessons and Dilemmas*, a respected professional study of the Cuban educational system made on the eve of the twenty-first century, Lavinia Gasperini remarks that Cuba "ranked first in math and science achievement, at all grade levels, among both males and females" (Latin America), and then she adds the following:

> The challenges are daunting, but then who would have predicted that Cuba—after a decade of economic turmoil—would have built the region's highest-achieving schools? The next few years are likely to be critical ones if Cuba's educational excellence is to be maintained, whether Cuba follows the path of other transitional economies and education systems or charts its own course. (p. 2)

Ten years later Cuba again achieved the best scores in the Segundo Estudio Regional Comparativo y Explicativo (SERCE; Second Comparative and Explanatory Regional Study) coordinated by the Latin American Laboratory of Evaluation of the Quality of the Education of the OREALC–UNESCO, which took place in 2006. For children of third and sixth grades, the study involved sixteen countries of Latin America and evaluated student performance in mathematics, languages, and sciences.

The *Education for All Global Monitoring Report in the World 2011*, an independent research and annual publication authorized by UNESCO, affirmed that Cuba led the region in investment in education with 13.8 percent of its gross national product devoted to education. Also, Cuba had the biggest percentage of qualified students with the maximum grade averages (more than 50 percent of the students got grades of four or above, out of five) and with the smallest proportion of schools with grade punctuations of one or less (EPT pp. 7–8).

According to Curry Malott, "Compensating for shortages of every sort imaginable, Cuba allocates from 11 to 10 percent of their GDP to education, which, compared to other Latin American and Caribbean countries, is high and 4 to 5 percent higher than that recommended by UNESCO."

The following facts and statistics serve as a summary of Cuba's educational achievements:

- Practically speaking, there is no illiteracy in Cuba.
- The Cuban population has a tenth-grade educational level, compared to a third-grade level in 1959.
- In a country of 11.2 million inhabitants, between 1960 and 2010 almost one million graduated from Cuban universities.
- The "Educate Your Child" program prepares families and communities for participation in early childhood education. This program of non-formal education has been an important factor in providing preschool education to almost all of the children who are not registered in formal early childhood education.
- Virtually no child repeats a grade, as evidenced by the fact that 99.4 percent of the children in primary schools are between the ages of six and eleven.
- Of the students who start primary school, 95 percent complete it, and the 5 percent who do not are then enrolled in, and graduate from, more than 400 special education schools, where 41,000 students with various disabilities prepare for integration into society.
- During the 2009–2010 school year, there was an average of 9.8 students per teacher in elementary schools and 10.3 at all educational levels.
- Throughout the country there is a network of more than 12,000 educational institutions, including child care centers, elementary schools, special education schools, basic secondary schools, pre-university schools, technical-professional schools, art schools, sports schools, and adult schools, with access guaranteed for the whole population.
- Each province has a university of pedagogical sciences, and under its aegis university professors are trained in all 169 municipalities.
- More than 117,000 educators have enrolled in masters of education sciences programs in these pedagogical institutions, and more than 22,000 have already attained that degree.
- More than 900 teachers earned doctorates in a scientific field.

- The educational attainment of Cubans has translated into a highly educated workforce: of all Cuban workers, 14 percent have a university degree.
- To ensure primary education is universal, there are 146 rural schools with a single student and 1,117 with five or fewer (Canfux 2008 p. 38).
- The literacy rate among fifteen- to twenty-four-year-olds is 99.96 percent.
- Graduates of basic secondary school (25–64 years old) constitute 77.58 percent of the general population.
- Graduates of pre-university school (25–64 years old) constitute 46.08 percent of the general population.
- Average level of schooling among workers is the eleventh grade.

(Santos and Lopez p. 392, citing data from the Cuban National Census of Population and Housings, 2002)

The Cuban government's efforts indicate a new relationship that needs to be articulated regarding education, the prevailing economic conditions, and new projects to develop the country's future. Despite past achievements, difficulties continue to rise in the early 2000s as Cuba faces new challenges in a global economy. There is a need to improve the educational system's quality in line with its universality. There is an emphasis in post-secondary studies on technical studies more in line with the real conditions of the Cuban economy and the demands of localities. The standards for final exams in mathematics, language, and history have been raised. Areas of study that have become more significant are agronomy, accounting, construction, and pedagogy (Barrios; Sánchez).

Álvarez Figueroa points out:

It is difficult to forget that the quality of the education has been affected less than the shrinkage of available resources. This is due to the creativity and efforts of educational personnel, Cuban families and to a strong movement of international solidarity that has replaced the absence of external financing with donations of texts, educational materials, equipment along with free technical assistance. (p. 126)

BIBLIOGRAPHY

Álvarez Figueroa, Oneida. *El sistema educativo cubano en los noventa*. Barcelona: Universitat Autónoma de Barcelona, Servei de Publicacions Universitat Autónoma de Barcelona: Departament de Sociologia, 1997.

Artiles Granda, Madeline. *Los cambios educativos en la Cuba de hoy. Retos del mundo actual*. Havana: Universidad de Ciencias Pedagógicas, 2009.

Barrios, Margarita. *Después de la Secundaria, ¿qué estudiaremos? Juventud Rebelde: Diario de la Juventud Cubana* (6 March 2010). Available from http://www.juventudrebelde.cu/cuba/2010-03-06/despues-de-la-secundaria-que-estudiaremos/.

Buenavilla, Rolando. *Historia de la pedagogía en Cuba*. Havana: Editorial Pueblo y Educación, 1995.

Canfux, Jaime. *Política y estrategia empleadas en la Campaña Nacional de Alfabetización de 1961*. Havana: Centro de Documentación del Ministerio de Educación, 1989.

Canfux, Jaime. *Situación presente de la educación de personas jóvenes y adultas en Cuba*. México: Centro de Cooperación Regional para la Educación de Adultos en América Latina y el Caribe, 2008.

Castro, Fidel. *La educación en la Revolución*. Havana: Instituto Cubano del Libro, 1974.

Castro, Fidel. *Primer congreso del Partido Comunista de Cuba: informe central*. Havana: Departamento de Orientación Revolucionaria del Comité Central del Partido Comunista de Cuba, 1975.

Chávez Rodríguez, Justo A. *Bosquejo histórico de las ideas educativas en Cuba*. Havana: Editorial Pueblo y Educación, 1996.

Gasperini, Lavinia. *The Cuban Education System: Lessons and Dilemmas*. Washington, D.C.: Education Reform and Management Team, Human Development Network-Education, World Bank, 2000.

Gómez Gutiérrez, Luis Ignacio. *El desarrollo de la educación en Cuba*. Havana: Conferencia Especial del Ministro de Educación en el Congreso Pedagogía, 2003.

González González, José, and Raúl Pedro y Reyes Velázquez. "Desarrollo de la educación en Cuba después del año 1959." *Revista Complutense de Educacion* 21, no. 1 (23 March 2010): 13–35.

Guadarrama, Pablo. *El pensamiento filosófico cubano (1900–1960)*. Villa Clara, Cuba: Universidad de Las Villas, 1998.

InfoCIP_Educación en Cuba_ la campaña infinita (Cronología de la educación cubana_ 1991–2000). Centro de Información para la Prensa, de la Unión de Periodistas de Cuba, 2003.

Informe de Seguimiento de la Educación para Todos en el Mundo 2011. In *Panorámica regional: América Latina y el Caribe*. Available from http://www.cubadebate.cu/wp-content/uploads/2011/03/gmr2011-region-lac-es.pdf.

Kolesnikov, Nikolái. *Cuba: educación popular y preparación de los cuadros nacionales: 1959-1982*. Moscú Progreso, 1983.

Lutjens, Sheryl L. *Cambios perdurables: La educación superior en Cuba en la década de los noventa*. Universidad Nacional Autónoma de México, 2004.

"El maestro emergente, solución puntual. Revista Electrónica." *Actualidades Investigativas en Educación*, 9, no. 2 (2009).

Malott, Curry. "Cuban Education in Neo-liberal Times: Socialist Revolutionaries and State Capitalism." *Journal for Critical Education Policy Studies* 5, no. 1 (May 2007).

Montalván, Olga. *De Conrado a Manuel*. Havana: Unión de Escritores y Artistas de Cuba, 1994.

Nieves Lamas González, Margarita de las. *Periodización del desarrollo de la superación de los docentes de la educación técnica y profesional de 1959 al 2000.* Vol. 6, no. 3. Havana: Universidad de Ciencias Pedagógicas. Available from http://www.pedagogiaprofesional. rimed.cu/vol6no3/margarita.htm.

Sabina, Elvira Martín. "Thoughts on Cuban Education." *Latin American Perspectives* 36, no. 2 (2009): 135–137.

Sánchez Zúñiga, Tayli R. *Continuidad de estudios: Luego del noveno grado, ¿qué?* (February 11, 2010). Available from http://www.cubaeduca.cu/index. php?view=article&catid=253%3Anacionales&id= 3694%3Acontinuidad-de-estudios-luego-del- noveno-grado-ique&format=pdf&option=com_ content&Itemid=153.

Santos Gutiérrez, Sinesio C., and Francisco López Segrera. *Revolución cubana y educación superior.* Avaliação: Revista da Avaliação da Educação Superior (Campinas), 2008.

Steele, Jen. "Yo, Sí Puedo: South-South Educational Collaboration in Practice." A Volume of Graduate Student Research. *Society for International Education Journal.* Available from http://www.tc.columbia.edu/ students/sie/journal/Volume_5/steele.pdf.

"Trigésima novena reunión de la mesa directiva de la Conferencia Regional sobre la Mujer de América Latina y el Caribe, Informe nacional de Cuba." Comisión Económica para América Latina y el Caribe (CEPAL), División de Asuntos de Género. (México D.F), 11–12 May 2006. Available from http://www.eclac.org/mujer/noticias/ noticias/1/24331/Cuba.pdf

Uriarte, Miren. "Holding to Basics and Investing for Growth: Cuban Education and the Economic Crisis of the 1990s." *Journal of Pedagogy, Pluralism, and Practice,* 2003. Available from http://www.lesley.edu/journals/ jppp/7/uriarte.html.

Varela Hernández, Miguel. *Sistemas educativos nacionales: Cuba.* Havana: El Ministerio de Educación and the Organización de Estados Iberoamericanos para la Educación, la Ciencia y la Cultura, 1995.

Velázquez, Ena Elsa. *La Educación en Cuba y los retos del personal docente.* Havana: Folleto del VII Congreso Internacional de Educación Superior, Palacio de la Convenciones, 2010.

EDUCATION: REVOLUTIONARY PERIOD: PHILOSOPHY

Susan J. Fernandez

The development of education after 1959 and the quest to mold a new society along the lines of revolutionary humanism.

The Revolution's commitment to education began during the guerrilla war, as the more educated guerrillas taught basic literacy and math skills to recruits and adult *guajiros* (peasants) in the countryside. The Program Manifesto of the 26th of July Movement (1956) set forth clear positions about the functions of education in society that were reinforced later through words, laws, and actions. Education is believed to serve the interests of the individual, the state, and society, and is seen as a human right as well as a national necessity.

Pragmatically, revolutionary Cuba holds traditional views regarding the political and economic value of education. From the perspective of nationality and citizenship, education is seen as a means of facilitating participation in the political and cultural life of the country. This idea is not revolutionary in itself, but once Cuba embarked on a dramatic economic and political transformation, education played an important role in preparing citizens to adapt to and adopt the new system. Other countries have recognized that education is an important component of economic development. In revolutionary Cuba, technical, scientific, and other formal and informal education preparations created a modern workforce capable of solving problems that arose during transitions from a U.S.-dominated market to a Soviet and Eastern bloc market and finally to a more global market.

Revolutionary leaders embarked on an aggressive campaign to expand education in 1959, starting with increasing literacy rates in urban and rural areas. Literacy centers were established in police stations, camps, and military headquarters to educate members of the military, supervised by the Directorate of Culture of the Rebel Army. Within the first year, a National Literacy Commission, local literacy boards, and a special census to identify and locate illiterate Cubans were initiated. The National Literacy Campaign was launched in 1961, and more than 250,000 professional teachers and young volunteers began teacher training as the Bay of Pigs assault began (April 1961). The methodology developed from the campaign, later termed "Yo! Sí Puedo" (Yes, I Can!), was so successful that it was approved by UNESCO for other countries, and Cubans later traveled throughout the world to teach this ten-week path to basic literacy.

The immediate goal of the campaign was to reduce the illiteracy rates of 11 percent in the cities and 41.7 percent in the countryside in rural areas (UNESCO 1965). Achieving that objective also bolstered other pragmatic and ideological revolutionary goals that underpinned the educational programs established and expanded by the Revolution. The campaigns that prioritized the acquisition of basic skills for the whole Cuban population did much more than raise literacy rates—they also demonstrated to students that the new government was committed to expanding opportunities and improving the lives of all Cubans. The nontraditional approach of bringing teachers for free to people's homes and workplaces confirmed that the working poor would no longer be ignored, and the campaign simultaneously incorporated them into the revolutionary society.

Teachers in the Literacy Campaign committed themselves to an altruistic, humanistic goal that likewise drew them more actively into the Revolution. Especially for those teachers who had lived almost exclusively in urban areas and were sent to teach in the countryside, it was expected that exposure to the lives of rural workers would build a sense of national solidarity and *conciencia* (consciousness). This awareness and empathy became part of the effort to build the Revolution's "New Man." To reinforce this commitment to change—from individualism and selfishness to a sense of community and solidarity—Literacy Campaign teachers were required to share in the work of their students at farms, factories, and other workplaces. Just as education had (and continued in the early 2000s to have) a relationship to the military since the armed phase of the Revolution, teaching and learning were also linked with labor. Many other revolutionary objectives—including economic independence, diversification of the economy, universal health care, mass participation in the revolutionary process, and reinforcement of a national cultural identity—also depend on the interrelationship between learning, work, and military preparedness and defense.

Improving education and educational opportunities is seen as integral to improving social justice and the standards of living for all Cubans. Basic literacy and advanced educational skills and options are as essential to the economic vision of a society building socialism as they should be to market or profit-based systems, but because the revolutionary government sees education as a human right and a responsibility of government, all costs are born by the state. Eliminating the private schools, which were widely seen as superior to the public schools, was an early step in bringing about uniformity in curricular and performance standards as well as universal access. As the government took control of the education system, classroom sizes were gradually reduced, pedagogies were defined, and regular review systems, teacher training, and teaching methods were introduced. Over the next few decades, the rural/urban disparities in literacy rates and achievement scores were eliminated (Gasperini pp. 14–15; Summit of the Americas). Although the overall standards, methods, and learning objectives are centralized, school principals retain the authority to evaluate and terminate teachers, which is one of several ways that the system was decentralized.

As the Literacy Campaign achieved success, the government built new schools for children in rural areas and extended education to adults at workplaces and public centers. School calendars were regularized to meet the production needs of rural and urban areas. The program to build rural schools and send more teachers to the countryside was part of a broader effort to provide more services and opportunities outside Havana, which was meant to slow the historic migration to a city unable to adequately serve new residents, and to demonstrate the government's commitment to rural workers.

UNICEF's 2003 *State of the World's Children Report* reaffirmed the success of Cuba's effort in

Teacher training in Minas del Frío, 19 October 1963. Many of the classes at the Minas del Frío school for rural teachers were held outdoors, using makeshift desks and benches provided by the students themselves. © BETTMANN/CORBIS

education, which already had been praised by many other national and international reports. In 2003 the Cuban adult literacy rate was 96 percent, compared with an average of 88 percent for all of Latin America and the Caribbean. As of 2003, a full 95 percent of Cubans reached at least grade five, whereas only 76 percent of those in the rest of region achieve that level (education to grade nine is mandatory) (UNICEF 2003). Other studies have demonstrated that Cuban third- and fourth-graders outscore their Latin American peers in language and mathematics (Partnership for Educational Revitalization in the Americas 2001). The Cuban education success story is so widely acknowledged that educators from all over the world traveled to Cuba in the early 2000s to study the system.

The government's perspective on the importance of education is evident in the expansion of higher education institutions. In 1958 there were three universities in Cuba; in 2011 forty higher education institutions offered degrees in teaching, scientific, medical, and other professions. Medical research in particular has yielded important exportable products and procedures. In addition to bringing thousands of medical students from other countries for full scholarship study in Cuba, the government has sent teams of doctors, nurses, and other medical practitioners throughout the world to provide health care and teach. Efforts have been made to extend the use of computers by medical practitioners and students, encouraging cooperative work in diagnosis, medical records maintenance, and treatment.

In Cuba's new educational system race, class, and gender were no longer barriers at any level of schooling, and access to higher education was based on merit and a demonstrated commitment to revolutionary goals (usually by proving participation in a revolutionary mass organization). Students were strongly encouraged to select fields of study that meet social needs as determined by the government—the primary employer. This was in keeping with the view that the education system should respond to the needs of society, and it was reflected in the allocation of the national budget to education: approximately 18.5 percent, in 2008 the highest percentage in the region (UNESCO 2008).

An example of the government's use of education to respond to social needs was the revival and revision of the undergraduate and graduate social work programs that began in 2000 that have been combined with technical training programs for youths in the sixteen to twenty-two age bracket. Social work students are trained to address social problems that have emerged since 2000, and they all engage in extensive field work that includes assessing community needs.

Educational programs and systems have been revised periodically since 1959. A 1971 congress on education and culture attended by teacher delegates resulted in curricula changes, improved teacher training, and the development of new texts, as well as extended classroom hours and years of study. Subsequent congresses continued to address problems and promote improvements.

In addition to the formal educational systems that have improved literacy dramatically for a large percentage of the population, the revolutionary government showed its commitment to continuing education and lifelong learning in other ways. Three state-controlled television channels provide educational programming such as *Universidad para Todos* (University for All). National and international conferences and festivals provide information and promote dialogue on a vast array of topics, including pedagogy, and educational programs in workplaces and communities are designed to encourage active learning.

The government dramatically expanded schools for the blind and others with learning impairments—in 2011 these schools numbered 429. In 1993 the Ministries of Education and of Public Health launched *Educa a Tu Hijo* (Educate Your Child), a program that provides parents with guidelines on age-appropriate skills development for preschool children outside daycare and kindergarten settings. The ministry also organizes preparedness workshops in communities in areas that might be threatened by natural disasters.

In the early twenty-first century Cuban schools and formal education programs were dealing with a number of challenging problems. Although resources for schools were a priority throughout the Revolution, the government had not always been successful in its ongoing efforts to provide and upgrade the latest technology. Limited access to the Internet and limited bandwidth were issues as of 2011 for academics and students. Fuel shortages were another problem; the government responded by replacing oil-based systems with solar panels to power the computers and televisions that were widely used in schools. The massive school building campaign of the 1960s through the 1980s slowed with the collapse of the Soviet Union, and the government fell behind in repairing existing facilities.

The U. S. embargo has affected educational programs in Cuba in several ways, from limiting access to the latest scientific and social science research and methodology to restricting purchases of educational tools and materials. Cuban officials argue that purchasing materials through Asian markets more than doubles the cost of freight, negatively affecting supplies.

Although the revolutionary government remained committed to providing universal education at every level and in every discipline, it was simultaneously promoting an economy that relies on tourism to earn foreign exchange. The lack of jobs in certain sectors and the lure of convertible currency in the tourist industry affected teacher and student commitments to secondary and higher education. The government acknowledged that there were graduates without jobs in their fields of study and asserted that the state cannot guarantee a job for every major. Leaders also argued that there were needs in certain scientific and technical areas that had not been filled. Like other developing countries, Cuba had experienced so-called brain drain as highly educated and skilled professionals emigrated to seek better opportunities elsewhere.

In the early 2000s, the La Escuela en el Campo project (School in the Countryside) was the subject of extensive debates about curriculum and setting. Some argued that the Cuban educational systems limit the level of debate and dialogue about national problems and/or emphasize an ideological commitment that minimizes professional options. Concerns were raised as well about the rigidity of the K-13 curriculum and the emphasis on basic skills. Such criticisms are not unique to the Cuban system, yet Cuba has unequivocally demonstrated gains that have made it the envy of other countries not only in the region, but also in other parts of the world.

BIBLIOGRAPHY

Abendroth, Mark. *Rebel Literacy: Cuba's National Literacy Campaign and Critical Global Citizenship*. Duluth, MN: Litwin Books, 2009.

Aquirno, R. *Cuba: Organization of Education, 1992–1994. Report of the Republic of Cuba to the 44th International Conference on Public Education*. Havana: Ministry of Education.

Carnoy, Martin. *Cuba's Academic Advantage: Why Students in Cuba Do Better in School*. Stanford, CA: Stanford University Press, 2007.

Cruz-Taura, Graciella. "Revolution and Continuity in the History of Education in Cuba." Paper presented at the 18th Congress of the Association of Cuban Economy, August 2008. Available from http://www.nacae.com/pdf/Cruz-Taura.ASCE18.pdf.

Gasperini, Lavinia. "The Cuban Educational System: Lessons and Dilemmas." *World Bank Country Studies* 1, no. 5 (July 2000).

Ginsburg, Mark, Carolina Belalcazar, Simona Popa, and Orlando Pacheco. "Constructing Worker-Citizens in/through Teacher Education in Cuba: Curricular Goals in the changing Political Economic Context." *The Politics of Education Reforms* 9, no. 2 (2010): 137–163.

González González, José, and Raúl Reyes Velázquez. "Desarrollo de la educación en Cuba después del año 1959." *Revista Electrónica* 9, no. 2 (30 August 2009): 1–28. Available from http://revista.inie.ucr.ac.cr/articulos/2-2009/archivos/cuba.pdf.

Jardines Méndez, José B. "Education in Network: Much More than Distance Education." Paper presented at the Congreso de la Sociedad Cuba de Bioingeniería, 2007. Available from http://www.hab2007.sld.cu/Members/anag/title-description/.

Partnership for Educational Revitalization in the Americas (PREAL). *Lagging Behind: A Report Card on Education in Latin America*. Santiago de Chile: Author, 2001. Available from http://www.thedialogue.org/PublicationFiles/LaggingFinal.pdf.

Leiner, Marvin, and Robert Ubell. *Children Are the Revolution: Day Care in Cuba*. New York: Viking Press, 1974.

Lutjens, Sheryl. *The State, Bureaucracy, and the Cuban Schools: Power and Participation*. Boulder, CO: Westview Press, 1996.

MacDonald, Theodore H. *The Education Revolution: Cuba's Alternative to Neo-liberalism*. London: Manifesto Press, 2009.

Ministerio de Educación de la República de Cuba. *Portal Educativo Cubano*. http://www.rimed.cu/.

Strug, David, and Walter Teague. "New Directions in Cuban Social Work Education." *Social Work Today* (2 September 2002). Available from http://www.redandgreen.org.

Summit of the Americas: Regional Education Indicators Project. "Achieving the Educational Goals," Santiago: Chile, 2001. Available from http://www.prie.oas.org.

UNESCO. *Report on the Method and Means Utilized in Cuba to Eliminate Illiteracy*, 1965. Available from http://unesdoc.unesco.org.

UNESCO. *Educación en Cuba: Regional Conference of Ministers and Education*. Havana: Empresa Impresoras Gráficas, 1979.

UNESCO. Institute for Statistics, 2008. Available from http://stats.uis.unesco.org.

UNESCO. *Report on the Method and Means Utilized in Cuba to Eliminate Illiteracy*, 1965. Available from http://unesdoc.unesco.org.

UNICEF. *State of the World's Children Report, 2003*, 2003. Available from http://www.unicef.org.

Uriarte, Mirem. "Holding to Basics and Investing for Growth: Cuban Education and the Economic Crisis of the 1990s." *Journal of Pedagogy, Pluralism, and Practice* 7 (May 2003). Available from http://www.lesley.edu.

Wald, Karen. *Children of Che: Childcare and Education in Cuba*. Palo Alto CA: Ramparts Press, 1978.

EDUCATION: LITERACY CAMPAIGN OF 1961

Mark Abendroth

A government project and mass movement to eliminate illiteracy.

Cuba's National Literacy Campaign took place in 1961, the Year of Education, with the goal of eliminating illiteracy in a single year. UNESCO reported that the campaign reduced Cuba's illiteracy rate from 23.6 to 3.9 percent (Lorenzetto and Neys).

PREPARATIONS

After Fidel Castro assumed power of the country following the successful overthrow of Fulgencio Batista (1901–1973) in 1959, the new government's Ministry of Education formed the National Commission for Literacy and Fundamental Education (CNAEF).

■ *See also*

Cuban Thought and Cultural Identity: Socialist Thought

Gender: Social Justice in the Revolutionary Period

Governance and Contestation: The Cuban Revolution

National summary of illiteracy in Cuba

Population	Number	Percentage
Estimated total	6,933,253	
Identified illiterate	979,207	
Became literate	707,212	72.22
Did not become literate	271,995	27.78
Illiteracy index		3.92

SOURCES: Hart, Armando. "Cuba Territory Free of Illiteracy: Report of the National Literacy Campaign." Havana, 22 December 1961. In the National Literacy Museum, Havana. As appears in Pérez Cruz, Felipe de J. *La Alfabetización en Cuba: Lectura Histórica para Pensar el Presente.* Havana: Editorial de Ciencias Sociales, 2001, p. 214.

Table 1

Minister of Education Armando Hart Dávalos stated that the Urgent Plan of Cuban Literacy would "involve the decided cooperation of the people through civic institutions, worker organizations, live classes, and volunteers in order to carry the interest and desire to learn reading and writing to the most remote corners of Cuba" (Toroella p. 39). In August 1959, about 400 young students became the instructors for the earliest pilot program of the campaign.

Two sources designed in 1960 became textbooks for the campaign. *Alfabeticemos* (Let's Teach Literacy) introduced literacy instructors to the political content of the Revolution and guided them on what and how to teach. The text summarized twenty-four themes and provided a glossary. *¡Venceremos!* (We Will Triumph!) was the primer that instructors used for lessons. The National College of Teacher Trainers, the CNAEF, and the Ministry of Revolutionary Armed Forces together designed the primer to address the economic, social, and political needs of the nation. Cuban educators applied a working draft of *¡Venceremos!* to a pilot program on 22 August 1960.

On 26 September 1960, President Fidel Castro (b. 1926) announced in New York before delegates to the United Nations that Cuba had set a goal of eliminating illiteracy in the coming year. Notices for the campaign appeared in print throughout Cuba, often with quotations from the Cuban national hero José Martí (1853–1895). The messages connected participation in the campaign with civic dignity and revolutionary courage. The year 1961 began with the United States ending diplomatic relations with Cuba and the campaign continuing in a pilot phase. On 5 January a counterrevolutionary band assassinated a young volunteer teacher named Conrado Benítez. When the campaign began in full, all volunteer instructors who left their homes to teach in rural areas were called Conrado Benítez *brigadistas*.

The National Commission for Literacy (the words "and Fundamental Education" had been dropped from its name) set May as the goal for full implementation of the campaign and organized itself into four departments. The Technical Department managed logistics for a mass movement among teaching and nonteaching personnel. The Publicity Department recruited instructors and urged illiterate people to accept instruction. The Finance Department managed revenues and expenses. The Publication Department printed instructional materials and other documents. Eighteen organizations in civil society, known as Integrated Revolutionary Organizations, assisted the departments.

Although illiteracy was worse in rural areas, urban neighborhoods also had illiterate residents. Volunteer instructors who taught in their own neighborhoods were called *alfabetizadores populares* (people's literacy teachers). Some were adolescents who had not received parental permission to teach in rural zones. They did not receive mass training, but they had ongoing coaching from professional teachers. The *brigadistas*, who had an average age of fifteen, needed orientation and training. The seven-day training of more than 100,000 volunteers began with a first cohort in mid-April and continued with others through August. The training site was Varadero Beach, a favorite destination for wealthy vacationers before the Revolution. The trainees learned how to use *Alfabeticemos* and *¡Venceremos!*; attended classes on revolutionary politics, personal conduct, and rural public health; and enjoyed recreation.

A MASS MOBILIZATION

The campaign became a mass movement with ongoing recruitment of instructors and students. Secondary schools closed in April, enabling students and teachers to join the campaign. Municipal councils of education identified illiterate adults and urged them to accept lessons. Each municipal literacy council supervised neighborhood commissions, which in turn monitored literacy units. According to plan, each literacy unit had one coordinator, one licensed teacher, twenty-five literacy instructors, and fifty illiterate students. The licensed teacher, called an *asesortécnico* (technical assessor), coached the twenty-five instructors.

There also were noninstructional roles connected to fundraising and transportation. Many of these workers came from the eighteen Integrated Revolutionary Organizations, including the Federation of Cuban Women and the Federation of Rural Worker Associations. Further help with local organizing came from the Committees for Defense of the Revolution (CDRs); these groups, which monitored for counterrevolutionary penetration at the block level of every neighborhood and small town, assisted in campaign tasks.

The campaign's budget provided materials to support instruction. Production of eyeglasses increased rapidly even though many opticians had fled the country after the Revolution. The government also purchased lanterns from China at reduced cost. Each brigadista received two complete uniforms and a monthly stipend for purchasing necessities.

DAILY WORK OF THE CAMPAIGN

The campaign put families at the center. Often, a single brigadista or people's literacy teacher instructed an entire family. Brigadistas and their hosting students usually had little in common: The brigadista typically was an adolescent from a relatively privileged urban home, and the students of all ages lived mainly in rural poverty that had existed for generations.

During the day, a brigadista worked with the host family on tasks in the fields or in the home. Each visiting teacher had a hammock that was issued during training. Female teachers slept in homes of designated families, and male teachers lived with the families whom they taught. At night the literacy lessons took place in the family's house under the Chinese lantern. The brigadistas learned about working the land and living without modern conveniences; the rural families learned how to read and write, and the lessons' content introduced them to agrarian reform and other projects. Many of these families had members who had fought in the Revolutionary War of 1956–1959, so they in turn had lessons to teach their instructors. The harsh conditions of rural life caused injuries and illnesses that resulted in the deaths of more than sixty brigadistas.

The campaign brought urban and rural Cubans together, and it also challenged assumptions about race and gender. Some white rural families in need of instruction resisted having a black instructor. Other families believed that urban adolescent girls could never handle rural living. Local campaign coordinators convinced many of these families to put aside their prejudices and to accept a brigadista who was black or female or both (Juan Luís Báez Martínez, personal communication). By the end of the campaign many prejudices had been destroyed as family-like bonds developed between brigadistas and their hosts.

INTENSIFIED EFFORTS

By mid-summer the government had become concerned that the campaign might not succeed by December. Between July and August, census workers increased the number of identified illiterate people from 735,426 to 985,322 (Comisión Nacional de Alfabetización, cited by Pérez Cruz p. 183). The Second Congress of Municipal Councils of Education convened in early September. There Raúl Ferrer coined the acronym *QTATA*, from "Que todo analfabeto tenga alfabetizador, que todo alfabetizador tenga analfabeto" (That every illiterate person has a literacy teacher, that every literacy teacher has an illiterate person). The term was used in radio broadcasts and on posters throughout Cuba.

Literacy parade, 1 May 1961. Young Cuban women carrying lanterns and giant pencils demonstrate in Havana during the 1961 literacy campaign. STF/AFP/GETTY IMAGES

For instructional help, the campaign turned to 30,000 workers called *brigadas Patria o Muerte* (Homeland or Death brigades). They continued to be paid while workers who stayed behind accepted extra hours. Most Patria o Muerte instructors traveled to rural zones, but some taught their coworkers at their work sites. On 18 September the government began to require all professional teachers to participate in the campaign. The Statistics Section of the campaign administration reported that 34,772 teachers contributed (Pérez Cruz p. 269).

COMPLETING AND CELEBRATING

On 5 November Melena del Sur became the first municipality to declare itself free of illiteracy. Other towns followed with their announcements. So-called acceleration camps formed wherever adults were struggling with the lessons. Every municipal literacy council wanted to finish in time for a national celebration before Christmas. On 26 November counterrevolutionary bands murdered a sixteen-year-old brigadista named Manuel Ascunce and the father of his host family, Pedro Lantigo. Like Conrado Benítez, Ascunce became a martyr. Castro and other leaders spoke of the need to finish the campaign successfully in solidarity with Ascunce's family.

Upon completing all lessons, each newly literate student wrote a letter to Castro. When their work was finished, brigadistas and their host families separated after having been together for months. Trains and buses took campaign participants to Havana for the final celebration held on 22 December. The celebration was in the Plaza of the Revolution at the statue of Martí. Approximately 308,000 instructors had worked for the campaign, and many were present (Fagen). Conrado Benítez brigadistas marched to the plaza in uniform, carrying Cuban flags and giant pencils.

At the campaign's end, 707,212 Cubans had become literate while 271,995, or 3.9 percent of the nation's population, remained illiterate (Hart Dávalos, cited by Pérez Cruz p. 214). Cuba had the highest literacy rate among all nations in Latin America. Out of a total of 5 million Cubans who were old enough, 1.25 million participated in the campaign either as an instructor or a student (Fagen).

It was not enough to leave newly literate people with only a first-grade level of reading and writing. When the campaign ended, the adult continuation program, the Battle for the Sixth Grade, began, and was followed in 1980 with a Battle for the Ninth Grade. The government also enforced compulsory education for all youth through ninth grade and ensured that every community had access to a school.

BIBLIOGRAPHY

Comisión Nacional de Alfabetización. *Alfabeticemos.* Havana: Imprenta Nacional de Cuba, 1961a.

Comisión Nacional de Alfabetización. *¡Venceremos!.* Havana: Imprenta Nacional de Cuba, 1961b.

Fagen, Richard R. *The Transformation of Political Culture in Cuba.* Stanford, CA: Stanford University Press, 1969.

Lorenzetto, Anna, and Karen Neys. *Methods and Means Utilized in Cuba to Eliminate Illiteracy.* Havana: Cuban National Commission for UNESCO, 1965.

Pérez Cruz, Felipe de J. *La Alfabetización en Cuba: Lectura Histórica para Pensar el Presente.* Havana: Editorial de Ciencias Sociales, 2001.

Toroella, Gustavo. "Veinte y cinco Preguntas al Dr. Armando Hart, Ministro de Educación." *Bohemia* 51–58 (1959): 38–41, 138.

■ *See also*

Cuban Thought and Cultural Identity: Socialist Thought

Economy: Special Period

Governance and Contestation: The Cuban Revolution

EDUCATION: SCHOOLS IN THE COUNTRYSIDE

Denise Blum

Rural boarding schools for secondary school students.

The School in the Countryside model refers to boarding schools for secondary school students with a curriculum that combines agricultural labor with academics. Escuela Secundaria Básica en el Campo (ESBEC) included seventh to ninth grades, and Instituto Preuniversitario en el Campo (IPUEC) tenth to twelfth grades. In 1971 the first ESBECs were created for ideological and pragmatic reasons: to absorb the highest population ever of secondary students and to immerse young people in rugged rural conditions that recall and remind students of the rebel army at the time of the triumph of the Revolution and of the

socialist values of cooperation, egalitarianism, hard work, solidarity, and sacrifice. From 1990 to 2010 the boarding schools were converted to IPUECs for older students and the junior-high students remained in the city. These boarding schools were in the process of being terminated as of the 2010–2011 academic year, mostly because of economic reasons.

After ninth grade, Cuban students typically opted for either technical-vocational high schools or the IPUECs. In other socialist and former socialist countries, students are mobilized for a week or more to the countryside to participate in agricultural labor. Cuba was the only country that provided high-school scholarships for all urban students to study and participate in agricultural labor while living in the countryside, a pivotal schooling practice to secure Marxist political-ideological formation. These schools also served local rural students. In the capital of each province, one high school was established for students with illnesses that impeded them from living and working in the countryside.

The Cuban government considered the IPUEC to offer the highest level of revolutionary learning, consistent both with Marxist philosophy and with Cuban historical roots. Fidel Castro noted that it unites fundamental ideas from two great thinkers: Karl Marx (1818–1883) and nineteenth-century Cuban literary figure, journalist, and political activist José Martí (1853–1895). "Both conceived of a school tied to work, a center where youth are educated for life. The product is holistic education and human development linked to productive, creative work, combining manual and mental labor" (Castro 1971).

The Marxist principles governing the ESBEC-IPUEC program included using education to eliminate labor and class divisions (including the rural and urban divide) by incorporating manual and mental labor; linking school to social, economic, political, and ideological goals; training new generations for work; educating a collectivist mentality and eliminating individualism; and including more structure and discipline while valuing the personality and potential of each student (García Galló 1971). These principles were already a part of an ongoing temporary mobilization of students for a month of agriculture labor, called the School to the Countryside, in the mid-1960s. The permanent ESBEC-IPUECs provided further political-ideological socialization for an extended period of time in a controlled environment.

The ESBEC-IPUECs were school complexes created for approximately six hundred students and about a hundred staff that included teachers, workers, cooks, nurses, and drivers. Each rural boarding school had dormitories, a library, classrooms, medical services, laboratories, a cafeteria, a kitchen, and recreational areas for sports and cultural activities. Barbers and hair stylists made weekly visits. Transportation services were available for teachers who traveled back

to the city each day and for transporting students to the city on weekends or twice a month, depending on the distance. In addition, each ESBEC-IPUEC had its own small parcel of land for which the students were responsible. Students participated in fieldwork Monday through Friday. Their fieldwork took place either in the morning or afternoon, according to their shift, and they would take academic classes during the other shift with short intervals for meals. From 5:00 p.m. to 8:00 p.m. was the *horario de vida* (personal time), which included sports, showering, and dinner; from 8:00 p.m. to 9:30 p.m. was *horario de autoestudio* (study hall); and at 10:00 p.m., *horario de sueño*, students were to be in bed with lights out. One night every week, usually Wednesdays, was reserved for recreation, therefore no study hall was scheduled. The itinerary for the ESBEC-IPUECs, based on the vision of ideologues (in consultation with experts in all disciplines), was precise and strictly practiced and reinforced constantly, instilling the values of the noble revolutionary: the new socialist citizen.

Fundamental to Marxist pedagogy, the collective was promoted in the structure of schooling. Students were organized into work brigades and students participated in regular assemblies and meetings to evaluate their intellectual and physical work as a collective. Sports and cultural activities were also channels for socialization in collectivism and emulation, a collective form of competition.

> This form of schooling, at least in structure, equalizes and inverts the hierarchical school structure. Students not only learn from reading and studying, but also from doing. In a society in which the manual work is, to a great extent, shared by all, the conventional class distinctions become blurred. And the school activities themselves—students and teachers working side by side with the *campesinos* [farmers], workers attending school—contribute greatly to the obliteration of the class lines based on manual versus nonmanual work distinctions.
>
> *Bowles 1971, p. 494.*

In addition, those teachers who lived on campus were able to establish personal relationships with students in an informal setting to better meet the students' needs and scaffold their learning accordingly.

In the 1990–1991 school year, the age range of students sent to the boarding schools for this honing process was changed to tenth to twelfth graders, with the junior high students schooled in the city. According to interviews with Ministry of Education officials, the switch was done primarily for two reasons. First, by boarding older students in the countryside, it was thought that productivity levels in agricultural labor would increase. The students were stronger physically and mature enough to handle the responsibility of the work. Second, it was thought that the pre-university students were more prone to "ideological contamination" in urban areas, where they were more exposed to influences from the outside world. Moreover, "material differences are more pronounced in the city" as well (Interview 10 December 1999). The government felt that the young peoples' ideological foundation would remain more intact in the countryside. Also, to maintain its labor force, the Cuban government did not want to lose its vanguard youth to the lures of a capitalist culture or illegal marketeering, which was more pronounced in the urban areas. Dropout rates had increased and the goal was to keep children in school and continue to solidify its base for the future of socialism.

Although some goals have been met, the vision and the realization of the IPUECs have diverged. Because of ongoing economic challenges, the conditions of the IPUECs became inadequate: Electricity and water were irregular at best and sometimes nonfunctioning for periods as long as a week. In 1991 one group of IPUEC students returned to Havana on foot, walking many miles in protest of the living conditions, vowing to never return. Parents complained about the deterioration of the schools, poor-quality food, sexual freedom, and inadequate supervision of students by their teachers. The separation of the young people from their families was criticized as changing family dynamics and having negative effects on the child's education. In response to the complaints, the minister of education at the time, Luis Gómez, criticized parents as "manifesting certain paternalistic attitudes" (Acosta 1998, p. 2).

Having one's child attend the IPUEC was not always the first choice, but to opt out carried a price. One woman stated, "Either you went to pre-university school in the countryside or you gave up the idea of going to the university. I had a really good grade average, but I decided to go to a technical school instead. It took me a little longer, but I was able to eventually study at the university" (Interview 18 March 1998). Attending the university also requires passing entrance exams, consideration of one's political-ideological character, and competing for the few openings that exist. The IPUEC was the natural path to take for those who wanted a university education, understood as an "incubator for revolutionary commitment" (Interview 25 February 1999). However, the unsatisfactory conditions rerouted a significant number of students into technical schools or to simply drop out.

While the average Cuban secondary student was expected to attend the IPUEC, many parents aspired to have their children attend the vocational schools (IPVCE; Instituto Preuniversitario Vocacional de Ciencias Exactas). However, considering that there is only one located in each province and admission is highly selective, parents with the financial means invested in tutoring. Since 1985 the schools have served tenth to twelfth grades (from 1974 to 1985, seventh to twelfth graders attended).

The IPVCEs emphasize the subject areas of mathematics and science. Students must maintain an 85 percent average in these focus areas or they will be dismissed. The IPVCEs' abundant and high-quality resources complement and stimulate the academic rigor expected of the students, which typically include more updated equipment and materials in the areas of computer and science labs and school libraries. Those who attend an IPVCE are more likely to acquire better jobs and/or be a part of the Cuban elite. The IPUECs and IPVCEs illustrate one of the ways the Cuban school system, in spite of the government's commitment to socialism, is still involved in the stratification of Cuban society.

The minister of education in 2010, Ena Elsa Velásquez, supported a restructuring that would eventually eliminate the IPUECs altogether (but not the IPVCEs) for city students but maintain them for schooling those in geographically isolated places. If school and society are mirror images, the elimination of this hallmark innovation in Cuba's education system may foreshadow a restructuring of Cuban society.

BIBLIOGRAPHY

Acosta, Dalia. "Boarding-School System Increasingly Unpopular." Inter Press Service (7 November 1998): 2.

Bowles, Samuel. "Cuban Education and Revolutionary Ideology." *Harvard Educational Review* 41, no. 4 (1971): 472–500.

Castro, Fidel R. "Prime Minister's School Dedication Speech" (4 April 1971). Available from http://lanic.utexas.edu/project/castro.

Garcia Galló, Gaspar J. "La escuela al campo." *Educación en Cuba* 1, no. 1, (January–February 1967): 9.

Interview with woman in Havana. Havana, 18 March 1998. This interview was conducted in confidentiality, and the name of the interviewee was withheld by mutual agreement.

Interview with staff member of Ministry of Education. Havana, 10 December 1999. This interview was conducted in confidentiality, and the name of the interviewee was withheld by mutual agreement.

Interview with staff member of Ministry of Education. Havana, 25 February 1999. This interview was conducted in confidentiality, and the name of the interviewee was withheld by mutual agreement.

EDUCATION: CUBAN SCHOOLS IN MIAMI

Uva de Aragón

Inés Morales

The Cuban influence on American education.

Although there are some antecedents, the history of Cuban and Cuban American education in the United States begins in the 1960s, for it was in the wake of the

■ *See also*

Cuban Adjustment Act

Diasporas: Waves of Immigration Since 1959

Miami

Cuban Revolution that a large-scale influx of Cuban immigrants arrived in southern Florida. Many of the exiles were families with small children, who attended the schools and had an impact on the system. Cuban educators also made significant contributions to the American education system almost from the start. Their efforts addressed every level of the educational system.

CUBAN EDUCATORS IN THE UNITED STATES

Since the Cuban Revolution, the Cuban migration to the United States has included a considerable number of people with teaching experience. In the 1960s, many of the exiles who left Cuba were middle-class professionals. There were also a great number of women with university degrees but little or no work experience. They all came from a tradition that highly valued education. However, the language barrier and, more important, the legal requirements for obtaining a license to teach in the state of Florida prevented these immigrants, even former teachers, from integrating right away into the American education system. In time, the public demand for qualified Spanish-speaking educators, combined with the teachers' own efforts in order to facilitate their entry into the schools, improved the situation.

In response to the demand, certain colleges and universitics throughout the United States granted scholarships to Cuban professionals and trained them to become certified in the United States. One of the earliest of these plans was the Cuban Teacher Retraining Program at the University of Miami, started in 1963, but other states followed suit. Therefore, some of the Cuban teachers who received such scholarships remained in the state of Florida, while others pursued their careers elsewhere.

As teacher assistants, certified teachers, and administrators, Cubans went on to play an important role in the education of children at elementary and secondary levels, as well as in the development of public education programs, particularly in the state of Florida. At a higher level, many Cubans have also made a difference in American universities.

PUBLIC SCHOOL SYSTEM

Many immigrant Cuban children in Florida, as well as generations of Cuban-American children born in the United States, attend or have attended public schools. The first waves of immigrants were political exiles who believed they would soon return to their homeland. Although they wanted their children to benefit from education in the United States, they also were interested in helping them preserve their own culture and language. The public school system, initially, was ill prepared to cope with the massive increase of students who spoke a different language and came from a different culture. Previously, the United States had considered bilingual education to be a transitional program to help integrate students into the monolingual, mainstream American culture. Cuban parents wanted more for their children. They finally persuaded Dade County (renamed Miami-Dade in 1997) educators to develop a bilingual system that would integrate English and preserve Spanish literacy.

The experiment was first attempted in 1963, at Coral Way Elementary in Little Havana, in which an alternative instructional program combining Spanish and English was introduced, first with the participation of Cuban aides and eventually with certified Cuban teachers. This led to the development of a curriculum as well as adequate teaching materials, again with the assistance of Cuban educators.

Eventually, the success of the Coral Way Elementary experiment encouraged other schools throughout Dade County to implement bilingual education programs of their own based on this model. Many Cuban teachers found employment in Dade schools, and some of them were asked to give workshops for their English-speaking colleagues designed to train them for the new bilingual education system. Although this process was not without its difficulties, by the 1970s bilingual education programs had been adopted by many schools in Dade County at all levels of the primary and secondary school system, and their curricula continued to be reworked and adjusted as its deficiencies became apparent and new needs emerged. Meanwhile, more and more Cubans arrived in southern Florida, and an increasing number of students and teachers from the island settled in counties adjacent to Dade, such as Broward and Monroe. Throughout this period of growth and change, the participation of Cuban and Cuban American teachers was essential. As more Hispanics arrived in the United States from different countries, the bilingual education system that started in Florida was adopted by other states. By the mid-1970s, bilingual education had become a recognized profession with its own professional organization, the National Association for Bilingual Education (NABE).

Another development in the realm of public education in Florida involved the creation of public charter schools, which offer free instructional programs with relative independence from the state public education system. In Miami-Dade County, the Lincoln-Martí private school system, founded by a Cuban educator in 1968, includes one charter school and about a dozen small private elementary schools, along with twenty daycare and preschool facilities. In 1999, the long-term Cuban American superintendent of Miami-Dade schools Octavio J. Visiedo helped establish the nationwide charter school system, Chancellor Academies.

The Cuban American National Council, a non-profit organization founded in 1974, whose president and CEO is the Cuban American Guarioné Díaz, has among its missions to serve as a resource center

Coral Way Elementary School. A Cuban teacher guides students at Coral Way Elementary School in Miami's Little Havana. In 1963, this school became the first to introduce an alternative instructional program combining Spanish and English, with the participation of Cuban teachers and aides. COURTESY OF THE CUBAN HERITAGE COLLECTION, UNIVERSITY OF MIAMI LIBRARIES, CORAL GABLES, FLORIDA

for Hispanic educational progress. Its network of preschools and schools helps to identify and support the educational needs of students—both Cuban and non-Cuban—who experience difficulty in regular classrooms.

PRIVATE SCHOOLS

Some of the refugee Cuban children who arrived in Florida, especially in the early stages of the exile, attended Roman Catholic parish schools; for many Cuban parents particularly wanted their children to have a religious education. In time, as Cuban immigrants in Florida recognized the possibility of long-term exile and became financially able to plan beyond mere survival, Cubans started founding private schools in Miami to assure that their children could receive an education more suited to their cultural and religious interests. In Miami, some of these schools continued the tradition of private Catholic education that existed in pre-revolutionary Cuba—for instance at well-known schools such as the Immaculata–La Salle High School in Coconut Grove, a coeducational school for grades nine through eleven, and Belén Jesuit Preparatory School in southwest Miami, a college preparatory institution of high academic standards, from which 100 percent of graduates advance to postsecondary education. Belén, an all-boys school, has an

enrollment of fifteen hundred students from sixth to twelfth grade, and although its student body is diverse, Cuban American students, teachers, and clergy constitute the majority.

Other new institutions were lay private schools, among them the above-mentioned Lincoln-Martí, whose network of schools covers much of Miami-Dade County. Many of these schools not only offer students a bilingual education but also preserve many Cuban cultural values—for instance, schools may celebrate and honor the January 28 birth date of José Martí, the apostle of Cuba's independence, and they are likely to serve Cuban food in the cafeterias. Although at the elementary level the curriculum does not include courses directly related to Cuba, information about the country and its culture is presented in Spanish classes and other courses, such as art and music. Some private high schools offer elective courses on Cuban history.

UNIVERSITIES

Three universities in Miami have particularly close ties to the Cuban and Cuban American community. The first of these is Miami-Dade College, founded in 1960 and presided over since 1995 by Eduardo Padrón, a Cuban by birth and a well-known educational leader. Miami-Dade College creates educational opportunities for many people, the majority of whom are from ethnic minorities. In addition to its formal programs of study, the two-year college offers technical, art, and clerical classes and sponsors cultural events directed to the community as a whole.

Between 1986 and 2009, Florida International University, a public university that grants postgraduate degrees and engages in important research programs, was headed by Modesto Maidique, a Havana-born professor and educational administrator. Florida International is closely linked to the Cuban American community in southern Florida through its faculty as well as its student population, and it has developed and maintained research projects and collections pertaining Cuba. In 1991, the Cuban Research Institute (CRI) was founded at Florida International. The CRI has distinguished itself for its close academic contact with Cuba and its forums for respectful discussion of controversial topics among Cubans from the island and the diaspora. Every two years the institute convenes the CRI Conference on Cuba and Cuban American Studies, which attracts Cubanists from top universities around the world, and since 2005, it has offered annually in December its Classically Cuban concert. The FIU library houses the Cristóbal Díaz Ayala Cuban and Latin American Popular Music Collection. The school itself has a high percentage of students of Cuban origin; many are the children or grandchildren of exiles from the 1960s, but many graduates and current students arrived in later waves of immigrants and come from modest families. Some are the first members of their families to attend a university.

A similar story can be told of the University of Miami, a private institution and the oldest of its kind in South Florida. Before the Revolution, many Cuban students attended this university, and the enrollment of Cuban and Cuban American students in its programs continues. Like Florida International University (its public counterpart), the University of Miami conducts cultural activities and research on Cuba. Its Cuban Heritage Collection, housed in the Otto G. Richter Library, is an important depository of Cuban books, documents, personal archives, photos, and memorabilia.

Outside the state of Florida, Cuban administrators have served in universities and public education programs and boards in places as far apart as Massachusetts and Texas. University professors of Cuban and Cuban American origin have also contributed to the development of research projects and institutes dealing with a variety of issues concerning not only Cuba but also Latin America and the United States.

BIBLIOGRAPHY

Beebe, Von N., and William F. Mackey. *Bilingual Schooling and the Miami Experience.* Coral Gables, FL: University of Miami, 1990.

De Aragón Clavijo, Uva. "Bright Minds." In *Greater Miami: Spirit of Cuban Enterprise*, edited by Miguel González-Pando, 70–79. Fort Lauderdale, FL: Copperfield, 1995.

González-Pando, Miguel, ed. *Greater Miami: Spirit of Cuban Enterprise.* Fort Lauderdale, FL: Copperfield, 1995.

ELPIDIO VALDÉS: A REVOLUTIONARY CARTOON HERO

Dean Luis Reyes

Popular Cuban animated character.

Elpidio Valdés is a fictional character created in 1970 by the Cuban cartoonist Juan Padrón (b. 1947) for the children's magazine *Pionero*. Originally a secondary character in a series about the adventures of the samurai warrior Kashibashi, Elpidio rapidly became the protagonist in his own series and Cuba's most popular comic strip character. In 1974 Elpidio vaulted into the movies, and for over thirty-five years he has been featured in more than twenty short films and three feature-length films. Since the 1970s he has served as an allegory of the Cuban character in mass popular culture.

Elpidio Valdés is a white peasant who joined up with the *mambi* forces fighting for Cuba's independence from Spain during the second half of the nineteenth century. In the early versions of his story, particularly in Cuba's first animated full-length feature film, *Elpidio Valdés* (1974), Elpidio embodied legitimate opposition to the Spanish authorities because of the creoles' lack of economic and civil rights. His movies evolved to incorporate anti-imperialist plots, as in *Elpidio Valdés contra dólar y cañón* (Elpidio Valdés versus the Dollar and the Cannon, 1983), as well as the theme of international solidarity, as in *Más se perdió en Cuba* (More Was Lost in Cuba, 1999), an account of the end of the wars of independence and the U.S. military intervention in Cuba. Elpidio's saga is told in chronological order, and the animated shorts follow comic narrative codes, whereas the three full-length films show greater dramatic complexity and a more formal structure. All of the films adhere to a visually realistic model of barely stylized, clean, conventional lines, with rounded figures and functional backgrounds that follow the limited animation method.

During the 1970s, the Elpidio series adapted the period's epic, nationalistic discourse prevalent in Cuban cinema, which explored the initial stages of the national independence movement, depicting the most memorable moments of that historical process. This discourse was seeking the origins of a national awareness, a Cuban character and a historical necessity for

See also

Cuban Thought and Cultural Identity: Costumbres in the Revolutionary Period

Education: Revolutionary Period

Spanish-American-Cuban War: 1898

Ten Years' War: 1868–1878

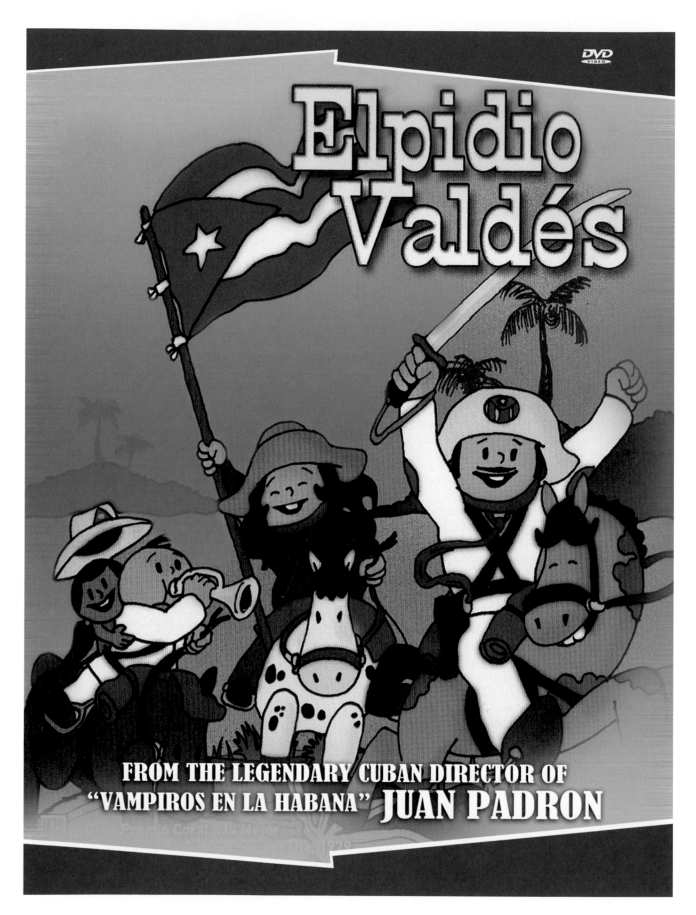

the founding of the nation, the turning point leading to the 1959 Revolution.

Within these efforts to construct the desired version of the nation's past, the essential contribution of Padrón and his *Elpidio Valdés* was an uninhibited, satirical treatment of the same themes that most films addressed in a serious, didactic tone. The saga of the rebel fighter began with the creation of a group of charismatic, witty characters. Two sides face-off (natives vs. foreigners, colonials vs. colonizers), but not in the simplistic, linear contradictions between negative and positive characters. Both sides are highly differentiated in their cultural attributes, so their conflicts can be interpreted not only as the disputes of historical adversaries, but within a wider cultural framework in which the principal clash is rooted in a confrontation between customs, habits, and ways of thinking. Jokes, constant mockery, satirical scenarios, and a general distancing from the solemnity of the official version of history are the stylistic hallmarks that define Padrón as a creator whose talent extends beyond episodic gags to concoct amusing, moving stories.

With the Elpidio series, Padrón appealed to the emotions of a mass audience, raising its self-esteem and allowing it recognition of its political tradition, thanks to the use of the genre's resources: the epic tales of a romantic hero and his adventures. These episodes usually depict feats of physical prowess and spectacular exploits of war. The views of Cuban generations born in and after the 1960s on the nation's wars for independence were influenced more by these films than by the Cuban history books they read in school.

Padrón's work developed from an already existing interest in finding new ways and more desirable patterns to express the realities of a socialist culture. These explorations originated with a critical debate over the bourgeois cultural legacy that minimized the role of popular and mestizo forms coming out of *creolism*. That is why Elpidio, even though he is white, participates in a multiracial environment in which blacks and mulattoes are his equals in the struggle.

Padrón made an invaluable contribution to national cinematography by decodifying the Cuban character in his portrayal of a popular and appealing character with whom the audience can identify. Elpidio's historical role is naturally accepted, but not because he has extraordinary qualities, and his heroic conduct is idealized, but not to the point of stereotyping. His films function as anthropological documentation that reconstructs customs and sheds light on the cultural evolution of the Cuban ethos.

From the perspective of the Elpidio saga, the Cuban national character radicalized its stance against foreign domination at the time of the wars of independence during the second half of the nineteenth century. The system of resistance that evolved into the qualities defined by Jorge Mañach in his essay *Indagación del choteo* (An Exploration of Irreverent Humor, 1928) dates from this period in Cuban history. Even when displayed clandestinely or suppressed in front of the colonial power, that resistance was characterized by the systematic devaluation of the ruling authority. The presumed identifier of Cuban culture as indomitable—an attribute that, in one way or another, generally develops in subaltern cultures—in Cuba expanded into a repertoire in which irony, humor, and mockery comprised the basic articulations of an ideology of resistance, which was essential for the public's identification with Elpidio Valdés.

The Elpidio films openly promote domestic values over foreign influence, demeaning the colonizer by mocking the voices and characters of the Spanish officers, the sworn enemies of the Cuban hero as well as sources of comedy themselves, while the Spanish private soldier is always portrayed as a subordinate completely uninterested in the reasons for the war. These depictions resulted in an uneasy reception of the Elpidio Valdés films in Spain. The films are even more scornful of unpatriotic Cubans, such as the *rayadillos* or creoles who work for the Spanish authorities; whereas the colonial officers escape more or less unscathed at the end of every skirmish, the mercenaries invariably are executed. The message is that there is no possible honor in treason.

In this way, Padrón transferred to mass culture the antihegemonic tradition of Cuba's popular culture. His cinematic work set the desirable tone for a paradigm of popular national animated films. Padrón also adapted his films to explicit militant ideological demands without sacrificing quality. That allowed him to introduce a new dimension of entertainment into the nationalist discourse that no other filmmaker had achieved. For these reasons, he is the national filmmaker best known to Cubans. Padrón's Elpidio Valdés is an essential symbol in the creole worldview, and his work is cherished by three generations of Cubans.

BIBLIOGRAPHY

Cobas, Roberto. "Notas para una cronología del dibujo animado cubano." *Cine Cubano* 110 (1984): 1–12.

Cobas, Roberto. "El dibujo animado en Cuba o la verdadera historia de Quijotes y Sanchos." In *Coordenadas del Cine Cubano 2*. Santiago de Cuba: Oriente, 2001.

Del Río, Joel. "Diálogo con Juan Padrón: El dibujo animado es el cine en estado puro." *Miradas: Revista del Audiovisual* (November 2005). Available from http://www.cinelatinoamericano.cult.cu/texto.aspx?cod=75.

Mañach, Jorge. "Indagación del choteo." In *Ensayos*. Havana: Editorial Letras Cubanas, 1999.

Planas Cabreja, Justo. "El reverso mítico de Elpidio Valdés." *La Gaceta de Cuba* (January–February 2010): 48–51.

Reyes, Dean Luis. "El etnocentrismo blando: Mambises y vampiros como guerrilla anticolonial en el cine de Juan Padrón." *Miradas: Revista del Audiovisual* (2010). Available from http://www.eictv.co.cu/miradas/.

Sotto, Arturo. "Juan Padrón: Un vampiro mambí o viceversa." *La Gaceta de Cuba* (May–June 2008): 11–14.

Opposite page:
Revolutionary cartoon hero Elpidio Valdés. Elpidio Valdés (right), a fictional character created in 1970 by the Cuban cartoonist Juan Padrón, became a symbol in mass popular culture for what it means to be Cuban. ELPIDIO VALDÉS. © VANGUARD CINEMA. USED WITH PERMISSION.

■ *See also*

Music: 1945–1959

Performing Arts: Cuban Forms of Popular Dance

Popular Songs of the 1920s

ENRIQUE JORRÍN AND THE CHA-CHA-CHA

Radamés Giro

The contribution of composer Enrique Jorrín to the musical genre known as the cha-cha-cha.

The composer and violinist Enrique Jorrín was born in Candelaria, Pinar del Río, on 25 December 1926, and died in Havana on 12 December 1987. He came to Havana in 1931 and in 1941 began studies at the Conservatorio Félix Alpizar (later the Conservatorio Amadeo Roldán.) That same year he joined the Orquesta Hermanos Contreras, led by the pianist and composer Silvio Contreras (1911–1972), and later played in the Artemisa, Idea, and Hermanos Peñalver orchestras until 1945, when he assumed leadership of Orquesta Selecciones del 45 and joined the Orquesta Arcaño y sus Maravillas.

From 1946 to 1953 Jorrín directed the Orquesta América, and in 1954 he established his own Orquesta Enrique Jorrín. In 1955 he took this orchestra to Mexico, where he remained until 1958. In Mexico he performed with the orchestra on radio station XEW. While in that country, he introduced the trumpet into his orchestra, changing the timbre of the ensemble in order to break the monotony of the *charanga*, a type of dance band in which the flute typically carries the melodic voice. In addition, he amplified the violins and the double bass to enlarge the sonic presence of the group in order to better handle the spacious ballrooms in which they were performing.

BACKGROUND

In 1942 Ninón Mondéjar (1914–2006) founded the Orquesta América, which included Enrique Jorrín among its musicians as musical director and arranger. In the 1940s young people's clubs sprang up, including Los Jóvenes del Silencio, Fraternidad Estudiantil, Inter Social, Silver Star, and Federación de Sociedades Juveniles (founded by Mondéjar). The Orquesta América wrote a *danzón* (national dance of Cuba) for each of these clubs with a sung refrain that mentioned the specific club's name. In the first part, the danzón was played with all of its sections, and in the second, the members of the whole orchestra sang the melody with lyrics that mentioned the names of those clubs.

Jorrín composed the danzones "Doña Olga" (which was a hit in the 1940s), "Liceo del Pilar," "Central Constancia," "Osiris," and "Unión Cienfueguera," to which he added another section, called a *montuno*. Mondéjar and Antonio Sánchez Reyes (1916–2001) (known as Musiquita), another member of América and composer of "Felicidades," did something similar,

as did Félix Reyna (1921–1998), composer of "Angoa," with Fajardo y sus Estrellas.

THE CHA-CHA-CHA

The claim that Enrique Jorrín was the creator of the cha-cha-cha fails to take into account that no musical genre springs out of the mind of a single creator. Nevertheless, history shows that there exist "genres created by popular composers attempting to respond to demands of business and fashion, who borrow different stylistic elements from other genres to restructure new ones; though these are almost always ephemeral, as they don't embody the experience of the people. Hence they call themselves 'creators' or 'inventors' of new forms, when they are simply remixing an already existing patrimony of the people. The mambo and the cha-cha-cha spring from these combinations" (León p. 42). According to this concept, Jorrín was not the creator of the cha-cha-cha, as has been claimed. As León indicates, it was the culmination of a process that went through many variations until a genre took shape.

Nor was Jorrín the one who brought singers back into the charanga orchestras. It should be recalled that the danzón, as performed with singer, had been in vogue since the era of the *danzonete*, from 1929 roughly to the 1950s. In fact, what Jorrín did was to have the three singers sing in unison, as previously they were soloists, as in the case of Pablo Quevedo (1907–1936), Fernando Collazo (1902–1939), and Dominica Verges (1918–2002).

The sung parts of the cha-cha-cha were characterized by the incorporation of some Spanish stylistic traits. Examples are the *chotis* in "Madrid," by Agustín Lara (1900–1970), and the *cuplé* in "Soy cigarrera," by José Padilla (1889–1960) (Torres 1998, p. 194).

So, then, when and where did the term *cha-cha-cha* arise? The term received an official imprimatur when it was used by the promoter Vicente Amores, president of the Amores de Verano Society and owner of the ballroom located at Prado and Neptuno. Mondéjar said that it was Amores who recruited "a group of girls who were very active, and who were the first to match the dance steps to the chorus that went *un, dos, chachachá*" (Acosta p. 96). The cha-cha-cha was in the air. In 1948 Jorrín recorded "Nunca," by the Mexican composer Guty Cárdenas (1905–1932), whose first part he played in its original style and whose second part he played in a more lively tempo.

However, the first works considered to be cha-cha-chas are those by Ninón Mondéjar, then leader of the Orquesta América. They are "Yo no camino más" and "La verde palmera real," recorded on the Panart record label in 1954. Prior to that, Jorrín had recorded "La engañadora" (The Deceiver, 1953) as *mambo-rumba*. But Jorrín and Mondéjar were not the only composers whose works América performed. The orchestra also played works by Félix Reyna ("Muñeca Triste"), Rosendo Ruiz Quevedo ("Rico vacilón"), and Antonio Sánchez Reyes ("Poco pelo") (Acosta p. 93).

"La engañadora" was born into this lineage, with an introduction and ending in a rumba tempo, which is why it bears the inscription of a mambo-rumba and, later, mambo-cha-cha-cha (during the peak of the mambo of Dámaso Pérez Prado) although it already had the characteristics of what would eventually be the cha-cha-cha. But included on the same record as "La engañadora" is "Silver Star," which became known as a danzón and which, in its vocal section, said that the cha-cha-cha was "the best dance of all." In Jorrín's same creative vein, América performed "El túnel," "Nada para ti," "Cógele bien el compás," and Sánchez Reyes's "Poco pelo" and "Yo sabía."

It was the Orquesta América that premiered "La engañadora" and spread the cha-cha-cha in other countries at the same time that Rosendo Ruiz (1918–2009) composed "Rico vacilón" (perhaps the best-known cha-cha-cha in the world), César Portillo de la Luz (b. 1922) composed "Chachachá de las pepillas," Richard Egües (1923–2006) composed "El bodeguero," and Félix Reyna composed "Muñeca triste" and "Pa' bailar." All of these pieces contributed to the popularity of the genre, thanks particularly to the success the Orquesta Aragón, from Cienfuegos, had among dancers, for which they were known as the *stylists* of cha-cha-cha. Other groups that spread the cha-cha-cha were the charanga orchestras of Neno González (1903–1986), Melodías del 40, Sensación, Fajardo y sus Estrellas, Maravillas de Florida, and Estrellas Cubanas. Musicians abroad took up the new genre, and in New York, Tito Puente (1923–2000) presented "¡Qué será!" and "Happy chachachá," and Ray Cohen offered "Chachachá de los pollos."

JORRÍN'S CONTRIBUTIONS

Jorrín gave cha-cha-cha the structure and style for which it became known, and the cha-cha-cha was the form he adopted for his creative work. In fact, he was not trying to create a new genre; no composer does (Martínez p. 307). However, Jorrín isolated the last part of the danzón and give it its own shape. He wrote an introduction of eight or sixteen measures, which meant that the pieces were shorter, distinguishing the cha-cha-cha from the danzón, even though it was derived from the latter's rhythm cell.

Jorrín was also the one who delineated the form later known as the cha-cha-cha by changing the rhythmic cell of the *güiro* (a percussion instrument with notches on one side), the vamp of the piano in the last part, and introducing a new rhythmic cell played by the *tumbadora* (conga drum), *timbales* (shallow, single-headed drums with metal casings), and the güiro. He also had the singers sing in unison. In the cha-cha-cha, the *tumbao* (the way of phrasing the basic rhythm on the piano or the bass) is basically percussive, in which the rhythmic element dominates over the melodic. This does not mean that the latter holds no interest but that the melodic element serves to

Dancing the cha-cha-cha, 1957. The cha-cha-cha, a Cuban dance promoted around the world by bandleader Enrique Jorrín and others in the 1950s, was a refuge for dancers because it was much easier to dance to than the frenetic mambo. THURSTON HOPKINS/PICTURE POST/ GETTY IMAGES

highlight the rhythmic and accompanies and supports the steps of the dancers.

In addition, Jorrín was the one most responsible for the cha-cha-cha attaining the popularity it enjoyed in its day, although it was the Orquesta Aragón that kept it in the hit parade the longest, for the Orquesta América, after returning from Mexico, no longer commanded the support it previously had from dancers. In 1975 Jorrín turned the group into a chamber orchestra devoted to playing cha-cha-cha.

"Cha-cha-cha was a refuge after the mambo"; their composers created a stylistics of charanga, without thinking that its sonic density would distinguish it from the mambo (Galán p. 211). The cha-cha-cha was a refuge for dancers in particular, for it was much easier to dance to than the frenetic mambo and so, from ears to hips to feet, it spread throughout the world.

SELECTED DISCOGRAPHY

Charangas de Siempre (2006).

Encuentro de Charangas (1999).

BIBLIOGRAPHY

Acosta, Leonardo. *Otra visión de la música popular cubana.* Havana: Editorial Letras Cubanas, 2004.

Betancourt Álvarez, Fabio. *Sin clave y bongó no hay son.* Medellín, Colombia: Editorial Universidad de Antioquia, 1993.

Castillo Faílde, Osvaldo. *Miguel Faílde, creador musical del danzón.* Havana: Editora del Consejo Nacional de Cultura, 1964.

Galán, Natalio. *Cuba y sus sones.* Valencia, Spain: Pre-Textos Literarios, 1997.

Gómez García, Zoila, and Victoria Eli. *Música latinoamericana y caribeña*. Havana: Editorial Pueblo y Educación, 1995.

Hernández, Erena. *La música en persona*. Havana: Editorial Letras Cubanas, 1986.

León, Argeliers. "Notas para un panorama de la música popular." In *Panorama de la música popular cubana*, compiled by Radamés Giro. 2nd ed. Havana: Editorial Letras Cubanas, 1998.

Martínez, Mayra A. *Cubanos en la música*. Havana: Editorial Letras Cubanas, 1993.

Rodríguez, Ezequiel. *El danzón: Iconografía, creadores e intérpretes*. Havana: Consejo Provincial de Cultura, 1967.

Roy, Maya. *Músicas cubanas*. Madrid: Ediciones Akdal, 2003.

Torres, Dora Ileana. "Del danzón cantado al chachachá." In *Panorama de la música popular cubana*, compiled by Radamés Giro. 2nd ed. Havana: Editorial Letras Cubanas, 1998.

Ulloa, Alejandro. *La salsa en Cali*. Cali, Colombia: Ediciones Universidad del Valle, 1992.

■ *See also*

Diasporas: Exiles in the Cuban Popular Imagination

Operation Pedro Pan

Performing Arts: Performance Art

ESCULTURAS RUPESTRES AND OTHER WORKS BY ANA MENDIETA

Laura Roulet

The life and work of artist Ana Mendieta who did a series of rock carvings in the caves of Jaruco Park, Cuba.

The *Esculturas Rupestres* (Rupestrian sculptures), a series of rock carvings named for Taínan goddesses, were created by Cuban American artist Ana Mendieta in 1981. They represent an extension of her earlier earth-body work and a spiritual homecoming for the artist, who was born in Cuba and sent to the United States as an adolescent under the auspices of Operation Pedro Pan.

CHILDHOOD AND FAMILY

Ana Mendieta was born on 18 November 1948, in Havana. She was the second daughter of Ignacio Alberto Mendieta de Lizáur and Raquel Oti de Rojas. Her father, Ignacio, worked as an attorney, and her mother, Raquel, was a chemist and researcher. Ana and her older sister Raquelín attended Catholic schools and enjoyed a comfortable, privileged upbringing. The family divided its time between a home in Vedado and vacations spent with relatives in a large family house on Varadero Beach. These summers spent in the water and sand with her cousins constituted an important point of reference for Mendieta's later body of work, which was composed mostly outdoors, in nature.

Both sides of the family had strong political roots. On her father's side was Carlos Mendieta, who served as president of Cuba (1934–1935), and on her mother's side was Oscar Maria de Rojas Cruzat, a Cuban general in the Spanish-American War. Mendieta's father was a supporter of the 26th of July movement. With the success of the Revolution in 1959, he was offered a job as assistant to Raul Roa y Garcia, minister of state. In 1961, when he refused to join the Communist Party, he lost his job and was blacklisted.

As the political climate shifted in the post-Revolutionary period, private schools were closed, and Mendieta's parents decided to send Ana and Raquelín to the United States through Operation Pedro Pan, a program sponsored by the Catholic Church and U.S. State Department to relocate to the United States more than 14,000 unaccompanied Cuban minors. On 11 September 1961, Ana and Raquelín flew to Miami. Because they had no relatives able to care for them in the United States, they were sent on to Dubuque, Iowa, where they were shuttled among three foster families and a boarding school over the next few years. This abrupt shift to a homogeneous, Midwestern American community caused a traumatic sense of alienation and dislocation for Mendieta that later found expression in her work.

In January 1965, Ignacio Mendieta was arrested for his political activities and sentenced to twenty years' imprisonment. In January 1966, the artist's mother and younger brother left Cuba on a Freedom Flight, reuniting with Ana and Raquelín in Cedar Rapids, Iowa. Ignacio was released in 1971 and finally rejoined his family in 1979.

EARLY WORK

By 1967, Mendieta had found focus as an artist and was studying painting at the University of Iowa, Iowa City. After completing a B.A. and M.F.A., she switched resolutely from painting to multimedia studies at the University of Iowa's newly established Center for New Performing Arts (CNPA) and Intermedia Program. To explain the multidisciplinary approach of the program, which combined visual art with dance, music, theater, and writing, Professor Hans Breder adopted the term *intermedia*, coined by the Fluxus artists to describe art that exists between or outside traditional art media. Visiting artists such as Robert Wilson, Vito Acconci, and Alan Kaprow, and the critic Lucy Lippard played a vital role in exposing students to avant-garde art forms of the 1970s.

Mendieta was adept at assimilating the contemporary movements of earth art, body art, feminism, and conceptualism and incorporating them into her own artistic practice. While still a student, she began producing mature work in performance art and the earth-body works known as *Siluetas* (silhouettes). She is quoted as saying:

The turning point in my art was in 1972, when I realized that my paintings were not real enough for what I wanted the image to convey—and by real I mean I wanted my images to have power, to be magic. I decided for the images to have magic qualities I had to work directly with nature. I had to go to the source of life, to mother earth.

Eshelman and Eshelman p. 70

The *Silueta* series includes ephemeral earth-body works Mendieta formed by incorporating her body or tracing her silhouette into the landscape. Most were created in private rituals as a way of investing her image with sacred qualities. Materials range from grass, flowers, sticks, and moss to those charged with spiritual meaning such as blood, water, and fire. Like the work of earth artists such as Richard Long (b. 1945), Mendieta's work was site-specific, used found materials from the environment, and was meant to meld back into its original natural state. The cycle of life, death, and regeneration replicated in nature can be related to her Catholic upbringing and also to a holistic sense of nature as the source of universal energy, a belief closer to Santería or pre-Columbian faiths.

In early performative work, Mendieta used materials derived in part from Santería such as blood, gunpowder, and earth as a means of reconnecting with her Cuban roots. Though raised a Catholic, she was exposed to Santería in her childhood through the beliefs of the household servants. In a 1972 performance, *Untitled (Death of a Chicken)*, she held a struggling, decapitated chicken, allowing its blood to splatter over her nude body. In this case, she drew on the powerful emotional effects of both the cathartic rituals of animal sacrifice in Santería and violent performances of contemporary artists such as the Viennese Actionists. A series of tableaux in 1973, addressing issues of rape and violence toward women, was contemporaneous with the social critiques of feminist artists such as Suzanne Lacy (b. 1945).

From 1971 to 1980, Mendieta traveled almost every summer to Mexico, either with a group of students or alone with Hans Breder. She viewed Mexico as a return to her source, a Spanish-speaking culture and natural world reminiscent of her childhood summers at Varadero. She created a large series of *Siluetas* in Oaxaca, San Felipe, La Ventosa, and archaeological sites near Oaxaca. Her performative earth-body works, using first her own body and then body substitutes and silhouette outlines, are documented on slides, video, and super-8 film.

In 1977, Mendieta completed her M.F.A. in multimedia and was awarded a small National Endowment for the Arts grant, which enabled her to move to New York City. Her new circles of friends included artists such as Ted Victoria (b. 1944), Mary Beth Edelson (b. 1933), Liliana Porter (b. 1941), Luis Camnitzer (b. 1937), and Nancy Spero (1926–2009), as well as members of the Cuban expatriate community.

Having been placed within the context of feminist art by the writer Lucy Lippard, Mendieta was invited to join the feminist art cooperative A.I.R Gallery, where she exhibited from 1979 to 1982. Mendieta's use of Great Goddess imagery, such as the photograph of herself covered in mud with arms upraised, against a tree trunk in *Tree of Life* (1976), related to the search for female prototypes and matriarchal antecedents in history explored by other feminist artists such as Edelson and Donna Henes (b. 1945). Mendieta also contributed to two issues of the feminist journal *Heresies*.

In 1979, she met the Minimalist sculptor Carl Andre (b. 1935). They began an on-again, off-again romantic relationship and creative partnership. Over the next six years, she and Andre exhibited jointly three times and traveled extensively, sharing a fascination with the Paleolithic and ancient art sites of Malta; Newgrange, Ireland; and Egypt.

Mendieta was interviewed by the filmmaker Estela Bravo for *Los que se fueron* (Those Who Left, 1980), a film about involuntary exiles sent from Cuba by their parents in Operation Pedro Pan. As travel restrictions were loosened under the Carter administration, Mendieta began to investigate the possibility of returning to Cuba. Her first opportunity came in 1980 through the Círculo de Cultura Cubana (Cuban Cultural Circle), which sponsored group tours and symposiums. Over the next three years she led several Círculo de Cultura Cubana tours, bringing American artists and scholars to the island, and then returned on her own at the invitation of the government to exhibit and create work.

LATE WORK AND DEATH

Mendieta was awarded a Prix de Rome and began a residency at the American Academy in Rome in October 1983. Installed in her first indoor studio, she was challenged to create more permanent work. She began a series of flat, horizontal sculptures composed of earth and sand mixed with binder, made to lie flush with the floor, and free-standing wood sculptures with designs carved or burned with gunpowder.

She and Carl Andre were married in Rome on 17 January 1985. They exhibited a jointly conceived portfolio of lithographs titled *Duetto pietre foglie* (Duet of Stone and Leaf) with their sculpture at the AAM (Architettura Arte Moderna) Gallery. On 8 September 1985 Mendieta died in a fall from the thirty-fourth floor window of the New York apartment she shared with Andre.

ESCULTURAS RUPESTRES

Mendieta was the first post-Revolution Cuban American artist to receive permission from the Cuban Ministry of Culture to exhibit and create work on the

island. Returning first out of longing to reconnect with her family and birthplace, she quickly developed ties within the art community. Between January 1980 and July 1983, she traveled seven times to the island, expanding on her knowledge of Cuban culture, particularly pre-Columbian art and Santería, a syncretic Afro-Cuban religion combining elements of Catholicism with West African Yoruba traditions.

Mendieta's second trip to Cuba, in January 1981, coincided with the *Volumen I* (Volume One) exhibit featuring the work of what would become known as *La generación de los ochenta* (the 1980s generation). The first generation raised under the Castro regime, these artists broke with the programmatic art promoted by the government in the 1970s. Mendieta befriended José Bedia (b. 1959), Juan Elso Padilla (1956–1988), Ricardo Rodriguez Brey (b. 1955), Flavio Garciandía (b. 1954), and Gustavo Pérez Monzón (b. 1956). Bedia, Rodriguez Brey, and Elso Padilla shared an interest in Santería and pre-Columbian culture; like Mendieta, they were incorporating rituals, materials, and imagery from those sources into their art. Bedia remembered Mendieta as part of the first rapprochement between Anglo and Latin American artists, describing her as a "connector" (Bedia, interview with author). She served as a bridge for them, demystifying the North American art world known to them only through magazines. She also helped them to secure artistic residencies in the United States. In turn, they facilitated her exploration of Afro-Cuban culture and helped her scout a location for the Rupestrian sculptures.

Aided by a Guggenheim Foundation fellowship, Mendieta returned in July 1981 to create the Rupestrian sculptures in the *Escaleras de Jaruco* (Stairs of Jaruco) located in Jaruco Park, about twenty miles from Havana. Choosing two sites in the mountainside, she carved a series of goddess sculptures into the soft oolitic limestone grottos. The creation myths of the Taínos, an indigenous tribe of the Caribbean, and those of other pre-Columbian Mesoamerican people center on caves as the birthplaces of humanity. Inspired by petroglyphs, Mendieta used the natural rock outcroppings to shape the outlines of the figures, which were scaled to her under-5-foot height. Sculptural volumes replace the voids of her *Silueta* (silhouette) forms, perhaps reflecting the artist's sense of psychological restoration in returning her work to Cuba.

Having researched the Taíno people, Mendieta saw herself as a cultural inheritor, identifying with their dislocation and near decimation within a generation of the Spanish conquest. Based on consultation with Yale University professor José Juan Arrom and the writings of Cuban scholar Lydia Cabrera, Mendieta named the carvings after Taínan goddesses: Maroya (Goddess of the Moon), Guabancex (Goddess of the Wind), Iyare (Mother), Guanaroca (First Woman), Alboboa (Beautiful One), Bacayu (Light of Day), Guacar (First Menstruation), Atabey (Mother of the Waters), and Itiba Cahubaba (Old Mother Blood).

Aware that few spectators would ever encounter the works in person, Mendieta documented the series in black and white photographs, 35mm slides, and super-8 film. She later printed and exhibited the series in large format 40 x 60-inch prints to convey the experience of seeing the works in life-size. She also received a grant from the New York State Council on the Arts to create photo etchings of the series, which she intended to print in book format with an introduction by Arrom. In her grant application, she wrote:

> It was during my childhood in Cuba that I first became fascinated by primitive art and cultures.... This sense of magic, knowledge and power found in primitive art has influenced my personal attitude toward art-making. For the past twelve years I have been working out in nature, exploring the relationship between myself, the earth and art. I have thrown myself into the very elements that produced me, using the earth as my canvas and my soul as my tools.

> *Clearwater p. 41*

To achieve a sense of intimacy, Mendieta cropped the photos so that each sculpture appears independently. The initial five sets of ten photo etchings were prepared on zinc plates and printed by the artist Luis Camnitzer in 1983. Although Mendieta had intended to print an edition of twenty, the project remained unfinished at her death; it was completed posthumously by Liliana Porter.

RETROSPECTIVE

In November 1987, the first Ana Mendieta retrospective opened at the New Museum of Contemporary Art in New York City. A comprehensive retrospective, *Ana Mendieta: Earth Body, Sculpture and Performance, 1972–1985*, was organized by the Hirshhorn Museum and Sculpture Garden in Washington, D.C., in 2004, with venues at the Whitney Museum of American Art, Des Moines Art Center, and Miami Art Museum. Her work has directly inspired homage by the Cuban collective Galería DUPP and the performance artist Tania Bruguera (b. 1968). No longer seen solely as feminist, Latina, or identity art, Mendieta's photography, sculpture, drawings, and films can be appreciated in multiple contexts for their groundbreaking originality. Mendieta assimilated many sources in creating works of transcultural expression, mediating between her native Cuba and adopted North America.

BIBLIOGRAPHY

Arrom, Juan José. *Mytología y artes prehispánicas de las Antillas.* Mexico City: Siglo Venitiuno, 1975.

Bedia, José, interview by Laura Roulet and Olga M. Viso. 9 August 2001, artist's studio, Miami, Florida.

Opposite page:
Tree of Life (1976) by Ana Mendieta (1948–1985). Ana Mendieta's use of goddess imagery, as seen in this 1976 photograph of the artist covered in mud with arms upraised against a tree trunk, a work called *Tree of Life*, related to her search for female prototypes and matriarchal antecedents in history. © THE ESTATE OF ANA MENDIETA COLLECTION. COURTESY GALERIE LELONG, NEW YORK

Bedia, José, follow-up telephone interview by author. 30 October 2003.

Cabrera, Lydia. *Leyendas cubanas*. Havana: Editorial Arte y Literatura, 1978.

Clearwater, Bonnie, ed. *Ana Mendieta: A Book of Works*. Miami, FL: Grassfield Press, 1993.

Eshelman, Clayton, and Caryl Eshelman, eds. "A Tribute to Ana Mendieta." *Sulfer* 22 (Spring 1988): 46–114.

Mosquera, Gerardo. *Ana Mendieta, Rupestrian Sculptures—Esculturas Rupestres*. New York: A.I.R. Gallery, 1981.

Viso, Olga M., ed. *Ana Mendieta: Earth Body, Sculpture and Performance, 1972–1985*. Washington, DC: Hirshhorn Museum and Sculpture Garden with Hatje Cantz, 2004.

■ *See also*

Faith: Catholicism

Music: Early History

ESTEBAN SALAS: AN EIGHTEENTH-CENTURY COMPOSER

Radamés Giro

The career of the first great Cuban composer.

When Alejo Carpentier was researching *La música en Cuba* (Music in Cuba, 1946) in the 1940s, he had no idea that he was going to rediscover the lost work of one of Cuba's most important composers, Esteban Salas y Castro (1725–1803). Carpentier's research led him to an 1855 article in *Semanario Cubano* (Cuban Weekly) containing a biographical portrait and a description of the works and the time at which they were composed; material contained in books of notes kept in the cathedral; and scores of Salas's music itself that had been forgotten. It was through Carpentier's discoveries that Salas's career and music became known.

Before Carpentier's discoveries, Esteban Salas was rarely mentioned. Salas was not as well known as Blas López, choirmaster at the Bayamo church in the late sixteenth and early seventeenth centuries, and Miguel Velázquez, choirmaster at Santiago during the sixteenth century, even though he lived in a more recent time than either of them. Laureano Fuentes Matons mentions Salas in his *Las artes en Santiago de Cuba* (The Arts in Santiago de Cuba, 1893). Not until the studies of Pablo Hernández Balaguer (1928–1966), however, was a more complete knowledge of Esteban Salas's role in Cuban musical history available.

BIRTH AND EDUCATION

At the time of Salas's birth the island was practically divided in two: the eastern and western departments. That geographical division also marked the stages of Salas's life: the first stage in Havana from the time of his birth until 1764; the second, from 1764 until his death in Santiago de Cuba. Esteban Salas was born in Havana on 25 January 1725 (Franco 1953). Little is known about his life and work there. At the age of nine he became a boy soprano in the chorus of the city's main church and began to study plainsong, organ, violin, counterpoint, and composition. In 1740 he enrolled in the San Carlos Seminary, where he studied philosophy, theology, and canon law. Little is known about his musical training or about other musicians who provided music for the Havana choir. However, Salas studied with Cayetano Pagueras, who had solid academic training and transmitted to Salas the technical command that is so obvious in all of his compositions.

An organist and composer, Pagueras came to Cuba in 1750, and he knew the latest trends in Spanish and Italian music. It is known that in 1792 and 1795, when Pagueras was precentor of the cathedral, he used to sell harpsichord music by the best composers that had come from Spain, and other kinds of church music, as well as music for secular concerts (Escudero Suástegui pp. 47–82). Pagueras worked with Salas in Havana until 1763.

MUSICAL INFLUENCES

After the Spanish conquest of the New World, the works of Palestrina, Francisco Guerrero, Tomás Luis de Victoria, and Cristóbal de Morales were brought to America and influenced New World composers. Mexico also provided music and items of worship to the choirs of Havana and Santiago de Cuba (Béhague pp. 26–89). Ships from the Canary Islands and other regions of Europe converged on Havana once a year, establishing a flow of products of every kind, including books and musical scores. From the time of Esteban Salas, Spanish culture permeated Italy as a consequence of Spain's occupation of half of that peninsula. So it is not surprising that Venetian publications of Spanish music, and those of Neapolitan composers as well, were sung in the Santiago de Cuba Cathedral and in Havana's major church.

These historical facts help explain the dual Hispanic-Italian influence found in Esteban Salas's style. The possible influence of Mexican *villancicos,* or Christmas carols, which predated by a century those produced by the Cubans, should not be discounted either. The presence in Salas's works of elements from two great eras in the history of music is due to his living at a time when Europe was converting the Baroque legacy into a new view of the world and musical experience, trends that Salas could not elude.

CHOIRMASTER OF THE SANTIAGO DE CUBA CATHEDRAL

In 1763 Bishop Pedro Agustín Morell de Santa Cruz appointed Salas to head the choir of the Santiago de Cuba Cathedral, and he arrived there in February 1764. He began as the interim choirmaster. To prove his competence, he directed a performance of "Ave

Maris Stella" for the town council and was provisionally awarded the title of choirmaster on 12 March. His permanent appointment to the post was granted by royal letters patent on 12 March 1769. Salas reorganized the choir and under his direction it came to have a roster of fourteen musicians.

The new auxiliary church, Iglesia del Carmen, was scheduled to be inaugurated on 16 July 1766, but an earthquake on 11 June destroyed almost the entire city, including the cathedral, its archives, and the new church. The reconstruction of the church buildings motivated Salas to compose the carol, "Pues la fábrica de un templo" (So the Building of a Church).

Salas's work can be divided into two categories, liturgical and nonliturgical music, although the latter could also be used in the liturgy. The difference is that the liturgical works have texts in Latin and the nonliturgical works are in Spanish. The first category contains psalms, litanies, settings of the "Salve Regina," and masses, and the second, *villancico*-style Christmas carols and *pastourelles* (a kind of ballad).

The carols, such as "Quién ha visto que en invierno" (Who Has Seen in Winter) and "Sobre los ríos undosos" (Over Winding Rivers) have a choral refrain, usually with solo parts, followed by the verses, almost always sung in unison, that end with a repetition of the refrain. Cantatas, such as "Saltando viene" (Leaping Along) and "Silencio, por si dormido" (Quiet, He May Be Sleeping), are short and include arias and recitatives, like the pastourelles. Traces of Spanish popular music are found in the villancicos and pastourelles. The liturgical music is basically restricted to the Spanish models that preserved the preclassical traditions, especially the Baroque.

The instrumentation most often used for the carols consists of two violas and one bass, adhering to the practices of *basso continuo*, although with classical accents. In liturgical music, it was more common to use only a bass instrument accompanying the voices while the parts written for solo instruments were generally simple, as was the custom in the Baroque period.

LATER LIFE

Salas was ordained as a priest on 20 March 1790 in a ceremony at the Iglesia de Dolores, and for the occasion he composed a villancico that was not a Christmas carol, "¿Quién es esta, cielos?" (Heavens, Who Is This?), and a *Stabat mater* consisting of fourteen movements.

In 1855, *Semanario Cubano* described Esteban Salas physically in the earliest known article about him:

> He had a small, lean body, a dark face, a high, wide, ample forehead, an indication of the great intelligence beneath, dark, large, almond-shaped eyes, an aquiline nose and lips a bit thick. He had a serious and circumspect but nevertheless affable and open-faced look, like that of any happy person . . . even his attire, which was that of priest . . . denoted his customary self-denial and his fervent desire to live the life of a poor man.

Salas was an educated man who composed and provided music for all the parishes in eastern Cuba, met the liturgical needs of the cathedral and its auxiliary

Studying music in Santiago de Cuba.
A music student practices piano at the Esteban Salas Conservatory in Santiago de Cuba. © MARKA/ALAMY

church, and taught plainsong, philosophy, and moral theology at the San Basilio seminary. As an old man, ill and poor, he composed his last villancico for Christmas 1801 (Carpentier 1972, p. 81). Carpentier offered the following evaluation of Salas's work: "All of Salas's scores are written with an astonishing professional confidence . . . Salas's *villancicos*—entirely different from the traditional Spanish polyphonic *villancico*—are finely crafted works, particularly accomplished . . . All in all, Salas was the classic composer within Cuban music."

SELECTED DISCOGRAPHY

Un barroco cubano del Siglo XVIII (1996).

Cuban Baroque Sacred Music: Esteban Salas (1997).

Esteban Salas: Baroque Cantatas from Santiago de Cuba (1998).

Esteban Salas: Cantus in honore Beatæ Mariæ Virginis (2002).

Esteban Salas: Passio Domini nostri Jesu Christi (2004).

Nativité à Santiago de Cuba (2001).

BIBLIOGRAPHY

Ardévol, José. *Música y revolución*. Havana: Ediciones Unión, 1966.

Béhague, Gerard. *Music in Latin America: An Introduction*. Englewood Cliffs, NJ: Prentice-Hall, 1979.

Béhague, Gerard. *La música en América Latina: (Una introducción)*. Translated by Miguel Castillo Didier. Caracas: Monte Ávila, 1983.

Carpentier, Alejo. *La música en Cuba*. Mexico City: Fondo de Cultura Económica, 1972.

Carpentier, Alejo. *Music in Cuba*. Translated by Alan West-Durán. Minneapolis: University of Minnesota Press, 2001.

Escudero Suástegui, Miriam Esther. *El Archivo de Música de la iglesia habanera La Merced: Estudio y catálogo*. Havana: Fondo Editorial Casa de las Américas, 1998.

Franco, José Luciano. "Esteban Salas, el compositor olvidado." *Carteles* (Havana) 46 (15 November 1953).

Fuentes Matons, Laureano. *Las artes en Santiago de Cuba*. Havana: Letras Cubanas, 1981.

Hernández Balaguer, Pablo. *El más antiguo documento de la música cubana y otros ensayos*. Havana: Letras Cubanas, 1986.

Hernández Balaguer, Pablo. *Los villancicos, cantadas y pastorelas de Esteban Salas*. Havana: Letras Cubanas, 1986.

Pérez Sanjurjo, Elena. *Historia de la música cubana*. Miami, FL: Moderna Poesía, 1986.

Torres-Cuevas, Eduardo, and Edelberto Leiva Lajara. *Historia de la iglesia católica en Cuba: La iglesia en las patrias de los criollos (1516–1789)*. Havana: Ediciones Boloña, 2007.

F

FAITH

Religion has played an important role in the spiritual and cultural life of Cubans. Although the indigenous peoples who lived on the island before the arrival of the Spanish had a coherent spiritual belief system, it was the clash and convergence of European Catholicism and African religions introduced by Cuba's slave population that have given Cuba a spiritual uniqueness. These Afro-Cuban religions are Regla de Ocha (Santería), Reglas de Palo, Abakuá, Arará, and Vodou. Other religions are Protestantism, Judaism, Spiritism, and Rastafari.

Like its cuisine and music, Cuba's religious manifestations bear the imprint of many parts of the world. Under Spanish colonialism, the Catholic Church was a powerful institution, and enslaved Africans were encouraged and coerced into converting to Catholicism. Protestantism and Judaism were forbidden, as were the different African religions of the enslaved.

Beginning in 1959, the Cuban Revolution, as a secular force, resulted in Cuba defining itself for decades as an atheist state. Cuba reclassified itself as a secular state after the fall of the Soviet Union. The relationship between the revolutionary government and different religions is central to several of the articles that follow.

FAITH: CATHOLICISM

Aurelio Alonso

The changing relations between the Roman Catholic Church and Cuban civil authorities.

Although it is unlikely that the Roman Catholic Church will ever single out Pope Alexander VI (1492–1503) for sainthood, he nonetheless played a decisive role in the history of Catholicism in the Spanish colonies in the New World, and, ultimately, in world history. His pontificate coincided with the arrival of Christopher Columbus on the islands that would later be called the Caribbean. In 1493, a year after the admiral's first voyage, the pope, in a show of force that went beyond matters of the faith, issued three papal bulls delimiting rights to the territories that had been or were yet to be conquered. They were assigned to Spain and, to a lesser extent, Portugal, and *a priori*

invalidated the claim of any other state to these lands. Since Spain's dominion over the American hemisphere had not yet extended from the Caribbean to the continent, the Crown could hardly imagine the significance that the discovery, and the support of the Spanish pope, would eventually acquire.

Alexander's most significant decree might well have been a fourth and less often-cited bull, issued toward the end of his pontificate. In 1501, in *Eximia Devotionis Sinceritas*, the pope granted in perpetuity to the monarchy of Castile and León the tithe that would serve as the primary rents to support the Church in the colonial territories, which the new colonists would also have to pay. Likewise, the pope delegated to the Crown the responsibility for "founding, endowing, and maintaining the churches." By that time, Columbus, on his fourth journey, had already explored the mouth of the Orinoco on the South American continent, and it was evident that the expanse of land to be conquered far exceeded the missionary capabilities of

CHRONOLOGY OF EVENTS

1493: Pope Alexander VI (Rodrigo Borgia) divides the New World between Spain and Portugal.

1501: Alexander VI makes Spain responsible for church organization in its colonies, granting it church tithes in perpetuity.

1508: Pope Julius II grants Spanish monarch control of church governance in New World.

1518: Pope Leo X establishes the Diocese of Cuba.

1689: Jesuits found Seminary of San Ambrosio in Havana.

1728: Dominican friars found the University of Saint Gerónimo of Havana.

1774: Seminary of San Carlos y San Ambrosio opens.

1838: Spanish government confiscates Church property.

1901: Cuban Constitution establishes religious freedom; Catholic Church receives recompense for property seized in 1838.

1925: Diocese of Cuba transferred from Santiago to Havana.

1946: Pope Pius XII names Manuel Arteaga Betancourt the first Cuban cardinal.

1959: Cuban Revolution establishes Communist government.

1961: Cuban government expels numerous priests, effectively ending private education.

1969: Cuban bishops issue pastoral letter against U.S. embargo of Cuba.

1975: Cuban Communist Party Congress proclaims atheism official stance of the state.

1986: Cuban Catholic Church holds conference on role of the Church in Cuba that includes bishops from throughout the Americas.

1993: Cuban bishops issue pastoral letter, "El amor todo lo espera" ("Love always hopes") identifying a spiritual crisis in Cuba.

1994: Pope John Paul II appoints Archbishop Jaime Ortega the first Cuban cardinal in thirty years.

1998: Pope John Paul II visits Cuba.

2003: Cuban bishops reaffirm concern for Cuba's spiritual future.

Pope Alexander VI. The Valencian pope Alexander VI (r. 1492–1503) played a decisive role in the history of Catholicism in the Spanish colonies in the New World.
© SCALA /ART RESOURCE, NY

Rome; at the same time Spain was seeking ideological support for its adventure in colonial domination and its positioning on the European stage.

It was not, however, the Borgia pope, who was murdered in 1503, but rather his successor Julius II (1503–1513) who would add a new twist to the story. With Julius the throne of Saint Peter returned to the control of the Italian nobility, and although he found the claims being pressed by the Spanish monarch distasteful, and despite great misgivings, Julius yielded to the pressures of King Ferdinand. In 1508 he issued the bull *Universalis Ecclesia Regiminio*, by virtue of which the Spanish king was recognized by the Church as the patron in perpetuity of the American lands. It was now the king's gift to appoint bishops, set the boundaries of dioceses, allocate the tithes set by the Crown, and assert other powers that subordinated the clergy to temporal authorities. In exchange, the temporal authority guaranteed the Church's mission of Christianizing the population in the colonies, and of excluding any other creed.

The final bull of Alexander VI had been the true starting point of royal patronage, which dominated the ideological panorama of the Latin American continent from then until the independence of the colonies at the beginning of the nineteenth century and in the cases of Cuba and Puerto Rico, until the end of that century. The legal-administrative machinery of Spanish colonial domination was comprehensive in scope, and citizenship status and the Catholic faith in Spanish America were, therefore, organically related.

CATHOLICISM AND COLONIAL CUBA

During the first half century of the occupation of the island, epidemics, abuse, and exploitation decimated the indigenous population. Estimated at 112,000 at the end of the fifteenth century, it shrank to 5,000 by the middle of the sixteenth. Along with the people, virtually all traces of indigenous culture and religion vanished. There was thus never a real possibility in Cuba for an indigenous-Christian syncretism to arise.

After seeing the lands rich in gold and silver that Hernán Cortés and Francisco de Pizarro acquired after their bloody campaigns to establish the viceroyalties in Mexico and Peru, the colonial powers rapidly lost interest in the islands. The main efforts of the colonial ecclesiastical establishment, and the focus of Catholic pastoral activity, accordingly took place in those areas. Havana flourished largely as the port of assembly for the treasure fleet, gathering and arming Spanish ships loaded with gold and silver arriving from Veracruz, Portobello, and Cartagena de Indias. But its religious life, outside the narrow circle of elites at the top of Havana society, was disorderly and impoverished, starting with the priests themselves: "a numerous, undisciplined clergy, living in a society filled with transients" (Maza Miquel 1999, p. 36).

However, the Church bowed to the diocesan synod of 1680 and the efforts of Bishop Compostela began to flourish on the colonial stage. The synod, convened by Bishop Juan García Palacios, for the first time, established programmatic regulations for the Church on the island, which the prelates, notably Diego Avelino Hurtado y Vélez and Jerónimo de Nosti y Valdés, took as a starting point for the expansion and consolidation of existing ecclesiastic structures and increasing religious influence on social life. In 1789 the diocese of Havana was born, separating it from the pastoral service of Santiago de Cuba, and the Church reached a period of splendor after the ordination of Juan José Díaz de Espada y Fernández de Landa as bishop. Espada played a decisive role in the development of civil institutions and further demonstrated his character through his support of Father Félix Varela

(1788–1853) and the whole generation that founded the idea of the nation. This splendor stopped abruptly, however, in the 1830s, after the death of Bishop Espada, due to circumstances that had little to do with religion. The Spanish crown was not going to permit a preponderance of a clergy inspired with a patriotic and independent spirit in its last American colonies (especially in Cuba). After Espada and until the end of Spain's colonial domination, the Spanish government made sure to appoint clergy that were loyal to the crown.

During that golden century, many hospitals, charitable, and educational institutions were founded, in particular the University of Havana in 1728, under the guidance of the Dominican friars, and the College-Seminary of San Carlos y San Ambrosio in 1774, from whose classrooms Varela would purge educational dogma. Obtaining exile in New York after being condemned to death by Ferdinand VII, along with the rest of the deputies to the Cortes of Cadiz of 1821, Varela would become a champion of the Cuban independence movement. At the same time, he was an exemplary figure as a theologian and pastor in New York's Catholic community, which was then beginning to swell with Irish immigrants.

Spain began to come to grips with its expulsion from its continental colonies by surging independence movements in which the native-born clergy played a significant role. At that time Cuba also had a relatively high proportion of native-born priests and religious figures. By the

Seminary of San Carlos y San Ambrosio. During the eighteenth century, numerous Catholic hospitals, charities, and educational institutions were established in Cuba, including the Seminary of San Carlos y San Ambrosio, founded in Havana in 1769. © CUBOIMAGES SRL/ALAMY

end of the eighteenth century, out of the fifty parishes in Cuba, forty-six were Creole. Having exhausted its gold and silver troves, the Spanish metropolis now clung to the Cuban colony, which supplied sugar as its economic mainstay after European demand swung toward Cuba in the wake of the Haitian Revolution.

Holding on to the Cuban colony meant, however, that forces for independence had to be neutralized, and for that Spain needed a Church that was politically accountable to it, without dissent. It thus temporarily left the two existing dioceses (Santiago and Havana) without an administration and separated Cuban priests from major ecclesiastical positions. The proportion of ultramontane Spanish clergy increased. By the time the wars for independence broke out in 1868, the Church acted as the most reliable institutional and ideological force for colonial power. "Until the end of the century, the top-level hierarchy of the Church would remain on the fringe of the great ideals for independence of the Cuban people. This was the era of an ungoverned, impoverished, and manipulated church . . . as an institution, the Church suffered a painful eclipse" (Encuentro Nacional Eclesial Cubano 1986, p. 35).

In 1838 Spain decreed the confiscation of Church lands and other property in order to cover the expenses of the Carlist civil war. Thus ties that had been justified in exchange for patronage began to unravel, and ecclesiastical ultramontanism, like its political counterpart, was left to the mercies of the liberal onslaught.

Over the course of the three decades of the struggle for Cuban independence, anticlericalism spread broadly in the ranks of those struggling for liberty in the broadest sense of the word. This stance chiefly reflected a rejection of the positions of the hierarchy and the political involvement of the clergy, rather than of Catholic religiosity per se, although it would be naive to believe that faith itself would not go through its own process of decline.

Even in the final years before the intervention of the United States in the war and the usurpation of independence, the bishop of Havana, Santander y Frutos, preached that "the insurrectionists harbored a satanic hatred against religion, that the population of his diocese was horribly indifferent to religious matters, and that not even the bitter suffering of war had drawn God closer to his Cuban flock" (Maza Miquel 1997, p. 354). Though this stance of the clergy would start to change after the Spanish defeat, the credibility of the bishops and the majority of the clergy was deeply damaged by their militant alignment with Spain.

THE SECULAR REPUBLIC

The Cuban republic born out of the struggle for independence was not actually independent; it was created within the framework imposed by U.S. intervention during the four postwar years. This was sufficient to establish the mechanisms that would ensure the highest level of dependency on the United States. As the Cuban historian Pedro Pablo Rodríguez put it, "the neocolonial model implanted in Cuba in 1902 was such a modern system of domination that it did not even require a relationship of colonial domination" (Rodríguez 1997–1998).

During the debates of the Constituent Assembly of 1901, the most controversial issue, apart from territorial concessions and the recognition of a U.S. right to intervene (the Platt Amendment), had two aspects connected with faith and the Church. First, there was a bitter, drawn-out debate about putting the words "God's blessing" at the beginning of the text of the constitution. Second, and of yet greater importance, was the explicit recognition of freedom of religion, which opened the space for Protestant missionaries arriving from the United States, including the separation of church and state, "which may not under any circumstances subsidize any religion." The public education system was defined as secular and was to be free of charge. At that time, except for Mexico, there was probably no country in Latin America that had distanced itself so far from the Spanish system of official religious belief.

The Church thus witnessed the birth of the republic at the beginning of the twentieth century from a much weakened institutional position and with fewer and more reluctant parishioners, who were highly skeptical of giving the Church a key role in national affairs.

Despite all this, economic support for the Church was strengthened when, prior to the withdrawal by the U.S. interventionist government (the protectorate), an indemnity of several million dollars was approved to pay for properties the Spanish Crown had confiscated from religious institutions six decades earlier. This indemnity would not be paid by the intervening power, but rather would come from the budget of the new republic, to which another million was added under the second intervention in 1909. This, possibly, was a way to compensate for the constitution's ending the monopoly over faith.

Schools would turn out to be the strongest link in the recovery of Catholicism. The public education system was well designed, but had to be implemented in a republic that had come into being with extremely precarious human and financial resources and in the context of a corrupt system in which politics had become a source of enrichment. Private schools had not been banned, and the Church was able to reopen the doors of the country to educational congregations. By 1914, the four schools for boys and a similar number for girls that existed at the beginning of the republic had grown to fifty-four schools, which included twelve working male congregations and twenty-four female congregations. By 1940 there were 112 schools run by religious communities (Montenegro González pp. 1057, 1068). Among the most significant male congregations in the educational system of the first republic, which most influenced the generation that would dominate the scene in the 1950s, were the Society of

Jesus, the Christian Brothers, the Pious Schools, the Marist Brothers, and the Salesians; the female congregations included Sacred Heart, the sisters of St. Ursula and St. Theresa, and the Dominicans. Relying on well-trained teachers with a well-established educational tradition, the religious orders shaped generations of the upper and middle bourgeoisie, children of professionals and politicians who wanted their offspring to have a privileged education, and some children from the poorer classes.

On the issue of religious liberty, there were no concordats or agreements that could have overturned the constitutional framework of 1901, which was in fact reproduced with few changes in the constitution of 1940. It can thus be said that Catholicism recovered its influence by means of its institutions, and chiefly among the dominant classes of society, although it had to do so with a clergy that was mainly of Spanish origin, and predominantly conservative, given the low level of national vocation to the priesthood.

When the uprising against the Batista regime began in 1956, the Church called on both sides to lay down their arms. Only the archbishop of Santiago de Cuba, Monsignor Enrique Pérez Serantes, along with some groups from Catholic youth organizations, dared to denounce the crimes of the Batista regime. Although they were a minority within the Church, many Catholics participated at various levels in activities against the Batista government, including José

Antonio Echeverría (1932–1957), founder of the Directorio Revolucionario Estudiantil (DRE; Revolutionary Student Directorate), who was killed during the assault on the presidential palace, which was carried out by the organization he founded and led.

FAITH AND THE REVOLUTION

When the Revolution triumphed in 1959, the Church had not yet undergone the renewal fostered by Vatican Council II, and it had no effective way to engage adequately with the changes that occurred in political and economic life or the main currents of social thought. For most of the population of believers this presented a dilemma: Catholicism or Revolution. Furthermore, the state's official assimilation of Marxism in its orthodox Soviet form, which by doctrine was atheist, further widened the impasse by framing it in terms of religion or revolution.

These tensions reached their peak between 1960 and 1962. Even though there was never any lack of voices, either from Catholic media and those of other religious creeds or from the Marxists, in one way or another they were able to keep a dialogue open. But beyond the commitments of the classes who ensured that ecclesiastical institutions would be supported, the churches "did not oppose the revolution primarily because it struck at the interests of the bourgeoisie and the empire but rather because it proposed a value system, an interpretation of reality, the concept of

Plaza and Church of St. Francis in Old Havana. HÉCTOR DELGADO AND ROLANDO PUJOL

the 'New Man,' and an educational project that were alternatives to those of the churches" (Girardi p. 109).

The power of the Revolution asserted itself in Havana in 1961 when the annual procession of Our Lady of Charity turned into a street rally against it. The government reacted by expelling one of the auxiliary diocesan bishops to Spain, along with 131 priests and other religious figures, mostly Spaniards. What followed was the preponderance of doctrinaire Marxist atheism, which would translate into years of discriminatory restrictions for believers and in particular for practicing Catholics.

A new stance by the bishops became noticeable in April 1969, in the first pastoral letter against the U.S. economic blockade of Cuba, which reads: "We condemn this unjust blockade which adds needless suffering and makes the quest for development ever more difficult. We therefore appeal to the conscience of those who are in a position to resolve this situation so that they can undertake decisive and effective actions to end this measure" (*La voz de la Iglesia en Cuba*, p. 175). In a second pastoral letter in September the bishops stated:

> We must approach atheists with all the fraternal respect and charity that a human being deserves, simply because he is human. We must not dismiss the honesty in his or her position ... nor must we eschew collaboration in the practical nature of our earthly ambitions .... There is a huge field of common commitment among all persons of good will whether they are atheists or believers.

La voz de la Iglesia en Cuba, p. 177

We can see that the Church took the initiative in demonstrating to the socialist state its disposition to harness change, a process initiated in the previous decade at the time it provided believers with a solution for the dilemma of religion or revolution. In this case, to provide a solution meant showing that in fact no such dilemma exists.

From the 1980s onward there was a clearly perceptible revival in religious spirituality in Cuba, of Catholic ecclesiastical and general religious activity, in contrast to what might be considered the two previous decades of retreat and withdrawal in the face of the ideological hegemony of atheism that had been enshrined at the first Cuban Communist Party Congress in 1975 and not revised until the fourth, held in 1991. *Revival* here refers to the clear signs, with proven data, of growth in the number of religious communities, the appearance of new expressions of faith, and the increasing number of people who are uninhibited in acknowledging themselves as believers. Since then it has become possible to speak of the "active engagement of religious institutions and movements in Cuban civil society" (Del Rey and Castañeda).

In its postrevolutionary ecclesiastical recovery, it was impossible for the Church to carry on the battle of ideas using the same methods it employed in

its recovery during the post-colonial republic. By establishing the public educational system as the only authorized one and confiscating private property in 1961, the revolutionary state deprived the Church of its key instruments of influence. Until the early 1990s, this new process of recovery occurred under far less favorable conditions and was further burdened with restrictions imposed by the project of official atheism.

The evolving stance of the Church in the 1980s, as reflected in the *Documento Final* of the Encuentro Nacional Eclesial Cubano (ENEC; the Cuban National Ecclesiastical Meeting) of 1986, had already provided hints of recovery in the Catholic presence. Around the same time, the book *Fidel and Religion* (1985) was published, the product of twenty-three hours of interviews with Fidel Castro by the Brazilian Dominican Frei Betto, in which the Cuban chief of state acknowledged that Cuba's socialist policy indeed contained elements that discriminated against religious belief and that these needed to be overcome. This statement was issued under circumstances that broadcast a willingness to change the policy.

AFTER THE COLD WAR

The visit of Pope John Paul II to Cuba in 1998 was a religious event of enormous relevance, but it took place within the context of what was already a full-fledged spiritual revival, and so cannot be considered a cause of the revival in the strictest sense. Nor was it a phenomenon arising from the Cuban economic collapse at the beginning of the 1990s, although this certainly was a contributing factor. The breakdown of the comprehensive package of social solutions to material problems was now intensifying the search for ways out, whether effective or symbolic.

The fall of the Berlin Wall in 1989 led to expectations of the imminent collapse of socialism worldwide, from which the Cuban experiment was not expected to be immune. A new pastoral document from the bishops in 1993, "El amor todo lo espera" (Love Always Hopes), provided yet another connotation for the *Documento Final*, with a local interpretation of Catholic social doctrine in the context of a world that was no longer bipolar and where the focus now had to shift to the failure of socialism and the coordinates for a new, alternative project that needed to be mapped out, while preserving a sphere of influence for Catholics.

In 1989 the country's ecclesiastical structure consisted of five dioceses and two archdioceses. The territorial and hierarchical configuration of the church had hardly changed in thirty years. By the end of 1998, however, there were eight dioceses and three archdioceses. As of 2010 there were six hundred churches, the number of priests had risen to over four hundred, and a new diocesan seminary was almost completed. The Catholic lay movement, which had become almost invisible, also revived during this period.

The appointment of Bishop Jaime Lucas Ortega y Alamino to cardinal in 1994, the first Cuban cardinal

Pope John Paul II in Havana, 25 January 1998. The visit of Pope John Paul II (r. 1978–2005) to Cuba in 1998 was a religious event of enormous relevance that took place within the context of what was already a full-fledged spiritual revival in the country. AP IMAGES/ DOMENICO STINELLI

since the death of Manuel Arteaga Betancourt in 1964, confirmed the institutional recovery and signaled the culmination of a maturation process that was required for the pope to be received in a "New Church" (Ortega y Alamino pp. 401ff.). It was a sign of recognition of the Catholic revival; the flock had been assigned a pastor, and the state an interface from the highest level of the ecclesiastical hierarchy. It meant that Cuba now had a clergy with an international presence. Catholics in Miami may practice in their local dioceses, but Ortega is a visible figurehead and interlocutor for all Catholic Cubans the world over.

For the pope's visit, one could see the Church and the Cuban socialist state working in coordination and toward the same purpose for the first time since 1959. The dilemma regarding who should get credit or blame for the success or failure of the visit vanished, because it was everyone's due for success while failure was only for the intransigents. Possibly for the first time in forty years, the people would find in the media a message different from the official one. The pope owned the media stage for five days.

In a conference in 2000 Cardinal Ortega affirmed:

Revolution in Cuba is, well, about nationhood, the future, and independence. The fact that divides the history of Cuba in the 20th century into two separate halves can be summarized in a single sentence: the triumph of the revolution, for in 1959 it was believed that, at long last, we had the authentic possibility of achieving the revolutionary project so often dreamed of [. . .] in everyday speech anyone can declare they are not a Communist, but not being Revolutionary involves a grave defect in the condition of citizenship itself.

Ortega Alamino p. 998

By contrast, the Cuban Catholic pastoral style remained as of 2011 typically church-centric. With the exception of a very small group of lay persons, the Cuban Catholic intelligentsia (lay persons and clergy), trained over the last few decades of the twentieth century, is guided in a highly orthodox manner by papal thought, which articulates the social doctrine of the Church. In Cuba, the orthodox homogeneity of the Catholic fundamentalist intellectuals competes with the homogeneity often attributed to the Marxist fundamentalist intellectuals. At times there seems to be more intransigence and exclusion, and less diversity, among the Catholics than among the Marxists, or at any rate, as much, since it is difficult to make comparisons.

When one states that normal relations exist between Church and State, it becomes necessary to define what *normal* means: Does *normal* mean consensual agreements regarding the nation's social project and an explicit cooperative relationship, or an understanding based on some combination of respect and tolerance between the state and the institution of civil society that has most systematically rejected an orderly accommodation with it? Perhaps people should speak of an *eventful normality*: Rather than being characterized by immobility, the proliferation of channels for understanding between Catholicism and the complex socioeconomic dynamics of the Cuban system is evident. This explains the government's acceptance in 2010 of a mediating role for the cardinal so that expressions of opposition would be tolerated and that a solution would be found involving the release of prisoners jailed for oppositional activities that violate current law. Catholicism has rescued its institutional influence, along with an important place in Cuban religious demography. The chief of state, Raúl Castro, along with other political figures, attended the inauguration of the new facilities for the Catholic seminary of Havana.

The space that has been restored is also shared more proportionally as of 2011 with Protestant denominations as well as with religiosity of African origin, which is not limited to practitioners of Santería and Palo Monte, in the rigorous sense, but which permeates in various degrees the subtleties of the Catholic faithful, even if the Catholic Church is doctrinally reluctant to acknowledge that these belief systems merit characterization as religious institutions. In any case, the spectrum of religion in Cuba in the early 2010s reflects a major achievement in the nation's history of overcoming discrimination and in nurturing a climate of religious liberty.

■ *See also*

Cuban Thought and Cultural Identity: Socialist Thought

Race: Race Relations after the Revolution

BIBLIOGRAPHY

Alonso Tejada, Aurelio. "La Iglesia y el contexto sociopolítico cubano: Antecedentes y perspectivas de la visita pastoral de Su Santidad Juan Pablo II." *Cuadernos del Aula Fray Bartolomé de las Casas* 3 (March 2000).

Alonso Tejada, Aurelio. *Iglesia y política en Cuba.* 2nd ed. Havana: Caminos, 2002.

Betto, Frei. *Fidel and Religion: Talks with Frei Betto.* Havana: Publications Office of the Council of State, 1987.

Céspedes García-Menocal, Carlos Manuel de. *Promoción humana, realidad cubana y perspectivas: Ponencia presentada en la Segunda Semana Social Católica, La Habana 17 a 20 de noviembre de 1994.* Caracas: Fundación Konrad Adenauer, 1996.

Céspedes García-Menocal, Carlos Manuel de. *Pasión por Cuba y por la Iglesia: Aproximación biográfica al P. Félix Varela.* Madrid: Biblioteca de Autores Cristianos, 1998.

Del Rey Roa, Annet, and Yalexy Castañeda Mache. "El reavivamiento religioso en Cuba." *Temas* 31 (October–December 2002).

Encuentro Nacional Eclesial Cubano. *Documento Final e Instrucción Pastoral de los Obispos.* Rome: Tipografía Don Bosco, 1986.

Fernández Santelices, Manuel. *Cronología histórica de Cuba (1492–2000).* Miami: Ediciones Universal, 2001.

Girardi, Giulio. *Cuba después del derrumbe del comunismo: ¿Residuo del pasado o germen de un futuro nuevo?* Madrid: Editorial Nueva Utopía, 1994.

Maza Miquel, Manuel P. *Entre la ideología y la compasión: Guerra y paz en Cuba, 1895–1903: Testimonios de los Archivos Vaticanos.* Santo Domingo: Instituto Pedro Francisco Bonó, 1997.

Maza Miquel, Manuel P. *Esclavos, patriotas y poetas a la sombra de la cruz: Cinco ensayos sobre catolicismo e historia cubana.* Santo Domingo: Centro de Estudios Sociales Padre Juan Montalvo, 1999.

Montenegro González, Augusto. "Vicisitudes de una comunidad eclesial (1898–1983)." In *Manual de historia de la Iglesia.* Vol. 10, *La Iglesia del siglo XX en España, Portugal y América Latina,* edited by Quintín Aldea Vaquero and Eduardo Cárdenas. Barcelona: Editorial Herder, 1987.

Ortega y Alamino, Jaime. *Te basta mi Gracia.* Madrid: Palabra, 2002.

Ramírez Calzadilla, Jorge. *Religión y relaciones sociales.* Havana: Academia, 2000.

Rodríguez, Pedro Pablo. "Modernidad y 98 en Cuba: Alternativas y contradicciones." *Temas* 12–13 (October 1997–March 1998).

Torres-Cuevas, Eduardo, and Edelberto Leiva Lajara. *Historia de la Iglesia Católica en Cuba: La Iglesia en las patrias de los criollos (1516–1787).* Havana: Ediciones Boloña/Ciencias Sociales, 2008.

La voz de la Iglesia en Cuba: 100 documentos episcopales. Mexico City: Obra Nacional de la Buena Prensa, 1995.

FAITH: AFRO-CUBAN RELIGIONS AND REVOLUTION

Juan Mesa Díaz

An overview of the relationship between the Cuban revolutionary state and Afro-Cuban religions since 1959.

African slaves living in Cuba and the religions they practiced were profoundly affected over the centuries by exposure to local religious practices, including Catholicism, Spiritism, and even Masonic rituals. Afro-Cuban religions became known as Regla de Ocha (Santería), Reglas de Palo Congo, Abakuá, and Arará. Followers of these religions were subjected to persecution, prohibition, condemnation, and rampant discrimination. Afro-Cuban religions survived in colonial and republican Cuba as a culture of resistance. Any religious display by Africans and their descendants in Cuba was condemned and suppressed. Slaves were only allowed to play drums (an important aspect of Afro-Cuban religious ceremonies) on 6 January—Three Kings Day, a major festival on the island and their only day of rest during the entire year. It was only in the *palenques* (hideouts of runaway slaves known as *cimarrones*) that they were able to find the freedom to express their religious consciousness freely, while in the *cabildos* (municipalities) they were able to do it in a more disguised fashion.

CONTINUED SUPPRESSION AFTER INDEPENDENCE

Independence and the birth of the republic in 1902 did not improve acceptance of Afro-Cuban religions. The political and cultural elites cut off Cuban culture from the African roots that fed it. The subjugation of Afro-Cuban religions led adherents to develop new methods of practicing their faith, while not openly identifying themselves to those outside their religious circles. Practitioners would set up highly visible altars with images of Catholic saints in their homes to quell others' suspicions about their faith. New musical expressions were elaborated so as to disguise the underlying religious significance and circumvent the bans prohibiting religious rituals. To this end, rudimentary fiddles and *güiros* (gourd instruments) were introduced in the place of the traditional *batá* drums, whose very distinctive sound could be easily identified. These clandestine incorporations of different aspects of Cuban culture have led some critics to try Afro-Cuban religions on the count of existing solely as syncretic cults, but this view fails to take into account the distinct manifestations of culture and philosophy that persevered through severe persecution.

The Constitution of 1940, and the short, corrupt, and indulgent democratic period that followed it, contributed in some way to creating a climate favorable to certain religious freedoms: Ceremonies could be held openly, displaying the batá drums was more accepted, and scholarly research became more prominent (and respectful). But many among the elite and middle classes (black and white) continued to be classist and discriminatory when it came to anything that appeared to have African origins.

AFTER THE REVOLUTION

The triumph of Fidel Castro's guerilla forces in January 1959 aroused enormous expectations among the disenfranchised Cuban populace and specifically among Cubans of African descent and those of mixed race. Meanwhile, radical changes in the country's economic, political, and social life were occurring. The revolution's socialist orientation "of the poor, by the poor, and for the poor" seemed to promise a leading role to those classes that had been previously marginalized by the successive governments since independence.

At that time, the great majority of those in the community who practiced Cuban religions of African origin were some of the most marginalized of all the disadvantaged social groups. During the 1960s the disadvantaged majority of Cuban society took on the new socialist project with unbridled enthusiasm, viewing it as a struggle to improve themselves and as an opportunity to fashion a society that accounted for them. However, the full-scale implementation of the revolution's policies (education, culture, public policy, political consciousness) carried with it to a large degree an abjuration of religious consciousness, since Marxist-Leninist thought is atheistic. While this massive and unconditional incorporation to the revolutionary ideology was embraced by many, the secular ideology promoted by the revolution was questioned and regarded with suspicion by a large part of the religious community, who viewed some of its approaches and measures as incoherent with the liberating discourse of the revolution and explicitly hostile to their religious beliefs.

During the 1970s, once the power of the revolutionary leadership was consolidated and with the support of the Soviet Union, the government's priority focused even more on the ensuring of a just and equitable society by rendering in Cuba an idealized Soviet-style monolithic unity of the people. With this push toward redefining Cuba as an egalitarian society, little effort was spent on acknowledging the cultural and ideological diversity of Cuba's citizens.

The Primer Congreso de Educación y Cultura (First Education and Cultural Congress) in 1971 set the standard for what afterward would be referred to, in cultural circles, as the *quinquenio gris* (Five Grey Years). This period was marked by open hostility toward all religious practices, but especially those of African origins, which were seen as obscurantist and showing ideological weakness. Afro-Cuban religions had become increasingly noticeable after the adoption of burdensome requirements for obtaining permission to perform religious ceremonies involving drum playing, celebrations, initiations, and sacrifices in the mid-1960s. The newly initiated wear white for a year, as well as necklaces and bracelets that make them visible and identifiable as *santeros* to the public at large.

These developments set the stage for the conflict between the revolutionary government and practitioners of Santería and Palo (both Afro-Cuban religions) and members of Abakuá (an Afro-Cuban male secret society). These communities had not anticipated that because of their religious status, they would continue to be relegated to exploitation and poverty in Cuba's new society, just as they had been marginalized before the Revolution. They could not, for example, understand the tacit prohibition against the initiation and consecration of the community members' underage sons into their ancestral religion. Practitioners of Afro-Cuban religions were also denied access to the teaching profession, as well as to posts of any significance in revolutionary organizations and at work centers; additionally, the mass media and official state propaganda disseminated by the revolutionary socialist government branded them unenlightened and superstitious. The regime always placed them on the side of delinquency, marginality, social unruliness, and maladaption. In that sense, when it came to this broad sector of society, the prejudices of the new rulers were not so very different from those of the old regime.

The overarching ideology of the revolutionary process included all citizens in its implementation of social justice, but conditioned that inclusion on the forswearing of religious beliefs and acceptance that those beliefs were remnants of a past that has been done away with forever. Afro-Cuban religions were officially recognized only as religious by-products, and they were referred to as syncretic cults and not fully developed religions. This classification promoted a misunderstanding of Afro-Cuban religions as an accumulation of fetishistic, animist, and primitive practices that lacked any philosophical foundation. By positing ritual objects as fetishes, a panoply of spirits as animism, and the sacrifice of animals as primitive, these critics overlooked the centuries-long philosophical and ethical underpinnings of these religions.

The principle of conditional inclusion of believers and the intellectual discrediting to which their religious expressions were subjected was noticed, with much apprehension, by the social corpus of practitioners: It meant possible ostracism and limited possibilities for social advancement. Believers assumed, once again, a defensive and secretive position as a culture of resistance—something in which they had centuries' worth of experience. Many believers came to understand the propaganda against them as representing an inability on the part of the revolutionary leadership to accept the slightest expression of cultural and ideological diversity.

The limited tolerance (or hostility) to Afro-Cuban religions contributed to misunderstandings. The flexibility toward social manifestations again resulted in a semi-clandestine practice of the religions. These government attitudes also contributed to a second diaspora, this time for religious reasons, which resulted in the establishment of these religions in unexpected places such as the United States, Spain, Mexico, Venezuela, Puerto Rico, and elsewhere.

DIALOGUE AND ACCEPTANCE

In the early 1960s the Revolution's cultural and academic institutions carried out research to recover cultural traditions, an undertaking that decisively contributed to ensuring that the legacy of Afro-Cuban religions would not be erased from the nation's historical memory during the Five Grey Years that lasted more than five years and at times was very bleak. The valuable contributions of Argeliers León (1918–1991) and Isaac Barreal (1920–1997), the founders and souls of the Instituto de Etnología y Folklore de la Academia de Ciencias de Cuba (Ethnology and Folklore Institute of the Cuban Academy of Sciences), and the work of Rogelio Martínez Furé (b. 1937) and the Conjunto Folklórico Nacional (National Folklore Group), were

instrumental in opening up a serious-minded space for the understanding of these religious expressions as a part of the national culture.

The socialist Constitution of 1976 proclaimed a state that was, denominationally speaking, atheistic, but which nevertheless did respect citizens' right to religious freedom. In the First Congress of the Communist Party of Cuba, the government laid out that "Respect for the right of citizens to profess and practice their religious beliefs is, of course, extended to those who follow syncretic belief systems" (p. 316). However, this support was immediately qualified:

The specific aspects of our policy concerning these systems of worship is directed at preventing antisocial behavior and activities that are harmful to the health and well-being of citizens, and that are contrary to public interest, activities and behaviors that were generated in the past under the cover of these religions and that today are still on evidence as the consequence of certain social conditions that the Revolution has overcome and banished forever.

The folkloric cultural values (music, dance, musical instruments, and so on) contributed by the ethnic groups represented in these religious groups should be assimilated, purging them of their mystical elements so that using their essence will not serve to sustain customs and beliefs that are incompatible with scientific truth.

pp. 316–317

This manner of top-down thinking and belief that scientific thought is superior to any other has Stalinist resonances in its harsh appraisal of Afro-Cuban religions and in its bureaucratic need to stamp out these beliefs. The message was clear that the government would showcase the folkloric aspects of Afro-Cuban religious culture as Cuban culture, while relegating the underlying body of belief to the absurd. Nevertheless, the stubborn reality that people would not stop being religious imposed itself, day after day.

Religious believers were not going to stop believing, and neither would they give up being part of a nation carrying out a distinct kind of social experiment, socialism with freedom of religious expression. The self-definition of the prevailing social system as liberating needed to be reexamined: Can believers be full members of a revolutionary society?

Tensions had to be overcome through dialogue. Dr. José Felipe Carneado (1915–1993), a skilled politician, contributed a great deal to this end. He was designated as head of the Oficina de Asuntos Religiosos del PCC (Cuban Communist Party's Office on Religious Affairs), a post he held from 1985 until his death in 1993. When he employed his negotiating skill, unlike the more dogmatic and bureaucratic ways of thinking prevalent within the party, a political will emerged within the government and religious denominations to work toward overcoming conflicts between them. Following a course that was increasingly open—and not free from dissension—between the 1990s and 2010, rapprochement set the standard for a new stage. The new accommodating approach was characterized by greater religious freedom, which translated into a climate of cordial respect and a greater awareness of the essence that underpins Afro-Cuban religious practices, accompanied by a reduction of prejudice. Greater religious tolerance led to a certain permissiveness in practice, some of it for monetary gain, some of it out of ignorance of traditions. The government promoted religious tourism, something that became more prevalent from the beginnings of the nineties, and greater commercialization of the religion became more widespread, with outrageous fees being charged for initiations or for the purchase of religious artifacts.

Several milestones attested to this new stage of religious tolerance: One of these was the visit of Alayeluwa Oba Okunade Sijuwade (Olobuse II) (b. 1930), the Ooni (emperor) of Ifé (the capital city of the Yoruba people), in 1987. A major religious figure from Nigeria, Olobuse II was treated almost like a head of state when he visited Cuba. Other important achievements were: the legalization in 1991 of the Sociedad Cultural Yoruba de Cuba (Cuban Yoruba Cultural Society) and its recognition as a religious institution since 2007; Communist Party bylaws in 1991 accepting the enrollment of religious believers into that organization; and the success of the first edition of Natalia Bolivar's book, *Los Orishas en Cuba* (The Orishas in Cuba, 1993), referring to the deities and spirits of the Yoruba belief system and its offshoots in the New World. The publication of *Fidel y la religión* (Fidel and Religion, 1985), by Frei Betto, also helped: With more than one million copies sold, it added new spark to the debate about religious beliefs. The pope's visit in 1998 contributed to the opening up of a space for all believers, although the pontiff refused to meet with practitioners of Santería and its high priests.

The full inclusion of Afro-Cuban practitioners into Cuban society ultimately validated their religious, cultural, and social importance as key participants in the creation of the revolutionary republic Martí envisioned, "*con todos y para el bien de todos*" (by all, and for the good of all). This inclusion of believers affected the ruling ideology and its leadership as well, liberating them from the ghosts of prejudice. An old Yoruban proverb, illustrating the importance of the inclusion of religious and cultural diversity, says it best: the water makes the stream, and the streams make the river.

BIBLIOGRAPHY

Betto, Frei. *Fidel y la religión*. Santo Domingo: Editora Alfa y Omega, 1985.

Bolívar Arostequi, Natalia. *Los Orishas en Cuba*. Miami: Libros Sin Fronteras Inventory, 1993.

Fernández Robaina, Tomás. *Hablen paleros y santeros*. 2nd ed. Havana: Editorial Ciencias Sociales, 2008.

Moore, Robin D. "Music and Revolution." In *Ay, Dios ampárame: Sacred Music and Revolution*. Berkeley: University of California Press, 2006.

Primer Congreso del Partido Comunista de Cuba. *Tesis y Resoluciones*. Havana: Dep. de orientación revolucionaria del Comité central del Partido Comunista de Cuba D.O.R., 1976.

Hagedorn, Katherine J. *Divine Utterances: The Performance of Afro-Cuban Santería*, especially chapters 6–7. Washington, DC: Smithsonian Institution Press, 2001.

Heran, Adrian H. *Cuba: Religion, Social Capital and Development*. Durham, NC: Duke University Press, 2008.

Kirk, John M. *Between God and the Party: Religion and Politics in Revolutionary Cuba*. Gainesville: University Press of Florida, 1989.

FAITH: ABAKUÁ SOCIETY

Ivor Miller

An initiation club for men in Havana and Matanzas, derived from the Ékpè leopard society of West Africa.

Abakuá, known by its members as *Ekório Enyéne Abakuá* (a group founded by a sacred mother that is called Abakuá), is a Cuban mutual aid society for men, whose ceremonial activities occur exclusively in the port cities of Cárdenas, Havana, and Matanzas. Popularly referred to as African Masonry, Abakuá is structured through lodges, the first of which was created in 1836 by its African-born founders who migrated from the Cross River region of southeastern Nigeria and southwestern Cameroon. In the 2010s, there were more than 150 functioning lodges with more than 20,000 members. Although it is a secretive initiation society, Abakuá has been referred to unofficially as a national symbol of Cuba, due to the participation of its members in the development of Cuban music, arts, and identity.

In the Calabar region, the Ékpè leopard society was the regulatory institution, in which councils of free-born titled members established the common laws of their communities and regulated trade throughout the region. Abakuá practice, which includes a ritual language, body-mask traditions, collective organization, percussive music, cuisine, cosmology, and gender relations, is best understood in relation to its African sources. Although it was created in the context of a slave society, Abakuá is not a slave culture, as is often assumed. Instead, following the Ékpè model, it was created by free-born Africans as a vehicle for jurisprudence and artistry.

In colonial Cuba, the Spanish government divided migrating Africans ethnically by encouraging those in urban areas to form *cabildos* (nation-groups).

These cabildos became important centers for the conservation of African languages and cultural practices. Carabalí peoples formed several cabildos by the 1750s, and titled members of the leopard societies were among them. The African-born Ékpè members were hesitant to initiate their Cuban-born sons, which explains why Abakuá was not established until the 1830s in Regla, a small town across the harbor from Havana.

Abakuá tradition has three lineages, the Efí, Efó, and Orú. Each is derived from an ethnic identity in the Cross River region, known today as Èfìk, Èfúùt, and Úrúán. The term *Abakuá* memorialized the Àbàkpà people of Calabar, who call themselves the *Quas*. The first lodge was known as *Efí Butón*, after the Òbútòng community in Calabar.

EARLY LODGE NAMES DOCUMENT CARABALÍ MIGRATION

As Carabalí organized themselves in western Cuba, they started using African names for areas of their environment. They renamed Havana *Núnkue*, interpreted into Èfìk as *nung nkwe* (I have also not seen), meaning that Havana was a new place to them. They called Regla *itiá ororó kánde*, interpreted into Èfìk as *itiat òyóyò Nkàndà* (the foundation of great Nkàndà); Nkàndà was a key Ékpè grade that was evoked during the foundational Abakuá ceremonies.

Abakuá lodges were created in western Cuba because many Cross River peoples lived there, but also because Calabar and Cuba shared a similar ecology. Both have estuary zones of mangrove swamps, manatees, crocodiles or alligators, and other fauna that have deep symbolism for Ékpè. Components missing in Cuba (e.g., leopards) were represented symbolically.

Throughout the nineteenth century, Cuban lodge names represented communities in the Calabar region, becoming indexes for source communities. For example, the Efí Abarakó Eta lodge founded in Regla in 1863 was likely named after the Calabar community called *Mbàràkòm*, a ward of Creek Town foundational to modern Èfìk Ékpè history. Cuban data supports this interpretation, because *Mbarankonó abarakó* is an Abakuá phrase. An Abarakó lodge also exists in Matanzas. The Efí Mbemoró lodge, founded in 1846 in Havana, refers to a riverside community in the Calabar region. For example, *Mbemong* (by the river) is an Èfìk settlement on the Great Kwa river, along the ancient trade route from Calabar to Oban and into Cameroun. The Havana lodge Ékuéri Tongó, established in 1848, refers to the Èfìk community of Ékórétònkó. Another Havana lodge, Ekerewá Momí, founded in 1863, is clearly derived from *Ekeng Ewa*, a family name from Henshaw Town, Calabar, where in Èfìk, *Ekerewá Momí* means "Ekerewá is here!" Such matter-of-fact interpretations of Abakuá lodge names were possible only through renewed contact with Calabar peoples.

According to Ékpè and Abakuá mythology, Ékpè was discovered or created in a fishing community in the estuaries of what is in modern times the Bakassi Peninsula, along the Cameroun-Nigeria border. Called *Usagaré* in Cuba and *Ùsàghàdè* (spelled on maps as *Usak-Edet* or *Isangele*) in Africa, this place is spoken of with reverence on both sides of the Atlantic.

The altar spaces in Abakuá lodges display objects that evoke Cross River cultural history. They often contain a seven-keyed lamellophone (*mbira* in Southern Africa) to represent the original music of Ùsàghàdè; in the Calabar region lamellophones were once common instruments. Abakuá altars also display the signature of their lodge, a magical sign—based upon the Nsìbìdì writing of the Cross River Ékpè practice—that is fully known only by the lodge leaders. Other common objects are the percussion instruments of Abakuá music, the *nkomo* drums (*ekomo* in Efik), *ekón* metal gong (*nkong* in Efik), and the two seed-filled rattles (*nsak* in Efik), the forms of which are nearly identical to Cross River Ékpè instruments. Showing the Catholic influence in Cuba, each lodge has a representative Catholic saint upon its altar. Because Cross River Ékpè practice is directly linked to that of the water spirit societies of each community (called *Ndèm* among the Efiks), the female saints are understood as cognates for the link between male Ékpè and female water powers.

ABAKUÁ BECOMES A UNIVERSAL INSTITUTION

Each generation of Abakuá leaders directed their lodge activities based upon their understanding of the teachings of the African founders, as well as upon the needs of the day. Whereas the African founders took decades to create a lodge for their own offspring, the Cuban Creoles decided that, in the face of the tremendous repression of African-derived institutions, they would best defend Abakuá by opening up their ranks to any qualified male, regardless of his ancestry. The first lodge of white males was created in 1863 by members of some of Cuba's elite families who, it was thought, could influence the dominant class perspective on this criminalized institution. The result was the universalizing of Abakuá, making it no longer the exclusive concern of African descendants, but of all communities in western Cuba.

The legendary founder of this movement was Andrés Petit (1830–1878), a leader in the Havana lodge named Bakokó Efó. In southwestern Cameroon, Bakoko is a Balondo-speaking group; migrants from there established a Bakoko settlement in Calabar. Petit was a free mulatto with strong ties to the Catholic Church and a leader of a Cuban-Kongo practice called *Kimbisa*, which he helped establish in Havana. Petit fused basic elements from the available initiation systems in Cuba to create spiritual practices without racial distinctions, so that all participants could coexist as spiritual family members, a radical move in a slave society. In 1857, Petit consecrated the objects for a new Abakuá lodge; after six years of selecting and organizing its first members, he initiated them in 1863. According to legend, with initiation fees paid by the whites, Petit bought the freedom of many enslaved people. In the process, he and his colleagues transformed Cuban society. The anthropologist Fernando Ortiz (1881–1969) labeled his movement the Reform of Petit (Ortiz 1954, pp. 70–71), and as late as 1996, Petit was referred to as "forger of the Cuban nation" (Mosquera p. 256).

Thus, in 1863, the first lodge of whites, called *Okóbio Mukarará Efó* (white brothers of Efó), was established. In Cuba, *okobio* is interpreted as "brother"; in Èfìk, as "it belongs to us" (figuratively, "brother"). In Balondo (Èfúùt), *mukara* is "white person." Soon afterwards, many Chinese descendants also joined Abakuá, so lodge members came from African, American, Asian, and European backgrounds.

Why did the white brothers want to join? One reason is that as in Freemasonry, Abakuá emerged as a parallel tradition of underground cells whose members participated in the anticolonial struggle. As the first War of Cuban Independence began in 1868, all the rebel leaders from across the island were members of Freemasonry lodges. Many Abakuá members in the Havana-Matanzas region were also Freemasons and used both institutions for organizing rebel activities.

In Calabar, for very different reasons, several European merchants were initiated by Ékpè leaders in the eighteenth and nineteenth centuries. In order to have the support of Ékpè councils while recouping fees from their local debtors, these whites paid high fees for membership but had no say in the actual functioning of Ékpè lodges and their ceremonial activities.

ABAKUÁ TITLES AND THEIR FUNCTIONS

No one has complete knowledge of Abakuá; initiation can be a lifetime process with many stages, each having rigorous protocols designed to safeguard knowledge of the society's inner mechanisms. Information about Abakuá practice, history, and mythology is compartmentalized into the teachings of each title; therefore, titleholders have specialized knowledge pertaining to their own functions. This collective practice is taught in debates between masters and apprentices who study for years to learn the language and its many interpretations.

Most young men are initiated when they are between seven and twenty-one years of age, with exceptions. Traditionally, once a neophyte asked or agreed to be initiated, a process of inquiry about his character and moral behavior began that could take up to two years. The mother of the neophyte had the final word on whether her son was morally qualified to join. If the neophyte was accepted, he was known as *ndisime* (accepted for initiation); in Èfìk, *nsidime* means "ignorant." Initiations take place every few years, or whenever several *ndisimes* are ready.

Because Abakuá initiations proceed as ritual-theater enactments of African foundation myths, Ortiz likened them to ancient Greek tragedies (Ortiz 1950). Each ceremonial action is meant to recreate the birth of Ékpè in Ùsàghàdè, West Africa, wherein a mystic Voice was heard coming from the river, but no man could find it. The Voice, known as the epicenter of Ékpè and Abakuá practice, was captured only when a royal female known as Sikán (from Nsikan, an Ìbìbìò name meaning "What is greater than God?") filled her water pot at the river, and the sacred fish known as Tánze (from Tánsí, an Éjághám name meaning "Lord Fish") entered it, eventually becoming incorporated into Ékpè.

Using a specific step-by-step process, Abakuá initiations narrate their epic myths through descriptive chanting and gestures. At the center of the story is Nasako, the diviner who foresaw the coming of the Voice, then organized local leaders into an Ékpè lodge and gave them titles that memorialize their contributions. For example, Abakuá processions moving to and from a nearby river led by the masquerade dancer Eribangando are performances that narrate the first appearance of this mask to defend Sikán as she left the river with the Voice. In another example, when the yellow and white chalk are introduced in Abakuá rites, the story of the title *Moruá Engomo* is enacted to explain how one ancestor brought the coded chalk into Ékpè practice. The chalk is used to draw magical symbols, known as *anaforuana* or *gandó* in Cuba, that authorize all ritual actions, just as a signature authorizes a bank transaction.

But the Cuban signs comprise a huge corpus; Lydia Cabrera collected more than 500 examples in her 1975 book *Anaforuana*. Paralleling the Abakuá language, these signs show little influence from Spanish or the Roman alphabet; instead, they are derived from the Nsìbìdì codes of the Cross River region, a form of secret communication through signs drawn, gestured, or spoken that is part of Ékpè practice. As Percy Talbot documented in the early 1900s, the Éjághám-speaking community of Oban had a complex system of Nsìbìdì signs that resembles those in Abakuá (Talbot).

Once initiated, the Abakuá neophyte is reborn as *abanékue* (or *obonékue*), in Èfìk meaning "admitted into Ékpè." *Abanékues* are highly regarded because they are the soldiers of Abakuá trained to carry on the tradition; if they excel, and a position opens when an elder titleholder dies, they may take it. Initiation in Abakuá is for life; as the Abakuá say, "what is written cannot be erased," a reference to the chalk marks made on the bodies of initiates.

The three categories of Abakuá titles are Obón, Indiobón, and Etenyén obón. In Èfìk, *obon* is "ruler" or "king," whereas *Etinyin* is "our father"; therefore *Etiyin Obong* would be "our father who governs us." *Indiobón* is likely derived from Ndian, the estuary

Abakuá initiation. An initiate wearing a blindfold participates in the 18-hour initiation ceremony. A man in front holds the ritual empegó drum, and behind the initiate is a representation of íreme, a spiritual figure from Abakuá. HÉCTOR DELGADO AND ROLANDO PUJOL

river in Cameroun where Ékpè was born, according to legend.

The following is a partial list of Abakuá titles, their functions, and West African sources:

Ìyámbà is the head of a lodge in both Cuba and West Africa. The word *Ìyámbà* is derived from Éjághám, where *ayamba* means "open the way"; it is a directive, so if one wants to enter a compound, one could say *a mba* (make us open the way); *Ìyámbà* is plural (let us open the way). The Ìyámbà Ékpè title means "the Ékpè that clears the way."

In Cuba, Íreme Anamanguí wears a black and white costume and is the only mask to work in the *nyóro* (funerary rites) where Nyámpe (Death) is a principal figure. In Calabar, the Nyàmkpè mask functions in the burial rites of an Ékpè titleholder, where *nyóró* dances are performed. In Arochuku communities up the Cross River, an Ékpè mask with a black and white body suit performs the same function while visiting the corpse during funerals.

In Cuba, Ekuenyón is remembered as a hunter who brought all the fees to the *baroko* of Usagaré, but as a special fee, he brought a leopard whose skin was used to cover all the instruments. To begin the ceremonies of some Cuban lineages, Ekuenyón stands at the entrance of the hall to summon the Voice of the leopard, the resonant sound

that authorizes all ceremonial acts. In West Africa, a hunter who killed a leopard and brought the animal intact to his paramount ruler would receive an Ékpè title for his actions. In the Oron communities on the Cross River, Èkpényòng was the name of an Ékpè title. In Cuba, as Ekuenyón is preparing a ritual drink called *mokúba*, he is referred to as *Ekuenyón Bakasi*, likely after the Bakassi Peninsula where the Ùsàghàdè community is located.

In Cuba, Íreme Éribángandó is a masquerade dancer who leads the processions. Mythically, this mask cleared the path for the Èfúùt (Efó) princess who, after discovering the Voice in an African river, brought it back to her community. Along the way, she was blocked by a serpent and a crocodile, the guardians of the sacred waters. In southwestern Cameroon, crocodile is *gando*, so Cubans interpret Eribá as the name of the ancestor who helped the woman escape Gandó the crocodile.

In Cuba, Íreme Mbóko represents the sugarcane, which he carries in one hand and with which he strikes those who do not perform their tasks well. In Èfik and Ìbìbìò, *mbòkò* means "sugarcane."

In Cuba, Íreme Nkóboro, referred to as the Abakuá police, is the masquerade performer who guards the Eribó (mother) drum in processions during initiations. In

Èfik communities, *Mkpokporo* (literally, skull) is the name of an Ùkwà war society mask that leads processions, guarding the female mask that comes afterwards.

In Cuba, the Fambá titleholder guards the entrance to the temple (Fambá) so that only those authorized may enter. In West Africa, *èfámbá* is a hidden display of Ékpè artifacts, originally assembled in a sacred forest, but among Calabar lodges, they are displayed inside an Ékpè hall. Èfámbá is the highest form of teaching in Ékpè, when the esoterics are revealed to those titleholders who make the appropriate sacrifices.

In Cuba, Mokóngo represents the jurisprudential aspect of Abakuá, as well as the military power to execute it. Mokóngo is a lodge leader mythically known for bravery, thus the famous term *Mokóngo Ma Chebere* (Mokóngo the valiant) that led to the Cuban popular phrase *qué Chébere* (how positive or wonderful). Among the Balondos (Èfúùt) of southwestern Cameroon, Mukóngo is an executive officer of the Ékpè society with a representative masquerade performance.

In Cuba, Moní Bonkó is the custodian of the Bonkó Enchemiyá drum, an early Èfik sacred object. In West Africa, Ebonkó is the Sacred Mother of Ékpè, who ultimately represents the life-giving and healing powers of the drum. Among the Èfúùt (Efó) people of Calabar and Cameroon, Muri is a title for the clan head; customarily, each Muri has the Ékpè title of Ebonkó, thus Muri Bonkó.

In Cuba, there are two titles with the name Moruá, Moruá Eribó and Moruá Yuánsa, both of which are masters of the coded sign language of Abakuá, known as Nsìbìdì in Africa. In Cuban lore, Moruá Eribó brought the chalk used to write the signs that authorize all ritual actions. Moruá Yuánsa is custodian of the music. In West Africa Ékpè, Mùrúàs are chanters who carry wooden rattles (*ekpat*) and perform Nsìbìdì, most commonly during the burial rites for an important elder, an Obong Ékpè. In West Africa as in Cuba, there are two types of Mùrúàs, known as *Mùrúà Nyàmkpè* and *Mùrúà Òkpòhò*.

In some Cuban lodges, Mosóko represents the bamboo stick in the ceremony. In Calabar, the bamboo stick is an important symbol representing the authority to display Ékpè masquerades. The staffs of titleholders are often made of bamboo for this reason.

In Cuba, Mosóngo is a title with custody of the Voice of the Leopard. In West Africa, Mosóngo is an Éjághám Ékpè title that is the equivalent of Ìyámbà, the administrative head of a lodge. Among the Àbàkpà (Qua-Éjághám) of Calabar, Mosóngo is a family name.

In Cuba, Nasakó is known as a diviner who learned from the oracle about the birth of Ékpè and organized those who became the first titleholders into the society. In West Africa, Nasakó was an ancestral god known by the Ngolo clan in Ndian Division in southwest Cameroon (and, by extension, the Oroko tribe) and exalted by the Ékpè society there. Moreover, the people of the Ngolo clan invoked the spirit of Nasakó whenever there was a serious problem in the land. There is also a traditional family lineage of Nasakó ancestry, called the *BoNasako* family (family of Nasakó).

NATIONAL AND POPULAR CULTURE

Having been well organized and kept underground in the colonial period, Abakuá was later celebrated as a culture of resistance in popular music. By the 1850s, Cuba's first national music, the *contradanza* and the related *danzón,* had titles and sonic elements that referred to Abakuá. During the Wars of Independence (1868–1898) popular theater also had many references to Abakuá masquerade performers as a symbol of *cubanía* (Cubanness). With the birth of the modern *son* with rumba sections in Havana in the 1910s, Abakuá codes and rhythms became essential to the genre. In the 1920s and 1930s, an artistic movement called *Afrocubanismo* emerged in Havana, seeking to define a national culture while drawing inspiration from the working-class cultures of African descendants.

Being anticolonial and endemic to Cuba, Abakuá became an important symbol for the *Afrocubanistas*, who included leading intellectuals such as Ortiz, Nicolás Guillén (1902–1989), Alejo Carpentier (1904–1980), and Lydia Cabrera (1900–1991); also participating were the composer Ernesto Lecuona (1895–1963) and the singer Rita Montaner (1900–1958), as well as the painter Wifredo Lam (1902–1982). All of them used Abakuá themes in their work as a key facet of Cuban identity.

Among the important musicians of Cuban popular music were Abakuá members Ignacio Piñeiro (1888–1969), a member of the Abakuá group Efóri Nkomón, who founded the *son* group Septeto Nacional in 1927, and Chano Pozo (1915–1948), a member of the Munyánga Efó group, whose compositions and performances with jazz great Dizzy Gillespie in the late 1940s helped create the bebop genre and established Afro-Cuban jazz globally. Following this legacy were the Abakuá musicians Julito Collazo (1935–2004), who migrated to the United States to play with Katherine Dunham's troupe in the 1950s, and Orlando (Puntilla) Ríos (1947–2008), who arrived in the 1980s. They among others extended the Abakuá musical impact on jazz music, setting the stage for unprecedented cultural exchanges between West African Ékpè and Cuban Abakuá members in the twenty-first century.

RECONNECTING THE ÉKPÈ-ABAKUÁ CONTINUUM

After recognizing Calabar place names and phrases in Abakuá chanting, leaders of the Èfìk National Association in the United States invited a contingent of Abakuá to their national meeting in 2001 in New York City, where the two groups exchanged songs, percussion music, and masquerade ensemble performances. The matter-of-fact recognition through the performance of inherited traditions by both groups led to a series of further encounters that escalated the transatlantic communications to extraordinary levels. In 2003, the Obong (Paramount Ruler) of Calabar, while meeting with Cuban Abakuá in the United States, called them his children and invited them to Calabar. In 2004, at the invitation of Donald Duke, governor of Cross River State, two Cuban Abakuá traveled to Calabar, where they were able to confirm that Ékpè and Abakuá practices were mutually intelligible. In 2007, Ékpè and Abakuá met onstage in the Musée Quai Branly in Paris for four command performances. These events inspired the Abakuá leaders in Cuba to reevaluate their inherited phrases and ceremonial actions based upon new information from West Africa.

■ *See also*

Language: Lucumí

BIBLIOGRAPHY
Books and Articles

Brown, David H. *The Light Inside: Abakuá Society Arts.* Washington, DC: Smithsonian Institution Press, 2003.

Cabrera, Lydia. *La sociedad secreta Abakuá: Narrada por viejos adeptos.* Havana: Ediciones C. R., 1958

Cabrera, Lydia. *Anaforuana: Ritual y símbolos de la iniciación en la sociedad secreta Abakuá.* Madrid: Ediciones Madrid, 1975.

Cabrera, Lydia. *La Regla Kimbisa del Santo Cristo del Buen Viaje.* Miami: Colección del Chicherekú en el exilio, 1977.

Kubik, Gerhard. "Lamellophone." In *The New Grove Dictionary of Music and Musicians,* 2nd ed., vol. 14, edited by Stanley Sadie. New York: Grove Press, 2001.

Matibag, Eugenio. *Afro-Cuban Religious Experience: Cultural Reflections in Narrative.* Gainesville: University Press of Florida, 1996.

Miller, Ivor. "A Secret Society Goes Public: The Relationship Between Abakuá and Cuban Popular Culture." *African Studies Review* 43, no. 1 (April 2000): 161–188.

Miller, Ivor. *The Voice of the Leopard: African Secret Societies and Cuba.* Jackson: University Press of Mississippi, 2009.

Mosquera, Gerardo. 1996. "Elegguá at the (Post?) Modern Crossroads: The Presence of Africa in the Visual Art of Cuba." In *Santería Aesthetics in Contemporary Latin American Art,* edited by Arturo Lindsay. Washington, D.C.: Smithsonian Institution Press.

Ortiz, Fernando. "La 'tragedia' de los ñáñigos." *Cuadernos Americanos* 52, no. 4 (July–August 1950): 79–101.

Ortiz, Fernando. *Los bailes y el teatro de los negros en el folklore de Cuba.* Originally published 1951. Havana: Letras Cubanas, 1981.

Ortiz, Fernando. *Los instrumentos de la música afrocubana,* vol. 4. Havana: Cárdenas y Cía, 1954.

Talbot, Percy Amaury. *In the Shadow of the Bush.* London: William Heinemann, 1912.

Thompson, Robert Farris. *Flash of the Spirit: African and Afro-American Art and Philosophy.* New York: Vintage, 1983.

Selected Discography

"Afro-Cuban Suite," 1989. *Dizzy Gillespie/Max Roach in Paris.* BMG Music. CD 09026-68213-2.

"Iya" and "Aguanille Bonko," 1992. *Irakere: Selección de exitos 1973–1978.* Havana: Areito.

FAITH: ARARÁ

Juan Mesa Díaz

A lesser-known religion related to the Ocha-Ifá and Vodou faiths that developed in Cuba.

Arará is an Afro-Cuban religion that combines elements of the Ocha-Ifá system as well as Vodou. While combining elements of both of these religions it still retains its own uniqueness. *Arará* is the umbrella term for people who were introduced into Cuba as slaves from the sixteenth into the nineteenth centuries. They came from the Ewé and Fon ethnic groups that were settled in Dahomey, West Africa, later known as the Republic of Benin. The term comes from a corruption of *Allada* (or Ardráh), a city-state that was conquered by the kingdom of Dahomey.

Along with Oyó and Benin, Dahomey rounded out the trio of cities on the west coast of Africa that were called the Brother Kingdoms, which served as the spiritual centers of the African religions that form the base of Arará. The Brother Kingdoms were founded by Oduduwa, the mythic ancestor of the Yoruba people, from the sacred city of Ilé Ifé in the ninth century. Oyó and Benin (to a lesser degree) became the centers for the Ocha-Ifá religion, while Dahomey was the center for Vodou.

Starting in the middle of the sixteenth century, absolute monarchy was the prevailing system in Dahomey. All the structures of power depended on the strictest obedience to the royal figure. The king himself granted titles of nobility and selected local chiefs from among the family patriarchs. Absolute power also manifested itself in the religious milieu. The king was also the high priest, and he appointed the priestly caste. In contrast to Benin and Oyó, any freedom of religious association based on region or lineage was totally forbidden in Dahomey.

In addition to Ewé and Fon, Dahomey was populated by Sahe, Ketu, Awori, Ife, Idaisa, Manigri, Ohori, Isa, Ifongin, and Ajase people, all of whom were of Yoruba origin. The differences between the Ewé-Fon and the Yoruba are both ethno-linguistic and religious, but the close proximity of the two groups within Dahomey resulted in Dahomey's religious system being permeated by Yoruba influence, something that clearly shows in the parallels between the governing and religious practices of both groups. Common traits from the two religious traditions (Vodou and Ocha-Ifá) include the significance of belonging to a noble bloodline; ancestor worship; ritual acts based on sacrifice; the consideration of man as a model figure that came out of divine creation, and his indissoluble link to God and his work; the coexistence of monotheism with polyatry; the importance of the word, silence, and corporeal expression within religious phenomenology; and the use of divination rites and medical practices derived from a coherent system of knowledge, which was interwoven with an elaborate and learned philosophy.

Although the mixture of the two religions began in Africa, it did not emerge as the unique religion of Arará until the Yoruba and Ewé-Fon peoples were brought to Cuba as slaves beginning in the sixteenth century. Ewé-Fon peoples were concentrated in the Matanzas province, as that was a major sugar-growing center that employed slave labor. Therefore, the religious practice of Arará was concentrated in Matanzas.

Slaves were not allowed to practice their African faiths openly, including Arará, so religious expression was secretive and highly family-oriented. Slaves worshipped in house temples that served as both a home and a temple. The family orientation and secrecy resulted in variation in the names of the deities and in the ritual practices. Diversity with linguistic variants and ritualistic differences are noticeable in house temples that are separated by just a few miles. They perpetuate regional differences that are found in Africa, as well as differing levels of cultural mixing and adaptation in each region of Matanzas itself.

The functions of the house temples include consecrations, ritual celebrations, works of appeasement, sacrifices, and mourning rites. They also serve as storehouses for ancestral culinary, musical, dance, and oral traditions, the crafting of musical instruments, and profuse and colorful ritual handicrafts. These, along with an associated pharmacopia of plants, animals, the use of water and stones, and the Fon language—at times intermixed with Yoruba—make this familial heritage one of the legacies of the Cuban nation and its traditional popular culture. Prominent house temples include temples in the town of Espíritu Santo founded by the Reyes family; the San Manuel house temple of the Baró family in Jovellanos; Ilé Amoreyé, created under the leadership of Florentin a Zulueta in Perico; and Ilé Moyokán, founded by Wenceslao Campos in the city of Cárdenas at the beginning of the twentieth century. These temples continued to exist in the early 2000s as evidence of the strong oral traditions that sustained them for centuries.

In Arará, the Supreme Being is identified with the entity known as Mawu-Lisa, interpreted as the primordial husband and wife, and the Creator is blended with Oloddumare, a similar Yoruba deity (some house temples are identified with Oduduwa) from the Ocha-Ifá tradition. Because Mawu-Lisa rarely intervenes in human affairs, he has no devotees. However, the link to terrestrial life is delegated to the *vodum* (spirits), who are organized within a pantheon accompanied by an elaborate liturgy. Among Arará practitioners, the term *vodum* (also *foldum*) refers to an invisible force and selective divine energy that intervenes in human affairs. It is analogous to the *loa* of Vodou or the Yoruba *orisha*.

There are many parallels between the Arará vodum and the Ocha-Ifá orishas. Eleggua is the Yoruba orisha of the crossroads and is identified with Afrá Kubije ga (in Matanzas), Jurajó Takuó (in the Baró house in Jovellanos), and Topo Yayino (in the Zulueta house). Oggún, the orisha of metals, and a complex creator-destroyer figure, is known as Gum in Matanzas's Arará worship, and Oguyé plays the same role in the Zulueta house temple in Jovellanos, while Aladekó presides in Perico and Ajodekó in the Baró house. Changó, another orisha, is identified with the Jebiosso cult in Matanzas, Cárdenas, and Jovellanos and with devotees of Accuoso in Perico. Yemayá, the orisha of motherhood and the ocean, is associated with Afrekete in Matanzas, Frekete in the Baró family temple and in the city of Cárdenas, and with the venerated Anamú in Perico.

The house temples of the Arará are designated by a word derived from Yoruba influence, Ilé, and their structure calls to mind the Ocha-Ifá house temples more than the Vodou's *oufò* (temple-altars). The presence of *poteau-mitan* (the vertical post at the physical and spiritual center of a Vodou temple) is not noticeable in the Arará case, nor are the altars similar.

The hierarchical structure of Arará's pantheon is closer to that of Ocha-Ifá, since Radá, Petró, and Congo (all Vodou cults) are not defined in Arará, as they are in Vodou. Neither do their rituals have much in common with these variations of Vodou. There are similarities, however, in the structure of the high priests between Arará and Vodou. In Arará, the Babamí is the high priest, and Iyalodú is his female equivalent. Bakú is the male or female assistant or initiate who is entrusted to handle various ceremonies. Vodou also has a hierarchy of people who assist in the ceremonies.

■ *See also*

Afro-Cuban Spirituality
in the Art of Manuel
Mendive

Food: Ritual Foods
and Afro-Cuban
Religious Traditions

Music: Afro-Cuban
Religious Influence on
Cuban Popular Music

La Virgen de la Caridad
del Cobre

For basic divination rites, *obi* (pieces of coconut) are used in the same way that they are in the Ocha-Ifá system, as well as *diloggun* (cowrie shells), along with interpretations of these rites that are identical to those in the Ocha subsystem. The calendar of their ritual celebrations fully coincides with the one adopted by the Ocha-Ifá system. It corresponds with the calendar of Catholic saints' days: Yemayá-Afrekete on 7 September, Changó-Jebiosso on 4 December (St. Barbara in the Catholic calendar), and Azojano and Babalú Ayé on 17 December (St. Lazarus in the Catholic calendar), among others.

As regards rites of initiation, the Arará stages are similar to those of Yoruba origin, with initial ceremonies that include cleansing baths, sequestration for several days, and year-long purification measures for new initiates. Arará initiations are traditionally familial. This peculiarity makes them seem exclusionary in the view of other denominations that have first opened themselves up to local communities and then have even extended their influence beyond the country's borders. Some branches of the traditional families have established themselves in Havana and even outside of Cuba, where they maintain a so-called semi-closed status that sets them apart and a close and almost subordinating link to their original family trees.

Arará musical traditions have maintained themselves throughout the centuries. As in Ocha-Ifá and Vodou, drums are used, but the drums are a different size, played on one side with both hand and a stick (usually three drums but possibly as many as five), and they are accompanied by an *ogán* (the metal part of a hoe) and an *acheré* (a type of rattle).

The biggest influence of Matanzas's Arará practices on the rest of the Afro-Cuban religions is rooted in the worship of Azojano (variously known as Azonhano, Azojuano, Olúo Popó, Xampaná, or Xampata). His equivalent in Ocha-Ifá is Babalú-Ayé (St. Lazarus in Catholicism). Also, the initiation and promotional ceremonies for Azojano are highly regarded, since the Arará are thought of as a depository of the secrets of this orisha (*loa, vodum*), given that they are the people that Babalú Ayé founded.

BIBLIOGRAPHY

Akinjogbin, I. A. *Dahomey and Its Neighbours, 1708–1818.* Cambridge, U.K.: Cambridge University Press, 1967.

Brandon, George. *Santeria from Africa to the New World: The Dead Sell Memories.* Bloomington: Indiana University Press, 1993.

Brice Sogbossi, H. *La tradición ewé-fon en Cuba.* Havana: Fundación Fernando Ortiz, 1998.

Guanche, Jesús. *Procesos etnoculturales en Cuba.* Havana: Editorial Letras Cubanas, 1983.

Mesa Díaz, J. "The Religious System of Ocha Ifá." In *Music in Latin America and the Caribbean*, vol. 2, edited by Malena Kuss. Austin: University of Texas Press, 2007.

FAITH: REGLA DE OCHA AND IFÁ

Alan West-Durán

An outline of major concepts and practices of Regla de Ocha (Santería) and Ifá religious traditions.

On the streets of Havana two men greet each other with "*¿Qué bolá, asere?*" In Cuban slang it means roughly "Wassup, bro?" The word *asere* is an Efik word from the Calabar region of West Africa. At one time it was used only by members of the Abakuá society, but it has in modern times gained general currency for most Cubans as meaning the equivalent of *brother, dear friend,* or *close buddy.* The two are joined by a female friend dressed all in white and wearing several brightly colored necklaces. On her left arm she sports a blue and white beaded bracelet. They cheerfully but respectfully acknowledge her with the term "*Iyawó!*" This greeting is reserved for those who are going through the one-year period after initiation into Regla de Ocha, a popular religion with profound African roots. All three decide to go to one of their homes to listen to music and drink some rum. They put on a CD that begins with a well-known tune, "La Negra Tomasa," which has a refrain that says, "*Esa negra linda, que me echó bilongo*" (That beautiful black woman has put a spell on me). *Bilongo* is a Kikongo word that resonates with the practices of Regla de Palo Mayombe, an Afro-Cuban religion of Congolese origins, which has a reputation for putting the spirits to work for one's benefit. As the three enjoy the music they reach for the bottle of rum, open it, and pour a little on the floor first, saying, "*¡Para los orishas!*" (For the orishas). These greetings, gestures, clothing, words, colors, and attitudes show ingrained African culture in Cuba, linguistically, religiously, and socially.

Nor is the African influence limited to Havana. Ninety miles away in Miami, during Thanksgiving 1999, a five-year-old boy washed ashore in a makeshift raft that came from Cuba. Of the fourteen who had been on the raft with him, twelve did not make it, including the boy's mother. His family in Miami took him in, and the fact that he had survived—with virtually no physical signs of travail—was viewed as a miracle by many Miami Cubans. They saw it as a sign that he had been protected by the Virgin of Charity (the orisha Oshún), who saved his life during the perilous journey. In effect they were saying that Oshún is the protectress of all Cubans, regardless of where they live. The term *orisha* is used as roughly equivalent to a Catholic saint, but they are not synonymous. Both Oshún, the orisha of fresh waters, and Yemayá, the mother orisha of the ocean, were invoked as guiding spirits for the boy who captured headlines for the next six months: Elián González.

Furthermore, exiled *santeros* (initiates of Regla de Ocha or Santería) claimed that Fidel Castro—who some claim is a secret santero—had offended Elegguá, the orisha of the crossroads, who is often depicted as a child. Some Miami Cubans saw Elián as a messenger of Elegguá and believed he had been chosen as the child who would overthrow Fidel. Was it a coincidence that Elegguá's colors are black and red, the same colors as Castro's 26th of July Movement?

The Virgin of Charity is Cuba's patron saint and legend says she rescued three men, all named Juan (a Spaniard, an Indian, and an African), from a terrible storm at sea in 1612, near the town of El Cobre (in eastern Cuba), where in modern times her shrine towers on a hill. Regardless of the political dimensions of little Elián's plight—of whether he should have stayed with family in Miami or be returned to his father in Cuba—Cubans from both sides of the Florida Straits had reason to believe that what had transpired showed signs of a divine imprint. And despite the Catholic imagery of the Virgin of Charity, the sheen of her fine golden-hued robe also speaks eloquently to the deeply embedded African beliefs that make her—and her sister Yemayá (the Virgin of Regla)—so beloved to many Cubans.

However, say Santería, Palo, or Abakuá to most people and if they don't react with a blank stare of incomprehension they will likely conjure up images of blood, animal sacrifice, violently writhing bodies, and strange rites that can do mental or physical harm to people. These Afro-Cuban religions, or as some prefer to say, these Cuban religions of African ancestry, are not cults with malevolent rituals but practices deeply embedded in West African thought, theology, and experience. By any definition of the word they are religions, with a profoundly spiritual view of the world buttressed by complex philosophical systems, centuries of intricate ritual, and practices that pragmatically and poetically tie everyday existence to the divine.

West African religions deeply influenced Cuban history and demography by way of the Atlantic slave trade, brought from the countries in modern times known as Ghana, Benin, Togo, Nigeria, Cameroon, and the Bantu-speaking regions of the two Congo states, Gabon, and Angola. Most but not all of the religions share some common traits: They are monotheistic, yet believe in a world of intermediary spiritual forces (*orishás*, *loas*, *mpungus*) that serve as translators between the human and divine. They attribute great significance to ancestral spirits that can guide the living, they are religions of initiation, and possession plays an important role. Their adherents believe in reincarnation, but not in the sense of coming back to the physical world in a body or object; instead one's spirit forms part of the cosmic flow of energy in the universe, becoming an ancestral presence that brings light (or not) to the living. The religions practice certain forms of divination, are involved in physical and spiritual healing, and employ sacrifice (some animal).

MERCEDITAS VALDÉS: AFRO-CUBAN FOLKLORIC SINGER

Merceditas Valdés (1928–1996) was an outstanding popular and folkloric singer and interpreter of Afro-Cuban vocal music, especially the music of Santería and rumba. At age twelve, she won awards in the Corte Suprema del Arte (Supreme Court of Art) competition for singing "Babalu" and Lecuona's "La Negra Merced," and she went on to learn and perform Yoruba sacred music. In the Radio Cadena Suaritos, accompanied by an orchestra directed by Obdulio Morales, including a *batá* drum ensemble led by Trinidad Torregrosa, Valdés pioneered radio broadcasting of that music. Later she worked with musicians such as Jesús Perez, her husband Guillermo Barreto, Raul Días, Pablo Roche, Ernesto Lecuona, Yoruba Andabo, and Mongo Santamaría. A decisive moment in her career came in 1944 when she met the esteemed Cuban ethnologist Fernando Ortiz (1881–1969), who asked her to work with him to demonstrate the influence of Afro-Cuban music at academic conferences. Ortiz nicknamed Valdés his "little Aché" (divine force). After that she recorded Cuban ritual music and toured in Europe, the United States, and South America.

Glenn Jacobs

Finally, these are not religions of salvation (that is, believers are not rewarded with a place in heaven if they have been virtuous or saved), but stress the living of a good life of self-realization and a good death here on earth.

THE ORIGINS OF THE OCHA-IFÁ SYSTEM

The most widely practiced of these religions is known as Regla de Ocha, also called Santería. Similar but not identical to it is the Ifá tradition, which has its own system of initiation and different types of divination, but is closely linked to the orishas. The popularity of the Ocha-Ifá tradition has much to do with Cuba's history of slavery. In the eighteenth century the predominant group of Africans came from the Congo-Angola region and in the early nineteenth century from the area of the Cross River (Calabar region). By the mid-nineteenth century one out of three slaves coming to Cuba was Lucumí, as the Yoruba people of Nigeria are known on the island. The preponderance of the Yoruba up to abolition in Cuba (and Brazil) explains their modern importance, along with the fact that Cuba was among the last countries to abolish slavery (1886). Overall, Yoruba peoples constituted only 9 percent of the enslaved Africans brought to the New World, but they were concentrated in three areas that still constitute an important African presence: Saint Domingue (modern Haiti), Salvador do Bahia (Brazil), and Cuba.

These peoples had long practiced a belief system related to Ifá and worship of the orishas. In the Yoruba tradition, *Ifá* refers to both a system of divination and the verses of the literary corpus known as the *Odú Ifá*, which is drawn upon during divination. Orúnmila (in Cuba Orula) is the orisha who presides over divination, and sometimes the name is used interchangeably with *Ifá*.

In Cuba these religions came into contact with other cultural and religious practices, particularly Catholicism and Spiritism, engendering new forms of spirituality that came about through what Cuban anthropologist Fernando Ortiz (1881–1969) called *transculturation*. In Cuba the Yoruba-based transculturation became known as Santería (way of the saints) or Regla de Ocha (rule or law of the orishas). The name *Santería* refers to the practice of resistance and re-elaboration by Cuban slaves in camouflaging their African beliefs through the imagery and symbols of Catholicism. So, for example, the orisha Changó, who is associated with thunder and lightning, music, and warriorhood, becomes syncretized with Saint Barbara, often depicted with a sword defending the faith. Her colors are red and white like Changó's, and she is also linked to lightning. In Cuba Saint Barbara and Changó are both honored on December 4.

THE ORISHAS: DEFINITIONS AND HISTORY

The term *orisha* has generated numerous misunderstandings. Many well-intentioned researchers have called them divinities or gods, which is not exactly accurate. Orishas are the varied and multifaceted manifestations of all the divine energies in the universe that together would constitute God, which is too vast for human capacities to comprehend, so people give names and attributes to these manifestations. It is the proliferation of names and orishas that erroneously gives the impression that Ocha is polytheistic. Others have characterized the orishas as guardian angels or saints (interpretations that both show Catholic influences), as well as representing natural forces (e.g., water, wind, lightning, fire, earth, and herbs), the latter not surprising for a religion born in rural surroundings and intricately entwined with nature.

Still others see the orishas as a metaphysical principle or as an archetype. As archetypes they are viewed as people, like ancestral spirits, but more powerful. They are described as personifications of certain personalities. An orisha materializes in the life, actions, and the personality of a person. They are role models: parent, sibling, public defender, psychologist, botanist, healer, spiritual advisor. This view is common because believers develop a definite personal relationship with their tutelary orisha, and the orisha becomes a member of the family.

The archetypal-personal view is logical because some orishas did exist as human beings. For example, Changó was a former king of Oyó and through his powers, gifts, and special abilities, after death became a revered ancestor and eventually became an orisha.

Orishas are like people in that they have frailties: Oggún can be overly impetuous, Changó can appear arrogant, and Yemayá too severe. The only orisha deemed to be above these weaknesses is Orula, who is impartial and not coincidentally is the orisha of divination, able to analyze one's destiny without bias.

The Yoruba Ifá tradition has a rich lore passed on orally about the orishas, including how they came to be, their relationships to other orishas, and stories about animals, nature, and how things were created or acquired certain traits, physical or otherwise. These stories, known as *pattakís*, usually have a moral to them and are often drawn upon in the divination process.

The complexity of what constitutes an orisha is understandable, given the vast web of interconnected energies in the world. But in no way does this complexity keep people from seeing the orishas' spiritual power with great clarity and faith or pleading with them to ensure that the *aché* they convey be shared with mortals, giving them good health, prosperity, a loving family, and steadfast friends. Orishas are ensured of remaining central to Cuba's cultural imaginary because of the heartfelt and intimate interactions between them and humans.

SANTEROS

Santeros (initiates of the religion) are monotheists, believing in a Creator, known as Olodumare, who after creating the universe retires from intervening directly in the world, but makes his/her presence felt through different manifestations of divine energy through the orishas. The orishas incarnate spiritual, natural, and other energies that surround mortals. They are conveyors of *aché*, the energy of the universe that gives life, makes events happen, transforms things, and imbues humanity with empathy, creativity, and joy.

Like any human, santeros want to receive aché so that their lives are blessed with good fortune (*iré*), patience, health (physical and mental), friends, family unity, spiritual peace, and an existence in harmony with nature, society, and family. In fact, *santeros* see the troubles of the world, whether personal, familial, or societal, as the product of imbalances between the natural, personal, societal, and spiritual worlds, and the importance of *aché* is to bring about harmony between those realms.

Thus, the words from one of the sacred *odus*, sayings that are part of the Ifá written corpus, admirably synthesize Ocha's worldview: "Nothing is more natural than the supernatural" (quoted in Mesa p. 58). Aside from the more obvious meaning of not seeing the natural and supernatural worlds as being radically separated, what the *odu* points to is a philosophical worldview that sees every aspect of human existence as interrelated, so that the natural world (plants, animals, minerals), humans, the ancestral spirits, and the orishas are all part of a cosmos that is both natural and divine, and gives humans the responsibility to keep these cosmic balances from being disrupted, damaged, or destroyed.

Regla de Ocha is a religion of initiations and the process centers on three steps toward full initiation: *los guerreros* (the warriors); *los collares* (the necklaces); and *el asiento* (full initiation). These initiations are spiritual milestones that show an increasing involvement with the religion; full initiation brings a person into the religious community of other santeros.

The Warriors An initiate receives the warriors as protection against danger, enemies, accidents, and physical attacks. This important ceremony involves not necklaces but actual objects that represent or contain the aché of the warrior orishas, who are Elegguá, Oggún, Ochosi, and Osun. Elegguá is usually received in the form of a cement head four to six inches in height, with cowrie shells representing the eyes, ears, and mouth. The head is hollow, and ritual materials are placed in it. The head is usually topped by a small blade or feather. Elegguá is usually kept right behind the front door of a house, as one of his functions is to guard a person's home.

Oggún and Ochosi are received in an iron three-legged cauldron. Inside the cauldron are the different metal implements associated with Oggún: knives, hammers, nails, horseshoes, and a tiny anvil. A metal bow and arrow represents Ochosi, the orisha of hunting. A person can receive the warriors through a *babalawo* in a ceremony called *Mano de Orula* (Hand of Orula) or through a *padrino* or *madrina* (godfather or godmother) in Ocha.

Finally, Osun is represented by a small metallic rooster atop a cup with a fringe of tiny bells. He is usually kept in a high spot within the house since he is a lookout to prevent any misfortune. Osun must never be allowed to tip over because that will bring ill fortune to the owner.

Receiving the Necklaces Receiving the necklaces is not a long and complicated ceremony. Usually, the necklaces of five major orishas are presented: Obbatalá, Changó, Yemayá, Ochún, and Elegguá. Each necklace confers upon its wearer the blessings of that particular orisha. For example, the red and white necklace of Changó helps with issues of power, passion, getting things done, and control of one's enemies. The all-white necklace of Obbatalá deals with the head, peace, and spiritual harmony.

Before the necklaces are given they are prepared and treated in different receptacles with different kinds of herbs and liquids in a process called *feeding the necklaces*. Before the rituals begin the *padrino* or *madrina* performs a reading with sixteen cowrie shells, using the Ifá corpus to find out about the person's life, problems, health, and so on and also to see if the ceremony should proceed or if anything special (some type of offering or sacrifice) needs to be made. Individuals do not select their *eledá* (their guardian orisha); the orisha selects them. To find a person's tutelary orisha one needs a reading done by a babalawo; however, in some house-temples the consultation is done by a santero who is a skilled oriaté (an interpreter of the shells). This latter practice is disapproved of by babalawos. If the *eledá* is not one of the five principal orishas of the necklaces, then an additional necklace is prepared and given to the wearer; thus if the guardian orisha is Obba, the initiate wears a necklace with purple and lilac beads, in addition to the other five.

The person receiving the necklaces must abstain from sexual activity a day before the ceremony. The person is given a cleansing bath with *omiero* (a liquid that contains holy water, crushed herbs, and small amounts of blood used to purify people during important ceremonies). Then he or she is dressed in white and given a *rogación de cabeza*, a spiritual cleansing of the head. This is followed by a ceremony in which the person kneels on a mat and receives one necklace at a time.

Necklaces are taken off while bathing, sleeping, or having sexual intercourse. If a necklace breaks, it must be brought back to the *padrino* or *madrina* so that it can be fixed and reconsecrated. A broken necklace is actually a good thing in that it serves as a warning, potentially saving its wearer from a calamitous event.

***El Asiento* (Full Initiation)** Receiving the necklaces and the warriors is likened to being halfway toward being an initiate. Many people choose to go through the first two steps and not the *asiento*, or full initiation. The full initiation is a major commitment of time and of money; moreover, many people may not feel spiritually ready for such a profoundly transformative experience.

The asiento takes roughly a week, but preparatory rituals take place days before: a *misa espiritual* (a spiritual mass), a shell reading, a look at the initiate's spiritual ensemble (*cuadro espiritual*), that is, the ancestors and other types of spirits that guide and protect a person (which reflects a Spiritist influence in Ocha, as does the spiritual mass). These preparatory rituals are performed for several reasons: to gain an immediate view of the initiate's spiritual state, to determine whether the initiation should take place (in some cases, the asiento is postponed), and to further spiritually cleanse and prepare the initiate for the upcoming days, which will be spiritually demanding.

These preparatory rituals are followed by a visit to a river, where the initiate pays respect to Oshún, the orisha of fresh waters. In this ceremony the *iyawó* wears old clothes, which are removed, symbolically enacting the removal of one's old life. The initiate bathes in the river and is then dressed in white. He or she gathers some of the river water as well as a stone, which are incorporated into upcoming rituals.

The next day is perhaps the most memorable, when the initiate is led, with eyes closed, into the *igbodu*, the sacred room. Here several santeros chant songs in Lucumí while a major santero shaves the initiate's head. Once the head is shaven a small incision is made on the top of the head and aché, a mixture of herbs, some from Africa, are placed into the incision. This is central to the initiation because santeros believe that any aché comes in through the head. This procedure follows Yoruba traditions by which the head is the seat of a person's character, inner being, and intelligence, and is linked spiritually to the heart and soul.

After this ceremony there is a lunch and a brief rest and soon after the major sacrifices begin, mostly of animals. Depending on the orisha into which the person is being initiated, the rituals will require certain animals, or fruits, candles, and so on. All of the creatures are then prepared and cooked and served as food to santeros, visitors, and the initiate over the next several days. Nothing goes to waste.

SACRIFICE AND HEALING

Animal sacrifice is probably one of the more controversial—not to mention sensationalized—aspects of Regla de Ocha. The sacrifices, however, are handled humanely and with great respect, and the cooked flesh of the animals is later consumed by santeros and visitors. The animals are ritually prepared and cleansed. Before they can be sacrificed, the permission of the orishas as well as the *egún* (ancestors) must be obtained, because human beings do not have the authority to destroy life. Permission to sacrifice animals is obtained through the mediation of two orishas: Elegguá and Oggún.

In his *Yoruba Beliefs and Sacrificial Rites* Nigerian scholar J. Omosade Awolalu defines several types of sacrifice, including thanksgiving and communion, votive (fulfilling a vow), propitiatory (for events such as failure of crops, plague, famine, and disease), preventive (to ward off danger and evil), substitutionary (to save one from premature death), and foundational (to bless the building of a house, a new business, or a marriage) (pp. 143–161). Santeros perform all of these ceremonies. The blood is fed to the orishas, and the flesh goes to nurture humans. However, as Alan West-Durán explains, the offerings do not belong to humans:

> What is involved is a real and symbolic exchange that seeks to create an equilibrium of cosmic forces, the creation (or reaffirmation) of a community, and the search for *aché* (the sacred life force). The *ebbó* (sacrifice) is ultimately a ritual of healing. The symbolic exchange is the giving of one life to sustain, nourish, and improve our own lives; the real exchange involves that precious loss in order to ward off obstacles, sickness, and death and create both health and peace of mind. "Life is but a process of giving in order to receive."

p. 629

Most *ebbós* are offerings of fruit, foods, candles, and the like, and it is important to remember that all major religions have sacrifice as central to their beliefs, sometimes symbolic, as in Christian communion, fasting, or giving up certain foods or preparing them in a special way, and these sacrifices seek to redress spiritual imbalances. *Santeros* take their sacrifices not only symbolically, but literally, and the intimate nature of these sacrifices—not to mention their physical proximity—makes them unique moments in which one may witness powerful spiritually charged cosmic energies in motion.

If one believes that the natural and supernatural worlds are entwined, then sacrifice can be understood as binding those two realms. In the belief that the plant, animal, human, and divine worlds are delicately balanced and interwoven, the notion of sacrifice as healing becomes more prominent. Santeros will often see illness as neither entirely physical nor entirely mental. This holistic approach does not mean *santeros* are not accepting of scientific approaches to healing. On the contrary, as healers *santeros* use both natural and scientific approaches to curing illness; for example, someone with cancer will be given herbal remedies, but will also be encouraged to see a doctor, and, if need be, undergo chemotherapy or radiation treatment. Accomplished santeros are knowledgeable herbalists and healers. They consult Osain, who is the orisha of herbs, and also draw on the vast empirical knowledge accumulated throughout the centuries by santeros and non-santeros alike. For example, the herb anis is associated with Oshún and is used for indigestion, gas, and exhaustion; *yerba buena* (spearmint) is linked to Yemayá and helps cure skin troubles and brings good luck. Likewise, the Ocha-Ifá tradition has no quarrel with evolution or other scientific advances concerning the earth or the universe, as do fundamentalist interpretations of Christianity and Islam.

THIRD AND FOURTH DAYS OF THE *ASIENTO*: DÍA DEL MEDIO AND DÍA DEL ITÁ

On the third day of the initiation the devotee is dressed in the ritual attire of his or her orisha. That morning the *iyawó* (initiate) is ritually bathed with *omiero* by his or her padrino or madrina and then dressed for the occasion. After this ceremony the *iyawó* can receive some visitors, albeit briefly. That day another ritual meal is shared with *santeros*, family, and close friends.

The following day, known as the *Día del Itá* (the Day of the Itá Reading), the devotee undergoes an extensive reading with the cowrie shells that pertain to each of the major orishas (Elegguá, Oshún, Changó, Yemayá, Obbatalá, and Oggún). This consultation, aside from looking at the initiate's past, present, and future, lays down a set of recommendations for his or her future life as a santero. There might be certain prohibitions regarding food, clothing, and certain activities (such as going to the beach, playing sports,

Opposite page:
Preparations for a ceremony. Santería practitioners prepare to hold an initiation ceremony in which goats will be sacrificed. HÉCTOR DELGADO AND ROLANDO PUJOL

or traveling over water). An initiate of Yemayá is often told to stop eating duck, because that is one of Yemayá's favorite foods, but other food prohibitions, against eggs or seafood, for example, might be invoked for health reasons.

The Itá is a long and complex consultation with the orishas about the initiate's life, health, family, job, and spiritual harmony. Close friends and family members can be present, as this consultation is a collective conversation about the initiate's life, its constraints, and how to change things so the person can live a better life. The Itá reading is done with cowrie shells, and because so many orishas are consulted, can take half a day or even longer.

During the Itá, a new name is chosen for the initiate, which will be in the Lucumí language, and a second orisha parent is determined. In future ceremonies the initiate is then referred to by the new ritual name. If a person is initiated into a female orisha, such as Ochún, then he or she also needs a father orisha, which could be Oggún, Ochosi, Elegguá, or any other of the male orishas. Conversely, if the person is initiated into a male orisha, then that person needs a mother orisha. This further reinforces the idea that the tutelary orishas serve as a spiritual family, echoing the godfather-godmother structure that guides the initiate during all phases of the initiation.

Following the Itá, the initiate, still dressed in white, spends the next three days on a mat (*estera*) in the throne room where the person was initiated, sleeping and eating on the mat and only leaving the area of the mat to go to the bathroom, accompanied by their padrino or madrina or a santero or assistant. The initiate can receive visitors, but this is kept to a minimum as the three days are supposed to be for reflection, for reading, for going over what was said in the Itá, and for speaking to the padrino or madrina about the practices of the religion, the meaning of different rituals, and the initiate's own doubts or questions about what he or she is experiencing.

On the seventh and final day, the *iyawó* is taken outdoors and accompanied by a santero to a market, where the person symbolically steals food from merchants (later paid for) to honor the fact that many santeros in the past were too poor to buy food. Then the person goes to a church, preferably one with many of the key saints that are syncretized with the major orishas (such as the Virgin of Charity, Saint Barbara, the Virgin of Mercedes, or the Virgin of Regla), where the *iyawó* prays and leaves offerings, usually candles. From there the person returns to the house-temple where the initiation took place, and the padrino then asks the orishas, through coconut divination, if he or she is satisfied with the initiation. If the answer is yes, then the *iyawó*, padrino, madrina, officiating santeros, and friends finish off with a celebratory lunch. If the answer is no, then the padrino or madrina must find out what else needs to be done (offerings, candles, a mass, or a sacrifice of some sort).

Once all these steps are completed the *iyawó* becomes someone born anew into Ocha, and as such is treated somewhat like a child. He or she must continue to wear white for a year (sometimes special dispensation is given for going to work in regular clothing and wearing white at home), including covering the head, and for the first three months the initiate must continue to eat meals on a mat and with a special cup and spoon (to show humility). Some time between three months to a year after the initiation a major *ebbó* (sacrifice) is performed to further the cleansing process. During this year the *iyawó* will also wear the *idé* (bracelet) of his or her orisha on the left wrist, as well as the orishas' necklaces. Except for important occasions, *iyawós* are supposed to be home by sundown and not go out at night.

As the initiate goes through the different steps toward full initiation, different readings are performed by the padrino or madrina, and all of the information is written down in a *libreta* (notebook). At the one-year birthday after initiation, the notebook is handed over to the *iyawó*. The birthday celebration is a party with drumming, food, and drink, during which other santeros and friends pay homage to the recent initiate and begin to form his or her greater spiritual family.

The remaining major ceremonies in the initiation are *tambores* (drumming ceremonies), in which the initiate is presented to the sacred *batá* drums. There are three tambores. The first two are offered to the padrino's and the madrina's orishas, and finally the initiate can offer his or her own tambor. In a tambor three batá drums are played, richly draped with colorful cloths, shells, mirrors, and bells, and a singer performs sacred chants. The *olubatá*, the drummers, have to be initiates as well and often require ten years or more of training to be able to play at rituals. The batá drums, which are also consecrated, cannot be played in nonritual circumstances or by non-initiates.

In the first tambor, the initiate is dressed in his or her ritual orisha attire and is kept in a separate room until formally presented to the consecrated drums. The initiate pays reverence to the drums by ritually bowing and then kissing them and laying his or her forehead on the drums while they are being played. The second and third tambores only require the person to dress in white. Non-initiates can come to a tambor but the person cannot dance in the circle of dancers, who are all santeros. A key aspect of the tambor is that some participants can bring down the spirit of an orisha by entering a trance state.

POSSESSION

Possession, like animal sacrifice, draws a lot of attention to the religion but is not a frequent occurrence. Usually, people with a special gift for *bringing down the saint* are invited to a tambor, and if things proceed as planned, they will receive the orisha being honored by the ceremony into their bodies. This usually takes place over a period of twenty to thirty minutes, with intense drumming, chanting, and dancing, ultimately producing a trance state in which the orisha inhabits the person. If the host is male and the orisha is female, his voice might go into a high-pitched

register or he will begin to flirt like a woman. At that point the person is dressed in the orisha's attire. Then the orisha moves about and talks to different people, providing information, giving advice, admonishing participants to desist in destructive attitudes. Sometimes an orisha can see a person's future as well and warn that person of an unforeseen danger. Usually the trance lasts one to three hours, sometimes longer. The host remembers nothing, and the experience is physically and spiritually exhausting. There is nothing demonic or crazed about trance, as is sometimes suggested, and those capable of bringing down an orisha are seen with great respect.

DIVINATION SYSTEMS

Regla de Ocha and Ifá use systems of divination to help initiates and non-initiates with their lives. Many people consult an *oriaté*, who is an expert interpreter of the literary corpus known as the *Odú Ifá* and the *odus*, or signs (from verses and sayings), that are indicated by the reading. Divination is not fortunetelling, but a way of helping people find balance between their different energies and worlds. The reading is a consultation with the sacred, in which one seeks guidance about acquiring aché and his or her intellectual, emotional, and spiritual levels are intensely engaged.

A common form of divination is called *obi*, performed with four pieces of coconut rind, where the brown or white side is interpreted after being tossed onto the floor or a mat. There are five variations, reading from a strong yes to a strong (or even dangerous) no. The *obi* is used in all major rituals to determine whether the orishas are satisfied with the offerings received and what must be done with the offerings after the ceremony is over. Both santeros and *babalawos* use the *obi*. It is used in addition to but never in place of the *diloggún*, the reading performed with cowrie shells.

The primary form of divination is the *diloggún*, which uses twenty-one cowrie shells. Five are set apart as witnesses. The other sixteen are tossed onto a mat, and depending on whether the open or closed side falls up or down, they are interpreted according to the Ifá corpus. Most signs come in pairs. So, for example, three open shells followed by two would be read as three-two, which signifies Ogundá Ejioko, a sign of tragedy, with karmic repercussions. Roughly, Ogundá Ejioko can be summarized by the saying, "You sow what you reap." The sign has three proverbs associated with it: With your tongue you make dangerous games; where there are arguments there can be no peace; and arguments bring bad spirits. For men this sign spells trouble with women, friends who might betray secrets, and being involved in a relationship that might bring misfortune (arguments, discord). For women the sign points to a past (or present) of physical or sexual abuse and the urgent need to end that abuse. The sign also warns a person who should take care of his or her health, particularly of the heart (because danger comes

through affairs of the heart). There are recommended offerings for those who receive this sign, primarily related to ancestral spirits. In this sign the ancestral spirits (the *egún*) demand something from the supplicant instead of simply offering help. If the person does not have a *bóveda* (an altar to honor and propitiate his egún), he should build one. If he has one, he should feed it further.

The diloggún is a consultation process. The reading is adapted to the person's personal circumstances: The oriaté and the person discuss the situation as the reading is going on, and when something negative appears, a solution is proposed. However, it is still in the hands of the person who went for the reading to act. He or she can choose to ignore the warnings or do nothing about solving the problem. If more than thirteen shells land face up, then the person is referred to a *babalawo*, a priest in Ifá, who is skilled in interpreting the full range of sixteen main signs (*odus*) with their 256 permutations. A babalawo also uses the *opele* chain, which has eight pieces of coconut or pods on a chain and is also read according to the sixteen major *odus* analogous to the sixteen cowrie shells. In addition, the reader uses the Tray of Ifá, a more complex form of consultation that is considered to be more accurate. It combines the use of sixteen *ikines* (kola nuts) and drawing lines on the tray to create the signs. The Tray of Ifá is deemed the most advanced method because it invokes Orula, the orisha of divination, who is present and considered less biased than ordinary orishas. The *opele* and the Tray of Ifá are only used by babalawos.

IFÁ INITIATIONS

The Ifá initiations are primarily two: the Mano de Orula (Hand of Orula) for men or Kofá de Orula (bracelet) for women, and full initiation. The former are three-day ceremonies in which the person receives Elegguá and the warriors (or has them refreshed if he or she is an Ocha initiate) and has an Itá reading performed by three *babalawos* done with the Tray of Ifá (and not with the cowrie shells as in the Ocha tradition). The latter is a more complete initiation into the mysteries of Ifá and takes a week, with some similarities to an Ocha initiation. The major difference is that when a person receives Ifá he or she does not become an initiate of a specific orisha, but of Orula. Once someone had done this, he or she is considered a babalawo. This requires years of study both before and after the ceremony if a person chooses to be a practicing babalawo. Becoming a babalawo signifies that a person has received the most rigorous training as a diviner, healer, and spiritual advisor.

In Cuba the babalawos gather annually from December 30 through January 1 to determine what is called *La Letra del Año* (Letter of the New Year). In this reading for the new year the babalawos determine which orishas will rule over the year (usually two) and issue warnings about world events, health, and even natural phenomena. (For 2010 they predicted major natural disasters just twelve days before Haiti was devastated by an earthquake that took over 200,000 lives.)

SANTERÍA AND CUBAN IMAGINARY

Many elements in Cuban life show the rich heritage of the Ocha-Ifá traditions. In music, aside from direct musical and rhythmic influences, there are countless songs about the orishas, ranging from Celina González's "¡Qué Viva Changó!" to "Soy Todo," by Los Van Van. Even Cuban rap artists have drawn heavily on Ocha, Palo, and Abakuá, among them Anónimo Consejo, Orishas, Obsesión, and Clan 537. Cuban films have made reference to Ocha directly or indirectly, in works ranging from *Cecilia Valdés* (1981) to *Strawberry and Chocolate* (1994) and from *Life Is to Whistle* (1998) to *Los dioses rotos* (2008). Cuba's literary culture is hugely indebted to Ocha (as well as Palo and Abakuá), as seen in the works of Alejo Carpentier (1904–1980), Nicolás Guillén (1902–1989), and Severo Sarduy (1937–1993) to Nancy Morejón (b. 1944), Excilia Saldaña (1946–1999), Georgina Herrera (b. 1936), and Teresa Cárdenas (b. 1970). In the visual arts the likes of Wifredo Lam (1902–1982), René Portocarrero (1912–1985), Mario Carreño (1913–1999), Roberto Diago (1920–1955), José Bedia (b. 1959), Manuel Mendive (b. 1944), Magda Campos (b. 1959), and Belkis Ayón (1967–1999) have drawn on the images and cosmology of these religions. And, of course, there has been no shortage of scholars who have studied the religions and their vast legacies: Fernando Ortiz, Lydia Cabrera, Rómulo Lachatañeré, Lázara Menéndez, José Luciano Franco, Teodoro Díaz Fabelo, Natalia Bolívar, and Rogelio Martínez Furé, just to name the most prominent.

How this religious tradition overcame the worst ravages of slavery, colonialism, and racism in order to survive and resist and then thrive is a remarkable story in itself. But beyond that, the Ocha-Ifá system, as well as other African-based religious traditions such as Regla de Palo, Abakuá, and Arará, began as and remained in the twenty-first century examples of a culture of resistance. They occupy a central position in defining Cuban national consciousness and provide a source of boundless creativity in Cuban art, culture, and identity.

BIBLIOGRAPHY

Awolalu, J. Omosade. *Yoruba Beliefs and Sacrificial Rites.* Brooklyn, NY: Athelia Henrietta Press, 1996.

Bolívar Aróstegui, Natalia. *Los orishas en Cuba.* Havana: Ediciones Union, 1990.

Cros Sandoval, Mercedes. *Worldview, the Orichas, and Santería: Africa to Cuba and Beyond.* Gainesville: University Press of Florida, 2006.

De la Torre, Miguel. *La Lucha for Cuba: Religion and Politics on the Streets of Miami.* Berkeley: University of California Press, 2003.

Opposite page:
Altar offerings. A small altar for Yemayá, the orisha of motherhood and the oceans, includes a doll wearing blue and white, Yemayá's colors, and offerings of flowers, seashells, and various maritime objects.
HÉCTOR DELGADO AND ROLANDO PUJOL

González-Wippler, Migene. *Santería: The Religion; A Legacy of Faith, Rites, and Magic*. New York: Harmony, 1989.

Mesa Díaz, Juan. "The Religious System of Ocha-Ifá." In *Music in Latin America and the Caribbean: Performing the Caribbean Experience*, vol. 2, edited by Malena Kuss. Austin: University of Texas Press, 2007.

Thompson, Robert Farris. *Flash of the Spirit: African and Afro-American Art and Philosophy*. New York: Vintage, 1984.

West-Durán, Alan. "Orishas after 9/11." In *Speaking desde las heridas*, edited by Claire Joysmith. Mexico City: Universidad Nacional Autónoma de México, 2008.

GLOSSARY OF TERMS

ngueyo initiate.

nkisi spirit of the dead that inhabits a *nganga*.

nfumbe bones of a dead person.

nganga physical receptacle of a spirit; also referred to as *prenda* in Cuba.

patipemba signatures, magic signs.

■ *See also*

Food: Ritual Foods and Afro-Cuban Religious Traditions

Music: Afro-Cuban Religious Influence on Cuban Popular Music

FAITH: REGLAS DE PALO CONGO

Natalia María Bolívar Aróstegui

An overview of the major variants of the Reglas de Palo Congo, Afro-Cuban religions based on religious beliefs and practices from the Congo-Angola regions of Africa.

Originating in the Great Lakes region of eastern equatorial Africa, many Bantu ethnic groups migrated to escape religious wars and the influence of other peoples, moving into the Congo River estuary and the highlands of the Cunene, Cuango, and Kasai rivers. Among those groups were some of Cubans' African ancestors, in coastal Angola almost to the mouth of the Kwanza River, and in a small territory covering the strip of present-day Democratic Republic of the Congo and the enclave of Cabinda, as well as a portion of the Republic of the Congo. Over time, these communities produced various embryonic state formations under the rule of a central authority called *manikongo* (king).

The oral tradition of the Bakongos—the generic name for the Bantu immigrants in that area—tells two stories about the formation of their kingdom. One relates that nine of the manikongo's nephews abandoned their uncle's clan and crossed the Zaire River to settle along the river bank, founding nine clans that were direct descendents of the monarch. According to the other story, after years of warring, Mtinu Wene, the first manikongo, settled south of the Congo River and distributed the conquered lands among his nine most courageous captains. Nine is a sacred number for these peoples.

SETTLEMENT AND ORIGINS IN CUBA

In the late sixteenth century hundreds of slaves destined for sugarcane, coffee, and tobacco plantations landed in Cuba. Upon their arrival, in honor of the nine sacred kingdoms, they created the first nine *nkisi* (sacred objects) of Cuba's Regla de Palo cults. Two of them, *ndumbo* (*nzinga*) and *manawanga* (*mariwanga*), were made in Pinar del Río; *mboma ndongo* in Havana; *nanga nsaya* and *mankunku* in Matanzas; *makaba* (*mbumba kuaba, kaba*) in Santa Clara; *ngumbi* (*nkindi*) in Camagüey; and the last two, *mbudi yamboaki nzinga* and *mbenza-bana*, in Oriente.

The believers' central religious concepts are the worship of dead spirits and mystic control over supernatural forces through the creation of magical objects known as *ngangas*, which are receptacles containing all mysteries and forces. This is the universe in miniature; ancestors and elements of nature are guided by Sambia, the supreme god who lives in the sky, does not come down to earth, and is not worshipped.

According to legends, Sambia created man in the sky and then lowered him to earth by a string hanging from a spider web. In the human spinal cord he embedded the mysteries of the road to be traveled; in the lines of the hand he engraved the text of existence; he blew into man's ear the soul and the intelligence to glimpse it; and he gave man life with blood that made the body shake.

NKISI AND NGANGA

The *nkisi* is the spirit living in the receptacle (nganga), the link between the living and the dead. The nkisi breathes, hears, and does what its master orders. The nkisi's life does not end; instead, it is transmitted to form a sort of lineage.

The word *nganga* means *maker* or *doer*. In Cuba ngangas or *prendas* are receptacles of different kinds that contain what Robert Farris Thompson (1984) describes as a microcosm, which is how those peoples perceive it. The physical form of a nganga may be a squash, a bundle made from tree bark or cloth, an iron or clay pot, or even a shell.

Believers make them from natural elements such as plants that serve as sustenance, cover, or medicine; animals and birds that are hunted for food; waters that quench their thirst; lands where they can rest and that bear fruit. The stars, elements, and natural phenomena also have their own powers and attributes: Whirlwinds

and comets bring misfortune, drought, hunger, and desolation; lightning is sacred and punishes human transgressions. For the Bakongos, the most important celestial bodies are the moon, the evening star, and the morning star. Each star is associated with a particular human activity. Thus, the beliefs taken to Cuba from the Manikongo kingdom are centered on the ngangas and nkisi, in veneration of Bakongo ancestors, nature, and spirits.

SIGNATURES (*PATIPEMBA, KATIKANPOLO MUNANTOTO*)

A signature or hieroglyph is a sacred engraving defined as the interior *I*. Each human being is identified with a signature, and each nganga or *nfumbe* is personalized with a symbol that is partly the product of interpretation—perhaps fantasy—but whose basic characteristics are similar to those of the individual's godparents. In the initiation rite, the tatas create a symbol that distinguishes this *ngueyo* from the initiates of other houses.

The circle is the basis of all Regla de Palo signatures, and it is divided into four parts by vertical and horizontal lines that cross at a right angle and through the center point. Above the line is *nzulu* (the sky) and below is *kumangongo* (the underworld); to one side is *ntoto* (the earth) and to the other *kalunga* (the sea).

For the Congos and their descendents, these separate regions are the visible world and celestial space, which is the dwelling place of gods, *npungus*, and the spirits of those who were once human beings.

REGLA DE MAYOMBE

Mayombe is a Congo word meaning magistrate, top leader, or governor, and it also serves as an honorific title. In Cuba, a *mayombero* is the sorcerer in the Congo tradition that worships the dead and natural spirits. Its followers are called *nganguleros* or *tatas* (fathers) and *yayis* (mothers).

Studies of Mayombería throughout the island show that its liturgy has been kept intact, its ceremonies have maintained the ancestors' characteristics, and its spread has given rise to other religious cults known as Brillumba, Shamalongo, and Kimbisa del Santo Cristo del Buen Viaje.

Their ngangas are small, as were those of previous clans, and easily carried from one place to another, depending on the nomadic herders' and gatherers' needs. Mayomberos do not worship more than one power at a time, unlike other cults born out of Regla de Mayombe. In Mayombería the main sacred object is *nsasi siete rayos*, a generic name given to all Regla de Mayombe ngangas. *Nsasi* means *leaders' burial place* as well as *antelope* or *deer* and is also the name

Regla de Mayombe ngangas. The central concepts of Cuba's Regla de Palo religions are the worship of dead spirits and mystical control over supernatural forces through the creation of magical objects known as ngangas, which are receptacles containing all mysteries and forces. HÉCTOR DELGADO AND ROLANDO PUJOL

of the microcosm that contains the main nkisi. Nsasi is located inside a fired clay pot sealed with earth that includes the bones of a dead person (nfumbe) and the bones of several animals, as well as water brought from particular places.

The collective's activities are based completely on the nganga, which symbolizes the clan's unity and confers upon the owner prestige and power over those around him. All social manifestations—art, economics, politics, war, religion—are subordinated to the advice of this receptacle's owner.

A consecration rite brings people together around the nganga. The rite's main feature is exchange of blood, the highest expression of family bonds and solidarity, but the Mayombero is careful about accepting a new godson, who must strictly observe a series of behavioral standards related to his family and public life. For Mayomberos, religious commitment is social responsibility. Before they are accepted, initiates must participate in various ceremonies: the prophesy of the initiation; purifying baths; animal offerings; entering the room; the reaffirmation ceremony; ritual body marking; and finally the toast and greeting.

A new Mayombero is sworn to only one power—because a person has only one head—to rule him and help him throughout his life with the most positive vibrations. Enclosed and sealed in the nganga, these vibrations will give him peace and guide him on the long road of life, and they will help him to die well.

REGLA BRILLUMBA

The Regla Brillumba appeared at the end of the nineteenth century in Matanzas province. It is a combination of Mayombe, Regla de Ocha, and Cuban spiritism. Sarabanda-Oggún, the lord of all metals, is the principal guide of Brillumberos.

When the enigmatic and reserved tatas were approached by religious people who already had taken an *orisha* (deity) but wanted to practice Regla de Palo, which was closely associated with the forces of nature, an interrelationship was established between Brillumba and Regla de Ocha. Some houses began to make ngangas containing fragments of the sacred objects of the initiates' orishas. These individuals received Congo names with surnames belonging to the original nganga. In this way, those who had an orisha in Regla de Ocha were satisfied, and the Mayomberos continued to practice rites in their pure form, as their godfathers had taught them.

Initiations in Brillumba houses differ in the ways their marks are made and in the instruments used to make them. The tatas once used rooster or sparrow hawk spurs to scratch in the marks, but this method fell into disuse; only houses with orthodox traditions or those in rural areas continued to employ them. Many initiations used to take place in the countryside, in private ceremonies attended only by the godfathers and the *bakonfula* (chosen leader), because they were considered rites of deep communion with the spirits.

REGLA DE SHAMALONGO (XIANMALONGO, MALONGO)

The name *Shamalongo* comes from *Xiamaloango*. To believers, *xian* (*shama*) is a spirit of great strength and complexity, but spontaneous, direct, and assertive, whereas *longo* (*loango*) is the name of the African land where this faith began.

This branch's activities are also strongly influenced by Regla de Ocha (also called Santería). Its followers identify with their orishas, and they work with flowers, plants, purifications, and prayers. Its nkisi have the same purpose as in other branches of Regla de Palo: to protect and bring prosperity to the owners and their godsons. Its ngangas are created in the same way as in Mayombe, as an offshoot, but in Shamalongo the nganga's interior reflects the spiritual to a greater extent, invoking protecting spirits, the first of which is from the Loango land. In Shamalongo as well as Brillumba, some of the ngangas contain magnets, horseshoes, crucifixes, firearms, and knives, as well as a bag with fourteen prayers to different saints that serve as spiritual guides.

Believers in Shamalongo are considered to be very spiritual. Generally, a person enters this branch as a son and later asks his godfather to make his nganga. They prepare the nganga together for spiritual purposes, and in that way, the initiate learns to relate to his spiritual guides and protectors through rituals, prayers, flowers, plants, and chants associated with spiritualist rites. Many initiates are not taught how to enter *nso-nganga*, and they are not taught the (*puya*) chants because these tend to exacerbate feelings and create squabbles based on the power of the predictions and their suggestive allusions.

REGLA KIMBISA DEL SANTO CRISTO DEL BUEN VIAJE

Regla Kimbisa del Santo Cristo del Buen Viaje is a totally Cuban innovation founded in the late nineteenth century by Andrés Facundo de los Dolores Petit (1829–1878), who was simultaneously a tertiary of the San Francisco Order of the town of Guanabacoa (a lay member of a Catholic order), a believer in Regla de Ocha, and a member of the Abakuá Secret Society. Although it has not been proven that Petit was also a Freemason, some characteristics of Masonry can be seen in Kimbisa liturgy and rituals.

Regla Kimbisa differs from Mayombe and Brillumba because its creator included some of the rituals and concepts of other Afro-Cuban religions, of spiritism, and of Catholicism. Thus, it could be said that if any Cuban religious practice is truly and deliberately syncretic, it is Regla Kimbisa. Petit promoted a message of universal brotherhood, respect for traditions and solidarity with the wider Abakuá family, devotion to ancestors (the source of wisdom and aid for their descendents), and communion with those ancestors and other good spirits through trances and Kimbisa's divination systems. These noble goals are reflected in the liturgy created by Petit; its prayers and exhortations urge followers to work and live with righteousness and kindness.

The Catholic saint Louis Bertrand (1526–1581) is the Kimbisa temples' guide, but his nganga is the main object of adoration. In the initiation ceremony, loyalty is sworn before the crucified Christ, who is present in all rituals. Followers always wear crucifixes containing magic powers. The deities revered by Kimbiseros are the most popular Catholic saints and their respective Yoruba orishas. Unlike believers in Santería and other Afro-Cuban religions, Kimbiseros do not usually employ sticks and powders in their activities; they prefer plants, flowers, and perfumes.

Kimbisa divinations utilize practices from Regla de Ocha and spiritism. A mat is placed on the floor along with a glass of water containing a basil leaf; predictions are made by means of coconuts, marine shells, mirrors, or trances.

First, neophytes must prove that they are honorable and irreproachably moral. For a period they are constantly observed to confirm that this is true; if it is so, the initiation goes forward. The initiation basically consists of a *rayamiento*: six marks for men and nine for women. But the interrogation to which the ngueyo is subjected regarding his or her reasons for joining, and the exhortations made after the initiation, clearly show that the new member is expected to behave with Christian altruism to fulfill the mission of caring for and curing bodies and souls.

WOMEN IN REGLA DE PALO

As in many other ancient religions, women, who are the universal source of life and the core of the family, are excluded or restricted from sacred magical rituals in Regla de Palo. Called *ndumbas* (women) and, depending on their status, yayis (mothers or godmothers), women do not play a leading role in important ceremonies such as making the ngangas, initiations, and sacrifices.

In Cuba three famous *yayis ngangas* are the subjects of legends: Manga Saya, Ña Filomena, and Ña Secundina. They created their own ngangas, following the customs of their native Africa. Manga Saya, a runaway slave from the Orozco sugar plantation in the Pinar del Río area, is famous for her regal manner and vast knowledge of plants' curative properties. Ña Filomena and Ña Secundina, two robust women with curative and resurrecting powers, were taken from the Congo as slaves in the mid-nineteenth century to the Santa Amalia sugar plantation in the town of Cimarrones, Matanzas. It is said that they restored breath to several men after nights of prayer, purification, and exorcism that returned the men to their earthly existence.

REGLA DE PALO DIVINATION SYSTEMS

Each variant of Regla de Palo has its own ways of predicting the future, advising initiates about their behavior, and solving the most complex and intimate problems.

In Mayombe, communication with the nfumbe's spirit is direct: The owner of the nganga speaks, reflects, and consults in close spiritual union with the supernatural force. Instruments employed for divination are the *mpaka* (bull or goat horn), the *vititi mensu* (horn sealed with a mirror), *fula* (gunpowder), the *nkulo* (calabash), a white plate, and a trance that occurs when the seer is possessed by the spirit living in the nganga. Contact with the magically empowered *mpaka* or *vititi mensu* is the most direct way to sense the vibrations emanating from the spirit inside of them. They speak simply and directly, offering guidance for the future.

Another popular method of divination session involves holding a white plate to the head, shoulders, chest, and legs of the person asking for advice. After holding it to the four cardinal points the tata passes the plate over the flame of a candle lit at the feet of the nganga, enveloping it in smoke. Diverse figures appear on the plate, which are interpreted in order to form advice.

When extrasensory powers to communicate with the spirit of the godfather's nganga are present, a ngueyo is prepared to serve as a *perro de prenda* (medium for the spirit of the dead) who, possessed and in a trance, predicts the future of the initiates and others attending the ceremony.

Brillumba uses the same divination methods as Mayombe but also interprets predictions through *nkobos*, which provide quick answers. *Nkobos* are open conches that are ritually prepared before use; they are read in the same way as Regla de Ocha's traditional *cauris* and are the link with the nganga's spirit, which is mute.

To read the oracle's message, followers of Shamalongo use the *mpaka* hung on a string, which begins to turn as soon as it enters into communication with the spirit. Through its vibrations and the extreme sensitivity of the tata or yayi, the spirit transmits advice and messages to the accompaniment of prayers, crucifixes, plants, flowers, incense, perfumes, essences that ward off bad influences, and purifications that bring light and positive vibrations to believers.

Followers of Regla Kimbisa del Santo Cristo del Buen Viaje devote themselves to curing, purifying, and exorcizing with all kinds of formulas that are exclusive to each case. In a trance, they are possessed by lofty spirits such as their spiritual guide Saint Louis Bertrand, other Catholic saints, virgins, archangels, Yoruba orishas, and nkisi. Among their divination

■ *See also*

Cuban Thought and Cultural Identity: Costumbres in the Republican Period

tools are coconuts; employed in the same way as in Regla de Ocha, the coconuts offer simple and direct results depending on the way they fall on the mat. In some houses a mirror is used to aid the godfather in predicting more clearly. As in Catholic rites, incense is burned to achieve good communication. To cast spells, talismans, amulets, safeguards, brews, and potions are directed to the archangel Michael, Saint Anthony, Saint Louis Bertrand, and Saint Benedict the Moor, who offer protection.

Although the forms adopted by these Regla de Palo branches are similar, in modern times some aspects of the divination and initiation rituals and ceremonies are omitted out of neglect, a desire to be modern, or inadequate knowledge of the more traditional practices. Both ignorance and the profit motive have caused considerable corruption of their practices. The beauty, mystical significance, and profound mysteries of the signatures (*patipemba*) have inspired many artists, but sadly, they have been used in all kinds of ways without the appropriate study or seriousness needed for their use in a respectful manner or popularization, even if for purely aesthetic purposes. Mayombe, Brillumba, Shamalongo, and Kimbisa belong to Cubans, like these lands where they became established and from which popular religious culture springs.

BIBLIOGRAPHY

Bolívar Aróstegui, Natalia, and Carmen González Díaz de Villegas. *Ta Makuende Yaya y Las Reglas de Palo.* Havana: Ediciones Unión, 1998.

Cabrera, Lydia. *Las Reglas de Congo: Palo Monte, Mayombe.* Miami: Colección del Chicherekú, 1979.

Farris Thompson, Robert. *Flash of the Spirit.* New York: Vintage, 1984.

Laman, Karl. *The Congo.* Vol. 3. Lund, Sweden: Håkan Ohlssons Boktryckeri, 1962.

Laman, Karl. *Dictionnaire Kokongo-Français* [1936]. Hants, U.K.: Gregg Press, 1964.

Manga Saya and Mancaperro families of Pinar del Río, and Batalla Sácara Empeño and Madioma Ca of Havana. Unpublished notebooks.

Ventura, Stefano. "Palo Monte y sus Reglas Rituales." Unpublished manuscript. Havana, 1968.

FAITH: SPIRITISM

Natalia María Bolívar Aróstegui

An overview of spiritism in Cuba and its relationship to Afro-Cuban religions.

Spiritism is a spiritual practice and belief system from the mid-nineteenth century based on communication with the spirit world, the law of cause and effect (karma), and free will and choice as integral to the spiritual evolution of human beings. Spiritists believe in reincarnation and, despite their deeply spiritual convictions, do not believe that spiritism is a religion. While perhaps not as widely practiced as in Brazil, spiritism in Cuba is often linked to Afro-Cuban religious practices, particularly Regla de Ocha (Santería) and Reglas de Palo. Scholars do not agree on how spiritism arrived in Cuba, but it likely arrived by the mid-1850s. There is, however, agreement that by the second half of the nineteenth century, Kardecian spiritism was noted on the island.

The doctrine of Kardecian spiritism was founded by Hippolyte León Denizard Rivail (1804–1869), known as Allan Kardec, an eminent French philosopher and educator who codified modern spiritism. Kardec laid the doctrinal foundation for what he termed *scientific spiritualism* and began to study that phenomenon. Fernando Ortiz points to the Spanish figure Amalia Domingo Soler (1835–1909), whom he describes as a great proponent of this eschatological doctrine in Spain, as being responsible for its dissemination in eastern Cuba, where many of her Spanish compatriots lived. Kardecian spiritism is "based on science with philosophical implications and moral consequences" (Hess p. 16). Kardec's philosophy (including reincarnation, the law of cause and effect, and free will and choice in the spiritual evolution of humans), which he considered scientific in its approach, owes much to Christian tenets. Yet there are many elements of Christianity that Kardec rejected: the divinity of Christ, the trinitarian concept of God (Father, Son, and Holy Ghost), and the divine nature of miracles (for Spiritists these are either natural or psychic phenomena). He also did not believe in a literal heaven and hell (Hess p. 17).

SPIRITUAL TENDENCIES

The different cultures that converged in Cuba gave rise to a variety of spiritist practices and rituals based on the belief in the continuation of existence after death. They could, as Ortiz proposes, be divided into those that believed in the visible apparitions or manifestations of spirits; those that favored the temporary possession of a living person by a spirit, that person serving as the spirit's channel of communication; and those that attributed unusual or inexplicable events to the actions of spirits.

Spiritism and Cuban religions of African origin provide a vast realm in which to study paranormal phenomena. In addition to those phenomena linked with extrasensory perception (telepathy, clairvoyance, precognition), there are others studied in modern times in the field of parapsychology. They include *médiumnidad* (the collection of faculties that allows a person to communicate with the world of spirits); communication with the spirit of a dead person believed to be trapped in the *nganga* (a cauldron infused with spiritual powers, often linked to the powers of spirits) of the Reglas de Palo Monte (a syncretic Caribbean

religion of Central African origin); and possession of initiates by their guardian *orishas* (spirits or deities that reflect one of the manifestations of God in the Yoruba spiritual or religious system) in the Regla de Ocha or Santería (a syncretic Caribbean religion of West African origin).

Cuban scholar José Millet describes the most significant tendencies of spiritism in Cuba. Among them are *Espiritismo de Mesa* or *Espiritismo Científico* (Table or Scientific Spiritism), considered a science following Kardecian principles, not a religion, whose supporters practice ritualism, an Anglican movement that emphasizes rituals and that tends toward Catholicism; *Espiritismo de Caridad* (Charity Spiritism), whose characteristics are similar to scientific spiritism and whose practices include the use of *el despojo* (cleansing) and *santiguación* (making the sign of the cross); *Espiritismo de Cordón* (Cord Spiritism), with a great richness of song and dance; *Espiritismo Cruzado* (Crossed or Mixed Spiritism), a mixture of Regla de Ocha or Santería, the Reglas de Palo Monte, Abakuá, Vodou, and Catholicism, among other beliefs; and *Bembé de Sao*, the precursor of Espiritismo Cruzado, emerging from the culture of the slave barracks, with an emphasis on religions of Bantu origin.

THE CORDONEROS OF ORILÉ

Espiritismo de Cordón first appeared in the Cauto region of the old Oriente province, possibly in Manzanillo, around the second half of the nineteenth century. It came to Bayamo around 1910, by which time it had developed as a ritualist version of Kardecian spiritism mixed with Catholicism and indirect influences from Protestantism and Afro-Cuban religions. *Orilé, lorile, olile,* and *oringue* are all variants of the same word that appears in the choral refrains of the *cantos de cordón* (cord chants). Its etymology could derive from *lori* (to turn quickly around in circles) and *ilé* (house), an allusion to the ritual, consisting in the gathering together of a chorus, functioning as the medium, that turns counterclockwise, the participants moving their arms up and down and pounding their feet rhythmically on the floor, to help bring down a spirit. Cordoneros practice other rites, including *martillos* (synchronized flapping of arms combined with heavy breathing), *despojos, santiguaciones,* baptisms, consultations, and spiritual masses.

SPIRITIST SYMBOLISM

Followers of the spiritual currents in Cuba—Espiritismo de Mesa or Espiritismo Científico, Espiritismo de Caridad, Espiritismo de Cordón, and Espiritismo Cruzado—devote a large amount of space for its altars, whether they are located in homes or the centers the followers attend. The altar, or sacred table, is the central element around which take place the various rituals and ceremonies such as cleansings, sacrifices, and consultations. The altars vary in structure and the way the elements are arranged on them according to the tastes of their owners as well as the requirements of the spirits that visit them. For believers, the altar is a microcosm and a catalyst of the sacred and symbolizes the place and the moment when a being becomes sacred.

An important element of an altar is water. Glasses or goblets filled with water symbolize abundance, immortality, and revelation. Water is also important symbolically as the source of life, means of purification, and center of regeneration. The crucifix is another important symbolic element of spiritism. Some researchers believe the horizontal beam of its crossbars corresponds to the passive principle, to the world of manifestations, while the vertical beam symbolizes the active principle, the world of transcendence and spiritual evolution.

Spiritists use *aguardiente* or other types of alcohol as creative inspiration and to symbolize the creative fire of life. Flowers, whose aroma represents the spiritual presence of souls, symbolize strength and express the different phases of the relationship between men and gods. Images and photographs hold life force, ensure family prosperity, and demonstrate continuity. Tobacco or incense represents the union of earth, heaven, and the spiritualization of man. The candle is ascendant life, the light of the soul in the strength of its ascent, the purity of the spiritual flame that rises to heaven, and the perennial nature of the individual's life at its zenith.

For Cuban spiritists, prayer is a person's expression of the intensity of faith and of his or her spiritual alignment. According to the oldest spiritist doctrine, all people have a good spirit that accompanies and protects them from birth onward. With men this entity establishes a sort of maternal relationship, that is, it seeks to guide the man it is protecting along the path of good and progress through the tests that life presents to him. This spirit is referred to as his Ángel Guardian, Ángel de la Guarda, or Buen Genio.

BIBLIOGRAPHY

Bachelard, Gastón. *El agua y los sueños.* Fondo de Cultura Económica, Spain, 1994.

Bermúdez, Armando Andrés. "La expansión del espiritismo de cordón." *Etnología y Folklore* 5 (1968): 5–32.

Hess, David J. *Spirits and Scientists, Ideology, Spiritism and Brazilian Culture.* University Park: The Pennsylvania State University Press, 1991.

Lago Vieito, Ángel. *Fernando Ortiz y sus estudios acerca del espiritismo en Cuba.* Havana: Centro de Investigación y Desarrollo de la Cultura Cubana Juan Marinello, 2002.

Millet Batista, José. *El espiritismo: variantes cubanas.* Santiago de Cuba: Editorial Oriente, 1996.

Ortiz, Fernando. "Orígenes de los cordoneros del Orilé." *Bohemia* 23 (July 9, 1950): 34–36, 105–107.

Reglamento del Consejo Supremo Nacional Espiritista. *Casa de los Espiritistas.* Havana, 1988. Mimeographed booklet.

FAITH: VODOU

Juan Mesa Díaz

An overview of the practice of Vodou in Cuba.

Vodou is a religion with roots in Haiti, where it originated among the Ewé-Fon ethnic groups brought to the island from Africa as slaves. *Vodou* is an umbrella term that embraces a range of beliefs and practices that derive from Ewé-Fon, Yoruba, Guinean, Congo, Angolan, and local (indigenous) religions. The word *vodou* is derived from the Fon word *vodun*, which means *spirit*. The religion is both monotheistic and incorporates polyatry—the worship of multiple deities and spirits that are the multiple manifestations of the spiritual power of God (known as Bon Dieu). It persisted through the difficult circumstances that slavery imposed on its followers. Even after Haitian independence in 1804, those who practiced Vodou had to overcome periodic campaigns against superstition conducted by the Catholic Church and the Haitian government, which entailed the imprisonment of priests and political persecution of the practitioners, as well as the destructions of temples, altars, and other venerated objects (Hurbon pp. 53–61).

The Haitian presence in Cuba dates back to the end of the eighteenth century and the beginning of the nineteenth century. At that time many French colonists who fled the Haitian revolution (1791–1804) settled in the eastern part of Cuba. However, it was not that wave of migration that brought Vodou to the largest island in the Caribbean. The Haitian religious traditions of African origin appeared in central and eastern Cuba in the beginning of the twentieth century, when tens of thousands of day laborers migrated, either temporarily or permanently, from Haiti to become cane cutters in the settlements that fed cane to the sugar mills in those areas.

The immigrants' manpower restored prosperity to an agricultural industry that had been devastated by the War of Independence and U.S. intervention. Between 1913 and 1921, about 50 percent of the 156,000 Caribbean immigrants who settled in Cuba were Haitian. From 1921 until 1930, the number of Haitians rose to some 114,000, most of whom settled in the *bateyes* (Cuban sugar mill towns) from Ciego de Ávila to Guantánamo (James, Millet, and Alarcón pp. 88–91). They founded close-knit rural communities that were typically located far from urban areas. They chose these locations to avoid the discrimination to which they were subjected. They were scorned for speaking a foreign language (Haitian Creole), for being willing to work for a much lower wage, and for practicing a religion that was considered satanic.

Permeated by the hegemony of the Catholic religion introduced through colonization, the syncretized figure of Bon Dieu is identified with the Ewé-Fon deity Mawu-Lisa, the Creator, who fashioned the *loas* (also spelled *lwas* or *luases*) to interact with humanity. The *loas* are divine emissaries to the world who operate in three realms: water, earth, and sky. In Haiti, this pantheist structure is organized into two overarching categories: Rada and Petro (Petwo in Haitian Creole). The Rada originated from the Ewé-Fon peoples of West Africa, whereas the Petro came from the Congo-Angola region of central Africa.

Rada and Petro represent characteristics of the human condition. The *Rada loas* represent good qualities such as benevolence, trust, community, and family; as a counterpoint, the *Petro loas* represent more negative qualities such as self-interest, skepticism, and aggression, which were used as tools to fight oppression and slavery during the colonial period. Rada is the most orthodox of the Ewé-Fon traditions, governed by the cult to the good Guinean loas; for Haitians, Guinea represents the African motherland and their spiritual resting place after death. Petro is regarded as the cult of the *criollo loas* (Caribbean-born of foreign descent), who are violent, bitter, and vengeful due to the suffering they endured as slaves on the New World side of the Atlantic. In addition, there are loas of death, the Gedé, who preside over the funerary rites of the Rada and Petro. These spirits take their name from important Africans who were defeated during the Dahomey wars and deported to Haiti. There are also loas of protection known as the Kongo loas.

Haitian Vodou spread widely in Cuba. Some researchers, therefore, refer to it as Cuban Vodou. Like the other Afro-Cuban religions practiced by slaves, Vodou was prohibited during colonial times and continued to be marginalized after the end of slavery in 1886, and the practice of Vodou became an expression of values and customs that remain outside the dominant culture.

The practice of Vodou is highly concentrated in the eastern part of the island, closest to Haiti, as well as the central region of Matanzas (a significant sugar-growing province). Specialists agree on classifying Cuba mainly as Rada territory, where practices are more noble, meaning in contrast to the violence attributed to Petro rites. Santiago de Cuba is the exception, defined by scholars as Rada-Petro.

Vodou is practiced in structures known as *oufò* (house temples). The structure of the house temple, known in Cuba as *hounfort or hounfour,* is similar to those in Haiti; the house temples are family-oriented and are passed down through family members. The temples are presided over by the *hougan* (*oungan* in Haiti, a Vodou priest) and the *manbo* (priestess). The *poteau-mitan* (a ritual tree trunk) serves as a bridge between the sky and the earth used by loas to move between the divine and human

Vodou ceremony, Havana. Cuban Vodou shares some elements with another Afro-Cuban religion, Regla de Ocha (Santería), and encompasses a variety of beliefs and practices across the island.
© MIREILLE VAUTIER/ALAMY

realms. It is there where the *vevé* (visual symbols that summon the Vodou loas) are traced in lime, ash, or flour to indicate the outline of the ceremony to be performed. In the temple, sacrifices are made, religious offerings are placed on the altars, the drum is played, and there are songs and dances for the loas, who manifest themselves as the believers go into spirit-possession trances.

Vodou has elements common to another Afro-Cuban religion known as the Regla de Ocha (Santería). The Vodou loas are roughly equivalent to the Regla de Ocha *orishas*, and several are known by similar names. The loa Legba, who mocks destiny by opening and closing opportunities, parallels the orisha of Eshu-Eleggua, whose purpose is the same. The loa Gu and the orisha Oggún represent labor and a warrior spirit in both pantheons and share an explosive character. This explosive nature leads certain sects to refer to them as *Criminel*, due to the Christian tendencies in the island's dominant culture to demonize energies that manifest themselves violently. Vodou's Marassa (meaning "twins") is similar to Regla de Ocha's *ibeyi*; similarly, Vodou's Erzilí Freda and Regla de Ocha's Oshún represent beauty, sensuality, and freshwater in both pantheons. The Gedé lead Vodou funerary rites and the cult to ancestors, like the *eggun* of Regla de Ocha.

Vodou's legacy in Cuba includes a religion known as Arará that combines elements of Regla de Ocha-Ifá and Vodou. The practices of Vodou and the Arará tradition centered in the province of Matanzas are distinct, with an absence of the Petro variant in Arará. The main similarity between them lies in their familial, almost hermetic, character, although they will readily offer occasional religious services to those outside the religious community as well.

The religion's legacy reaches as far as Havana, where in the 1980s several *hounfour* were established in downtown Havana, Old Havana, and San Miguel del Padrón, enriching the culture of those areas with its dance and musical traditions. Haitian and Cuban migrations and their influence in other countries have produced a new religious denomination in the United States, Orisha-Vodou. It was established in the community of Olatunji Village in South Carolina in the 1980s and persisted into the early twenty-first century.

BIBLIOGRAPHY

Brandon, George. *Santeria from Africa to the New World: The Dead Sell Memories*. Bloomington: Indiana University Press, 1993.

Hurbon, Laënnec. *Los misterios del vudú*. Barcelona: Ediciones Grupo Zeta, 1998.

James, Joel, José Millet, and Alexis Alarcón. *El vodú en Cuba*. Santiago de Cuba: Editorial Oriente, 1988.

FAITH: PROTESTANTISM IN CUBA

Luis Martínez-Fernández

Protestantism, the faith of an estimated 600,000 to 800,000 Cubans.

Catholic Christianity came to Cuba with the first Spanish colonizers in the early 1500s. The Spanish principle of *pureza de sangre* (purity of blood) banned non-Catholics and Muslim and Jewish converts from settling in Spain's colonies. Protestants were considered heretics and could neither travel nor settle in the Spanish colonies because their presence was seen as an obstacle to the religious purity that Spain wanted to establish there.

Political-religious conflicts between Protestant northern Europe and Catholic southern Europe in the 1500s and 1600s were played out throughout the Caribbean, where contending European naval forces and corsairs fought for control of territory, trade, and navigation routes. Spaniards derided Protestant corsairs, pirates, and filibusterers as heretics and Lutherans. Another form of foreign intrusion consisted of smuggling activities that included the importation of banned Protestant bibles and tracts.

The first recorded Protestant services in Cuba took place in 1741 in Guantánamo Bay as the English admiral Edward Vernon (1684–1787) attempted to wrest Cuba from Spain. Twenty years later, British forces captured Havana and occupied the city and its environs for eleven months. Anglican priests conducted services at the San Francisco convent chapel and other Catholic places of worship.

Beginning in the 1820s, Protestantism became entangled with the island's political and social struggles. Abolitionism, for example, was championed by some Protestant Britons, most saliently by David Turnbull (c. 1794–1851), who served briefly as Havana's British consul. Spanish authorities claimed that the illegal distribution of so-called adulterated bibles sparked slave uprisings. Due to the Catholic Church's increasing conservatism and loyalty to the Spanish Crown, many Cuban intellectuals and patriots assumed anticlerical positions and in some instances developed an appreciation for Protestantism as a source of freedom and liberal influences.

With Cuba's growing integration into the North Atlantic commercial networks, British, German, and American Protestants began settling on the island, establishing communities in Havana's suburbs during the 1840s and 1850s. There was also a growing floating Protestant population consisting of sailors, merchants, and tourists. Because of prohibitions against non-Catholic religious ceremonies, they were unable to attend services or participate in the sacraments of baptism, communion, marriage, and burial. Many drifted from their faith; others sought religious services clandestinely. Visiting clergymen, mostly naval chaplains, discreetly officiated at religious ceremonies. The most troubling issue for resident or visiting Protestants was the prohibition on burials of non-Catholics in consecrated grounds.

Resulting from Spain's declaration of religious tolerance in 1869, Cuba's first Protestant mission began in 1871, when the Episcopalian Reverend Edward Kenney (1848–1899) began his work in Havana. The mission held English-language services in rented hotel rooms and had a significant ministry among the sick, mostly victims of yellow fever and other tropical diseases.

Protestantism was practiced by Cubans in exile communities that emerged during the late nineteenth-century wars for independence in Key West, Tampa, Philadelphia, and New York. The first Cuban exile congregation was under Reverend Joaquín de Palma (1823-1844), and it met in Santiago Church in New York City. Many of the members and leaders of exile congregations held anti-Spanish sentiments and, in many cases, were actively involved in the struggle for independence. Work led by Cuban preachers for Cuban congregations on the island started when exiled Protestants returned to Cuba in the mid-1880s. Among them

were the missionaries Pedro Duarte (Episcopalian), Enrique Someillán (Methodist), and Alberto J. Díaz (Episcopalian, later Baptist). By the time U.S. forces occupied Cuba at the end of the War of Independence in 1898, most U.S. Protestant denominations had already established footholds on the island. To avoid competition, denominational leaders carved out spheres of influence in 1902. Protestantism appealed mostly to working-class Cubans, though curiously, Cuba's first president, the long-exiled Tomás Estrada Palma (1832–1908), was a Protestant with Quaker links. By 1910, there were about 200 Protestant churches with an estimated 10,000 members (Pérez 1995, p. 64).

During the first few decades of the Republican era, Cuban ministers clashed with more conservative U.S.-born ministers and denominational leaders, and many resigned in protest. The Americanization of Protestantism pushed many denominations to support U.S. interests and values. The Quakers, for example, established a meeting house and school in Banes, on land owned by the United Fruit Company; the future president Fulgencio Batista (1901–1973) studied there. In the 1930s, Cuban clergymen began to assume control of most Protestant congregations. Several Protestants played leading roles in the revolutionary struggle against Batista, among them the Baptist school teacher Frank País (1934–1957), Commander Huber Matos (b. 1918), and the underground leader Faustino Pérez (1920–1992).

Cuban Evangelical Christians. A vibrant house-church movement developed among Cuban Protestants during the first decade of the twenty-first century. These evangelical Christians worship in a Havana residence in 2007. © ROBERT WALLIS/CORBIS

Whereas the Catholic Church assumed a critical and combative position against Fidel Castro's revolutionary government, Protestant denominations mostly adapted to the new climate, generally supporting the revolutionary regime; some U.S. pastors, however, were imprisoned or forced to leave Cuba. In the immediate aftermath of the Bay of Pigs invasion in April 1961, Castro nationalized all private schools, including those run by the Catholic Church and Protestant churches. Hostile to all religious activities, the Cuban state was officially declared atheist in 1976. Throughout the first three decades of the Revolution, believers endured harassment and discrimination and had few opportunities to congregate and worship, but continued to do so.

In the mid-1980s, Cuba assumed a more tolerant view on religion, and Fidel Castro met with Protestant leaders in 1984. Later, as Cuba entered the traumatic experience of the Special Period (1991), the state further softened its stand on religion, even allowing believers to join the Communist Party of the secular Cuban state. The dismal material conditions and despair of the Special Period sparked a renewal in spirituality, with Cubans joining the Catholic Church and Protestant denominations by the tens of thousands. Over 700 new Protestant churches were established between 1992 and 1997 (Rifkin). Pentecostal churches in particular increased in popularity. Estimates put the number of Protestants in 2010 at between 600,000 and 800,000, with Baptists being the single largest denomination, followed by Pentecostal denominations (U.S. Bureau of Democracy, Human Rights, and Labor). The Cuban Council of Churches (CCC) is the government-sanctioned organization that includes most of the Protestant denominations; CCC membership confers legal status, and nonmember organizations are subject to official harassment. In the 2000s, a vibrant house-church movement began to develop.

BIBLIOGRAPHY

Corse, Theron. *Protestants, Revolution, and the U.S.-Cuba Bond.* Gainesville: University Press of Florida, 2007.

Martínez-Fernández, Luis. *Protestantism and Political Conflict in the Nineteenth-Century Hispanic Caribbean.* New Brunswick, NJ: Rutgers University Press, 2002.

Pérez, Louis A. Jr. "North American Protestant Missionaries in Cuba and the Culture of Hegemony, 1898-1920." In *Essays on Cuban History: Historiography and Research*, edited by Louis A. Pérez Jr. Gainesville: University Press of Florida, 1995.

Pérez, Louis A. Jr. *On Becoming Cuban: Identity, Nationality and Culture.* Chapel Hill: University of North Carolina Press, 1999.

Ramos, Marcos Antonio. *Panorama del protestantismo en Cuba.* San José, Costa Rica: Editorial Caribe, 1986.

Rifkin, Ira. "Cuba's Other Christians: Island's Protestant Population is Climbing" Updated February 16, 1998. Available from http://www.jewishcuba.org/protestant.html.

U.S. Bureau of Democracy, Human Rights, and Labor. "International Religious Freedom Report, Cuba 2010." Updated November 17, 2010. Available from http://www.state.gov.

Yaremko, Jason M. *U.S. Protestant Missions in Cuba: From Independence to Castro.* Gainesville: University Press of Florida, 2000.

FAITH: RASTAFARI

Katrin Hansing

The emergence and development of the Jamaican Rastafari movement in socialist Cuba.

Over the past eighty years, the Jamaican Rastafari movement has gained a wide international following. Recognized as one of the leading Afro-Caribbean religions and popular cultural trends in the world, Rastafari communities can be found all over the Americas and in many parts of Africa, Europe, and Australasia. Crossing geopolitical, linguistics, and ideological boundaries, Rastafari also emerged in Cuba.

RASTAFARI'S EMERGENCE AND GROWTH IN CUBA

Rastafari first entered Cuba in the late 1970s via a number of different agencies, most notably reggae music. Reggae, which still gets little air time on local Cuban radio stations, was introduced by sailors and foreign students. Listeners recorded reggae music off Jamaican and Floridian radio programs, and these recordings were played and circulated at private reggae parties, mainly in Havana and Santiago, creating new fans and a new underground music circuit.

At the time, English was not widely spoken in Cuba, so comprehension of the music's lyrics was limited, and most fans were unaware that there was a religion and social movement connected to the music. This changed as increasing numbers of Anglo-Caribbean (especially Jamaican) students went to Cuba to study in the 1980s. Although these students were not Rastas, they did bring with them basic knowledge about the Rastafari movement and their own islands' histories and cultures. Due to the haphazard manner in which Rastafari was introduced to the island, coupled with the lack of access to Rasta networks outside Cuba, the movement grew slowly throughout the 1980s, picking up pace with the beginning of the Special Period in the early 1990s.

Cuba's economic crisis and the subsequent economic opening, especially in the form of tourism and remittances, made access to foreign information, ideas, and styles easier and broader. Although the state maintained its firm grip on official cultural production, it could not control the inflow of goods and cultural trends from abroad. Young people especially adopted foreign styles and bolder forms of self-expression, growing dreadlocks and asking family and friends abroad to send Rasta-related literature, videos, and clothes.

In addition, a small group of religious Rastas from the English-speaking Caribbean who came to study in Cuba in the mid-1990s began meeting with Cubans, sharing their knowledge and beliefs in a more organized manner. By 2010, there was a sizeable group of religious Rastas in Havana, many of whom were engaged in spreading their faith across the island.

RASTAFARI A LA CUBANA

Generally speaking, Rastafari in Cuba is a predominantly urban, male, Afro-Cuban youth movement. Most adherents are from socioeconomically marginalized urban neighborhoods and work as artisans, musicians, or in the informal sector. Due to the disorganized ways in which the movement was introduced on the island, Cubans have been exposed to Rastafari in a haphazard manner.

The lack of centralized structure, leadership, and general access to information in the Cuban movement, as well as the language barrier, has meant that people simply choose those elements of Rastafari that most appeal to them and reinterpret them to fit their own needs and circumstances. As a result, three broad Rasta identifications have emerged:

1. *Rasta as religion* includes individuals who follow the movement's religious beliefs and teachings, adhering to a strict vegetarian diet and conservative dress code.
2. *Rasta as philosophy* includes people who are mainly interested in the movement's philosophical and political ideas and teachings on equality, liberty, justice, and antiracism.
3. *Rasta as fashion/style* refers to people who are mainly attracted to Rastafari's hair and body culture, reggae music, and popular culture; among these Rastas there is a subgroup, called *Rasta jineteros*, that has assumed the Rasta look in order to attract tourists' black-market exchanges.

There is enormous diversity within these dominant Rasta manifestations; many Rastas copy, alter, and fuse different Rastafari components with elements from other cultural systems. For example, many Cubans combine elements from Rastafari's religious

Cuban Rastafarian. By wearing dreadlocks and African-inspired accoutrements and styles of clothing, Rastafarians in Cuba defy dominant European standards of beauty and challenge old stereotypes about blackness.
© ROLF BRENNER/ALAMY

and philosophical beliefs and practices with elements from Afro-Cuban religions such as Santería and Palo Monte, creating new forms of Rastafari and cubanizing the movement.

Despite the different ways in which the movement has been individually adopted, defined, and expressed in Cuba, a number of commonalities do exist among Rastas on the island. Apart from their share dreadlock image, most adherents share a common understanding of what their so-called Babylon in Cuba is.

BABYLON IN CUBA

In most societies where Rastafari is present, the term *Babylon* is usually equated with oppression and injustice and most often associated with capitalism, racism, and the police. In theory, Rastafari and Cuba's revolutionary doctrine and principles are surprisingly similar. What then is Babylon in Cuba?

Despite the revolutionary government's efforts to create a more just and equal society, socioeconomic inequalities in Cuba were never completely eliminated. Indeed, since the beginning of the Special Period, these inequalities increased, producing new social discrimination, a resurgence of racial prejudices, and public frustration. Moreover, governmental control and the lack of freedom of expression have allowed little room for open public debate and constructive criticism of the system and its policies.

■ *See also*

The Poetry of José Kozer

In the eyes of most Rastas, Cuba's official ideology and rhetoric on behalf of humanity, justice, and the people are hypocritical. Young, black, and marginalized Rastas brought up to believe that all Cubans are equal have found that some Cubans are more equal than others. In their view, Cuba is neither the multiracial democracy nor the egalitarian society it claims to be, and it is the power of this myth and the system that propagates it that Rastas call Babylon.

RASTA, RACE, AND RESISTANCE

In the context of growing social inequalities and racial discrimination, Afro-Cubans are questioning what it means to be black in Cuba. Rastafari offers an alternative view of race, blackness, Africa, and *cubanidad* (cubanness)—a view that is antiracist, yet at the same time recognizes the importance of Africa and people of African descent. The movement's ability to convey its positive identification with blackness through various symbolic forms—aesthetically, musically, bodily, and spiritually—has led many Cubans to identify with the culture and use it as a means to examine and express what blackness means to them. For example, by wearing dreadlocks and Afrocentric clothing, Rastas not only defy and question dominant European aesthetic norms and standards of beauty but also reevaluate and challenge old stereotypes about blackness. Reggae concerts are evolving into new black cultural spaces in which Rastafari fashion, news, and knowledge are shared, shown off, and exchanged; reggae itself is an important vehicle through which individual ideas about blackness are articulated and other sensitive social issues are addressed. In these spaces a growing sense of shared black identity is discovered and created.

In light of Cuba's economic crisis, historically complex race relations, and persistent problems of racial discrimination, Rastafari contributes to raising awareness about social issues, and in so doing it offers a counternarrative to the official discourse on race, equality, and what it means to be Cuban.

BIBLIOGRAPHY

Barrett, Leonard. *The Rastafarians*. Boston: Beacon Press, 1977.

Campbell, Horace. *Rasta and Resistance: From Marcus Garvey to Walter Rodney*. London: Hansib, 1985.

Chevannes, Barry. *Rastafari Roots and Ideology*. Syracuse, NY: Syracuse University Press, 1995.

Hansing, Katrin. *Rasta, Race and Revolution: The Emergence and Development of the Rastafari Movement in Socialist Cuba*. Berlin: Lit Verlag, 2007.

Murrell, Nathaniel Samuel, William D. Spencer, and Adrian Anthony McFarlane. *The Rastafari Reader: Chanting Down Babylon*. Kingston, Jamaica: Ian Randle Publishers, 1998.

FAITH: JUDAISM

Ruth Behar

The Jewish diaspora of Cuba or the Jewish presence in Cuba.

Since the time of Columbus's first voyage, Jewish *conversos* were present in Cuba. *Conversos* were Jews who had converted to Catholicism in the era of the Inquisition rather than face expulsion from Spain. Luis de Torres (d. 1493), a Jewish converso, traveled with Columbus to Cuba as a translator in 1492, under the assumption that his knowledge of Hebrew, Aramaic, or Arabic would prove helpful in communicating with the natives.

But the true history of the Jews in Cuba—as openly practicing Jews—began much later, when three distinct Jewish groups took form: American Jewish expatriates who settled in Cuba after the War of 1898, as Spanish colonial rule ended and U.S. postcolonial domination took root; Sephardic Jews who arrived in Cuba from Turkey as early as 1904 and continued in greater numbers following the dissolution of the Ottoman Empire; and Ashkenazi Jews, mostly from Poland, who came after the passage of the 1924 Immigration and Nationality Act, which imposed a quota on their immigration to the United States. Polish Jews settled in Cuba in such large numbers that Cubans assumed all Jews on the island came from Poland. The term *polaco* (Pole) became interchangeable with the word *Jew*. It is the term still used in Cuba to refer to a Jewish person, even someone of Sephardic background or any native-born Cuban with Jewish ancestry.

The American Jews were wealthy enough to maintain American schools and hire English-speaking rabbis for their synagogues. In contrast, the Sephardic and Ashkenazi from Europe arrived in Cuba penniless. Initially, many thought of Cuba as a transitory location, as Hotel Cuba, but when it became clear that the island was not an easy stepping-stone to reach the United States, they began to aspire to be Cuban and viewed Cuba as their promised land. In the early years these immigrants worked as peddlers. They took their wares to cities, to towns and villages, and to sugar mills in the countryside, establishing a Jewish presence even in remote areas of the island.

Over time, the immigrants prospered. By 1950 about 15 percent had become wealthy merchants who owned large stores and wholesale enterprises. But the majority ran small mom-and-pop shops in Old Havana and provincial cities and towns. They and their first-generation offspring created an impressive range of educational, social, and cultural institutions. They built Jewish cemeteries in small and large cities in Cuba and founded Jewish schools and newspapers in which every ideological and religious position was represented—from Zionist to communist.

Five synagogues existed in Havana. The oldest was the Chevet Ahim, built by Sephardic Jews in 1914, on a street that could not have been more ironically named: the Street of the Inquisitor. In the mid- to late 1950s, the Jews of Havana demonstrated their desire for a permanent place on Cuban soil by building three new synagogues: Adath Israel, an Orthodox synagogue; the Patronato, a Jewish community center; and the Centro Sefaradí, a Sephardic temple, completed as members faced the new reality of having to utter their last goodbyes. There were also, by this time, synagogues in Santa Clara, Camagüey, and Santiago de Cuba, and Jewish associations across the island.

When the Revolution began in 1959 most of the Jews supported Fidel Castro, but by 1961, as more private businesses, including mom-and-pop shops, were nationalized by government militia, their Jewish owners chose to leave, many on the very days they lost their stores. Some went to New York and New Jersey, but most of the community landed in Miami with the other Cuban exiles, where the tropical climate made them feel more at home. They had to remake their identity as *Jubans*, creating an in-between sense of themselves as people who felt connected to both the Jewish and the Cuban diaspora in the United States.

The dissolution of the Jewish community in Cuba was swift and intense, like a lit candle snuffed by the wind. Of the 15,000 to 20,000 Jews who had been in Cuba, only about 2,000 chose to remain: one-tenth of the Jewish community. In the heyday of socialist revolutionary ideology, Jewish faith and practice diminished, though many continued to adhere to their traditions by buying meat in the kosher butcher shop in Havana (which never shut down after the Revolution) and quietly celebrating the beginning of Shabbat with bowls of lit oil, in the absence of candles.

After the collapse of the Soviet Union this small community experienced a renaissance in the early 1990s. As the door to religious freedom swung open, Jews and descendants of Jews in Cuba began to return to their Jewish identity and faith, bringing their non-Jewish spouses and children along on their roots quest. Jewish American philanthropists and organizations sent educators, economic aid, food and clothing, and organized humanitarian missions that brought Jewish Americans into contact with the newly arisen Jewish community on the island. After decades of being out of touch with the contemporary global Jewish community, the Jews of Cuba were able to learn Hebrew and Jewish history, undergo conversion to Judaism, be circumcised, celebrate bar and bat mitzvahs and Jewish weddings, and even migrate to Israel. The Jews who remain in Cuba guard the Jewish legacy and keep it from

Jewish family in Cuba (1936). A Polish and Russian Jewish family poses for a photograph shortly after their arrival from Eastern Europe in the small town of Agramonte, Cuba. PHOTO COURTESY OF RUTH BEHAR

disappearing. They chant from Torahs brought from Poland and Turkey. Upon them has fallen the burden of preserving the scattered bits and pieces of Jewish life, the archaeological relics that have survived: wine cups, mezuzahs, a ketubah (Jewish marriage contract), family photographs, a tattered shirt from Auschwitz.

Notable personalities of the Jewish Cuban experience include Fabio Grobart (née Abraham Simjovitch), born in Bialystok, Poland, in 1905, a founding member of the Cuban Communist Party in 1925; Enrique Oltuski, born in Havana in 1930, who fought with Che Guevara in Santa Clara during the Cuban Revolution; Jaime Sarusky, born in Havana in 1931, a journalist and novelist who received the Cuban National Literature Award in 2004; José Miller, born in Yaguajay in 1925, and Adela Dworin, born in Havana in the 1940s, whose outreach to Jewish Americans, as past and current presidents of the Patronato synagogue, are responsible for the Jewish renaissance in revolutionary Cuba; José Kozer, born in Havana in 1940, a poet who left Cuba in 1960 for the United States and writes only in Spanish and has authored more than fifteen collections of verse; and Bernardo Benes, born in Matanzas in 1934, a banker and civic leader in Miami, who met with Fidel Castro in 1978 to negotiate the release of 3,600 Cuban political prisoners.

BIBLIOGRAPHY

Behar, Ruth. *An Island Called Home: Returning to Jewish Cuba.* New Brunswick, NJ: Rutgers University Press, 2007. In Spanish, *Una isla llamada hogar.* Barcelona: Linkgua Ediciones, 2010.

Bejarano, Margalit. *La comunidad hebrea de Cuba: La memoria y la historia.* Jerusalem: Avraham Harman Institute of Contemporary Jewry, Hebrew University, 1996.

Bettinger-López, Caroline. *Cuban-Jewish Journeys: Searching for Identity, Home, and History in Miami.* Foreword by Ruth Behar. Knoxville: University of Tennessee Press, 2000.

Corrales, Maritza. *The Chosen Island: Jews in Cuba.* Chicago: Salsedo Press, 2005.

Levine, Robert M. *Tropical Diaspora: The Jewish Experience in Cuba.* Gainesville: University Press of Florida, 1993.

FEFU AND HER FRIENDS (MARÍA IRENE FORNÉS)

Laura G. Gutiérrez

The play Fefu and Her Friends, *by María Irene Fornés, as an example of strangeness.*

Cuban American playwright, theater director, teacher, and mentor María Irene Fornés was born in Havana, Cuba, on 14 May 1930. *Fefu and Her Friends* is her most important contribution to U.S. avant-garde theater, for which she won an Obie in 1977. Very early into the play Fefu says to Christina, one of the titular friends: "I'm strange, Christina. But I am fortunate in that I don't mind being strange." Soon after, another of the friends, Cindy, tells Fefu that even if she were not strange she would still love her, to which Fefu responds: "You would not know it was me if I weren't the way that I am." These quotations are important for several reasons. Fefu's pronouncements are related to several of her eccentricities, especially the so-called game she plays with her husband, which entails Fefu shooting at him, purportedly with blanks. She always misses her target, although he still falls. This game becomes an important element in the play's structure and thematic content.

The concept of strangeness can also be extrapolated to discuss Fornés and her awkwardness within Cuban American culture and contemporary avant-garde theater. One way to begin to evaluate her contributions is to recognize that Fornés refrained "from adopting identity markers and labeling herself a Latina playwright" (Gutiérrez p. 613).

Fornés is part of the Cuban diaspora; she has lived in the United States since the age of fifteen, yet her theatrical work resists facile classifications. Her characters are seldom ethnically marked, and her plays often lack content that is traditionally (perhaps stereotypically) considered Cuban American or Latino. The lack of easily identifiable *cubanía* (Cubanness) or *latinidad* (Latinness) allows Fornés's playwriting to extend beyond the confines of Latino cultural production. Some critics have studied her theatrical work within the context of Latino cultural

studies, but, more often than not, it is her role as mentor for younger playwrights that situates her within the Latino tradition.

In "Feeling Brown," a 2000 article for *Theatre Journal,* Latino queer theorist and critic José Muñoz proposes a model of latinidad based on a "structure of feeling," as opposed to identifying a cultural production's latinidad solely on thematic content or the presence of Latina or Latino characters. According to an often-repeated anecdote about *Fefu and Her Friends'* creative evolution, Fornés would listen to the emotionally charged *boleros,* recorded by legendary Cuban singer Olga Guillot (1922–2010), when she was writing about the characters' suffering. The bolero is a Cuban musical form often with mournful melodies, and lyrics that depict scorned and suffering lovers. Thus, as Muñoz points out, if the strict notion of latinidad is understood more broadly as a modality, Fornés's plays are representative of "a specifically Latin/o *manera de ser* (way of being) wherein her avant-gardism can be considered transcultural" (Muñoz p. 73).

Moreover, the idea of "strangeness" in Fornés's work can be conceptualized as a dimension of queerness. However, the notion of *queer* as used here should not be read as a reference to Fornés's sexual orientation. Although the avant-garde playwright is a lesbian (and there is a lesbian subtheme in *Fefu and Her Friends*), Fornés does not self-identify as one nor does she create exclusively lesbian-themed plays, another example of her resistance to easy categorization. Fornés, like her play's main character, Fefu, is "strange" and does not fall neatly into normative categories of identity politics or cultural expectations. In that sense, her strangeness (queerness) and her specifically transcultural avant-gardism are important categories of analysis from which to rethink Fornés's work.

The now defunct theater company the New York Theater Strategy was the first to produce *Fefu and Her Friends* for the stage. This performance took place on 5 May 1977 at the Relativity Media Lab in New York City, under the direction of the playwright herself. After that, *Fefu and Her Friends* was staged numerous times by regional and university-based theater companies, both in the United States and in Canada. It is set in New England in the spring of 1935 and centers on eight women at Fefu's house who gather to work on a performance that will be part of a fundraising effort. As the play's narrative unfolds, the audience becomes acquainted with the women, who are all suffering emotionally and, in the case of Julia, who is confined to a wheelchair, physically. The audience's awareness of the characters' suffering is revealed early in this three-part play (the script refers to "parts" rather than acts), and continues to be built up as the play progresses. Fornés introduces her characters as they arrive, two or three at a time. Meanwhile Fefu runs around, preparing lunch, fixing the toilet, but she still has time to offer her opinions. Some of Fefu's pronouncements about relationships, especially between men and women, shock her friends, as does the shooting game she plays with Phillip, her husband. However, while Fefu may appear "strange" to her friends for articulating her thoughts about how loathsome women are, there are some moments that subtly (or not) complicate her position. Fornés's seemingly simplistic characterizations underscore Fefu's complicated position and develop an important theme in the play: There is always another side to each individual, one that others may not see, which, in turn, complicates the way that humans relate to each other. Fornés suggests that people must want to recognize others and be recognized themselves, no matter how revolting it may be, a process metaphorically exemplified in *Fefu and Her Friends* in the reference to picking up and turning over a stone only to reveal worms crawling and fungi growing on the other side.

The second part divides the audience into four groups and contains four scenes, each one performed for one section of the audience. In this part the play brings the complexly drawn characters closer to audience members. The proximity is literal as well as metaphorical as the staging structurally brings the audience closer to the characters in each of the scenes, as if they are observing an almost secretive dialogue between them.

Scene one features Emma and Fefu and takes place on the lawn. Fefu confides to Emma that she is in constant yet distorted pain, then she exits to gather everyone for a round of croquet. Scene two takes place in the study where Christina and Cindy discuss the idea of being swept off one's feet (literally and metaphorically) and Fefu's "strangeness," all before Fefu interrupts to invite them to join in the game. Scene three features Julia in the bedroom hallucinating—she suffers from a traumatic event that has rendered her "crippled." Sue briefly appears toward the end. In the fourth scene former lovers Paula and Cecilia negotiate their present relationship. Sue and Fefu make brief appearances.

The last part brings the entire audience together and opens with all the women in the living room where they rehearse for the fundraising performance. After the rehearsal some of them exit the stage by going to the kitchen or elsewhere in the house.

The scene culminates with a discussion, bordering on argument, between Fefu and Julia; they discuss how tired they are, each in her own way. They seem to lack the will to live. The discussion escalates when Fefu accuses Julia of pretending to be unable to walk, saying that she saw Julia walk to the kitchen to fetch some sugar. Later Fefu asks for forgiveness for being so rude and then goes to get her gun, which surprises Cecilia and Christina, who have come in to the living room. Fefu informs them that she needs to clean the gun and then exits. A gunshot rings out, and the play ends with Fefu coming back holding a rabbit, which she drops as soon as she sees Julia shot in the head and dead.

In her 1996 *Maria Irene Fornes and Her Critics*, Assunta Bartolomucci Kent observes that feminist critics have interpreted the play variously, some using gynocentric or material feminism approaches. Kent suggests that opting for one critical paradigm in reading Fornés's richly layered and provocative play, particularly its ambiguous ending, forecloses any possibility of understanding Fornés's critique of human relationships and social identities. The ambiguous ending of *Fefu and Her Friends* allows for different interpretations and underlines the performative dimensions contained within and beyond the play. The play stresses the complexity of different types of relationships, between male and female, for example, or between character and audience. On one level there is an intra-performative dimension in the play itself, with the women gathered in Fefu's house to rehearse a performance. Thus, if viewers understand *performative* as relating to staging, the play's third part, as well as other references to the fictional performance, all make visible the fine line between so-called real life and theater. The third part's rehearsal can be read as a meta-commentary on the illusory nature of theater while it pinpoints the theatrical dimensions that occur in real life.

The play has a second and less obvious performative dimension, which leads to the ambiguous ending. Fefu shocks her friends at the beginning of the play with her wild statements about desire and revulsion—then leaves the stage with her gun, followed by a shot that we later learn is part of a game she plays with her husband. The audience is brought back to this so-called game at the end, except that here Fefu has shot at a rabbit, yet Julia bleeds and dies. The game has finally crossed over to real life and has garnered consequences—or perhaps not. One brilliant aspect of Fornés's play is its open ending, which allows for the performance to continue after the curtain drops as different audiences continue to discuss the play's ending, revealing yet another aspect of performativity: The play continues via conversations and critical analyses. Herein lies the power of Fornés's work—its potential for societal transformation by way of an ongoing dialogue.

BIBLIOGRAPHY

Fornés, María Irene. *Fefu and Her Friends*, 1977. New York: PAJ Publications, 1992.

Gutiérrez, Laura G. "María Irene Fornés." In *Latino and Latina Writers*, edited by Alan West-Durán. 2 vols. New York: Charles Scribner's Sons, 2004.

Kent, Assunta Bartolomucci. *Maria Irene Fornes and Her Critics*. Westport, CT: Greenwood Press, 1996.

Muñoz, José Esteban. "Feeling Brown: Ethnicity and Affect in Ricardo Bracho's *The Sweetest Hangover (and Other STDs)*." *Theatre Journal* 52 (2000): 67–79.

℮ FILM

Although the Cuban film industry began with the creation of the Instituto Cubano del Arte e Industria Cinematográficos (ICAIC; Cuban Institute of the Cinematographic Arts and Industry) in 1959, generations of Cuban filmmakers and technicians had long before set the stage for its development. Film has been one of Cuba's favorite forms of cultural consumption. In the beginning, this popularity was primarily due to its proximity to the United States, one of the largest production centers in the world; later on it was due to the extraordinary boost the industry received after 1959. After the triumph of the Revolution, film was one of the main faces of Cuba's new social process internationally. In the Cuban diaspora, in turn—and despite the obstacles to development created by the industrial structure of film—numerous producers have achieved works that round out this face of the nation. Today, film is one of the most dynamic sectors of cultural creativity on the island. Works produced by the youngest producers are especially notable.

Along with studies addressing the historical development of Cuban film, these essays analyze some of Cuba's most important films and filmmakers. Issues covered include eroticism, gender, race, emigration, nationalism, urban poverty, and the critique of ideology and socialism.

FILM: EARLY HISTORY TO 1930

Luciano Castillo

The beginnings of Cuba's film industry.

On January 24, 1897, the Frenchman Gabriel Veyre (1871–1936) held Cuba's first public viewing of a film at Cinematógrafo Lumière, located at 126 Prado Street in Havana. Cuba was one of the first Latin American countries to show movies, which were regarded as foreign intruders attempting to impose themselves on the public's customs and habits. On February 7, a Sunday morning, Veyre filmed Cuba's first movie, *Simulacro de incendio* (Fire Drill), at El Comercio Central Fire Station to satisfy the curiosity of the eminent Spanish actress María Tubau (1854–1914), who was a hit at the nearby Tacón Theater. In the next year José Esteban Casasús (1871–1948) filmed and acted in the short *El brujo desapareciendo* (The Disappearing Magician, 1898), which was sponsored by a brewery. It was the first film directed by a Cuban.

Although the new invention caused some stir among audiences and the press, initially it was rejected because of the dominance of live theater. The seasons for stage productions followed one after the other, without interruption, especially at the famous Alhambra Theater. At this men-only playhouse the foundations were laid for a type of popular theater that in great measure influenced the films produced during the first half of the *Siglo de Lumière*, as the Mexican cinematographer Arturo Ripstein (b. 1943) dubbed it. Negative stereotypes of the mixed-race woman, the Spaniard, and the dark-skinned Cuban of African descent transferred to the screen and became key characters.

EARLY FILM COMPANIES

One figure dominated Cuban cinema during the first decade of the twentieth century, and his preeminence extended throughout almost the entire silent film era: Enrique Díaz Quesada (1883–1923), a filmmaker from Havana with an unbridled passion for the new art. It is unknown who produced the first filmed news report in Cuba, but in all probability it was Díaz Quesada. Beginning in 1906 he presented local news under the title *Cuba al día* (Cuba Today). These shorts were the earliest precursors of newsreels on the island.

Díaz Quesada enjoyed the patronage of the indefatigable Pablo Santos and Jesús Artigas. Together they formed a small Italian film distribution company; on April 29, 1908, the Compañía Cinematográfica Habanera (Havana Film Company) opened its doors. Better known as Santos y Artigas, the company became the first distribution house to directly import movies to Cuba, and it also rented, sold, and purchased movie equipment and supplies. When the shrewd Santos and Artigas (who also ran a famous circus) became aware of the lucrative possibilities of the movie business, they decided to produce Díaz Quesada's films. Thanks to their financial support, Díaz Quesada was able to make several well-known films, including *Manuel García, o El rey de los campos de Cuba* (Manuel García, or the King of the Cuban Countryside, 1913); the first full-length *criollo* feature film, *El capitán mambí, o Libertadores y guerrilleros* (The Mambi Captain, or Freedom Fighters and Guerillas, 1913); *La manigua, o La mujer cubana* (The Jungle, or the Cuban Woman, 1915); and *La hija del policía, o En poder de los ñáñigos* (The Police Officer's Daughter, or In the Power of the Ñáñigos, 1917).

CHRONOLOGY OF EVENTS

1897: First films shown in Cuba.

1932: First sound movies made in Cuba.

1937: Ernesto Caparrós makes first feature-length film, *La serpiente roja* (The Red Snake); Manuel Alonso produces first sound cartoon.

1938: First film production company, Películas Cubana S.A. (PECUSA), releases its first films.

1949: La Universidad de La Habana creates Department of Cinematography, begins Cuban film archive.

1950: La Productora Fílmica Cubana (PROFICUBA) founded.

1952: Cuban filmmakers establish Patronato Pro Fomento de la Industria Cinematográfica.

1954: Manuel Alonso directs *Casta de roble* (Lineage of Oak).

1956: Nuestro Tiempo, affiliated with Communist Party, releases *El Mégano*.

1959: Revolutionary government creates Instituto Cubano del Arte e Industria Cinematográficos

(ICAIC; Cuban Institute for Cinematographic Art and Industry, a.k.a., Cuban Film Institute), under Alfredo Guevara's direction, creating state film-making monopoly.

1961: Castro delivers "Words to the Intellectuals" speech subsuming art to the revolution.

1965: Santiago Álvarez, Cuba's leading documentary filmmaker, makes *Now* on discrimination in U.S. set to music of Lena Horne.

1968: Havana Cultural Congress celebrates Cuban films; Tomás Gutiérrez Alea's *Memorias del subdesarrollo* (Memories of Underdevelopment) released to international acclaim.

1969: Julio García Espinosa publishes *Por un cine imperfecto* (For an Imperfect Cinema).

1975: Sergio Giral begins his cycle of films on Cuba's African heritage with *El otro Francisco* (The Other Francisco).

1979: Pastor Vega's controversial *Retrato de Teresa* (Portrait of Teresa) explores machismo; annual Festival Internacional del Nuevo Cine

Latinoamericano (International Festival of New Latin American Cinema) begins in Havana.

1980: Controversy over the making of Humberto Solás's *Cecilia* (released 1981) leads to the removal of Alfredo Guevara as head of the ICAIC and his replacement by Julio García Espinosa.

1991: Controversy over *Alicia en el pueblo de Maravillas* (Alice in Wonderland) leads to Espinosa's resignation as head of the ICAIC; succeeded by Omar González.

1994: Tomás Gutiérrez Alea's and Juan Carlos Tabío's *Fresa y Chocolate* (Strawberry and Chocolate) addresses homosexuality in modern Cuba, and is the first Cuban film nominated for an Oscar.

2001: Juan Carlos Cremata's *Nada Más* (Nothing More) wins numerous international awards.

2006: With the government again allowing the production of independent films, Alejandro Moya's *Mañana* (Tomorrow) enjoys great popularity.

With the financial backing of Santos and Artigas and help from his brother Juan, Díaz Quesada set up Cuba's first film studio on the flat roof of a house on Jesús del Monte Road. Like Méliès's and Edison's ateliers, the studio had a glass roof and walls, and not even the dark storm clouds threatening torrential tropical downpours held up filming. The film lab and other facilities were located on the ground floor. Of the vast number of *Cuban Pathé* films (as they were christened in Camagüey) produced, only one minute has survived: the short feature *El parque de Palatino* (Palatino Park, 1906).

Shortly before Díaz Quesada's premature death, another pioneer, Ramón Peón García (1897–1971), emerged and eventually became one of the most enduring figures in the history of Latin American cinema. Formerly an accountant from Havana, Peón had tried his hand at various acts in the entertainment industry—tap dancing, performing illusions, and giving magic lessons—before he became interested in cinema and debuted as a producer with the film *Realidad* (Reality, 1920). By the time Peón appeared, only about twenty films had been produced in Cuba. During the 1930s, Peón directed more films than anyone else: eleven fiction films out of a total of thirty-nine, or 28 percent of the total. (Díaz Quesada had made sixteen films with plots, out of the twenty-five that were filmed between 1907 and 1920.) During his cinematographic career, which developed in Cuba, the United States, Venezuela, and above all, Mexico,

Peón shot a great number of films of various genres, developing sound technical skills. Some said he was an exceptional professional; others, particularly in Mexico, criticized him as an overly eager moviemaker because of the speed with which he turned out films.

The March 1920 edition of the magazine *Cine-Mundial* published the only news about what may have been the first animated cartoon produced by a Cuban: *Conga y Chambelona* (1919), directed by the painter and cartoonist Rafael Blanco (1885–1956), was presented around this time at a private showing in New York City, where it had been completed. A satirized José Miguel Gómez (1858–1921), a former president of the Cuban Republic, is the main character in this short. The drawings of the cartoons for the film show Blanco's talent for lively lines, bold strokes, and unusual solutions that so impressed his admirers.

PEÓN AND BPP PICTURES

With help from a new patron, the wealthy Arturo del Barrio (1907–1950), Ramón Peón (1897–1971) and the Spanish movie critic and producer Enrique Perdices (1901–1979) founded BPP (Barrio-Peón-Perdices) Pictures. (The word *pictures* suggests the post–World War I invasion of Cuban movie screens by North American cinema, which had pushed out battle-weary European film.) Under the pseudonym Guy de Pelletier, the outstanding journalist and movie critic Gonzalo de Palacio (1896–1992) produced the melodrama *El veneno de un beso* (The Poison of a Kiss, 1929), the first film of BPP. In the surviving fragments of this film—which has subtitles in English as well as Spanish, for U.S. distribution—there is a certain carefulness in the settings, lighting, and acting, which is restrained. Two others who joined the team that produced *El veneno de un beso* were Ernesto Caparrós Oliver (1907–1992), who was born in Camajuaní, and the mostly unknown Max Tosquella (1890–1975), who was affectionately called "the Jules Verne of Cuban cinema" because of his determination to build a movie city—a miniature Hollywood with studios, restaurants, housing, and a shopping center—whose profits would be invested in criollo films. His fanciful plans were passed from one government to another and never realized.

In 1930 the newspaper *El Mundo* announced a contest for the best original Cuban-themed movie plot, which would be filmed in natural settings. The winning story was *La Virgen de la Caridad* (Our Lady of Charity), by Enrique Agüero Hidalgo (1890–1975). Hidalgo was a railroad worker and passionate film buff who had published movie reviews in the press; he also is considered Cuba's first film historian. Peón had barely read the plot before he decided to make it BPP's second production. The diverse cast was made up of actors who had broad theatrical experience and others who had emerged from the discover-the-artist competition that *El Mundo* had sponsored. *La Virgen de la Caridad*, which premiered September 8, 1930, at the Rialto movie house, was an interesting film, technically speaking. It marked the end of silent Cuban films and the close of the first chapter in Peón's filmography.

In the early 2000s, *La Virgen de la Caridad* is considered a classic of the early period of Ibero-American movies. Despite its simple, melodramatic storyline and its technical flaws, it stands up well against the other works produced by the minor Cuban film companies of the era. The French film historian Georges Sadoul (1904–1967), invited by the Instituto Cubano del Arte e Industria Cinematográficos (ICAIC) to attend a private viewing of *La Virgen de la Caridad*, described it in his *Diccionario de Films* (1981) as "a good achievement for a rather conventional screenplay (within a weak national production field), due to its authentic scenery and social types" (p. 332). Another attendee at this showing was the Catalán photographer Néstor Almendros (1930–1992), who called Peón "the Cuban D. W. Griffith" (p. 300).

Arturo Agramonte (1925–2003), cameraman and Cuban cinema historian, defined film production on the island during the first fifty-eight years of the twentieth century as "the cinema of dreamers," not because film itself is something that exists between actual experience and dreaming, but because it is made by people who have dreamed of seeing a film on the big screen (Interview directed by Arturo Arias Polo 1989).

■ *See also*

Governance and Contestation: The Republic: 1902–1952

Television: Beginnings and Development

BIBLIOGRAPHY

Agramonte, Arturo. *Cronología del cine cubano*. Havana: Ediciones ICAIC, 1966.

Agramonte, Arturo. Interview directed by Arturo Arias Polo. In "Los soñadores." *Hacienda memoria*. Havana: Televisión Universitaria, 1989.

Agramonte, Arturo, and Luciano Castillo. *Ramón Peón, el hombre de los glóbulos negros*. Havana: Editorial Ciencias Sociales, 2003.

Agramonte, Arturo, and Luciano Castillo. *Entre el vivir y el soñar: Pioneros del cine cubano*. Camagüey, Cuba: Editorial Ácana, 2008.

Almendros, Néstor. *Cinemanía*. Barcelona: Editorial Seix Barral, 1992.

Sadoul, Georges. *Dictionnaire des films*. Paris: Editions Microcosme/Senil, 1981.

FILM: 1931–1959

María Caridad Cumaná González

Cuban film from the introduction of sound to the Revolution.

The arrival of talking pictures placed yet another obstacle in the path from scattered Cuban filmmaking to a stable film industry. The main difficulties were the following:

- Political, economic, and social frustration following the overthrow of the government of Gerardo Machado in 1933 and the coup d'état headed by Sergeant Fulgencio Batista
- The new technical complexity of filmmaking after the introduction of sound and the high costs of the necessary equipment
- Control of the Cuban market by North American film distributors along with the presence of successful Mexican, Argentinean, and Spanish films
- A lack of well-trained technicians and professionals, as well as of screenwriters with a good sense of the requirements of film.

SOUND FILM IN THE 1930s

The first Cuban musical short subject, *Maracas y bongó*, appeared in 1932. Directed by Max Tosquella with cinematography by Ernesto Caparrós, the film synthesized the formula that would characterize most Cuban productions in the years to follow: a simple love triangle set in the communal courtyard of a Havana *solar* or tenement populated by Cuban stereotypes such as the mulatta, the pimp, and the local policeman on his beat, all of whom sing well-known pop tunes. Years later, in 1937, Caparrós would direct the first feature-length Cuban sound film, *La serpiente roja* (The Red Snake), with a script by Félix B. Caignet.

The first Cuban sound film production company with industrial ambitions was Películas Cubana S.A. (PECUSA), with a plan for series production. Its first two films, which enjoyed large and lasting success, were Ramón Peón's *Sucedió en La Habana* (It Happened in Havana) and *El romance del palmar* (Romance under the Palm Trees), both in 1938. These were followed in 1939 by Mexican director Jaime Salvador's *Mi tía de América* (My [Latin] American Aunt), *Estampas habaneras* (Havana Scenes), *La última melodía* (The Last Melody), and *Cancionero cubano* (Cuban Songbook). The stylistic features of these films reveal their roots in theater and radio. By the time it shut its doors in 1940, PECUSA had made six films.

Another effort of the 1930s was that of Compañía Habana Industrial Cinematográfica (CHIC; Havana Industrial Cinema Company), which set up its own studio and sought the help of North American technicians. Its first film was *Ahora Somos Felices* (We're Happy Now, 1938), made by the U.S. director William Nolte with Cuban technicians.

In 1938, the Partido Socialista Popular founded the newspaper *Hoy* (Today), whose archives are of significant social and documentary value. *Hoy*'s photographer José Tabío, along with his cousin José Álvarez Tabío and other collaborators, founded Cuba Sono Films to make interview-documentaries about current social struggles. Among these were *Azúcar amargo* (Bitter Sugar), *Desfile obrero del 1ro de Mayo* (Workers' May Day March), *Desalojo del Hato del Estero* (Eviction from Hato del Estero), and *La lucha del pueblo cubano contra el nazismo* (The Cuban People's Fight Against Nazism).

CUBAN FILM IN THE 1940s AND 1950s

The plots of Cuban films in the 1940s and 1950s are generally considered to be inadequate, although there were some attempts to make works with historical-literary ambition. Cuba's national hero José Martí and novelist Cirilo Villaverde's nineteenth-century masterpiece *Cecilia Valdés* both inspired efforts, in 1942 and 1949, with disastrous results. A film treatment of Martí worthy of mention is *La rosa blanca: momentos en la vida de José Martí* (The White Rose: Episodes in the Life of José Martí, 1954) begun in late 1953 under the direction of the Mexican Emilio "El Indio" Fernández with cinematography by his compatriot Gabriel Figueroa. The result was a rigid and uneven film, which despite its technical quality and flashes of style fell far short of expectations.

The most ambitious effort of the 1950s was mounted by Manuel Alonso. Alonso, who initially came to public attention as an illustrator and made the first Cuban sound cartoon, *Napoleón, el faraón de los sinsabores* (Napoleon, the King of Troubles, 1937), sought to monopolize the resources of Cuban cinema.

He directed *Siete muertes a plazo fijo* (Seven Deaths on the Installment Plan, 1950), the best Cuban film up to that time, with a cinematic idiom approaching the level of Hollywood's B movies. His 1954 rural melodrama *Casta de robles* (Lineage of Oak) surpassed his previous work and is regarded as the best sound film of the prerevolution period. It recreates the bitter life of a poor country family, with implicit elements of social comment. Alonso was the first Cuban director with a clear desire to express himself in a cinematic idiom.

The year 1950 also saw the emergence of the LASPES studio, formed by Lázaro Prieto, Manuel Pellón, and Manuel de la Pedrosa, and soon renamed La Productora Fílmica Cubana (PROFICUBA), a company that achieved mediocre results. Among its titles were *Música, mujeres y piratas* (Music, Women, and Pirates, 1950), *Príncipe de contrabando* (Prince of Smugglers, 1950), and *Olé Cuba* (1957). Some productions by Salvador Behar, mostly directed by Raúl Medina, reveal a higher level of resources. These include the 1950 films *Rincón criollo* (Criollo Corner) and *Qué suerte tiene el cubano* (Cubans Are Lucky). Setting a record for Cuban filmmaking, 1950 saw fourteen films produced in all, though mostly of low quality.

A special case is that of Juan Orol, originally from Spain, resident in Mexico, and an exemplar of the worst filmmaking in Cuba before 1959. The films Orol directed on the island were *Siboney* (1940), *Sandra, la mujer de fuego* (Sandra, Woman on Fire, 1953), *El sindicato del crimen o La antesala de la muerte* (Murder, Inc., or the Prelude to Death, 1954), *La mesera del café del puerto* (Waitress at a Dockside Café, 1955), *Un farol en la ventana* (A Lamp in the Window, 1957), and *Tahimí, la hija del pescador* (Tahimi, the Fisherman's Daughter, 1959). Their inconsistency, absurdity, and poor quality cannot be overstated.

CUBA AND FOREIGN OR COPRODUCTIONS

Cuba was a propitious location for Cuban-Mexican coproductions, especially in the 1950s. These films made ample use of the most folkloric aspects of Cuban music and landscapes, almost always featuring popular dancers, singers, and musical groups of the moment. Juan J. Ortega made eight films, beginning with *El ángel caido* (The Fallen Angel, 1949). His sumptuous color film *Tropicana* (1956) showcased the spectacular productions of that cabaret and drew some critical attention. Another Mexican, Adolfo Fernández Bustamante, made a film inspired by Ernersto Lecuona's zarzuela *María La O* (1947). In 1954, Argentine-born Tulio Demichelli made *Un extraño en la escalera* (Stranger on the Steps) and *Más fuerte que el amor* (Stronger than Love), among others of more or less importance. Alfredo B. Crevenna filmed the ambitious *Yambaó* (1957) in color, featuring the dancer Ninón Sevilla. The Argentinean film industry also joined with Cuban cinema when Luis Bayón Herrera filmed *A La Habana me voy* (Bound for Havana) in 1948.

**Filmmaker Juan Orol
(1897–1988).** CHISTIAN
FAURE/CLASOS.COM/
LATINCONTENT/GETTY IMAGES

Hollywood made use of Cuban locations as well. John Huston filmed part of his *We Were Strangers* (1949) in Cuba, with a plot inspired by an incident in the struggle against the Machado government. Obvious historical distortions, as well as errors in atmosphere and in representation of the Cuban character, marred Huston's film, which was inferior to his work up to that time. In 1955, another famous director, Fred Zinneman, began an ambitious film version of Ernest Hemingway's literary classic *The Old Man and the Sea*. After Zinneman bowed out, the film was completed in mediocre fashion by John Sturges, filming on the coast of Peru.

In 1959, with the newly triumphant revolution in full swing, Sir Carol Reed came to Cuba from England to film an adaptation of Graham Greene's international spy novel *Our Man in Havana*, produced by Columbia Pictures. It was not one of the famous director's most outstanding works.

During the administration of President Carlos Prío Socorrás (1948–1952), representatives of the private Cuban film companies established a Patronato Pro Fomento de la Industria Cinematográfica. After the 1952 coup d'état, the Patronato's assets were inherited by Comisión Ejecutiva para la Industria Cinematográfica (CEPLIC; Executive Committee for the Film Industry), but poor results led to the dissolution of CEPLIC and the creation of an autonomous body, the Instituto Pro Fomento de la Industria Cinematográfica (INFICC).

INFICC was created on February 27, 1955, by Decree-Law No. 2135 of President Fulgencio Batista and was placed under the direction of Manuel Alonso, who thus came to control the resources for film production in Cuba. He in turn put them up for auction and they were bought by Octavio Gómez Castro, head of the Mexican company Distribuidora Peli-Mex. Thus the basic means of production for Cuban filmmaking passed into the hands of the industry's major rival. The number of Mexican productions filmed in Cuba grew, and Cuban studios devoted themselves almost entirely to the business of coproduction.

One curious case was that of Mario Barral, a theater, radio, and television figure who in 1956 began a project of making English-language films for distribution in U.S. movie houses. The first and only result of this unusual initiative, *Backs Turned*, shows surprising creative ambitions. The story follows a bizarre day in the life of a middle-class man who wonders why people turn their backs on the misfortunes of others. Critics, while pointing out certain deficiencies, praised the attempt at a more artistic kind of cinema. Barral's next effort, *Con el deseo en los dedos* (1958; With Desire in the Fingers) was a painful failure, made with enormous enthusiasm but with almost no resources by a group of actors and technicians who aspired to making art cinema. However, nothing could rescue the work, based as it was on a pretentious and absurd script.

CUBAN INITIATIVES TO PROMOTE CUBAN FILM

In 1949 the University of Havana opened a Department of Cinematography, including a Filmoteca to archive copies of early Cuban films, which years later passed into the hands of the Cinemateca de Cuba created by the Revolution. The department's courses and other events, which stimulated appreciation of quality films with little commercial distribution, express the desire in this period for the presence and (if it had been possible) successful creation of better Cuban cinema.

Another important initiative was the founding in 1951 of the first Cinemateca de Cuba, which showed films of high artistic value, under the direction of Germán Puig with the support of the influential French cinephile Henri Langlois, cofounder and director of the Cinématèque Française. Despite its precarious condition and irregular performance, the Cinemateca too was an example of the importance that film—an art felt to be emblematic of the modern spirit—had for the nation's intellectuals.

The film section of the cultural society Nuestro Tiempo, affiliated with the Communist Party (which was outlawed after Batista's 1952 coup d'état), carried out a serious program of deepening cultural interest in film. It published basic texts, stimulated criticism in its magazine, and organized interesting discussions about the art of cinema. The practical result of these concerns was the making, in 1956, of a dramatic 16-millimeter short *El Mégano*, which revealed the difficult lives of the charcoal makers of the Zapata Swamp. Seized by Batista's police and later rescued, this film, along with the work of Cuba Sono Films in the 1930s, is one of the essential antecedents of a spirit of creation in the service of society and in defense of social justice, which in turn gave life to future Cuban cinema.

BIBLIOGRAPHY

Agramonte, Arturo, and Luciano Castillo. "Ernesto Caparrós: El hombre orquesta del cine cubano." In *Coordenadas del cine cubano*, vol. 1, edited by Reynaldo González, 43–61. Santiago de Cuba: Editorial Oriente, 2001.

Agramonte, Arturo, and Luciano Castillo. *Ramón Peón, el hombre de los glóbulos negros*. Havana: Editorial de Ciencias Sociales, 2003.

Chanan, Michael. *Cuban Cinema*. Minneapolis: University of Minnesota Press, 2004.

Douglas, María Eulalia. *La tienda negra: El cine en Cuba, 1897–1990*. Havana: Cinemateca de Cuba, 1996.

Douglas, María Eulalia. "Ángel y demonio: Molina y Alonso." In *Coordenadas del cine cubano*, vol. 1, edited by Reynaldo González, 62–67. Santiago de Cuba: Editorial Oriente, 2001.

Douglas, María Eulalia. "Etapas temáticas del cine cubano." In *Coordenadas del cine cubano*, vol. 1, edited by Reynaldo González, 90–106. Santiago de Cuba: Editorial Oriente, 2001.

Garcia Osuna, Alfonso J. *The Cuban Filmography, 1897 Through 2001*. Jefferson, NC: McFarland, 2003.

González, Reynaldo. *Cine Cubano: Ese ojo que nos ve*. San Juan, PR: Editorial Plaza Mayor, 2002.

Kriger, Clara, and Alejandra Portela. *Cine latinoamericano*. Vol. 1, *Diccionario de realizadores*. Buenos Aires: Edicones El Jilguero, 1997.

Paranaguá, Paulo Antonio, ed. *Le cinéma Cubain*. Paris: Centre Georges Pompidou, 1990.

Piñera Corrales, Walfredo, and María Caridad Cumaná González. *Mirada al cine cubano*. Brussels: Edición OCIC, 1999.

Valdés Rodríguez, José Manuel. *Ojeada al cine cubano: 1906–1958*. Havana: University of Havana Press, 1963.

FILM: 1959–1989

Michael Chanan

The film institute of the revolutionary government.

This article encompasses the first thirty years of the Cuban Film Institute, Instituto Cubano del Arte e Industria Cinematográficos (ICAIC). It discusses the ideological battles of the early years under the leadership of Alfredo Guevara against sectarians of both right and left, Cuban films' international successes; the defense of the ICAIC's autonomy in the quinquenio gris (the Five Grey Years of the early 1970s), the crisis occasioned by the film *Cecilia* (1981) when Alfredo Guevara was ousted, and the resurgence of ICAIC following the appointment of Julio García Espinosa as his successor.

FREEDOM FROM FOREIGN CONTROL

The creation in Cuba during 1959 of a state film institute was an act of will and defiance: the will to create a film industry where the objective conditions for it hardly seem to exist and defiance toward the hitherto overweening control of Cuban cinema exhibition by the major U.S. distributors. The revolutionary government's first decree in the cultural field was the establishment of ICAIC (Instituto Cubano del Arte e Industria Cinematográficos; Cuban Institute for Cinematographic Art and Industry), initially set up to take over the property of leading figures in the island's small film business who quickly fled the scene in the wake of Fulgencio Batista's hasty exit. But film had been a central site of cultural resistance for urban middle-class intellectuals during the 1950s, and a close reading of the founding decree reveals a good deal about the politics, intelligence, and intentions of its authors. The provisional government was not yet publicly known as socialist in its leanings, but its approach would not have been taken by an administration that just happened to acquire a film studio without knowing what to do with it. On the contrary, the new government's actions exhibited a clear understanding of the character of the forces that had prevented the growth of an independent film industry in Cuba until then; in fact, the actions were based on an analysis of the structure needed to establish an industry that might be able in the future to escape those forces.

SUBSIDY AND AUTONOMY

Growing out of the film unit set up by the rebel army after the seizure of power to make documentaries explaining policies in key areas like agrarian reform, the new institute was subsidized but granted considerable autonomy under the direction of a kind of Cuban John Grierson figure, Alfredo Guevara, a member of Fidel Castro's inner circle who argued for a cinema of art, not propaganda. The institute would not be controlled by government bureaucrats but self-managed by the filmmakers; later on it would come under the Culture Ministry rather than the Ideological Office of the Party Central Committee, which controlled broadcasting and the press. Subsidy meant it was free from the immediate pressures of the market, and Guevara publicly defended the institute's liberal distribution policies against Communist Party hard-liners such as Blas Roca (1908–1987) and also supported the stylistic freedom of its own directors. No attempt was made to impose stylistic models, least of all Soviet-style socialist realism, which Cuban filmmakers found aesthetically unconvincing and even anathema, nor was the ICAIC to be in the business of making genre movies that simply swapped the goodies and the baddies (although they inevitably made some of those, too). As a result, in the words of Gerardo Chijona, a second-generation ICAIC director, Cuban filmmakers were "the spoiled children of Latin American cinema" (Venegas p. 38).

The institute not only clashed with hard-line Communists but also the liberal bourgeoisie, among whom cinema played a deeply symptomatic role as a marker of individual rather than collective aspiration. Issues came to a head in 1961, when the ICAIC declined to exhibit a short independent documentary called *P.M.* because it seemed to them ideologically ambiguous, too subjective in its rendering of the black lumpenproletariat. The resulting commotion led to a meeting in which Castro gave the speech known as "The Words to the Intellectuals," where he pronounced the formula that henceforth defined cultural policy: "dentro de la Revolución, todo; contra la Revolución, nada," or "within the Revolution, everything, against it, nothing." (For the circumstances of this speech, its relation to cinema, and the historical detail summarized in the present essay, see Chanan 2004, pp. 133–141 and passim.) The formula turned out to be ambiguous. On the one hand, it led to attacks on those who openly criticized the Revolution. On the other hand, however, as Ambrosio Fornet observed, "The fact is that, in the context of a state

of siege, aesthetic discourse, perhaps because of its own polysemic nature, delights in the license of this 'inside' where everything—or almost everything—is permitted." Nor are the limits ever fixed, because "the 'everything' permitted is not a permanent right but an arena of conflict that must be renegotiated every day, with no quarter granted to the bureaucracy and with the temptation of irresponsible whimsy firmly resisted" (Fornet pp. 11–12). Responsible whimsy, however, is another matter, and there is a strand running through Cuban cinema even in the early 2000s that gently satirizes the more surreal aspects of everyday life in revolutionary Cuba.

NEW CUBAN CINEMA

When the Revolution took power in 1959, cinema was at a peak of popularity. Box office earnings in 1960 reached 22.8 million pesos from roughly 120 million admissions; for a population of around seven million, this gives a national cinema-going average of seventeen visits annually (more than in the United Kingdom, for example). The institute extended this audience by introducing mobile cinemas in the countryside. And with new films from the United States officially unobtainable (although some always managed to enter through the back door and would later circulate on videocassette), the institute brought in films from everywhere else— Europe East and West, Latin America, Japan— and thus the Cuban audience came to see a much wider range of world cinema than was usual almost anywhere.

But if the ICAIC turned Cuban cinema into a state monopoly, then in the process it also opened this space up to domestic production, and within a few years the institute's directors began to win awards at international film festivals for films that combined neorealism, experimentalism, and fervor in a series of films by directors, including Tomás Gutiérrez Alea, Julio García Espinosa, Humberto Solás, Manuel Octavio Gómez, Santiago Alvarez, and others. All of them belonged to a generation schooled in a highly syncretistic culture that celebrated rumba and surrealism, Yoruba gods and Catholic transcendentalism, in equal measure, and paid aesthetic homage equally to Eisenstein and Chaplin, Hollywood and Italian neorealism, the French New Wave, and Brazilian Cinema Novo. In 1968 Cuban cinema was not only identified with the worldwide radical ferment of that memorable year, but with titles released that year such as *Memorias de subdesarollo* (Memories of Underdevelopment) and *Lucía*, by Alea and Solás, respectively, in which the aesthetic of the European avant-garde is metamorphosed through a kind of revolutionary transfiguration, while Santiago Álvarez, the boldest of innovators (*Now* [1965], *LBJ* [1968], *Hasta la victoria siempre* [1967], etc.), reinvented the newsreel, the compilation film, the travelogue, and every other documentary genre he laid hands upon in an irrepressible frenzy of filmic bricolage licensed by that supreme act of bricolage, the Cuban Revolution.

Audience Impact With films like these, the white building at the corner of Twenty-third and

Santiago Álvarez (1919–1998). Filmmaker Santiago Álvarez reinvented the newsreel, the compilation film, the travelogue, and every other documentary genre he laid his hands on in an irrepressible frenzy of filmic bricolage.
© RIA NOVOSTI/ALAMY

with this impact. In 1969 Julio García Espinosa wrote a crucial manifesto, "Por un cine imperfecto" (For an Imperfect Cinema), which reflected the Communist island's unique position but was also taken up more widely. Warning against the technical perfection that after ten years now began to lie within the reach of Cuban filmmakers, he argued that they should resist the temptation of what would only be a subindustrial cinema that could never achieve the polish of the real McCoy; moreover, it would be self-defeating, because cinema of that kind only induced audience passivity, whereas a more experimental, indeed Brechtian, cinema, which resisted convention and upset orthodox representation by demonstrating its own methods of construction, opened up spaces for the viewer's involvement and participation.

A Haven for Nonconformity Events toward the end of the decade, including the death of Che Guevara in Bolivia, shook the Cuban Revolution hard. Economic errors were made; critics and nonconformists, including homosexuals, were victimized. The ICAIC in this period constituted a space of safety, providing haven for gays and long-haired young artists like the musicians who were invited to set up the Grupo Sonora Experimental in 1970, some of whom, like Pablo Milanès, had been in work camps; it also provided a home for polemical intellectuals such as the writer Jesús Díaz when the journal he edited, *Pensamiento Crítico* (Critical Thought) was closed down a short while later. Outside the ICAIC, the country turned in on itself; hard-liners, confident of Moscow's backing, held the reins of power.

Several filmmakers turned to allegories of national identity. The black director, Sergio Giral, initiated a cycle of films, beginning with *El otro Francisco* (The Other Francisco, 1975) which asserted Cuba's African heritage by deconstructing and then reassembling the history of slavery. Alea's historical allegory, *La ultima cena* (The Last Supper, 1976), and Solas's *Cecilia* (1981) were part of this trend. Others played safe by recounting tales of revolutionary heroes in adaptations of Hollywood genres. These films included *El hombre de Maisinicú* (The Man from Maisinicú, 1973), by Manuel Pérez, and *El Brigadista* (The Literacy Teacher, 1977), by Octavio Cortázar, both powerful films in themselves but hardly examples of imperfect cinema. The high value placed on documentaries and newsreels ensured not only that a second generation of young filmmakers was brought into the institute but that these newcomers faced direct encounter with a constantly evolving reality. Occasionally they ran into trouble. Even Sara Gómez, an outstanding representative of the black intelligentsia, whose films deal with the essence of Cubanía in all its manifestations, including music, Afro-Cuban religions, and the culture of marginal communities, was forced to abandon a projected trilogy of documentaries that touched on the excesses of machismo

Twelfth in Havana's Vedado district threw down an exhilarating and infectious experimentalist challenge to the hegemony of the culture industry headquartered in Hollywood, a challenge that was also expressed in the pages of the institute's important journal *Cine Cubano*. The results so intrigued the audience that they began to change their viewing habits; for example, they started taking documentaries seriously, especially those of Álvarez. In the 1970s, ICAIC researchers found that sometimes people went to the movies because they wanted to see the new Álvarez and would then stay and watch whatever feature was shown after it—a complete inversion of normal cinema-going behavior. The institute took advantage of the public's interest to produce a whole series of feature documentaries by diverse directors at a time when documentary elsewhere had practically disappeared from cinema screens.

Havana began to draw leftist artistic intelligentsia around the world that was celebrated at the Havana Cultural Congress of 1968, and the freedom and originality of the new Cuban films had much to do

and the persistence of racism. The issue of machismo would burst onto the screen in the New Wave realism of one of the most successful of Cuban films, Pastor Vega's *Retrato de Teresa* (Portrait of Teresa, 1979), which provided the stimulus for wide debate about the double oppression of Cuban women.

Havana: A Film Capital The ICAIC was autonomous but centrally funded on a fixed annual budget. For seven million pesos (a fraction of the budget for a Hollywood blockbuster), it managed to produce a handful of features annually, as well as documentaries, a weekly newsreel, and even some animated cartoons. (Production levels in the 1970s reached around half a dozen features per year, and forty or more documentaries of varying length; the numbers would be exceeded slightly in the 1980s). When the end of the 1970s saw Cuba cautiously opening up again, the ICAIC played a leading role with the creation of the International Festival of New Latin American Cinema in 1979, held ever since in Havana every December. Since very few films made in Latin America, and especially not those that espoused any kind of revolutionary politics, were seen in any country other than their own, Havana became Latin America's capital of cinema, practically the only city where everything made worth seeing could be seen. And it was a home away from home for many who, like several Chilean filmmakers after the coup of 1973, were forced into political exile.

Crisis and Renewal The 1980s began with an unexpected crisis, when Humberto Solás undertook the most ambitious film project that the ICAIC had yet attempted, an epic adaptation of the nineteenth-century Cuban novel, *Cecilia Valdés*. The production tied up so much of the institute's production capacity that it caused chagrin among other filmmakers. Furthermore, when Solás presented a somewhat idiosyncratic, Freudian interpretation of the classic novel that, for all its visual splendors, disconcerted both traditionalists and the popular audience, the disunity among the filmmakers enabled Alfredo Guevara's old enemies to mount a rearguard attack when the project proved an expensive flop and edge him out of power.

His successor was García Espinosa, who quickly brought fresh vision, pursuing a policy of low budget production, democratizing the institute's internal decision-making process, and giving directors of a new generation a chance to prove themselves. What emerged was a new genre, what might be called the sociocritical comedy, which met with huge popular success. Juan Carlos Tabío scored an immediate hit with *Se permuta* (House for Swap) in 1983, a satire on the intractable problem of overcrowding in Havana. A year later *Los pájaros tirandole a la escopeta* (Tables Turned), by Rolando Díaz, a comedy of generational conflict in which a son forbids his mother of having a relationship with the father of the woman he himself is in love with, drew an audience

of two million—one-fifth of the entire population—in the space of two months.

Some of these films continued the experimentalism of the earlier period. Juan Carlos Tabío's *Plaff!* of 1988 brings back the hilarious illogic of zany Hollywood comedy in a new context, where self-reference crosses with Brechtian distanciation (alienation) to produce a new brand of self-reflexive laughter about bad habits of thinking. It, too, was a huge success. Other new directions followed. Jesús Díaz began as early as 1985 by confronting the fractious issue of the split with the Cuban emigré community in the United States with a thoughtful film called *Lejanía* (Distance). At the end of the decade, another new talent emerged with a powerful allegory on generational conflict in the shape of *Papeles secundarios* (Secondary Roles), by Orlando Rojas. These were difficult films for reviewers in the state-controlled press, but they pointed in a direction that would soon become predominant. However, the institute would not escape the crisis that hit Cuba following the collapse of Communism in Eastern Europe and the Soviet Union itself in 1989–1991, which would heavily curtail production and bring about the economic emigration of many ICAIC personnel.

Jesús Díaz (1941–2002). In 1985, Cuban author and filmmaker Jesús Díaz confronted the fractious issue of the split with the Cuban emigré community with a thoughtful film called *Lejanía* (Distance). © LEBRECHT MUSIC & ART

BIBLIOGRAPHY

Burton, Julianne. "Cuba." In *The New Latin American Cinema: An Annotated Bibliography of English-Language Sources, 1960–1976*. New York: Cineaste, 1976.

Castro, Fidel. "Words to the Intellectuals." In *Radical Perspectives in the Arts*, edited by Lee Baxandall. Harmondsworth, U.K.: Penguin, 1972.

Chanan, Michael. *Cuban Cinema*. Minneapolis: University of Minnesota Press, 2004.

Espinosa, Julio García. "Por un cine imperfecto" *Cine Cubano*, no. 66–67 (1969). Translated as "For an Imperfect Cinema" in *Jump Cut*, no. 20 (May 1979) and in *Twenty-five Years of Latin American Cinema*, edited by Michael Chanan. London: British Film Institute, Channel Four, 1983.

Fornet, Ambrosio. "Introduction." *Bridging Enigma: Cubans on Cuba*. Special issue, edited by Ambrosio Fornet. *South Atlantic Quarterly* 96, no. 1 (1997): 1–15.

Myerson, Michael. *Memories of Underdevelopment: The Revolutionary Films of Cuba*. New York: Grossman, Pelican, 1973.

Venegas, Cristina. "Filmmaking with Foreigners." In *Cuba in the Special Period: Culture and Ideology in the 1990s*, edited by Ariana Hernandez-Reguant. New York: Palgrave Macmillan, 2009.

■ *See also*

Cuban Thought and Cultural Identity: Socialist Thought

Cuban Thought and Cultural Identity: The Internet Experience in Cuba

The Films of Jorge Molina and Eduardo del Llano

Gender: Women Behind the Camera

Governance and Contestation: The Cuban Revolution

Suite Habana (Fernando Pérez)

FILM: 1989–2010

Ann Marie Stock

The movement of Cuba's cinema into a global audiovisual era.

In fall 2010 the director Esteban Insausti (b. 1971) and editor Angélica Salvador (b. 1975) were in Venezuela *blowing up* their first feature—that is, transferring *Larga Distancia* (Long Distance) from digital format onto celluloid for 35-millimeter projection. With its reliance on new technologies for its creation, its theme of emigration driving the narrative, a New York–based Cuban playing the lead role, and coproduction as the financing mechanism, this film project demonstrates the very long distance that Cuban filmmaking has come since 1989.

Film has been a key arbiter of Cuban revolutionary identity; "Cuban cinema," Tomás Gutiérrez Alea stated, "was born with and thanks to the revolution." It is through the medium of cinema that notions of citizenship have been defined and promoted, relationships to the state have been negotiated, and alliances have been forged. The cultural project that began in the late 1950s, wielding a camera to help construct a new nation, continued into the twenty-first century—but with significant changes.

FILM IN THE SPECIAL PERIOD

Following the breakup of the Soviet Union, Cuba plummeted into a full-scale crisis. During the so-called Special Period that began in 1991, severe shortages prevailed. With foodstuffs unavailable, gas pumps empty, and shop windows bare, it was inevitable that reverberations would be felt in the film world. It was at this difficult moment that a polemic reverberated through the Instituto Cubano del Arte e Industria Cinematográficos (ICAIC, National Film Institute): In *Alicia en el pueblo de Maravillas* (Alice in Wondertown, 1991), Daniel Díaz Torres (b. 1948) satirizes his nation's precarious economy and his compatriots' growing disenchantment with socialism. Although written in the late 1980s, before the force of the Special Period had destabilized the island, the film's critique hit a nerve, and the ICAIC came under fire. Heated criticism resulted in the resignation of the institute's president, Julio García Espinosa (b. 1926), and a proposal for a merger of the ICAIC and the National Institute of Radio and Television (ICRT). Alfredo Guevara, one of the ICAIC's founders, returned to lead the institute through this tumultuous time, and although he and his colleagues managed to resist the merger, the incident left the ICAIC significantly weakened.

During the Special Period some ICAIC filmmakers explored the uncertainty of the time: Enrique Colina (b. 1944) with *El rey de la selva* (King of the Jungle, 1991), Pastor Vega (1940–2005) with *Vidas paralelas* (Parallel Lives, 1993), Julio García Espinosa with *Reina y rey* (Queen and King, 1994), and most notably, Fernando Pérez (b. 1944) with *Madagascar* (1994). The dire economic conditions caused ICAIC's filmmaking activity to slow and stop completely. The Noticiero ICAIC Latinoamericano, after thirty years of uninterrupted production under the direction of Santiago Álvarez (1919–1998), ceased to exist, and documentary production slowed dramatically. The Animation Studio managed to keep its doors open, but only by contracting with foreign clients. Feature film production plummeted, bottoming out in 1996, when not a single feature was made. The future of the ICAIC and the nation's revolutionary cinema was tenuous at best. No longer could the state-backed institute afford to hire and train the island's emerging cineastes, procure and maintain the equipment necessary for costly 35-millimeter production, and invest in films that had little hope of breaking even.

Circumstances in Cuba and within the ICAIC necessitated a new economic model. Financing through coproduction, an arrangement involving at least one partner from another country, helped stretch the institute's limited resources. Spain, Mexico, Venezuela, France, Germany, Nicaragua, and other countries invested capital to create coproductions such as *Adorables mentiras* (Adorable Lies, 1991), by Gerardo Chijona (b. 1949); Vega's *Vidas paralelas*; *El siglo de las luces* (Explosion in a Cathedral, 1992), by Humberto Solás (1941–2008); *Fresa y chocolate* (Strawberry

Filmmaker Enrique Colina. Enrique Colina, director of *Entre ciclones* (Between Cyclones), examines a film strip in an editing room at the Cuban Institute of Art and Cinematography on 6 May 2003. AP IMAGES/ CRISTOBAL HERRERA

and Chocolate, 1994), by Gutiérrez Alea and Juan Carlos Tabío; *Derecho de asilo* (Right of Asylum, 1994), by Octavio Cortázar (1935–2008); Tabío's *El elefante y la bicicleta* (The Elephant and the Bicycle, 1994); García Espinosa's *Reina y rey*; Gutiérrez Alea and Tabío's *Guantanamera* (1995); *Pon tu pensamiento en mí* (Think About Me, 1995) and *Amor vertical* (Vertical Love, 1997), by Arturo Sotto (b. 1967); Díaz Torres's *Kleines Tropicana* (Tropicanita, 1997); Chijona's *Un paraíso bajo las estrellas* (Paradise Under the Stars, 1999); and Vega's *Las profecías de Amanda* (The Prophecies of Amanda, 1999). The increasing reliance on coproduction compelled filmmakers to blend markers of *cubanía* with transnational signs to satisfy a wider audience. At times the signature Cuban humor delighted, and at other times it merely circulated stereotypes and clichéd depictions of the island. Regardless of the trajectory of individual films, taken together they positioned Cuban filmmakers increasingly as auteurs alert to opportunities beyond the island and attentive to market forces, and they engaged Cuban audiences in seeing themselves in new ways.

In experimenting with new production models, the ICAIC targeted one initiative at young filmmakers. A call for proposals offered $10,000 to each of three aspiring directors whose individual short films would be compiled into a single feature-length film. The project was designed to stimulate emerging audiovisual artists while generating a low-cost film. Pavel Giroud (b. 1973), Lester Hamlet (b. 1971), and Esteban Insausti were selected, and their shorts were combined to create *Tres veces dos* (Three Times Two, 2004). Although occasional initiatives such as this one provided incentive and opportunities to up-and-coming filmmakers, their sporadic nature limited their impact.

AUDIOVISUAL INNOVATIONS AND ALTERNATIVES

Coinciding with these efforts were shifting demographics. Industry filmmakers had aged, and increasingly, headlines lamented the deaths of pioneers, including Gutiérrez Alea, Álvarez, and Vega. As a result of all these factors, the state's role in film production and circulation shifted. Whereas the ICAIC constituted the principal venue for Cuba's filmmakers from the 1960s through the 1980s, this ceased to be the case when innovative audiovisual endeavors began outside the industry's purview.

A series of organizations established in the late 1980s and early 1990s tested and refined new modes of film production and dissemination. The Escuela Internacional de Cine y Televisión, Instituto Superior de Arte, Taller de Cine de la Asociación Hermanos Saíz, Movimiento Nacional de Video, video club movement, Televisión Serrana, and others trained emerging filmmakers, embraced video technology, and established partnerships with island

and international organizations. In documenting this period and proving the efficacy of new production modes, they demonstrated that working outside state institutions did not mean working at cross-purposes with them.

The same period also witnessed a technological revolution. Digital cameras and PC-based editing proliferated around the world. So too did VCRs, DVDs, PCs, CDs, and the Internet. The introduction of new technologies in Cuba provided an attractive alternative to the costly industry equipment and infrastructure. Satellites began to beam films to Cuba from all over the world. A network of official and unauthorized video and DVD rental shops cropped up. Films passed easily from one person to another, from one home to the next, increasingly circulated on hard drives and flash drives. The Internet also became an important avenue for film sharing. After 1989 Cubans revolutionized the ways in which they produce and disseminate audiovisual material and communicate with audiences both at home and through cyberspace.

A NEW GENERATION OF FILMS OUTSIDE IN THE STREETS

Like previous generations of Cuban cineastes, new artists began wielding cameras to create films, but many did so from outside state institutions. Lacking opportunities within the industry, determined entrepreneurs sought funding, established contacts, and procured equipment. Out of necessity, and working with limited budgets, this new generation became adept at *resolviendo*—devising creative solutions. One strategy was to forge partnerships; another was to experiment with new technologies. These efforts revolutionized the ways in which films were made and marketed in Cuba.

Works created in this style share common features: All relied on new technologies for their creation, often in conjunction with traditional approaches; all were financed with low budgets; and all benefited from local-local and local-global partnerships. Included are features, animation, documentaries, experimental works, and music videos that vary greatly. Some reveal the influence of popular culture. Ernesto Piña Rodríguez (b. 1980) recast Japanese *manga* to comment on the uniquely Cuban transportation mode the *camello* (camel-backed trailers) in *EME 5* (2004). Alejandro Pérez (b. 1964) featured Cuba's acclaimed a capella group Vocal Sampling as they performed the Eagles' "Hotel California" in a video clip (2009). And both Juan Carlos Cremata (b. 1961) and Alfredo Ureta (b. 1971) employed road movie conventions in *Viva Cuba* (2005) and *La mirada* (The Gaze, 2010), respectively.

Some audiovisual artists explored the creative process in their work. In *Habanaceres* (2001), Luis Leonel León (b. 1971) illuminated the changing role of Cuban artists by intercutting portrayals of four

leading cultural figures. In *Las manos y el ángel* (Hands and the Angel, 2002), Esteban Insausti crafted an innovative portrait of the musician Emiliano Salvador by inflecting the film language with jazz techniques. Carlos Barba (b. 1978) paid tribute to notables in Cuba's film world in several documentaries. And in *Oda a la piña* (Ode to the Pineapple, 2009), Laimir Fano (b. 1981) drew upon Cuban poetry, music, and dance to explore what it means to lose one's rhythm, to be out of step.

The theme of emigration recurs. Although the phenomenon of migration affects people the world over in this global era, the subject of emigration resonates uniquely for Cubans. Humberto Padrón (b. 1967) broached the subject in *Video de familia* (Family Video, 2001), in which the trope of a home video serves to scrutinize family dysfunction. Aram Vidal (b. 1981) took advantage of his stay in Mexico while working on an advanced degree to capture the reflections of Cuban residents of Mexico City in *Ex Generación* (2006). Gustavo Pérez (b. 1962) probed the experiences of six Russian women who fell in love with Cuban men and subsequently relocated to the island in *Todas iban a ser reinas* (All Were Going to Be Queens, 2006). Alina Rodríguez (b. 1984) framed the issues in terms of internal migration: *Buscándote Havana* (Looking for You, Havana, 2006) exposes the plight of Cubans who move from the provinces to the island's capital only to occupy a peripheral position there.

The most distinctive feature of the new generation was its insistence on pushing the limits. Many filmmakers did this by tackling subjects once considered taboo. Besides emigration, new films dealt with mental illness (*Existen* [They Exist], Esteban Insausti, 2005), censorship (*Zona de silencio* [Zone of Silence], Karel Ducases, 2007), prostitution (*Sexo, historias y cintas de video* [Sex, History, and Videotape], Ricardo Figueredo, 2007), homosexuality and transgendered identity (*Ella Trabaja* [She Works], Jesús Miguel Hernández Bachs, 2007), the challenge of finding meaningful work (*Como construir un barco* [How to Build a Boat], Susana Barriga, 2007), drug use and abuse (*Todo por Ella* [All for Her], Pavel Giroud, 2002), inadequate housing (*Las camas solas* [Lonely Beds], Sandra Gómez, 2006), inconsistencies between what is practiced and what is preached (*Utopía*, Arturo Infante, 2004; *Monte rouge*, Eduardo del Llano, 2005), and violence (*La guerra de las canicas* [The War of the Marbles], Adrián Ricardo Hartill and Wilbert Noguel, 2008; *La bestia* [The Beast], Hilda Elena Vega, 2007). In focusing on the island's disenfranchised sectors and reporting what had gone unmentioned in the mass media, these works posed challenges to dominant state discourse. Heated debate often accompanied the screenings and then continued in email exchanges and on blogs. Many of these artists probed problems in their midst not with the intention of undermining revolutionary accomplishments, but rather to foster

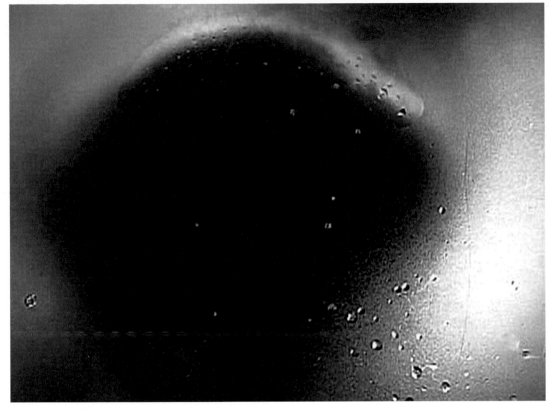

On the Ball (2000). Still from *On the Ball* (2000), a short video by Felipe Dulzaides (b. 1965). This still is a close-up of a mouth breathing heavily on the camera lens. Dulzaides belonged to a generation of video artists in the late 1990s that focused on body images in their art. Dulzaides's work often depicts simple acts that take on larger meaning through repetition.
© FELIPE DULZAIDES

awareness and explore solutions. Actor-director Jorge Perrugoría affirmed this tendency in an interview filmed by Todd Green and Hans Dudelheim: "I think Cuban film has a commitment with society. . . . It's the commitment of artists to not only entertain but also to make people think, reflect, and question reality—which is the only way of changing or improving it."

TAKING STOCK

A great deal changed in Cuban filmmaking between 1989 and 2010. What was once a concertedly national cinema evolved into a decidedly transnational audiovisual praxis. No longer was the ICAIC the privileged purveyor of Cubanness; a series of organizations and individuals began to participate in this endeavor from various locales. Whereas to be considered a Cuban creator once implied rootedness on the island, by 2010 this was no longer the case. So-called round-trip-ticket artists such as Zulema Clares (b. 1973), Miguel Coyula (b. 1977), Tané Martínez (b. 1981), and others could work both in Cuba and from the diaspora. Greater access to the medium, proffered by new technologies and partnerships, democratized representation and yielded multiple and sometimes contradictory visions of what it means to be Cuban. Predictably, these diverse and divergent perspectives resulted in clashes, and yet, while emerging audiovisual artists explored new modes and tackled topics not previously treated in their nation's films or mass media, their stance vis-à-vis state institutions was not necessarily oppositional. In

fact, some artists worked in state institutions as well as on their own street projects (Eduardo del Llano, Karel Ducases, and Enrique Molina, to name only a few). Indeed, the ICAIC actually contributed to bringing about many of these changes, among them establishing a series of festivals—the Muestra in Havana being the most significant—to showcase the work of emerging audiovisual artists. So the voices of these nonstate actors, sometimes amplified and echoed by state actors and agencies, were making themselves heard.

It appeared unlikely during the Special Period that Cuban stories would make their way to the screen. In fact, Fernando Pérez recalled thinking that *Madagascar*, created during the bleakest moment in Cuba's recent history, would be his last film, and then, against all odds, he went on to make four more films. That is not to say all challenges have been surmounted, or that Cuba's audiovisual future is guaranteed. Problems persist. And yet, the resilience of Cuban culture is noteworthy. As Esteban Insausti remarked in an interview in 2006, "in this country right now, where there are difficulties distributing powdered milk and buying gasoline, the fact that films are being made is a miracle" (Stock 2006).

BIBLIOGRAPHY

Douglas, María Eulalia, Sara Vega, and Ivo Sarría, eds. *Producciones del Instituto Cubano del Arte e Industria Cinematográficos, 1959–2004.* Havana: Cinemateca de Cuba, ICAIC, 2004.

Gutiérrez Alea, Tomás. "Respuesta a *Cine Cubano.*" In *Cine y revolución en Cuba*, edited by Santiago Alvarez et al. Barcelona: Editorial Fontamara, 1975.

Perrugoria, Jorge, in interview by Todd Green and Hands Dudelheim. Unpublished film recording. Havana, December 2004.

Stock, Ann Marie. "An Interview with Esteban Insausti." *Cuban Cinema Classics* 6, 2006.

Stock, Ann Marie. *On Location in Cuba: Street Filmmaking during Times of Transition.* Chapel Hill: University of North Carolina Press, 2009.

■ *See also*

El Super (León Ichaso)

FILM: CUBAN CINEMA OF THE DIASPORA

Juan Antonio García Borrero

The question of Cubanness vis-à-vis Cuban cinema made outside the island.

Films made by Cubans outside the island have been absent from the majority of academic studies concerning Cuban cinema. Such research is still dominated by what one might call *icaicentrism*—a tendency to view the history of Cuban cinema as if it were the history of the Instituto Cubano del Arte e Industria Cinematográficos (ICAIC; Cuban Institute of Cinematographic Art and Industry). The ICAIC, created on 24 March 1959, was the first new agency of the revolutionary government related to culture. In light of Benedict Anderson's oft-cited thesis, which argues that a nation is, above all, an "imagined community," it is not so absurd for Cubans, Mexicans, Argentines, or Venezuelans to imagine themselves as Latin Americans who share the same language, the same economic hardships, and a common goal: the immediate improvement of those societies that over the centuries have suffered the consequences of colonialism. That subaltern nationalism allowed for the birth and consolidation of a regional cultural identity and, in the case of cinema, a common ideology that tended to mask disparities between the homeland and the diaspora.

Scholars in the field of cinema studies have thus tended to overlook Cuban cinema produced or made by those residing outside the island, who imagine themselves as part of a community that need not even be perceived physically. Specifically, the subjective link that binds a Cuban who lives in Cuba with another residing in Miami and a third trying to survive in Madrid goes beyond the tangible space they inhabit or that they are prevented from inhabiting; it even extends beyond the possible ideological differences they debate. The uniting factor (up to the point of their likely political divergence) is the sense of belonging to something that cannot be seen, but only felt. In those cases, the nation overcomes the palpable limits of the archipelago to become that lucid image that the scholar Ana López has proposed: the image of a greater Cuba. Nevertheless, studies of Cuban cinema concentrate only on what is created on the physical island.

THE 1960s AND 1970s

In the first three decades after the revolution, understandings of cinema generated on the island and in the diaspora existed in precise counterpoint. Ideology was the driving force behind most films of this period, sometimes legitimizing the Republican past, as in *La Cuba de ayer* (The Cuba of Yesterday, 1963), by Manolo Alonso, sometimes demonizing the present, as in *La verdad de Cuba* (The Truth of Cuba, 1962) and *Cuba, satélite 13* (Cuba, Satellite 13, 1963), both by Manuel de la Pedrosa. It was not until the mid-1970s that works of cinema filmed in the diaspora began to show collective growth as well as diversification of subject matter. This transformation is directly connected to the creation of the Cuban Cultural Center of New York, founded in 1973 and headed for ten years by Iván Acosta (b. 1943), which inspired a group of artistic projects that for the first time took cinema seriously. The center brought together a group of actors (Orestes Matacena, Rubén Rabasa, Raymundo Hidalgo-Gato, Rolando Barral, Clara Hernández), playwrights (Iván Acosta), cinematographers (Ramón F. Suárez), editors (Gloria Piñeyro), and producers (León Ichaso, Orlando Jiménez Leal, Jorge Ulla, and Camilo Vila, among others) who facilitated the production of several films.

One of the first was *Guaguasí* (1977), a feature film shot in the Dominican Republic under the direction of Jorge Ulla. In addition to the actors associated with the center, the cast included Andy García (at that time still listed in the credits as Andrés García) in his debut. *Guaguasí* won the Silver Award at the Philadelphia Film Festival and was submitted for consideration as the Dominican Republic's offering in the Academy Awards' Best Foreign-Language Film category. The film tells the story of a peasant who joins the insurrectional struggle against Cuban leader Fulgencio Batista, but who, once the revolutionary triumph is achieved, gets dragged along by the violence of social change and gradually grows disenchanted. Camilo Vila's *Los gusanos* (The Worms), which premiered in October 1977 and was rereleased in 1980 for technical reasons, was another significant moment in film production. Recontextualizing *The Victors*, a play by the French existentialist Jean-Paul Sartre, the film narrates the adventures of a troop of exiles who return to the island with the goal of rescuing an officer and are captured by the revolutionary forces.

Of all the films made during this period, the one with the greatest impact is *El súper* (The Super, 1979), by León Ichaso and Orlando Jiménez Leal, based on the play of the same name by Iván Acosta. Widely recognized, it earned the Grand Prize at the 1979 Mannheim-Heidelberg International Film Festival in Germany and was screened at the Venice International Film Festival that year. The film looks at the difficult lives of a Cuban exile family in New York City, marking perhaps the first time a Cuban filmmaker portrayed exile as something other than an automatic form of improvement or salvation. Ichaso (b. 1948) is the most prolific director of the group in terms of feature films: *Crossover Dreams* (1985), *Sugar Hill* (1993), *Azúcar amarga* (Bitter Sugar, 1996), *Piñero* (2001), *El cantante* (The Singer, 2006), and *Paraíso* (Paradise, 2009). Not all deal with Cuban themes, but his Cuban trilogy (*El súper*, *Azúcar amarga*, and *Paraíso*) attempts to capture the turning points of Cuban life, both on and off the island.

THE 1980s

In the 1980s films made by Cubans in the diaspora were even more thematically diverse. Although the anti-Castro focus did not disappear, as indicated by the documentaries of Néstor Almendros, Orlando Jiménez Leal, and Jorge Ulla, among others, directors addressed new problems. Almendros (1930–1992), one of the great cinematographers and a collaborator of the French director François Truffaut, finished two projects during the 1980s that gave rise to much discussion. The first, made in France under the French title *Mauvaise Conduite* (1984) and released in the United States as *Improper Conduct*, deals with the so-called moral purges, beginning in 1964, of those considered to have engaged in improper conduct and whom the government sent to camps known as Unidades Militares para la Ayuda de Producción (UMAP; Military Units to Aid Production); the film specifically addresses the regime's mistreatment of gays. *Nadie escuchaba* (1987), made in the United States, where it was released as *Nobody Listened*, exposes human rights abuses in Cuba.

The mass exodus of Cubans during the Mariel Boatlift in 1980 earned the attention of more than a few filmmakers. Some films, such as Ulla's *En sus propias palabras* (In Their Own Words, 1980), offer a testimonial gaze that tries to record the arrival of compatriots to the United States. Others take a comedic look at the impact on the Cuban community of the arrival of the *marielitos*, as in *¡Qué caliente está Miami!* (Miami Is So Hot!, 1980), by Ramón Barco, with Blanquita Amaro. In a more reserved reflection, Miñuca Villaverde's *Ciudad de carpas* (Tent City, 1984), addresses the situation of those who, once in the United States, had to wait for an official pronouncement as to their status. Iván Acosta's *Amigos* (Friends, 1985) is the first (and possibly the only as of 2011) fictional feature film to explore the challenge faced by those Cubans stigmatized as *marielitos* in gaining entry into the society of the so-called historic exiles—who immediately noted the economic, and even ethnic, differences between themselves and the new arrivals and at first showed more fear than solidarity. Acosta also made *Candido: Hands of Fire* (2005), a video documentary about the great Cuban conga player.

THE 1990s AND EARLY 2000s

The Mariel phenomenon has remained an obsession of Cuban filmmakers. The award-winning documentary by Lisandro Pérez-Rey, *Más allá del mar* (Beyond the Sea, 2003), explores that migratory event twenty years later, appealing to the memories of some of its protagonists and presenting photos and images from that time. The particular characteristics of the later 1994 wave of migration, known as "the crisis of the rafters," inserted a new subject into the films of the diaspora, though not until 2006 did the short film *Pies secos, pies mojados* (Wet Feet, Dry Feet), directed by Carlos Gutiérrez and with performances by Francisco Gattorno and Jorge Luis Álvarez, give the subject dramatic significance. Two documentaries on this subject are *¿Adios patria?* (Farewell Homeland?, 1996) by Alex Antón and Joe Cardona, and *Marcadas por el paraíso* (Marked by Paradise, 1999) by Mari Rodriguez Ichaso, which focuses on the perspective of women. Cardona has made documentaries about the Pedro Pans (1999), referring to the 1960–1962 operation supported by the U.S. government in which thousands of parents in Cuba voluntarily sent their children into exile in Miami, as well as the Cuban national hero José Martí (2002), and the famed salsa singer Celia Cruz (2008).

Perhaps the most important film of the Cuban diaspora in the early twenty-first century is *Memorias del desarrollo* (Memories of Development, 2010), by Miguel Coyula, a young filmmaker living in New York. Although the film is not exactly a sequel to *Memorias del subdesarrollo* (Memories of Underdevelopment, 1968), by Tomás Gutiérrez Alea, almost unanimously considered the most significant work in the history of Revolutionary film, the tendency to think of the two films as two sides of the same coin is inevitable. Coyula's film tries to undo the habitual, reflexive language used to speak of Cuban cinema by combining flashbacks, daydreams, and visions; live-action, animation, and newsreel footage; multiple locations and multiple languages. Furthermore, Coyula performed multiple roles: writer, director, editor, photographer, and musician. His film challenges assumptions as far as what makes a Cuban project Cuban.

Two Cuban American women filmmakers, Ruth Behar and Vivien Lesnik Weisman, also merit attention. Behar's *Adio Kerida* (Goodbye Dear Love, 2002), a documentary about her family (in the United States) and the Jewish community in Cuba, is a film about memory and faith, with a poetic sensibility. Lesnik's 2007 documentary *The Man of Two Havanas* deals with the life of her father, Max Lesnik, who fought with the 26th of July Movement but later opposed the Revolution and fled to Miami, where he founded the magazine *Réplica*. His opposition to the embargo and refusal to join in the vehement anti-Castro sentiment of Miami's Cuban exile community was costly: Bombs were placed in the magazine's offices on eleven occasions. Notwithstanding the seriousness of the film's themes—politics, exile, terrorism, revolution—it is made with a large dose of humor and compassion.

In terms of both subject matter and form, the cinema of the Cuban diaspora remains a field ripe for scholarly attention. One of the most intriguing issues is the effectiveness of a concept of Cuban cinema that considers only the territorial, ethnic, and ideological aspects of the work without also analyzing the place of diasporic Cuban cinema in the evolving global world of art and ideas.

BIBLIOGRAPHY

García Borrero, Juan Antonio, ed. "Cine cubano: Nación, diáspora e identidad." Festival Internacional de Cortometraje y Cine Alternativo de Benalmádena, Spain, 2006.

Johnson, Mariana. "Imperfect Distance: Contemporary Cuban Film and Media Across the Florida Straits." Ph.D. diss., New York University, 2006.

López, Ana. "Cuban Cinema in Exile: The Other Island." *Jump Cut* 38 (June 1993): 51–59. Available from http://www.ejumpcut.org.

■ *See also*

Economy: Special Period

Film: 1989–2010

THE FILMS OF JORGE MOLINA AND EDUARDO DEL LLANO

Alberto Ramos Ruiz

Two independent filmmakers whose work embodies a challenge to the production model, aesthetic project, and ideological discourse of the Cuban film industry.

The work of Jorge Molina (b. 1966) represents a true anomaly in the history of national cinema. Under the auspices of his alma mater—the Escuela de Cine y Televisión de San Antonio de los Baños (EICTV; San Antonio de los Baños International School of Film and Television), from which he graduated in 1992 and for which he later performed a variety of intra- and extracurricular roles—Molina created visionary and provocative films, including eight fiction shorts, two documentaries, and one full-length feature, *Molina's Ferozz* (2010; *Ferozz: The Wild Riding Hood*, 2010). This is no small accomplishment for any producer in Cuba after the fall of the socialist bloc; the Film Institute itself acknowledged the blows the industry took in the way of a drastic reduction in film production and the exodus of technicians and artists due to the economic crisis of the 1990s and its aftermath.

Filming with a minimal amount of capital contributed by friends, nongovernmental agencies, and occasional funding from regional film organizations, such as Cinergia, Molina made his presence felt with his inventiveness, passion, and an encyclopedic knowledge of the history of film. Ignored by the Cuban audiovisual industry—for which his no-holds-barred exploitation of certain of the most difficult and disturbing varieties of film genre (particularly gore and porn) is clearly a scandalous transgression against the socialist moral ideal—Molina instead was transformed into its *enfant terrible* and a point of reference for new generations of Cuban filmmakers.

His films are nothing short of interior voyages toward knowledge through the experience of pleasure and desire, a carnal knowledge in which sex elicits psychological pain, and frequently conjures up his male protagonists' repressed demons or alter egos, an array that includes serial killers, the sanctimonious, ex-cons, and petty thieves, won over by the shapely bodies of insatiable women who look like they have come from the Mexican *film noir* of Juan Orol. Groveling whores, shameless schoolgirls, old hussies, and ghostly virgins—the gallery of women is worthy of the great filmmakers to whom Molina continuously alludes and pays homage. It is a cosmopolitan genealogy that he proudly declared himself heir to, one that includes Whale, Romero, Hooper, Cronenberg, Jodorowsky, Franco, Bava, Franju, Argento, and Fulci, among others. He confessed that his style amounts to a love of allusions, whose origins go back to a precocious love of cinema; based on it, in postmodern fashion, he constructed his hallucinatory trash interpretations of the classics. *El hombre que hablaba con Marte* (The Man Who Spoke with Mars, 2009), for example, is a masterly *tour de force* in which *Psycho*, *Vertigo*, and *The Shining* converge, together with references to Wong Kar-wai, the culture of the serials, and American detective films of the 1930s.

If, as the title of one of artist Francisco José de Goya y Lucientes's etchings says, "the sleep of reason produces monsters," then sex, according to Molina (in a long tradition going back to Buñuel and terminating in trash and countercultural films) is responsible for unleashing these monsters in all their destructive violence. As the director himself made clear, moving from this to horror, or rather the horrific, as part of the human experience requires but a single step. But it is a step of great consequence, bearing the context in mind. In contrast to the brief, insipid bedroom scene that has been de rigueur in films both inside and outside of Cuba, Molina's are hotbeds of blood and desire, of voluptuous nudes and never-ending copulation, of torn bodies, martyrs in the name of passion, suspended between dreaming and wakefulness, in that confused zone from which the darkest instincts emerge and in which the abominable and bestial rule. As far as that goes, the very name of his production company, La Tiñosa Autista (The Autistic Vulture) offers an interpretation worth taking into account, since it not only sums up, in the figure of the carrion bird, the choice of that which is supposedly disagreeable and aberrant, but also his lack of interest in the immediate reality of contemporary Cuba and in the institutional discourse of film on it.

Unlike Jorge Molina, whose world essentially feeds on cinematographic tradition, the points of reference of Eduardo del Llano (b. 1962) include his own written work and the legacy of Cuban radio and television sketches, as well as the literature and theater of the absurd. A 1995 graduate of the University of Havana with a degree in art history, del Llano became well known as a writer in Cuba and abroad, where several volumes of his short stories and novels have been published. He was also the founder of the theater group Nos-y-otros (1982–1997), which revolutionized the comedy scene with its enthusiasm for satire of politics and high culture. In addition, he worked as a scriptwriter for important Cuban directors such as Fernando Pérez, Daniel Díaz Torres, and Gerardo Chijona.

In 2004 del Llano's production company Sex Machine released *Monte Rouge*, the first in a series of ten shorts devoted to Nicanor O'Donnell, the enlightened antihero who is an incarnation of the Cuban common man and his daily struggles ("Each of us carries a Nicanor inside us," the theme song says). By late 2010, nine installments had been completed. Del Llano surrounded himself with a team of regular collaborators that included Luis Alberto García and Néstor Jiménez, popular Cuban actors cast in the respective roles of Nicanor and Rodríguez, Nicanor's eternal antagonist.

The character Nicanor first appeared in del Llano's fiction, in such works as the novel *La clessidra de Nicanor* (Nicanor's Hourglass, 1997) and the short story "Los viajes de Nicanor" (Nicanor's Journeys, 2000). For that reason, the film series can be seen as an extension of del Llano's journey as an author and scriptwriter. A good part of this trajectory is framed inside sociopolitical comedy, the most memorable example of which bears del Llano's stamp as scriptwriter: *Alicia en el pueblo de Maravillas* (Alice in Wondertown, 1991, directed by Daniel Díaz Torres). This surrealistic satire concerns the imperfections of socialism and caused an unheard-of crisis of confidence between the Revolution's leadership and the Instituto Cubano del Arte e Industria Cinematográficos (ICAIC) that pushed the institute to the edge of dissolution.

If indeed *Monte Rouge* generated some momentary discomfort, the fact is that the nine chapters were screened and honored at film festivals and were extensively circulated throughout the country, thanks in good measure to the wonders of digital technology but also to a higher threshold of official tolerance, compared to the violent campaign to discredit and censure *Alicia* in the early 1990s. Compared with that film, the Nicanor series is much more daring and transparent in its criticism of the dysfunctional nature of Cuban socialism. By the time viewers have

Filmmaker Eduardo del Llano (b. 1962), 26 February 2005. Eduardo del Llano's short film *Monte rouge* (2004), a satire about Cuba's state security apparatus, broke taboos by criticizing the Cuban government. REUTERS/ CLAUDIA DAUT/LANDOV

reached the ninth installment, what they see through del Llano's relentless camera leads to something that is more than eloquent. Here is a superficial inventory of themes: paranoid vigilance (*Monte Rouge*), absence of economic realism (*High Tech*, 2005), the trivialization of history (*Photoshop*, 2006), the infantilization of the media (*Homo Sapiens*, 2006), the vice of unanimity (*Intermezzo*, 2008), the silence of the press (*Brainstorm*, 2009), the frustration of initiative (*Pas de Quatre*, 2009), double standards (*Aché*, 2010), and the syndrome of suspicion (*Pravda*, 2010). The director's strategy remains invariable: to naturalize the absurdity of the situations Nicanor finds himself in, to the point of irrationality, which becomes unbearable and enlightening. His work is comparable to the Polish absurdist playwright Slawomir Mrozek if he were rewritten by Brecht, the latter providing stylized dialogs infused by a pompous rhetoric that infiltrates and degrades Cubans' speech. Songs are also a Brechtian device. The lyrics of the introductory ballad continue throughout the series while the musical setting, like the different incarnations of Nicanor, changes in every episode, including rock, tango, *guaracha*, and *ranchera*. The song for the closing credits, on the other hand, delivers a recapitulation with a "moral."

Regarding Mrozek, his influence is evident in the elegance of narrative design and a sad disenfranchised humor, typically East European, which excuses our catharsis in the name of intelligence.

BIBLIOGRAPHY

Goldberg, Ruth. "Sex and Death, Cuban Style: The Dark Vision of Jorge Molina." In *Fear Without Frontiers: Horror Cinema across the Globe*, edited by Steven Jay Schneider. Godalming, U.K.: FAB Press, 2003.

■

FLORIDA

Gerald E. Poyo

Florida's important role in Cuba's independence from Spain.

During the final third of the nineteenth century, Florida's Cuban communities played an important role in promoting and inciting the Cuban independence movement against Spain. Florida's prosperous cigar manufacturing centers with dozens of Cuban-owned factories and a mostly Cuban workforce supported a militant nationalist movement that continually provided resources for revolutionary propaganda and insurrection, support unmatched even by wealthier communities in New York and other centers.

Key West and Jacksonville hosted the first nationalist communities during the 1870s and early 1880s, but a fire that destroyed one-third of Key West in 1886 expanded the Cuban presence in Florida. Cigar entrepreneurs searching for new locales in which to build their factories moved to the Tampa Bay area and Ocala, where thousands of workers supported the establishment of new nationalist centers. Among the many insurgent leaders who repeatedly visited Florida to raise funds for the rebellion was Francisco V. Aguilera (1821–1877), vice president of the Cuban republic-in-arms, who in 1874 characterized Key West as the *baluarte de la libertad* (bulwark of liberty), a term that described Florida's communities more generally. Florida's leaders, especially those in Key West, regularly and with pride applied this sobriquet to their community throughout the struggle for independence. The discourse of revolution in Florida became more radical in the 1880s, and the posture eventually was embraced by Cuba's most celebrated nationalist figure, José Martí (1853–1895), whose leadership inspired the second war of independence against Spain. Writing in 1900, the Methodist reverend Manuel Deulofeu declared these communities to be the "most firm and powerful supporters of rights and liberties" (Deulofeu p. 5). Later writers cemented Floridians' historical place as central and indispensable actors in Cuba's independence struggle.

NATIONALIST COMMUNITIES

Cuban communities harnessed a patriotic spirit that imbued family households, political clubs, social organizations, newspapers, cigar factory floors, and schools with a deep commitment to the nationalist cause. Intimate dinner conversations at home among family members expressed and transmitted patriotic values and aspirations for a future that included Cuba. The Club Patriótico Cubano (1869) and Asociación Patriótica del Sur (1874) and the newspapers *El Republicano* (1870) and *La Igualdad* (1876) were the first such enterprises in Key West, which inspired similar clubs and newspapers throughout the nineteenth century in Jacksonville, Tampa, and Ocala. Though men led most political organizations and published the newspapers, women formed their own grassroots organizations, including Hijas de la Libertad (1878) in Key West, which raised funds through bazaars, patriotic celebrations, and direct appeals. In the cigar factories *lectores* read novels, plays, and newspapers to workers as they rolled cigars, constantly reminding them of their nationalist obligations to the homeland. In bars, cafes, social clubs, and on street corners in fiery speeches, nationalist orators solidified community claims to identity and culture, often becoming celebrities in their own right. New insurgent generations emerged from Cuban schools that promoted exile culture, values, and political perspectives among the young. In 1871, Cubans in Key West founded the Instituto San Carlos, which among other activities provided their children schooling in a totally Cuban environment. Though they were welcome at San Carlos school, many black and mulatto Cubans in Key West preferred their own school, El Progreso. Informal schools organized in New York, Tampa, and Key West encouraged tobacco workers and others to advance their education and embrace nationalist ideals.

Enduring public rituals and patriotic symbols also enhanced nationalist culture. Each historical era produced martyrs and heroes who became the subjects of annual commemorations and processions. Monuments offered a visual reminder of their exile reality, especially the obelisk dedicated to Cubans killed in the anti-Spanish struggles erected in Key West's cemetery in 1892, which serves in the early 2000s as a reminder of the nineteenth-century exile experience. The innumerable ways exiles raised awareness of the Cuban question played a critical role in maintaining loyalty to the homeland and an exile consciousness that became a central feature of community life.

DEFENDING THE *BALUARTE*

Despite many challenges, Florida's leaders maintained the integrity of their communities and ensured the endurance of the nationalist cause. Throughout the 1880s, the expanding Florida cigar industry attracted not only Cubans but also thousands of Spanish workers who mostly expressed ambivalence or open opposition to Cuban independence. Spanish immigrants threatened the demographic dominance of Cuban

workers, and many brought radical labor ideologies, particularly anarchism, that challenged nationalist ascendancy. Nationalists blocked Spanish immigration through various strategies, including pressing factory owners to reject Spanish employees and encouraging Cuban-dominated unions to prohibit Spanish membership. They also formed vigilante organizations that intimidated arriving Spaniards.

These strategies often caused division in their communities. During early 1887, nationalists in Ybor City sought to block Spaniards from entering the factories, but Tampa's Board of Trade reacted by intimidating and expelling Cuban nationalists, hoping to avoid the escalating ethnic conflicts that threatened economic disruptions. Particularly distressing to the nationalist leadership was the growing number of traditionally nationalist Cuban workers attracted to anarchist ideas. The Havana-based anarchist newspaper *El Productor* regularly criticized the nationalist press, and numerous labor newspapers edited by Cubans supporting the labor movement appeared in Key West and Ybor City, including *El Ecuador* and *La Revista de Florida* (Ramón Rivero y Rivero), *La Tribuna del Trabajo* (Carlos Baliño), *El Pueblo* (Martín Morúa Delgado), and *El Buñuelo* (Enrique Creci). Though divisive debates among Cuban nationalist leaders about the wisdom of challenging the Spanish community and criticizing Cuban anarchists threatened dangerous political splits and the viability of the nationalist message, *El Yara* (José D. Poyo) and *La Propaganda* (José R. Estrada) continually reinforced the nationalist discourse. After Spanish repression of the anarchist movement in Havana in the early 1890s, many Cuban and Spanish anarchists concluded that

only the island's independence from Spain offered the possibility of sufficient freedom to promote their cause, defusing tensions in exile and opening the way for renewed unity in the nationalist community.

Cubans also protected their nationalist communities through participation in Florida politics. They learned to use the political system to promote their own local economic and social interests, but also harnessed their electoral power to encourage Anglo-American support, or at least tolerance, for their nationalist projects. When Cubans arrived in Key West during the 1870s, they entered a community deeply engaged in post–Civil War Reconstruction politics. Allowed to vote after only six months' residence, white and black Cubans initially joined the dominant Republican Party, which appointed many Cubans to federal, county, and city offices, including county judges, justices of the peace, and customs house officials. In the 1875 city council elections, Carlos Manuel de Céspedes, the son of Cuba's insurgent president, was elected mayor. Cubans also became active in the Democratic Party when it gained ascendancy in Florida.

For the most part, local interests determined Cuban party affiliation, and only threats to their ethnic and especially nationalist interests mobilized and united them in the political arena. In 1884, Cubans elected Fernando Figueredo (1846–1929) to the Florida legislature after an unprecedented and aggressive campaign by local officials to arrest and prosecute activists involved in launching an expedition by the guerrilla Carlos Agüero (d. 1885). Likewise, in 1889, the Cuban voters elected Manuel Patricio Delgado and Manuel Moreno to both Monroe County seats in the legislature in response to another effort by local officials to punish nationalists for pressing local cigar manufacturers to donate to an expedition. The next year, José Pómpez also won election to the assembly. In each case, Cubans responded to perceived threats to their nationalist interests with a unified ethnic vote that sent Cubans to the state legislature.

REVOLUTION

Throughout the 1870s, Key West nationalists did what they could to support the Cuban rebellion. With the Spanish undefeated, the war ended in 1878 with a treaty known as the Zanjón Pact; a new outbreak, *La guerra chiquita* (The little war), also supported by Florida, raised the hopes of revolutionaries before it too was defeated. After Cuba was finally pacified in 1880, most Cubans in the exile communities lost confidence in revolutionary solutions, and many embraced political reforms in exchange for peace promised by Spain. Key West activists, however, rejected Cuba's pacification, insisting the war had not ended but was simply in abeyance. José Francisco Lamadríz (1814–1892), José Dolores Poyo (1837–1911), and Fernando Figueredo took the lead in reorganizing and promoting revolutionary activities and convincing cigar workers and manufacturers to continue to back nationalist goals. The eldest, Lamadríz, an attorney, had been involved in separatist politics in New York since the 1850s, and in the 1870s he sided against the conservative sectors that sought negotiated peace and pacification. Much admired as an experienced, credible, and committed insurgent, Lamadríz moved to Key West in 1879. A community organizer, reader in the cigar factories, and editor of nationalist newspapers, Poyo arrived in Key West in 1869 and became a master propagandist and intransigent revolutionary. For twenty years his newspaper *El Yara*, founded in 1878, maintained a constant drumbeat for revolution and opposing compromises with Spain. Also in 1878 he founded a secret organization, Orden del Sol, to encourage the formation of patriotic clubs dedicated to provoking revolution in Cuba. Figueredo, who worked as a bookkeeper in the cigar factories, was a military veteran who arrived in Key West after participating in Antonio Maceo's failed effort to revive the dying insurrection known as the Protesta de Baraguá. The three rejected out of hand reformers' calls for Cuban autonomy within the Spanish empire as a viable alternative to absolute independence, and in 1880, they organized Key West for what turned out to be an eighteen-year fight against Spanish colonialism.

The nationalist community's revolutionary strategies included funding guerrilla operations, organizing expeditions for invasion, and urging the formation of revolutionary cells in Cuba. Its members appealed to military veterans of the Ten Years'

War, especially Máximo Gómez (1836–1905) and Antonio Maceo (1845–1896) in Honduras, to head a new revolutionary effort. Initially, two other veterans, Carlos Agüero and Ramón Bonachea (1845–1885), took up the torch and received financial support in Key West to establish guerrilla operations in Cuba while they waited for Gómez and Maceo to commit. Many in Key West also urged the use of dynamite as a so-called scientific tool of warfare, manufacturing it in their homes and smuggling it into Cuba for the insurgents. Before long, the two guerrilla leaders lost their lives in Cuba, but Gómez and Maceo promised an invasion to carry on the work of the martyred fighters. Key West's cigar workers and manufacturers provided tens of thousands of dollars for the Gómez-Maceo initiative, but they too failed, never landing in Cuba. To make matters worse, the Key West fire in 1886 left thousands of workers unemployed, increasingly attracted to anarchist labor organizing, and in no mood or position to continue donating resources to the nationalists.

Lacking the financial means to raise expeditions, nationalist leaders embraced a new strategy promoted by a new breed of insurgent activists who had operated in Cuba as bandits and fled to Florida in the mid-1880s. Politicized by listening to revolutionary *lectores* and orators in the Key West and Ybor City cigar factories, reading the nationalist newspapers, and simply experiencing the nationalist ambience, these men proposed raising funds for the revolution by kidnapping and ransoming wealthy plantation owners in Cuba. Though some traditional leaders in Key West expressed discomfort with this strategy, Poyo and Juan Fernández Ruz, a Ten Years' War veteran, dispatched an expedition led by former bandits Manuel García (1851–1895) and Manuel Beribén. Within days of landing Spanish soldiers killed Beribén, but García—who became popularly known as *Rey de los campos* (King of the countryside)—for the next eight years in the name of *Cuba libre* kidnapped and ransomed wealthy individuals and sent funds to his supporters in Key West.

In late 1889, nationalists in Key West again refined their strategies and turned to encouraging and supporting the establishment of revolutionary cells in Cuba, an effort organized by a new secret society known as the Convención Cubana, also led by Lamadríz, Poyo, and Figueredo. In early 1890, Maceo received an amnesty and returned to Cuba feigning reconciliation with Spain and conspiring to spark an uprising. He contacted insurgents throughout the island, including Manuel García, and asked nationalists in Key West and Tampa to prepare an expedition to support the insurrection. Veterans Perico Torres and Rosendo García led the organizing efforts, but after learning of the conspiracy, Spanish authorities ordered Maceo to leave Cuba, forcing the Florida exiles to abandon preparations.

Cuban market in 1762 during the English occupation of the island, but they were later blocked in favor of Spanish merchants.

AFRO-CUBAN CUSTOMS

From the end of the eighteenth century, Cuba was profoundly transformed by the establishment of the plantation model for producing sugar. The conversion of the island into the world's principal exporter of sugar created lavish fortunes for a few, but it also reduced the production of food for the internal market, creating an excessive dependence on imports that continued into the early twenty-first century.

Sugar plantations required a large slave population, generating a demand for food that farmlands dedicated mostly to sugarcane could not satisfy. The best solution in terms of price, food preservation, transportation, and nutrition was massive importation of dried beef from the United States, Argentina, and Uruguay, and of salted cod from Canada, Europe, and the United States. These two foods were the basis of the slaves' daily fare. The dried beef encouraged the Cubans' fondness for meat, even at the lowest levels of the social ladder. Cod, rice or corn, and plantains or tubers filled out the diet of slaves, as well as peasants and the urban poor. In modern times, a range of African foods that arrived on the slave ships are eaten in Cuba, including *quingombó* (okra), *frijol de carita* (seasoned black-eyed peas), sesame seeds, varieties of *ñame* (yam) and *malanga*, *banano* (a type of banana), and guinea fowl.

Vestiges of African cuisine were preserved because many slaves worked as cooks in the houses of affluent whites, and other blacks and free mulattoes worked as street vendors, selling the sweets they prepared. Although most of these dishes remain only for use in Afro-Cuban religious rituals, some African food traditions endure in Cuban cooking in modern times.

The African predilection for *papillas* (a puree made of boiled tubers, legumes, or cereals with rice or corn) can be seen in the Cuban customs of eating native tubers and cooking dried corn kernels that have been ground into a flour and then combined with other ingredients; this tradition contrasts with the Latin American custom of making tortillas and *arepas* (cornmeal rolls). Also particular to Cuban cuisine is the practice of seasoning one type of food after it has been cooked with the sauces of another food, as is typical in the preparation of rice, which is flavored after cooking with the marinade from the main dish. Unripe plantains are cut lengthwise for frying then pounded before returning them to the pan, in the Congolese style; ripe plantains are sliced into cross sections, in the Yoruba style.

PREVAILING CUSTOMS

The combination of these diverse culinary influences produced food customs widespread throughout Cuba. One example is the traditional Cuban Christmas dinner, which consists of well-roasted pig, turkey, stewed guinea fowl and chicken, white rice, and black beans; a salad made of lettuce, tomato, and radishes; and, for dessert, *turrones* (nougat candies), *membrillos* (quinces), hazelnuts, walnuts, *buñuelos* (fritters), coffee, and a Cuban cigar. This is primarily a banquet of Spanish and Arab lineage, with the addition of the native Cuban cigar, African guinea fowl, and coffee, and the Mesoamerican turkey, tomato, and black beans.

The Cuban habits of consuming large amounts of fat and preparing mixed rice dishes comes down from the Arab-Andalusians, who tended to fry their foods, and the Africans, who added fat to foods to increase their fat content; this was a custom from southern Spain, as well as the Gold Coast of Africa. The most common forms of cooking in Cuba are frying, from the Andalusians, and boiling, from the indigenous peoples, Andalusians, and Africans. Roasting is associated with emblematic dishes eaten on special days—pork and red snapper.

Characteristic of Cuban gastronomy is its liberal use of a variety of spices. Since the sixteenth century, Spanish ships consecutively known as the *Nao de China* (galleon from China) embarked from the Philippines laden with cinnamon, pepper, cloves, nutmeg, anise, ginger, saffron, and sesame seeds and landed in Acapulco before continuing on to Havana. Foods grown in Europe—garlic, onions, thyme, marjoram, oregano, cumin, sage, mustard, and vinegar—arrived with the Spanish fleets.

The introduction of sugarcane stimulated Cubans' sweet tooth. It is still common to find sweet commingling with sour in the same dish, a custom brought by the Arabs to Andalusia, and sweet with salty, which was typical of European cooking at the time of the Spanish arrival in Cuba. The amalgam of this cuisine is shown in the typical fritters, sweetened or plain, made of flour from indigenous tubers.

Preference for meat reduced fish to a lower status. Because fishing was more costly than cattle farming, it was only in the nineteenth century that the waters of Campeche and Florida began to be fished, and the catches were consumed by the affluent along with the great variety of meat. Until then, only Cubans living near rivers ate the later extinct freshwater fish.

The extravagant oligarchy frequently combined French and *criollo* dishes and service styles, although they preferred the criollo. The protocol for serving, following Andalusian etiquette, began with soups, broths, or hotpot stews as appetizers, meat or fish—or both—for the main course, and sweets with lots of sugar to finish. Casseroles, known as the *entrante* (starter) and later as an entrée, were served after the fish but before the roasted meat. Dinner concluded with strong black coffee, cigarillos and cigars, and toothpicks artistically decorated with colored feathers.

Coffee is still a widespread habit, and it is obligatory for hosts to offer it to guests. Drinks were chilled with ice from the nineteenth century on, when ice was imported from New England wrapped in bags filled with sawdust.

BIBLIOGRAPHY

Aguilera Pleguezuelo, José. *Las cocinas árabe y judía y la cocina española*. Málaga, Spain: Editorial Arguval, 2002.

Atkins, Edwin F. *Sixty Years in Cuba*. Cambridge, MA: Riverside Press, 1926.

Ballou, Maturin M. *Due South: Or, Cuba Past and Present*. 10th ed. Cambridge, MA: Riverside Press, 1898.

Cárcer Disdier, Mariano de. *Apuntes para la historia de la transculturación Indoespañola*. Mexico City: Universidad Nacional Autónoma de México, 1995.

Cassá, Roberto. *Los indios de las Antillas*. Madrid: Editorial Mapfre, 1992.

Chateausalins, Honorato Bernard de. *El vademécum de los hacendados cubanos o guía práctica para curar la mayor parte de las enfermedades*. Havana: Imprenta de Manuel Soler, 1854.

Coloma Garcés, Eugenio de. *Manual del cocinero cubano*. 2nd ed. Havana: Imprenta de Spencer, 1856.

Colón, Cristóbal. *Diario de a bordo*. Madrid: Ediciones y Distribuciones Promo Libro, 2003.

Fernández de Oviedo, Gonzalo. *Sumario de la natural historia de las Indias*, edited by José Miraud. Mexico City: Fondo de Cultura Económica, 1950.

Guerra, Ramiro, ed. *Historia de la nación cubana*. 10 vols. Havana: Cultural S.A., 1952.

Hammer, Karl, Miguel Esquivel, and Helmmut Knupffe. *Origin, Evolution and Diversity of Cuban Plants Genetic Resources*. Haberstadt, Germany: Buch-und Offsetdruck Lüders D-O.3600, 1992.

Hazard, Samuel. *Cuba a pluma y lápiz*. 3 vols. Havana: Cultural S.A., 1928.

Hyatt, Pulaski F., and John T. Hyatt. *Cuba: Its Resources and Opportunities*. New York: J. S. Ogilvie Publishing Company, 1898.

Legrán, José P. *Nuevo manual del cocinero cubano y español*. Havana: Imprenta y taller de encuadernación La Fortuna, c. 1880.

Le Riverand, Julio. *Historia económica de Cuba*. 4th ed. Havana: Instituto del Libro, 1974.

Marrero, Leví. *Cuba: Economía y sociedad*. 15 vols. Madrid: Editorial Playor S.A., 1977.

Moreno Fraginals, Manuel. *África en América Latina*. Mexico City: Siglo XXI, Editores S.A. and UNESCO, 1977.

Nobiatur, J. F. *El agricultor, horticultor, jardinero e higienista agrícola cubano*. 4 vols. Havana: Imprenta de Rosendo Espina, 1877–1879.

Ortiz, Fernando. *Los negros esclavos*. Havana: Editorial de Ciencias Sociales, 1975.

Pezuela, Jacobo de la. *Diccionario geográfico, estadístico, histórico de la Isla de Cuba*. 4 vols. Madrid: Imprenta del Establecimiento de Mellado, 1863.

Ramírez Corría, Filiberto. "La cultura condumial de los aborígenes cubanos." *Revista Universidad de La Habana* (March–April 1963): 143–163.

Sauer, Carl O. *The Early Spanish Man*. Los Angeles: University of California Press, 1966.

Tabío, Ernesto E., and Estrella Rey. *Prehistoria de Cuba*. Havana: Editorial de Ciencias Sociales, 1985.

Triay, José E. *Manual del cocinero criollo*. Havana: La Moderna Poesía, 1921.

FOOD: REPUBLICAN PERIOD

Joshua H. Nadel

The creation of Cuban national cuisine in the nineteenth and twentieth centuries.

Between 1990 and 2010, scholars from Sydney Mintz to Arjun Appadurai and Jeffrey Pilcher argued convincingly for food's importance to understanding both societies and nationalism (see Pilcher 1998; Appadurai; Mintz). What humans eat is an everyday, subconscious marker of identity that helps to shape ideas of self and nation; put another way, food is a form of what Michael Billig calls "banal nationalism" (Cusack). According to Blanche Zacharie de Baralt, who wrote the first Cuban cookbook for a foreign audience, cuisine is a "psychological aspect" of a country, representing a "synthesis of its civilization" (p. 8). Thus, changes in the way that people eat—how they cook their food, the mealtime ritual, what they ingest—implicate and reflect a host of other changes. In this light, Fernando Ortíz's definition of Cuban identity in terms of food bears even more significance. For the famed Cuban sociologist, the *ajiaco* represented the very creation of the nation: a long-simmering stew of indigenous and African vegetables, European meats, "mysterious spices" from China, and technology from the United States that produced something uniquely Cuban (Ortíz). Created from the multiple influences comprising Cuba, the *ajiaco* in turn sustained these influences and defined the continual process of cultural creation and re-creation. The creative process that culminated in what in the early 2000s is considered Cuban cuisine began the moment that Spaniards arrived on the island in 1511. Over the course of the next four centuries, cooks mixed elements of African, indigenous, European, and Asian food cultures to create food that was recognizably Cuban.

VARIETY AND AVAILABILITY OF FOODS

From the available evidence, in terms of the variety of food and caloric intake, on average Cubans in the early twentieth century ate well. Rice, beans, milk, vegetables, meat, and tubers were all readily available, and the Cuban diet was among the healthiest in the Americas. For example, in 1913, the average Cuban ate 60 pounds of meat per year. By 1918, this number had risen to 124 pounds per year, making Cuba the sixth largest per capita consumer of meat worldwide, behind Australia, New Zealand, the United States, Argentina, and Canada. By 1926, however, likely due to the downturn in sugar prices in the 1920s, meat consumption had dropped to below 60 pounds (*Anuario estadistico*; Lipman; Cuban Economic Research Project).

Though the data for the pre-Revolutionary era are not systematic, estimates for per capita caloric consumption range from 2,610 to 2,918 calories per day in the prewar era and hover around an average of 2,700 calories per day for the period from 1946 to 1949 (Schroeder; Office of Population Research; Food and Agricultural Organization of the United Nations 1946, 1952). According to the 1947 *Population Index*, Cuba ranked in the top twenty nations in terms of caloric intake and was behind only Argentina in Latin America (Office of Population Research, 1947). Yet in 1951, the International Bank for Reconstruction and Development estimated that between 30 and 40 percent of Cuba's urban population—and over 60 percent of the rural population—was malnourished (IBRD). Nevertheless, throughout the early twentieth century, a diverse array of meats, grains, tubers, vegetables, and beans comprised the Cuban diet, the basis of which was formed in the pre-Colombian era. (For more on per capita food consumption, see Cuban Economic Research Project.)

Prior to the arrival of the Spanish, Taíno foodways rested mainly on tubers such as boniato (white sweet potato), cassava (manioc), malanga (similar to taro), and ñame (yam); squash, peppers, corn, and beans; and animal protein from fish, turtles, crocodiles, and rodents (Rouse; Cassá; Keegan; Lamarche). Of these foods, the most important was cassava, which was made into bread and had religious value as well. The Taíno also cultivated fruits such as pineapple and guava. To this rich and varied diet, the Spanish both added and subtracted. Indigenous animal protein sources were hunted to extinction shortly after Spanish arrival, but others quickly took their place. Pigs, goats, and cattle all survived (with varying degrees of difficulty) in the Caribbean, as did chicken. Europeans added onions, garlic, olive oil, wheat, and chickpeas. From Africa came bananas, plantains, okra, pigeon peas, cabbage, and rice, among other important crops. Cultivation methods also played an important role, with the indigenous *conuco* mounds often replicated by enslaved Africans in their provision grounds.

Ingredients are one factor, however, and cuisine is another. Although people on the island were likely eating Cuban food as early as the 1500s—*ajiaco* often

is considered a descendant of the *olla española*, but it may also derive from the Taíno pepperpot—its codification and identification as Cuban began only in the nineteenth century. Cookbooks and recipes—printed in magazines, written on scraps of paper, handed down orally—played a crucial role in this transition, beginning in the mid-nineteenth century. Cookbooks perform a number of roles. At the most basic level, they play a supporting role in the domestic sphere by providing advice and instruction to family cooks. Their use implies literacy, which in turn suggests a level of education or social class. Yet recipes and literacy have a dialogic relationship: Illiterate cooks pass on recipes for people to write down, whereas literate people might read recipes to cooks. At the same time, they also provide a window into the past by displaying the types of food eaten—and considered appropriate—at a certain moment in time. Thus, over an extended period of time, cookbooks "reflect shifts in the boundaries of edibility" (Appadurai p. 3). The development of Cuban cookbooks may reflect the growing Cuban national consciousness of the era: The first compilations of recipes appeared in the period between Narciso López's failed filibustering expeditions in 1850 and 1851 and the boiling over of nationalist sentiment of the Ten Years' War in 1868. By the twentieth century, cookbook authors reflected a Cuban consciousness—one that was at once cosmopolitan and nationalist that culminated with the consolidation of the Cuban Revolution.

COOKBOOKS IN CUBA

The first cookbooks published in Cuba appeared in the 1850s. In the period between the *Manual del cocinero cubano* (Manual of Cuban Cuisine) in 1856 and the Cuban Revolution in 1959, roughly twenty cookbooks were published—not including new editions and reprints. These manuals, as that is essentially what cookbooks are, can be broken down into two rough categories: instructive and constructive. The former compiled all sorts of recipes, including Cuban food, or they highlighted a particular item (such as dessert, see *La sagüera, Utilisima colección ampliada de recetas probadas* [La sagüera, The Latest Expanded Collection of Proven Recipes, 1923]) or technology, such as an electric stove. Constructive cookbooks, by contrast, actively sought to define Cuban cuisine both to Cubans and to the world. There is a good deal of crossover in these categories: In one way or another they all defined Cuban cooking—if not Cuban cuisine—at a particular moment in time. That is, they all give a taste of the types of food served on Cuban tables.

Nineteenth Century From available sources, there were four cookbooks published in Cuba during the nineteenth century. Eugenio de Coloma y Garcés published the *Manual del cocinero cubano* (Manual of the Cuban Chef) in 1856, with a second edition the following year. The *Nuevo manual del cocinero cubano y* *española* (New Manual of the Cuban and Spanish Chef) by J. P. Legran and *Nuevo manual de la cocinera catalana y cubana* (New Manual of Catalan and Cuban Chef) by Juan Cabrisas were published in 1857 and 1858, respectively. Finally, Enrique Langarika's *El cocinero de los enfermos, convalecientes y desganados* (The Chef for the Sick, Convalescent, and the Listless), containing recipes aimed at healing the sick, was printed in 1862.

These four cookbooks fall into the instructive category. They compiled recipes for cooks in Cuba rather than offering only recipes for Cuban food. They offered little in the way of commentary about the importance or history of particular dishes. Rather than promoting Cuban food above others, the *Manual del cocinero cubano*, the *Nuevo manual del cocinero cubano y española*, and the *Nuevo manual de la cocinera catalana y cubana* incorporated Cuban cooking alongside continental cuisine, identifying Cuban dishes with phrases such as *a la criolla, a lo guajiro,* and *cubano*. Legran's book is also replete with recipes such as rabbit *a la española*, chicken *a la rusa*, bacalao *a la vizcaína*, and tongue *a la mejicana*. In other words, alongside Cuban cuisine, they included popular dishes from continental Europe and the Americas. Coloma y Garcés and Legran appeared to be more interested in selling cookbooks, offering recipes that would "bring good results" that the "general public" would appreciate (Legran). For Cabrisas, success was measured by whether he could provide recipes to please Spaniards and Cubans alike (Cabrisas; Dawdy).

At the same time, however, the three works—excluding Langarika—began the process of identifying Cuban food. Each book included a special section on Cuban desserts. Coloma y Garcés provided "the method for making sweets with all the fruits of this fertile soil," whereas Legran devoted his section to "sweets, cakes, and botilleria [bottling] in the Cuban style" (Coloma y Garcés; Legran). Moreover, both offered tips for adapting foreign recipes and foods to the Cuban tropical climate.

Perhaps more importantly, these early authors set in motion the process of compiling recipes from different regions of the country. According to Jeffrey Pilcher, this is one of the most important roles of cookbooks; by "encouraging the interchange of foods," they "help unify a country" (p. 3). Dishes that in the early 2000s are considered quintessentially Cuban appeared in multiple versions. Legran, for example, presented *picadillo* (ground or shredded beef sautéed with onion, green pepper, green olive, cinnamon, and cumin), fish *matancera* (from Matanzas), and pork chops *a lo guajiro* (peasant style). He also included recipes for three versions of *ajiaco*: *ajiaco, ajiaco de "tierra dentro"* [sic], and *ajiaco de Puerto Principe* (Camagüey). These dishes all have the same basic ingredients—boniato, ñame, onion, tomato, garbanzo beans, plantains, and chayote—but they reflect regional variation in taste, usually in the types

of meat added to the pot. At the same time, by placing them in one source, Legran united them as national foods. Similarly, Coloma y Garcés instructed cooks on recipes from the city of Trinidad, *ajiaco de monte, picadillo,* and *lechón a lo guajiro* (peasant-style suckling pig). For his part, Cabrisas explains many of the Cuban ingredients to his audience and includes recipes of African provenance such as *fufú*—a dish most commonly consisting of a mashed starch (primarily plantains in Cuba) served with rice and meat. Cabrisas offered two recipes: one of plantain and malanga and one of ñame, both of which he shaped into small balls and suggested serving either in soup or with *quimbombó* (okra) *criollo*.

Twentieth-Century Instructive Cookbooks If nineteenth-century cookbooks placed Cuban food on the table, the development of Cuban cooking to the level of cuisine began in earnest in the twentieth century. This should not be surprising: Independence brought about a greater pride in, and effort to define, all aspects of Cuban culture. At the same time, however, Cuban desire to identify the nation with the modern currents coming from the United States and Europe created a simultaneous cosmopolitanism that was reflected in food. Cookbooks and, increasingly in the twentieth century, recipes in magazines were an important indicator of this duality.

As in the nineteenth century, the majority of cookbooks and recipes remained steadfastly instructive. Recipe authors sought to modernize Cuba through cooking, providing quicker recipes using canned goods or electric stoves and increasingly bringing scientific precision into the kitchen. These changes signified Cuban acceptance of modernity and implied an adaptation of foreign norms. With the coming of the Cuban Revolution, food writers eschewed foreign food even as they embraced modern technology.

Most cookbooks of the early twentieth century fell into the instructive category, presenting Cuban and foreign dishes side by side. Of books such as María Antonieta Reyes Galivan y Moenck's *Delicias de la mesa* (Delicacies of the Table, 1923), Ernestina Varona de Mora's *Manual de la cocina moderna* (Manual of Modern Cooking, 1932), Berta Crespo y Setien's *El arte de bien guisar; o La cocina practica en Cuba* (The Art of Good Taste; or Practical Cooking in Cuba, 1926), Dolores Alfonso Rodríguez's *La cocina y el hogar* (The Kitchen and the Home, 1931), and Nitza Villapol's *Cocina al minuto* (Cooking in a Minute, 1954), none focused solely on national dishes. They included the island's food among the foreign recipes more as a reflection of what people ate than as an attempt to define a Cuban cuisine. That is, for example, in most twentieth-century Cuban cookbooks, *picadillo* shared the page with Chateaubriand, and *ajiaco* with lobster bisque. As in the nineteenth century, authors made no explicit effort to define Cuban food, save to append *a lo cubano* or *criollo* to a particular dish.

Dolores Alfonso y Rodríguez's *La cocina y el hogar* (1931), for example, advertised its "more than 1,500 recipes" on the cover. Like a later version of Legran's *Nuevo manual*, it eschewed both introduction and commentary. Instead, Alfonso, who was a professor of cooking and baking at the Escuela del Hogar in Havana, offered advice on other topics: how to master the "true art" of setting the table; how to invite guests to a dinner party (some "invitations should not be made by phone but rather in writing"); and how many servants were needed for an event. Because her book was aimed at social occasions for the middle and upper classes, the fact that Alfonso included Cuban recipes along with continental fare is important. Placing *sofrito* (the base of much Cuban cuisine: a sauté of finely chopped onion, pepper, garlic, spices, and occasionally tomato) on the same page as *salsa parisien* and in the same section as béchamel, and *ropa vieja* (Cuban-style brisket) together with "Roastbeef" [sic] suggests that Cubans proudly saw their cuisine as worthy of being served at dinner parties. At the same time, her work shows Cuba to be cosmopolitan in taste: Alfonso's fifteen daily menus include a little of everything, from shrimp cocktail to *ajiaco* and *boniato* to spaghetti with meatballs.

Twentieth-Century Constructive Cookbooks
José E. Triay, the editor of the Havana newspaper *El Diario de la Marina*, originally published the *Manual del cocinero criollo* (Manual of Creole Cuisine) in 1903, a second edition of which appeared in 1914. More than earlier Cuban cookbooks—and most that came after—his book justified its inclusion of Cuban food as spurred in part by the need to refine national cuisine in light of the "increased travel, frequent visits by foreigners and new hotels" (p. 8). Moreover, although it recognized Havana's cosmopolitan nature and palate, it also included dishes "so appreciated by our grandparents" that they were "conserved in their primitive simplicity" in the rural districts of Cuba.

Triay's book is most important for compiling regional variations of Cuban dishes. Triay listed two types of *olla cubano* and five *ajiacos*, as well as recipes for six different Cuban styles of soup, from *sopa de ajiaco* (made with the broth of *ajiaco*) to *sopa ala Habanera*. Similarly, Triay brought together *picadillos* from around the island, including *picadillo matancero*, *picadillo criollo*, and an haute cuisine version, *picadillo* with truffles for a turkey stuffing. Crucially, in Triay's book, foods of African provenance were included for the first time in the twentieth century, incorporating the immense influence of enslaved people on the Cuban pantry—and reflecting greater acceptance of Afro-Cubans in the aftermath of independence. To

Ropa vieja. Ropa vieja, a popular Cuban stew made of shredded beef in tomato sauce with peppers and onions, was brought to Cuba by immigrants from the Canary Islands. LEW ROBERTSON/GETTY IMAGES

that end, Triay offered three types of *fufú*, as well as okra in two different regional styles. Along with African food, he devoted entire sections to "the meat of the poor"—*tasajo* (salted meat) and *bacalao* (salt cod), which was "served equally on rich and poor tables." In describing for his presumably Cuban readers the range of *picadillos*, the importance of *tasajo* to peasants, and the popularity of *bacalao*, Triay codified these foods as acceptable for all Cubans to eat, thus unifying the country through the humble food of the rural poor and people of African descent.

If uniting the country through food was Triay's goal, Blanche Zacharie de Baralt's was to put the country's best food forward. Her 1931 *Cuban Cookery: Gastronomic Secrets of the Tropics, with an Appendix on Cuban Drinks* could easily be mistaken for a text that sought to exoticize Cuba for a foreign audience (along the lines of travel guides of the period), but Baralt's credentials as a Cuban nationalist could not be criticized; an earlier book describes in detail her friendship with José Martí, the apostle of Cuban independence. In any case, Baralt's cookbook is an early example of a constructive book: it explicitly purported to compile Cuban recipes, proudly placing on foreign tables "the typical [dishes] of the country ... which are well worthy of being known and relished by a wider public" (p. 7). She recognized with pride the multiple influences on Cuban food, "directly derived from Spain" but "modified and refined" by indigenous ingredients, as well as African and Asian methods and ingredients. Perhaps to make Cuban cuisine seem a little more "civilized," however, Baralt could not leave out the possibility that Cuban food had a "French touch imported from Santo Domingo" (p. 9).

Like Triay, Baralt offered some commentary on her dishes, explaining to her foreign audience that, for example, salt cod *a la vizcaína*, though Spanish, was "so typical that to omit it might be considered a sin" (p. 36) and that *picadillo*, "a homely dish," was "served at all Cuban breakfast tables" (p. 51). She also analyzed some regional variations on dishes, calling attention to the facts that, for example, Habaneros preferred black beans, whereas Santiagueros and eastern Cubans preferred the red kidney bean. This explained the difference between *moros y cristianos* (Moors and Christians, i.e., black beans and rice) and *congri* (red beans and rice). In large measure, Baralt did outside Cuba what José Triay did inside it—explain how particular foods were important to Cuban eaters, thus incorporating them into a developing Cuban cuisine.

COOKBOOKS AND MODERNIZATION OF THE KITCHEN

In the 1920s, a major shift began in Cuban cookbooks and kitchens. Recipes became more standardized, with measurements such as teaspoons and tablespoons replacing less technical quantities such

as *some* and *a bit*. But this process took more than a decade to complete. Still in 1930, for example, a recipe for "Roast Beef con Verduras" that appeared in the magazine *La Mujer* called for the cook—presumably a woman—to "choose a nice piece of beef roast of a few kilos [un par de kilos]," put it in a roaster with "a little" *manteca*, and roast it in an oven that was "bien caliente"—very hot ("El restaurant en el Hogar," p. 17).

The increasing rationalization and mechanization of the kitchen was spurred in part by new technologies. General Electric began exporting electric stoves to Cuba in the middle of the 1920s, marking a turning point in cooking technology and science. Cubans saw this as a positive change that brought modernity to the nation. In 1929, the Cuban Electric Company and General Electric published *El arte de cocinar electricamente* (The Art of Electric Cooking) in Havana to teach the modern Cuban woman how to cook both efficiently and well on electric ranges. Each section contained very specific instructions on how to prepare food in an electric oven (or on the range top), as well as a quick guide on efficiency and the types of pots and pans to use. The recipes barely touched on dishes that might be considered Cuban cuisine. Indeed, the only recognizably Cuban- (or Spanish-) influenced dish in the cookbook is "Superior Chicken and Rice." Apple compote was not indigenous to the island, nor were strawberry shortcake and bran muffins. As later authors pointed out, a generation of Cubans began to think of hamburgers and macaroni and cheese as Cuban. These recipes represented the cosmopolitanism that existed within Cuban nationalism: Tying the nation gastronomically to Europe and the United States validated Cuba.

But the dishes in *El arte de cocinar electricamente* represented Cuban aspirations to modernization. The precise measurements of ingredients and temperatures signaled a rationalization of cooking techniques. A recipe for grilled chops, for example, called for the cook to place the meat on the broiling pan and cook at 400 degrees Fahrenheit for fifteen to eighteen minutes per pound for rare, at 450 degrees for eighteen to twenty minutes for medium, and twenty to twenty-five minutes per pound for well (General Electric p. 36). For macaroni and cheese, the recipe called for "2 cups cooked macaroni, 1½ cup white sauce, 1 cup grated cheese," and instructed women to mix the ingredients together and bake at 450 degrees for twenty minutes (p. 48). Precision became the norm as kitchens became modernized, and Cubans strove to make their nation both rational and modern.

MAGAZINE FOOD COLUMNS: FROM INSTRUCTIVE TO CONSTRUCTIVE

By the mid-1940s, cooking columns had become an important source for recipes and cooking advice. The weekly articles printed in magazines such as

Vanidades, Ella, and *Bohemia* could provide much more up-to-date information about new technologies and cooking news from abroad. Their series regularly reprinted recipes from sources such as *Women's Home Companion, Ladies Home Journal, Good Housekeeping, Avon Improved Cookbooks,* and *Quick and Easys for Brides,* and occasionally included Cuban food in their pages. They helped to elucidate what Cubans ate but usually were more instructive than constructive of Cuban cuisine.

The most representative—and long-lived—of these columns, "El menú de la semana" (The Weekly Menu), ran in *Bohemia* from 1946 until 1960. It provides an excellent source for examining changes in Cuban cuisine from the mid-1940s until immediately after the Revolution. The series proffered recipes from around the world, emphasizing foods that could be made quickly and often using canned and bottled ingredients; it compiled recipes from different parts of Cuba; and it offered advice on how to use a wide range of kitchen implements, from electric stoves to pressure cookers and electric mixers. For much of its existence, "El menú de la semana" was instructive in nature. Cuban recipes such as stuffed snapper, *moros y cristianos,* and *arroz con pollo* appeared alongside meatloaf, barbecued chicken with sauce made from Libby's or Hunts tomato sauce, corn dogs, spaghetti with meatballs, and hamburgers. This variety reflected the Cuban taste for the foreign, the fact that so-called American dishes were less time consuming to prepare, and, more broadly, Cuban aspirations to modernity; it certainly was neither revolutionary nor nationalist.

Nevertheless, "El menú de la semana" and other cooking series did give recipes for Cuban dishes, and in February 1959, one month after the Cuban Revolution successfully ousted Fulgencio Batista, the author of "El menú de la semana," Adriana Loredo, (a pseudonym for the Cuban poet Rosa Hilda Zell, 1910–1971) suddenly rejected the instructive cosmopolitan style for a more constructive, distinctly Cuban approach. She altered the tenor of the column to glorify the Revolution and highlight women as its unsung heroes, and she chastised those who complained about the scarcity of meat (*Bohemia* October 9, 1960). The series increasingly came to be about economization for the nation. By grinding meat, Loredo wrote, its use became more varied and would last longer: *Picadillo* one night became meat sauce for spaghetti the next, or meatballs one night could be hamburgers the next. She began to write proudly about Cuban products—shrimp from Matanzas, boniato and plantains, ñame, yucca, and malanga—whereas before she had rarely mentioned them.

Loredo railed against the United States as well. In 1960, she published an article that sought to allay fears about food shortages due to the end of imports from Cuba's "imperialist neighbor." With

the U.S. boycott of Cuba, she wrote, it was time to take stock of what "they sent us" and "how they sent it to us" to see "in reality what we are losing." Butter, she argued, would be available directly from New Zealand until the Cuban dairy industry began producing enough to meet domestic consumption. Powdered milk produced in Cuba, she told her readers, was just as healthful as either fresh or tinned milk, and much easier to store (*Bohemia* November 13, 1960). Not only would the Revolution survive without U.S. products, she seemed to be saying, it would thrive.

Eventually "El menú de la semana" was replaced by "Ud. puede cocinar sano y sabroso" (You Can Cook Healthy and Flavorful), penned by the television cooking personality and cookbook author Nitza Villapol (1923–1998). The new column was even more constructive than its predecessor. Villapol stressed woman's role as nourisher of the country,

Moros y Cristianos. The Cuban version of the Caribbean staple beans and rice is known as Moros y Cristianos (Moors and Christians), a name that reflects the hue of the two basic ingredients, black beans and white rice. © ART OF FOOD/ALAMY

highlighted the need to economize in the kitchen, and underscored the importance of using local products. Each recipe in the new column had both a healthy purpose—for the good of Cuban families—and a national one: to provide jobs, defend the culture, or conserve resources. She urged her readers to purchase less expensive cuts of meat, which are healthier than filet mignon and steak. She advised readers to ask for "the least expensive varieties" of fish (*Bohemia*, November 29, 1960). Along with these tips, Villapol noted that her recipes could be made with food easily found in the market, which was to say local products. She suggested new uses for pressure cookers: Instead of just beans and soup, pressure could be used to cook meats in order to save "time and ... fuel" (*Bohemia* January 15, 1961). Thus, Villapol sought to make the kitchen a place of nationalist sentiment. To make this point more explicit, she published recipes with which to "toast the honor of the men and women who help produce our sugar and also our allies who consume it" (*Bohemia* July 2, 1961). The column reminded readers that before the 1898 to 1902 U.S. occupation Cubans had always eaten fish on Christmas Eve and urged her compatriots to return to the practice, pointing out that by "reviving old recipes and mealtime customs, we can help conserve our traditions" (*Bohemia* December 18, 1960).

From 1856 until 1961, cookbook authors and food journalists used their pages to both reflect and shape Cuban diets. They instructed cooks on the basics of continental and Cuban dishes, modernized and standardized the kitchen, and placed national dishes on the same table with foreign cuisine, showing their pride in the *patria*. They also constructed a national cuisine by incorporating African and indigenous elements, bringing together regional dishes, and revising Cuban tastes to reflect growing national pride and shrinking culinary possibilities. Over the course of little more than a century, cookbooks brought together the diverse ingredients and influences on the island to forge a cuisine reflecting the island's history: cosmopolitan but distinctly Cuban.

BIBLIOGRAPHY

Anuario estadistico de la República de Cuba. Havana: Imprenta El Siglo XX, 1915.

Appadurai, Arjun. "How to Make a National Cuisine: Cookbooks in Contemporary India." *Comparative Studies in Society and History* 30, no. 1 (January 1988): 3–24.

Baralt, Blanche Zacharie de. *Cuban Cookery: Gastronomic Secrets of the Tropics, with an Appendix on Cuban Drinks*. Havana: Editorial Hermes, 1931.

Cabrisas, Juan. *Nuevo manual de la cocinera catalana y cubana*. Valladolid, Spain: Editorial Maxtor, 2010.

Cassá, Roberto. *Los indios de las Antillas*. Madrid: Editorial Mapfre, 1992.

Coloma y Garcés, Eugenio. *Manual del cocinero cubano*, 1856.

Cuban Economic Research Project. *A Study on Cuba*. Coral Gables, FL: University of Miami Press, 1965.

Cusack, Igor. "African Cuisines: Recipes for Nation-Building?" *Journal of African Cultural Studies* 13, no. 2 (December 2000): 207–225.

Dawdy, Shannon Lee. "La Comida Mambisa: Food, Farming, and Cuban Identity, 1839–1999." *New West Indian Guide* 76, no. 1–2 (2002): 47–80.

Food and Agricultural Organization of the United Nations. *World Food Survey*. Rome: Author, 1946.

Food and Agricultural Organization of the United Nations. *Second World Food Survey*. Rome: Author, 1952.

General Electric. *El arte de cocinar electricamente*. Havana: Author, 1929.

International Bank for Reconstruction and Development (IBRD). *Report on Cuba*. Washington, DC: Author, 1951.

Keegan, William F. "The Caribbean, including Northern South America and Lowland Central America: Early History." In *The Cambridge World History of Food*, edited by Kenneth F. Kiple and Kriemhild Coneè Ornelas. Cambridge, U.K.: Cambridge University Press, 2000.

Lamarche, Sebastián Robiou. *Taínos y Caribes: Las culturas aborigines antillanas*. San Juan, Puerto Rico: Editorial Punto y Coma, 2003.

Legran, J. P. *Nuevo manual del cocinero cubano*. Madrid: Agualarga Editores, 2005.

Lipman, W. H. "Meats—The Present Aspect of Supply, Conservation and Development." *American Journal of Public Health* 9, no. 8 (August 1919): 575–580.

Loredo, Adriana. "El menú de la semana." *Bohemia* (1946–1960).

Mintz, Sidney W. *Tasting Food, Tasting Freedom*. Boston: Beacon Press, 1996.

Office of Population Research. "Food, Income, and Mortality." *Population Index* 13, no. 2 (April 1947): 96–103.

Ortíz, Fernando. "Los factores humanos de la cubanidad." *Revista Bimestre Cubana* 45 (1940): 161–186.

Pilcher, Jeffrey M. *¡Que Vivan los Tamales!: Food and the Making of Mexican Identity*. Albuquerque: University of New Mexico Press, 1998.

Pilcher, Jeffrey M. "The Caribbean from 1492 to the Present." In *The Cambridge World History of Food*, edited by Kenneth F. Kiple and Kriemhild Coneè Ornelas. Cambridge, U.K.: Cambridge University Press, 2000.

"El restaurant en el Hogar." *La Mujer* 2, no. 24 (November 15, 1930).

Schroeder, Susan. *Cuba: A Handbook of Historical Statistics*. Boston: G. K. Hall & Company, 1982.

Triay, José *Nuevó manual del cocinero criollo*. 2nd ed. Havana: La Moderna Poesia, 1914.

Villapol, Nitza. "Ud puede cocinar sano y sabroso." *Bohemia* (1960–1962).

FOOD: REVOLUTIONARY PERIOD

Guillermo Jiménez

Issues in food supply and rationing from 1959 to the early 2000s.

The supply of food in Cuba, characterized by chronic deficits and a rationing system that covers the entire population, has been among the most challenging issues faced by the revolutionary government since 1959. The modalities for food production and distribution were disrupted early in the Revolution, as Cuba abruptly shifted from a private property system to a state-run economy and also experienced the rupture of economic ties with the United States.

Nevertheless, during the Revolution's first thirty years, or what is known as the revolutionary period, Cuba managed to achieve internationally acceptable nutrition indexes that were within the reach of all strata of the population, thanks to a substantial rise in the income levels of a majority of persons with low purchasing power and high levels of malnourishment. At the same time, the rationing system guaranteed food in equal quantities and at moderate prices for all. That system, which remained in place more than five decades later, gave rise to a monotonous and restricted diet in terms of the quantity, quality, variety, and choices of traditional foods, even while it led to the disappearance of other foodstuffs.

After 1990 Cuba faced another set of drastic changes in its economic and nutritional structure. The disappearance of the Soviet Union and the European socialist states created a situation that was even more critical than what had come before; it is officially referred to as the Special Period and remained in effect as of 2011.

ORIGINS OF THE SHORTAGES

Shortages first appeared in 1961, when there was a boom in demand coupled with a drop in production and an interruption of indispensable imports from the United States. The revolution extended the payments for minimum wage, pensions, pregnancy, illness, and a one month vacation; it suppressed seasonal wages and payments for land use or share-cropping; and it made education and public health care free of charge, while creating any number of jobs needed in order to eliminate unemployment (the main socioeconomic problem at that time). Also established was the state-run Consumo Social, which delivered free food to schools, hospitals, asylums, homes for the elderly, and other similar facilities. The meals were also sold at low cost at day care centers and workers' canteens. All of this was done, however, without having established a productive foundation that could support it adequately. The traditional availability of foodstuffs was no match for the purchasing power thus generated. Between 1959 and 1961 the population consumed so much beef that per capita consumption figures grew by a factor of one and a half.

This production deficit was coupled with the abrupt rupture in trading relations with the United States, which hitherto had been Cuba's primary foreign supplier and had provided virtually all the country's food imports. Rice, lard, wheat, and wheat flour were staples of the diet, and in that order accounted for over half of all imports; they were also the items that registered the highest growth rates in consumption.

Cuba was also the largest customer for U.S. agriculture and livestock exports to Latin America. In spite of Cuba's small population, its disproportionate dependency on the United States made it that country's seventh-largest purchaser of foodstuffs, and the first on a per capita basis.

When the United States cut its imports of sugar on 4 July 1960 and suppressed them altogether in December 1961, it deprived Cuba of its chief source of the hard currency needed to buy food from the United States. As early as October 1960 the United States forbade exports to Cuba and in May 1964 foodstuffs was formally included. Thus began the U.S. policy of *bloqueo* (or blockade, as the Cubans call it) or of *embargo* (as the people in the United States call it), a policy that remained in effect as of 2011.

The absolute production levels achieved before 1959 were eventually surpassed for most foods during the next thirty years. The same did not hold true, however, for per capita consumption levels. This situation was caused by several factors, including demographic growth that nearly doubled the baseline population, low yields in certain crops, and absolute declines in output with regard to others. Increased food security was not achieved either, since the country was unable to shake free of the high dependency on imports that had existed since colonial times.

RATIONING

In order to cope with the food shortages, a food-rationing system was launched on 13 March 1962. The entire population was guaranteed access to food through individual allocations of egalitarian quotas distributed through state-owned establishments, though privileging the capital and major locations, ill and disabled persons, pregnant women, infants, and the elderly. From that time forward prices remained moderate and virtually unchanged, because they were subsidized by the state budget to an amount estimated in 2009 at US$800 million.

Although there was some pretense that this was to be a temporary measure and would include only a few foods, after 1971 it covered them all, and the system remained in effect as of 2011. Throughout those decades the system used a variety of cards, vouchers, and

Food rations. Cuban Juan Carlos Montes is shown in 1993 with his ration of food for the month (left) and, twelve years later, in 2005, with another month's ration. AP IMAGES/JOSE GOITIA

coupons, including in the early 2000s the supply booklet, sometimes simply called the booklet. Every household is required to purchase its foods from a specific retailer, where an employee makes a handwritten entry in a booklet duly noting the ration quota in question.

In 1973, in the face of a sharp contraction in food output precipitated by high inflation, as an alternative to rationing for the first time state-run markets were authorized to exist in which a wider range of higher-quality foods could be sold but at higher prices. Other measures eliminated gratuities, linked wages to productivity, and differentiated wages as a function of qualifications and experience. All of these measures led to something of a boom in food availability that lasted up to the mid-1980s.

Cuba's rationing system has been less flexible and longer lasting than those instituted in the United States and Great Britain during World War II, in the Soviet Union, or in Francisco Franco's Spain. It allows no discretion for individualities or exceptions, and it does not permit the beneficiary to select options on the basis of personal interests and inclinations; it also rejects the principle of differentiation with regard to quality, choice, and purchasing power. Its extreme egalitarianism has served to discourage worker productivity, and it has led to widespread bartering for food, with the inevitable rise of the black market and speculators.

REVOLUTIONARY PERIOD

The Revolution substantially transformed the structure of Cuba's land ownership, whose unproductiveness and absenteeism had been among the highest in Latin America. Large *latifundios* (estates), idle lands, and misappropriated properties were expropriated and confiscated, and a fraction of the land was distributed

among the campesinos who worked on them, but did not own them; the bulk of the lands ended up being managed by the state, whose share of land ownership increased until it reached 82 percent in 1990 (Nova González p. 38).

Some campesinos organized into cooperatives, particularly after 1976. Others stayed on as individual producers; despite being fewer in number and possessing a much smaller expanse of land, of poorer quality, and despite lacking raw materials, machinery, and qualified personnel, they have generally produced larger harvests than the state entities. The latter, by contrast, have generally obtained higher yields, except in certain categories such as potatoes and sweet potatoes during certain periods.

The wide range of less-grueling, better-paid jobs induced a huge rural migration to urban areas and the chronic impoverishment of the rural workforce. This process in turn was aggravated by an aging population and the never-ending exodus of youth to the cities in order to study or report for the draft. Most of them would not return to their place of birth. Prior to 1959, Cuba was a nonindustrialized nation, with a little over half of its population living in rural areas; this figure shrank to 31 percent in 1981 and to 24.1 percent by 2002 (according to the respective censuses of 1981 and 2002) (ONE 2002, p. 173).

In order to address this situation, from the 1960s to the 1990s urban workers were transported to rural areas during the peak labor demand periods, and they were paid wages equal to those at the work center from which they came. The lack of qualifications and inexperience of these workers damaged crops and harvests, raised costs, depressed productivity, and in general contributed to inefficient management.

Simultaneously, traditional modes of production were transformed. Technology and agricultural know-how were disseminated: Mechanization was encouraged, along with the use of agricultural chemicals, attention to plant health, and manipulation of animal and plant genetics. Irrigation was ensured through an infrastructure based on numerous dams; and the cattle breeding stock was upgraded, as were the methods of feeding animals.

The production of animal protein was an early high priority, pursued through defined strategies. Increasing the output of milk, eggs, and the harvesting of fisheries was a higher priority than the production of beef and poultry. Vegetable proteins were neglected, however; for instance, the black bean (a staple) crop began to decline, even though prior to 1959 the harvest had been able to meet national demand.

Livestock was lavished with the highest levels of attention and investment, but the results fell far short of the effort. The great challenge was discovering the country's own sustainable system to produce animal feed in a tropical environment. An artificial insemination program was launched in 1962 to transform Brahmin cattle into a primary dairy producer. By the late 1980s a majority of the Cuban herd consisted of Holstein cross-breeds.

In 1967 the nation's livestock herd reached a historical peak. Despite an enormous investment and technological effort, after 1978 the herds began to shrink due to low breeding rates. Average weights began to shrink as well. Likewise, dairy production had been rising, but in 1983 the trend began to reverse, and yields per cow dropped to an average of barely 2 liters per day during that decade (Nova González p. 25).

This period saw successes in the production of eggs, fish, citrus, and pork and, more modestly, in dairy products and vegetables, principally tomatoes, potatoes, and rice. Nevertheless, the levels for certain basic foodstuffs plunged far below those of 1958, such as corn, beans, coffee, and root crops (except for potatoes), which, together with beef and rice, fell on a per capita basis. As for fruits, a few new strains of banana proved to be weak producers.

Imports supplied part of the deficit, but they did not resolve it. Rice provides an example, despite the fact that output tripled, and an equivalent amount was imported. Something similar occurred with milk,

Havana's Cuatro Caminos market. Various types of markets provide a broader range of products than the rationing system. Such markets sell food that is left over after sales obligations to the state have been met.
© DESMOND BOYLAND/ REUTERS/CORBIS

Table 1

Selected livestock production

	Unit of measurement	1946[1]	1950s[2]	1964[3]	1988[4]	2000[5]	2007[6]
Beef	Thousands of animals	4,115.7	4,042.1[8A]	5,776.4[9]	4,926.8	4,110.2	3,787.4
Pork	Thousands of animals	1,344.0	1,285.8[8A]	827.6[9]	1,168.7	1,221.7	1,868.6
Milk	[7]	408,159.4		225,978.0	918.7	614.1	485.1
Poultry	Thousands of animals	7,146.0			27,307.8	13,232.0	29,412.8
Eggs	Million units	78.4		297.5	2,459.8	1,453.8	2,351.7
Fish	Metric Ton		8,499.0[8B]	22,941.5	178,940.9	122,457.6	48,804.4
Shellfish	Metric Ton			13,472.0	52,614.6	39,801.5	13,339.8

SOURCE: [1] Memoir of the National Agricultural Census: 163, 166, 168; [2] Ministry of Finance. General Directorate of Statistics. Statistical Yearbook of Cuba 1957: 103, 105, 119; [3] Central Planning Board, Statistical Bulletin 1964, 21, 23; [4] State Statistical Committee. Statistical Yearbook of Cuba 1988: 329, 334, 335, 336, 356; [5] National Statistical Office. Statistical Yearbook of Cuba 2000: 211, 213, 214; [6] National Statistical Office. Statistical Yearbook of Cuba 2007: 240, 241; [7] Unit of measure: one thousand liters until 1964, and thousands of tons thereafter; [8A] Year 1952. Statistical Yearbook of Cuba 1957, 104, 105; [8B] Year 1955. Statistical Yearbook of Cuba 1957, 119; [9] National Tally 1961. Central Planning Board, Statistical Bulletin 1964, 21.

beans (the object of large-scale importation, nearly approaching the figures for total consumption), spices, and coffee. There was no relief on other items, such as root crops (which are not traded on global markets) or corn imports (which were geared toward animal feed) or fruits.

The role formerly reserved for the United States as a food supplier was filled by the Soviet Union, which provided two-thirds of total imports, with other socialist countries contributing on a smaller scale. The Soviet Union offered Cuba generous terms of trade, supplying wheat and flour, corn, rice, barley, oats, peas, animal and vegetable fats, dairy products, preserved meats, fish (fresh, frozen, and salted), potatoes, onions, raisins, spices, and baby food.

Imports of wheat and flour tripled after 1959, and dairy and vegetable imports doubled, while imports of fats rose by two-thirds and preserved meats by one-third. Wheat become the single most important food item traded with the Soviets, as rice had formerly been in trade with the United States.

THE SPECIAL PERIOD

As the Revolution entered its fourth decade, it faced the most difficult circumstances in its history with regard to feeding the population: it was squeezed between the disappearance of the Soviet Union and the European socialist countries, and the intensification of the U.S. embargo or blockade. This catastrophe converged in setbacks to both the absolute and relative production of basic foodstuffs. After 1976 agricultural production geared toward food had displayed a rising trend, but by 1986 the impact of low productivity and declining outputs for several basic foodstuffs was inescapable. The yields for many crops, such as rice, beans, tomatoes, onions, peppers, and others, were among the lowest on the continent by 1988.

The breakup of the Soviet Union unleashed a chain reaction through the Cuban economy and lay waste the agricultural sector. Food output and imports collapsed for a short time. The vulnerability of the agricultural production sector became apparent: Its growth and development had been built on the foundations of a high dependency of imported raw materials and agricultural machinery. The historical subordination to imported food, which increased during the revolutionary period, became even more intense.

The model of a state-run agriculture pursued up to that point became unsustainable. This system had dedicated cultivation areas on average six times larger than those of the United States and Western Europe to single-crop agriculture, with few crop rotations, highly centralized management systems, low utilization of resources and the labor force, high costs, and losses subsidized by the state budget.

The average consumption of fertilizers was twice that of the United States. Machinery utilization rates were extremely low. In addition, as the number of workers grew, their productivity declined even as wages and labor qualifications rose. By the beginning of the 1990s the gross national product had collapsed by more than one-third. In the food sector output fell by half, due to the meager availability of national and imported raw materials and the lack of materials for

Selected agricultural output

Table 2

	Unit	1945[1]	1957[2]	1977[3]	1988[3]	1994[4]	2000[4]	2007[5]
Rice	Ton	62,862.8	27,161.7[6]	455,774	488,857	226,095	305,915	47,532
Corn	Ton	221,731.8		16,342	35,521	73,623	203,758	19,449
Black beans	Ton	26,479.3		3,230	14,840	10,771	59,590	3,013
Coffee	Ton	30,749.4	12,122.5[7]	16,826	28,801	--------	---------	---------
Yams	Ton	157,772.6		67,624	163,546	133,414	219,530	48,152
Potatoes	Ton	56,217.5		154,856	276,750	188,334	367,856	38,836
Plantains	Ton	----------		85,543	142,435	217,619	402,006	90,233
Bananas	[8]	7,911,627		134,462	202,628	143,060	185,115	76,424
Citrus	Ton	----------		225,884	981,009	504,991	898,510	257,191
Oranges	[9]	2,458		159,686	507,711	256,435	440,764	181,996
Vegetables	Ton	----------		326,212	675,597	332,164	1,460,497	499,988
Tomatoes	Ton	----------		160,252	335,012	95,876	338,542	74,429

SOURCE: [1] Memoir of the National Agricultural Census: 186, 203, 190, 206 and 210, 188, 218; [2] Ministry of Finance. General Directorate for Statistics. Statistical Yearbook of Cuba 1957: 186, 187, 190, 191; [3] National Statistics Committee. Statistical Yearbook of Cuba 1988: 316; [4] National Statistical Office. Statistical Yearbook of Cuba 2000: 205; [5] National Statistical Office. Statistical Yearbook of Cuba 2007: 235; [6] Harvest of 1952-1953; [7] Harvest of 1955-1956; [8] Bunches, 1945 and Metric Tons thereafter; [9] Thousands of Units until 1957 and Metric Tons thereafter.

containers, particularly with regard to dairy, tomato, and wheat flour products.

Annual food imports fell to nearly one-third of the previous level. Prior to 1959 food imports had covered one-third of consumption; now they had to cover more than half, and even then they only managed to make up for one-third of demand.

The most acute situation came between 1991 and 1994, as agriculture imploded and the import capacity of the country fell to one-fourth, and as the U.S. cutoff intensified after 1992. Accordingly, the rationing quota was subjected to such a drastic curtailment that it failed to satisfy even the minimum basic needs of the population. This situation led to nutritional deficiencies that caused multiple cases of epidemic neuropathy between 1991 and 1992.

Economic reforms did not lag far behind, and they began to have an impact in several areas between 1993 and 1995, sparking a recovery to some extent. State lands were distributed to private individuals; nonstate food markets with no price controls were authorized; and the private sales of handmade crafts were legalized. In order to raise productivity, in certain sectors productivity was linked to wages, with the delivery of in-kind benefits or foreign or national currency. Finally, Cuba entered into new partnerships with foreign investors, for example, with Israel for citrus, China and Vietnam for rice, and Canada for vegetables.

The most far-reaching reform was the legalization of holding foreign currency, leading to free circulation of the dollar, with a floating exchange rate that was always far above the national currency. Thus a unique situation arose in which there were two currencies in circulation: one national, the other foreign.

LAND REFORM

The structure of landholding once again was reformed during the Special Period. The state's share and the scale of land owned by the state were reduced to one-fourth, whereas the land held by cooperatives and private hands increased. The "usufruct" (or right to exploit and enjoy) for a little less than half of the best land in the country, at that time held by the largest state farms, was sold off along with their assets to cooperative entities made up of former wage earners. These were obligated to sell their output to the state, which continued to set purchasing prices and the list of items to be cultivated and which continued to exercise oversight as if they were still state lands.

Various cooperative and individual landholdings endured, while new owners of small plots and gardens appeared in urban environs. In one type of cooperative, the campesino transfers the land to the cooperative entity, which in turn distributes profits among its members; in another type, which is majority-owned,

Table 3

Land distribution in Cuba and use according to type of landholding and enterprise or economic entity as of December 31, 2007
THOUSANDS OF HECTARES

	TOTAL	STATE	NON-STATE			
			Total	UBPC	CPA	CCS & Private
TOTAL	10,988.6	6,088.9	4,899.7	2,804.8	692.8	1,402.1
AGRICULTURE AREA	6,619.5	2,371.2	4,248.3	2,448.2	585.8	1,214.3
Cultivated	2,988.5	694.2	2,294.3	1,189.9	305.3	799.1
Non-Cultivated	3,631.0	1,677.0	1,954.0	1,258.3	280.5	415.2
NON-AGRICULTURAL AREA	4,369.1	3,717.7	651.4	356.6	107.0	187.8

SOURCE: National Statistical Office. Statistical Yearbook of Cuba, 2007, 226.

the campesino has a freehold possession and joins in order to receive certain services.

Until 2009, even though the abovementioned cooperatives held only one-fourth of Cuba's cultivable land, they produced over one-half the country's coffee, cocoa, beans, corn, fruit, and honey, as well as something less than one-half of the output of root crops and vegetables, livestock and pork, and nearly one-third of dairy products, which by 2010 had grown to nearly one-half the total. For its part, the state sector remained the producer of the majority of poultry and citrus products, which were generally subsidized by the state budget. As of 2010, two-thirds of foodstuffs were produced by private campesinos associated in cooperatives, despite the limitations imposed by a shrinking workforce and the lack of adequate inputs and machinery.

These circumstances led to a return of organic, ecological agriculture. Known as urban agriculture, this movement engages urban residents in the production of foodstuffs that are essential for self-supply in noncultivated surrounding areas. This modality has been successful, in part because of the high salaries received by its workers. It is based on self-sufficient, diversified agriculture on small plots near large consumption centers, using few or no imported raw materials, with no agricultural chemicals, and using animal power. It stimulates the use of technologies that are commensurate with local resources, the recycling of animal and vegetable waste to be used as fertilizer, the biological control of pests, the diversification of species and breeds in the different plots, and the use of alternative energy sources.

Although Cuba has yet to return to the levels of food output attained in 1989, this strategy has increased agriculture and livestock production by one-third since 2000, thanks to higher yields (as compared to 1995) for all foods except milk, beef, pork, and citrus. The largest gains were registered in bananas, *malanga* (taro), onions, and peppers. Nevertheless, the yield for most crops remained still below the worldwide average, except for potatoes and beans.

Harvests larger than those for 1989 were reaped for the categories of vegetables, corn, beans (the item with the highest increase in output), plantains, onions, root crops, sweet potatoes, tomatoes, and peppers. Other foodstuffs, such as rice, by 2010 had yet to reach their historical levels, while some items such as citrus and fruits in general were approaching them.

The categories of foodstuffs that displayed the highest recovery levels during this period were vegetables (which showed significant growth), root crops, *guayabas* (guava), and pork. The sector restored its former production levels for beer, confectioneries, and refined vegetable fats, and the dairy industry was reengineered so that it could use soy, particularly in the production of yogurt.

Cuba's production shortcomings increased dependency on imports, which rose in the category of the foods that make up the basic consumer basket: rice, milk, beans, fats, fish, and chicken. Since 2002 Cuba even imported sugar, after having been the world's largest exporter for over a century and a half.

The nonavailability of animal protein was a major challenge during the Special Period. The fish harvest fell to less than one-third of its former levels, and even so the catch was mostly derived from aquaculture. Cuba's production of beef, milk, and poultry collapsed to one-half the former figure, while the size of its cattle and hog herds, as the poultry flock, dropped. The decline was especially sharp with regard to cattle. Pork was the only category to display a modest recovery, growing by about one-half, largely because of private activity.

COMMERCIAL AND CURRENCY REFORMS

Various types of markets were established that provide a broader range of products than the rationing system and without its quota restrictions; these markets, however, are differentiated on the basis of currency types and regulated prices. Thus, national currency markets exist alongside markets that accept hard currencies for agriculture and livestock products. The former system includes rationed products, which are stocked in extremely limited supply and are still governed by low prices, virtually unchanged from those of fifty years earlier. The system also includes private markets that can set their prices freely, rather than having established prices; these were restored in October 1994 after having been abolished in 1986. There is also a system of state markets with prices that are higher than those for rationed products but lower than in the private markets. Finally, there are a few other less significant markets.

The private markets are supplied by cooperative and private entities. These sell whatever is left over after their sales obligations to the state have been met, with the exception of beef, dairy products, and potatoes.

The state markets are supplied by state-run agricultural enterprises. Their prices cannot be higher than certain regulated limits. They were created in 1999 in order to encourage lower prices in foods. This objective was not achieved, since what they offer, even though it may be less expensive, cannot compete with the private markets in terms of quantity, quality, variety, or service.

Apart from these national-currency agricultural markets, a vast network of state stores was organized than provide all kinds of food, without any restrictions and offering a wide range of largely imported items, including certain basic goods and necessities that are available only at those stores. The cost of goods from these stores is payable in hard currency and at progressively higher prices.

Never before had such a broad array of supply systems been adopted, with such disregard for the egalitarianism assured by rationing or allowing for such differentiation on the basis of income and consumption. In a situation that is quite extraordinary for modern Cuba, the purchasing power of most Cubans in the early twenty-first century is too low for the food that is actually available. Despite the infamously meager quotas of the rationing system, for most people it is simply out of the question to acquire complementary foods at the private agriculture and livestock markets or even at state markets. The hard currency markets are even more inaccessible. The quota for black beans, for example, which amounts to 10 ounces a month, costs $0.80 in the rationing system; however, for a similar quantity, one would have to disburse fourteen times as much ($11.50) on the private agricultural market, or thirty-nine times as much ($31.50) at the foreign exchange stores, according to the exchange rates of October 2010 for the Cuban convertible peso.

CUBA-U.S. TRADE

Although the vicissitudes of trade with the United States have certainly left their mark on the culinary habits of Cubans since the mid-eighteenth century, their impact was never so far-reaching as during the decades following the Revolution. The U.S. embargo on food, which came into law in 1964, was tightened in October 1992 through the Cuban Democracy Act, known as the Torricelli Act, which forbids trading with U.S. subsidiaries from which soy, wheat, sunflower and palm oil, corn, and rice were being purchased in third countries. In March 1996 this law was reinforced with the Cuban Liberty and Democratic Solidarity Act, or the Helms-Burton Act, which allowed prosecutions under U.S. law of foreign companies trading with Cuba.

Paradoxically, it was during the presidency of George W. Bush (2000–2008), and the strictest period of the blockade or embargo, that influential congressmen from both parties in the agricultural states managed to insert a wedge into the ban on agricultural sales to Cuba. The first food shipments since 1964 thus took place on 15 December 2001, under onerous conditions, since U.S. banks were forbidden from supporting the deals with loans, requesting cash payment, and transporting the goods under U.S.-flagged vessels.

In June 2004, President Bush tightened the embargo policy. Three laws were passed that limited travel by Cuban Americans to the island, banned cash remittances, and restricted the conditions for trade in food. Under the new legislation, U.S. exporters must request licenses from the Departments of the Treasury and Commerce; the letter of credit is difficult to process, since there are no banking relationships; and shippers must obtain the authorization of the Department of the Treasury in order to come to Cuban ports and their ships must return unladen.

The Cuban government retaliated for the U.S. sanctions on European banks operating with Cuba by banning the circulation of dollars in November 2004. These had now be exchanged for a new currency, the convertible peso (or CUC), which was subject to a 10 percent levy and other taxes, which add up to 18 percent, thus raising the cost of living. Subsequently this 18 percent was lowered approximately to an exchange rate of 10 percent for all foreign currencies in March 2011 (Medina Villaveirán).

Until that point, about one-third of Cuban agricultural and livestock products were being brought in from the United States. Imports of corn, wheat, soy, poultry, and rice in particular were growing. After the restrictions of 2004, Cuba cut back on its purchases from the United States, diverting them to markets that were less restrictive and offered credit facilities. The prices for these items increased considerably, and

Cuba was forced to pay its import bill up front. Even so, food imports from the United States rose considerably, from $173 million in 2002 to $962 million in 2008 (ONE 2009, p. 179). After that, however, imports were reduced. There is no historical precedent for such a long-standing policy of unilateral food exclusion. Every year since 1992 the UN General Assembly has discussed the termination of the policy. In 2010, there were 187 countries that voted for it to end, with two against, and three abstentions.

CULINARY HABITS

The ongoing shifts in the production, importation, and distribution of food transformed Cuban cooking, with an impact surpassed only by the experience of the aboriginal culture when the Spanish arrived over four centuries ago. Gastronomic changes that had stabilized during the first three decades after the Revolution (1959–1989) suffered yet another severe upheaval with the Special Period, and Cubans once again were forced to adapt to customs and habits that in the past would have seemed unusual.

The rationing system allowed little room for gastronomic individuality and initiative, and it became difficult to indulge in special tastes and the orthodox preparation of traditional recipes. Much of Cuba's gastronomic heritage has disappeared, including the main recipes of the traditional cuisine that filled the island's tables for centuries. Quite aside from gastronomic issues, the cumulative impact of rationing over the life of nearly three generations of Cubans has influenced their national identity and shaped an egalitarian idiosyncrasy in the nation's collective consciousness. Meanwhile, such groceries as can be found in the rationing book continue to hold sway over Cuban palates, whereas those that are not included have faded from culinary memories.

The most remarkable survivor has been that tenacious staple, rice, which was guaranteed throughout the rationing of both periods and became the daily fare of the entire population. In the early 2000s, a rice shortage was nothing less than a national drama. The almost total disappearance of corn, meanwhile, meant that the campesinos were forced to substitute it with rice. As compensation, however, they received more animal protein, which hitherto had been off-limits for them, as well as bread, fish, and a few other new items. Beef, the preferred food of Cubans since the sixteenth century, has been the most controversial item. During the revolutionary period the quota was 0.65 kilograms, but deliveries were drawn out over seven to nine days. Per capita consumption ranged between 29.9 and 34.7 kilograms, less than the 50 to 55 kilograms recommended by the Food and Agriculture Organization of the United Nations (Nova González p. 179). During the Special Period, beef all but disappeared from the rationing system, although it eventually resurfaced in the form of low-quality ground beef mixed with soymeal, subsequently substituted by imported poultry. As of 2011, beef was sold only at the foreign currency stores at outrageous prices. Since pork was freely sold at high prices, albeit in the national currency, Cubans consumed more pork than beef, as was customary during the sixteenth century.

During the revolutionary period, protein was supplied with various kinds of fish and with an excessive consumption of eggs. By necessity, both fish and eggs became a much larger part of the Cuban diet than they had been in the past. Milk was distributed only to children, pregnant women, the ill, and the elderly. Cubans never ate so much fish as during the revolutionary period. The catch was guaranteed by a fleet of state-of-the-art trawlers (nonexistent in 2011) that roiled out the extent of the world's seas. During the Special Period the egg quota was reduced, whereas milk was maintained only for the ill and for children up to the age of seven. Shortages of fish, by contrast, were remedied through the farming of aquaculture species that Cubans do not particularly like.

The food groups not included in the state rationing system have been roots, fruits, vegetables, and spices, which are rarely distributed and even then in a very restricted range. Nevertheless, during the Special Period these products reemerged in the private market sector and at the convertible currency stores. The shortages of fats meant that the population was compelled to reduce its intake of fried foods, and, as noted earlier, the Cuban diet no longer includes the customary quantities of rice and beef. The flavor palette was also curtailed, given the shortage of traditional spices and dressings, which the convertible currency stores subsequently brought back to the market. The most commonly used condiments were peppers (*ají*), garlic, onion, salt, citrics, wine, vinegar, mayonnaise, mustard, soy sauce, and the ubiquitous tomato sauce, which found its way into the least likely dishes.

Imports were the key variable that determined the contents of a Cuban's pantry. A shortage of black or red beans in the Soviet Union, the legumes most delectable to a Cuban, might require using chickpeas as a substitute. Rising imports of Soviet wheat multiplied the consumption of bread and pastas. Pasta restaurants, serving pastas manufactured by several factories set up for the purpose, spread throughout the country, and from that point onward pasta became part of the national menu. Pizzas, which were formerly unknown, became the preeminent fast food.

As has happened elsewhere, the food shortages stimulated the imagination and inventiveness of Cubans, who took refuge in ersatz versions of culinary favorites. Coffee was the most noteworthy practice of this during the revolutionary period, when it was heretically mixed with things such as wheat or ground peas in order to expand its volume. Then, during the Special Period, soybean derivatives were substituted for dairy products and were used to eke out meat supplies while enriching their nutritional value.

Huge volumes of cold beverages continued to be consumed, and beer was drunk since the beginning of the twentieth century as a companion for meals (unlike the beer-drinking countries of Europe, where beer tends to be consumed at times other than meals). To offer a visitor coffee, whether pure or mixed, even in the early 2000s, remained the primary social ritual of the Cuban host.

THE TWENTY-FIRST CENTURY SITUATION

For the first time since 1959 there was widespread social differentiation in Cuba based on nutritional options. Even though the rationing system offered few choices during the revolutionary period, its regulated quotas, however imperfect, ensured the availability of the minimum needed for the entire population.

The limited rationing system that existed in Cuba as of 2011 was insufficient to maintain a proper diet, and it did not provide an acceptable level of nutrition. The calories provided through this system were officially estimated at one-half the recommended intake. A rough guess is that most people could make the foods distributed through rationing last barely ten days, or at best fifteen, for the most temperate.

In order to supplement their meager diets, Cuban consumers were hard-pressed to acquire foreign currency, whether through legal means or otherwise, in order to obtain foods that were obtainable only at hard currency stores. But not everyone had this option. According to official estimates, only 40 to 50 percent of the population had access to hard currency, whereas the Comisión Económica para América Latina (CEPAL), the economic commission of the U.N. for Latin America and the Caribbean, estimated the figure at 60 percent.

The incongruity between getting paid one's income in a devalued national currency while having to pay one's expenses in a more highly valued foreign currency is the main problem in contemporary Cuban life: It deranges the organization of society, spreads labor indiscipline, contributes to declines in productivity and output, and serves as an incentive to crime. As of 2011, the government had expressed its willingness to take gradual steps to rectify this situation.

Along with these circumstances, there were the continuing ramifications of the global financial crisis that began in 2008, which caused price spikes in global food markets while at the same time depressing the income derived from imports and services. These setbacks coincided with the widespread crop damage in Cuba caused by three hurricanes in 2008, which were immediately followed by one of the most intense droughts on record. In 2009 food imports contracted by more than one-third, and agricultural production also dropped sharply.

The production of food, together with the reduction of food imports, was proclaimed as the number one problem facing Cuba. The most far-reaching

decisions that were taken in this regard concerned the delivery of lands, which was an ongoing process. As of the end of 2009, a little more than half of the state lands that were idle or had been overtaken by weeds were delivered to some 100,000 producers. These lands were given under the legal figure of a *usufructo,* or grant for exploitation. At the same time, some campesinos saw increases for the purchase prices for their agricultural products, and inefficient state agricultural enterprises were suppressed.

There was an ongoing effort to abolish the rationing system, along with the canteens and messes of work establishments where one-third of the population were able to lunch at a moderate price (and who would be compensated with payments to subsidize a modest diet).

On another note, the suppression of approximately one-fourth of all jobs was planned, along with cuts in the state budget and subsidies and plans for the eradication of the twin currency systems. On July 2010 it was officially announced that between October 2010 and March 2011 500,000 jobs would be supressed. These were enormously complex processes, whose execution provided a glimpse into the transcendent changes yet in store.

BIBLIOGRAPHY

American Association for World Health. *Bloqueo de alimentos y medicinas: El impacto del embargo de EE.UU. en la salud y la nutrición en Cuba: Resumen ejecutivo.* Washington, DC: Author, March 1997.

Asociación Nacional de Economistas y Contadores de Cuba. *Informe de la ANEC para reunión de la FAO.* Havana: ANEC, 1996.

Baisre Álvarez, Julio A. *La pesca marítima en Cuba.* Havana: Editorial Científico-Técnica, 2004.

Castro, Fidel. *La agricultura en Cuba: Selección temática.* 3 vols. Havana: Editora Política, 1996.

Castro, Raúl. "Discurso el 20 de diciembre del 2009 en la clausura del IV período ordinario de sesiones de la Asamblea Nacional del Poder Popular." *Granma,* 21 December 2009.

Comisión Económica para América Latina. *La economía cubana: Reformas estructurales y desempeño en los noventa.* 2nd ed. Mexico City: Fondo de Cultura Económica, 2000.

Comisión Económica para América Latina. *Política social y reformas estructurales: Cuba a principios del siglo XXI.* Mexico City: Fondo de Cultura Económica, 2004.

Comité Estatal de Estadísticas. Havana: CEE, annual series.

Cornide Hernández, María Teresa. *Las investigaciones agropecuarias en Cuba cien años después.* Havana: Editorial Científico-Técnico, 2006.

González, Alfredo, ed. *La ganadería en Cuba: Desempeño y desafíos.* Havana: Instituto Nacional de Investigaciones Económicas, 2004.

Instituto Nacional de Reforma Agraria. *Memorias: Primer Fórum Nacional sobre Reforma Agraria.* Havana: Instituto Nacional del Libro, 1960.

Junta Central de Planificación. *Series estadísticas de las importaciones de productos alimenticios 1959–1968.* Havana: JUCEPLAN, 1969.

Medina Villaveirán, Ernesto. "Acuerdo No. 30/11 del Comité de Política Monetaria del Banco Central de Cuba. 12 de marzo de 2011." *Granma,* March 14, 2011.

Mesa-Lago, Carmelo. *Breve historia económica de la Cuba socialista: Políticas, resultados, y perspectivas.* Madrid: Alianza Editorial, 1994.

Mesa-Lago, Carmelo. *Economía y bienestar social en Cuba a comienzos del siglo XXI.* Madrid: Editorial Colibrí, 2003.

Mesa-Lago, Carmelo. "Problemas sociales y económicos en Cuba durante la crisis y recuperación." *Revista de la CEPAL* (August 2005): 86.

Nova González, Armando. *La agricultura en Cuba. Evolución y trayectoria (1959–2005).* Havana: Editorial de Ciencias Sociales, 2006.

Obra Revolucionaria. *Primera Reunión Nacional de Producción.* Havana: Imprenta Nacional de Cuba, August 26, 27, and 29, 1961.

Oficina Nacional de Estadísticas. *Anuario Estadístico de Cuba.* Havana: Combinado Poligráfico Alfredo López, annual series.

Oficina Nacional de Estadísticas (ONE). *Informe nacional: Censo de población y viviendas 2002.* Havana: ONE, September 2005.

Oficina Nacional de Estadísticas (ONE). *Anuario Estadístico de Cuba 2009.* Havana: ONE, 2010.

La Producción Agrícola y Animal en Cuba. Havana: Impresora Universitaria André Voisin, 1967.

Rodríguez Nodal, Adolfo. "La agricultura urbana en Cuba: Impactos económicos, sociales, y productivos." *Revista Bimestre Cubana* (January–June 2004): 103–124.

Valdés Paz, Juan. *Procesos agrarios en Cuba 1959–1995.* Havana: Editorial de Ciencias Sociales, 1997.

Valdés Paz, Juan. *Los procesos de organización agraria en Cuba, 1959–2006.* Havana: Fundación Antonio Núñez Jiménez de la Naturaleza y el Hombre, 2009.

■ *See also*

Faith: Abakuá Society

Faith: Regla de Ocha and Ifá

Faith: Reglas de Palo Congo

FOOD: RITUAL FOODS AND AFRO-CUBAN RELIGIOUS TRADITIONS

Natalia María Bolívar Aróstegui

The significance of food in Afro-Cuban religious rituals.

Three religious systems with African influence are widely practiced in Cuba, a result of the presence of thousands of slaves forcibly transported from the west coast of Africa. These religions are monotheistic, naturalist, and based on oral tradition, and none has a single, centralized hierarchy. Each has a supreme god that is part of a complex spiritual world mediated by *orishas,*

GLOSSARY OF TERMS

Abasí The supreme god of the Abakuá Secret Society.

Brillumba A well-known branch of Regla de Palo; also means skull, spirit.

Kimbisero One who believes in Regla Kimbisa del Santo Cristo del Buen Viaje, a Regla de Palo cult founded in Cuba by Andrés Facundo Petit.

Mayombero A follower of Mayombe, one of the Regla de Palo cults.

Nsasi The name used for all the *ngangas,* or principal receptacles used in Mayombe; spirit.

npungus, nkisis, and other deities that are intermediaries between the supreme god and the people.

The most important legacy of these religions is a vast mythology with an infinite number of situations and interpretations. The deities have virtues and defects similar to those of humans, and believers seek their favor in order to improve their lives on earth or to gain access to significant prophecies through oracles or omens.

Although Afro-Cuban deities bear no resemblance to the Penates, the ancient Roman household gods that ensured an adequate supply of food and drink for families, there is a strong link between food and their worship; at every major ceremony, dining and specific foods play a central role. There is no parallel to the Christian sacrament of communion, in which a food representing, or believed actually to be, God is consumed, but many foods are reserved for specific gods and are eaten during ceremonies held in their honor, while others are expressly forbidden. Most of the preferred foods are tubers and fruits native to the Americas and exported to Africa, as well as some originally from Africa that were brought to the New World, such as yams. Poultry and lamb are among the most frequently consumed meats, as well as eggs and seafood.

These three Afro-Cuban religions hold collective meals as part of their initiation ceremonies. In Regla de Ocha, also called Santería, when the food is served a portion is saved as an offering to the orishas, in rigorous hierarchical order. In Regla de Palo Monte animals are sacrificed to the gods and then eaten; the diners sit in a semicircle, and a chorus leader sings the virtues of the menu. Those initiated into the Abakuá Secret Society dance around a large common pot.

REGLA DE OCHA OR SANTERÍA

Each orisha or deity has a favorite dish for some special reason, explained in the *pattakíes* or legends of Afro-Cuban culture. The orishas are masters; they supervise and favor certain human activities and materials, and they have certain responsibilities. Eggún prefers a Cuban stew called *ajiaco*, Elegguá likes coconut, Oggún likes aguardiente (a distilled spirit), Ochosi prefers venison, Oddúa eats pigeons, Yemayá likes watermelon, Obatalá eats any white-colored food, Ochún likes honey, Changó prefers bananas, Babalú Ayé likes beans, Yewá prefers fish, and Oyá likes eggplant.

Some dishes are used only as offerings, either because many of their ingredients are inedible or because they are not cooked. Such preparations have the generic name of *addimú* and are placed on altars, near running water, under a sacred tree, or any place commanded by the honored orisha. Among the terms used for these offerings, it is easy to distinguish between the ones that Africans make to their orishas, the ones created in Cuba, and the ones that were brought from Africa but significantly modified by the Cuban independence fighters, including drinks such as *kasimbanjoó*, made from cane juice, sour orange, and *piña ratón*, an edible bromeliad; and *cheketé*, prepared with roasted and fermented corn, lemon verbena tea, sour orange, and molasses.

Food prohibitions are indicated in the messages, or *oddunes*, in the *Ifá* and *Diloggún* prophecy systems. Oddunes reveal to the believer what could be described as a life pattern, providing a vision of what is operating and exerting influence on the believer. Restrictions are linked to the deities' likes and dislikes, described in relevant *pattakíes*. On a more subjective and individual level, strict observance may be interpreted as the believer's desire to attract

the deities' favor and satisfy personal needs with their help. For example, the oddún of *Ifá Obbara Melli* prohibits eating cornmeal in all its forms, as well as eggs, squash, lamb, okra, bananas, and any other food enjoyed by Changó.

REGLAS DE PALO MONTE

The day a *ngueyo*, or initiate, is born, a drink called *chamba* is prepared; it is used as a toast from the tata or yaya (from the father or mother) to guests from other houses. To a base of *malafo*, or aguardiente, the *Mayomberos* add cayenne peppers, hot sauce, garlic, grains of paradise, ginger, grated sticks, and *fula* or gunpowder, among other ingredients. *Brillumberos* and *chamalongos* also add cooking wine, cognac, cinnamon, basil, sacred root, incense, and some other ingredients, depending on the customs of the respective temples. The chamba prepared by *kimbiseros* also contains candle scrapings, a little tobacco, and pieces of cascarilla, the *pemba* or gypsum used in all rites and recovered by the *dimanga* or scribe, in order to ensure direct communication with the *nfumbe* or dead person and the spirits of deceased elders.

The food placed on the *ngangas* is a sacrificed animal. On occasion *plazas* of various fresh fruits are placed in a circle around the ngangas. Signatures are scratched into the ground, and participants ask how many days the offering should remain and where to throw away the fruits when that period has ended. There is always whispered singing to the ngangas when the food is offered and when it is thrown away or buried, as well as when the initiates and elders gather to eat.

Ceremonial offerings of food. Santería followers offer food to Saint Barbara during a ceremony in Santiago de Cuba in December 2009.
AP IMAGES/JAVIER GALEANO

For spiritual communion with the deities and the nganga, sacrificed animals are cooked and served at a ceremony called *cumbite saura*. The diners sit in a circle on the ground, around the cooks and their pots, and pass the plates from left to right. When everyone has taken his portion the people begin to eat, while the leader of the singing explains how the food was made and praises the results. The food eaten on this occasion is a sort of stew shared by the initiates, guests, and religious elders. Usually white rice, thick black beans, lamb roasted over charcoal, rooster fricassee, yucca with garlic sauce, and lettuce and tomato salad are also served. Malafo is drunk from gourds. At the end, the *Bakonfula*, or chosen leader, takes a little of the food to the woods, so that Sambia and the spirits are aware of this act of communion.

In contrast to Mayombe and Brillumba, in Regla Kimbisa the most important ceremonies are the initiation or *Jubileo de Padres*, the day of Santo Cristo del Buen Viaje; October 9, the festival of Santo Cristo del Buen Viaje's sponsor and guide, San Luis Beltrán; the end of the Old Year; and the start of the New Year.

On September 5, father and mother teachers, as the elders are called in Regla Kimbisa, bury crucifixes that are magic, according to Andrés Facundo del Cristo de los Dolores Petit, the founder of the cult, at the foot of a ceiba, a tree sacred in all Afro-Cuban religions—replacing the African baobab in the liturgy—for a period of seven days. After burying them, believers clean themselves with the leaves of the white cedar, which have great purifying powers. At midnight a sacrifice is made to Sarabanda, and a ritual meal is held inside the temple, headed by twelve father and mother teachers, recalling Christ's Last Supper with his disciples. After that, a large dinner is given for all the believers who belong to the temple. Finally, a receptacle is circulated among the participants for washing their hands, while they sing, "Let's take away the table, let's take it away."

The most important banquet within Regla Kimbisa is the Dinner of the Dead, on December 31. The *fundamento*, or sacred objects, are revealed; candles are lit; deceased ancestors are prayed and sung to for hours; and the ceiba and the nganga receive sacrifices. On one side of the temple a chalk circle is drawn, and inside it is placed a pot of rice, beans, and pork. Everyone dances and sings around this circle, while also taking some food from the pot with their fingers and eating it until the pot is empty. The ceremony generates an intimate communion with the dead. At dawn, the poultry is killed and cooked, and the ceremony is repeated to satisfy the spirits, who view their followers' joy approvingly.

ABAKUÁ SECRET SOCIETY

Abakuá's austere nature is reflected in various aspects, including the ritual meal on the day a new member is initiated or sworn into the society. This initiation ceremony is popularly known as the appearance of the *iremes* or *diablitos* (little devils). In elegant clothing, believers perform an intricate mimetic dance through which they purify and cleanse themselves of evil and communicate with their dead ancestors who were virtuous members of the society.

Huge pans of boiling oil are placed inside the circle formed by the participants; while black-eyed pea fritters are cooked in the oil, the participants pass around a gourd filled with aguardiente. To make the fritters, which are quite tasty, the black-eyed peas are soaked all night, washed several times the next day, strained, and crushed in a mortar with garlic. Salt, pepper, and a little water are added to this paste, and then it is fried in spoonfuls in a lot of lard or in a cast-iron fryer.

The initiates are served a sacramental drink called *aguañusosó*, made from aguardiente, salt, seven finely chopped herbs, grated pieces of seven sacred woods, peanuts, ginger, banana, grated yam, and other ingredients. When the initiate drinks it, he communes with Abasí, with the spirits of his fellow members, and with his brothers. Without breaking the circle, believers and initiates pass around a second gourd filled with *uriabón*, the food offered at the feast; they dance around the marks made on the ground with gunpowder and then offer food to the dead, the four winds, and the four cardinal points. By that time, the sorcerer Nasakó will have tasted and approved the food cooked by the *nkandembo*.

That food is cooked in a large pot, with everything that has been served as an offering: yams, bananas, rooster or goat, and, in small amounts—so they do not spoil the flavor—herbs, sticks, tobacco, and cascarilla. The nkandembo's magic lies in attaining the exact amount of each ingredient, so as not to offend the palate. According to legend, Nasakó cooked the first meal and put the first nkandembo in charge of making the sacred food from then on.

Generally, these rituals are carried out once a year. They begin at midnight and end before the first morning light, because the so-called worldly party begins at dawn and ends at sundown. There is a round table, beautifully decorated, with Olofi-Sambia-Abasí-God at the head and surrounded by saints, orishas, nkisis, and npungus, enjoying the delicacies that nature provides and forgetting about squabbles, conflicts, and quarrels. All of humanity enjoys an unforgettable banquet.

BIBLIOGRAPHY

Angarica, Nicolás Valentín. "Manual del oriaté." Havana, 1955. Available at http://www.scribd.com/doc/20770141/Manual-de-El-Oriate-Con-Odduns.

Bolívar, Natalia, and González Díaz de Villegas, Carmen. *Mitos y Leyendas de la comida afrocubana.* Havana: Ciencias Sociales, 1993.

Bolívar, Natalia, and González Díaz de Villegas, Carmen. *Afro-Cuban Cuisine: Its Myths and Legends.* Havana: José Martí, 1998.

FOOD: FOOD SHORTAGES AND GENDER

Catherine Krull

The early 2000s Cuban food shortages and women's lives.

On 8 November 2008 the third catastrophic hurricane in two months hit Cuba. Damage to infrastructure and an already shaken food system was extensive—exceeding $10 billion, one-fifth of Cuba's annual GDP. Anxiety increased as Cubans despaired over widespread destruction of recently re-sown fields, a dislocated economy's ability to import food, and a broken transportation system's capacity to distribute foodstuffs. Complicating recovery, the hurricanes occurred concurrently with the genesis of a global financial crisis, while the decades-old U.S. embargo exacerbated shortages in Cuba. However, this crisis was not Cuba's first confrontation with acute scarcities. With the onset of the Special Period (1990–1994), domestic food production fell by more than one-half while imports declined by 30 percent. During this time Cubans consumed 57 percent less protein and 51 percent fewer calories than the daily recommended minima. The state reacted, but formal mechanisms to meet the dearth of food and other essential items proved inadequate. Not surprisingly, given that economic crisis has long politicized Cuban women's daily lives, women were expected to fill the gaps left by the state. Accordingly Cuban women have become adept at dealing with food shortages, assuming an increased workload, and navigating daily challenges in a society in which gender equity and family survival are often at odds.

HOW CUBA'S FOOD SUPPLY FALLS SHORT

The 1959 Revolution brought Cubans promised education, health care, housing, and food. The state made food accessible through a ration system (roughly one-half of the daily caloric intake), subsidies, price controls, and distribution programs at workplaces and schools. Agricultural markets, primarily government owned and operated, offered produce at low fixed prices. Because Cuba imports significantly more food than it produces (a ratio of 4:1), macroeconomic mechanisms looked to increase supplies: generating hard currency by redirecting the economy from sugar production to services, import substitution, and large-scale agricultural restructuring, including urban agriculture programs. But Cuban agriculture underperformed. Moreover, these mechanisms have habitually flagged during economic crises, as in the early 1990s and post-2008, necessitating state-enacted emergency measures, including some counter to revolutionary principles.

With the Soviet Union's collapse and a simultaneous crash of the international sugar market, Cuba's standard of living plummeted; 89 percent of its exports and imports were lost and within two years its economy contracted by 35 percent. By 1993, Cuba's gross domestic product (GDP) decreased by 60 percent. A 1992 government-implemented austerity program, the so-called Special Period in a Time of Peace, included emergency measures to withstand an exceptionally serious economic crisis. This program kept hospitals and schools open, increased foreign investment, expanded the tourist industry to generate hard cash, and legalized the use of U.S. currency. Urban agriculture was also heavily promoted. However, these measures did not overcome scarcities, and, on the whole, families coped on their own. The efficiency of these emergency measures was severely compromised when the U.S. federal government enacted the 1992 Torricelli and the 1996 Helms-Burton laws to tighten sanctions.

Between the late 1990s and 2008, the economy improved, with food and other essential items more plentiful. Several emergency measures taken in the early 1990s were rescinded, including the U.S. dollar-based dual economy. But just as Cubans began experiencing relative abundance, the island suffered three catastrophic hurricanes: Gustav (30 August 2008), Ike (8 September 2008), and Paloma (8–9 November 2008). Housing, roads, local industry, and electrical systems across the island sustained extensive damage, and the food system and infrastructure were decimated; all sectors of production—fruit, vegetable/tuber, grain, avian, and porcine—reported significant losses. An estimated 4,000 metric tons of reserve foodstuffs were lost in damaged storage facilities during Ike alone. For months markets sat empty or, in those few that were open, with only limited items available. Scarcity caused price inflation. Many food items doubled in value (guava) or tripled (onions). Others like black beans and avocados reached unprecedented prices. In many ways, post-hurricane food disruptions mirrored the worst of the Special Period.

Again the state introduced emergency measures, including price-fixing and planting quick-to-grow vegetables in fields and vacant urban areas. Landmark decisions increased the number of private small businesses and distributed tens of thousands of acres of farmland into private hands and cooperatives. In 2009, the state cancelled the majority of free worker lunches and closed most canteens—saving $350 million. On September 13, 2010, the government announced that one-half million public-sector workers would be laid off—10 percent of Cuba's wage-earners—to revitalize a stagnating economy. Despite these sweeping state measures, Cuba still experienced acute

Damage from Hurricane Paloma. Just as Cubans began experiencing relative abundance, the island suffered three catastrophic hurricanes. The last of these, Hurricane Paloma (8–9 November 2008) destroyed this family's home in Santa Cruz del Sur. SVEN CRUETZMANN/ MAMBO PHOTO/GETTY IMAGES

food problems: In the 2009–2010 period, adding to inefficient domestic production and distribution, imports decreased by 37 percent owing to poor sugar harvests, lost revenues from tourism, and global rice shortages. These difficulties, alongside recent government cuts—like the lunch program—unduly affected Cuban women.

HOW FOOD SHORTAGES SHAPE WOMEN'S LIVES

From the onset, Fidel Castro argued that a successful revolution depended on freeing "women from domestic slavery, to create conditions . . . to participate as much as possible in production" (Castro 1963). Yet Cuba's recurring economic/food crises have rendered women's public participation precarious, their home life more labor intensive, and their ability to contribute to their community limited by the challenge of everyday survival. With fewer resources, household work, especially acquiring and preparing food, has become more laborious and stressful. Cuban women are expected to assume these responsibilities while maintaining paid employment and community participation. And they have typically sacrificed more during the most acute crisis periods.

For example, in 1993 the majority of the fifty thousand Cubans who temporarily suffered optical or peripheral sensory damage by epidemic neuropathy (caused by nutritional deficiency and significant weight loss) were women between the ages of twenty to sixty-four years of age (Román pp. 13, 25). Indeed, the incidence of females between the ages of twenty-five and forty-four contracting the disease were twice that of males in the same age group; the gap primarily explained by the tendency of women to give up their own portions of food to other family members (Krull and Kobayashi). It is not surprising then that the least likely to contract the disease were adolescents and children younger than fifteen years of age, pregnant women, and the elderly (Román p. 14).

Results from research conducted in Havana between 2001 and 2010, which involved 30 focus groups, 25 weekly 24-hour use-of-time diaries, and 35 unstructured face-to-face interviews, indicated that a typical day for most women entails eight and a-half hours at paid employment and another seven obtaining food, cooking and preparing meals, looking after family members, doing laundry, and housecleaning. Transportation consumes another hour.

Hence, women's work exceeds fifteen hours per day, one-fourth spent feeding their families. Women who kept daily use-of-time diaries for a study conducted in Havana claimed no free time or counted night-time sleep as free-time activity. Reflecting women's burden, 45 percent of employed women reported no help with domestic and childcare work; 10 percent described partner/husband assistance; and only 2 percent said their sons helped. Conversely, more than one-third of employed women relied on female relatives, typically mothers or daughters, to help with household work. This assistance reflects the gendered nature of work as female relatives contribute to household labor—acquiring and preparing food, cleaning, and childcare—while male partners/husbands assist primarily with childcare (see Krull and Kobayashi; Eckstein and Krull; Krull and Davidson).

HOW WOMEN RESPOND TO FOOD SHORTAGES

Although recurring economic crises have intensified the politicization of Cuban women, they are not passive victims of circumstance. They resist, act politically, take on the burden of excessive workloads, and collectively strategize and cooperate to survive the crisis and protect their gains in other state services. Women's first response to shortages is characteristically to alter their patterns of consumption by reducing their own food intake so their family has more, changing their diets by not eating meat, for example, or eating only evening meals. Another strategy sees family members move in together—what Cubans jokingly call an extended family by necessity—to stretch food budgets and supplies. It is economical and less work to cook for more, and it means more people to perform household tasks. Generally speaking, however, rather than creating possibilities for restructuring gendered domestic roles, food shortages reinforce gendered divisions. The idea of women as domestic experts is entrenched in Cuban society, thus solidarity with female neighbors and coworkers has been an effective strategy. A bag of tomatoes is shared. Coworkers living in different areas of Havana might acquire different products from local markets, and exchanges are arranged. When food is particularly scarce, a collective stew might be made whereby neighbors contribute whatever ingredients they possess.

With food products unavailable or financially inaccessible through conventional channels, many women use the black market. Black-market trading, however, is perceived as both counterrevolutionary and in opposition to revolutionary and familial duties. Women rationalize this conflict by creating boundaries: Purchasing milk, eggs, or other necessary items that are in short supply or expensive is acceptable; luxury purchases like lobster, shrimp, or expensive foods marketed for foreigners is excessive. Stealing from the workplace for family consumption or black-market selling remains taboo. Yet even then, necessity is taken into consideration. Many Cubans receive remittances from relatives living abroad, allowing some women to minimize black-market purchases. Many families depend on remittances; hence, migration becomes a longer-term strategy to overcome difficult economic circumstances at home. Medical, environmental, and other humanitarian endeavors by Cubans sent abroad have allowed some families to increase their incomes. Beyond direct financial benefits from transnational strategies, family member migration also means fewer mouths to feed and, naturally, more rations for the rest of the family.

Cuban women have become highly efficient at surviving in a crisis, but shortages and disruptions can only be sustained for limited periods before affecting their health and ability to participate fully in society. Cuba's food system remains vulnerable to environmental shocks, domestic economic fluctuation, and global economic and political trends. The 2008 hurricanes demonstrated this fact with their repeated shocks to agriculture and the Cuban economy. Rising international food prices and the global economic crisis threatened the sustainability of the ration system. Coupled with massive layoffs, the Cuban government has been faced with the daunting challenge of initiating needed economic reforms aimed at increasing food security, efficiency, and distribution during a global crisis without compromising revolutionary gains in education, health, equity, and social welfare. Cuban women faced various kinds of uncertainty that would test their capacity to adapt to shifting food landscapes.

BIBLIOGRAPHY

Castro, Fidel. Speech given at the closing of the Congress of Women of the Americas (Havana, January 16, 1963). Available from http://www.marxists.org/history/cuba/archive/castro/1963/01/16.htm.

Castro Ruz, Raul. July 26 Commemorative Address (Holguín 2009). Available from http://hcvanalysis.wordpress.com/2009/07/30/cuba-raul-castros-speech-at-july-26th-celebration-in-holguin/.

Eckstein, Susan Eva. *The Immigrant Divide: How Cuban Americans Changed the U.S. and Their Homeland*. New York: Routledge, 2009.

Eckstein, Susan, and Catherine Krull. "From Building Barriers to Bridges: Cuban Ties Across the Straits." *Diplomacy & Statecraft* 20, no. 2 (2009): 322–340.

Food and Agriculture Organization Trade Database. Imports: Commodities by Country: Cuba (1989–1994). Updated December 2010. Available from http://faostat.fao.org/desktopdefault.aspx?pageid=342&lang=en&country=49.

"Información a nuestro pueblo." *Granma*, September 30, 2009.

Krull, Catherine, and Melanie Davidson. "Adapting to Cuba's Shifting Food Landscapes: Women's Strategies of Resistance." *Cuban Studies* 42 (2011).

Krull, Catherine, and Audrey Kobayashi. "Shared Memories, Common Vision: Generations,

Sociopolitical Consciousness and Resistance among Cuban Women." *Sociological Inquiry* 79, no. 2 (2009): 163–189.

Román, Gustavo C. "An Epidemic in Cuba of Optic Neuropathy, Sensorineural Deafness, Peripheral Sensory Neuropathy, and Dorsolateral Myeloneuropathy." *Journal of the Neurological Sciences* 127 (1994): 11–28.

Weinreb, Amelia Rosenberg. *Cuba in the Shadow of Change: Daily Life in the Twilight of the Revolution.* Gainesville: University Press of Florida, 2009.

Wright, Julia. *Sustainable Agriculture and Food Security in an Era of Oil Scarcity: Lessons from Cuba.* London: Earthscan, 2009.

G

GALLO AMARILLO (MARIANO RODRÍGUEZ)

Dannys Montes de Oca Moreda

Mariano Rodríguez's Gallo Amarillo *(1956) painting and its Cuban roots, tradition, and modern sense of culture.*

The work of painter Mariano Rodríguez (1912–1990) transcends Cuban art and culture because of its diverse themes and their interrelationship. The rooster, in particular, has become an emblematic figure. Rodríguez himself explained that the rooster theme came to him as he observed his backyard and became fascinated by the bird's grace, movement, and composure, but it is not clear when he first featured a rooster in his painting. The artist states that he exhibited his first oils of roosters in 1940 at the National Capitol Building ("a red rooster, a white one, and one from behind"), possibly for the collective show *300 años de arte en Cuba* (300 Years of Art in Cuba), having already painted "a pile of watercolors using a live rooster as a model" (Garzón Céspedes pp. 87–88). Given the appearance of the poetry and art journal *Espuela de plata* (1939–1941), founded by Mariano along with poet José Lezama Lima (1910–1976) and critic Guy Pérez Cisneros (1915–1953), it seems 1939 was the starting point for this theme. The journal's title, which translates as "Silver Spur," transforms the fighting cocks' accessory into an aesthetic symbol and likely inspired Mariano's connection to and subsequent exploration of the theme. Without a doubt, portraying the rooster in a variety of colors, with many formal interpretations and poetic fantasies, was a great aesthetic exercise that eventually took on a life of its own; in the long run, Mariano identified with the rooster's symbolism, and the rooster became an icon of Cuban culture's universality.

The intrigues and myths that are often associated with this bird, which is unable to fly and can only lift itself up, conjure a telluric yet spiritual image. As part of Cuba's Hispanic and Christian heritage, the rooster appeared on the weathervanes of towers and cathedral domes greeting the sun during the period of the Cuban Republic. The rooster also embodied the spirit of that 1938 generation of poets and painters, the avant-garde to which Mariano belonged and which, full of hope, created the equally symptomatic *Espuela de plata*. Because of its apparently low level of aggressiveness, the rooster is associated with alertness, activity, and games, although its popular image in Cuban tradition signifies male sexual potency. Thus, it is not only an element recovered from Cuba's domestic, rustic origins, oral traditions, and imaginaries, but also a significant component of the island's diverse modern social imaginary. (The symptomatic and emphatic use of animals that attain a symbolic dimension is also apparent in other painters of that generation: Carlos Enríquez's horses, Fidelio Ponce's and Amelia Peláez's fish, Eduardo Abela's cows, and Wifredo Lam's birds.)

Rodríguez's roosters, still sculpted in the style of Mexican murals or classic Picassos and very decorative, displayed insubordination in their attempts to escape a threshold limited by fences or grates. Their beauty and nobility seemed to be intrinsic to the garden or surrounding yard, but their spurs, beaks, combs, and Egyptian eyes revealed a desire to transcend that space and time. In the 1950s, relationships of forms and symbols culminated in the representation of the winged (and unrepresentable) figure of the orisha Osaín. This development activated a latent animism suggesting a rooster that seems to rise up and achieve a mythic dimension.

Gallo amarillo (Yellow Rooster, 1956), more than any other painting, typifies a symbol of sunlight, a model of vigilance and activity that compares and contrasts it with the idea of the feminine as an ancestral domain, a life-generating source of nourishment. The painting is usually interpreted as an iconic version of latent cultural machismo; however, in Mariano's pictures, women preceded the alpha-male rooster, which in turn is subordinated in many of its early appearances.

■ *See also*

Visual Arts: Republican Period

Nonetheless, although the rooster/male would like to understand and rule woman's world of forms and games, his space is equally equidistant and transcends his subsequent relations with femininity. The game consists of placing them together and separated, in subjecting them to the seduction that each wields over the other. Woman is not a single identity, but becomes universal in her diversity; the rooster, in the case of *Gallo amarillo*, is emblematic, a unity of the diverse, bolstered by strength and masculinity that is complementary rather than exclusive. These are nonantagonistic poles in time and in Mariano's life, an equilibrium of forces coming together, forming a voluptuous femininity that is a complement to the rooster's masculinity.

Gallo amarillo is the incarnation of the symbolic rooster, refracted and variable. It is the most sweeping and explicit example of the rooster's formal and symbolic progressive integrity. It summarizes all of Mariano's searches and periods of experimentation up to that time, at a moment in which the artist exhibited the possibilities of combining the figurative and the abstract as a model that moves beyond form into the formless or that returns from the formless back to form. For that reason, *Gallo amarillo* is also a paradigm for subsequent paintings; it is the end, the beginning, the point of return, and representative of its own ontogeny. It includes both an anatomical rooster and stylization, as well as a set of boomerangs. The boomerang is an element that appears in Mariano's work as a formal solution for certain figurative elements and conceptual references that, in *Gallo* (Rooster), *Gallo amarillo*, *Gallo rojo* (Red Rooster), and *El hombre del bumerán* (The Boomerang Man), all from 1956, achieve a paradigmatic dimension. Beyond suggesting movement and displacement, the rooster's feathered body becomes the incarnation of the island's national and ecumenical spirit. Its legs, a strength born of the earth, whose spurs appear multiplied like knives and blades, are those of a generation still active. Its Egyptian eye—previously a universal primitive incarnation, now an Afro-Cuban vigil—syncretizes the rooster's Catholic affiliation.

Popular Cuban religious beliefs appear in Mariano not only in references to his Catholic affiliation but also in references to Afro-Cuban religion, as seen in works such as *Ireme* (1948), *Diablito* (Little Devil)

and *Bembé* (both from 1949), and *Elegguá*, *Osaín*, and *Babalú Ayé* (all from 1958). The red crest, the predominance of yellow, the nuances of grays, greens, and blues, all speak to Mariano's use of color, of the value of color in his aesthetic ideology.

Gallo amarillo also announces change: light, hope, and the dawn of a liberating and tenacious era and of a generation that tests itself in battle. It is a rooster to be admired, a triumphant rooster that, like a bull in the ring, is not allowed defeat and proudly displays an infinite certainty of victory, a boldness both provocative and majestic.

In the end, *Gallo amarillo* is Mariano, who lived his life courageously, a long and prodigious life of art, politics, and community, and who bequeathed to Cuba a symbol and an entire social imaginary of its modernity. This was a different modernity—diverse, transgressive, usurping, and given to the universal. With his roosters, he helped create what poet Cintio Vitier (1921–2009), quoting José Lezama Lima, called "that myth that we were missing, the myth of insularity with its diverse interpretations, an active reversal of perennial assimilations, a theology to which we are inevitably linked by frontiers of water" (Vitier p. 76).

BIBLIOGRAPHY

Garzón Céspedes, Francisco. "Barcos que ganaban y perdían batallas." In *La memoria y el juicio*. Santiago de Cuba: Editorial Oriente, 1981.

Merino Acosta, Luz. "Mariano Rodríguez: La identidad del color." In *Mariano*. Madrid: Centro Cultural del Conde Duque, 1998. Catalog.

Montes de Oca Moreda, Dannys. "Tema, discurso, y humanidad en Mariano Rodríguez." In *Mariano*. Seville: Escandón Impresores, 2003.

Pérez Cisneros, Guy. *Evolución de la pintura en Cuba*. Havana: Dirección General de Cultura, Ministerio de Educación, 1959.

Portuondo, José Antonio. "Mariano: Gallos y Masas." In *Morón: Dirección de artes plásticas y diseño*. Havana: Ministerio de Cultura, 1982. Catalog.

Veigas Zamora, José. *Mariano: Catálogo razonado: Pintura y dibujo, 1936–1949*. Vol. 1, Havana: Ediciones Vanguardia Cubana, 2007. Catalog.

Vitier, Cintio. "Para llegar a Orígenes." In *La aventura de Orígenes*. Havana: Editorial Letras Cubanas, 1994.

Opposite page:
Gallo amarillo (1956) **by Mariano Rodríguez (1912–1990).** Mariano Rodríguez's *Gallo amarillo* (Yellow Rooster) is an icon full of references to deep Cuban roots, tradition, and a modern sense of culture and its universal scope and importance. COURTESY OF THE ESTATE OF MARIANO RODRÍGUEZ

GENDER

Cuban studies related to gender span both social and humanistic sciences in various disciplines. Published topics have covered women, the women's movement and its associations, feminism, masculinity, sexism, violence, and sociability.

The diverse themes of the essays that follow cover the fields of history, literature, sociology, film, and the human involvement in sociocultural processes. While written from a Cuban experience, the essays provide a global overview of the manner in which human relations have been constructed from the sixteenth century to 2010. This timeframe covers three periods of society that extend over more than five centuries and range from the colony, through the republic in its first fifty years, to the later period of the Revolution of 1959. Many fundamental changes took place during this time.

Beginning in 1959, women became more visible in academic publications, but it was not until the last decades of the twentieth century that gender studies began to look at history from the perspective of women. Literature is still lacking, however, on basic studies that analyze different dimensions of the way in which mutual interactions between human beings have evolved.

GENDER: COLONIAL PERIOD TO 1920

María del Carmen Barcia Zequeira

An examination of social relations based on sexual differences and power relationships from the sixteenth to the twentieth century in Cuba.

Gender relations in Cuba have taken place within the context of extremely complex changes in Cuban society, in phases that span more than four centuries, through the transition from colony to republic and on a stage swept by two wars of independence. Gender relations in Cuba can be understood historically by describing the fundamental changes that occurred during the different stages, and the symbolic aspects of each period. This article suggests the following three periods: sixteenth century to 1750; 1750 to 1880; and 1880 to 1920.

FROM THE SIXTEENTH CENTURY UNTIL 1750

In early colonial society there were few women on the island. Conquistadors were men who left their wives and children behind and, upon settling on a new space, seized the native population and divided the land among themselves, though not all of it, since some land remained in the hands of the *cabildo* (town council), also controlled by this founding group. In due course, the conquistadors brought over their spouses or sought women on the island, and in one way or another they started families. Other settlers followed, and proceeded along the same lines.

The first population census were carried out by the Catholic bishops during their pastoral visits. They counted the number of residents, who in 1570 numbered no more than one thousand, and who even by 1608 numbered only 1,109. These statistics included families, and therefore suggest the presence of women. The documents and public records of the first centuries of the colonial period reveal a substantial number of women submitting petitions for land and authorization to develop their own businesses. For Havana

alone, there are 308 petitions by women between 1567 and 1660. Among these, there were few indigenous females and only a few free African women, known as *horras*. As might be expected, most of the women listed were white.

At least until the first half of the eighteenth century, the relatively precarious economic and demographic conditions of the island encouraged a certain degree of social equality between men and women. There are a number of examples. In the middle of the sixteenth century, farm property in Havana was granted to Catalina Martín, an indigenous woman. Inés de Gamboa was granted concessions to the site of Canímar and on the plain of Macurijes, in what later became the province of Matanzas, in order to herd her cows. Andrea del Corral offered to have fifty yearlings weighed at the butcher's for feeding the city of Havana. Costanza de Cárdenas, María Ruiz, and Catalina Alvarez owned frigates, while Juana García, an African, "fed white people" and sold wine. These and other women engaged in manufacturing and trade and were entrepreneurs, either in partnership with their husbands or sons or in their own right; they belonged to various social strata and classes and operated in public life with direct, personal petitions to do so.

Given their living conditions and activities, men had a shorter life expectancy than women, and widows were common. The high ratio of females to males prompted women to remarry or enter into consensual relationships that were socially acceptable.

Some upper-class women held eminent political positions, either standing in for or acting on behalf of their husbands in the performance of official duties. Such was the case of Doña Guiomar de Guzmán in Santiago de Cuba, who in 1540 assumed the political position left vacant by the death of her first husband, the auditor Pedro de Paz. In 1545, upon her third marriage, to Juanes de Avilés, governor of Santiago de Cuba, she acquired considerable wealth and began to play a major role in the political life of the *villa* (Pichardo Viñals pp. 42–56). Isabel de Bobadilla served as governor of the island when her husband, Hernando de Soto (d. 1542), set off to explore Florida. Nothing comparable to the behavior and impact of these women would occur in the following historical periods.

FROM 1750 TO 1880

During the latter half of the eighteenth century, disruption in the relatively equitable situation discussed above occurred, since the economic power of the island's patriarchy was by now well established. In this different context, women were gradually relegated to the domestic sphere, where their roles were defined as wives and mothers.

Yet even in this hegemonically masculine context, there were certain female transgressions between public and private space. Such was the case of the Marchioness de Jústiz de Santa Ana, who drafted a "Memorial" addressed to Carlos III (r. 1759–1788), which conveyed Havana women's views on the English occupation and scolded the cowardly and venal conduct of royal officials (Campuzano pp. 18–22). In 1808, another woman, writing anonymously but describing herself as "una fiel havanera a sus paisanas" (a loyal Havanera to her fellow country-women), published a proclamation denouncing the Napoleonic invasion of Spain (Granillo p. 67). Barely two years later, Manuela Mozo de la Torre, wife of Sebastián Kindelán, governor of Santiago de Cuba, defended her husband against accusations of his being a French sympathizer, as charged by Bishop Joaquín de Osés y Alzúa (Orozco p. 125). But such instances of outspoken behavior by women were exceptions.

By the latter half of the seventeenth century, the population of the island had increased rapidly due to the African slave trade, which continued until the 1860s. The island's population also increased due to the massive immigration of Spaniards, which began in the 1860s. The natural demographic growth of the population occurred only among the strata of free blacks and mulattoes.

The high ratio of males to females at this time encouraged extramarital consensual relationships, parallel to legal marriage, resulting in a high number of children born out of wedlock. According to the census of 1846, for instance, nearly 46 percent of all children belonged in this category. The ratio was higher among blacks and mestizos, since nearly 76 percent of baptized children belonged to that group.

Travelers to Cuba noticed how women shopped sitting in their carriages, wearing delicate gauze dresses and using the Victorian language of fans to seduce eligible young bachelors. They also referred to mothers who were concerned about the good order of their household, the education of their children, and keeping their pantries full. With less interest, travelers noted that along with these women, there were many African, free mulatto, or slave women, as well as poor whites, who were in charge of washing, cooking, sewing, nursing other women's infants, midwifery, teaching the alphabet at the schools of their female friends, and selling seasonal foods on the street. Some even owned small businesses; they were money-lenders, rented shops, and owned slaves. Their fathers, brothers, husbands, and sons worked at all available occupations and also engaged in certain professions: they were tailors, pall-bearers, carpenters, blacksmiths, masons, blood-letting practitioners, dentists, veterinarians, port foremen, and distinguished musicians, and some got to own houses, ranches, pastures, and coffee plantations.

In the middle of the nineteenth century, the discourse of domesticity spread, reinscribing the patriarchal view that women were inferior to men and were little more than an instrument of reproduction, destined to perpetuate the species. Although this view (which was similar to that of other societies) was vague in the lower classes, it was accepted by the elite families and middle classes, for whom female symbology was personified by the "queen of the house," whose purpose in life was motherhood, the schooling of children, and household management. To be patient, self-sacrificing, and passive, to preserve honor, and to provide consolation in distress, first for the husband and then for the children, were seen as the supreme feminine virtues. Accordingly, a woman's role was confined to the domestic sphere, in which there was little room for autonomous social, cultural, or labor objectives. Female education was directed toward the fulfillment of women's domestic obligations.

Women lacked legal status, regardless of social origin or skin color. In this regard, they occupied a space comparable to that of slaves, who were represented by their masters or by the authorities. Whether white, mulatto, or black, rich or poor, women were represented under the law by their fathers, husbands, or adult sons, and they constantly saw themselves foiled in exercising the paltry rights granted to them by existing patriarchal legislation. The activities of these women as they sought to safeguard their competence formed an imaginary practically unknown, woven into the complicated fabric of colonial society. This effort is evident in their divorce suits, the recourse established only for cases of confirmed adultery or extreme physical abuse. At this time divorce meant only a "separation of bodies," which prohibited sexual intercourse; it did not deal with other domestic issues such as property and custody of children (Hernández Fox pp. 39–58). Before a divorce judgment was handed down, the woman bringing suit was placed in a public or private house or locked up like an object under safekeeping. If and when a woman managed to obtain a divorce decree, she was despised, as was the experience of Baldomera Fuentes, who was fired from her teaching position (Provencio and Andreo pp. 241–261).

During the Ten Years' War (1868–1878), many women were insurrectionists and saw their children die of hunger and disease; these women cared for the sick and wounded and even engaged in combat operations. In exchange for their participation, however, they did not get the same social recognition as men. In 1869 Ana Betancourt lodged a claim with

URSULA COIMBRA PÉREZ DE VALVERDE: CHAMPION FOR WOMEN OF COLOR

Ursula Coimbra Pérez de Valverde (1865–?) was a primary school teacher; she also taught English, French, and piano. She was the daughter of Mariano Coimbra, an outstanding musician, poet, and Cienfuegos patriot. She married Nicolás Valverde and served as a promoter, editor, and outstanding journalist for *Revista Minerva* (Minerva Magazine) during its two stages. Her work was directed at women of color, with the basic goal of encouraging them to study, at the same time that it informed them of all their rights and prerogatives. All her articles were written under the pen names Cecilia, during the 1880s, and La Sibila in the early years of the republic. Her colleagues considered her to be a heroine, believing that she was inspired by the century's ideas, so that mulatto and black women would be able to emerge from their oppression.

María del Carmen Barcia Zequeira

the assemblymen of Guáimaro for the civil rights of women. During those years, slaves who served in the insurrectionist camp were freed, but the subordinate status of women remained unchanged. Despite these inequities of the patriarchal system, after a decade of struggle in which women had taken radical positions, a change in the life and aspirations of Cuban women was brought about.

FROM 1880 TO 1920

In the 1880s, a variety of changes were introduced into Cuban society, the most significant of which, from a social standpoint, were the abolition of slavery and the mass immigration of Spaniards. The white population grew rapidly, while the black and mulatto populations stabilized through natural demographic growth.

In the political arena, these years were defined by the War of Independence (1895–1898) and the Hispano-Cuban War (1898), whose outcomes transformed the life of many citizens and served as a catalyst for bringing women into public life. Particularly in the labor and intellectual spheres, the wars shattered the established norms of social behavior and opened new opportunities for the participation of women, both within and beyond Cuban borders. Women contributed significantly to the war effort. They not only performed services similar to those they provided in the previous war, but some even served as officers of the Liberation Army.

The upper and middle classes continued to assert that wives should be the harmonious complement of their husbands, properly educated and instructed to serve their spouses and teach their children. During this period, progressive women's schools were founded, such as the one started by the eminent Cuban pedagogue María Luisa Dolz, with the purpose of developing capable female citizens. However, these opportunities were limited to the elite families.

Despite the objective and subjective obstacles imposed on them, some women joined the workforce and entered the public sphere. They worked as teachers, midwives, nurses, sales clerks, telegraph operators, and typists, thus serving beyond the realm of household chores (Barcia pp. 298–317). According to the period's conservative view, women should only engage in salaried work to meet the special needs of their families, but not as an aim in itself, as a condition or as an achievement toward her financial or social emancipation. In 1899, women comprised 10.7 percent of Cuba's total labor force, a rate that remained constant throughout this period.

By the end of the nineteenth century, women appeared in public spaces, such as cafes and professional associations, which had formerly been off-limits to them if they were unescorted. They also entered the universities to follow career paths, graduating as pharmacists or physicians, and they traveled as professionals in their own right and even in the company of male colleagues. They expressed their own opinions publicly; that is to say, they were free to contradict male opinions, to resist or transgress sex-linked subordination, and they also enjoyed small liberties.

Feminist values became more widespread throughout the island, a development that contributed to women leaving Cuba to live elsewhere. Women like Emilia Casanova (wife of Cuban novelist Cirilo Villaverde and an activist and fundraiser for the War of Independence in her own right) distinguished themselves in the United States in the 1850s. Indeed, one important outcome of the struggle against Spain was increased emigration to the United States, which jumped significantly during the years before the War of Independence. At this time, Cubans founded more than one hundred revolutionary clubs, many of which were organized or chaired by women (Casasús pp. 265–269, 385–387).

The Cuban Independence War produced sharp disruptions on many levels, and it, of course, had an influence on gender relations. The economic and social situation forced women into the workplace, but also into beggary and prostitution. The women who had participated in the national emancipation process felt ready for gender emancipation and were in fact eager to exercise their democratic rights as equal citizens alongside the men.

Liberal behavior codes were introduced, first during the U.S. occupation (1898–1902) and subsequently during the establishment of the neocolonial republic (1902). Increasing numbers of women took on various occupations and jobs. For example, the container department of the Crusellas y Hno factory was staffed by women, some of whom were black or mestizas. Other women, trained in the 1890s at Domitila García de Coronado's typesetting school, worked as typesetters at many of the printing shops. In Cárdenas, the magazine *Página azul* (Blue Page) was printed in a shop where five women worked (Barcia p. 303).

The feminization of the teaching profession was evident during the early years of the republic, especially in the primary schools. The demand for teachers caused the development of an academic curricula designed to train women. Courses were offered in six provinces on the island; the courses in Havana were conducted at the Teatro Martí (Barcia p. 292). In 1899, Harvard University offered summer courses on its main campus in Cambridge, Massachusetts; since 47.2 percent of the students selected were women, the program was structured to include contacts with the women's clubs of Boston. This educational resource and their experience in the United States contributed to the development of feminist ideas in Cuba (Pérez pp. 35–55).

WOMEN DISTINGUISH THEMSELVES IN FIELDS OTHER THAN EDUCATION

Another key area of employment for women was nursing. By 1902, the seven existing schools in Cuba had graduated 23 professionals and had 205 alumni (Barcia p. 304). Women also published newspapers and magazines for white intellectuals (whether *criollos*, or descendents of Spaniards), as well as for blacks and mulattoes.

As more women entered the workforce, domestic duties needed to be handled differently. Caring for the infants of working mothers, for instance, became a problem, since in 1904 Havana had only two daycare centers for children under the age of six. Some progressive women began to support women with fewer financial resources and lower educational levels. Using the slogan "For the Cuban Woman," they founded the Sociedad Protectora de Sirvientas y Artesanas La Caritativa (Charitable Society for the Protection of Servants and Artisans), which was directed by Dolores Laseville de García. Thus, a new social vision developed regarding working women (Barcia p. 307).

The fact that marriages occurred between men and women with similar profession suggests the recognition of female success in public life, as well as respect for women's financial independence. All these transformations served to establish new gender relationships.

It is likely that the lower classes, whose members worked simply to earn a living, had a better understanding of women in the workforce than the wealthier classes did. But it must also be noted that in marriages where both parties were financially solvent, many women left their profession to devote themselves to caring for their children and household duties.

Despite the increasing numbers and contributions of women in the health and educational fields, still some thinkers voiced criticism. For example, in the magazine *La Higiene*, Dr. Manuel Delfín used the epithet *marimachos* (butch) for women who presumed to occupy traditionally male roles in public life, accusing those who allow women this freedom of being "enemies of our social regeneration" (Barcia p. 322). Undeterred, in 1912 women demanded the right to vote and other civil rights, action that led to the emergence of three feminist parties (Caraballo y Sotolongo pp. 41–50).

Women's demands, which were ultimately approved between 1917 and 1934, had been under discussion since the closing years of the nineteenth century. During the Constitutional Assembly in January 1901, men of such prestige as General José Lacret Morlot, Miguel Gener, and Salvador Cisneros Betancourt proposed that women be granted the right to vote, but only nine legislators voted in support of the idea. After this setback, a group of distinguished women began making the case for a feminist conference. The magazine *Cuba libre* (Free Cuba) reported that the conference would be held in Havana in 1904, and it would address civil rights issues, improvements in the financial condition of women, and other concessions that would endow them with the same legal rights enjoyed by women in other countries.

From 1904 on, the debate focused on how to reform the outdated civil code, including laws governing divorce, which had been addressed as early as 1896 when it was included in the insurgents legislation and covered by Miguel de Carrión in the pages of the journal *Azul y rojo* (Blue and Red). Opposing views appeared in *El Nuevo Criollo* (New Criollo) and in the magazine *Minerva*, because black and mestizo women believed that that law was detrimental to their interests.

The feminist positions were reinvigorated in 1910 and circulated in the printed media, as for example, the magazines *Fémina* and *Minerva*. In 1913, two newspapers were founded in order to spread Cuban feminism: *La luz* (The Light), edited by Amalia Mallén de Ostolaza and published by a branch of the National Party, and *El feminista*, the mouthpiece of the Cuban Feminist Party. Thus, this period between the colony and the republic became the harbinger of substantial changes, not only in the political sphere, but also in gender relations.

BIBLIOGRAPHY

Archives of the Office of the City Historian. *Actas trasuntadas del cabildo de la Habana.* 18 vols. Havana, 1550–1699.

Barcia, María del Carmen. *Capas populares y modernidad en Cuba.* Havana: Editorial de Ciencias Sociales, 2009.

Campuzano, Luisa. *Las muchachas de la Habana no tienen perdón de Dio.* Havana: Ediciones Unión, 2004.

Caraballo y Sotolongo, Francisco. *Mujeres: ¡A las urnas y al hogar!* Havana: Librería Cervantes, 1918.

Casasús, Juan J. E. *La emigración Cubana y la independencia de la patria.* Havana: Editorial Lex, 1953.

Cruz Martínez, Dania de la. *Movimiento femenino Cubano.* Havana: Editora Política, 1980.

Cruz Martínez, Dania de la, and Marcos D. Arriaga. *María Luisa Dolz: Documentos para el estudio de su labor pedagógica y social*. Havana: Editorial Academia, 1990.

Duby, Georges, and Michelle Perrot, eds. *Historia de las mujeres en Occidente*. 5 vols. Madrid: Editorial Taurus, 1993.

Estrade, Paul. "Los clubes femeninos en el Partido Revolucionario Cubano (1892–1898)." In *Anuario del Centro de Estudios Martianos*, no. 10. Havana: Centro de Estudios Martianos, 1987.

Fernández Robaina, Tomás. *Bibliografía de la mujer Cubana*. Havana: Biblioteca Nacional José Martí, 1985.

González Pagés, Julio Cesar. *En busca de un espacio: Historia de mujeres en Cuba*. Havana: Editorial Ciencias Sociales, 2003.

Granillo, Lilia. "Feminist Background from 1808: The Proclamation of a Habanera." *Review of Social Sciences and Humanities* A–27 (May–September 1989): 67–73.

Hernández Fox, Leonor A. *El divorcio en la sociedad Cubana (1763–1878)*. Havana: Editorial de Ciencias Sociales, 2007.

Orozco, María Elena. *Ana Manuela Mozo de la Torre: Los acentos de una mujer*. Santiago de Cuba: Editorial Oriente, 2007.

Pérez, Louis A. Jr. "The Imperial Design: Politics and Pedagogy in Occupied Cuba 1899–1902." In *Essays on Cuban History: Historiography and Research*. Gainesville: University Press of Florida, 1995.

Pichardo Viñals, Hortensia. "Una mujer en la conquista de Cuba: Doña Guiomar de Guzmán." In *Temas históricos del oriente Cubano*, edited by Fernando Carr Parúas. Havana: Editorial de Ciencias Sociales, 2006.

Provencio, Lucía, and Juan Andreo. "Una vida de horizontes y fronteras: Baldomera Fuentes: Mujer y maestro." In *Mujer, cultura, y sociedad en América Latina*, edited by Roland Forgues. Pau, France: Université de Pau et des pays de l'Adour, 1998.

Rojas, María Teresa de. *Indice y extractos del archivo de protocolos de la Habana*. 3 vols. Havana: Burgay y Cía, 1950–1957.

Scott, Joan. "Gender: A Useful Category of Historical Analysis." *American Historical Review* 91 (1986): 1053–1075.

GENDER: THE WOMEN'S SUFFRAGE MOVEMENT IN CUBA

K. Lynn Stoner

The demand for women's rights and universal suffrage in Cuba between 1920 and 1940.

In 1901, as Cubans turned their attention to forming a modern state that many hoped would embrace progressive ideals such as sovereignty, liberty, racial equality, and workers' rights, the matter of women's rights inevitably arose. The recent wars for independence had uniquely prepared women and their supporters to demand suffrage and social reforms, because women had spent the previous thirty years at war for *Cuba libre*. The prominence of female independence fighters in the Cuban national struggle, the fact that the desire for independence was informed by aspirations for social justice and democracy, the centrality of individual liberty and national sovereignty to the formation of a new national identity, and the convergence of national and international women's movements pushed women's rights to the forefront of nation building. Thus Cuban women were poised to demand full citizenship with all its privileges and responsibilities when Cuban administrations were installed. The struggle for suffrage provides a segue into an examination of the female experience between 1898 and 1940. Women's rights activists believed that only through the vote could women of all races and classes chart their course in the emergent nation.

The path to suffrage was not long but it was circuitous, involved as it was with controversies between political parties and the struggle to overthrow the autocratic leader Gerardo Machado (1925–1933). Nearly all participants in the women's movement, whether they were from conservative Catholic associations such as the Damas Isabelinas or the more liberal social democratic organizations such as the Asociación Nacional Feminista, supported women's suffrage. Only those associated with the Partido Socialista Popular (PSP; the Cuban Communist Party), rejected democracy and universal suffrage as tools of an illegitimately imposed state and evidence of U.S. domination. Political and cultural divisions did weaken the women's movement, but these did not center on the matter of suffrage. Rather, they formed around issues such as the rights of illegitimate children, aid to prostitutes, venereal disease, and sexual double standards for women and men. Suffrage, by contrast, united women in a campaign built around democratic principles.

THE EARLY SUFFRAGE MOVEMENT

Following independence in 1902, war widows sought work and their husbands' pensions since their husbands had died defending Cuba's freedom. The economy, however, could not sustain employment for all able-bodied men, much less women. War widows without a trade or who did not have children able to support them were forced onto the streets by the thousands to beg or prostitute themselves. Unemployment also affected educated women seeking jobs as teachers, business staff, nurses, journalists, typesetters, seamstresses, entertainers, social workers, and maids. It fell to bourgeois women, who had the luxury to attend meetings and raise money, to act in the cause of resolving the pressures of women's unemployment, poor education, and political exclusion.

By 1912 numerous women's clubs had formed throughout the island, and at first they reflected the ideas of the local membership rather than a united national cause. Clubwomen were the first to ask the government to provide women's health facilities, women's education, and provisions for war orphans and widows. In general, these women also agreed that Cuban feminism differed fundamentally from U.S. and European feminisms, in that motherhood and femininity, not gender equality or challenges to men's authority, were the foundations of women's rights. By 1917 the clubs were sufficiently established with reliable memberships and goals to consider a national movement for women's rights.

THE WOMEN'S MOVEMENT AND THE VOTE

Women organized a national movement amid the embarrassment of government failures and foreign domination. Cuban officials not only served primarily themselves and their class, they gave preference to U.S. business investors, disadvantaging Cuban workers in the process. Unrest grew as labor organizations were attacked by the national police and military. Successive presidents responded to opposition with violence, which caused some Cubans to wonder whether they could govern themselves. From the chaos, the women's movement not only insisted that Cubans could govern but laid out principles by which they should do so. In 1917 from among the clubs, two Havana associations, the Comité de Sufragio Femenino and the Partido Nacional Sufragista, formed to advance the terms of women's political participation on a national level. Both associations adopted the republican ideals of individual rights, women's rights as citizens, and a constitution that would guarantee them.

By the end of 1917, the Comité de Sufragio Femenino and the Partido Nacional Sufragista had merged to form the first major political association of the women's movement: the Club Femenino de Cuba. Its initial objectives were to end prostitution, establish women's prisons, and win women's rights. Leading members of the club also engaged in important resistance operations against President Alfredo Zayas Bazán (1921–1925). They blamed him for corruption and the subversion of democracy. They joined the Veterans of Independence Association to demand the *regeneration* of Cuba, meaning the end of corruption and cronyism. By 1923, the leaders of the club agreed to enhance their efforts by bringing together a national women's movement. They invited representatives from all the women's clubs and associations from around the nation and through democratic procedure defined the goals of a national campaign. This action was the first democratic process in Cuban history, but it was not an entirely harmonious affair. Religious and conservative women clashed with free-thinking progressives who challenged traditional marriage values and the inheritance rights of illegitimate children.

The Club Femenino de Cuba formed the umbrella organization, the Federación Nacional de Asociaciones Femeninas, which planned and carried out the First National Women's Congress in April 1923. Under the leadership of Pilar Morlon de Menéndez, the Federación set an agenda and invited participation from every women's organization, feminist or not. The idea was to accurately balance diverse women's views and not rush forward with a predominance of feminist representatives. Thirty-one organizations attended, and their agendas ranged from the non-political to the conservative (Damas Isabelinas) to the militantly progressive (Club Femenino de Cuba). Delegates spoke on themes such as suffrage, the adultery law, the rights of illegitimate children, public welfare programs, prostitution, drugs and alcohol, fair wages for women, school curricula, women's education, feminism, and the beautification of the city of Havana.

This democratic approach exposed deep divisions among Cuba's female leaders and resulted in the more progressive proposals losing support. Yet the congress was successful. It resolved to establish women's and children's courts, a welfare system, moral and material aid to working women, the equalization of women's legal status, civic activities, action against social vice and crime, an end to the adultery law, and women's suffrage.

In 1925, Gerardo Machado of the Liberal Party took office as president. He promised to root out corruption, develop the economy, ensure peaceful political competition, and abrogate the Platt Amendment; he also promised to serve only one four-year term. The Club Femenino could not allow such an optimistic moment to escape, so the membership organized a second national congress in April 1925 to attract Machado's allegiance and to assure legislation that would give women the political participation and social change they wanted. As in the first congress, speakers took the stage to convince their fellow delegates, the press, the public, and officeholders of the logic of their demands. This meeting, however, was different from the first, because the conservative women came prepared to destroy any radical resolutions aimed at rights for illegitimate children or changes in public policy on prostitution. The meeting resulted in a show of hostility toward the radicals, provoking a walk-out of women such as Ofelia Domínguez Navarro, the major proponent of the rights of illegitimate children. The Second National Women's Congress finally agreed to emphasize women's suffrage and social welfare. It resolved to advance women's education, cultural events, charity, and research on childhood diseases, and agreed to create maternity hospitals subsidized by federal government funding and oversee the moral justification of political movements, which meant that women would speak out against political corruption and the government's violation of human rights.

WOMEN'S SUFFRAGE AND THE CRISIS IN DEMOCRACY

In 1927 a political crisis forced the women's movement to take a position either for or against President Machado, who had canceled democracy for what he called "the strict enforcement of law and order." That year Machado, encouraged by his support base and with the endorsement of the three largest political parties (an arrangement he called *cooperativismo*), decided to amend the Constitution of 1901 to extend the presidential term from four to six years to allow him to remain in office until 1934. To make sure of loyal congressional support, he outlawed all political parties except the faithful Popular, Conservative, and Liberal parties, a move that violated the constitution. He courted women's support by saying that after his term, he would step down and allow for a free election in which women would participate.

Responding to the crisis, all female activists gave priority to the vote. They attempted to force Machado to include women's suffrage in his reform package as proof that he was a democrat and not a dictator for life. But Machado gave suffrage scant attention, and the Constitutional Assembly approved the most grievous departures from participatory government, including outlawing opposition parties and extending presidential terms without having to get public approval through referenda. The issue of votes for women was laid aside for a later national referendum. At this point, most organized women withdrew their support for Machado.

Between 1927 and 1933, Cuba collapsed into an undeclared civil war brought on by the constitutional crisis and the economic depression. New recruits joined the insurrection. Students and members of the bourgeoisie united with the working class against what they saw as a dictator who used deadly force against citizens. Women who had believed they could set an example of democratic process were rendered irrelevant in an environment of insurgency. In 1928, members of the Club Femenino who supported liberal, broad, democratic, and social reforms organized the Alianza Nacional Feminista (ANF), calling themselves the new *mambisas* (revolutionary fighters), and they invited women from the working classes to join their ranks. The organization lasted for two years before the most radical elements broke away in 1930 over a disputed election for the association's president. Ofelia Domínguez Navarro and a group of radicals formed the Unión Laborista de Mujeres that served the insurgency as lawyers, propagandists, and mobilizers. That same year a moderate group of women organized the Lyceum Lawn and Tennis Club, a noncombative organization that adhered to liberal democratic principles and provided scholarships and educational opportunities for women. It also invited individuals from every political path to speak in its gracious surroundings.

Women were divided over the means of opposing Machado, but this did not mean that they remained in their homes and submitted to his increasingly brutal law-and-order tactics. María Collado was perhaps the only stalwart who remained in the Ministry of Labor, serving as an inspector who went into factories to investigate violations of labor codes, salary contracts, and health conditions. The rest of the activist women found ways to subvert Machado's government. Elena Mederos de González and Hortensia Lamar joined the middle- and upper-class ABC Sociedad Revolucionaria, a violent underground organization known for its urban sabotage and assassination campaigns. Their work was not visible until Lamar became a major negotiator for Machado's ouster. Ofelia Domínguez Navarro went to prison four times and was exiled once for her visible and boisterous resistance. Genteel ladies were known to carry pepper in their pockets when they went shopping in case they encountered mounted policemen chasing students or workers. They threw the pepper up the noses of the horses to help the young people escape.

The fact that members of the women's movement splintered into various factions of the resistance meant that the ABC, Machado, and the mainstream political parties, the Directorio Estudiantil Universitario (DEU; University Student Directorate), the Unión Nacionalista (UN; National Union), and the PSP, all had to guarantee women's rights if they desired female support. While the Communists did not discuss women's suffrage but did guarantee women's presence in the leadership, all others advocated suffrage. Thus the crisis in democracy was a catalyst for women's voting rights.

The configuration of women's resistance differed from that of men's. Women joined in underground movements and risked their lives organizing strikes and demonstrations, writing propaganda flyers, and standing before troops who were prepared to mow them down at funerals of fallen protestors. However, they did not participate in gangster-like shootouts with the authorities. More than men they made spectacles of the government's failures to abide by the constitution. Asserting their own feminine moral authority, they attempted to shame the president, the police, and the congress, sometimes appearing in the public galleries of the congress and exposing the bruises across their backs as evidence of police brutality, demanding that law and order be applied to the government. They formed a nonaligned organization called Mujeres en Oposición (Women of the Opposition) that expressed popular outrage at Machado's repression. They carried the coffin of a university student shot to death by the police. They turned funeral eulogies into political excoriations, and they interrupted theater events with performances of their own as they rose to accuse the government and its officials of the miscarriage of justice and perversion of their responsibilities.

Their trump card was the humiliation of public men. Like men, they went to jail. They were, however, assassinated in fewer numbers.

In 1932 and 1933, popular resistance to Machado was overwhelming. Unable to smother popular unrest and with Washington's support of him waning, Machado resigned in August 1933. Commander of the Armed Forces Fulgencio Batista helped appoint Ramón Grau San Martín president on 9 September 1933. Grau was a radical and a noncommunist reformer. He began issuing executive decrees aimed at social restructuring and redistributing wealth. Between 9 September and 15 January 1934, when he was forced from office by Batista, Grau established the eight-hour workday, distributed land, nationalized the labor force, and granted women the vote. Six years later under Batista's stern leadership, Cubans prepared to write their own constitution that would cleanse the old one of U.S. tutelage and Machado's reforms. Votes for women, decreed in 1934 in time for that year's elections, sent seven women into the House of Representatives, and suffrage was guaranteed in the 1940 Constitution, as were rights for illegitimate children.

Women's rights and suffrage came with the rejection of a dictatorship and the struggle for democracy. It was born with the post-independence generation eager to see the promises of José Martí fulfilled and to sanctify the blood of their mothers. Women proved themselves worthy of full citizenship as educators, businesswomen, journalists, civil servants, laborers, union organizers, entertainers, artists, and, later, insurgents.

BIBLIOGRAPHY

Domínguez Navarro, Ofelia. *50 años de una vida*. Havana: Instituto Cubano del Libro, 1971.

Lamar, Hortensia. *La mujer y la vida moderna*. Havana: Labor Escolar, 1928.

Mederos de Fernández, Rafaela. *La Mujer en el frente social de Cuba: Recopilación de 44 años de labor, 1894–1938*. Havana: Editora de Publicaciones Virtudes, 1939.

Miller, Francesca. *Latin American Women and the Search for Social Justice*. Hanover, NH: University Press of New England, 1991.

Prados-Torreira, Teresa. *Mambisas: Rebel Women in Nineteenth-Century Cuba*. Gainesville: University Press of Florida, 2005.

Stoner, K. Lynn. *From the House to the Streets: The Cuban Woman's Movement for Legal Reform, 1898–1940*. Durham, NC: Duke University Press, 1991.

Stoner, K. Lynn, ed. *The Women's Movement in Cuba, 1898–1958: The Stoner Collection on Cuban Feminism*. Microfilm, 13 reels. Woodbridge, CT: Scholarly Resources/Primary Source Media, 1987.

Torriente, Loló de la. *Mi casa en la tierra*. Havana: n.p., 1956.

Torriente, Loló de la. *Testimonio desde dentro*. Havana: Editorial Letras Cubanas, 1985.

GENDER: THE ROLE OF WOMEN IN THE STRUGGLE AGAINST BATISTA

Gladys Marel García Pérez

Gender and power relationships understood in biology and symbolically.

The assumption that the world of women is part of the broader world of mankind makes it possible to understand the study of humanity from the viewpoint of gender and power relationships, quite above and beyond sexist conceptions. The revolutionary generation of the 1950s provided the context for a gradual transformation of discriminatory power relations governing the place of women and youth in the family, society, and politics, thus making it possible for women to make a qualitative leap after the triumph of the Revolution of 1959.

REPUBLIC AND REVOLUTION

Following the coup d'état that returned him to power in 1952, Fulgencio Batista abrogated the Constitution, banned political parties, established an autocratic regime, and set up an antagonistic situation between the government and the people. The rebellion against the military coup involved the organization of emerging power groups, under the leadership of the so-called *Generación del '50* (Fifties Generation). This activity occurred in a climate of widespread dissatisfaction and a deep feeling that nothing in Cuba was the way it should be. The mindset of this generation, heirs to the *Generación del '30* (Thirties Generation), reflected several strains of thought, including José Martí's ideas on liberty and social justice, European and Latin American cultural currents carrying ideas of reform and transformation, and the socialism of the Russian Revolution. From the perspective of gender relations, the ideals and actions of the Generación del '50 were symbolically linked to the liberation and social justice movements that challenged the Batista regime.

In 1927 the Grupo Minoristas (Minority Group) appeared, which defined itself as a "group of intellectual workers" because they were "representative of the majority of the population" (Rexach p. 64; Sabas p. 1). Among their members, Mariblanca Sabas Alomá and Emilio Roig de Leuschering worked to maintain equitable gender relations between themselves and the other members of the group. Another creation amid the effervescence of the time was the founding of the Havana Lyceum by Berta Arozena and Renée Méndez Capote. Méndez had been involved in the creation of the Madrid Lyceum and had personally experienced discrimination by the highest social classes after her divorce, when her situation went

■ *See also*

Constitution of 1940

Governance and Contestation: Insurrection, 1952–1959

Governance and Contestation: The Republic: 1902–1952

The Machado Dictatorship Falls: August 1933

Figure 1

Total population of Cuba by sex (1919–1953)

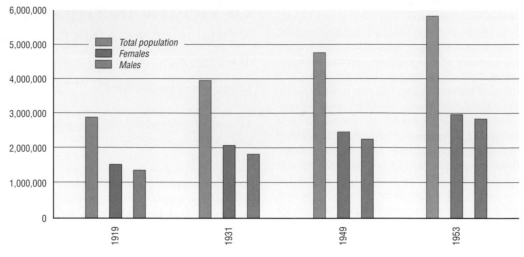

SOURCE: Cuban census of 1919, 1931, 1949, and 1953.

from that of a "rich woman to the lifestyle of a working woman" (Méndez p. 67). Lyceum members held Sabas Alomá in high regard as an intellectual symbol, and together with male literary affiliates, they championed the cause of equal rights for women; working together, they declared that the plentitude of tasks of the "human community" were for men and women to do together.

The National Feminist Alliance was also created in 1928, composed of women from different political ideologies. Elena Mederos was elected secretary, and another prominent member was the militant socialist Ofelia Domínguez. Elena Mederos, Cuba's official delegate to the Inter-American Women's Commission, represented cultural currents in the United States; identified with the feminist perspective promoted by the Woman's National Party of the United States (Guerrero pp. 46–49). Meanwhile María Gómez Carbonell carried on the ideological concepts purported by Fulgencio Batista's "revolución del 4 de septiembre," following the confrontation with the repressive government of General Gerardo Machado. These women generally reflected U.S., Spanish, Soviet, and European political trends.

After Batista seized power in 1934, women insurrectionists opposed to his regime joined Joven Cuba (Young Cuba), which had a left-wing leadership. Previously various women of the Directorio Estudiantil Universitario (DEU del '30; University Student Directorate) and its Directorio Feminino (Women's Directorate) preserved the slogan of "total and definitive regime change" and transferred their field of activities to the political arena. They joined the women's section of Partido Revolucionario Cubano (PRC; Cuban Revolutionary Party), more commonly known as the Partido Auténtico (Authentic Party), which governed

between 1944 and 1952 and was characterized by dishonesty and corruption.

The Constitution of 1940 guaranteed a state of law that included the civil and political rights of women as citizens; in practice, however, what prevailed were laws passed by men. Ordinary people increasingly steered clear of politics. In response to this pattern, Eduardo Chibás organized the Partido del Pueblo Cubano (Ortodoxo) (PPC[O]; Party of the Cuban People [Orthodox]) and brought in women such as Carmen Castro, the secretary-general of Socorro Rojo Internacional (International Red Aid) with whom he had collaborated in the struggle for civil, political, and union rights. She was a member of the national executive directorate of the Ortodoxos and served as an active participant in the creation of the worker, peasant, and youth sections.

THE STRUGGLE AGAINST BATISTA (1952–1959)

On the morning of the coup d'état of 10 March 1952, women and men mobilized and converged upon Havana's Colina Universitaria (University Hill) and barracks throughout the country, seeking arms to take up against Batista; they later made up the critical mass of insurrectionary organizations under the leadership of the Generación del '50. The vanguards of this diverse movement were Rafael García Bárcena, José Antonio Echeverría, Fidel Castro, Carmen Castro, and Aída Pelayo, who respectively organized the Movimiento Nacional Revolucionario (MNR; National Revolutionary Movement), the Directorio Revolucionario 13 de Marzo (13th of March Revolutionary Directorate), the Movimiento Revolucionario 26 de Julio (MR-26-7; 26th of July Movement), and the Frente Civico de Mujeres Martianas (Martí

Women's Civic Front [Martianas]). Other women's groups in the Generación del '50 included Mujeres Oposicionistas Unidas (United Women's Opposition), directed by Marta Fryde; the Frente de Mujeres Cubanas (Cuban Women's Front) directed by Gloria Cuadras in the province of Oriente; and in the United States the women's section of MR-26-7 in New York City, and the Frente Cívico de Mujeres Martianas of Tampa. In Cuba neither the MR-26-7 nor the DR had specifically female sections.

In the ongoing debates between Ortodoxo youth and the women's section of that party, Carmen Castro Porta, Pastorita Núñez, and Fidel Castro stood out for their championing of the insurrectionary struggle against the regime. These two women and Marta Frayde organized the Ortodoxo women into the civic front known as *las Martianas* (inspired by José Martí). Women from the Partido Auténtico also joined the Martianas, as did women from the MNR and others, including workers, homemakers, and students with no party affiliation. Women from the Lyceum would join later on.

The Frente Cívico de Mujeres Martianas (Civic Front of the Martianas) objective was to engage in activities with the insurrectionary organizations in order to overthrow Batista and install the people's power in the form of a popular revolutionary government. The Front promoted the ideas of José Martí; it opposed overtures to the regime by the partisan political opposition favoring civic dialogue; and it provided aid to political prisoners and their families, among other activities. Fidel Castro proposed a merger of the front and MR-26-7 to Carmen Castro Porta, but the incomprehension of the leaders charged with this effort forestalled it.

The women who were actively involved in or leading the insurrection escalated their efforts, going from organizing strikes and demonstrations from their vantage point within student groups (Federación de Estudiantes Universitarios [FEU], Asociaciones de Alumnos de los Institutos, Escuelas de Segunda Enseñanza) to joining the actual armed conflict, which was led by the action section of the Revolutionary Directorate. Ester Lina Milanés, who was brutally tortured, was among those who distinguished themselves in conflict. In the provinces and regions women also helped create the guerrilla front of the Directorate in Escambray.

WOMEN IN LEADERSHIP AND POWER ROLES

Eva Jiménez exemplifies the engagement of Cuban women who joined an array of insurrectionary groups whose membership consisted exclusively of women or was mixed or who were politically active in groups of both kinds. In the 1930s she was associated with the politician Eduardo Chibás and subsequently with Fidel Castro. After the coup d'état she joined the MNR and, along with Rafael García Bárcena,

MARIBLANCA SABAS ALOMÁ

Mariblanca Sabas Alomá (1901–1983), a poet and journalist, was one of the founders of the Grupo Minorista (Minority Group, 1927), a leftist social, literary, and political organization. Sabas Alomá opposed the regimes of Gerardo Machado and Fulgencio Batista from a revolutionary standpoint. She also rebelled against the discriminatory limitations established by male hegemony, and she predicted early on that the twentieth century would be transformational in the emancipation of women.

Sabas Alomá advocated radical reform in all parts of society, from changes in family relationships to reorganization of governmental structures and the state. In her writings published in Cuba and abroad, she denounced social injustice, affirmed the principles and ideals of feminism, and fought for recognition of the civil, social, and political rights of women. She argued that salaried employment for women was essential to their achieving liberation from and equality with men. In her view, the feminist struggle should welcome support from men.

BIBLIOGRAPHY

Cairo, Ana. *El Grupo Minorista y su tiempo*. Havana: Editorial de Ciencias Sociales, 1978.

Sabas Alomá, Mariblanca. *Feminismo: Cuestiones sociales y crítica literaria*. 1930. Santiago de Cuba: Editorial Oriente, 2003.

Stoner, K. Lynn. *From the House to the Streets: The Cuban Woman's Movement for Legal Reform: 1898–1940*. Durham, NC: Duke University Press, 1997.

Unruh, Vicky. *Performing Women and Modern Literary Culture in Latin America: Intervening Acts*. Austin: University of Texas Press, 2006.

Gladys Marel García-Pérez

organized the plan to assault the headquarters of the Ciudad Militar de Columbia (Military Citadel of Columbia) in Havana, but the plan was aborted, and she was captured along with other conspirators in April 1953.

Through these actions Jiménez was the first woman to confront Batista by participating in a plan to attack military headquarters. She secured the involvement of other women, represented by the Martianas and by the women's section of the Partido Ortodoxo (whose general secretary, as well as the secretaries for organization and propaganda, engaged in protests against her imprisonment as well as that of García Bárcena). After serving her sentence, Jiménez emigrated to Mexico, joining Fidel Castro there. She returned to Cuba after the *Granma* expedition, and during 1957 and 1958 she was once again a crucial actor in the insurrectionary plots undertaken by the Martianas and the Revolutionary Directorate.

Margot Machado, the leader of the MR-26-7 in the Cuban province of Las Villas and in Venezuela,

Figure 2

Population of Cuba by age and sex (1919–1953)

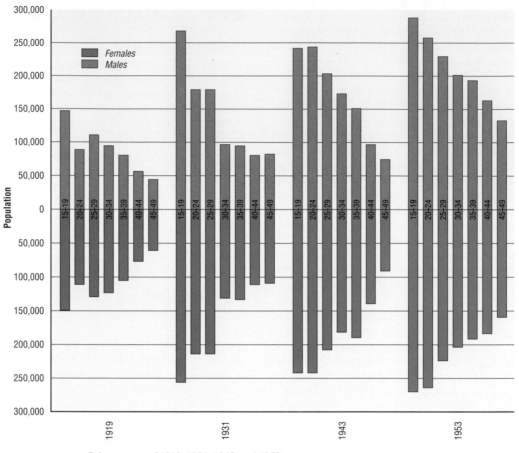

SOURCE: Cuban census of 1919, 1931, 1943, and 1953.

Population of Cuba by sex and level of education, 1953

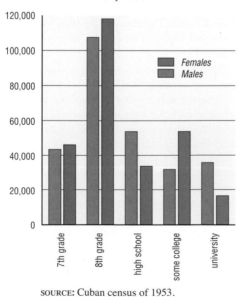

Figure 3   SOURCE: Cuban census of 1953.

was a widow who also headed her own household on the principle of equality with her children, with regard to both their work and in their struggle for liberty, democracy, and social justice. The idea of participating in the *mambisa* (insurrectionist) family thus took on another level of meaning in the light of the woman-mother fighting in the wars of independence. She represents changes in sensibilities and psychology that were also manifested in the political and social activity of other women at this time—women who were perhaps not even aware that along with the men they were in fact launching a process that would break down gender and power relationships and reconstruct them on the basis of equity.

Machado internalized the concept of *patria* (homeland) meaning *pueblo* (people), more through sentiment than through a rational process. José Martí's paradigms of liberty and social justice inspired Machado's and many other families to join the struggle against Batista and seek the restoration of democracy. She, as a teacher and provincial inspector of the Ministry of Education, held a post that allowed her to influence the teachers in her jurisdiction (most of whom were women, as elsewhere in Cuba) with her knowledge, honesty, and justice, while enabling her to circulate through the insurrectionist network in the province, promoting patriotic morals in society.

Despite all the changes that were occurring at the time, instances of discrimination continued. At the meeting on the Sierra Maestra convened by Fidel Castro in order to establish the Mariana Grajales Squad (1958), for instance, the physicians in the insurrectionary forces strenuously opposed allowing women to participate in armed combat, based on arguments having to do with female sensibilities, biological weakness, and physiological issues such as menstruation. Faustino Pérez, from the national directorate of the MR-26-7, argued in favor of integration, as did Fidel Castro; Castro declared that since women had been fighting alongside men to defend their rights, it was essential for men and women to keep on earning those rights together in combat. This approach was sustained after the triumph of the Revolution.

In the region of Cárdenas, as another example of contradictions around equality, the MR-26-7 was directed by a twenty-year-old woman who worked closely with the leaders of clandestine and guerrilla elements—but during some meetings with personalities of the region she was discriminated against on account of her sex and age. She sometimes needed to have another well-established male political figure, Dr. Enrique Sáez, the chief of the civic resistance, accompany her. One guerrilla chief questioned her leadership by asking Amador del Valle, chief of the action, militias, and guerrillas division, "Who is the boss, you or her?" to which he answered "she" (García-Pérez 2005, p. 27).

To demonstrate the youth of the women who participated in the insurrection a survey of seventy-five insurrectionary women conducted in 1955 (the year the insurrectionary network spread throughout the entire country) found that 53.5 percent were between the ages of fifteen and twenty-four. Some 70.7 percent lived in Cuba, whereas the remainder mostly lived in Miami and New York. Most were white, and most belonged to the MR-26-7 (García-Pérez 1999, pp. 129–130).

Conducted under the lead of Díaz Vallina, a larger survey of 675 insurrectionary and opposition women found that in terms of occupation, the highest percentages were engaged in household work, studies, office work, technical skills, and teaching. Their ideals were based on the political and social thought of José Martí. In concrete terms, they wanted to overthrow Batista, to achieve national economic independence, to implement the ideals of the Verguenza contra Dinero (Shame against Money)

Ortodoxo Party, remove corrupt governments, and end injustice; 7.5 percent of them advocated the ideal of a socialist society. The women interviewed reflected the Martí-inspired social conscience of freedom within a democracy that all Cubans could participate in.

Some 23 percent were familiar with or participating in women's organizations such as the Martí Civic Women's Front, the Daughters of Acacia, the Lyceum, or the United Women's Opposition. With regard to the insurrectionary struggle, 51 percent of these women affirmed that it drew no distinctions between them and the men. Being a student, male or female, also permitted more freedom of action, as they did not have the responsibility of providing for a family, and they were protected by their comrades. Some 48.75 percent considered that the struggle had made conditions more difficult for them since they lacked family support, or they felt rejected by their colleagues and had been assigned less important duties.

Nearly 93.75 percent of these women held the view that women had not tabled feminist demands in order to join the opposition movement but rather were struggling for social and political benefits on behalf of all the people, in working for the triumph of democracy, liberty, respect for human rights, and the full dignity of all human beings.

In January 1959 the revolutionary government appointed the first woman to hold a senior, national-level government post in Cuba: Elena Mederos became the minister of social welfare. Mederos was a distinguished figure from the Lyceum who had joined the insurrection. Other women who participated in or led the insurrectional project as leaders of a clandestine web, guerrillas, or from exile that later assumed positions in policy or the revolutionary government include: Celia Sánchez, Raquel Pérez, Margot Machado, and Pastorita Núñez (in government); Haydée Santa Maria, Vilma Espin, Gladys Marel García, Mirta Rodriguez Calderón, and Norma Porras (in cultural institutions and political organizations).

Women's engagement in the insurrection cannot be studied as a phenomenon that is somehow separate from or independent of the engagement of men. They acted together; men and women redefined themselves in terms of each other and achieved a balance that brought them ever closer to the goal of equity.

In their clandestine and guerrilla life, women liberated themselves from male hegemony over family and society; they shook off obsolete norms of social behavior and served alongside men in various public ways. These actions laid the groundwork for new assumptions about gender and power that made possible a women's revolution within the Revolution of 1959.

BIBLIOGRAPHY

Sources

Castro Porta, Carmen, Aída Pelayo, et. al. *La lección del maestro*. Havana: Editorial de Ciencias Sociales, 1990.

Coffigny Leonard, Olga. "Mujeres parlamentarias cubanas (1936–1958)." *Boletín Novedades Bibliográficas* 3 (2009).

Díaz Vallina, Elvira, et al. "La mujer revolucionaria en Cuba durante el período insurreccional 1952–1958." Archives of the University of Havana, Faculty of Philosophy and History, 1995.

García-Pérez, Gladys Marel. "Género, historia, y sociología: Cuba Siglo XX: Mujer y revolución: Algunos apuntes sobre estudios de casos y familias a partir de la perspectiva de la nación y la emigración." *Santiago* 86 (January–April 1999): 114–134.

García-Pérez, Gladys Marel. *Crónicas guerrilleras de Occidente*. Havana: Editorial de Ciencias Sociales, 2005.

García-Pérez, Gladys Marel. "Cuba, siglo XX: historia de vida y familia." *Revista Brasileira do Caribe* 8, no. 16 (January–June 2008): 377–395.

García-Pérez, Gladys Marel. "Mujer y Revolución: Una perspective desde la insurgencia cubana (1952–1959)." In *1959: Una rebelión contra las oligarquías y los dogmas revolucionarios*. Havana: Ruth Casa Editorial, Instituto Cubano de Investigación Cultural Juan Marinello, 2009.

Guerrero, Maria Luisa. *Elena Mederos: Una mujer con perfil para la historia*. Miami: Ediciones Universal, 1991.

Leyva Pagán, Georgina. *Historia de una gesta libertadora 1952–1958*. Havana: Editorial de Ciencias Sociales, 2009.

Méndez Capote, Renée. *Amables figuras del pasado*. Havana: Editorial Letras Cubanas, 1981.

Meyer, Eugenia. *El futuro era nuestro: Ocho cubanas narran sus historias de vida*. Mexico City: Universidad Nacional Autónoma de México, 2007.

Pérez, Louis A. Jr. *On Becoming Cuban: Identity, Nationality, and Culture*. Chapel Hill: University of North Carolina Press, 1999.

Rexach, Rosario. "El Lyceum de Havana como institución cultural." In *Dos figuras cubanas y una sola actitud: Félix Varela y Morales*. Miami: Ediciones Universal, 1991.

Sabas Alomá, Mariblanca. *Feminismo: Cuestiones sociales y crítica literaria*. Havana: Editorial Hermes, 1930.

Scott, Joan. "Gender: A Useful Category of Historical Analysis." *American Historical Review* 91, no. 5 (December 1986): 1053–1075.

Further Reading

Barcia, Maria del Carmen. "La familia: Historia de su historia." In *La familia y las ciencias sociales*, edited by Ana Vera Estrada. Havana: Centro de Investigación y Desarrollo de la Cultura Cubana Juan Marinello, 2003.

Domínguez Ofelia. *50 años de una vida*. Havana: Instituto Cubano del Libro, 1971.

Lamas Marta, ed. *El género: La construcción cultural de la diferencia sexual*. Mexico, PUEG, 1996.

Segura Bustamante, Inés. *Cuba Siglo XX y la generación de 1930*. Santo Domingo: Editora Corripio, 1987.

GENDER: SOCIAL JUSTICE IN THE REVOLUTIONARY PERIOD

Gladys Marel García Pérez

Gender, identity, and the activities of women in Cuba from 1959 to 2010.

The Cuban Revolution of 1959 launched a new cycle in the history of the republic, but the assumptions underlying the qualitative leap toward the construction of new roles and gender and power relations had already started during the preceding stage of national liberation. (With regard to social issues, *gender* and *power* refer to subjective human identities whose social constructs and ideas are manifested through symbols.) Most families, in their quality as collective structures, were in the vanguard of society, as were the individual women and men who comprised them, and they had already organized into popular revolutionary groups. They challenged old social norms, and in their day-to-day lives they broke down discriminatory behavior that subordinated women to male hegemony, race, and youth.

REVOLUTION AND SOCIAL JUSTICE: 1959–1960

Between 1959 and 1960, the example of liberating youth had seeped through every stratum and sector of Cuban society. The patriotic cultural identity that arose under the aegis of the republic was a harbinger of the movement for liberty and social justice and was manifested in the unity of the popular masses. The dams of youth were bursting open, sweeping away obsolete family patterns, and exacerbating disobedience and rebellion against paternal hegemony and its restrictions on the free will of the children. Patriarchal molds shaping marital relations began to fall apart, to the extent that they discriminated against or questioned the emancipation of women or applied unequal rules of behavior for men, women, lesbians, homosexuals, whites, and blacks.

In the social arena, the oppressive and subordinate roles and relationships of women were yielding to changes in law and public policy. Women were acquiring new roles and methods for engagement, in step with the rhythm of the real-life changes occurring in the political organization of society.

The original platform of the Revolution did not include women's demands. Women were not involved in drafting it, nor were they aware that they needed to crystallize their role as the vanguard of that segment of society. At this time, Cuban women were not attached to feminist ideas: Indeed, to some extent, they even rejected such ideas, seeing them as the bearers of a nationalist patriotic identity and a cultural mindset in search of social justice that did not include their demands with regard to women. Nevertheless, their active participation in the network of the liberation movement, on the island as well as in the diaspora and in the rebel army, gave women the authority and right to demand the construction of new and more equitable relations.

After 1959, the women's movement showed signs of continuity across the various strands of thought— nationalist patriotic, leftist, U.S., orthodox Soviet (Martínez)—that were manifesting themselves in women's organizations and institutions. In 1960, after the organization of the Women's Congress in 1959, these groups joined to form the Federación de Mujeres Cubanas (FMC; Federation of Cuban Women).

WOMEN'S ORGANIZATIONS AND INSTITUTIONS: 1959–AUGUST 1960

Combatant women wanted to engage in the Cuban revolutionary project on an equal footing with men. This objective included members of the Frente Cívico de Mujeres Martianas (Martí Women's Civic Front), Frente de Mujeres Cubanas en Oriente, and the Mujeres Oposicionistas Unidas (United Women's Opposition). Those women who were part of the policy team, in the provinces as well as in the municipalities, participated under the hegemony of the largely male leadership of the Movimiento Revolucionario 26 de Julio (MR-26-7; 26th of July Revolutionary Movement). The MR-26-7 (whose leaders seized power with a revolutionary army and government) and the Directorio Revolucionario 13 de Marzo (13th of March Revolutionary Directorate) were the main organizations during the first stages of the Revolution. Neither of these groups had a women's section, whereas those of the traditional parties were, in practice, nonfunctional.

During the first months of 1959, differing approaches were taken by the Frente Cívico de Mujeres Martianas, which followed radical leftist thought inspired by José Martí (1853–1895), and the Mujeres Oposicionistas Unidas, whose members came from a variety of orientations, such as those of the Mariana Grajales Squadron and the Lyceum. The Lyceum was a cultural and social women's society founded in Havana in 1929 by Berta Arozena and Renée Méndez Capote. It was modeled after the Lyceum of Madrid and promoted the progress of women's rights and the diffusion of culture (Guerrero pp. 64–67). These groups played a prominent role in the civic institutions that supported the insurrectionary movement.

In January 1959, Elena Mederos (1900–1981), a distinguished figure in the Lyceum, was appointed minister of social welfare of the revolutionary government (Guerrero). Several Lyceum graduates also joined the leadership of this entity, including Elena Mouré, who held the title of vice minister. The Frente Cívico de Mujeres Martianas dissolved on 28 January of its own accord. The Frente de Mujeres Cubanas de

Latin American Women's Congress, Santiago, Chile, 1959. Vilma Espín (standing right), delivers a report on the Cuban revolution and its programs. Facing her in the first row are (from left to right) Aleyda March, Cachita Abrahantes, and Gladys García. COURTESY OF GLADYS MAREL GARCÍA PÉREZ

Oriente and the executive arm of the Mujeres Oposicionistas Unidas continued to be engaged in various institutional roles, and its leaders on the left convened a national conference for April 1959.

The Frente Democrático de Mujeres (Democratic Women's Front), which was linked to the Soviet socialist–inspired Partido Socialista Popular (Popular Socialist Party), did not play a significant role in the liberation phase. Neither did other women's social, cultural, and political associations, whose records are preserved in the "Associations" section of the National Archives of Cuba.

In early January, the Células Revolucionarias de Base (Revolutionary Base Cells), which was in fact the MR-26-7 in Havana, organized the Casas del 26" (Houses of the 26th) group, which later spread throughout the country. At the same time, the group established its own Sección Femenina (Women's Section) with the Brigada Femenina of the Células Revolucionarias de Base. That leadership split off in March and, under the guidance of Ernesto "Che" Guevara (1928–1967), organized the Brigada Femenina Revolucionaria (Women's Revolutionary Brigade). This grassroots group, which was the largest such group by the summer of 1959, participated in the November Women's Congress in Chile, and set the stage for the Federación de Mujeres Cubanas.

Both the Sección Femenina and the Brigada Femenina Revolucionaria of the MR-26-7 were organizers of mass movements. As such, they were involved in the dispute between two alignments: The first sought a nationalist revolution, and the other sought a radical nationalist revolution inspired by the ideas of José Martí, which would in due course lead to a Cuban socialism. Neither favored Soviet socialism (García 2009).

The main activities of the Brigada Femenina Revolucionaria involved supporting the laws set forth in the Moncada Program (Castro 1960), supporting the revolutionary government and the Ministry of Social

Women's Revolutionary Brigade, 1959. Women who joined the Women's Revolutionary Brigade were trained to march in rallies and support the government through various forms of mass activity and mobilization. COURTESY OF GLADYS MAREL GARCÍA PÉREZ

Welfare through all kinds of mass activity and mobilization, and, in particular, supporting agrarian reform through mobilizations in the agricultural cooperatives and people's farms. The Brigada Femenina Revolucionaria also engaged in housing campaigns, civilian and military training of women, the redevelopment of the poor and insalubrious neighborhood of Las Yaguas, the rehabilitation of prostitutes and thieves, and the *campaña de alfabetización* (literacy campaign) in the capital and on the island of Turiguanó in the province of Camaguey. In the face of the organizational power of the domestic workers in the Brigada Femenina Revolucionaria, Fidel Castro provided Brigada Femenina with two hundred volunteer teachers from the Minas del Frío School in the Sierra Maestra to help the brigade organize the Escuela de Instructoras Revolucionarias (School for Revolutionary Teachers), which would prepare housemaids for this effort.

The leadership of the Brigada Femenina Revolucionaria founded and held executive offices within the Congreso de Mujeres Cubanas (Congress of Cuban Women) and in the management of the Milicias Nacionales Revolucionarias (Revolutionary National Militias). Based in the National Capitol and in the Fifth District of Havana, the congress assembled a variety of social sectors and segments, including cigar-rollers and shoe saleswomen. At their general assembly, they elected two delegates for the Latin American Women's Congress in Santiago, Chile, held in November 1959: Gladys García, the president of the brigade, and the sailor Orquídea Pérez.

The Federación de Mujeres Cubanas was officially established in 1960. The members of the Sección Femenina and the Brigada Femenina Revolucionaria of the MR-26-7, the Directorio Revolucionario 13 de Marzo, and the Frente Cívico de Mujeres Martianas were absent from its founding leadership.

CUBAN GENDER STUDIES

Since the early 1990s, Cuban researchers and thinkers across a range of disciplines have used the category of gender in various ways. A distinction can be drawn between two basic approaches: one that speaks of *gender* in referring to women, and another that refers to the cultural construction of sexual differences in social relationships between the sexes, that is to say, the cultural symbolization of sexual differences. There are different interpretations of how these approaches are to be pursued.

For social historian Joan W. Scott, identifying the social relations between the sexes and showing that there is not a different world of women set apart from the world of men and that information about women necessarily implies information about men, makes it possible to dismiss the notion of two separate spheres. This approach allows for the existence of systems of social or sexual relationships and is a way of taking ownership of the theoretical debate.

Scott proposes a definition of gender with two different, though analytically interconnected, parts. At the heart of her definition is a holistic connection between two ideas: "gender is a constitutive element of social relationships based on perceived differences between the sexes, and gender is a primary way of signifying relationships of power" (Scott p. 1067).

Marta Lamas, who views Scott's concept as valid, believes that even though there is some risk that women's studies will perpetuate the fiction that the experiences of one sex have little or nothing to do with those of the other, this is the approach that provides the most comprehensive understanding of social relations between the sexes (Lamas 1996, pp. 265–302).

LANGUAGE DIFFERENCES, ANALOGIES, AND CONCEPTUAL CONFUSION

During the 1970s, Western academic feminism promoted the use of the category of *gender* with the intention of drawing a distinction between social and cultural constructs and biological constructs (Lamas 1986). These scholars also pursued the scientific objective of obtaining a better understanding of social reality. Subsequently, the use of this category led to the recognition of a range of methods for the interpretation, symbolization, and organization of sexual differences in social relationships and shaped a critique of the existence of a feminine essence. The term *gender* became popular during the 1990s, although the distinction is often evaded and the words *gender* and *sex* are used interchangeably.

In her 1996 essay "Usos, dificultades, y posibilidades de la categoría género" (Uses, Difficulties, and Possibilities of the Categories of Gender), Lamas analyzes Scott's key essay (1986), which sets forth various ways in which the concept of gender is used and explains how the search for academic legitimacy led female students of the 1980s to substitute *gender* for *women.* In these cases, as Lamas explains, the use of the concept of *gender*, which is more neutral and objective than that of *women*, makes it possible to adapt to the terminology of the social sciences. Furthermore, this approach avoids the constraints of the politics of feminism, which according to Scott reduces gender to a concept associated with the study of issues that exclusively concern women or are directly related to issues of children, the family, and ideology. Lamas concludes that for purposes of the current debate, Scott's analysis has some key merits, which include rejecting the notion that the binary opposition has a fixed and permanent nature, allowing historical approaches and the deconstruction of terms of sexual difference, clarifying the debate, and suggesting linkages to power.

MANIFESTATIONS OF CUBAN HISTORIOGRAPHY

In Cuba, the transformations and new constructions of gender relations were launched in 1959 within a context that had the primary objective of achieving revolutionary change. The analysis of social relationships during the first few decades of the Revolution was based on the use of the category of social class. It was not until the 1990s that the concepts of community and gender occupied a broader space.

During the 1960s and 1970s, Cuban journalism increased the visibility of women and the women's movement. There was a proliferation of articles on women's engagement in the wars of national liberation, from the wars for independence up to the Revolution. There was also work analyzing feminism and women's rights, legislation, legal status, education, employment, and suffrage, along with women's roles in organizations and literature, their sources of employment, and prostitution. There was a further focus on the roles of worker and peasant women, and on female prison inmates (Pérez 1976; De la Cruz).

In the 1960s, Cubans did not talk explicitly about the liberation or emancipation of women, but general and sectoral public policies were initiated that corresponded to the overall economic and social strategy. The objective was to create conditions for justice in social development, with a real impact on the life and subjectivity of Cubans, while starting the process of transforming discriminatory mindsets with regard to gender relations (Figure 1).

Beginning in the 1960s, the creation of children's circles (day care) became indispensible, as was the residential and dormitory system. These activities gave women access to the workplace and training, as well as political office, while encouraging nonsexist socialization. There was a sense that Cuban men and families supported these changes, a sense reinforced by the passage of new laws that broadened women's participation and protected their rights, including nondiscriminatory labor legislation that promoted equality of wages, promotions, benefits, and training (Fernández 1996, pp. 18–23). These actions were not

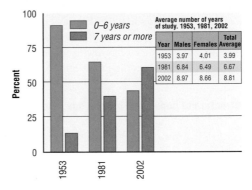

Structure of the population by years of schooling, 1953, 1981, 2002

Figure 1

SOURCE: Albizu-Campos E., J. J. and G. Rodriguez G. following ONE. "Los censos de población y viviendas en Cuba, 1907–1953". Havana: ONE-UNFPA. 2007, Table 36; CEE, "Censo de Población y viviendas, 1981. República de Cuba. Volumen 16". Comité Estatal de Estadísticas. Havana: June 1984.; Table 8, pp. 16–17 and Table 38, pp. 151–152 and 160–161; ONE, "Censo de Población y viviendas. Cuba, 2002. Informe nacional". Oficina Nacional de Estadisticas. Havana, September 2006, Table II.2, p. 206 and Table II.2, p. 317–319.

inspired by gender theories or feminism; rather, they arose as the result of actual social practice at various historical points in time.

Over time, women began to bring all these forces together in the theory and practice underlying a coherent set of demands. Lourdes Fernández affirms that "these actions were a requirement of feminism, even though at the time people still weren't talking about gender perspectives or studies" (1996, pp. 18–23). She writes that it was at the Second FMC Congress (1975) that the term *equality* began to be used due to a growing awareness of "problems of existing inequality, stereotypes, and prejudice derived from the condition of gender" (1996, pp. 18–23).

Some major legislation was enacted in the 1970s. Legal reforms included the Law on Maternity (1974), the Family Code (1975), the Law on Occupational Safety and Health (1977), and the Law on Social Security and the Penal Code (1979). Nevertheless, this long process kept running into obstacles due to a persisting discriminatory mindset among families, men, and even some women. This was despite the fact that Cuban law and the 1992 Cuban constitution prohibited discrimination against women and placed no express restrictions on their civil status and despite the clear intention to create conditions that would implement the principle of equality through social mechanisms to promote and advance policies that benefit women. Along with literacy and the universal availability of free, egalitarian education, women have attained achievements that give them a privileged place in contemporary social life (Figures 2 and 3).

According to studies by sociologist Dayma Echevarría, after 1975 there was a growing awareness that not all women were exercising their right to equality.

Subjective forms of discrimination, which are much more difficult to eradicate, lingered. Along with the political and legal recognition of this issue, there was a boom in academic studies. Echevarría adds that, as of the mid-1980s, some 37.7 percent of Cuban women were employed, comprising 56 percent of the technical and professional labor force of the country

Figure 2

Structure of population by age, sex, and years of schooling, 1953

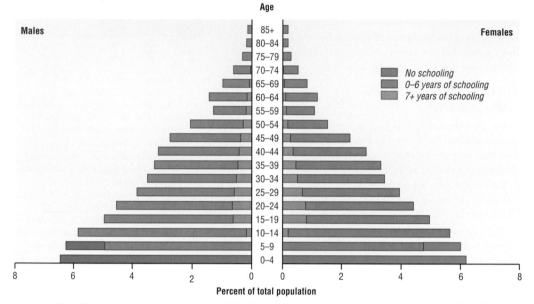

SOURCE: Albizu-Campos E. J.C. y G. Rodríguez. ONE. "Los censos de población y viviendas en Cuba,1907-1953." Havana: ONE-UNFPA, 2007, Table 36, p. 376.

Figure 3

Structure of population by age, sex, and years of schooling, 2002

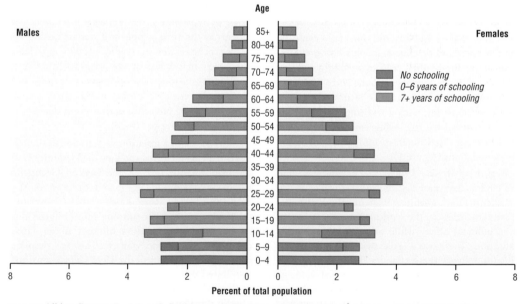

SOURCE: Albizu-Campos E., J.C. y G. Rodriguez. ONE, "Censo de población y viviendas. Cuba, 2002. Informe nacional". Oficina Nacional de Estadísticas. Havana: September 2006, Table II.2, p. 206 and Table II.1, p. 317–319.

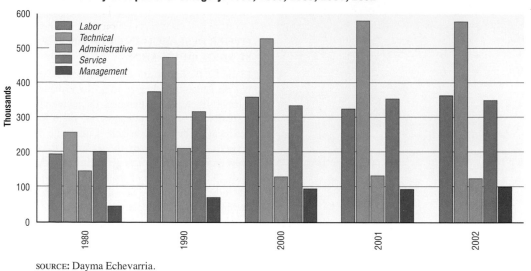

Female workers by occupational category: 1980, 1990, 2000, 2001, 2002

SOURCE: Dayma Echevarria.

Figure 4

(Comité Estatal de Estadísticas p. 206). Their prominence in public life has become an undeniable fact (Figure 4).

The United Nations proclamation of the Decade of Women (1975–1985) encouraged the boom in research at Cuban academic institutions, which was promoted by the FMC. Women's studies departments and programs were established at various universities. Echevarría draws attention to the strengthening of institutional support at this time, with other researchers getting involved in the subject and the variable of gender being included in the research agenda.

Various activities took place in the mid-1980s that influenced new approaches and encouraged the adoption of new theoretical perspectives. Women, blacks, and youths were promoted to management jobs. There was also a foreign influence, thanks to the links Cuban scientists and personalities involved in women's studies programs had forged with foreign institutions. In addition, exchange forums were organized under the auspices of the Women's Department at the University of Havana and the Cuban Academy of Sciences. The Women's Houses and Family Houses were created in 1991, as was the FMC's Center for Women's Studies. Gender studies after the late 1980s, and even more so in the 1990s, specifically analyzed feminist theory, prejudice against feminists, and gender perspectives.

The economic crisis of the 1990s exposed the raw differences in male and female survival strategies and their different options in gaining access to power in order to influence decision making (Fernández 2000; Núñez 2003). Gender studies scholars in Cuba are currently exploring a range of subjects in the humanities, as well as in the social sciences and other scientific disciplines. These included topics related to gender,

Women employed in the economy by type of occupation
WOMEN AS A PERCENT OF THE WORKFORCE

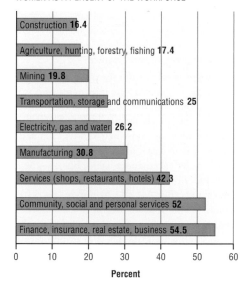

Figure 5

SOURCE: Oficina Nacional de Estadisticas (ONE), 2008. *Anuario Estadístico de Cuba*. 2007. In: Echevarría, Dayma and Ileana Diaz. *Empleo y dirección en Cuba: una mirada desde la perspectiva de género*. Centro de Estudios de la Economía Cubana. Universidad de La Habana, 2010.

generation, and social justice; feminist thought; sexuality and couples; the family; violence; power, gender, and subjectivity; health; prostitution; homosexuality; communications media; and masculinities.

In the field of literature, Luisa Campuzano at the Women's Studies Program of the Casa de las Américas

Vilma Espín and Fidel Castro, 1998. Vilma Espín (1930–2007), the wife of Raúl Castro and longtime head of the Federation of Cuban Women, joins her brother-in-law at the closing of the 1998 World Solidarity Meeting of Women in Havana. ADALBERTO ROQUE/GETTY IMAGES

fostered debates and exchanges among Cuban writers throughout the Americas and Europe. This program also engaged in information exchanges with regard to women and the historical and cultural environment of Cuba, Latin America, and the Caribbean, along with issues of gender and ecosystems; ecofeminism; eco-critiques of women's output in literature and art; thought and myth about women and nature; and the culture and history of rural women.

Ongoing research from the perspective of gender relations aimed to incorporate it into "social-historical structures, along with the categories of class, race, and generation, and to clarify how the subjectivities of women and men are constructed, how each acts out its engagement in social life, and how they interrelate with each other" (Fernández 1996, pp. 18–23). This effort includes the research of the historian María del Carmen Barcia. But not all Cuban scholars delved in depth into gender roles and relations using a symbolic and nonsexist approach. This boom in research and its findings influenced the sphere of communications, television programming, and other methods of communication, with the ultimate objective of contributing to the advancement of society.

The impact of the economic crisis of the 1990s, with all its troubles and constraints, fell most heavily on women in their multidimensional condition as workers, mothers, and homemakers. In 1997, women's participation in the state civilian sector was 42.5 percent, with 22.9 percent in the private sector. In 2007, of the country's technicians and professionals 66.6 percent were women, along with 70 percent and 72 percent of education workers and educators, respectively (ONE 2008; Echevarría and Díaz) (Figure 5).

The 1999 Report on Human Development issued by the United Nations Development Program ranked Cuba in twenty-first place on a global index of empowerment of women and fifty-third on the development index for women.

OTHER RESEARCH IN CUBA ON THE SUBJECT OF WOMEN

In the 1970s, Juan Carlos Alfonso, Sonia Catasús, and Niurka Pérez Rojas began using the variable of sex to uncover interesting differences in demographic data, even though at that time none of them had a gender focus. When that variable is used, the differences between sexes revealed by the statistical data begin to show an approximation to gender only in the early or mid-1980s. The study of women in Cuban literature and other areas of the social sciences also began to manifest itself at this time.

Cuban sociologist Niurka Pérez published the first work based on life histories, *El hogar de Ana* (Ana's Home, 1986). Her team in the field of sociological research (1983–2010) produced outstanding work. Their main approaches to the subject focused on the issue of agrarian women in the family and in society. Her fieldwork, which was conducted in several regions of Cuba, explored gender relations in the family and in the workplace, and at the credit and services cooperatives, the agriculture and livestock cooperatives, and the sugarcane cooperatives. Although initially associated with the American sociologist Carmen Diana Deere, this team conducted comparative studies that were discussed at national and international forums by experts from the United States, Nicaragua, Great Britain, and other countries.

Miriam García and Dayma Echevarría conducted important research on the subject of labor; their work incorporated the issues of power relationships and decision making. As of 2011, this team was conducting research on the engagement of women in the rural economy as part of the reality of life in Cuba, with a priority on participation in mass organizations, such as the FMC and the credit and services cooperatives. This research proposed to study the relative weight of women's work in the household and in the national agriculture and livestock system, as well as their interrelationships and their engagement in manufacturing and marketing. These researchers were also tracking expressions of inequality and subordination, while suggesting approaches to developing policies on gender.

The work of the sociologist Marta Núñez includes research on the different ways in which Cuban intellectuals approach the study of gender perspectives and relations, as well as studies on the topic of women from the mid-1980s to the early 1990s.

Many of the problems that impacted women in the early 2010s were dependent on Cuba's economic recovery. Others were a function of subjective factors. A gender perspective makes it possible to analyze cultural, economic, political, and ideological relationships in a real society. Such an approach fulfills the need to understand these relationships in a sociohistorical context along with the categories of class, race, and generation, and sheds light on how subjectivities interact and how they are constructed and have an impact on everyday life.

Between the 1960s and the early 2010s, Cuba made progress in gender equity. Transforming deep-rooted stereotypes and concepts that date back centuries in the subjectivity of Cubans was understood, however, to be a much slower process.

The early twenty-first century saw a proliferation of gender studies in Cuba, as well as the application of a wide array of methodological approaches, which created opportunities in the sciences, communications media, and Cuban life. Most of this work was published in journals, and there was an obvious shortage of books that compiled this work. Nevertheless, ever more thought and reflection was taking place in public spaces, and there was a continuing effort to promote change in people's attitudes, in policies, in cultural products, and across all spheres of reality, in order to continue promoting social equity.

Despite the changes produced by a process that was already underway for a half century, patriarchal patterns were manifested in the culture and values perpetuated by social and individual subjectivities and in the lack of adequate levels of awareness of ongoing expressions of discrimination. These inequities were most obvious in the sphere of the private life of families and couples and in access to leadership positions in the political and economic arenas.

BIBLIOGRAPHY

Álvarez, Mayda. "La revolución de las cubanas: 50 años de conquistas y luchas." *Temas* 56 (2008): 67–77.

Barcia, María del Carmen. *Mujeres al margen de la historia.* Havana: Editorial de Ciencias Sociales, 2009.

Castro, Fidel. *La historia me absolverá.* Havana: Editora Política, 1960.

Comité Estatal de Estadísticas. *Anuario Estadístico de Cuba, 1987.* Havana: Author, 1987.

De la Cruz, Dania. *Movimiento femenino cubano: Bibliografía.* Havana: Editora Política, 1980.

De Lauretis, Teresa. *Technologies of Gender: Essays on Theory, Film, and Fiction.* Bloomington: Indiana University Press, 1987.

Domínguez García, Maria Isabel. "La mujer joven hoy." *Temas* 5 (1996): 90–37.

Echevarría, Dayma. "Empoderamiento femenino en Cuba: Situación actual y estudios sobre el tema." PowerPoint presented at Alfa Project, Empoderimento de Mujeres Brainstorming & Planning Meeting, Torino, Italy, 15–21 November 2004. Available from http://www.saa.unito.it/alfa1/spanish/planificacion_material.htm.

Echevarría, Dayma, and Ileana Díaz. "Empleo y dirección en Cuba: Una mirada desde la perspectiva de género." Havana: Center for Study of the Cuban Economy, University of Havana, 2010.

Espin, Vilma. *Informe de Cuba: Primer Congreso Latinoamericano de Mujeres.* Havana, 1959. Pamphlet.

Fernández, Lourdes. "¿Roles de género? ¿Feminidad vs. Masculinidad?" *Temas* (Havana) 5 (1996): 18–23 .

Fernández, Lourdes. "Roles de género y mujeres académicas." *Revista de ciencias sociales* (University of Costa Rica) 42, no. 88, II (2000): 63–75.

García Pérez, Gladys Marel. "Mujer y Revolución: Una perspectiva desde la insurgencia cubana (1952–1959)." In *1959: Una rebelión contra las oligarquías y los dogmas revolucionarios.* Havana: Instituto Cubano de Investigación Cultural Juan Marinello/Ruth Casa Editorial, 2009.

Guerrero, María Luisa. *Elena Mederos: Una mujer con perfil para la historia.* Washington, DC: Office of Human Rights, 1991.

Lamas, Marta. "La antropología feminista y la categoría 'género.'" *Nueva antropología: Estudios sobre la mujer: Problemas teóricos* 30 (1986): 173–198.

Lamas, Marta. "Usos, dificultades, y posibilidades de la categoría género." In *El género: La construcción cultural de la diferencia sexual,* edited by Marta Lamas, 265–302. Mexico City: M.A. PUEG, 1996.

Martínez Heredia, Fernando. *El ejercicio de pensar.* Havana: Instituto Cubano de Investigación Cultural Juan Marinello/Ruth Casa Editorial, 2008.

Mesa Castillo, Olga. "La situación jurídica de la mujer en Cuba." In *Diversidad y complejidad familiar en Cuba.* Havana: Center for Demographic Studies of the University of Havana and the Ibero-American Institute of Family Studies, Bogota, Colombia, 1999.

Núñez, Marta. "Gender Studies in Cuba: Methodological Approaches, 1974–2001." *Gender and Society* 17, no. 1 (February 2003): 7–31.

Oficina Nacional de Estadística (ONE). *Anuario Estadístico de Cuba, 2007.* Havana: Author, 2008.

Padula, Alfred. "Gender, Sexuality, and Revolution in Cuba." *Latin American Research Review* 31 (1996): 226–235.

Pérez, Louis A., Jr. *The Cuban Revolutionary War, 1953–1958: A Bibliography.* Metuchen, NJ: Scarecrow Press, 1976.

Perez, Louis A., Jr. *On Becoming Cuban. Identity, Nationality, and Culture.* Chapel Hill: University of North Carolina Press, 1999.

Pérez Rojas, Niurka. *El hogar de Ana.* Havana: Editorial Ciencias Sociales, 1986.

Pérez Rojas, Niurka, and Miriam García Aguiar. "Mujer de campo: Campesina, cooperativista, y obrera-cooperativista cubana." In *Mujer y género: Potencial alternativo para los retos del nuevo milenio,* edited by Irene Pineda Ferman. Managua, Nicaragua: Universidad Centroamericana, 1997.

Scott, Joan W. "Gender: A Useful Category of Historical Analysis." *American Historical Review* 91, no. 5 (1986): 1053–1075.

Vasallo, Norma. "La mujer cubana ante los cambios económicos: Impactos en su subjetividad." In *Hacia una mutación de lo social: Europa-América Latina.* Zaragoza, Spain: Egido Editoria, 1999.

Vasallo, Norma. *Subjetividad social femenina en diferentes roles y generaciones.* Havana: Editorial Ciencias Sociales, 1999.

GENDER: FEMINISM AND MASCULINITY IN THE REVOLUTIONARY PERIOD

Julio César González Pagés

Changing gender roles after 1959, including discussion of the development of gender studies in Cuba.

The Federación de Mujeres Cubanas (FMC; Federation of Cuban Women) was the third twentieth-century attempt by the women of Cuba to form a mass association. The first two attempts took place in 1921 with the creation of the Federación Nacional de Asociaciones Femeninas de Cuba (National Federation of Women's Associations of Cuba) and in 1947 with the Federación Democrática de Mujeres Cubanas (Democratic Federation of Cuban Women).

Founded on 23 August 1960, the FMC is the only women's organization in the country as of 2011. It was created by forty women's associations that had been established in previous decades and it brought together a broad range of women, including intellectuals, peasants, workers, housewives, and religious professionals. Vilma Espín Guillois was elected as the FMC's first president and served as its leader until her death in 2007. During the 1960s, the word *federada* (federated) replaced the word *feminista* (feminist). Through the voice of its president, this organization sought to break away from the old "capitalist feminism" in order to create a new paradigm for women: the socialist woman.

By the 1960s, when the FMC was created, Cuban women had achieved many of the aspirations postulated by liberal feminism. Among other achievements, women had obtained laws that allowed them to exercise their right to vote and get divorced, as well as advanced labor legislation. The government of General Fulgencio Batista (1901–1973) placed the highest number of women in political positions in Latin America during the 1950s (González Pagés 2005, pp. 168–174).

The new model of the socialist woman broke with the model of the liberal feminist, who saw her goal solely in terms of legal equality. The socialist woman postulated that equality under the law was not the same as equality in life and, therefore, proposed a social project that would integrate women to sectors where they had not played a prominent role. This new revolutionary feminism, with its worker-peasant discourse, encouraged a collective rather than an individual struggle. The struggle to eliminate gender gaps was therefore combined with the class struggle. Cuban feminism of the 1960s and 1970s sought to lend visibility to sectors not yet vindicated by international feminism.

Young female peasants were the first to join this new project. Some thirteen thousand young women from every province in the country came to Havana to study dressmaking as part of a strategy that would also enhance their cultural and educational training (Espín p. 12). Using a special method known as *Ana Betancourt*, dental work, medical checkups, and courses to build self-esteem were set up for peasant women in an effort, for the first time in the history of Cuban feminism, to create leaders from a group other than middle-class urban women.

This project was extended to other sectors, such as *domésticas* (domestic workers) and *criadas* (servants), as women working in such services were called. Yet another even more daring idea, given its moral and religious connotations, was redirecting prostitutes or sex workers as taxicab drivers, while also allowing them to go to school (Espín pp. 17–18).

The FMC used new methods for communication, such as the publication *Revista mujeres* (Women's Magazine), which started to feature on its covers women who had been previously ignored, due to their occupation (workers and peasants), race (black), or social status (marginalized lower-class sectors). Thanks to this effort, a substantial nucleus of women in the country was incorporated into the task of organizing the communities, particularly in the bases that were created at neighborhood levels.

ELIMINATING GENDER GAPS

The changes in the social structure brought with it the passing of laws encouraging the entry of women into new jobs. With this in mind, the Labor Code was revised and prohibitions and restrictions were eliminated to give women free access, also women's employment commissions were established at all levels. Conditions in the national health system were modified, so that women could freely manage their fertility and how many children they wanted, as well as other aspects of their sexual and reproductive health.

Through its delegations at neighborhood levels, the federation undertook ventures that made change possible in many of the negative aspects of daily life for a Cuban family. Children were offered the advantage of new projects, such as street plans, in which boys and girls exchanged new family roles. Homemakers took courses that allowed them to acquire new skills for community-type jobs. During the 1970s, women became key collaborators in education and culture in the so-called battle for sixth and ninth grades.

But culture was not the only area where change was to originate, which is why a Family Code was enacted on 14 February 1975, the first of its kind in the country. Comprising 166 articles, it regulates the institutions of family, marriage, divorce, parent-child relationships, obligatory food support, adoption, and guardianship. Before its approval it was discussed at workers' assemblies and mass organizations, where lively debates took place, concerning the emancipating nature of some of its articles, and the official adult age for men and women was set at eighteen.

The Family Code became one of the laws a couple must comply with when marrying, which is why some of its articles are read at the wedding. After 2005, under the leadership of the FMC and with the support of the Ministries of Justice and Social Security, and the Centro Nacional de Educación Sexual (CENESEX; National Center for Sex Education) among others, the code underwent a thorough review in order to bring it up-to-date with regard to many current issues facing women in the Cuban family. Issues concerning sexual choices and sexual rights, emigration, old age and the aging of the Cuban population, child abuse, and other highly sensitive social issues were included in the updated version of the Family Code.

Since the promulgation of Cuba's new constitution in 1976 and its amendment in 1992, the FMC has struggled to establish other rights, such as the access of women to all government jobs and positions, public administration, manufacturing, and services. The Asamblea Nacional (parliament) also established the Comisión Permanente de Atención a la Infancia, la Juventud y la Igualdad de Derechos de las Mujeres (Permanent Committee on Care of Children, Youth, and Equal Rights for Women).

In compliance with the agreements of the Fourth Global Conference on Women of the United Nations, held in Beijing in 1995, government committees were established and were endorsed by a resolution of the Council of State on 7 April 1997. These agreements were published by the FMC and consist of ninety measures that are described as "the cornerstone of the development of policies for women, and provide continuity to the progress and development of gender equality in our country" (FMC p. 35).

The FMC has been the organization most responsible for the achievements made by Cuban women at the end of the twentieth century. A few figures can serve to illustrate this point. In 2008, women accounted for 42.5 percent of the state's workforce, and 64.6 percent of workers in the technical and professional sectors. Furthermore, the Cuban parliament holds fourth place in the world for representation of women (FMC, UNFPA, and ONE p. 19). Since the 1980s, the policy of quotas for women promoted by the Communist Party of Cuba, as well as the struggles led by the FMC, have enabled the steady rise of women in the distribution of power at the highest levels of the state, the party, parliament, and mass organizations.

Regardless of the praiseworthy implications of statistics and the country's progress on social issues, there are, as of 2011, many issues yet to be addressed, particularly among professional women, whose most urgent aspirations are not well represented in the FMC. In the sectors of peasant, blue-collar workers, and homemakers, the federation's work is highly valued on account of its continuing engagement with communities and the problems of daily life. Likewise, the comprehensive transformation that has taken place in favor of women has provoked a *machista* backlash from a broad sector of men who jealously watched the changes in their colleagues. Such films as *Lucía* (Humberto Solás, 1969) and *Retrato de Teresa* (Pastor Vega, 1978) criticized such attitudes.

The rise of international tourism led the agencies involved in the industry to promote an image of Cuban women that is closer to that of the tourism industries of other countries of the region, which present women as exotic and sexual objects, coupled with an increase in prostitution or sex work. The use of images, often dichotomized, of women described as the revolutionary ideal, like those from the Nueva Trova movement, contrasts with the erotic and sexual-object take on women of salsa, reggae, and pop groups. Even in radio station or television programs one can hear the song "María del Carmen," by Noel Nicola, which highlights an ideal that hews closely to the revolutionary *compañera*, alongside "La Bruja," by José Luis Cortés, in which women are presented as *jineteras* (prostitutes).

GENERATING A NEW DISCOURSE

The conferences on Ibero-American Women and Communications are the longest-running forum for debate and controversy on gender in Cuba. At their first meeting in Havana in 1993, they gathered a broad array of specialists from different branches of knowledge with a focus on gender. A group was created on 15 March 1994, under the name of MAGIN Steering Committee (on the same date in 1939 when Ernestina Otero launched the Asociación Nacional Femenina de Prensa [National Women's Press Association]). The MAGIN group took its name from the Greek word for imagination. It sought to carry on the work of the association, which had hitherto been limited to a few executive meetings, in a more effective manner. The MAGIN Steering Committee was established after several consultations among the participants, who chose the image and discourse to be represented and planned courses, workshops, and seminars for the future. The idea was to generate a new debate in the Cuban media and break away from the old patterns of masculinity and femininity for all products.

One of the MAGIN-organized events with significant impact was the workshop on Gender in Social Communications: A New Focus (18–22 July 1994), which gathered some sixty communications experts from around the world. With such key themes as the division of labor in the Cuban family and gender gaps and disparities, Cuban and United Nations experts complied with the opinion of gender expert Patricia Anzola that "the news may be sexless, but they're handled with gender" (MAGIN 1994).

The MAGIN Steering Committee also coordinated self-esteem workshops for communicators, as well as courses for personal development, which included topics such as sexism in language and how a project should be structured in order to be understood or financed.

The MAGIN Steering Committee encompassed a diverse group of organizers, journalists, and communicators, among whom the following should be mentioned: Mirta Rodríguez Calderón, Xiomara Blanco, Irene Esther Ruiz, Carmen María Acosta, Norma Guillard, Belkis Vega, Niurka Pérez Rojas, Irma Armas, Nora Quintana, Magalys García, Rosalía Arnaez, and Teresita Segarra. A plan to turn the committee into an association in November 1994, through which a national conference would elect a board of directors and establish bylaws, was, however, never carried out.

These first efforts by MAGIN to address gender issues helped to promote the work of other organizations. Led by the FMC, university chairs for women's studies programs were encouraged throughout the country's universities, and the Centro de Estudios de la Mujer (Center for Women's Studies) was founded in 1997. These groups organized workshops, seminars, and conferences that motivated people to keep this issue on their agenda. The Gertrudis Gómez de Avellaneda Chair at the Instituto de Literatura y Lingüística (Institute for Literature and Linguistics) and the Programa de Estudios de la Mujer (Program for Women's Studies) at Casa de las Américas are two examples of the advancement of women's studies programs at Cuba's academic institutions.

MASCULINITY IN THE DEBATE

In the last two decades of the twentieth century, workshops, seminars, and conferences on the status of men in Cuba began to be sponsored. Starting in 1994, a nongovernmental organization called the Movimiento Cubano por la Paz (Cuban Movement for Peace) convened national-level meetings through its Gender and Peace Committee. These included Masculinities and Struggles for the Emancipation of Women (1994) and Masculinities and Violence (1996) (González Pagés 2010, pp. 7–10). Until 2005, this committee organized seminars for social workers, university students, police, inmates, local leaders, and so forth, with the common purpose of discussing their key issues and proposing alternatives for change.

Academically focused masculinity studies in Cuba have been launched chiefly by women. Professor Patricia Arés of the Universidad de La Habana has been particularly prominent in this effort. Among the men, professors Carlos A. LLoga Domínguez (Universidad de Oriente in Santiago de Cuba), Víctor Hugo Pérez Gallo (Instituto Superior Minero-Metalúrgico de Moa in Holguín), and Julio César González Pagés (Universidad de La Habana) are noteworthy in terms of the volume and impact of their work. Academic programs in this field include the diploma in gender and communications from the Instituto Internacional de Periodismo "José Martí" (José Martí International

Journalism Institute), as well as the master's degree programs in gender studies at the Universidad de La Habana. Groups focused on masculinity studies have emerged in other provinces, among which the Equidad group at the Universidad de Oriente is most prominent.

The First Cuban Working Session in the Study of Masculinities, conducted in Havana in June 2006 with the participation of several academic institutions, made a theoretical and scientific discussion possible through conferences, workshops, and presentations. More importantly, the event revolutionized the subject throughout the entire country. The researchers Oscar Ulloa, Yarlenis Meste, and Maite Pérez expressed the view that "the subject of men and their changes, distress, limitations, and costs, has pierced the walls of academia to become an issue for everyday discussion" (González Pagés 2010, p. 16).

Inspired by the event and its success and as part of a broader effort to spark new debates on masculinities in other Latin American countries, the Red Iberoamericana de Masculinidades (Iberoamerican Masculinities Network) was launched in November 2007. This network is an academic study-group with members from twenty-eight countries in the region, committed to help prevent gender violence by men as its fundamental concern. In Cuba, the network is represented by the group Masculinidades en Cuba (Masculinities in Cuba), which is made up of graduates in academic tracks such as social communications, history, sociology, and anthropology. The most discussed issues are those related to violence, migration, race, sexuality, and sports.

BIBLIOGRAPHY

Arés Munzio, Patricia. "Virilidad ¿Conocemos el costo de ser hombres?" *Revista sexología y sociedad* 2, no. 5 (August 1996): 18–21.

Díaz Vallina, Elvira, and Julio César González Pagés. "The Self Emancipation of Woman." In *Cuban Transitions at the Millennium*, edited by Eloise Linger and John Walton Cotman. Largo, MD: International Development Options, 1999.

Espín Guillois, Vilma. *Informe centrales de los congresos de la FMC*. Havana: Imprenta Central de la FAR, 1990.

Federación de Mujeres Cubanas (FMC). *Plan de Acción Nacional de Seguimiento a la Conferencia Mundial sobre la Mujer de Beijing*. Havana: Editorial de la Mujer, 2002. Available from http://www.undp.org.cu/documentos/genero/PAN.pdf.

FMC, UNFPA, and ONE. "Mujeres Cubanas 1958–2008: Estadísticas y realidades." Havana: FMC, UNFPA, and ONE, 2008.

González Pagés, Julio César. *En busca de un espacio: Historia de mujeres en Cuba*. Havana: Editorial de Ciencias Sociales, 2005.

González Pagés, Julio César. *Macho, varón, masculino: Estudios de masculinidades en Cuba*. Havana: Editorial de la Mujer, 2010.

Jorné, Laurette Sé. *Mujer Cubana en el que hacer de la historia*. Mexico City: Editorial Siglo Veintiuno, 1980.

MAGIN. "Género en la comunicación social: Un nuevo enfoque. Memorias." Havana: MAGIN, 1994.

Molyneux, Maxine. "State, Gender, and Institutional Change. The Federación de Mujeres Cubanas." In *Hidden Histories of Gender and the State in Latin America*, edited by Elizabeth Dore and Maxine Molyneux. Durham, NC: Duke University Press, 2000.

Smith, Lois M., and Alfred Padula. *Sex and Revolution: Women in Socialist Cuba*. New York: Oxford University Press, 1996.

Stoner, K. Lynn. *From the House to the Streets: The Cuban Woman's Movement for Legal Reform, 1898–1940*. Durham, NC: Duke University Press, 1991.

GENDER: TRENDS IN WOMEN'S WRITING AFTER THE REVOLUTION

Luisa Campuzano

General trends in the writings of Cuban women after 1959 and their intersections with worldwide feminist currents.

Two periods in the evolution of Cuban women and the literature written by women since 1959 can be clearly identified. The first began with the success of the Revolution and ended with the collapse of socialism and the Soviet Union. The second began at that time and continues into the early 2000s, when the global economic crisis seems to be ushering in a new stage.

ASCENT WITHOUT A FEMINIST CONSCIOUSNESS: 1959–1991

The Revolution provided Cuban women the opportunity to take on roles and achieve unimaginable advancements in a patriarchal society. In 1966, Fidel Castro was already affirming: "the most revolutionary thing the revolution is doing is ... the revolution that is taking place in the women of our country" (Castro 1966, "Discurso"). But the fiction writing of that period does not evince these substantial changes in women's circumstances and in the shape of society, nor does it give signs of a new consciousness among male authors.

Backed by legislation aimed at promoting equal rights between the sexes and by policies and programs that favored women, within three decades Cuban women achieved great progress, which placed them in advantageous positions relative to other Latin American women (and to Cuban men as well). This is particularly the case in education and science, fields in which they soon surpassed men (*Mujeres*

passim). However, discrimination was still present in the workplace, and men still avoided promoting women to positions of leadership. In politics, women were not elected or appointed to first-rank positions. Cultural patterns that reinforced female subordination remained in place, and the so-called double shift (referring to women working a full day of paid work and then another full day of domestic work) continued to hinder the achievement of equality. Furthermore, women assumed that everything they had obtained was a concession rather than an achievement, more of a way to contribute to the development of the Revolution than to their own emancipation. There was no gender or race consciousness, only class consciousness. People talked not about differences but about unity. All belonged to a nation that had to be united as a single unit (Campuzano 1997, pp. 52–58).

In the 1970s and 1980s, the production of Cuban literature did not match the proliferation of women's writing that took place in other Latin American countries in the heat of the women's liberation movement of the late 1960s and the rise of feminist theories and critique. In Cuba, the women's movements went almost totally unnoticed, and where they had some resonance, it was mostly due to their political dimension rather than their specific social demands. Feminism underwent the same process as any other political or philosophical doctrine. People were living in a large vacuum of theory, and non-Marxist contemporary literary criticism was considered suspect.

The work produced by Cuba's female authors—whether they were established authors at the time of the Revolution or new writers—typically followed the norms of the patriarchal national canon, which was reinforced by the work of male writers who cultivated virile, martial themes. The major themes were the so-called hard years, the war and the fight against bandits (Capote pp. 20–23), referring to the fight against counterrevolutionary bands in the Escambray mountains in the early 1960s. Confronting this discourse of epic nationalism, the individual and social transformations triggered by incorporating women into public life were not considered interesting. For this reason, if one were to read many Cuban authors of both sexes, one might erroneously conclude that nothing worth telling, nothing novel-worthy, happened in the lives of women during those three decades.

Literary genres traditionally considered to be female, such as confessional literature and children's and young adult literature, were cultivated successfully and creatively by a good number of female authors. But it was in the fantasy genre, which allowed them to shrewdly mock the realist boundaries imposed by more fashionable subjects (Garrandés pp. 116–128), and in poetry (especially among the youngest writers) that female authors came closer to expressing the profound changes the Revolution had produced in their surroundings, as well as within themselves (Campuzano 1988, pp. 66–104).

■ *See also*

Cuban Thought and Cultural Identity: Socialist Thought

Dreaming in Cuban (Cristina García)

Governance and Contestation: The Cuban Revolution

Sexuality: Jinetera in the Special Period

Sexuality: Revolutionary Period

EMPOWERMENT OF WOMEN BEGINS: 1991–2010

After the fall of the Berlin Wall in 1989 and the collapse of the Soviet Union in 1991, the island underwent a deep economic crisis that demanded many sacrifices of the population, especially women. Despite its progresses, Cuba continued to be a country of deep-rooted patriarchal culture, and women continued to be responsible for taking care of their families. A serious setback in priority areas such as food and employment took place. Education and health care, which were considered the Revolution's greatest accomplishments, were at risk. All spheres of life were seriously eroded, and the sustained and drastic moral, social, and political consequences have continued into the early 2000s.

But it was precisely in that moment that a gradual empowerment of women began, which started with the raising of their consciousness and utilization of their abilities—first to survive, and later to achieve new positions and take on more challenges (Campuzano 1996, pp. 4–10). It is not surprising that, with the crisis of the mid-1990s, there was an explosion of short-story collections and novels written by women. By the late 1990s, this had become one of the distinctive features of Cuban turn-of-the-century literature.

Almost at the same time, a well-documented and polemical critique started to emerge (Araújo 1997a), and within cultural and academic circles a movement was launched that led to the creation of formal spaces dedicated to women's studies, with bibliographic support and the enthusiastic participation of feminists in the Americas and in Europe, with whom ongoing dialogue was initiated. The first conferences and courses on feminist theory and women's literature were organized, and the first anthology of Cuban women writers, *Estatuas de sal* (Pillars of Salt, 1996), was published. For the first time, two magazines also organized special issues, one on Cuban women, *Temas* 6 (1996), and one on women's cultural works, *Unión* 1 (1997). These female writers received coveted literary prizes and began to find their niche within foreign publishing houses. The very fact that a good number of the main characters in these texts are women writers signaled a change.

The *Novísimas* The works by the first generation, the *novísimas* (newest) (Araújo 1997b, pp. 28–29)—made up of female authors born in the 1960s and 1970s for the most part—covered various social and moral aspects of the crisis and its repercussions in the public and private sphere: shortages, the resurgence of economic disparities in a society that had been programmatically equitable, opportunism and the double standard, and the reemergence of prostitution and the *jineteras* (young prostitutes), who were turned into the symbol of the Special Period. These authors also cover, either directly or indirectly, the subject of emigration and what it unleashes: the anxiety of the traveler and the administrative red tape; the rafters—present in the male storytelling but dealt with by female writers from a more critical point of view; the period after migration; the permanent unease and the emigrant's sense of not ever truly belonging; and, especially, the struggles of those who stayed behind, including works by women who write from the viewpoint of their torn families. Subjects that had not been addressed or had been considered taboo reappeared, such as female homoeroticism (Fowler pp. 141–160), domestic violence, and pedophilia. Almost all female writers avoided approaching these subjects directly. They were treated obliquely, touched on, or alluded to with humor or irony.

The *Posnovísimas* The youngest women writers, the *posnovísimas* (post-newest) (Redonet pp. 68–75), avoid all reference to social context and address themes of individuality, self-knowledge, and doubt, expressed through forms of powerful and remarkable creativity. They are, moreover, very productive, and it was predicted that before long they would make their presence known in bookstores and in Cuban and foreign publisher catalogs. Their subversive, transgressive texts are developed in closed or marginal spaces inhabited by solitary, self-destructive individuals who have built themselves an alternative life, alienated from norms and connections to society and authority: strange, dirty, and sometimes deformed young men and women who give themselves over to sex, alcohol, or drugs and who are only interested in themselves, literature, or films.

To the extent that cultural forms not only reproduce but also *produce* reality, the writings of the *novísimas* and *posnovísimas* represent important spaces of confrontation and struggle for interpretative power, literary acts charged with historicity, and artistic declarations in a dynamic relation with social transformations (Campuzano 2004, pp. 142–168).

RECOMMENDED READING

Alabáu, Magali. *Hemos llegado a Ilión*. Coral Gables, FL: La Torre de Papel, 1995. Poetry.

Alonso, Dora. *Ponolani*. Havana: Ediciones Gente Nueva, 1966. Short stories.

Araújo, Nara. *El alfiler y la mariposa*. Havana: Letras Cubanas, 1997. Essay.

Bobes, Marilyn. *Alguien tiene que llorar*. Havana: Casa de las Américas, 1995. Short stories.

Cabrera, Lydia. *Ayapá: Cuentos de Jicotea*. Miami: Ediciones Universal, 1971. Short stories.

Fernández Pintado, Mylene. *Anhedonia*. Havana: Ediciones Unión, 1999. Short stories.

García, Cristina. *Dreaming in Cuban*. New York: Knopf, 1992. Novel.

García-Marruz, Fina. *Visitaciones*. Havana: Ediciones Unión, 1970. Poetry.

Llana, María Elena. *Casas del Vedado*. Havana: Letras Cubanas, 1983. Short stories.

Loynaz, Dulce María. *Fe de vida*. Pinar del Río, Cuba: Ediciones Centro Hermanos Loynaz, 1994. Memoir.

Mateo, Margarita. *Ella escribía poscrítica.* Havana: Casa Editora Abril, 1995. Essays.

Méndez Capote, Renée. *Memorias de una cubanita que nació con el siglo.* Santa Clara, Cuba: Universidad Central de las Villas, 1963. Memoir.

Montero, Mayra. *Del rojo de su sombra.* Barcelona: Tusquets, 1992. Novel.

Morejón, Nancy. *Richard trajo su flauta y otros argumentos.* Havana: Instituto Cubano del Libro, 1967. Poetry.

Portela, Ena Lucía. *Djuna y Daniel.* Havana: Ediciones Unión, 2007. Novel.

Rodríguez, Reina María. *Foto del invernadero.* Havana: Casa de las Américas, 1998. Poetry.

Rubiera, Daysi. *Reyita, sencillamente.* Havana: Prolibros, 1997. Testimonial.

Saldaña, Excilia. *Mi nombre: Antielegía familiar.* Havana: Ediciones Unión, 1991. Poetry.

Suárez, Karla. *Silencios.* Madrid: Ediciones Lengua de Trapo, 1999. Novel.

Vega Serova, Anna Lidia. *Bad Painting.* Havana: Ediciones Unión, 1998. Short stories.

BIBLIOGRAPHY

Araújo, Nara. "Women and Literature: Feminism and Feminist Literary Criticism in Cuba from Colonial Times to the Revolution." In *The Women, the Writer, & Caribbean Society: Essays on Literature and Culture,* edited by Helen Pyne-Timothy. Los Angeles: UCLA Center for African American Studies, 1997a.

Araújo, Nara. "Proyección y perfil de la crítica feminista del Caribe." In *Mulheres e literatura: (Trans) Formando identidades,* edited by Rita Teresinha Schmidt. Porto Alegre, Brazil: Universidade Federal do Rio Grande do Sul, 1997b.

Campuzano, Luisa. "La mujer en la narrativa de la Revolución: Ponencia sobre una carencia." In *Quirón o del ensayo y otros eventos.* Havana: Letras Cubanas, 1988.

Campuzano, Luisa. "Ser cubanas y no morir en el intento." *Temas* 5 (January–March 1996): 4–10.

Campuzano, Luisa. "Cuba 1961: Los textos narrativos de las alfabetizadoras: Conflictos de género, clase, y canon." *Unión* 9, no. 26 (January–March 1997): 52–58.

Campuzano, Luisa. "Literatura de mujeres y cambio social: Narradoras cubanas de hoy." In *Las muchachas de Havana no tienen temor de Dios: Escritoras cubanas, siglo XVIII al XXI.* Havana: Ediciones Unión, 2004.

Capote, Zaida. "Cuba, años sesenta: Cuentística femenina y canon literario." *La Gaceta de Cuba* 1 (January–February 2000): 20–23.

Castro, Fidel. "Discurso pronunciado por Fidel Castro Ruz, presidente de la República de Cuba, en la clausura de la V plenaria nacional de la FMC, en el Estadio 'Sandino' de Santa Clara, Las Villas, el 9 de diciembre de 1966, 'Año de la Solidaridad'." Discursos e intervenciones del Comandante en Jefe Fidel Castro Ruz, presidente del Consejo de Estado de la República de Cuba. Available from http://www.cuba.cu/gobierno/discursos.

Fowler, Víctor. "En apenas una década ..." In *La maldición: Una historia del placer como conquista.* Havana: Letras Cubanas, 1998.

Garrandés, Alberto. *El concierto de las fábulas: Discursos, historia, e imaginación en la narrativa cubana de los años sesenta.* Havana: Letras Cubanas, 2008.

Redonet, Salvador. "Otro final promisorio: (Post) novísimos ¿y/o qué?" *Unión* 22 (January–March 1996): 68–75.

Valdés, Teresa, and Enrique Gomáriz, eds. *Mujeres latinoamericanas en cifras: Cuba.* Santiago de Chile: Instituto de la Mujer (Spain) FLACSO, 1993.

Yáñez, Mirta, and Marilyn Bobes, eds. *Estatuas de sal: Cuentistas cubanas contemporáneas.* Havana: Ediciones Unión, 1996.

GENDER: WOMEN BEHIND THE CAMERA

Danae C. Diéguez

The cinema of women directors in Cuba, a revision of the canon.

A review of works produced by the Instituto Cubano de Arte e Industria Cinematográficos (ICAIC; Cuban Institute of Cinematographic Art and Industry), founded in March 1959, highlights the low turnout of women filmmakers. Although modern Cuban history emphasizes women's participation in public life as another revolution within the Revolution, the film industry perpetuated the traditional distribution of roles, restricting women to the occupations they had always performed: makeup, costume design, acting, and editing.

An analysis of women's underrepresentation as film directors in Cuba clearly reveals the nation's gender inequalities and consequently probes the question of whether their themes and aesthetic judgments suggest the existence of a *women's cinema*, or that at least reveals a subjectivity committed to women's narratives. Charting a course through a body of films directed by women does not mean, per se, that a feminine gaze exists, but it allows us to revisit the consideration of a number of works that have been overlooked within the cinematographic canon, based on a discrimination paradigm.

In order to understand how women became film directors in Cuba, it is necessary to extend beyond the films produced by ICAIC, since other production companies that, unlike ICAIC, did not envision cinematic work as an art or as an industry sponsored women who chose film directing as their career.

The Estudios Fílmicos de las Fuerzas Armadas Revolucionarias (FAR; Revolutionary Armed Forces Studios) and the Estudios Fílmicos de la Televisión (Television Film Studios) represent the emergence of some female directors whose work is today highly regarded within Cuban cinematography.

PIONEERS

In the 1960s, Sara Gómez (1943–1974) began directing documentaries at the ICAIC. This genre became the preferred medium for most female filmmakers, and Gómez used it to deal with some of her fundamental themes: the individual who experiences the revolutionary process from a marginal position, the machismo that survives in the construction of a new society, and the conflicts this entails for women who enter the public sphere as their pathway to autonomy. Documentaries such as *Mi aporte* (My Contribution, 1972) and *Guanabacoa, crónica de mi familia* (Guanabacoa, Chronicle of My Family, 1966) reveal topics and processes of self-representation with which Cuban film had not yet experimented. In the first documentary, Gómez appears within a group of women who question what it means for them to be a part of the Revolution. While these women have conquered the public sphere, the domestic sphere continues to uphold and legitimize the sexist roles that lead women to the experience of the second shift.

Her incisive look into this matter, her continuous questioning of how far had things truly changed in the symbolic imaginary in regards to women's positions and status in the new emerging society, made Gómez a pioneer in these subjects, which she developed through several different angles in other documentaries. *Guanabacoa, crónica de mi familia* is an autobiographical film about Gómez's family and about herself in that context: a black middle-class woman. It is a personal dissection of class, gender, and race, in which her self-reflective gaze constitutes a different point of view in the country's documentary tradition. Gómez is considered the first female Cuban filmmaker; she has produced some eighteen documentaries and one fictional film: *De cierta manera* (One Way or Another), finished in 1974 by Tomás Gutiérrez Alea (Titón) and Julio García Espinosa after Gómez's death from an asthma attack. This film, the first feature-length fictional work to be directed by a woman in Cuba, returns to the topics covered in Gómez's previous documentaries and insists on addressing the creation of "the new woman" within socialist society. It also continues an aesthetic search fundamentally based on the elimination of montage as a narrative resource and the articulation of documentary and fiction elements in the development of the plot.

In 1978 Marisol Trujillo directed her first documentaries at the ICAIC: *Lactancia* (Breastfeeding) and *El sitio en que tan bien se está* (It's a Good Place to Be), and in 1977 Rebeca Chávez helped direct a Latin American ICAIC news program; while at Estudios Fílmicos de las Fuerzas Armadas Revolucionarias (FAR) in 1976, the filmmaker Belkis Vega directed the documentary *Ustedes, esta generación* (You, This Generation). These women started their careers as documentary directors, but each followed a different path. One of the core subjects around which many of their offerings revolve is the epic and its narration through the film text. Filmmakers such as Vega and Chávez have added to this subject—which has been characteristic of Cuban cinema—a cinematographic body of work that offers a glimpse into the Cuban epic from a perspective (re)presenting subjects ignored by history and, in some cases, women left on the sidelines of epic narrative. Examples include the documentaries *Cuando una mujer no duerme* (When a Woman Doesn't Sleep, 1986), by Chávez, or *Mujeres, simplemente* (Simply Women, 1980), by Vega, or *Esa mujer de tantas estrellas* (That Woman of So Many Stars, 1987), by the filmmaker Mayra Vilasís, who began her career at the ICAIC as a documentary director in 1985.

The work of Marisol Trujillo has women's issues as a central topic. Her most celebrated work is *Mujer ante el espejo* (Woman in the Mirror, 1983), about the sacrifices a female dancer must make in order to succeed professionally and personally, which include the stoic care of her body. Trujillo portrays the dancer's body as the domain where the public and private spheres come together and clash: her desire to perform a leading role as a ballet dancer and her desire to become a mother. In other documentaries, such as *Oración* (Prayer) and *Mujer junto al faro* (Woman By the Lighthouse), both from 1984, Trujillo's point of view is again committed to the female universe. Trujillo left several unfinished projects that covered this same theme; one of them, the script for a feature-length fictional film dedicated to children, was meant to be a work of science fiction. She stopped filming in the early 1990s.

THE 1980s

In the 1980s the work of several female directors became prominent. One of them was Mayra Vilasís, born in 1944, a director with a feminist outlook who addressed women's issues in Cuban cinematography and who also wrote several essays on the subject; she once said that in Cuba "it is easier for a woman to become an airplane pilot than a film director." Vilasís died in 2002, before she was able to finish a feature film dedicated to Gertrudis Gómez de Avellaneda, a female Cuban writer of the nineteenth century.

Editors such as Miriam Talavera at the ICAIC and sound engineer Lizette Vila, who came from the FAR Studios, also directed their own projects in this decade. Vila produced pioneering work on subjects such as HIV, gender violence, and sexual diversity, demonstrating a concern for issues that had been ignored and that would be subsequently addressed by other filmmakers.

Although there is scant data about women directors in television, particularly in television drama, as of 2010 there were approximately fifteen female directors working in this sector, which shows it has been a less complex media for them. Female television directors have explored women's issues that have not been represented in the movie industry. One of these themes is eroticism, a topic on which some producers have a unique viewpoint. The visually lyrical *Te llamarás Inocencia* (You Will Be Called Innocent), by the producer Teresa Ordoqui for Estudios Fílmicos de la Televisión in 1989, is considered the second full-length fiction film directed by a woman, within a larger cinematographic perspective other than ICAIC. As of 2010, television directors such as Elena Palacio and Magda González Grau, among others, were not only dealing with themes related to symbolic violence and women's relationship with their bodies, but also using the medium to challenge the discursive boundaries between filmmaking and television.

THE 1990s AND AFTER

The film *Mujer transparente* (Transparent Woman), produced by ICAIC in 1990, consisted of five stories that addressed women's issues from different perspectives. It included three short films directed by women who previously worked as assistant directors or documentary filmmakers: *Adriana* by Mayra Segura, *Julia* by Mayra Vilasís, and *Laura* by Ana Rodríguez. The film provided several women with the opportunity to direct, and also used women's voices to present unresolved social conflicts. It addresses subjects such as the invisibility of housework and the second shift; desire and pleasure in older women; and women who take charge of their lives and thus disrupt the larger social mandate to subordinate individual needs to patriarchal expectations. These themes are particularly evident in the film's last two stories—*Zoe*, directed by Mario Crespo, and *Laura*, directed by Ana Rodríguez.

In the 1990s, thanks to videotape technology, filmmakers from the film industry started directing. Gloria Arguelles (who worked as an editor), Marina Ochoa, Lourdes de los Santos, and Gloria Rolando (who produced her own documentaries from her independent video production company on topics such as race) are directors who have turned documentary production into works noteworthy within the study of Cuban cinema. Although not always focused on women's issues, these directors produced films that should be taken into account in any analysis of gender equality in Cuban film and video industries. Such an analysis, however, is thwarted by the difficulty in constructing a bibliography: It is hard to identify the work of all the female filmmakers who have directed independent films and who come from other production companies.

In 1999, the director Belkis Vega produced a television version of the play *La casa de Bernarda Alba* (The House of Bernarda Alba), which was screened at movie theaters. In 2002, using a much more cinematographic mise-en-scène, she filmed the play *Santa Camila de la Habana Vieja* (Saint Camille of Old Havana) for television, a work that also premiered at movie theaters. In 2009, the director Rebeca Chávez,

who had started off with two short fiction films in the 1990s, released her first feature film, *Ciudad en rojo* (City in Red), an ensemble cast production that addresses the revolutionary epic, especially the clandestine struggle in the province of Santiago de Cuba in the days preceding the January 1959 victory. In a 2006 documentary about Cuban lives and the Revolution, the television director Consuelo Elba made *Mujeres de la guerrilla* (Guerilla Women, 2006); telling the story of ten former female guerrilla combatants of the Revolution, she describes their humble origins, the events that led them to join the struggle, and subsequent incorporation into society.

THE NEW GENERATION

The democratization of new technologies and the creation of film schools allowed young female filmmakers access to positions in film directing, as well as other positions in the movie industry, such as cinematography, a specialization that had historically discriminated against women in the industry. Film directors such as Patricia Ramos, with her short fiction films *Na-Na* and *El patio de mi casa* (The Patio of My House, 2008); Susana Barriga, with her documentaries *Cómo construir un barco* (How to Build a Boat, 2008), *Patria* (Fatherland, 2008), and *The Illusion* (2009); Heidi Hassan, with her short fiction film *Tierra roja* (Red Earth, 2008) and documentary *Tormentas de verano* (Summer Tempests, 2009); and Daniellis Hernández, with her documentary *Extravío* (Lost, 2008) address such themes as emigration from the perspective of children, female emigration, female eroticism thwarted by domesticity, self-representation as a search for identity, and race, among others. Their work reveals an aesthetic search for a new language that breaks away from the customary narrative of Cuban cinema. Even younger artists, such as Alina Rodríguez, Milena Almira, and Jessica Rodríguez, among others, address some of Cuba's controversial subjects: the migration from the country to the city, social abandonment, marginality, and transvestism. Marilyn Solaya based her 2010 documentary *En el cuerpo equivocado* (In the Wrong Body) on the story of

Approximate numbers of women filmmakers in Cuba, by studio affiliation

	1960	1970	1980	1990	2000
ICAIC	1	3	4	8	5
Estudios Fílmicos de FAR		1	2	3	Studio closed
Estudios Fílmicos de Televisión			1	6	15
Independent and other institutions				4	More than 20

SOURCE: Danae C. Dieguez.

Figure 1

Cuba's first transsexual, in which she depicts how the protagonist ends up trapped by the traditional stereotypes that the woman's realm is a domestic one.

The new generation takes up themes with greater self-assurance, perhaps to some degree based on their growing numbers and their independence from institutions (see Figure 1). In 2000, fifteen women were creating films at Estudios Fílmicos de Televisión—Xiomara Blanco, Mirta González Perera, Consuelo Elba, Consuelo Ramírez, Virgen Tabares, Belkis Vega, Mariela López, María de los Ángeles Núñez Jauma, Elena Palacios, Yaíma Pardo, Marta Recio, Magda González Grau, Milena Almira, Heiking Hernández, and Gretel Medina—as compared to just one woman in 1980. They work independently, and their projects search for a repositioning of subjects that have been absent from the images about the nation, as well as examine new points of view about gender relations within a cultural and social context.

FILMOGRAPHY

Selected Films

Chávez, Rebeca. *Cuando una mujer no duerme* (1985). ICAIC, Documentary.

Chávez, Rebeca. *Rigoberto* (1985). ICAIC, Documentary.

Chávez, Rebeca. *Una más entre ellos* (1988). ICAIC, Documentary.

Chávez, Rebeca. *La fidelidad* (1992). ICAIC, Drama.

Chávez, Rebeca. *El triángulo* (1992). ICAIC, Drama.

Chávez, Rebeca. *Con todo mi amor, Rita* (2000). ICAIC, Documentary.

De los Santos, Lourdes. *Sara González* (2003). ICAIC, Documentary.

De los Santos, Lourdes. *Del Río Zaida* (2004). ICAIC, Documentary.

Gómez, Sara. *Guanabacoa: Crónica de mi familia* (1966). ICAIC, Documentary.

Gómez, Sara. *En la otra isla* (1968). ICAIC, Documentary.

Gómez, Sara. *Una isla para Miguel* (1968). ICAIC, Documentary.

Gómez, Sara. *Año uno* (1972). ICAIC, Documentary.

Gómez, Sara. *Atención prenatal* (1972). ICAIC, Documentary.

Gómez, Sara. *Mi aporte* (1972). ICAIC, Documentary.

Gómez, Sara. *De cierta manera* (1974). ICAIC, Drama.

Ochoa, Marina. *Blanco es mi pelo, negra mi piel* (1997). ICAIC, Documentary.

Ochoa, Marina. *Julieta busca a Romeo* (1998). ICAIC, Documentary.

Pérez, Niurka. *Mujer imagen* (1994). ECITVFAR, TV documentary.

Pérez, Niurka. *Zaida* (1994). ECITVFAR, TV documentary.

Pérez, Niurka. *Mujeres diferentes* (1997). ECITVFAR, TV documentary.

Rodríguez, Ana. *Laura* (segment of *Mujer transparente*) (1990). ICAIC, Drama.

Segura, Mayra. *Adriana* (segment of *Mujer transparente*) (1990). ICAIC, Drama.

Solaya, Marilyn. *Mírame mi amor* (2001). ICAIC, Documentary.

Solaya, Marilyn. *En el cuerpo equivocado* (2010). ICAIC, Documentary.

Talavera, Miriam. *Un, dos, eso es* (1986). ICAIC, Documentary.

Talavera, Miriam. *Yo soy Juana Bacallao* (1986). ICAIC, Documentary.

Trujillo, Marisol. *Lactancia* (1978). ICAIC, Documentary.

Trujillo, Marisol. *El sitio en que tan bien se está* (1978). ICAIC, Documentary.

Trujillo, Marisol. *Canción feliz* (1983). ICAIC, Documentary.

Trujillo, Marisol. *Mujer ante el espejo* (1983). ICAIC, Documentary.

Trujillo, Marisol. *Mujer junto al faro* (1984). ICAIC, Documentary.

Trujillo, Marisol. *Oración* (1984). ICAIC, Documentary.

Vega, Belkis. *Mujeres, simplemente* (1980). Estudios Fílmicos FAR, Documentary.

Vega, Belkis. *María Luisa* (1985). Estudios Fílmicos FAR, Documentary.

Vega, Belkis. *Simplemente mujer* (1996). Estudios de la Televisión, TV documentary.

Vega, Belkis. *De domésticas a compañeras* (1998). Estudios de la Televisión, TV Documentary.

Vega, Belkis. *La casa de Bernarda Alba* (1999). Estudios de la Televisión, TV Drama.

Vega, Belkis. *Santa Camila de la Habana Vieja* (2002). Estudios de la Televisión, TV Drama.

Vila, Lizette. *Y hembra es mi alma* (1994). Productora de documentales UNEAC Huròn Azul, Documentary.

Vila, Lizette. *Otra mujer sin rostro* (2006). Proyecto Palomas, Documentary.

Vila, Lizette. *Rasgando velos* (2006). Proyecto Palomas, Documentary.

Vilasís, Mayra. *Yo soy la canción que canto* (1985). ICAIC, Documentary.

Vilasís, Mayra. *Visión de Amelia* (1986). ICAIC, Documentary.

Vilasís, Mayra. *Esa mujer de tantas estrellas* (1987). ICAIC, Documentary.

Vilasís, Mayra. *Con luz propia* (1988). ICAIC, Documentary.

Vilasís, Mayra. *Momentos de Tina* (1988). ICAIC, Documentary.

Vilasís, Mayra. *En casa de Haydée* (1989). ICAIC, Documentary.

Vilasís, Mayra. *Julia* (segment of *Mujer transparente*) (1990). ICAIC, Drama.

Vilasís, Mayra. *Cuerdas en mi ciudad* (1995). ICAIC, Documentary.

Independent Films of the 2000s

Almira, Milena. *El grito* (2008). Facultad de Arte de los Medios de Comunicación Audiovisual, ISA, Drama.

Almira, Milena. *Alina, 6 años* (2009). Drama.

Barriga, Susana. *The Illusion* (2009). Escuela Internacional de Cine y Televisión de San Antonio de los Baños, Documentary.

Castellanos, Adriana. *El pez de la torre nada en el asfalto* (2008). Facultad de Arte de los Medios de Comunicación Audiovisual, ISA, Drama.

Hassan, Heidi. *Tierra Roja* (2008). Drama.

Hernández, Daniellis. *Extravío* (2008). Escuela Internacional de Cine y Televisión de San Antonio de los Baños, Documentary.

Ramos, Patricia. *El patio de mi casa* (2008). Escuela Internacional de Cine y Televisión de San Antonio de los Baños, Drama.

Rodríguez, Alina. *El color de Elisa* (2009). Drama.

Vega, Belkis. *El futuro es mi sueño* (2006). Documentary.

Vega, Hilda Elena. *La Bestia* (2008). Facultad de Arte de los Medios de Comunicación Audiovisual, ISA, Drama.

BIBLIOGRAPHY

Chanan, Michael. *The Cuban Image: Cinema and Cultural Politics in Cuba.* London: British Film Institute, 1985.

Chanan, Michael. "Otra mirada." *Cine Cubano* 127 (1989): 29–37.

Colaizzi, Giulia. "El acto cinematográfico: Género y texto fílmico." *Lectora* 7 (2001): v–xiii.

Diéguez, Danae C. "Cine de mujeres en Cuba: ¿Atisbos de un contracine?" In *Conquistando la utopía: El ICAIC y la Revolución 50 años después.* Havana: Ediciones ICAIC, 2010.

Diéguez, Danae C. "¿Voces de mujeres o mujeres para ser miradas?" *Mujeres* (1 June 2011): 14–17. Available from http://www.mujeres.co.cu/articulo. asp?a=2011&num=522&art=12.

Doane, Mary Ann. *The Desire to Desire: The Woman's Film of the 1940s.* Bloomington: Indiana University Press, 1987.

García Borrero, Juan Antonio. "Sara Gómez (I)," n.d. Available from http://cine-cubano-la-pupila-insomne. nireblog.com.

García Borrero, Juan Antonio. "Sara Gómez (II)," n.d. Available from http://cine-cubano-la-pupila-insomne. nireblog.com.

García Borrero, Juan Antonio. *Guía crítica del cine cubano de ficción.* Havana: Editorial Arte y Literatura, Havana, 2001.

García Borrero, Juan Antonio. "La mujer en el cine cubano." March 25, 2010. Available from http://cine-cubano-la-pupila-insomne.nireblog.com/.

Khun, Annette. *Cine de mujeres: Feminismo y cine.* Madrid: Cátedra, Signo e Imagen, 1991.

Lauretis, Teresa de. *Alicia ya no: Feminismo, semiótica, cine.* Valencia, Spain: Ediciones Cátedra, 1992.

Mulvey, Laura. *Placer visual y cine narrativo.* Valencia, Spain: Fundación Instituto Shakespeare/Instituto de cine y RTV (Documentos de trabajo), 1988.

Pastor, Brígida M. "Del margen al centro: Cuba y el nuevo cine latinoamericano." *Razón y Palabra* 46 (August–September 2005). Available from http://www. razonypalabra.org.mx/anteriores/n46/bpastor.html.

Siles Ojeda, Begoña. "Una mirada retrospectiva: Treinta años de intersección entre el feminismo y el cine." *Caleidoscopio* 1 (March 2000).

Vilasis, Mayra. "Por una mirada divergente." *Temas* 5 (January–March 1996): 164–171.

GENDER: GENDER ROLES IN UNION CITY: A CASE STUDY

Yolanda Prieto

■ *See also*

Diasporas: Cubans Abroad, Post-1959

The role of gender in the development of the Cuban community of Union City, New Jersey, since 1959.

Cuban immigration to the United States dates to the nineteenth century, when the majority of the *criollo* elite were involved (though the working class still emigrated in greater numbers). During the Republican period this migratory flow continued. The 1930 U.S. census revealed a notable increase in the ratio of Cuban-born males to females as compared to 1920; indeed, the male preponderance was the highest of any foreign-born group in the United States (Aja Díaz pp. 100, 104).

According to the scholars Gerald Poyo and Lisandro Pérez, Cuban emigrants in the 1930s, 1940s, and 1950s were motivated in part by social discontent that encouraged migration to the traditional destination cities that had a favorable labor market (New York, Tampa, and Miami), where Cuban culture and identity are also present (Poyo and Pérez cited in Aja Díaz p. 104). The revolutionary movement of the 1950s, which had its roots in the 1930s, prompted Cubans to leave for the United States in search of political refuge. The immigrants of the 1950s were part of an organized campaign aimed at ending Fulgencio Batista's regime, and their network reached into many cities in the Americas (López Rivero). No information about the migratory chains or kinship networks was collected before 1959, and research on gender relations in Cuban immigrant communities is sparse.

The 1950 census counted 32,200 persons of Cuban origin in the United States. The number of Cubans registered as immigrants in the period 1946 to 1950 increased by 132 percent from 1941 to 1945 (when it totaled 10,807 persons), and between 1951 and 1955 the number doubled, surpassing the levels of the nineteenth-century tobacco migration to Florida. From 1956 to 1958, the census shows that 40,267 Cubans entered the United States as immigrants. During those years the Cuban immigrant community was concentrated in New York City, where other Caribbean immigrants had relocated for jobs. Women outnumbered men in this wave of migration, which reinforces the theory of a work-related migration from

Cuba (Aja Díaz p. 105). Study of the development of Cuban settlements abroad, and particularly in the United States, shows that women played a vital role in daily life, in economic growth, and in social integration into the communities where they typically settled as part of a family.

Although Miami is the heart of the Cuban population in the United States, from the mid-1960s to the mid-1980s Union City, New Jersey, was home to the second-largest concentration of Cubans in the country; many people referred to it as "the second capital of exile." Cubans moved to Union City from New York City, where they had arrived as economic immigrants in the 1940s, long before the Cuban Revolution. In Union City they sought a quieter environment and better schools for their children, following in the footsteps of German, Irish, and Italian immigrant groups.

Before 1959 Cuban women in Union City worked in factories and in small family businesses together with their husbands and other family members. They rarely remained housewives, which had been the norm in Cuba except for a handful of female professionals and impoverished women who needed to work. The Cuban ideal, particularly for the middle class, was for women to be supported by their fathers or husbands; in the United States, in contrast, it was commonplace for women to work.

The Cuban Revolution in 1959 triggered a massive exodus to the United States. The majority of immigrants landed and stayed in Miami, and the resulting economic, demographic, and social pressures in Miami-Dade County led the U.S. government to establish the Cuban Refugee Program to relocate immigrants to other states. Many chose to go to New Jersey, especially to Union City, where a small Cuban community already existed. Some went there to reunite with family members, and many were attracted by the city's plentiful work opportunities, mainly in the textile and embroidery industries. The vibrant Cuban community grew up on the banks of the Hudson River and flourished until the late 1980s; after building successful businesses in Union City, many wealthy or retired Cubans moved to Miami or to more affluent suburbs in New Jersey. The economic growth of Union City attracted the attention of researchers, who found that women were pivotal to the development of the Cuban community in Union City.

LATE 1970s AND EARLY 1980s

Interviews conducted by Yolanda Prieto with 107 Cuban women in Union City from 1979 to 1980 revealed that they had a higher rate of participation in the local workforce than white women and women in other minority groups (Prieto 2009). Most of them had arrived in the mid- or late 1960s, and some of them before 1959. They came from the middle and working classes. Many arrived with their families after Cuba's 1968 revolutionary offensive nationalized small businesses. Almost half of them had finished high school and some had college degrees.

In 1980 Cuban women in the United States had the highest rate of workforce participation at 55 percent, compared to 40 percent of Puerto Rican women and 49 percent of Mexican women. The figure for American-born women as a whole was 50 percent. In the state of New Jersey, however, the numbers were even higher for Cuban women: 59 percent of them participated in the workforce, compared to 43 percent of Puerto Rican women, 52 percent of Mexican women, and 50 percent for the U.S. female population as a whole. In 2000, the level of participation in Hudson County, New Jersey, where Union City is located, had dropped to 44 percent, for several reasons: the population of Cuban women was older, and many had retired; there were fewer jobs available; and as the Cuban community was dispersed in the 1980s, there were fewer young immigrants to replace the older ones (U.S. Bureau of the Census 2000).

There are several factors that help to explain Cuban women's higher level of workforce participation. Union City had plenty of manufacturing jobs in the 1960s, but in the 1980s many of the manufacturing enterprises moved to areas where labor was cheaper. In addition, the Cuban women in the Union City study were older than average, with an average age of 49.7 as compared to 40.0 for Cuban women in the United States as a whole, an average age of 27.8 for Latinas in the United States, and an average age of 33.8 for the entire female population of the United States (U.S. Bureau of the Census 1970). The higher age of Cuban women in New Jersey might indicate that this group was at its productive peak, and, therefore, its participation in the labor market was higher.

When participants in the study were asked why they worked and why they thought so many Cuban women worked, they responded that they wanted to help their families financially and to regain the middle-class status they had had in Cuba or to achieve that status for the first time, as immigrants. The United States offered them social mobility through work—an opportunity that the Revolution had destroyed in Cuba. It can be argued that there was an ideological motive for the intense participation of the first postrevolutionary wave of Cuban female immigrants in the workforce.

One of the women interviewed (Elsa, 47, a married white factory worker from Pinar del Río) said that she had to work because it was the only way for her family to get ahead: "We Cubans like success. . . . We want to give our children a good education. We are also saving money to buy a house in Miami. This country has given us so much: shelter from communism, work, and the opportunity for our children to succeed" (Prieto 2009, p. 70).

TEN YEARS ON: 1990

Ten years after the original study, the research was repeated with a smaller sample of women with similar characteristics (Prieto 1995, pp. 47–59). The main focus of the second study was gender dynamics within the family, covering issues from women's attitude to work to their relationships with their husbands and children. Did Cuban women feel liberated by their employment outside the home? How did their husbands and children feel about their work?

For the most part, daughters admired their mothers and regarded them as role models. For the women workers, employment had an intrinsic value that fostered a feeling of independence. When one interviewee was asked if she would keep working if she did not need the money, she replied, "Of course I would. I'd go crazy if I stayed at home all the time. Besides the money I make, I have friendships at work, and it keeps me entertained." Another woman said, "I love to work. Work makes me feel satisfied, genuine. Work is a central part of my life" (Prieto 2009, pp. 72–73). Marina (59, white, divorced), originally from Havana and then an editor for a Spanish book publisher in New York City, replied:

> Work makes life colorful. In Cuba, it was not common for women to work, although in my case I was a teacher. But things are different here. Most Cuban women work and are very active. I'm not saying this because I have a good job. I also worked in a factory when I arrived in the United States. I believe that work, no matter what kind of work it is, is good for people.
>
> *Prieto 1995, p. 52*

In addition to appreciating work as a means to help their families and to reclaim or obtain middle-class status, the interviewed women cited feelings of accomplishment, independence, and usefulness. Their daughters agreed that women should have careers; indeed, they could not see themselves without a mission in life beyond the confines of the family. At the same time, the daughters also cherished the family values they had learned from their mothers. Of the subjects who were married, most of their husbands supported the different role of women in the United States, but some were still reluctant to have their women work outside the home. Without a doubt, Cuban women have changed more rapidly than Cuban men in accepting their new roles in U.S. society.

THE 2000s

In a third, follow-up study of the Union City Cuban community conducted from 2000 to 2005, the research sample included women who had arrived in the United States after the 1990s, and in contrast to participants in the earlier studies, most of these women had been professionals in Cuba. Some of them had found jobs in the United States, but not in their own fields because of the language barrier; others were taking intensive English classes to expand their opportunities in the job market. Having grown up with the Revolution, they believed that women had the right and the duty to develop as human beings, and that entailed employment outside the home. The group included physicians, college professors, engineers, and artists. They said they had left Cuba for economic reasons, and their attitudes toward work and life in the United States in general were not influenced much by politics or ideology. One of the interviewed women—Esperanza, 41, a divorced mulata Spanish teaching assistant originally from Havana—said:

> My reasons for coming to this country were mostly economic. Most of the people who come here now feel that way. I am not very interested in politics. I was well respected as a physician in Cuba. I enjoyed my work. But I couldn't live on my salary! People who earned dollars working in hotels made more than I did. Life here is hard. I am studying so I can recertify my degree. I must keep on going and not lose hope. I truly miss Cuba, but I had no future there.
>
> *Prieto 2009, p. 81*

Like their predecessors in the 1970s, 1980s, and 1990s, the women interviewed in the early 2000s demonstrated great integrity in their work ethic and determination to fight odds. Whether they worked to help support their families or because they valued employment as a central factor in their personal development, Cuban working women have been mainstays in the Cuban communities in the United States.

BIBLIOGRAPHY

Aja Díaz, Antonio. *Al cruzar las fronteras*. Havana: Editorial CEDEM, 2009.

Domínguez, Virginia, and Yolanda Prieto. *Guest Editors, Sex, Gender, and Revolution*. Pittsburgh, PA: University of Pittsburgh Press, 1987.

López Rivero, Sergio. "Emigración y Revolución (1955–1958)." In *1959: Una rebelión contra las oligarquías y los dogmas revolucionarios*. Havana: Ruth Casa Editorial, 2009.

Pérez, Lisandro. "Immigrant Economic Adjustment and Family Organization: The Cuban Success Story Re-examined." *International Migration Review* 20 (Spring 1986): 4–20.

Prieto, Yolanda. "Reinterpreting an Immigration Success Story: Cuban Women, Work, and Change in a New Jersey Community." Ph.D. diss., Rutgers, State University of New Jersey, 1984.

Prieto, Yolanda. "Continuity or Change? Two Generations of Cuban American Women." *New Jersey History* 113, no. 1–2 (1995): 47–59.

Prieto, Yolanda. *The Cubans of Union City: Immigrants and Exiles in a New Jersey Community*. Philadelphia: Temple University Press, 2009.

U.S. Bureau of the Census, *Basic Demographic Characteristics*. Washington, DC: U.S. Department of Commerce, 1970.

U.S. Bureau of the Census. *Census of Population, 1980: General Social and Economic Characteristics*. Vol. 1, Series, PC-80-1 C1. Washington, DC: U.S. Department of Commerce, 1983.

U.S. Bureau of the Census. *Census of Population, 1980, General Social and Economic Characteristics, New Jersey*. Washington, DC: U.S. Department of Commerce, 1983.

U.S. Bureau of the Census. *Sex and Age by Employment Status, Racial or Ethnic Groupings, Hudson County, New Jersey*. Washington, DC: U.S. Department of Commerce, 2000.

■ *See also*

Cuban Thought and Cultural Identity: Costumbres in the Republican Period

Visual Arts: Republican Period

■

LA GITANA TROPICAL AND THE ARTISTIC INFLUENCE OF VÍCTOR MANUEL

Carlos M. Luis

The career of the artist primarily responsible for introducing modern art to Cuba in the 1920s, including his most iconic painting.

Víctor Manuel (1897–1969) was a Cuban painter who introduced to Cuba the styles of modern art he had studied during his travels to Europe. He is known primarily for his landscapes, both rural and urban, as well as his portraits of women's faces. One of his most famous works is a portrait in oil on wood titled *La gitana tropical* (Tropical Gypsy), completed in 1929. This painting is an important work in the Cuban avant-garde as a representative of the modernist movement of the last decade of the nineteenth century and the first decades of the twentieth.

To understand the importance given to this painting in the development of Cuban modern art, one must consider its historical context. Víctor Manuel was a painter who worked outside the restrictions of academic painting and became a spokesman for the incipient school of young artists struggling to shape a new style in Cuban art. His model was in the style of the French painter Paul Gauguin, which was already surpassed by the Europeans moving toward dadaism, futurism, cubism, expressionism, surrealism, and abstractionism. Even in some Latin American countries, such as Argentina, Brazil, and Uruguay, painters such as Alejandro Xul Solar (1887–1963), Tarsila do Amaral (1886–1973), and Joaquín Torres García (1874–1949), respectively, were finding other modes

of expression, more aligned with art developments in Europe. Mexican painters, who exercised considerable influence in Cuba, were at that time preoccupied with the adoption of a national language—a focus that permeated the development of the Cuban avant-garde. Gauguin thus served as a role model for many Cuban artists aiming to portray these national sentiments, with Víctor Manuel becoming one of the standard-bearers of this effort.

INFLUENCE OF EUROPEAN MODELS

The first two decades of Víctor Manuel's life coincided with a period of turmoil for a country attempting to emerge from the political and cultural domination of the United States. He studied at Havana's San Alejandro Academy of Fine Arts, but found the atmosphere stifling. Following his first personal exhibition at Havana's Galería San Rafael in 1924, he travelled to Paris in search of an environment more conducive to artistic experimentation. It was in Paris that he began to study the modern artistic trends, the primitive painters of the Renaissance, and the postimpressionists. His work began to evolve at this time to reflect these European influences.

Manuel returned to Cuba in 1927, where he participated in the pioneering Arte Nuevo exhibition in Havana. The aim of this exhibition was to show that Cuban artists finally were adopting the new artistic trends practiced by Europeans. This exhibition represents the introduction of modern art to Cuba. Víctor Manuel travelled to Paris again in 1929, joining other Cuban modernist artists such as Eduardo Abela (1889–1965) and Amelia Peláez (1896–1968), who were also living and exhibiting in Paris at the time.

LA GITANA TROPICAL

Manuel painted his famous *La gitana tropical* in 1929 while living in Paris. The painting is a portrait of a young woman of mixed racial heritage. The delicate melancholy of her expression has drawn comparisons with Leonardo Da Vinci's famous painting, *Mona Lisa*.

The importance of *La gitana tropical* lies in its discovery of a pictorial language that attempted to promote in Cuba a step forward in the direction of the aims of the avant-garde. A style based on Gauguin gave this painting a particular flavor that was also prevalent in some Mexican painters of the time. But if in the French master this flavor was more inclined toward the representation of the primitive, in Víctor Manuel's case the main idea was to portray within the parameters of a modernist style the main features of an idealized woman who could be more representative of an American paradigm. Painted with vivid colors, the *La gitana tropical* will arguably remain in the history of Cuban painting the icon that opened the doors to a more experimental practice of art.

LATER YEARS

Manuel's influence continued to be felt in Havana in the 1930s and the 1940s, with his participation in the newly created Estudio Libre para Pintores y Escultores, an organization founded by Abela in 1937. Despite its short duration, this organization gave new impetus to modern art in Cuba by teaching upcoming artists styles that were rejected by the San Alejandro Academy.

Manuel's influence waned during a period of artistic upheaval in the 1950s. At that time a group of young painters and sculptors, known as the group of the eleven, promoted abstractionism, leaving behind those who initiated the avant-garde in the 1930s and 1940s, Víctor Manuel among them. Manuel responded by producing what is considered by some to be his most adventurous work—his series of nocturnal streets. In these paintings, he departed from the old themes of gypsies and peasants, displaying a forceful use of brushstrokes and colors. By comparing these paintings with some that were done elsewhere in Europe and the United States during this same period, one could arrive at the conclusion that his sense of rebellion was still very much alive. Yet, in spite of the constant repetitions of the same icons, one can discover in his paintings a sense of humor reflecting a certain ironic eroticism.

BIBLIOGRAPHY

Lastra, Luis. "Víctor Manuel: Trascendencia de la libertad." Exhibition Catalogue. Miami: Alfredo Martínez Gallery, no date.

Lezama Lima, José. "Otra página para Víctor Manuel." In *Obras completas*, vol. 2. Mexico City: Aguilar, 1977.

Pérez Cisneros, Guy. "Víctor Manuel y la pintura cubana contemporánea." In *300 años de arte en Cuba*. Havana: Universidad de La Habana, 1941.

Rigol, Jorge. *Víctor Manuel*. Havana: Editorial Letras Cubanas, 1990.

Zéndegui, Guillermo de. "Víctor Manuel: Un innovador de la pintura cubana." Inaugural Catalogue. Miami: Museo Cubano de Arte y Cultura, 1982.

■ *See also*

Cuban Singers in the United States

Diasporas: Cubans Abroad, Post-1959

Miami

GLORIA AND EMILIO ESTEFAN: LATIN MUSIC'S POWER COUPLE

Celeste Fraser Delgado

Singer and producer who pioneered Cuban crossover into global pop.

In the 1980s Gloria Estefan and her husband, Emilio Estefan Jr., with the Miami Sound Machine (MSM), discovered a formula for producing hits by combining elements of traditional Cuban music with current trends in global pop. During the following three decades, the pop star and producer/promoter applied that formula to a wide range of Latin American musical traditions and shifting pop trends. The Estefans' success created opportunities for other Latin artists to break out of local markets and reach pan–Latin American and global audiences.

CROSSOVER

Gloria Estefan and the Miami Sound Machine reached a global audience with a Miami sound: American pop with English lyrics and Cuban flourishes. Born in Havana in 1957 and raised in Miami, Estefan remained as of 2011 the most successful Latin artist to cross over to mainstream pop. She was one of the top-selling pop acts of any origin, with more than ninety million albums sold worldwide. Early hits such as "Conga" (1985) and "The Rhythm Is Gonna Get You" (1987) were essentially disco tunes accented by Cuban percussion and elements such as Conga's famous *tumbao*, played by Cuban pianist Paquito Hechavarría. The Miami sound was created by three MSM band members, known as the Three Jerks, who also served as producers: Joe Galdo, Rafael Vigil, and Larry Dermer.

Originally in the lineup as a percussionist, Emilio Estefan Jr. quit playing to concentrate on managing, producing, and promoting the band. Born in Havana in 1953, Estefan arrived in Miami as a teenager. He founded the Miami Latin Boys in 1974, then changed the band's name when Gloria joined two years later. To spotlight his wife's role, Estefan later changed the name again to Gloria Estefan and the Miami Sound Machine.

A solo artist from 1989 on, Gloria Estefan continued to release dance tracks, such as "Get on Your Feet" (1989). As a songwriter, she favored soft rock and had several hit ballads, including "Don't Wanna Lose You" (1989) and the anthem "Coming Out of the Dark" (1990), penned after she recovered from a spinal injury suffered in a tour bus accident in 1990.

The Estefans departed from the Miami Sound with *Mi tierra* (1993). Gloria's first solo album in Spanish featured original boleros and romantic ballads in the style of pre-revolutionary Cuban music. The musicians included venerable Cuban players such as bassist and Mambo King Israel "Cachao" López as well as Irakere alumni saxophonist Paquito D'Rivera and trumpeter Arturo Sandoval. This retro Cuban project appealed to both Latin American and mainstream audiences, selling 1.2 million copies in the United States and millions more internationally.

CROSSBACK

In April 1990 Emilio Estefan Jr. opened Crescent Moon Studios, a suite of business offices and state-of-the-art recording studios in southwest Miami. There he put together a roster of songwriters and producers to record not only Gloria Estefan, but other artists as well. Early on, Jon Secada matched Gloria Estefan's crossover success, selling more than twenty million albums. Like the Estefans, Secada was born in Havana and raised in Miami. His biggest hits were soulful ballads released in both English and Spanish: "Just Another Day" ("Otro día mas sin verte," 1991) and "If You Go" ("Si tu vas," 1994).

Estefan's team also produced local Miami artists such as African American soul singer Betty Wright as well as Miami-based Cuban acts, such as Cachao and the newly arrived *guajira* singer, Albita. These efforts did not achieve commercial success.

Still, Emilio Estefan's accomplishments with Gloria Estefan and Jon Secada earned him a reputation as the so-called godfather of Latin pop, both in the benevolent sense that he could make a singer a star and in the Mafia-inspired myth that he could end the career of any musician or producer who crossed him. Eager to win Estefan's favor, aspiring artists, producers, and songwriters trekked to Crescent Moon Studios from across Latin America. Many of these artists were not looking to cross over into the global, English-speaking market. Instead, they came to Miami to cross back to Latin American markets—to reach audiences across the hemisphere rather than being restricted to their home countries.

Through the crossback phenomenon, a formula was developed for the use of traditional Latin American music in Latin pop similar to the use of Cuban music in the creation of the crossover Miami sound. Key elements of the traditional music were removed from the traditional context and applied as decoration to dominant pop trends. Estefan's team at Crescent Moon applied this formula with varying degrees of artistic and commercial success with artists from Mexico (Thalía, Alejandro Fernandez, Cristian Castro), Colombia (Shakira, Carlos Vives), Panama (Los Rabanes), and Peru (Gian Marco). Because Cuban popular music has such a long history as a source material in American and Latin American pop, Estefan's team also mined less familiar Latin American musical traditions for fresher sounds.

LATIN BOOM

The success of the crossback phenomenon did not divert from the Estefans' crossover efforts. Emilio Estefan played a supporting role in the explosive introduction of Puerto Rican singer Ricky Martin to English-speaking audiences, which led stars such as Marc Anthony and Jennifer Lopez to book Crescent Moon for their crossover bids, too. Conversely, English-speaking stars such as Madonna, Lenny Kravitz, and Will Smith made the trek to southwest Miami in search of a Latin tinge for their pop songs.

The mass media proclaimed a Latin boom, and Emilio Estefan joined a cadre of music industry figures,

latin and mainstream, determined to capitalize on the surge of interest in Latin pop by creating a lasting institution. In 2000, the newly formed Latin Academy of Recording Arts and Sciences (LARAS) broadcast the first annual Latin Grammys on CBS. Some critics derided the show as the "Grammilios" because many of the featured artists were associated with Estefan, who was also named the first LARAS "Person of the Year."

POLITICS

Throughout her career, Gloria Estefan has made anti-Castro politics part of her performance. In 1995, she performed her protest song "Oye Mi Canto" (Hear My Song) for 16,000 Cuban refugees being held on the U.S. naval base in Guantánamo, Cuba. That same year, she appealed to the Pope to pray for Cuba's freedom during a performance at the Vatican. In June 2001, she performed on the *Today Show* wearing a t-shirt that proclaimed "Cuba B.C." (Before Castro). Although Estefan has never collaborated with a Cuban artist who maintains ties with the Castro regime, neither she nor Emilio has joined the Miami Latin music industry in excluding artists who remained in or retained ties with Cuba. In fact, both Gloria and Emilio Estefan have made public statements supporting the right of Cuban nationals to

Emilio and Gloria Estefan, 2007. Gloria Estefan and her husband, Emilio Estefan Jr., discovered a formula for producing hits by combining elements of traditional Cuban music with current trends in global pop. ROB VERHORST/REDFERNS/GETTY IMAGES

perform in the United States on the basis of freedom of speech.

Despite a long tradition of political lobbying in Washington, D.C., by anti-Castro exiles, Emilio Estefan concentrated his political influence on the federal government's promotion of Latin music. He was appointed by George W. Bush to the President's Committee for Arts and Humanities in 2001 and was called upon throughout the Bush administration to produce musical presentations at the White House for Hispanic Heritage Month and Cinco de Mayo. The Estefans also hosted a dinner at their home for Barack Obama after his presidential election.

BORROWING FROM CUBA'S MUSICAL PAST

Gloria Estefan continued to alternate albums in English and Spanish. In 2007 she returned to Cuban source material with *90 millas* (90 Miles), a reference to the distance between Cuba and the United States (at Key West). Where *Mi tierra* consisted primarily of love songs, *90 millas* offered original versions of pre-revolutionary dance styles, such as *son* and *danzón*.

This album coincided with a documentary video produced by Emilio Estefan exploring the influence of Latin music in the United States. Both album and film included Cuban musical legends such as Paquito D'Rivera, Arturo Sandoval, Cachao, and Generoso Jiménez, as well as other Latin stars such as Carlos Santana, Papo Lucca, and Jose Feliciano. Rather than a simple act of nostalgia, *90 millas* explicitly recognizes the creation of retro-Cuban sound in the diaspora.

At the same time, Gloria Estefan continued to insert herself in the broader trends of global pop; as of February 2011, she was working with hip-hop producer Pharrell Williams. Both Gloria and Emilio Estefan formed strategic collaborations with songwriters, musicians, and producers from across the hemisphere, crossing over and back across the traditions of Cuba, Latin America, and the United States.

SELECTED DISCOGRAPHY
Gloria Estefan and Miami Sound Machine
Gloria Estefan. *Cuts Both Ways* (1989).

Gloria Estefan. *Into the Light* (1991).

Gloria Estefan. *Mi tierra* (1993).

Gloria Estefan. *Hold Me, Thrill Me, Kiss Me* (1994).

Gloria Estefan. *Abriendo puertas* (1995).

Gloria Estefan. *Destiny* (1996).

Gloria Estefan. *Gloria!* (1998).

Gloria Estefan. *Alma Caribeña* (2000).

Gloria Estefan. *Unwrapped* (2003).

Gloria Estefan. *90 millas* (2007).

Gloria Estefan and Miami Sound Machine. *Let It Loose* (1987).

Miami Sound Machine. *Miami Sound Machine* (1978).

Miami Sound Machine. *Miami Sound Machine* (1982).

Miami Sound Machine. *Rio* (1982).

Miami Sound Machine. *Eyes of Innocence* (1984).

Miami Sound Machine. *Primitive Love* (1985).

Emilio Estefan Jr. Producer Credits
Cuban Artists
Albita. *No se parece a nada* (1995).

Albita. *Una mujer como yo* (1997).

Arturo Sandoval. *Trumpet Evolution* (2003).

Cachao. *Master Session Volume 1* (1994).

Cachao. *Master Session Volume 2* (1995).

Celia Cruz. *Siempre viviré* (2000).

Cheito. *Cheito* (1994).

Jon Secada. *Jon Secada* (1992).

Jon Secada. *Heart, Soul, & a Voice* (1994).

Jon Secada. *Better Part of Me* (2000).

Other Artists
Alejandro Fernandez. *Me estoy enamorando* (1997).

Carlos Vives. *Amor de mi tierra* (1999).

Carlos Vives. *Déjame entrar* (2001).

Jennifer Lopez. *On the 6* (1999).

Jennifer Lopez. *Let's Get Loud* (2000).

Madonna. *Evita: Music from the Motion Picture* (1997).

Marc Anthony. *Marc Anthony* (1999).

Paulina Rubio. *Pau-Latina* (2004).

Ricky Martin. *Ricky Martin* (1999).

Ricky Martin. *Sound Loaded* (2000).

Ricky Martin. *Almas del silencio* (2003).

Shakira. *Dónde están los ladrones?* (1995).

Thalia. *En éxtasis* (1995).

Thalia. *Amor a la mexicana* (1997).

BIBLIOGRAPHY

Aparico, Francis R. *Listening to Salsa: Gender, Latin Popular Music, and Puerto Rican Cultures.* Hanover, NH: Wesleyan University Press, 1998.

Cepeda, Maria Elena. "'Columbus Effect(s)': Chronology and Crossover in the Latin(o) Music 'Boom.'" *Discourse* 23, no. 1 (Winter 2001): 63–81.

Estefan, Emilio Jr. *Ritmo al éxito: Cómo un inmigrante hizo su sueño americano.* New York: Celebra, 2010.

Fraser Delgado, Celeste. "Los Producers." *Miami New Times* (September 6, 2001).

Fraser Delgado, Celeste. "Rewrapping Gloria." *Miami New Times* (September 25, 2003).

Morales, Ed. *The Latin Beat: The Rhythms and Roots of Latin Music, from Bossa Nova to Salsa and Beyond.* Cambridge, MA: Da Capo Press, 2003.

Pérez-Firmat, Gustavo. *Life on the Hyphen: The Cuban-American Way.* Austin: University of Texas Press, 1994.

GÓMEZ, GUILLÉN, GIRAL: THREE UNDERAPPRECIATED FILMMAKERS

Odette Casamayor-Cisneros

Disquieting glimpses of post-revolutionary Cuban society in the works of three black filmmakers.

Aesthetic innovation and radical examination of racial problems, marginalization, history, and popular culture in post-revolutionary Cuba are key elements in the filmography of three black filmmakers: Sara Gómez, Nicolás Guillén Landrián, and Sergio Giral. Through the years, their work did not receive the attention it deserves on the island or internationally, but in the early 2000s some interest was being expressed. The work of these filmmakers challenges dominant views of reality and examines the persistence of marginalization and racism in the socialist society. Their film perspectives are unusual given that black Cubans were almost exclusively depicted in the context of slavery and/or revolutionary heroism.

SARA GÓMEZ (1943–1974): COMPLEX MARGINALITY

Sara Gómez explored the persistence of marginality and racism, within the political context of the revolutionary government that dedicated significant legislative, economic, and pedagogical efforts to their eradication. In *De cierta manera* (One Way or Another), Gómez analyzes these contradictions through the love story of Mario and Yolanda. The mulatto Mario lives in a Havana slum that is in the process of being renovated by the revolutionary government. He is hesitant to join the Abakuá's brotherhood, a strictly male secret society of African origin. Yolanda is a white middle-class teacher. She does not understand the characteristics of the marginal enclave where her school is located, which is Mario's environment. The couple's disagreements are driven by machismo, racism, and cultural stereotypes.

Gómez's support for the revolutionary project shaped her perspective. In the 1960s, at the Instituto de Etnología y Folklore (Institute of Ethnology and Folklore), Gómez studied popular culture, religions, and Cuban marginalized populations. Later, as assistant director at the Instituto Cubano de Arte e Industria Cinematográficos (ICAIC), she became Cuba's first female film director. Her work conveyed her social and ethnographic viewpoint and constant concern for the everyday life of Cubans.

Her interest in the individual, commonly minimized within the collective tasks of the revolution, dominates documentaries such as *En la otra isla* (On the Other Island, 1968). In this film, Gómez interviewed youths who were being rehabilitated on the Isla de Pinos (Isle of Pines)—christened the Island of Youth by authorities, since youth reeducation centers were installed there. Racist prejudices are denounced by a black tenor discriminated against by his colleagues. Toward the end of the interview, the young singer wonders if he might someday be allowed to perform *La Traviata*. In the prolonged silence that follows, the filmmaker underscores, as in *De cierta manera*, a sense of inconclusion, the absence of a definitive answer to these racial and social problems.

Gómez also used this expressive silence at the close of the documentary *Guanabacoa: Crónica de mi familia* (Guanabacoa: Chronicle of My Family, 1966), in which she presents the complexity of socioeconomic conditions of black Cubans through the history of her own family. Here, Gómez leaves the viewer with another unanswered question, this time regarding how far black Cubans should go in transforming themselves to fit the new social standards. The film asks if black Cubans should abandon their beliefs and popular culture and whether they should recognize their history as marginalized subjects.

Gómez mixed fiction with documentary and analytical interrogation in order to expose the subjectivity of the Cuban people. In *De cierta manera* viewers see her skillful juxtaposition of documentary scenes expressing outward social change with fictive ones revealing individual internal transformations. One of the most interesting experiments of Cuban cinema, this film—Gómez's only feature-length fiction film and the first by a woman in Cuba—was not completed by the director, who died in 1974. The editing was completed thanks to the collaboration of fellow filmmakers Tomás Gutiérrez Alea, Julio García Espinosa, and Rigoberto López.

NICOLÁS GUILLÉN LANDRIÁN (1938–2003): ABSURDITY, UNDERDEVELOPMENT, REVOLUTION

Nicolás Guillén Landrián died poor and professionally unacknowledged in Miami. Despite their high aesthetic level and poetic sharpness, most of his documentaries were received with suspicion in Cuba, possibly due to his complicated representation of Cubans during the revolutionary period.

Coffea Arábiga (1968) was commissioned by the ICAIC to document the Havana Cordon, an intensive late-1960s campaign to develop the coffee-growing industry around the capital. The disruptive, quizzical editing is startling, eliciting both justifications and questions regarding the agricultural projects promoted, at times arbitrarily, by the government. With dizzying speed, a fragmented reality emerges in which popular culture, traditional and modern coffee-growing techniques, the benefits of the revolution, the anachronism

■ *See also*

Film: 1959–1989

Film: Cuban Cinema of the Diaspora

Race: Race Relations after the Revolution

Sugar: Representation in Cuban Culture

Sexuality: Gay and Lesbian Representation in Cuban Art, Film, and Literature

of both the U.S. presence in Cuban society in the prer-evolutionary era and the Soviet presence afterward, all interact in a way that is apparently unconnected with history and everyday urban and rural life. For example, a Soviet woman is hastily interviewed and responds in Russian, inserting information heard on the radio. (Previously, a black woman brushed her hair while the soundtrack played radio melodramas.) Similarly, while a narrator emphasizes the importance of the sun in agriculture, the Soviet woman protects herself with a parasol, in a Havana neighborhood where architecture reminiscent of the U.S. presence predominates.

Coffea Arábiga opens with laudatory verses to the triumphant nation, written by Nicolás Guillén Batista (1902–1989), the director's uncle and Cuban national poet. Thus, the film focuses on the people, more than the product, that led the ICAIC to commission this documentary. Who are Cuba's coffee producers? The people are no longer an indistinct mass as they are typically portrayed; in this film, the anonymous subject acquires not only a face but a particular gaze, directed toward the viewer. Like Sara Gómez, Guillén examines individuals, showing that their private lives are not accessible through preconceived messages and slogans. Both Gómez and Guillén are suspicious of generalizations; rather, they are obsessed with the reality that lies beneath the intricate text woven by people's gestures and thoughts and by popular imaginary. At the end of *Coffea Arábiga*, public cheers for the revolutionary leaders are mixed with the drums of the *tumba francesa*—music of Haitian origin that is especially widespread in eastern Cuba, where the largest coffee plantations have been located since the end of the eighteenth century. But this is no chorus of triumphal ecstasy. The filmmaker plays the Beatles' song "The Fool on the Hill" over images of Fidel Castro. The censorship of Guillén's work has been superficially explained by how the song is juxtaposed with Castro's image. But the filmmaker's use of a song by a rock group banned in Cuba at the time overshadows the message of the lyrics, which resonate with the revolutionary gesture itself. The choice could also be taken as criticism of the bureaucratization of the original dream that drove the revolutionary process and was backed by the popular majority.

This complex vision of the revolution and its international context hits the viewer in *Desde La Habana ¡1969!* (From Havana, 1969!, 1969). Containing no direct dialogue, the film delivers an explosion of images and sounds that disallow a single or overarching interpretation of reality. Guillén exposes the paradoxes of these images from an existentialist point of view. The phrase "Mother Nature's Son" from the Beatles song of the same name, is followed by images of U.S. nuclear bombs dropping on Japan. A continuation of the messages begun in *Coffea Arábiga*, this film uses Beatles music to denounce crimes perpetrated in Vietnam, the repression of civil rights demonstrators, and the U.S. tolerance of the Ku Klux Klan. The same United States is shown to be a paragon of development that put the first man on the

moon. Guillén uses the first images of Tomás Gutiérrez Alea's *Memorias del subdesarrollo* (*Memories of Underdevelopment*, 1968) to question the meaning of development, accompanied by the beat of drums played by Afro-Cubans. The original idea of these images has been attributed to Guillén, and this sequence certainly reflects his dizzying aesthetic. In *Desde La Habana* such images appear linked to the agricultural work, through which development would be achieved. The film also presents the situation prior to 1959 (a pseudo-republic, a succession of dictators, economic misery, and racial segregation), all reasons and justifications for the revolutionary triumph. History is needed to counter national amnesia (one of the characteristics of underdevelopment recreated in *Memorias*). Fidel Castro reappears at a podium, giving a diatribe in response to the deaths of Ernesto Guevara and Camilo Cienfuegos, commanders with whom he had shared leadership. Also heard are his exhortations to the coffee growers. Sometimes, the technical commentaries about the coffee production appear absurd, as do the testimonies of Cubans before and after 1959. The film is dominated by the absurd, passing through reality compressed between destruction and the birth of a new world. "Everybody's got something to hide, except me and my monkey," is a phrase repeated in the film. Except for existence itself, irreducible because a person either exists or does not, everything has a hidden meaning: the photographs, supposedly a faithful reflection of reality or the letters that make up a phrase. Reality is not cohesive but fractured. The films of Nicolás Guillén Landrián emanate from this nervous decomposition. To accept his schizophrenic viewpoint is to renounce the contemplation of chaos and jump into it, experiencing it. His work inspires questions rather than enforcing indoctrination. It did not meet the expectations of a government attempting to do away with uncertainty and chaos.

Los del baile (The Dancers, 1965) is dedicated to popular music, specifically the Mozambique, created by "Pello el Afrokán" in the 1960s. Although of marked African derivation, the Mozambique was overwhelmingly accepted as a national rhythm. However, the film's intense soundtrack does not express revolutionary euphoria. The director brings together images of Cubans removed from the epic context: dancing, drinking beer, celebrating Carnival. Mostly blacks and mulattoes, they also appear in domestic scenes, sometimes with melancholy expressions. Guillén captures their penetrating gaze. He traces the pain of a wound open since slavery forward into the present: It marks a pervasive sadness that persists as long as blackness, conceived in terms of otherness, continues to determine status in Cuban culture and society.

Racial, economic, and social marginality in times of revolutionary transformation is also recreated in the earlier *En un barrio viejo* (In an Old Neighborhood, 1963). This documentary depicts the difficult transition toward socialism. It shows a militia squadron passing through a humble Havana neighborhood, poor children for whom the revolution promises brighter futures, white middle-class residents approached by a beggar, black workers with a somber or tired gaze, Soviet insignias beside the Cuban flag. Juxtaposed with images of the Catholic Church is a religious ceremony of African origin in which whites also participate and where the camera focuses on portraits of leaders and revolutionary posters hanging on the walls. The documentary finishes with the words "THE END, but it isn't the end."

In *Ociel del Toa* (1965; the Toa is the mightiest river in Cuba, located in the east of the island), Guillén Landrián captures the facial expressions and body language of the peasants whose meager lives are documented through the young Ociel. This perspective is polemical since it reveals these peasants' views of hard work, recreation, their religion, and the eruption in their lives of revolutionary measures such as mandatory education and the prohibition of cockfighting. The film searches for an expressive authenticity of subjects marginalized by geographical remoteness. Rather than a celebration of the revolutionary epic, the film conveys uncertainty. This is exemplified by the undefined space toward which Ociel's boat navigates. Ociel, in the final intertitles, is not an optimistic hero or thankful for the revolutionary changes, but rather a mere mortal with basic existential concerns. He asserts that he has never seen death, because it cannot be touched, seen, or heard.

Taller Claudio A. Camejo: Línea y 18 (Claudio A. Camejo Workshop: Línea and 18th Streets, 1971) reproduces the dialogue of workers in a bus factory, but viewers do not hear clearly what they say. The absurd overcomes their words: propagandist language accompanied by concise explanations from the spokesperson, interrupted by factory sounds, contradictory musical themes, and incomprehensible messages. Chaos permeates this film, in which workers as individuals purposely disappear inside a flood of noises and empty phrases. This documentary was made in 1971, the year of the Primer Congreso de Educación y Cultura (First Congress for Education and Culture), when the ideological and moral parameters of the new society were dictated.

Much of Nicolás Guillén Landrián's work was censored. He did not offer the clarity or the explanations of reality that cultural institutions expected, particularly in documentary film, which was appreciated for its mobilizing potential and testimonial and didactic values. To the contrary, his work constituted a vivid recreation of a fruitful chaos: the revolution in the haste of its first moments.

The director was imprisoned more than once. His health deteriorated, and he was shut away in psychiatric institutions. In 1989, he emigrated. After more than a decade of exile, Guillén directed his last documentary, *Inside Downtown* (2001), in which he once again addressed his inquisitor's gaze toward the social contradictions and marginalized individuals hidden behind the orderliness and luxury of Miami.

SERGIO GIRAL: EXISTENTIAL GAZE AT SLAVERY AND RACIAL MIXING

Sergio Giral (b. 1937) also lived in Miami after 1991. He had previously lived in the United States during his childhood but returned to Havana after the triumph of the revolution and collaborated with the ICAIC, where he enjoyed a successful career.

María Antonia (1990), his last feature-length film made in Cuba, contains transgressions incompatible with prevailing ethical and ideological standards under the socialist regime. The film ends with an image of a beautiful mulatto woman getting out of a foreign car and disappearing into a poor neighborhood. A group of pioneer children shares the scene, representing the future promised by the revolution. The woman, ornately dressed in an evening gown though it is daytime, could represent prostitution, which was invisible in Cuba prior to the Special Period (the 1990s, after the collapse of the Soviet Union). This is María Antonia, whose tragic love relationship with the boxer Julián the film depicts. Based on the theatrical piece of the same name by Eugenio Hernández Espinosa, the film version emphasizes the marginality and the burden of racial and gender stereotypes that, in a story set in a poor neighborhood of Havana in the 1950s, allude to a situation that persists in present-day Cuba, despite the revolution.

Giral highlights the role of Afro-Cuban religions in marginal communities. The movie conveys the *patakíes* (legends) that express the cosmological foundation of the Regla de Ocha or Santería worldview. What to do with such persistent myths becomes the central question in Giral's work. María Antonia brings certain myths forward to the present: those of the *orisha* (Yoruba deity) Oshún and those of Cecilia Valdés, the tragic mulatta immortalized in the nineteenth century by novelist Cirilo Villaverde. The film also deconstructs these myths. From its opening sequences, irrespective of orders and hierarchy, the protagonist blasphemes the orishas that rule the consciences in her community and rejects the role society assigns to her. She murders Julián then dies at the hands of Carlos, another lover. If she had allowed herself to be taken away by Carlos, she would have improved her life. But the protagonist negates her image: She transforms herself from passive object into active subject. It is not the new lover who will transform her existence. He kills María Antonia by her own provocation, not spontaneously. Nor do the orishas change her destiny, despite the ceremonies and offerings dedicated to them. With her actions and her death, María Antonia disrupts the reproduction of the image of the Cuban mulatto woman at the mercy of other people's decisions. However, she is not able to completely erase the myth, also incarnated by the young mulatto woman of the 1990s who appears at the end of the film. It is left to the spectator to decide whether new María Antonias will perpetuate the irreverence—that is, if they are not already doing so by existing in broad daylight, before the young pioneers, in a revolutionary society.

In *El otro Francisco* (The Other Francisco, 1974), the analysis of myths is explicit. Based on the novel *Francisco*, written in 1838 by the abolitionist Anselmo Suárez y Romero, the film establishes, through a voiceover narrator, that Giral's intention is to reveal the "other Francisco," which the nineteenth-century author would not, or could not, reveal. Fragments of the novel, read in an exaggerated melodramatic tone suitable to the literary romanticism of its time, are juxtaposed with explanations of the real motives behind the abolitionist ideas of the *criollo* sugar barons who were acolytes of Domingo del Monte (1804–1853), an abolitionist and literary critic and promoter. For them, the black man was not a human being, only—as a slave—an obstacle to the island's development. Giral shows how blacks were manipulated through the use of different myths and stereotypes. Suárez's Francisco is a noble savage whose suffering is caused by a despot master, not by a complicated sociopolitical and economic system. His passivity is dismantled in the film by its depiction of blacks who take their destinies into their own hands. Giral's Francisco does not commit suicide but rather dies in resistance during a revolt. The action is transferred to the enslaved masses who become the real protagonists of the film.

In his other feature-length movies, *Rancheador* (Slave Hunter, 1976), *Maluala* (1977), and *Plácido* (1986), Giral pursues the rehabilitation of black Cubans in national history, presenting them from an existential perspective. In *Maluala* this perspective reveals the essential humanity of runaway slaves and their settlements—making clear their relevance to the contemporary revolutionary context in which these movies were produced. The music and dances, the beautiful images of the runaway slaves' all-out rebellion, and the plasticity of the scenes dignify black Cubans, who become here an absolute, transcendent human presence, rather than mere objects. This reality crushes the Spanish commander, defeated by the runaway slaves of the Maluala settlement. At the end of the film, he screams desperately, trapped in the popular tumult of the blacks and mulattoes celebrating in the streets with Afro-Cuban dances. His scream cuts across the years.

While Giral's films about slavery crudely portray subhuman blacks, according to the white perspective, in *Plácido* and *María Antonia* the analysis also touches on the issues of racial mixing. Giral brings out the meaning of the intermediate status of the mulatto, located between two worlds and stigmatized as a racial outcast and also as a legal outcast in the case of the nineteenth-century poet Gabriel "Plácido" de la Concepción Valdés (1809–1844). Giral extends these concerns about the mulatto subject to the current situation in the United States, where he developed his first feature-length film in exile, *Dos veces Ana* (Two Times Ana, 2010), the story of two Hispanic mulatto women.

CURRENT TRANSGRESSIONS

The work of Gómez, Guillén, and Giral illuminates the complexity of marginality, racial inequalities, and popular culture in post-revolutionary Cuba. The problems that accompanied the transformation into the ideal "New Man" outlined by Che Guevara, especially in marginalized sectors of the population, dominate their filmography. Their works are daring aesthetic experimentations, significant in their combining of fictional and documentary film.

Though these filmmakers were much overlooked, in the early 2000s a critical interest in them testified to the continued force of their legacy. In 2002 and 2003, important discussions were devoted to Nicolás Guillén Landrián during the ICAIC's Muestra de Jóvenes Realizadores (Young Directors Showcase). In addition, in 2005, the ICAIC organized a symposium about Sara Gómez.

SELECTED FILMOGRAPHY: SARA GÓMEZ

Plaza Vieja (1962, documentary).

El solar (1962, documentary).

Iré a Santiago (1964, documentary).

Excursión a Vueltabajo (1965, documentary).

Guanabacoa: Crónica de mi familia (1966, documentary).

. . . Y tenemos sabor (1967, documentary).

Una isla para Miguel (1968, documentary).

En la otra isla (1968, documentary).

Isla del Tesoro (1969, documentary).

Poder local, poder popular (1970, documentary).

Un documento a propósito del tránsito (1971, documentary).

De bateyes (1971, documentary).

Atención prenatal (1972, documentary).

Mi aporte (1972, documentary).

Año uno (1972, documentary).

Sobre horas extras y trabajo voluntario (1973, documentary).

De cierta manera (1974, fiction).

SELECTED FILMOGRAPHY: NICOLÁS GUILLÉN LANDRIÁN

Congos reales, Patio Arenero (1962, documentary).

Un Festival (1963, documentary).

El Morro (1963, documentary).

En un barrio viejo (1963, documentary).

Homenaje a Picasso (1965, documentary).

Los del baile (1965, documentary).

Ociel del Toa (1965, documentary).

Retornar a Baracoa (1966, documentary).

Coffea Arábiga (1968, documentary).

Desde la Habana¡1969! (1969, documentary).

Recordar (1970, documentary).

Taller Claudio A. Camejo: Línea y 18 (1971, documentary).

Nosotros en el Cuyaguateje (1972, documentary).

Para construir una casa (1972, documentary).

Un reportaje sobre el puerto pesquero (1972, documentary).

Inside Downtown (2001, documentary).

SELECTED FILMOGRAPHY: SERGIO GIRAL

Inseminación artificial, El Testigo (1963, documentary).

Cimarrón (1967, documentary).

Gonzalo Roig (1968, documentary).

Un relato sobre el jefe de la columna cuatro (1972, documentary).

Qué bueno canta Usted (1973, documentary).

El otro Francisco (1974, fiction).

Rancheador (1976, fiction).

Maluala (1977, fiction).

Techo de vidrio (1982, fiction).

Plácido (1986, fiction).

María Antonia (1990, fiction).

La imagen rota (1995, documentary).

Dos veces Ana (2010, fiction).

SELECTED BIBLIOGRAPHY

Chanan, Michael. *Cuban Cinema.* Minneapolis: University of Minnesota Press, 2004.

Gónzalez Pérez, Tomás. "Sara, One Way or Another." In *AfroCuba: An Anthology of Cuban Writing on Race, Politics and Culture,* edited by Pedro Pérez Sarduy and Jean Stubbs. Melbourne: Ocean Press; New York: Latin American Bureau, 1993.

"De cierta Sara." *La Gaceta de Cuba* 4 (July–August 1999), 42–49.

Egusquiza, George, and Víctor Jiménez. *Nicolás: El fin pero no es el fin* Miami: Coincident Productions and Village Films, 2005. Documentary film.

García Yero, Olga. "Desde Camagüey, 2009: Más de cuarenta años después." At *Cine Cubano, la pupila insomne.* http://cine-cubano-la-pupila-insomne. nireblog.com/post/2009/03/16/nicolas-guillen-landrian-en-la-mirada-de-olga-garcia-yero.

Giral, Sergio. "Images and Icons." In *AfroCuba: An Anthology of Cuban Writing on Race, Politics and Culture,* edited by Pedro Pérez Sarduy and Jean Stubbs. Melbourne: Ocean Press; New York: Latin American Bureau, 1993.

López, Ana M., and Nicholas Peter Humy. "Sergio Giral on Filmmaking in Cuba: An Interview." In *Cinemas of the Black Diaspora: Diversity, Dependence, and Oppositionality,* edited by Michael T. Martin. Detroit: Wayne State University Press, 1995.

Kaplan, E. Ann. "The Woman Director in the Third World: Sara Gómez's *One Way or Another* (1974)." In *Women and Film: Both Sides of the Camera,* by E. Ann Kaplan. New York and London: Methuen, 1995.

Muller, Alessandra. *Sara Gómez: An Afro-Cuban Filmmaker.* Cuba/Switzerland: Amka and Iceberg Films, 2005. Documentary film.

"Número Especial Sara Gómez." *Cine Cubano* 127 (1989).

Reyes, Dean Luis. "Nicolás Guillén Landrián: El iluminado y su sombra." *La Gaceta de Cuba* 1 (January–February 2005).

Zayas, Manuel. *Café con leche* Havana: Escuela internacional de Cine y Televisión, 2003. Documentary film.

GOVERNANCE AND CONTESTATION

Cuban history is often interpreted through the types of governments Cuba has had and the ways in which people have tried to change them. Spanish colonial authorities established an administrative system in Cuba that still influences the country's political culture. In the 1800s, Cuban rebels attempted to overthrow the Spanish colonial government and develop an independent republic. U.S. intervention established still another influence on the governance of Cuba. Even today, Cuban government ministries still impose regulations that have roots in the U.S. military government of the early 1900s.

In the 1930s, an authoritarian government rose, coupled with a broad-based opposition that included intellectuals and key members of the military. Like many other countries, popular nationalism had its heyday in Cuba and culminated with the adoption of the 1940 constitution, a progressive document heavily influenced by Cuban communists that prohibited discrimination on the basis of race, gender, religion, and class. The suspension of this constitution by Fulgencio Batista in 1952 fed the flames of a revolutionary movement that led to the Revolution of 1959.

Although its leaders had promised elections and a restoration of separation of powers, the revolutionary government quickly consolidated its regime and soon aligned with the Soviet Union. Cuba's government has been marked by centralized power as well as bureaucratic and authoritarian rulers. Tales of heroism have characterized contestation of these governments as has the popular notions of "one hundred years of struggle," suggesting that it was the revolution that finally fulfilled the quest of the war of independence from Spain. Debates, however, continue about the place of social justice, democracy, and social and human rights.

GOVERNANCE AND CONTESTATION: COLONIAL PERIOD

Guadalupe García

The Spanish colonial government in Cuba and efforts to balance the interests of the monarchy and the needs of island residents.

Following its initial exploration and settlement in the early sixteenth century, the Spanish Crown established the island's colonial government in order to further its constantly evolving interests in the Americas. Resident responses to the changing interests of the Spanish monarchy similarly reflected the needs of the island's inhabitants, composed of *peninsulares* (Spanish-born Cubans), *criollos* (island-born Cubans of Spanish descent), African-descended peoples (slave and free), and European and Caribbean immigrants. Given the demographic differences within the island's population, it is not surprising that resident interests often diverged from those of the colonial administration. The resulting government attempted a careful balance between the needs of the empire and those of its colonial subjects with varying degrees of success, at least until the final war of independence in 1898 effectively ended colonial rule.

SIXTEENTH CENTURY

Until the latter half of the sixteenth century, Cuba remained a backwater of the Spanish empire, with a weak government structure. European exploration had quickly exhausted the island's mineral reserves and led to the extermination of the island's indigenous population, effectively destroying two of the most highly sought-after commodities in the Americas. The island was unable to compete with Mexico and Peru for settlers and thus relegated to a secondary position within the empire's newly conquered territories, with little administrative governance. Its government structure was instead the result of an early expedition led by Diego Velásquez de Cuéllar (1465–1524), who, along with subsequent settlers, established seven *villas*: San Cristóbal de la Habana, Baracoa, Bayamo, Trinidad, Sancti Spiritus, Camaguey, and Santiago de Cuba. The primary function of these villas was to aid the Crown in controlling trade and production in their respective hinterlands. As the first governor-general representing the Crown, Velásquez named each town's *regidores* (municipal council members) and *alcaldes* (magistrates), who together made up the membership of the *cabildo* (council), Cuba's earliest form of government. Other officials also involved in colonial governance were the *alguacil* (sheriff), *escribano* (notary), and *procurador* (attorney).

Cuba remained under the jurisdiction of the Royal Audiencia of Santo Domingo, the court of the Spanish Crown in the Americas. (The *audiencia* was subdivided into four archdioceses, of which Cuba's, established in 1522, was further divided between Santiago in the east and Havana in the west.) Colonial subjects' attempts to bypass the audiencia in protest of royal policies led them to Spain: It was to the Crown and the Council of the Indies, formally created in 1524, that Cuba's earliest residents directed their appeals. This early form of contestation stemmed from residents' desires to safeguard their own interests by establishing the importance of the island, despite depopulation, vis-à-vis the rest of Spain's possessions. In Havana, where from 1520 to 1540 the population declined by as much as 80 percent, residents correctly surmised that the town's inability to compete with Spain's larger territories would diminish its significance within the colonial nexus and jeopardize its future standing.

Formal Spanish presence on the island, however, was about to increase. During the latter half of the sixteenth century, as Europe's geopolitical struggles were mirrored in the threats the island faced by pirates, corsairs, and foreign armies, Havana took on economic, military, and political importance, thus propelling Cuba to the forefront of the Spanish empire's attention. The city's location in the Caribbean basin made it a natural stopover for ships making their way to and from the Iberian Peninsula, and its natural harbor quickly solidified Havana's importance in world commerce at the same time that it increased the island's susceptibility to attack. The Crown responded by aggressively attempting to increase the island's population. Whereas the New Laws of 1542 prohibited the passing down of the encomienda labor system elsewhere in the Americas, it remained a hereditary enterprise in Cuba. The Cáceres Ordinances of 1574 also ensured that, pending the approval of the cabildo, land grants would honor right of first entry. Both measures were attempts to ensure a stable and permanent population in Cuba. The Cáceres Ordinances would eventually be ratified and reversed during the eighteenth century, when the cabildo experienced an overall loss of power.

SEVENTEENTH AND EIGHTEENTH CENTURIES

During the late sixteenth and early seventeenth centuries, Cuba reaped the benefits of royal importance as a result of Havana's port and Spain's development of a fleet system. By 1607, Havana had displaced Santiago de Cuba as the island's capital city. Yet despite Havana's growing prominence in the Atlantic, Cuba remained on the periphery of an empire more concerned with its mainland American territories and its European political struggles. Under the Hapsburgs during the seventeenth century, a relative lack of oversight allowed Cubans to function largely on a local level and encouraged them to develop trade alliances across the Atlantic. Cuban government, however, was directly influenced by Europe's geopolitical situation,

CHRONOLOGY OF EVENTS

1492: Christopher Columbus (Cristóbal Colón) claims Cuba for the Spanish crown.

1511: Diego Velásquez de Cuéllar, the first governor, begins Spanish settlement of Cuba.

1514: Havana founded.

1522: Royal Audiencia of Santo Domingo, divided into archdioceses.

1524: Crown and Council of the Indies created.

1552: Governor moves residence from Santiago to Havana; slave trade restricted to Havana.

1574: Cáceres Ordinances formulated.

1607: Havana officially named capital of Cuba.

1762: British capture Havana; return it to Spain the following year.

1764-65: Spain allows expansion of Cuban trade.

1774: Spanish duties on Cuban imports rescinded.

1777: Spain grants Cuba an independent colonial administration under a Governor-General.

1789: All Cuban ports opened to slave trade.

1811: Spain abolishes slave trade, except in Cuba.

1812: Aponte Rebellion.

1825: Powers of Cuba's Governor-General expanded.

1834: Cuba's Governor-General granted near total power.

1837: Cuban representation in Spanish Cortes ended.

1844: Conspiración de La Escalera.

1868: Ten Years' War begins.

1886: Slavery abolished in Cuba.

1895-1898: Spanish-American-Cuban War.

1898: Treaty of Paris ends Spanish rule of Cuba.

and by the eighteenth century, the Bourbon dynasty was sitting on the Spanish throne. The following reorganization of the Americas, Cuba included, was a harbinger of things to come. Vast social and economic changes had taken place across the island and would have a direct impact on its political administration. Trade in tobacco, sugar, and hides had expanded to complement the economic importance of Havana's port, making the island potentially much more lucrative for the new Bourbon monarchy.

The economic importance of Cuba underscored the monarchy's need to neutralize any potential threat emanating from either external forces or from mismanagement under the Hapsburgs. The colonial administration quickly went about attempting to curb local power and end local initiatives. In 1717, it established a royal monopoly on tobacco and, in 1740, created the Real Compañía de Comercio de La Habana, which had almost exclusive rights to all trade and commerce between Spain and Cuba. The economic changes complemented political ones. Cuban officials were replaced with military administrators that tended to favor peninsulares in an attempt to ensure the island's loyalty to the Crown. Cubans did not sit idly as the changes took place. Accustomed to the caprices of the Crown, they were also painfully aware that the new changes tipped the political and economic scales in favor of peninsulares and reinforced the political privilege that Havana had always enjoyed at the expense of the island's outlying regions (especially that of Santiago de Cuba). *Vegueros* (planters) protested the new royal monopoly in an armed confrontation that successfully removed the colonial authorities in charge of the Real Factoría de Tabacos. Smuggling, always a form of economic protest, also continued. Trade networks established between Cuba, Jamaica, and Saint-Domingue, especially, served Cubans trying to find ways around depressed prices on Cuban exports and the inflated prices of European goods.

Bourbon policies, however, were not immune to external changes. On June 6, 1762, Spain's participation in the Seven Years' War (1756–1763), which involved all the European powers, spilled into the Caribbean with the British assault on Havana. The following occupation of the city revealed a myriad of problems with colonial rule. For the Crown, the city's capitulation exposed the failure of its existing system of defense and the need to step up its militarization efforts, while for residents of the city, the British occupation underscored the limitations of Spanish colonial policies and trade restrictions. Once Spain recovered Havana under the 1763 Treaty of Paris, Charles III reorganized his Spanish possessions with the aim of curbing colonial discontent and ensuring Spanish hegemony. Royal decrees were issued in 1784, 1788, and 1790, allotting a total of 290,000 *duros* (Spanish currency of the time) to the fortification of Havana (compared with a total of only 146,000 duros for the effort in Santiago de Cuba). Militarization of the city took place on an unprecedented scale: Not since the sixteenth century had Havana experienced such large-scale efforts to ensure its safety. Militarization also complemented the expanding sugar industry, which predated the British occupation, and helped finance the sugar magnates that would define the future economy of the island.

The Crown's reorganization also included revising the existing taxation system and abolishing the monopoly on trade. In 1764, Cuba was allowed to trade with seven other Spanish cities, effectively ending the trade monopoly by the Spanish city of Cadíz. Legal trade with Spain's other Atlantic possessions soon followed, and Spanish duties on Cuban imports were subsequently rescinded in 1774. Moreover, the primacy of Havana came to an end as other Cuban ports in Santiago de Cuba, Trinidad, and Batabanó were allowed to conduct trade. The British occupation also radically affected the slave trade. In 1740,

King Charles III of Spain. King Charles III (r. 1759–1788), in hunting garb in a portrait by the Spanish artist Francisco Goya. MUSEO DEL PRADO MADRID/COLLECTION DAGLI ORTI/THE ART ARCHIVE/THE PICTURE DESK, INC.

the slave trade had become a monopoly of the Havana Company, which produced wide fluctuations in the number of slaves imported. The British occupation, however, had increased the number of slaves significantly as a result of new trade policies. The increase in slave numbers further stimulated the island's already expanding sugar economy with significant repercussions for nineteenth-century Cuba.

NINETEENTH CENTURY

By the nineteenth century, Cuba was distributing its exports among the United States, Spain, England,

Germany, and France, as well as other, smaller markets. Its newfound splendor and economic prosperity significantly affected how Cubans responded to colonial rule. Between 1776 and 1825, most of the region had shed colonial rule. Cuba, however, remained a stronghold of Spanish colonialism. The colony's reliance on sugar and slaves and the effects of the Haitian Revolution, which began with a slave rebellion in 1791, played a major role in Cubans' ambivalence toward independence. That is not to say that nationalism was not a prevalent aspect of nineteenth-century Cuba. On the contrary, discontent with colonial policies was expressed through various channels—including traditional forums for political expression, such as expatriate communities' social and political clubs, as well as those that facilitated a more nuanced form of Cuban nationalism. Spanish cultural traditions such as bullfighting and cockfighting, for example, quickly fell out of vogue and were replaced by activities such as baseball. (That baseball was more closely aligned with the cultural practices of the United States should not be viewed as the trading of one hegemon for another. Rather, the shedding of Spanish traditions was a form of Cuban self-definition in defiance of its colonial government.) Proto-nationalist sentiment, however, was not enough to eradicate Cuban planters' fears of what independence might mean for Cuba's economy if its slaves were freed, not to mention the potential destabilizing effects on racial hierarchies.

For the African-descended population in Cuba, the increase in sugar cultivation in the late eighteenth and early nineteenth centuries was an omen of things to come. Cuba had benefited from the 1789 decision to open Cuban ports to the free trade in slaves. Even after Spain banned the slave trade in 1811, Cuba continued the practice illegally. By 1846, 36 percent of the Cuban population lived under the yoke of slavery. Another 17 percent were the free descendants of Africans, a group especially targeted by colonial legislation—restrictions on where they could live, what they could wear, and how and where they could congregate—aimed at ensuring the administration's control over Cuba's increasingly diverse populations. Free people of African descent nonetheless found ways around Cuba's racial hierarchies, often choosing to incorporate themselves into existing colonial structures. For example, many took advantage of the opportunity for upward social mobility provided by joining colonial militias. In Havana, some two-thirds of all African-descended households had family members who served in the black and mulatto colonial militias. By allowing African-descended peoples to participate in colonial structures, the government was able to incorporate a potentially dangerous population into the hegemonic society.

Slaves were another matter altogether, as they had limited channels for expressing political discontent outside armed rebellion. Slave revolts were

Manaca Iznaga plantation. The main house and other structures of the old Manaca Iznaga sugar plantation still stand in the Valle de los Ingenios near Trinidad. © SAMI SARKIS PHOTOGRAPHY/ ALAMY

a constant concern for colonial administrators, who feared not only the possibility of revolt and its eco nomic consequences, but also the political implications of anticolonial sentiment across cross-sections of the Cuban population. Two potentially destabilizing events with respect to slavery and abolition occurred in 1812 and 1844. The first, the Aponte Rebellion, was a revolt by a population of slaves and free people of color against the Spanish Crown. The other, known as the Conspiración de La Escalera (Ladder Conspiracy), elicited a harsh crackdown by colonial authorities fearful that a planned revolt would undermine colonial rule.

Colonial fears would come to fruition in 1868 with the beginning of the Ten Years' War. The insurgency's commitment to emancipation, though still ambiguous in 1868, nonetheless contributed to the eventual abolition of slavery in 1886 by forcing the Spanish administration to address the issue. Prior to abolition, the Moret Law of 1870 provided a free-womb clause granting freedom to children born of slave mothers after 1870. It further provided freedom for slaves of the Spanish royalty, slaves sixty years of age or older, and those who had fought on the side of Spain during the war. The 1878 Pact of Zanjón effectively ended the Ten Years' War and the insurgency's initial call to arms, but there was no stopping the tide of independence. Armed revolts again took place between 1879 and 1880 and 1895 and 1898. The Treaty of Paris in 1898 brought an end to the final war of independence and effectively ended Spain's dominion over Cuba, albeit not before the United States intervened in the fighting and established a new form of indirect governance over the island.

BIBLIOGRAPHY

Childs, Matt D. *The 1812 Aponte Rebellion and the Struggle against Atlantic Slavery.* Chapel Hill: University of North Carolina Press, 2006.

Ferrer, Ada. *Insurgent Cuba: Race, Nation, and Revolution, 1868–1898.* Chapel Hill: University of North Carolina Press, 1999.

Fuente, Alejandro de la. *Havana and the Atlantic in the Sixteenth Century.* Chapel Hill: University of Chapel Hill Press, 2008.

Keuthe, Allan J. *Cuba, 1753–1815: Crown, Military, and Society.* Knoxville: University of Tennessee Press, 1986.

Le Riverend, Julio J. *La Habana: Biografía de una provincia.* Havana: Imprenta El Siglo XX, 1960.

Le Riverend, Julio J. *Breve historia de Cuba.* Havana: Editorial de Ciencias Sociales, 1974.

Pérez, Louis A. Jr. *On Becoming Cuban: Identity, Nationality, and Culture.* Chapel Hill: University of North Carolina Press, 2001.

Pérez, Louis A. Jr. *Cuba: Between Reform and Revolution*, 4th ed. New York: Oxford University Press, 2011.

Roig de Leuchsenring, Emilio. *La Habana, apuntes históricos*, 2nd ed. Havana: Oficina del Historiador de la ciudad, 1964.

Scott, Rebecca J. *Slave Emancipation in Cuba: The Transition to Free Labor, 1860–1899.* Princeton, NJ: Princeton University Press, 1985.

Wright, Irene Aloha. *The Early History of Cuba, 1492–1586.* 1916. Reprint, New York: Octagon Books, 1970.

GOVERNANCE AND CONTESTATION: THE REPUBLIC: 1902–1952

David C. Carlson

The multi-party republic of Cuba (1902–1952).

From independence on 20 May 1902 until a military coup 10 March 1952, Cuba experienced a fifty-year period as a republic, characterized by considerable and rapid economic and demographic growth but also by periodic political violence and systemic crises that led to ruptures in constitutional governance.

THE MEDIATED REPUBLIC

The first thirty-two years of the republican period (1902–1934) are often referred to as the mediated republic or neocolonial era because the United States exerted a de facto protectorate status via the 1901 Platt Amendment. Large landowners, merchants, bankers, sugar-mill owners, and a class of professional politicians exerted oligarchic control over the republic until the economic crisis of the 1920s. From 1925 to 1933, Gerardo Machado y Morales (1871–1939; pres.1925–1933) ruled in an increasingly authoritarian manner until political unrest and popular revolt forced him from office in the 1933 revolution. After a brief reformist period in 1934, there came a seven-year interregnum dominated by the military leader Fulgencio Batista Zaldívar (1901–1973; pres. 1940–1944, 1952–1959), in which the developmentalist state intervened in the economy and interceded in conflicts between elites and popular sectors. The 1940 constitution codified this modern, progressive, interventionist state. Control of state machinery enabled professional politicians to distribute favors and wealth to clients, and the substance of politics became rife with corruption, graft, and *gangsterismo* tainted by scandal and thuggery. Finally, the political system became largely discredited by the 10 March 1952 coup d'état when Batista returned to power through a military putsch.

THE EARLY REPUBLIC

On 20 May 1902, the first U.S.-occupation government ended, and Cuba became an independent republic with long-term New York resident Tomás Estrada Palma (1832–1908; pres. 1902–1906) as its first president. Estrada Palma's government ratified three treaties with the United States.

First, the Permanent Treaty implemented the Platt Amendment that had previously passed at the 1901 constitutional convention as a precondition to independence. Second, the 1903 Reciprocity Treaty provided preferential trade relations whereby Cuban sugar entered the United States at a discount, and U.S. manufactured goods entered Cuba with a tariff reduction of 20 to 40 percent. The agreement underlay a rebuilt and expansive sugar monoculture economy after the War of Independence, and facilitated U.S. capital investment and dominance of Cuban markets. By 1911, U.S. investment capital surpassed $200 million and continued to grow (Pérez p. 152; Whitney p. 23). Third, as a further stipulation of the Platt Amendment, the United States leased Bahía Honda and Guantánamo Bay for naval installations under the 1903 Cuban-American Permanent Treaty.

Economic Growth Sugar production boomed, from 888,000 tons in 1902 to 2.5 million tons on the eve of World War I (WWI) in 1913. After WWI, in 1919 Cuba exported 77 percent of its sugar output—approximately one-fourth of world production—to the United States (Whitney p. 24). Sugar mill construction expanded into previously untapped frontier regions of Camagüey and Oriente in the east. There, sugar companies amply supplied with foreign investment, such as from the North American United Fruit Company, erected some of the largest mills ever built. North American capitalists by the 1920s owned 60 percent of the sugar industry and predominated in other key industries and services.

Immigration from Spain, which had risen in the 1880s and early 1890s, resumed on a large scale. Approximately 700,000 Spaniards, primarily from the northwest and Canary Islands, immigrated as temporary sojourners and permanent residents between 1902 and the end of WWI (Whitney p. 24). The expanding sugar economy brought in laborers from the British West Indies and Haiti, particularly during the boom years of sugar production during WWI known as the Dance of the Millions. Although these cane workers were thought of as temporary migrants, many of them stayed and created permanent communities in Cuba.

The Second U.S. Occupation The Platt Amendment made the United States the ultimate arbiter of an untested and chaotic political system often characterized by infighting, cronyism, nepotism, and corruption. In the 1905 elections, Estrada Palma exercised his control of the presidency to manipulate the electoral system so that voting fraud assured his reelection. Election chicanery provoked an armed revolt, the so-called August Revolution, by the Liberal Party. Estrada Palma, unable to suppress the uprising, dissolved the government and summoned the United States to resume control. A second U.S. occupation of Cuba ensued, from 1906 to 1909.

First, the U.S. secretary of war William Howard Taft (1857–1930) governed Cuba. Soon, however, Minnesota judge and governor of the Panama Canal Zone Charles E. Magoon (1861–1920) acted in the provisional capacity. While governor, Magoon established public works, a permanent Cuban armed forces, and a civil service. Later, this civil employment became a feature of political corruption known as *botellas* (bottles), in which officials received salary compensation

CHRONOLOGY OF EVENTS

1898: Treaty of Paris grants Cuba independence from Spain.

1901: Cuban Constitution adopted; U.S. Congress passes Platt Amendment claiming right to intervene in Cuban affairs.

1902: U.S. occupation of Cuba ends; Tomás Estrada Palma inaugurated as president of Cuban republic.

1903: Reciprocity Treaty establishes preferential trade between U.S. and Cuba; Cuban-American Permanent Treaty gives U.S. control of Guantánamo Bay.

1906: The U.S. occupies Cuba through 1909.

1912: Government efforts to crush the Partido Independiente de Color (PIC) leads to the killing of several thousand black and mixed-race Cubans.

1916: February Revolution against President Mario García Menocal leads to U.S. military intervention; U.S. troops remain until 1922.

1925: General Gerardo Machado y Morales elected president.

1933: Economic crisis leads to the overthrow of President Machado, followed by the Sergeants' Revolt led by Fulgencio Batista and the brief reform presidency of Ramón Grau San Martín.

1934: Batista overthrows Grau and effectively rules Cuba through 1944.

1940: New, more democratic, constitution adopted; Batista elected President.

1944: Grau elected president.

1952: Batista overthrows the government of President Carlos Prío Socarrás shortly before election.

1953: Fidel Castro leads attack on Moncada army barracks; arrested, tried, amnestied, and exiled.

1956: Castro returns to Cuba, launches revolution.

1959: Batista flees Cuba; Castro takes power.

---

for jobs that they did not fulfill. During the U.S. occupation, people of color grew increasingly dissatisfied with their marginalization amid a climate of nativism and resentment directed at Spanish merchants and immigrants, and subtle and explicit racist sidelining of blacks within the republic. Founded in 1907, the Agrupación de Color, later the Partido Independiente de Color (PIC), tried to mobilize black and mixed-race Cubans against manifestations of racist hostility and deprecation.

The November 1908 elections, held under North American occupation and tutelage, resulted in the victory over Conservatives of Liberal candidate José Miguel Gómez (1858–1921; pres. 1909–1913). The second U.S. occupation ended in 1909.

The 1912 Race War During the 1912 election campaign, the incumbent Gómez administration faced an armed protest by the PIC. Gómez had voted in favor of the Platt Amendment, but his campaign rhetoric extolled nationalism and independence from U.S. influence. To repress the rebellion, he sent in the newly created armed forces and militia. The republican state crushed the PIC and, especially in Oriente province, tried to expiate the specter of rebellion and race war with a heavy hand. In repressing rebellion, the republic's military meted out racist terror, and the *guerrita de doce* (War of 1912) saw massacres and extra-judicial executions. At least 3,000 black and mixed-race Cubans were killed during this period (Gott p. 124). U.S. marines intervened on a limited scale, occupying some U.S.-owned sugar mills and railways during the revolt.

Menocal and the Dance of the Millions The U.S.-educated, Conservative presidential candidate Mario García Menocal (1866–1941; pres. 1913–1921), who had been a manager at the enormous U.S.-owned Chaparra sugar mill, won the November 1912

elections and was reelected in 1916. During WWI the price of sugar surged. Sugar mill owners greatly expanded production, borrowing heavily from banks, to meet the increased demand and reap higher profits. This period, known as the Dance of the Millions, fed a boom-bust cycle that had far-reaching effects when recession after WWI led to a precipitous drop in prices.

In 1916 Menocal was reelected through fraudulent means. Liberal opponents launched another revolt, known as the February Revolution or *la Chambelona*, after popular Liberal campaign songs with derisive lyrics. Occurring at the same time as U.S. interventions in nearby Haiti and the Dominican Republic, the revolt led to a third Platt-sanctioned intervention of U.S. marines. Some U.S. troops remained in eastern Cuba until 1922. In early 1917 the United States declared war against Germany, and Cuba followed suit the next day.

The prosperity of the boom years quickly ended after the war. Sugar prices plummeted from a high of 22 cents a pound in mid-1920 to 8 cents by September and 3.8 cents at the end of the same year (Pérez 2010, p. 170). Large loans hedged against the high prices led to insolvency, runs on banks, and ruination. Political crisis shortly followed. Under the Platt Amendment, the Warren G. Harding (1865–1923; pres. 1921–1923) administration dispatched General Enoch H. Crowder (1859–1932) aboard the USS *Minnesota* to Havana harbor as the special representative of the United States in Cuba. He remained until 1923, whereupon he became U.S. ambassador. The intellectual Liberal president Alfredo Zayas (1861–1934; pres. 1920–1924) served a single term underscored by extreme nepotism and corruption, as the state patronage distributive mechanisms became more crucial for political elites in assuring social status amid the economic downturn.

Fulgencio Batista (1901–1973). Fulgencio Batista waves to supporters in Havana on 5 April 1952. When it became apparent that Batista stood little chance of winning the 1952 election, he seized control of the government with the support of a group of allies in the military. KEYSTONE-FRANCE/GAMMA-KEYSTONE VIA GETTY IMAGES

The *Machadato*, 1925–1933 The youngest general of the War of Independence (1895–1898), Gerardo Machado (1871–1939; pres. 1925–1933), a former mayor of Santa Clara, began his presidency with a Platform of Regeneration: support of no reelection for presidential terms and pushing a reformist, nationalist agenda of infrastructure improvement, promotion of education, economic diversification away from sugar monoculture, and abrogation of the Platt Amendment. His administration began many projects to stimulate capitalist development, including construction of the central highway, which was seen as an alternative to the foreign-owned railroads, as well as many public buildings in Havana. Protectionist measures promoted nascent national industries. Machado repressed labor organization, suppressing strikes and outlawing unions, which derived influence from both craft traditions and militant Iberian anarchism. Machado's agents, the *porra*, became a secret police directed against Machado's opponents in an ever more repressive and authoritarian pattern as Cuba slid into the Great Depression.

The onset of worldwide economic crisis came to Cuba early and hit the nation hard. Sugar prices declined drastically. Growers produced less sugar and threw many out of work to join the expanding numbers of unemployed and underemployed workers. Machado, who had pledged to serve a single term,

decided the dire situation required him to extend the term of office in order to ameliorate the crisis. Through bribery and emoluments to co-opt opponents, combined with intimidation of enemies, the Liberal, Conservative, and Popular parties formed a *cooperativismo* pact for the 1928 elections with Machado as the only candidate for a six-year term.

COLLAPSE OF THE PLATTIST REPUBLIC, REVOLUTION OF 1933

Between 1929 and 1933 the Cuban gross national product declined 11 percent per year. The United States increased tariffs on Cuban sugar to protect domestic beet sugar producers. Sugar prices fell to a 1933 low point of .97 cents a pound, and production levels declined precipitously as sugar became more expensive to cultivate and process than what it could recoup on the market. In three years, the state's revenues fell from $90 million in 1928 to $47 million. State employees by 1933 had not been paid in six months; their back wages, $9 million in total, represented one-fifth of the state budget. Unemployment rose steeply. Hunger stalked the land. Opposition to Machado mounted (Pérez 2010, pp. 191–193; Whitney pp. 58–62).

Membership in unions grew, reinvigorating the first national labor federation, the Confederación

Nacional Obrera de Cuba (CNOC) founded in 1925. Strikes, marches, demonstrations, and other forms of resistance proliferated in the face of Machado's heavy-handed attempts at repression. Membership grew in the small Communist Party founded by the student leader Julio Antonio Mella (1903–1929), who was assassinated in Mexico City either at the behest of Machado or by Stalinists for deviating from the Moscow line. Middle-class opposition included the Directorio Estudiantil Universitario (DEU) that produced several influential reformist and nationalist political figures such as Antonio Guiteras (1906–1935), Eduardo Chibás (1907–1951), and Carlos Prío Socarrás (1903–1977; pres. 1948–1952). The green-shirted, quasi-corporatist ABC Sociedad Revolucionaria (ABC Revolutionary Society), so named for its clandestine ten-member cellular structure, included many young professionals and intellectuals. ABC and other militant organizations carried out a terrorist campaign of bombings and assassination in a plan to bring about Machado's downfall or provoke U.S. intervention. Armed bands operated in the countryside.

Machado's feared porra arrested, tortured, and murdered opponents. Machado's former occupation—*carnicero* (butcher)—became in the early 1930s a sobriquet that referred to his brutal methods. Late in 1930 Machado suspended constitutional guarantees, closed the University of Havana, and censored newspapers. The CNOC carried out repeated strikes directed against the Machado government, and each was met with violence and repression. An incipient civil war overtook the nation.

The U.S. presidential administration of Franklin D. Roosevelt (1882–1945; pres. 1933–1945) dispatched Sumner Welles (1892–1961) in 1933 as ambassador and mediator to broker a change of government. Roosevelt distanced U.S. foreign policy from past interventionism and shortly formulated the Good Neighbor Policy vis-à-vis Latin America. Nonetheless, given U.S. economic, political, and strategic interests in Cuba, a naval flotilla of thirty warships awaited orders to move in. Machado stubbornly refused to resign, and opposition renewed in the form of a general strike. Finally, by August 1933, believing that the United States would intervene, the military rose against Machado and installed the ABC Society's Carlos Manuel de Céspedes y Quesada (1871–1939; pres. 1933), a U.S.-born son of Carlos Manuel de Céspedes, the so-called Padre de la Patria who initiated the rebellion against Spain in 1868. His appointment placated Washington. Machado flew into exile. Mobs vented their wrath against people associated with Machado; reprisal killings, looting, and acts of revenge followed.

The following month, September 1933, the so-called Sergeants' Revolt of noncommissioned officers and enlisted ranks against the officer corps, led by a mixed-race army stenographer from Oriente, Fulgencio Batista, overthrew Céspedes. A tenuous alliance between the military rebels and the DEU formed a five-man junta known as the Pentarchy. This collective executive council led in turn to the appointment of Ramón Grau San Martín (1887–1969; pres. 1933–1934, 1944–1948), a popular professor, as president. Guiteras, a nationalist and socialist, became minister of the interior.

This four-month *government of a hundred days* enacted many reform laws that became codified seven years later in the progressive 1940 constitution. Such enactments of the revolution included female suffrage and the right of women to hold elected office, workers' rights to organize, a minimum wage law, and the eight-hour workday. The government intervened in labor disputes to mediate favorable terms for strikers, passed a law requiring that half the workers at minimum should be Cubans (the Fifty Percent Law), and banned the common practice of paying workers in company scrip redeemable only at company stores. The Fifty Percent Law was seen as a way of curbing not only Spanish and U.S. influence in the economy but also the Chinese and West Indian (Haitian, Barbadian, and Jamaican) populations. Such radical measures distanced the revolutionary government from the middle and upper classes. The deposed officers and the ABC Society hewed to U.S. interests and revolted against the Grau government. In foreign policy, Cuba formally and unilaterally abrogated the Platt Amendment. Sumner Welles recommended U.S. intervention and responded to the reformist policies by withholding U.S. recognition, thereby signaling Washington's displeasure with the revolution. In spite of its opposition to the revolution, the Roosevelt administration later acceded to the abrogation of the Platt Amendment.

In early 1934 Batista orchestrated a new coalition with the opposition that led to the downfall of the Grau government. Batista effectively ruled behind the scenes for the next six years via caretaker presidencies: Carlos Mendieta (1873–1960; pres. 1934–1935), José Barnet (1864–1946; pres. 1935–1936), and Miguel Mariano Gómez (1889–1950; pres. 1936), who was impeached for opposition to Batista and replaced by Federico Laredo Brú (1875–1946; pres. 1936–1939). In 1934 Mendieta signed a new reciprocity treaty with the United States that renegotiated the terms of the Guantánamo Bay lease. Guiteras and young radicals formed the Joven Cuba (Young Cuba) movement, and political violence and repression continued, particularly into 1935. In that year police shot and killed Guiteras, and many other leftists also died violently. Others journeyed to Spain after July 1936 to fight on behalf of the beleaguered Spanish Republic in the civil war there (1936–1939). Out of power, by 1937 Grau San Martín had organized the Partido Revolucionario Cubano-Auténtico after a period in exile in Mexico. The Auténticos absorbed many members of the Joven Cuba movement. In a 1938 compact Batista obtained the acquiescence of the communists in exchange for legal recognition of the party, offering an electoral path and support for elements of the labor reforms of 1933 to 1934. The Confederación de Trabajadores de Cuba (CTC) subsumed the earlier CNOC labor federation.

THE 1940 CONSTITUTION

After a series of delays, constitutional delegates replaced the obsolete Plattist 1901 constitution with a new basic document, the progressive 1940 constitution. This basis of laws, promulgated by July 1940, recognized equality among all Cuban citizens, reaffirmed the rights of women to vote and hold office, and accorded the state the right to intervene in the national economy while upholding the right to private property. It approved a range of civil liberties and supported many of the labor rights from 1934, including the right to workers' compensation, the right to organize and go on strike, maximum working hours, and a basic minimum wage. Subsoil rights accrued to the nation-state, and there were limitations on foreign ownership of land and other resources. A democratic and progressive educational system formed part of the constitution's provisions as well. Batista, the populist military leader, remade himself as a democratic presidential candidate against the Auténtico rival, Grau. Batista won a clean and honest election and served as president from 1940 to 1944.

In December 1941 Cuba declared war on the Axis powers. Cuba supplied sugar to the Allies, with the United States paying fixed prices of 2.65 cents per pound for the crop (Pérez 2010, p. 215). Cuban *colono* sharecroppers and sugar mill owners reaped the largest harvests since the bleak Depression-era year of 1930. Cuba offered ports, bases, and facilities to the U.S. military conducting U-boat operations in the Atlantic and Caribbean and also in transit to the battlefronts. In exchange, the United States supplied weapons and aircraft to the Cuban armed forces. In 1944 Grau won the presidential elections handily in a campaign that recalled his role in the events of 1933. Batista left for Daytona Beach, Florida, after peacefully handing the presidential sash to Grau and placidly vacating the presidential palace. Yet, the onset of the Auténtico government fomented a crisis in confidence in the political system and party structure that later manifested itself in the 1952 coup and the armed movement that arose to challenge it.

THE AUTÉNTICO YEARS, 1944–1952

Grau San Martín, elected president for a four-year term, presided over a government of self-interested, unscrupulous, and corrupt office holders. Auténticos in power engaged in all manner of corruption, graft, and misappropriation of funds in a recrudescence of the worst features of the republic's nepotism and cronyism. A violent, swaggering, mafia-style *gangsterismo* of machine politics and party officials as criminal operatives fed public exasperation and completed the discrediting of the political system. One scandal after another revealed the once idealistic Auténticos as unprincipled, voracious grifters. Indeed, with the end

of World War II, North Americans returned as tourists to Cuba where they reeled down the streets in pursuit of sun, rum, and transgression of the social constraints of home. North American Mafiosi who had first come to Cuba during the 1920s and Prohibition now returned to invest in gambling, hotels, sex trafficking, and vice. This pernicious influence continued apace into the 1950s, particularly with the return of Batista after 1952.

The dissident Eduardo Chibás, who emanated from the DEU opposition to Machado, broke with the party in 1947 to found the Partido del Pueblo Cubano (Ortodoxo). Carlos Prío Socarrás won the 1948 presidential elections. He had cofounded the anti-Machado DEU while a law school student and later served as Grau's labor minister in a post–World War II purge of communists from the CTC. Some accounts paint Prío's government as the pinnacle of corruption, but it may have been the lofty but hypocritical rhetoric against political gangsterism colliding with the stark realities of its continued practice that most rankled observers.

Chibás took to the radio airwaves to denounce the Auténticos. His party adopted the broom as its symbol; they intended to sweep the corrupt from office and clean up the political system. A new generation of young professionals joined the Ortodoxos, including a Havana lawyer from Baní in Oriente province, Fidel Castro Ruz (b. 1926; prime minister 1959–1976; pres.1976–2006), who emerged from the violent netherworld of student politics. Chibás accused Prío's education minister of taking money earmarked for school breakfast programs. The minister vehemently denied the charge and threatened libel unless proof could be produced. In August 1951, unable to provide the proof he had promised, Chibás shot himself after a radio broadcast.

1952 COUP D'ÉTAT: BATISTA'S UNDEMOCRATIC REGIME

In the 1952 elections, it appeared that Batista, who had returned to politics as a senator in 1948, stood no chance of winning. Instead of running, Batista seized control of the national government, with the help of his military allies, forcing Prío from office and ending constitutional government in Cuba. Few rallied to save the Auténticos. The public greeted the news of the coup with exasperation and disgust at the government's corruption, yet a powerful sense of indignation at the deferred promises of the 1940 constitution gained currency. Batista promised stability and a return to democratic elections by 1954, and the United States recognized his government. Historians mark the end of the republic with Batista's reemergence as a national political figure in the coup d'état. In 1953, the centennial of José Martí's 1853 birth, the Ortodoxo Fidel Castro led an audacious if ill-advised, almost suicidal assault on the Moncada army barracks in Santiago de Cuba during carnival, on 26 July. His arrest and his defense summation at the end of his trial ("History

Will Absolve Me") gained him notoriety and stature in the emerging anti-Batista struggle of the 1950s that led to the Cuban Revolution.

BIBLIOGRAPHY

Aguilar, Luis E. *Cuba 1933: Prologue to Revolution.* New York: Norton, 1972.

Ameringer, Charles D. *The Cuban Democratic Experience: The Auténtico Years, 1944–1952.* Gainesville: University Press of Florida, 2000.

Argote-Freyre, Frank. *Fulgencio Batista.* Vol. 1, *From Revolutionary to Strongman.* New Brunswick, NJ: Rutgers University Press, 2006.

Ayala, César J. *American Sugar Kingdom: The Plantation Economy of the Spanish Caribbean.* Chapel Hill: University of North Carolina Press, 1999.

Barcia Zequeira, María del Carmen, Gloria García and Eduardo Torres Cuevas. *La historia de Cuba.* Vol. 3, *La neocolonia: organización y crisis desde 1899 hasta 1940.* Havana: Instituto de Historia de Cuba, 1998.

Beals, Carleton. *The Crime of Cuba.* Philadelphia: J. B. Lippincott, 1933.

Benjamin, Jules R. *The United States and Cuba: Hegemony and Dependent Development, 1880–1934.* Pittsburgh, PA: University of Pittsburgh Press, 1977.

Bronfman, Alejandra. *Measures of Equality: Social Science, Citizenship, and Race in Cuba, 1902–1940.* Chapel Hill: University of North Carolina Press, 2004.

De la Fuente, Alejandro. *A Nation for All: Race, Inequality, and Politics in Twentieth-Century Cuba.* Chapel Hill: University of North Carolina Press, 2001.

English, T. J. *Havana Nocturne: How the Mob Owned Cuba and then Lost It to the Revolution.* New York: William Morrow, 2008.

Gott, Richard. *Cuba: A New History.* New Haven, CT: Yale University Press, 2004.

Ibarra Guitart, Jorge Renato. *La mediación del 33: Ocaso del machadato.* Havana: Editora Política, 1999.

Jenks, Leland Hamilton. *Our Cuban Colony.* New York: Vanguard Press, 1928.

López Civeira, Francisco. *Cuba entre 1899 y 1959: Seis décadas de historia.* Havana: Editorial Pueblo y Educación, 2007.

McGillivray, Gillian. *Blazing Cane: Sugar Communities, Class, and State Formation in Cuba, 1868–1959.* Durham, NC: Duke University Press, 2009.

Moore, Robin. *Nationalizing Blackness: Afrocubanismo and Artistic Revolution in Havana, 1920–1940.* Pittsburgh, PA: University of Pittsburgh Press, 1997.

Pérez, Louis A. Jr. *Cuba under the Platt Amendment, 1902–1934.* Pittsburgh, PA: University of Pittsburgh Press, 1986.

Pérez, Louis A. Jr. *Cuba and the United States: Ties of Singular Intimacy.* 2nd ed. Athens: University of Georgia Press, 1990.

Pérez, Louis A. Jr. *On Becoming Cuban: Identity, Nationality, and Culture.* Chapel Hill: University of North Carolina Press, 1999.

Pérez, Louis A. Jr. *Cuba: Between Reform and Revolution.* 4th ed. Oxford, U.K.: Oxford University Press, 2010.

Riera, Mario. *Cuba política, 1899–1955.* Havana: Editora Modelo, S.A., 1955.

Schoultz, Lars. *That Infernal Little Cuban Republic: The United States and the Cuban Revolution.* Chapel Hill: University of North Carolina Press, 2009.

Shaffer, Kirwin R. *Anarchism and Countercultural Politics in Early Twentieth-Century Cuba.* Gainesville: University Press of Florida, 2005.

Stoner, Lynn K. *From the House to the Streets: The Cuban Women's Movement for Legal Reform, 1898–1940.* Durham, NC: Duke University Press, 1991.

Thomas, Hugh. *Cuba: The Pursuit of Freedom.* New York: Da Capo, 1998.

Whitney, Robert. *State and Revolution in Cuba: Mass Mobilization and Political Change, 1920–1940.* Chapel Hill: University of North Carolina Press, 2001.

Zanetti Lecuona, Oscar. *Los cautivos de la reciprocidad. La burguesía cubana y la dependencia comercial, 1899–1959.* Havana: Empresa de Producción de la Educación Superior, 1989.

GOVERNANCE AND CONTESTATION: INSURRECTION, 1952–1959

Gladys Marel García Pérez

Insurrection against the Batista regime as the first phase of the Cuban Revolution, leading to the overthrow of Fulgencio Batista.

When Fulgencio Batista finished his presidential term in the 1940s, he moved to Daytona Beach, Florida, where he lived until his return to Cuba in order to participate in the 1952 presidential elections. When it became clear that he had no chance of winning he led a coup d'état on 10 March 1952 against president Carlos Prío, with the support of U.S. and Cuban economic interests. Determinant in the coup's success was support for Batista by three military groups: hard-line young officers and cadets; active captains and lieutenants, known as tank officers; and retired officers.

The citizenry recalled the violence of Batista's previous coup in 1934 and his regime's repression, but the crisis faced by political parties, especially the Partido del Pueblo Cubano (Party of the Cuban People), known as the Ortodoxos (or Orthodox Party), following the death of its leader, Eduardo Chibás, left a leadership vacuum. No political party led the people when they headed toward the universities and barracks demanding weapons to fight the insurrectionists; the chiefs of the regiments at Matanzas and Santiago de Cuba resisted, but were overcome.

The Federación Estudiantil Universitaria (FEU; Federation of University Students) in Havana and Santiago de Cuba and the secondary education institutes

■ *See also*

Che Guevara and the New Man

The Cuban Revolution of 1959

History Will Absolve Me (Fidel Castro)

The Politics and Death of Eduardo Chibás

Santa Clara's Leoncio Vidal Park

Santiago de Cuba

(high schools) across the island went on strike. The Central de Trabajadores de Cuba (CTC; Confederation of Cuban Workers) released a statement that morning, calling for a general strike. The Federación Nacional de Trabajadores Textiles y Henequeneros (Federation of Fiber and Textile Workers) upheld it for a few weeks, led by their secretary general Pascasio Linares, along with provincial labor leaders of plantation and factory federations. Meanwhile, workers from the Cuban Electric Company began to sabotage electrical, telephone, and telegraph lines in several parts of the country.

INSURRECTIONAL ORGANIZATIONS: STRATEGY, TACTICS, AND RELEVANT ACTIONS

The task of channeling the rebellion was assumed by the so-called Generación del '50, which Gladys Marel García-Pérez defines as consisting of people of different ages and social classes who saw themselves as being linked by a community of interests as a starting point, a similar frame of mind, and by the momentum of events that swept them along into a plan that eventually led to a revolution. The opposition parties adopted the electoral route, and those favoring an insurrectional struggle broke off from the Auténtico (Authentic) and Ortodoxo parties. The main pro-insurrection organizations were the FEU, subsequently led by José Antonio Echeverría, the founder of the Directorio Revolucionario (Revolutionary Directorate); the Movimiento Nacional Revolucionario (National Revolutionary Movement), headed by Rafael García Bárcena; the Triple A and the Organización Auténtica (Authentic Organization), led by Aureliano Sánchez Arango and Antonio Varona, respectively; the Movimiento Revolucionario, later known as the MR 26 de Julio (MR-26-7; 26th of July Revolutionary Movement), headed by Fidel Castro; and the Frente Cívico de Mujeres Martianas (Martí Women's Civic Front), organized by Aida Pelayo and Carmen Castro Porta. Justo Carrillo's Acción Libertadora (Liberating Action) operated along with the Los Puros military movement, headed by Colonel Ramón Barquín. They all had a common strategy for overthrowing the regime, but used different tactics.

DIRECTORIO REVOLUCIONARIO

The Directorio and the MR-26-7 spearheaded the insurrection, along with the Mujeres Martianas, who supported and participated in all the insurrectional organizations. The FEU's approach in the early years of revolt was mass mobilization; starting in 1954, it played the main civic and political role in demonstrations and rallies. Out of this activity had come the armed action group known as the Directorio Revolucionario, founded by José Antonio Echeverría in 1955 to confront the police forces and strike at the upper echelons of power.

The Directorio's executive committee planned an attack on the Presidential Palace on 13 March 1957, with the goal of killing Batista, which they believed would spark an armed popular uprising in Havana. In addition to the attack itself, the plan included a support operation and a takeover by José Antonio Echeverría of the radio station Radio Reloj. The General Staff of the Revolutionary Armed Forces would be established on the hilltop at the university's entrance, to direct the actions, to take over the radio stations and newspaper offices, and to call the population to a general strike.

After speaking to the Cuban people on the air, Echeverría left the station and headed toward the university, but when he stepped into the street, he was shot down by police from a moving patrol car. Batista undertook to demonstrate his military strength, sending a column of tanks and armored cars into the streets as reinforcements against insurrectionary activity an hour after the failed attack. Meanwhile, the Directorio survivors fled the Presidential Palace and left the university in the evening.

Weeks later, the Directorio's top leaders were murdered by the repressive forces of the police at a Havana apartment at 7 Humboldt Street. The Directorio then incorporated guerrilla warfare in its tactics, with the creation of the Frente Nacional del Escambray (Escambray National Front) later in May. The national executive committee of the DR sent its commander, Eloy Gutiérrez Menoyo, to Escambray, at the end of September 1957, with military equipment for the guerilla leaders in Santi Spiritus. Eloy was to return to Havana but instead stayed in Escambray and months later was appointed the head of the front.

In January 1958 Faure Chomón, general secretary of the Directorio's national executive board, officially announced the organization's founding, and a month later he headed an expedition on a boat called the *Scapade*, which sailed for Nuevitas, in Camagüey province, subsequently heading for the mountains in Las Villas province.

The plan for the landing of the *Scapade* was to divide the expeditionary force into two groups. One would leave for Havana and the other for Sierra del Escambray. After disembarking, Rolando Cubela was named head of the front and maintained an encampment separate from Gutiérrez Menoyo, who had established contact with representatives of the Organización Auténtica. The national executive committee called a meeting in Cubela's camp, unaware of a conspiracy led by Carlos Prío, now the leader of the Organización Auténtica, who wanted to establish a new military presence in Escambray. Before attending this meeting, Menoyo stopped and disarmed six members of Cubela's troop. During the meeting Menoyo asserted that they wanted to create a fourth organization in the area independent of the existing ones, though maintaining cooperation. This political maneuvering led to the withdrawal of Menoyo and his soldiers from the front of the DR 13 de Marzo and the creation of the Frente

Unido, later known as Segundo Frente de Escambray (Rodríguez Loeches pp. 273–274).

The Directorio's executive board, as a member of the Frente Cívico Revolucionario based in Caracas, denounced Prío's maneuver, for betraying the "Unity, to the Homeland and the Revolution by endangering the cause of the Revolution" (Rodríguez-Loeches pp. 268–284).

In a manifesto called Proclamation of Escambray, the Directorio announced its platform and urged the continuation of the freedom movement initiated in 1868 and developed by José Martí, Antonio Guiteras, and José Antonio Echeverría among the peoples of the Caribbean and the Americas, guided by Latin American leaders such as Simón Bolívar, Francisco Morazán, Augusto Sandino, and Leonardo Ruiz Pineda. The proclamation described the need to enforce the fundamental principles of the Revolution, based on the 1940 Constitution of Cuba and the creation of a party or united movement after taking power.

MR-26-7: INSURRECTION AND GENERAL STRIKE

The strategy of Fidel Castro and the MR-26-7 leaders was to combine armed struggle and revolutionary general strikes. This concept was the methodological key that integrated tactics with success in leading large segments of the population into the struggle to overthrow the regime. Coordinated rebel assaults in July 1953, on the Moncada Garrison in Santiago de Cuba and the Carlos Manuel de Céspedes Garrison in Bayamo, were the first attempt to arm the Cuban people and call for a general strike, but the plan failed and the survivors of the attack, including Fidel Castro and his brother, Raúl Castro, were sent to prison.

An amnesty for political prisoners in 1955 did not apply to those who had attacked the Moncada Garrison, but the FEU, led by José Antonio Echeverría, the Frente Cívico de Mujeres Martianas, the Frente de Mujeres Cubanas de Oriente, and other groups, waged a successful campaign for their release, which included rallies, radio programs, and press releases. A public demonstration gathered to welcome them upon their release.

In June 1955, after leaving prison, Fidel Castro reorganized MR-26-7, appointing national and provincial representatives. A few weeks later he went to Mexico City to prepare for an expedition to Cuba by sea on a cabin cruiser named *Granma* purchased a year later. With Juan Manuel Márquez, he created MR-26-7 branches in Mexico City and the United States. This network was later extended to other cities in the Americas, the Caribbean, and Europe.

The clandestine military apparatus on the island of Cuba operated as an action and sabotage unit, whose brigades were later transformed into militia units. After the *Granma* landed in December 1956, the expeditionary members organized the MR-26-7 Revolutionary Army, continuing the guerrilla warfare tactics of the Cuban Liberation Army. Later on, they operated in columns and positions.

On 30 November 1956 the mobilization of the MR-26-7 in all provinces across the island began in support of the landing, projecting the combatants against the police in Santiago de Cuba and in Guantánamo, where they maintained a general strike. After these events, the MR-26-7 national coordinator Frank País restructured the organization's social class foundation, establishing the Sección Obrera (Workers' Section), the Movimiento de Resistencia Cívica (Movement of Civic Resistance), and the Frente Estudiantil Nacional (National Student Front). He organized trial runs for a national strike supported by armed actions and was thereafter killed in July 1957 in Santiago de Cuba. This action resulted in a spontaneous popular strike, called the August strike, which spread across the country. Following this experience, the Dirección Nacional del Movimiento organized another strike on 9 April 1958. It failed in its objective and sparked an army offensive and a counteroffensive by the rebel army.

País was a mediating force in relations and differences of opinion between the urban underground leaders and the political and military guerrilla leadership in the mountains, although the differences were not fundamental, since both groups had the same combined methods of tactics and struggle. The death of País left a vacuum in the movement's civilian-military coordination, and after the failure of the 9 April strike, a controversy arose over the strikes supporting the armed struggle or vice versa. This controversy was addressed at the May 1958 meeting of the national MR-26-7 leadership at Altos de Mompié, in the Sierra Maestra, resulting in the leadership's political and military hegemony. Also significant at this meeting was the position put forward by Commander Daniel, Frank País's replacement, that the movement should achieve liberation from Yankee domination and be a revolution based on José Martí's political ideas, rather than aspire to Soviet alignment.

REBEL ORGANIZATIONS: UNITY AND INSURRECTION

Between 1952 and 1957, the consolidation of forces in favor of the insurrection—as demonstrated in the attacks on military buildings, strikes, fighting with the army in guerilla fronts and with the police in the cities—converged in an insurrectional unity between the DR 13 de Marzo and the MR-26-7 at first, and by the end of 1958, these forces joined the national reformists in the Frente Cívico Revolucionaro, or Pacto de Caracas.

Rafael García Bárcena—an insurrectionist during the revolutionary attempt of 1930 and an opponent of Batista's regime—organized an attack on Camp Columbia in Havana, with students, workers, professionals, soldiers, and one woman, Eva Jiménez.

Fidel Castro (b. 1926) with his commanders. Revolutionary leader Fidel Castro (standing center) meets with the leaders of his guerrilla army at a secret base in June 1957. The group includes his brother Raúl Castro (kneeling in the foreground) and Ernesto "Che" Guevara (second from left). © BETTMANN/CORBIS

A Batista infiltrator informed on the attackers, and they were intercepted on Sunday, 4 April 1953, on the way to the camp. Several combatants were harassed and abused by the police. Bárcena and Jiménez then defied the army officers and presented a strong challenge during their trial by denouncing the mistreatment they had received and defending the legality of the rebellion.

In July, the attacks on the Moncada and Bayamo garrisons took place, with Fidel Castro leading several male commando units and also bringing along two women, Haydée Santamaría and Melba Hernández, who served as nurses. Although the attacks resulted in a military reverse, they became a revolutionary milestone and provided a platform for political success when Castro presented the Revolution's action program in his defense plea, which came to be known as *La historia me absolverá* (*History Will Absolve Me*), a radical nationalist revolutionary document.

The increasing number of strikes making economic demands transformed workers' consciousness in 1955, as it happened with the sugar workers, who were demanding payment of the differential at the end of the year. The strike's leaders, Conrado Bécquer and Conrado Rodríguez, in coordination with José Antonio Echeverría and the FEU, planned and organized the strike and turned it into a strong movement of labor and political demands that involved direct confrontation with the police. Several FEU leaders went to various provinces and sugar mills to lend their

support to the union leaders. This worker-student rebellion shut down the main cities. The island had risen up and the strike was transformed into a political force, threatening to prevent the start of the sugar harvest in January. Batista was forced to negotiate and make concessions.

Months later, the leader of the Auténtico movement, Reynold García, led a group in the attack on the Goicuría Garrison in Matanzas. But they had been betrayed, and when they entered the garrison's yard on 29 April 1956, machine guns opened fire, killing them all.

The landing of the *Granma* cabin cruiser in December 1956 continued the tactics of the 1953 attacks on the Moncada and Bayamo garrisons, as agents of change for the dynamics of the liberation movement. In August 1956, the FEU and the MR-26-7 declared their unity in the so-called Mexico Letter, a document pledging joint action against Batista and signed by José Antonio Echevarría and Fidel Castro. Each organization would develop its own plans in support of an uprising on the island: MR-26-7 would carry out the *Granma* landing, and the Directorio Revolucionario would attack the Presidential Palace.

The *Granma* did not land on 30 November 1956, the date set for insurrectional support all over the country, but the regime failed to kill the expedition members when the cruiser did land on 2 December. The inefficiency of Batista's counterinsurgency plan made it possible for the revolutionaries to establish a guerrilla stronghold and initiate the process leading to the breakdown of the Republican army.

The most heroic and significant actions of this time in the cities were the Directorio's attack on the Presidential Palace in March 1957, which shook the country and stirred Havana, and an uprising in the city of Cienfuegos on 5 September. On the day of the uprising, the officers and soldiers of the Marina de Guerra, supported by the combatants of the MR-26-7, attacked the military garrisons and gave the arms to the people. The regiments of Matanzas and Las Villas fought against the rebels, and the city was bombarded and gunned by the regime's Air Force.

AN EXPANDING REVOLUTION: LEADERSHIP AND PRINCIPLES

Anti-Batista political leaders Raúl Chibás and Felipe Pazos met with Fidel Castro in the Sierra Maestra on 28 July 1957 and created the Frente Cívico Revolucionario (Revolutionary Civilian Front) and signed the Sierra Manifesto, opposing a military junta, foreign mediation, or any interference and intervention by any other country in Cuba's internal affairs. The Frente specifically denounced the U.S. Marines' occupation of the Yateras Aqueduct, one of the pro-intervention maneuvers undertaken by Batista and the U.S. ambassador Earl Smith.

In October 1957 a unity pact was signed in Miami that created the Junta de Liberación Cubana (Cuban Liberation Board). The board, made up of representatives of the Autenticos and the Ortodoxos, DR 13 de Marzo, FEU, two labor unions, and MR-26-7, had the objective of coordinating opposition forces and forming a government once the regime was overthrown. However, major sections of the Sierra Manifesto—opposition to foreign intervention in Cuba's affairs and to a military junta—were not included. This omission sparked an ideological schism reflected in the positions of parties, insurrectional organizations, and the national leadership of the MR-26-7.

Felipe Pazos and Lester Rodríguez, delegates of the MR-26-7 abroad, had not asked for authorization from the national executive board of the MR-26-7 to sign the pact. Before the document reached the board, the information was leaked to U.S. newspapers, which published the news. On behalf of the executive board, Castro emphatically denounced the representatives in the Junta for modifying the manifesto's principles, and he asked Pazos and Rodríguez to change the points of the pact and to establish the unification basis of the Sierra Manifesto.

Batista's strategy, after the overthrow of the Prío government in 1952, had been to reorganize the political parties and reinstate constitutional normality, announcing elections for November 1954 and promoting a government coalition. The opposition leader, Ramón Grau San Martín, declared his intention to

Arrival of Cuban rebels in Havana, 1959. Cuban rebels parade down the street after their arrival in Havana in 1959. © LESTER COLE/CORBIS

run for the presidency, but the Ortodoxos' persistent reluctance to participate in the elections held him back. For Grau, the problem was merely the historical differences between himself and Batista, two political principles, two manners of government representing the old debate over the ideological legacy of the revolution against Gerardo Machado y Morales in 1934. Grau decided to abstain from running.

By calling for elections in November 1958, Batista attempted to prolong his regime until 24 February 1959—at which time his supporter Andrés Rivero Agüero, whose candidacy had been the result of manipulated elections, would be inaugurated as president. But this tactic was met with an uproar of sabotage activity all over the island: The rebel forces operating in Oriente, Camagüey, Las Villas, and Pinar del Río provinces; the rebel columns in Havana and Matanzas; and the clandestine military apparatus all carried out acts of sabotage at the polls and against government representatives.

After the split of the Miami Pact, efforts were continued to forge a common revolutionary front. Luis Buch, coordinator of the Comité del Exilio (Exile Committee) of MR-26-7, carried out negotiations, with all sectors and opposition organizations participating in support of a document written by Castro and distributed in 1958 to those opposition groups as well as to news agencies and the media in Venezuela and the Americas. The fundamental aspects of the document were: acceptance of armed struggle and the mobilization of resources for a general strike and joint armed insurrection; and a consent that upon the fall of Batista, a provisional government would take control of the country and would guarantee the punishment of war criminals and would take steps to achieve economic, social, and institutional progress in Cuba.

In their first meeting in Caracas to approve the document, the opposition representatives agreed to call their new organization the Frente Cívico Revolucionario and move their headquarters to Miami, Florida. José Miró Cardona was chosen as its leader. The Partido Socialista Popular (People's Socialist Party) was denied membership because it did not support the insurrection policy, preferring the possibility of a negotiated political settlement with the Batista government.

Delegates of the member organizations planned to travel to the Sierra Maestra in September and October 1958, but the rebel army's final offensive prevented the trip. Only Manuel Urrutia and Luis Buch were able to make the trip, and a government-in-arms was set up.

FALL OF BATISTA AND TAKEOVER BY REVOLUTIONARY FORCES

As general secretary and commander-in-chief of the MR-26-7, Fidel Castro called a meeting of the organization's national executive board in La Rinconada, in the Sierra Maestra, for 18 December 1958, to analyze the Batista regime's imminent demise, the course of the war, the final offensive strategy, and the designation of the revolutionary government's Council of Ministers. The general command, members of the national executive board, and provincial coordinators of MR-26-7 and the Movimiento de Resistencia Cívica participated.

They resolved that on 24 February 1959, Manuel Urrutia would be sworn in as president of the Republic in Arms in the town of Baire. But when Batista fled the country in the early morning of 1 January 1959, events were accelerated. At 8 a.m. of that morning, Urrutia heard the news over the radio and went with Luis Buch, a member of the new Council of Ministers, to the Radio Rebelde station in Altos del Escandel.

A few hours later, Fidel Castro, Urrutia, Raúl Chibás, and Luis Buch arrived at the Santiago de Cuba radio station, and around 11 p.m. or midnight, they appeared at the Santiago de Cuba city hall, where Manuel Urrutia was proclaimed provisional president of the revolutionary government before a large crowd. Then Urrutia traveled to Havana.

Previously, several opposition leaders had held talks at the Presidential Palace, occupied at the time by the Directorio Revolucionario. Commanders Guillermo Jiménez of the Directorio, Ernesto "Che" Guevara, and Camilo Cienfuegos asked for the palace to be turned over to MR-26-7 forces, and the Directorio, functioning as a revolutionary unit, relinquished the premises for the inauguration of the new president and the cabinet ministers and withdrew its forces. Commander Camilo Cienfuegos took charge of the building and its internal operation.

Outside the Presidential Palace, people had been gathering on streets and in public squares, and the huge crowd flocked to the building, cheering the president. Urrutia spoke of the spirit of the law in the 1940 Constitution and the goals of the revolutionary government. On 8 January, Fidel Castro and the Freedom Caravan entered Havana, as thousands of people with red-and-black flags and armbands hailed the realization of their dream to change the country's fate.

REASONS FOR THE SUCCESS OF THE REVOLUTION

There were several factors that led to the success of Castro and MR-26-7:

1. Unity among the driving forces integrating a broad social base;

2. Creation of an army and militia that confronted and broke down the regime's military apparatus;

3. A network of financial and promotional support within the country, among Cuban exiles and immigrants in the Americas and Europe;

4. The structuring of MR-26-7 upon a social basis, integrated social classes and sectors in the national, provincial, and municipal framework of the clandestine and guerrilla organizations, including the Sección Obrera, the Frente Estudiantil Nacional, the Movimiento de Resistencia Cívica, the middle class, the patriotic bourgeoisie, civilian institutions, professional, fraternal and religious organizations, housewives, revolutionary cells with a network of families, sympathizers, social activists, and women's brigades, as well as branches in cities abroad;

5. Appropriate options and conjunctions of methods and forms of armed struggle and revolutionary general strikes, with tactical flexibility;

6. Exact evaluation by the movement as a whole of class interests in all segments and social sectors, and the correct analysis of national and international realities;

7. Revolutionary experience among similar driving forces: workers, professionals, rural and farm workers, students, the middle class, and the patriotic bourgeoisie;

8. An understanding on the part of the international community and the promotion of a powerful national and international media campaign in the Americas; an

underground press; and Radio Rebelde in communication with Venezuela, Colombia, and ham radio operators;

9. The achievement of unity among the armed forces, including members of the regime's army and navy who conspired against Batista, as well as various insurgent or opposition political groups in the Cuban community abroad, such as the Junta de Liberación Cubana (Miami Pact) and the Frente Cívico Revolucionario (Caracas Pact) that supported the establishment of the revolutionary government headed by Manuel Urrutia;

10. The neutralization of the U.S. government's supply of arms and airplanes to Fulgencio Batista as well as the neutralization of its diplomatic support of Batista's strategy to stay in power until February 1959;

11. Financial support for arms purchases through tax collection, with Pastorita Núñez heading up the rebel army's tax mechanism in liberated zones, Haydée Santamaría in Miami on behalf of the MR-26-7's national leadership, and Alberto Fernández among the sugar mill owners; and

12. The promotion of the Revolution's platform of laws and reforms, demanded for decades by Cubans advocating the establishment of an independent republic dedicated to social justice, economic reconstruction, and the struggle for self-determination and sovereignty.

BIBLIOGRAPHY

Barquín, Ramón. *Las luchas guerrilleras en Cuba: De la colonia a la Sierra Maestra.* Vols. 1–2. Madrid: Playor, 1975.

Batista, Fulgencio. *Piedras y leyes.* Mexico City: Ediciones Botas, 1961.

Batista, Fulgencio. *Respuesta.* Mexico City: Manuel León Sánchez, 1960.

Buch, Luis M. *Gobierno Revolucionario Cubano: Génesis y primeros pasos.* Havana: Editorial de Ciencias Sociales, 1999.

Castro Porta, Carmen. *La lección del Maestro.* Havana: Editorial de Ciencias Sociales, 1989.

Castro Ruz, Fidel. *La historia me absolverá.* Havana: Editora Política, 1967.

Castro Ruz, Fidel. "Carta a los dirigentes oposicionistas que firmaron el pacto de Unidad en Miami." In *Diario de la revolución cubana,* edited by Carlos Franqui. Paris: Ruedo Ibérico, 1976.

Castro Ruz, Fidel. *La victoria estratégica: Por todos los caminos de la Sierra.* Havana: Oficina de Publicaciones del Consejo de Estado de la República de Cuba, 2010.

Chomón, Faure. *El asalto al Palacio Presidencial.* Havana: Editorial de Ciencias Sociales, 1969.

De la Osa, Enrique. *En Cuba: Tercer tiempo, 1952–1954.* Havana: Editorial de Ciencias Sociales, 2007.

Dorschner, John, and Roberto Fabricio. *The Winds of December.* New York: Coward, McCann, & Geoghegan, 1980.

Echeverría, José A. "Constitución del Directorio Revolucionario." In *13 documentos de la insurrección.* Havana: Delegación del Gobierno del Capitolio Nacional, 1959.

Franqui, Carlos. *Diario de la revolución cubana.* Paris: Ruedo Ibérico, 1976.

García Olivera, Julio. *José Antonio Echeverría: La lucha estudiantil contra Batista.* Havana: Editora Política, 1974.

García Olivera, Julio. *Contra Batista.* Havana: Editorial de Ciencias Sociales, 2006.

García Pérez, Gladys Marel. *Insurrection and Revolution: Armed Struggle in Cuba, 1952–1959.* Translated by Juan Ortega. Boulder, CO: Lynne Rienner Publishers, 1998.

García Pérez, Gladys Marel. "Mujer y revolución: Una perspectiva desde la insurgencia cubana (1952–1959)." In *1959: Una rebelión contra las oligarquías y los dogmas revolucionarios,* Ruth Cuadernos no. 3. Havana: Ruth Casa Editorial, 2009.

Glennon, John P., and Ronald D. Landa. *Foreign Relations of the United States, 1958–1960,* Vol. 6: *Cuba.* Washington, DC: U.S. Government Printing Office, 1991.

Guevara, Ernesto. *La guerra de guerrillas.* Havana: Departamento de Instrucción del MINFAR, 1959.

Guevara, Ernesto. *Escritos y discursos.* Vols. 1–2. Havana: Editorial de Ciencias Sociales, 1972.

Guevara, Ernesto. *Pasajes de la guerra revolucionaria: Cuba 1956–1959, edición anotada.* Havana: Editora Política, 2001.

Pacheco, Judas M., Ernesto Ramos Latour, and Belarmino Castilla. *Daniel, comandante del llano y de la sierra: Biografía.* Havana: Editora Política, 2003.

Pérez, Louis A., Jr. *Army Politics in Cuba, 1898–1958.* Pittsburgh, PA: University of Pittsburgh Press, 1976.

Pérez, Louis A., Jr. *Ser Cubano: Identidad, nacionalidad, y cultura.* Havana: Editorial Ciencias Sociales, 2006.

Ramos Latour, René (Comandante Daniel). "Polémica." In *Diario de la revolución cubana,* edited by Carlos Franqui. Paris: Ruedo Ibérico, 1976.

Roa, Raúl. *El fuego de la semilla en el surco.* Havana: Editorial Letras Cubanas, 1982.

Rodríguez-Loeches, Enrique. *Bajando del Escambray.* Havana: Editorial Letras Cubanas, 1982.

Shayne, Julie D. *The Revolution Question: Feminisms in El Salvador, Chile, and Cuba.* New Brunswick, NJ, and London: Rutgers University Press, 2004.

Smith, Earl, E. T. *El cuarto piso.* San Juan: Cultural Puertorriqueña, Editora Corripio, 1963.

Sweig, Julia E. *Inside the Cuban Revolution: Fidel Castro and the Urban Underground.* Cambridge, MA, and London: Harvard University Press, 2002.

GOVERNANCE AND CONTESTATION: THE CUBAN REVOLUTION

Velia Cecilia Bobes León

The establishment and development of Cuba's revolutionary government from 1959 to the early 2000s.

Cuba, constitutionally, is a socialist state directed by the Communist Party; its legislative branch is the National Assembly of Popular Power, whose deputies are elected every five years and who in turn elect the Council of State. Executive power is in the hands of the Council of Ministers. Fidel Castro held the positions of president of the Council of State, the Council of Ministers, and first secretary of the Partido Comunista de Cuba (PCC; the Cuban Communist Party) from the founding of these institutions until July 2006, when he transferred these authorities to his brother Raúl Castro.

These governmental institutions had their origins in the Revolution of 1959 and thus reflect the political, economic, social, and cultural transformation processes launched by the Revolution. The result is a one-party system with noncompetitive elections, a highly centralized economy run by state planning, and a society that is mobilized around the goals and objectives set by the state. Despite the fact that these features have remained virtually intact for over five decades, a variety of political processes and junctures have produced changes that can be grouped broadly into three distinctly identifiable periods, as described below.

THE FOUNDING STAGE

The overthrow of General Fulgencio Batista's regime, and the rebel army's seizure of power on 1 January 1959, occurred within a context marked by extremely complex internal and external circumstances. Internally, the armed struggle in the Sierra Maestra was coupled with intensive popular mobilization that involved a variety of strategies, groups, and political alignments, including civil protests demanding the restoration of the Constitution of 1940 and democratic institutions, strikes, rallies, and violence in the cities.

From an international point of view, the new government was establishing itself just as the Cold War was escalating, and against a historical background of dependency on and contentious relations with the U.S. government. This antagonism intensified with the process of expropriations the new government set into motion upon seizing power. The U.S. government first responded to the Cuban nationalization of the large U.S.-based companies by suspending the annual sugar quota in July 1960 (which the Soviet Union swiftly agreed to purchase), and then imposed a trade embargo in October 1960. The Cuban government, for its part, went on to sign trade and cultural agreements with countries in the socialist camp. In January 1961, Cuba and the United States finally broke off diplomatic relations. These differences with the United States form the essential background necessary to understanding Cuba's political processes and governance; likewise, they are critical elements in the legitimization of the Cuban system.

The new institutions were established within this context, along with the simultaneous enactment of a group of economic and social measures that were becoming radicalized with extraordinary speed. These measures included the Agrarian Reform Law; cuts in telephone, electricity, and rent rates (1959); the nationalization of foreign property, banks, and large national enterprises; and the Urban Reform Law (1960). All of these led, on the one hand, to a redistribution of income that helped raise the standard of living, and, on the other, to an increase in the concentration of state control over property and the economy on the other.

The transformation of the political order began with the proclamation of a provisional revolutionary government (which included figures from a range of political orientations). This government reaffirmed the validity of the Constitution of 1940, relieved the president, the vice president, governors, mayors, and council members of their offices, and appointed Fidel Castro as commander-in-chief of the armed forces. It also dissolved the Congress, the army, and the police; transferred legislative authority to the Council of Ministers (appointed by decrees); and abolished the emergency tribunals and installed the revolutionary tribunals in their place. These measures were sanctioned by the Basic Law of the Republic (7 February 1959), which replaced the Constitution of 1940, albeit while preserving most of its articles; it made the prime minister the leader of the government. Fidel Castro was appointed to that office on 13 February.

Shortly thereafter (October 1959) the minister of defense was replaced by the minister of the Fuerzas Armadas Revolucionarias (FAR; Revolutionary Armed Forces). Out of this would arise the G-2, as an embryonic Ministry of the Interior in charge of internal security. The National Revolutionary Militias were founded in October 1959 in the face of the first backlash from an internal counterrevolution as well as threats from the U.S. government. This institution provided the populace with military training and organization, and it amounted to a military force that complemented the regular army. These militias were of vital importance at a time when the army and the security agencies were still in their organizational stages. They played a prominent role during the U.S. Bay of Pigs invasion in April 1961, at which point Fidel Castro proclaimed the socialist character of the revolution.

Once it had eliminated the mechanisms for representation—such as elections, political parties, and the Congress—the new government was now distinguished by its dynamism, high degree of improvisation, mobilization of the masses, and direct communications between the leadership and its bases (or grass roots). The first local governments, the Juntas de Coordinación Evaluación e Inspección (JUCEI; Coordination and Inspection Boards), were established in 1961, followed by the Poder Local (Local Authorities) in 1966; nevertheless, these institutions operated on the principle of centralization and subordination to the central executive authority.

Once socialism had been proclaimed and the alignment with the Soviet bloc openly acknowledged, the new governmental authority (which arose from a variety of political forces) focused on achieving unity. The process of integrating and unifying political organizations (such as the Popular Socialist Party [communist], the Student Directorate, and the 26th of July Movement) began in July 1961 with the creation of the Organizaciones Revolucionarias Integradas (ORI; Integrated Revolutionary Organizations), which were replaced in 1963 by the Partido Unido de la Revolución Socialista (PURS; United Party of the Socialist Revolution). This effort culminated in 1965 with the founding of the Partido Comunista de Cuba (PCC), which from then on into the early 2000s was the only political party in Cuba. It was through this process that the new authority consolidated its base under the leadership of Fidel Castro.

The strategy of revolutionary unity meant that the scope and reach of social organizations had to be transformed. This action occurred rapidly and deliberately. The various autonomous organizations of civil society (business associations, neighborhoods, artists, and the like) vanished, while the leadership of the Federación Estudiántil Universitaria (University Students' Federation) and the Cuban labor unions were grouped into the Central de Trabajadores de Cuba (CTC; Cuban Workers Center) and the *new* mass organizations of the Revolution were created.

The year 1960 witnessed the founding of the Federación de Mujeres Cubanas (Cuban Women's Federation), the Comités de Defensa de la Revolución (CDRs; Committees for the Defense of the Revolution), and the Asociación de Jóvenes Rebeldes (Rebel Youth Association), which in 1962 would change its name to the Unión de Jóvenes Comunistas (UJC; Young Communists Union). In 1961 various sectoral groups appeared, such as the Asociación Nacional de Agricultores Pequeños (ANAP; National Association of Small Farmers) and the Unión de Escritores y Artistas de Cuba (UNEAC; Union of Writers and Artists of Cuba). Subsequently, other professional and student organizations (elementary and high school) began to appear, completing the process to organize and control the entire society across all its various sectors.

The mass organizations were designed to ensure the rapid, massive incorporation of the population in defense, political support, and economic and social activities. They were the cornerstone of the mobilization scheme that would play a central role in Cuban politics after 1959. The sheer number of these organizations reflected the imperative of encompassing the entire society, while the styles, methods, and operating mechanisms were geared toward controlling collective action and subordinating its purpose to the goals of the revolution. Accordingly, they contributed to the generation and consolidation of the power of the new regime.

With regard to their structure and operations, these organizations were at first unstable and disorganized. They were characterized by a high degree of innovation and improvisation, with some degree of self-determination and a high level of convening capacity. The membership demonstrated a high degree of spontaneity even as it served as a visible symbol of identification, commitment, and loyalty to the new order.

During this period, even though the institutionalization of power was precarious and limited, communications between the leaders (Fidel Castro in particular) and the people were fluid and took place through gigantic rallies, where the most important laws were voted on or approved by acclamation. This governing style decisively concentrated and personalized power in the person of Fidel Castro, whose charisma and ability to stir up the enthusiastic support of the masses were essential to the legitimizing of a government that, at that time, lacked a legal foundation. Amid the widespread belief that the old republican order was exhausted and corrupt, political discourse centered on the ideals of sovereignty and social justice. The performance of the new government gave credibility to these grounds for legitimization: both in its unwavering resistance to U.S. hegemony and in the benefits that economic redistribution measures evidently brought to the great majority. Accordingly, when the Revolutionary Offensive was launched (1968), eliminating the country's small businesses, the new economic model was justified as part of a broader effort to eliminate inequalities, close the gaps in the standards of living among the various groups and social classes, and narrow differences between the countryside and the city.

The new government was conspicuously slow and inefficient with regard to the constitution of its own legal and regulatory framework, and it appeared to show an utter lack of interest in or even a disdain for legality. This, however, did not significantly affect its legitimacy, since this leadership was rooted not in law but in the Revolution itself (and in the rights that were achieved through it).

Between 1960 and October 1965, when the newspaper *Granma* was founded as the official

COMITÉS DE DEFENSA DE LA REVOLUCIÓN (CDRs)

In the wake of the Cuban Revolution in 1959, the new government fostered the creation of mass organizations as channels for citizen participation. As a result organizations were created for women (FMC) and small farmers (ANAP), while others were revamped to the new realities, such as those created for students (FEU) and workers (CTC). The largest, and most comprehensive in scope are the Comités de Defensa de la Revolución (CDRs; Committees for the Defense of the Revolution), a network of neighborhood committees set up originally on every block to prevent foreign and counterrevolutionary threats and attacks, especially against bombs that were frequently used on stores, factories, and other buildings. A local CDR is made up of a president, a vice president, a director of vigilance, a secretary, and a director of finances.

The CDR system was created on 28 September 1960 as the tension between the Cuban and U.S. governments became increasingly confrontational. When the United States invaded Cuba at the Bay of Pigs (Playa Girón), the CDRs were instrumental in containing the opposition in other parts of the island not directly affected by the invasion. During the early 1960s, when internal military opposition was a threat, the duties of vigilance were paramount. Critics say that the CDRs are a form of political vigilance and an unwanted intrusion in a person's privacy. During the Mariel Boatlift crisis in 1980, CDRs were involved in the harassment of those who chose to leave Cuba for the United States; CDR members pelted homes with rocks and bottles, and physically assaulted and injured emigrating Cubans (García p. 62). Even in the twenty-first century, CDR members rotate guard duty (staying up all night) as part of their civil defense mission. CDRs are the main logistical vehicle for mass political mobilizations such as marches, major speeches, May Day celebrations, and large demonstrations. The logistics of major celebrations (CDR Anniversary, Children's Day) are handled by the CDRs, as are any elections and voting for the Poder Popular (Popular Power), where an individual residence is chosen as the head office during the vote.

By 1976, the CDR boasted almost 5 million members, some 80% of the adult population of the island (Domínguez p. 262). As military threats subsided in the late 1960s, the CDRs began to take on many other functions: vaccination campaigns to fight infectious diseases or epidemic outbreaks (dengue, SARs, HIV/AIDS), donation of blood, and recycling of glass and other materials. Since the early 1960s, the CDRs have run the exemplary parent program to ensure that children go to school and pass their grade. More recently, CDRs have been helpful in dealing with crime and prostitution.

Identity verification for legal transactions such as weddings, divorces, job applications, inheritance claims, and requests for emigration are channeled through the CDRs. CDRs are also involved in providing a character reference for those seeking certain important jobs. Among its community functions are the distribution of certain goods (televisions, refrigerators, telephones, mattresses during a hurricane) when appropriate and according to either need or merit.

Additional tasks coordinated by the CDRs include organizing volunteer work on weekends. In the late 1960s they were used as part of Cuba's 10 million-ton sugar harvest program, which ultimately failed to meet its goal. Later on they helped mobilize the population for building new housing; nowadays, the voluntary labor is more restricted to the block where people live. Tasks like weeding, cleaning of sidewalks, sweeping, and other elements of public hygiene are performed by CDR members. One of the major tasks undertaken is the mobilization of people and resources during hurricanes to ensure a minimum of loss of life and property; the CDRs have been praised by international relief agencies for this type of work.

BIBLIOGRAPHY

Domínguez, Jorge. *Cuba Order and Revolution*. Cambridge, MA: Harvard University Press, 1978.

García, María Cristina. *Havana USA: Cuban Exiles and Cuban Americans in South Florida 1959–1994*. Berkeley: University of California Press, 1996.

Gray, Alexander, and Antoni Kapcia, eds. *The Changing Dynamic of Cuban Civil Society*. Gainesville: University Press of Florida, 2008.

mouthpiece of the PCC, all of the media (print, radio, and television) passed into the hands of the state, meaning that free and independent channels for public opinion disappeared. Furthermore, the school system was nationalized, making education not only free of charge but universal, standardized, and state-operated at every level. The combination of these factors favored the generation of a broad national consensus on the revolutionary process and its leader.

Nevertheless, upon examining this consensus, one must not dismiss the existence of an opposition movement in that very same year of 1959. The radicalization of the revolutionary process, as well as its origins in a broad array of organizations and political orientations, led to an intense power struggle in which allegiances and loyalties were constantly being redefined. Despite Fidel Castro's success in securing the support of a great majority of the people, the first few years of his government were marked by clashes

CUBANO

MANTEN LAS LUCES DE TU CASA APAGADAS DURANTE LA NOCHE, COMO REFLEJO DE TRISTEZA.

DRE handbill. This handbill was circulated by the Directorio Revolucionario Estudiantil (DRE), a counterrevolutionary group involved in the movement to oust Batista. The DRE later turned against Fidel Castro and advocated sabotage. The handbill suggests actions that ordinary Cubans can take to subvert the government, in this case, leaving lights on to drain electricity. © HOLLY ACKERMAN, PH.D.

en cambio...

DURANTE EL DIA ENCIENDE TODAS LAS LUCES QUE PUEDAS, PARA CONSUMIR MAS ELECTRICIDAD, DURANTE LAS HORAS DE FUNCIONAMIENTO DE LAS INDUSTRIAS.

Directorio Revolucionario Estudiantil

between supporters of the Revolution and diverse opposition groups who squared off, often violently, against the government, with the support of the United States. This support, together with the rupture in diplomatic relations and the embargo, contributed to bolstering the nationalist components of the ideology and the symbolic identification of the state project with the homeland and the nation. Indeed, the sense of being under siege by the United States persists as of 2011.

Emigration was yet another form of opposition that became apparent very quickly. Although support for the Revolution was virtually unanimous at the outset, embraced as much by the upper classes, intellectuals, and businessmen, as by the great mass of the people, by the end of 1959 and throughout the entire decade of the 1960s a huge exodus occurred. Between 1959 and 1975, migratory waves of some 555,000 people, mostly drawn from the middle and upper classes, left for the United States. This mass exodus of the regime's opponents was stimulated and favored by U.S. government programs and policies, including the political refugee status conferred on Cubans beginning in 1961, and Cuban Adjustment Act, which after 1966 made it possible for these immigrants to obtain legal resident status after one year. Paradoxically, these measures actually served to foster homogeneity in the political alignment of those who stayed behind and unity around the state project. Thus a consensus emerged on the basis of various combined elements: negative perceptions of how the democratic institutions of the old order were functioning; the mobilization of nationalistic impulses; the positive impact of the redistribution and social security measures that meant an increase in levels of equity and social justice; the leader's charisma; and the export of dissidents.

INSTITUTIONALIZATION

During the 1970s changes became apparent in both the institutional order of the Revolution and its economic model. On the one hand, there was an institutionalization process coupled with a decline in mobilization activities; on the other hand, faced with the failure of the Ten Million Ton Harvest (1970) and, generally speaking, of the entire economic strategy of the 1960s, in 1976 the System for Direction and Planning of the Economy was launched in an effort to raise efficiency and reestablish the principle of compensation according to a person's work. These internal changes occurred within an international context that included increasing rapprochement with the Soviet Union and the socialist bloc; the acceptance of Cuba in the international Council for Mutual Economic Assistance (known as Comecon) in 1972; a decline in Cuban support for Latin American guerrilla movements; the incursion of the army into various African conflicts; a certain measure of détente in relations with the United States; and the stirrings of the first dialogue with the Cuban émigré community in the United States.

Although these changes had actually started earlier, a juncture can be clearly identified in the approval of the socialist Constitution of 1976 and the establishment of the so-called Organs of Popular Power. The draft Constitution was discussed at worker and neighbor assemblies throughout the country and voted on in a referendum in February 1976. This Magna Carta conferred legality and continuity on the political system and recognized the PCC as the (only) party of the working class and as the lead entity of Cuban society. This Constitution declares that the Cuban state is a socialist worker and peasant state and authorizes Marxist-Leninism as the official ideology. It endorses a hierarchical structure of the country's political institutions, in which the party is superior to all other organizations, state entities, and the armed forces. It emphasizes equality as a basic right of all Cubans and conditions the exercise of their civil and political rights on the defense of the socialist state. Likewise, it recognizes that the mass organizations (protected and stimulated by the state) perform state functions.

These precepts strengthened the guidance and leadership role of the PCC over society. The mass organizations began to assimilate operating mechanisms and management styles that were actually appropriate to government entities; their leadership was professionalized and their activities routinized. Mobilizations to the countryside and volunteer work were cut back, and the unions were increasingly guided by an identification of the interests of the workers with those of the state. These organizations operated on the basis of a vertical hierarchy in which they were the metaphorical gears implementing centrally determined economic policies.

The professionalism of the armed forces (FAR) also increased, and the militias were transferred to the FAR Reserves. This meant replacing the old form of popular mobilization for defense with an institutional style that was more consistent with military traditions. At the same time, many reservists were drafted in the troops sent to Africa, principally Angola. The prestige of the military grew throughout this period, associated precisely with its successes in the African campaigns. In 1980 some Milicias de Tropas Territoriales (MTT; Territorial Militias) reappeared; they were now much better organized but less spontaneous and more closely associated with the regular troops than their predecessors of the 1960s.

The process of political institutionalization—pursued through a resolution of the first PCC Congress (1975)—culminated with the establishment of a popular power system that was based on assemblies at the municipal, provincial, and national levels. In December 1976 the National Assembly of Popular Power was proclaimed the country's highest legislative body, thus placing the legal order on a more solid constitutional footing (based on suffrage), which was rooted in a new political-administrative division that reorganized the six old provinces into fourteen new ones in order to strengthen the principle of territorial representation.

The electoral system thus approved was based on the principle of representation and indirect elections at the provincial and national levels. At the district level voting was direct. From there the municipal delegates elected the provincial delegates, who in turn elected the deputies. In the National Assembly, the deputies elected the Council of State (the body of the assembly between legislative sessions, and the collegiate representative of the state and the government) who in turn elected their president, who then nominated the Council of Ministers (the executive branch) and the judicial branch (president, vice president, and justices of the Supreme Court, the attorney general, and the deputy attorneys general of the Republic). The lists of candidates are prepared by a PCC-led candidacy commission consisting of territorial representatives from the mass organizations. This system forbids electoral campaigning and mandates regular accountability to the voters, while upholding the principle that mandates can be revoked.

Among the shortcomings of popular power that have been repeatedly pointed out, its very low capacity for actually governing deserves highlighting. The assembly meets infrequently (twice a year), and its debates tend to be formalistic; very few measures proposed by the top leadership of the country fail to get approved; local entities have very little autonomy; the legislative branch is supplanted by the executive; and indirect elections and PCC-manufactured candidacies are undemocratic. The establishment of the Organs of Popular Power implied a change in the style of government. Direct contacts were replaced by representation and electoral participation, and power was decentralized, which meant a diminution of personalization and identification with the figure of Fidel Castro. These years marked a transition from a scheme centered on the mobilization of the masses toward a politics that is more routinized, bureaucratized, and formal. These changes have been interpreted in various ways. While some analysts (Marifeli Pérez-Stable, for example) have argued that this was the culmination of the revolutionary period as such, others (including Jorge I. Domínguez) have pointed to the end of charisma and the beginning of legal legitimacy; still others (Juan Valdés Paz among them) have seen this as an election-based reformulation of consensus governance.

Beyond the debates, there is little doubt that the PCC, with its constitutional mandate to define the general objectives of all policies of the country, enhanced and legalized its status as the leader of society and its highest political authority. At the same time, the constitutional concept of the unitary state (similar to the Soviet model) limited the differentiation of its functions by encouraging a concentration of offices and roles in the same persons, while fostering the rise and entrenchment of the administrative bureaucratic elite. The media, which during this period were completely in state hands and under the ideological control of the PCC, served as an echo chamber for the official party line.

The establishment of a new constitutional legality also led to a transformation in the forms of legitimacy itself. Socialist legality now began to serve as the basis of the state and its institutions. Even though the Revolution remained the ultimate reference point for legitimization, the emphasis shifted to Marxism-Leninism. As events have shown, despite the institutionalization of the regime, Castro's charisma has continued to serve as a foundation for legitimacy. Indeed, during times of crisis, it has turned out to be an irreplaceable weapon in reformulating the consensus.

During this stage, consensus was obtained through an ideological dogmatism that insisted on unanimity and cohesion; the tendency for social homogenization rather than the expression of a diversity of interests persisted. Although mobilization diminished, it never vanished entirely; there were still exhortations to mass participation and engagement as shows of support for and allegiance to the revolutionary project, such as that which occurred during the months the Elián González affair lasted in 1999 and 2000.

Although the government had managed to eliminate violent opposition by the 1970s, emigration continued to provide evidence of disaffection. In 1980 over 125,000 people (from all social strata and backgrounds) departed from the port of Mariel, a phenomenon that was unusually spectacular for the sheer number of people who left over a very short period of time as well as the atmosphere of internal confrontation that surrounded the event: Those who expressed their intent to emigrate were treated not just as opposition but as traitors to their country and were insulted and humiliated in official acts of repudiation, which likewise served as a tangible reaffirmation of the loyalty of those who stayed behind. After Mariel, the exodus continued both through legal and illegal means.

RECTIFICATION AND THE SPECIAL PERIOD

At the end of the 1980s, in an international context marked by the initiation of processes of opening and change in the Soviet Union and the Soviet socialist countries, international détente, and the end of the Cuban military adventure in Africa, the Cuban leadership set about its task of recovering the original sources of the Revolution and the proposals of its early years in order to ensure the continuity of the regime and recycle the underlying consensus. This was to be accomplished through the Process for the Rectification of Errors and Negative Tendencies.

The strategy chosen for this, as outlined at the Third PCC Congress (1986), insisted on the importance of a socialist (Marxist-Leninist) orientation and emphasized the leadership role of the PCC. There were signs that the economic model of the 1970s was no longer working. There was also evidence of a fraying consensus, failing mechanisms of integration, and eroding bases of revolutionary legitimacy (as evidenced not only in the change in the social composition of migration, but in the appearance of new youth identities and cultural alternatives and the rise of the first human rights organizations inspired by the process of opening in the Eastern Bloc countries). As a result, a decision was made to return to older styles and strategies, which in effect meant reinvigorating the mobilization of the masses and reviving revolutionary morale.

From an institutional standpoint, the rectification process did not introduce major changes. Rather, what it did was to prepare and mature the proposals that finally crystallized in the constitutional reforms of 1992. Between 1986 and 1993 the PCC's organizational charts were restructured, and at the Fourth Congress (1991) an accord was reached to reduce the provincial committees and cut down the number of secretariats and departments of the Central Committee. The PCC was redefined more inclusively as the party of the Cuban *nation*, and it jettisoned the principle of atheism (by allowing believers to join).

The Popular Councils were created in an effort to enhance the decentralization of the organs of popular power and increase citizen involvement in state activity. These were established at the territorial level and had the executive authority to address and make decisions on economic and social problems in the locality. Paradoxically, along with this process of political decentralization of the bases, rectification, by dismantling the planning system and reviving the special plans managed at the discretion of the support team of the commander-in-chief, introduced a greater personalization of power and an increase in the centralization of the economy. With regard to the mass organizations, the rectification proposal was geared toward reinvigorating them. The unions would be in charge of setting a socialist example and reducing material incentives, while the other organizations would focus on reviving techniques for mobilizing participation while beginning to criticize the formal and bureaucratic plans that had hindered the government's capacity for social mobilization and agitation. In an attempt to strengthen control, Rapid Response Brigades and the Association of Revolutionary Veterans were created to maximize commitment and confront potential counterrevolutionary protests.

The arrest and execution by firing squad of General Ochoa and several high-ranking officers of the FAR and the MINIT (Ministry of the Interior) in 1989 further eroded the legitimacy of institutions and the credibility of their leaders. Although the case was handled as an issue of individuals' moral corruption, in truth the process involved a far-reaching reorganization of the security apparatus. This resulted in downgrading the Ministry of Interior while granting the army a much larger role and prominence in politics and national life.

Under these conditions, there was an obvious need to rearticulate a consensus that was showing signs of weakness. The focal points for this rearticulation were the recovery of nationalism, the rejection of the Soviet model, the return to the original thinking of the Revolution, and the proposal for self-critiques by Cuban society. In the search for endogenous sources of legitimization, this discourse moderately circumscribes Marxism-Leninism in order to reach back into the nation's history. In the face of the crisis and self-critique of international socialism, there was an effort to go back to the revolutionary origins of the state and emphasize the uniqueness of Cuba's own process while reinforcing Fidel Castro's charisma as the basis of legitimacy.

The new model continued to politicize the economic environment. Volunteer work was saved, labor contingents were established, and the micro-brigades were revived. The results of this new experiment overlapped with the new crisis in the Cuban economy, caused by the dissolution of Comecon and the end of the Soviet subsidy. Only a few years after it was set in motion, the crisis made it necessary to rectify the rectification, and in 1990 the government declared the beginning of the Special Period during Peacetime.

In 1991 the authorities convoked the Fourth Congress of the PCC to engage in a public debate on the main political and economic guidelines for the next five years. Worker and neighbor assemblies gathered the opinions of the public and verified that there was indeed a widespread social demand for broadening democracy, increasing the representativeness of the Poder Popular and voting mechanisms. The Congress ended with a suggestion that a proposal for reform be prepared, and indeed in 1992 the National Assembly approved a constitutional reform along with a new electoral law. The former modified the articles that established the foundations of the state. It defined the PCC as *martiano* (after José Martí) and Marxist-Leninist and as the vanguard of the Cuban nation and the leading force in society and the state. It also removed the principles of unity of power and democratic centralization; eliminated the principle of scientific atheism; reformulated socialist property as "the ownership of all the people over the basic means of production"; and recognized small private property holdings and the possibility for state property to be transferred to real persons or corporate entities. These constitutional changes provided legal recognition to the Popular Councils, while they eliminated the municipal and provincial executive committees, which were replaced by administrative councils. For its part, the electoral reform provided for the direct election of provincial delegates and deputies to the National Assembly, albeit through closed nominations (for both the candidates and the offices they were running for).

In this new context the mass organizations heeded calls to strengthen their vigilance and combativeness, reject crime and the counterrevolution, and safeguard labor and social discipline. Only the unions (CTC), through the Worker Parliaments, maintained a critical stance (and not very energetic) against the adjustment measures.

At this point, with the emergence of different kinds of autonomous associations at the beginning of the 1990s, there was a renaissance of civil society, that is, affiliations more or less tolerated by the state. These include nongovernmental organizations dedicated to research, popular education, and community and neighborhood issues; lay organizations connected with churches and religious cults; and a large number of small dissident groups (human rights groups, relatives of political prisoners, independent journalists associations, and so forth).

Although the political and institutional changes were moderate, the Economic Reform of 1993 pointed toward a broader transformation of the model: It included the promotion and acceptance of foreign investment (whether private capital or mixed) in various sectors; legalized self-employment and the possession of foreign currencies, the opening of the internal market, and massive cooperatives for agricultural and livestock production; provided the rationale for restructuring the state apparatus and implementing a fiscal policy; and reduced the number of state jobs. One of the peculiarities of this process has been that the military has surfaced as a leader of the new economic strategies. The army has created companies engaged in tourism and foreign trade, where the concept of entrepreneurial perfectionism has developed as a model of efficiency and productivity. When the defense budget was cut as a result of the end of the Soviet subsidy, many officers were recycled into management positions with these companies, and subsequently rose to the most important institutions of the government.

Among the social consequences of the Special Period, the growth in inequality stands out. The existence, side by side, of foreign exchange and national currency markets (with the latter certainly depressed to minimum levels of subsistence) has led to a differentiation in consumption patterns, based on income obtained through family remittances since possession of dollars was legalized. This has stimulated the proliferation of illicit activities such as prostitution and has increased marginalization. Add to this the persistence of what has been there all along but that without a doubt is going through a new boom: the underground economy, the black market, and the diversion of state resources, which emerge as alternative survival strategies that intersect the new logic of social life. The Helms-Burton Law aggravated the situation by tightening the blockade while conditioning its lifting on a regime change in which neither Fidel nor Raúl Castro may govern.

The meaning of these changes has been interpreted in quite different ways. The debate includes authors such as Rafael Rojas (who speaks of "post-communism") and Eusebio Mujal León (who speaks of "post-totalitarianism"), while others refer to the "beginning of a transition," without saying precisely where that transition leads. But there is general agreement that these are in fact important changes. The consensus has undergone fractures and a rearrangement. Even though the adjustment measures should not be seen as the sole driving cause of changes in Cuba, they have certainly undermined the egalitarian redistribution policies that caused people to believe in the values of equity and social justice at the very heart of the nation's legitimizing discourse.

The first direct elections for Cuba's National Assembly were held in February 1993. Despite a 99-percent turnout rate, only 88 percent of the voters voted for the full list (as called for by official propaganda). The government considered these results an indicator of a continuing consensus around the goals of the Revolution and as a major success, since the elections were held at the worst moment of the economic crisis.

There are, however, other elements that lead one to temper such optimistic estimates, even though Cubans' electoral choices continue to hew closely to the proposals advanced by the governing power. New forms of dissent had appeared since 1991, along with the growth in emigration. During 1994 as the economic crisis hit the hardest, a number of incidents related to the intent to leave the island escalated into the 5 August rioting near El Malecón (the sea wall) in Havana. This event lasted only a few hours and was controlled with a minimum of police repression thanks to the involvement of loyal civilian groups. The official explanation insisted that this was a group of lumpenproletariat and marginal individuals egged on by the enemy; however, it was in fact a manifestation of popular discontent, showing a fracture in the people's support of the revolutionary project. Occurrences like this (never seen in Cuba after 1959, nor repeated since) make it possible to think in terms of the erosion of mechanisms of control and of flaws in the social integration system.

Furthermore, the uncertainty and lack of clarity that arrived with the Special Period were accompanied by increasing social diversity, which in and of itself reflected a reshuffling of the consensus, which could no longer be based on social uniformity and homogeneity. The signs of fracture were also evident in the growth and diversification of dissident organizations. For a time these organizations enjoyed a relative boom, culminating in the Proyecto Varela (Varela Project): a citizens' initiative that managed to collect the ten thousand signatures required by the Constitution in order to promote a referendum on legislation for freedom of expression and association, for Cubans to establish their own businesses, for amnesty for political prisoners, and for the promulgation of a new electoral law. These organizations took a serious blow in the spring of 2003, however, when more than seventy of their members were imprisoned and charged with being mercenaries at the service of the United States.

Some of Cuba's subsequent constitutional amendments occurred in this context. In 2002, the National Assembly approved a constitutional reform law, which declared that socialism was irrevocable, thus armoring the Constitution against any possibility of changes. To the extent that economic conditions were improving as a result of the reforms (and strategic alliances with new international partners), there was indeed a gradual recovery of authority and, consequently, increased repression of these dissident groups. After the Elián affair the government launched a Battle of Ideas to recover its mobilizing capacity.

The sudden illness of Fidel Castro forced the leader to transfer his power to his brother Raúl (second secretary of the PCC, vice president of the Council of State, and minister of the Revolutionary Armed Forces). Since then there have been no transformations in the political sphere. Instead there has been a recycling of the elites, clearing the ranks of high government offices for a return of the historical leadership and placing many generals in key positions. These moves indicate a decline in the mobilizing style and the twilight of the Battle of Ideas. New adjustment measures have been put into effect in the face of yet another extremely serious economic crisis. Despite the fact that he no longer holds the reins of government and is not the president of the Councils of State and of the Ministers, Fidel Castro is still the first secretary of the PCC, and his important personal charisma and moral authority continue to be a pillar of legitimization. He has never ceased to have a presence, whether through the publication of his reflections or in the media's exploitation of his public appearances.

In November 2010, the government announced that the Sixth PCC Congress would be held in April 2011, to conduct an in-depth review of the nation's economic strategy. According to the documents circulated in early 2011 for discussion among the citizenry, this so-called updating of the model includes labor reforms that were anticipated to eliminate more than one million government jobs while authorizing new self-employment activities and the creation of cooperatives; an expansion of the modes of foreign and mixed investment; and a review of social policy with a view to "eliminating illicit gratuities" and an end to state paternalism and egalitarianism. These measures were expected to deepen the erosion of mechanisms that were essential to legitimizing the socialist system, such as the state's provision of minimum levels of basic consumer goods, housing, health, and education through a social security policy based on criteria of universality, solidarity, and equality, the result of which has been one of the most egalitarian and homogenous societies on the continent. The new circumstances spark reflection on the new tensions created when the phenomena of inequality associated with these adjustment measures are introduced into society, particularly on the legitimizing discourse of the political order, which, although it has been modified, is still squarely based on the concept of social justice as an achievement of the Revolution and socialism.

The forms of legitimization have continued to be premised on the Revolution as the founding act of the state and as the condition of its sovereignty, even while there has been an effort to broaden the inclusive character of its ideology and institutions. However, the crisis has obliged it to restate the Revolution's achievements in a version that restricts them to those in education, health, and social security. The mottoes of the day reflect that effort. With the loss of such reference points, there is yet again a resort to nationalism. The call now is to "save the Homeland, the Revolution, and Socialism." Allusions to abundant future and idyllic visions of long-term development have been replaced with a more realistic perspective that underscores the difficulties to be faced and the adversity that results as much from the structural deformities of the Cuban economy as from recurring natural disasters, the tightening of the blockade, and the collapse of the international socialist system.

BIBLIOGRAPHY

Bell Lara, José, Delia L. López, and Tania Caram. *Documentos de la revolución cubana 1959*. Havana: Editorial de Ciencias Sociales, 2006.

Bobes, Velia C. *Los laberintos de la imaginación: Repertorio simbólico, identidades, y actores del cambio social en Cuba*. Mexico City: El Colegio de México, 2000.

Bobes, Velia C. *La nación inconclusa: (Re)Constituciones de la ciudadanía y el cambio social en Cuba*. Mexico City: FLACSO, 2007.

Buch Rodríguez, Luis M. *Gobierno revolucionario cubano: Génesis y primeros pasos*. Havana: Editorial de Ciencias Sociales, 1999.

Constitución de la República de Cuba. Havana: Revolutionary Orientation Directorate of the Cuban Communist Party, 1976.

Dilla, Haroldo, ed. *La democracia en Cuba y el diferendo con los Estados Unidos*. Havana: Centro de Estudios de América, 1995.

Dilla, Haroldo, ed. *La participación en Cuba y los retos del futuro*. Havana: Centro de Estudios de América, 1996.

Domínguez, Jorge I. *Cuba: Order and Revolution*. Cambridge, MA: Harvard University Press, 1978.

Domínguez, Jorge I. *Cuba: Internal and International Affairs*. Beverly Hills, CA: Sage, 1982.

Fernández, Damián. *Cuba and the Politics of Passion*. Austin: University of Texas Press, 2000.

Halebsky, Sandor, and John M. Kirk, eds. *Cuba in Transition: Crisis and Transformation*. Boulder, CO: Westview Press, 1993.

Ley Electoral de 1992. Available from http://www.cubanet.org.

Ley de Reforma Constitucional, 2002. Available from http://www.cubanet.org.

Mesa-Lago, Carmelo. *Cuba in the 1970s: Pragmatism and Institutionalization.* Albuquerque: University of New Mexico Press, 1978.

Mesa-Lago, Carmelo, ed. *Cuba after the Cold War.* Pittsburgh, PA: University of Pittsburgh Press, 1993.

Pérez, Lisandro, ed. *Transition in Cuba: New Challenges for U.S. Policy.* Miami: Florida International University, 1993.

Pérez-López, Jorge, ed. *Cuba at a Crossroad.* Gainesville: University Press of Florida, 1994.

Pérez-Stable, Marifeli. *The Cuban Revolution: Origins, Course, and Legacy.* New York: Oxford University Press, 1993.

Rojas, Rafael, and Velia C. Bobes, eds. *La transición invisible: Sociedad y cambio político en Cuba.* Mexico City: Océano, 2004.

Valdés Paz, Juan, ed. *La transición socialista en Cuba: Estudio sociopolítico.* Havana: Editorial de Ciencias Sociales, 1994.

"LA GUANTANAMERA"

Olavo Alén Rodríguez

A simple song turned into the symbol and emblem of the Cuban nation.

The song known as "La Guantanamera" or "Guajira Guantanamera" is one of the most powerful symbols of Cuban culture, not only within Cuba but also throughout the world. It is worth noting, though, that the song's title and chorus, which have remained intact in its many versions, refer specifically to a peasant woman from the eastern province of Guantánamo, not to all Cuban women.

Other songs whose lyrics refer to Cuba and its beauty more generally—such as "Cuba, que linda es Cuba" (Cuba, How Beautiful Is Cuba)—have not had the same wide and lasting appeal, and even very famous Cuban songs that have also become symbolic of Cuban culture such as "Canto Siboney" (Siboney Song), "Son de la Loma" (From the Hills), and "El Manicero" (The Peanut Vendor) are not so immediately recognizable by international audiences, nor have they spawned as many versions as "La Guantanamera." The reasons for the immense popularity of "La Guantanamera" lie in the complex history of a simple song.

HISTORY

In his book *La música en Cuba* (Music in Cuba, 1945), Alejo Carpentier (1904–1980) discussed the powerful influence of the Spanish *romancero*, an old Spanish ballad style. "Cuba is one of the New World countries that has best preserved this tradition," he wrote (p. 23), offering several examples of which this is the last:

Recently, a Havana radio station made a popular hit of a peasant song entitled "Guantanamera," which had been brought to the capital by authentic singers. Verses were set to its tune, narrating the latest current events. The music for "Guantanamera's" first two lines was nothing other than the tune of the very old Spanish ballad "Gerineldo," in its version from the Spanish region of Extremadura.

Carpentier p. 24

The reference is to CMQ's radio program *El suceso del día* (The Event of the Day), broadcast from Monte and Prado streets in Havana. Two years previously, Joseíto Fernández had been hired to join the program and sing his already popular melody.

THE SONG

"La Guantanamera" (or "Guajira Guantanamera," which is its original title) was composed in 1928 by the Havana songwriter Joseíto Fernández Díaz (1908–1979), who sang it in public for the first time accompanied by Alejandro Riveiro's group. Fernández was invited to sign a contract with the radio station precisely because of the popularity he achieved with that song.

The musical genre known as *guajira* (peasant-style) is a variation of the *canción cubana* (Cuban song) that emerged in Havana and whose lyrics depict scenes of the Cuban countryside. This type of music typically utilizes the melodies, rhythms, harmonic sequences, and musical traits of Cuba's rural dwellers, who divide geographically into two groups, eastern region and western region. The first group generated its own music style known as *son*, and the second did the same with the *punto guajiro*. Fernández alluded to both types of rural music in "La Guantanamera," taking the distinctive *tumbaos* (repetitive rhythmic and harmonic patterns) of the east to shape the chorus and the tonal style of the west to create the melody.

Fernández was not the first to fuse these two rural musical styles. Ignacio Piñeiro (1888–1969), a Havana composer who had created the mixed genre known as *guajira-son*, preceded him, and undoubtedly Fernández followed Piñeiro's lead out of admiration. Nevertheless, "La Guantanamera" is neither *son* nor *tonada*; it is a *canción cubana* in the form of a *guajira*. The song's importance stems from the fact that it depicts rural Cubans in an artistic way.

Carpentier held that the music in the first part of "La Guantanamera" was taken from a very old Spanish ballad, but the melody and the rhythm with which it moves are too Cuban to have resulted from a *romancero*. Rather, the connection is lyrical, through the utilization of the *décima* (a ten-line rhyme scheme comprised of eight-syllable lines) as a literary resource. This makes it possible for all Cubans to identify with it, despite its region-specific title. Furthermore, "La

■ *See also*

Music: 1900–1945

Music: *Nueva Trova* (New Song): Music of the Cuban Revolution

Versos sencillos (José Martí)

Guantanamera" was created using an economy of means: a harmonic sequence of only three chords (tonic-subdominant-dominant) atop a simple *tumbao sonero*. All this made it easy for diverse Cuban populations to accept it.

THE EVENT OF THE DAY

The 1940s have been called the Golden Age of Cuban radio. There was a great deal of competition among radio stations, but CMQ was undoubtedly the listeners' favorite because of the popular program *El suceso del día* (The Event of the Day), which broadcast the most scandalous and hair-raising news sung to the tunes of popular melodies.

This was the first popular use of "La Guantanamera"; the day's news was adapted to the melody of the song then used as the radio show's closer, which Fernández sang (López p. 143). This routine was unprecedented, and the program had great social impact. All of Cuba listened to "La Guantanamera" for seventeen years to learn about the most gruesome recent incidents in the country. A news bulletin reported the effect it had on one listener in Sancti Spiritus on 5 August 1948:

> Seventeen-year-old Elia Rosa Acosta was listening to the radio with her grandmother while "La Guantanamera" was being played; she started feeling so anguished that she went into her room, took some poison, and lay down on her bed awaiting death. Her state was critical when her grandmother found her and took her to the first aid station. She is not expected to survive.
>
> *Díaz Ayala p. 199*

"LA GUANTANAMERA" GETS A NEW IMAGE

In the 1950s the Cuban songwriter Julián Orbón (1925–1991) wrote a substantial number of songs with a strong Cuban flavor. The clear influence of Hispanic music in his works is uniquely blended with rhythmic and style elements taken from Afro-Cuban music. He was one of the most promising alumni of the Grupo Renovación Musical (Musical Revival Group) directed by José Ardévol.

A great admirer of the literary work of the revolutionary José Martí (1853–1895), Orbón adapted "La Guantanamera" to Martí's *Versos sencillos* (Simple Verses), which were well known in Cuba, especially among the younger generations. Beginning the melody in the middle of Fernández's original version allowed Orbón to set only six verses to music. Also, instead of the ten-line stanzas Fernández had used, Orbón took the four-line stanzas used by Martí and repeated the first two lines of each. This version of "La Guantanamera" was heard by Orbón's student Héctor Angulo when he visited the maestro's home in the Vedado neighborhood of Havana in the 1950s.

In 1959 Angulo won a scholarship from the new revolutionary government to study music at the Manhattan School of Music in New York. With his mind filled with the social ideas prevalent in Cuba after the Revolution, he was drawn to intellectual and left-wing circles in New York City. The break in diplomatic relations between the United States and Cuba made Angulo's financial situation precarious, and in 1962 he accepted a position as a counselor at the Camp Woodland summer camp in upstate New York. There he organized an impromptu choir of teenagers, teaching them songs including Orbón's version of "Guajira Guantanamera," for which he wrote a guitar accompaniment reminiscent of Fernandez's Cuban radio performances.

Angulo used only three stanzas from Martí's *Versos sencillos*, and the stanzas he selected did not follow the order in Martí's work; indeed, they belong to three different *Versos*. The purpose of this arrangement was to present an image of Martí clearly associated with the revolutionary ideas set forth by the Cuban Revolution. This is how the new lyrics for "La Guantanamera" were passed on for posterity.

They read:

> Yo soy un hombre sincero,
> De donde crece la palma
> Y antes de morirme quiero,
> Echar mis versos del alma.
>
> Mi verso es de un verde claro
> Y de un carmín encendido
> Mi verso es un ciervo herido
> Que busca en el monte amparo.
>
> Con los pobres de la tierra
> Quiero yo mi suerte echar
> El arrollo de la sierra
> Me complace más que el mar.
>
> [I am a sincere man,
> From where palm trees grow
> And before dying I wish to
> Free the verses in my soul.
>
> My verse is a light green
> And a bright red
> My verse is a wounded deer
> Who seeks shelter in the woods.
>
> With the poor people of the earth
> I want to share my fate
> The mountain creek
> Pleases me more than the sea.]

While visiting Camp Woodland that summer, the famous American folksinger Pete Seeger (b. 1919) heard the choir sing Angulo's version of "La Guantanamera." He enquired about the writer of the verses, whom he did not know, and was given a recording of the choir's performance. Later, the song entered Seeger's own repertoire and became one of his personal hits, especially after he sang it in concert at Carnegie Hall in New York City on 8 June 1963.

The philosophical universality of its new verses, together with its praise for the honesty and simplicity that should characterize humankind, brought "La Guantanamera" worldwide acclaim. Seeger sang it during his tour of several socialist countries in Europe, including the Soviet Union and Czechoslovakia, where the popular Czech singer Karel Gott adopted it, reinforcing the song's image as an emblem of progressive music coming out of revolutionary Cuba. "La Guantanamera" was added to the repertoires of many celebrated singers in the Latin world, in Anglo culture, and in the distant cultures of Europe. It has been popularized by diverse groups such as the Sandpipers in the United States, Los Cinco Latinos in Argentina, Marco Antonio Muñiz in Mexico, and Dámaso Pérez Prado's Orquesta in Cuba, among others.

Thus did Fernández's "Guajira Guantanamera" become richer over time due to the work of prestigious musicians who added the elements it needed to become a powerful emblem of the Cuban nation.

BIBLIOGRAPHY

Angulo, Héctor. Interview by Olavo Alén Rodríguez. Havana, 24 September 2010.

Carpentier, Alejo. *La música en Cuba*. [1945]. Havana: Editorial Luz-Hilo, 1961.

Díaz Ayala, Cristóbal. *Música cubana, del Areyto al Rap Cubano*. Miami: Ediciones Universal, 2003.

López, Oscar Luis. *La radio en Cuba*. Havana: Editorial Letras Cubanas, 2002.

GUANTÁNAMO

David C. Carlson

Cuba's southeastern-most province and, since 1902, site of a U.S. Navy base.

The name *Guantánamo* often brings to mind the U.S. naval installation on the Windward Passage between Cuba and Haiti—site of the prison for detainees from early twenty-first century U.S. wars in the Middle East and Central Asia—or perhaps the *guajira Guantanamera* chorus to the famous folk song dedicated to a Cuban countrywoman, but Guantánamo properly includes southeastern Cuba's broad and deep bay, a city of almost 250,000 inhabitants, and, since 1976, the mountainous southeastern province where the Caribbean Sea and Atlantic Ocean meet.

GEOGRAPHY

Guantánamo province is among the most diverse in Cuba, with a circum-Caribbean population that includes descendants of Spaniards, Africans, francophone and anglophone West Indians, and Haitians, as well as indigenous inhabitants. Some of Cuba's most pristine wilderness and most unusual flora and fauna are to be found in the Alejandro von Humboldt and UNESCO Biosphere Reserves in the Nipe-Sagua-Baracoa mountains. The predominantly agricultural economy is devoted to cultivation of coffee, cacao, bananas, and plantains, and less than 2 percent of Cuban sugar production. Valley (*cuenca*) soils surrounding Guantánamo Bay exhibit salinity damage from prolonged use of irrigation. The Cuban Ministry of the Revolutionary Armed Forces (MINFAR) maintains a security zone around the perimeter of the U.S. base installation at the lower part of the bay, contributing to a pronounced military presence. During much of the 1960s, the decade immediately following the Revolution, there was considerable tension and even shooting incidents with base guards, but in the late twentieth century there were regular, routine meetings between Cuban and North American personnel. The Cuban government insists on the return of the base area to its sovereignty, but as of 2010 the United States continued to occupy the post under the 1934 lease, which states that both parties must agree to alter arrangements.

Guantánamo's distinctiveness is rooted in geography and history. The farthest eastern end at the Punta Maisí forms a rugged peninsula of the Sagua-Baracoa Massif and the Sierra del Purial mountains. The northern coast around Baracoa and the Bay of Honey has the highest rainfall in Cuba and lush tropical vegetation. The southern Windward Passage, including the area surrounding the U.S. base, lies in a semi-desert arid rain shadow characterized by thorny scrub vegetation. In 1494 Christopher Columbus anchored in the sheltered bay during his second voyage. Baracoa is thought to be Cuba's oldest permanent settlement, dating to its 1511 foundation by Spaniards under Diego de Velásquez. It may be the oldest colonial city in the Américas; certainly it rivals settlements in Hispaniola with similar claims. Baracoa was for a long time very isolated, and the Guantánamo region as a whole remained a sparsely populated hinterland of Santiago de Cuba throughout the colonial period. During the age of sail, ships of all kinds—including pirate ships—put into the bay for careening and to obtain salt to preserve food during voyages. Much of modern-day Cuba's sea salt production emanates from Caimanera and Boquerón inside the bay.

COLONIZATION

The mountainous regions of Tiguabos and Yateras have a population of Taíno descendents. Since Bartolomé de las Casas in the sixteenth century, Cuba's own indigenous peoples have been commonly understood to be entirely extinct. Certainly the chief Hatuey led fierce Arawak resistance against the Spanish before his capture and execution. From July to December

■ *See also*

Governance and Contestation: Insurrection, 1952–1959

Platt Amendment

Race: Racial Issues during the Transition to Independence

Rafter Crisis: 1994

Spanish-American-Cuban War: 1898

Map showing location of U.S. naval base Guantánamo Bay.

1741, during the War of Jenkins's Ear—one of a series of Anglo-French-Spanish wars in the eighteenth century—a British invading force from Jamaica led by Vice-Admiral Edward Vernon (1684–1757) and General Thomas Wentworth landed in Guantánamo Bay (anglicized as *Walthenham*) after being repulsed from Cartagena de Indias on the coast of South America in May.

The British intended to march overland against the powerful fortress that defended Santiago de Cuba, seize that strategic port, and use it as base of operations to conquer the rest of Cuba, or hive off the island's eastern end to control the Windward Passage. Santiago's governor, Francisco Caxigal de la Vega (b. 1715), the garrison commander Carlos Riva Agüero, and regional militia composed of white and mixed-race settlers, free blacks and mulatos, and Indians commanded by Pedro Guerra from the *hato* (ranch land grant) of Guantánamo and Marcos Pérez from the village San Anselmo de Tiguabos, fell back into the interior from whence they launched ambushes and surprise raids against the English camps. When the British sick list grew to more than 2,000 soldiers and sailors—half the total invasion force—they abandoned the bogged-down campaign. At this early date there was mention of a village, Santa Catalina, at the rapids and waterfalls—*saltadero*—of the Guaso River. In time, the crown militia became a paramilitary force to track fugitive runaway slaves—known as *cimarrones*—who fled into the Sagua-Baracoa mountains.

The wars of the Haitian Revolution (1791–1804) led to the immigration of several thousand French colonists from Saint-Domingue and Spanish Creoles from Santo Domingo to Cuba. The majority of this cohort of migrants settled around Santiago de Cuba, between El Cobre and Santa Catalina, where there were many coffee plantations of the model abandoned in nearby Haiti. Archaeological sites of 117 early nineteenth-century coffee farms scattered across the mountainous uplands of the Sierra Maestra to Tiguabos and Yateras in Guantánamo are in the early 2000s a UNESCO World Heritage site and part of the project to record the transatlantic slave trade and the African diaspora in the New World. The infusion of francophone migrants amid the earlier Creole population transformed the culture of Cuba's southeast. Travelers reported that French and a Haitian *krèyol* were spoken by planters and slaves. The region's geographic isolation meant that slaves often ran away and formed fugitive settlements (*palenques*) in the mountains. Militia patrols—often staffed by mestizos, mulattos, and free blacks—attempted to suppress this slave resistance, which approached a continuous battle between 1815 and 1838. Archaeological surveys have limned four concentrations of *palenques*: the Sierra Maestra south of Bayamo, the uplands near Mayarí, the rugged mountains between Santiago de Cuba and Guantánamo, and—by far the largest—between Guantánamo and Baracoa.

Santa Catalina del Saltadero was officially founded the same year (1819) as Cienfuegos, which derived some settlers from French Louisiana and

Spanish Florida after their cession to the United States by the Adams-Onís Treaty. Both Cuban settlements commanded bays as strategic and commercial outlets. By 1857 the Havana- and Santiago de Cuba–based English merchant house Brooks and Company had built the region's first railway, connecting Santa Catalina to Caimanera on the bay, and steamer service to Santiago de Cuba. As a result, the slave-cultivated sugar and coffee production of the region grew in the 1860s as an enclave economy attached to Santiago and primarily Catalan merchant firms via Guantánamo Bay. In 1870 Santa Catalina was officially renamed Guantánamo and the city adopted a coat of arms emblazoned with a beehive at the confluence of two rivers framed by sugar cane, coffee trees, and tobacco. Guantánamo City outgrew Baracoa, and by the 1860s its environs had the highest per capita ratio of slaves of any eastern Cuban district.

When Cuba's first war of independence (1868–1878) broke out, proindependence advocates likened Guantánamo to a *little Spain* due to the planters' loyalty to the colonial metropolis. Regional militia ejected separatists from the district. In 1871 the Liberation army generals Máximo Gómez (1836–1906) and Antonio Maceo (1845–1896), whose plans to carry the anticolonial rebellion into western Cuba had been frustrated by lack of supplies and internal opposition within the separatist leadership, led an invasion of the Guantánamo region. During the remainder of the Ten Years' War and the successive Little War (1879–1880) desultory fighting destroyed much of the coffee production in the district, though the sugar sector on the plain around the bay was better protected from insurgent depredations. Years of anticolonial conflict destabilized the slave system, and endemic banditry arose in the region.

INDEPENDENCE

In 1895 the War of Independence began with simultaneous risings in Guantánamo and other eastern locales. During the war Pedro Agustín Pérez—scion of the family that historically had commanded the pro-Spanish militia—led local separatists. The remoteness of Guantánamo made it ideal as entry point for prominent separatist exile leaders. Maceo and Flor Crombet (1850–1895) landed at Duaba in Baracoa and moved inland under constant pursuit. José Martí (1853–1895) and Gómez landed at Cajobabo near the Punta de Maisí on the southeastern coast. Martí died in battle 19 May 1895 near Bayamo, but Gómez and Maceo managed to organize a rebel column to invade western Cuba in October. The *mambí* army subjected many sugar mills in Guantánamo to payment of war taxes, but most remained under Spanish control throughout the war. In 1896 Spanish forces carried out *reconcentración*, their population-removal counterinsurgency strategy in the district.

During the War of 1898 a small U.S. naval flotilla commanded by Captain Bowman McCalla (1844–1910) bombarded Spanish positions in Guantánamo Bay and cut the transatlantic cable as part of blockade operations. Two Cuban officers joined the North Americans and established communications, apprising them of the disposition of Cuban and Spanish forces in the district. On 9 and 10 June 1898 the first marine battalion landed on the eastern shore of the bay and fought skirmishes with Spanish troops. Cubans cooperated in these operations. The U.S. Navy established a safe harbor that was used as a coaling station throughout the summer of 1898 and as the base of operations for the U.S. invasion of Puerto Rico in July. When the war's focus shifted to Santiago de Cuba and its immediate environs after the landing of the U.S. Army Fifth Corps at Daquirí and Siboney, Guantánamo was relegated to a peripheral role, but the effects of *reconcentración*, combined with the wartime blockade, and epidemic disease outbreaks led to the deaths of approximately 10 percent of the region's population from disease and malnutrition in July and August 1898.

THE U.S. NAVAL BASE AND OFF-SHORE PRISON

After the U.S. occupation of Cuba (1899–1902) ended with the imposition of the Platt Amendment and de facto protectorate status mediating effective sovereignty, the presidential administrations of Theodore Roosevelt (1858–1919) and Tomás Estrada Palma (1832–1908), signatories to the Permanent Treaty, established the peculiar lease agreement for the U.S. installation at Guantánamo Bay. U.S. strategists wanted to establish permanent naval bases and stations in the Caribbean as part of the "navy second to none" project, particularly with the acquisition of Panamá and the building of the interoceanic canal, which lay some 800 nautical miles from Guantánamo. In 1912, during peasant unrest and the uprising of the black Cuban political party, the Independientes de Color, political and racial violence accompanied by massacres in rural areas of Oriente jarred the Guantánamo region. U.S. marines dispatched from the base occupied Caimanera, Guantánamo City, several U.S.-owned sugar mills, and the railway links in the basin surrounding the bay. After the 1933 revolution overthrew the authoritarian president Gerardo Machado, abrogating the Platt Amendment, the Cuban government and the United States updated the lease agreement in a 1934 treaty. The terms called for full U.S. jurisdiction and control of the base area, which can be terminated only by consensus of the two nations, and in lieu of the original yearly payment of $2,000 in gold, an annual rent check of $4,085 issued by the U.S. Treasury. The Cuban government has refused to cash the checks since the revolution because it insists on the return of the base area.

The U.S. base—the oldest on foreign soil, and thus the first in the postwar "empire of bases" worldwide—covers an area of 45.4 square miles (117.6 sq km). It underwent considerable development and

U.S. Naval Station Guantánamo Bay (GTMO). GTMO is the oldest U.S. base on foreign soil and thus the first in the postwar "empire of bases" worldwide. The base covers an area of 45.4 square miles, shown on the map in pink.

© MAPS.COM/CORBIS

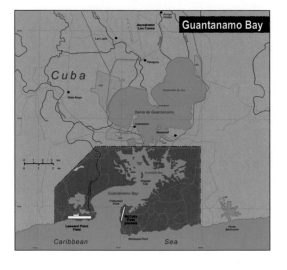

expansion during World War II—when the Caribbean was a theater of the Battle of the Atlantic—along with bases in Panamá, Roosevelt Roads in Puerto Rico, and Trinidad, and again later during the Korean War, because the bay boasts excellent harbors and other naval advantages in the strategically important Windward Passage. A substantial economy servicing the base arose in Caimanera and Guantánamo, and West Indians and Haitians migrated to the district to work alongside Cubans on sugar mills and as base workers. Prostitution drew women bereft of job and educational opportunities from Cuba's impoverished eastern province, and large red-light districts developed in Caimanera and Guantánamo. The infusion of West Indians into the established Creole and French society, combined with North American influence and Haitian *bracero* (temporary worker) communities, gave Guantánamo a pronounced pan-Caribbean culture. In the early 2000s there are cultural associations that reflect this diversity.

During the Cuban revolutionary struggle against the Fulgencio Batista (1901–1973) regime in the 1950s, the U.S. possession of the base at Guantánamo Bay came under opposition scrutiny and debate because it symbolized U.S. military and institutional ties with the Cuban armed forces. There was considerable subversive activity at Guantánamo, including theft of equipment from the base, and some dependents of U.S. personnel joined the Cuban rebels. By 1958 Raúl Castro commanded the Frank País Second Front that extended the armed guerrilla movement into the Sierra de Cristal. M26 rebels, subjected to air strikes that threatened to distance rural supporters from the guerrillas by U.S-equipped Cuban pilots, abducted North American citizens, sailors, and marines as so-called human shields to inhibit or halt aerial bombardment. This *Operación Antiaerea* ended diplomatically with the intercession of Fidel Castro and U.S. State Department officials. After Batista's ousting and the consolidation of the revolutionary

government, the U.S. base was the site of several provocations during the deterioration of U.S. and Cuban relations, particularly in the lead up to and aftermath of the April 1961 Bay of Pigs/Playa Girón invasion and the October 1962 Missile Crisis. In 1964 Cuba cut off potable water supplies to the base from the Yateras River and demanded return of the territory to national sovereignty.

Since the Cuban Revolution social indices have improved, but Guantánamo has remained the island's poorest region through 2010. Many *guantanameros* have migrated in search of better prospects. Tensions between the base and the surrounding area have eased since Cold War–era military exercises and support operations ended there.

GTMO, as the Guantánamo base is called, has been used during U.S. military operations in the Caribbean and also for housing refugees. After the Haitian military overthrew Jean Bertrand Aristide (b. 1953; pres. 1990–1991, 1994–1996, 2001–2004) in 1991, thousands of Haitians fled in small boats. By February 1992 more than 12,500 refugees picked up at sea by the U.S. Coast Guard were living in a tent city at the GTMO base. (George H. W. Bush's EO 12807 later ordered that Haitians rescued on the high seas be returned to Haiti.) When U.S. Operation Uphold Democracy (1994) restored Aristide to power temporarily, GTMO served as a forward base and continued to house 21,638 Haitians and up to 32,780 Cuban rafters (*balseros*) picked up by the U.S. Coast Guard and Navy during the immigration crisis of 1994 to 1995.

In the aftermath of 11 September 2001, in 2002 the GTMO base became an offshore prison for captives from U.S. foreign wars and counterterrorism operations. The presidential administration of George W. Bush (b. 1946; pres. 2001–2009) selected Guantánamo Bay to house the prisoners—termed *illegal combatants* in order to deny them Geneva Convention protections—in the belief that the lack of official relations between Cuba and the United States and the unique base lease agreement rendered the area a legal black hole where neither U.S. laws and regulations nor Cuban sovereignty or oversight applied. By 2003 up to 660 detainees were housed at small prison facilities built at Guantánamo and manned by Joint Task Force Guantanamo personnel. Court cases eroded the administration's contentions that GTMO was an exclusionary zone not subject to national and international laws: In *Rasul v. Bush* (2004) the Supreme Court dismissed arguments that the base lay beyond U.S. law; *Hamdan v. Rumsfeld* (2006) ruled that the executive branch could not try captives in military commissions (whereupon the U.S. Congress passed the Military Commissions Act, which essentially provided that power to the administration); *Boumediene v. Bush* (2008) held that the detainees had rights to some habeas corpus protections given that the base is effectively controlled by the United States. President

Barack Obama (b. 1961; pres. 2009–) pledged to close the GTMO base's prison facilities and transfer the detainees to the United States, but as of November 2010 it had not occurred.

GUANTÁNAMO CULTURE

Guantánamo has figured prominently in Cuban cinema as a quasi-mythological source of origins, as in Tomás Gutiérrez Alea's east-to-west road-trip film *Guantanamera* (1994) and Humberto Solás's west-to-east *Miel para Ochun* (2001, Honey for Ochun), which ends in Baracoa. Guantánamo has been home to several prominent Cubans, including athletes and musicians, and to distinctive rhythms, dance styles, and cultural forms such as the *son changüí* and *tumba francesa*. As of 2010, urban Guantánamo preserved an architectural heritage of some late-nineteenth-century houses and commercial buildings; an early twentieth-century public market; the Salcines Palace, surmounted by Italian sculptor Américo Chini's statue *La Fama* (a popular informal symbol of the city); Casa de la Trova and Casa de Cultura; and the Cosmonaut Hall, which houses the reentry capsule from the 1980 Soyuz 38 space mission manned by the *guantanamero* cosmonaut Arnaldo Tamayo (b. 1942), the first Latin American, Caribbean, Cuban, and person of salient African ancestry launched into space.

BIBLIOGRAPHY

Alonso Coma, Ismael. *Historia de Guantánamo: El camino hacia la plantación, 1494–1842*. Guantánamo, Cuba: Editorial El Mar y la Montaña, 2009.

Barreiro, José. "Survival Stories." In *The Cuba Reader: History, Culture, Politics*, edited by Aviva Chomsky, Barry Carr, and Pamela María Smorkaloff. Durham, NC: Duke University Press, 2003.

Boti Barreiro, Regino Eladio. *Guantánamo: Breves apuntes acerca de los orígenes y fundación de esta ciudad*. Santiago de Cuba: Editorial Oriente, 1985.

Carlson, David C. "In the Fist of Earlier Revolutions: Postemancipation Social Control and State Formation in Guantánamo, Cuba, 1868–1902." Ph.D. diss., University of North Carolina at Chapel Hill, 2007.

Cruz Ríos, Laura. *Flujos inmigratorios franceses a Santiago de Cuba*. Santiago de Cuba: Editorial Santiago de Cuba, 2006.

Gott, Richard. *Cuba: A New History*. New Haven, CT: Yale University Press, 2004.

Hazard, Samuel. *Cuba with Pen and Pencil*. 1870. Reprint, Oxford, U.K.: Signal Books, 2007.

La Rosa Corzo, Gabino. *Runaway Slave Settlements in Cuba: Resistance and Repression*. Translated by Mary Todd. Chapel Hill: University of North Carolina Press, 2003.

Lipman, Jana K. *Guantánamo: A Working-class History between Empire and Revolution*. Berkeley: University of California Press, 2009.

Miranda Bravo, Olga. *Vecinos indeseables: La base naval de Guantánamo*. 2nd ed. Havana: Editorial de Ciencias Sociales, 2008.

Portuondo Zúñiga, Olga. *Una derrota británica en Cuba*. Santiago de Cuba: Editorial Oriente, 2000.

Sánchez Guerra, José. *El azúcar en el valle de los ingenios guantanameros*. Guantánamo, Cuba: Editorial El Mar y la Montaña, 2003.

Schwab, Stephen Irving Max. *Guantánamo, USA: The Untold History of America's Cuban Outpost*. Lawrence: University Press of Kansas, 2009.

Worthington, Andy. *The Guantánamo Files: The Stories of the 774 Detainees in America's Illegal Prison*. London: Pluto Press, 2007.

GUERRILLERO HEROICO (ALBERTO KORDA)

Alan West-Durán

A brief cultural history of a famous revolutionary photo.

Few images have attained the universal recognition and dissemination of Alberto Korda's photo of Ernesto "Che" Guevara. As an emblem of Cuba and its revolution, the photo is unparalleled in its ability to communicate so much to so many. Emblazoned on flags, banners, T-shirts, book covers, posters, even sneakers and bathing suits, the image of the *Guerrillero Heroico* (Heroic Guerrilla) has become a ubiquitous and richly layered symbol to millions around the world. To say the Korda photo and its subsequent re-elaboration, reframing, and sometimes distortion is instantly identifiable still begs the question of what the image signifies.

CHE: A COMPLEX SYMBOL WITH DIVERGENT MEANINGS

To many, the Che of this image is a symbol of defiance and rebellion, the face of a hopeful warrior of change, a man who gave up a comfortable middle-class existence to become a revolutionary, a relentless fighter for justice who overcame the physical limitations of his asthma to become a guerrilla, fighting a brutal and corrupt dictatorship, and then after assuming power relinquishing the privileges of a top government figure to join wars of liberation in Africa and Latin America, ultimately giving his life in Bolivia. This Che is the daring romantic, the radical prince of the poor and downtrodden, the utopian visionary, the believer in selfless devotion to a cause that will change the world.

To others, Che means something else: He is an apostle of violence, who led many astray in seeking social change through bloodshed that caused the deaths of many thousands; a ruthless Communist who did not flinch in suppressing any kind of political opposition, a purveyor of totalitarian beliefs.

■ *See also*

Che Guevara and the New Man

Che Guevara, Social and Political Thought

Governance and Contestation: Insurrection, 1952–1959

Governance and Contestation: The Cuban Revolution

Visual Arts: Photography

Visual Arts: Revolutionary Period

Guevara was the special prosecutor overseeing the trials and executions of the worst human rights offenders of the Batista regime. Between eight hundred and five thousand men were judged and executed, earning Che the moniker Butcher of La Cabaña, the colonial fort where he was headquartered. These trials were popular among Cubans, but the international outcry forced the Cuban government to stop them.

To his detractors, Che is the architect who took the island from neo-colony of the United States to client state of the Soviet Union, thus trading one form of dependency for another. He is the reckless guerrilla adventurer who did not heed the advice from his own book *Guerrilla Warfare* (1960) and bungled attempts in the Congo and Bolivia, wasting resources and lives, including his own. In addition, he is the government minister who engineered Cuba's rapprochement with the Soviet Union and with it economic policies that have haunted Cuba into the twenty-first century: an over-centralized centrally planned economy that is inefficient and leads to rationing. Some argue that Guevara's emphasis on "moral incentives" and the creation of the "New Man" from his essay "Man and Socialism in Cuba"—both noble goals—left a legacy of workers who feel little incentive to produce when there is no material compensation for their efforts. His critics point out he was the inspiration for the revolutionary offensive of 1968 that completely abolished small business and private property, and only in the 1990s were attempts made to correct the overzealous role of the state in the economy.

The reality, as always, is somewhere between these two, and the Korda photo is both a template and a warning of what human beings bring to certain images that can represent their deepest desires, fears, and dreams. These opposed views alert all people to how images can be decontextualized and manipulated and serve as a wider warning for how post-1959 Cuba can be misinterpreted or misunderstood, willfully or not. For those who see Che as a champion for justice, equality, and the rights of the poor, Korda's photo fulfills an element of hero worship that every society creates through historical narratives, superhero figures, or athletes. Conversely, to those who despise him, Che represents the perfect villain, where all that has gone wrong in Cuba can be apportioned to an image.

THE STORY BEHIND THE IMAGE

But why this photo of Che? Certainly there are many shots of Che that reveal his qualities: the guerrilla fighter on a horse in the Escambray mountains, with his beret, rifle on the shoulder, and trademark cigar (1958); the wounded Che in front of a tank during the battle of Santa Clara (1958); a smiling and engaged Che during press conferences in Havana post-1959; his appearance before students where he seems to have an aura about him captured admirably by Chinolope (1962); or his U.N. speech in 1964, statesmanlike, a bearded Cary Grant in fatigues. All of them show

his youth, vitality, movie-star good looks, and revolutionary fervor, but none has achieved the afterlife of Korda's *Guerrillero Heroico*.

It is unlikely, however, that Korda's image would have resonated so deeply if another Che photo had not been circulated: the Freddy Alborta (1932–2005) photo taken in Vallegrande Hospital, Bolivia, after Che's death, his eyes open, Christ-like, which English writer John Berger compared to Andrea Mantegna's *Lamentation over the Dead Christ* (1506). Here, the physical resemblance of Che to Jesus, both martyrs to a cause, merges into an ideal of Che that became known as Chesucristo, and retrospectively begins placing Korda's photo in a timeless realm. One could argue that Korda's shot was prophetic, that one can already see in Che's eyes his own martyrdom some seven and a half years later.

Guerrillero Heroico was shot on 5 March 1960 by Alberto Díaz Gutiérrez (1928–2001), who went by the name of Korda. The picture was part of his coverage of a memorial to the victims of the *La Coubre* explosion, in which a French ship carrying Belgian arms to Cuba had exploded in Havana harbor, killing some seventy-five people. Che attended the memorial service, where Jean-Paul Sartre and Simone de Beauvoir were also present. As Fidel spoke, Che briefly came to the dais, where Korda took two quick shots. One was unusable because the top of someone's head appears over Che's right shoulder, the other needed to be cropped for full effect.

The usable shot has the profile of a man on the left and a small palm tree on the right. The cropped sides of the image are telling and reveal something about Che's past, present, and future. The man on the left was Jorge Ricardo Masetti (1929–1964), an Argentine enchanted by Cuba's revolution, who first interviewed Che in the Sierra Maestra during the revolutionary war against Batista, stayed on, and became one of the founders of Prensa Latina, the news agency founded after Fidel's takeover. Masetti, under direct supervision from Che, helped start a guerrilla *foco* (insurrectionary nucleus) in Argentina in 1964, which was ill-executed and ended in the guerrillas' defeat and Masetti's death. Masetti's son, Jorge, became a spy and counter-intelligence agent for Cuban state security, performing his duties in Latin America and Angola. He was married to the daughter of Tony de la Guardia, who was executed during the Ochoa Trial of 1989, and subsequently fled to Paris, where he published *El furor y el delirio* (1999), a tell-all tale of his experiences that contains damaging accusations about Cuba's clandestine foreign policy. In Paris he worked with Canek Sánchez Guevara (b. 1974), Che's grandson and a heavy metal musician, debunking the myth of his grandfather.

The right side of the photo (with the palm tree) betrays a tropical environment, a reminder of Che's guerrilla days in the Sierra. The palm tree is of course the national tree of Cuba, symbolic of Che's adopted homeland. In the middle of a cloudy, indistinct day, almost as if he were floating in space, Che's look is stern. According to Korda, Guevara was understandably angry, determined and resolute in his outrage and desire to avenge those who died from this heinous act. Korda rightfully saw there was no news value to the image, but good fashion photographer that he was, he knew that he had captured something special: the defiant look, the steely determination, the flowing hair joining with his beard that looks like the mane of a lion, the sleek look of his bomber jacket, the ever-present beret with the star.

THE AFTERLIFE OF THE IMAGE

For years Korda told a story about the image languishing in oblivion until Italian publisher Giangiacomo Feltrinelli (1926–1972) was given two prints of the photo in 1967 and then made a fortune reprinting it throughout the world, first in poster format. But Ziff and others have proven the image was already used in the Cuban press by April 1961 and that Korda often gave prints of the photo to friends and intellectuals he met when they came to Cuba. *Paris Match* published the photo in August 1967, and Irish artist Jim Fitzpatrick admits to using the image for posters he designed before Che's death as well.

At any rate, Che's death (9 October 1967) certainly propelled the dissemination of the image globally, through Feltrinelli himself (who used the image on the cover of *The Bolivian Diary*, which came out in 1968 and to which he owned the world rights) and via Fidel Castro's speech of 18 October 1967 at the Plaza de la Revolución, where over one million Cubans heard him give the sad news of Che's death to the backdrop of a forty-foot banner of Korda's image turned into a two-toned giant poster. The use of Korda's shot for Fidel's speech should indicate that the Cuban government knew this image would someday have enormous political value. From there it became one of the most widely displayed images for revolutionary movements, used in the colorful posters produced by the Havana-based Organización de Solidaridad con los Pueblos de Asia, África y América Latina, better known as OSPAAL (founded in 1966; Organization of Solidarity with the Peoples of Africa, Asia, and Latin America), as well as for the covers of its magazine *Tricontinental*.

By 1968 Che's image could be seen on the streets of Berkeley, Berlin, Paris, Tokyo, Mexico City, Accra, Lagos, Santiago, and even swinging London, competing with images of the Beatles. It was an image that fit into the times: counterculture revolt, hip manifestations of rebellion, new attitudes toward sexuality and marriage, exploration of new forms of spirituality, a questioning of authority, new movements for black and women's liberation. But even those who wore Che T-shirts for overtly political reasons, particularly in the West, had little idea of the sacrifices Che made for

his ideals in terms of family life, health, and material comforts.

CHE RECYCLED AND TURNED INTO POP BRANDING

By the late 1960s Che's image was being used for posters and paintings. The Cuban artist who was probably most responsible for bringing Che into a pop idiom was Raúl Martínez (1927–1995), an abstract painter before the revolution, but later best known for his tropical pop version of the *Lucía* (1968) film poster. Martínez depicted Che in collective portraits that dealt with the revolution but also as sole subject, availing himself of the Warholian technique of repeating (and varying) a sole image (as was done with Marilyn Monroe, Jackie Kennedy, and Mao). By introducing Che as a pop image done with beautifully bright colors and with an edge of playfulness, but always respectful of Che's political significance, Martínez certainly paved the way for the pop dissemination of Che in the 1970s and beyond, and for his commodification as well.

Guerrillero heroico. This portrait of Ernesto "Che" Guevara, shot in 1960 by Cuban photographer Alberto Korda, has become one of the most iconic images of the twentieth century. © 2011 ARTISTS RIGHTS SOCIETY (ARS), NEW YORK/ADAGP, PARIS. © BANQUE D'IMAGES, ADAGP/ART RESOURCE, NY.

Beginning in the 1970s and 1980s, decades characterized by a waning of the revolutionary spirit, Che's image was used more irreverently. Korda's Che appeared with a pie on his face on the cover of *National Lampoon* magazine (January 1972), with Mickey Mouse ears, and superimposed on Liberace's ornate clothes and ringed hands (2002), with the caption "A Revolution in Rhinestones." Other uses were more confrontational, like Oleg Atbashian's depiction of Che's face as a skull with the hair and the beret intact, with the caption "Che Is Dead—Get Over It!"

Aside from the photo's more traditional use on T-shirts, banners, and berets, Che started to become a brand image, appearing on lighters, cigarette boxes, mouse pads, clocks, handbags, ice cream, wine, beer, a rum-and-cola mix, condoms, bathing suits, and even Smirnoff's vodka. The latter ad prompted a lawsuit by Korda in which he won $50,000 in damages, which he donated to the Cuban health-care system.

THE COMMODIFICATION OF CHE AND ULTIMATE LEGACY

Che as commodity or brand image raises important questions about politics, art, and commerce. Most visitors see Che images everywhere in the early 2000s in Cuba, from T-shirts to ash trays to murals and photos on school walls. He is still the quintessential image of the revolution, now over a half century old. As Michael Casey observes, one of the beauties of branding is that different people bring different meanings to a brand: to one person, Che could mean hip rebellion, to another a figure of defiance faced with the inequities of globalized capitalism, to yet another a symbol of hope and change.

For Cuba's aging revolution, Che's eternal visage of youth is a ubiquitous reminder of the revolutionary ardor, passion, and youth of the 1960s, the so-called golden years of the Revolution. Since he has long passed, it is easier to disconnect Che from the current policies and realities of the Cuban regime. This can cut both ways, however, as his utopian vision makes a stark contrast to the current pattern of shortages, erratic food supply, and collapsing infrastructure. Because he was from Argentina but fought in Guatemala, Cuba, the Congo, and Bolivia, it is natural to give Che a pan-Latin or even global significance. And yet he remains undeniably tethered to Cuba, invoked daily by Cuban schoolchildren as part of their revolutionary pledge of allegiance, his ever-present portrait hanging in schools, factories, and offices.

That Che continues to fascinate people more than forty years after his death is obvious from the fact that several motion pictures were made about him in the first decade of the 2000s, the best being the *Motorcycle Diaries* (2004), by Walter Salles Jr., and *Che* (2008), by Steven Soderbergh. Interestingly, none of the films focuses on Che as minister or governmental official, his role in Cuba from 1959 to 1964.

Jean-Paul Sartre (1905–1980) once said that Che was "the most complete man of our age" (Löwy p. xxxi). Does Korda's Che capture in a photograph the "New Man" Che hoped the revolution would create? And what exactly does Sartre mean by the compliment—that Che was able to bridge the gap between the intellectual and the man of action; that he was the seamless synthesis of theory and practice; that he was a unique fusion of compassion, indomitable will, and selfless sacrifice?

Is Che a martyr? In religious terms, martyrs are those who bear witness to the truth of their faith. What truth did Che witness and why did it kill him? Or is Che a martyr in the way that Albert Camus (1913–1960) wrote: "Martyrs, my friend, have to choose between being forgotten, mocked or used. As for being understood: never." It does not seem likely that Che will be forgotten. Mocked and used, undoubtedly (Camus quoted in Casey p. 110). As future generations face the terrible consequences of economic or environmental devastation, the harsh realities of oppression, misery, and disease, and the prickly dilemmas of power and how it can shatter lives, the image of Che will offer to many the hope that people can change their world and live their lives with dignity.

BIBLIOGRAPHY

Anderson, Jon Lee. *Che Guevara: A Revolutionary Life*. New York: Grove Press, 1997.

Casey, Michael. *Che's Afterlife: The Legacy of an Image*. New York: Vintage Books, 2009.

Guevara, Ernesto. *Che Guevara Reader: Writings on Politics and Revolution*, 2nd ed., edited by David Deutschmann. New York: Ocean Press, 2003.

Löwy, Michael. *The Marxism of Che Guevara: Philosophy, Economics, Revolutionary Warfare*. 2nd ed. Lanham, MD: Rowman & Littlefield, 2007.

Ziff, Trisha, ed. *Che Guevara: Revolutionary and Icon*. New York: Abrams Image, 2006.

H

HAVANA

The personality of the city of Havana is portrayed in a diversity of themes. It was a main port of call in Hispanic Atlantic commerce within the Americas and the administrative center of the plantation economy, at a time when it was the crossroads between Europe, the Far East, and North and South America, bringing together many ethnic groups.

Art from the time the English held Havana provides a realistic vision of the city, including the works of local artisans. The European contra dance prevailed at the city's dances, accompanied by orchestras of blacks and mulattos. In this way, the nation soon became criollo, *then Cuban. The nineteenth century brought the* habanera *musical genre, as well as opera and zarzuela. A vibrant theater and ballet culture later emerged.*

Havana's urban culture evolved; it expanded into a contemporary and cosmopolitan city, with a landscape featuring the landmark fortresses of El Morro and Cabaña. As the wealthy moved west, the common people expanded in all other directions. A mix of different architectural types and styles appeared in new developments: Neoclassical, Catalan Modernism; Beaux Arts Eclecticism, Art Deco, and the Modern Movement.

In the twentieth century, Havana came under U.S. influence. Middle and upper classes from the United States flocked to the district of El Vedado in east Havana, bringing a rise in movie theaters, luxury hotels, cabarets, and casinos where wealthy Cubans and foreigners were entertained. The telephone, radio, television, and other forms of technology appeared.

Plans for new popular housing and the eradication of unsanitary neighborhoods took into account sociocultural concerns. Emigration patterns changed, and religion was recognized and blended into cultural, musical, dance, and oral traditions. The 1990s saw investment in tourism, condominiums for foreigners, and commerce.

HAVANA: ARCHITECTURAL DEVELOPMENT AND CITY PLANNING

Mario Coyula-Cowley

Architecture and city planning of Havana in the nineteenth and twentieth centuries.

In its evolution up to the mid-twentieth century, Havana was initially more Spanish in composition and character. It was increasingly influenced later by the United States and also more modern than most other important Latin American cities. Prior to the Revolution, Havana was essentially a European city settled in the Caribbean. Its silhouette, rhythm, urban texture, and scale were distinctive. With few changes, the urban center had narrow streets with small, compact blocks; low buildings with high ceilings; partition walls; and narrow, deep lots that meant a large number of facades facing the street. An extensive lower-middle class gave form to the city, following the spirit of petit-bourgeois decorum. Its growth

449

CHRONOLOGY OF EVENTS

1791: Construction is completed on two emblematic buildings, the Palacio del Gobernador (Governor's Palace) and the Palacio del Segundo Cabo (Second Lieutenant's Palace) in the Plaza de Armas.

1797: Construction of the city's walls is completed.

1806: Espada Cemetery opens. It is the first disposal place for the dead in Latin America lying outside church buildings and is also the first neoclassical work in Cuba.

1819: Regular steamship service between Havana and Matanzas starts. It is the first in Latin America.

1827: The population outside the city walls exceeds that inside the walls.

1827–1840: A program of urban reform in Havana is carried out.

1830: Construction inside the safety zone of La Muralla is authorized.

1833: A cholera epidemic strikes Havana; there are 8,000 deaths in three months. Leading families begin to settle in El Cerro.

1836: The Fernando VII aqueduct is completed.

1837: A rail line is opened between Havana and Bejucal. It is the first in Latin America and seventh in the world. Tacón Boulevard is opened. Ferry service between Havana and Regla begins. This is the peak year for the importation of slaves.

1847–1860: Forty-eight thousand Chinese coolies enter Cuba as a substitute for African slaves.

1848: Public gas lighting is installed.

1849–1850: Antonio Meucci invents the telephone in Havana's Teatro Tacón. The Havana Expansion Plan is drafted by Mariano Carrillo de Albornoz. Havana reaches Galiano, covering 1.56 square miles (4 sq km) with 140,000 inhabitants.

1851: Telegraph service commences.

1859: Luis Yboleón's El Carmelo urban development plan is introduced.

1860: The El Vedado urban development begins, following the same design as El Carmelo.

1861: A new building code is implemented that stands until 1963. Francisco de Albear proposes a malecón (jetty) that would run from La Punta to Belascoaín.

1862: A horse-drawn omnibus service is initiated. The population outside the city walls is twice the size of that inside the walls.

1863: Demolition of the city walls begins. Havana-Marianao railway begins running.

1864: Recreational bathing pools open along El Vedado coastline.

1868: El Grito de Yara (The Cry of Yara) marks the beginning of the Ten Years' War.

1869: A telegraph between Havana and Key West is opened; it is the first international line in the world.

1870: The Moret Law, a free-womb statute, liberates the children of slaves. Havana reaches Belascoaín, covering 2.73 square miles (7 sq km) with a population of 170,000.

1874: Francisco de Albear makes the first topographical map of Havana and proposes a suburb with octagonal blocks like Barcelona's Cerdà Plan.

1879–1880: The Little War is fought.

1881: Telephone service starts in Havana.

1883: The urban development of Medina starts, as an expansion of El Vedado.

1889: Electric street lighting, the first in Latin America, is introduced.

1890: Havana reaches Infanta, covering 3.9 square miles (10 sq km) with 200,000 inhabitants.

1893: Francisco de Albear's aqueduct, a masterwork of Cuban engineering, is inaugurated.

1895–1898: The War of Independence is fought.

1896: Spanish captain-general Valeriano Weyler issues the Edict of Reconcentration, which forces more than 300,000 peasants to move into cities and towns to cut off their support to insurgents. About 100,000 die of hunger and disease.

1897: The first Cuban film, one minute long, is shown.

1898: The United States offers to purchase Cuba from Spain. The U.S. battleship *Maine* explodes in the Bay of Havana; the United States enters into war with Spain, which is defeated. A peace treaty is signed between the two countries without participation of the Cuban Liberating Army. The first U.S. intervention in Cuba begins. A Parisienne car built in France is the first automobile introduced in Cuba. Havana, including satellite towns, has 253,011 inhabitants.

1900: Cuban Fencer Ramón Fonst is the first Latin American Olympic champion.

was by addition, without major demolitions of the core built stock. All of this contributed to the city's rich mixture of styles and periods and to its specific urban image. In the twentieth century, the city began to relate to the sea when the Malecón—its iconic, S-shaped coastal avenue of a little more than four miles—was built.

URBAN AND ARCHITECTURAL TYPOLOGY IN THE NINETEENTH CENTURY

The focus of colonial-era buildings was the patio—positioned to one side and elongated in low-income homes, and centrally situated and surrounded by wide galleries with double-height ceilings in upper-class houses. This model of columned galleries extended to porches facing the plazas, which projected over the public space like a roofed continuation of the access streets. The predominant architecture was baroque from the end of the eighteenth century into the early decades of the nineteenth, followed by neoclassical style. Both were very restrained. The neogothic style was less widespread; some examples of it appeared toward the middle of the nineteenth century, almost all of them religious in nature. Beginning in the second half of the eighteenth century, the city expanded beyond its defensive walls, which were already obsolete when they were finished in 1797. Their demolition began in 1863.

Havana Expands: El Cerro Starting in the first third of the nineteenth century, white *criollo* families of local nobility began to move southwest to El Cerro. There, a new type of residence emerged, the *casa-quinta*, or neoclassical villa with gardens. The rise, apogee, and decline of El Cerro all occurred during the

1901: Construction begins on the Malecón, which will reach Calle Crespo the following year. The first electric streetcar in Latin America is introduced.

1902: The U.S. intervention ends; the first Cuban government takes power.

1902–1912: Official records show that 660,958 immigrants arrived in Cuba, 68 percent of them European.

1904: A count finds 2,839 rooming houses in Havana.

1905: A Master Plan is drafted by Raúl Otero.

1906: The Little War of August sparks the second U.S. intervention.

1906–1940: The new University Hill campus of the University of Havana is built.

1907: The first X-ray department in Latin America opens. A census reports that Havana has 302,526 inhabitants; Cuba has slightly more than 2 million.

1908–1913: A sewer system is constructed. It is designed for a population of 600,000 (double the existing population). For the first time anywhere, an air-shield or pneumatic excavation technique is used for the siphon under the bay.

1909: El Malecón reaches Belascoaín.

1910: Automatic telephone service is introduced, before New York.

1913: Domingo Rosillo flies from Havana to Key West; it is the first international flight from Latin America.

1915: The Cuban peso is created, at par with the U.S. dollar.

1916: El Malecón reaches San Lázaro. An electric train from Casablanca to Hershey (later to Matanzas) is initiated; it is the oldest of its kind still in operation.

1918: A divorce law is passed, the first in Latin America.

1919: Pedro Martínez Inclán presents his proposal for a Master Plan. Havana has 363,506 inhabitants. Cuba produces one-fourth of sugar production worldwide.

1920: Fortunes are made in what is called the Dance of Millions as the price of sugar rises with dizzying speed; however, prices fall violently later in the year, introducing the Vacas Flacas (Thin Cows) period.

1922: Eduardo Montoulieu presents his Master Plan. El Malecón reaches Calle 23. The first radio broadcast from Cuba is made.

1925–1928: The Havana Design Plan, directed by J. C. N. Forestier, is carried out. Havana has 562,009 inhabitants.

1927: The monumental staircase of the University of Havana is completed.

1928: Havana has 580,950 inhabitants.

1929: The National Capitol Building is inaugurated. Lutgardita, a working-class subdivision, is inaugurated. The 700-mile Central Highway opens.

1930: El Malecón reaches G Street, in El Vedado.

1947: The Radiocentro Building is completed. It was the first Modern public building in Cuba, fueling the quick development of a new downtown district in La Rampa.

1948: Luyanó Workers Barrio is completed, with eight apartment buildings and two hundred houses.

1950: Television arrives.

1952: Fulgencio Batista leads a military coup. The Horizontal Properties Act propels the construction of high-rise condominium buildings.

1954: The Insured Mortgages Promotion Act (Fomento de Hipotecas Aseguradas) unleashes dozens of new developments of single-story homes.

1955: El Malecón reaches Paseo. The National Planning Board is created.

1955–1958: A Master Plan for Havana, directed by Josep Lluís Sert, with Paul Lester Wiener, Paul Schulz, Mario Romañach, and others, is carried out.

1959: January 1 witnesses the triumph of the Cuban Revolution.

1960: The Urban Reform Act is passed.

1963: The Havana Building Code (a revision of the 1861 Code) goes into effect.

1963–1964: The first Master Plan for Havana since the victory of the Revolution is proposed and approved.

1968: A revolutionary offensive nationalizes all private businesses and services.

1971: The Microbrigade Movement, a massive program in which government employees build their own flats with heavy state support, begins.

(CONTINUED ON PAGE 452)

nineteenth century, when Havana achieved many firsts in urban development for Latin America. These technological innovations represented a precursor of the heavy investment in urban infrastructure that made impressive urban growth possible from the beginning of the twentieth century.

El Vedado In 1859 the El Carmelo housing development was launched near the western shore and set apart from the city. This core area expanded with the same layout until it constituted the most important and progressive part of Spanish colonial urban development in Cuba, called El Vedado. It was built on a grid plan, with square blocks and lots arranged in a swastika shape. Here, for the first time, homes were separated from the street by a tree-lined *parterre*, a low fence, a five-meter garden, and a four-meter entry portal on the ground floor. One-third of the parcel had to be left unbuilt. This urban development was traversed perpendicularly from the sea by two broad, tree-lined avenues. Some blocks were reserved for tree-dotted plazas, creating the *parque republicano* (republican park) style.

The Avenues Havana grew following a finger-like pattern along old rural roads, creating a metropolitan area by the mid-twentieth century. These roads were converted to paved thoroughfares bordered by double-height porticos with continuous colonnades, the *calzadas*. Shops and services were housed on the ground floors, with residences above. This pattern was formalized in the Ordinances of 1861. In downtown Havana, the calzadas performed as linear centers that simultaneously divided and united the urban fabric whose dominant function was residential.

CHRONOLOGY

(CONTINUED FROM PAGE 451)

1976: A new Constitution is adopted and the Asemblea Nacional de Poder Popular (National Assembly of the People's Power) is established.

1982: In December, UNESCO designates as a World Heritage Site the walled city of Old Havana, plus the expansion strip in the nineteenth century previously occupied by the walls and fortresses of the colonial defensive system.

1985: The General Housing Act is adopted.

1986: New urban regulations and a new building code go into effect.

1987: The process known as Correction of Errors and Negative Trends begins in Cuba in response to *perestroika* in the Soviet Union. The Group for the Integral Development of the Capital (Grupo para el Desarrollo Integral de la Capital) is created. A strong construction boom in the capital begins. A revitalization of the Microbrigades and the creation of Social Microbrigades is implemented.

1988: A revision of the General Housing Act is adopted. The first three Integrated Neighborhood Transformation Workshops (Talleres de Transformación Integral del Barrio) are established in the neighborhoods of Atarés, Cayo Hueso, and La Güinera.

1990: People's Neighborhood Councils are created in Havana. An opening to foreign investment is initiated.

1991: The Panamerican Games are played in Havana. The Panamerican Village in Cojímar is built; it is the first attempt in Cuba to reinterpret traditional urban development. The year marks the official start of the Special Period.

1992: The 1976 Constitution is revised.

1993: Ownership of dollars by Cubans is legalized. Private work is authorized for services, including food services, arts, and trades. In October, Decree #143 is approved, authorizing the Office of the Historian of the City of Havana to conduct business and to use the proceeds to finance its rehabilitation and restoration projects.

1994: The Community Architect program starts. Lengthy, scheduled blackouts are implemented. In the crisis of the boat people, nearly 40,000 emigrate by water to the United States. Facing the lack of public transportation, Havana establishes the Metrobus service, popularly known as the *camellos* (camels) for the buses' hunch-back shape.

1995: La Güinera is selected as one of the fifty best community development projects in the world on the fiftieth anniversary of the United Nations.

1996: The Group for the Integral Development of the Capital and the Integrated Neighborhood Transformation Workshops are recognized in the Habitat II Summit in Istanbul as one of the Best Practices in community development in the world.

1997: On April 22, Decree #217 regulating migration to Havana is issued.

1998: New Urban Development Regulations for Plaza Municipality are introduced. The pope visits Cuba in January and offers mass in the Plaza of the Revolution. At the 6th Congress of the Writers and Artists Union (Unión de Escritores y Artistas), architectural and urban problems are discussed for the first time.

1999: Montecarlo Palace, the first condominium for foreigners built in Cuba by a joint venture, sets the stage for real estate agencies. The World Monuments Fund designates the National Schools of Art in Cubanacán as having international architectural relevance.

2000: In May a suspension of the sale of new condominiums to foreigners is ordered; they remain available for rent. Havana has 2.2 million inhabitants, but its population is beginning to decrease.

THE TWENTIETH CENTURY

In 1902 the direct intervention of the United States in Cuba ceased. During the first third of the twentieth century, demographic growth was enormous. In the first twenty-five years of the century, more Spanish immigrants arrived in Cuba than during the entire colonial period. An impressive economic boom—known as the Vacas Gordas (Fat Cows)—fed a construction boom. The first decade witnessed a short period of art nouveau influence, more Catalan than Belgian or French, but it was the eclectic architecture of the Beaux-Arts School, and especially minor eclecticism, which made up the central mass of Havana and almost all of Cuba's cities. By the second decade of the century, the development of Miramar had started. This elegant new neighborhood across the Almendares River, all along the western shore, utilized the same checkerboard pattern as El Vedado, but with larger lots and more vegetation. The beautiful Quinta Avenida (Fifth Avenue) was its green backbone, a thoroughfare that connected with the Country Club subdivision (later Cubanacán), a development even farther west and home to the very wealthy. There, the Spanish American grid gave way to an Anglo-Saxon layout of winding streets, along City Beautiful lines.

Havana has an important art deco heritage, in both geometrical and streamline variants, added from the late 1920s through the early 1940s. This architecture marks a switch from European to U.S. influence, which in Cuba coincided approximately with the end of the Republic of Generals and Doctors—that is, the displacement of the old oligarchy exercising direct political power. During this period Havana and Buenos Aires were considered the two leading cities of Latin America. The shift from eclectic architecture to modernism occurred between the world wars and followed a path that was far from straight. Eclecticism and art deco coexisted with neocolonial style, vernacular U.S. architectural style, and what was known as modern monumental, of fascist and futurist inspiration.

The Plan for the Project of Havana, carried out under the direction of Jean-Claude Nicolas Forestier between 1925 and 1928, followed an academic aesthetic with its grand diagonals and rotundas. In contrast, the Master Plan that would be undertaken thirty

years later by a team directed by Josep Lluís Sert was deeply influenced by the International Congresses for Modern Architecture and the contemporary example of Chandigarh. The model was no longer Nice, but rather Las Vegas. Despite certain achievements, this plan distorted the character and scale of the city and discarded an important part of its historical heritage. The Sert plan remained unfinished as, indeed, did Forestier's.

In the post–World War II period, several dozen suburban subdivisions appeared under the terms of the Insured Mortgages Promotion Act (1954), and the Vedado shore began to sprout condominium towers, taking advantage of the Horizontal Properties Act (1952). All of this further reinforced the primacy of the capital city as the great, glittering head of a small and poor country. In the 1950s a group of important Cuban architects was able to adapt the iconoclastic spirit of the modernist movement to Cuba's climate, context, and cultural identity. These creators left their mark on the students and young architects of that era, when the artistic vanguard dovetailed with the revolutionary one. They would fill the void left by the masters a short time after the triumph of the Revolution— at least for a while.

The Century's Second Half The search for architectural excellence within modernity that marked the 1950s continued until well into the second half of the 1960s, incorporating a structural expressionism with a strong brutalist component. The Havana of 1959 contained just over one-fifth of the country's six million residents. The new government halted the land

speculation that had begun to adulterate neighborhoods like El Vedado. State construction was directed toward the national network of provincial capitals and intermediate cities, along with new rural villages. This neglect of the capital added to the physical and social deterioration that had already begun, but it also stemmed the flow of internal migration toward the capital.

The legendary Unidad #1 (Unit 1) of East Havana (1959–1961) was as of 2011 the best public housing project ever built in Cuba. Energy, creativity, and innovation marked the 1960s, with other superb works such as the Cubanacán Schools of Art and the José Antonio Echeverría University Campus (Ciudad Universitaria José Antonio Echeverría). Most important of all, the general level of design and execution throughout the entire country was high. Cuba's subsequent centralization of power reduced architecture to massive-scale construction with just a few repeated styles, devoid of cultural intent.

In the 1970s new public housing projects were built in the capital by the *microbrigades*, a form of sweat equity with heavy state support. The architectural model was always the same: five-story buildings without any defined urban structure, devoid of services, technical networks, or public spaces. Many people got a roof over their heads, but an appreciable difference arose between the traditional city and these amorphous constructions. The program later languished, but at the end of the 1980s it had a short resurgence. Ironically, housing ceded priority to other social programs and the expectations of many people were disappointed who had joined the microbrigades to receive a dwelling.

These developments all coincided with the late arrival of postmodernism, taken up by a group of young architects hungry for change. At the beginning of the 1990s the collapse of the Soviet Union led to a terrible crisis. Known as the Special Period, this era left many projects half built. The nation's impoverished postmodernism reappeared later in a *blanda* (soft) architecture for tourism and condominiums for foreigners.

Implementing the Revolution At the beginning of the 1970s, the presence of inherited physical structures gave the illusion that little had changed in the capital, above all in the downtown area. But already many businesses and services, all state-owned since 1968, had been closing due to the scarcity of supplies. Their spaces were given over to people in need, who turned them into precarious dwellings. The grandeur of the great old department stores and commercial streets was degraded. Along with the deliberate national policy of urbanizing the countryside came a corresponding, spontaneous *ruralization* of the city. Little by little, the original facades became hidden by junk architecture. By contrast, the best new projects were built principally on the outskirts of the city, or even in the country; they thus had little impact on the urban image.

These physical changes reflected changes in values, customs, and behaviors. Until the beginning of the 1990s Havana had received little internal migration, while it had experienced considerable losses to emigration abroad. But in the middle of the decade, there was an increase in internal migration, which flooded the precarious residences. Decree #217 of 1997 attempted to regulate movement toward the capital. However, this did not curb the influx into the city of unemployed people with low levels of education and few skills.

A Moving Center A new, phantom, suburban area arose in the West, automobile-dependent and serving a relatively wealthy, corporate, largely foreign constituency and a dollar economy: the Miramar Trade Center, in Monte Barreto. Begun in the 1980s, this mixed Cuban-foreign investment hosted seven hotels and eighteen square blocks of office buildings and shops that had been partially built by 2010. With this de-centered downtown, which lacks the urban functions that comprise a living city (housing with local residents, shops in Cuban regular currency, cultural and sports facilities, historic sites or landmarks), centrality has completed a journey, from the port and the plazas of the old walled city to the west along Calle Obispo and its small businesses in the nineteenth-century European style; the Manzana de Gómez (Gomez Block), at the turn of the twentieth century, following the model of the grand European commercial galleria with interior streets, and the whole Parque Central (Central Park) area; the American-style department stores of the 1940s and 1950s, at Galiano

and San Rafael; and the commercial calzadas along the avenues of downtown Havana. In the mid-twentieth century, the cosmopolitan center of modernity, La Rampa, appeared where El Vedado abutted downtown Havana, reinforced by University Hill, home to the University of Havana.

Architecture Deteriorates, Population Declines
The early twenty-first century found Havana to be a city preserved by omission. An important exception to this neglect is the work of the Office of the Historian in Old Havana, which had managed to reconcile preservation and restoration of its architectural heritage and public spaces through a form of self-management in which economic, urban, cultural, and social interests coexist. But apart from investments to attract hard currency, deterioration was growing more acute in the rest of the city and its infrastructure, and neither the government nor the public had the resources to preserve and restore them.

At the dawn of the new century, the population of Havana was 2.2 million—one-fifth of the nation—but already by 2009 it had decreased to 2.14 million. This worrisome decrease was linked to emigration overseas, an aging population, and low birthrate. Inequality was rising and was finding geographical expression: The traditionally privileged character of the coastal zone—the *Franja Azul* (the Blue Strip)—was reinforced, in contrast to Havana's *Sur Profundo* (Deep South), poorer both in the past and in the early 2000s. These are some of the problems that must be confronted, with the challenge of maintaining the Revolution's social achievements while reclaiming moral and ethical values, and building an economy to sustain them.

BIBLIOGRAPHY
Basic Works

Martín, María Elena, and Eduardo Luis Rodríguez. *Havana, Cuba: An Architectural Guide | La Habana: Guía de Arquitectura.* Seville, Spain: Junta de Andalucia, Consejeria de Obras Publicas y Transportes, Direccion General de Arquitectura y Vivienda, 1998.

Scarpaci, Joseph, Roberto Segre, and Mario Coyula. *Havana: Two Faces of the Antillean Metropolis.* Chapel Hill: University of North Carolina Press, 2002.

Segre, Roberto. *Transformación Urbana en Cuba: La Habana.* Barcelona: Gustavo Gili, 1974.

Venegas, Carlos. "Havana between Two Centuries." Special issue on Cuba. *Journal of Decorative and Propaganda Arts* 22 (1996): 13–23.

Complementary Works

Cluster, Dick, and Rafael Hernández. *The History of Havana.* New York: Palgrave Macmillan, 2006.

Coyula, Mario. "Los Muchos Centros de La Habana." In *VII Encuentro Internacional de Revitalización de Centros Históricos: La Arquitectura de Hoy, entre la Ciudad Histórica y la Actual,* 59–69. Mexico City: Centro Cultural de España en México, 2009.

Griffith, Cathryn. *Havana Revisited.* New York: Norton, 2010.

Moreno Fraginals, Manuel. *Cuba/Spain, Spain/Cuba: Common History*. Barcelona: Grijalbo Mondadori, 1995.

Rodríguez, Eduardo Luis. *La Habana: Arquitectura del Siglo XX*. Barcelona, Spain: Blume, 1998.

Segre, Roberto. *Arquitectura y Urbanismo de la Revolución Cubana*. Havana: Pueblo y Educación, 1989.

Segre, Roberto. "Iconic Voids and Social Identity in a Polycentric City: Havana from the 19th to the 21st Century." In *Ordinary Places, Extraordinary Events: Citizenship, Democracy, and Public Space in Latin America*, edited by Clara Irazábal. London: Routledge, 2008.

Weiss, Joaquín. *Arquitectura Colonial Cubana: Siglos XVI al XIX*. Havana: Letras Cubanas, 2002.

Zardoya, María Victoria. "Las Calzadas, Arterias Vitales de La Habana." *Arquitectura y Urbanismo #2/99* (1999): 27–34.

Havana: Atlantic Center of Shipping, Commerce, and Building

Arturo Sorhegui D'Mares

The center of Spanish commerce in the Atlantic from the sixteenth through the eighteenth centuries and the hub of Cuba's plantation economy at the beginning of the nineteenth century.

Among all of the cities of the Americas the personality of Havana stems from its position as the main Atlantic port of call for Spanish commerce from 1561 onward and its social and economic capacity for transformation. By the end of the eighteenth century, this masthead of the plantation economy had evolved into the principal exporter of sugar to the global market. This evolution was linked to the process of European expansion, which had begun at the end of the fifteenth century. With the advent of ocean navigation that opened the Atlantic realm, the European powers commenced a colonial project over a greater distance than any realized during classical or medieval times. This project favored a new Atlantic orientation, in contrast to pre-Hispanic populations, whose civilizations had been built upon the Pacific corridor.

VITAL MARITIME PASSAGES AND TRADE ROUTES

Part of the new concept of territorial settlement in Spanish America resulted in the founding of cities in the Caribbean. These island settlements would guarantee continuous maritime communication with Spain and serve as centers of Spanish colonial expansion onto the continent. The first of these settlements was La Isabela, founded in 1493 on the island of Hispaniola, in what was later the Dominican Republic. Around 1502 Santo Domingo was established on the west coast of the Ozama River, on the southern part of the island, and became the principal port for the Spanish presence in the Americas.

The history of Havana in its modern location, on the bay of the same name, is linked with the initiation in 1519 of the conquest of Mexico. After Hernán Cortés founded the city of Veracruz on the eastern coast of Mexico in 1519, Havana was relocated from the south of the island to its permanent location on the north coast, at the command of the entrance to the Gulf of Mexico (the Yucatán Channel) and the exit from it (the Straits of Florida). Havana would thus become the bulwark for the maintenance of communication between Spain and the future Viceroyalty of New Spain (founded in 1534).

The new potential for Spanish wealth, arising from the 1521 conquest of Mexico and enhanced by the 1532 conquest of Peru, led to conflicts among European powers over who would control the Caribbean. French privateers took the first actions, followed by the English and Dutch. Spain responded by creating a system of fleets in 1561 and, at the end of the century, a network of fortifications that included Havana, Veracruz, Cartagena de Indias (on the coast of modern-day Colombia), and Portobelo (on the northern coast of the Isthmus of Panama), in addition to sites on Puerto Rico, Hispaniola, and other points around the Caribbean.

Under the new system, two fleets left for Spain each year. One, designated the galleon fleet, was charged with receiving shipments of silver from Peru. It journeyed from the Peruvian port of Callao to Panama City, on the Pacific, from whence notice was sent overland to Portobelo, on the Atlantic. A ship in Portobelo then conveyed this message to the Spanish fleet stationed in Cartagena. The fleet set sail for Portobelo, calculating for the time it would take to move the shipment across the Isthmus of Panama by mule. The cargo was then transferred to Havana by way of Cartagena. The second fleet, after reaching the port of Veracruz, would head for Havana, where it would join the galleon fleet to begin the return voyage to Spain. Havana Bay was the only enclave where the two fleets met up; their stays could last more than three months. As a result, the city became the principal port of call for commerce in the Indies and replaced Santo Domingo as the home port for the Spanish presence in the Americas. In the seventeenth century the number of vessels arriving at Havana Bay averaged about one thousand a year. This number would nearly double in the following century.

As a result of a royal decree in 1561 by Philip II of Spain, Havana became the home of a system of fortifications constructed to defend its bay. This included the Morro and Punta castles, built at the end of the sixteenth and beginning of the seventeenth centuries,

See also

Ecology and Environment: Colonial Period

Governance and Contestation: Colonial Period

**Map showing
location of Havana**

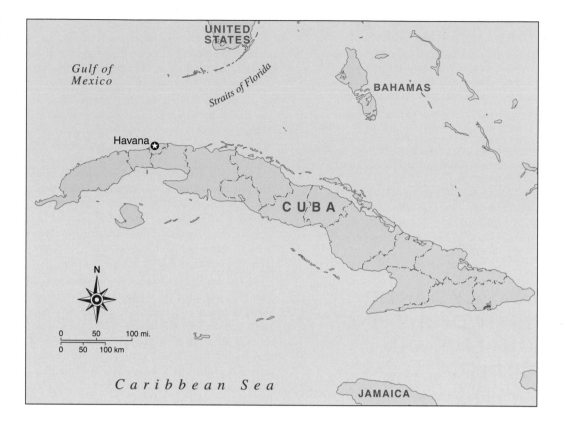

and later those of San Carlos de la Cabaña and Atarés, built in the 1760s. The establishment of systematic funding from the coffers of colonial Mexico also provided for the building of a copper foundry, a shipyard, and an aqueduct. A concession of extraordinary permits was granted to dispatch individual warships to Mexico and the Canary Islands to insure the provisions of the crews and passengers of the fleets. Also created as part of this project was La Real Compañía de Comercio de La Habana, the sole commercial company to be established by Spain in the Americas; it was founded in 1740.

Between 1570 and 1630 Havana had the highest population growth of any city in the Americas, thus creating ample opportunities for commerce. In a 1969 study Jorge Hardoy and Carmen Aeronovich noted that Havana's growth rate for those years reached 20 percent, as compared to 6.6 percent for Cartagena de Indias and 13 percent for Durango, the silver-mining town in New Spain. In contrast to Cartagena de Indias, Veracruz, and Panama City, three of the major port cities of the sixteenth century, Havana sustained its growth rate through the eighteenth century: According to the census of 1774, the inhabitants of the city numbered 75,618, even without counting its sizeable rotation of seamen, military, and other visitors.

The elimination of the fleet system in 1774 and of the remittance of *situados* (payments from the Mexican treasury) at the beginning of the nineteenth century brought an end to Havana's status as a port of call in the Indies. However, these changes did not, as one might assume, curtail the city's population and economic growth. Rather, after 1791 conditions in Havana favored the establishment of a plantation economy on a grand scale and Cuba replaced Haiti as the main supplier of sugar and coffee to the world.

NINETEENTH-CENTURY HUB

Beginning around the turn of the nineteenth century, Havana evolved into the main port of Cuba's plantation economy. Whereas the amount of sugar that Havana exported between 1760 and 1763 did not exceed 4,000 boxes annually, between 1796 and 1800 that number reached an average of over 30,000 boxes a year. In the case of coffee, which was introduced late to the island, 50,000 arrobas (a Spanish unit of weight equal to about 25 pounds) of the bean left Havana in 1804, whereas the average between 1815 and 1820 surpassed 120,000 arrobas. Before the occupation of Havana by the British, the sugar mills extended radially out from the city, west to Jaimanitas, south to Calabazar, and east to the area next to Guanabacoa. This extension of intensive systems of coffee and sugar production to rural areas previously dominated by livestock grazing was a revolution of sorts, increasing the population surrounding Havana and supporting the development of the plantation economy. According to Juan Pérez de la Riva's 1975

Havana Harbor. The harbor as it appeared in the nineteenth century, in an illustration by E. Wullmann. © GIANNI DAGLI ORTI/CORBIS

study, the population grew in its initial centers in Guanajay, Güines, Jaruco, Santiago de las Vegas, and Matanzas to an average density of approximately seventy inhabitants per square kilometer in just over 1,600 square kilometers. Without this expansion, the conversion of Cuba into the largest global producer of sugar would have been impossible.

Between 1792 and the end of the 1830s, public docks were extended along the coast, more comprehensively arrayed along the central part of the bay. The new demands for handling goods were reflected in the installation on the Luz dock of a crane, known simply as *the machine*, which evolved into a 32-meter-high masting machine (for installing masts on vessels). In 1824 the shipping agents whose services were most favored by foreign ships, Carlos Drake and Charles Mitchell, built a wooden warehouse on the Caballería dock, on which davits (cranes that project over the sides of ships) had recently been installed. In 1819 the first steamboat service was launched between Havana and Matanzas. Attesting to the port's activity, Joel Roberts Poinsett, who served as the U.S. envoy extraordinary and minister plenipotentiary to Mexico in the 1820s, noted after visiting Havana: "I have never seen in any U.S. port, with the exception of New York, so many boats or such bustle of business; and in New York it isn't concentrated in one single place, as it is here" (Poinsett p. 280).

Competition from Europe, where beet sugar was produced with salaried labor, forced plantations in western Cuba to modernize so as to reduce costs. Toward that end, construction of a railroad—the second in the Americas and the seventh in the world—began in 1837, and a system of vacuum boilers and centrifuges was installed in the sugar mills. In addition, a modern system of docks and warehouses was introduced in Havana Bay that consisted of a system with facilities for the integrated loading, unloading, and storing of cargo known internationally as *English docks*. Between 1845 and 1860, approximately five million pesos were invested in Havana Bay to build five docks specifically for this purpose.

The evolution of the port over the course of the nineteenth century had an enormous impact on the city itself. As the city lost its standing as the juncture of commerce in the Indies, the docks ceased to be the driving force in the transformation of the surrounding urban area. Instead, developers, who had amassed wealth under the plantation economy, became the dominant group in Havana. By the end of the nineteenth century, planters and merchants exerted political influence through the Real Consulado (Royal Consulate), the Real Junta de Fomento (Royal Development Board), and the Real Sociedad Económica (Royal Economic Society). These groups were critical to the superseding of military construction by civil

■ *See also*

Governance and Contestation: Colonial Period

Spanish-American-Cuban War: 1898

Ten Years' War: 1868–1878

construction. From the high social position that they had recently attained, as noted by Arturo Sorhegui in a 2009 article, elite inhabitants of Havana sought to create a city that matched the image they were advocating: a city of new public spaces, broad avenues, and improved urban conditions.

BIBLIOGRAPHY

Braudel, Fernand. *Civilization and Capitalism, 15th–18th Century*. New York: Harper & Row, 1982.

Chaunu, Pierre Huguette. *Seville et l'Atlantique, 1504–1650*. 8 vols. Paris: Armand, 1955–1959.

Elliot, John. *En busca de la historia atlántica*. Las Palmas de Gran Canaria, Spain: Ediciones del Cabildo de Gran Canaria, 2001.

Elliott, J. H. *The Old World and the New 1492–1650*. Cambridge, U.K.: Cambridge University Press, 1970.

Guimerá, Agustín, and Fernando Monge, eds. *La Habana, puerto colonial (siglos XVIII y XIX)*. Madrid: Fundación Portuaria, 2000.

Hamilton, Earl J. *War and Prices in Spain, 1651–1800*. Cambridge, MA: Harvard University Press, 1947.

Hardoy, Jorge E., and Carmen Aeronovich. "Escalas y funciones urbanas en América Hispana hacia el año 1600." In *El proceso de urbanización en América desde su orígenes hasta nuestros días*, edited by Jorge E. Hardoy and Richard Schaedel. Buenos Aires: Instituto Torucate di Tella, 1969.

Knight, Franklin W., and Peggy K. Liss, eds. *Atlantic Port Cities: Economy, Culture, and Society in the Atlantic World, 1650–1850*. Knoxville: University of Tennessee Press, 1991.

Le Riverend, Julio. *La Habana, espacio y vida*. Madrid: Editorial MAPFRE, 1992.

Marrero, Leví. *Cuba: Economía y Sociedad*. 15 vols. Río Piedras, Puerto Rico: Editorial San Juan, and Madrid: Editorial Playor, 1972–1992.

Pérez de la Riva, Juan. "El país de La Habana en los albores del siglo XIX, según Antonio del Valle." *Revista Economía y Desarrollo* 29 (Havana) (May–June 1975).

Pezuela, Jacobo de la. *Diccionario Geográfico, Estadístico e Histórico, de la Isla de Cuba*, vol. 3. Madrid: Imprenta del Establecimiento Mellado, 1863.

Poinsett, Joel Roberts. *Notas sobre México*. Traducción de Pablo Martínez del Campo. Mexico: Editorial Jus, 1950. First English edition, 1824.

Sauer, Carl Ortwin. *The Early Spanish Main*. Berkeley: University of California Press, 1966.

Sorhegui, Arturo. *La Habana en el Mediterráneo Americano*. Havana: Imagen Contemporánea, 2007.

Sorhegui, Arturo. "Puerto de la Habana: De principal enclave del comercio indiano, a cabecera de una economía de plantación." *Revista Honda* 26 (Havana) (2009).

Wallerstein, Immanuel. *The Modern World-System: Capitalist Agriculture and the Origins of the European World-Economy in the Sixteenth Century*. New York: Academic Press, 1976.

Wright, Irene A. *The Early History of Cuba, 1492–1586*. New York: Macmillan, 1916.

HAVANA: EL MORRO AND LA CABAÑA

Carlos Venegas Fornias

The fortifications El Morro and La Cabaña in Havana.

The natural advantages of the port of Havana include a promontory on its eastern side that protects the harbor from strong ocean winds. The location has housed a defensive acropolis, lighthouse, and navigation watchtower. The promontory emerges from the sea as a wall of rock and rises to about 250 feet (70 m.), and it is separated from the city by a canal that feeds into the bay. The first Spanish inhabitants called these naturally occurring features of the terrain El Morro and La Cabaña. They provide a view of the entire ocean horizon, the port, and its surroundings and support two of the most valuable fortifications the Spanish Empire built in the Americas.

Havana Bay, known as the *llave del Nuevo Mundo* (Key to the New World), was converted into a stronghold in the second half of the sixteenth century, protecting the sea route to the Indies from pirate attacks. In 1586 Spanish king Phillip II, threatened by the English, charged Maestre de Campo Juan de Tejeda and engineer Juan Bautista Antonelli (1550–1616), born in Gatteo, Romagna (present-day Italy), to design a defense system for the two main gateways to Spain's New World possessions, the Caribbean Sea and the Gulf of Mexico. The men worked under the supervision of the chief engineer of the kingdom, Tiburcio Spanoqui (1541–1606). However, Antonelli was the true author of the plan and design for the main fortifications. Following a long voyage of reconnaissance, he drew up maps and layouts for all the *llaves* or keys, the strategic locations for controlling navigation.

Appointed governor of Cuba by the king, Tejeda returned to Havana. In 1589, Antonelli began the construction of the Castillo de los Tres Reyes del Morro (Castle of the Three Kings at El Morro) at the entrance to Havana Bay, a lengthy undertaking on which his nephew, Cristóbal de Roda, collaborated.

The fortification began operation as a defensive installation in 1615, once the barracks and interior church were finished, although its moat was still not completed. The moat was dug out of the rock itself and not finished until 1630. With more than forty cannons in place, the fort was considered during the seventeenth century to be the largest in the Americas. Its construction was accomplished using forced labor from throughout the world: African slaves; privateers and pirates from France, England, Holland, and the Maghreb; and prisoners from the Americas. The roots of this collaboration seemed to be implicit

Morro Castle. Morro Castle, a fortress built in 1589, protects the entrance to Havana Bay. © JOSE FUSTE RAGA/ CORBIS

in the structure's very name, taken from the Christian Epiphany—the adoration of the three kings who came from the ends of the gentile world.

Antonelli designed El Morro in an innovative style. He altered the pure and closed geometric forms of the Italian school so as to adapt them to the promontory's irregular terrain and to increase its firing capacity. Although based on a triangular figure, this is only shown uniformly at its earthen facade, with two bastions, known as Tejeda and Austria, as well as the moat. The other facades are broken down into walls and elevated terraces that look out over the sea at different levels that coincide with the irregular angles of its rocky site. The fortress was able to defend the city for a century and a half, but its purpose was, above all, to protect access to the bay by cross-fire with the La Punta fort, which was situated at the opposite end of the bay. It was, however, unable to stop more than twelve thousand English soldiers in 1762 from landing, who succeeded in laying siege to the city and occupying it.

THE INFLUENCE OF THE FRENCH SCHOOL OF MARQUIS DE VAUBAN

The capture of La Cabaña hill hastened the defeat of Havana, since from it the English were able to bombard El Morro and the city. This danger was understood as far back as the sixteenth century, and an attempt was made to defend the hill by keeping the site covered with thick, impregnable evergreen vegetation. Barely a month before the invasion, French engineer Francisco Ricaud de Tirgale had drawn up a plan to equip La Cabaña hill with a fort. In 1763, once Havana was

restored to Spain, Charles III sent the Count of Ricla (1720–1780) as its governor, accompanied by the engineering brigadier Silvestre Abarca in order to modernize the system of fortifications.

During the eighteenth century, Spain and France, united by the dynastic ties of the House of Bourbon, acted as allies. French engineers participated in the reorganization of the Spanish corps of engineers. Havana's defense was discussed at a council of generals in Madrid, and the French army's field marshal, Marquis de la Valliere (1644–1710), drew up a plan that was delivered to Abarca so that he would have the opportunity to modify it when he arrived in Havana. Abarca altered certain aspects that did not match with reality. But he did agree on the plan for a large fort at La Cabaña, which he built in a manner similar to that proposed by Ricaud in 1761.

The construction of the Castillo de San Carlos of La Cabaña (San Carlos Castle), named in honor of King Charles III, was started in 1763 and finished in 1774. Its construction followed the principles developed by military engineer Sebastián Le Prestre Vauban (1633–1707), who had improved on the techniques employed for defensive bulwarks since the seventeenth century by using the trench fortification style and forward batteries to facilitate arms fire from the structure's flanks. No one else had applied these trends so strictly within Spain's colonial realm. The Castillo de San Carlos was a complex fortification, the product of a specialized academic culture, based on models that left little room for improvisation, and in spite of its large dimensions, it was semi-underground and partially hidden from view. Its dynamic ground plan was shaped like a crown, outlined by ravelins and bastions protected by a wide moat. The staircases, passageways, depositories, and cisterns allowed for the lodging and mobility of troops. It was prepared for mining, enabling its destruction in case of the danger of falling into the hands of an aggressor.

The fort acted as the center of the city's protection system from its highest point. It acted in concert with El Morro, which was rebuilt at the same time to enlarge its barracks. These structures were supported by two other forts, Príncipe and Atarés Castles, which were outside of the area walled in by the earthen section. The mobilization of troops inside the four forts kept the city from being besieged and conquered. Tradition has it that King Charles III, upset by its fourteen-million peso price tag, asked for a telescope so he could look at it from his court in Madrid. However, research into this matter has shown the true cost to have been 3,526,463 pesos. The Castillo de San Carlos de la Cabaña occupied a premier place among American fortresses, boasting 178 cannons and the ability to garrison almost two thousand men.

SIGNALS

El Morro's role as a lighthouse preceded the site's use for defense and continues into the twenty-first century. Since the middle of the sixteenth century a whitewashed tower has stood on this point, in which residents viewed sea traffic and which allowed ships to identify the entrance into the bay from the high seas. A firewood-fueled lighthouse was built inside the fortress's most prominent bastion in the beginning of the eighteenth century but was destroyed by attacking British troops in 1762. Innovations for the beacon light were introduced in the nineteenth century, first through the shift to oil fuel and then, in 1824, with a revolving harbor beacon.

Around 1840 a decision was made to equip the light with one of the lenses created by French engineer Juan Agustín Fresnel (1788–1827). These were considered the best in the world and were much used in European ports, but they were little used in the Americas due to their high cost. A new tower in the form of a monumental Doric column was built to house the new Fresnel lens. Some 70 feet (21 m.) high, in the style of the columns of the famed temples of Pesto, the column was named after the governor of the island, Leopoldo O'Donnell (1809–1867), in honor of his success in stamping out the recent slave uprisings. The new lighthouse combined technical progress and classical style, and it affirmed modern slavery. It was inaugurated in a solemn ceremony attended by the governor, the archbishop, ten brigadier generals, consuls from twelve different countries, and thirty-seven local nobles. The beacon continued to function without interruption until the following century. Its energy source was first replaced by oil and then in 1940 by electricity.

Although it had no lighthouse, La Cabaña served as the stage for another memorable light show during the 1858 celebrations of the birth of Spanish prince Alfonso. The fort shone in the night thanks to a powerful battery—the first time electric lights were used publicly in the country. The battery, invented by the French physicist Jean-Luc Bouzon, was introduced into the Americas by Carlos Sánchez Benítez, who taught telegraphy at Havana's preparatory school. Hundreds of people congregated on the docks and on the nearby seashore to gaze at the spectacle, and a transparent tapestry some 135 feet (41 m.) high was decorated and lit up to welcome Queen Isabella II of Spain.

These fortifications also communicated messages that affected the city's daily life. Rows of small flags hung at El Morro indicated, through their color and placement, the number, type, and ports of origin of approaching vessels. This signal code was followed, with much interest, from balconies and windows of homes and businesses, and lithographic depictions were made for sale to the public. La Cabaña, for its part, fired a cannon to announce the opening and closing of the city wall gates. After the physical demolition of the wall surrounding Havana in 1865, the daily custom of firing the *cañonazo de las nueve* (the 9:00 p.m. cannonade) still lived on. This audible, surviving symbol of the military past allows residents to set their watches.

THE SYMBOLS

El Morro and La Cabaña became symbols of Spanish power at the entrance to the empire's most-coveted port. Ships had to greet them with salvos upon entering the bay, and monarchy's flags waved from their heights. El Morro's walls, rising directly from the rocks and battered by the waves, provided a traditional image expressive of the domination and resistance associated with medieval castles. La Cabaña, by contrast, with its hidden structures that left only a continuous and uniform horizontal wall visible, produced a less intense effect at first glance. Some popular old verses speak to the transcendence awakened by the image of the entrance channel to Havana, so rigorously protected by both castles, so central to the identity of the colonial city:

> Tres cosas tiene La Habana
> que no las tiene Madrid.
> Son el Morro, La Cabaña,
> y ver los barcos salir.
>
> (Havana has three sights
> That Madrid does not provide.
> El Morro and La Cabaña,
> and boats sailing out on the tide.)

During the nineteenth century, these great fortifications fell into disuse due to progress made in artillery range. But they continued to perform other functions. Their prisons and dungeons were an important component from their beginnings, and they amassed dark memories of imprisonments and executions. This is especially true for La Cabaña, which, despite not being the scene of military battles, was used, starting with the wars of independence, as a prison for domestic repression. After the end of Spanish colonial domination of the island, both fortresses served as symbols of Cuba's sovereignty. This change was most strongly manifested by El Morro, which in 1902 was selected as the site for the official raising of the Cuban flag for the first time since U.S. troops had withdrawn, in full view of the entire city.

With the passage of time and as its military role grew weaker, the fortified hill changed roles: Instead of being admired from the outside, it became the preferred place from which to view the profile of the growing city. By the middle of the nineteenth century, the urban landscape captured from there in lithographs and photographic panoramas was frequently reproduced and constituted the symbolic image of modern Havana, with the silhouette of its most important buildings along the horizon. During the last decades of the twentieth century, the recreational and visual possibilities of the complex were greatly developed, and the two fortresses—both included, along with Old Havana, on the World Heritage list—became museums and cultural centers. After 1986 they became the Parque Arqueológico Morro-Cabaña (Morro-Cabaña Archeological Park). This park draws people who enjoy its numerous activities.

BIBLIOGRAPHY

Blanes Martín, Tamara. *Castillo de los Tres Reyes del Morro de la Habana: Historia y arquitectura.* Havana: Letras Cubanas, 1998.

Pérez Guzmán, Francisco. *La Habana clave de un imperio.* Havana: Editorial de Ciencias Sociales, 1997.

Ramos Zúñiga, Antonio. "Tres ejemplos de la fortificación caribeña: Los castillos del Morro de la Habana, Santiago de Cuba y San Juan de Puerto Rico." *Revista de la Universidad de Oriente* 76 (Santiago de Cuba) (July–December 1993): 53–80.

Roig de Leuchsenring, Emilio. *Los monumentos nacionales de la República de Cuba.* Vol. 3. *Fortalezas coloniales de La Habana.* Havana: Publicaciones de la Junta Nacional de Arqueología y Etnología, 1960.

Segre, Roberto. "Significación de Cuba en la evolución tipológica de las fortificaciones coloniales de América." *Revista de la Biblioteca Nacional José Martí* 2 (Havana) (May–August 1968): 5–46.

HAVANA: HAVANA AS CULTURAL CENTER

Zoila Mercedes Lapique Becali

The city as a cultural beacon and a center for art, performance, publishing, and modern media.

Havana's destiny was sealed when the daring Spanish pilot Antón de Alaminos discovered the gulf stream that originates in the Gulf of Mexico in 1517. From that point on, this would be the obligatory and shortest return route to Spain. In 1519, the conquest of Mexico by Hernán Cortés (1485–1547) turned the port of Carenas, or La Habana, into the connecting point and center of operations to the territories of the continent, or Terra Firma, as it was known then. The original village had been founded on the southern coast, and was successively moved northward, first along the banks of the Chorrera (Almendares) River to a place later known as Puentes Grandes. Shortly thereafter, it was relocated to the mouth of that river. Finally, in 1519, the village was settled at its present location next to the great bay, known at that time as the port of Carenas. The city is exposed to the Gulf of Mexico on an exceptionally long strip of shoreline, whose outline resembles the shape of a shell. Its strategic geographic position, facing the Straits of Florida and the Old Bahama Channel, made it the new communications route for the Spanish Fleet system, covering the Route to the Indies between the New World and the ports of Seville and Cádiz. The port city of Havana was regarded as "the Royal Road to the Indies" from the Andalusian ports.

HAVANA AS A HUB OF ENTERTAINMENT, ART, AND ARCHITECTURE

For five or six months at a time, sailors, soldiers, and travelers flocked the streets of the port, where taverns and inns thrived with services and entertainment (food, games, music, and dance). Thus Havana perfected its role as a focal point generating and spreading these activities. Like ancient Rome, Havana was both a city and a world unto itself. Everything came to Havana and Havana gave back to the world everything it received.

Indigenous and African dances (such as the *folia*, the *chaconne*, the *zarabanda*, the *zarambeque*, and others known as "dances from the Indies") traveled back to Spain with sailors and soldiers, and were represented in the literature of the Golden Age in Spain. The dances later spread through the Americas and Europe, and some were introduced into the Baroque Suite in Europe.

Havana's first visual reference and unique background are its fortifications, with designs that embody and conform to the principles of defense developed by French military engineer Sébastien Le Prestre de Vauban (1633–1707). It is not by chance that those old castles appear on the first coat of arms of the city, surrounding a golden key, the key to the Gulf of Mexico, which represents the geographical position of the island of Cuba. Thus, in 1592, the village is designated as a city by a royal decree of Philip II (r. 1556–1598). It is also recognized as the key to the New World and the bastion of the West Indies, a city described by German scientist Alexander von Humboldt as a town half hidden by a forest of ships' masts and sails.

■ *See also*

Día de Reyes en la Habana (Víctor Patricio de Landaluze)

Performing Arts: Dance: Ballet

Performing Arts: Opera

Performing Arts: Theater: Republican Period

Three Kings Day procession in Old Havana. Costumed marchers parade through a narrow street in Old Havana on 6 January, Three Kings Day. HÉCTOR DELGADO AND ROLANDO PUJOL

During the colonial period, the streets were ablaze with festival lights, in celebration of coronations, weddings, and births of the royal house. Processions went down the streets honoring the different patron saints, while the *horras* (free black women) came out to dance in both religious and profane festivities. Havana developed thanks to the construction of the fortresses of El Morro and La Punta, the growing sugar industry, and the cultivation of the tobacco plant, which was legally exported to Spain in the form of leaves, snuff, rolled, and paste. Havana was a port city with a cosmopolitan character.

ARTISANS AND SHIPBUILDERS

In Havana of the sixteenth and seventeenth centuries, the silversmiths and craftsmen of the guild of San Eloy showed remarkable skills. The guild took its name from the bishop of Noyon (France), Saint Eloy (588–659), who practiced as a goldsmith long before being appointed a bishop and was active into the nineteenth century. Among their works, still highly prized today, is a filigree silver cross made by the first silversmith of the city, Gerónimo de Espellosa, and donated by the deacon of the Cathedral of Havana to the Church of Icod de los Vinos in the Canary Islands.

In the eighteenth century, Havana had one of the largest shipyards, where the finest vessels of the Spanish Armada were built on templates crafted from the precious woods of Cuba. They also exported chests known as *Havana boxes*. The skill of these carpenters also meant that the city had magnificent artisans to build high-quality houses and furniture.

IMAGES OF HAVANA IN EUROPEAN ART

In 1762, Havana was besieged and captured by the British. The invading forces stayed in the city for eleven months, ultimately withdrawing in exchange for Florida and after destroying the shipyards in order to prevent further construction of ships for the Spanish Armada. The siege and fall of the city are memorialized in a set of copper-plate engravings in London. The first series, with twelve naval scenes, was based on oil paintings by Dominic Serres (1719–1793), a London-based French painter of martial themes, who was inspired by the drawings that his partner, English lieutenant Philip Osbridge, made during the capture of the city. Some of the engravings depict a partial view of Havana from the sea. Vistas of the city during the English occupation were drawn by Elias Durnford (1739–1794). The two series are significant because they portray the city in a realistic manner and eschew the fantasies indulged in by other European engravers, who copied each other and produced their work without ever having visited Havana. In the English prints there are no onion domes topped by a chess rook, nor are there the unexplainable steeples on the rooftops of houses, churches, and convents, repeatedly seen in the aforementioned engravings. In the work of Serres and Durnford, the world could finally see the jewel the British acquired for their crown as it really was. For his part, the young Havanan engraver Francisco Javier Báez (1746–1828) captured the moment in which the English expelled Bishop Morell de Santa Cruz from his home, for resisting the invasion.

PUBLISHING

A short-lived gazette was first published in Havana in 1764. Twelve years later the printing press of Esteban José de Boloña was inaugurated. A more stable *Gaceta de La Habana* was established in 1782. Cuba's first scientific book, a treatise on the abundance of fish in Cuban waters, was published in 1787 by Antonio Parra and was illustrated with metal engravings by his son, Manuel Antonio. The *Papel Periódico de La Habana* (Periodical Paper of Havana) was first published in 1790. The Patriotic Society was established in 1793, followed by the Economic Society of Friends of the Country. In the same year, the *Calendario Manual y Guía de Forasteros* (Calendar Manual and Guide for Foreigners) was published. The *Papel Periódico de La Habana* of 29 July 1792 describes the progress in the capital and the works of art and architecture made by Havanan craftsmen.

DANCE, MUSIC, AND THEATER

Public and private dances were organized, at which a Spanish-tempered French *contredanse*, with music performed by black and mulatto orchestras, ruled supreme. The dance known as the *habanera* emerged in the nineteenth century. This genre traveled throughout the Americas and above all to Spain, where it filled the grand stage of the lyric theater, opera, and zarzuela. Few productions did not have at least one *habanera*, right up to the zarzuelas and *sainetes* of the twentieth century, including *Luisa Fernanda* (1932), by Moreno Tórroba (1891–1982). In 1875, Georges Bizet's opera *Carmen* was performed around the world with a habanera sung by a sensual cigar-roller. The habanera also became part of the high-art music of the nineteenth and twentieth centuries, registering unforgettable moments. The *danzón* became Cuba's national dance, travelled to Mexico—as happened later with the bolero and the mambo by Pérez Prado (1916–1989)—and from Havana and Mexico was performed throughout the globe.

The Coliseum Theater was built in 1776 on the Alameda de Paula, staging plays, opera, and above all, the scenic *tonadilla*. It was quickly followed by other theaters in the Italianate architectural style, unquestionably the finest of the age. The most important Cuban theater in the first half of the nineteenth century was the Gran Teatro de Habana (Grand Theater of Havana, 1837), which played host to the most notable lyric, ballet, and theater companies that visited the island. Havana was a transit or departure point for foreign companies arriving from Europe, whether on their way to Mexico or the United States. Havana hosted musical performances of the highest order and became a mandatory stage for international debuts and premieres. Other theaters were built in Havana or existing buildings were adapted for the stage, such as Villanueva, Payret, Irijoa, Jané, Torrecillas, Albizu, and Trotcha, the latter in Vedado.

The Alhambra Theater, where notable Cuban bufo actors performed, was founded at the close of the nineteenth century.

In 1918, a group of women founded the Sociedad Pro Arte Musical (Musical Arts Society) to offer concerts and recitals by the best national and international performers of the day. A few years later, the Auditorium Theater was inaugurated in Vedado as a venue for these concerts and for opera and ballet performances. The brothers Fernando (b. 1914) and Alberto Alonso (1917–2008) became famous at this theater, as did the *prima ballerina assoluta* Alicia Alonso (b. 1920), who was later acclaimed as the world's finest interpreter of *Giselle*, as well as other ballets by renowned choreographers of the twentieth century. After a long decline, the 1950s saw the rise of countless *salitas* (little theaters), which staged plays of major importance, as much for the performances as for the plays themselves, by Cuban and world playwrights alike.

MODERN TECHNOLOGIES

Havana has been a beneficiary of the most important inventions and technological advances, which made their way rapidly to the city, where they served as beacons for the rest of the island and for other countries in the hemisphere. One of the first modern technologies to appear in Havana was an early version of the telephone invented by the Italian-born Antonio Meucci (1808–1889) around 1850 so he could do his job as a stagehand, mechanic, and special-effects technician at the Tacón theater. Within a few years, Havana had horse-drawn public transportation, aqueducts, and electrical lighting.

On 24 January 1897, a motion picture screened in Havana for the first time, with great success. The 1906 documentary *El parque de Palatino* (Palatino Park) was the first motion picture made in Cuba. Huge crowds went to the movies every day, and Havana became the place to see European and American movies in Cuba. Such was the interest of Cuban fans of the seventh art that the city was obliged to build new and improved movie theaters, featuring all the technical advances of the age, in order to satisfy the rising demand.

Radio, a vitally important communications media, was launched in Havana in 1922 and became Cubans' medium of choice, since it is able to reach even the remotest corners of the country. A similar phenomenon occurred with television, which was launched in Havana in 1950, after the United States, Mexico, and Argentina.

THE IMPRESSIONS OF FOREIGN VISITORS

Throughout its history, Havana has received visits from notable personalities in the world of politics, history, and art, who have fallen for its charm. Other visitors came to recover their health, pass through on their way to other destinations, or conduct business. Havana was considered one of the finest of Spain's colonial cities in the Americas. Havana's charm was captured by the Spanish poet and dramatist Federico García Lorca (1898–1936), who, after a visit in the 1930s, just a few years before he was murdered, was claimed to have said: "si me pierdo, que me busquen en La Habana" (If I disappear, look for me in Havana) (Consejo Nacional de Cultura).

BIBLIOGRAPHY

Arrate, José Martín Félix de. *Llave del Nuevo Mundo antemural de las Indias Occidentales: La Habana descripta, noticias de su fundación, aumentos, y estados.* Havana: Imprenta Andrés Pego, 1876.

Artiles, Jenaro. *La Habana de Velázquez.* Cuadernos de historia Habanera. Havana: Municipality of Havana, 1946.

Bachiller y Morales, Antonio. *Apuntes para la historia de las letras y de la instrucción pública en la isla de Cuba.* 3 vols. Havana: Cultural, S. A., 1936.

Barras y Prado, Antonio de las. *La Habana a mediados del siglo XIX.* Madrid: Imprenta de la Ciudad Lineal, 1925.

Consejo Nacional de Cultura. *El poeta en La Habana: Federico García Lorca 1898–1936.* Havana: Author, 1961.

González del Valle, Francisco. *La Habana en 1841.* Havana: Office of the Historian of the City, 1952.

Humboldt, Alexander von. *Ensayo político sobre la isla de Cuba.* Havana: Editorial Cultural S.A., 1930.

Leal Spengler, Eusebio. *La Habana intramuros.* Havana: Office of the Historian of the City, 1975.

Leal Spengler, Eusebio. *La Habana: Ciudad antigua.* Havana: Editorial Letras Cubanas, 1988.

Roig de Leuchsenring, Emilio. *Historia de La Habana.* Havana: Municipality of Havana, 1938.

Roig de Leuchsenring, Emilio. *La Habana: Apuntes históricos.* 3 vols. Havana: National Cultural Council, 1963.

Rousset, Ricardo V. *Anales de la fundación de La Habana en su cuarto centenario.* Havana: Imprenta La Prueba, 1919.

Serres, Dominic. *Engravings of the Capture of Havana in 1762 by Dominic Serres.* Havana: José Martí National Library, 1962.

Torre, José María de la. *Lo que fuimos y lo que somos o La Habana antigua y moderna.* Havana: Imprenta de Spencer, 1857.

Urrutia Montoya, Ignacio José. *Teatro histórico, jurídico, y político militar de la isla Fernandina de Cuba y principalmente de su capital La Habana.* Havana: Imprenta Andrés Pego, 1876.

Valdés, Antonio José. *Historia de la Isla de Cuba y en especial de La Habana.* Havana: Imprenta Andrés Pego, 1877.

Wright, Irene A. *Historia documentada de San Cristóbal de La Habana en el siglo XVI, basada en los documentos originales existentes en el Archivo General de Indias en Sevilla.* Havana: El Siglo XX, 1927.

HAVANA: HISTORY OF URBANIZATION, HOUSING, AND PUBLIC SERVICES

Guillermo Jiménez

Urbanization, public services, important buildings, and the houses of the rich and poor, from colonial days to the early 2000s.

Although the date on which the city of Havana was founded is uncertain, it has officially been established as 16 November 1516. The city was originally founded on the southern coast, but was later relocated to the north, where it was built twice on the banks of different rivers until it was seated at the mouth of the harbor. In the early 2000s, Havana had more than two million inhabitants. As of 2011, it contained one-fifth of the country's population with a density thirty times greater than the national average, exhibited diverse architectural styles and epochs, and faced severe housing problems.

THE COLONY

The city was confined behind walls from 1674 to 1863 to protect it from pirates. The walled city was known as *Havana Vieja* (Old Havana) or *Intramuros* (Inside-the-Walls), and the section on the outskirts of the walls was known as *Extramuros* (Outside-the-Walls). For two and a half centuries, the city's only remarkable buildings were three military fortresses: Castillo de la Fuerza (built 1558–1577), Castillo de El Morro (built 1589–1630), and Castillo de San Salvador de La Punta (built 1590–1630).

It was not until the sugar boom at the end of the eighteenth century that this village of adobe and palm-thatch huts stirred from its lethargy. The first boulevards such as the Alameda de Paula were constructed in Intramuros, and what is in modern times called Paseo del Prado was constructed in Extramuros. A few streets were paved, and the Palacio de Gobierno and the Palacio del Segundo Cabo, paradigms of the Cuban baroque and the archetypes of future seigniorial mansions, were also built. During these years, the population of Havana (51,307 in 1792) grew larger than that of Philadelphia (42,444 in 1790) and New York (33,131 in 1790) (Boyer and Davies; Venegas Fornias p. 137).

The most outstanding of the few public works built during the city's first three centuries were the three aqueducts. The Zanja Real, the first aqueduct in the New World, was built in 1566. It had an open canal that ran 6.8 miles (11 km) from the Almendares River and remained in service until 1835, when it was replaced by the piped aqueduct of Ferdinand VII. The aqueduct designed by Havana engineer Francisco de Albear (1816–1887) was inaugurated in 1893; it is widely considered a world masterpiece of nineteenth-century engineering.

Beginning in 1839, horse-drawn omnibuses and urban railroads travelled throughout Havana. The telegraph was installed in 1853, and an underwater cable joined Havana and Florida in 1867. The public gas lamps of 1846 were replaced in 1889 by electric lights operated by the U.S. American Light and Power Company. In 1881, the U.S. company Edison Telephone Exchange introduced the telephone, a concession that was later transferred to the Western Electric Company.

THE REPUBLIC

Following independence in 1898, an urban development fever spread in Havana, starting in Marianao, which until then had been an aristocratic neighborhood. It reached a peak between 1913 and 1920, when the world price of sugar shot up from 1.95 per pound to 11.95 per pound. The Great Depression subsequently slowed the sector until after World War II (1939–1945), when an economic resurgence occurred, but that only benefited the middle and upper classes. After 1861, Spanish ordinances set aside lands in urbanized areas, known as *repartos*, for use as communal assets, the green areas and colonnaded porticoes that caused the writer Alejo Carpentier (1904–1980) to christen Havana as a *city of columns*, in a famous essay. In 1901, the U.S. government began construction of the most symbolic of the avenues of Havana, the Malecón, along the shoreline, which was built intermittently and not completed until 1959. During the 1920s, the two main government facilities, the Presidential Palace (1920) and the Capitol (1929), were erected. In the 1950s, two tunnels were built for automobile traffic, one running under the Almendares River and the other beneath the bay.

In 1899, only half of Havana's homes had running water; three percent had some kind of washroom or bathroom, only 48 percent of which had toilets. The city's sewer system was built with the support of the United States between 1908 and 1912; by the 1930s, however, a mere 10 percent of Havana's households had managed to connect to it. New aqueducts were built in Guanabacoa (1907), Cojímar (1908), Marianao (1916), Regla (1918), and Cuenca Sur (1956), while the Albear system was expanded three times between 1908 and 1948.

In 1901, an electric tramway was inaugurated by the U.S. firm Electric Bond and Share. The tram was replaced in 1950 by a bus company owned by the American William Pawley (1896–1977), the emissary the United States sent to Fulgencio Batista (1901–1973) in December 1958 to urge him to step down as head of state.

The U.S. firm ITTC, which had held the concession for the telephone monopoly since 1909, launched long-distance telephone service that same year. It installed the first automatic global network in 1910 and, in 1921, laid out a submarine cable to Florida. In the mid-1920s, Havana was the Latin American city with the highest number of telephones per capita, at seventy-five per one hundred residents; however, after 1952, the number of telephones dropped to one for every ten residents.

THE REVOLUTION

Although virtually the entire population became homeowners after the Revolution of 1959, the housing deficit continued to increase. Population growth, disrepair due to a lack of maintenance, and the postponement of new housing projects in the capital in favor of rural housing and other social projects aggravated the shortages. To address the demand for housing in Havana, existing units were subdivided, lofts were created in colonial houses with high ceilings, and establishments were restored under precarious conditions. The freedom to change addresses or to expand, rebuild, sell, inherit, donate, or build other structures was restricted, and there were further restrictions on internal migration from the provinces, which accounted for one-third of the population. As a result, the city's houses and their residents remained unchanged through space and time. Most urbanization took place on the idle land east of Havana, with builders taking advantage of facilities offered by the bay tunnel and other existing infrastructure. Buildings were erected to fill the empty spaces inside the *repartos* of the 1950s. The seats of political and administrative power were installed in the Plaza of the Revolution, which had been designed and built in the 1950s under the name of the Civic Plaza.

The prefabricated building sector expanded, but the quality of construction and urban planning was poor, and a rigidly monotonous anti-aesthetic architectural design became widespread (from which only a few exceptional buildings managed to break free, such as the Coppelia ice creamery, the Pabellón Cuba, the Las Ruinas restaurant, and the Convention Palace). The city's eastern aqueduct was built in 1972, the Gato aqueduct in 1987, and some sections of the Albear were repaired in 2000, but most of the water-system networks still needed to be restored as of 2011. All homes received chlorinated water through utility pipes, as of 2011, but only 60 percent were connected to the old sewer system, the two submarine drainages, or the processing tanks built in 2000.

Some other public services fell far behind. The availability of digitization and mobile phones, for example, lagged, and the economic crisis frustrated a project to build a subway. In the early 1980s a proposal was initiated to construct a subway system with service between Naranjito, Vedado, and Havana Vieja. However, due to much higher than anticipated costs, Soviet backing of the project was withdrawn in 1987 right before construction had been scheduled to begin.

HOUSING FOR THE POOR

The standard dwelling for the poor during Havana's colonial period was the *bohío,* the thatched hut of the indigenous people so typical of the Cuban landscape or some variation thereof using mixed and tamped clay, adobe, and palm fronds for roofing. Recently arrived slaves were housed in the *barracón,* a large, undivided building that also served as the home of rural slaves throughout the nineteenth century. From the sixteenth century onward, housing shortages were endemic and rents were high. In order to expand the city, powerful individuals resorted to arson to force blacks and mestizos off the land so they could build on the devastated properties.

By the end of colonial rule, thousands of campesinos had been thrown off their lands; Cuba's war with Spain for independence in 1898 drove many of these campesinos into Havana, where the housing shortage left many homeless. Even though rents were extraordinarily high and there was tremendous overcrowding, there were only three occasions during which neighborhoods for worker housing were subsidized. The economic depression of the 1920s and 1930s aggravated this situation. One-third of the population of Havana, overwhelmingly black, was ill-housed in dilapidated old mansions that were sectioned off into tiny, unhealthy dwellings known since colonial times as *solares,* whose rent nevertheless ate up half the occupants' income. For the most unfortunate among the populace, there was a proliferation of indigent *barrios.*

In 1939, widespread social unrest led to the approval of a Law on Rentals that offered tenants some protections. None of the successive administrations would dare repeal the law despite the power of the Urban Property Center of Havana, which sought unsuccessfully to legalize evictions, raise rents, and invalidate renters' rights. The Urban Property Center (founded in 1881 and active until the early years of the revolutionary government) was an organization supported by many property owners. These owners had accumulated large investments in real estate as the chronic instability in sugar's world price made them reluctant to invest their profits in the sugar industry even though it was more lucrative and also monopolized credit bank. Real estate was made even more attractive as an investment since there were no financial markets in which to invest. By the 1950s, nearly 90 percent of the occupants of houses were rent-paying, nonproprietor tenants.

Although the 1939 Law on Rentals prevented rent increases in buildings constructed before that date, it actually aggravated the housing shortage. In the 1950s, a little over one-third of the dwellings in Havana consisted of a single room, while only a little more than half the city's residences had their own bathroom, with slightly less than one-third in disrepair. The revolution eradicated most of the indigent

barrios but very few of the *solares,* which in the 1980s still accounted for 13 percent of homes.

THE HOUSES OF THE RICH

The first signs of social differentiation appeared in the first half of the sixteenth century, when wealthy residents began to build houses out of stone, brick, lime, and timber in the area where the Castillo de la Fuerza (the first fortress in America) would be built, subsequently spreading out to the site of the future Plaza de Armas. They congregated in the Plaza Vieja after the seventeenth century and around the plaza of the Cathedral after 1720, and by the end of the eighteenth century they lined the Alameda de Paula.

Ostentatious mansions flourished in the seventeenth century. These often had a Moorish influence; were two stories high; had windows and balconies of carved wood, tile roofs, and a rectangular central patio with a fountain, surrounded by galleries that led to the rooms. The first floor was used for hallways, coach stalls, a sitting room, offices, and storerooms, while the upper floor had bedrooms, a bathroom, the kitchen, and the dining room. During the first half of the eighteenth century, the tobacco boom gave rise to huge fortunes, which underwrote titles of nobility and luxurious mansions. These houses now featured a mezzanine to shelter the household slaves, shimmering marble on the floors and staircases, iron replacing wood, terraced roofs replacing tiles, and high gables and windows with grillwork and Venetian blinds to provide light and air to the interior.

Such structures were jammed together on narrow streets with no green areas. The upper classes lived side-by-side with the lower classes, and colonnades harbored the vendors and merchants, since there was no neighborhood equivalent to the West End of London (Hazard, vol. 1, p. 62). Like the colonial homes of British North America, these mansions often had offices and storerooms.

For a brief time, the rich of Havana managed to isolate themselves in El Cerro, the most elegant *barrio* of the nineteenth century. Yet regardless of how far they extended the city out toward Extramuros, the undignified vestiges of the old ruinous dwellings would continue to importune them, like a curse, until 1959. During the republic, new *barrios*—El Vedado, Miramar, and El Country—would arise in the west.

THE EXCLUSIVE BARRIOS

The most exclusive *reparto* of the bourgeoisie was Country Club Park, which was laid out on lands surrounding the golf club founded in 1903 by Frederick Snare, an American engineer, golf champion, and a future builder of major Cuban construction projects. In order to urbanize this area, Snare set up a corporation in 1914 with his fellow Americans Norman Davis (undersecretary of state under President Woodrow Wilson) and Robert M. Orr, and the Canadian James

A new hotel in Miramar. This hotel was under construction in 2001 in Havana's Miramar, an elegant district that became popular with Havana's elite during the 1920s. AP IMAGES/JOSE GOITIA

M. Hopwood, all partners in the Trust Company of Cuba, a Cuban branch of the House of Morgan, which was chaired by Davis.

El Vedado was the first *reparto* designed to modern urban standards. Even though its development began in 1859, its age of splendor really dates to 1910, when it displaced the erstwhile aristocratic Paseo del Prado. Inevitably, El Vedado began to decline after World War II under the encroachment of new buildings, businesses, and *solares*. The construction boom of the 1950s took place in this area, which included the city's tallest buildings. Wealthy families tended to move to other luxury *barrios* further west, although the two most powerful clans, Lobo and Batista-Falla, continued to live there.

Miramar extended the outskirts of the city beyond the Almendares River. The brothers Luís and Leonardo Morales Pedroso (an engineer and an architect, respectively) owned property in the area, which they designed and promoted in 1911. Leonardo was Cuba's most important architect of the bourgeoisie during the first third of the twentieth century.

The Havana Biltmore was the last *reparto* built after the end of World War II. It was promoted by the Americans John M. Bowman and Charles Flynn, horseracing and casino partners in Havana. Bowman had been the owner of the Bowman Biltmore Hotel chain, the largest of the 1920s,

and the co-owner of the famous Biltmore Hotel in Miami.

When the owners of these Miramar mansions fled the country, the Revolution converted the buildings to schools and student dormitories. In the early 2000s, they functioned as offices, shopping malls, hotels, modern buildings for foreigners, and diplomatic embassies. The most noteworthy architectural achievements of this period are the Instituto Superior del Arte (Higher Institute for Art), which was built over the gardens of the Country Club, and the restoration of Old Havana, which was designated a United Nations World Heritage site in 1982.

BIBLIOGRAPHY

Benz Arrate, José M. "La Habana colonial durante el siglo XIX." Pts. 1 and 2. *Revista nacional de la propiedad urbana* 21, no. 250 (December 1954); 22, no. 251 (January 1955).

Boyer, Richard E., and Keith A. Davies. *Urbanization in 19th Century Latin America: Statistics and Sources.* Los Angeles: Latin American Center, University of California, 1973.

Castro, Martha de. "Contribución al estudio de la arquitectura Cubana." Ph.D. diss., Universidad de La Habana: Imprenta La Verónica, 1940.

Chailloux Cardona, Juan M. *Síntesis histórica de la vivienda popular.* Havana: Jesús Montero, 1945.

Clark, William J. *Commercial Cuba: A Book for Business Men*. New York: Scribner's, 1898.

Costa, Octavio R. "El Centro de la propiedad urbana de La Habana." *Diario de la Marina* (May 23–30, 1954).

Cuevas Toraya, Juan de las. *500 años de construcciones en Cuba*. Madrid: Chavín, Servicios Gráficos y Editoriales, 2001.

Hazard, Samuel. *Cuba a pluma y lápiz*. 3 vols. Havana: Cultural S.A., 1928.

Inclán Lavastida, Fernando. *Historia de Marianao*, 2nd ed. Marianao, Cuba: Editorial El Sol, 1952.

Jiménez Soler, Guillermo. *Las empresas de Cuba 1958*, 4th ed. Havana: Editorial de Ciencias Sociales, 2008.

Jiménez Soler, Guillermo. *Los Propietarios de Cuba*, 3rd ed. Havana: Editorial de Ciencias Sociales, 2008.

Leal Spengler, Eusebio. *La Habana: Ciudad antigua*. Havana: Editorial Letras Cubanas, 1988.

Lloyd, Reginald. *Impresiones de la República de Cuba en el siglo veinte*. London: Gresham Press, Unwin, 1913.

Marrero, Leví. *Cuba: Economía y sociedad*. 15 vols. Madrid: Editorial Playor S.A., 1977.

Oficina Nacional de Estadísticas. *Informe nacional: Censo de población y viviendas, 2002*. Havana: ONE, September 2005.

Oficina Nacional de los Censos Demográfico y Electoral, Tribunal Superior Electoral. *Censos de población, viviendas, y electoral, enero 28 de 1953*. Havana: Fernández y Compañía S en C, 1955.

Pezuela, Jacobo de la. *Diccionario geográfico, estadístico, histórico de la isla de Cuba*. 4 vols. Madrid: Imprenta del Establecimiento de Mellado, 1863.

Quintana, Nicolás. "Evolución histórica de la arquitectura en Cuba." In *La enciclopedia de Cuba*, vol. 5, edited by Vicente Báez. Madrid: Editorial Playor, 1978.

Roig de Leuchsenring, Emilio. *La Habana: Apuntes históricos*. 3 vols. Havana: Editora del Consejo Nacional de Cultura, 1963.

Segre, Roberto. *La vivienda en Cuba en el siglo XX*. Mexico City: Editorial Concepto S.A., 1980.

Segre, Roberto. *Arquitectura y urbanismo de la Revolución Cubana*. Havana: Editorial Pueblo y Educación, 1995.

Venegas Fornias, Carlos. *Cuba y sus pueblos: Censos y mapas de los siglos XVIII y XIX*. Havana: Centro de Investigación y Desarrollo de la Cultura Cubana Juan Marinello, 2002.

Weiss, Joaquín. *Medio siglo de arquitectura cubana*. Havana: Imprenta Universitaria, 1950.

Weiss, Joaquín. *La arquitectura colonial Cubana*. Havana-Sevilla: Instituto Cubano del Libro and Junta de Andalucía, 1996.

Wright, Irene A. *Historia documentada de San Cristóbal de La Habana en el siglo XVI*. 2 vols. Havana: Imprenta el Siglo XX, 1927.

Wright, Irene A. *Historia documentada de San Cristóbal de La Habana en la primera mitad del siglo XVII*. 2 vols. Havana: Imprenta el Siglo XX, 1930.

HAVANA: URBAN AND SOCIAL HISTORY IN THE TWENTIETH CENTURY

Rafael M. Hernández Rodriguez

Social geography and urban culture of the capital city since Cuban independence.

During the colonial era Havana's strategic position made it a crossroads for commerce among Europe, Africa, Asia, and the Americas. Havana thus developed a cosmopolitan society of descendants of people from various places, including Europeans, Africans, Chinese, Arabs, Jews, and North Americans. After years of independence struggles, the military intervention of the United States (1898–1902) brought about the new Cuban republic, and a Havana looking to the North emerged with the new century.

SOCIAL GEOGRAPHY AND URBAN CULTURE

By 1902 the Havana elite had already moved from the old city to El Cerro and, to the west, El Vedado. During the 1920s they moved to Miramar, and during the 1940s and 1950s to Biltmore and Country Club. They gathered in private clubs whose names painted a group portrait: Havana Yacht Club, Vedado Tennis Club, Havana Biltmore Yacht and Country Club, Miramar Yacht Club, and Casino Español Club. In these enclaves—which after the 1959 Revolution became social clubs for unions—the elite played cricket and tennis, sailed their yachts, drank and played cards. A North American influence took shape in buildings such as the Lonja de Comercio (Commerce Exchange), the train terminal, and other later buildings in the art deco style, such as the López Serrano (at L and 13th Streets), the Bacardí (near Parque Central), and the América movie theater on Avenida Galiano. However, it was in the eastern zone of El Vedado, located near the Hotel Nacional, the university, and Avenida Paseo, in modern buildings such as the Focsa and luxury hotels named Capri, Riviera, and Hilton, that this American Havana was established by upper- and middle-class Cubans.

On Havana's numerous radio stations, residents encountered the rich universe of Cuban music, which assimilated the heritage of Spain, Africa, and North America. Tourists in huge numbers brought the customs, lifestyles, and consumption style typical of the North, which caught on among city residents. The thousands of U.S. citizens residing in the capital had access to numerous English-language periodicals, as well as radio, television programs, and films from the United States—sometimes, as Louis Pérez Jr. notes in *On Becoming Cuban* (2008), even before these reached certain parts of the United States itself. Through these forms of exposure, Havana assimilated U.S. culture—its standards of business efficiency, technological modernity, and household comfort, as well as its favored types of entertainment and pastimes, most especially baseball.

In luxury hotels and cabarets called Montmartre and Sans Souci, gambling rooms proliferated, where Cubans and wealthy foreigners socialized with mafia bosses such as Meyer Lansky, Lucky Luciano, and Santo Trafficante Jr. Cubans and foreigners enjoyed games of chance such as the lottery and the numbers and placed bets at the Marianao horse-racing track and a dog track in the beach rotunda across from the Havana Yacht Club. However, many visitors thought of the city less as the Monte Carlo of the Antilles than as the bordello of the Caribbean. In this pre-1959 Havana, prostitution was not limited to a particular neighborhood but went on in brothels all over town: in the exclusive Casa Marina, near Maceo Park in Malecón; Calle Pajarito south of the Carlos III market; the neighborhood of Colón adjacent to the commercial center at Galiano and San Rafael; Barrio Chino (Chinatown), where the infamous Shanghai Theater presented live sex shows and pornography; and, for the cheapest sex, the nightclubs of Playa de Marianao and Avenida del Puerto.

The center of Havana, which in 1900 was located in the area surrounding the Teatro Tacón (later called the Gran Teatro) and the Parque Central, moved in the 1940s and 1950s to the Galiano and San Rafael area, where the commercial sector was growing to be the most vigorous in the capital. During that period the city was more heterogeneous than in the early 2000s, with more highly demarcated zones. Working-class neighborhoods were dotted with shops and gathering places: small corner stores, grocery stores, bars, produce stands, the lottery and numbers desk, *frita* (fried meatball) and oyster stands, laundries, the neighborhood cinema.

As the wealthy city expanded toward the east, the working-class city moved out in all other directions. South of Miramar, Marianao grew, beginning with the settlements west of the Almendares River, including working-class neighborhoods such as Pogolotti and La Lisa. In the far south of the city, other similar neighborhoods multiplied, such as Lawton, El Diezmero, Arroyo Apolo, Mantilla, and Vibora Park. Old enclaves outside the old city, to the southeast and the east, such as Atarés, joined small villages later connected by urban corridors on the borders of the old avenues of Jesús del Monte, Bejucal, and Luyanó, secondary arteries that united old Havana with villages such as El Calvario, Párraga, and San Miguel del Padrón. On the other side of the bay, the seaside villages of Guanabacoa, Regla, Casablanca, centers of popular Afro-Cuban religions, maintained connections to the city via small boats that crossed the bay incessantly. According to one study, in the 1940s, 18 percent of all Cubans lived in this Greater Havana (Scarpaci, Segre, and Coyula).

La Timba. Havana residents who lacked the means to pay rent settled in precarious huts of cardboard and planks in neighborhoods such as La Timba. COURTESY OF THE CUBAN HERITAGE COLLECTION, UNIVERSITY OF MIAMI LIBRARIES, CORAL GABLES, FLORIDA

As with other cities in the hemisphere, by mid-century an underground city had sprung up in Havana. Many old colonial mansions, as well as new buildings in downtown Havana and other areas, sheltered poor tenants in unsanitary and overcrowded conditions. Those who lacked the means to pay rent settled in precarious huts of cardboard and planks, in neighborhoods such as Las Yaguas, Llega y Pon, El Romerillo, La Timba, Coco Solo, and Palo Cagao. This squalid city, side by side with the city of theater marquees, nightlife, and commerce, revealed an ever more acute social polarization.

THE REVOLUTION AND BEYOND

The social struggles of workers and students, which had not ceased since the first decades of the century, erupted following the overthrow of Gerardo Machado into a bloody civil war (1933–1935) (Tabares del Real). Although it was thwarted, this revolution gained women the vote and led to a new constitution that enshrined this and other new civil rights.

The Revolution of 1959 had a profound and wide-ranging impact on Havana's society and urban culture. The new government proclaimed free access to blacks and whites at all beaches and recreational areas. A program of urban reform nationalized apartment buildings and reduced rents by half, created a community housing plan, and eradicated more than thirty unsanitary neighborhoods. Those Havana residents who became militiamen, literacy instructors, teachers, volunteer cane harvesters, and coffee pickers became aware of living in the privileged capital of a poor country; they witnessed rampant hunger, curable diseases, and illiteracy in the countryside. As Oscar Luis López noted in his 1998 book, Havana had 123 cinemas as compared to no more than three or four in most provincial capitals, and 36 radio stations out of the total 66 in Cuba. This new awareness, together with the radical ideology of the Revolution, resulted in social policies that were more favorable to the rest of the country.

With its special connection to the United States lost, Havana established new ties with Eastern Europe. The showcase of Cuban capitalism was transformed. Among the many changes noted by Dick Cluster and Rafael Hernández, the Sears-Roebuck chain, new models of cars, casinos, cockfights, and the numbers game all disappeared. The brothels closed and the exclusive clubs were thrown open to all, as were the private schools, which had been nationalized. In the expensive shops, Omega and Rolex watches were replaced by the less-expensive Poljot and Raketa. The bookstores sold European, Cuban, and Latin American literature, as well as the works of Mao, Lenin, Marx, and Martí, at giveaway prices.

Between 1959 and 1962 the city was abandoned by its elite, and the poor took over their formerly exclusive spaces. After agrarian reform and the nationalization of large businesses in 1960, owners of property, factories, and luxury stores emigrated, as later did the Jewish and Arab proprietors of the businesses on Calle Muralla. Chinese laundries, *frita* stands, produce stands, and corner stores survived in the hands of small shopkeepers until 1968, when they were also nationalized. Between the 1960s and 1980s, equitable gains were made in Havana residents' standard of living, rate of employment, public health, and access to education. Rents dropped along with the prices of rationed basic foodstuffs, public transportation, books, and even dining out. Kindergartens, schools, university centers, hospitals, theaters, museums, libraries, and bookstores multiplied. The cultural life of the city became more diversified and democratic: ballet, modern dance, art, and vanguard film became available for popular consumption, with screenings of films from the Soviet Union and Eastern Europe, Japan, Italy, France, England, Spain, and Latin America. Stores were filled with Russian televisions and canned meats; Bulgarian jams, vegetable preserves, and wines; blenders and records from East Germany and Czechoslovakia. In the streets, Lada, Moskvitch, and Volga automobiles from Russia proliferated. This encounter left its mark on Cuban culture. Cubans could study the Russian, Czech, German, and Serbo-Croatian languages for free. Tens of thousands of Cubans went to study in the Soviet Union and its Eastern European satellites, and some, particularly men, married natives from Warsaw or Prague.

Beginning in the 1970s, Cuba, and primarily Havana, produced an ever greater number of doctors, teachers, art instructors, and sports coaches, who became an exportable surplus. Workers in Havana came into contact with a greater variety of cultures than ever before. In addition to civil and military cooperation with countries in Africa, the Middle East, and Central America, the University of Havana welcomed thousands of foreign students—Angolans, Palestinians, Ethiopians, Afghans, Ukrainians, and Vietnamese.

In the Cuba of 1958, barely 11 percent of the population was practicing Catholics, 6 percent identified themselves as Protestant, and the majority professed a popular faith, a blending of African religions (Santería, Palo Monte, Abakuá) with elements of Christianity and spiritualism. With the Revolution, popular religions were legitimized as a part of the cultural heritage, in its music, dance, and oral traditions. But the conflict between the Catholic Church and the Revolution and its adoption of an official ideology that proclaimed atheism prompted many Havana residents to renounce their beliefs or not to practice them from that point forward.

THE CRISIS OF THE 1990s

Provoked by both internal and external causes, particularly the 1991 collapse of the Soviet Union and dissolution of the Eastern Bloc, the nation was in crisis during the 1990s. In Havana (and in all of Cuba) the standard of living dropped by 30 percent as a result of reductions in the energy supply, food, and transportation, with everyone having to ride bicycles. The black market, unemployment, and inequality increased. This massive decline triggered a migratory wave, the *balsero* (rafter) crisis of 1994. Although much less than in any Latin American capital, sex and drug markets catering to the tourist trade became more common than ever before in post-1959 Cuba. The government authorized the circulation and exchange of convertible currency, self-employment, a free market for agricultural and manufactured products, and foreign investment. These freelance activities, together with tourism and remittances received from family members outside the country, became a greater portion of the income of families in Havana. Although affected, health, education, and social security services were nonetheless maintained.

The slow economic recovery at the end of the century brought with it a resurgence of the Parque Central area, with its nightlife and attractive hotels, as the center of Havana. Thanks to the reinvestment of tourist dollars, the old city, deteriorating for decades, revived somewhat, although the same was not true for the rest of the capital, where homes suffered from overcrowding and lack of maintenance.

At the beginning of the twenty-first century, the society and culture of Havana, with a population of 2.2 million, underwent yet another uncertain and difficult transformation. The number of mechanics, electricians, carpenters, masons, taxi drivers, barbers, and others who work for themselves once again grew, and the number of students in Havana's universities increased. Small produce markets appeared again and vehicle traffic picked up on Havana's streets, including bicycle taxis, 1940s Chevys, and horse-drawn carriages. As in days gone by, the city continued to be characterized by these curious means of transportation, its cosmopolitan atmosphere, and especially, the *bulla*, the whirl and bustle that has always pervaded life in Havana.

BIBLIOGRAPHY

Cluster, Dick, and Rafael Hernández. *The History of Havana*. New York: Palgrave Macmillan, 2006.

Hernández, Rafael. *Looking at Cuba: Essays on Culture and Civil Society*, translated by Dick Cluster. Gainesville: University Press of Florida, 2003.

Iglesias Utset, Marial. *Las metáforas del cambio en la vida cotidiana: Cuba 1898–1902*. Havana: Ediciones Unión, 2003. Translated by Russ Davidson as *A Cultural History of Cuba during the U.S. Occupation, 1898–1902* (Chapel Hill: University of North Carolina Press, 2011).

López, Oscar Luis. *La radio en Cuba*, 2nd rev. ed. Havana: Letras Cubanas, 1998.

Ojeda, Jorge Pavez. *El Vedado: 1850–1940: De monte a reparto*. Havana: Centro Juan Marinello, 2003.

Pérez, Louis A., Jr. *On Becoming Cuban: Identity, Nationality, and Culture*. Chapel Hill: University of North Carolina Press, 2008.

Pérez, Louis A., Jr. *Cuba: Between Reform and Revolution*, 4th ed. New York: Oxford University Press, 2011.

Scarpaci, Joseph, Roberto Segre, and Mario Coyula. *Havana: Two Faces of the Antillean Metropolis*, rev. ed. Chapel Hill: University of North Carolina Press, 2002.

HEALTH AND HEALTH CARE

Cuba has a long and well-established history in medical science. Its development can be traced back to the nineteenth century, when a generation of physicians was culturally formed and professionally trained abroad, principally in France and the United States, a tradition that continued through the middle part of the twentieth century.

That the celebrated health-care system in the early Cuban republic was concentrated in urban centers, to the neglect of rural areas, was a manifestation of the larger social inequalities of the post-colonial society and a source of mounting discontent. With the triumph of the Cuban Revolution in 1959 and the subsequent emigration of vast numbers of physicians and health-care workers, the Cuban health system reorganized around egalitarian norms. After the revolution, medicine was as important as it had been in the republic, celebrated as a singular achievement of Cuban socialism.

As the essays that follow indicate, Cuba was particularly successful in projecting a global presence in health care, as a result of dispatching thousands of physicians, nurses, and health-care technicians to Third World countries and giving students from all over the world educational opportunities.

HEALTH AND HEALTH CARE: INTRODUCTION

Ester R. Shapiro

Cuba's integrative public health framework.

The Cuban Revolution's success in improving health for all Cubans—termed a paradox for achieving with far fewer economic resources health outcomes comparable to wealthy nations—is among the most admired of its social reforms. Although pre-1959 Cuba had one of the most advanced health systems in the region, medical care was influenced by U.S. and French models that failed to address Cuban realities, with significant economic, geographic, and racial disparities. Postrevolutionary Cuba has substantially improved its health status, as measured by World Health Organization (WHO) indices of morbidity (disease burden), mortality (causes of death and years of life), and health equity as measured by universal access to primary care. Cuba protected these gains while facing significant economic hardships due to the collapse of the Soviet Union, the continuation of the U.S. blockade, and the global economic crisis of the early 2000s. When half the island's physicians and most medical school faculty left after 1959, Cuba faced a challenging yet transformative opportunity to reorganize health care in line with revolutionary goals. Starting in 1959, the Cuban Revolution used principles of health as a human right, equitable access that systematically addressed existing economic and geographic disparities, centralized government responsibility and control, and application of high-quality research evidence to implement an evolving, multisectoral health systems transformation that emphasized community-based primary care and was responsive to changing Cuban realities (Rojas Ochoa).

Cuba's accomplishments are best understood using global health promotion and human development frameworks that recognize that both individual and population health result from burdens and resources in multiple systems, requiring attention to public health, community education and mobilization, and health-care system reforms (Hadad Hadad and Valdés Llanes; Spiegel and Yassi; WHO). These models understand health outcomes to be determined by social factors such as education, housing, employment, and environmental quality; by health-care organization, quality, and access that favors primary care and education; and by individual participation and engagement across personal, family, and community levels in promoting health and preventing illness. Human development economic frameworks (UNDP) argue that social investments in health, education, and employment offer better indicators of population quality of life than do measures of gross national product. With far smaller per-capita income and health expenditures, Cuba's investments in education and health have resulted in indicators such as life expectancy and infant mortality that are comparable to those in the world's wealthiest nations.

Cuba's achievements have generated considerable debate among health policy analysts who study them. Cuba's national health system is organized under the Ministry of Public Health, with three levels—national, provincial, and municipal—linked to levels of political organization. The system provides primary care (family doctors and interdisciplinary teams focused on homes and neighborhoods and schools and workplaces), secondary care (polyclinics), and tertiary care (hospitals and specialized services). Health psychology and family-based behavioral health is integrated into every level of care (Louro Bernal and Serrano Patten). Cuba's integration of public health and civic engagement has made the nation a global leader in primary care and in specialties, including HIV/AIDS prevention and treatment, hurricane and disaster response, and targeted infectious disease response (as in dengue outbreaks). The use of mass media and neighborhood organizations in public health education and mobilization, as well as the deployment of providers as educators and researchers, has generated model programs linking individual and collective health promotion, prevention, and treatment.

Cuba's approach required reorganization of medical and provider education, with social and family primary-care medicine foundational. Cuban doctors and other providers are trained as experts on whole patients in family and community contexts, conducting home visits in interdisciplinary teams and working in community settings as well as polyclinics. Although the Cuban health-care system supports specialized care, by intention and economic necessity it places greater emphasis on doctor-patient relationships than on high-technology or specialty care. Cuba has also made significant investments in health research using science to guide innovation. Health research is conducted in primary care settings, specialty hospitals, and specialized biotechnology centers, which have played a critical role in developing affordable medications and equipment for national use and regional sales. Cuba's integrative approach protected population health outcomes even during the worst of the nation's economic crisis in the 1990s (the Special Period in a Time of Peace), when resources, including basic medical supplies, were often unavailable.

By placing health at the center of revolutionary values and planning, Cuba has produced a unique form of articulate, critically engaged health citizenship. Cubans are remarkably informed about health concerns and vocal about the accomplishments and faults of their health system. The importance of health awareness is reinforced throughout society, with educational campaigns that employ government media and community outreach as well as provider relationships. Cuba faces the same challenges of managing chronic diseases and caring for aging populations that wealthier countries face, with far less access to high-technology specialty care and material limitations at every level, greatly compounded by the expense of bypassing the U.S. blockade. Enduring economic stresses of everyday life increase the chronic illness burden, compounded by high costs of improved nutrition and high rates of smoking. Ironically, researchers documented a temporary drop in chronic diseases associated with excess calories and cigarettes, including diabetes and heart disease, during the Special Period (Franco et al.).

In dealing with the continuing economic hardships that affect Cubans' quality of life, the Cuban health provider's revolutionary responsibilities require careful testing of relationships to determine which concerns can be discussed openly and which must be managed through the informal economy, *sociolismo* (associate or friendship networks; a play on *socialism*), and the constant process of *resolver* (solving problems or making do). Economic constraints intensified by the global economic crisis and the continued U.S. blockade impose barriers to achieving individual and population health goals.

These economic hardships are frequently discussed privately but seldom directly acknowledged in provider and policy forums. Cuba's two currencies, one national (peso) and one for foreign exchange (CUC), have created new forms of inequality because some people benefit from family remittances or access to CUC through formal employment or the informal economy. Recognizing economic limitations, the Cuban government continues to invest in health policies that protect the revolutionary vision in which every Cuban enjoys good health as a social responsibility and a human right.

■ *See also*

Science and Technology in Cuba

BIBLIOGRAPHY

Franco, Manuel, Pedro Orduñez, Benjamin Caballero, and Richard Cooper. "Obesity Reduction and Its Possible Consequences: What Can We Learn from Cuba's Special Period?" *Canadian Medical Association Journal* 178, no. 8 (2008): 1032–1034.

Hadad Hadad, Jorge Luis, and Elías Valdés Llanes. "La protección social en salud como enfrentamiento a una crisis económica." *Revista Cubana de Salud Pública* 36, no. 3 (September 2010).

Louro Bernal, Isabel, and Ana Serrano Patten. "La investigación familiar y el valor de la metodología cualitativa para el estudio del afrontamiento a la enfermedad sicklemica." *Revista Cubana de Salud Pública* 35, no. 1 (March 2009).

Mason, Susan, David Strug, and Joan Beder. *Community Health Care in Cuba*. Chicago: Lyceum, 2010.

Rojas Ochoa, Francisco. "La salud pública revolucionaria cubana en su aniversario 50." *Revista Cubana de Salud Pública* 35, no. 1 (March 2009).

Spiegel, Jerry M., and Annalee Yassi. "Lessons from the Margins of Globalization: Appreciating the Cuban Health Paradox." *Journal of Public Health Policy* 25 (2004): 85–110.

United Nations Development Programme (UNDP). *The Real Wealth of Nations: Pathways to Human Development*. New York: Palgrave Macmillan, 2010.

Whiteford, Linda, and Lawrence Branch. *Primary Health Care in Cuba: The Other Revolution*. Lanham, MD: Rowman & Littlefield, 2008.

World Health Organization (WHO). *The World Health Report: Primary Care Now More than Ever*. Geneva, Switzerland: Author, 2008.

HEALTH AND HEALTH CARE: PRE-1959

Jennifer Lambe

Health and health care in Cuba from the early colonial period, with a particular emphasis on the 1899–1959 period.

Health and health care were closely tied to the changing political circumstances of Cuba's prerevolutionary history. This relationship was manifest throughout the colonial and national periods, from the dependence of early medical practice on the sugar-slave complex to debates over Cuban sovereignty with respect to yellow fever in the late nineteenth and early twentieth centuries. Health and health care constituted a crucial arena of political contestation and nationalist assertion, and mobilizations around medicine were thus strongly connected to independence, antidictatorial, and revolutionary struggles.

EARLY COLONIAL PERIOD

During the early colonial period, the island in general and health care in particular suffered imperial neglect. This weakness of institutional medicine created an opening for extra-institutional and non-European healing. Though steps toward the formation of an official field of health care were taken with the naming in 1634 of Havana's first *protomédico*, a physician charged by the Spanish Crown with regulating medical services, the office remained vacant for several decades after his death. Hospitals, which originated in military health facilities or religious charity initiatives, were notoriously inadequate and in poor condition.

SUGAR BOOM; MEDICAL EXPANSION

This chronic medical underdevelopment began to be reversed with the late-eighteenth-century boom of sugar production and slavery in Cuba. Tomás Romay Chacón (1764–1849) was the critical medical innovator of this period. Most celebrated for his smallpox vaccination campaign, he also advocated for broader reforms, including the secularization of medicine. His career was closely tied to the expansion of African

Nuestra Señora de las Mercedes Hospital in Havana. The former Nuestra Señora de las Mercedes Hospital in Havana, inaugurated in the 1880s, was demolished in 1957. COURTESY OF THE CUBAN HERITAGE COLLECTION, UNIVERSITY OF MIAMI LIBRARIES, CORAL GABLES, FLORIDA

slavery, which he hoped to rationalize and put under the oversight of modern medical science. Like other physicians of the time, Romay's professional ascension depended on a close relationship to the expanding slave forces on sugar plantations. Many doctors in training gained clinical and surgical experience and enhanced their professional reputations in tours of duty on plantations. By the 1840s the University of Havana was graduating increasing numbers of native-born physicians thanks to the growth prompted by sugar in the previous decades. Some have argued that Cuba in this period represented a "laboratory of modernity" due to the intermingling of medical advancement and racial subjection in the sugar-slave complex (López Denis; Palmer).

The founding of the Real Academia de Ciencias Médicas, Físicas y Naturales de La Habana in 1861 marked the inauguration of a national medical and science field. As elsewhere, the ascendance of bacteriology proved a boon to the medical and associated professions. The spirit of association during this period was also galvanized by the emergence of an expanded civil society after the Ten Years' War (1868–1878) (Funes Monzote). Science and medicine acquired an increasingly public and political character, not only through the involvement of doctors in the revolutionary struggles of the time, but also in the significance attached to medicine as a barometer of Cuba's capacity for national sovereignty (Funes Monzote; Espinosa). This period saw the emergence of an oversupply in Havana's medical personnel due to the increased

importance of medical education as an avenue of social mobility. An influx of Spanish immigrants in the last third of the nineteenth century led to the founding of *centros regionales*, or ethnic centers, with their own mutualist clinics in which members paid a small monthly fee to receive subsidized health care and some social services.

YELLOW FEVER; MEDICAL INTERVENTION

Despite the consolidation of a Cuban medical profession in the latter part of the nineteenth century, the prevalence of poorly understood diseases remained an obstacle to the advancement of health care. In the 1870s, Carlos J. Finlay (1833–1915), a Cuban physician and scientist, began experiments on the etiology and course of yellow fever. By 1881 he had arrived at the conclusion that yellow fever transmission could best be explained in terms of an insect vector, specifically the mosquito *Aedes aegypti*, which spread the disease by biting first an infected and then a healthy person. Finlay's innovative research was mostly ignored or belittled until the U.S. occupation following the War of Independence of 1895–1898.

Anxiety over several prior yellow fever epidemics in the Caribbean and Gulf of Mexico region was a motivation behind the U.S. decision to intervene in the War of Independence. Yellow fever control became a justification for U.S. intervention after the defeat of the Spanish in 1898 and would remain a point of contention between the United States and a fledgling sovereign Cuba (Espinosa). The health

CUBA

officials of the occupation government first moved to eradicate yellow fever in Cuba through improved sanitation. The failure of these projects led occupation officials in 1900 to establish the Yellow Fever Commission, headed by Walter Reed (1851–1902), which eventually recapitulated Finlay's earlier path from bacteriological to vector explanations for the spread of yellow fever. The health officials of the occupation's Sanitary Department mounted an exhaustive attack on the mosquito in Cuba with impressive success. Though this work retroactively vindicated the earlier hypotheses of Finlay and others, Reed received—and continues to receive—the credit for this discovery outside Cuba.

The U.S. concern for yellow fever control in Cuba was enshrined in the Platt Amendment (1901), which forced a sanitation clause upon the Cuban Convention. The debate over yellow fever reflected Cuban concern about U.S. infringements on Cuban sovereignty and a fundamental divergence of opinion on yellow fever; in Cuba, yellow fever was understood to affect mostly foreigners and thus did not represent a critical health issue, whereas the United States considered the disease to be a top priority. Subsequent instances in which Cubans were believed to have neglected the sanitation standards mandated by the Platt Amendment generated tensions between Cuba and the United States, contributing to a second U.S. occupation in 1906. The 1906–1909 provisional governorship of Charles E. Magoon (1861–1920) abolished municipal health boards and transferred control over public health to the National Board of Sanitation, headed by Finlay. This nationalization of sanitation led to a swift and successful campaign against yellow fever.

The public health programs of the U.S. occupation governments, however, were not merely extensions of imperial power. Once yellow fever had been targeted, both Leonard Wood (1860–1927), military governor during the first U.S. occupation from 1899–1902, and then Magoon moved to more ambiguously humanitarian interventions in public health, including anti-tuberculosis campaigns and hospital rebuilding. It was during this period that an impressive decline in the Cuban mortality rate began, following the demographic and epidemiological catastrophe of the independence war.

Despite the efforts of many Cuban physicians, however, official corruption undermined many public health endeavors during the Republican period. Hospital administrative positions were often acquired through cronyism, and bribes and sinecures were the order of the day. Meanwhile, the highest quality medical care was restricted to proliferating clinics in ethnic centers. Poorer *habaneros* and rural Cubans were forced to resort to less-developed public health institutions, and, outside of Havana, health care arrangements for the nonelite tended to be ad hoc.

The international prevalence of eugenics during this period also impacted the development of the medical field in Cuba. In the early decades of the twentieth century, two Cuban physicians, Domingo F. Ramos (1884–?) and Eusebio Hernández (1853–1933), developed the French-influenced discipline of homiculture. Ramos became a principal advocate of eugenics in Cuba and Latin America at large. As elsewhere in Latin America, homiculture incorporated environmental as well as biological (breeding) solutions in targeting the problems of alcoholism, venereal disease, and sanitary conditions in cities. In contrast with Ramos's more narrowly racist and biological view, which dominated this early period of Cuban eugenics, Hernández's vision of a socially attuned eugenics movement and medical establishment would resurface in the 1930s (García González and Álvarez Peláez).

THE REVOLUTIONARY REPUBLIC

Obstetrician and eugenicist José Chelala-Aguilera was representative of a new generation of physicians and medical students whose views on medical care were radicalized by the experience of university agitation in the 1920s and mobilization in the Revolution of 1933, which toppled president Gerardo Machado (1871–1939). In the course of the struggle, this cohort came to assume the leadership of the medical establishment but remained divided between those physicians who sought more propitious conditions for private medical practice through an attack on the established centros regionales and others who favored social medicine. A significant step toward the emergence of this new bloc of physicians, united around their opposition to the ethnic centers but otherwise quite diverse in ideological orientation, was the formation of the Federación Médica de Cuba (FMC) in 1925. The attack was launched in an FMC strike against the Centro Gallego, an ethnic association of Spaniards, which had come to be seen as a bastion of Spanish privilege. Medical strikes coincided in some cases with the movement against the regime of Machado and general anti-Spanish sentiment in Cuba. In the course of the struggle, a more radical group split off. This left wing of the medical movement favored greater attention to social medicine, medical ethics, and the rights of patients.

Medical strikes continued under the regime of Colonel Fulgencio Batista (1901–1973), who had deposed President Ramón Grau San Martín (1887–1969) in a 1934 coup. Severe repression greeted medical strikers under his watch. By the end of the March 1935 strike, the FMC had been declared illegal, and it did not reappear again for several years. The fortunes of all factions in the FMC were subject to quick change during this period. During an upswing in the late 1930s and early 1940s, the FMC successfully lobbied for restrictions on the centros regionales, a single professional post for physicians, a minimum wage, physician retirement plans, and compulsory physician federation, though some of these victories evaporated in later years.

Despite the participation of the FMC in formulating national policy in the early 1940s, its members tended not to address the most glaring inadequacy of institutional health care in Cuba: medical concentration in Havana and other large urban centers, to the detriment of the health of rural, nonelite Cubans (Danielson). Only the more radical members of the FMC entertained proposals that would aid nonwealthy patients on a national scale, and one such project for a national mutuality of medical assistance was quickly defeated in the FMC. Thus, though institutional health care supported by the government expanded after the Revolution of 1933, its extension or quality did not improve significantly for neglected groups outside the cities.

EXTRA-INSTITUTIONAL HEALING

Since colonial times, popular healing had been a primary recourse for many inhabitants of the island in case of illness. Colorful figures stand out in the long history of *curanderismo*, or folk healing, in Cuba: from Juan Chambombián (*el médico chino*, [the Chinese doctor]), who was tried for the illegal practice of medicine, to the *Hombre Dios* (Man God) Juan Manso, who emphasized spiritual cures for physical ailments in the late nineteenth and early twentieth centuries. The multifaceted healing practices that had emerged throughout Cuba during the colonial period also became the target of popular racist anxieties, as in the African *brujo* (witch) scares from the 1900s into the 1920s. Several decades later, the radio host Clavelito (1908–1975) was able to parlay his adaptation of hydrotherapeutic healing into fame and popularity across wide sectors of the Cuban populace (Román). There is no simple story to tell about these diverse popular healers, who were frequented not only by the poor, black, and rural Cubans who had little access to other medical care, but also by wealthy and middle-class white *habaneros*.

HEALTH INDICATORS; STRUCTURAL LEGACIES

While it is difficult to assess the health profile of all regions of Cuba prior to 1959, some general patterns can be emphasized. Due to sanitation and medical technology improvements, a steady decline in mortality statistics characterized the period from 1899 to 1959. From 15.18 deaths per thousand people in 1906, the mortality rate had dropped to 4.93 by 1958, one of the lowest rates in the hemisphere (Hernández p. 543). Similarly, the infant mortality rate registered a significant decline during the years of the Republic, from 58.5 per thousand in 1926 to 33.7 in 1958 (Hernández p. 544). A large number of physicians and greater development of health services compared to other Latin American countries contributed to strong health indicators. By 1953, Cuba's life expectancy at birth, 58.8 years, was one of the highest in Latin America, though life expectancy in Havana, at 62.7 years, indicates disparities between Havana and the rest of the country (Díaz-Briquets p. 111). The regional distribution of hospital beds in 1958 is further testament to the urban-rural divide in pre-1959 health care: Havana's 9.6 beds per 1,000 population stood in stark contrast to the other provinces, whose beds per 1,000 population ranged from 1.9 to 2.7 (Díaz-Briquets p. 107).

On a structural and administrative level, the corruption, graft, and inefficiency that pervaded health care throughout the Republican years, with a brief intermission around the Revolution of 1933, provided ideological fodder for the continued politicization of health care after 1959, particularly in the underserved rural areas. Those FMC physicians with more radical agendas quickly became disillusioned by the evident gap between rhetoric and reality under the administrations of Grau and Carlos Prío Socarrás (1903–1977), much as their predecessors had been under the *caudillos* of the early Republic and under Gerardo Machado and Fulgencio Batista. After 1959, centralization and extension into the rural areas of Cuba early on became the solutions to the chronic shortcomings of Cuban health care.

BIBLIOGRAPHY

Danielson, Ross. *Cuban Medicine*. New Brunswick, NJ: Transaction Books, 1979.

Delgado García, Gregorio. *Temas y personalidades de la historia médica cubana*. Cuadernos de Historia de la Salud Pública, no. 72. Havana: Consejo Nacional de Sociedades Científicas del Ministerio de Salud Pública, 1987.

Díaz-Briquets, Sergio. *The Health Revolution in Cuba*. Austin: University of Texas Press, 1983.

Espinosa, Mariola. *Epidemic Invasions: Yellow Fever and the Limits of Cuban Independence, 1878–1930*. Chicago: University of Chicago Press, 2009.

Funes Monzote, Reinaldo. *El despertar del asociacionismo científico en Cuba, 1876–1920*. Havana: Centro Cultural Juan Marinello, 2004.

García González, Armando, and Raquel Álvarez Peláez. *En busca de la raza perfecta. Eugenesia e higiene en Cuba (1898–1958)*. Madrid: CSIC, 1999.

Hernández, Roberto E. "La atención médica en Cuba hasta 1958." *Journal of Inter-American Studies* 11, no. 4 (October 1969): 533–557.

López Denis, Adrián. "Melancholia, Slavery, and Racial Pathology in Eighteenth-Century Cuba." *Science in Context* 18, no. 2 (2005): 179–199.

López Sánchez, José. *Cuba, medicina y civilización: Siglos XVII y XVIII*. Havana: Editorial Científico-Técnica, 1995.

McGuire, James W., and Laura B. Frankel. "Mortality Decline in Cuba, 1900–1959: Patterns, Comparisons, and Causes." *Latin American Research Review* 40, no. 2 (2005): 83–116.

Palmer, Steven. "From the Plantation to the Academy: Slavery and the Production of Cuban Medicine in the Nineteenth Century." In *Health and Medicine in the Circum-Caribbean, 1800–1968*, edited by Juanita De Barros, Steven Palmer, and David Wright. New York: Routledge, 2009.

Roig de Leuchsenring, Emilio. *Médicos y medicina en Cuba: Historia, biografía, costumbrismo.* Havana: Museo Histórico de las Ciencias Médicas "Carlos J. Finlay," 1965.

Román, Reinaldo. *Governing Spirits: Religion, Miracles, and Spectacles in Cuba and Puerto Rico, 1898–1956.* Chapel Hill: University of North Carolina Press, 2007.

■ *See also*

Cuban Thought and Cultural Identity: Socialist Thought

Gender: Social Justice in the Revolutionary Period

Governance and Contestation: The Cuban Revolution

Science and Technology in Cuba

HEALTH AND HEALTH CARE: REVOLUTIONARY PERIOD

P. Sean Brotherton

Development of the health care system after the Revolution of 1959.

The history of the development of Cuba's health care system can be divided into three periods: the Republic Period (1902–1959); the Socialist Revolutionary Period (1959–present day); and within the latter period, the Special Period in Time of Peace (1991–present day). Throughout the Socialist Revolutionary Period, the Cuban government focused on health as a defining characteristic of its socioeconomic and political reform. The public health system underwent three distinct phases of reform in the creation of a comprehensive health care and prevention program that encompasses the physical, social, and psychological needs of individuals. These phases are the *policlínico integral* (integral polyclinic program); the Medicina en la Comunidad; and the Programa del Médico y la Enfermera de la Familia (MEF; Family Physician and Nurse Program).

The earliest stage of establishing primary health care in the postrevolutionary period, the *policlínico integral*, launched in 1964, provided outpatient care in order to decentralize the services traditionally provided by hospitals. It served medically marginalized groups in both rural and urban areas. A general restructuring of the polyclinics' operations occurred in 1976 under the Medicina en la Comunidad. This program was praised because it viewed health as a function of the biological, environmental, and social well-being of individuals. In the 1980s, the government suspected that the structure of medical services and education in Cuba needed fundamental change. Given that the pattern of morbidity and mortality in Cuba had slowly changed from diseases of poverty (for example, parasitic and infectious diseases) to diseases of development (heart disease and cancer), the needed

change required preparing better-equipped primary-care family doctors to address the populations' changing health needs. Out of this process emerged the primary healthcare system, the Programa del Médico y la Enfermera de la Familia (MEF), created in 1984 and still in effect in the early 2000s.

HEALTHCARE SERVICES AFTER 1959

Shortly after the 1959 Cuban Revolution, the emphasis of the new government was on dismantling discriminatory practices and making universal provisions for basic needs and health care. Of the 6,300 physicians in Cuba in 1959, only 3,433 remained in 1967, many having left principally for the United States and Spain. In addition, in 1960, only sixteen professors remained at the one medical school in the country, in Havana (Gilpin and Rodriguez-Trias p. 4). Severely hampered by this loss of medical professionals, the government initially encountered difficulties in extending health care to marginalized groups in urban and rural locations and in maintaining the existing state-run health services in the city of Havana. Two other health systems, the *mutualistas* (mutual benefit societies) and private health care, were left intact temporarily to help handle the severe shortage of medical personnel; however, by 1970, they had been phased out—either closed or changed into public facilities and integrated into the state-run services.

After 1961, the Soviet Union helped Cuba to enact its plan for a revolutionized healthcare system. For example, Soviet physicians and allied health professionals from other socialist countries compensated for Cuba's shortage of doctors and medical professors. In 1964, the Havana Medical School graduated 394 physicians; by 1971, 30 percent of all university students were studying medicine, and new medical schools were being built to accommodate the growing student body across the country (Danielson p. 184).

Following the Czechoslovakian model of health planning, which concentrated the administration of health care in one governing body with an administratively decentralized delivery system, Cuban public-health officials formed the Sistema Nacional de Salud (SNS; National Health System). The SNS is organized at three levels: national, provincial, and municipal. The national level is represented by the Ministerio de Salud Pública (MINSAP; Ministry of Public Health), which coordinates all services pertaining to health and health care and fulfills the methodological, regulatory, coordination, and control functions for the whole country. Provincial and municipal levels are represented by public-health offices, which are under the direct financial and administrative authority of their respective provincial and municipal councils. All levels integrate the basic functions of public health: treatment, health protection, long- and short-range planning, and scientific improvement of health workers.

Integral Polyclinic Program (1960s) In 1964, the integral polyclinic program (*policlínico integral*) was the first health-services program implemented. The four founding principles of the new revolutionary primary healthcare system were:

1. The health of all people is the full responsibility of the state
2. Universal coverage is guaranteed to all persons without discrimination
3. People must participate actively to assure and maintain high health levels
4. Preventive care is the primary goal of health care

The polyclinic system was designed to provide, integrate, and address these founding principles through the provision of four basic services in a specifically defined area and population: clinical services (for example, curative-preventive care); environmental services (hygiene and sanitation); community health services (health promotion campaigns); and related social services (social workers).

Between 1962 and 1970, the number of polyclinics in the country steadily rose from 161 to 308, and by 1976, there were a total of 344 fully staffed and operating polyclinics in the country and an additional 140 rural medical posts (Gilpin and Rodriguez-Trias pp. 4–6). The polyclinic's health coverage was subdivided on a regional basis into sectors, each with about 30,000 inhabitants served by health teams that included preventive and curative wings. Polyclinics typically offered primary care specialists, including several internists, a pediatrician, an obstetrician-gynecologist, a dentist, a nurse, and a social worker. Polyclinics also offered clinical outpatient services designed to prevent illness and to improve the quality of public health.

The foremost objective of the integral polyclinic was to reduce the morbidity and mortality from communicable diseases, which were a major health problem in Cuba in the 1960s. Public health officials believed that continuous care by the same health team promotes a better understanding of the patients and their environments. Such an understanding, health officials thought, would be effective in addressing the physical and social causes of the patients' illnesses. By 1970, the following health programs were already being implemented, in an elementary form, in every municipal polyclinic:

1. Comprehensive attention to women
2. Comprehensive attention to children
3. Comprehensive attention to adults
4. Hygiene and epidemiological surveillance
5. Dental care
6. Postgraduate training programs for medical staff

As part of the general initiative to stimulate popular participation in the revolutionary objectives, the government created new organizations in the 1960s that brought people together on a territorial and functional interest-group basis. For example, the Comité de Defensa de la Revolución (CDR; Committee for the Defense of the Revolution), Federación de Mujeres Cubanas (FMC; Federation of Cuban Women), and the Federación de Trabajadores de Cuba (CTC; Cuban Labor Federation) were among many organizations that encouraged the adult population to actively participate in revolutionary reform. Youth were organized into political groups during their schooling; primary school children formed the Unión de Pioneras de Cuba (UPC; Cuban Pioneers' Union), and older students belonged to the Federación Estudiántil de la Enseñanza Media (FEEM; Federation of Secondary School Students), the Federación Estudiántil Universitaria (FEU; University Students' Federation), or the Unión de Jóvenes Comunistas (UJC; Union of Young Communists). The formative role of these organizations was, and continued into the early 2000s to be, to instill the values of the Revolution and to promote participation in health education, literacy training, and other social activities that sought to incorporate the wider community in the state's various campaigns for reform. These campaigns included mass immunization programs, blood donations, and disease-control campaigns such as hygiene and sanitation lessons.

The organization of groups proved to be practical and efficient. During the October Missile Crisis in 1962, for example, MINSAP needed to organize people to give blood so that the country would have a sufficient reserve in case of emergency. Within ten days, the CDR had mobilized 8,000 Cubans to give blood. A well-known example of widespread participation in disease control was the involvement of mass organizations in the polio vaccination campaigns of the early 1960s. These campaigns were carried out throughout the entire country in as little as seventy-two hours. As a result, polio was completely eliminated from Cuba by 1963, years ahead of the United Sates.

In spite of these exhaustive campaigns and the optimistic efforts of the integral polyclinics, the program was not entirely successful in dealing with the burgeoning health needs of the population, which for many years had been without basic health services. Cuban public-health officials found problems with the system. First, a shortage of medical personnel specializing in primary health care meant that a different physician treated the same patient from one visit to another. This situation reduced the chances that a particular doctor would be familiar with a particular patient's life history. Second, physicians did not work in health teams as originally planned, and as a result, the interdisciplinary component believed necessary to address health issues was absent. Third, health care tended to be primarily curative, and physicians lacked the appropriate doctor-patient-community relationship required for the new socialist society. The poor training of primary healthcare workers led to an increased number of patient cases referred to secondary specialists and to more people in hospital emergency rooms. The shortage of physicians entering primary health care resulted from the lack of opportunities in advanced teaching and training at the primary health level. There was little incentive, therefore, for professionals and technicians to enter this specialty.

Medicine in the Community (1970s) The year 1970 marked a shift to a second, distinct stage in the development of the public health system. In 1969, the government enacted the Ten-Year Health Plan, which sought to carry out various health initiatives from 1970 to 1980. One of the priorities of the plan was screening for asymptomatic diseases. Health-related activities were thus directed at enriching and developing principles that sought to provide therapy and investigate hidden morbidity. The latter required the health teams to work on highlighting the social morbidity that contributed to nontransmissible chronic illnesses and their risk factors. This meant giving priority to the treatment of healthy people who exhibited risk factors for certain diseases or disorders over those individuals who were healthy but exhibited low risk factors. For example, the 1970s public health campaigns, as evinced in health promotion ads, started targeting smoking and lifestyles such as unhealthy diets and sedentarism.

The Medicine in the Community program, also known as the *policlínicos comunitarios*, was first tested in the Policlínico Alamar in 1974. It incorporated existing health programs from the *policlínico integral* system. Polyclinic teams were assigned to a sector of the population such as infants or the elderly that was defined by its high-risk assessment. This arrangement allowed medical services to be dispensed through a system of continuous assessment and risk evaluation (CARE) of the patient population, known by the Spanish term *dispensarización*. This community-based model of primary care provided integrated health programs carried out by health teams that sought to determine the health status of the at-risk population for targeted health programs; define the social, economic, psychological, and biological variables in the health-illness process; and analyze the needs and resources available.

During the 1970s, in collaboration with the World Health Organization (WHO) and the Pan American Health Organization (PAHO), Cuba created a number of national public-health campaigns targeted at lowering infant mortality. In 1977, MINSAP established a series of objectives to be met by all primary healthcare centers nationwide:

- Early detection of pregnancy (before the third month)
- Early consultation with the obstetrical health team (also before the third month)

- Provision of at least nine prenatal examinations and consultations for women in urban areas and six for women in rural areas
- Education about hygiene, health during pregnancy, childbirth, and child care
- Special prenatal attention to women considered to be high obstetrical risk
- Psychological counseling with regard to childbirth
- Instruction in birth exercises
- Provision that all births take place in hospitals

Consistent with its objective to manage the country's infant mortality rate, the government also began targeting perinatal diseases and congenital problems, the main causes of infant death. Perinatal intensive-care units were created in all maternal and infant hospitals, and therapeutic abortions were strongly advised for mothers found through genetic screening to be carrying babies with congenital abnormalities.

Utilizing the extensive network of mass organizations, specifically CDRs and the FMC, MINSAP trained *brigadistas sanitarias* (health brigade members) to assist polyclinic staff in seeking out pregnant women. The aim was to target expectant mothers and discuss with them the need to go for medical consultation and to monitor women who failed to show up for scheduled appointments. In addition to basic health coverage, all women who were pregnant or breast-feeding were provided supplemental food rations and vitamins. Furthermore, measures were taken by the Cuban government to improve children's life expectancy from birth. For example, the use of facilities such as maternity homes guaranteed that nearly 100 percent of babies were born in hospitals with staff trained to detect all birth-related problems. Maternity homes, an integral part of the primary health care system, are residential facilities with medical attendants where pregnant women go when they reach approximately thirty-seven weeks. There they await birth in the company of other women, free of the responsibilities of maintaining a household. After delivery, mothers and their babies generally go home on the first postpartum day and are visited in their homes by a family doctor and nurse every day for the next ten days. Additionally, a doctor or nurse schedules a minimum of two monthly pediatric visits along with one home visit.

The development of maternal-infant healthcare programs was carried out against a background of broad socioeconomic changes that redefined traditional female roles in a revolutionary context. The government made a concerted effort to facilitate this transformation, which Fidel Castro referred to as a "revolution within a revolution." In 1976, the constitution codified women's equal rights in marriage, employment, wage equity, and education. This was matched by the massive extension of public daycare facilities and a 1974 maternity law that guaranteed women paid maternity leave and the right to take time off from work to attend to their children's healthcare needs.

Significantly, the FMC provided women with a collective voice and ensured their full and equal participation in the revolutionary movement. A well-known indicator of women's changing role in postrevolutionary Cuba was the birth rate in the first two decades after the Revolution, which steadily declined after 1963, representing one of the lowest in Latin America. By 1979, the birth rate had dropped to 18.0 per 1,000 inhabitants from 28.3 per 1,000 before the Revolution (Werner). Although the revolutionary government provided birth control at low cost to women who wanted it, it conducted no public campaign to promote family planning. Such a remarkable decline in the birth rate without even trying, while other countries such as Mexico used high-pressure tactics without success, indicates that the socioeconomic pressures that supported having many children had been mitigated, and women were beginning to assess for themselves the advantages of smaller families.

Although the maternal-infant healthcare programs were successful in lowering infant morality, the overall achievements of the primary-health program quickly fell short of its objectives. Several studies illustrated that the community health teams were not adequately trained to screen the population for certain ailments (Díaz-Briquets pp. 118-19; Santana 1987, p. 117). Specifically, chronic illnesses such as cancer and high blood pressure, along with related heart diseases, were not adequately detected and thus not treated. Cuban primary public-health professionals commented that there were inequalities between the care offered at the training polyclinics—the centers associated with teaching hospitals (less than 10% of the clinics in the country)—and the care in nontraining polyclinics. In addition, health teams were unable to effectively address the behavioral determinants of ill health, including smoking, alcoholism, and promiscuity, that put people at risk. Some healthcare teams' lack of familiarity with the communities in which they worked meant that they were unable to identify other important social problems, thus impeding a holistic and integrative approach to health care. The lack of personalized medical attention by the same health teams resulted in the persistence of symptomatic visits, which were treated as acute episodes, without an examination of the relationship between the illness and its broader biological, emotional, or social origins.

In conclusion, public-health officials determined that the community medicine program lacked the tools to provide an integrative evaluation that took into consideration all the factors affecting the well-being of patients. Doctors ended up having a passive role in the polyclinics, waiting for morbidity to arrive instead of seeking out, preventing, and controlling

their patients' health problems after a careful analysis of the morbidity of the population. Given these problems, public-health officials instituted a curriculum that extended medical education from six to ten years. The new curriculum required six years of undergraduate and predoctoral medical education and a four-year residency in Medicina General Integral (MGI; General Comprehensive Medicine), thus eliminating the distinction between the practice of general medicine and specialization. This meant that medical students would graduate as Médicos Generales Básicos (MGB; Basic General Physicians).

Family Physician and Nurse Program (1980s)
In the 1980s, considered the most ambitious period in the development of Cuba's national health ystem, MINSAP created the Programa del Médico y la Enfermera de la Familia (MEF; Family Physician and Nurse Program). This program, launched in 1984, called for family physician-and-nurse teams to live and work in small clinics known as *consultorios* on the city block or in the rural community they serve. The MGI residency provides specialized training in primary health care, including a rotation in each of the primary care specialties—internal medicine, pediatrics, obstetrics, and gynecology—as well as a rotation in neighborhood-based clinics, supervised by family physicians.

By the end of 1985, the MEF had expanded to include 10,000 physicians; by 2009, it included 34,261 physicians overseeing 100 percent of the population (MINSAP 2009). Physician-and-nurse health teams (*equipos básicos de salud*) are stationed in small clinics all over Cuba known as *consultorios del médico de la familia* that each serve 120 families, approximately 600 to 700 persons. Each *consultorio* is located in a designated health area (*área de salud*) that is attended by the physician-and-nurse team. In the organization, the MEF calls for family physician-and-nurse teams to live and work on the city block or in the rural community in which they serve. Moreover, physician-and-nurse teams are stationed in every factory and school. The role of the new family physicians, following the MEF training manual (*Programa de Trabajo del Médico y Enfermera de la Familia, el Políclinico y el Hospital*) issued by MINSAP in 1988, was to carry out clinical and social-epidemiological vigilance of the population, promote health, and prevent disease by working in tandem with the community. As stipulated in the MEF work manual, the specific functions of the participating health professionals are:

1. To promote health through education, lifestyle changes, and an improvement in hygienic and sanitary habits and conditions
2. To prevent illness and conditions dangerous to health
3. To guarantee early diagnosis and comprehensive outpatient and inpatient medical care over time

4. To develop community-based rehabilitation for the physically or psychiatrically disabled

5. To aid the social integration of families and communities

6. To complete residency training in family practice with scientific excellence and a willingness to serve humanity

7. To do research that responds to the health needs of the population

The local *consultorio* is the pillar of the primary healthcare system because it works at the level of a specifically defined community and acts as an intermediary between the community, the local polyclinic, the municipal and provincial hospitals, and the national health system. This organization permits all health initiatives to be specifically tailored to the needs of local communities. Although their role as specialized centers continues to be crucial, secondary and tertiary institutions have adjusted their structural and functional framework to meet the demands posed by the multilevel, comprehensive, integrated healthcare delivery approach.

The design and structure of the MEF allows for greater accessibility to healthcare services and a closer relationship between health teams and their patients. This makes it possible for health teams to obtain a more intimate knowledge of their patients, enabling family physicians to better comprehend their patients' psychological and physical problems and then provide immediate and continuous care. Community participation in healthcare initiatives and the healthcare decision-making process is crucial to the MEF. The earlier creation of popular councils (*poderes populares*) in 1976 theoretically gave citizens more grassroots involvement in the government's decision-making process. For example, to allow citizens to take a greater part in what Fidel Castro referred to as the "defense of health," *consultorios* were strategically placed in an area circumscribed by one or more mass organizations.

Going beyond the community primary-health services provided in the past, the *consultorios* are supported by a massive expansion of secondary and tertiary healthcare institutions. In the 1980s, for example, Cuba's national health system made significant financial investments in state-of-the-art tertiary care institutions such as the Hermanos Ameijeiras (Clinical Surgical Hospital) and the Centro de Investigaciones Médico-Quirúrgicas (CIMEQ; Center for Medical Investigation and Surgery), and research facilities such as the Centro de Ingeniería y Biotecnología (CIGB; Center for Genetic Engineering and Biotechnology). These institutions offer a wide range of healthcare services, including organ transplants, in-vitro fertilization, laser surgery, and magnetic resonance imaging (MRI); they also have been involved in the development of genetic engineering and biotechnology and the production and research of vaccines and pharmaceuticals.

Acting as an intermediary between the *consultorios* and tertiary institutions, a complex network of local polyclinics and municipal hospitals provide laboratory, ancillary, and emergency-room services, as well as supervision, teaching, and subspecialty consultation. To facilitate this organization, each polyclinic in every municipality oversees ten to fifteen *consultorios* that form a basic working group known as a *grupo básico de trabajo*. Each polyclinic is staffed with a specialist in internal medicine, a pediatrician, an obstetric-gynecologist, a psychologist, a dentist, a supervising nurse, a social worker, a statistician, and an epidemiological-and-hygiene technician. All public health services are institutionally integrated, both horizontally and vertically. For example, under the MEF a physician can refer a patient to the services in the polyclinics, which in turn can make referrals to a municipal hospital. The family physician is always the patient's primary provider and is consulted during diagnosis and treatment. Moreover, the family physician is required to follow up on patients who have been treated at other levels of the health system, such as at polyclinics and hospitals. In this way, the family physicians never lose contact with their patients, even if the patients are admitted to an intensive-care unit. Physicians also can make suggestions on the treatment of their patients while they are in more specialized institutions.

A unique aspect of the MEF is its consideration of the family as the basic unit of attention. This allows health teams to consider the repercussions of the problems of the individual on the family as a whole, and vice versa. Furthermore, ideally, the family is an integral part of all prevention, treatment, and rehabilitation of health problems. One of the hallmarks of the MEF is the introduction of at-home treatment, based on the family physician's judgment, the patient's condition, and the family members' ability to care for the patient at home. This approach reduces the high costs incurred by admitting and treating people unnecessarily in local hospitals, thereby freeing up the total number of beds available. Furthermore, at-home treatment, when appropriate, encourages patients and their families to participate more fully in healthcare activities and therefore take greater responsibility for their own health.

The scheduling of physicians' hours is determined by patients' needs rather than a predetermined structure. However, in a typical day the family physician-nurse team conducts morning office hours (usually from 8 a.m. to 1 p.m.) in the *consultorio* for routine visits and checkups. In the afternoons (usually, from 1 p.m. to 5 p.m.), the health teams carry out home and field visits known as *en el terreno* (literally, in the field). Physician-and-nurse health teams follow a number of health programs set out by the ministry guidelines for primary health care (*atención primaria de salud*). In theory, the family physician is required to see every patient in his or her *área de salud* at least twice a year. The physician is also required to maintain a *ficha familiar*, which is a record of preventive services and conditions for all patients in their area. This record is updated and reviewed at least monthly with a clinical supervisor who is an academically based family physician. Acute and chronic health problems are coordinated in a database at municipal, provincial, and national levels of MINSAP. The monitored services and conditions include prenatal and natal care; immunizations; cancer screening by smear and mammography; risk factors such as smoking, hypertension, and follow-up for chronic conditions; and psychosocial problems and sources of stress in the family or at work.

CHALLENGES TO HEALTH CARE IN THE SPECIAL PERIOD (1990s)

After the crumbling of the Soviet bloc in 1989, the Cuban government declared that socialism was under siege, and in 1991, it formally announced the beginning of the *Período Especial en Tiempos de Paz* (Special Period in Time of Peace, hereafter, *período especial*). During this period of economic upheaval, Cuba's socialist healthcare system has been affected by market-based reforms and the government's pursuit of a dual economy in Cuban pesos and U.S. dollars or, since November 2004, its equivalent, *pesos convertibles*. These new economic reforms, complicated by the U.S. government's tightening of economic sanctions against the island, have undermined individuals' health by limiting the availability of food, medicines, and medical equipment.

MINSAP reported that between 1989 and 1993 the total expenditures in hard currency for the health sector dropped from U.S.$227 million to $56 million. In 1990, the country imported approximately U.S.$55 million in medical and pharmaceutical products; by 1996 this figure had dropped to U.S.$18 million, a decrease of around 67 percent (Dunning p. 8). This decline in medical and pharmaceutical imports seriously compromised many physicians' treatment options. With a reduction in therapeutic options, and growing numbers of nonfunctioning medical equipment in the country's hospitals, the capacity of secondary and tertiary institutions to undertake high-technology procedures decreased significantly.

The agricultural-nutritional crisis also affected the health of the population, as a critical shortage of petroleum and the growing scarcity of replacement parts for antiquated Soviet technology brought the agricultural industry to a grinding halt in the early 1990s. Food production plummeted. In 1993, an epidemic of neuropathy, which led to thousands of people temporarily losing their vision, was due in part to nutritional deficiencies that resulted from the drop in per-capita daily food consumption from 3,100 calories in 1989 to less than 1,800 in 1993 (PAHO; Chomsky).

In 1991, MINSAP drafted the document *Objectives, Aims, and Guidelines for Improving the Health of the Cuban Population 1992–2000* to define the state's health goals to be achieved by the year 2000. In this document, the ministry designated biotechnology and high-technology medicine as priority sectors for continued investment, despite the general program of economic austerity measures in the national health system. These strategies, the government argued, were part of the greater plan to build Cuba's economy and, ultimately, make the island more self-sufficient. First, they were a means to address the local shortage of pharmaceutical products created by the cessation of Soviet aid and the U.S. embargo. Second, they aimed to capitalize on their newly acquired high-technology medical capabilities.

Despite these larger macroeconomic strategies to sustain the national health system, the devaluation of the peso-based salary and the state's withdrawal from various sectors of the economy (not only health care) mean that Cubans have to engage in a complex web of informal practices in a thriving non–state-regulated economy to mitigate the increased pressures in daily life. These practices, often classified as *lo informal* (informal), depend on a network of client-based relations with individuals known as *socios* (informal partner or affiliate), or an economy of favors. These activities include, but are not limited to, the *bolsa negra* (black market), which includes informal trading in basic medical provisions (e.g., medicine, medical supplies, and access to medical services).

This situation is exacerbated by the legalization and circulation of the U.S. dollar shortly after the economic crisis began, which has effectively destabilized the state's ability to control wealth and income disparity in the population. For instance, shortly after the circulation of the U.S. dollar was legalized, the Cuban government quickly opened stores tellingly named *tiendas recaudadoras de divisas* (TRDs; stores for the recuperation of hard currency). Popularly referred to as *chopins*, these stores sell a host of basic goods as well as luxury items (e.g., TVs, refrigerators, and stereos) at significantly marked-up prices. Changes to the country's foreign-investment laws also led to the creation of several joint-venture socialist corporations such as Cubanacán's *Turismo y Salud* (Tourism and Health) that offer a wide range of health services, international pharmacies, and optometry clinics, all catering to a clientele with hard currency.

Engaging in *lo informal* to obtain foreign currency (*divisa*) is a proactive strategy to secure therapeutic recourses that the state can no longer provide. In the 1990s, Cubans found themselves increasingly relying on an expanding network of state-sponsored and informal options in biomedical, spiritual, and alternative medicine to achieve personal definitions of health and wellbeing. It became evident after the visit of Pope John Paul II to Havana in 1997, when the pope publicly condemned the socialist government for curtailing religious expression in Cuba, that faith-based healing has increasingly become part of people's health-seeking behavior. For example, people turn to syncretic religious practices such as Santeria, among other religious groups, to solve both health-related and spiritual problems, which are often intimately connected. Although the Cuban government previously espoused a militant atheism, after 1997 it started to ignore open religious worship. Equally important is the fact that the practice of medicine has begun to change, with the government actively promoting the use of natural and traditional medicine as part of a strategy to provide the population with more healthcare options.

HEALTH CARE IN THE TWENTY-FIRST CENTURY

In the post–cold war era, the reconfiguration of global relations has meant that Cuba, as a result of its disadvantaged position, must respond to external global factors and shift domestic state policies in the health arena. Although Cuba boasts one of the highest physician-per-inhabitant ratios in the world, the massive deployment of doctors on foreign missions throughout the 2000s—to participate in the *Misión Barrio Adentro* (Inside the Neighborhood) in Venezuela, for example—has left noticeable gaps in the country's domestic primary healthcare programs.

In his 26 July 2007, address to the nation, the acting president Raúl Castro called on Cubans to hold meetings to discuss the country's most pressing problems. In the public community meetings that ensued, citizens were increasingly vocal about the daily constraints they encountered in trying to solve their immediate health problems. In an ironic twist, the departure of thousands of physicians to engage in humanitarian work in other parts of the globe has left their own patients without the personalized care that had been the hallmark of the MEF.

In March 2008, President Raúl Castro announced that the MEF would be reorganized to address some of the structural and staffing problems that resulted from the increasing demand for the country's primary healthcare physicians and auxiliary health staff in foreign countries. Rather than emphasize *consultorios*, the capstone of Cuba's primary-health sector, polyclinics were to take on a considerably more important role. The aim of these changes, health officials noted, was to strengthen their roles in the communities they served and to add a host of specialty services previously available only in hospitals, including X-rays, ultrasounds, psychiatry, and cardiology, among others. Cuban health officials increasingly assert that it is the success of the primary-health programs of the past, such as the MEF, that makes it possible for Cuba to begin the process of restructuring health care to meet the populations' new health needs.

BIBLIOGRAPHY

Brotherton, P. Sean. "Macroeconomic Change and the Biopolitics of Health." *Journal of Latin American Anthropology* 10, no. 2 (2005): 339–369.

Brotherton, P. Sean. "We Have to Think Like Capitalists but Continue Being Socialists: Medicalized Subjectivities, Emergent Capital, and Socialist Entrepreneurs in Post-Soviet Cuba." *American Ethnologist* 35, no. 2 (2008): 259–274.

Chomsky, Aviva. "The Threat of a Good Example: Health and Revolution in Cuba." In *Dying for Growth: Global Inequality and the Health of the Poor*, edited by Jim Yong Kim, Joyce V. Millen, Alec Irwin, and John Gershman, 331–357. Monroe, ME: Common Courage Press, 2000.

Dalton, Thomas C. *Everything within the Revolution: Cuban Strategies for Social Development Since 1960.* Boulder, CO: Westview Press, 1993.

Danielson, Roswell S. *Cuban Medicine.* New Brunswick, NJ: Transaction, 1979.

Delgado García, Gregorio. *Desarrollo histórico de la salud pública cubana en el período revolucionario socialista.* Havana: Editorial Mimeografiada, 1990.

Delgado García, Gregorio. "Etapas del desarrollo de la salud públic revolucionaria cubana." *Revista Cubana de Salud Pública* 22, no. 1 (1996): 48–54.

Díaz Novás, José. "La familia como unidad de atencion." *Revista Cubana de Medicina General Integral* 5 (1989): 231–234.

Díaz Novás, José, and José A. Fernández Sacasas. "Del policlinico integral al médico de la familia." *Revista Cubana de Medicina General Integral* 5 (1989): 556–664.

Díaz-Briquets, Sergio. *The Health Revolution in Cuba.* Austin: University of Texas Press, 1983.

Dunning, Thad. "Structural Reform and Medical Commerce: The Political Economy of Cuban Health Care in the Special Period." Latin American Studies Association Conference, Washington, DC, 2001.

Eckstein, Susan Eva. *Back from the Future: Cuban under Castro.* Princeton, NJ: Princeton University Press, 1994.

Feinsilver, Julie. *Healing the Masses: Cuban Politics at Home and Abroad.* Berkeley: University of California Press, 1993.

Feinsilver, Julie. "Overview of the Cuban Health System." In *Community Health Care in Cuba*, edited by Susan E. Mason, David L. Strug, and Joan Beder. Chicago: Lyceum 2009.

Gilpin, Margaret. "Cuba on the Road to a Family Medicine Nation." *Family Medicine* 21 (1989): 405–471.

Gilpin, Margaret, and Helen Rodriguez-Trias. "Looking at Health in a Healthy Way." *Cuba Review* 7 (1978): 3–15.

Jardines Méndez, José B. "Cuba: El reto de la anteción primaria y la eficiencia en salud." *Revista Educación Médica Superior* 9, no. 1 (1995).

Jova Casañas, Rodolfo, and René Pradrón Martinez. "El medico de la familia. Estudio preliminar en Ciudad de la Habana." *Revista Cubana de Salud Pública* 13 (1989): 128–137.

Kirkpatrick, Anthony F. "Role of the USA in Shortage of Food and Medicine in Cuba." *Lancet* 348 (1996): 1489–1491.

Macdonald, Theodore. *A Developmental Analysis of Cuba's Health Care System Since 1959.* Lewiston, NY: Edwin Mellen Press, 1999.

Ministerio de Salud Pública (MINSAP). *Programas básicos.* Havana: Author, 1976.

Ministerio de Salud Pública (MINSAP). *Fundamentación para un nuevo enfoque de la medicina en la comunidad.* Havana: Author, 1977.

Ministerio de Salud Pública (MINSAP). *Salud para todos: 25 años de experiencia cubana.* Havana: Author, 1983.

Ministerio de Salud Pública (MINSAP). *Médico de la familia: Información estadística.* Havana: Author, 1988.

Ministerio de Salud Pública (MINSAP). *Evaluación estrategias de salud todo en el año 2000: Informe de Cuba 1990.* Havana: Author, 1991.

Ministerio de Salud Pública (MINSAP). *Analisis del sector salud en Cuba—Resumen ejecutivo.* Havana: Author, 1996.

Ministerio de Salud Pública (MINSAP). *Programa nacional de medicina tradicional y natural (MTN).* Havana: Author, 1997.

Ministerio de Salud Pública (MINSAP). *Carpeta methdológica de atención primaria de salud y medicina familiar, VII reunión metodológica del MINAP.* Havana: Author, 2001.

Ministerio de Salud Pública (MINSAP). *Anuario Estadístico de salud.* Havana: Author, 2009.

Nayeri, Kamran. "The Cuban Health Care System and Factors Currently Undermining It." *Journal of Community Health* 20 (1995): 321–335.

Ordónez Carceller, Cosme. "La medicina en la comunidad." Havana: Ministerio de Salud Pública, 1976.

Orozco Muñoz, Calixto. "Reflexión acerca de la labor del médico de la familia." *Revista Cubana de Medicina General Integral* 12 (1996): 34–78.

Pan American Health Organization. *Country Health Profile: Cuba.* Washington, DC: Author, 2001.

Perez, Cristina. *Caring for Them from Birth to Death: The Practice of Community-Based Cuban Medicine.* Lanham, MD: Lexington Books, 2008.

Santana, Sarah. "The Cuban Health Care System." *World Development* 15 (1987): 113–125.

Santana, Sarah. "Whither Cuban Medicine? Challenges for the Next Generation." In *Transformation and Struggle: Cuba Faces the 1990s,* edited by Sandor Halebsky and John M. Kirk. Boulder, CO: Westview Press, 1990.

Werner, David. "Health Care in Cuba Today: A Model Service or a Means of Social Control." In *Practicing Health for All,* edited by David Morley, Jon Rhode, and Glen Williams, 15–37. New York: Oxford University Press, 1983.

Whiteford, Linda M., and Laurence G. Branch. *Primary Health Care in Cuba: The Other Revolution.* New York: Rowman and Littlefield, 2008.

HEALTH AND HEALTH CARE: HIV/AIDS

Ester R. Shapiro

Cuba's integrative, yet controversial, response to HIV/AIDS.

Cuba's response to the global HIV/AIDS epidemic has been called both "the most admired" and "the most hated AIDS programme in the world" (Burr) for its reliance on signature revolutionary principles of health as a human right and government responsibility; on evidence-based planning that integrates public health, health and sexuality education, and health care; and on multisector mobilization to meet these goals. Internationally recognized as a model public health and prevention-based approach to infectious disease control, Cuba's HIV/AIDS program has successfully applied a multisector scientific approach to the evolving, rapidly changing understanding of transmission, prevention, and treatment involving the whole society (Gorry et al.).

Since emerging in the early 1980s as a mysterious, highly infectious disease and terrifying death sentence, HIV/AIDS has consistently exposed enduring social inequalities through its pathways of infection and access to treatment. HIV/AIDS has become a chronic, largely manageable though costly illness in developed countries and continues to create enormous burdens of disease, devastation, and death in low-resource countries. Reviled early in the epidemic for emphasizing public health disease-control principles and creating sanatoria for mandated quarantine and treatment of seropositive individuals, by 2010 Cuba's integrative approach was considered visionary for successfully controlling the epidemic and providing universal treatment while limiting violations of individual rights and involving individuals living with HIV in prevention and health education (Anderson 2009a; Castro, Khawja, and González Nuñez).

INFECTION AND EARLY POLICY

Using the most recently available data from the World Health Organization (WHO) and analyses of policies (Anderson 2009b; Gorry; WHO 2008; Perez et al.), Cuba has been shown to be effectively monitoring evolving knowledge regarding the epidemic to identify and treat seropositive individuals while preventing infections in vulnerable populations. In sub-Saharan Africa, some countries report 20 to 25 percent of adults as seropositive, low rates of access to antiretroviral treatment, and high death rates. The Caribbean is the second most affected region, with 2 percent of adult populations recorded as seropositive in the Bahamas, Haiti, and the Dominican Republic, but less than 0.1 percent reported seropositive in Cuba. Placing incidence rates in perspective, Cuba

■ *See also*

Cuban Thought and Cultural Identity: Socialist Thought

Governance and Contestation: The Cuban Revolution

Sexuality: Revolutionary Period

has an adult HIV prevalence rate of 52 (per 100,000), compared to 2,807 for the Bahamas; 3,377 for Haiti; 1,036 for the Dominican Republic; 454 for Brazil; and 598 for Venezuela, using the same metric (WHO 2008). According to most recent reports, in 2008 Cuba had 6,200 individuals living with HIV, about 80 percent of them men who have sex with men and 20 percent women infected through heterosexual contact (WHO 2008). Through Cuba's universal access to health care via primary care, use of biotechnology to develop national HIV testing of vulnerable populations, intensive education and nearly universal drug treatment for all seropositive individuals, and broad-based public education campaigns with accessible, very low-cost condoms, the signature Cuban multisectoral approach to health has generated one of the world's success stories in learning from, as well as managing, the epidemic.

Initially misidentified as the gay plague due to high incidence in men who have sex with men, globally HIV/AIDS has been transmitted through social pathways that reflect particular cultural and population realities and social vulnerabilities, exposing sexual attitudes and practices and highlighting care of marginalized groups. Cuba created the National AIDS Commission in 1983, the first in the world, two years before the first case of HIV infection was detected on the island, in a husband and wife returning from an African international mission. Because the first Cuban cases emerged in a nonmarginalized group, it became far easier to communicate that HIV/AIDS prevention should target all sexual relationships. Starting in 1986, Cuba was among the first countries globally to test blood supplies for HIV and destroy all untested blood products. Cuba's strict public health policies targeting infection control during the initial phases of the AIDS epidemic, which included mandatory isolation of HIV-positive individuals and strict contact tracing, were controversial. These measures were considered rights violations by some U.S. and European critics more concerned about individual privacy and stigma than about other health and human rights considerations such as disease control, universal access to health care, and government protection from workplace discrimination. As Cuban and global researchers learned more about HIV/AIDS transmission and treatment, policies protecting both individual and public health were altered correspondingly. Mandatory quarantine ended in 1989, and AIDS patients were permitted contact with their families, but still required to live in sanatoria until 1993, when an ambulatory care system was initiated; that was the current standard of care in 2010.

Cuba's response to the HIV/AIDS epidemic has been complicated by the realities of economic crisis and the U.S. blockade, particularly when the Soviet Union's withdrawal of favored trade and subsidies significantly reduced Cuba's economy. Zidovudine (AZT) was recommended as monotherapy for AIDS patients beginning in 1987, and the research base for understanding maternal transmission during childbirth evolved during the early 1990s. An ambulatory care system introduced in 1993 was expanded in 1998. By 1995 laboratories nationwide were using Cuban-manufactured HIV test kits. In 1996, after researchers at the International AIDS Conference presented data recommending Highly Active Antiretroviral Therapy (HAART), Cuba purchased Antiretroviral Therapy (ARVT) drugs for all children with AIDS and their mothers at a cost of US$14,000 per person per year, which was especially costly considering the depth of Cuba's economic crisis. Cuba relied on some global nongovernmental donations while working with its biotechnology research sectors to develop its own drug regimens. In 2001 Cuba began manufacturing its own antiretroviral drugs and distributing them free to those who needed them and, by 2003, had achieved universal antiretroviral treatment. In 2010 only HIV-positive patients who are unable to manage their medication treatment on an outpatient basis were required to live in sanatoria, though some chose to reside there in part because of benefits such as access to higher-quality food and shelter and convenient specialized care. In April 2008 there were 220 people living at Havana's Sanatorio del SIDA de Santiago de Las Vegas (AIDS Sanatorium of Santiago de Las Vegas), and Cuba had twelve sanatoria around the country (Gorry 2008).

SOCIAL AND CULTURAL FACTORS

Cuba's program has been globally recognized as offering a unique balance of universally accessible health care, extensive education of HIV-positive individuals regarding their rights and responsibilities in treatment and prevention, and public education campaigns (Anderson 2009a, 2009b; Castro, Khawja, and González Nuñez). Historically, Cuba's social agreements have been characterized by an acceptance of openly expressed heterosexuality and culture of machismo, acceptance of multiple sexual partners for men (and, increasingly, for women), and limited but expanding tolerance of homosexuality. Since the Revolution, these evolving social trends have combined with government control that limits intravenous drug use and access to travel, focusing Cuba's epidemic on men who have sex with men (80% of the infected population per Gorry and Ochoa Soto and Rojo Pérez), but with a growing risk to young women in heterosexual relationships (Castro, Khawja, and González Nuñez). Cuba has an open attitude toward sexuality throughout the life span and begins sex education in grade school. Cultural norms traditionally have encouraged multiple partners, supported by widely available contraception and free abortions. Although Cuba has a history of homophobia, homosexuality and sexual diversities are increasingly accepted and have been the subject of government media campaigns. Although the Revolution radically transformed women's public roles as workers and officials, sexual and family roles remain traditional. Men who have sex with men remain a vulnerable population in Cuba, accounting for 84 percent of infected individuals as of December 2007 data (Gorry). However, women infected through heterosexual contact are among the most rapidly growing vulnerable groups, as are sexually active young people who are likely to have sex with foreigners or multiple partners. Men over sixty are emerging as a growing affected population; they are most likely to appear with full-blown AIDS at the time of testing (Gorry). These changing social realities have initiated a new phase in addressing social attitudes and behaviors that interfere with condom use and responsible sexuality. Seropositive individuals are increasingly participating in community education efforts and play a growing role in primary prevention and education as peer educators.

EDUCATION AND PREVENTION PROGRAMS

Cuba's integration of prevention and treatment relies on a strong intersectoral approach that includes health and public health sectors and community responses that involves peer educators as well as experts. Cuba continues to test high-risk individuals, including young people, pregnant women, men who have sex with men, and health workers. For individuals identified as HIV positive, sexual partners are identified and strongly encouraged (though not legally required) to be tested. HIV-positive individuals undergo a mandatory

six-week course called "Living with AIDS" presented by health providers and peer educators that emphasizes the individuals' responsibility to care for their own health and that of others. In contrast to approaches focused on protecting individual privacy rights, Cubans living with HIV/AIDS are strongly encouraged to disclose their status to sexual partners and are acknowledged as a first line of defense in preventing infection.

Global HIV/AIDS prevention programs recognize that social attitudes toward sexuality and toward marginalized populations play a role in HIV/AIDS transmission, and Cuban government-controlled media have unique access to channels for public education. In 2006 Cuban television aired the telenovela *La otra cara de la luna* (The Dark Side of the Moon), which told the stories of five individuals who met during a course on living with AIDS and continued working as social educators while meeting for mutual support and sharing ongoing dramas in their lives. The telenovela was pioneering in its presentation of dilemmas of intimacy, sexuality, health, and HIV in contemporary Cuba. It became a topic of nationwide discussion for its stories of a sixteen-year-old schoolgirl infected in her first sexual relationship with an older man; a heterosexual male construction worker who fell in love with an HIV-positive man; a professional woman infected through a heterosexual affair at work in the midst of marital conflicts; and a young man neglected by his mother who became involved with an older woman tourist.

Local AIDS Prevention Efforts, 21 February 2007. The owners of a hair salon in Havana participate in the "Women and AIDS" initiative by offering literature and information on HIV/AIDS and other sexually transmitted diseases. © EPA/CORBIS

In Cuba, antihomosexual attitudes have diminished somewhat but remain a significant force, and they have played a role in the lack of acknowledgment of risky sexual practices for men who have sex with men. One important cultural and legal resource in promoting tolerance of sexual diversities has been Cuba's Centro Nacional de Educación Sexual (CENESEX; National Center for Sex Education), directed by Mariela Castro, Raul's daughter and Fidel's niece. CENECEX has been at the forefront of advocacy for gay, lesbian, bisexual, and transgendered individuals and their rights in Cuba, including legal recognition of civil unions, assisted reproduction for lesbians, and government-supported gender reassignment surgery.

Condom use in Cuba has significantly increased, and the government has made available very low-cost condoms throughout the island. However, the general population continued in the early 2000s to see condom use as interfering with sexual pleasure, and safe sexuality is the focus of public health education campaigns in the media and communities as well as by health care providers. Although women made enormous political and economic gains during the Revolution, persistent gender-traditional roles in the home and in intimate relationships make it difficult to require condom use during sex. Enduringly, Cuba's commitment to health as a government responsibility and a human right and its high social valuing of collective responsibility and solidarity has given the Cuban program to control HIV/AIDS a unique history of successes, even as it strives to meet new challenges presented by the evolution of a sexually transmitted chronic disease that is managed at great social cost.

■ See also

Cuban Thought and Cultural Identity: Socialist Thought

Economy: Special Period

Education: Revolutionary Period: Stages of Educational Reform

Governance and Contestation: The Cuban Revolution

The World and Cuba: Cuba and Africa

The World and Cuba: Cuba and Socialist Countries

BIBLIOGRAPHY

Anderson, Thomas. "HIV/AIDS in Cuba: A Rights-based Analysis." *Health and Human Rights* 11, no. 1 (2009a): 93–104.

Anderson, Thomas. "HIV/AIDS in Cuba: Lessons and Challenges." *Revista Panam Salud Publica* 26, no. 1 (2009b): 78–86.

Burr, Chandler. "Assessing Cuba's Approach to Contain AIDS and HIV." *Lancet* 350 (30 August 1997): 647.

Castro, Arachu, Yasmin Khawja, and Ida González Nuñez. "Sexuality, Reproduction and HIV in Women: The Impact of Antiretroviral Therapy on Elective Pregnancies in Cuba." *AIDS Journal* 21, supp. 5 (2007): S49–S54.

De Arazoza, Héctor, Jose Joanes, Rachid Lounes, et al. "The HIV/AIDS Epidemic in Cuba: Description and Tentative Explanation of Its Low HIV Prevalence." *Biomedical Central Infectious Diseases* 7 (9 November 2007): 130.

Gorry, Conner. *Cuba's HIV/AIDS Strategy: An Integrated, Rights-Based Approach.* Havana: Oxfam International, 2008.

Mason, Susan. "HIV/AIDS in Cuba." In *Community Health Care in Cuba,* edited by Susan Mason, David Strug, and Joan Beder. Chicago: Lyceum, 2010.

Ochoa Soto, Rosaida, and Nereida Rojo Pérez, eds. *Investigaciones sobre VIH en el contexto de la salud pública cubana.* Havana: Centro Nacional de Prevención de las ITS-VIH/SIDA, 2006.

Pérez, Jorge, Daniel Pérez, Ida Gonzalez, et al. *Approaches to the Management of HIV/AIDS in Cuba.* Geneva, Switzerland: World Health Organization, 2004.

World Health Organization (WHO). "Cuba: Epidemiological Fact Sheet on HIV and AIDS." Geneva, Switzerland: Author, 2008.

HEALTH AND HEALTH CARE: MEDICAL DIPLOMACY AND INTERNATIONAL MEDICAL EDUCATION

Julie M. Feinsilver

Cuba's role as a major purveyor of health care and medical education to developing countries.

Medical diplomacy—the provision of medical assistance to simultaneously produce both health benefits and improved government-to-government relations—has been a key instrument of Cuba's foreign policy since the beginning of the Revolution. Cuba first provided disaster-relief assistance to Chile after the great earthquake of May 1960 and again after Chile's February 2010 earthquake, when it sent a team of eighty doctors. In the fifty years between those two earthquakes in Chile, Cuba became a major purveyor of health care and medical education to developing countries. Cuba's medical assistance for both short-term emergencies and long-term health-system development has aided tens of millions of people in 107 countries throughout the world. In an effort to contribute to the sustainability of this medical assistance, between 1961 and 2010, Cuba also provided free medical education for tens of thousands of foreign students; in 2010, it was training more than 50,000 future doctors from all over the world. At the 2009 Summit of the Americas, President Barack Obama said that the United States could learn from Cuba's experience.

ORIGINS OF CUBA'S MEDICAL DIPLOMACY

Cuba began conducting medical diplomacy for humanitarian reasons. Its leaders believed that health is a basic human right, not only for Cubans, but for all peoples of the world. They also believed that Cuba owed a debt to humanity for assistance the nation received during the Revolution and that it could be repaid by providing medical assistance to other countries. Because Cuba faced hostility and a trade embargo from the United States, the search for other allies rather than just a single benefactor was an important geopolitical reason to conduct medical diplomacy. Over time, it became evident that the provision of medical assistance to other countries brought Cuba increased symbolic capital (influence, prestige, and goodwill) on the world stage, which in turn created many more allies and led to material capital such as trade, credit, and aid. Therefore, symbolic and material capital accumulation also became reasons to conduct medical diplomacy.

A factor that allowed Cuba to become a major player in the international health arena, apart from vision and political will, was the creation of a free, universal health care system that provided a credible model for health care delivery at considerably lower costs per capita than other countries with comparable health indicators. Cuba's achievement of key health indicators (infant mortality at birth and life expectancy) on a par with those of developed countries—particularly the United States, with which Cuba competes in this area for ideological and moral superiority—further cemented Cuba's standing and lent credibility to its offer of assistance to others. Cuba's decision in 1978 to produce an additional 10,000 doctors to support a major expansion of its medical diplomacy efforts and its goal of becoming a world medical power foreshadowed the massive expansion of medical education for foreign medical students in the 2000s.

MEDICAL DIPLOMACY ACTIVITIES

The primary elements of Cuba's medical diplomacy include disaster relief, medical care in host countries and in Cuba, medical education, and specialized training in Cuba and in the host countries. This training occurs either in medical schools Cuba helped establish or via on-the-job training in hospitals or polyclinics. Having become very successful in running vaccination, disease eradication, and health promotion campaigns, these programs too have been part of Cuba's various medical diplomacy instruments, along with more administrative and organizational activities such as the development of epidemiological surveillance systems, strategic planning, operations research, and the establishment of Programas de Salud Integral (Comprehensive Health Programs), as of 2010 in forty-five countries around the world. Most of these medical diplomacy instruments have been part of Cuba's offerings for decades and continue to be key to Cuba's success in this field.

Although Cuba's first medical diplomacy activity was conducted in Latin America, this mode of soft-power politics was consolidated in Africa in the 1960s, 1970s, and early 1980s. The first long-term medical brigade sent abroad was to Algeria in 1963, when fifty-six doctors and other health workers went on a fourteen-month assignment. Thereafter, Cuba conducted medical diplomacy alongside its military support for liberation and anti-apartheid movements in Africa and Vietnam in the 1960s and 1970s and as part of its more traditional diplomatic efforts. With the triumph of the Sandinistas in Nicaragua in 1979, Cuba began large-scale medical diplomacy activities there and began to turn more attention to Latin America. It should be noted that Cuba provided medical assistance to other countries whether or not it had diplomatic relations with them. For example, Cuba provided disaster relief to Somoza's Nicaragua after the 1972 earthquake that destroyed a large part of the capital Managua and to the Chamorro government to which the Sandinistas had lost the elections in 1990.

Surprisingly, from 1976 through 1981, Cuba implemented a disproportionately larger civilian aid program (particularly medical diplomacy) than did its more developed trade partners, the Soviet Union and the Eastern European countries. In 1979, Cuban civilian aid workers comprised 19.4 percent of the total provided by these countries, although it had only 2.5 percent of the population. Moreover, from 1983 through 1985, Cuba sent abroad almost as many health workers in absolute numbers as China did from 1963 through 1986. These endeavors quickly generated considerable symbolic capital that translated into political backing in the United Nations General Assembly, as well as material benefits in the case of Angola, Iraq, and other countries that could afford to pay fees for professional services rendered, though the charges were considerably below market rates (Feinsilver 1993, pp. 159, 160, 183–186, 201; Feinsilver 2006, p. 92).

The rise to power of Hugo Chavez in Venezuela in 1999 ushered in a new era of regional solidarity, which gave Cuba the opportunity to vastly expand its medical diplomacy. With their new alliance Alianza Bolivariana para los Pueblos de Nuestra América (ALBA; Bolivarian Alliance for Latin America and the Caribbean), Venezuela and Cuba aimed at uniting and integrating Latin America in a social justice–oriented trade and aid bloc. Through ALBA, Chavez financed Cuba's medical diplomacy with member states (especially Bolivia) and other countries, particularly under the eyesight saving and restoration program Operation Miracle. Under this program, from 2005 to 2010, more than 1.8 million operations were conducted free of charge to patients, either in Cuba or in one of the sixty-one eye surgery centers established by Cuba in various countries in Latin America, the Caribbean, and Africa (Feinsilver 2010, pp. 160–161). Cubans even restored the eyesight of the Bolivian soldier who killed Che Guevara in 1967.

Beginning in 2000, Venezuela and Cuba signed various cooperative agreements whereby Cuba received 90,000 barrels of oil per day at US$25 a barrel, a fraction of the market rate, and got preferential pricing for exports of professional services (primarily oil-for-doctors, though teachers and other professionals were included). These deals also included joint investments in strategically important sectors for both countries and the provision of lines of credit to Cuba. Cuba provided

INTERNATIONAL COLLABORATIONS

Internationalism in Cuban education has manifested itself through the presence of large contingents of the nation's teachers as collaborators in foreign schools. Examples include the Destacamento Pedagógico Ernesto Che Guevara (Ernesto Che Guevara Teaching Detachment) in Angola (1978) and the Destacamento Augusto César Sandino (Augusto Cesar Sandino Detachment) in Nicaragua (1980), among others.

During the 1970s and 1980s, thousands of young people coming from a score of Third World countries completed their secondary education on the Isle of Pines (later renamed the Isle of Youth). Hundreds of them continued their education in Cuban universities as well.

The Escuela Latinoamericana de Medicina (ELAM; Latin American School of Medicine), founded in 1999, merits special mention. As of 2010, it had graduated 8,594 professionals from 54 different countries of Latin America, the Caribbean, Africa, and the United States, with 40 students from the United States obtaining medical degrees.

Another distinguished arena of educational collaboration, the Escuela Internacional de Educación Física y Deporte (EIEFD; International School of Physical Education and Sport) was established in 2000. It has graduated hundreds of students coming from seventy-one countries, most from Latin America.

Also worthy of note is Yo Sí Puedo (Yes, I Can), a literacy program that has been applied in nineteen countries. Created by Cuban educational specialists, the program has successfully taught three and a half million people to read and write.

All in all, hundreds of thousands of students from different countries have undertaken general and specialized studies, and even obtained further professional training, in Cuba since 1959. In addition, hundreds of specialists from abroad have collaborated with the Cuban educational system through universities and other teaching and research centers.

Justo Alberto Chávez Rodríguez

medical services (about 30,000 doctors and other healthcare workers), fully equipped diagnostic and rehabilitation centers (600 of each) for rural and urban marginal communities in Venezuela, and full scholarships to study in Cuba for 10,000 Venezuelan medical and nursing students and in Venezuela for 40,000 medical students and 5,000 healthcare workers. Cuba's medical export earnings in 2006 in the oil-for-doctors deal amounted to US$2.3 billion (28% of total export earnings), a figure greater than nickel and cobalt and tourism exports. By 2008, the export of professional services (mostly medical) totaled US$5.6 billion and accounted for 69 percent of export earnings (Mesa-Lago). On November 8, 2010, Cuba and Venezuela signed a new ten-year general cooperation agreement.

After the Non-Aligned Nations Meeting in Malaysia in 2003, Cuban medical teams began working in far-flung locations such as Timor-Leste (East Timor) in Southeast Asia and the Pacific island countries of Nauru, Vanuatu, Kiribati, Tuvalu, and the Solomon Islands. None of these nations is in Cuba's strategic areas of interest, but each one has a vote in the United Nations General Assembly, and that fact is strategically important as Cuba has garnered the support of all of the world's countries except Israel and Palau in condemning the U.S. embargo of Cuba in that forum. This is symbolically as well as politically important for Cuba.

DISASTER RELIEF

Cuba has been quick to mobilize well-trained disaster-relief teams for many of the major disasters in the world, including earthquakes in Chile, Nicaragua, China, Turkey, Armenia, Iran, Pakistan, and Haiti; the tsunami in Indonesia; hurricanes in the Caribbean and Central America; floods in Pakistan, Guyana, Bolivia, Peru, and China; dengue epidemics in Brazil, El Salvador, Ecuador, Nicaragua, and Honduras; cholera epidemics in Peru and Haiti; and the nuclear disaster at Chernobyl. Over a twenty-year period, Cuba treated more than 20,000 children from the Ukraine, Russia, and Byelorussia for post-Chernobyl radiation-linked illnesses. Despite hostile relations with the United States, Cuba offered to send more than 1,500 specially trained doctors with medical supplies to New Orleans after Hurricane Katrina, but the Bush administration did not accept the offer.

When the January 2010 earthquake struck Haiti, Cuba immediately dispatched a disaster-relief medical brigade (sixty doctors) to supplement their existing 400-strong medical team and over more than 500 Haitian graduates of Cuban medical schools who worked with them. Because the Cuban doctors had already established the Programa de Salud Integral in all ten departments (administrative units) in Haiti and teams of Cuban doctors had worked in the country since 1998, they were the first to respond to the Haitian earthquake. At the end of 2010, they were still in Haiti providing medical care with financial support from Norway (via two agreements for US$850,000 each) and Venezuela, as well as an agreement with Brazil to jointly build three hospitals there.

MEDICAL EDUCATION

Although Cuba had been educating doctors from other countries since 1961 (more than 12,000 graduates by 2010), it was not until after Hurricanes Georges and Mitch struck Haiti and Central America in 1998 that Cuba established a medical school on the island specifically to train foreign doctors using the community-based medical education model to teach primarily primary health care. In 1999, Cuba opened the Escuela Latinoamericana de Medicina (ELAM; Latin American Medical School) to train physicians to rebuild the healthcare systems damaged by those disasters and to make Cuba's medical assistance elsewhere sustainable. The six-year program is free of charge to the students, who must come from underprivileged backgrounds and must promise to return to their communities to provide healthcare services upon graduation. Students spend the first two years at ELAM and then go to another of Cuba's twenty-two medical schools connected to hospitals and polyclinics for community-based medical education and hands-on internships.

In the 2009 to 2010 academic year, 51,648 medical students from Latin America, the Caribbean, Africa, the Pacific Islands, and the United States were in training either in Cuba or in their own countries under the tutelage of Cuban professors in Cuba's Universidad Virtual de Salud (UVS; Virtual Medical School). Of that total number, only 8,170 were enrolled in ELAM, as the bulk of medical education has shifted to community locations. Thus, 12,017 foreign medical students were in the Nuevo Programa de Formación de Médicos Latinoamericanos (New Program to Train Doctors; polyclinic-based) in Cuba. The bulk of foreign medical students (29,171) were being trained in their home countries by Cuban medical brigades under the UVS modality. Finally, 1,118 foreign medical students were matriculated under other projects, and 1,172 were studying for medical technician careers (Feinsilver 2010).

Cuba's UVS was established in 2006 to meet increased demand stipulated in the Cuba-Venezuela accords. The plan was to train 100,000 doctors for the developing world over a ten-year period, as well as 40,000 Venezuelans and 5,000 Bolivians. However, given enrollments in 2010, it appeared likely that this number would be surpassed if the dropout rate were to remain at levels of about 20 to 25 percent the first year and 6 percent the second year (Borroto Cruz and Salas Perea p. 40).

The UVS extends the scope of training Cuba can offer to students while increasing its capacity to provide medical services to patients, and it affords more nontraditional students and low-income students the opportunity to study medicine in their own communities. The UVS uses the tutorial method, whereby a Cuban doctor who has been given pedagogical training tutors a small number of students while providing medical care to their communities. The students learn in their communities, clinics, and classrooms during their first three years of study and have the benefit of various pedagogical materials, including Web-based tools. Graduates of this program are *Médicos Integrales Comunitarios* (comprehensive community doctors) trained in primary health care with emphasis on health

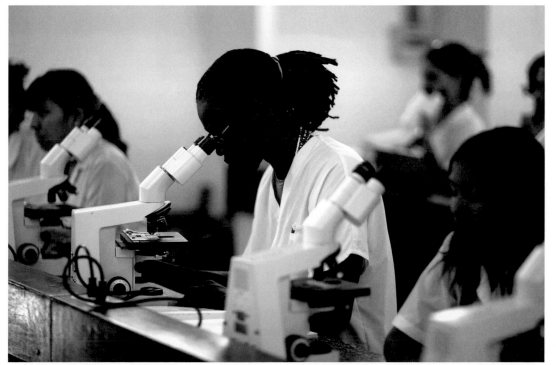

Latin American School of Medicine. Jamar Williams (center) from Brooklyn, New York, attends class at the Latin American School of Medicine in Havana in 2006. JOE RAEDLE/GETTY IMAGES

Medical school graduation. Medical students from Cuba and twenty-six other countries attend their graduation ceremony in Havana on 22 AUGUST 2006. ADALBERTO ROQUE/AFP/ GETTY IMAGES/NEWSCOM

promotion and disease prevention, which is most appropriate for the type of environment in which they will work and the health issues they will confront. However, these students are expected to improve their skills through lifelong learning opportunities and, at some point, study in Cuba to deepen and broaden their knowledge.

Over the years, Cuba has helped establish medical schools in Angola, Yemen, Guyana, Ethiopia, Guinea Bissau, Uganda, Ghana, Gambia, Equatorial Guinea, Haiti, Venezuela, East Timor, and Zanzibar. The humanitarian benefits to these nations are enormous but so are the symbolic benefits to Cuba (prestige, influence, and goodwill). Moreover, the political benefits could be reaped for years to come as students trained by Cuba with Venezuela's support become health officials and opinion leaders in their own countries. As of late 2010, some of the 50,000 foreign scholarship students who trained in Cuban universities since 1961 (11,811 as doctors) were in positions of authority and responsibility in their own countries (Feinsilver 2010, p. 166).

Medical diplomacy has been an integral part of almost all the agreements that Cuba has made with other developing countries. As a result, Cuba has positively affected the lives of millions of people per year. At the same time, Cuba's medical diplomacy with countries whose governments had not been sympathetic to the Revolution—Pakistan, Indonesia, Guatemala, Honduras, and El Salvador, to name only a few—has led to improved relations and trade with those countries. It also has led Latin American and Caribbean leaders to press U.S. president Barack

Obama to normalize relations with Cuba. Medical diplomacy has helped Cuba garner symbolic capital well beyond what would have been possible for a small, developing country, and it has contributed to making Cuba a player on the world stage.

In the early 2000s, medical diplomacy also has been instrumental in providing considerable material capital (aid, credit, and trade), as the oil-for-doctors deal with Venezuela demonstrates. In 2009, medical-pharmaceutical exports were second only to nickel, rising from US$297 million in 2008 to US$520 million in 2009. During this period, medical-pharmaceutical exports to ALBA countries increased by 22 percent (Feinsilver 2010, p. 172). This trade has helped keep the Revolution afloat in trying economic times.

BIBLIOGRAPHY

Anderson, Tim. *The Doctors of Tomorrow: The Timor L'este-Cuba Health Cooperation.* Documentary film. University of Sydney, 2008.

Borroto Cruz, Eugenio Radamés, and Ramón Syr Salas Perea. "National Training Program for Comprehensive Community Physicians, Venezuela." *MEDICC Review* 10, no. 4 (Fall 2008): 35–42.

Brotherton, P. Sean. "'We Have to Think like Capitalists but Continue Being Socialists': Medicalized Subjectivities, Emergent Capital, and Socialist Entrepreneurs in Post-Soviet Cuba." *American Ethnologist* 35 no. 2 (2008): 259–274.

Brotherton, P. Sean. "Fueling la Revolución: Transactional Humanitarianism, Medical Diplomacy and 'the Struggle for Socialism' in 21st-Century Cuba." Paper presented at the Measure of a Revolution, Cuba, 1959–2009 Conference, Kingston, Canada, May 9, 2009.

Feinsilver, Julie M. *Healing the Masses: Cuban Health Politics at Home and Abroad.* Berkeley: University of California Press, 1993.

Feinsilver, Julie M. "La diplomacia médica cubana: Cuando la izquierda lo ha hecho bién." *Foreign Affairs en Español* 6, no. 4 (October–December 2006): 81–94.

Feinsilver, Julie M. "Médicos por petróleo: la diplomacia médica cubana recibe una pequeña apoyo de sus amigos." *Nueva Sociedad* (Buenos Aires) no. 216 (July–August 2008): 107–122.

Feinsilver, Julie M. "Cuba's Health Politics at Home and Abroad." In *Socialist Register 2010: Morbid Symptoms: Health under Capitalism*, edited by Leo Panitch and Colin Leys, 216–239. London: Merlin Press, 2009.

Feinsilver, Julie M. "Fifty Years of Cuban Medical Diplomacy: From Idealism to Pragmatism." *Cuban Studies* 41 (December 2010).

Giraldo, Gloria. "Cuba's Piece in the Global Health Workforce Puzzle." *MEDICC Review* 9, no. 1 (Fall 2007): 44–47.

Kirk, John M., and H. Michael Erisman. *Cuban Medical Internationalism: Origins, Evolution, and Goals.* New York: Palgrave Macmillan, 2009.

Mesa-Lago, Carmelo. "The Cuban Economy in 2008–2009: Internal and External Challenges, State of the Reforms and Perspectives." International Seminar on Cuba, Tulane University and Centro de Investigación y Adiestramiento Político Administrativo, San Jose, Costa Rica, 3–4 February 2009.

HISTORY WILL ABSOLVE ME (FIDEL CASTRO)

María de los Angeles Torres

Speech given by Fidel Castro in his defense on charges brought against him by the Batista government.

On 26 July 1953, 170 men and women led by Fidel Castro Ruz (b. 1926) stormed the military barracks in Santiago de Cuba in an attempt to overthrow the rule of Fulgencio Batista (1901–1973). At his trial, Castro gave a self-defense that included his blueprint for the future of Cuba; his speech was later published as a pamphlet with the title "History Will Absolve Me."

Simultaneous actions took place at Santiago's Military Hospital and courthouse and in the city of Bayamo. By every military calculation, all four actions were failures. Six men died in battle and fifty-five others were killed after being captured; the rest were imprisoned and charged with armed insurrection against the state, including Castro. The actions, however, marked a historic change in tactics from electoral to armed struggle to oust Batista. Batista, the populist sergeant who had shepherded an insurrection that toppled the liberal government of President Gerardo

Machado (1871–1939) in 1933, maintained military control until he was elected president from 1940 to 1944 and left the country until 10 March 1952 when he staged his own military coup. He suspended the 1940 Constitution and substituted a series of new decrees that gave him the power to suspend civil and political rights. Those who had sought relief through elections were left with little hope of reforming the system through peaceful means.

Castro's trial began in September 1953. The trial provided Castro with a national stage in which he could condemn the regime and present his political platform to the people of Cuba. In it he detailed his actions, justified his right to rebel, and outlined his vision for the future of Cuba. His legendary self-defense was later published and circulated under the title "History Will Absolve Me." In it, Castro claimed that history would justify his actions and be his ultimate judge.

The first part of the trial, conducted on 21 September, was a public hearing. Castro turned his accusers into the accused when he questioned a government witness about the mistreatment and torture of prisoners. He was subsequently removed from the courtroom and only allowed to deliver his defense behind closed doors.

On 16 October, Castro gave his famous speech, some four hours long, that constitutes the heart of "History Will Absolve Me." He began with an explanation of why he was defending himself instead of being defended by a lawyer. He detailed how he was denied adequate legal counsel in that he was not permitted to meet with his lawyer in private, and he was denied access to legal documents and books. He added, "only one who has been deeply wounded and seen his country so forsaken and its justice so vilified, can speak at a moment like this with words that spring from the blood of his heart and the essence of truth" (Deutschmann and Schnookal p. 46). He continued with the plans of his armed actions, including how many weapons were procured, how they trained the group, and the nature of their support. In part these details were elaborated as a defense against accusations that he had been financed by the ousted president Carlos Prío (1903–1977). But perhaps most importantly, it demonstrated that he had popular support from many sectors of the Cuban population.

THE MANTLE OF HISTORY

Castro next addressed why he believed armed struggle would succeed. He argued that there were multiple examples in human history, and specifically Cuban history, which showed that when a struggle is noble and justified, even poorly armed and ill-prepared men can be victorious against powerful armies.

For Castro, history thus became a powerful resource and legitimating image that formed part of a national narrative to justify present action for the

Fidel Castro's deposition. Fidel Castro (seated in center) gives a deposition to law-enforcement authorities after leading an attack on the military barracks in Santiago de Cuba in July 1953. AFP/GETTY IMAGES/ NEWSCOM

sake of the future. He summoned past national heroes such as Antonio Maceo (1845–1896), a general from Cuba's war of independence from Spain, and especially Jose Martí (1853–1895), the political organizer and leading thinker of the independence movement, in his attempt to demonstrate that he was taking up the historical mantle to lead the struggle for an independent Cuba.

Castro believed that the struggle would also succeed because people were living under intolerable conditions. Unemployment was close to 20 percent. There was a housing shortage, and only 58.2 percent of Cubans had electricity (only 9% in the countryside), and only about one-third had running water. He pointed to Cuba's lack of educational opportunities—particularly for the rural poor—and suggested that this was yet another problem around which people would agree that an alternative was needed. There would be widespread support for his programs, which would include land redistribution, worker profit sharing, and the return to the public of properties and resources stolen by Batista. Agrarian and educational reforms would be the cornerstone of his platform. (Social justice was indeed at the heart of Castro's future policies and was one of the enduring legacies of the revolution.)

Beyond his ideas about the country's severe domestic problems, Castro believed the revolution would succeed because Cubans longed for a country free of foreign control. At the time, U.S. companies controlled 40 percent of raw sugar production, 50 percent of public railways, 25 percent of all bank

deposits, and 90 percent of public utilities. Foreign holdings, particularly those from U.S. citizens, would be nationalized, as would the electric and telephone companies. Castro's revolution would be the culmination of Cuba's one hundred years of struggle, dating back to 1868, the beginning of Cuba's first war for independence.

THE 1940 CONSTITUTION

The guiding thread of Castro's speech was the Constitution of 1940. The violation of the constitution's spirit provided the basis for claiming that Batista's government was not legitimate, and its restoration became one of the promises Castro made to the Cuban people.

By most legal standards, the 1940 Cuban constitution was one of the most progressive documents in the Americas. It included individual rights as well as economic and social ones. It began with guaranteeing equality to everyone regardless of race, gender, religion, and class. Every citizen had the right to a job as well as to fair compensation for work done. It framed a nationalist agenda that even prescribed that every class taught on any Cuban subject had to be taught by teachers born in Cuba with textbooks also written by island-born Cubans.

The document also called for a democratic state in which there would be a separation of powers and where people were guaranteed individual liberties as well as the right to vote. The death penalty was outlawed except in military courts.

About midpoint in the speech, Castro switched from detailing historical events and the island's social ills to telling a political allegory of Cuba's fate in disregarding the constitution and the rights of the people. He said:

> Let me tell you a story. Once upon a time there was a republic. It had its Constitution, its laws, its freedoms, a President, a Congress, and Courts of Law. Everyone could assemble, associate, speak and write with complete freedom. The people were not satisfied with the government officials at that time, but they had the power to elect new officials. . . . Public opinion was respected and heeded and all problems of common interest were freely discussed. There were political parties, radio and television debates and forums and public meetings.

He continued:

> One morning the citizens woke up dismayed; under the cover of darkness, while the people slept, the ghosts of the past had conspired and had seized the citizenry by its hands, its feet, and its neck. That grip, those claws were familiar: those jaws, those death-dealing scythes, those boots. No; it was no nightmare; it was a sad and terrible reality: a man named Fulgencio Batista had just perpetrated the appalling crime that no one had expected.

Deutschmann and Schnookal, pp. 89–90

The crime, according to Castro, was Batista's dismissal of the Constitution of 1940. He then elaborated arguments about the right to revolt and concluded his speech with the stirring line "History will absolve me."

Castro's speech was not recorded, but he later reconstructed its content, which was smuggled out of prison and published as a widely circulated pamphlet. The speech helped solidify Castro's status as the leader of the revolutionary movement.

Castro was sentenced to fifteen years in prison but was granted amnesty by the Batista government in May 1955 along with the other revolutionaries. Castro regrouped with his followers in Mexico and later staged a successful insurrection against Batista that allowed Castro to take power in January 1959.

THE REVOLUTIONIZING OF CUBAN SOCIETY

After assuming power, Castro immediately began to implement the promises he had expressed in "History Will Absolve Me." One of the revolutionary government's first acts was to reinstate the Constitution of 1940. Social justice measures designed to benefit the millions of Cuba's poor were swiftly enacted. Society's obligation to the poor was an historic and a moral commitment, reflecting Castro's training under the Jesuits, who were leading proponents of social justice for the poor.

In May 1959, Cuba enacted an agrarian reform law. The government also nationalized key sectors of the economy and attempted to reduce Cuban dependency on sugar by introducing a diverse industrialization program. In 1960 housing legislation was enacted and rents drastically reduced. Unemployment was reduced as people were hired to work in different state enterprises. Despite the flight of doctors and teachers, health and education became priorities of the regime; the medical system was socialized and a literacy campaign was launched in 1961.

Absent from early revolutionary policy was the restoration of the democratic articles of the 1940 Constitution, especially elections. As early as spring 1959, Castro claimed that it was senseless to hold elections, since the majority of the people supported the revolutionary government; in order to have elections there would have to be opposition, which he argued did not exist or was the discredited remnants of Batista's political allies. More important than holding elections, he said, was the restoration of social justice and public morality to the Cuban body politic. To those critics who accused the government of being infiltrated by Communists, he responded that those critics represented the class interests of the enemies of the Revolution; in Castro's mind, the crowds who assembled to hear him speak represented the true voice of the people, the true democracy.

Addressing those who claimed he had betrayed his own platform, Castro declared in this speech, delivered on 28 July 1959, that Cuba was a true democracy. He added, "Those who want to know what a true democracy is should come to Cuba . . . a democracy so pure and clean that the democracy born of our revolution reminds us of the first democracies in the world, the Greek democracy, in which the people debated and decided on their fate in the public square."

As peaceful and armed opposition mounted, the Castro government tightened the reins of control. The right to rebel, so eloquently defended by Castro in his 1953 speech when he declared that revolution was the right of those who were attempting to restore the constitution, was denied to those who rebelled against him. Indeed, many faced summary trials and were condemned to death by firing squads or were given long prison terms. In "History Will Absolve Me," he argued that the right to revolution was established in Article 40 of the 1940 Constitution. This right was based in the ideas put forth in the French philosopher Charles Louis de Secondat Montesquieu's *The Spirits of Laws*, which posited that power lay in the sovereignty of people, not in one person's interpretation of the law. Castro had reminded the judges of the military tribunal overseeing his case that even philosophers in ancient China and India upheld the right to resist arbitrary authority. It was a principle that could be found in political writings of the classical Greeks and Romans and then throughout the Middle Ages, including the writings of Thomas Aquinas (c. 1225–1274). He also made references to the writings of John Milton (1608–c. 1674), Jean-Jacques Rousseau (1712–1778), and John Locke (1632–1674), citing their legacies in the narratives of the people of France and the North American colonies that justified their popular revolutions by claiming the right to rebel against despotic governments.

Another point of contention after Castro gained power became the protection of freedom of expression that had been guaranteed by the 1940 Constitution. In 1961, the government withdrew from circulation *PM*, an eighteen-minute film by Alberto "Sabá" Cabrera Infante and Orlando Jiménez Leal about nightlife in Cuba, shot in a bar in which mainly Afro-Cubans were amicably dancing and drinking. The seeming frivolity of the film, which was released the same month that United States–backed Cuban exiles attempted a takeover of Cuba in the ill-fated Bay of Pigs campaign, was viewed by some as an affront to revolutionary ideals. A heated debate about the role of art in the revolution ensued, parts of which were published in *Lunes de revolución*, the cultural supplement of the major newspaper of the time. The debate ended with a meeting two months later between writers and intellectuals in which Castro pronounced that *dentro de la revolución todo, afuera de ella nada* (within the revolution everything, outside of it, nothing). This speech became known as "Las palabras a los intelectuales" (Words to the Intellectuals).

HISTORY AS JUDGE

The clampdown on individual freedoms and failure to hold elections led critics of the regime's growing radicalization to claim that the revolution had been betrayed. However, a closer reading of the philosophical underpinnings of Castro's conception of history as expressed in "History Will Absolve Me" suggests an authoritarian, not-so-democratic understanding of social processes.

Classical views of history as literary genre and intellectual pursuit entwined with the law had evolved by the eighteenth century to a stance in which historical narrative was expected to put forth evidence and witnesses as proof of its veracity. In 1769, the Jesuit Henri Griffet was one of the first to articulate this development, when he compared history to a judge. The German philosopher Georg Hegel (1770–1831) further developed this idea when he declared history to be the world's court of justice as well as final judgment, which emphasized the judge's sentence, not necessarily the process of carefully evaluating evidence.

Castro summoned history as his judge in his 1953 speech, stating that the military judges who were overseeing his trial were illegitimate because they represented an illegitimate government. In effect, by invoking the Cuban historical past of figures such as Martí, Carlos Manuel de Céspedes, and Maceo, defenders of Cuba's sovereignty and freedom from foreign dominance, Castro condensed legal doctrine and historical discourse to say that his actions would be decided by a "higher court," declaring, "History will absolve me" (Deutschmann and Schnookal, p. 105).

In this way, his conception of history is closer to Hegel's than it is to the historiography evolved from evidentiary practices. For Hegel, the movement of history was toward the realization of world spirit and individual freedom. Castro emphasized history's movement toward judgment (social justice), which brings him closer to the "final judgment" view of history that has profound roots in Christian theology. Hegel's idea of history has dual dimensions: He secularizes the Christian teleology of a final goal but then theologizes the movement of history. "History Will Absolve Me" does likewise; its teleology is social justice, and its theology is the idea of Christian brotherly love under the guise of revolutionary solidarity.

History from this perspective is an unmediated force that holds the power to absolve human behavior and actions. There is a universal history that stands above human action but is not entirely indifferent to it. History has the power to judge and to decide what is right and wrong, and from Castro's point of view this meant being able to decide which deeds had been done for the good of others and which were undertaken for the self-interest of a few. History also had the power to absolve; in particular, Castro claimed the blessings of Cuban history and its national heroes, Martí, Céspedes, and Maceo.

One can argue that history as judge is a process that is not participatory. There is no structure in which to develop collectively an ethical code through which personal behavior could be socially mediated. This lack of mediation leaves society bereft of any concrete way to decide the rules with which to gather proof or debate the meanings of those historical proofs and their ethical implications.

It is difficult to reconcile the concept of history as judge with the democratic ideals of the Constitution of 1940. A more democratic understanding of history would not give history the role of judge but rather one of facilitator: a view of history that creates a space in which contested memories—personal, public, cultural—and narratives of history can be debated and reinterpreted.

"History Will Absolve Me" is an important, passionate, and richly complex document of Cuban history. One can argue that it is a prophetic document, which was subsequently vindicated by the course of Cuba's post-1959 revolutionary history, or it can be viewed as a document that betrayed the democratic promise of the 1940 Constitution. More important is to understand that as a speech, as a call to political action, as a vision of the historical forces that have shaped Cuba, it will continue to offer insights about Cuba's search for sovereignty, social justice, and democracy.

BIBLIOGRAPHY

Castro, Fidel. Speech given on 28 July 1959. Castro Speech Database. Available from: http://lanic.utexas.edu/project/castro/db/1959/19590728.html

Deutschmann, David, and Deborah Shnookal, eds. *Fidel Castro Reader*. Melbourne, Australia: Ocean Press, 2007.

Ginzburg, Carlo. "The Judge and the Historian." *Critical Inquiry* 18, no. 1 (Autumn 1991): 79–92.

Liss, Sheldon. *Roots of Revolution: Radical Thought in Cuba*. Lincoln: University of Nebraska Press, 1987.

Miller, Nicola. "The Absolution of History: Uses of the Past in Castro's Cuba." *Journal of Contemporary History* 38, no. 1 (2003): 147–162.

HOLGUÍN

José Vega Suñol

The third-largest province in Cuba.

The territory that comprises the province of Holguín was populated by the first inhabitants of the island, who were present when Christopher Columbus arrived in Bariay Bay on the northeast Atlantic coast of Cuba in 1492. Several archeological sites have uncovered evidence of Indo-Hispanic contact, signs of the transcultural coexistence of the two groups from the earliest colonial settlement. The parish archives of Holguín testify to the presence of Indians into the middle of the eighteenth century. The legacy of the indigenous cultures shaped the regional identity. Holguín was part of the area known for the indigenous *caney* longhouses and *bohío* huts, *yucca* (yucca or cassava) and the *casabe* bread made from it, and the indigenous language that survives in the names of places, flora, and fauna.

DEMOGRAPHY

After the town of Bayamo was founded in 1513 and land was granted to Captain García Holguín, the area was named after him around 1545. The farming area became a population center subordinate to Bayamo and was officially established as the town of Holguín on 4 April 1720. In 1752 it was designated as a city and jurisdiction, the fourth of its kind in the eastern dominions after being separated from Bayamo. In 1878 it became a municipality. From its extensive territory new municipalities were established at the end of the nineteenth and the beginning of the twentieth centuries, including Gibara, Puerto Padre, Banes, and Antilla. In 1976 Holguín became a province with an administrative-political center in the city of Holguín. At the beginning of the twenty-first century Holguín was Cuba's fourth-largest city, with close to 300,000 citizens, and Holguín province was Cuba's third largest province, with 1,013,600 inhabitants (Oficina Nacional de Estadísticas 2004).

The ethnohistorical roots of Holguín's population are Spanish, primarily from peninsular Spain and its provinces, especially the areas of Castile and Andalucia, with a notable influx of immigrants from the Canary Islands continuing from the eighteenth century to the early twentieth century. The Spanish-descended population of Bayamo and other nearby towns added to Holguín's makeup, which had become a differentiated identity type by the eighteenth century. Native Cubans descended from that early mix have played a leading role for more than 200 years in a long process of regional ethnic construction.

The population has mainly increased through endogamous marriage—either legal or common law. The residents refer to themselves as *Holguinero, Cuban*, and *white* (owing to the area's relatively low population of African origin). Ethnic groups from Africa have little representation in the ethnic-racial makeup of Holguín because the area was not engaged in economic activities that required large slave populations, though households did use slaves for domestic purposes until 1886.

Small farmers have played an important role in the history and cultural formation of the region. Tenant farmers, tobacco growers, ranchers, and cooperative farmers have been active during all stages of Holguín's social history. Small farmers tended to have large families and long family lineages, and the region has a traditional patriarchal culture that sees the man as the head of public and family life. Small farmers also have forged the traditional culture of the palm-thatched wood house, the plow and the hoe, the sombrero and the machete, the *guateque* (the celebratory binge), the *punto cubano* (Cuban peasant music), the wake, and a rich oral history. This cultural mix pervades Holguín.

At the beginning of the twentieth century significant ethnodemographic changes occurred with the arrival of thousands of immigrants, mostly Spanish, and also several thousand workers from the anglophone and francophone Caribbean, who were hired as laborers for the sugar industry; these people totaled 21,790 immigrants by 1931. They settled around sugar mills and in adjacent rural locations, living in bunkhouses or huts in the middle of the sugarcane fields. There were also Chinese and Arab immigrants (principally Syrians and Lebanese), who for the most part settled in urban areas and set up restaurants and retail businesses. The new ethnic groups established cultural communities and contributed to the mix their religious ideas, foods, dances, and music. Many of their descendents formed part of Holguín's populace at the outset of the twenty-first century.

GEOGRAPHY AND INDUSTRY

Holguín's local heritage is defined by its diversity and unique attractions. Its geography and national parks—including the Maniabón mountain group, the Cristal and Nipe mountain ranges, Cristóbal Colón Park, and

■ *See also*

Diálogo Agreement

Ecology and Environment: Revolutionary Period

Ten Years' War: 1868–1878

The World and Cuba: Cuba and Spain in the Colonial Period

The World and Cuba: Cuba and Spain in the Post-Colonial Period

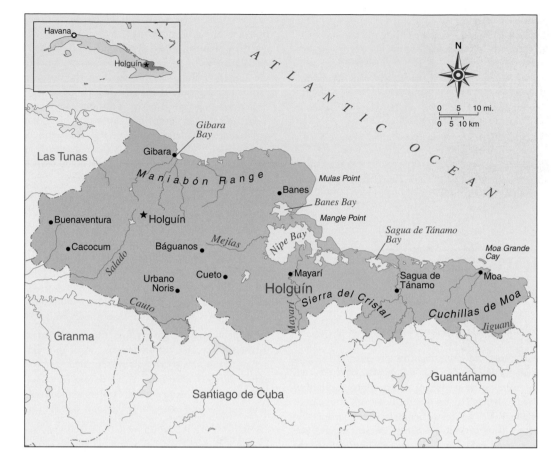

Alejandro de Humboldt Nature Park—make Holguín a destination for ecological tourism.

Holguín's fine architecture dates from the colonial period. Among the most significant buildings are the Church of San Isidoro; the Church of San Fulgencio of Gibara; the La Periquera building, an example of local neoclassic style; the Holguín-Gibara defense walls (from the wars of independence); the art deco Suñol Theater; the steps of La Loma de La Cruz; the Municipal Palace of Banes; the old Marist Brothers school; the V. I. Lenin Hospital; and the Velasco House of Culture. Also noteworthy are Holguín's colonial town center with its systems of plazas and the colonial center of Gibara. The historic centers of Antilla and Holguín have a mix of styles, whereas rationalist architecture is especially pronounced in the Peralta and El Llano de Holguín precincts of Holguín and in the Rollo Monterrey neighborhood in Moa.

The area's industrial heritage began in the nineteenth century with the Santa Lucia sugar mill, one of the most important factories in the history of sugar in Cuba, and grew with the founding of half a dozen large sugar mills in the early twentieth century. This expansion was promoted by U.S. companies such as the United Fruit Company, the Atlantic Fruit Company, and the West Indies Company, among others, which had acquired immense parcels of lands aided by U.S.

military occupations in the 1899–1902 and 1906–1909 periods. New settlements that grew up around these centers followed North American patterns visible in the architecture, the educational system, Protestant churches, and a commercial network that catered to high levels of consumption among the upper-classes of these communities. Macabí and Preston were the classic models of the refinery-town culture, but it extended throughout the entire region. There are commendable examples of wooden architecture around the province's sugar mills, in the eastern part of the city of Banes, and in the historical-architectural complex of Birán, birthplace of the Castro Ruz family.

Northeast Cuba has the country's richest mineral deposits. In the first half of the twentieth century, the area's mineral industry received a boost from investments by U.S. companies that targeted the extraction of manganese, iron, and nickel. Three new mining towns sprang up: Felton, Nicaro, and Moa on the Atlantic coast. In the early 2000s, nickel was the principal natural resource exported from Cuba, placing Holguín at the forefront of the national economy.

Coffee farmers left their mark on part of the province's eastern region. French colonists who came from Haiti in the late eighteenth century and settled in the mountains of Santiago de Cuba and Guantánamo helped expand coffee farming to the

districts of Sagua de Tánamo and Mayarí in the early nineteenth century. In the early 2000s, these municipalities continued that coffee-growing tradition. Sagua de Tánamo boasts the *tumba francesa*, a drumming, song, and dance style that began on coffee plantations and was recognized by UNESCO.

CULTURE

The success of the Cuban Revolution in 1959 prompted the sociocultural development of the region. The prestigious Rodrigo Prats Theater was founded in 1962 and the Holguín Choral Society in 1964. A system of institutions for arts education was formed, including the Escuela Profesional de Música José María Ochoa (José María Ochoa Professional School of Music) and the Escuela Vocacional de Arte (Vocational School of Art). Museums of history and natural sciences (Museo de Historia, Museo de Ciencias Naturales), cultural centers in all the municipal capitals, a provincial television station, video rooms, and dozens of computer clubs were established. The Ediciones Holguín publishing house was founded to promote authors from the region, and magazines such as *Ambito*, *Diéresis*, and *Historia de Holguín* appeared. After the inauguration of the Casa de Iberoamérica in 1993, the city promoted two international events that attracted both Cubans and foreigners: the May Festivals and the Iberoamerican Cultural Festival held in October.

The province has four universities offering degrees in medicine, education, engineering, economics, and humanities, as well as a school of physical education. Late 1990s and early 2000s urbanization developed areas such as the Lenin District, the Plaza of the Revolution environmental site, and the Nuevo Holguín, Pedro Díaz Coello, and Villanueva districts.

Holguín is known for its artists and historians. Members of the literary and arts communities enjoy local, national, and international recognition. Notable musicians include the singer, guitarist, and composer known as El Guayabero (Faustino Oramas, 1911–2007) and the famous baritone Raúl Camayd (1937–1991), founder of the most prestigious lyric company outside Havana. In literature, the award-winning writers Lourdes González (b. 1952) and Manuel García Verdeccia (b. 1953) stand out, and in painting, Cosme Proenza (b. 1948) and Armando Gómez (b. 1941), among many others. In history and culture, Holguín is a bastion of Cuban cultural identity.

BIBLIOGRAPHY

Corella, Cosme Casals, and Manuel Antonio Fernández Domínguez, eds. *Biodiversidad y Turismo 2006*. Santiago de Compostela: Grafinova S.A., 2007.

Oficina Nacional de Estadísticas. *Censo de población y viviendas: Cuba 2002*. Havana: Author, 2004.

Peña Obregón, Ángela Cristina. *Holguín en dos siglos de arquitectura*. Holguín, Cuba: Ediciones Holguín, 2001.

Valcárcel Rojas, Roberto. *Banes precolombino. La ocupación agricultora*. Holguín, Cuba: Ediciones Holguín, 2002.

Vega Suñol, José. *Región e identidad*. Holguín, Cuba: Ediciones Holguín, 2002.

Vega Suñol, José. *Norteamericanos en Cuba. Estudio etnohistórico*. Havana: Colección La Fuente Viva, Fundación Fernando Ortiz, 2004.

INDAGACIÓN DEL CHOTEO (JORGE MAÑACH)

Marta Lesmes Albis

Jorge Mañach and the tradition of Cuban thought.

Prose that reflected on the Cuban condition, particularly the essay, has had a constant presence in the history of Cuban literature. With the advent of the neocolonial republic in 1902, the island's thinkers expressed themselves on matters of Cuban culture, sovereignty, and uniqueness as a new nation in texts that added a rich formal diversity to the genre. One of its most important examples is *Indagación del choteo* (Investigation into Choteo), by Jorge Mañach (1898–1961), which was based on a lecture Mañach gave in 1928 at the eminent Institución Hispano-Cubana de Cultura (Hispano-Cuban Cultural Institution), founded by Fernando Ortiz (1881–1969). Mañach's essay has deep roots in a tradition that included nineteenth-century figures such as José Antonio Saco (1797–1879). With *Memoria sobre la vagancia en la isla de Cuba* (Report on Vagrancy on the Island of Cuba, 1829), Saco was one of the first writers to express concerns similar to those discussed by Mañach in the second decade of the twentieth century, such as the absence of authority and the lack of popular respect toward the social hierarchies.

The word "choteo" is a Cuban expression that refers to an irreverent humor that mocks everything, where nothing is sacred. It has a democratic element in that it often mocks the powerful, but on the other hand it can merely express a devastating and cynical disenchantment with any public institution or authority. This disenchantment is rooted in Cuba's frustrated quest for national sovereignty following the end of Spanish colonial rule in 1898. Upon Cuba's recognition as an independent nation in 1902, a great inter-

nal debate arose over the new reality of the island, presumably independent but with its sovereignty compromised by interference from the U.S. government. The United States had intervened in the war between Spain and Cuba, opportunistically snatching the Cuban victory at the last moment for its own interests. After establishing official governance of the island, the United States forced Cuba to accept the Platt Amendment, which permanently limited Cuba's national sovereignty. Thus, as the country recovered in the first decades of the twentieth century from the material calamities of the war (1895–1898), Cuba had to acknowledge that its quest for real independence had been frustrated. In addition, the burdens of a distorted society and a fragile economy inherited from Spanish colonization did not disappear with the advent of the republic, and this legacy presented serious obstacles to the full economic, political, and social development of the country. These sentiments were expressed by "analysts of the national condition" such as Francisco Figueras (1880–1960), Manuel Villaverde (1881–1962), José Antonio Ramos (1890–1930), Jesús Castellanos (1878–1912), and Fernando Ortiz (Ubieta pp. 70–72).

The study of *choteo* was pursued from different angles by writers of the first Republican generation such as Ortiz and Castellanos. Works such as Ortiz's *Entre cubanos (Psicología tropical)* (Among Cubans [Tropical Psychology], 1913) and Ramos's *Manual del perfecto fulanista* (Manual of the Perfect So-and-So, 1916) deal with the subject later addressed by Mañach, who in "Nuestro prestigio humorístico" (Our Comedic Prestige, 1925) introduced his own preliminary thoughts on humor (Lesmes pp. 40–42).

DEFINING CHOTEO

In the introduction, Mañach attempts to define choteo through its etymology, but it is clear right away that the exercise is futile, because none of the terms he examines—the Andalusian words *choto* and *chotar*, the Lucumí (the Yoruba dialect used in Afro-Cuban Santería liturgy) words *soh* and *chot*, and the Fang (a West African language group from Gabon) term

Author Jorge Mañach (1898–1961), 1944. With the essay *Indagación del choteo* (1928), Jorge Mañach established himself as a pioneer in the reason-based analysis of the national identity and culture of Cuba. GEORGE SKADDING/TIME LIFE PICTURES/GETTY IMAGES

Affable by nature and social habit, Cubans tend toward familiar mannerisms, which is evident in their casual forms of address (as in the use of the Spanish *tú*, the informal *you*), a symptom of the "egalitarian instinct" (Mañach 1955, p. 71).

HISTORICAL CIRCUMSTANCE AND BEHAVIOR

Mañach emphasized social factors that favor the emergence and permit the presence of choteo in Cuban society, the most important being the behavior of the island's people within their historical circumstances. His reflections drew much attention when he stated the following:

> There is a relationship of reciprocal influence between the character and the experience of the people. If the national character models its history in its own way, I also believe that the history itself leaves its mark on the character. Perhaps this is due to a fact that to my mind is very evident: that the national character is not as fixed as some may suppose.
>
> *(1955, p. 73)*

Considering historical events as determining the attitude of the people and their ability to respond to the events in which they are immersed in each time period allowed Mañach to use a dynamic definition of identity, insofar as it is seen as part of a process and not as an unchangeable phenomenon.

Mañach's concept of the Cuban people is also important. He admits the relevance of the momentous era of their struggle for independence, as if that were the point after which one could speak of a real Cuban people. It is precisely those historical events that provided the context for the appearance of the expressions that were predecessors of choteo—irony and mockery—which were used by Cubans during the nineteenth century as weapons against the colonial regime. With the advent of the Republic, irony was set aside, according to Mañach, and mockery held sway until the revolution of the 1930s, a period whose dramatic bias tempered Cubans' desire to turn to laughter whenever they wanted to question the established order.

For Mañach, choteo has a double effect on Cuban society. When it serves to loosen tensions or to protest the inappropriate conduct of legal or government representatives, choteo is a positive instrument for regulating social conduct. However, it also has served as a negative demonstration of "an alarming moral and social state" (Mañach 1955, p. 79); this is the real reason for Mañach's very detailed reflection on Cuban society. He writes, "the choteo has tended to infuse in our people the fear of all noble forms of distinction—the fear of being 'too' intellectual, too spiritual, too polite, and even too sensitive or elegant" (1955, p. 80). Negative choteo is "largely responsible

chota—shed light on the subject. Faced with this problem, Mañach resorts to recounting the most common meanings of choteo—"not taking anything seriously" and "making fun of everything." These meanings, in their absolute quality and their systematic nature, stand for the representation of a specific idea: social contravention of the principle of authority.

Next, Mañach delves into a study of the phenomenon. He recognizes two levels of the display of choteo: The first is more outward and less injurious, caused by somewhat careless behavior, whereas the second is deeper, "perhaps a perversion of the former" (Mañach 1955, p. 54). Mañach turns to explaining the process that leads to choteo. The seed is found in laughter, a quality unique to humankind that distinguishes people from all other species. Next comes mockery, which through satire, irony, or parody constitutes a form of protest against the socially empowered or authorized. Choteo is not the same as the wit of the *criollo*, which is a virtue rather than a defect and appears only from time to time. Mañach finds that choteo, in contrast, is a constant reprehensible attitude, a systematic negative behavior that originates in an individual's attempts to maintain independence from the established social order. Mañach leaves no room for doubt when he writes, "The Cuban's independence leads him to abolish authority, even in social dealings" (1955, p. 70).

for the sluggishness with which we have progressed toward the achievement of a certain social and cultural decorum" (Mañach 1955, p. 79). The basis of this analysis of choteo is found in Mañach's earlier essay "La crisis de la alta cultura en Cuba" (The Crisis of High Culture in Cuba, 1925), which identifies the problems that impede a socially accepted and hierarchically shared order in which reason displaces instinct in human conduct and intellect and culture are recognized as the governing elements of Cuban society. These conclusions were subjected to a new analytical perspective in *Indagación del choteo*.

METHOD AND SOURCES

Indagación del choteo is a work of sociopsychological observation, an exploration of the national identity. Its goal is to analyze social conduct in Cuba in order to reach critical conclusions about the consequences of this conduct, as well as to propose a solution in the best interests of the nation. Mañach used both "empirical and logical" methods (Mañach 1955, p. 50) in his investigation. Instead of starting with lofty abstractions, his work focused on an analysis of specifics, expressed using clear, simple terms.

Mañach used a variety of sources. He appears to have taken his study of the actual forms of socialization from George Simmel's *Sociology* (1908). The influence of Henri Bergson on Mañach's work can be seen particularly in his use of "intuitionism," which stands in contrast to the positivism that Mañach renounces in his writing; nevertheless, he establishes positivism as one of the fundamental pillars of his analysis at a time when its methodological implementation in the contemporary Latin American essay was harshly criticized. Intuitionism (moral intuitionism) is based on a reasoning logic that states our awareness of values is intuitive and that our understanding of objective facts of morality cannot be reduced to natural facts. Positivism is the perspective that the scientific method is the best way to understand nature and society and is unconcerned with grand philosophical explanations. The positivism in *Indagación del choteo* was disparaged as detrimental to efforts to establish values for a higher educational system that was in desperate need of revision. But part of his assessment of choteo is supported by a positivist perspective that Mañach cannot avoid using. The phenomenological current, considered to be the most consistent in Mañach's thinking, is made up of distinct aspects: On one hand, it is influenced by the anthropological concerns of Max Scheler (1874–1928), Scheler's interest in culture, and his theory of values, which Mañach applies to his various contemplations; on the other hand, it demonstrates Mañach's proximity to the ideas of José Ortega y Gasset (1883–1955) that relate to "vital reason."

Mañach considered choteo "a typically Cuban form of relating," and given the absence of previous studies on the subject, his analysis is as unique as the manifestation of national identity itself. In "Image of Ortega y Gasset," Mañach wrote that "to know is to relate ideas—the word 'reason' [*razón* in Spanish, which carries the double meaning of *reason* and *ratio* in the mathematical sense] means nothing else" (Mañach 1956, p. 111). Mañach applied the concept of relating for the first time in *Indagación del choteo*. In formulating a thesis using a method based on relationships, Mañach became a pioneer of the method in Latin America, with Ortega y Gasset as one of his main points of reference (Fabelo Corzo).

CALL FOR REASON-BASED ANALYSIS

Mañach's overall goal was the opposite of what choteo proposes. He pursued a critical sensibility founded in reason, the defense of the capacity of the individual to evaluate in order to understand and respect, and the substitution of behavior based on instinct by behavior based on reason. He argued that the hour was at hand when we should be "critically joyful, judiciously bold, and conscientiously disrespectful" (Mañach 1955, p. 83). Cuban society urgently needed to recover a sense of authority that had been lost gradually over time when the historical link with Spanishness was broken. In order to reverse that disaster, Mañach urged that education and culture should take up the leading role that the intellectual vanguard (despite its differing and even contradictory political and ideological affiliations) had assigned to them.

The explanation of choteo as a destabilizing element and a regulator of authority found its justification in the principle that reason must impose itself over any expression not governed by its authority. The existence of choteo is based on the inability to comply with hierarchies, and it is sustained by various factors explained in a positivist light, such as the deterministic role of climate and geography in Cuban behavior. Choteo was one of the serious consequences of the worst aspects of Spanish heritage in the Cuban cultural legacy.

Among the most respected opinions on the importance and repercussions of *Indagación del choteo* was that offered by Manuel Pedro González, who wrote,

> It appears impossible that such a serious and evocative study could be undertaken on such an unsuitable subject.... Mañach ran up against the difficulty in, and at the same time the advantage of, venturing into an absolutely virgin territory, not tread upon by anyone, and he gives us a complete analysis of it, which we believe will be difficult to improve upon.
>
> *González 1930, p. 100*

The critic Andrés Valdespino commented: "Unlike any other of his other works, here Mañach presents this fluctuation in his personality between the attraction to certain characteristics of the criollo mind—an attraction that reflects the Hispanic roots of his temperament—and the rejection of these same characteristics by his intellectual training" (Valdespino p. 76).

With *Indagación del choteo* Mañach broke new ground in expressing his philosophical ideas through reason-based analysis of the national identity and culture of Cuba. For his work, Mañach received two stamps of approval: first, as one of the best Spanish-language writers in Latin America, and second, as one of the most modern thinkers of his time. Both for the elegance of his prose and for his enlightened ideas on a complex subject rarely explored, Cuban reflective prose, *Indagación del choteo* is considered "one of the authoritative essays of the Republic" (Díaz p. 95).

BIBLIOGRAPHY

Díaz, Duanel. *Mañach o la República*. Havana: Letras Cubanas, 2003.

Fabelo Corzo, José Ramón. *Los valores y sus desafíos actuales*. Havana: Editorial José Martí, 2003.

González, Manuel Pedro. "En torno a los nuevos." *Hispania* 2 (March 1930): 100.

Lesmes, Marta. "Jorge Mañach y nuestro prestigio humorístico." *En Extramuros* 6 (April 2001): 40–42.

Mañach, Jorge. "La crisis de la alta cultura en Cuba." [1925]. In *Ensayos*, edited by Jorge Luis Arcos. Havana: Editorial Letras Cubanas, 1999.

Mañach, Jorge. "Indagación del choteo." [1955]. In *Ensayos*, edited by Jorge Luis Arcos. Havana: Editorial Letras Cubanas, 1999.

Mañach, Jorge. "Imagen de Ortega y Gasset." *Revista Cubana de Filosofía* 13 (January–June 1956): 104–125.

Ubieta, Enrique. "El ensayo y la crítica." In *Historia de la literatura cubana*, vol. 2. Havana: Letras Cubanas, 2003.

Valdespino, Andrés. *Jorge Mañach y su generación en las letras cubanas*. Miami, FL: Ediciones Universal, 1971.

ISLA DE PINOS

Julio César González Laureiro

Isla de Pinos, renamed Isla de la Juventud in 1978, a less developed island than other Caribbean islands.

Located about 62 miles (100 km) off Cuba's southern coast, opposite the Gulf of Batabanó, Isla de Pinos (literally, Isle of Pines) was named for the pine forests, which covers much of its surface. Its status is that of a special municipality (as opposed to a province) of Cuba; Nueva Gerona is the capital and largest city. With an area of 1,182 square miles (3,601 sq. km.), it is the largest island in the Canarreos Archipelago, the second-largest Cuban island, and the sixth-largest in the Greater Antilles. Despite its size, several fac-

tors have limited the island's population growth and development as compared to other Caribbean islands: the shallow seabed of its insular platform, the lack of a port or waterway to allow communication with the outside, and economic dependence on Havana. During the nineteenth century, Spain valued the island as a link to the Greater Antilles and defended it against England's threat of occupation.

EARLY HISTORY

Discovered on 13 June 1494 by Christopher Columbus, who named it La Evangelista, the island was inhabited by indigenous groups that predated agriculture and pottery. Cave drawings discovered on the island attest not only to the indigenous people's highly developed pictorial skills but have been variously interpreted as pertaining to a lunar calendar, an astronomical observatory, a temple of the dead, a temple honoring the sun, as well as indicating an understanding of the development of the human fetus. Awarded by royal decree to the oligarch Alonso de Rojas in 1573, the island was neglected until the nineteenth century except as a stopover or meeting place for privateers and pirates. Their presence accounts for many of the names given to locations on the island, such as Laguna de los Bucaneros (Buccaneer Lagoon), Estero de los Corsarios (Privateer Estuary), and Cayos del Mallorquín (Majorca Keys). In 1792 Isla de Pinos had a population of 86—55 men, 16 women, and 15 children—whose main economic activity was raising cattle.

In 1830 Spain fortified its claim to the island by founding Reina Amalia, which it also hoped would spur the island's economy. Residents prepared products made from pine sap and quarried marble from Sierra de Caballos; in the 1860s the Sociedad de Fomento Pinero (Pinero Development Society) was founded to further activities such as those associated with navigation, tile factories, medicinal baths and spas, logging, and sugar production. Scant records of the island's development leave many questions as to how the settlers fared, but one 1875 report by a Spanish officer on the island's sugar industry enumerates such obstacles as a lack of knowledgeable workers, poor communications, the need to bring workers and supplies over from Cuba, malfunctioning equipment, and difficulties of making timely repairs. One grower, as the officer recounted, complained of reduced capital as a result of eight years of coping with such obstacles and the high cost of delivering sugar to market (Núñez Jiménez pp. 431–432). Moreover, water needed for agricultural development was in short supply, and aid promised to the settlers was not forthcoming.

An 1877 census indicates that the territory had 2,478 inhabitants, but many of these were temporary residents such as military personnel and prisoners—both common criminals and political opponents sent to the island as a confinement area. Notable among the political prisoners held there were José Martí,

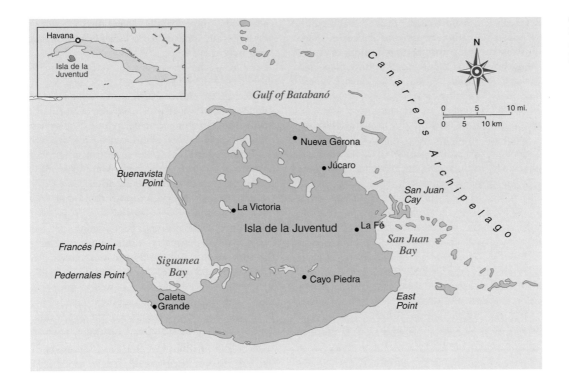

Map of Isla de Pinos, also known as Isla de la Juventud

Raimundo Cabrera, and Evangelina Cossío Cisneros. Cossío Cisneros participated, together with several deportees, in an 1896 uprising against colonial authorities in Nueva Gerona. Cossío Cisneros was arrested and taken to the Casa de Recogidas (Women's Detention Center) in Havana, but she escaped with the help of several U.S. journalists and arrived in New York in 1897. Her case became legendary, attracting support for the rebels' cause.

U.S. PRESENCE

In 1898, under the Treaty of Paris, Spain ceded control of Cuba to the United States, and in 1902 the United States granted Cuba its independence while retaining the right to intervene under the Platt Amendment. U.S. companies ended up controlling more than half the land of Isla de Pinos, which was sold as small lots in installments and options. Hundreds of families from the United States settled in Nueva Gerona and Santa Fe and founded the communities of Columbia, McKinley, Palm Grove, West Port, San Francisco, and Santa Barbara. Using the U.S. dollar as legal currency and producing goods for the U.S. and Havana markets, this new community generated new economic and social dynamics. Residents founded ten churches, nine schools with American teachers, two newspapers, one bank, several hotels, and many businesses and community organizations. As Irene Wright observed in *Cuba*, American residents "made the Isle of Pines an American community in everything except political status" (p. 322).

The initial U.S. interest in the island stemmed from its efforts to establish strategic enclaves in the Caribbean. However, taking note of the island's geography, the secretary of the navy in a 1903 report rejected the notion that the island would be useful for this purpose. The U.S. citizens on the island, though they constituted only about 13 percent of its population, sought to claim the territory, campaigning against U.S. plans to relinquish it and attempting an uprising to annex the island in 1904. In 1907 the Supreme Court ruled that the United States had no legal right to Isla de Pinos, which "under the provisions of the Platt Amendment and the Constitution of the Republic of Cuba, is de facto under the jurisdiction of the Republic of Cuba" (*Pearcy v. Stranahan*, 205 U.S. 257 [1907]). After the ratification in 1925 of the Hay-Quesada Treaty, which recognized Cuban sovereignty over Isla de Pinos, and a 1926 hurricane that damaged the island, the majority of the U.S. settlers abandoned the land. They left their mark on its architecture, agriculture, and diverse population, which in addition to Antilleans included Europeans and Japanese who had visited the island looking to buy land or find employment.

PRESIDIO MODELO

The idea of building a model prison on Isla de Pinos, postponed since the term of President José Miguel Gómez (1909–1913), was fulfilled in 1925 during the term of President Gerardo Machado (1925–1933). The Presidio Modelo building, following architectural plans conceived by the English social reformer Jeremy Bentham (1748–1832), was panoptic or circular in shape, with a capacity for approximately 5,000 inmates. It became the new standard of Cuban penitentiary reform and reflected Cuban theorists' study of European criminal anthropology.

Intended for common criminals as well as political prisoners, the prison at one time housed the journalist Pablo de la Torriente Brau, the author of *La Isla de los 500 asesinatos* (The Island of 500 Murders) and *Presidio Modelo* (Model Prison). Once convicts disembarked on the Columpo dock and arrived at the prison to begin their period of incarceration, they were subjected to a regimen of work and brutal punishment that often led to death. The Pinero Civil Registry includes hundreds of files pertaining to cases of mental illness and deaths among the prisoners. By the time the prison was closed in 1967, there had been 839 deaths, 433 of which occurred while Machado was in office. In 1938, when the Code of Social Defense came into effect, abolishing the Iberian penal legislation, the name of the prison was changed from Presidio Modelo to Reclusorio Nacional para Hombres (National Penitentiary for Men); the Superior Committee for Social Defense was also created, limiting the powers of prison directors and their subordinates.

The 1940s and early 1950s were characterized by numerous legal proceedings stemming from disorder in the prison. Stories of the manufacture and use of handmade weapons, of the proliferation of prohibited gambling, and of gangsters blackmailing their victims from behind bars made the front page of newspapers. After the 1952 coup led by Fulgencio Batista, the military personnel deposed by the Code of Defense returned to head the prison. They were later judged and sentenced by the Revolutionary Court for new crimes against the inmate population. Fidel Castro prepared the final version of "La historia me absolverá" (History Will Absolve Me), the speech he delivered in court in his own defense on charges of leading the attack on the Moncada Barracks while incarcerated in the prison in 1954.

REVOLUTIONARY ERA

The Cuban Revolution brought many changes to Isla de Pinos, not least of which was the takeover of the prison by its political prisoners. In June 1959 a referendum in Nueva Gerona eliminated the free-trade zone status, which had been given to the island in 1954 in an attempt to stimulate its economy, and established new strategies for development of the island. These included promoting agriculture, cattle farming, industry, and tourism, as well as plans for reforestation and deactivation of the prison. It continued to serve as the National Penitentiary for Crimes against the Safety of the State until 1967; in 1973 it was converted into a museum, and in 1978 it was named a national monument.

Given the island's sparse population, the government called on Cuban youth to aid in its development; they began arriving on the island in 1960. That year the first ranch for breeding cattle was established; in 1967 the first dam was opened; in 1971 the first rural school was opened; and in 1977 large numbers of foreign students began arriving, primarily from Africa and Latin America. In 1976 the Canarreos Archipelago adopted new political and administrative divisions, and the island was given the status of special municipality. As such, it began participating in government at the national level and endeavored to end its historical isolation, to overcome its geographical limitations, and to integrate the island into Cuban

Presidio Modelo. During the 1950s, Fidel Castro and other rebels were imprisoned at the Presidio Modelo, a Panopticon-style prison on the Isla de la Juventud, formerly known as the Isla de Pinos. AP IMAGES

life. In 1978, during the Eleventh Youth and Student Festival, the government changed the island's name to Isla de la Juventud (Isle of Youth).

Further changes followed. Citrus plantations were established, reservoir capacity was expanded, dozens of schools were built, and industry and tourism, centered in Cayo Largo, increased. However, after the thousands of Cuban and foreign students who arrived on the island in the 1970s graduated, this population was not replenished, and the huge citrus production of the past began to fall off. Because its economic outlook and growth remained uncertain, the Isla de Pinos may stay, as Ofelia Rodríguez put it in 1929, a "sleeping beauty."

BIBLIOGRAPHY

Gort, Sergio A., et al. *Isla de la Juventud: Su naturaleza*. Havana: Editorial Científico-Técnica, 1994.

Hevia, Aurelio. *Los derechos de Cuba sobre la Isla de Pinos*. Havana: Imprenta "El siglo XX," 1924.

Marrero, Leví. *Cuba: Economía y sociedad*, vol. 2. Madrid: Editorial Playor, 1974.

McManus, Jane. *Cuba's Island of Dreams: Voices from the Isle of Pines and Youth*. Gainesville: University Press of Florida, 2000.

Núñez Jiménez, Antonio. *Isla de Pinos: Piratas, colonizadores, rebeldes*. Havana: Editorial Arte y Literatura, 1976.

Pérez, Louis A. Jr. *On Becoming Cuban: Identity, Nationality, and Culture*. Chapel Hill: University of North Carolina Press, 2008.

Rodríguez Acosta, Ofelia. *Apuntes de mi viaje a Isla de Pinos*. Havana: Montiel y Co. Impresores, 1929.

Sorhegui, Arturo, and Mirna Quiñones. *El tratado Hay Quesada: Consideraciones históricas. Revista de la Biblioteca Nacional José Martí* 1 (January–April 1980): 151–171.

Torriente Brau, Pablo de la. *La isla de los 500 asesinatos*. Havana: Nuevo Mundo, 1962.

Wright, Irene Aloha. *Cuba*. New York: Macmillan, 1910.

LA ISLA EN PESO (VIRGILIO PIÑERA)

Víctor Fowler Calzada

One of the most influential poems in Cuban literature.

La isla en peso (Island in the Balance), a long poem published in 1943, is considered a canonical work of modern Cuban literature and remains one of its most debated and influential texts. Its author, Virgilio Piñera (1912–1979), was also a fiction writer, playwright, and critic who introduced European avant-garde genres and styles to Cuba, especially the theater of cruelty and the theater of the absurd. As a

playwright Piñera was seen as the leader of modern theater on the island. Absurdity, violence, and cruelty are central elements in Piñera's fiction, conveying an existentialist notion of being. Piñera's poetry was influenced by the works of his contemporaries Emilio Ballagas (1908–1954) and José Lezama Lima (1910–1976); afterward he adopted the prosaic, colloquial language and the use of the grotesque characteristic of the so-called anti-poetry.

Piñera's poem is characterized by the triumph of chaos, hopelessness, disgust, and eroticism. These qualities constituted a break from the authors who appeared in the influential journal *Orígenes*, who viewed their work as an act of giving sense to the nation. The first six lines of *La isla en peso* describe the island thus:

> La maldita circunstancia del agua por
>   todas partes
> me obliga a sentarme en la mesa del café.
> Si no pensara que el agua me rodea como
>   un cáncer
> hubiera podido dormir a pierna suelta.
> Mientras los muchachos se despojaban de sus
>   ropas para nadar
> doce personas morían en un cuarto por
>   compresión.

> [The damned circumstance of water everywhere
> forces me to sit on the coffee table.
> If I did not believe that water engulfs me
>   like cancer
> I could have slept like a baby.
> While the youths were taking their clothes
>   off to swim
> twelve people were dying in a room by
>   compression.]

LEZAMA, PIÑERA, AND LITERARY DISILLUSION

One must go back to one of Lezama's most important texts, *Coloquio con Juan Ramón Jiménez* (Colloquium with Juan Ramón Jiménez; 1937), to understand the enormous rupture Piñera's opening represents. *Coloquio* is a foundational document out of which the poetry of the Grupo Orígenes emerged fewer than ten years later. In his imagined conversation with the Spanish poet Juan Ramón Jiménez, Lezama listens and tries to respond, presenting his own theory about his country, to the historical tensions—the escape from Spanish colonialism in 1898 and the subsequent U.S. occupation—that it was still wrestling with as it strove to find its final structure as a nation. Lezama's theory is unique in that it does not offer a pragmatic approach for moving forward (through social action and the formation of political parties) from the present circumstances to the desired goal; rather, it offers a philosophy of a culture rooted in the history of poetry,

 See also

Governance and Contestation: The Republic: 1902–1952

Indagación del choteo (Jorge Mañach)

Literature: Poetry in the Republican Period

The Orígenes Group and Journal

which from that starting point proposes the construction of meaning destined to take shape in writing. Such a writing project intends to create myths that could propose future qualities and spaces for the confluence of the nation and its constituents.

For Lezama, the creative act of writing poetry is the highest step humans can reach in their journey to God. The Catholic foundation of his conceptualization explains this fanciful mix, in which collectivity must first pass the test of nation-building before reentering (through death) the body of God the Creator. From a historical perspective, the process meant going back to the "period of splendor" of the nineteenth century, when the desire to build the nation drove the *criollo* bourgeoisie to start a war that jeopardized and sacrificed its privileges in exchange for liberation from Spanish control.

Lezama formulated a positive response to the long chain of frustration, skepticism, and confusion that characterizes a large number of Cuban texts written during the first years of the Republic, such as *Entre cubanos (Psicología tropical)* (Among Cubans [Tropical Psychology], 1913), by Fernando Ortiz; *La decadencia cubana* (Cuban Decadence, 1915), by Enrique José Varona; *El manual del perfecto fulanista* (How to Be the Perfect So-and-So, 1916), by José Antonio Ramos; *El manual del perfecto sinvergüenza* (How to Be the Perfect Scoundrel, 1922), by José M. Muzaurieta; *La escudilla de Diógenes: Etopeya del cínico* (Diogenes' Shield: Portrait of a Cynic, 1924), by Fernando Lles; and *La crisis de la alta cultura en Cuba* (The Crisis in Cuban High Culture, 1925), by Jorge Mañach. These texts pulsated with the fundamental suspicion of Cuba's inability to become an independent, modern nation. Their disillusion is in stark contrast to the title of a speech given by Diego Vicente Tejera in 1897 in Key West, Florida, to his fellow exiled supporters of independence: *La capacidad cubana* (Cuba's Ability).

La isla en peso may be considered a summary as well as a multiplication of this suspicion and disillusion. Referring to the connection between Piñera's corrosive vision and the extent of disillusion among the intellectuals of the First Republic, Antonio José Ponte, in *El libro perdido de los origenistas* (The Lost Book of the *Orígenes* Writers, 2002), makes a bitter joke: "It is impossible to define [Piñera] without having first defined Lezama, which means having defined *Orígenes*, having defined the Republic, having defined Martí, etc. etc. etc., till the beginning of time."

As is evident from the opening of *La isla en peso* quoted above, the poem lacks any myth of insular happiness, coherence, or progress. Despite being one of the most accomplished poems of all Cuban literature, it presents the island's condition as a "damned circumstance," something that "engulfs like cancer," a thought that becomes such torture that it disrupts sleep. Lines 5 and 6 contrast the lyrical beholding of the seminude bodies of young people against the overcrowding of poor neighborhoods. The happiness of eroticism contrasts with misery; the transcendent freedom that the ocean symbolizes (communion between man and nature) stands in opposition to suffering, a type of suffering that extends across time. Since presumably those twelve people are struggling to enter into a small space until they are crushed to death, readers are obliged to imagine the presence of a terrible "outside" that forces them to seek shelter, even if it costs them their lives. From that point on, there is no amenable place upon which the symbolic tale of the nation can rest.

At the end of the first stanza, Piñera introduces the idea of a past coherence and perfection that have been lost: "Una taza de café no puede alejar mi idea fija, / en otro tiempo yo vivía adánicamente. / ¿Qué trajo la metamorfosis?" (A cup of coffee cannot drive off my fixed idea, / I used to have a heavenly life. / What brought on the metamorphosis?) The second stanza suggests that such a time corresponds to the moment in which "the combinations" were formed. But then an interruption appears that destroys this design: the black race (illustrated by dance, music, eroticism, rum). This interruption elicits the historical and cultural contradictions of the forced importation of Africans to Cuba, scrambling any pretense of remembering Cuba as a wholesome spiritual homeland; the nation, in its roots, keeps secrets of ferocity and crime. This can be viewed in part as an address to *origenista* poets who would like to represent Cuba as a raceless spiritual Eden without violence or barbarism; on the contrary, any sign of black culture (dance, music, eroticism, rum) will always be a reminder of white/Spanish colonial violence and a sort of marker of Cuban historical and cultural contradictions.

> La eterna miseria que es el acto de recordar.
> Si tú pudieras formar de nuevo aquellas
>   combinaciones,
> devolviéndome el país sin el agua,
> me la bebería toda para escupir al cielo.
> Pero he visto la música detenida en las caderas,
> he visto a las negras bailando con vasos de ron
>   en sus cabezas.
>
> [The eternal misery that remembering carries.
> If only you could form those combinations
>   again,
> and return to me the country without the
>   water,
> I would drink it up to spit it into the sky.
> But I have seen the music stand silent on
>   the hips,
> I have seen black women dance with cups of
>   rum balanced on their heads.]

PIÑERA'S VISION OF CUBANNESS

Piñera's interpretation of "the national" here is complex. From a chronological standpoint, African slaves, through their work, created the country's wealth, thus allowing the splendor of nineteenth-century Cuban culture. Yet this is the very source of its contamination, and the effort to build the nation is broken as a result of this hostile conjunction ("but") that introduces a dissipating otherness and crushes any attempt at mental elaboration. As it continues to excavate history, the lyric voice finds new interruptions at the end of the fourth stanza:

> Pienso en los caballos de los conquistadores
> cubriendo a las yeguas,
> pienso en el desconocido son del areíto
> desaparecido para toda la eternidad,
> ciertamente debo esforzarme a fin de poner
> en claro
> el primer contacto carnal en este país, y el
> primer muerto.

> [I think of the conquistadors' stallions
> mounting the mares,
> I think of the alien *areíto* tune
> wiped out for eternity,
> I surely have to make an effort to make clear
> the first carnal contact in this country, and the
> first death.]

Against the efforts made by the *Orígenes* writers to present a mythical national history, Piñera's imagery evokes the violent destruction of the native peoples (*areíto* is indigenous music) and the cruelties of slavery. He points to mixtures that impede any thought of purity and cancel the presumption of any homogenous identity. He suggests that the refinements of Cuban patriots, especially the founding fathers of the nineteenth century, are mere copies of European models. Under the surface is the fear that the violence and mixing of the past and the present misery and disintegration might be discovered. Thus later in the poem Piñera transforms the symbol of the sun as the giver of light and warmth into a monstrous and invasive light that suffocates and exposes any secret or intimacy. The arrival of the noonday sun is far from pleasant, but rather triggers chaos and panic:

> ¡Hay que tapar! ¡Hay que tapar!
> Pero la claridad avanzada, invade
> perversamente, oblicuamente,
> perpendicularmente,
> la claridad es una enorme ventosa que chupa
> la sombra,
> y las manos van lentamente hacia los ojos.
> [...]
> Son las doce el día.

> Todo un pueblo puede morir de luz como
> morir de peste.

> [We must cover up! We must cover up!

> But the advancing light, it invades
> perversely, oblique, perpendicularly,
> the clarity is an enormous sucker that sucks up
> the shade,
> and the hands move slowly toward the eyes.
> [...]

> It is twelve noon.

> An entire town can die from light as it would
> from a plague.]

Contrasted to the Christian metaphor of *light* as a weapon against *darkness*, in Piñera's poem light passes through shadows to expose the occult, the secrets; there are no places to hide and all becomes public, because the past surfaces again and again. Thus the idealized notion of the nation is shown to rest on a foundation of silence regarding past violence and non-homogenous races. The living are prisoner to ancient crimes, but they are also held captive to the currents of sensuality in a group historically repressed. The bars of this "prison" are made up of Cuba's tried past but, in the body of Piñera's work, the cell of this "prison" is paradoxically also a stage of pleasure, sensuality, dance, naïveté, and simplicity.

As the poem continues, it becomes clear that the "cancer" of the first stanza of the poem affects all people, average and educated. All are intertwined in the contradiction between European reason and Caribbean sensuality:

> [E]n esta hora del cáncer un extranjero llegado
> de playas remotas
> preguntaría inútilmente qué proyectos tenemos
> o cuántos hombres mueren de enfermedades
> tropicales en esta isla.
> Nadie lo escucharía: las palmas de las manos
> vueltas hacia arriba,
> los oídos obturados por el tapón de la
> somnolencia,
> los poros tapiados con la cera de un fastidio
> elegante
> y de la mortal deglución de las glorias pasadas.

> [...]
> ¡Pueblo mío, tan joven, no sabes ordenar!
> ¡Pueblo mío, divinamente retórico, no sabes
> relatar!
> Como la luz o la infancia aún no tienes un
> rostro.

> [At this time of cancer a foreigner from faraway
> beaches
> would pointlessly ask what projects we have
> or how many men die of tropical diseases on
> this island.
> Nobody would listen to him: the palms of
> hands turned upward,

ears clogged by the plug of somnolence,
pores blocked by the wax of an elegant
      fastidiousness
and by the fatal swallowing of past glories.

[...]
My people, so young, you don't know how to
      give orders!
My people, divinely rhetorical, you don't know
      how to tell a story!
Like light and like childhood, you still don't
      have a face.]

PIÑERA'S CRITICS

If there is any work that established the enormous gap between Piñera's work and that of the Grupo Orígenes, it is *La isla en peso*. Gastón Baquero and Cintio Vitier, two of the most important poets and essayists of the Lezama group, harshly criticized it to the end of their days. In "Tendencias de nuestra literatura" (Trends in Our Literature), a 1943 essay, Baquero regards Piñera's poem as an imitation of *Cahier d'un retour au pays natal* (Journal on a Return to the Native Land), a poem by the African-Martinican poet Aimé Césaire. Fragments of Césaire's poem, which is emblematic of the negritude movement, appeared in Spanish in Cuba in 1943; the previous year Piñera had translated it (from the French) for *Poeta*, a short-lived journal he had founded after breaking away from another journal, *Espuela de Plata*. Baquero writes that *La isla en peso* is:

> Full of a primitive vitality we do not possess, with colors we do not possess, with a will to act and a reaction we do not possess. It is precisely the opposite island to the one defined by our status as eager for problems, for history, for conflict, which makes us live more "civilly," more in the spirit of civilization and nostalgia.
>
> *p. 481*

The Cuba of Piñera's vision, he says, "is the island of an Antilleanness or Martinicanness that does not reflect us, does not belong to us" (p. 481).

Vitier's equally hostile judgment had graver consequences. Piñera's text was excluded from two important anthologies: *Diez poetas cubanos* (Ten Cuban Poets, 1948) and *Cincuenta años de poesía cubana* (Fifty Years of Cuban Poetry, 1953). These collections were the most serious efforts yet on the part of the *origenistas* at creating a canon. Piñera's poem was also attacked in *Lo cubano en la poesía* (Cubanness in Poetry, 1970): "The tone and the theory of this poem make evident the influx of visions like Aimé Césaire's in *Retorno al país natal*, which could never belong to us. ... Our blood, our sensitivity, our history, lead us along very different paths" (Vitier 1970, p. 481).

EXILE, RETURN, OSTRACISM, AND REDISCOVERY

From early on Piñera positioned himself as a solitary outsider in the Cuban literature of his time, a fate that stuck with him until the end. In 1946 he went into exile in Buenos Aires, where he met the Polish fiction writer Witold Gombrowicz, also living in exile there, as well as the members of the translation committee for Gombrowicz's modernist novel *Ferdydurke*. In 1952 he published a novel, *La carne de René* (René's Flesh), and during a stay in Havana in 1955, he helped José Rodríguez Feo in the creation of the journal *Ciclón*, for which he served as a correspondent. In 1956, back in Argentina, he published his *Cuentos fríos* (Cold Stories). He returned to Havana in 1958.

After the Cuban Revolution, Piñera wrote for the newspaper *Revolución*, especially the weekly cultural section *Lunes de Revolución*, which was closed in 1961. He was named director of Ediciones R in 1961 and held this position until the publishing house closed in 1964. His *Teatro completo* (Complete Plays) was published in 1960, his novel *Pequeñas maniobras* (Little Maneuvers) in 1963, and *Cuentos completos* (Complete Stories) in 1964. In 1968 he was awarded the Casa de las Américas prize in theater for *Dos viejos pánicos* (Two Old Men in a Panic), and in 1969 a personal anthology of his poetry, *La vida entera* (The Whole Life), was published. Piñera's last contribution to Cuban culture was the staging of *El encarne* (The Incarnation, 1970). After the 1971 imprisonment and interrogation of playwright Heberto Padilla for the supposed counterrevolutionary tone of his works, Piñera was no longer permitted to have his plays staged, to publish his books, or to leave the island. He died, ostracized, in 1979.

The appearance of *Un fogonazo* (An Explosion) in 1987 denotes the reincorporation of Piñera and his works into the nation's cultural realm and the beginning of his impact on younger writers. After the enlarged edition of Piñera's *Poesía completa* came out in 1982, the stage was set to confront once again the legacy of both Piñera and his perpetual adversary José Lezama Lima, who had suffered the same cultural ostracism, from 1973 until his death in 1976. In Cuba's literary renewal of the 1980s, both authors were hoisted like flags in a gesture aimed at the most critical, radical, and politicized positions concerning the relations between the act of writing and the cultural limits of the socialist project and at large of Cuban society. After 1959, the work of Piñera and Lezama could be analyzed as two answers to the same question. In 1994 Damaris Calderón, writing in *Virgilio Piñera: Una poética para los años 80* (Virgilio Piñera: A Poetics for the 1980s), drove a wedge into the celebrations of the fiftieth anniversary of the founding of *Orígenes*:

> Moving away from the contributions of the *Orígenes* writers, from its astonishing project of an insular theology—this group's defining

feature and biggest mistake—we begin to see in this same drive a revision of the Cuba built on mythology, on story-telling, on the paradisiacal as a category or emblematic value of that which is Cuban. The key to this revision: Virgilio Piñera.

In Cuba's changed conditions, Piñera and his poem were resurrected.

BIBLIOGRAPHY

Abreu, Alberto. *Virgilio Piñera: un hombre, una isla.* Havana : Ediciones Unión, 2002.

Anhalt, Nedda G. de, Víctor Manuel Mendiola, and Manuel Ulacia, eds. *La fiesta innombrable: Trece poetas cubanos.* Mexico City: Ediciones El Tucán de Virginia, Fundación E. Gutman, 1992.

Arrufat, Antón. *Virgilio Piñera: entre él y yo.* Havana: Ediciones Unión, 1994.

Baquero, Gastón. "Tendencias de nuestra literatura." *Anuario Cultural de Cuba (1943).* Havana: Úcar, 1944.

Cabrera Infante, Guillermo. *Vidas para leerlas.* Madrid: Alfaguara, 1992.

Calderón, Damaris. "Virgilio Piñera: una poética para los años 80." Paper presented at the Coloquio por los 50 años de *Orígenes*, Havana, 1994.

Cristófani Barreto, Teresa. *A libélula, a pitonisa: Revoluçao, homossexualismo e literatura em Virgilio Piñera.* Sa-o Paulo, Brazil: FAPESP, Iluminuras, 1998.

Díaz, Duanel. *Límites del origenismo.* Madrid: Colibrí, 2005.

"Dossier Virgilio Piñera." *Diario de Poesía* 51 (1999): 7–35.

Espinosa, Carlos. *Virgilio Piñera en persona.* Havana: Ediciones Unión, 2003.

Molinero, Rita, ed. *Virgilio Piñera: La memoria del cuerpo.* San Juan, Puerto Rico: Editorial Plaza Mayor, 2002.

Piñera, Virgilio. "Ballagas en persona." *Ciclón* 1, no. 5 (September 1955): 41–50.

Piñera, Virgilio. "La vida, tal cual." *Unión* 3, no. 10 (1990): 22–36.

Ponte, Antonio José. "La lengua de Virgilio." Matanzas, Cuba: Ediciones Vigía, 1994.

Ponte, Antonio José. *El libro perdido de los origenistas.* Mexico City: Editorial Aldus, 2002.

Vitier, Cintio, ed. *Diez poetas cubanos, 1937–1947.* Havana: Orígenes, 1948.

Vitier, Cintio, ed. *Cincuenta años de poesía cubana (1902-1952).* Havana: Dirección de Cultura del Ministerio de Educación, 1953.

Vitier, Cintio. *Lo cubano en la poesía.* Havana: Instituto del Libro, 1970.

J

JOSÉ MARTÍ: EXILE IN NEW YORK

Oscar Montero

The experience of Cuba's foremost patriot while in exile in New York City starting in 1880.

On the northbound M7 bus, as it turns from Sixth Avenue to run along the southern edge of New York City's Central Park, west to Columbus Circle, riders are greeted by the sight of José Martí's equestrian statue, framed by those of Simón Bolívar and José de San Martín. At the end of its brief run through Central Park South, as the M7 approaches Columbus Circle, another monument juts out of the trees in the park. "Columbia Triumphant" consists of a huge gilded figure, atop a five-story-high monolith. At its base a youth stands on the prow of a boat, as if poised between the past and the future, holding his arm high and making the victory sign. These grand allegorical gestures on the 1913 Beaux-Arts monument pay homage to the sinking of the battleship *Maine* in Havana's harbor in 1898.

It takes the bus only a few minutes to go from the heroic trio centered by the statue of Martí to the *Maine* monument, but the history those monuments evoke reaches from the beginning of Cuba's war of independence, marked by Martí's death in the battlefield in 1895, to the beginning of the Spanish-American War in 1898, the end of Cuban independence, and the beginning of the United States as the world power of the twentieth century. These are beginnings and endings worth remembering through the perspective of Martí's experiences and through his work during the fifteen years he lived in New York City.

When Martí came to New York in January 1880 at the age of twenty-seven, the brand-new elevated railway roared down Ninth Avenue, frightening horses and showering sparks of coal dust. Although

he traveled frequently, New York City was Martí's home base. New York might have been something of a home, as much of a home as an exile can make in the great city. Martí's goal was a heroic return to Cuban soil, which was, if not home, certainly the only *patria* he ever wanted. New York was the awesome capital of wealth he inhabited out of necessity. Yet the city offered a place to work and a refuge, however precarious and transitory.

Exile became for Martí "the condition of the poet and the revolutionary" (Díaz-Quiñones p. 31). He arrived in New York on 3 January 1880, onboard the steamer *Francia*, which had left the French port of Le Havre less than two weeks before. He had visited Paris and was now arriving in New York, exiled, *desterrado* rather, banished, from Cuba and having overstayed his welcome in Mexico, Guatemala, and Venezuela. Volumes have been written about Martí's New York years, especially after the appearance of a seminal work on the subject, *José Martí: Epic Chronicler of the United States in the Eighties*, by Manuel Pedro González, published in 1953 to commemorate the centennial of Martí's birth. The statuary figure of heroic proportions and the "epic chronicler of the United States" and of "our America" are well known not just to scholars but also to millions of other people, including schoolchildren in Cuba and orating politicians from Albuquerque to Caracas; less is said, however, about the small, intense man who dodged the harrowing traffic of Broadway, who ran up the stairs to his office on 120 Front Street, right where it crosses Wall Street, who managed to become for a while, perhaps despite himself, like millions of others, something of a New Yorker. In New York, Martí, revolutionary hero, unequaled chronicler of the Americas, radical poet, also helped to define a nascent Latino consciousness in the United States.

VISION OF THE FUTURE AND SENSE OF IDENTITY

Martí was both a nineteenth-century hero and a poet with a fearful vision of the century to come. It was a vision crafted for the people Martí himself called *los latinos, la gente latina*, Latin people. By *latinos* Martí

CHRONOLOGY

1853: 28 January: José Julián Martí y Pérez born in Havana.

1868: Carlos Manuel de Céspedes proclaims Cuban independence, beginning the Ten-Years' War.

1869: Martí arrested for treasonable activities and sentenced to six years imprisonment.

1870: Martí's father arranges commutation of sentence; José Martí deported to Spain. While in Spain he will publish *El presidio político en Cuba*, an intense account of his experiences in a Spanish prison in Cuba, intending to publicize Cuba's plight under colonial rule.

1875: Martí moves to Mexico to write and teach.

1877: Marries Carmen Zayas Bazán.

1878: Ten-Years' War ends; Martí returns to Cuba and gets job as teacher.

1879: The Little War breaks out near Santiago de Cuba; Martí arrested for conspiracy and deported.

1880: Martí moves to New York and devotes himself to writing.

1882: Publishes *Ismaelillo*, considered key text in *modernismo* (modernist) movement.

1889: Writes *Cuba and the United States*.

1891: Joins Patriotic Cuban League; publishes *Versos sencillos* and important essay, "Nuestra América."

1892: Founds the Cuban Revolutionary Party and begins publication of *Patria*.

1894: Formulates the "Fernandina Plan" aimed at launching a revolution in Cuba.

1895: January: Despite seizure of arms by the U.S. government, Martí continues with plans for his revolution.

1895: March: Lands in Cuba.

1895: April: Proclaimed Major General of Liberating Army.

1895: 19 May: Martí killed at the Battle of Dos Ríos.

---

meant people from Latin America, wherever they might be: Mexico, New York, Tampa, or Key West. One may certainly argue that the terms *latino* and *Latin people* in the work of Martí are far removed from contemporary debates around the notion of *Latino-America*, which negotiate the question of national identity and its relationship to Latin Americans' many diasporas. It may seem simplistic to suggest that Martí's own ideas about *Latinity* and identity prefigure the contemporary debates of the late twentieth and early twenty-first centuries. In Martí's use of *los latinos*, however, there is a sense of identity that still resonates, that is, identity as the sharing of values—cultural and even spiritual values—and the sharing of common purposes beyond the geographic and political limitations imposed by a person's discrete, and sometimes limiting, identities.

Martí's sense of identity had its core in Cuba—his own heart he called it—but it was quick to embrace Puerto Rico and the Dominican Republic, the countries of some of Martí's most loyal allies. It expanded to embrace the idea of an Antillean coalition and then came to include all of "our America." Martí's idea of identity was also a plea for human solidarity across all borders, a plea as urgent in the early twenty-first century as it was when it was uttered in a world that only wistful nostalgia could imagine as a simpler time. For Martí, *cosmopolitanism* was more than a chic buzzword among his contemporaries. He took its root to heart: cosmos, the universe, where everyone must live regardless of which flag each chooses to wave.

In March 1882, in New York City, Martí published a slim volume titled *Ismaelillo* inspired by his three-year-old son Pepito, who arrived in the city with his mother, Martí's wife Carmen Zayas-Bazán,

in December of that year. The book, which at first circulated among the poet's friends, ultimately revolutionized Spanish American poetry, ushering in what would later be called *modernismo*. Also while in New York, Martí in 1891 published a small edition of his *Versos sencillos* (Simple Verses), a lyrical autobiography that eventually became one of the best-known collections of verse ever written in the Spanish language. In Martí's writings, whether speeches given to cigar workers or essays written for the Latin American press, there recurs a call for commitment and compassion, praise for the life of the mind, sustained warning against the traps of materialism, and stoic faith in the betterment of humankind. These are familiar topics, but Martí stated them with brilliant, enduring urgency.

Looking at population figures, many see the United States in the process of becoming a Latin nation. But what is more important than census statistics is the question of what kind of nation might that be. Whatever the answer, the fact is that individuals such as Martí should figure prominently in the culture of the United States. They should figure prominently in the curricula of U.S. teaching institutions, not only as representative men but also as important figures in serious scholarship and debate. Such an inclusion requires work in translation, interpretation, critical thinking, and teaching.

Martí believed that the sovereignty of a nation guaranteed the rights of its citizens, but he mistrusted the flag-waving nationalism of the demagogue. He believed that all nations should share a vision of universal harmony. From the perspective of the early twenty-first century, such an idea may seem as naive as the pipe dream of a belated romantic, but for Martí it held real promise. He believed in democratic ideals, but from his vantage point in New York City, he also saw quite a different picture of a working democracy. Martí's gaze on New York and on U.S. politics and culture was sustained for fifteen of his most productive years. He observed the culture of the metropolis like no one else writing in Spanish. His gaze provides a sharp evaluation of the best and the worst that the United States has to offer.

THOUGHTS ON MANY ISSUES HEWN IN THE CITY

Martí's thoughts on wealth, on race, on eminent North Americans, on the expanding role of the United States, and on death and transcendence were shaped by his experience in New York City. At times the style of Martí's writing may seem as distant from the world of the early twenty-first century as the steam locomotive and the telegraph. Yet on many issues, Martí's words are sharp and fresh, certainly more powerful in their way than the ready-made prattle coming at people from every angle. Martí wrote about righteousness and values, but he stood solidly on the side of the weak, the dispossessed, and the disenfranchised. Yet Martí's writing is not about victims but about power, which can be harnessed through wisdom.

For Martí, the classroom is a privileged space, the core of what used to be called *civilization*, which to him did not mean elitism and exclusion but uninhibited cooperation across every arbitrary boundary conjured by the human mind. The classroom encompasses and transcends the privacy of the home and the duties of the public sphere. For Martí, it is the place in which people learn to tolerate and love one another in a way that may be powerful and revolutionary. Martí taught in various New York City institutions, and the role of education is central in his ideological agenda. In 1890, Martí and Rafael Serra (1858–1909), also exiled in New York, founded a new school called *La Liga* (the league), where "whites and blacks may sit together" (*donde se sientan juntos blancos y negros*) (González Veranés p. 18).

Martí wrote about many subjects during his years in the city he called the *Iron Babel*, in honor of its architecture and its status as the colossal entry to the United States for legions of immigrants. In 1883, three years after Martí's arrival in the city, the Brooklyn Bridge opened, a spectacular achievement celebrated by thousands of people. Martí was there, holding his young son on his shoulders so the child could see over the heads of the jubilant crowd. Coney Island dazzled visitors with garlands of electric lights and unheard-of marvels: Martí was there, alone in the crowd. Criminal trials, labor strikes, art exhibits, political turmoil, elections, the death of a poet, the assassination of a president, a funeral in Chinatown, the latest feats of reconstructive surgery: Martí covered all these topics and then some.

José Martí (1853–1895) monument, Havana. Workers repair a massive statue of Cuban writer and national hero José Martí in Havana in 2010. Although he lived most of the last fifteen years of his life in New York, the core of Martí's sense of identity was rooted in Cuba. CHRISTIAN SCIENCE MONITOR/GETTY IMAGES

In various articles published all over Latin America, Martí wrote on Ralph Waldo Emerson, Walt Whitman, Henry Wadsworth Longfellow, Ulysses S. Grant, "Buffalo Bill" Cody, and Jesse James. Martí also wrote about Henry James and Henry Garnet, the latter a son of runaway slaves who became U.S. ambassador to Liberia. No other Latin American writer knew the glories and the shames of the United States as well as Martí. He wrote in awe of the democratic process and in horror of other forces that he saw transforming the city and the American nation in disturbing ways, dividing rather than uniting people.

Martí marveled at the wealth of New York City but wearied of the city's infatuation with luxury. A few years before Thorstein Veblen published *The Theory of the Leisure Class* (1899), in which he coined the expression *conspicuous consumption*, Martí looked in disbelief as New York's *Anglomaniacal rascals* (*bellacos anglómanos*) showed off their wealth with lackeys in full livery, buckles on their shoes, silk stockings, and red frock coats (*Obras completas*, vol. 13, p. 436). The vain display of luxury brings with it a chilly harshness that turns neighbors into spectators, Martí wrote. In some of his essays, he contrasts the positive values of the United States, such as a spirit of cooperation in the midst of disaster, with a newly acquired hunger for luxury and pomp. Charmed by the getting and spending of the well-heeled residents, newly arrived immigrants threw themselves into the task of accumulating wealth and enjoyment of their new fortunes. People of modest means were enticed to hock their souls for the sake of displaying cheap versions of the trappings of wealth.

Martí believed that race prejudice, whatever forms it might take, whatever excuse might be used to justify it, had no place in a democracy. Martí feared for the United States, where he saw racism thriving like a weed. He feared that if Cuba remained divided by its own prejudices, it would never be a democratic republic. In Cuba and in the United States, Martí witnessed the abominable treatment of people of African descent. In New York, he learned of the U.S. military campaigns designed to dispossess and subjugate Native Americans. In his own body, he felt the sting of misunderstanding, disdain, and exclusion.

MARTÍ ON U.S.–LATIN AMERICAN RELATIONS

Beginning in the fall of 1889, representatives of the United States and Latin American nations met in Washington to consider economic and political issues that affected the entire hemisphere. Eager to impress the Latin nations, the federal government chartered a luxurious train that took delegates on a grand tour of the nation, covering some 5,000 miles. The train proved to be a public relations disaster, domestically and internationally. Nevertheless, it achieved its goal in displaying advances in technology and comfort never before seen by most of the delegates.

Each Latin American nation brought its own agenda to Washington, and its delegates were unlikely to fall in line behind Martí, in spite of his prestigious position as consul of Uruguay, Argentina, and Paraguay in New York. Yet, as a delegate to the international congress, Martí underscored the fact that for the United States, hemispheric unity was less about transnational cooperation than about ensuring its dominant position in the economic and political future of the Latin nations. As Martí saw it, delegates were literally being taken for a ride in a fancy train, and he said so, in no uncertain terms. His best-known essay on this topic is "Our America" (1891), a cry from the heart to confront the imminent expansion of the United States not with arms but with a radical rethinking of the very idea of a Latin American identity—Bolívar's dream of political unity recast as a project of Latin American solidarity, strong enough to counteract, if not stop, the advances of "the colossus of the North."

Martí's admiration for democracy in the United States, for the richness of the country's resources, for its boundless energy, and for its writers, orators, and reformers, is evident in many of his writings. But Martí was also a witness to the radical alteration and at times the destruction of democratic ideals on many fronts. He wrote with vision about such a transformation, as a warning to those whose awe at the technological brilliance and boundless wealth of *El Norte* might lead them to an uncritical imitation.

Martí spent his last birthday, 28 January 1895, hiding at a friend's house on West Sixty-fifth Street, in the heart of Manhattan, fearful that his plans for an invasion of Cuba might be again discovered and destroyed. Earlier that month, U.S. authorities had stopped an expedition that was ready to sail from the coast of Florida, not far from Jacksonville. Arms and supplies, costing thousands of dollars, were confiscated. Devastated by this turn of events, Martí nevertheless gathered new resources and quickly organized a second expedition, vastly reduced in scope, to land in Cuba and join local insurgents in the unfinished struggle for its independence from Spain.

On 11 April 1895, in a torrential rainstorm that nearly capsized their small craft, Martí along with Dominican general Máximo Gómez and four other men landed at a remote beach not far from Guantánamo. After some five weeks on the move, the insurrectionists made their way to the heart of Cuba's Oriente region, camping near Dos Ríos. Around noon, on 19 May 1895, against orders issued by General Gómez to keep away from the front lines, Martí and a single aide found themselves alone in enemy territory. Martí galloped on, while the aide, uncannily named Angel de la Guardia (Guardian Angel), followed close behind. Seconds later, Martí was shot by a Spanish sniper hiding in the underbrush. A Cuban scout, working for the Spanish authorities, finished him off with his Remington rifle. Martí's doomed charge is captured in the statue in Central Park. Angel de la Guardia was wounded but survived to tell Gómez, and history, what happened.

Martí's writings in New York are a warning to any newcomer who might too easily and too uncritically imitate the values and customs of the emerging U.S. consumer culture, divorced from what he saw as the moral core of any nation: a respect for universal freedom and equality for all. Martí warned his Latin readers, without resorting to the cliché that all that glitters is not gold, that their stores of spirit are a treasure to be unearthed and cherished. His voice still urges that people should search for those sources and use them for their own survival and for the benefit of all.

BIBLIOGRAPHY
Works by and about Martí

Abel, Christopher, and Nissa Torrents, eds. *José Martí: Revolutionary Democrat*. Durham, NC: Duke University Press, 1986.

Belnap, Jeffrey, and Raúl Fernández, eds. *José Martí's "Our America": From National to Hemispheric Cultural Studies*. Durham, NC: Duke University Press, 1998.

Camacho, Jorge. *José Martí: Las máscaras del escritor*. Boulder, CO: Society of Spanish and Spanish-American Studies, 2006.

Cañas, Dionisio. *El poeta y la ciudad: Nueva York y los escritores hispanos*. Madrid: Cátedra, 1994.

Díaz-Quiñones, Arcadio. *Sobre los principios: Los intelectuales caribeños y la tradición*. Bernal, Argentina: Universidad Nacional de Quilmes Editorial, 2006.

Ette, Ottmar. *José Martí, apóstol, poeta, revolucionario: Una historia de su recepción*. Translated by Luis Carlos Henao de Brigard. Mexico City: Universidad Nacional Autónoma de México, 1995.

Fountain, Anne. *José Martí and U.S. Writers*. Gainesville: University Press of Florida, 2003.

González, Manuel Pedro. *José Martí: Epic Chronicler of the United States in the Eighties*. Chapel Hill: University of North Carolina Press, 1953.

González Veranés, Pedro N. *La personalidad de Rafael Serra y sus relaciones con Martí* (lecture at the cultural institute Club Atenas). Havana: La Verónica, 1942.

Guerra, Lillian. *The Myth of José Martí: Conflicting Nationalisms in Early Twentieth-Century Cuba*. Chapel Hill: University of North Carolina Press, 2005.

Hidalgo Paz, Ibrahim. *José Martí, 1853–1895: Cronología*, 2nd ed. Havana: Centro de Estudios Martianos, 2003.

Kirk, John M. *José Martí: Mentor of the Cuban Nation*. Tampa: University Presses of Florida, 1983.

Mañach, Jorge. *Martí: Apostle of Freedom*. Translated by Coley Taylor. New York: Devin-Adair, 1950.

Martí, José. *Obras completas*, 27 vols. Havana: Editorial de Ciencias Sociales, 1975.

Martí, José. *Ismaelillo; Versos libres; Versos sencillos*. Edited by Iván A. Schulman. Madrid: Cátedra, 1987.

Martí, José. *Diarios de campaña*. Edited by Mayra Beatriz Martínez and Froilán Escobar. Havana: Casa Editora Abril, 1996.

Montero, Oscar. *José Martí: An Introduction*. New York: Palgrave Macmillan, 2004.

Pérez, Louis A., Jr. *Cuba: Between Reform and Revolution*, 4th ed. New York: Oxford University Press, 2011.

Pérez, Louis A., Jr., ed. *José Martí in the United States: The Florida Experience*. Tempe: Arizona State University, ASU Center for Latin American Studies, 1995.

Ramos, Julio. *Divergent Modernities: Culture and Politics in Nineteenth-Century Latin America*. Translated by John D. Blanco. Durham, NC: Duke University Press, 2001.

Rodríguez, Pedro Pablo. *De las dos Américas: Aproximaciones al pensamiento martiano*. Havana: Centro de Estudios Martianos, 2002.

Rodríguez-Luis, Julio, ed. *Re-reading José Martí (1853–1895): One Hundred Years Later*. Albany: State University of New York Press, 1999.

Rojas, Rafael. *José Martí: La invención de Cuba*. Madrid: Editorial Colibrí, 2000.

Santí, Enrico Mario. "*Ismaelillo*, Martí y el modernismo." In *Escritura y tradición: Texto, crítica y poética en la literatura hispanoamericana*. Barcelona: Laia, 1988.

Schulman, Iván A. "Desde los Estados Unidos: Martí y las minorías étnicas y culturales." *Los Ensayistas* 10–11 (March 1981): 139–152.

Toledo Sande, Luis. *Basket of Flames: A Biography of José Martí*. Translated by Pamela Barnett Idahosa. Havana: Editorial José Martí, 2002.

Veblen, Thorstein. *The Theory of the Leisure Class*. Originally published in 1899. New York: Modern Library, 1934.

Vitier, Cintio, and Fina García Marruz. *Temas martianos*, 2nd ed. Río Piedras, Puerto Rico: Ediciones Huracán, 1981.

Works by Martí in English Translation

The America of José Martí: Selected Writings. Translated by Juan de Onís. New York: Noonday Press, 1953.

Inside the Monster: Writings on the United States and American Imperialism. Edited by Philip S. Foner. Translated by Elinor Randall, with additional translations by Luis A. Baralt, Juan de Onís, and Roslyn Held Foner. New York: Monthly Review Press, 1975.

José Martí: Major Poems; A Bilingual Edition. Edited by Philip S. Foner. Translated by Elinor Randall. New York: Holmes & Meier Publishers, 1982.

José Martí Reader: Writings on the Americas, 2nd ed. Edited by Deborah Shnookal and Mirta Muñiz. Melbourne: Ocean Press, 2007.

José Martí: Selected Writings. Edited and translated by Esther Allen. New York: Penguin Books, 2002.

José Martí: Thoughts on Liberty, Government, Art, and Morality, 3rd ed. Edited and translated by Carlos Ripoll. New York: Editorial Dos Ríos, 1995.

Martí on the U.S.A.. Edited and translated by Luis A. Baralt. Carbondale: Southern Illinois University Press, 1966.

On Art and Literature: Critical Writings. Edited by Philip S. Foner. Translated by Elinor Randall, with additional translations by Luis A. Baralt, Juan de Onís, and Roslyn Held Foner. New York: Monthly Review Press, 1982.

On Education: Articles on Educational Theory and Pedagogy, and Writings for Children from "The Age of Gold." Edited by Philip S. Foner. Translated by Elinor Randall. New York: Monthly Review Press, 1979.

Our America: Writings on Latin America and the Struggle for Cuban Independence. Edited by Philip S. Foner. Translated by Elinor Randall, with additional translations by Luis A. Baralt, Juan de Onís, and Roslyn Held Foner. New York: Monthly Review Press, 1977.

Political Parties and Elections in the United States. Edited by Philip S. Foner. Translated by Elinor Randall. Philadelphia: Temple University Press, 1989.

Versos sencillos / Simple Verses. Translated by Manuel A. Tellechea. Houston: Arte Público Press, 1997.

JOSÉ MARTÍ: POLITICAL ESSAYS

Pedro Pablo Rodríguez

The experiences and writings that defined the political ideology of one of Cuba's foremost patriots.

After the failure of the Ten Years' War (1868–1878) and the Little War (1879–1880), the Cuban patriot forces suffered deep divisions, and their most prominent leaders went into exile. In Cuba, the colonial Spanish government authorized the existence of political parties. The Liberal Autonomist Party supported the goal of autonomy under Spanish sovereignty and tended to capitalize on nationalist sentiment. It systematically prevented access to the colonial government; that was solidly controlled by the Constitutional Union Party, which favored keeping Cuba fully under the Spanish monarchy.

The island underwent a profound economic and social transformation in which the merchants, money lenders, and slave suppliers used their capital to take over the sugar industry and mechanize it, eliminating the old planters and forming large factories called *centrales*. These interests accepted the abolition of slavery, which finally came in 1886, and directed a large part of Cuban exports of crude sugar and leaf tobacco—both raw materials—to the United States. The country moved toward giant sugarcane plantations, a one-crop economy, and a single market, signs that pointed to a new dependent relationship with the United States.

Various attempts to renew the armed fight for independence were unsuccessful, mainly because they involved plans designed and executed by emigrants who had little or no contact with the island, and also because of the divisions among the patriot leaders and their failure to offer a plan for the republic to address the demands and needs of the majority.

MARTÍ'S CALL TO REVOLUTION

The young José Martí (1853–1895) was sent to Spain after being sentenced to manual labor for his political ideas. In Spain, he was able to complete his studies in law, philosophy, and religion in 1874 before living in Mexico and Guatemala, where he became a writer and well-known figure in intellectual circles. In 1878, he returned to Havana, the city of his birth. He immediately began to conspire against the colonial government and the following year was again deported to Spain. He escaped to New York, where he joined the Revolutionary Committee that directed the Small War from abroad. When the war ended he lived for six months in Caracas during 1881 then returned to New York, where he lived for most of the rest of his life.

From his first public discourse before Cuban emigrants in 1880, Martí proclaimed the need for a "revolution of reflection," not of anger, and his conviction that the "people, the grieving mass" are the real leaders of revolutions (Martí 1963–1965, vol. 4, pp. 192–193). Firm in his stance as an advocate of independence, in 1884 he separated from the movement led by the patriot military leader General Máximo Gómez (1836–1905), who appeared to be positioning himself as a *caudillo*, or political-military leader.

After staying away from the political environment of the exile community for several years, Martí returned to the public stage at the end of the 1880s. By that time he was well-known; his poetry and his article about the United States had been published in twenty Latin American journals. His ideas now fully mature, he began to draft a plan of transformation for Cuba, the Caribbean, and all of the Americas. Beginning in 1892, he dedicated the rest of his life to the practical achievement of this plan.

THE CUBAN REVOLUTIONARY PARTY

The political action strategy devised and pursued by Martí required first the unity of the Cuban patriot forces. To achieve this, with support from the emigrant community in New York, he created the Cuban Revolutionary Party in early 1892. The party platform stated that the party's goal was to attain Cuban independence and "to encourage and aid in the independence of Puerto Rico" (Martí 1963–1965, vol. 1, p. 279), the other Spanish colony in the Caribbean at that time. According to its secret bylaws (1963–1965, vol. 1, pp. 281–282), the party was comprised of groups of exiles in base cells called clubs that had been forming since the time of the Ten Years' War. The clubs were voluntarily formed by their members and had only to accept the platform and bylaws of the party. The presidents of all the local clubs made up the party's governing council, and the delegate and treasurer, the party's only officials, were chosen annually by the membership. Martí himself was successively reelected delegate until he was killed in battle in 1895.

Based on the Cuban patriotic tradition and incorporating modern political practices, Martí's party sought to dissolve regional, racial, and class differences, as well as divides between the educated and the uneducated and civil leaders and military leaders. The clubs contributed funds to purchase arms and resources for a renewed armed fight against colonialism.

Martí called this war a war of love, not hate. It was unavoidable because the Spanish government would not make any concessions to Cuban interests, much less allow independence through agreements. Though Martí said that armed warfare was necessary, he insisted that it did not entail hatred for Spaniards and that Spaniards living on the island would continue to have a place in the republic that would be founded after victory. Both the party and the conflict itself, described by Martí as a war "of republican methods and goals" (1963–1965, vol. 1, p. 279), should move toward creation of the republic, which he frequently referred to as "new." In his numerous references to the republic, Martí also noted the profound changes that he believed would be required in Cuba because of its own developmental needs and in order to avoid repeating the errors committed by other Latin American republics.

"NUESTRA AMERICA"

In January 1891 Martí published in New York and Mexico the essay "Nuestra America" (Our America), later considered one of the key writings of his ideology. In it he roundly criticized the continental republics for maintaining the characteristics they had as colonies and for imposing European and U.S. models without considering a land's own history, traditions, social psychology, and identity: "Hamilton's decree cannot stop the plainsman's pony in mid-bolt. A phrase from Sieyes does not quicken the stagnant blood of the Indian race" (Martí 1963–1965, vol. 6, p. 17). He proposed that the natural man (the Indian, the black, and the peasant), cast aside after separation from Spain, should be valued, and that regional identity should be acknowledged if solutions were to be found. "To know is to decide," he wrote (Martí 1963–1965, vol. 6, p. 18). His support for the native did not mean a return to the pre-Hispanic past or a withdrawal from modernity but rather that a new nation would do well to consider the native element with an open mind and incorporate aspects favorable to "our America."

In "Nuestra America" he also repeated what he had been saying in his writings since the 1880s: that the sovereignty of the people of America was threatened by the increasing power of the United States, which was disdainful of nations it considered weak or backward. According to Martí, monopolies controlled the life of the northern nation, seeking to satisfy their needs for consumer markets and suppliers of raw materials and food. As a modern money-based oligarchy, he said, they had eroded the democratic foundations from which the United States had arisen. These expansionist sectors of the United States would take advantage of the internal weaknesses of Latin American republics caused by their failures to adapt their social and economic models, imposing U.S. control and new domination. Two years before, in 1889 in Washington, D.C., Martí had emphatically denounced the International Conference of American States assembled at the behest of the United States in order to "establish an alliance against Europe" (1963–1965, vol. 6, p. 46). For similar reasons, in his role as representative of Uruguay (he served in New York as consul for Uruguay, Argentina, and Paraguay), before the Monetary Conference of American Republics, Martí opposed the U.S. plan for a common regional currency.

He criticized the fledgling monopolies: "The monopoly is seated, like an implacable giant, at the door of all the poor" (Martí 1963–1965, vol. 10, p. 84). And he thought that the accelerated formation of monopolies in the United States was distancing the nation from its democratic traditions, creating an *Anglomaniacal* aristocratic class that had to be confronted by the joint action of farmers, workers, small business owners, and free-market capital—the healthy part of the nation, and potential allies in the interests of "our America." This view explains his admiration for American intellectuals such as Ralph Waldo Emerson and Walt Whitman, whom he appreciated not just for their literary accomplishments, which he made known to Spanish-speaking readers, but also for their antislavery and democratic opinions and their expression of the popular culture of the United States.

Martí saw, then, the relationship between Cuban national circumstances and the new South American and global conditions that were emerging at the beginning of the nineteenth century. Cuban independence—and Puerto Rican independence—were not matters of concern for only the two islands, but events with global reach that would contribute to global balance: "We are balancing the entire world, not just the two islands that we are going to liberate" (Martí 1963–1965, vol. 3, p. 142). For Martí it was essential to impede the expansion of U.S. imperialism to prevent the domination and subordination of Latin America; in his view, Spanish possessions in the Antilles were the first step in the U.S. march on South America.

These objectives of his political strategy were laid out in a letter to a Mexican friend, which remained unfinished because of his death in combat the following day: "What I have done until now and what I will do is for this: to in timely fashion, with the independence of Cuba, prevent the United States from falling upon our American lands with this great force. This had to be done in silence, and indirectly, because there are things that, in order to be achieved, must be done in secret" (Martí 1963–1965, vol. 6, p. 168).

VISION FOR CUBA AND LATIN AMERICA

Martí spent the last three years of his life tirelessly spreading his ideas among his followers through speeches, party documents, personal letters, circulars, and numerous writings printed in *Patria*, a newspaper he published in New York. At the same time, he organized the Cuban Revolutionary Party, fostered a vast conspiratorial network within Cuba, and gathered resources to send expeditions to the island to hasten a quick victory in order to avoid both enormous losses of life and property and the interference of the U.S. government.

The great task of unifying the patriots meant confronting the caudillo and regionalist elements in the Cuban social psychology and political culture of the time, as well as the racism against blacks and mulattos based on centuries of slavery that had been incited under colonialism to terrorize the white population

with the threat of vengeful insurrections. Aware of the effects of the years of slavery and discrimination, Martí insistently fought the notion of racial superiority and inferiority, affirming that "there are no races; there is only the different modifications of man, in details of habit and form that do not change what is equal and essential, according to the climate and history in which he lives" (Martí 1963–1965, vol. 28, p. 290). Therefore, the Cuban republic had to offer full justice to black and mulatto Cubans who had suffered from racism.

In Martí's plan, the free republic in Cuba would be a nation of peace, work, and equality, achieved through the implementation of a social and economic plan that envisioned a large class of peasant landowners, suppliers of abundant food and raw materials to spark industrial development on an agricultural base. Foreign trade would be expanded to the largest possible number of nations and would no longer depend on just one or two products (as was the case with raw sugar and leaf tobacco). A strong sense of homeland and knowledge and defense of local identity would have to be sustained through modern education, which would emphasize science without neglecting spiritual development and individuality. Education would combine study with work, both to avoid elitist upbringing and to maintain harmony with the needs and characteristics of society.

Understanding the modern class struggle inherent in industrial capitalism (which he had denounced in his stories about the United States), Martí believed that a just Cuban republic free of the dominance of caste oligarchy could lead to united action with a free Puerto Rico and the Dominican Republic, and perhaps even Haiti. Such Caribbean unity would make more feasible the union of all the peoples of Latin America, which was desirable and necessary because of the commercial and territorial expansion of the United States. Thus he proclaimed in "Nuestra America," "We must move forward in close ranks, like silver in the veins of the Andes" (Martí 1963–1965, vol. 6, p. 16).

It is no accident, then, that in outlining the goals of the new struggle in his Montecristi Manifesto, Martí wrote that it "is a far-reaching human event and a timely service that the judicious heroism of the Antilles lends to the stability and just interaction of the American nations and to the still unsteady equilibrium of the world" (Martí 1963–1965, vol. 4, p. 101).

BIBLIOGRAPHY
Primary Works

Martí, José. *The America of José Martí*. Edited by Federico de Onis. Translated by Juan de Onis. New York: Noonday Press, 1953.

Martí, José. *Obras completas*. 27 vols. Havana: Editorial Nacional de Cuba, 1963–1965.

Martí, José. *Obras completas*. Vol. 28. La Habana: Instituto Cubano del Libro, 1973.

Martí, José. *On Education: Article on Educational Theory and Pedagogy, and Writing for Children the Age of Gold*. Edited by and introduction by Philip S. Foner. Translated by Elinor Randall. New York: Monthly Review Press, 1979.

Martí, José. *On Art and Literature: Critical Writings*. Edited by and introduction by Philip S. Foner. Translated by Elinor Randall, Luis A. Baralt, Juan de Onis, and Roslyn Held Foner. New York: Monthly Review Press, 1982.

Martí, José. *Political Parties and Elections in the United States*. Edited by Philip S. Foner. Havana: José Martí Publishing House, 1988.

Martí, José. *Political Parties and Elections in the United States*. Edited by and introduction by Philip S. Foner. Philadelphia: Temple University Press, 1989.

Martí, José. *José Martí Reader: Writings on the Américas*. Edited by Deborah Shnookal and Mirta Muñíz. Introduction by Iván A. Schulman. Melbourne: Ocean Press, 1999.

Martí, José. *José Martí: Selected Writings*. Edited and translated by Esther Allen Witham. Introduction by Roberto González Hechevarria. New York: Penguin, 2002.

Secondary Works

Armas, Ramón de. *La revolución pospuesta: Contenido y alcance de la revolución martiana por la independencia*. Havana: Centro de Estudios Martianos, 2002.

Armas, Ramón de, and Pedro Pablo Rodríguez. "El pensamiento de José Martí y la creación del Partido Revolucionario Cubano." In *Historia de Cuba, Las luchas por la independencia nacional y las transformaciones estructurales, 1868–1898*, ed. Instituto de Historia de Cuba. Havana: Editora Política, 1996.

Fernández Retamar, Roberto. *Introducción a José Martí*. Havana: Editorial Letras Cubanas, 2001.

González, Manuel P. *José Martí: Epic Chronicle of the United States in the Eighties*. Chapel Hill: University of North Carolina Press, 1953.

Hidalgo Paz, Ibrahim. *José Martí: Cronología 1853–1895*. Havana: Centro de Estudios Martianos, Editorial de Ciencias Sociales, 1992.

Ibarra, Jorge. *José Martí, dirigente político e ideólogo revolucionario*. Havana: Centro de Estudios Martianos, 2008.

Kirk, John M. *José Martí: Mentor of the Cuban Nation*. Tampa: University Presses of Florida, 1983.

Le Riverend, Julio. *José Martí: Pensamiento y acción*. Havana: Centro de Estudios Martianos, Editora Política, 1982.

Mañach, Jorge. *Martí, Apostle of Freedom*. Translated by Coley Taylor. New York: Devin-Adair, 1950.

Rodríguez, Pedro Pablo. *De las dos Américas*. Havana: Centro de Estudios Martianos, 2003.

Roig de Leuchsenring, Emilio. *Martí Anti-imperialist*. Havana: Instituto del Libro, 1967.

Toledo Sande, Luis. *Basket of Flames*. Translated by Pamela Barnet. Havana: Editorial José Martí, 2002.

Turton, Peter. *José Martí: Architect of Cuba's Freedom*. London: Zed Books, 1986.

Vitier, Cintio. *Vida y obra del apóstol José Martí*. Havana: Centro de Estudios Martianos, 2004.

JOSÉ MARTÍ: WRITINGS FOR AND ABOUT CHILDREN

María de los Angeles Torres

The role of Martí's children's literature and writings about education in the Cuban national identity.

Children held an important place in José Martí's vision of the Cuban nation. He wrote for them and about them, as well as on the topic of education. These writings shaped not only the Cuban national identity, but also the sense of belonging to a Latin American culture. In 1889, while living in New York, Martí published *La Edad de Oro* (The Golden Age), a magazine for young readers that included Martí's original stories, essays, and poems as well as translations of great works. In the opening issue—which was to be followed by only three more—Martí stated that his purpose was to help "children of the Americas ... learn how people lived in the past, and today in America, and in other lands." He was also interested in teaching children about science and nature and encouraging their enjoyment of fantasy and magic.

In *La Edad de Oro* young readers encountered Latin American history as told through Martí's stories of three heroes of the Latin American wars of independence: the Venezuelan general Simón Bolívar, the Argentine general José de San Martin, and the Mexican priest and rebel Miguel Hidalgo. Martí's essay about Bartolomé de las Casas, the sixteenth-century Spanish friar who defended the rights of indigenous peoples and denounced their abuse by colonial authorities, details the young friar's struggle to treat Indians as human beings, recounting the legends and real-life struggles of the native peoples of Latin America. Other articles discussed struggles for independence in other lands, such as that of the Annamese (Vietnamese) against the French; the anthropological history of human dwellings; and scientific breakthroughs and inventions, as in one essay about the 1889 Paris world industrial exposition and another detailing the history of forks and spoons. Fantasy stories included "El camarón encantado" (The Enchanted Shrimp) and "Meñique" (about a Tom Thumb–like hero), Martí's Spanish versions of French stories by Édouard de Laboulaye. A poem inspired by the American writer Ralph Waldo Emerson presents a quarrel between a mountain and a squirrel, emphasizing the value of individual differences and talents. The magazine also printed Martí's poem "Los zapaticos de rosa" (The Rose-Colored Slippers), which many Cubans have learned by heart. Dedicated to a Mademoiselle Marie (María Mantilla, Martí's goddaughter in New York City), the poem celebrates empathy and generosity.

Martí's political writings pressed for Cuba's independence from Spain and the building of a uniquely Cuban nation. His children's stories are more universal, expressing curiosity alongside the desire for freedom; through explorations of different cultures and moments in history, he finds strong parallels in different human experiences. The characters in Martí's children's literature include heroes and ordinary folk from all over the world as well as enchanted animals. Although most of them are male, females are not absent. Martí expresses a modern admiration of inventions and industrial progress and also stresses the virtues of generosity and charity. He teaches the value of empathy as a way to develop a nonjudgmental and more egalitarian view of human history. With his stories, Martí gives children a special lens through which to view and understand humanity.

CHILDREN AND NATION BUILDING

Martí saw children as the essential players in constructing new nations. Thus their education and preparation for adulthood were an essential part of nation building. Like the eighteenth-century French philosopher Jean-Jacques Rousseau, Martí believed that educators must appeal to children's natural curiosity and urge to experiment. Their lively imaginations and impetuosity were to be encouraged rather than stifled by rote memorization. He saw it as essential for children to learn science as well as to deepen their automatic appreciation of nature. Martí also believed that education must be universal and secular, with girls as well as boys entitled to be educated. He revered the work and ideas of Peter Cooper, the nineteenth-century American industrialist and philanthropist and founder of the Cooper Union in New York City, who believed that all children are entitled to a free education and that those who have been educated have an obligation to teach others. Martí tied the destiny of a nation to its individuals. Happiness, another important Renaissance concept, was central in Martí's writings about education: "The happiness of a nation was a direct result of the level of education of its citizens" (p. 175). Above all, the education of children was nation building. Just like the North American philosopher and educator John Dewey in later years, Marti believed that democracies could exist only if there was an educated citizenry. "An instructed people will always be strong and free," he observed, arguing that "the best way to defend our rights is to know them well....When all men know how to read, all men will know how to vote" (1979, p. 91).

Although Martí believed in a universally shared humanity, he also saw certain distinct national characteristics as being shaped by culture and geography. People are in part a product of their backgrounds and regions and the specific needs arising from these contexts. After years in the United States—New York was his home base from 1881 until his death in 1895—during which he observed both U.S. culture and that of the Cuban exile community, Martí concluded that

Latin Americans were not only unappreciated but demeaned. He worried that the children of Cuban exiles would lose their national character if they were educated in the United States, becoming estranged from themselves. This was not the poetic Martí but the cultural nationalist Martí, the author of the 1891 essay "Nuestra America," who saw stark cultural differences between the United States and Latin America. Martí the immigrant exile battled to preserve a cultural identity in the midst of discrimination and racism, calling for children to be educated in the language, history, and culture of their homeland. Cuban educators applied Martí's ideas about how to teach Cuban children in exile to the curricula of Cuban schools. Indeed, the 1940 constitution required that all courses on any Cuban topic be taught by teachers born in Cuba and with books written by Cubans.

MARTÍ'S LEGACY

Martí's children's literature influenced, even shaped, the Cuban imagination. *Platero y yo*, a series of prose poems by the Spanish writer Juan Ramón Jiménez (1881–1958) that tell the story of a man and his donkey, became a classic in Cuba. Jiménez was steeped in Martí's legacy of combining romanticism with *modernista* expressive innovations. In the 1950s the book *Había una vez* (Once Upon a Time), by Ruth Robes Masses and Herminio Almendros, followed the model of Martí's *Edad de Oro*, bringing together original stories and poems as well as translations of classic tales. The lyrical and fantastical stories and fables became a classic of children's literature. The poetry of Cuban writer Mirta Aguirre (1912–1980), also in the spirit of Martí, entertained children with wordplay.

After the 1959 revolution, there was a special emphasis on children's literature, as children were then viewed playing a special part in building a socialist nation. In books such as *Cuentos de heroes* (Stories about Heroes), sacrifice and love of the nation are values central to each story. *Cuentos para ti* (Stories for You) is also a compilation of stories by various authors that emphasize the socialist work ethic of cooperation and personal sacrifice.

Like Martí, some authors appreciated childhood not just as a pedagogical project but as a realm of imagination to be approached respectfully and tenderly. Eliseo Diego (1920–1994), one of Cuba's greatest poets, expressed this view. In the early 1960s he was named director of the Department of Children's Literature and Narratives for the National Library. In this post, Diego developed courses on childhood and children's literature. But unlike Martí, who looked ahead to children's futures, Diego asked teachers to consider students not as they will be but as they are. Nevertheless, his emphasis on the present left room for imagining a future, as is seen in his *Sonar despierto* (Dreaming while Awake), and as such was able to reconcile the two temporalities in Martí's thoughts about children.

Beginning with *La Edad de Oro*, whose stories and lyrical poems have lulled multiple generations of Cuban children to sleep, Martí's journey into the world of children and their imaginations instilled values and social attitudes that found their way into a national sense of being Cuban.

BIBLIOGRAPHY

Diego, Eliseo. *Un hondo bosque de sueños: Notas sobre literatura para niños.* Havana: Ediciones Unión, 2008.

Martí, José. *On Education: Articles on Educational Theory and Pedagogy, and Writings for Children from "The Age of Gold."* Translated by Elinor Randall. Edited by Philip S. Foner. New York: Monthly Review Press, 1979.

Martí, José. *La Edad de Oro.* Madrid: Mondadori, 1990.

LA JUNGLA AND THE ARTISTIC DEVELOPMENT OF WIFREDO LAM

Graziella Pogolotti

One of Cuba's most important twentieth-century avant-garde artists and analysis of his most important work.

Like the Martinican poet Aimé Césaire (1913–2008) and the Cuban fiction writer Alejo Carpentier (1904–1980) before him, in 1941 Wifredo Lam (1902–1982) set out on his *retour au pays natal*. He had been living in Europe for eighteen years—first in Spain and then in France—where he accumulated an artistic education, underwent tumultuous personal experiences, and, without yet being fully aware of it, completed an in-depth voyage into his cultural memory. He was just about to give definite form to his major work and achieve full visibility in the turbulent landscape of twentieth-century avant-gardism.

EARLY LIFE

According to Esteban Montejo, the protagonist of *Biografía de un cimarrón* (Biography of a Runaway Slave, 1966) by Miguel Barnet, at the outskirts of Sagua la Grande in north-central Cuba there were several sugar mills that were active during the time of slavery and even after slavery was abolished. The production system implemented at the sugar mills resulted in a population composed of African descendants, Chinese workers, and whites who were in charge of administration and small business. A culture was thus forged and along with it, customs, lifestyles, and

■ *See also*

Faith: Regla de Ocha and Ifá

El monte (Lydia Cabrera)

Race: The Chinese in Cuba

Visual Arts: Republican Period

a type of spirituality with close ties to the world of nature. Wifredo Lam was born in Sagua la Grande in 1902 to a Chinese father and a black/white mestizo mother. He spent the early years of his childhood in that town, and his deepest personal memories were formed there.

Lam's date of birth places him right in the middle of the generation that led the Cuban avant-garde revolution during the second decade of the twentieth century. This revolution was oriented toward the renewal of artistic languages and, above all, to a reinterpretation of the process of formation of the Cuban nation and culture. The fundamental volteface in this process took the form of a new appreciation for cultures of African origin. The work of the Cuban anthropologist Fernando Ortiz (1881–1969), which was ongoing at the time, presented scientific foundations for overturning the still-latent stereotypes of colonialist tradition that had created an insuperable contradiction between civilization and barbarism. Ortiz's cultural perspective acknowledged the intrinsic significance of expressions that had come out of Africa.

Practices that had originated in Europe and Africa were not locked in airtight compartments, though Africans did keep many of their rituals secret. Blending of cultures was manifested in religious syncretism, in the popular imaginary, and in dance music. Poets and composers started to explore ways in which black rhythms could be incorporated into high-culture traditions from Europe.

EUROPE

Lam was not in Cuba, however, when the rediscovery of complex hidden networks inside the nation's cultural framework began. Nor was he in Havana in 1927 when the art nouveau exposition announced his contemporaries' avant-garde experimentation. From Sagua de la Grande, Lam had gone to Havana to study law to fulfill his family's aspirations, but his vocation as an artist was already decided. He enrolled in the San Alejandro Academy and traveled to Madrid in 1923, carrying with him a modest stipend of 30 pesos that had been awarded to him by his native city.

In Spain he stubbornly held to mastering traditional styles in the face of the interwar European artistic revolution. He perfected his craft. His speech acquired traces of a Madrid accent. He studied great masters such as Hieronymus Bosch (1450–1516) and Pieter Brueghel (c. 1525–1569), who were examples of a heretic kind of Otherness. While in Spain he also suffered ordeals in every aspect of his life. Surprised by the pro-Franco military uprising, he took the side of the Republicans. Under the onslaught of bombs, he wore a militia uniform and worked in an arms factory, and he suffered from extreme hunger in the besieged city. His wife and son died of tuberculosis. One chapter of his life was over, forever.

In 1938, like many Civil War refugees, Lam left Spain for Paris, where he had his decisive encounter with Pablo Picasso (1881–1973). The man from Málaga, creator of *Guernica* (1937), must have sympathized with the Cuban painter who had endured the worst of the tragedy in Spain. Already at the height of his fame, Picasso opened doors for Lam. He put him in contact with art dealer Pierre Loeb (1897–1964) and above all (and paradoxically) introduced him to the rigorous study of African art. Lam's enlightenment occurred at the right moment. He upended his style, abandoning all academic formulas and changing his palette, and began a series of maternal scenes that captured the volumetric dimensions of breasts and buttocks. With this leap in the dark, Lam achieved success in the Paris art market.

Nevertheless, the war was following him because of his role in the antifascist struggle. Lam could not remain in Nazi-occupied France, so he headed south, where the Vichy regime did not offer any guarantees, either. In Marseilles he embarked on a difficult return trip that—in another fortuitous accident—provided him with very valuable experience. In the stampede to the United States brought about by World War II, it was customary to cross the Atlantic to New York and from there go on to Havana, but refugees coming out of Marseilles had to endure a long voyage across the Caribbean by way of Césaire's Martinique and the magical island of Haiti, which for Carpentier was the center of the kingdom of the world.

RETURN TO CUBA

For some artists who had been nourished by Parisian avant-gardism, the war and fascism in Europe prompted a revelation of aspects specific to the Caribbean island world. With this return to original sources, they made use of a vision and a sensibility enriched by surrealism, the most influential cultural movement of the twentieth century, which fomented repercussions in art and, well beyond that, in the way people perceived reality. Surrealism's recovery of oneiric potential, myths, and an intangible, prevailing collective memory was momentous. In addition, its interest in psychoanalysis led eventually to an anthropological approach to cultures, particularly those that were considered primitive. In Cuba, Alejo Carpentier had become interested in this area of knowledge, beginning with his initial research during the 1920s. In the early 1940s the teachings of the renowned Fernando Ortiz engendered the studies of Lydia Cabrera (1899–1991), a disciple of his who explored the paths of the national imaginary, juggling scientific method, informants' evidence, and literary vision. In 1940 Cabrera published *Cuentos negros de Cuba* (Black Tales from Cuba), a canonical text for island literature.

When Lam returned to Cuba, he had no connections in the intellectual community. He did share their poverty, though, and this led him to settle in Havana's

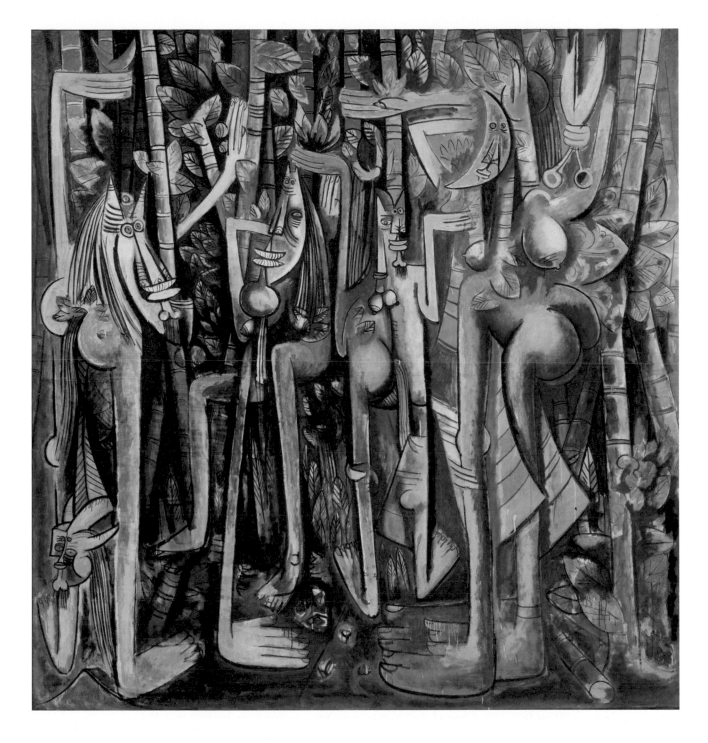

outskirts, in the Marianao district, a true reservoir of living, popular traditions. Out of the way of the war in Europe, Havana was a cosmopolitan environment that afforded ample opportunity for the exchange of avant-garde ideas. It reproduced, on a minor scale, the phenomenon of the heretics and the persecuted, individuals who had withdrawn to the New World and left their marks on New York City, Mexico, and Haiti. Under these exceptional circumstances, Lam recaptured the cross-cultural mythical world of Africa

through the popular route of his immediate environs and the educated route via experts such as Ortiz and Cabrera, as well as through a dialogue with Carpentier, who was following a similar path in his work as an editor and musicologist.

LA JUNGLA

After arriving late to the avant-garde movement and following a long, slow process, with a single leap Lam became a leader among Latin American artists.

Synthesizing what was most important in European trends in thinking with the Caribbean imaginary, in 1943 he painted *La jungla* (The Jungle; New York Museum of Modern Art) and *La silla* (The Chair; Havana Museum of Fine Arts), works that complement and shed light on each other.

La jungla is not a depiction of a rainforest or woods. Associated with the tropics, it depicts an intricate undergrowth of diverse plants that have not been tamed or put in place by the hand of man. *Jungla* is a common term, a catch-all word used by Lam to inform his countrymen, and outsiders, about the peculiar environment known in Cuba as *el monte*, or dense tropical vegetation. This environment is in the innermost part of Cuba—a historical refuge for runaway slaves, a swamp to hide in—and in the outskirts of cities and towns, where it extends into front yards and backyards. It is a sacred environment. Philosophically, *el monte* is the tangible representation of an intimate, dialogical relationship between Man and Nature, a mediator with the *orishas* (gods) to whom respect and obedience is due, and with whom one establishes an exchange of offerings and favors.

Life and death coexist in the monte countryside, where trees serve as a dwelling place for the gods and wild herbs provide both remedies and harmful substances. This imaginary is inhabited by stories—sometimes contradictory—that have been transmitted through oral tradition and impart values that govern the behavior of human beings. The gods' incarnations are represented in an extensive form of storytelling (the *patakíes*) and in an iconography of syncretic origin (a visual legacy of the Roman Catholic calendar of saints) whose syncreticism was a strategy for survival.

Pervaded by the culture of surrealism, Lam ruled out the use of that iconography, which is recognizable only to Cubans who practice it. He did not aspire to illustrate a mythology. For Lam, *La jungla* is the countryside, a natural site, the privileged environment of the spirit where gods and human beings live together in harmony, where life and death are inseparable, along a continuum, and where there is transcendence and routine, wild thickets and tilled land. Philosophically, this countryside reveals a conception of the world in which the dualism inherited from Western tradition has been abolished. Judeo-Christian notions of sin and its consequences and the feeling of guilt disappear, because in the animist pantheon, the gods are also sinners and deceivers. The debate between good and evil moves from the abstract to the concrete, and transgression receives its punishment in the realm of deeds.

To express this world visually, Lam made use of his apprenticeship in European avant-gardism, employing the essential lessons of Picasso and the surrealists. From Picasso he had learned that a painting is, above all, a flat surface that does not reproduce reality in an illusionist manner. The laws of composition are derived from that idea and deployed in *La jungla* in a profuse horizontality that devours empty space. With attempts at individuality suppressed, human figures synthesize, with their pronounced forms, what Lam learned from African sculpture. Those interchangeable profiles, in a dialogue with Nature, restore the active presence of mystery.

As a background for *La jungla*, the tightly compressed mass of sugarcane plants evokes man's action in planting, cultivating, and harvesting it. Thus the gods accompany every task, even on the borders of the modernity brought by sugar production. The idea that the jungle is not virgin rainforest is corroborated by another fundamental work that Lam painted during his prolific period of 1943: *La silla*. Another function is found for this everyday piece of furniture: Appearing in the middle of the composition, the chair suggests an altar surrounded by vegetation typically found in backyards of homes on urban outskirts. The fear of empty space and the chaos of plants have disappeared, but herb doctors will continue to find remedies for illnesses and protection from curses.

CREATING A CULTURE

During the difficult years after Lam's return to Cuba, he worked in the type of yard depicted in *La silla*. Dispensing with an easel, canvases, and frame, he stretched brown paper—the kind used to wrap packages—across the floor. On a very modest scale, still not enough to ensure a stable income, he began to enter the New York market. He was discriminated against in his own country because he was black, and his participation in the Spanish Civil War barred him from traveling to the United States, so he had to work through intermediaries, with all the risks that entailed. Nevertheless, self-discovery, that is to say, the uncovering of memory and the discovery of his essential culture, made up his mind. The future was written on his painting *La jungla*. Images that were increasingly free of localist references, of solitary birds suspended in the air of infinite spaces, predominated in his work.

After the war, Lam returned to Europe. His immersion in the jungle—image and symbol of a buried memory that was personal yet collective—had contributed to the drafting of a world unknown until then. Cultures become recognizable and open to dialogue through syntheses crafted by writers and artists. The blending of European avant-gardism and anthropological studies occurred under circumstances favorable for overcoming the distance between high and popular culture. The profile of each culture results from a construct, a crystallization of an imaginary. The Caribbean was being created through the work of Lam, Carpentier, and Césaire.

Once Lam had resettled in Paris and achieved a firm footing in the art market, he worked tirelessly in the solitude of his Albisola-Mare studio but never again lost contact with the island of his birth.

He went back to Cuba many times. He exchanged ideas with his friends using his own Esperanto comprised of expressions from Madrid, Italianisms, and French words. He took great pains in preparing, with a masterly hand, splendid Cuban dishes. But the fundamental lesson learned at the time of the marvelous re-encounter in the 1940s was forever defined by the jungle scrubland.

BIBLIOGRAPHY

Benítez, Helena. *Wifredo Lam: Interlude Marseille.* Copenhagen: Blondal, 1993.

Cabrera, Lydia. *El monte.* Havana: Editorial Letras Cubanas, 1993.

Fouchet, Max Pol. *Wifredo Lam.* Barcelona: Ediciones Polígrafa S.A., 1976.

Laurin Lam, Lou. *Wifredo Lam: Catalogue Raisonné of the Painted Work*, Vol. 1: *1923–1960.* Lausanne, Switzerland: Editions Acatos, 1996.

Laurin Lam, Lou, and Eskil Lam. *Wifredo Lam: Catalogue Raisonné of the Painted Work*, Vol. 2: *1961–1982.* Lausanne, Switzerland: Editions Acatos, 2002.

Noceda Fernández, José Manuel. *Wifredo Lam en las colecciones cubanas.* Havana: Artecubano Ediciones, 2002.

Noceda Fernández, José Manuel, ed. *Wifredo Lam: La cosecha de un brujo.* Havana: Editorial Letras Cubanas, 2002.

Ortiz, Fernando. *Visiones sobre Lam.* Havana: Fundación Fernando Ortiz, 2002.

K

KID CHOCOLATE

Elio Menéndez

First Cuban world champion of boxing.

It is impossible to discuss Cuban boxing, regardless of the period or forum, without paying homage to Eligio Sardiñas Montalvo (1910–1988), the legendary Kid Chocolate. In addition to being an exceptional fighter, Chocolate was charismatic, which explains why after only thirteen matches in New York City rings, the doors of the hallowed Madison Square Garden were opened to him. Previous boxing greats, including Jack Johnson (1878–1946) and Harry Wills (1889–1958), finished their careers without ever having a match at the Garden; Kid Chocolate was the first black fighter welcomed there.

WORLD CHAMPION

Kid Chocolate gave Cuba its first world champion title in boxing on 15 July 1931, when he scored a TKO during the seventh round of a fifteen-round battle against the holder of the lightweight juniors title, Benny Bass (1904–1975). On 13 October 1932, he knocked out Lew Feldman (b. 1908) after twelve rounds, and the New York Commission on Boxing awarded Chocolate the featherweight title that Christopher "Battling" Battalino (1908–1977) had given up. The United States Boxing Association did not recognize New York's title, awarding the world featherweight title to Tommy Paul (1909–1991). Despite enormous efforts to arrange a match between Kid Chocolate and Paul to share the title, Paul's managers refused.

Prior to that, on 12 December 1930, Kid Chocolate had fought for the featherweight crown that was, at that time, held by Battling Battalino. Battalino retained the title through the fight officials' so-called generosity—a deliberately long count that saved him from a knockout in the first round. The bout ended with an infamous two-votes-to-one decision vehemently protested by fans and some sportswriters.

In November 1931, four months after he dethroned Benny Bass, Kid Chocolate challenged the Italian American fighter Tony Canzoneri (1908–1959) for the lightweight title. The boxing magazine *The Ring* named that bout one of the best in boxing history. The two-votes-to-one decision in favor of Canzoneri split experts and fans into two camps. Fans carried the two so-called little giants out of the Garden on their shoulders.

OUTSTANDING FIGHTS

Although the fights with Bass and Feldman earned him titles, Kid Chocolate did not regard them as his most significant bouts. He preferred his draw with Joey Scalfaro (b. 1903) when he debuted at Madison Square Garden on November 30, 1928; his victory over the Jewish boxer Al Singer (1909–1961) at the Polo Grounds on 29 August 1929; and his memorable fights against the Englishman Jack Kid Berg (1909–1991) and Italian-American Tony Canzoneri, on 7 August 1930, and 20 November 1931, respectively.

The ten-round draw with Scalfaro was particularly memorable. Amazed to find that his dream of fighting at the Garden had come true, Kid Chocolate was taken unawares by a blow during the first round just after he left his stool. The blow left him stunned, but he fought on until the eighth round, driven on by instinct. The draw verdict satisfied most people.

Maintained over the course of forty-five fights in the times' Mecca of boxing—New York City and Madison Square Garden—Kid Chocolate's undefeated record was brought to an end by Jack Kid Berg. The two-to-one vote in favor of Berg surprised Berg himself. But far from diminishing his prestige, Kid Chocolate's defeat made Chocolate even more popular.

Chocolate was not a boxer with a refined technique. He was creative, and he did what others could not because he was a genius. Chocolate never lost a match in Cuba, not even during his five years (1920–1925) participating in championships organized for kids who sold the *La Noche* newspaper on the street (Chocolate made his debut when he was ten years old and weighed only 55 pounds) or during his semi-professional career (1925–1928).

■ *See also*

Sports: Boxing Before 1959

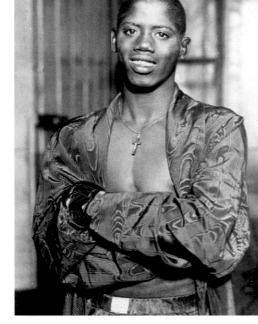

Kid Chocolate. Boxer Eligio Sardiñas Montalvo (1910–1988), better known as Kid Chocolate, in New York City before a fight, 9 September 1929. AP IMAGES

■ *See also*

Faith: Vodou

Literature: Fiction in the Republican Period

black musicians of the time. He was an elegant man both in the ring and on the street—a fashion magazine named him the best-dressed man in the world—and he was known for having taken to Havana the first Packard automobile.

Chocolate spent his last years in his home in the Havana suburb of Almendares. Those who were at his bedside related that when he was near death, he sat up, lifted his closed fists up to his face, grappled with the guard on duty, and toppled over one last time (personal account made to the author by close friend of Kid Chocolate, Alejandro Lugo 1988). Eligio Sardiñas Montalvo died on 8 August 1988.

BIBLIOGRAPHY

Knuchel, Stefano, and Iván Nurchis. *Knockout.* Documentary film. ANKA Films, October 2002.

Menéndez García, Elio. "No hay olvido para el Kid." *Semanario LPV* (August 8, 1988).

Menéndez García, Elio, and Víctor Joaquín Ortega. *El boxeo soy yo.* Havana: Editorial Orbe, 1981.

From 1 August 1928, the date of his debut at Mitchell Fields, New York, when he knocked out Eddie Enos in the second round, to 18 November 1938, when he left Havana after draws against Nick Jerome, the Kid fought in 136 bouts. He won 120 matches, suffered ten defeats, and had six ties. Of the ten defeats, only two were knockouts: on 24 November 1933, his second confrontation with Canzoneri, and thirty-four days later, when Frankie Klick defeated him in seven rounds.

Only Canzoneri and Klick knocked out Chocolate, and these losses occurred after his star was fading, following a bohemian tour through Europe. After he lost to Klick, the Cuban fighter's career languished in second-rate venues. During his decline, he won thirty-nine fights, lost three, and had five draws. His abilities failed because of the physical deterioration that resulted from his disorderly life. Five years after he lost to Klick on 18 December 1938, Chocolate retired from fighting after the draw against Jerome.

POPULARITY OUTSIDE THE RING

From humble origins in Havana's El Cerro neighborhood, where he sold newspapers and shined shoes as a boy, Kid Chocolate became both Cuba's most universal athlete and an international star. The most demanding and varied audiences bowed at his feet. In New York City he was one of the greats on the sports pages, and he brought traffic to a standstill when he appeared in public. He was acclaimed in Paris, where he enjoyed the friendship of the singers Carlos Gardel (1887–1935) and Maurice Chevalier (1888–1972), and he prided himself on his links with the most elite

■

THE KINGDOM OF THIS WORLD (ALEJO CARPENTIER)

Anke Birkenmaier

Carpentier's seminal work of Latin American literature depicting the Haitian Revolution.

First published in Spanish in 1949, *El reino de este mundo* (best known in its English translation, *The Kingdom of This World*, 1957), by Alejo Carpentier (1904–1980), will probably remain one of Latin America's all-time bestsellers. Generations of college students have been taught this fictionalized account of the Haitian Revolution told from the point of view of the slave Ti Noel, who witnesses between 1757 and 1820 some of the key moments of the slave revolution, including the poisoning campaign of the one-armed Mackandal, the sermon of the Jamaican Bouckman and the uprising of thousands that followed, and the brutal reign of King Henri Christophe over the northern half of Haiti. With this novel, Carpentier established reworkings of history and the concept of the *marvelous real* as the primary concerns of a new Latin American novel that was to begin its rise to international prominence. Mario Vargas Llosa (b. 1936), Gabriel García Márquez (b. 1927), and Carlos Fuentes (b. 1928) hailed the novel for its formal perfection and declared Carpentier, along with Jorge Luis Borges (1899–1986), one of their models.

THE MARVELOUS REAL

The first Spanish edition of the book was accompanied by a prologue in which Carpentier explained how the Americas were essentially different from Europe, arguing that "because of the virginity of its landscape, because of its formation, because of its ontology, because of the Faustian presence of the Indian and of the Black, because of the Revelation its recent discovery constituted, because of the fertile racial mixtures it favored, the Americas are far from having used up their wealth of mythologies" (p. 31). The Americas, that is, offered a unique history and landscape that compared favorably to what were to him the sterile attempts of French surrealists to uncover the poetry of the subconscious through automatic writing and other means. The *marvelous real* was for Carpentier that moment in which the particular qualities of Latin America revealed themselves to the observer:

> The marvelous begins to be marvelous in an unequivocal way when it arises from an unexpected alteration of reality (a miracle), from a privileged revelation of reality, from an illumination that is either unusual or singularly favorable to the unnoticed riches of reality, from an amplification of the scale and categories of reality, perceived with particular intensity by means of an exaltation of the spirit that leads it to a kind of "limit-state."
>
> *Prologue, p. 29*

Strikingly, Carpentier's explanation of the marvelous is couched in religious terms: Faith is crucial to understanding the presence of the marvelous in Latin America, as it referred to the belief in whatever reality is established collectively. In this way, Carpentier extended the notion of the marvelous from the supernatural to myth and also to states of ecstasy, as they occur during Vodou ceremonies or in moments of mystical out-of-body experiences. He thus adopted an anthropological notion of the marvelous real, one guided by his interpretation of the history of Haiti. Yet, even though Carpentier distanced his vision of Latin America from French surrealism, he combined knowledge of the avant-garde, of French anthropology, and of Oswald Spengler's morphology of cultures in *Der Untergang des Abenlandes* (1918, 1922; *The Decline of the West*, 1926, 1928) to conclude that the Americas offer all the advantages of a culture at the height of its inner possibilities and none of the disadvantages of the technological modernity that had brought European states to the brink of self-destruction.

Carpentier omitted the prologue from subsequent editions and translations, republishing it only in 1967 in changed form as part of the essays of *Tientos y diferencias* (Approaches and Distinctions). Yet it became recognized as one of the first theoretical statements about the magical realism of Latin American fiction, and academic controversies centered on the differences between Borges's notion of the fantastic, Carpentier's marvelous real, and García Márquez's magical realism. For better or worse, magical realism became a distinctive label for Latin American fiction, one that identified it as representing the West's *other* in mythical tales of violence and miracles, and Carpentier's prologue, together with essays by Franz Roh, Angel Flores, and Luis Leal, was read as one of its foundational statements (Zamora and Faris pp. 75–125).

***THE KINGDOM OF THIS WORLD* AND SURREALISM**

To be sure, at the time of its publication, the novel was innovative in more ways than one. Its vocabulary was charged with antiquated terms that made its language seem baroque and dense; its structure was complex with short chronological chapters grouped in four parts that were separated by large intervals; and the images it used were strongly infused with surrealism. The story depicted scenes in the life of the slave Ti Noel and his master Monsieur Lenormand de Mézy, at whose farm the first rebellion under Mackandal had historically originated. In an early draft of the novel, the protagonist was initially a stranger visiting Haiti (much as Carpentier himself had visited in 1944). However, Carpentier eventually adopted the narrative perspective of someone on the margins of history who comes to participate in revolutionary struggle (Campuzano). This preference for the perspective of an anonymous slave was complemented by a pronounced taste for surreal juxtapositions. In the famous first chapter, for example, the master goes to see a barber, and his head comes to lie in proximity to the wigged wax heads in the window, which in turn appear next to the pigs' heads at the butcher next door, and finally, next to a shop with French newspapers depicting the soon-to-be-decapitated king of France. The juxtaposition of heads is premonitory of the revolutionary events that later invert the power relation between master and slave; it points in a playful way to what is behind the appearances of colonial Haitian society. The surrealists would also have liked Carpentier's taste for destruction and for the charm of the relics of old times, as in the final scenes in which the green coat that had belonged to King Henri Christophe is worn by the old slave in combination with an old straw hat he has transformed into a Napoleonic two-cornered hat.

But more importantly, Carpentier's view of the phases of the Haitian Revolution in *The Kingdom of this World* is a cyclical one, and a departure from Hegelian or Marxist historical materialism (González Echevarría). In affirming the necessity for societies to renew themselves periodically, Carpentier possibly was inspired by Roger Caillois's essay "Théorie de la fête" (Theory of the Festival, 1939), which argued that world history is marked by eras of chaos and eras of order and that feasts celebrate the remembrance of the dialectic relation between the two. Carpentier knew

Alejo Carpentier (1904–1980). Alejo Carpentier's historical novel *El reino de este mundo* (The Kingdom of This World), first published in Spanish in 1949, is a fictionalized account of the Haitian Revolution told from the point of view of a slave. AFP/GETTY IMAGES/NEWSCOM

Caillois and was in contact with other members of the College of Sociology while he lived in Paris in the 1930s. Although in the prologue to *The Kingdom of this World*, Carpentier reclaims American independence from Europe and especially from French surrealism, he still combined research into Latin American history with an avant-garde rhetoric and historic philosophy very much en vogue in Europe.

In his years in Paris, Carpentier worked for French radio with friends he had made in surrealist circles (Robert Desnos and Paul Deharme, among others). While working in radio, he learned to view Latin America from a distance. He also was friends with many Latin Americans living in Paris and read Latin American history and literature extensively, as well as European travelers' tales and anthropological accounts. He became familiar with Georges Bataille's and Michel Leiris's fascination with non-European cultures, and he contributed to their journal *Documents*, a heteroclite publication on archaeology, modern art, and anthropology. It was during his years in Paris that Carpentier formed a new interest in Latin America as a culture in its own right, inspired just as much by European philosophy and avant-garde currents as by his readings in Latin American history.

THE NEW LATIN AMERICAN NOVEL

In choosing to write on a historical topic such as the Haitian Revolution, Carpentier helped to inaugurate what Carlos Fuentes called the "new Latin American novel," which is marked by an emphasis on the rewriting of Latin America's history, and on the creation of a "new" language to render what was perceived as uniquely Latin American. This language included archaisms just as well as oral and pop culture elements, plotlines that were not tied to main characters, and stream-of-consciousness techniques. It also brought with it a critical questioning of the possibility of writing or rewriting history. In many of the Latin American boom novels, power—political or narrative—became contested, and the lines between myth and truth blurred. For the critic Seymour Menton, the *new historical novel* of Latin America, as exemplified by Carpentier's fictions *The Kingdom of this World* and *El arpo y la sombra* (1979; *The Harp and the Shadow*, 1990), is therefore distinguished from the nineteenth-century historical novel by the ultimate impossibility of ascertaining the true nature of history, by an increase in intertextual references and metafictional instances. In *The Kingdom of this World*, Carpentier's claim to historical truth is further emphasized in his subtitle, *relato* (tale) instead of *novela* (novel). As González Echevarría, Emma Speratti Piñeiro, and Angela L. Willis have shown in their studies of chronicles, histories, and biographies of the Haitian Revolution, the details of historical events and characters in Carpentier's book were not invented. The tale-like quality of the book derives from the intricate way in which the oral story-telling tradition of the slaves is interwoven with colonial historiography, and the focus is set on events of collective coming together.

Carpentier's view of slave culture and syncretic religion changed during the sixteen years between his first novel, *Ecue-Yamba-O* (1933), and *The Kingdom of this World*. In *Ecue-Yamba-O*, Carpentier had rendered the life of a rural black family in contemporary Cuba and had adopted an outsider's perspective on the customs and everyday life of blacks in Cuba, their rivalries with Jamaican and Haitian sugarcane cutters, and their attempts to escape to the city for a better life. The membership of the main character Menegildo in an Afro-Cuban secret society ultimately causes his death, and the Vodou rituals practiced by Haitian workers are depicted as fearsome and dangerous. In *The Kingdom of this World*, by contrast, Vodou is described as a community-creating force, as highlighted in the scenes in which the slaves secretly meet and sacrifice a pig before rebelling under Bouckman, and in the nativity scene in which the slaves' belief in the metamorphoses of Mackandal is eventually rewarded by his sudden appearance among them.

INFLUENCE ON FICTION AND SCHOLARSHIP

Carpentier's view of Latin American history as inspired by myth and religion led his emphasizing the importance of Vodou in the course of the Haitian Revolution. In contradistinction to C. L. R. James's *The Black Jacobins: Toussaint L'Ouverture and the San Domingo Revolution* (1938, 1963), Carpentier considered the spiritual solidarity forged in Vodou rituals, chants, and legends as more decisive in the slaves' struggle than the leadership of Toussaint L'Ouverture (1743–1904), Jean-Jacques Dessalines (1758–1806), or Alexandre Pétion (1770–1818), who are barely mentioned in *The Kingdom of this World*. Such a view of the Haitian Revolution, hinging more on religious rituals and folklore than on social and economic history, is provocative even in the early 2000s. Contemporary historians of Haiti such as Michel-Rolph Trouillot quote Carpentier in passing as part of a club of writers fascinated with the legacy of Henri Christophe, but they avoid analyzing Vodou as a factor in the slave revolution.

A fresh look at Carpentier's *The Kingdom of this World* makes readers appreciate the relevance of the historical vision of Latin America expressed in it. Although it seems outdated to claim that Latin American reality is inherently different by virtue of its nature and racial mixing, Carpentier's critical assessment of history through fiction has not lost its appeal. Especially among Cuban writers, there was during and immediately following Carpentier's lifetime a surge of historical novels such as *El mar de las lentejas* (1979; *The Sea of Lentils*, 1991) and *Mujer en traje de batalla* (Women in Battle Dress, 2001) by Antonio Benítez Rojo (1931–2005); and *El mundo alucinante* (1966; *Hallucinations*, 1994), by Reinaldo Arenas (1943–1990). In addition to its indubitable influence on the historical novels that followed, *The Kingdom of this World* has had a lasting impact on scholarship on the history of the Haitian Revolution by academics such as Michel-Rolph Trouillot, David Patrick Geggus, Sibylle Fischer, and Laurent Dubois. More than ever, Carpentier's so-called tale is read today as literature and at the same time as a pointed statement on the history of the Haitian revolution and its relevance in Latin America. With respect to the marvelous real, even those writers of the Latin American Boom who were eager to distinguish themselves from their predecessors—the McOndo group, the Crack writers in Mexico, and dirty realist writers such as the Cuban Pedro Juan Gutiérrez (b. 1950)—would probably agree that Carpentier is unequalled among them.

BIBLIOGRAPHY

Birkenmaier, Anke. *Alejo Carpentier y la cultura del surrealismo en América Latina.* Colección Nexos y Diferencias. Madrid: Iberoamericana-Vervuert, 2006.

Caillois, Roger. "Théorie de la fête." *Nouvelle revue française* 27 (1939): 863–882.

Caillois, Roger. "The Sacred as Transgression: Theory of the Festival." In *Man and the Sacred.* Translated by Meyer Barash. Urbana: University of Illinois Press, 2001. 97–128.

Campuzano, Luisa. "Un libro y muchos destinos." *Revolución y cultura* 4 (2009): 44–48.

Carpentier, Alejo. *El reino de este mundo.* Mexico City: Ediapsa, 1949.

Carpentier, Alejo. *The Kingdom of This World.*. Translated by Harriet de Onis, Introduction by Edwidge Danticat. New York: Farrar, Straus and Giroux, 2006.

González Echevarría, Roberto. *Alejo Carpentier: The Pilgrim at Home.* 2nd ed. Austin: University of Texas Press, 1990.

MacAdam, Alfred. "Prologue to *The Kingdom of This World* (1949)." *Review: Latin American Literature and Arts* 47 (1993): 28–31.

Menton, Seymour. *Latin America's New Historical Novel.* Austin: University of Texas Press, 1993.

Speratti-Piñero, Emma Susana. *Pasos hallados en El reino de este mundo.* Mexico City: Colegio de México, 1981.

Trouillot, Michel-Rolph. *Silencing the Past: Power and the Production of History.* Boston: Beacon Press, 1995.

Willis, Angela. "Paulina Bonaparte en *El reino de este mundo* de Alejo Carpentier." *Revolución y Cultura* 1 (January–March 2004): 23–27.

Zamora, Lois Parkinson, and Wendy Faris, eds. *Magical Realism: Theory, History, Community.* Durham, NC: Duke University Press, 1995.

N

0   25   50 mi.

0   25   50 km

Gulf of Mexico

Straits of Florida

24°N

Havana

Colorados Archipelago

San José de las Lajas

Matanzas

Cárdenas

Sabana Archipelago

Artemisa

Cordillera de Guaniguanico

Pinar del Río

Broa Gulf

Batabanó Gulf

Santa Clara

Guadiana Bay

Zapata Peninsula

Cienfuegos

22°N

Guanahacabibes Peninsula

Bay of Pigs

Sancti Spíritus

Cape San Antonio

Nueva Gerona

Corrientes Bay

Cape Corrientes

Francés Cape

San Felipe Cays

Canarreos Archipelago

Trinidad

Isla de la Juventud

...go Cay

Cuba

Elevation in Feet

3,000
2,000
1,000
500
100
0

20°N

Cities

⊗ National capital

• Other city

Cayman Islands

18°N

Caribbean Sea

86°W   84°W   80°W